The SAGE
Handbook of
Social Research
Methods

(65101

The SAGE
Handbook of
Social Research
Methods

Edited by
Pertti Alasuutari,
Leonard Bickman,
Julia Brannen

SAGE Publications
Los Angeles • London • New Delhi • Singapore

Editorial arrangement and Introduction © Pertti
    Alasuutari, Leonard Bickman, Julia Brannen 2008
Chapter 2 © Alan Bryman 2008
Chapter 3 © Marja Alastalo 2008
Chapter 4 © Martyn Hammersley 2008
Chapter 5 © Karen Armstrong 2008
Chapter 6 © Pekka Sulkunen 2008
Chapter 7 © Ann Nilsen 2008
Chapter 8 © Celia B. Fisher and Andrea E. Anushko 2008
Chapter 9 © Howard S. Bloom 2008
Chapter 10 © Thomas D. Cook and Vivian C. Wong 2008
Chapter 11 © Ken Kelley and Scott E. Maxwell 2008
Chapter 12 © Giampietro Gobo 2008
Chapter 13 © Linda Mabry 2008
Chapter 14 © Jane Elliott, Janet Holland and Rachel
    Thomson 2008
Chapter 15 © David de Vaus 2008
Chapter 16 © James A. Bovaird and Susan E.
    Embretson 2008
Chapter 17 © Susan A. Speer 2008
Chapter 18 © Edith de Leeuw 2008

Chapter 19 © Andrea Doucet and Natasha Mauthner 2008
Chapter 20 © Joanna Bornat 2008
Chapter 21 © Janet Smithson 2008
Chapter 22 © Suzanne E. Graham, Judith D. Singer and
    John B. Willett 2008
Chapter 23 © Rick H. Hoyle 2008
Chapter 24 © Stephen G. West and Felix Thoemmes 2008
Chapter 25 © Charles Antaki 2008
Chapter 26 © Matti Hyvärinen 2008
Chapter 27 © Kathy Charmaz 2008
Chapter 28 © Lindsay Prior 2008
Chapter 29 © Christian Heath and Paul Luff 2008
Chapter 30 © Janet Heaton 2008
Chapter 31 © Angela Dale, Jo Wathan and Vanessa
    Higgins 2008
Chapter 32 © Erika A. Patall and Harris Cooper 2008
Chapter 33 © Jane Fielding and Nigel Fielding 2008
Chapter 34 © Ann Cronin, Victoria D. Alexander, Jane
    Fielding, Jo Moran-Ellis and Hilary Thomas 2008
Chapter 35 © Manfred Max Bergman 2008
Chapter 36 © Amir Marvasti 2008

First published 2008

SAGE Publications Ltd
1 Oliver's Yard
55 City Road
London EC1Y 1SP

SAGE Publications Inc.
2455 Teller Road
Thousand Oaks, California 91320

SAGE Publications India Pvt Ltd
B 1/I 1 Mohan Cooperative Industrial Area
Mathura Road
New Delhi 110 044

SAGE Publications Asia-Pacific Pte Ltd
33 Pekin Street #02-01
Far East Square
Singapore 048763

Library of Congress Control Number: 2007929185

British Library Cataloguing in Publication data

A catalogue record for this book is available from
the British Library

ISBN 978-1-4129-1992-0

Typeset by CEPHA Imaging Pvt. Ltd., Bangalore, India
Printed in Great Britain by The Cromwell Press Ltd, Trowbridge, Wiltshire
Printed on paper from sustainable resources

Contents

Notes on Contributors

Marja Alastalo is post-doctoral Research Fellow in the Department of Sociology and Social Psychology, University of Tampere, Finland. She is interested in history of research methods and sociology of knowledge and science. Currently she is doing research on the processes of harmonizing social statistics in the European Union.

Pertti Alasuutari, PhD, is Professor of Sociology and Director of the International School of Social Sciences at the University of Tampere, Finland. He is editor of the *European Journal of Cultural Studies*, and has published widely in the areas of cultural and media studies and qualitative methods. His books include *Desire and Craving: A Cultural Theory of Alcoholism* (SUNY Press, 1992), *Researching Culture: Qualitative Method and Cultural Studies* (SAGE, 1995), *An Invitation to Social Research* (SAGE, 1998), *Rethinking the Media Audience* (SAGE, 1999), and *Social Theory and Human Reality* (SAGE, 2004).

Victoria D. Alexander is Senior Lecturer in Sociology at the University of Surrey, and is interested in sociology of the arts, sociology of cultural organizations, and visual methods. She is author of *Museums and Money* (Indiana University Press, 1996), *Sociology of the Arts* (Blackwell, 2003), and co-author of *Art and the State* (Palgrave Macmillan, 2005).

Charles Antaki, PhD, is Professor of Language and Social Psychology at the University of Loughborough, where he is a member of the Discourse and Rhetoric Group. He is Associate Editor of *Research on Language and Social Interaction*, and among his books are *Identities in Talk* (SAGE, 1998; with Susan Widdecombe) and *Conversation Analysis and Psychotherapy* (CUP, 2007; with Anssi Perakyla, Sanna Vehvilainen, and Ivan Leudar). He has published widely on language and interaction.

Andrea E. Anushko, MA is a graduate student in the applied developmental psychology program at Fordham University and the project coordinator for the Fordham Resident Alcohol Prevention Program at the Center for Ethics Education. Her research interests include language development and early education.

Karen Armstrong is Professor of Cultural Anthropology at the University of Helsinki, Finland. Her research focuses on politics and the narrative construction of national identity. She is the author of *Remembering Karelia* (Berghahn, 2004), and is currently doing research on the relation of American Samoa to the US nation-state.

Manfred Max Bergman is Professor of Sociology at Basel University, Switzerland. His areas of specialization are political sociology and research methods. His research interests relate to stratification, identity, and inter-group relation, and his recent publications focus on poverty, stratification and mobility, mixed methods research, and data quality.

Leonard Bickman, PhD, is Professor of Psychology, Psychiatry and Public Policy. He is Associate Dean for Research and Director of Center for Evalution and Program Improvement, Peabody College of Vanderbilt University.

Howard S. Bloom, Chief Social Scientist for MDRC, specializes in the design and analysis of experimental and quasi-experimental studies of causal effects. He has conducted a number of such studies and has written widely on methodologies for them.

Joanna Bornat is Professor of Oral History in the Faculty of Health and Social Care at the Open University. She has researched and published in the areas of oral history and ageing for a number of years. Her current research interests include the secondary analysis of archived data.

James A. Bovaird is Assistant Professor of Quantitative, Qualitative, and Psychometric Methods (QQPM) in the Department of Educational Psychology at the University of Nebraska-Lincoln. As a quantitative psychologist (University of Kansas, 2002), his research focuses on the application of latent variable methodologies to novel substantive contexts and the evaluation of competing latent variable methodologies in situations of limited inference.

Julia Brannen is Professor of the Sociology of the Family, Institute of Education, University of London. Her main interests are in research methodology; the family lives of parents, children, and young people; and the relation between paid work and family life. She is a co-founder and co-editor of the *International Journal of Social Research Methodology*. Books include: *Mixing Methods: Qualitative and Quantitative Research* (Ashgate, 1992), *Connecting Children: Care and Family Life in Later Childhood* (Falmer, 2000), *Young Europeans, Work and Family* (Routledge, 2002), *Rethinking Children's Care* (OUP, 2003), *Working and Caring over the Twentieth Century* (Palgrave, 2004), and *Coming to Care* (Policy Press, 2007).

Alan Bryman is Professor of Organisational and Social Research, Management Centre, University of Leicester. His main research interests lie in research methodology, leadership, organizational analysis, and Disneyization. He is author or co-author of many books, including: *Quantity and Quality in Social Research* (Routledge, 1988), *Social Research Methods* (OUP, 2001, 2004), *Business Research Methods* (OUP, 2003), and *Disneyization of Society* (SAGE, 2004). He is co-editor of *The SAGE Encyclopedia of Social Science Research* (SAGE, 2004), *Handbook of Data Analysis* (SAGE, 2004), and the forthcoming *Handbook of Organizational Research Methods* (SAGE, 2008).

Kathy Charmaz is Professor of Sociology and Coordinator of the Faculty Writing Program at Sonoma State University. Her books include *Good Days, Bad Days: The Self in Chronic Illness and Time* (Rutgers, 1993) and *Constructing Grounded Theory: A Practical Guide through Qualitative Analysis*, published by SAGE, London, and has co-edited the forthcoming *The SAGE Handbook of Grounded Theory*. She received the 2006 George Herbert Mead award for lifetime achievement from the Society for the Study of Symbolic Interaction.

Thomas D. Cook has a BA from Oxford and a PhD from Stanford and is a Professor of sociology, psychology, education and social policy, and Joan and Serepta Harrison Chair in Ethics and Justice at Northwestern University. His main interests are in social science methodology and contextual influences on adolescent development.

Harris Cooper is Professor of psychology and Director of the Program in Education at Duke University. His research interests include research synthesis methodology and applications of social psychology to education policies and practices.

Ann Cronin, BSc, PhD (Surrey) is Lecturer in Sociology at the University of Surrey. She teaches a variety of courses relating to social theory, methodology, and the substantive topics of gender and sexuality. Her research interests lie in the social construction of sexual identities and qualitative methodologies.

Angela Dale is Professor of Quantitative Social Research at the Centre for Census and Survey Research, University of Manchester. She is Director of the ESRC's Research Methods Programme and heads a team providing support for government datasets as part of the UK's Economic and Social Data Service. From 1993 to 2003, she led the academic team responsible for the development and dissemination of samples of microdata from the UK Census of Population.

Andrea Doucet is Associate Professor in the Department of Sociology and Anthropology, Carleton University, Ottawa, Canada. She is the author of *Do Men Mother?* (University of Toronto Press, 2006) and over two dozen book chapters and articles on mothering and fathering, gender equality and gender differences, and methodology and epistemology.

Jane Elliott, PhD, is reader of Research Methodology and Principal Investigator of the 1958 and 1970 British Birth Cohort Studies at the Centre for Longitudinal Studies at the Institute of Education, University of London. She has a long-standing interest in combining qualitative and quantitative methodologies and has published in the areas of methodology, gender, and employment. Her book *Using Narrative in Social Research: Qualitative and Quantitative Approaches* was published by SAGE in 2005.

Susan E. Embretson is a Professor of psychology at the Georgia Institute of Technology. Her interests span modern psychometric methods (e.g. item response theory), cognitive and intelligence, and quantitative methods, and her main research program has been to integrate cognitive theory into psychometric models and test design.

Jane Fielding is Senior Lecturer in Quantitative Sociology, University of Surrey, and teaches statistics and computing at both undergraduate and postgraduate levels. Recent research projects, supported by funding from the Environment Agency, include flood warning for vulnerable groups and the public response to flood warning and, more recently, a study of environmental inequalities. Her particular interest is in mapping and measuring environmental inequalities using geographical information techniques. She was also a co-holder on an ESRC Methods Programme project (2002–2005) exploring the integration of quantitative and qualitative methods in an investigation of the concept of vulnerability.

Nigel Fielding is Professor of Sociology and co-Director of the Institute of Social Research, University of Surrey. His research interests are in qualitative research methods, mixed methods research design, and new technologies for social research. His books include *Linking Data* (SAGE, 1986; with Jane Fielding), a study of methodological integration; *Using Computers in Qualitative Research* (SAGE, 1991; edited with Raymond M. Lee), an influential book on qualitative software; *Computer Analysis and Qualitative Research* (SAGE, 1998; with Raymond M. Lee), a study of the role of computer technology in qualitative research; and *Interviewing* (SAGE, 2002; editor), a four volume set; he is currently co-editing the *Handbook of Online Research Methods* (SAGE).

Celia B. Fisher holds the Marie Doty Chair in Psychology at Fordham University where she also directs the Center for Ethics Education. Her professional interests are in developing ethical standards for the discipline of psychology and federal guidelines for the protection of vulnerable populations in research.

Giampietro Gobo, PhD, is Associate Professor of Methodology of Social Research and Evaluation Methods, and Director of the ICONA (Centre for Innovation and Organizational Change in Public Administration) at the University of Milan, Italy. Among the founders of the *Qualitative Methods* research network of ESA (European Sociological Association), he has been its first chair. Associate Editor of the *International Journal of Qualitative Research in Work and Organizations*, member of the editorial boards of *Qualitative Research* and *International Journal of Social Research Methodology*, he has published over fifty articles in the areas of qualitative and quantitative methods. His books include *Ethnography into Practice* (SAGE, 2007), and he has co-edited *Qualitative Research Practice* (SAGE, 2004; with Clive Seale, Jaber F. Gubrium, and David Silverman).

Suzanne E. Graham is an Assistant Professor at the University of New Hampshire. She is interested in applying methods of longitudinal data analysis to questions about mathematics course taking and achievement among secondary school and college students.

Martyn Hammersley is Professor of Educational and Social Research at the Open University. His early research was in the sociology of education. Much of his more recent work has been concerned with the methodological issues surrounding social and educational enquiry. His most recent books are *Taking Sides in Social Research* (Routledge, 2000); *Educational Research, Policymaking and Practice* (Paul Chapman, 2002); and *Media Bias in Reporting Social Research? The Case of Reviewing Ethnic Inequalities in Education* (Routledge, 2006). He is currently working on the issue of research ethics.

Christian Heath is Professor at King's College London, and leads the Work Interaction and Technology research group. He specializes in video-based studies of social interaction drawing on ethnomethodology and conversation analysis. He is currently undertaking projects in areas that include health care, museums and galleries, and auctions.

Janet Heaton, BA (Hons), is Research Fellow at the Social Policy Research Unit, University of York. She is the author of *Reworking Qualitative Data* (SAGE, 2004), and has published a number of articles based on her mainly qualitative research on health and social care services for patients and their families in the UK.

Vanessa Higgins is based at the Centre for Census and Survey Research, University of Manchester, where she works for ESDS Government, providing support for research and teaching using the large-scale government datasets. Prior to this, Vanessa worked at the Office for National Statistics and also on a number of policy-led research projects within academic settings.

Janet Holland is Professor of Social Research and co-Director of the Families and Social Capital ESRC research group at London South Bank University. She also co-directs *Timescapes: Changing Relationships and Identities through the Life Course*, a multi-university, large-scale qualitative longitudinal study. Research interests cover youth, education, gender, sexuality and family life, and methodology, and she has published widely in these areas. Examples are *Sexualities and Society* (Polity Press, 2003; edited with Jeffrey Weeks and Matthew Waites);

Feminist Methodology: Challenges and Choices (SAGE, 2002; with Caroline Ramazanoglu); and *Inventing Adulthoods: A Biographical Approach to Youth Transitions* (SAGE, 2007; with Sheila Henderson, Sheena McGrellis, Sue Sharpe, and Rachel Thomson).

Rick H. Hoyle is Research Professor of psychology and neuroscience at Duke University, where he is Associate Director of the Center for Child and Family Policy and Director of the Office of Data, Methods, and Research Facilities in the Social Science Research Institute. His methodological interests include the strategic application of structural equation modeling to longitudinal and complex cross-sectional data in the social and behavioral sciences, with a particular focus on statistical strategies for managing the detrimental effects of measurement error.

Matti Hyvärinen is an Academy of Finland Research Fellow, University of Tampere, Department of Sociology and Social Psychology. His current project, *The Conceptual History of Narrative*, aims to capture the changing and different uses of narrative in literary, social, and historiographical theory and analysis. He also leads the Politics and the Arts research team at the Finnish Centre for Excellence in Political Thought and Conceptual Change. He is a co-editor of the electronic volume *The Travelling Concept of Narrative* (2006) at http://www.helsinki.fi/collegium/e-series/volumes/index.htm. Recent work includes *Acting, Thinking, and Telling: Anna Blume's Dilemma in Paul Auster's In the Country of Last Things* (*Partial Answers* 4:2, June 2006). Website: http://www.hyvarinen.info.

Ken Kelley is an Assistant Professor in the Inquiry Methodology Program at Indiana University, where his research focuses on methodological and statistical issues that arise in the behavioral, educational, and social sciences. More specifically, Dr. Kelley's research focuses on the design of research studies, with an emphasis on sample size planning from the power analytic and accuracy in parameter estimation approaches, and the analysis of change, with an emphasis on multilevel change models nonlinear in their parameters.

Edith de Leeuw is an Associate Professor at the University of Utrecht, Department of Methodology and Statistics and a member and Senior Lecturer of the Interuniversities graduate school for psychometrics and sociometrics in the Netherlands. Her most recent publications focus on children as respondents, survey nonresponse, survey data quality, and comparative research.

Paul Luff is Reader of Organisations and Technology at King's College, University of London. His recent publications include *Technology in Action* (Cambridge University Press, 2000; with Christian Heath) and numerous articles in journals and books. He is co-editor of *Workplace Studies: Recovering Work Practice and Informing System Design* (Cambridge University Press, 2000).

Linda Mabry, Professor of Education at Washington State University Vancouver, specializes in qualitative research methods in research and evaluation and in the assessment of student achievement K-12. She has conducted studies for the US Department of Education, National Science Foundation, National Endowment for the Arts, and others, publishing a number of articles and books. She is a member of the Board of Trustees for the Center for the Improvement of Educational Assessments, and a former member of the Board of Directors for the American Evaluation Association. Her most recent book (co-authored) is *RealWorld Evaluation* (SAGE, 2006).

Amir Marvasti is Assistant Professor of Sociology at Penn State Altoona. His research focuses on social construction and representation of deviant identities in everyday life. He is the author of *Being Homeless: Textual and Narrative Constructions* (Lexington Books, 2003), *Qualitative Research in Sociology* (SAGE, 2003), and *Middle Eastern Lives in America* (Rowman & Littlefield, 2004; with Karyn McKinney). His articles have been published in the *Journal of Contemporary Ethnography, Qualitative Inquiry*, and *Symbolic Interaction*.

Natasha Mauthner is a Senior Lecturer at the University of Aberdeen, where she teaches courses on qualitative research methods, and gender, work, and organization. She has published extensively on methodological and epistemological issues in qualitative research. Much of this work has focused on the links between reflexivity, research practice, and the construction of knowledge, and the implications for data analysis, data archiving, and the politics of research management. Her empirical research has focused on issues of gender, work, and family and has been published in a number of publications including *The Darkest Days of My Life: Stories of Postpartum Depression* (Harvard University Press, 2002).

Scott E. Maxwell is Fitzsimons Professor of Psychology at the University of Notre Dame. He received his Ph.D. from the University of North Carolina at Chapel Hill, and is currently editor of *Psychological Methods*.

Jo Moran-Ellis is Senior Lecturer in the Department of Sociology, University of Surrey. Her research interests are primarily in the areas of childhood studies and research methods, especially mixed and multiple methods. Her recent projects include a reflexive methodological study looking at integrating methods (the PPIMs study), public attitudes toward research governance, and studies of children's mental health services.

Ann Nilsen is Professor of Sociology at the Department of Sociology, University of Bergen, Norway. Her areas of interest include biographical and life course methodology, cross-national research, gender studies, and environmental sociology. In addition to books and articles in Norwegian and international journals, her publications include a recent co-edited book *Young People, Work and Family: Futures in Transition* (Routledge, 2002). She is currently writing a book on American pragmatist thought and biographical research.

Erika A. Patall is a graduate student in Social Psychology in the Department of Psychology and Neuroscience at Duke University. Her research interests include research synthesis, as well as the nature of motivation and the relationship between motivation and academic achievement.

Lindsay Prior is Professor of Sociology at Queen's University, Belfast. He is the author of *Using Documents in Social Research* (SAGE, 2003), and has contributed to various handbooks and edited collections in the field of social research methods.

Judith D. Singer is the James Bryant Conant Professor of Education at Harvard University and former academic Dean of the Harvard Graduate School of Education. As one of the nation's leading applied statisticians she is primarily known for her contributions to the practice of multilevel modeling, survival analysis, and individual growth modeling.

Janet Smithson is a post-doctoral Research Fellow in the Schools of Law and Psychology at the University of Exeter. She has worked on a variety of national- and European-funded research projects, using both qualitative and quantitative research methods. Her main research interests are in cross-national comparative research on work–family, youth, transitions to adulthood and parenthood, gender and discourse, and qualitative methodology. She is currently working on a Nuffield-funded study 'The common law marriage myth and cohabitation law revisited' with Anne Barlow and Carole Burgoyne, University of Exeter.

Susan A. Speer is a Senior Lecturer in Language and Communication in the School of Psychological Sciences at The University of Manchester. Her research interests include conversation analysis, medical interaction, and gender and sexuality (especially transgender). Her book *Gender Talk: Feminism, Discourse and Conversation Analysis* was published by Routledge in 2005. She is Principal Investigator on the project 'Transsexual Identities: Constructions of Gender in an NHS Gender Identity Clinic', which is part of the ESRC's Identities and Social Action Research Programme. She is currently working with Elizabeth Stokoe (Loughborough University) on an edited collection, *Conversation and Gender*, for Cambridge University Press.

Pekka Sulkunen, PhD, is Professor of Sociology at the University of Helsinki, Finland. He has published widely in the areas of alcohol and addiction studies and social theory. His books include *The European New Middle Class* (Avebury, 1992) and *Constructing the New Consumer Society* (Macmillan, 1997, edited).

Hilary Thomas is Professor of Health Care Research in the Centre for Research in Primary and Community Care, School of Nursing and Midwifery, University of Hertfordshire. She was previously Senior Lecturer in the Department of Sociology, University of Surrey. Her substantive research interests include the sociology of health and illness, particularly reproduction and women's health, and recovery from illness and injury. She was convenor of the BSA Medical Sociology Group (1991–1994) and president of the European Society for Health and Medical Sociology (1999–2003).

Felix Thoemmes is a graduate student in the Department of Psychology at Arizona State University with an interest in Latent Class Models, the history of statistics, and some aspects of evolutionary psychology.

Rachel Thomson is Professor of Social Research in the Faculty of Health and Social Care at the Open University. Her research interests include youth transitions, gender/sexual identities, and social change, and she has published widely in these fields. She is part of the team that conducted a 10-year qualitative longitudinal study of youth transitions (Inventing Adulthoods) and is currently researching the transition to motherhood. Forthcoming publications include *Researching Social Change: Qualitative Approaches to Personal, Social and Historical Approaches* (with Julie McLeod) published by SAGE in 2008.

David de Vaus is Professor of Sociology and Dean of the Faculty of Humanities and Social Sciences at La Trobe University, Australia. He is the author of a number of internationally renowned books on research methods including *Surveys in Social Research* (Routledge, 2001) and *Research Design in Social Research* (SAGE, 2001). His main areas of research are family sociology, living alone, life course transitions, and the sociology of ageing. Further details are available at http://www.latrobe.edu.au/humanities/devaus.html.

Jo Wathan is Research Fellow at the Cathie Marsh Centre for Census and Survey Research. She works as a member of two data support teams for British cross-sectional microdata: ESDS Government and the Samples of Anonymised Records Support team. She also teaches classes on statistical software and secondary analysis.

Stephen G. West is currently Professor of psychology at Arizona State University, and was the editor of *Psychological Methods* for six years. His research interests are in field research methods, multiple regression analysis, longitudinal data analysis, and multilevel modeling.

John B. Willett is Charles William Elliot Professor at Harvard University Graduate School of Education. He is interested in all things quantitative, particularly statistical methods for analyzing the timing and occurrence of events; methods for modeling change, learning, and development; and longitudinal research design.

Vivian C. Wong is training to be a Research Methodologist in the field of education. Her interests include examination of the following areas: recent shifts in methodology choice in education; empirical tests of quasi-experimental designs such as regression-discontinuity (RD), abbreviated interrupted time series, and difference-in-differences designs; and issues in implementation and analysis of regression-discontinuity studies.

Social Research in Changing Social Conditions

According to Herbert Blumer (1969), methodology refers to the 'entire scientific quest' that has to fit the 'obdurate character of the social world under study'. Thus methodology is not some super-ordained set of logical procedures that can be applied haphazardly to any empirical problem. In short methodology constitutes a whole range of strategies and procedures that include: developing a picture of an empirical world; asking questions about that world and turning these into researchable problems; finding the best means of doing so – that involve choices about methods and the data to be sought, the development and use of concepts, and the interpretation of findings (Blumer 1969: 23). Methods *per se* are therefore only one small part of the methodological endeavor.

In producing this book we address the methodology of social science research and the appropriate use of different methods. The contributors describe and question different phases of the research process with many focusing upon one or more methods, often in combination with others. What unites their contributions is the way they relate the discussion of method to the broader

methodological work in which they were engaged. Thus, the contributors draw not only upon their own research experiences but relate their discussions in Blumer's terms to the larger issue of *strategy*, that is tailoring methodological processes to fit the empirical world under study.

Across the social sciences and humanities, there are differences in the development and popularity of particular methods, differences that are also evident cross-nationally. From the 1930s onward survey research and statistical methods have assumed a dominant position, whereas qualitative methods have gained ground more recently. There has also been a recent resurgence of interest both in the social sciences and humanities in quantitative methods and in mathematical modes of inquiry, for example, fuzzy logic (Ragin 2000). Mixing different methods (e.g. Goldthorpe et al. 1968) and the innovative use of statistical analysis (e.g. Bourdieu 1984) are not, however, recent phenomena. The growth of explicit interest in mixed-methods research designs dates from the late 1980s, resulting in a number of specialist texts (Brannen 1992, Bryman 1988, Creswell 2003,

Tashakkori and Teddlie 2003) but the practice has historically been intrinsic to many types of social science research. In qualitative research, many researchers have incorporated several quantitative approaches such as cross-tabulation of their data (Alasuutari 1995, Silverman 1985, 2000); and some have adopted a multivariate approach (Clayman and Heritage 2002). In 1987 Charles Ragin published his text on qualitative comparative methods (Ragin 1987), which lies in between qualitative and quantitative methods and draws upon logic rather than statistical probability. Historically there has been a plurality of practices of social research.

What distinguishes the social sciences today is a positive orientation toward engaging in different types of research practice. Present-day scholars undertaking empirical research view methods as tools or optics to be applied to several different kinds of research questions that they and their funders seek to address in carrying out research. Coding observations and subjecting them to statistical processes is one way of creating and explaining patterns. Case study and comparative approaches are others: the explication of the logic that brings together the clues about a case and has an explanatory purpose with reference to other cases. These two approaches can also be combined as in embedded case studies that employ both a case study design and a survey design.

Although qualitative and quantitative methods have evolved from very different scientific traditions as, among others, Charles Ragin (1994) points out, from the viewpoint of how empirical data are used to validate and defend an interpretation, they form a continuum. It can be argued that the two concepts, 'qualitative' and 'quantitative', are not so much terms for two alternative methods of social research as two social constructs that group together particular sets of practices (see Chapter 2). For instance, quantitative research draws on many kinds of statistical approaches and is not necessarily epistemologically positivistic in orientation. While the social survey is the current dominant, paradigmatic form, there is no uniform 'quantitative research'. Similarly,

there is no uniform 'qualitative research' either. Because much of the craft of empirical social research cannot be classified as either qualitative or quantitative, an increased permissiveness toward mixing methods and questioning of the binary system formed by the terms 'qualitative' and 'quantitative' are welcome trends.

In this new paradigmatic situation many contemporary scholars no longer regard it as reasonable to divide the field of methodology into opposing camps. On the one hand, researchers are willing to learn more about the possibilities of applying survey methods and statistics to their data analysis. On the other hand, what is known as 'qualitative research' has gone a long way since Malinowski's (1922) principles of ethnography or Glaser and Strauss' (1967) grounded theory. Different methods of analyzing talk, texts and social interaction have multiplied the 'optics' available to scholars who want to study social reality from different viewpoints.

This book charts the new and evolving terrain of social research methodology in an age of increasing pluralism. By putting together different approaches to the study of social phenomena within a single volume, the Handbook serves as an invaluable resource for researchers who wish to approach research with an open mind and decide which methodological strategies to adopt in empirical research in order to understand the social world. Given the scope of the field of social research methodology, this volume concentrates on mapping the field rather than discussing each and every aspect and method in detail. In this way the Handbook serves not only as a manual but also as a roadmap. If and when the reader wants to learn more about a particular aspect of methodology or method, he or she can consult other literature.

CHALLENGING THE PROGRESS NARRATIVE

Why social research seems to be heading toward greater open-mindedness in methodological strategies can easily be interpreted as proof of scientific progress. It is tempting to think that after decades of hostility between different methodological camps, notably between qualitative and quantitative researchers, we have now finally acquired the wisdom to see that the best results can be achieved by addressing different ways of framing research questions and by bringing to bear the means to ensure the validity of data analysis and interpretation. This may imply the use of a mixed method design; in qualitative research it may mean employing innovative approaches such as hypermedia or, in social surveys, multi-mode approaches. When researchers adopt new methods they will require the guidance of methodological texts. The Handbook represents our attempt to provide such guidance.

When discussing developments in social research methodology, it is also common to justify change through a narrative in which problems and omissions in past research practices and paradigms have led to new approaches. For instance, in the influential *Handbook of Qualitative Research* Denzin and Lincoln recount the development of qualitative research in terms of a progress narrative (Denzin et al. 2000). According to them, the history of qualitative research in the social and behavioral sciences consists of seven moments or periods: the traditional (1900–1950); the modernist or golden age (1950–1970); blurred genres (1970–1986); the crisis of representation (1986–1990); the postmodern, a period of experimental and new ethnographies (1990–1995); post-experimental inquiry (1995–2000); and the future (2000–). As informative as their description of the development of qualitative research is, their story also testifies to the problems and dangers of such a narrative. Despite their caveats, their progress narrative functions implicitly as an enlightenment discourse, suggesting where up-to-date, well-informed researchers should be heading if they are not already there and likewise identifying exemplary studies that represent the avant-garde or the cutting edge of present-day qualitative research. It is hardly a surprise that the researchers in question are a very

small band and that practically all of them are American, because both authors come from the United States. Moreover, the closer to the present, the more frequently there are new moments, and the narrower the group.

To follow suit in this book, it would be quite easy to find good reasons for arguing that the methods represented here are a natural outcome of scientific progress in social research methodology. One such argument may be that scientific progress constitutes the closure of the gap between qualitative and quantitative methods; that by pursuing a multi-method approach we can best tackle the tasks of the social sciences in today's society.

Even though we are not unsympathetic to such a view, there are also problems with that argument. Unlike natural science, whose development can be described as the vertical accumulation of knowledge about the laws of nature, human sciences are quite different. They are more like a running commentary on the cultural turns and political events of different societies, communities, institutions and groups that change over time. Social science research not only speaks to particular social conditions; it reflects the social conditions of a society and the theories that dominate at the time. Because there is no unidirectional progress in social and societal development, the theoretical and methodological apparatus available to social scientists change as they too are shaped by historical, structural and cultural contexts. The notion that eventually methodology may consist in a collectively usable toolbox of methods is illusory. Methodological traditions vary across societies and they are also subject to fashion with some more popular at one moment in time and in a particular context than others. In any case it is rare for a wholly new method to be developed.

METHODOLOGICAL PLURALISM AND EVIDENCE-BASED RESEARCH

From this viewpoint, changes in social research must always be seen in their social and historical contexts. Thus, our assumption that there is a trend toward greater permissiveness in methodology stems from our own experience as scholars working in countries that belong to the Organisation for Economic Co-operation and Development (OECD)[1]. In addition, our experience stems from primarily following the English language literature. According to our analysis, that trend is due to the position that social research has been required to adopt. During recent decades, the OECD countries have experienced a climate of increased accountability in public expenditure and a requirement that research should serve policy ends and 'user' interests[2]. In particular the promotion and dominance of the concept of new public management by the OECD and its member countries is a key factor. As part of the growing pervasiveness of neoliberal principles, public policy decisions are required to be grounded in evidence-based, scientifically validated research. This has also led to developments in social science research: the 'systematic review' process, one of the catchwords also promoted by the OECD, has become a major area of methodological investment in the social sciences.

For instance in the United States, although the emphasis on policy is not as strong, the tradition of action research and the accountability of research to a diversity of 'user' groups is longstanding. Program evaluation is a significant player in the policy environment. Most government agencies require that their demonstration programs be evaluated. One research agency, the Institute of Educational Sciences, has in the last few years shifted to rigorous randomized experiments. There are forces promoting evidence-based treatments in health, mental health and education. Even though the evidence-based medicine approach originated in Great Britan, the United States is emphasizing the existence of such evidence in the funding of health and mental health services. The U.S Department of Education, through its No Children Left Behind programme is requiring quantitative evidence of academic improvement. The establishment of the Campbell Collaborative, modeled after

medicine's Cochrane Collaborative, focuses on systematic evidence of the effectiveness of programs in mental health, education and criminal justice. At the federal level of government the agencies themselves are now responsible for providing formal reviews of their agency's performance through the Government Performance and Results Act (GPRA).

The systematic review of social research evidence is widespread in quantitative research whose quality is seen to be measurable in 'scientific terms'. Systematic review is also being applied to qualitative research, a process that is requiring researchers in this genre to develop more rigorous and convincing arguments for their evidence as well as criteria against which such studies may be measured.

Social research is also affected by the increasing prevalence of *cross-disciplinary* pilot or applied projects that serve as tools to develop solutions to social, economic and environmental problems. Typically such projects, often developed in co-operation between public, private and civil society sectors, include a practical research element and the evaluation of results. One of the aims is to generate 'best practices' that are to be promoted worldwide[3]. Such a model for the improvement of governance creates new roles and requirements for social research. The close co-operation of researchers with policy-makers and the merging of the roles of project manager and researcher challenge the ideals of rigorous science, thus creating an increased interest in action research methodology. Second, the evaluation of pilot or demonstration projects has contibuted to the further development of a whole evaluation research industry. Additionally, the marketing of such pilot projects as best practice creates an aura of research as scientifically systematic, although the emphasis is on practical, policy-directed research.

The growing market for policy-directed and practice-oriented social research does not necessarily or directly affect academic social science the same way in all contexts. In some contexts universities need to complement shrinking public funding with money from external sources, while in other countries such as the UK universities are increasingly being seen and run as businesses, with research income from external sources sought at 'full economic cost'. Within Academe, one consequence of the growing market of policy-directed research is that the position of traditional disciplines is weakened as a result of the growth of cross-disciplinary theme-based research programmes, which are fishing in the new funding pools of research and development. This, in turn, affects the field of methodology. Cross-disciplinary applied research improves the transfer of knowledge between hitherto bounded disciplines, thus constructing methodology as an arena and area of expertise that spans disciplines. In some ways, this has also meant that methodology has become a discipline in itself, or at least it has assumed part of the role of traditional disciplines. Vocational apprenticeships conducted within a particular discipline have been overtaken by training courses for the new generation of researchers who are schooled in a broad repertoire of methods. While it is always useful to master a large toolbox of methods, the danger is that without a strong link between theory and practice via a particular discipline, for example sociology, people lack what C. Wright Mills (1959) called the 'sociological imagination'. As methodology acquires a higher status across all the social sciences and more emphasis is placed on *displaying* methodological rigour, there is the need to be mindful of Lewis Coser's admonition to the American Sociological Association in 1975 against producing researchers 'with superior research skills but with *a trained incapacity to think* in theoretically innovative ways' (Coser 1975).

THE RELEVANCE OF QUALITATIVE RESEARCH

In recent years advanced capitalist societies have indeed witnessed increasing method-ological pluralism and a resurgence of interest in quantitative methods. This development, however, must be seen against the larger picture in which qualitative research can be placed at the forefront, because qualitative methods have gained popularity particularly during the past two or three decades. Despite increasingly pluralist attitudes toward quantitative methods, a major proportion of British sociologists, for instance, conduct qualitative inquiries. A recent study shows that only about one in 20 of published papers in the mainstream British journals uses quantitative analysis (Payne et al. 2004). The figures are about the same in Finland (Räsänen et al. 2005), and the same trend, a forward march of qualitative research particularly from 1990s onward, can also be detected in Canada (Platt 2006) and the U.S. (Clark 1999).

The increase in the popularity of qualitative methods has coincided with new theoretical trends that have many names. One talks, for instance, of a linguistic or cultural turn, or about interpretive social science. Overall, we could say that constructionist approaches have gained ground from scientific realism and structural sociology. Along with this paradigm shift, personal experience, subjectivity and identity have become key concerns for many social researchers. For instance in British sociology, as Carl May (2005: 522) points out, 'after the political watershed of the early 1980s, much explicitly Marxist analysis disappeared, to be subsumed by social constructionism and postmodern theoretical positions that also privilege subjectivity and experience over objectification and measurement'. He emphasizes that in different ways, subjectivity seems to have been one of the central concerns of British sociology since the 1980s, which according to him also explains the popularity of qualitative investigation. Indeed, a recent study shows that only about one in 20 of published papers in the mainstream British journals uses quantitative analysis (Payne et al. 2004).

An interest in cultural studies and constructionist research grew up out of a desire by social scientists to distance themselves from economistic Marxism and structural sociology, particularly in the UK. Other political influences were also important. For example, under the influence of the Women's Movement in the 1970s feminist social scientists sought to address gender inequality and to focus upon women's perspectives in public and private spheres. By the early 1980s qualitative research had established a foothold, and by the early 1990s qualitative methods had become mainstream in Finnish sociology (Alastalo 2005) and pervasive in the UK. Theory-wise, different strands of constructionist thought have gained popularity, and the development has meant an increased interest in questions of identity.

In the United States qualitative research developed particularly in response to 'scientistic' sociology and to research techniques that require a deductive model of hypothesis testing. The more inductive approach of qualitative research was seen not only as a better way to explain social phenomena by understanding the meaning of action, but it was also seen as a way to 'give voice' to the underdog, to help see the world from the viewpoint of the oppressed rather than the oppressor (Becker 1967, Becker and Horowitz 1972). Like European sociology, the rise of qualitative research has meant a trend 'away' from determinism to active agency and to questions of subjectivity.

It seems that the increased interest in qualitative research is partly due to recent policy changes, which have foregrounded questions of subjectivity in many ways. For instance, when public services are marketized or privatized and citizens are turned into customers, there is demand for expertise on subjectivity (Rose 1996: 151). Sometimes the link between policy changes and an increasing demand for qualitative research can be quite direct. For instance, when the deregulation of the Finnish electronic media system started during the first part of the 1980s, YLE, the national public broadcasting company quickly launched a fairly big qualitative research program to study the audiences, their way of life and viewing preferences to fight for its share of the audience. There appears to be a similar link between media research and changes in media policy throughout the OECD countries: while the deregulation of public broadcasting, promoted and reviewed by the OECD (OECD 1993, 1999), was started during the 1980s, reception studies and qualitative audience research gained in momentum from the 1970s onward[4]. For the most part, however, the increased interest in subjectivity and identity construction within academic (qualitative) research is only indirectly related to its policy relevance.

THE IMPORTANCE OF REFLECTIVITY

All in all, social research is being forced to perform a more strategic role in society than hitherto. Our argument is not that this strategic role is the sole determinant of developments in social research, or the kinds of research methods that are used. However, we think it is important for social scientists to be conscious of the social conditions of our profession. In that way we are likely to be better equipped to meet the changing demands upon us, for instance the need to argue for the methodological strategies we employ and the way we interpret our data. On the one hand, we need to retain a sense of integrity about the claims we make for our research evidence while, on the other, we need to take part in a dialogue with the funders and users of social research. Reflectivity about the position of social scientists and their public role will enable them to retain a critical edge toward research.

Under the present conditions in which social research has an increasingly close link with policy-makers and methodology is assuming higher status in the social sciences, it is more important than ever to emphasize that methods cannot be seen as separate from the 'entire scientific quest' and should include the inspiration of theory. This is the spirit of this book. It is meant to be an aid to researchers in their attempt to perform innovative research. As researchers have always known, one of the keys to good research is to challenge one's own assumptions and to carry out the study in such a way that the data have the possibility of surprising the researcher.

USING THE HANDBOOK

The Handbook is structured around the different phases of the research process: research design, data collection and fieldwork, and the processes of analyzing and interpreting data. First, however, it begins with several chapters of more overarching importance that set out some important current issues and directions in social research: such as the history and present state of social research, the debate about research paradigms, the issue of judging the credibility of different types of social science research, and the importance now being placed upon research ethics.

The contents of the Handbook have several features that are not present in all such texts. As well as ranging widely across the field of social research methodology, we have been selective in including a number of chapters that discuss the combining of qualitative and quantatiative methods and integrating different types of data. The book is also particularly strong in its section on data analysis and includes four chapters on the analysis of quantitative data, five devoted to qualitative data analysis, and three to the integration of data of different types. It also covers the secondary analysis of qualitative and quantitative data with one chapter on meta-analysis, and another on writing up and presentation of social research.

NOTES

1 Originally set up in 1947 with support from the United States and Canada to co-ordinate the Marshall Plan for the reconstruction of Western Europe after World War II, today the OECD consists of 30 member countries sharing a commitment to democratic government and the market economy. It plays a prominent role in fostering good governance in the public service and in corporate activity and helps governments to ensure the responsiveness of key economic areas with sectoral monitoring. By deciphering emerging issues and identifying policies that work, it helps policy-makers adopt strategic

orientations. It is well known for its individual country surveys and reviews.

2 European Union funding requires research that produces 'impacts' and addresses the concerns of the social partners.

3 For this task, there is an international Best Practices database, maintained by the United Nations, UNESCO and non-profit organizations (http://www.bestpractices.org/index.html).

4 For the development of qualitative audience research, see Alasuutari 1999.

REFERENCES

Alastalo, Marja (2005) *Metodisuhdanteiden mahti: Lomaketutkimus suomalaisessa sosiologiassa 1947–2000 [The Power of Methodological Trends: Survey Research in Finnish Sociology 1947–2000]*. Tampere: Vastapaino.

Alasuutari, Pertti (1995) *Researching Culture: Qualitative Method and Cultural Studies*. London: Sage.

Alasuutari, Pertti (1999) 'Three Phases of Reception Studies.' Pp. 1–21 in *Rethinking the Media Audience: The New Agenda*, edited by Alasuutari, Pertti. London: Sage.

Becker, Howard S. (1967) 'Whose Side Are We On?' *Social Problems* 14(3): 239–47.

Becker, Howard S. and Irving Louis Horowitz (1972) 'Radical Politics and Sociological Research: Observations on Methodology and Ideology.' *Americal Journal of Sociology* 78(1): 48–66.

Blumer, Herbert (1969) *Symbolic Interactionism: Perspective and Method*. Berkeley, CA: University of California Press.

Bourdieu, Pierre (1984) *Distinction: A Social Critique of the Judgement of Taste*. London: Routledge & Kegan Paul.

Brannen, Julia (1992) *Mixing Methods: Qualitative and Quantitative Research*. Aldershot: Avebury.

Bryman, Alan (1988) *Quantity and Quality in Social Research*. London: Unwin Hyman.

Clark, Roger (1999) 'Diversity in Sociology: Problem or Solution?' *American Sociologist* 30(3): 22–41.

Clayman, Steven E. and John Heritage (2002) 'Questioning Presidents: Journalistic Deference and Adversarialness in the Press Conferences of U.S. Presidents Eisenhower and Reagan.' *Journal of Communication* 52(4): 749–75.

Coser, L (1975) 'Presidential address: Two methods in search of a substance.' *American Sociological Review* 40(6): 691–700.

Creswell, John W. (2003) *Research Design: Qualitative, Quantitative, and Mixed Methods Approaches*. 2nd ed. London: Sage.

Denzin, Norman K. and Yvonna S. Lincoln (2000) 'Introduction: The Discipline and Practice of Qualitative Research.' Pp. 1–28 in *Handbook of Qualitative Research*, 2nd ed., edited by Denzin, Norman K. and Yvonna S. Lincoln. Thousand Oaks: Sage.

Glaser, Barney G. and Anselm L. Strauss (1967) *The Discovery of Grounded Theory: Strategies for Qualitative Research*. Chicago: Aldine Transaction.

Goldthorpe, John H., David Lockwood, Frank Bechhofer and Jennifer Platt (1968) *The Affluent Worker: Industrial Attitudes and Behaviour*. Cambridge: Cambridge University Press.

Malinowski, Bronislaw (1922) *Argonauts of the Western Pacific*. London: G. Routledge & Sons.

May, Carl (2005) 'Methodological Pluralism, British Sociology and the Evidence-based State: A Reply to Payne et al.' *Sociology* 39(3): 519–28.

Mills, Wright C. (1959) *The Sociological Imagination*. New York: Oxford University Press.

OECD (1993) 'Competition Policy and a Changing Broadcast Industry.'

OECD (1999) 'Regulation and Competition Issues in Broadcasting in the Light of Convergence.'

Payne, Geoff, Malcolm Williams and Suzanne Chamberlain (2004) 'Methodological Pluralism in British Sociology.' *Sociology* 38(1): 153–63.

Platt, Jennifer (2006) 'How Distinctive Are Canadian Research Methods?' *Canadian Review of Sociology & Anthropology* 43(2): 205–31.

Ragin, Charles C. (1987) *The Comparative Method: Moving Beyond Qualitative and Quantitative Strategies*. Berkeley: University of California Press.

Ragin, Charles C. (1994) *Constructing Social Research: The Unity and Diversity of Method*. Thousand Oaks: Pine Forge Press.

Ragin, Charles C. (2000) *Fuzzy-Set Social Science*. Chicago: University of Chicago Press.

Rose, Nikolas (1996) *Inventing Our Selves: Psychology, Power, and Personhood*. Cambridge, England; New York: Cambridge University Press.

Räsänen, Pekka, Jani Erola and Juho Härkönen (2005) 'Teoria ja tutkimus Sosiologia-lehdessä [Theory and research in the Sosiologia journal].' *Sosiologia* 42(4): 309–14.

Silverman, David (1985) *Qualitative Methodology and Sociology: Describing the Social World*. Aldershot: Gower.

Silverman, David (2000) *Doing Qualitative Research: A Practical Handbook*. London: Sage.

Tashakkori, Abbas and Charles Teddlie (2003) *Handbook of Mixed Methods in Social and Behavioral Research*. London: Sage.

Directions in Social Research

What is the state of the art of social research? What are its new directions in terms of methods, credibility, ethical questions, and its relationship to the users of research? As was discussed in the introduction, to understand better the current trends we need to place them in historical and societal context. Social research does not only follow its own logic of scientific progress but rather responds to and at times also influences social change.

Part I of this book discusses the current state of social research and places it in historical context. The chapters approach the present condition of social research from different angles and complement each other in producing a picture of the field, in which some of the earlier controversies or tensions are left behind and new ones emerge.

It is interesting that methodology, as the means of knowing, has become a forum for furious disputes, generally known as the paradigm wars. More generally, there is a tendency in the field of social science for researchers to define themselves and the other in terms of differentness. As Alan Bryman argues in Chapter 2, while these differences are referred to as paradigms or philosophical positions in practice they often represent technical decisions about the use of methods – qualitative or quantitative. In a similar vein, Marja Alastalo points out in Chapter 3 that the paradigm wars between qualitative and quantitative methods have

contributed to an exaggerated distinction between two camps, when in fact social researchers using quantitative methods have always been innovative and pragmatic in applying different approaches. Because of the focus upon differences *between* methodologies, we tend to miss the continuing diversity that exists *within* qualitative and quantitative research. On the other hand, as Bryman (Chapter 2) notes, there is a hierarchy of status given to particular research designs within the quantitative tradition in which experimental methods with their superiority in offering causal explanations are positioned at the top. In contrast, qualitative research is represented by diversity rather than hierarchy. The trend is, however, towards an increase in the explicit use of mixed methods research designs and a growing pragmatism and diversity in the ways in which such researchers view the integration of qualitative and quantitative data.

Why is it, then, that the self-identity of social researchers is caught up in the idea of incommensurable paradigms, which tends to exaggerate differences and downplay diversity and a pragmatic use of methods? One possible explanation is given by Marja Alastalo in Chapter 3, in which she laments the scarcity of empirical research about the history of social research. Instead, method textbooks, for instance, contain histories of methodological development that aim at legitimating the writers' own approaches.

Such descriptions tend to paint a picture of the field in black and white and ignore details that do not fit nicely into stereotypical representations of the different camps. For instance, in many accounts of the history of social research, the contradiction between case study and statistical methods is presented in terms of differences of tradition in the universities of Chicago and Columbia. Such accounts ignore the fact that the Chicago School, often mentioned as the birthplace of case study, also contributed to quantitative social research, and the Columbia School was a dominant force in the development of qualitative research. All in all it is evident that despite the paradigm wars between case study and statistical research, or qualitative and quantitative approaches, in actual practice many social researchers have always been quite flexible in applying different methods.

Currently methodological pluralism is on the rise, and this development calls for a rethinking of the nature of research, both quantitative and qualitative, and of how it can be assessed. Reflecting the exaggerated contrast drawn between qualitative and quantitative methods, it is often suggested that quantitative research has a clear set of assessment criteria, whereas in the case of qualitative inquiry no agreed validity criteria are available. However, Martyn Hammersley argues in Chapter 4 that the general standards in terms of which both the process and products of research should be judged are the same whichever approach is employed. Hammersley stresses that whether we are talking about quantitative or qualitative inquiry, there cannot be tests that *measure* validity; there is substitute for judgement.

In addition to aiming at true findings or conclusions in their inquiries, social researchers also need to think about the questions they pose in their research. From which perspectives are they relevant, and whose interests does the knowledge produced serve? In light of Michel Foucault's (Foucault 1977, 1980a, 1980b) point about the power-knowledge couplet, it is evident that no neutral observer position exists. Instead, forms of knowledge imply and produce forms and relations of power. However, this does not mean that researchers can select a standpoint and an audience of their own choice and only produce knowledge that serves interests of which they approve. First, as Karen Armstrong (Chapter 5) remarks, researchers are dependent on research funding; this affects the topics they study and often reflects the influence of dominant interests in society. Second, the audiences of ethnography with which Armstrong deals are increasingly global. The text may be written from a perspective of a Western academic – 'we' – but as Armstrong points out, the audience may be any number of people with an interest in the place, the topic, or for other reasons. Ethnographers – and other social researchers – are faced, therefore, with the situation in which data are collected from a variety of people who themselves have a variety of interests, while a variety of readers bring their own interests to understanding the text. Thus the work produced will be read for its relevance by readers who assign meaning to it according to their own evaluations.

The observation that social research has an increasingly diverse audience and serves the interests of a diversity of social groups, as reflected in the trend towards participatory methods, is part of the general picture of the changes taking place in the role of social inquiry in advanced capitalist societies. These changes are outlined from different perspectives by Marja Alastalo (Chapter 3), Pekka Sulkunen (Chapter 6) and Ann Nilsen (Chapter 7). As Pekka Sulkunen discusses, there has been a major trend over the last three decades from Mode 1 'pure' science to Mode 2 knowledge production, in which the latter relies on pragmatic criteria of evaluation and is trans-disciplinary (Gibbons et al. 1994).

This change in the role of social science knowledge in society is part of the regime change from Keynesian liberalism to neoliberalism, in which there has been a move from 'resource steering' to 'market steering' within public administration and in the privatization of many public services. The change has affected social research in several ways. On the one hand, structural functionalism and other holistic theories of society, which served the interests of Keynesian-planned economy, have been challenged by constructionist approaches, which direct attention to questions of subjectivity and identity. Because the regulation of human beings is increasingly based on one's own ability to foresee and manage 'choices', there is demand for expertise in subjectivity (Rose 1996: 151). Consequently, qualitative research has gained in momentum from the 1970s onwards. On the other hand, the requirement that public policies and practices are grounded in evidence-based, scientifically validated research has also gained in momentum, since the early 1990s (Dixon-Woods et al. 2006: 27). That is one reason why there is increased demand for quantitative research skills. Under these conditions it is predictable that along with the attitude of methodological pluralism there continues to be tension between realist and constructionist approaches, as discussed by Ann Nilsen in Chapter 7.

Albeit the role of social research in society is changing, its importance is not decreasing. As Celia B. Fisher and Andrea E. Anushko (Chapter 8) argue, increased public recognition of the value of social research has been accompanied by a heightened sensitivity to the obligation to conduct social science responsibly. Insuring ethical competence in social research is a difficult task for social researchers and for institutional review boards. Social scientists are additionally challenged because of the historical biomedical bias in the way in which ethical questions are perceived and handled. More generally they are challenged by increased open access to information (Freedom of Information laws) and increased legal protection of informants.

REFERENCES

Dixon-Woods, Mary, Sheila Bonas, Andrew Booth, et al. (2006) 'How Can Systematic Reviews Incorporate Qualitative Research? A Critical Perspective.' *Qualitative Research* 6(1): 27–44.

Foucault, Michel (1977) *Discipline and Punish: The Birth of the Prison.* London: Penguin Books.

Foucault, Michel (1980a) *The History of Sexuality/Vol. 1. An Introduction.* New York: Vintage Books.

Foucault, Michel (1980b) *Power/Knowledge: Selected Interviews and Other Writings, 1972–1977.* Brighton, Sussex: Harvester Press.

Gibbons, Michael, Camille Limoges, Helga Nowotny, et al. (1994) *The New Production of Knowledge: The Dynamics of Science and Research in Contemporary Societies.* London: Sage.

Rose, Nikolas (1996) *Inventing Our Selves: Psychology, Power, and Personhood.* Cambridge, England; New York: Cambridge University Press.

The End of the Paradigm Wars?

Alan Bryman

INTRODUCTION

The term 'the paradigm wars' is not easy to pin down, in that there is likely to be some debate about which paradigms were involved and the dates signalling the beginning and the end of the conflict (in addition, of course, the matter of whether there really has been a cessation of hostilities). One of the main meanings of the term in social research and kindred fields is the reference to the debates that have raged about the merits and assumptions of quantitative and qualitative research, although alternative terms are sometimes employed to express these contrasting positions. This is certainly the meaning that can be gleaned from such prominent writers as Hammersley (1992) and Oakley (1999). This was also one of the battle lines in an article by Gage (1989) which was one of the earliest uses of the term, although he employed alternative terms to quantitative and qualitative research.

The paradigm wars in this sense centre on the contrasting epistemological and ontological positions that characterize quantitative and qualitative research and their various synonyms. At the level of epistemology, there is the issue of desirability of a natural

scientific programme for social research, as against one that eschews scientific pretensions and the search for general laws and instead emphasizes humans as engaged in constant interpretation of their environments within specific contexts. This contrast is one that is frequently drawn up in terms of a battle between positivist philosophical principles and interpretivist ones, based on general theoretical and methodological stances, such as phenomenology, symbolic interactionism and a *verstehende* approach to social action. At the ontological level, there is a contrast between a belief that there is a social realm waiting to be uncovered by the social researcher and which exists externally to actors and on the other hand a domain that is in a continuous process of creation and recreation by its participants. This contrast is often drawn up in terms of a contrast between objectivist and constructionist accounts of the nature of society. Quantitative research is typically associated with a positivist and objectivist stance, while qualitative research is associated with an interpretivist and constructionist one. However, the often stark contrasts that are sometimes drawn up in accounts of the differences between quantitative and qualitative research possibly exaggerate the differences between them.

It is striking that this contrast is drawn up in predominantly philosophical terms. The presence or absence of quantification, as symbolized by the terms quantitative and qualitative research, is not the issue that is the focus of conflict between the warring parties; rather, quantification and its absence act as ciphers for the underlying philosophical issues. Had the issue that divides the parties simply been a technical matter of the desirability or otherwise of quantification, it is likely (or at least possible) that the differences between the proponents of quantitative and qualitative research would not have been as intractable as they have been. It is the fact that debate about quantitative and qualitative research is to do with such fundamental philosophical matters as how humans and their society should be studied and the very nature of 'the social' that has contributed towards making the paradigm wars so resistant to mediation, although the parties sometimes alternate between philosophical and technical discourses (Bryman, 1984, 1988). Quite why philosophical issues became entwined with matters of research practice to this degree is unclear. One factor may be that drawing on philosophical ideas provided an intellectual rationale and legitimacy to qualitative research as it emerged from the shadows of quantitative research in the 1970s. Indeed, our understanding of quantitative research and its philosophical bases and biases is largely founded on the account of it provided by qualitative researchers since that time (Brannen, 2006). Quantitative researchers tend to be less reflective than qualitative researchers concerning the fundamental nature of their approach.

THE ISSUE OF INCOMPATIBILITY

The association of the two approaches with the idea of paradigms represented an implicit reference to the influential work of the American historian of science Thomas Kuhn (1970). Kuhn memorably argued that a science proceeds through successive scientific revolutions whereby one paradigm of scientific understanding is replaced by another. A paradigm, then, represents a cluster of beliefs about the proper conduct of science. One further important element in Kuhn's argument was that paradigms within a field are incompatible. Their fundamental beliefs cannot be reconciled. There is no common ground between paradigms in terms of their underlying tenets.

One of the over-riding implications of construing quantitative and qualitative research as paradigms in Kuhn's sense, and therefore as incompatible approaches, was that this implied to many commentators that it was not appropriate to combine them in an investigation. In other words, it denied the legitimacy of conducting a research project in a manner that combined, say, a survey with unstructured interviewing or with any other research method associated with qualitative research. While the term 'paradigm wars' may seem a rather dramatic – some might say overly dramatic – way of characterizing the debates that were going on about methodological issues, it does give a sense of the intensity of these debates.

Whether it is justifiable to treat quantitative and qualitative research as paradigms is a separate issue. It is probably the case that it is quite inappropriate to designate them as paradigms because neither of them can be viewed as indicative of the normal science of a discipline, which is how Kuhn employed the term, although it has to be recognized that his use of the term was somewhat slippery. Quantitative and qualitative research are probably closer to being 'pre-paradigms'. As Kuhn noted: 'it remains an open question what parts of social science have yet acquired … paradigms at all' (1970: 15). However, the language of scientific paradigms is deeply ingrained in many discussions of social research methods and even when the term is not used, there is a sense that the 'paradigmatic mentality' (Hammersley, 1984) lies behind those discussions. Moreover, the notion of incommensurability is deeply ingrained so that any recourse to the language of paradigms tends to be associated with a sense of the differentness and incompatibility of approaches.

One of the most influential statements revealing a preoccupation with paradigms is Burrell and Morgan's (1979) account of the ways in which organization theory could be viewed in terms of four distinct paradigms. Two of the paradigms they identified – the functionalist and interpretive paradigms – correspond closely to quantitative and qualitative research. For these authors, the four paradigms 'define four views of the social world based upon different meta-theoretical assumptions with regard to the nature of science and society' (1979: 24) and as such are incompatible.

It is this sense of paradigm incompatibility that lies at the heart of the paradigm wars. The discussions about quantitative and qualitative research tended to be underpinned by a sense of their incompatibility, as long as the debates about them remained at the level of what Burrell and Morgan refer to in the above quotation as 'meta-theoretical assumptions'. In fact, as I noted in my early discussions of these issues, writers on these issues were not consistent about the levels at which they explored quantitative and qualitative research (Bryman, 1984, 1988). While the discussion sometimes operated at an epistemological level, and as such was concerned with 'meta-theoretical assumptions', it also sometimes took place at a technical level. At this latter level, the debate about quantitative and qualitative research was fundamentally concerned with the technical merits and limitations of each of the two approaches and the research methods with which they tend to be associated.

The distinction between epistemological (along with ontological) and technical levels of the debate is crucial from the point of view of the paradigm wars and the prospects for their resolution. At the epistemological and ontological levels there is an incompatibility of fundamental assumptions in terms of what should be regarded as acceptable knowledge and how society and its institutions should be characterized (although some positions may be more determinative with regard to research approach than others). At the technical level, the differences are more to do with the character of the data generated by the research methods associated with quantitative and qualitative approaches and their relevance to different kinds of research questions or roles in the overall research process (Bryman, 2004).

THE RISE OF MIXED METHODS RESEARCH

A crucial stage in the paradigm wars, and more particularly in the production of some respite in hostilities, has been the emergence of mixed methods research. By mixed methods research I am referring to research that combines quantitative and qualitative research. This has become the most common meaning of the term (Tashakkori and Teddlie, 2003). Of course, it is possible to mix quantitative research methods and it is also possible to mix qualitative research methods, so that the mixing is *within* a quantitative or a qualitative strategy. Indeed, each of these is quite a common occurrence, but the term 'mixed methods research' tends to be used to represent the mixing of research methods that cross the quantitative-qualitative divide.

Mixed methods research should not be regarded as a new approach, even though some writers are characterizing it as a third way of conducting social research (e.g. Creswell, 2003). For example, Fine and Elsbach (2000) have noted that some of the early classics in social psychology were notable for their employment of both quantitative and qualitative methods. Such classic studies as *Marienthal* (Jahoda et al., 1972), a study of a community with a high level of unemployment and originally published in German in 1933, is a veritable smorgasbord of data sources, some of which are quantitative and some qualitative.

The early existence of mixed methods studies might seem to be inconsistent with the paradigm wars and their timing, as outlined above. If there are early mixed methods classics such as these, can it make sense to date the paradigm wars from the 1970s and to associate the hostilities with the rise of qualitative research? The answer resides in large part in the rise of quantitative research as the dominant approach to the collection and analysis of data in the years after the Second World War. While this research strategy was especially dominant in North America, it held sway in many other countries as well, such as the UK. Qualitative research continued to enjoy support and to be practised but it was often regarded as unscientific and as merely occupying a preparatory role for the conduct of quantitative social research.

We can see such a perception if we briefly examine the chapter headings of *Methods in Social Research*, a key text published in 1952 by William Goode and Paul Hatt. This book was significant for two reasons. First, it was written by two leading figures in the field. Both authors were distinguished American social researchers who also had made significant contributions to social research methodology and to substantive areas. Second, the broad structure formed a kind of template that many other research methods texts would follow over the succeeding years.

Three things are striking about this chapter layout. First, virtually the first third of the book in terms of the number of chapters concerns issues to do with the scientific method. Not only are there references to science and scientific method but we also see key terms often associated with the approach – references to facts, hypotheses, proof, and testing. These activities were seen as the very stuff of scientific method at the time. Second, most of the following chapters are based on the discussion of methods that are associated with the implementation of the scientific method in social research – questionnaires, interviews, probability ideas and sampling, and scaling. Third, there is just one chapter – Chapter 19 – that includes a discussion of methods that stand outside the mainstream methods with their scientific connotations. This chapter covers the discussion of qualitative research and the examination of single cases. However, it is telling that unlike

other chapters presenting specific methods, this one is about *problems* in qualitative and case analysis. In other words, the chapter is not just an exposition of these methods but a critique of them as well. Even the chapter on observation (Chapter 10) was not concerned with observation of the participant observation kind but that associated with structured observation – a quantitative approach to observation. This brief examination of a key text provides a small insight into the marginal status of qualitative research in the past.

An interesting insight into this neglect of qualitative research during these years is provided by Savage's (2005) examination of the *Affluent Worker* studies conducted in Luton in England in the 1960s (Goldthorpe et al., 1966). In various reports of their findings, the *Affluent Worker* researchers emphasized findings that could be expressed in statistical terms. These were findings that reflected a high level of consistency between coders. As a result, the authors tended to ignore:

> the more qualitative features of the interview and concentrating on those aspects of the respondent's testimony which could be quantified ... In the process, a huge amount of evocative material was left 'on the cutting room floor'. Having gathered rich qualitative material, the researchers then effectively stripped out such materials in favour of more formal analytical strategies when they came to write up their findings. (Savage, 2005: 932)

Savage observes that his re-analysis of the qualitative data did not lead him to cast doubt on the broad conclusions Goldthorpe et al. proffered, such as their significant findings concerning the prevalence of instrumentalism among a broad swathe of the work force. However, there is evidence from the transcripts and the field notes that both the respondents and their interviewers thought in different ways about class from the researchers, especially David Lockwood, who was a member of the team and a prominent theorist of social stratification in the 1960s. It is plausible that had the researchers not been so clearly locked into a quantitative research approach, they might have taken the qualitative nuances in their data more seriously. The general point is that Savage's exercise sheds light on the relatively low esteem in which qualitative research was held at the time.

It is difficult and probably impossible to chart the point that qualitative research came out of the shadows and closer to the mainstream, although it is questionable how far it has entered the mainstream in North America. From 1970 onwards, there is evidence of a growing number of books (Filstead, 1970; Schwartz and Jacobs, 1979). Journals with a qualitative research emphasis began to appear: *Qualitative Sociology* was started in 1978 and *Urban Life and Culture* (later named *Urban Life* and then *Journal of Contemporary Ethnography*) began life in 1972. The reasons probably had a lot to do with a certain amount of disillusionment in some quarters regarding the utility of quantitative research and its outcomes. Critiques of the quantitative research orthodoxy like those written by authors like Cicourel (1964) and Phillips (1971, 1973) probably played a significant role in the rise of qualitative research, although qualitative research itself was not immune to their critical gaze. Further, as previously suggested, the growing awareness of theoretical ideas and philosophical positions that offered an alternative viewpoint to the positivist position that was seen as the motor behind quantitative research probably played a significant role and almost certainly accounts for the way in which quantitative and qualitative research became entangled with philosophical issues. Along with a growing awareness of theoretical ideas and philosophical positions that offered an alternative to positivism, it served to legitimate the use of qualitative methods in the face of the hegemony of quantitative research.

Thus, although there is evidence of earlier generations of researchers combining quantitative and qualitative research, the emergence of the paradigm wars was a product of the way in which philosophical issues became attached to research methods and the domination of social research by quantitative research.

There is little doubt, as previously noted, that there has been an increase in interest in and use of mixed methods research. I conducted a content analysis of articles using a mixed methods approach covering the period 1994–2003. This research is described in Bryman (2006a) but one unreported finding relevant to the present discussion is that if we compare the number of articles which combined quantitative and qualitative research in 2003 with the number in 1994, there was a threefold increase. However, it would be wrong to depict the paradigm wars as having totally come to an end. The growth of mixed methods research may give the impression that there has been an abatement in the hostilities but that is not the case.

THE CONTINUED EXISTENCE OF PARADIGM DISPUTES

In the rest of this chapter, I will draw attention to three areas which suggest that there are lingering signs of paradigm hostilities. In other words, although mixed methods research represents a sign that one of the main cleavages in the paradigm wars has been bridged, this is not to say that paradigm disputes have been totally resolved. First, it is important to appreciate that there are fundamental differences *within* both quantitative and qualitative research. Insofar as quantitative and qualitative research might be described as paradigms, these represent what could be termed 'intra-paradigmatic differences'. Second, there are some fairly fundamental differences among social and other researchers concerning how mixed methods research should be viewed. Third, there are signs in fields that are very adjacent to social research that the dust has not settled on the paradigm wars and that in fact there are occasional paradigm skirmishes. Each of these three areas will form the basis for the remainder of this chapter.

Intra-paradigmatic differences

Quantitative research is sometimes viewed as though it is a monolithic, undifferentiated approach that is completely imbued with positivism. However, there is a growing recognition of a post-positivist position that, while it shares many of positivism's basic tenets, it differs in certain respects. Post-positivism differs in its more accommodating stance towards qualitative data, which are given short shrift in traditional positivist conceptions other than in a very limited role. It typically shares with positivism the view that there is a reality that is independent of and external to the researcher but tends to recognize that reality can only be understood in a limited way because that understanding derives from the researcher's conceptual tools. As such, post-positivism accommodates many of the critiques of the positivist view of science by recognizing that there cannot be theory-neutral observation (Wacquant, 2003).

Further, there are fundamental differences in some areas of social research, such as social psychology, between those who prioritize experiments and those who include non-experimental research methods, such as the sample survey, within their purview. For the former, it is not possible in non-experimental research unambiguously to attribute causality to relationships between variables, whereas the second group accepts that causal impacts can be gleaned through statistical controls. As an example of the former position, an experimentalist writes:

> For strict experimentalists, factors that differentiate participants (e.g., sex, gender, religion, IQ, personality factors), and other factors not under the control of the researcher (e.g., homicide rates in Los Angeles), are not considered independent and thus are not interpreted causally. However, in some research traditions, variables under experimental control sometimes are suggested as causes. ... Owing to the possibility of ... third-variable causes, causal inferences based on correlational studies are best offered tentatively. (Crano, 2004: 484)

It is precisely for this reason, that a hierarchy of research methods is sometimes presented which implies that evidence from experimental studies is or should be at the top after systematic reviews of experiments (Becker and Bryman, 2004: 57). Arguably, the 'research traditions' (to use Crano's term)

associated with experimentalists and non-experimentalists do not warrant the appellation 'paradigms'. On the other hand, they do reflect a fundamental difference in the degree to which a strict positivist position should be followed and what value can and cannot be placed on non-experimental investigations. Such considerations also elide with disciplinary contexts, in that a view like Crano's is more likely to be associated with a discipline like psychology which has a strong inclination towards experiments.

However, there are even more intra-paradigmatic differences within qualitative than within quantitative research. A glance at the latest edition of the *Handbook of Qualitative Research* (Denzin and Lincoln, 2005b) displays an extraordinary and apparently growing diversity of approaches within the qualitative research community. At one point in the volume, Denzin and Lincoln (2005a: 24) outline a table that presents this diversity. They delineate several paradigms (their term) that share three features – relativist ontologies, interpretivism at the epistemological level, and interpretive and naturalistic methods. They then outline several paradigms that share these three criteria but differ in other fundamental ways, including constructivism, feminism, ethnic, Marxist, cultural studies and queer theory.

Other writers have drawn attention to additional basic differences among qualitative researchers. Charmaz (2000, 2005) discusses a basic difference between objectivist and constructivist stances within expositions of and studies using grounded theory. Whereas the former is founded on the assumption that there is an 'external world that can be described, analyzed, explained, and predicted' (2000: 524), a constructivist grounded theory 'recognizes that the viewer creates the data and ensuing analysis through interaction with the viewed' (2000: 523). A further fundamental difference between forms of or approaches to qualitative research centres on the approach to the use of language. Much qualitative research treats language as a mechanism for understanding the social world, so that interviewees' replies are treated as a means of understanding the topics about which they are asked questions. For researchers working within traditions like conversation analysis and discourse analysis, language is a topic in its own right. It is viewed as constitutive of social reality and is a form of action in its own right, not simply a window on action. Given these different stances on the role of language in social research, it is not too fanciful to suggest that they represent paradigmatic differences in the ways in which social reality should be apprehended. For example, the conversation analyst's disinclination to take context, as identified by researchers, into account in examinations of talk is in stark contrast to the significance of context for many qualitative researchers (Schegloff, 1997). For example, Morse (2001) talks about evidence of a degree of 'paradigm asynchronicity' when referring to the rise of a debate within qualitative research implying that approaches like grounded theory and narrative analysis are less rigorous than conversation analysis.

Differences in positions on mixed methods research

Mixed methods research has attracted a variety of positions on its prospects and on what it can and cannot achieve. Some writers have been extremely resistant to the idea that quantitative and qualitative research might be combined. Smith and Heshusius (1986) have provided one of the strongest and clearest statements of such resistance. These authors argue that treating quantitative and qualitative research as compatible and therefore as combinable neglects the fact that they are based on fundamentally different and irreconcilable foundations. Theirs is an example of what I have referred to as the 'paradigm argument', which stresses the differences between quantitative and qualitative research in terms of foundational assumptions about the nature of knowledge rather than in terms of technique (Bryman, 2004). The paradigm argument rests upon another argument which is often employed in such discussions. This is the 'embedded methods'

argument which depicts research methods as associated with a set of epistemological assumptions. A research method is thus a cipher for underlying philosophical ideas. Smith and Heshusius write:

> This disregard of assumptions and preoccupation with techniques have had the effect of transforming qualitative inquiry into a procedural variation of quantitative inquiry. ... That certain individual procedures can be mixed does not mean that there are no differences of consequence. (1986: 8, 9)

This is in reality a re-statement of the bases on which the paradigm wars were waged. It depicts two irreconcilable sides, so that no fraternizing with the enemy is legitimate.

In recent years, this position on mixed methods research has become less frequently voiced and in its place an attitude of pragmatism has permeated the field. Initially, this sense of a pragmatist position was most often in evidence in the more applied fields in the social sciences, such as evaluation research. Indeed, practitioners from such fields have been especially prominent advocates of and writers on mixed methods research (e.g. Greene et al., 1989). Essentially, the pragmatist position either ignores paradigmatic differences between quantitative and qualitative research or recognizes their existence but in the interests of exploring research questions with as many available tools as possible, it shoves them to the side. For example, Maxcy (2003: 79) argues that pragmatism 'seems to have emerged as both a method of inquiry and a device for the settling of battles between research purists and more practical-minded scientists. The point about pragmatism is that in place of an emphasis on philosophical issues and debates that were a feature of the paradigm wars and which were the province of the 'research purists' to which Maxcy refers, issues to do with the mixing of methods become matters of technical decisions about the appropriateness of those methods for answering research questions. Issues to do with the appropriateness of research methods for answering research questions or ensuring continuing funding in the modern competitive academic environment became the criteria for judging the desirability or otherwise of mixing methods, rather than philosophical principles.

In 2003, I interviewed 20 UK social scientists who were known to be mixed methods research practitioners. The details of this research can be found in Bryman (2006b). The pragmatist stance was very much in evidence among these researchers. In the words of one of my interviewees: 'So we've taken that pragmatic decision to do it that way because that'll generate something that either method, standing alone, is not gonna give us' (quoted in Bryman, 2006b: 117). Another referred to the fact that he/she was located in an entrepreneurial research centre where 'there's always been so much more of a pragmatic approach to doing things' (quoted in Bryman, 2006b: 117). On other occasions, it was striking that although the term 'pragmatism' was not employed, it could be clearly discerned in interviewees' replies. One interviewee replied that the crucial issue was:

> attempting to better understand what it is you're trying to understand, and in that way, you then have to ask how appropriate are the sorts of methods I'm using and are they going to give me the information to understand what it is I'm researching? (Quoted in Bryman, 2006b: 117)

Further evidence of the sidelining of philosophical issues among many mixed methods researchers is that the previously mentioned content analysis revealed that only 6 percent of the 232 articles examined referred to epistemological or ontological issues or to paradigm conflicts in the combined use of quantitative and qualitative research (Bryman, 2006a). The coding of this dimension required only a mention of these issues; it was not concerned with the way in which the issue was couched. Thus, the coding was neutral about whether paradigm issues were depicted in articles as impeding or irrelevant to the combination of the mixing of quantitative and qualitative research. This finding provides further suggestion that mixed methods researchers adopt a pragmatic view of the research process that

prioritizes finding out whatever is needed to address the researcher's objectives.

As such, there would seem to be two distinct stances on mixed methods research: one which emphasizes paradigm differences between quantitative and qualitative research and which stresses their incompatibility, and another which emphasizes a pragmatist position of depicting research as using whichever research methods are most appropriate regardless of the supposed epistemological location. These might usefully be labelled the *paradigmatic* and *pragmatic* stances on the prospects of doing mixed methods research, although these do not exhaust the range of possibilities (Greene and Caracelli, 1997).

The growth of mixed methods research has to a significant extent occurred because the pragmatic stance became ascendant in the years after Smith and Heshusius articulated their views, although it is important to appreciate that similar views continued to be expressed (e.g. Buchanan, 1992). However, the very surge of interest in doing mixed methods research has been accompanied by assessments of its prospects and potential. One of the themes that can be discerned among these appraisals is some recourse to paradigmatic arguments. Three examples can be used to illustrate this point. Sale et al. (2002) write that because they represent different paradigms with contrasting epistemological positions, quantitative and qualitative research involve the study of different phenomena and therefore cannot be compared. This means that they cannot be used for exercises like triangulation of findings, but can be employed to study complementary issues. This argument does not represent an outright rejection of mixed methods research at all, but it does imply that there are limits to its use. A second example is Giddings' (2006) suggestion that mixed methods research 'is positivism dressed in drag'. As she puts it: 'mixed methods dwells within positivism; the 'thinking' of positivism continues in the 'thinking' of mixed methods. … [It] rarely reflects a constructionist or subjectivist view of the world' (2006: 200). The point here is very consistent with Smith and Heshusius's concerns in that Giddings is arguing that in the service of mixing methods, qualitative research becomes what they called in the quotation above a 'procedural variation' of quantitative research. The concern here seems to be that by colonizing qualitative research, mixed methods research may marginalize philosophical traditions that have come to the fore in recent years and which have drawn significantly on qualitative methods (e.g. critical approaches, interpretivism). A similar kind of concern has been expressed by Howe (2004) who argues that in mixed methods research, qualitative methods have become adjuncts to quantitative ones. He suggests that such research is founded on the same epistemological principles as quantitative research and argues for mixed methods research that draws explicitly on interpretivism. We see here a clear example of a paradigmatic stance on mixed methods research.

The point of this brief discussion of these views that are critical of the use of mixed methods research is that they imply that paradigmatic views of the approach have not gone into abeyance and indeed may be involved in something of a renaissance in response to its growing prominence. What we see here as well is a suggestion that the paradigm wars are not over or that clashes continue even when a truce has been declared.

Paradigm wars in applied fields

It is very striking that, as previously noted, applied fields like evaluation research and nursing research have been very receptive to mixed methods research, as can be seen when the contents of the *Handbook of Mixed Methods in Social and Behavioral Research* (Tashakkori and Teddlie, 2003) are examined. However, at the same time, some applied fields continue to provide something of a battleground in which clashes akin to the paradigm wars can be encountered.

One of the most prominent forms of what I am suggesting here is the rise of systematic review in areas that overlap with social research, such as health research, education, social policy research, and organization studies. In these fields, systematic review is sometimes promoted as a yardstick for conducting literature reviews and, as previously noted, is often regarded as occupying the top spot in hierarchies of evidence in fields like social policy research (Becker and Bryman, 2004). It has emerged out of medical research, where it has been used to inform evidence-based medical decision-making. In this field, meta-analyses of trials and other kinds of investigation have become gold standards on which important decisions rest. Systematic review draws on and incorporates many of the insights and procedures with which meta-analysis is associated. Indeed, it is to all intents and purposes a form of systematic review.

Systematic review has been defined as: 'a replicable, scientific and transparent process, in other words a detailed technology, that aims to minimize bias through exhaustive literature searches of published and unpublished studies and by providing an audit trail of the reviewer[']s decisions, procedures and conclusions' (Tranfield et al., 2003: 209). Systematic review begins with an explicit statement of the purpose of the review and specifies the criteria by which studies are to be included in the review. The issue of criteria operates on at least two levels. One is that the criteria should specify such things as the limits in terms of geography and time. The other is that the reviewer should specify quality criteria, that is, that only research that meets the pre-set criteria should be included in the review. This has become one of the most contentious areas of systematic review because it has sometimes been viewed as discriminating against the inclusion of qualitative studies within its purview, because they cannot meet the criteria that are specified which presume that the studies derive from quantitative research. Further, qualitative research, until fairly recently, has been viewed as less obviously capable of synthesis than quantitative research. These features have resulted in considerable interest since the late 1990s in the development of quality criteria for qualitative studies to inform their inclusion or exclusion from systematic reviews and of approaches to aggregating qualitative studies. The issue of synthesizing qualitative studies has been explored in terms of both aggregating qualitative studies with quantitative ones and aggregating qualitative studies in domains where most of the literature draws on qualitative evidence.

Two things are relevant to the discussion of the supposed termination of the paradigm wars. One is that the systematic review approach is very much predicated upon principles that can be traced to a quantitative research stance and its association with positivism. These principles include an emphasis on: transparency, replicability, and the application of apparently neutral procedures. These principles can then be deployed against conventional reviews to suggest that they are lacking in rigour and are biased. For example, Tranfield et al. write: 'applying specific principles of systematic review methodology used in the medical sciences to management research will help in counteracting bias by making explicit the values and assumptions underpinning a review' (2003: 208). There is a glimpse in these discussions of the remnants of paradigm war issues or at least the potential for them. For example, Hammersley has argued that systematic review 'assumes the superiority of what … can be referred to as the positivist model of research' (2001: 544). Much like in qualitative research, the reviewer is almost seen as a contaminant whose biases and predilections have to be minimized. Hammersley also observes that evidence is not typically presented to suggest that systematic reviews are superior to non-systematic (increasingly called 'narrative') reviews. Instead, narrative reviews are condemned by innuendo – they are not systematic, they do not use explicit procedures, etc.

Hammersley (2001) also argues that it is not easy to see how qualitative studies fit with a systematic review approach. In fact, one of the most notable aspects of the discussion of systematic reviews in the social sciences since he wrote this article is the growing discussion of ways of making qualitative research amenable to systematic review. As previously noted, this includes developing quality criteria specifically for qualitative studies and mechanisms

for synthesizing such studies. However, at the time of writing there has been no agreement about either of these areas. Instead, there has been a proliferation of attempts to specify quality criteria for qualitative research, both within and beyond the context of systematic review (Bryman, 2006b; Dixon-Woods et al., 2004; Spencer et al., 2003). Also, several approaches to synthesis have been promoted but there is little consensus about which to use or when (Sparkes, 2001). The approaches include: meta-ethnography; content analysis; and critical interpretive synthesis (Dixon-Woods et al., 2006; Mays et al., 2005). In itself, the lack of agreement concerning how qualitative studies can best be incorporated into systematic reviews is not a problem. However, it does make it difficult for qualitative researchers to acquire legitimacy beyond the qualitative research community for their literature reviews. This is not unlike the situation that pertained in the early years of the paradigm wars when, from the point of view of many qualitative researchers, quantitative researchers were perceived as defining what constituted an appropriate approach to the research process.

What is not clear is how far the predilection for systematic reviews will diffuse beyond the applied fields where it has been especially promoted. Systematic review works best when research questions are of the 'what works?' kind but in less applied fields this kind of research question is uncommon or unlikely. The main point that is being registered at this juncture is that the creation of a contrast between systematic and narrative reviews, along with the problems of incorporating qualitative studies into the former, reveals vestiges of issues that were long associated with the paradigm wars.

A further example of a resurgence of paradigm hostilities can be found in educational research. In this field, there has been a recognition in both the USA and the UK that there have been attempts to restrict the acceptability of empirical research to just studies that conform to what is taken to be scientific research. Feuer et al. (2002) note that in the context of educational research in the USA, 'scientifically based research' has become a watchword for what is to be treated by government departments as valid and acceptable knowledge. The authors counted no fewer than 111 references to the term in the No Child Left Behind Act of 2001. Scientifically based research perhaps unsurprisingly rests on the same or at least similar principles to those that have long been held among quantitative researchers in the social sciences. As Hodkinson (2004) notes, this valorization of a set of epistemological principles means that methodological procedures associated with certain research methods come to be seen as the ones most likely to generate acceptable knowledge. A similar kind of stance could be discerned in the UK in the Tooley report (Tooley with Darby, 1998). This report provided a critique of much educational research in the UK largely using principles associated with quantitative research to criticize qualitative studies. These discussions have caused considerable consternation among educational researchers and others working within a qualitative research tradition (e.g. Hodkinson, 2004; Lather, 2004; Ryan and Hood, 2004). The subtext of much of this discussion is to argue against the tendency to attach greater value to a set of methodological principles and to carve out some space for qualitative investigations in the face of a perceived hostility.

As Hammersley has acknowledged, the creation in the education field of an orthodoxy around so-called scientific research principles 'may amount to a new round in the paradigm wars' (2005: 141). However, Hammersley writes that it is doubtful whether this means that a period of paradigm peace has been shattered because there have been other paradigmatic battles. He mentions the battle over postmodernism as one such area. This is an important point. It is easy to view the paradigm wars purely in terms of quantitative and qualitative research and their various synonyms. However, these were never the only ways of conceiving of paradigm conflicts. It is worth recalling that in Burrell and Morgan's (1979) scheme there were four paradigms and only two of these mapped onto the quantitative-qualitative distinction. In many fields, the existence of a critical paradigm, as noted by Denzin and Lincoln (2005b) and mentioned above, has been a constant companion to the quantitative and qualitative ones (see, for example, Deetz, 1996). While critical studies tend to be associated with qualitative approaches, this need not be so (Morrow and Brown, 1994).

CONCLUSION

In this chapter, I have sought to outline the grounds on which it is sometimes claimed that the paradigm wars have come to an end. At a superficial level, there has been something of a lessening of hostilities around the quantitative-qualitative divide. At this level, the rise of mixed methods research and a commitment to pragmatism would seem to act as a high-profile indicator of this détente. However, the evidence that the paradigm wars have come to an end can be countered with some trends that point in the opposite direction. I have mentioned three areas that suggest this: the continued presence of intra-paradigmatic differences; the existence of different stances on mixed methods research; and signs of paradigm wars in applied fields that are adjacent to social research. Thus, even the rise of mixed methods research has not brought the paradigm wars to an end, although it may have lessened the mutual hostility.

The issue then becomes does the continued presence of paradigm divergences matter? Some social scientists may feel uncomfortable about the lack of resolution to some of the main debates in the area of social research methodology. For others, the existence of competing paradigmatic positions is a cause for celebration and offers the opportunity to examine the social world through different lenses. Such a stance may reflect the way in which although postmodernism is often regarded as having lost its potency as a force within social theory, its influence still lingers in diverse ways (Bloland, 2005). It may be that postmodernism's commitment to the co-presence of different ways of viewing the world and the diffusion of constructivist ideas has resulted in a greater tolerance of such paradigm diversity.

ACKNOWLEDGEMENTS

I wish to thank Martyn Hammersley for discussions of some of these issues as well as for his comments on this chapter. His ideas greatly helped to sharpen my thoughts on many of these topics, although I alone am responsible for the deficiencies in this chapter. I also wish to thank the Economic and Social Research Council for funding the research project 'Integrating quantitative and qualitative research: prospects and limits' (Award number H333250003) which made possible the research on which parts of this chapter are based.

REFERENCES

Becker, S. and Bryman, A. 2004. *Understanding Research for Social Policy and Practice*. Bristol: Policy Press.

Bloland, H.G. 2005. 'Whatever happened to postmodernism in higher education?' *Journal of Higher Education* 76: 121–150.

Brannen, J. 2006. 'Mixed Methods Research: A Discussion Paper' *NCRM Methods Review Papers*: ESRC National Centre for Research Methods.

Bryman, A. 1984. 'The debate about quantitative and qualitative research: a question of method or epistemology?' *British Journal of Sociology* 35: 75–92.

Bryman, A. 1988. *Quantity and Quality in Social Research*. London: Unwin Hyman.

Bryman, A. 2004. *Social Research Methods*. Oxford: Oxford University Press.

Bryman, A. 2006a. 'Integrating quantitative and qualitative research: how is it done?' *Qualitative Research* 6: 97–113.

Bryman, A. 2006b. 'Paradigm peace and the implications for quality'. *International Journal of Social Research Methodology* 9: 111–126.

Buchanan, D.R. 1992. 'An uneasy alliance: combining qualitative and quantitative research'. *Health Education Quarterly* 19: 117–135.

Burrell, G. and Morgan, G. 1979. *Sociological Paradigms and Organisational Analysis*. London: Heinemann.

Charmaz, K. 2000. 'Constructivist and objectivist grounded theory' in Denzin, N.K. and Lincoln, Y.S. (eds.) *The Sage Handbook of Qualitative Research*. Thousand Oaks, CA: Sage.

Charmaz, K. 2005. 'Grounded theory in the 21st century' in Denzin, N.K. and Lincoln, Y.S. (eds.) *The Sage Handbook of Qualitative Research*. Thousand Oaks, CA: Sage.

Cicourel, A.V. 1964. *Method and Measurement in Sociology*. New York: Free Press.

Crano, W.D. 2004. 'Independent variable in experimental research' in Lewis-Beck, M.S., Bryman, A. and Liao, T.F. (eds.) *The Sage Encyclopedia of Social Science Research Methods* (Vols. 1–3). Thousand Oaks, CA: Sage, pp. 483–4.

Creswell, J.W. 2003. *Research Design: Qualitative, Quantitative, and Mixed Methods Approaches*. Thousand Oaks, CA: Sage.

Deetz, S. 1996. 'Describing differences in approaches to organizational science: rethinking Burrell and Morgan and their legacy'. *Organization Science* 7: 191–207.

Denzin, N.K. and Lincoln, Y.S. 2005a. 'Introduction: the discipline and practice of qualitative research' in Denzin, N.K. and Lincoln, Y.S. (eds.) *The Sage Handbook of Qualitative Research*. Thousand Oaks, CA: Sage.

Denzin, N.K. and Lincoln, Y.S. 2005b. *The Sage Handbook of Qualitative Research*. Thousand Oaks, CA: Sage.

Dixon-Woods, M., Cavers, D., Agarwal, S., Annandale, E., Arthur, A., Harvey, J., Hsu, R., Katbamna, S., Olsen, R., Smith, L.K. and Sutton, A.J. 2006. 'Conducting a critical interpretive synthesis of the literature on access to healthcare by vulnerable groups'. *BMC Medical Research Methodology* 6: 35.

Dixon-Woods, M., Shaw, R.L., Agarwal, S. and Smith, J.A. 2004. 'The problem of appraising qualitative research'. *Quality and Safety in Health and Social Care* 13: 223–225.

Feuer, M.J., Towne, L. and Shavelson, R.J. 2002. 'Scientific culture and educational research'. *Educational Researcher* 31: 4–14.

Filstead, W.J. 1970. *Qualitative Methodology: First-hand Involvement with the Social World*. Chicago: Markham.

Fine, G.A. and Elsbach, K.D. 2000. 'Ethnography and experiment in social psychological theory building: tactics for integrating qualitative field data with quantitative lab data'. *Journal of Experimental Social Psychology* 36: 51–76.

Gage, N. (1989). 'The paradigm wars and their aftermath: a 'historical' sketch of research on teaching since 1989'. *Educational Researcher* 18: 4–10.

Giddings, L.S. 2006. 'Mixed-methods research: positivism dressed in drag?' *Journal of Research in Nursing* 11: 195–203.

Goldthorpe, J.H., Lockwood, D., Bechhofer, F. and Platt, J. 1966. *The Affluent Worker: Industrial Attitudes and Behaviour.* Cambridge: Cambridge University Press.

Goode, W.J. and Hatt, P.K. 1952. *Methods in Social Research.* New York: McGraw-Hill.

Greene, J.C. and Caracelli, V.J. 1997. 'Defining and describing the paradigm issue in mixed-method evaluation' in Greene, J.C. and Caracelli, V.J. (eds.) *Advances in Mixed-Method Evaluation: The Challenges and Benefits of Integrating Diverse Paradigms.* San Francisco: Jossey-Bass.

Greene, J.C., Caracelli, V.J. and Graham, W.F. 1989. 'Toward a conceptual framework for mixed-method evaluation designs'. *Educational Evaluation and Policy Analysis* 11: 255–274.

Hammersley, M. 1984. 'The paradigmatic mentality: a diagnosis' in Barton, L. and Walker, S. (eds.) *Social Crisis and Educational Research.* London: Croom Helm.

Hammersley, M. 1992. 'The paradigm wars: reports from the front'. *British Journal of Sociology of Education* 13: 131–143.

Hammersley, M. 2001. 'On 'systematic' reviews of research literatures: a 'narrative' response to Evans & Benefield'. *British Educational Research Journal* 27: 543–554.

Hammersley, M. 2005. 'Countering the 'new orthodoxy' in educational research: a response to Phil Hodkinson'. *British Educational Research Journal* 31: 139–155.

Hodkinson, P. 2004. 'Research as a form of work: expertise, community and methodological objectivity'. *British Educational Research Journal* 30: 9–26.

Howe, K.R. 2004. 'A critique of experimentalism'. *Qualitative Inquiry* 10: 42–61.

Jahoda, M., Lazarsfeld, P.F. and Zeisel, H. 1972. *Marienthal: the Sociography of an Unemployed Community.* London: Tavistock.

Kuhn, T.S. 1970. *The Structure of Scientific Revolutions.* Chicago: University of Chicago Press.

Lather, P. 2004. 'Scientific research in education: a critical perspective'. *British Educational Research Journal* 30: 759–772.

Maxcy, S.J. 2003. 'Pragmatic threads in mixed methods research in the social sciences: the search for multiple modes of enquiry and the end of the philosophy of formalism' in Tashakkori, A. and Teddlie, C. (eds.) *Handbook of Mixed Methods in Social and Behavioral Research.* Thousand Oaks, CA: Sage.

Mays, N., Pope, C. and Popay, J. 2005. 'Systematically reviewing qualitative and quantitative evidence to inform management and policy-making in the health field'. *Journal of Health Services Research and Policy* 10: S6–S20.

Morrow, R.A. and Brown, D.D. 1994. *Critical Theory and Methodology.* Thousand Oaks, CA: Sage.

Morse, J.M. 2001. 'A storm in an academic teacup'. *Qualitative Health Research* 11: 587–588.

Oakley, A. 1999. 'Paradigm wars: some thoughts on a personal and public trajectory'. *International Journal of Social Research Methodology* 2: 247–254.

Phillips, D.L. 1971. *Knowledge from What? Theories and Methods in Social Research.* Chicago: Rand McNally.

Phillips, D.L. 1973. *Abandoning Method.* San Francisco: Jossey-Bass.

Ryan, K.E. and Hood, L.K. 2004. 'Guarding the castle and opening the gates'. *Qualitative Inquiry* 10: 79–95.

Sale, J.E.M., Lohfeld, L.H. and Brazil, K. 2002. 'Revisiting the quantitative-qualitative debate: implications for mixed-methods research'. *Quality and Quantity* 36: 43–53.

Savage, M. 2005. 'Working-Class identities in the 1960s: revisiting the Affluent Worker study'. *Sociology* 39: 929–946.

Schegloff, E.A. 1997. 'Whose text? Whose context?' *Discourse and Society* 8: 165–187.

Schwartz, H.D. and Jacobs, J. 1979. *Qualitative Sociology: A Method to the Madness.* New York: Free Press.

Smith, J.K. and Heshusius, L. 1986. 'Closing down the conversation: the end of the quantitative-qualitative debate among educational researchers'. *Educational Researcher* 15: 4–12.

Sparkes, A. 2001. 'Myth 94: qualitative health researchers will agree about validity'. *Qualitative Health Research* 11: 538–552.

Spencer, L., Ritchie, J., Lewis, J. and Dillon, L. 2003. *Quality in Qualitative Evaluation: A Framework for Assessing Research Evidence.* London: Government Chief Social Researcher's Office.

Tashakkori, A. and Teddlie, C. 2003. *Handbook of Mixed Methods in Social and Behavioral Research.* Thousand Oaks, CA: Sage.

Tooley, J. and Darby, D. 1998. *Educational Research: A Critique.* London: Ofsted.

Tranfield, D., Denyer, D. and Smart, P. 2003. 'Towards a methodology for developing evidence-informed management knowledge by systematic review'. *British Journal of Management* 14: 207–222.

Wacquant, L.J.D. 2003. 'Positivism' in Outhwaite, W. (ed.) *The Blackwell Dictionary of Modern Social Thought.* Oxford: Blackwell.

The History of Social Research Methods

Marja Alastalo

Not only theories but also methods change in the course of history and these changes have had consequences for what is known about societies. However, less attention is paid to the history and formation of research methods than to the history of theoretical ideas and the thinking of key scholars (Platt, 1996: 1). There has also been a related tendency to discuss methods and methodological issues on a rather abstract and philosophical level, instead of studying what has actually been done.

In this chapter my aim is to briefly outline the history of social research methods on the basis of earlier accounts of that history. I try to cover the wide-ranging and incoherent histories of both quantitative and qualitative research methods. The focus is unavoidably but regrettably in the Anglo-American traditions. The Anglo-American social research is often a starting point that is taken for granted (Alasuutari, 2004). To compensate the brevity of this text an extensive listing of references in the history of social research methods is provided.

In this chapter social research is understood as empirical research on the society that can also be conducted in other institutions than universities[1]. By the concept of 'method' I refer to techniques of gathering and analyzing data. I also make an analytical distinction between 'a method of data collection' and 'a method of analyzing data', because changes in the methods of data collection and the methods of analysis have not occurred simultaneously. Textbooks also often focus on either specific methods of gathering data (e.g. Gubrium & Holstein, 2002; Kvale, 1996) or methods of analysis (Hardy & Bryman, 2004) and they may contain different sections for each (Denzin & Lincoln, 2000a). Methodology is often understood and defined as a normative attempt to find and discuss 'the good and the bad practices'. However, here methodology is understood as a research performed on research methods. 'Sociologists study man in society; methodologists study the sociologist at work' (see Lazarsfeld, 1993a: 236).

VARIATIONS IN THE HISTORY OF SOCIAL RESEARCH METHODS

The history of social research methods has been told in many ways and with different emphases for different purposes. Basically two types of histories can be found: in addition to actual studies on the history of methods, method textbooks, for instance, contain histories of methodological development that aim at legitimating the writers' own approaches. Research on the history of research methods has been rare compared with the numerous brief accounts in method textbooks.

A comprehensive history of social research methods is still unwritten because social research is fractured and exercised in various disciplines and on all continents. Even the most extensive histories have concentrated on one country and on a certain period of time (e.g. Bulmer, 1985; Kent, 1981; Oberschall, 1965; Platt, 1996, 2006b). In most cases, historical research on methods has focused on a limited period prior to the 1960s, which means that very little research has been conducted on the second half of the twentieth century. According to Jennifer Platt there is a shortage of serious historical work on empirical research and its methods since the 1930s (Platt, 1996: 4).

A great deal of the historical research has focused on the rise of statistical thinking and the formation of survey research. History and formation of qualitative methods is less studied than the history of survey methods, although a number of articles have also been written on the developments in qualitative methods (e.g. Platt, 1983, 1986, 2002; Vidich & Lyman, 1994)[2]. Historical overviews of some quite prominent subfields of qualitative research – such as ethnography and feminist research – still remain unwritten.

The emergence of qualitative research methods is often told in the textbooks on qualitative methods (e.g. Bogdan & Taylor, 1975; Denzin & Lincoln, 2000). The stories of the emergence are sometimes called origin myths. In an origin myth the method at hand is told a glorious history. These origin myths typically cover a long time-span. Thus, for instance qualitative methods are often said to stem from Max Weber's thinking and the Chicago School. This story has been disproved by showing that actually there was no continuity from Weber to the Chicago school (Platt, 1983). Another characteristic feature of an origin myth of qualitative methods is that the writer's own approach is contrasted to the claimed weaknesses of quantitative methods that are criticized for not being able to tackle the current challenges[3].

The histories of social research methods are not written in a vacuum, but always in a specific temporary-spatial context. The concurrent methodological disputes, controversies and conflicts have often guided the choice of focus in the histories of research methods. Despite the good intentions of the author there is always the possibility of a teleological interpretation and overdetermination of the course of history. That is why past events are inevitably seen to lead to the current state of art: 'It is observable that much writing about the history of sociology (…) starts from the moving frontier of contemporary, and works forward to it from ancestors chosen for their perceived contemporary relevance' (Platt, 1996: 3). Another tendency has been to narrate the history of a discipline as a progress narrative, where science is assumed to develop through successive and increasingly comprehensive paradigms (see Alasuutari, 2004)[4].

AN OUTLINE OF THE HISTORY OF SOCIAL RESEARCH METHODS

The roots of social research methods go back to the seventeenth century, when evidence based science started to take shape (see e.g. Oakley, 2000: 73–160). It is often claimed that the rise of capitalism with the processes of urbanization and industrializations gave impetus for empirical social research. A special need for knowledge of society is said to have arisen. 'Almost the very day on which the European feudal order suffered its first political defeat became the birthday of the first sociographic study' (Zeisel, 2002: 100).

In the following, the history of social research will be reviewed from the beginning of the twentieth century to the turn of the millennium. My aim is to trace both the continuities and discontinuities and to present an outline of the history, drawing on earlier research.

The methods of social research before the First World War

A prehistory of qualitative methods has not been traced to the same extent as the prehistory of the survey, and especially the formation of ideas that led to the rise of modern statistics and statistical institutions, which have been carefully studied (Höjer, 2001; Lazarsfeld, 1977; Porter, 1986; Stigler, 1986; Zeisel, 2002). Also the history of empirical social research and the formation of social survey from the end of the nineteenth century to the First World War in particular are outlined in several countries (Abrams, 1981; Converse, 1987, 11–53; Kent, 1981,1985; Marsh, 1982; Oberschall, 1965; Young, 1949). With few exceptions (e.g. Converse, 1987; Young, 1949) these histories discuss the course of events in Europe, as the roots of empirical social research actually lie in Europe, not America:

> All European countries have conducted empirical social research for nearly 200 years. As a matter of fact, many of the techniques which are now considered American in origin were developed in Europe 50 or 100 years ago and then they were exported from the United States after they had been refined and made manageable for use on a mass scale. (Lazarsfeld, 1965: v.)

The pioneer surveys in Britain and Germany dealt with poverty and the material and moral living conditions among working class and agricultural labour (Oberschall, 1965: 3). The aim was to provide information on contemporary social problems. The pioneers of social survey had various backgrounds from non-academics, such as Charles Booth and Seebohm Rowntree, to the classics of sociology such as Max Weber,

who also conducted a considerable amount of empirical research during his career (Lazarsfeld, 1993b: 283–298).

The pioneers did not aim at testing theories but collecting facts and sometimes also changing the state of affairs. At that time even the idea of collecting empirical material on ordinary people for research was novel. The early studies were influenced by various Christian, philanthropic and socialist ideas but also scientific ideas from statistics to national economy. The social reforms suggested by Booth and his successors are often interpreted as early steps taken towards the welfare state. In these interpretations the divergent suggestions – such as the segregation of the casual poor to 'labour colonies' and the loafers to detention centres – are forgotten (Kent, 1985: 55).

The early social survey in America was influenced by the European counterpart and at least one part of it has been defined as a social movement 'dedicated to putting science (…) in the service of social reform' (Converse, 1987: 21). In addition to the social surveys in the United States, election and opinion polls also started to evolve very early (Hoinville, 1985: 106). So, the new ideas of studying and describing the society were applied and advanced by various actors and for various interests.

Neither the methods of data collection nor the methods of analysis in the pioneer surveys meet the definition of the modern survey. The data collected in the early surveys can be considered miscellaneous because structured questionnaires were not yet an established mode of data collection. For example Booth, with his assistants, 'used a variety of methods, consulting existing statistics, conducting interviews with informants, and making countless observations of real conditions' (Converse, 1987: 15). What was characteristic of Booth and also of Max Weber was that they collected the data from informants instead of relying on the poor people themselves. Weber assumed that direct interviewing was impossible with low-income people because they were not able to describe their own situation. Later Weber changed his mind on this and became convinced that also low-income people are able to speak for themselves and thus they can be directly interviewed (Lazarsfeld, 1993: 286, 290).

Catherine Marsh (1985) has noted that even the idea of a respondent who is both a subject of the study and an informant at the same time was slow to develop. Once the ideas of direct data collection and interviewing were invented, researchers started to pay attention also to the questionnaire design and question wording.

These early surveys were not sample surveys, so in this respect too they differed from the modern surveys. Probability sampling was invented in statistics at the turn of the century, but the usefulness of sampling was not found in social research. The pioneers of survey aimed at covering everyone in the area that was chosen. This led to the encyclopaedic endeavours where huge amounts of data were collected. A.L. Bowley discovered the useful properties of probability sampling for social research. He applied probability sampling for the first time in his study of five English towns in 1915.

The methods of analysis were also elementary before the First World War. The data drawn from various sources were usually counted, classified and presented in percentage tables and sometimes in cross-tabulations. Early surveys have been criticized for being unsophisticated as they did not connect with the developments in correlational techniques that were invented by the turn of the century (Selvin, 1985).

According to Catherine Marsh, major advances in the survey technology were already made before the First World War (Marsh, 1982: 27). By major advances Marsh means the idea of probability sampling, the use of structured questionnaires, and the basic tools of statistical analysis such as correlation and regression coefficients. However, these innovations did not spread overnight. It took a long time before these methodological inventions were refined operational and widely accepted as self-evident established practices. Backward technical conditions are probably one explanation for the slow

diffusion of these ideas. For instance, most tabulations were carried out by hand, because machines for sorting and counting punch-cards were rare and mainly used by statistical offices. Random sampling was also technically difficult as it was laborious to compile lists of people suitable for sampling.

The imperfection of the methods used was not the only weakness of the early British social surveys; they were also often both conceptually and theoretically vague. As Raymond Kent has put it:

> Investigators did attempt to explain their findings by looking for causes, but the attempt was not very successful. (…) What they failed to realize was that explanation of the facts could never be based on yet more facts. Such an explanation was always a question of interpretation of the facts, and for that they would have needed the kind of theories being proposed by political economists and academic sociologists of the day. (Kent, 1985: 68.)

In the Continent attempts to combine theory and methods in empirical research were made in the field of sociology. The first method textbook *The Rules of Sociological Method* by Emile Durkheim was published in 1895 in French. Later on Max Weber wrote some methodological texts[5]. Because of the language barrier these texts did not influence the Anglo-American tradition before they were translated into English at the end of the 1930s and 1940s (see Platt, 1996: 69–70, 117–119 on the reception of these classics). In the United States the European tradition was seen through the contemporary frame. For example, Emile Durkheim's *Suicide* was presented as an early example of quantitative reasoning conducted in the Lazarsfeldian style (Selvin, 1958; also Madge, 1963; Riley, 1963).

The interwar period: A tension between case study and statistical method

Most writings on social research methods from the 1920s onwards deal with the development of methods in the United States. According to Jennifer Platt this emphasis can be considered justified because after the First World War American sociology 'became dominant quantitatively and qualitatively' (Platt, 1996: 2). Platt emphasizes the importance of American development by saying that 'the directions in which they (national sociologies, MA) have moved cannot be understood without understanding what happened in America, even if they have often reacted strongly against American influence in general, as well as particular American tendencies' (Platt, 1996: 2). This influence already began during the interwar period, but had the strongest impact after the Second World War.

The studies dealing with the history of social research during the interwar period have concentrated on the Chicago School and also on the research conducted in Columbia University. Otherwise the interwar period has not been paid much attention to (Bulmer, 1984; Harvey, 1987; Platt, 1996: 4)[6]. Despite the scarcity of research on this era, quite remarkable changes happened within both quantitative and qualitative methods. The debate from the 1920s onwards took place between – in terms that were in use then – the case study and statistical method. The frontline between case study and statistical methods is typically drawn between the universities of Chicago and Columbia. The terms 'quantitative' and 'qualitative' were not commonly used at that time, although they have been employed when the developments in the 1920s and 1930s have later been described.

Case study was used to refer to the collection and presentation of detailed, relatively unstructured information from a range of sources. As a scientific enterprise the case study was as much associated with social work as with sociology (Platt, 1992: 19). The concept of case study originates from the case work techniques developed by social workers. The influence of case reports was twofold: first they provided social researchers a model of reporting their fieldwork and second they were a source of data for social researchers. In addition, case study was rooted in the clinical methods of doctors, the methods of historians and anthropologists and qualitative

descriptions provided by basically quantitative researchers such as Le Play (Hammersley, 1989: 93). As a consequence of this diversity there was not any shared understanding of case study as a method (Platt, 1992).

The Chicago School is often mentioned as a birth home of case study and it is strongly identified with the birth of qualitative methods. Following from this emphasis *The Polish Peasant in Europe and America* by Znaniecki and Thomas has been presented as a foremost landmark of the Chicago School. No doubt it deserves to be praised. It moved academic sociology towards the empirical world and 'attempted to integrate theory and data in a way no American study had done before' (Bulmer, 1984: 45). Its importance was already acknowledged in 1937, when members of the American Sociological Association nominated it as the most influential sociological monograph (Hammersley, 1989: 71).

However, the situation in Chicago was more complex in that statistical methods and case study were seen both as complementary and as opposing approaches[7]. There were researchers (such as Ernest W. Burgess) who advocated a research style where after analyzing the symbolic culture and subjective meanings in a single case, a study was continued with statistical methods to search for more general patterns (Bulmer, 1984: 151).

The Chicago School also contributed to quantitative social research, as some prominent figures of survey – for instance William Ogburn, Samuel Stouffer and L.L. Thurnstone – worked there[8]. The technique of mapping was especially elaborated in the field of urban studies. Mapping was a simple quantitative technique where any available data were used to make maps of the city to show population density, the distribution of nationalities, land values, businesses and so on. Ernest Burgess contributed to census statistics by formulating the basic principles of modern census tract statistics and is recognized as the father of the idea. L.L. Thurnstone made advances in developing attitude measurement scales and in the analysis of such data (Bulmer, 1984: 151–89)[9].

The Chicagoans' contributions to statistical methods discussed above shows that it is misleading to equate the Chicago School merely with qualitative methods (see also Platt, 1996: 264–65). Considerable advances in statistical methods were also made outside Chicago during the interwar period. Statistical methods were widely practised by social surveyors, social researchers, pollsters and market researchers; all of them made methodological contributions. At that time these fields were not separate but there was interaction as, for instance, some of the academic social researchers worked in community survey programmes and then moved back to the university[10]. Also, at least some of the academic departments and research institutes appear to have formed multidisciplinary – before the word was invented – environments, where social scientists, statisticians and psychologists met.

In the interwar years the development of sampling techniques continued, as did the discussion on the use and choice of sampling methods which were far from being matters of course. By the end of the 1930s probability sampling became customary. Furthermore, advances were made by Louis Guttman and Rensis Likert in the attitude scaling techniques as they both invented scales which still carry their names (for details see Converse, 1987: 54–76).

Not surprisingly, these advances were not mobilized simultaneously in different disciplines and non-academic environments. They were also slow to spread, which can at least partly be explained by the material prerequisites of the time: 'Tasks now routinely carried out by computer were then done by hand, very laboriously. (…) Quantitative analysis required much more intensive use of manpower than is the case today' (Bulmer, 1984: 169).

Regarding these developments there is one study from Europe: *Marienthal* (Jahoda et al., 2002), published in Austria in 1933, which is worth mentioning. This study which became a classic of social research dealt with unemployment during the depression in an industrial village. The study combined various data types such as life histories, time sheets, school essays, meal records and statistical data. The authors – Marie Jahoda, Paul Lazarsfeld and Hans Zeisel – crystallized the atmosphere of the moment:

> But there is a gap between the bare figures of official statistics and the literary accounts, open as they invariably are to all kinds of accidental impressions. The purpose of our study of the Austrian village, Marienthal, is to bridge this gap. (Jahoda et al., 2002: 1)

The study is said not to be directly influenced by American sociology or German social research (Fleck, 2002: viii). This conclusion is difficult to draw from the book itself because it is unconventional in a sense that there are no references. As an afterword, there is a short history of sociography by Hans Zeisel where he writes about 'the American survey'. This proves that the authors were at least to some extent aware of American social research and the writings of the Chicago School. However, it can be said with certainty that this trio influenced American social research more thoroughly after their immigration to the United States in the 1930s[11].

All in all, it would probably be more apt to refer to both traditions in plural and speak about case studies and statistical methods. This would also direct more attention to the obvious diversity within the traditions, even though a similarity is found between the sides of the controversy as both of them are said to have adhered to the realistic approach (Hammersley, 1989). In America, the controversy between case study and statistical methods faded away before the Second World War (Platt, 1992). The case study vanished for decades and the conceptual repertoire changed so that the concept of 'statistical methods' was replaced by the concept of survey without the epithet 'social'.

From the 1940s to the end of the 1960s: The rise of survey

The Second World War can be considered as a watershed in the sense that almost everything written on social research methods in the after-war period has focused on survey methods from different angles. Like the economic depression of the 1930s in America stimulated social research, the Second World War also fuelled empirical research and especially the diffusion of survey methods.

The two volumes of *The American Soldier* are often recognized as the keystones of modern survey (Stouffer et al., 1949a, 1949b). They belong to the monumental four-volume research entitled *Studies in Social Psychology in World War II*, which were published in 1949–50. The huge volumes consisted of reanalysis and rewriting of the data collected during the wartime by the Research Branch of the Army.

> With data gathered from individuals largely by written questionnaires, Stouffer and his colleagues tried to capture some of the dynamic influence of group membership and context on individual perceptions, attitudes, opinions, morale, adjustment, and behaviours. Though they had few means of measuring group process directly, through tireless replication and imaginative analysis, they were able to cast some light on the interplay between individual and group characteristics. (Converse, 1987: 220)

Most of the reviewers noticed the contributions *American Soldier* made to social research. According to Platt the significance of the study was that it established survey as the leading method of data collection (Converse, 1987: 217–24; Madge, 1963: 287–332; Platt, 1996: 60–61).

If methodological advances were made in empirical research, the logic of survey analysis was recorded and established in method textbooks. Since the 1940s several influential textbooks were published (Lundberg, 1942; Jahoda et al., 1951a,b; Hyman, 1960) and they spread widely outside America[12]. In his textbook *Social Research* (1942) Georg Lundberg formulated the steps to be taken in most advanced level scientific research: 'The working hypothesis; the observation and recording data; the classification and organisation of the data collected; generalisation to a scientific law, applicable to all similar phenomena in the universe studied under given conditions'.

Lundberg considered his model apt to social as well as to natural sciences (Platt, 1996: 78). Afterwards Lundberg has been labelled as an extreme operationalist and his approach has been criticized for being atheoretical (Platt, 1996: 93)[13].

These decades are widely recognized as the heyday of survey. However, surprisingly, some of the best-known method textbooks do not focus in a blinkered way only on the collection of survey data (Jahoda et al., 1953a, 1953b; Riley, 1963; Selltiz et al., 1961; Young, 1949). On the contrary, the use of historical and personal documents, statistical data and field observation are also presented extensively, but when the focus turns to the methods of analysis then most of the pages are reserved to statistical methods. There were also exceptions to the dominance of survey analysis in the 1940s and 50s. For instance William Whyte used participant observation and attempted to systematize the case study method (Platt, 1996: 62–63).

After the war a change happened in social research in relation to theory. The British interwar sociology has been described in this way: 'These individuals who conducted survey before 1939 were not for the most part consciously trying to develop or test sociological theory. Their motives lay elsewhere but the end result of their endeavours was often the formulation of ideas and theories' (Kent, 1985: 52). This statement appears also to be apt of the American counterpart. After the war empirical research was often explicitly grasped as an effort to test a theory. However, a slightly different conception of theory is implicated by Stouffer and Lazarsfeld whose main goal, according to Converse was to keep the scientists shuttling back and forth between theory and data (Converse, 1987: 219).

The controversies within survey are seldom taken into consideration either in origin myths or in the critiques of survey. In reality, in the 1940s and 50s, there were tensions and disagreements on various issues. For example, the usefulness of statistical tests in social sciences was disputed (Morrison & Henkel, 1970) and there was no consensus on whether questionnaires should be based on open-ended or structured questions. Jean M. Converse claims that the controversy ended up in the structured questionnaires' favour, but not by evidence (Converse, 1984, 1987). Many of these controversies can be interpreted as consequences of strong departmental traditions, which also influenced the style of analysis that was preferred (Platt, 1996: 133).

Simultaneously with the rise of popularity also the critique of survey increased. Because of his central position in the field, Paul Lazarsfeld was one of the main targets. 'Great man theories of history may be unfashionable, but they are hard to avoid here; the whole pattern of publication after the war is marked by Lazarsfeld's influence' (Platt, 1996: 61). Altogether his reception, as it has emphasized only his impact on survey methods, is criticized to have been lopsided compared to his contribution (Platt, 1996: 64). It has not been remembered for instance that he insisted that quantitative and qualitative analysis should be combined (Boudon, 1993: 23) and that he promoted research on the history of social research.

Herbert Blumer, the inventor of symbolic interactionism, criticized statistical methods since the end of the 1920s. In the mid 1950s he targeted his critique especially on 'variable sociology' as a method of data collection and analysis and he saw Lazarsfeld as the main proponent of survey research. Blumer defined the process of interpretation as 'the core of human action' and considered variable sociology incapable of catching its essence. Blumer saw the potential of 'variable sociology' as very restricted. He notes that it is applicable to 'those areas of social life and formation that are not mediated by an interpretative process' but gives no examples of what such might be (Blumer, 1956; see also Hammersley, 1989: 113–36.) Despite his searing criticism against survey, Blumer did not suggest an alternative way of doing social research as he conducted very little empirical research himself (Platt, 1996: 120)[14].

In 1959 in *The Sociological Imagination* C. Wright Mills attacked what he called 'abstracted empiricism'. Again Lazarsfeld

was seen as its leading exponent. A few years later in *Method and Measurement* Aaron Cicourel discussed the problems that come up when sociologists try to measure meaningful action. He did not even intend to offer a solution either; if anything he called for clarification of sociological theory (1964: iii). Since the 1950s Howard S. Becker contributed to the use of qualitative methods and especially to participant observation with his studies on collective action: 'I conceive of society as collective action and sociology as the study of the forms of collective action' (Becker, 1970: v). Becker's methodological writings differed from the ones mentioned above as he did not concentrate on dissecting the weaknesses of the survey method. All these researchers prove that besides the mainstream of survey, there were efforts towards more qualitatively orientated methods of social research. Textbooks on qualitative methods did not appear until the end of the 1960s, when *The Discovery of Grounded Theory* was published (Glaser & Strauss, 1967).

In the late 1960s and 70s it was common to claim that there is a connection between functionalism and survey method since they were the leading tendencies in the post-war social research. These views rested on the assumption that '(t)he relationship between method and theory is one of elective affinity, but not symmetrical: theory is more fundamental, and leads to the corresponding method or (...) the epistemological leads to the technical' (Platt, 1996: 106). Later on Jennifer Platt claims that it was more of a coincidence that functionalism and survey dominated at the same time and there is no causal or logical connection between them (Platt, 1996: 113–17; 2006a).

Treating three post-war decades together gives necessarily a rough-grained picture. It does not do justice to the variety of social research during this period. For instance, the year 1960 has sometimes been considered a watershed, because, first, the pioneers, e.g. Lazarsfeld, Stouffer and Likert, were no longer active in survey work and, second, the modern survey had also been established in an institutional sense (Converse, 1987: 381). Anyway in the 1960s survey methods were widely exercised and had such a dominant position in the field that it provoked an increasing amount of criticism.

The 1970s and 1980s: The paradigm war

The beginning of the 1970s can be considered as a turning point, when the unexplored era of social research methods begins. Not much is known about the formation of research methods from 1970 onwards. After the turn of the decade, the discussion on research methods became structured by the quantitative-qualitative distinction. The whole period is known for this debate.

In this debate, strong epistemological assumptions were made about methods. Consequently, they were described to be rooted in contradictory epistemological traditions. Positivism as an epistemological stance was firmly connected to quantitative methods and to survey. Correspondingly the arising qualitative methods were related to the traditions of phenomenology and hermeneutics. Following from these epistemological assumptions quantitative methods, especially survey, and qualitative methods were conceived of as incompatible. In these critiques positivism became a new nickname for survey; such a labelling had not been made by the critics of the 1950s and 60s. At this point the concept of a paradigm was also employed to refer to the opposite nature of the qualitative and quantitative traditions.

Positivism is an example of a label that is given to a tradition from the outside. It is well known that there is no shared understanding of 'positivism', but numerous contradictory ways of using the term. In fact, there have been several distinct debates on social research and positivism in the course of the twentieth century (Bryant, 1985; Halfpenny, 1982; an insightful summary of survey critiques is presented by Marsh, 1982: 48–68).

In the textbooks of qualitative methods the authors' own approach since the 1970s was often justified by contrasting it

to the weaknesses of survey (Bogdan & Taylor, 1975). As a reaction to the mushrooming survey critiques the textbooks of survey methods also started to go through and to reply to these critiques (e.g. De Vaus, 1995: 7–10; Marsh, 1982).

If the tension between the quantitative and qualitative approaches is seen characteristic to this period, that is not all; one should also remember that both approaches have transformed. From the survey textbooks and empirical articles it can be inferred that more complicated methods of multivariate analysis were applied to survey data. In the beginning of the decade new opportunities opened up for quantitative analysis along with the development of computers:

> The development of electronic computers has led to tremendous advances in survey analysis. Not only has it resulted in great ease in tabulation but, more importantly, it has led to the use and development of high-powered multivariate statistical procedures. Before the advent of computers, the enormous amount of computation required for multivariate statistical analyses in large-scale surveys limited the use of these methods drastically. Multivariate methods were employed by only a few survey researchers, and even they had to restrict their analyses severely. (Moser & Kalton, 1986: 432)

Furthermore the methods of survey data collection have been shaped by the evolution of techniques, which for instance led to the emergence of the new forms of computer-assisted interviewing. In addition, more substantial work has been done to improve the questionnaire design (for a summary of this research see Schaeffer & Presser, 2003). What is often forgotten is the importance of data archives especially for the use of survey. Data archives highly increased the availability of survey data and made the secondary analysis attainable.

In a review on the history of qualitative methods the time-span from 1970 to 1986 has been designated as a period of 'blurred genres'. This refers to the situation where 'qualitative researchers had a full complement of paradigms, methods, and strategies to employ in their research'

(Denzin & Lincoln, 2000b: 15). On the list a wide range of theories is mentioned such as symbolic interactionism, ethnomethodology, critical theory, feminism and neo-Marxist theory. Furthermore Denzin and Lincoln remind us that 'diverse ways of collecting and analysing empirical materials were also available, including qualitative interviewing (…) and observational, visual, personal experience, and documentary methods' (Denzin & Lincoln, 2000b: 15). Exceptionally, the authors draw attention to computers that were also beginning to influence the methods of qualitative data analysis. Surprisingly, they do not recognize the impact of new technical devices (such as tape recorders and video cameras) on the methods of data collection[15].

All in all, during these two decades qualitative methods were established in several method textbooks and journals that certainly do not make up a coherent unity. The naturalistic, postpositivistic and constructionist traditions of thinking have been seen as distinctive to qualitative methods of this period. By the 1980s the linguistic turn started to challenge the more naturalistic lines of thinking. The linguistic turn probably also directed the attention from the qualitative-quantitative divide for instance to the controversies within qualitative methods.

There is some indication that at this point the American and European methodological traditions differentiated at the level of empirical research. In America the success story of survey methods continued and there was serious work done to advance the methods of survey research. In Britain, and maybe more generally in Europe, survey methods gained a bad reputation in academic research and the listings of their failings started to spread (see e.g. Marsh, 1982). In the beginning of this period the quantitative and qualitative traditions were defined as incompatible, but as time went by the juxtaposition was questioned and by the end of the 1980s the possibility of mixing the methods was taken under consideration (e.g. Bryman, 1988). For example David Silverman (1985) 'radically' suggested combining quantitative and qualitative analysis of qualitative data.

From the 1990s onwards: Unavoidable fragmentation?

Apparently, the most difficult task for a historian is to try to find current patterns. Every reader can make a trial and try to figure out the essential trends of contemporary social research after reading this handbook. However, two tendencies of the evolution of social research methods since 1990 will be discussed here with some, but not systematically selected evidence. The first one is the fragmentation or diffusion of methodological approaches, and the second one is the increasing tolerance between various methods of analysis and data collection.

I claim that the differentiation of methodological approaches has continued to escalate both within qualitative and quantitative methods since the beginning of the 1990s. There are highly specialized approaches within both traditions – one can specialize in conversation or correspondence analysis, choose to construct a structural equation or multilevel models or end up with one of the many variations of discursive or narrative analysis, just to mention a few alternatives. The increasing number of analytical approaches can partly be seen as a consequence of interaction between different disciplines and traditions. Simultaneously, numerous narrowly focused textbooks and journals have emerged to institutionalize them.

The abundance of different methodological and theoretical approaches or traditions comes out clearly from the periodization of qualitative methods presented by Norman Denzin and Yvonne Lincoln (2000b). They divide the field of qualitative methods since 1986 into four separate, but partly overlapping, phases that relate to successive waves of epistemological theorizing that have ensued a crisis of representation. Each of the 'moments', as they are called, cover only a few years and take different stances to the crisis representation.

The four moments are the crisis of representation, the postmodern period of experimental ethnographic writing, the post-experimental moment, and the future. The crisis of representation is associated with some methodological texts (e.g. Clifford & Marcus, 1986; Turner & Bruner, 1986) that made research and writing more reflexive and conscious of questions of gender, class and race. As the crisis of representation meant that researchers were not any longer seen able to capture the lived experience, it changed the relations of fieldwork, analysis and scientific writing. This led to the search for new models of truth, method and representation. The postmodern period of experimental ethnographic writing struggled with the triple crisis of representation (i.e. crisis of representation, legitimation and praxis). In this moment effort was made to search for more local and small-scale theories instead of grand narratives and writers also looked for new ways of composing ethnography. According to Denzin and Lincoln the post-experimental moment and the future were upon 'us' by the turn of millennium. In the post-experimental phase researchers try 'to connect their writings to the needs of a free democratic society' and to answer to the demands of a moral qualitative social science (Denzin & Lincoln, 2000a, 16–18; 2000b).

Even though this delineation has been criticized (e.g. Alasuutari, 2004), it proves that the field appears quite complex even to the insiders. The complexity of the qualitative methods is also pointed out by Jaber Gubrium and James Holstein (1997). Their overview is illuminating also historically as it goes to the roots of diverse lines of qualitative methods and takes into account the European tradition. What is still missing is a corresponding study of the ramifications of quantitative methods since the 1970s.

Concurrently with this fragmentation, tolerance between different methodological approaches seems to have slightly increased. A growing amount of methodological texts have been published during this period first exploring and pondering the possibility of mixed methods research (usually asking

whether qualitative and quantitative methods can be combined) and later on more confidently proclaiming the use of mixed methods research (Brannen, 1992, 2005; Tashakkori & Teddlie, 1998). The number of textbooks that include chapters on both qualitative and quantitative traditions has recently increased (e.g. Bernard, 2000; May, 2003). Also the new *Journal of Mixed Method Research* is an indicator of this kind of change. In its very first number, the journal presents an outline of a transition in relation to mixed methods research as well as a detailed analysis of various types of multi-methods research (Morgan, 2007). This tendency has been interpreted as a sign of increasing popularity of a more pragmatic approach to research methods (Tashakkori & Teddlie, 1998).

These two tendencies raise two questions. First, the motto of mixed methods approach has proclaimed a 'dictatorship of the research question' in the choice of research methods (Tashakkori & Teddlie, 1998: 20–22), but how can one rationally choose the method in a situation where it is impossible even to master the whole spectrum of alternatives by names? Second, is the suggested tolerance between the various methodological traditions only superficial? Is dialogue and deeper understanding between the diverse lines of thinking on research methods possible[16]?

THE ACTUAL USE OF DIFFERENT METHODS

So far the evolution of social research methods has been the centre of attention and very little has been said about the actual use of research methods. However, there are some empirical studies that have grasped the actual use of different research methods, mainly during the post-war decades. They will be shortly discussed to shed more light on some points of the history that have been dealt with earlier on in this chapter.

These studies are indicative of the proportions of the different research methods at various points in time (Snizek, 1975;

Wells & Picou, 1981; cf. Platt, 1996: 124–25; Bechhofer, 1996; also Platt, 2006b). Most of the studies draw on analyses of journal articles and cover a time-span from the end of the 1930s to the mid 1970s; only one of the studies goes back to the interwar decades.

However, regardless of the differences in the periods and categorizations of the research methods, the main results are parallel. Not surprisingly, the studies show the rise of survey and other methods based on quantification especially in the leading journals of sociology in America during the post-war decades. But they also show that survey methods never – not even in the 1950s and 60s – were the only ones applied. Other apparently more qualitative approaches such as 'observation', 'the interpretative method' and 'the qualitative method' were always used to some extent, although clear trends can be found in popularity of the different methods in America. One of the studies also shows that a small amount of experimental research was published around the Second World War (Wells & Picou, 1981). Because the experimental approach never gained success in social research, it is easily forgotten in method histories that it was regarded a promising – and sometimes even only rigorously scientific – method supported, for example by Samuel Stouffer.

Quite recently, on the basis of studying journal articles and conference abstracts the decline of survey and more sophisticated statistical methods has been shown in Britain (Bechhofer, 1996; Payne et al., 2004). This data on the actual use of methods also provides some evidence for the assumption that social research has gone to different directions in America and Europe.

Given the attention that these studies have directed to the quantitative-qualitative divide, they appear to be motivated by contemporary methodological debates. Yet most of the articles have been descriptive, and attempts to explain the changes in the popularity of particular research methods have been rare. Not even sloppy explanations drawing on the concepts of science studies, like 'paradigm', can be found.

CONCLUSION AND DISCUSSION

Up to now sociologists have scarcely occupied themselves with the task of characterising and defining the method that they apply to the study of social facts. (Durkheim, 1982: 48)

Since Durkheim's time social scientists have spared no effort when writing on research methods. Enormous amounts of methodological texts have been written and also numerous controversies have arisen on methodological issues.

The twentieth century has been a period of great expansion and institutionalization for social research and its methods. To summarize, not only the methods as such but also the relationships of different methods and methodological approaches have changed considerably during the period considered here. There have also been numerous methodological debates both within the quantitative (e.g. on probability sampling, questionnaire construction, statistical testing and causality) and qualitative approaches (Denzin & Lincoln, 2000b). Less attention is often paid to these controversies than to the dispute that is now being referred to as the paradigm war and which has drawn most of the attention.

There are some issues that seem to occur frequently in methodological writing. One is the relationship between theories and methods and another is the relationship of qualitative and quantitative methods (in whatever ways they are called). The first one is here passed by with only wonder as to whether there has been a shift in the interrelations between methods and theories during the past decade or two so that methods are more frequently seen as matters of a technical nature, not as theories of reality in themselves.

The controversy between qualitative and quantitative approaches is the most discussed topic; it has come up frequently with different names (case study vs. statistical method, participant observation vs. survey, qualitative vs. quantitative) (cf. Platt, 1996: 45). The divide has not only split methods textbooks and teaching but also the research on social research methods. There are only very few texts that even try to cover both approaches.

This divide has also drawn attention from the attempts being made to combine the two approaches. The earliest attempts to bridge the gap between qualitative and quantitative methods, that was just about to become important, were made in the 1930s. For instance, Hans Zeisel concluded his history of sociography in a way that still sounds familiar: 'The task of integration lies still ahead'.

An interesting question is why methods, the means of knowing, have become a subject of furious disputes – or wars. Why have just methods been so emotionally loaded for such a long time? Ann Oakley has suggested that the paradigm war is to continue as long as there are communities that take sides (Oakley, 2000: 41–42). Another reason may be that research methods have been connected with theoretical approaches. Similarly, as the rise of survey methods was connected with the rise of structuralist-functionalist approach, the rise of qualitative methods has been concomitant to the expansion of constructionism.

This chapter has largely drawn on studies in the history of methods. From time to time the importance of such a research has been noticed. Paul Lazarsfeld was one of the first people who recognized the need for research on research methods. He even wished that 'perhaps soon a historian of empirical sociology will be an acknowledged specialist of his own, where familiarity with contemporary work, skill in archival inquiry, and creativity in interpretation will be equally required' (Lazarsfeld, 1972: xv).

One can doubt whether the history of methods will ever be a specialist area or even whether it should be one. Yet research on social research methods is needed to prevent the origin myths or other empirically ungrounded narratives from becoming the only versions of the course of history. If any version of history can be considered partial, one can remember Jennifer Platt's comforting words that '(p)robably it is most fruitful to see the attempts to write the history of empirical social research as a necessarily continuing discussion' (Platt, 1996: 4).

ACKNOWLEDGEMENTS

I wish to thank the editors of this book and the anonymous referee for the valuable comments on this chapter. I also wish to thank the Academy of Finland for funding (the project number 114638) which made possible the writing of this chapter.

NOTES

1 Martin Bulmer has discussed the terminological differences between 'social research', 'sociology' and 'social science' in the British context and notes that they are indicative of underlying tensions. According to Bulmer there has been a discontinuity between sociology and empirical research as the latter cannot be treated as a part of the former, because of both intellectual and institutional differences (Bulmer, 1985: 4–5).

2 Here I must remind of the importance of Jennifer Platt's work in this field. She has not only spoken for the empirical research on the methods history, but also conducted a significant amount of research in this area.

3 Similarly, the formation of survey is often told in the method textbooks in a way that can be viewed as an origin myth. An origin myth of survey can begin, first, with the ancient censuses; second, with the history of statistics; or third, from the early (British) social surveys. These histories may contain leaps of hundreds of years and they are often quite brief listings of methodological improvements and the most important empirical studies.

4 Paradoxically researchers of the history of methods have seldom paid any attention to the methods of their own research – neither in the sense of data collection nor analysis – or to methods used in this kind of historical research more generally. However if the methods are explicated, the datasets drawn on typically consist of empirical research (journal articles), method textbooks, interviews and syllabi.

5 Weber's three methodological writings originally published between 1904 and 1917 were translated and edited into English in 1949 under the title *Methodology of the Social Sciences* by Edward A. Shils and Henry A. Finch.

6 The notion of 'school' is discussed e.g. by Bulmer (1984: 2–3) and Platt (1996: 230–37).

7 An anecdote is told that in the 1930s in Chicago 'baseball sides at the annual faculty-student picnic were chosen to represent case study vs statistical method' (Platt, 1992, 19). Martyn Hammersley discusses at length the case study vs statistical method controversy focusing especially on the argument between Herbert Blumer and Georg Lundberg

(Hammersley, 1989: 92–112). He notes that in this debate 'we can see the emergence of many arguments that are used today by the advocates of qualitative and quantitative approaches' (Hammersley, 1989: 111–12).

8 William Ogburn, trained in Columbia, was appointed to Chicago to strengthen the quantitative side of the department of sociology in 1927. That same year the psychologist L.L. Thurnstone was also nominated as associate professor of psychology. Bulmer notes these nominations as signs of the collective commitment to excellence, because they were made despite the diversity in the department's interests (Bulmer, 1984: 170–72, 176). Ogburn was spokesman for the use of statistical methods, as he wrote that 'a body of knowledge ought not to be called science until it can be measured' (Hammersley, 1989: 95).

9 Charles E. Merriam's and Harold F. Gosnell's study *Non-Voting* (1924) has been celebrated because of its complex and innovative research design and data collection which was based on personal interviews as well as written questionnaires. Gosnell is usually given merit for the methodological expertise. Despite its high quality the study is seldom recognized in the histories of survey (Converse, 1987: 79–83; also Bulmer, 1984: 164–69).

10 The career of Samuel Stouffer can be considered as an example of such interaction. He graduated from Chicago, worked in the Research Branch of the US Army, and ended up at Harvard.

11 *Marienthal* was translated into English as late as in 1972, although it was reviewed in various journals in a number of languages at the time of publication (Fleck, 2002).

12 These textbooks spread in several editions. There is even a legend that modern sociology was founded in Norway when during the Second World War Lundberg's *Social Research* was found in the backpack of a member of the resistance movement, who had died in the combat (Eskola, 1992: 260).

13 These characterizations were made by social scientists interviewed by Platt in the beginning of the 1980s, so they do not necessarily correspond to the reception of Lundberg's writing at his own time.

14 Again this may be a statement that is not signed by everyone, e.g. Martin Hammersley has extensively written on Blumer's alternative (1989: 155–220).

15 One can ponder whether it is apt to refer to this as a period of 'blurred genres' or whether the label is due to lack of research on developments in qualitative methods.

16 Frank Bechhofer describes the British situation in the mid 1990s in this way: 'There is no sign of a move away from two empirical cultures within the discipline, one growing the other static, with little communication between them' (Bechhofer, 1996: 588). By 'growing' Bechhofer refers to qualitative and by 'static' to quantitative 'empirical culture'.

REFERENCES

Abrams, Philip (1981) *The Origins of British Sociology: 1834–1914*. Chicago: The University of Chicago Press.

Alasuutari, Pertti (2004) The Globalization of Qualitative Research. In Clive Seale et al. (eds.) *Qualitative Research Practice*. London: Sage, 595–608.

Bechhofer, Frank (1996) Quantitative Research in British Sociology: Has It Changed Since 1981? *Sociology*, 30(3), 583–591.

Becker, Howard S. (1970) *Sociological Work. Method and Substance*. New Brunswick: Transaction Books.

Bernard, H. Russell (2000) *Social Research Methods: Qualitative and Quantitative Approaches*. Thousand Oaks: Sage.

Blumer, Herbert (1956) Sociological Analysis and the 'Variable'. *American Sociological Review*, 21(6), 683–690.

Bogdan, Robert & Taylor, Steven J. (1975) *Introduction to Qualitative Research Methods. A Phenomenological Approach to Social Sciences*. New York: Wiley & Sons.

Boudon, Raymond (1993) Introduction. In Teoksessa Boudon, Raymond (ed.) *Paul F. Lazarsfeld. On Social Research and Its Language*. Chicago: University of Chicago Press, 1–29.

Brannen, Julia (ed.) (1992) *Mixing Methods:Qualitative and Quantitative Research*. Aldershot: Avebury.

Brannen, Julia (2005) Mixing Methods: The Entry of Qualitative and Quantitative Approaches into the Research Process. *International Journal of Social Research Methodology*, 8(3), 173–184.

Bryant, Christopher G.A. (1985) *Positivism in Social Theory and Research*. New York: St. Martin's Press.

Bryman, Alan (1988) *Quality and Quantity in Social Research*. Unwin Hyman, London.

Bulmer, Martin (1984) *The Chicago School. Institutionalization, Diversity, and the Rise of Sociological Research*. Chicago: The University of Chicago Press.

Bulmer, Martin (ed.) (1985) *Essays on the History of British Sociological Research*. Cambridge: Cambridge University Press.

Cicourel, Aaron (1964) *Method and Measurement*. New York: The Free Press.

Clifford, James & Marcus, George E. (eds.) (1986) *Writing Culture: The Poetics and Politics of Ethnography*. Berkeley: University of California Press.

Converse, Jean M. (1984) Strong Arguments and Weak Evidence: The Open/Closed Questioning Controversy of the 1940s. *Public Opinion Quarterly*, 48(1B), 267–282.

Converse, Jean M. (1987) *Survey Research in the United States.Roots and Emergence 1890–1960*. Berkeley: University of California Press.

Denzin, Norman K. & Lincoln, Yvonna S. (eds.) (2000a) *Handbook of Qualitative Research* (2nd edn). Thousand Oaks: Sage (1st edn 1994).

Denzin, Norman K. & Lincoln, Yvonna S. (2000b) Introduction. The Discipline and Practice of Qualitative Research. In Norman K. Denzin & Yvonna S. Lincoln (eds.) *Handbook of Qualitative Research* (2nd edn). Thousand Oaks: Sage, 1–28.

De Vaus, D.A. (1995) *Surveys in Social Research* (4th edn). London: Routledge.

Devine, F. & Heath, S. (1999)*Sociological Research Methods in Context.* Houndmills: Palgrave.

Durkheim, Emile (1982) *The Rules of Sociological-Method and Selected Texts on Sociology and Its Method.* London: The Macmillan Press Ltd.

Eskola, Antti (1992) Sosiologian uudistuminen 1950-luvulla. In Alapuro, Risto, Alestalo, Matti & Haavio-Mannila, Elina (eds.) *Suomalaisen sosiologian historia.* Porvoo: WSOY, 241–285.

Fleck, Christian (2002) Introduction to the Transaction Edition. In Marie Jahoda, Paul Lazarsfeld & Hans Zeisel (eds.) *Marienthal.The Sociography of an Unemployed Community.* New Brunswick: Transaction Publishers, vii–xxx.

Glaser & Strauss, Anthony (1967) *The Discovery of Grounded Theory. Strategies for Qualitative Research.* New York: Aldine.

Gubrium, Jaber F. & Holstein, James A. (1997) *The New Language of Qualitative Method.* New York: Oxford University Press.

Gubrium, Jaber F. & Holstein, James A. (eds.) (2002) *Handbook of Interview Research: Context and Method.* Thousand Oaks: Sage.

Halfpenny, Peter (1982) *Positivism and Sociology: Explaining Social Life.* London: Allen & Unwin.

Hammersley, Martin (1989) *The Dilemma of Qualitative Method.Herbert Blumer and the Chicago Tradition.* London: Routledge.

Hardy, Melissa & Bryman, Alan (eds.) (2004) *Handbook of Data Analysis.* Thousand Oaks: Sage.

Harvey, Lee (1987) *The Myths of the Chicago School of Sociology.* Aldershot: Avebury.

Hoinville, Gerald (1985) Methodological Research on Sample Surveys: a Review of Developments in Britain. In Martin Bulmer (ed.) *Essays on the History of British Sociological Research.* Cambridge: Cambridge University Press, 101–120.

Hyman, Herbert H. (1960) *Survey Design and Analysis. Principles, Cases and Procedures.* Third Printing. Glencoe: The Free Press (Orig. 1955).

Höjer, Henrik (2001) *Svenska siffror: nationell integration och identifikationgenom statistic 1800–1870.* Hedemora: Gidlunds.

Jahoda, Maria, Deutsch, Morton & Cook, Stuart W. (1953a) *Research Methods in Social Relations with Especial Reference to Prejudice. Part I: Basic Processes.* New York: Dryden Press.

Jahoda, Maria, Deutsch, Morton & Cook, Stuart W. (1953b) *Research Methods in Social Relations with Especial Reference to Prejudice. Part II: Selected Techniques.* New York: Dryden Press.

Jahoda, Marie, Lazarsfeld, Paul & Zeisel, Hans (2002) *Marienthal.The Sociography of an Unemployed Community.* New Brunswick: Transaction Publishers (Orig. 1933).

Kent, Raymond (1981) *The History of British Empirical Sociology.* Aldershot: Gower.

Kent, Raymond (1985) The Emergence of the Sociological Survey, 1887–1939. In Martin Bulmer (ed.) *Essays on the History of British Sociological Research.* Cambridge: Cambridge University Press, 52–69.

Kvale, Steinar (1996) *InterViews. An Introduction to Qualitative Research Interviewing.* Thousand Oaks: Sage Publications.

Lazarsfeld, Paul F. (1965) Preface. In Oberschall, Anthony (ed.) *Empirical Social Research in Germany 1848–1914.* Paris: Mouton & Co, v–viii.

Lazarsfeld, Paul F. (1972) Foreword. In Teoksessa Oberschall, Anthony (ed.) *The Establishment of Empirical Sociology. Studies in Continuity, Discontinuity, and Institutionalization.* New York: Harper & Row, vi–xvi.

Lazarsfeld, Paul F. (1977) Notes on the History of Quantification in Sociology – Trends, Sources and Problems. In Kendall, Maurice & Plackett, R.L. (eds.) *Studies in the History of Statistics and Probability vol. II.* London: Charles Griffin & Company limited, 213–270 (Orig. 1961).

Lazarsfeld, Paul (1993a) Methodological Problems in Empirical Social Research. In Boudon, Raymond (ed.) *On Social Research and Its Language.* Chicago: University of Chicago Press, 236–254.

Lazarsfeld, Paul (1993b) Max Weber and Empirical Social Research. In Boudon, Raymond (ed.) *On Social Research and Its Language.*Chicago: University of Chicago Press, 283–298.

Lundberg, George (1942) *Social Research: A Study in Methods of Gathering Data.* New York: Green & co.

Madge, John (1963) *The Origins of Scientific Sociology.* London: Tavistock publications.

Marsh, Catherine (1982) *The Survey Method. The Contribution of Surveys to Sociological Explanation.* London: George Allen & Unwin.

Marsh, Catherine (1985) Informants, Respondents and Citizens. In Martin Bulmer (ed.) *Essays on the History of British Sociological Research.* London: Cambridge University Press, 206–227.

May, Tim (2003) *Social Research: Issues, Methods and Process* (3rd edn). Buckingham: Open University Press.

Mills, Wright C. (1977) *The Sociological Imagination*. Harmondsworth: Pelican Book (Orig. in 1959).

Morgan, David L. (2007) Paradigm Lost and Pragmatism Regained. Methodological Implications of Combining Qualitative and Quantitative Methods. *Journal of Mixed Methods Research*, 1(1), 48–76.

Morrison, Denton & Henkel, Ramon E. (eds.) (1970) *The SignificanceTest Controversy – A Reader*. Chicago: Aldine.

Moser, Claus & Kalton, Graham (1986) *Survey Methods in Social Investigation* (2nd edn). Aldershot: Gover.

Oakley, Ann (2000). *Experiments in Knowing.Gender and Method in Social Sciences*. Cambridge: Polity Press.

Oberschall, Anthony (1965) *Empirical Social Research in Germany 1848–1914*. Paris: Mouton & Co.

Payne, G., Williams, M. & Chamberlain, S. (2004). Methodological Pluralism in British Sociology. *Sociology*, 38(1), 153–163.

Platt, Jennifer (1983) Weber's *verstehen* and the History of Qualitative Research: The Missing Link. *British Journal of Sociology*, 26(3), 448–466.

Platt, Jennifer (1986) Qualitative Research for the State. *Quarterly Journal of Social Affairs*, 2, 87–108.

Platt, J. (1992) 'Case Study' In American Methodological Thought. *Current Sociology*, 40(1), 17–48.

Platt, Jennifer (1996) *A History of Sociological Research Methods in America 1920–1960*. Cambridge: Cambridge University Press.

Platt, Jennifer (2002) The History of Interview. In Gubrium, Jaber F. & Holstein, James A. (eds.) *Handbook of Interview Research: Context and Method*. Thousand Oaks: Sage, 33–53.

Platt, Jennifer (2006a) Functionalism and the Survey: The Relation of Theory and Method. In Williams, M. (ed.) *Philosophical Foundations of Social Research Methods*. London: Sage, 217–251 (orig. in *Sociological Review*, 34(3), 501–536).

Platt, Jennifer (2006b) How Distinctive are Canadian Research Methods? *Canadian Review of Sociology and Social Anthropology*, 43(2), 205–231.

Porter, Theodore M. (1986) *The Rise of Statistical Thinking 1820–1900*. Princeton: Princeton University Press.

Riley, Matilda White (1963) *Sociological Research I. A Case Approach*. New York: Harcourt, Brace & World, Inc.

Schaeffer, Nora Cate & Presser, Stanley (2003) The Science of Asking Questions. *Annual Review of Sociology*, 29, 65–88.

Selltiz, Claire, Jahoda, Marie, Deutsch, Morton & Cook, Stuart W. (1961) *Research Methods in Social Relations*. New York: Holt, Rinehart and Winston.

Selvin, Hanan C. (1958) Durkheim's *Suicide* and Problems of Empirical Research. *American Journal of Sociology*, 63(6), 607–619.

Selvin, Hanan C. (1985) Durkheim, Booth and Yule: the Non-diffusion of an Intellectual Innovation. In Martin Bulmer (ed.) *Essays on the History of British Sociological Research*. Cambridge: Cambridge University Press, 70–82.

Silverman, David (1985) *Qualitative Methodology and Sociology. Describing the Social World*. Aldershot: Gover.

Snizek, W.E. (1975) The Relationship between Theory and Research: A Study in the Sociology of Sociology. *Sociological Quarterly*, 16, 415–428.

Stigler, Stephen M. (1986) *The History of Statistics: The Measurement of Uncertainty Before 1900*. Cambridge: Harvard University Press.

Stouffer, S.A., Suchman, E.A., de Vinney, L.C., Star, S.A. & Williams, R.M. (1949a) *The American Soldier vol. I. Adjustment during Army Life*. Princeton: Princeton University Press.

Stouffer, S.A., Suchman, E.A., de Vinney, L.C., Star, S.A. & Williams, R.M. (1949b) *The American Soldier vol. II. Combat and Its Aftermath*. Princeton: Princeton University Press.

Tashakkori, Abbas & Teddlie, Charles (1998) *Mixed Methodology. Combining Qualitative and Quantitative Approaches*. Sage: Thousands Oaks.

Turner, Victor W. & Bruner, Edward (eds.) (1986) *The Anthropology of Experience*. Urbana: University of Illinois Press.

Vidich, Arthur J. & Lyman, Stanford M. (1994) Qualitative Methods: Their History in Sociology and Social Anthropology. In Norman K. Denzin & Yvonna S. Lincoln (eds.) *Handbook of Qualitative Research* (2nd edn). Thousand Oaks: Sage, 23–59 (2nd edn 2000).

Wells, R.H. & Picou, J.S. (1981) *American Sociology: Theoretical and Methodological Structures*. Washington DC: University Press of America.

Young, Pauline V. (1949) *Scientific Social Surveys and Research. An Introduction to the Background, Content, Methods, and Analysis of Social Studies* (2nd edn). New York: Prentice-Hall (1st edn 1939).

Zeisel, Hans (2002 [1930]) Afterword. Toward a History of Sociography. In Jahoda, Marie, Lazarsfeld, Paul & Zeisel, Hans (eds.) *Marienthal. The Sociography of an Unemployed Community*. New Brunswick: Transaction Publishers, 99–125 (orig. 1933).

Assessing Validity in Social Research

Martyn Hammersley

Much discussion of how validity should be assessed in social research has been organized around the distinction between quantitative and qualitative approaches, with arguments over whether or not the same criteria apply to both. It is often suggested that quantitative inquiry has a clear set of assessment criteria, so that readers (even those who are not researchers) can judge the quality of such research relatively easily, whereas in the case of qualitative inquiry no agreed or easily applicable set of criteria is available. While this is often presented as a problem, some qualitative researchers deny the possibility or even the desirability of assessment criteria.

In this chapter I will argue that this contrast between the two approaches is, to a large extent, illusory; that it relies on misleading conceptions of the nature of research, both quantitative and qualitative, and of how it can be assessed. I will suggest that the general standards in terms of which both the process and products of research should be judged are the same whichever approach is employed. Furthermore, when it comes to more detailed criteria of assessment these need to vary according to the nature of the conclusions presented, and the characteristics of the specific methods of data collection and analysis used. In the course of the chapter, I will raise questions about both older positivist conceptions of quantitative research, and of how it should be assessed, and those more recent relativist and postmodernist ideas, quite influential among qualitative researchers, which reject epistemic criteria of assessment, and perhaps even all criteria.

In the first section, I will examine the criteria normally associated with quantitative work. This discussion will raise several questions. One of these concerns *what* is being assessed, and the need to make some differentiation here, notably between assessing findings and assessing the value of particular research techniques. Another issue relates to what is meant by the term 'criterion' and what role criteria play in the process of assessment. In the second half of the chapter I will examine some of the arguments in the qualitative research tradition about how studies ought to be evaluated.

QUANTITATIVE CRITERIA?

If we look at the methodological literature dealing with quantitative research, and indeed at many treatments of the issue of validity in relation to social inquiry more generally, several standard criteria are usually mentioned. These concern three main aspects of the process of research: measurement, generalization, and the control of variables.

In relation to measurement, the requirements usually discussed are that measures must be reliable and valid. Reliability is generally taken to concern the extent to which the same measurement technique or strategy produces the same result on different occasions, for example when used by different researchers. This is held to be important because if researchers are using standard measurement devices, such as attitude scales or observation schedules, they need to be sure that these give consistent results. Furthermore, it is often argued that any measure that is not reliable cannot be valid, on the grounds that, if its results are inconsistent, the measurements it produces cannot be consistently valid. As this argument indicates, validity of measurement is seen as important by quantitative researchers, even though it is usually taken to be more difficult to assess than reliability. Indeed, given the link between the two criteria, reliability tests are often treated as one important means for assessing validity. Nevertheless, separate validity tests may also be used, for instance checking whether different ways of measuring the same property produce the same findings, or whether what is found when measuring the property in a particular set of objects is consistent with the subsequent behaviour of those objects. These tests are often described as assessing different kinds of validity, in this case convergent and predictive validity[1].

On the basis of this initial discussion, we can identify a first key question to be applied in

assessing the validity of quantitative research: were the measurement procedures reliable and valid? And it is often suggested that, in evaluating a study, the way to go about answering this question is to ask whether reliability and validity tests were carried out, and whether the scores on these tests were high enough to warrant a positive evaluation. This, then, is one set of commonly used criteria.

The second key area to which well-known criteria of assessment relate concerns the generalizability of the findings. This is an especially prominent issue in the context of survey research, where data from a sample of cases are often used as a basis for drawing conclusions about the characteristics of a larger population. In this context, the issue is relatively clear: are the statements made about the sample also true of the population? Short of investigating the whole population, which would render sampling pointless, there is no direct means of answering this question. However, statistical sampling theory provides a basis for coming to a reasonable conclusion about the likely validity of inferences from sample to population. If the sample was sufficiently large, and was drawn from the population on the basis of some kind of probability sampling, then a statistical measure can be provided of how confident we can be that the findings are generalizable. The criteria involved here then, are the sampling procedures employed and the results of a statistical significance test[2].

The final area where quantitative criteria are well established concerns whether variables have been controlled in a sufficiently effective manner to allow sound conclusions to be drawn about the validity of causal or predictive hypotheses; this sometimes being referred to as causal validity. Experimental designs employing random allocation of subjects to treatment and control groups are often seen as the strongest means of producing valid conclusions in this sense. However, statistical control, through multivariate analysis, is an alternative strategy that is employed in much social survey research. Moreover, with both forms of control, statistical tests are often applied to assess the chances that the results were a product of random error rather than of the independent variable. Here, then, the criteria concern whether physical or statistical control was applied, and the confidence we can have in ruling out random error.

Undoubtedly the most influential account of evaluative criteria for quantitative research that draws together these three different aspects into a single framework is that developed by Campbell and his colleagues (Campbell 1957; Campbell and Stanley 1963; Cook and Campbell 1979). This distinguishes between internal and external validity, where the former is usually seen as incorporating measurement and causal validity, while external validity refers to generalizability[3]. Campbell et al.'s scheme was originally developed for application to quasi-experimental research, but it has subsequently been applied much more widely.

There is no doubt that these three issues are potentially key aspects of any assessment of validity in quantitative research, and perhaps in social inquiry more generally. However, there are a number of important qualifications that need to be made.

First, we must be clear about what we are assessing. There is confusion in much discussion of measurement between a concern with assessing the findings of the measurement process and assessing the measurement technique or strategy employed. Validity relates only to the former, while reliability concerns the latter. We can talk about whether the findings are or are not valid, but it makes no sense to describe a measurement technique as valid or invalid, unless we are adopting a different sense of the term 'validity', using it to mean 'appropriately applied'. It is, of course, true that we should be interested in whether a measurement technique consistently produces accurate results. In fact, as is sometimes done, there would be good reason to define 'reliability' of measurement techniques as the capacity to produce consistently valid measurements[4].

Second, it is misleading to believe that there can be different *types* of validity. Validity is singular not multiple; it concerns whether the findings or conclusions of a study are true. The three aspects discussed above refer to areas where error can undermine research conclusions. For example, what was referred to as 'causal validity' is concerned with threats to valid inferences about causality arising from confounding factors. Furthermore, the distinction between types of measurement validity actually refers to ways in which we can assess whether our measurements are accurate. There is also the problem that the distinction between internal and external validity obscures the fact that 'causal validity' implies a general tendency, for the cause to produce the effect, that operates beyond the cases studied (Hammersley 1991). As a result, internal validity is not distinct from external validity.

Rather than differentiating types of validity, we need to distinguish between the different sorts of knowledge claim that studies produce. There are three of these: descriptive, explanatory, and theoretical[5]. Recognizing the particular sort of conclusion a study makes is important because each of the three types of knowledge claim has different requirements, and therefore involves somewhat different threats to validity. This is true even though there is some overlap caused by the way that these types of knowledge are interrelated: descriptive claims are required as subordinate elements in the other two kinds; and explanations always depend upon implicit or explicit theoretical knowledge[6].

In assessing the validity of descriptions, we must be concerned with whether the features ascribed to the phenomena being described are actually held by those phenomena, and perhaps also with whether they are possessed to the degrees indicated. Also of importance may be whether any specification of changes in those features over time, or any account of sequences of events, are accurate.

In assessing the validity of explanations we first of all need to consider the validity of the subordinate descriptions: those referring both to what is being explained and to the explanatory forces that are cited. Second, we must assess the validity of the theoretical principle that provides the link between proposed cause(s) and effect(s). Third, we need to consider whether that theoretical principle identifies what was the key causal process in the context being investigated.

Finally, in judging the validity of theoretical conclusions, we will also need to assess the validity of any descriptive claims on which they rely, both about the causal mechanism involved and about what it produces. In addition, we will need to find some means of comparing situations in which it does and does not operate, and of discounting other factors that could generate the same outcome.

There is also variation in the threats to validity operating on different sources of evidence, and this variation must also be taken into account in assessing knowledge claims. What is involved here is partly that some methods have distinctive validity threats associated with them. For example, if we rely on the accounts of informants about some set of events, then we must recognize that there are distinctive potential biases operating on these accounts, in addition to those operating on researchers' interpretations, for example, to do with whether the informant is able or willing to provide accurate information in relevant respects. By contrast, in the case of direct observation by a researcher only one of these two sources of bias operates. (At the same time, it is perhaps worth underlining that closely associated with many sources of bias are sources of potential insight, for instance, informants may be able to recognize what is going on in ways that are less easily available to an external researcher.)

Equally important is the fact that particular threats to validity vary in degree across methods. Reactivity is little or no threat with some sources of data, such as the use of extant documents or covert observation of public behaviour. By contrast, it is a very significant danger in the case of laboratory experiments, where subjects' actions may be shaped by the experimental setup and by the appearance and behaviour of the experimenter. At the same time, we should note that what is threatened by reactivity, the extent to which we can safely generalize our findings from the situations studied to other relevant situations in the

social world, is an issue that is relevant to all kinds of research, even those that manage to achieve low reactivity (Hammersley and Atkinson 2007: chapter 1).

In summary, then, validity is a crucial standard by which the findings of research should be judged, and it is a single standard that applies across the board. However, what is required for assessing likely validity varies according to the nature of the findings, and also according to the research methods employed. From this point of view, the argument that qualitative and quantitative approaches require different assessment criteria is defective both in drawing a distinction where none exists and in obscuring more specific and essential differences (in relation to types of knowledge claim and specific data sources).

Another important point relates to the notion of assessment criteria. There is sometimes a tendency within the literature of quantitative methodology to imply that there are *procedures* which can tell us whether or not, for instance, a measure is valid. Thus, reliability and validity tests are often said to *measure* validity. However, they cannot do that. They can give us evidence on which we can base *judgements* about the likely validity of the findings, but they cannot eliminate the role of judgement. Similarly, the use of experimental control, and random allocation of subjects to treatment and control groups, does not *guarantee* the validity of the findings; nor does the absence of these methods mean that the findings are invalid, or even that the studies concerned provide us with no evidence. In fact, there are usually trade-offs such that any research strategy that is more effective in dealing with one threat to validity generally increases the danger of other validity threats. Furthermore, making sound judgements about validity relies on background knowledge, both about the substantive matters being investigated and also about the sources of data and methods of investigation employed. This means that there will be significant differences between people in how well placed they are to assess the validity of particular sets of research findings effectively. The relevant research community necessarily plays a crucial, but by no means infallible, role here.

For all these reasons, it is misleading to talk about *criteria* of assessment, if by that is meant a universal and rigorous set of procedures that, if applied properly, can in themselves, and with certainty, tell us whether or not the findings of a study are valid. This notion is a mirage. How we assess research findings must vary according to the nature of the knowledge claims being made and the methods employed. Furthermore, this assessment will always be a matter of judgement that relies on background knowledge and skill.

QUALITATIVE CRITERIA?

Not surprisingly, much thinking about the assessment criteria appropriate to qualitative research has taken the quantitative criteria mentioned in the previous section as a key reference point. Some commentators have attempted to translate these criteria into terms that can be applied to qualitative work (see, for example, Goetz and LeCompte 1984). Others have replaced one or more of them by some new criterion, or have added extra ones to the list (see, for example, Lincoln and Guba 1985 and Lather 1986, 1993). Often, additions have been motivated by a belief that research is not just about producing knowledge but should also be directed towards bringing about some improvement in, or radical transformation of, the world. Sometimes, this is linked to the idea that application of knowledge is the primary means of testing its validity, but this argument is not always present. Indeed, increasingly in recent years, among qualitative researchers, there have been challenges to epistemic criteria, with the proposal that these be replaced by practical, ethical, and/or aesthetic considerations (see Smith and Deemer 2000; Smith and Hodkinson 2005).

Of central importance in these developments have been philosophical arguments about foundationalism, as well as political and ethical arguments about the proper purpose of research. Epistemological foundationalism was a strong influence on the development of ideas about criteria of assessment within social science research in the first half of the twentieth century, and it underpins some discussions of the concepts mentioned in the first part of this chapter. Foundationalism claims that what is distinctive about science, what makes the knowledge it produces superior to that available from other sources, is that it can rely on a foundation of absolutely certain data, from which theoretical conclusions can be logically derived and/or against which they can be rigorously tested. Very often, these data are seen as being produced by experimental method, but what is also often stressed is the requirement that the process of inquiry follows an explicit set of procedures that are replicable by others.

However, by the 1950s, most arguments for the existence of an epistemological foundation had been effectively undermined within the philosophy of science (Suppe 1974), though the impact of this on social research was delayed until the following decades. The claim that there could be perceptual data whose validity is simply given, and the idea that any particular set of data will only validate a single theoretical interpretation, were both challenged. Particularly significant was the account of scientific development presented by Thomas Kuhn, in which the older view of science as involving a gradual accumulation of facts on the basis of solid evidence was overturned. In its place, Kuhn presented a picture of recurrent revolutions within scientific fields, in which one framework of presuppositions, or 'paradigm', that had previously guided research was rejected and replaced by a new paradigm that was 'incommensurable' with the old one (Kuhn 1970). In other words, Kuhn emphasized discontinuity, rather than continuity, in the history of science, in the fundamental sense that later paradigms reconceptualized the field of phenomena dealt with by earlier paradigms, in such a manner that even translation from one to the other could be impossible. Rather, what was involved, according to Kuhn, was more like conversion to a new way of looking at the world, or gaining the ability to speak a different language[7].

These developments led the way for some qualitative researchers to argue that older conceptions of validity, and of validity *criteria*, are false or outdated[8]. Many commentators claimed that we must recognize that there are simply different interpretations or constructions of any set of phenomena, with these being incommensurable in Kuhn's sense; they are not open to judgement in terms of a universal set of epistemic criteria. At best, there can only be plural, culturally relative, ways of assessing validity. This argument, variously labelled 'relativism' or 'postmodernism'[9], was reinforced by claims from feminists, anti-racists, and others. They argued that conventional social science simply reproduces the dominant perspectives in society, that it marginalizes other voices that rely on distinctive, and discrepant, epistemological frameworks. From this point of view, the task of social science should be to counter the hegemony of dominant groups and their discourses, and thereby to make way for marginalized discourses to be heard and their distinctive epistemologies to be recognized. In this way, the original conception of epistemic criteria, and perhaps even the very notion of validity or truth, are rejected as ideological and replaced by a political, ethical or aesthetic concern with valuing, appreciating, or treating fairly, multiple conceptions of or discourses about the world.

These critics of assessment criteria claim then, that since there can be no foundation of evidence that is simply given and therefore absolutely certain in validity from which knowledge can be generated, or against which hypotheses can be tested, then all knowledge, in the traditional sense of that word, is impossible. We are, to quote Smith and Hodkinson (2005: 915) 'in the era of relativism'. This means that we must recognize that any claims to knowledge, including those of researchers, can only be valid within a particular framework of assumptions; or within a particular socio-cultural context. And, as already noted, some writers have concluded from this that the main

requirement is to challenge claims to universal knowledge and to celebrate marginalized and transgressive perspectives, perhaps in the name of freedom and democracy. Here, ethics and politics are foregrounded. Along these lines, Denzin and Lincoln argue that the criteria of assessment for qualitative research should be those of a 'moral ethic (which) calls for research rooted in the concepts of care, shared governance, neighbourliness, love and kindness' (Denzin and Lincoln 2005: 911).

Closely related to this line of argument is an insistence on seeing all claims to knowledge as intertwined, if not fused, with attempts to exercise power. Thus, the work of social scientists has often come to be analyzed both in terms of how it may be motivated by their own interests and/or in terms of the wider social functions it is said to serve, in particular the reproduction of dominant social structures. In the context of methodology, this has involved an emphasis on the senses in which researchers exercise power over the people they study; and this has led to calls for collaborative or practitioner research, in which decisions about who or what to research, as well as about research method, are made jointly with people rather than their being simply the focus of study. Indeed, some have argued that outside researchers should do no more than serve as consultants helping people to carry out research for themselves. These ideas have been developed within the action research movement, among feminists, and are also currently very influential in the field of research concerned with the lives of children and young people (see Reason and Bradbury 2001 and MacNaughton and Smith 2005). Almost inevitably, this breaking down of the barriers between researchers and lay people, designed to undermine any claim to authority based on expertise, leads to epistemic judgements being made in ways that diverge from those characteristic of traditional forms of research (qualitative as well as quantitative), and/or to them being mixed in with or subordinated to other considerations.

The problem with much of this criticism of epistemic criteria is that we are presented with contrasting, old and new, positions as if there were no middle ground. Furthermore, the irony is that the radical critique of foundationalist epistemology inherits the latter's definition of 'knowledge'. Foundationalists define 'knowledge' as being absolutely certain in validity. The critics show, quite convincingly, that no such knowledge is possible. But why should a belief only be treated as knowledge when its validity is absolutely certain? There is a third influential tradition of philosophical thinking, fallibilism, that is at odds with both foundationalism and relativism/scepticism. This position can be found in the writings of some contemporaries of Descartes, such as Mersenne, in the work of pragmatists like Peirce and Dewey, and in the philosophy of Wittgenstein. From this point of view, while all knowledge claims are fallible – in other words, they could be false even when we are confident that they are true – this does not mean that we should treat them as all equally likely to be false, or judge them solely according to whether or not they are validated by our own cultural communities. While we make judgements about likely validity on the basis of evidence that is itself always fallible, this does not mean either that validity is the same as cultural acceptability or that different cultural modes of epistemic judgement are all equally effective. Furthermore, in the normal course of making sense of, and acting in, the world we do not (and could not) adopt those assumptions[10].

Where the sceptical/relativist position challenges the claims of science to superior knowledge, the fallibilist position does not do this, although it insists on a more modest kind of authority than that implied by foundationalism. It points to both the power of, and the limits to, scientific knowledge (Haack 2003). The normative structure of science is designed to minimize the danger of error, even though it can never eliminate it. Moreover, while science can provide us with knowledge that is less likely to be false than that from other sources, it cannot give us a whole perspective on the world that can serve as a replacement for practical forms of knowledge. Nor, in the event of

a clash between the latter and scientific findings, can it be assumed that science must always be trusted. From this point of view, science, including social science, becomes a more modest enterprise than it was under foundationalism. But, at the same time, the specialized pursuit of knowledge is justified as both possible and desirable. By contrast with relativist and postmodernist positions, fallibilism does not reduce the task of social science to challenging dominant claims to knowledge or celebrating diverse discourses. Nor is it turned into a practical or political project directly concerned with ameliorating the world.

From this point of view, then, epistemic assessment of research findings is not only possible but is also the most important form of assessment for research communities. Moreover, while judgements cannot be absolutely certain, they can vary in the extent to which we are justified in giving them credence. In my view, it also follows from this position that the findings from qualitative research should be subjected to exactly the same form of assessment as those from quantitative studies, albeit recognizing any differences in the nature of the particular knowledge claims being made and in the particular methods employed.

OTHER RECENT DEVELOPMENTS

Within the last decade there has been a revival of older, positivist ideas about the function and nature of social research, and about how it should be assessed. With the rise of what is often referred to as the new public management in many Western and other societies (Pollitt 1990; Clarke and Newman 1997), along with the growing influence of ideas about evidence-based policy-making and practice, there have been increasing pressures for the reform of social research so as to make it serve the demands of policy and practice more effectively. These pressures have been particularly strong in the field of education, but are also increasingly to be found elsewhere[11]. The task of research, from the viewpoint of many policy-makers today, is to demonstrate which policies and practices 'work', and which do not; and this has led to complaints that there is insufficient relevant research, and that much of it is small-scale and does not employ the kind of experimental method that is taken to be essential for identifying the effects of policies and practices. To a large extent, this attitude reflects the fact that evidence-based practice has its origins in the field of medicine, where randomized, controlled trials are common[12].

At the same time, there have been attempts on the part of some qualitative researchers to show how their research can contribute to evidence-based policy and practice, and also to specify the criteria by which qualitative studies can be judged by 'users'. For example, in the UK two sets of assessment criteria for qualitative research have recently been developed that are specifically designed to demonstrate how it can serve policy-making and practice. The first was commissioned by the Cabinet Office in the UK from the National Centre for Social Research, an independent research organization (Spencer et al. 2003). These authors provide a discussion of the background to qualitative research, and of previous sets of criteria, before outlining a lengthy list of considerations that need to be taken into account in assessing the quality of qualitative research. They take great care in making clear that these should not be treated as a checklist of criteria that can give an immediate assessment of quality. However, perhaps not surprisingly, the authors have been criticized, on one side, for producing too abstract a list of criteria and, on the other, for providing what will in practice be used as a checklist, one which distorts the nature of qualitative research[13].

Another recent set of criteria for assessing research emerged in the field of education (Furlong and Oancea 2005). While it was not restricted to qualitative research, being concerned with 'applied and practice-based educational inquiry' more generally, the authors clearly had qualitative work particularly in mind. This venture had rather different origins from the first, and differs significantly in character. The project was commissioned by the UK Economic and Social Research Council, and the background here was very much recent criticism of educational research for being of poor quality and little practical relevance. At the same time, a prime concern of the authors seems to have been to provide criteria for use in the upcoming Research Assessment Exercise (RAE) in the UK, a process that is used to determine the distribution of research resources across universities. A longstanding complaint on the part of some educational researchers has been that the RAE uses traditional scholarly criteria of assessment that discriminate against applied work directed at practitioner audiences. And there has been much discussion of how this alleged bias can be rectified. In addressing the problem, Furlong and Oancea produce four sets of criteria. The first is epistemic in character, being concerned with issues of validity and knowledge development. More striking, however, are the other three sets of criteria: technical, practical, and economic. Here educational research is to be judged in terms of the extent to which it provides techniques that can be used by policy-makers or practitioners; the ways in which it informs, or could inform reflective practice; and/or the extent to which it offers 'added value' efficiently[14].

There is an interesting parallel between the emphasis placed by Furlong and Oancea on non-epistemic criteria and the move, outlined earlier, on the part of some qualitative researchers to abandon epistemic criteria completely. While many of the latter are hostile to the pressure for research to serve evidence-based policy-making and practice (see, for instance, Lather 2004), there is what might be described as a 'third way' approach championed by some, notably those associated with the tradition of qualitative action research. This redirects the pressure on research for policy- and practice-relevance away from a positivist emphasis on the need for quantitative methods to demonstrate 'what works' towards a broader view of worthwhile forms of research and of the ways in which it can shape practice. It is seen as playing a much more interactive and collaborative role, at least in relation to practitioners 'on the ground'. Advocates of this sort of position, such as John Elliott, are as critical of 'academic' educational research as the advocates of the new positivism. Where they differ is in the kind of research they believe is needed to inform policy-making and practice (see Elliott 1988, 1990, and 1991; see also Hammersley 2003).

We can see then, that besides divergent philosophical orientations between and among quantitative and qualitative researchers, equally important in shaping ideas about how social research should be assessed are views about its social function. In crude terms, we can distinguish four broad positions. First, there are those who see most social science research, especially that located in universities, as properly concerned exclusively with producing knowledge about human social life whose relevance to policy and practice is indirect, albeit not unimportant. Second, there are those who share the belief that social research must retain its independence, rather than being subordinated to policy-making or professional practice, but who regard the criteria of assessment as properly political, ethical, and/or aesthetic. For example, the task may be viewed as to 'disturb' or 'interrupt' conventional thinking in a manner that is not dissimilar to Socratic questioning, in its most sceptical form. Third, there are those who, while they see the purpose of social science very much as producing knowledge, insist that for this to be worthwhile it must have direct policy or practice implications: the task is to document what policies and practices 'work'. Finally, there are those who doubt the capacity of social science to produce knowledge about the social world, in the conventional sense of that term, and who believe the task of social researchers is to work in collaboration with particular groups of social actors to improve or transform the world[15]. Clearly, which of these stances is adopted has major implications for the question of how research should be evaluated.

Another recent development that has important implications for assessing the validity of research findings is a growing movement among some groups of social scientists towards championing the integration of quantitative and qualitative methods (see Bryman 1988; Tashakkori and Teddlie 2003a). 'Mixed methods' research is promoted as capitalizing on the strengths of both approaches. And this movement raises at least two issues of importance in the present context. First, there is the question of what sort of philosophical framework, if any, should underpin mixed methods research, since this has implications for how findings should be assessed. After all, simply combining the various types of validity identified by both quantitative and qualitative researchers produces a formidable list (see Teddlie and Tashakkori 2003: 13). A number of alternative ways of formulating mixed methods research as a 'third way' have been proposed, from the idea of an 'aparadigmatic' orientation that dismisses the need for reliance on any philosophical assumptions at all to the adoption of one or another alternative research paradigm, such as pragmatism or 'transformative-emancipatory' inquiry (see Teddlie and Tashakkori 2003b). It should be noted, though, that the reaction of many qualitative researchers to mixed methodology approaches is that, in practice, they force qualitative work into a framework derived from quantitative method, of a broadly positivist character. And there is some truth in this.

A second issue raised by mixing quantitative and qualitative approaches concerns whether new, distinctive, criteria of assessment are required, for instance relating specifically to the effectiveness with which the different kinds of method have been combined. Here, as elsewhere, there is often insufficient clarity about the difference between assessing research findings, as against assessing the effectiveness with which particular research projects have been pursued, the value of particular methods, the competence of researchers, and so on. Moreover, there is also the question of whether combining quantitative and qualitative methods is always desirable, and of whether talk about mixing the two approaches does not in effect embalm what is, in fact, too crude and artificial a distinction.

CONCLUSION

Clearly, the assessment of research findings is not a straightforward or an uncontentious matter. In this chapter I began by outlining the criteria usually associated with quantitative research, and noted serious problems with these: that there is often confusion about what is being assessed, and a failure to recognize differences in what is required depending upon the nature of the knowledge claim made and the particular research method used. In addition, I argued that it is not possible to have criteria in the strict sense of that term, as virtually infallible indicators of validity or invalidity. Judgement is always involved, and this necessarily depends upon background knowledge and practical understanding.

In the second half of the chapter, I considered the relativist and postmodernist views that are currently influential among many qualitative researchers. These deny the relevance of epistemic standards of assessment, in favour of an emphasis on political, ethical, or practical ones. I tried to show how this stems from a false response to the epistemological foundationalism that has informed much thinking about quantitative research. Instead, I suggested that what is required is a fallibilist epistemology. This recognizes that absolute certainty is never justified but insists that it does not follow either that we must treat all knowledge claims as equally doubtful or that we should judge them on grounds other than their likely truth.

Of course, discussion of these issues never takes place in a socio-cultural vacuum, and I outlined some recent changes in the external environment of social science research, in the US and the UK and elsewhere, which have increased demands that they demonstrate their value. I examined a couple of the responses to these pressures, in terms of attempts to develop criteria that should be used to assess the quality of qualitative research. Finally, I considered the implications of the growing advocacy of 'mixed methods' research, which in some respects is not unrelated to these external pressures.

We are a long way from enjoying any consensus among social scientists on the issue of how social research ought to be assessed. However, the differences in view cannot be mapped onto the distinction between quantitative and qualitative approaches, even though the argument is often formulated in those terms. It is essential to engage with the complexities of this issue if any progress is to be made in resolving the disputes.

NOTES

1 These commitments to reliability and measurement validity, and distinctions between types of validity, are spelled out in many introductions to social research. For a recent example, see Bryman 2001: 70–4. As Bryman indicates, the checking of reliability and validity in much quantitative research is rather limited, sometimes amounting to 'measurement by fiat'.

2 Of course, there are many other issues that survey researchers take into account, not least non-response.

3 The different accounts produced over several years allocate measurement somewhat differently: see Hammersley 1991.

4 On the considerable variation in definitions of 'reliability' and measurement 'validity', see Hammersley 1987.

5 There are also value claims: evaluations and prescriptions. I am taking it as given that research cannot validate these on its own: see Hammersley 1997.

6 The last of these claims is controversial: there are those, particularly among commentators on historical explanation, who deny that explanations always appeal to theoretical principles. For a discussion of this issue, see Dray 1964.

7 For valuable recent accounts of Kuhn's complex, and often misunderstood, position, see Hoyningen-Huene 1993, Bird 2000, and Sharrock and Read 2002.

8 For an extended account of a more moderate position, see Seale 1999.

9 Smith 1997 and 2004 distinguishes between his own relativist position and that of some postmodernists. However, the distinction is not cogent, in my view (Hammersley 1998). At the very least, there is substantial overlap between relativist and postmodernist positions.

10 For a sophisticated recent fallibilist account in epistemology, see Haack 1993.

11 On the history of these developments in the UK, see Hammersley 2002: chapter 1. On parallel changes in the US, see Feuer et al. 2002, Mosteller and Boruch 2002, and Lather 2004.

12 For these arguments, see, for example, Oakley 2000 and Chalmers 2003; see also Hammersley 2005.

13 See Kushner 2004; Murphy and Dingwall 2004; Torrance 2004. One critique has dismissed it as a 'government-sponsored framework' (Smith and Hodkinson 2005: 928–9).

14 Hammersley 2006 provides an assessment of the case put forward by Furlong and Oancea for these criteria.

15 These four positions are intended simply to map the field; many researchers adopt positions which combine and/or refine their elements.

REFERENCES

Bird, A. (2000) *Thomas Kuhn*, Princeton, Princeton University Press.

Bryman, A. (1988) *Quantity and Quality in Social Research*, London, Allen and Unwin.

Bryman, A. (2001) *Social Research Methods*, Oxford, Oxford University Press.

Campbell, D. T. (1957) 'Factors relevant to the validity of experiments in social settings', *Psychological Bulletin*, 54, 4, pp. 297–312.

Campbell, D. T. and Stanley, J. (1963) 'Experimental and quasi-experimental designs for research on teaching', in N. L. Gage (ed.) *Handbook of Research on Teaching*, Chicago, Rand McNally.

Chalmers, I. (2003) 'Trying to do more good than harm in policy and practice: the role of rigorous, transparent, up-to-date evaluations', *Annals of the American Academy of Political and Social Science*, 589, pp. 22–40.

Clarke, J. and Newman, J. (1997) *The Managerial State*, London, Sage.

Cook, T. D. and Campbell, D. T. (1979) *Quasi-Experimentation: Design and Analysis Issues for Field Situations*, Boston, MA, Houghton-Mifflin.

Denzin, N. K. and Lincoln, Y. S. (2005) 'The art and practices of interpretation, evaluation, and representation', in Denzin, N. K. and Lincoln, Y. S. (eds.) *Handbook of Qualitative Research*, 3rd edition, Thousand Oaks, CA, Sage.

Dray, W. (1964) *Philosophy of History*, Englewood Cliffs, NJ, Prentice-Hall.

Elliott, J. (1988) 'Response to Patricia Broadfoot's presidential address', *British Educational Research Journal*, 14, 2, pp. 191–4.

Elliott, J. (1990) 'Educational research in crisis: performance indicators and the decline in excellence', *British Educational Research Journal*, 16, 1, pp. 3–18.

Elliott, J. (1991) *Action Research for Educational Change*, Milton Keynes, Open University Press.

Feuer, M. J., Towne, L. and Shavelson, R. J. (2002) 'Scientific culture and educational research', *Educational Researcher*, 31, 8, pp. 4–14.

Furlong, J. and Oancea, A. (2005) *Assessing Quality in Applied and Practice-focused Educational Research: A Framework for Discussion*, Oxford, Oxford University Department of Educational Studies.

Goetz, J. P. and LeCompte, M. D. (1984) *Ethnography and Qualitative Design in Educational Research*, Orlando, Academic Press.

Haack, S. (1993) *Evidence and Inquiry*, Oxford, Blackwell.

Haack, S. (2003) *Defending Science – Within Reason*, Amherst, NY, Prometheus Books.

Hammersley, M. (1987) 'Some notes on the terms "validity" and "reliability"', *British Educational Research Journal*, 13, 1, pp. 73–81.

Hammersley, M. (1991) 'A note on Campbell's distinction between internal and external validity', *Quality and Quantity*, 25, pp. 381–7.

Hammersley, M. (1997) *Reading Ethnographic Research*, 2nd edition, London, Longman.

Hammersley, M. (1998) 'Telling tales about educational research: a response to John K. Smith', *Educational Researcher*, 27, 7, pp. 18–21.

Hammersley, M. (2002) *Educational Research, Policy-making and Practice*, London, Paul Chapman.

Hammersley, M. (2003) 'Can and should educational research be educative?', *Oxford Review of Education*, 29, 1, pp. 3–25.

Hammersley, M. (2005) 'Is the evidence-based practice movement doing more good than harm?', *Evidence and Policy*, 1, 1, pp. 1–16.

Hammersley, M. 'Troubling criteria: a critical commentary on Furlong and Oancea's framework for assessing educational research', forthcoming British Educational Research Journal, 2008.

Hammersley, M. and Atkinson, P. (2007) *Ethnography: Principles in Practice*, 3rd edition, London, Routledge.

Hoyningen-Huene, P. (1993) *Reconstructing Scientific Revolutions: Thomas S. Kuhn's Philosophy of Science*, Chicago, University of Chicago Press. (First published in German in 1989.)

Kuhn, T. S. (1970) *The Structure of Scientific Revolutions*, Chicago, University of Chicago Press.

Kushner, S. (2004) 'Government regulation of qualitative evaluation', *Building Research Capacity*, 8, May, pp. 5–8.

Lather, P. (1986) 'Issues of validity in openly ideological research: between a rock and a soft place', *Interchange*, 17, 4, pp. 63–84.

Lather, P. (1993) 'Fertile obsession: validity after poststructuralism', *Sociological Quarterly*, 34, pp. 673–93.

Lather, P. (2004) 'This *is* your father's paradigm: Government intrusion and the case of qualitative research in education', *Qualitative Inquiry*, 10, pp. 15–34.

Lincoln, Y. S. and Guba, E. G. (1985) *Naturalistic Inquiry*, Beverley Hills, Sage.

MacNaughton, G. and Smith, K. (2005) 'Transforming research ethics: the choices and challenges of researching with children', in A. Farrell (ed.) *Ethical Research with Children*, Maidenhead, Open University Press.

Mosteller, F. and Boruch, R. (eds.) (2002) *Evidence Matters: Randomized Trials in Education Research*, Washington D.C., Brookings Institution Press.

Murphy, E. and Dingwall, R. (2004) 'A response to 'Quality in Qualitative Evaluation: a framework for assessing research evidence", *Building Research Capacity*, 8, May, pp. 3–4

Oakley, A. (2000) *Experiments in Knowing: Gender and Method in the Social Sciences*, Cambridge, Polity Press.

Pollitt, C. (1990) *Managerialism and the Public Services*, Oxford, Blackwell.

Reason, P. and Bradbury, H. (eds.) (2001) *Handbook of Action Research: Participative Inquiry and Practice*, London, Sage.

Seale, C. (1999) *The Quality of Qualitative Research*, London, Sage.

Sharrock, W. and Read, R. (2002) *Kuhn: Philosopher of Scientific Revolution*, Cambridge, Polity.

Smith, J. K. (1997) 'The stories educational researchers tell about themselves', *Educational Researcher*, 26, 5, pp. 4–11.

Smith, J. K. (2004) 'Learning to live with relativism', in H. Piper and I. Stronach (eds.) *Educational Research: Diversity and Difference*, Aldershot, Ashgate.

Smith, J. K. and Deemer, D. K. (2000) 'The problem of criteria in the age of relativism', in N. K. Denzin and Y. S. Lincoln (eds.) *Handbook of Qualitative Research*, 2nd edition, Thousand Oaks, Sage.

Smith, J. K. and Hodkinson, P. (2005) 'Relativism, criteria, and politics', in Denzin, N. K. and Lincoln, Y. S. (eds.) *Handbook of Qualitative Research*, 3rd edition, Thousand Oaks, CA, Sage.

Spencer, L., Ritchie, J., Lewis, J. and Dillon, L. (2003) *Quality in Qualitative Evaluation: A Framework for Assessing Research Evidence*, London, Cabinet Office. Available at: http://www.policyhub.gov.uk/docs/qqe_rep.pdf (Accessed 13.02.2006).

Suppe, F. (ed.) (1974) *The Structure of Scientific Theories*, Chicago, University of Chicago Press.

Tashakkori, A. and Teddlie, C. (eds.) (2003a) *Handbook of Mixed Methods in Social and Behavioral Research*, Thousand Oaks, CA, Sage.

Teddlie, C. and Tashakkori, A. (2003b) 'Major issues and controversies in the use of mixed methods in the social and behavioral sciences', in Tashakkori and Teddlie (eds.) *Handbook of Mixed Methods in Social and Behavioral Research*, Thousand Oaks, CA, Sage.

Torrance, H. (2004) ' "Quality in Qualitative Evaluation" – a (very) critical response', *Building Research Capacity*, 8, May, pp. 8–10.

Ethnography and Audience

Karen Armstrong

INTRODUCTION

The ethnographic method results in an analysis of society which is built up from small facts and details. It brings the distant near to point out something not realized before, much like poetry does in a different genre (Heidegger 1971). In ethnography, the data are generally gathered from what people say and do in certain situations in order to illuminate broader comparative questions. The contemporary expansion of the audience[1] for ethnographic writing affects the contextualization of data by the researcher and raises questions about the relation of theory to audience. I will use some examples from anthropology to explore issues that are widespread in qualitative research to argue that, while the move to 'critical ethnography' raised issues about representation, it did not fully address the relation of ethnography to audience.

The problem of audience is apparent already when collecting ethnographic data. Typically, the researcher is a participant in the immediate situation, translating it later into a text. Implicit in this activity – talking, performing, writing – there is an audience; only some things are said to certain audiences, and other things are understood even if not said. In most cases, the audience is expected to do some of the work. What happens between the speaker's intention and the audience's understanding is a matter of interpretation. For example, the Xavante of Brazil perform dances for audiences of tourists in Brazil that could be interpreted to be invented tradition (Graham 2005). What the Xavante perform, however, is not intended to be measured as being true or not. They choose to perform as they do because they would insult the ancestors if they performed the full traditional rituals for outsiders. When non-Brazilian audiences appreciate their performance, the Xavante interpret the response to mean that their culture is recognized by outsiders as meaningful. In other situations, fragments of a narrative, or just allusions to a story, circulate among Quechua speakers in Peru, while place names summarize a moral story for the Western Apache (Becker and Mannheim 1995; Basso 1996). The fragments or names provide a cue; the audience does the work of understanding and creating meaning. As can be seen in these examples, being positioned as an insider or outsider affects audience and meaning.

The problem of audience appears again during the writing process. Whenever ethnographers write up their data they engage in an act of recontextualization (Duranti 1986: 244) by setting contextual clues, always selective, for the intended audience to judge the analysis. In anthropology, the ethnography (or monograph) is considered to be the account that pulls together the bits and pieces of data into a single whole. An ethnography is, by definition, comparative; it should address central questions about the nature of human existence through a specific society and its cultural system. Therefore, the audience is assumed to be both specific (academic, place, etc.) and general in the sense that anyone may engage with the broader questions addressed.

No good ethnography is self-contained. Implicitly or explicitly ethnography is an act of comparison. By virtue of comparison ethnographic description becomes objective. Not in the naïve positivist sense of an unmediated perception – just the opposite: it becomes a universal understanding to the extent it brings to bear on the perception of any society the conceptions of all the others (Sahlins 1996:10).

There have been ongoing debates about the goals of ethnography. These debates are commonly related to changing historical conditions and the need for social scientists to analyze what is going on in the contemporary world. In the past, situations like colonialism generated the need for new theoretical and methodological approaches. It seems appropriate, now that we live in a world connected by the Internet, mobile phones, web cameras, extensive media coverage, and so on, that we should rethink problems of method as related to audience. This is especially true for anthropology since the 'natives' are professionals in many fields, including anthropology.

In the most general sense, anthropologically informed ethnography is based on long-term fieldwork, and participant observation in a society other than one's own has been assumed and prioritized. Participant observation includes the assumption of a measure of fluency in the language of the society being studied, spending enough time among the people in order to know how they live, what they say about what they do, what they actually do, what they believe, and their system of valuation. The fieldworker may include archival and statistical data and discuss the influence of national and international organizations. Apart from these general procedures, it can be said that there is no distinct *object* of the anthropological fieldwork method (Faubion 2001: 39, my emphasis). What remains constant is the recurring problem of self and other: how do we know what we know, how do we assume to speak for others, and who is the audience being addressed? The first two issues have been addressed as problems of validity and representation; to address the third it is useful to begin by looking at the relation of theory to audience.

THEORY AND AUDIENCE

The sociologist, Arto Noro (2001, 2004), argues that there are three genres of sociological theory, each with an intended audience. One is general theory; theories of this type pose questions about how society in general is constituted and try to answer the questions. General theory is directed toward a scientific audience and aims for an interpretative synthesis by referring to earlier questions, which are readdressed to contemporary events. A second genre is research theory; this level consists of research projects that address or test the propositions of general theory and, in turn, provide material for general theory (2001: 1–2). As Noro points out, there is a significant relationship between these two. They lose their common ground only when research theory turns into administrative research or when general theory becomes philosophy. Research theory supplies material for general theory and is intended for a scientific audience; alternatively, it is directed toward specific social problems and is intended for instrumental use (for example, in forming social policy). Noro calls the third genre 'Zeitdiagnose'; this is theory that focuses on a diagnosis of the times we live in. Zeitdiagnose is directed toward a 'group-We' audience and intends to encourage 'us' to think about our situation and perhaps to change it accordingly.

Noro claims that Zeitdiagnose became popular in sociology in the 1980s and 1990s with books about risk society and modern identity (e.g. Beck 1992, 1994; Giddens 1991, 1992, among others)[2]. The key characteristic of Zeitdiagnose is that it offers an insight, understanding or vision (Noro 2001: 5) about our own times, something we have an inkling about but cannot name without the synthesis provided by the author. Zeitdiagnose tends to be openly normative and political (ibid.). Such texts are intensely seductive because they tell us who 'we' are, although these theories cannot be used in the interpretation of empirical evidence because we would find in the material what the diagnoses have already named. As Noro says, the end result would be poor mimesis (2001: 11).

As the audience for ethnographic research becomes global and less contained, there can be problems with the goals of research theory and Zeitdiagnose theory. These issues were anticipated in early discussions of the object of ethnographic research and the use of analytic concepts.

THE SCIENTIFIC AUDIENCE: EARLY STUDIES

Ethnographies tend to fall into the above classification of theories. An early example of an ethnography framed by general theory is *Seasonal Variation of the Eskimo* by Marcel Mauss in collaboration with Henri Beuchat (1979[1950]). It is based on field research by Beuchat and others and organized around Emile Durkheim's concept of social morphology to discuss the influence of seasonal variation on both social and cultural elements in Eskimo society and to propose that there may be similar variation in other societies. As with any good ethnography, details about culture (house styles, naming practices, hunting, etc.) and society (winter and summer social groups) are presented to argue the larger comparative point of social morphology.

The concept of culture was the general theory in American anthropology of the same period where cultural relativism focused on breaking the evolutionary model, a move which was especially relevant in the context of American society. Franz Boas and his students typically made visits to the field to collect cultural data and material artifacts. Much of their work was based on textual material collected from various North American Indian groups in order to record so-called aboriginal culture. This has been labeled 'salvage ethnography' because they were aware that most of the groups had been decimated by war with the American government at the end of the nineteenth century and they understood that what they were witnessing had been influenced and broken down by historical events. Nevertheless, they were looking at these groups to identify specific culture traits and their local patterning, not as an evolutionary process or a comparison of the primitive with the civilized.

One student of Boas, Paul Radin, did extensive fieldwork among the Winnebago for nearly 50 years and wrote a book for the method of studying culture (1987[1930]). Radin did not deny history, but he denied comparisons of cultures as being more or less advanced in direct or implicit comparison to 'us.' He was critical, therefore, of those who followed Malinowski's universalistic and functional style of description of 'primitives': '...whereas I see no necessity for proving that culture is culture, they apparently feel that it is incumbent upon them to laboriously demonstrate that, among primitive people, we are dealing with human beings who think as we do, feel as we do, and act as we do' (Radin 1987[1930]: 257). Radin's method argued for a study of culture based on 'reconstruction from internal evidence.'

> The task, let me insist, is always the same: a description of a specific period, and as much of the past and as much of the contacts with other cultures as is necessary for the elucidation of the particular period. No more. This can be

done only by an intensive and continuous study of a particular tribe, a thorough knowledge of the language, and an adequate body of texts; and this can be accomplished only if we realize, once and for all, that we are dealing with specific, not generalized, men and women, and with specific, not generalized, events. (ibid. 184–85)

Radin was critical of the categories imposed by universalistic theory, although he recognized that his method was similar to that of Marcel Mauss: 'In elucidating culture we must begin with a fixed point, but this point must be one that has been given form by a member of the group described, and not by an alien observer' (ibid. 186). To demonstrate his method, Radin uses one Winnebago man's (John Rave's) account of his conversion to the Peyote Cult. Radin traces themes in the narrative and, along with other native texts and his own observations, Radin shows how Rave's account is similar to and different from previous Winnebago practices. Radin thus analyzes how Rave could change his beliefs and still remain within the general Winnebago cultural framework. While the analysis remains self-contained (about the Winnebago), the method of eliciting native accounts of specific events and tracing how certain themes are replicated remains valid today.

Boas and his students often commented on issues in American society, especially about race or in their role as experts on Native American society. It has always been the practice of social science research to comment on contemporary issues; however, such comments are not the same as Zeitdiagnose when they are based on empirical research and linked to general theory (Noro 2001). A notable exception, Margaret Mead, came close to Zeitdiagnose in her popular writing and in her widely read ethnography, *Coming of Age in Samoa: A Psychological Study of Primitive Youth for Western Civilisation* (2001 [1928]). This book – not written strictly for a scientific audience – caused furor inside and outside academic circles. Mead used her ethnographic knowledge about Samoa as a basis for a critique of American culture, and wrote the book for an American general

audience[3]. The book presents the transition from youth to adulthood in Samoan culture as being easy and without the stress and rebellion found in American society. By using the contrast of Samoan culture, Mead proposed that the stress experienced in American adolescence had social and cultural causes which might be altered (see the discussion in Marcus and Fisher 1986; Stocking 1992). A friend of Mead, Edward Sapir, immediately complained that a student of culture cannot use what he knows as medicine for society (Handler 1986). Mead's book has generated enormous commentary, the most famous being numerous books and articles written by anthropologist Derek Freeman to disclaim the validity of Mead's ethnographic method and data (e.g. Freeman 1983, 1999, 2001). George Marcus and Michael Fisher argue that Mead failed because cultural juxtapositioning between 'us' and 'them' requires equal ethnography among 'us' (1986: 138). In the same period, Mead also wrote an ethnographic report on Samoa for the Bishop Museum in Hawai'i: *Social Organization of Manu'a* (1969[1930]). This is a standard research report about social organization (chiefs, titles, land arrangements) that does not attract much attention apart from an audience of anthropologists.

Coming of Age in Samoa reached an audience beyond the US. It remains significant in Samoa today, especially in American Samoa where Mead did fieldwork on the island of Ta'u in Manu'a. And, because texts extend beyond the moment of their production (Ricoeur 1991), *Coming of Age* continues to frame the meaning of anthropology *in* Samoa and *of* Samoa; my presence there in 2005 generated discussions of the book and the purpose of anthropology. *Coming of Age in Samoa* is cited by the American Samoan representative to Congress, Faleomavaega Eni Hunkin, as an insult to Samoan culture (Tavita 2004). He is upset by Mead's categorization of Samoa as a primitive society and by her discussion of Samoan sexuality. Perhaps more importantly, Manu'a was at one time the sacred center of an elaborate hierarchical culture and Mead does not recognize this in the popular *Coming of*

Age (although she does recognize it in *Social Organization of Manu'a*). Faleomavaega feels that the world continues to get the wrong image of Samoa because, he claims, the book is taught in introductory courses of anthropology at American universities. Derek Freeman does not escape criticism either; he is accused of depicting Samoan culture as being excessively violent. Both anthropologists are criticized for their reduction of Samoan culture. Samoan culture is not represented according to Samoan norms; that is, the Samoan voice is missing. In the research and writing process Samoans were typed by anthropological categories and Samoans today reject the gloss.

Edward Sapir was a contemporary of Radin and Mead, also a student of Boas, and a linguist. Sapir noted that all people use general categories as a way of making sense of a huge amount of personal experience. Because of this general tendency, he was wary of concepts (such as 'motivation') because they are generalizations that are imposed on our perception of objects and events, useful for talking about, in an analogical sense, the actual phenomena but removed from the phenomena (Preston 1966: 1115). Concepts tend to become endowed with what Sapir called a 'peculiar quality of self-determination' (ibid. 1115). Social scientists tend to prefer concepts and categories because they offer precision and clarity and in fact Sapir was criticized for his lack of theory and refusal of categories (ibid. 1105). However, when the categories are given prime importance, the researcher tends to use people selectively and only insofar as they provide new material for the categories. Sapir insisted that this was wrong, that 'the categories must be distinctively meaningful in and therefore derived from, the particular milieu, so that they will accurately describe the milieu' (ibid. 1120). For Sapir, the locus of culture is in individuals and the experience of actual individuals brings the researcher closest to the inherent structure of culture. He demonstrated this in his analyses of life histories (Sapir 1922, 1995[1938]). As Sapir defined method, you have to know the

overt forms (census materials, economic flow, geography, language, material culture, etc.) as well as how the forms are lived by individuals, which Sapir called the analysis of variation (Preston 1966: 1127). The cultural relativism of Radin and Sapir proposed a method that was based on internal evidence in order to avoid imposing categories on other cultures, with a focus on engaged individuals; this method was later criticized as being too particularistic.

Regarding audience, Radin and Sapir preferred to rely on texts, which turn out to have a longer 'shelf life' than concepts. The present-day Winnebago, or the Tikopians described so thoroughly by Raymond Firth, do not care about the concepts used by the anthropologists or their interpretations. The 'native' audience today is interested in these old ethnographies for their descriptive value as historical documents; they give them their own interpretation.

In another school, methods were developed to break out of the particularistic view and to address contemporary issues through general theory. Beginning in the 1940s, the so-called Manchester School of anthropology, headed by Max Gluckman, defined what became called situational analysis (a slightly different version was called social drama by his student, Victor Turner). Most of these anthropologists were working in Africa and trying to develop theories and methods appropriate for analyzing colonial relations. Gluckman (1958 [1940]) insisted that Europeans and Africans had to be seen as a total system, not as isolated groups. This could be done through the analysis of situations or events where problems would become apparent; the concept of 'social fields' was used to recognize the unbounded nature of social relations. Victor Turner used this method to show the symbolic importance of events – for example, rituals or conflicts – for individual participants. In four volumes about the Ndembu (cf. 1957, 1962, 1967, 1968) Turner demonstrates, through the personal stories of named individuals, how cultural categories sustain a given social structure through an intermingling of meanings. For Turner, a social drama, which is often a moment of conflict, reveals a 'moment of translucence' when the positions and conflicts among the involved individuals become apparent. Turner (1957) concluded that changes brought by colonial rule exacerbated the internal contradictions in Ndembu social structure. Whereas the contradictions caused by residence and decent could be tolerated or resolved before, they often collapsed into unrestrained conflict under colonial rule. Along with his analysis of conflict, Turner looked for replication in the symbols and concepts used by individuals in Ndembu society. Key (or root) metaphors were defined by Turner as those that occur at different times in different situations to structure meaning.

In a review of the Ndembu work, Mary Douglas claimed that Turner solved the problem of validation once and for all, although she worried about what the named individuals would think about their stories being public. 'It should never again be permissible to provide an analysis of an interlocking system of categories of thought which has no demonstrable relation to the social life of the people who think in these terms' (Douglas 1970:303).Whereas Sapir and Radin focused on culture as a system, Turner linked culture to practice, to the concept of society, and to universal questions. All these authors were attempting to address broader contemporary issues – the decimation of North American indigenous groups and the disruption caused by colonialism in Africa. The intended audience consisted of academics and possibly administrators. Mary Douglas' comment about named Ndembu individuals seems to anticipate that the audience was not going to be so contained in the future.

CRITICAL ETHNOGRAPHY

The emergence of a self-consciousness regarding 'self and other' in the last quarter of the twentieth century altered the way anthropologists and sociologists write ethnography and deal with data and representations of others (see, for example, Gubrium and Holstein 1997). 'Critical ethnography' introduced reflexivity about what 'we' do and cast a critical eye on writing practices, fieldwork topics and research sites. In anthropology, the emphasis has been on the production of ethnography, especially the relation between the fieldworker and those being researched. Two popular books, Paul Rabinow's (1977) *Reflections on Fieldwork in Morocco*, and *The Headman and I* by Jean-Paul Dumont (1978), opened up the reflexive question in the US about the relation between the researcher and his or her informants[4]. These were followed by *Writing Culture* (Clifford and Marcus 1986) and *Anthropology as Cultural Critique* (Marcus and Fischer 1986). *Writing Culture* was a collection of articles that questioned how the process of writing established a self/other relationship in ethnographic description. It questioned the notion of ethnographic authority and how the 'I' of the anthropologist had fashioned the 'we' or the 'other' of the 'natives.' *Anthropology as Cultural Critique* called for a more politically active engagement of anthropologists in the issues of their times. Following these, anthropology was challenged to drop the 'savage slot' and to undertake critical research about the contemporary world (Trouillot 1991: 40). These works, and many others, opened an experimental current that continues today (e.g. Carucci and Dominy 2005). As a result there have been various efforts in writing, such as teamwork between the anthropologist and the interlocutor in order to produce 'dialogue' or 'polyphony,' with different measures of success (Faubion 2001; Marcus and Mascarenhas 2005). Topics have broadened to include the contemporary world of elites, corporations, medicine, law and environmental issues, to name a few. Along with the focus on new topics, George Marcus (1998) talks about the 'complicity' of the fieldworker regarding his or her relation with the events or people being studied while others talk about 'emergent practices' (Mauer 2005: 1). Like Zeitdiagnose, these authors aim to study issues that they are involved in and to take a political, often a moral, position in order to describe what these times are like.

The valuation of the sites of research has also been redefined. Akhil Gupta and James Ferguson (1997) critiqued the place orientation of anthropology and called for research that was not so place dependent. Since we live in a world of transnational flows, refugees, and exiles, a researcher should adjust his or her methods appropriately. For George Marcus (1998), multi-sited ethnography recognizes that individuals in today's world are on the move; the anthropologist therefore tracks these individuals and their networks. James Faubion (2001: 52) notes that, although this type of research is easily justified, it has remained largely an ideal model since it is hard to find the time or funding to do it in practice. And even if funded and attempted, Ghassan Hage (2005) found that there are many pitfalls, primarily the exhaustion of the ethnographer and the unhappy expectations of reciprocity by individuals who expect him to take them seriously, not just to drop in for a short visit. Faubion suggests an alternative, that fieldwork might 'proceed cross-sectionally and sequentially,' and ends his review of American anthropology strongly in the spirit of Zeitdiagnose: 'modernity is … many things; and it is up to the cultural (and social) fieldworker to explore, describe and diagnose at once what such a multi-scalar assemblage of artifacts is, or what it might be' (Faubion 2001: 52).

The resultant political positioning generally puts the weight on categories or concepts like 'power,' 'hybridity,' and 'race,' and uses individuals to fill in the story. One example is a book about multi-sited memory and identity in the border region of Trieste that 'breaks with relativism' because it is 'not a standard ethnography of empathy' but 'an ethnography of complicity' (Ballinger 2003: 7). The author analyses how average citizens make sense of history by assimilating the events of their lives into long-standing narratives that 'are legitimated or authorized precisely in moral terms' (2003: 9). Asked to tell about the events of 1943–45, the speakers are said to draw the listener (anthropologist) in, so that the anthropologist shares their complicity in the violent events being described, while at the same time the narrators deny their own complicity (2003: 147). The author reports to a professional audience and determines the truth of the narratives. But, were life story narratives appropriate for talking about the tensions of state formation? It is likely that a different genre or domain was being addressed by her interlocutors and here is where, again, the problem of audience appears. Despite the attention paid to writing, topics and place, critical ethnography has not addressed adequately the relation of theory to method or the issues of ethnographic competence and intended audience.

ETHNOGRAPHIC COMPETENCE

The subject matter for anthropology has always been global but today its institutions, practitioners and audiences are also global (Lederman 2005: 321). The same can be said for the other social sciences and this expanded situation has implications for the methods used as well as for reception. However, with the exception of linguistic anthropology, very little of the discussion about fieldwork and representation addresses the need for new methods to interpret the data (e.g. Briggs 1986; Silverstein and Urban 1996). Although critical ethnography – and taking a political and moral stand – is often the goal, how do we know – and can we know? – the truth and intentionality intended by our interlocutors?

The move to critical ethnography defined privileged sites and privileged topics with sometimes unanticipated results. For example, the site of Asale Angel-Ajani's research reveals a preference for certain sites, the problem of speaking for someone else, and the problem of audience. Angel-Ajani's research with women prisoners in Italy, most of whom were from Africa, put her in the position of listening to dramatic testimony of chaos and violence, where what the prisoners say often does not seem to be 'really real.' She argues that in such situations the listener cannot assume to be an expert or authority; instead, the focus should be on critical reception, on actually listening to what is being said (2004: 142). Ironically, when she presented her data at a conference the academic audience rejected the prisoners' stories as implausible. Angel-Ajani suspects that the stories would have been accepted if they had been situated in a privileged site, such as a refugee camp or a women's shelter (ibid.).

Questions about intentionality raise issues about audience and code that have been addressed by discourse analysis in productive ways. Charles Briggs reviews the problems inherent in the interview as a genre. Briggs criticizes the assumption that acceptable questions are semantically transparent, that the respondent's assumptions will match those of the researcher (Briggs 1986: 50). He goes on to demonstrate the significance of reference, indexicality, code and social relations in interview situations. Responses can address a given subject from many different points of view (ibid. 54) and with differing amounts of detail. Radin argued that no one can say everything about the topic in answer to a question (1957[1927]: 16); there is always a selective process, a partial answer. Add to this the fact that any researcher exerts a certain amount of control over the situation so that often one's interlocutors are trying to give the appropriate answer to what they understand is the intended question. In other words, there is a large gap between intention and meaning which allows room for the researcher to impose an external meaning onto a response. A reliance on interviews, without being aware of the nature of speech acts, often reinforces our preconceptions rather than raising new questions (Briggs 1986: 119). However, interviews do not have to be thrown into the scrap bin. The aim of Briggs' book is to show that they require rhetorical competence: an understanding of the modes of verbal interaction among the group being studied, the context and indexical meanings for what is being said, and the fact that speech has the possibility to create or transform a given state of affairs (ibid. 45–46).

Because of the creative/transformative nature of speech, intentionality and truth are not as straightforward as question and answer sessions might suppose. In spoken language, not only do we communicate messages, we communicate how to interpret those messages, sometimes with additional devices (tone, body language, etc.) to modify the meaning. As has been shown in conversation analysis and linguistic anthropology, acts of speaking and interpretation are partly constructed by the audience's response and, in fact, we would not be able to communicate without others to carry, complete, expand and revise our messages (Duranti 1993: 226). Even the simplest routine like the opening of a telephone call is a joint activity between speaker and audience. When the audience is cooperative this work is hardly recognized. However, when the message is open to dispute speakers use other techniques such as verbal indirection, where the meaning is not in the text alone, the speaker avoids full responsibility for what is said, and the audience is actively involved and compelled to interpret the referent and the meaning (Brenneis 1987: 504).

If a message has multiple goals, how is it to be understood? Sometimes speakers seem to be exploiting the truth rather than to use it as the criterion for interpretation. The goal might be to make truth irrelevant or to make the audience at least partly responsible for what is being implied (Duranti 1993: 233). If a researcher does not fully account for the audience, he or she might suppose that the analysis is immune to the consequences of interpretation due to the geographical and institutional distance from their subjects (ibid. 229). As this distance breaks down, however, the notion of being objective is harder to maintain. According to Duranti, the emphasis must come away from the speaker and move instead to the 'coordinated role played by the addresses or audience in any kind of communicative act' (ibid. 237). And beyond this, truth has a different meaning across sociocultural domains such as domestic, political and ritual domains, so that an ethnographer's observations must be grounded in a careful analysis of discourse patterns according to the appropriate domain audience.

The issue of audience turns the attention from ethnographic authority (even a reflexive one) to that of ethnographic competence. One must be competent in order to understand the subtle signals and shifts that are occurring during the research. An example of this is John Haviland's (1991) recording and analysis of the life story of Roger Hart, an Australian aboriginal man. Haviland demonstrates how the discourse constitutes – brings into existence – a coherent view of personal identity that goes to the heart of the problem of individual participation in a cultural order. Using the actual text (which was also video-recorded), Haviland demonstrates how others participated in the performance (including the anthropologist), the immediate context for what Roger Hart says, as well as the background issues for why he says what he says at this point in time. The multiplicity of voices and the message of the story replicate the themes of ambivalence which surround the topic of aboriginality in Australia (Haviland 1991: 347).

Likewise, an analysis of a misunderstanding – a failure of competence – can open up problems of intention as Johannes Fabian (1995) found in a conversation he had while doing fieldwork in Zaire. In an interview with a woman leader of a charismatic prayer group, the woman insists, by coming back to the topic and addressing it openly, that they discuss why Johannes Fabian is no longer a Catholic. The ensuing conversation is full of evasion and a certain level of embarrassment on the part of the anthropologist. Both were speaking Swahili – a language in which Fabian is very competent – so there was not a language problem. As Fabian realized, it was a problem of intention. He understood the conversation as an interview, while she was trying to engage him in testimony (1995: 46). It is an example of how one cannot assume that the context is given; rather, Fabian argues, context works in a dialectical, not a logical-methodological way (ibid. 48).

The contradictions in narratives about colonial memories encountered by Andrea Smith (2004) were in fact examples of Bahktin's idea of heteroglossia. On the one hand, informants told her that in colonial Algeria people were 'all the same, a melting-pot,' and on the other hand they told stories about an ethnic hierarchy and tensions due to ethnic intermarriage. Her examples show that memory is narrated contingent on audience and on distinct voices. For a general audience, Algeria was a melting pot, as the story is replicated in official histories and discussions. But when talking about personal history and personal experience, people used the first person 'I' and spoke about a colonial experience marked by ethnic divisions and class. Distinct voices index a distinct orientation; neither version is intended to be the absolute truth (Smith 2004: 265).

When the focus is on universal concepts such as 'power' or 'race,' combined with a Zeitdiagnose purpose to describe 'what these times are like' it is easy to read motives into informants' answers. Ethnographic competence – the recognition of multiple voices, intention and heteroglossia – draws attention to the intended meaning and audience of the speakers as well as to the work being done by the audience.

INSIDERS AND OUTSIDERS

Due to the reflexive turn in ethnography, it is not possible to produce texts without considering the relation of authors to their subjects. Anthropology has generally practiced the interpretative project of translating the concerns of the research site and a certain group for an audience unlikely to encounter them directly (Lederman 2005: 322). However, an important historical shift has occurred so that it is often no longer clear who is a cultural insider and who is an outsider. The situation of 'translation' is changing as 'insider' anthropologists become more common and because publications circulate beyond limited audiences. One way around translation can be seen in the recent collaborative work between the anthropologist George Marcus and a Portuguese nobleman, Fernando Mascarenhas. Their email exchanges are reproduced with little editing and no interpretation as an example of the 'shifting "politics" between the tradition of letters in Portugal and the tradition of interviewing in anthropology' (Marcus and Mascarenhas 2005: xv). The intended audience remains narrow: an academic audience interested in the study of elites or the general problems of 'the presentation of ethnography expressed through the relations that produce it' (ibid. xvi).

Another possibility is that one's ethnographic competence will be used by the subjects of the study for their own purposes. This often occurs when the researcher has worked in an area over a long period of time. Glenn Petersen has done research in Micronesia for 30 years, but as he notes, 'since Micronesians know about Micronesia, they have neither need for nor much interest in my ethnography; they already know about themselves, to put it simply' (2005: 312). While his writing gave him ethnographic authority with a scholarly public (mostly outside Micronesia), the Micronesians put more value on his competence, that is, how they could make use of his outside experience. Competence means taking into account all the 'messy' parts: disagreements, the tensions that link hierarchy and equality, and the discrepancies of everyday experience (Petersen 2005: 315). For Petersen, a good ethnographer knows about life as the individuals in the community experience it, and therefore knows something about the effect of cultural contradictions on their lives (ibid. 316). Competence is gained by recognizing the complexities, not glossing them over with general concepts. This was, after all, the point of practice theory, when Pierre Bourdieu quoted Jean-Paul Sartre: 'Words wreck havoc when they find a name for what had up to then been lived namelessly' (Bourdieu 1977: 170). Practice brings the contradictions to the surface, as Gluckman recognized; practice theory recognizes the political implications of categorization and

internal critique (Kapferer 1997: 20). Naming creates authority; competence is the ability to live according to local systems of significance.

CONCLUSION: ACCOUNTING FOR AUDIENCE

Accounting for an expanded audience is a measure of the goals of the research and whether it addresses problems – even if unwittingly – defined by interests or categories that frame the results. If the ethnographic method aims to study every possible group and site, the goal of the research is a critical issue. One danger is that ethnography becomes a form of spying; another is that it reproduces dominant interests and discourses. The question of dominant interests is relevant in Finland, for example, where much of the research funding comes from the state and where the state often determines (beforehand) the topics that it will fund. Research theory, as defined earlier, can address two audiences: a scientific or an administrative audience. In many cases, research questions are designed for topics about which the state needs information (such as prison populations, area studies or Islam). The researcher in these cases is defined as an expert, despite the fact that expert predictions have proven to be unreliable and, ultimately, unaccountable for their errors (Menand 2005). Even when one avows to be critical – as in critical ethnography in the US – the research questions and results may unwittingly replicate central problems in American society (power, race, ethnicity, gender) in other places if one does not listen carefully to what is being said within the context of another social setting. This is what Louis Dumont meant when he warned that anthropology should not be subjected to non-anthropological concerns (Dumont 1986). Dumont argued that the proper study of society was based on enriching general theoretical questions through detailed ethnography in order to determine the valuations that *distinguish* one research context from another.

Zeitdiagnose has its own pitfalls. Because it is aimed at identity audiences, it is often based on fieldwork 'at home' and written for a defined 'we.' Since the content is already known, the only novelty is in the production, in the way the argument is written (Siikala 2004: 202). It is inevitable that certain identity audiences will have priority over others depending on the location and interests of the major publishing houses. As ethnographic texts become accessible – especially through the Internet – they are not tied to the frame of academic judgment or to a particular 'we.' If Zeitdiagnose defines a 'we' it runs the risk of excluding others since any 'we' implies a 'not-we' (Urban 1996).

General theory is written for a global scientific audience. When Marshall Sahlins states that comparison is at the heart of ethnography he is talking about general theory, not the comparison of 'these to those.' At the level of general theory, broad questions are addressed concerning the nature of society, the relationship of individuals to social structures, the way reciprocity creates social relations, the processes of social change, etc., and are argued with detailed ethnographic data. The questions can be revisited and revised in all sites as historical changes affect the nature of society and social relations. Ethnographies like *The Fame of Gawa* by Nancy Munn (1992[1986]), Marshall Sahlins' *Anahulu* (1992) or *Feast of the Sorcerer* by Bruce Kapferer (1997) are explorations of general questions such as (respectively) value and reciprocity, cosmology and contact between different cultural orders, and sorcery's relation to the conditions of human existence. These questions can be explored anew in new sites, with new data, according to new circumstances, because no one instance of a phenomenon accounts for all its dimensions (Kapferer 1997: 302).

For example, when Bruce Kapferer writes about sorcery in Sri Lanka he breaks the category expectations of sorcery, which are 'deeply engaged in the very aims and methodology of anthropology,' while at the same time avoiding the 'dark cave of methodological relativism' (1997: 11, 13).

Kapferer makes an ethnographically informed argument about the general possibilities of sorcery – it is directed to the contradictions and discordances of life worlds – while acknowledging distinctions in Sri Lankan practices (ibid. 11, 15). Sri Lankan sorcery is not another example of exotic otherness; sorcery is a practical discourse about 'human-generated social and political realities,' part of the general problematic of 'the alienating and constituting forces of power' (ibid. 7, 303). Kapferer breaks with the category because categories structure the interpretation, as Sapir warned. At the same time, Kapferer avoids the particularistic view of cultural relativism and the moral positioning of Zeitdiagnose. Sorcery is not analyzed to determine the truth about violence and power; rather, it demonstrates the anguish of human beings in a social and political world (ibid. 25). When ethnography addresses general questions the audience is 'human beings' and there is the possibility to debate and disagree. The intent is *relevance* not truth; thus, it allows the possibility for a voice (response) for a global audience.

The move to critical ethnography opened the question of audience. Since that time, information has become more widely available, making the problem of audience more pronounced in all aspects of the research project. So long as the audience was primarily a scientific one, there were guidelines about how the analysis should be read and judged – often for the way it addressed problems within an academic discipline. However, it is less likely today that the audience will be so narrow; in fact, it is quite likely that the audience will be any number of people with an interest in the place, the topic, or for many other reasons. It means that one's writing is read increasingly by 'an undisciplined audience' (Lederman 2005: 323). We are faced, therefore, with the situation where we collect data from a variety of people who themselves have a variety of interests, and publish our analyses in a variety of sites for a variety of readers, each of whom brings his or her own interests to the text. The text always escapes the author. The work produced will not be read conclusively; it will be read for its relevance by readers who assign meaning to it according to their own valuations.

NOTES

1 A caveat is necessary here: the 'native' audience is not necessarily a recent phenomenon. It has been common in Finland for a long time for the general public to read ethnology and folklore texts, among others, about themselves. However, while the audience is 'native,' the writing is among 'insiders' and does not raise the issue of 'self and other' in the same way as when the researcher is from another culture.

2 These works are part of 'reflexive modernity' and, in fact, 'modernity' is marked by reflexivity. The implications of how the information flow makes the world 'modern' and 'reflexive' on an institutional level, and the impact on anthropology, are discussed by John Knight (1992).

3 There are no footnotes or references, as would be expected in scientific writing, although there is an explanation of the methodology in an appendix.

4 The reflexive turn in American anthropology happened in the context of Project Camelot and the Vietnam War. Both events opened debates about the purpose of anthropological research: was it to supply information for the CIA and the US military? Rabinow refers to the American political context in the introduction to *Reflections on Fieldwork in Morocco*.

REFERENCES

Angel-Ajani, Asale 2004 'Expert Witness: Notes Toward Revisiting the Politics of Listening.' *Anthropology and Humanism* 29(2): 133–144.

Ballinger, Pamela 2003 *History in Exile: Memory and Identity at the Borders of the Balkans*. Princeton: Princeton University Press.

Basso, Keith 1996 *Wisdom Sits in Places: Landscape and Language among the Western Apache*. Albuquerque: University of New Mexico Press.

Beck, Ulrich 1992 *Risk Society: Towards a New Modernity*. London: Sage.

Beck, Ulrich 1994 *Ecological Politics in the Age of Risk*. Cambridge: Polity.

Becker, Alton and Bruce Mannheim 1995 'Culture Troping: Languages, Codes, and Texts.' In, *The Dialogic Emergence of Culture*, edited by Bruce Mannheim and Dennis Tedlock. Urbana: University of Illinois Press, pp. 237–252.

Bourdieu, Pierre 1977 *Outline of a Theory of Practice*. Cambridge: Cambridge University Press.

Brenneis, Donald 1987 'Talk and Transformation.' *Man*, New Series 22(3): 499–510.

Briggs, Charles 1986 *Learning How to Ask*. Cambridge: Cambridge University Press.

Carucci, Lawrence and Michèle Dominy 2005 'Anthropology in the 'Savage Slot': Reflections on the Epistemology of Knowledge.' *Anthropological Forum* 15(3): 223–233.

Clifford, James and George Marcus (eds.) 1986 *Writing Culture: The Poetics and Politics of Ethnography*. Berkeley: University of California Press.

Douglas, Mary 1970 'The Healing Rite (review article).' *Man*, New Series 5(2): 302–308.

Dumont, Jean-Paul 1978 *The Headman and I*. Austin: University of Texas Press.

Dumont, Louis 1986 *Essays on Individualism: Modern Ideology in Anthropological Perspective*. Chicago: University of Chicago Press.

Duranti, Alessandro 1986 'The Audience as Co-Author: An Introduction.' In, *Special Issue: The Audience as Co-Author*, edited by Alessandro Duranti and Donald Brenneis. *Text* 6–3.

Duranti, Alessandro 1993 'Truth and Intentionality: An Ethnographic Critique.' *Cultural Anthropology* 8(2): 214–245.

Fabian, Johannes 1995 'Ethnographic Misunderstanding and the Perils of Context.' *American Anthropologist* 97(1): 41–50.

Faubion, James 2001 'Currents of Cultural Fieldwork.' In, *The Handbook of Ethnography*, edited by Paul Atkinson, Amanda Coffey, Sara Delamont, John Lofland and Lyn Lofland. London: Sage Publications, pp. 39–59.

Freeman, Derek 1983 *Margaret Mead and Samoa*. Cambridge, MA: Harvard University Press.

Freeman, Derek 1999 *The Fateful Hoaxing of Margaret Mead: A Historical Analysis of her Samoan Research*. Boulder: Westview Press.

Freeman, Derek 2001 'Words have no Words for Words that are not True': A Rejoinder to Serge Tcherkézoff.' *Journal of the Polynesian Society* 4: 301–311.

Giddens, Anthony 1991 *Modernity and Self-Identity*. Stanford: Stanford University Press.

Giddens, Anthony 1992 *The Transformation of Intimacy*. Stanford: Stanford University Press.

Gluckman, Max 1958[1940] *Analysis of a Social Situation in Modern Zululand*. Manchester: Manchester University Press.

Graham, Laura 2005 'Image and Instrumentality in a Xavante Politics of Existential Recognition: The Public Outreach Work of Eténhiritipa Pimentel Barbosa.' *American Ethnologist* 32(4): 622–641.

Gubrium, Jaber and James Holstein 1997 *The New Language of Qualitative Method*. New York: Oxford University Press.

Gupta, Akhil and James Ferguson (eds.) 1997 *Culture, Power, Place: Explorations in Critical Anthropology*. Durham: Duke University Press.

Hage, Ghassan 2005 'A not so Multi-Sited Ethnography of a not so Imagined Community.' *Anthropological Theory* 5(4): 463–475.

Handler, Richard 1986 'Vigorous Male and Aspiring Female: Poetry, Personality and Culture in Edward Sapir and Ruth Benedict.' In, *Malinowski, Rivers, Benedict and Others*, edited by George Stocking. Madison: University of Wisconsin Press, pp. 127–155.

Haviland, John 1991 ' "That Was the Last Time I Seen Them, and No More": Voices Through Time in Australian Aboriginal Autobiography.' *American Ethnologist* 18(2): 331–361.

Heidegger, Martin 1971 *Poetry, Language, Thought*, translated by Albert Hofstadter. New York: Harper and Row.

Kapferer, Bruce 1997 *Feast of the Sorcerer: Practices of Consciousness and Power*. Chicago: University of Chicago Press.

Knight, John 1992 'Globalization and the New Ethnographic Localities: Anthropological Reflections on Giddens's *Modernity and Self-Identity*.' *Journal of the Anthropological Society of Oxford* 23(3): 239–251.

Lederman, Rena 2005 'Challenging Audiences: Critical Ethnography in/for Oceania.' *Anthropological Forum* 15(3): 319–328.

Marcus, George and Michael Fisher 1986 *Anthropology as Cultural Critique*. Chicago: University of Chicago Press.

Marcus, George 1998 *Ethnography Through Thick and Thin*. Princeton: Princeton University Press.

Marcus, George and Fernando Mascarenhas 2005 *Ocasião: The Marquis and the Anthropologist, A Collaboration*. Walnut Creek, CA: Alta Mira.

Mauer, Bill 2005 'Introduction to "Ethnographic Emergences".' *American Anthropologist* 107(1): 1–4.

Mauss, Marcel (in collaboration with Henri Beuchat) 1979 [1950] *Seasonal Variations of the Eskimo: A Study in Social Morphology*, Translated with a Foreword, by James J. Fox. London: Routledge and Kegan Paul.

Mead, Margaret 1969 [1930] *Social Organization of Manu'a*. Bernice B. Bishop Museum Bulletin 76. Honolulu, Hawaii: Bishop Museum Reprints.

Mead, Margaret 2001[1928] *Coming of Age in Samoa: A Psychological Study of Primitive Youth for Western Civilisation*. New York: Harper Collins (Perennial Classics).

Menand, Louis 2005 'Everybody's an Expert: Putting Predictions to the Test.' Book Review in *The New Yorker*, December 5: 98–101.

Munn, Nancy D. 1992[1986] *The Fame of Gawa: A Symbolic Study of Value Transformation in a Massim (Papua New Guinea) Society*. Durham: Duke University Press.

Noro, Arto 2001 'Zeitdiagnose' as the Third Genre of Sociological Theory?' Paper presented at European Sociological Association Conference, Helsinki, August 28.

Noro, Arto 2004 'Sosiologian Kolmio: teoriat, käytöt ja yleisöt' ('A Sociological Triangle: Theory, Use and Audience'), unpublished paper.

Petersen, Glenn 2005 'Important to Whom? On Ethnographic Usefulness, Competence and Relevance.' *Anthropological Forum* 15(3): 307–317.

Preston, Richard J. 1966 'Edward Sapir's Anthropology: Style, Structure, and Method.' *American Anthropologist* 68(5): 1105–1128.

Rabinow, Paul 1977 *Reflections on Fieldwork in Morocco*. Berkeley: University of California Press.

Radin, Paul 1957 [1927] *Primitive Man as Philosopher*. New York: Dover Publications.

Radin, Paul 1987 [1930] *The Method and Theory of Ethnology*. South Hadley, MA: Bergin and Garvey.

Ricoeur, Paul 1991 *From Text to Action: Essays in Hermeneutics, II*, translated by K. Blamey and J. B. Thompson. Chicago: University of Chicago Press.

Sahlins, Marshall 1992 *Anahulu: The Anthropology of History in the Kingdom of Hawai'i. Volume One, Historical Ethnography*. Chicago: University of Chicago Press.

Sahlins, Marshall 1996 [1993] *Waiting for Foucault*. Cambridge, UK: Prickly Pear Press.

Sapir, Edward 1922 'Sayach'apis, a Nootka Trader.' In, *American Indian Life*, edited by Elsie Clews Parsons. New York: Viking.

Sapir, Edward 1995 [1938] Foreword. *Left Handed, Son of Old Man Hat*, Recorded by Walter Dyk. Lincoln: University of Nebraska Press.

Siikala, Jukka 2004 'Theories and Ideologies in Anthropology.' *Social Analysis* 48(3): 199–204.

Silverstein, Michael and Greg Urban (eds.) 1996 *Natural Histories of Discourse*. Chicago: University of Chicago Press.

Smith, Andrea 2004 'Heteroglossia, "Common Sense," and Social Memory.' *American Ethnologist* 31(2): 251–269.

Stocking, George 1992 *The Ethnographer's Magic and Other Essays in the History of Anthropology*. Madison: University of Wisconsin Press.

Tavita, Terry 2004 'Faleomavaega Tackles Mead-Freeman Debate.' *Samoan Observer Online*, 25 October.

Trouillot, Michel-Rolphe 1991 'Anthropology and the Savage Slot: The Poetics and Politics of Otherness.' In, *Recapturing Anthropology: Working in the Present*, edited by Richard G. Fox. Santa Fe: School of American Research Press, pp. 17–44.

Turner, Victor 1957 *Schism and Continuity in an African Society: A Study of Ndembu Religious Life.* Manchester: Manchester University Press.

Turner, Victor 1962 *Chihamba, the White Spirit.* Manchester: Manchester University Press.

Turner, Victor 1967 *The Forest of Symbols: Aspects of Ndembu Ritual.* Ithaca: Cornell University Press.

Turner, Victor 1968 *The Drums of Affliction: A Study of Religious Process among the Ndembu of Zambia.* Oxford: Clarendon Press.

Urban, Greg 1996 *Metaphysical Community.* Austin: University of Texas Press.

Social Research and Social Practice in Post-Positivist Society

Pekka Sulkunen

Scientific methods are not tool kits that researchers can select to suit their tastes and preferences to compete with other techniques contending to reach the truth. Research instruments in sociology are no more than in other sciences independent of concepts and problematics from which they emerge, and they in turn structure the questions and theoretical concepts that they can be used to deal with. Instead of a choice of methods it is more appropriate to talk about 'styles of reasoning', like Ian Hacking (1990: 6), who has argued that although the social world is constructed differently by different styles of reasoning, this is not to say that the constructions are arbitrary. It simply means that, for example, an explanation or prediction formulated in probabilistic quantitative terms already implies a great deal about the world in its concepts which, in turn, are integrated with a statistical methodology. The same reality represented in another vocabulary and through a biographical or ethnographic methodology would look different but still be no less true.

How should we classify such styles of reasoning in sociology, and how could we explain or understand the reasons for such differences? In this article I argue that a major change in sociological styles of reasoning took place in the late 1970s and early 1980s both in the way sociology began to conceptualise the social world and in the way sociological research was related to social practices or policy-making. One apparent indication of the new style of reasoning was the boost in qualitative research and the accompanying 'cultural' or 'linguistic' turn in sociology (see Chapter 1). These changes reflect the role that social sciences first had in the three post-war decades and then lost when the welfare state construction period had attained maturity.

REPRESENTATIONAL, EPISTEMIC AND POSITIONAL DIMENSIONS OF KNOWLEDGE

Sociological studies tell about social reality in three different ways. First, they report knowledge about social realities. This knowledge depends on their conceptual framework and on their instruments of observation such as ethnography, media analysis or the survey technology, but within the constraints of the concepts and instruments, knowledge it is (Bhaskar 1975). This is the *representational dimension* of knowledge. For example, a study on the relationship between social capital and social exclusion might be made with statistical methods, which require that the abstract categories 'social capital' and 'social exclusion' are operationalised as measurable indicators that describe individuals or collectivities. Most likely, a fair amount of drug users would be found among the most excluded. Another study might compare Western countries and come to the conclusion that most of them apply strict prohibitions on a selection of pharmaceuticals – not all, like alcohol, but many such as opiates, cocaine, amphetamine or MDMA ('ecstasy'). Possession, distribution, production and import of the prohibited drugs are legal offences with penal consequences. The role of the criminal justice system as the interface between the state and the drug user in many ways operates as a mechanism of exclusion. The term 'prohibition' is also an abstract category and describes at least part of the same reality as the quantitative study, but from a completely different angle. Finally, a third study, made with ethnographic methods, could analyse the social relationships in the different types of public social and health services offered to illicit drug users, and find that at the low-threshold needle exchange clinic the (often voluntary) social workers are allies of their clients, trying to help them to get medication and other help, whereas the workers at the substitution treatment clinic require a great deal of 'motivation' and effort from their clients, often with the consequence that they are felt to be part of the penalising control system rather than a help. Again, we are observing mechanisms of exclusion, including social capital and the lack of it, but from a completely different angle than the other two studies. All of them report facts that

represent the same reality, but within very different styles of reasoning and methods.

Second, the style of reasoning itself tells us about society. The three studies of social exclusion, with their different methods and concepts, involve very different problematics although their subject matter is at least partly the same. The first probably would be built on communitarian hypotheses on how social relationships support people in their self-control, autonomy and integration into educational and work life. The second would raise different kinds of questions concerning the authority of the state, the basis of selecting some pharmaceuticals as legal and others as illegal, and the intended and unintended consequences of prevention efforts. The third would pay attention to the fact that social capital may be of very different kinds, and that it is not entirely an independent variable in the processes of social exclusion but depends, instead, on power relationships in society. All three studies involve moral investments in the way they categorise their observations, they represent not only the reality as facts but also wider frameworks in which they see society, the state, the individual and the interface between citizens and the public powers. In other words, they are motivated by different interests of knowledge.

The interests of knowledge which define the needs and dispositions to explain and understand what happens in society determine the types of questions that can be asked about social reality: the *épistème*, to use Michel Foucault's term (Foucault 1966: 197). Let us call this the *epistemic dimension* of socio-logical knowledge. *Épistèmes* themselves are social facts that represent the relations of domination in the given society. The master example is Foucault's own account of the history of Western science and its ways of relating human culture and nature. It evolved from classifying and representing the natural world, including humans, in the natural history of the seventeenth and eighteenth centuries, to the study of exchange and utility in mercantilist and physiocratic economics, to the focus on work in classical economic theory, and finally to the complete separation between human and natural sciences towards the end of the nineteenth century. A similar example is Ian Hacking's analysis of the discovery of probability and stochastic processes in the early nineteenth century. This opened up whole new areas of scientific research concerning populations and mass phenomena. Such grand transformations of the *episteme* reflect society's interests in itself and its natural environment in wide philosophical terms, but as the three examples above point out, the kinds of questions society asks of itself are also reflected in research designs in a smaller scale, and the designs and questions themselves tell us something important about society.

Third, sociological studies report through their form and scientific practice quite special facts about society, namely facts about the relationship between sociologists themselves and the object of their study. This we can call the *positional*, or the *sociology of knowledge dimension* of sociological facts (Bourdieu 1982). The division of sciences into disciplines in itself is an important fact about the society that engenders it. The fact that social sciences are today separated from natural sciences, and split into sub-disciplines each with their own dominant styles of reasoning, is not simply a consequence of the accumulation of knowledge but also a real factor which has an impact on what new knowledge it can produce. Another division, especially important in sociology, is the way that scientific knowledge is entangled with but sometimes also opposed to practical knowledge about society, held by ordinary people, by policy-makers, by the media and other significant institutions.

All these three dimensions must be accounted for when we discuss the relationship between social science and social practice. Sociological studies should not be read only as reports about their objects, but symptomatically, as manifestations of the power fields of knowledge in which they operate, and of their relationships to these fields.

In all three respects the social sciences in advanced capitalist societies have undergone a transformation which we must clearly understand to see precisely what practical role they potentially serve today.

PLANNED ECONOMY AND MODE 1 SOCIAL SCIENCE

When the architect of the British welfare state, Sir William Beveridge, envisioned the state's role in the post-war society he considered that the 'spectacular achievements of the war-time planned economy' (Beveridge 1944: 120) measured by the GNP and employment should be applied to the economy in peace, which also could benefit from state regulation, and not only by means of income redistribution. The state's aim was no longer to minimise public spending but to optimise all spending in society, in regard to available labour power by means of 'manpower budgeting'. The state budget should be measured to maintain full employment but not to exceed the national manpower capacity. The Keynesian principle of full employment was translated into income equalisation in social policy and growth was its primary objective. Thus planning was not uniquely a Socialist idea; a plan designed and supervised by the centralised national state was a generally accepted European model of industrial development.

The planning did not only cover infrastructure, regional policy, monetary and fiscal policy, but also the ways in which people should lead their lives. The Swedish Alva and Gunnar Myrdal (1934) had in their famous population policy programme proposed that the state should root out bad habits among its citizens and teach them good manners. People had to be trained to take care of their households and bring up their children, although the important and complicated task of education should primarily be yielded up to professionals in nursery schools and other institutions. The state had to make people conscious of their real interests. Psychological research about happiness was needed to discover what makes life worth living according to people themselves, and the institutions of society should be formed on the basis of these observations.

The sociology associated with the *plan* was an exemplary case of what Gibbons et al. (1997) call Mode 1 science. Knowledge production in Mode 1 takes place at a distance from the context of application, as 'pure' science at the far end of the continuum from research to 'development'. Mode 1 knowledge production respects rigorous disciplinary boundaries. Its canon of accountability and quality control dictates that only intra-disciplinary expert authority is qualified to judge the validity of knowledge, the merits of the scientists and the value of their work. Mode 1 science is enclosed in the universities, and – the authors claim in a second book (Nowotny et al. 2001) – in fact not accountable at all in practical terms, such as outcomes in welfare or as impact in policy effectiveness.

Nowotny et al. (2001: 63) explain that the positivist virtue of a completely self-controlling, context-free science was cultivated in a context that had an unlimited appetite for meaning and certainty already from the eighteenth century, when Western society was experiencing an enormous wave of modernisation. The same explanation holds even more emphatically for the post-war decades in Western countries where progress, change for the better, lurked in the future biographies of not only the elites but of the great majority of people. Post-war industrialisation was particularly dramatic for Europe which, with the exception of England and Belgium, was still a continent dominated by small-holding agriculture on the eve of the Second World War. Germany, Denmark, Netherlands and Sweden all had well over one-fifth of their labour force employed in agriculture; Spain and the eastern countries including Finland had well over one-half. Thirty years turned first the west and then the central and eastern part of Europe to economies dominated numerically by the industrial working class, the peaks reaching up to almost half of the total (civilian) labour force (48.5 percent in West Germany in 1970)[1].

The post-war industrialisation produced a phenomenal growth in consumption possibilities with no parallel in human history, not relatively speaking and certainly not in absolute terms. The earlier consumer booms of the eighteenth century in England (McKendrick et al. 1982; Mukerji 1983) and still in nineteenth-century Europe (Williams 1982) were limited to small elites, but the new industry-based consumer society was a phenomenon of the masses and encompassed the structural foundations of industrial society. In retrospect this change was so drastic that it has been given dramatic names, such as the European golden era (Therborn 1995), the golden years of capitalism (Hobsbawm 1994), the glorious thirty years (Fourastié 1979) or even the second French revolution (Mendras 1988). It changed the make-up and technology of everyday life. It reconfigured both social structures and people's way of thinking about themselves and about their relationships with others. It brought to ordinary people a quantity and diversity of goods, pleasures and uses of time that either had never existed before or had only been accessible to the very privileged. Luxury was democratised and became part of everyday life. The pleasures of consumption and sensuality became publicly presentable, in everyday life as well as in the media and in marketing, whereas they had earlier been excluded from public discourses and left to the private sphere. The Weberian values of industrial society – frugality, industriousness and achievement orientation – were replaced by post-industrial or post-modern values that stress pleasure for its own sake and cherish its public presentation as much as they spurn its public control. The romantic ethos of capitalism seemed to get the upper hand.

At the same time parliamentary institutions were consolidated in all Western countries. Europe only gradually recovered from quasi-totalitarian war-time regimes, the USA from an era of ultra-nationalistic anti-communist suspicion. Value conflicts over religion, nationalism, the family, sexuality and many forms of consumption and culture gained political platforms and turned into protests and counter-protests or moral panics (Cohen 1972).

The appetite for meaning and certainty was not only of a psychological nature. The plan was a central instrument in progressive national industrial policies, and the plan required reliable and impartial information for its material. Also the moral ambivalences needed to be formulated in a language and described more systematically than with anecdotal accounts by journalists and writers or movie directors. The appetite was not only for meaning and certainty; it was also for information.

Population statistics had already a solid foundation from the late nineteenth and early twentieth century. To a lesser extent this was true also for economic and labour statistics. However, household consumption data only began to become available in the 1950s. Income and mobility surveys have an even shorter history, and individual data on specific consumption patterns (such as alcohol), sexual behaviour, political opinions and attitudes about this or that aspect of every-day life, which today are routinely provided by Eurostat, European Science Foundation, and national statistical offices, or which are industrially produced and commercialised by private 'research' companies, were still in the 1960s a rarity provided by specially funded academic research programmes. All this information required a conceptual portrayal of society – a language to describe its direction of change, and to interpret its relevance.

Even though the epistemic dimension of the sociology associated with the plan was strongly normative – preparing the good life for all – any sociology of knowledge was an alien, if not hostile, idea to Mode 1 knowledge production. Science that speaks with the voice of disciplinary authority does not highlight its subject and the subject's relationship with the reality it speaks about. To take an example from the natural sciences, the mapping out of the human genome is a collective project which advances at every new step independently of who makes that step and independently of what the consequences of the genome project will be for diagnostic practices, for treatment methods, for the lives of people with known genetic disorders, and for the lives of many other people who live with them. In the same way, one might think that if basic social

science research could detect the determining elements in human social conduct, it does not matter who participates in the production of that knowledge, and from what point of view.

Instead of engaging in the question of standpoints of knowledge, there was a strange cleavage between 'Grand Theory' and 'Abstracted Empiricism' (Mills 1959) prevalent in sociological texts of that era. The highly technical vocabulary of the former and the bureaucratic ethos of the latter appear quite distinct from each other, theory representing 'basic' or pure science with disinterested motives (beyond the interest in the establishment of the discipline itself) while the empirical researchers apply their measurements and methods to practical social issues of integration, cohesion, equality, crime prevention, youth work, health promotion, etc. Neither theory nor empiricism left much room to *human agency*, with understandable aspirations, goals and hopes. For empiricist as well as theoretical sociologists, Mills argued, the object of knowledge is *social action* – what makes members of society act in a meaningful and orderly way *from the point of view of society*. According to Mills, it was the task of emancipating social science to help out people who 'need, and feel they need ... a quality of mind that will help them to use information and to develop reason in order to achieve lucid summations of what is going on in the world and of what may be happening within themselves' (p. 5). That quality of mind, the *sociological imagination*, is offered to them by the critical sociologist who is capable of using the classical tradition to translate private problems to public issues and vice versa.

THE NEOLIBERAL TURN AND MODE 2 SOCIAL SCIENCE

By the 1970s social research in accordance with Mode 1 knowledge production was criticised increasingly often. One of the objects of critique was the problematic assumption about objective knowledge independent from the viewpoint of the knower. One solution has been to make explicit 'whose side we are on', as Howard Becker, the famous American sociologist of deviant minorities, asked in 1966, and argued that it is the task of the sociologist to side with the 'underdogs', the drug users, prostitutes, ethnic minorities or extremely poor people. The voice of such people is not heard in the media; they are not seen in the halls of power, and thus information about their lives must be produced by professional sociologists who are explicitly equipped with methodologies to make that information available (Becker 1970). But as Alvin Gouldner (1970) remarked in a famous and influential debate with Becker, such a position does not solve the problem itself, created by the division of labour between pure academic science and applied research. Being on the side of the underdog is in itself an ambiguous position. What is an underdog? There is always somebody above every overdog, and thus if we study drug users, for example, even the local police officer – an obvious overdog to the addicts – is under the authority of the police headquarters, of the municipal council, the President of the local Lions Club, and many others, not least the legislator who decided that drug use is illegal and thus a police affair. Moreover, Gouldner argued that even when sociologists take the underdog point of view they, knowingly or not, serve a constituency on whose interest their career possibilities depend.

A major blow to Mode 1 social science came from social constructionism, which pointed out that there cannot be any pure social science knowledge independent from ordinary people's everyday knowledge about society. Anthony Giddens (1979: 245–253) gave this point a famous formulation in his state-of-the-art review of social theory by saying that the twentieth-century trend in social science has been to increasingly account for the fact that people always already, without any interference from social scientists, possess enormous amounts of knowledge about society. A landmark volume to realise this had already appeared in 1966: *The Social Construction of Reality* by Berger and Luckmann (1987). They had argued that

not only do people know a great deal about their society – obviously, in order to go to school, to be employed or be an employee, to be husband and wife, to make one's way in modern traffic, to be a consumer, a political or a social citizen, one has to know a very complicated set of rules and norms – but that the whole social structure is based on such shared knowledge. Thus the proper approach to the analysis of social structure is not abstract measurement such as statistics on income distributions or class divisions but sociology of knowledge.

Once it was recognised that people know a great deal about social life, and that social scientists' knowledge is part of the same 'stock of social knowledge' in which other people also live, it is easy to dismiss Mode 1 science as an illusion. There is no pure social science, independent of the context of application, because the scientists' knowledge is itself part of the context: it serves to define situations, to conceptualise social issues and to establish selections of feasible policy options, to exclude others and so on. Social sciences are permanently challenged by everyday thought, they cannot in actual fact justify themselves only with disciplinary canons, and their academic authority is constantly questioned. Such a view stresses the positional, or sociology of knowledge-dimension of social science: scientific concepts, methods and language which produce and express facts also reflect the relationship between the scientists and their object, the people they study. Sociology committed to this view always faces what is called 'the reflexivity problem'. If social reality is significantly influenced by what people think or believe about it, and these beliefs are influenced by the believers' interests, social scientists contribute to the shaping of this reality in a way that also is infected with their interests. In what way, then, can sociologists claim that their knowledge is superior or somehow less influenced by their situation than other knowledge? Berger and Luckmann said that sociology of knowledge is 'like trying to push a bus in which one is riding' (1987: 20). To pretend that disciplinary social science is somehow neutral and virtuously outside of social reality, even in its basic theoretical part, is to make a fallacious claim of objectivity and a rather dubious attempt to cover up its partiality. Recently this view has been profusely advocated by Michael Burawoy (2005).

When Giddens made his observation that social sciences tend towards a recognition of the importance of everyday knowledge, he was in fact pointing at a major change in the relationships between social science and social practice that was occurring in *all* its three dimensions: representational, epistemic and sociology of knowledge, in the post-positivist transition. In representational terms, the so-called cultural, semiotic or linguistic turn drew sociologists' attention to critical analyses of meaning in peoples' everyday life, in the media, in cultural products and also in social science itself. In Erik Allardt's terms (2006), the hermeneutic pole in social science gained dominance vis-à-vis its complementary opposite, the positivist vision. It was observed that beyond what was taken for fact there is a complex web of communication, from statistics collectors' concepts and classifications, to respondents' interpretations and responses to them, to statistical analysis and interpretation of results by researchers and by their readers. No part in this web can be taken for granted as evident and obvious. In cultural and media studies the same ambiguity of meaning appeared in many forms. Semioticians talked about the 'referential fallacy' (Greimas and Courtès 1979), media researchers focused on the user perspective, i.e. the interaction between the media and the audience (Sulkunen and Törrönen 1997; Alasuutari 1995), and literary criticism followed Roland Barthes (1977: 142–48) in believing that the 'author is dead' – the 'meaning' of literary texts escapes the intentions of their authors, and in the extreme case it even escapes the text itself. Meaning became a problem, the object of study, the referent, instead of being simply the medium of facts.

Why? It has by now become established that the end of the 1970s marked an end of a historical period in advanced capitalist countries if we look at it from the perspective of the principles of governance. Nikolas Rose and Peter Miller (1992) have associated this change with the Foucauldian idea of governmentality, the internalisation of power by its subjects in modern society, and found its locus in the changing role of the state. Since then, an extensive literature has demonstrated that essential reforms in public management (itself a new term signalling the change) have taken place in advanced capitalist states, at times to a point where the state seemed to be withering away from capitalism altogether. Luc Boltanski and Ève Chiapello (1999), on the other hand, have studied business management doctrines and found that a similar re-organisation has taken place in the private sector even earlier. In fact, the new style of governance has shifted from business to public management with more or less success. Michael Power (1997) has confirmed this phenomenon and used the term *The Audit Society* to describe the essential change that has occurred to the role of social sciences in the new mode of power: evaluation, of which auditing is one especially important part. Using the term coined by Gibbons and associates (1997), it depicted the change from Mode 1 to Mode 2 knowledge production. In contrast with Mode 1 'pure' science, Mode 2 knowledge production takes place in the context of application; it is transdisciplinary and it is directly accountable also on grounds of its practical usefulness (Nowotny et al. 2001: 220).

. Boltanski and Chiapello concluded that by the mid-1970s industrial life had entered a deep management crisis in OECD (all Organisation for Economic Co-operation and Development) countries. The bureaucratic management structures that had been copied from the military were inadequate for performance and unacceptable from the point of view of the increasingly educated labour force. The response was to create more democratic participatory work organisations, flexible employment schemes, subcontracting, autonomous quality circles or teams, outsourcing and competition within companies. The new organisational form was no longer the hierarchy but the network, and its node was the project: a task-based uniquely funded team with autonomous leadership, targets and a deadline. Control was no longer directed from central management down to the divisions, departments and the shop-floor stewards; from now on it was not only internalised in the employees' own individual interest but also externalised to peers and to competitive relationships between operational units and profit centres.

The public management doctrines that were adopted in a short time-span in the mid-1980s in the OECD and its member countries applied the same principles to state and local government. Similar problems of bureaucratic management were to be eliminated as in the private sector, but a moral dimension was also important: citizens should no longer be seen as subjects of the state; they were put in the position of clients, and the public service-providing agencies were re-organised to meet requirements that are often called *the three Es*: *E*conomy (ensuring the best possible terms for endowed resources, implying competition between service producers), *E*fficiency (producing more value for money) and *E*ffectiveness (ensuring that outcomes conform to intentions) (Power 1997: 50). The central government is no longer authorised to issue norms to local officials and service producers such as hospitals, schools, day care services etc., but only information and advice, and resources now measured to output rather than needs.

FROM THE GOOD LIFE TO GOOD PRACTICES

Governance – or management, borrowing again the language from the business world – by information is often used to describe the new power structure. A better term to highlight the moral dimension of the change would be 'governance by programmes' or 'frameworks which have replaced the plan'. The moral and political authority of the state does not suffice to define what the good society is, what kind of life is good or bad or how to solve problems.

There is no willingness to prescribe norms of how and what we should or should not do. Nevertheless, the political responsibility has to be attested and the officials have to be given grounds for decisions about how to direct the state's money to different purposes, among other things. Frame laws and programmes that define goals, recommendations for programmes and criteria for standards are needed to achieve the purposes mentioned above. In very many areas supra-national bodies define the targets. For example in the European Union framework programmes are formulated on many issues: development of technology, employment, prevention of exclusion, regional development, promotion of health, prevention of drug problems and harmonization of education and many other things. These are again translated to national strategies, policy programmes and eventually to short-term action plans. Local and regional governments insert these to their own objectives and action plans. The formulations of these goals are of very general nature in the programmes and their accentuations usually correspond to those of the general public administration thinking: in alcohol and drug programmes the goals are the responsibility of citizens themselves, initiative, networking and relying on the support of neighbourhood communities, to name just a few.

From the epistemic point of view, governance by programmes and frameworks rather than by plans means that society asks itself different kinds of questions than before. Social sciences that were attached to the plan were expected to say what happens if we do X, and what should be done to make Y happen. Now the questions are: in regard with the *three Es*, which of the projects A, B, C … N meet best the objectives of the programme? For example, the objective might be to minimise alcohol-related problems. The central government does not have the means at its disposal to reduce alcohol consumption in the country, or is reluctant to use such policy instruments (price increases, permitted hours of sale and other regulations of the market); instead it asks local communities, non-governmental organisations (NGOs), businesses, labour unions, churches, etc. to establish innovative projects and have them evaluated for economy, efficiency and effectiveness (Sulkunen 2006).

The central concept in goal and framework management, 'innovation', has been used in the science and technology policy already for a long time. The administration cannot predetermine the results of the researchers or the direction of the development interests of companies, but it can take a stand on the direction of the development in general and make strategic policy definitions. New ideas come from the 'grassroots level', from fieldworkers and citizens themselves. Transferred to social policy, the pattern of 'innovation thinking' has assimilated traits of romantic rationalism: people are thought to be creative and the solutions have to be given space to develop and grow upwards from down under. The researchers should evaluate and strengthen these tendencies instead of planning. The primary tasks of evaluation are surveillance of expenses, ensuring quality and supervision of observance of rules and regulations: tasks which used to belong to inspectors and superintendents of state governance. Often they include, though, more ambitious goals of generalisation, which are called recognizing good practices.

The expressions 'good practice' and 'what works' originate from prison administration (Garland 2001), and from there they have spread to social work and public administration in general. This manner of speech is an application of solution-oriented therapy or pedagogy, which detaches itself from analysing reasons of problematic behaviour and instead concentrates on the recognition of the effects of alternative action models. The search for reasons is, according to this perspective, not only a waste of time but it might also have negative effects. When criminals learn about the causes of their behaviour, those causes become 'vocabularies of motive', justifications and rhetoric for escaping responsibility (Sykes and Matza 1957).

The recognition of good and working practices is pragmatic thinking. The behaviour of a person is a sum of such complicated factors, that the practical social work in prisons, for example, cannot commit only to one or a few explanation models and their conclusions concerning *clients*. It is more useful to observe the effects of the existing methods of *social work itself* and choose the methods that seem functioning and cost-effective. The innovation thinking is dressed in the rhetoric of good practice, and it leads to a sort of new social Darwinism. Clients and employees are given free hands to invent new kinds of action models, mutations, and eventually the most fit among them are chosen for additional refining on the basis of expert reports. Evaluation is then considered the unbiased and unemotional mechanism of social and natural selection.

The other side of pragmatic thinking is moral neutrality. Assumption that the methods of social work or the alternatives for control policies could be evaluated only in regard of their functionality and effectiveness, presupposes a strong unanimity of goals – the employment, health and security of the population being considered good objectives and repeated offences a bad one, for example. In programme rhetoric neutrality leads to abstracticism and definitional – and at the same time administrative – ambiguity. Promotion of health is a good example of this. Another is management of security. This rhetoric calls the acts of officials with a general name that has a morally neutral flavour. It is easy for everyone to accept, but at the same time it expands the range of goals of the officials and experts and blurs the boundaries of their actions. The other moral points of view related to the matter – the customers' freedom of choice or the sense of justice of many citizens demanding more severe punishment for criminals, for example – can be forgotten from the standpoint of effectiveness.

THE FICTIONS OF EVALUATION RESEARCH

From the point of view of the sociology of knowledge, governance by programmes positions the sociologist in a new relationship with social practice, exactly like Nowotny et al. (2001) describes it as characteristic of Mode 2 knowledge production. Social research operates in the context of application; it is not constrained by disciplinary boundaries and the criteria of its accountability are less academic than practical: tell us what works, and we shall be pleased *not* to know why something else might *not* work.

If the idea of 'pure science' in the positivist Mode 1 knowledge production was an illusion, but an illusion in a real context with real consequences, are the ideals of Mode 2 social science more realistic and convincing? To some extent the answer is positive: social science that operates in a context and is aware of its own vested interests is more honest about itself and potentially also more relevant than social science built on the fiction of basic science and applied research. However, also Mode 2 science attached to the programme rather than to the plan has its illusions, as real as the fiction of Mode 1 science but in a different context and with different consequences. The first illusion arises from the logic of governance by programmes itself: abstract objectives.

Programme and evaluation rhetoric make politics look rational, and hierarchical decision-making just like business management. But what does state need this rhetoric for? Why is it impossible for example for a ministry to decide on its strategy in alcohol policy and to follow that strategy in financing and other solutions? One reason for this is the pursuit of political neutrality already discussed above. The ministry does not want to decide or it considers itself incapable to dictate how municipalities, organisations, companies – or other ministries – should act in order to decrease problems caused by alcohol consumption. To preserve the autonomy of those actors the policy goals are defined with abstract concepts, of which employment, health and security are the most central ones. It is always possible to reach unanimity concerning those goals, even though the moral or power resources would not always suffice to make concrete policy decisions. The rhetoric of 'what works' and 'best practices'

reflects what we have called the Ethics of Not Taking a Stand, quoting a fieldworker we interviewed on how she advises parents to behave in the drug issue: 'The most ethical stand is not to take a stand at all, the parents should decide this for themselves' (Määttä et al. 2003).

Abstraction has also another legitimating function. It protects the sphere of intimacy, which was the historical goal of the welfare state: the self-responsibility of citizens, individual agency and commitment to good choices to promote a person's own health, security and well-being. This is not limited to rhetoric or ideological speech, but it is part of the everyday life of advanced capitalist society. For example, the health care expert system is relatively helpless if the patient is unwilling to co-operate: 'only the medication that is taken will help'. But you cannot force anyone to co-operate. You cannot get overweight under control unless consumers eat less. Disciplining consumers' food choices directly would be felt as unacceptable paternalism. They will have to take responsibility for their own choices.

In programmes with very concrete targets such as weight loss the outcomes are easily measured. However, in many cases standards of performance are more ambiguous, and the audit or evaluation of efficiency and effectiveness is in fact a process of defining and operationalising them, often with perverse effects on the actual operation of the system. A good example is research evaluation. In theory, university departments and research institutes are expected to produce relevant good quality research, but the auditing criterion: articles published in refereed journals, leads to an increase in the number of such journals, with the consequence that fewer people read them and the social relevance of research results declines. Nevertheless, money is invested in them because the effective alternative, such as taxing food or alcohol, is not included in the repertoire of acceptable policies.

Governance by programmes and frameworks thus supports what Nowotny et al. (2001) consider the key features of the

Mode 2 science. Abstract objectives of evaluation research in the context of application encourage transdisciplinarity and pragmatic division of labour. When the interest is not directed at explaining behaviour nor even at the mechanisms of effects of the measures taken, but only at the effectiveness of the alternative action models, there is no need for the research of alcohol problems, youth culture or deviant behaviour but for skilful evaluation researchers who can flexibly move from one substance area to another. Corresponding abstracticism is visible in the training of fieldworkers and their division of work. As the French sociologist Robert Castel (1981: 135–44) has claimed, the professionalisation of social work has not actually led to the often anticipated medicalisation nor specialisation of other kind. Instead there has developed a paraprofessional mixed type, the general task of which is social control.

The abstracticism of goal and framework management has resulted in efficiency and effectiveness becoming passkey concepts that are applied everywhere. Sometimes, however, they misrepresent the reality that they are supposed to evaluate. For example, every society will need to take care of addicts in some way. For the clients' welfare as well as for the institutions – the police, social offices, penal and medical institutions – the most relevant questions relate not to outcomes in terms of recovery but to the division of labour between controlling and helping professions. This, however, is not an issue of performance but of ethics and values. Constrained to evaluating efficiency and effectiveness, Mode 2 social science may in fact sustain inefficient responses instead of asking pragmatically relevant questions about their rationale.

THE RETURN OF CAUSALITY AND ITS OLD PROBLEMS

The second illusion of the new mode of practical social science arises from the requirements of efficiency and effectiveness. Both are based on the notion of causality. The concept of

effect is a part of the equipment of science, as well as of everyday thinking. We light the lamp, roast the ham, start the car, give an advice to another person or call a meeting assuming on the basis of our prior experience, that a certain state of affairs will follow. We do not usually ask why it results from that action. Only when the lamp does not get lighted, the ham does not roast or advice or invitation are not followed, do we start investigating the error. Even then we don't have to know much about the mechanisms of the causal chain, but we can lean on our prior experience. We routinely change the bulb, check the fuse and the position of the ignition key or whether our advice or invitation has actually been received. Only in very exceptional circumstances do we have to lean on expert support, that is to say we utilise research-based knowledge to explain the mechanism between the cause and the effect and this directs us to look for the error in the different parts of the chain.

In evaluation research the primary interest of knowledge is similar to our everyday causal thinking. The interest of knowledge is not to establish general laws about social life but to verify whether the action causes the desired effect or not. This could be called clinical causal thinking. Its objective is not to explain the mechanisms of effects, but only to test pragmatically if they are there, how much they vary and are there possibly some ill effects. Medicine that is based on evidence and the medicine-influenced social policy of the same type are examples of clinical causal thinking[2]. Still, clinical causal thinking has similarly limiting logical conditions as the causality tests of the research laboratories. The cause and the effect have to be logically independent and empirically dependent on one another; the cause factor has to be adjustable in an unambiguous and measurable manner; and the effect of other variables has to be eliminated experimentally or statistically. Also there have to exist unambiguous means for measuring the effect, which has to follow the cause temporarily.

Some clinical medical research is able to come up with these expectations. The medicament will stay the same in spite of who it is given to and who hands it out, and the human body is approximately the same in different circumstances. Usually it is possible to control the effect of differences with the reliability that meets the expectations of the practice. In social work and social policy the conditions of clinical research can be measured up only in exceptional circumstances. As Tom Erik Arnkil and Jaakko Seikkula (2005: 60) have claimed, a psychosocial work does not move from a certain place, actor or situation to another remaining the same, as medication. No 'method' or 'model' can be independent of the agent who delivers it, who receives it, or that would be conceptually independent of the effect it aims at.

Evaluation is usually performed in a situation where a test or even comparative configuration of any kind is not possible. Ordinarily the evaluator is contacted when the funding of the project has already been granted, its staff and principal idea are decided, and the fieldwork of the project has already partly started. Some vested interests have already been created, the good-willing mission is an inspirational source for action, and there is no time or resources for comparison presupposed by a real evaluation of effectiveness. The expectation of establishing causality turns into a thin fiction.

CONCLUSION AND DISCUSSION

In this article I have discussed the relationship of social science to social practice, and argued that a radical paradigm shift occurred in the 1980s in all advanced capitalist countries from the positivist mode associated with the idea of the plan to a more context-based science attached to governance by programmes and frameworks. The change reflects the new practices of governance that were introduced at the same historical period in the business world as well as in public management. In social science knowledge production the shift corresponds to a transition from what Gibbons et al. (1997) call a transition from Mode 1 to Mode 2 science.

This shift has had implications at three levels: referential (what is studied), epistemic (what kinds of questions are asked) and sociology of knowledge in a narrow sense (position of scientists in relation to the object of their research and to those whose knowledge needs they serve).

I have also argued that Mode 1 social science was a deviation rather than a long tradition in modern social science. It was associated with governance by plan in the post-war decades of state-driven industrialisation and construction of the welfare states. It had important functions in providing a conceptual portrayal of society and the theoretical framework for growing needs for monitoring and information, which now are mostly covered by information systems other than the social sciences. However, Mode 1 social science was also an illusion, and many social scientists and critics were aware of this.

The shift to Mode 2 science was a reaction to internal developments within the social sciences but more importantly it reflects the epochal change in the logic of governance in capitalist societies from the plan to programmes and frameworks. This change is deeply rooted in the structure of capitalist societies which stress individuality and autonomy of agents. Fixity on abstract targets, good practices and causal relationships in Mode 2 science are fictions too, but on the other hand, science which is aware of its own context has a greater critical potential and capacity to act as 'public sociology' than a discipline that is divided between pure science and applied research.

NOTES

1 Therborn 1995, table 4.4, p. 66, and table 4.6, p. 69.
2 The so-called Cochrane-library collects the results of clinical treatment research, evaluates their validity and draws conclusions on the probabilities of the effects of the methods. Corresponding work has been done in social policy under the name of Campbell-cooperation.

REFERENCES

Alasuutari, Pertti (1995) *Researching Culture. Qualitative Method and Cultural Studies.* London: Sage.

Allardt, Erik (2006) 'The Twofold Nature of Sociology: Positivistic and Hermeneutic', *International Journal of Contemporary Sociology*, 43(2): 248–61.

Arnkil, Tom Erik and Seikkula, Jaakko (2005) *Dialoginen verkostotyö. (Dialogical meetings in social networks.)* Helsinki: Tammi.

Barthes, Roland (1977) *Images, Music, Text. Essays.* London: Fontana.

Becker, Howard S. (1970) 'Whose Side are We On?', in Douglas, Jack D. (ed.) *The Relevance of Sociology.* New York: Appleton-Century-Crofts. pp. 99–111. (1st edn, 1966.)

Berger, Peter and Luckmann, Thomas (1987) *The Social Construction of Reality.* Harmondsworth: Penguin Books. (1st edn, 1966.)

Beveridge, William (1944) *Full Employment in a Free Society.* London: George Allen & Unwin.

Bhaskar, Roy (1975) *A Realist Theory of Science.* Leeds: Books.

Boltanski, Luc and Chiapello, Ève (1999) *Le nouvel esprit du capitalisme.* Paris: Nrf Essais.

Bourdieu, Pierre (1982) *La leçon sur la leçon.* Paris: Éditions de Minuit.

Burawoy, Michael (2005) 'American Sociological Association Presidential Address: For Public Sociology', *The British Journal of Sociology*, 56(2): 259–94.

Castel, Robert (1981) *La gestion des risques. De l'anti-psychiatrie à l'après-psychanalyse.* Paris: Éditions de Minuit.

Cohen, Stanley (1972) *Folk Devils and Moral Panics.* London: MacGibbon and Kee.

Foucault, Michel (1966) *Les Mots et les Choses.* Paris: Gallimard.

Fourastié, Jean (1979) *Les trente glorieuses.* Paris: Fayard.

Garland, David (2001) *The Culture of Control: Crime and Social Order in Contemporary Society.* Oxford: Oxford University Press.

Gibbons, Michael, Limoges, Camille, Nowotny, Helga, Schwartzman, Simon, Scott, Peter and Trow, Martin (1997) *The New Production of Knowledge. The Dynamics of Science and Research in Contemporary Societies.* London: Sage. (1st edn, 1994.)

Giddens, Anthony (1979) *Central Problems in Social Theory: Action, Structure and Contradiction in Social Analysis.* London: Macmillan Press.

Gouldner, Alwin W. (1970) 'Anti-Minotaur: The Myth of a Value-free Sociology', in Douglas, Jack D. (ed.) *The Relevance of Sociology.* New York: Appleton-Century-Crofts. pp. 64–84.

Greimas and Courtès (1979) *Sémiotique - dictionnaire raisonné de la théorie du langage.* Paris: Hachette.

Hacking, Ian (1990) *The Taming of Chance.* Cambridge: The Cambridge University Press.

Hobsbawm, Eric John (1994) *Age of Extremes: the Short Twentieth Century 1914–1991.* London: Abacus.

McKendrick, Neil, Brewer, John and Plumb, J.H. (1982) *The Birth of a Consumer Society. The Commercialization of Eighteenth-Century England.* London: Hutchinson.

Mendras, Henri (1988) *La seconde révolution française 1965–1984.* Paris: Gallimard.

Mills, C. Wright (1959) *The Sociological Imagination.* New York: Oxford University Press.

Mukerji, Chandra (1983) *From Craven Images: Patterns of Modern Materialism.* New York: Columbia University Press.

Myrdal, Alva and Myrdal, Gunnar (1934) *Kris i befolkningsfrågan (Crisis in the Population Question).* Stockholm: Albert Bonniers förlag.

Määttä, Mirja, Rantala, Kati and Sulkunen, Pekka (2003) 'The Ethics of Not Taking a Stand. Dilemmas of Drug and Alcohol Prevention in a Consumer Society – a Case Study', *International Journal of Drug Policy*, 15(5–6): 427–34.

Nowotny, Helga, Scott, Peter and Gibbons, Michael (2001) *Re-Thinking Science. Knowledge and the Public in an Age of Uncertainty.* Cambridge: Polity Press.

Power, Michael (1997) *The Audit Society. Rituals of Verification.* Oxford: Oxford University Press.

Rose, Nikolas and Miller, Peter (1992) 'Political Power Beyond the State: Problematics of Government', *The British Journal of Sociology*, 43(2): 173–205.

Sulkunen Pekka (2006) 'Projektiyhteiskunta ja uusi yhteiskuntasopimus', in Rantala Kati and Sulkunen, Pekka (eds) *Projektiyhteiskunnan kääntöpuolia (The Flip-side of the project society).* Helsinki: Gaudeamus.

Sulkunen Pekka and Törrönen Jukka (1997) 'Constructing Speaker Images: The Problem of Enunciation in Discourse Analysis', *Semiotica*, 115(1–2): 121–46.

Sykes, Gresham and Matza, David (1957) 'Techniques of Neutralization: A Theory of Juvenile Delinquency', *American Sociological Review*, 22(6): 664–73.

Therborn, Göran (1995) *European Modernity and Beyond. The Trajectory of European Societies 1945–2000.* London: Sage.

Williams, Rosalind H. (1982) *Dream Worlds. Mass Consumption in Late Nineteenth-Century France.* Berkeley: University of California Press.

From Questions of Methods to Epistemological Issues: The Case of Biographical Research

Ann Nilsen

INTRODUCTION

There is a long tradition of research from biographical approaches[1] in sociology. Many and varied studies have been carried out from this perspective over time. My concern in this chapter is however not to outline the history of empirical studies in the field. Rather the intention is to focus on some of the methodological debates that have been prominent during different phases from the 1920s to the present. These discussions are of interest in their own right. They are also important because different methodological perspectives invite focus on different aspects of social reality. Biographical research is also a good *case*[2] to highlight important features of a wider methodological debate. Even though this chapter has no ambition of addressing the history of these debates in the social sciences in a broader sense, discussions in biographical research cannot be explored without reference to the wider field of methodological questions.

The history of the shifts in topics for debate in biographical research is set within the wider field of qualitative research. A number of different qualitative methods exist. A focus on biographical research highlights issues that have been important in different phases of the development of these methods. It demonstrates very clearly the main change in discussions; from method and methodological concerns in the early days, to more epistemological and ontological questions that have come to dominate the field from the 1980s onwards. These debates form the parameters between which methodological debates are set and are important for understanding the types of discussions that have dominated many areas of the social sciences, sociological biographical research in particular, over the time period. Thus the different sections in the chapter will highlight debates with reference to ontological/epistemological foundations of methodological discussions that were important in different phases.

In order to set the discussion within the wider context of methodological issues, the starting point here is a brief overview over some main lines of questions and concepts associated with the methodological debates.

TERMS AND CONCEPTS IN METHODOLOGICAL DISCUSSIONS: A BRIEF OVERVIEW

The meaning of the term 'method' has changed over time. The earliest book on social research methods: Emile Durkheim's *The Rules of Sociological Methods* (1972 [1895]), was not widely known in the English-speaking academia until its translation into English in 1938. Durkheim's objective was to write a text to discuss methods explicitly (Durkheim 1972, p. 19)[3]. As Platt (1996, p. 252) observes in a discussion about changes in interpretation over time, Durkheim's work in the English-speaking world came to be associated with method and the kind of multivariate analysis advocated by Lazarsfeld and his colleagues in the 1950s because of the use they made of his writings in their discussions on *method as technique* (Kaplan 1964).

Methodology is a concept often used synonymously with the term method[4]. Whereas the term 'method' in most cases refers to procedures or techniques for gathering evidence, methodology has a wider meaning. For the current purpose a definition of methodology that highlights the wider field of discussions about methods, and the relationship between method and theory, will be referred to. Kaplan (1964) gives the following definition of methodology: 'I mean by *methodology* the study – the description, the explanation, and the justification – of methods, and not the methods themselves' (p. 18). On the aim of methodology he continues: '[…] the aim of methodology is to help us to *understand*, in the broadest possible terms, not the products of scientific inquiry but the process itself' (Kaplan 1964, p. 23). Harding (1987) discussing these issues along the same lines, broadens the meaning of methodology even more when she observes that, 'A *methodology*

is a theory and analysis of how research does or should proceed; it includes accounts of how the general structure of theory finds its application in particular scientific disciplines' (p. 3). The connection between methods, methodology, epistemology[5] and ontology, is complex and is often debated in writings about method. For Harding this relationship can be thought of as concentric circles where method forms the inner circle and ontology the outer (ibid). This could in some instances be thought to imply that choices of methods bring with them certain methodological and epistemological assumptions. However, in discussions about the quantitative-qualitative divide in social science methods, the claim that choice of method implies certain epistemological underpinnings, is but one of several standpoints in the debate (see e.g. Platt 1996; Bryman 2004).

Throughout the history of the social sciences one of the most salient debates in the field of research methods has been that discussing the 'quantitative-qualitative' divide. Even though the general understanding of the distinction between the two involves techniques for collecting and analysing data, the boundaries between them are not as clear-cut if aspects of methodology and epistemology are brought to bear on the discussion (Brannen 1995; Bryman 2004). As Platt (1996) points out in writing on the history of methods discussions in America, the terms and concepts for describing methods have changed over time. The quantitative-qualitative divide was described in terms of 'case studies vs. statistical methods' before World War II. 'Survey' was in this period used to describe a method in studies of whole communities, whereas its modern use is associated with large-scale statistical studies. The term 'case study' derived from social workers' cases that were used by sociologists as data at a time when the boundaries between social work and sociology were not clearly defined (Platt 1996; Levin 2000). Life histories were used synonymously with case studies (Platt 1992, 1996). When the focus shifted in the 1950s from *what data was about* to the *way it was collected,* the debates changed and what was earlier known as case studies now known as 'qualitative' research. In circles where quantitative methods were regarded as the only truly objective methods for collecting objective data, qualitative methods were thought of as useful only in initial stages of a study.

Current discussions about the quantitative-qualitative issue are more open to bridging the divide where data and methods are concerned (Brannen 1995; Bryman 2004). Bryman (2004) points out how different ways of approaching the discussion are decisive of whether multi-strategy research is deemed possible or not. If the divide is seen in terms of methods for collecting and analysing data – the technical version – the gap is easy to bridge. However, if the quantitative-qualitative divide is referred to in terms of different epistemologies, multi-method approaches are not easy to apply. This latter point goes to the heart of the discussion in this paper; different epistemological positions invite different standpoints to what data is, and indeed also whether the very term 'data' is considered valid.

BIOGRAPHICAL MATERIAL

One definition of a biographical account is *a story told in the present about a person's experiences of events in the past and her or his expectations for the future* (Nilsen 1997). The term 'biographical material' does however cover a wide range of empirical evidence: personal letters, diaries, photographs, written autobiographical accounts (life stories) and more (Plummer 1983, 2001; Roberts 2002). In this paper the discussion is focused on research material stemming from interviews.

Life stories come in many varieties and one way of classifying is offered by Plummer (2001)[6]. He makes a distinction between *long* and *short* stories, where the first is the full-length story of one person's life, and the latter is based on more stories. A further distinction is related to the 'depth' of the accounts and is between *comprehensive, topical* or *edited* life stories. The comprehensive is a story of one

person's life in depth where the subject's voice is at the centre. A topical story focuses on one particular issue in persons' lives and is aimed at researching a particular area of life whereas edited stories leave the researcher's voice at the forefront. Plummer also makes a distinction referring to researcher 'interference' with accounts; *naturalistic stories* are spontaneously given accounts, researchers have not prompted them. Researched accounts are those that researchers have asked informants to provide, and reflexive stories are those where researchers reflect on their own partaking in the creating and constructing of a story (Plummer 2001, pp. 19–35). In current research there might be a focus on single individuals or groups of individuals such as families (Brannen et al. 2004), or as in the case of Bertaux and Thompson's study of social mobility in families (1997) and Bourdieu's study of socially excluded people in France, focusing on issues such as social class and try and map out meaning behind statistics (Bourdieu et al. 1999).

Ways of analysing such material varies with the overall approach taken by the researcher, as well as the purpose for having collected it to start with. When using biographical material other sources of data are inevitably drawn on to map out and understand the different layers of context lives are embedded in (Nilsen and Brannen 2005). In spite of this paper focusing mainly on one perspective in particular, it is nevertheless clear, as the following will demonstrate, that there is no such thing as one correct way of approaching biographical research material, and as the method has evolved into multiple ways of collecting biographical material, methods of analysis have also become many and varied.

An important theoretical influence for the discussion in this paper is the tradition from which biographical research originates: American pragmatism as developed by Peirce and Mead, especially with reference to notions of self and the social world as well as the type of ontological perspective that informed the works of these two (Lewis and Smith 1980). This perspective has been influential in most European approaches to biographical research, although as the following discussion will highlight, other epistemological standpoints and theoretical approaches have become more prominent over time.

THE MAKING OF A SOCIOLOGICAL METHOD: CHICAGO CA. 1920

One of the most comprehensive sociological studies to date is W. I. Thomas and F. Znaniecki's *The Polish Peasant in Europe and America* published in five volumes (1918–20)[7]. It is a study of Polish migrants in Poland and in Chicago, where they settled upon arrival in the USA. Based on a number of sources of data such as official documents and statistics, it also included personal letters, diaries and one autobiographical account: that of the peasant Wladek. For many reasons the study was not fully recognised as the accomplishment it was until nearly 20 years after it was published. In 1938 the American Sociological Association elected the study as one of the greatest works in sociology. The appraisal proceedings were convened by Herbert Blumer and were published in 1939. The book makes fascinating reading for anyone interested in social science methodology as the discussions in the panel are quoted verbatim.

The debates were set in a time period when positivism[8] defined the boundaries of what was to be considered science. Dilemmas discussed at the appraisal proceedings included whether 'subjective factors' should play a role in social science research, and if so, how was this to be accomplished? Following from this, another question – that of whether and to what extent 'human documents' could be considered reliable sources of data – became central. Wladek's autobiographical account, the first ever to be used as a sociological source of data, was especially scrutinised with reference to whether or not it could be considered *reliable*.

The underlying ontological premise in positivistic thinking is that reality is *fixed* and exists independent of human observation and interpretation[9]. According to this position, the role of any scientific endeavour is to uncover the basic laws that govern any phenomenon under scrutiny. Thus Thomas and Znaniecki, in keeping with their time, sought through the study of Polish immigrant society in Chicago and in Poland, to uncover 'laws of social becoming'. Such laws were sought by focusing on the objective (values) and the subjective (attitudes) sides of social life. The insistence on including subjective factors in social analysis was new at the time the study was carried out. It had the potential to undermine one of the basic premises of positivist social science: that objective facts alone could constitute the data studies were to be based upon. Their methodological principle was formulated as follows: *The cause of a social or individual phenomenon is never another social or individual phenomenon alone, but always a combination of a social and an individual phenomenon* (Blumer 1979 [1939], p. 9). Their standpoint was contrary to positivist social science also in that they did not see physics as the paradigmatic science the social sciences should model itself on:

> [...] while the effect of a physical phenomenon depends exclusively on the objective nature of this phenomenon and can be calculated on the ground of the latter's empirical content, the effect of a social phenomenon depends in addition on the subjective standpoint taken by the individual or group toward this phenomenon. (Thomas and Znaniecki 1918, p. 38 cited in Blumer 1939, p. 11)

The epistemological basis of pragmatist thought as represented by Peirce and Mead (Lewis and Smith 1980) could be thought of as a form of *processual* realism in that it does indeed presuppose independent reality, but this reality is not fixed as in positivist thinking. Reality itself changes in time and humans as social beings create reality as a collective activity. In contrast to a constructionist position, which highlights the social constructed nature of reality and rejects any independent qualities of it, the form of realism found in Peirce and Mead defined itself in contrast to their contemporary variety of constructionism, namely *idealism* (Lewis and Smith 1980). Drawing this parallel is reasonable because what idealism and constructionism share is a set of questions starting from epistemological foundations rather than ontology; 'what can be known' is the idealist/constructionist epistemological question, whereas 'what is there' is a realist ontological approach. Starting enquiry from the former blurs the boundaries between ontology and epistemology in that reality is seen only in terms of knowledge as expression of what is known – language.

The transcript of the conference proceedings following Blumer's critique demonstrates how the discussion and comments centred very much on the value of subjective data, and to what extent these could be regarded as 'scientific'. Indeed Blumer himself maintains that the human documents used by Thomas and Znaniecki could not be tested in a scientific way, and that their claim to have developed concepts from the empirical material could consequently not be regarded as valid (Blumer 1939, pp. 109–111). The discussion is interesting for several reasons, not least because some of Blumer's viewpoints anticipate his later writings. During the discussion he refuses to enter into a debate about validity, and concludes that his viewpoints coincide with those of Thomas and Znaniecki in that he believes the ultimate test of theory is whether it makes sense in relation to the data to which it refers (Blumer 1939, p. 115). This position is contrary to a strict positivist standpoint, where validity criteria are related to a theory's capability to *predict* in research beyond a single study[10]. The discussion in the panel thus demonstrates how *The Polish Peasant* as an example of empirical research challenged mainstream thought in the social sciences of its day. It did so by emphasising the need for research to include subjective accounts in empirical studies in order to make sense of the social world, and in doing so, it also challenged core discussions not only about questions of method, but also by moving the discussion into the realm of epistemological and methodological issues.

Anglo-American social research from the forties onwards entered into a phase where statistical methods became the dominant way of studying social phenomena (Platt 1996). A positivist way of thinking social science formed the epistemological basis of these methods[11]. When new technology made it feasible to handle large quantities of data within a shorter time-span, it became easier to focus on sophisticated statistical techniques for analysing data rather than questioning the validity of the data itself, or discussing design of studies or ontological and epistemological foundations for social research more generally. The phase when questions of *method as technique* (Kaplan 1964) were predominant lasted well into the seventies. As Blumer remarks in his foreword to the 1979 edition of the *Appraisal of The Polish Peasant*,

> It is believed today that generalizations are to be sought and that analyses are to be made in the form of relations and correlations between 'objective' variables. Further, even when sociological scholars are sensitive to so-called subjective factors, they are highly unlikely to rely on letters and life histories to catch such factors. (Blumer 1979, p. xi)

The situation was however not as bleak throughout the whole period as this suggests. Herbert Blumer's own work is but one example of alternative ways of thinking about social science and questions of method. In 1956 he published an article called 'What is wrong with social theory?' where he raised issues that had been touched upon in the *Appraisal* procedures. Some of the questions he did not want to explore during that discussion were developed in this paper. He sought to draw boundaries between the social sciences and the natural sciences by examining notions of theoretical concepts in both. For the social sciences to develop on its own terms and in order to free itself from the paradigmatic status that classical physics still enjoyed, he suggested that concepts in the social sciences be termed and treated as *sensitising concepts* in contrast to the *definite concepts* characteristic of the natural sciences (Blumer 1954). The former are theoretical concepts that indicate a direction in which to look, rather than concepts with strict definitions that tell you precisely what to look for, which is what definite concepts do.

Throughout his career Blumer sought to challenge 'variable sociology' by doing empirical studies that were in keeping with his notions that sociology was to be centred on studies of social interaction[12]. His naming of *symbolic interactionism* as a strand of sociology that developed the heritage from G.H. Mead's *social behaviourism* is evidence of this. Blumer's symbolic interactionism has been very influential for the development of biographical research, not least in the work of Norman Denzin. This will, however, be the topic of a later section.

Other alternative strands of thought existed, also in American sociology. The most radical critique of the situation in the social sciences came from a scholar who by many was regarded as an outsider but whom nevertheless made his mark in a distinctive way.

POSITIVISM CHALLENGED: THE SOCIOLOGICAL IMAGINATION

C. Wright Mills published *The Sociological Imagination* in 1959, three years before his death in 1962. The ideas presented in this book were developed throughout his career as an empirical researcher and a critic of much of his contemporary researchers' work. He was especially critical of the dominance of what he on the one hand called 'The Theory' which referred to a tendency to seek explanations for social phenomena in large bodies of thought known as 'Grand Theory' of the Parsonian variety, and on the other hand what he called 'The Method': statistical techniques for analysing huge datasets. The most prominent advocate of the latter was one of Mills' earlier superiors, Paul Lazarsfeld. Mills' critique was grounded in an alternative vision of what sociology was to be about. The historical period known as the cold war did not take kindly to a politically radical figure such as Mills. However, he was a productive empirical researcher and studies such as *White Collar* and *The Power Elite* received wide acclaim.

Even though Mills himself did not carry out biographical research in the tradition of

Thomas and Znaniecki, his thoughts on what empirical material sociology should concern itself with, emphasised the value of such data. In early writings he outlined thoughts about methodological issues (Mills 1940) that were later presented more extensively in *The Sociological Imagination*. Mills' work moved the discussion from method as technique, to the realms of methodology and epistemology. Very much influenced by American pragmatist thought and also by Karl Mannheim's sociology of knowledge, his views on social reality coincided with those of Mead in that he thought of the self as *in process* in social contexts that were also in continual development, hence his insistence on the proper subject for sociological study to be *the intersection between history and biography*. Only in studying the actions, thoughts and feelings of individuals and contextualising them in particular moments in history, can sociology fulfil its potential:

> [The sociological imagination] is the capacity to range from the most impersonal and remote transformations to the most intimate features of the human self – and to see the relations between the two. Back of its use there is always the urge to know the social and historical meaning of the individual in the society and in the period in which he has his quality and his being. (Mills 1980 [1959], p. 14)

Evident in this are his notions of theory that were closely linked to his thoughts on methodology and his epistemological and ontological beliefs. As to the latter he can be characterised as a realist of the variety found in the pragmatism of Peirce and Mead meaning that he thought of social reality as existing beyond human interpretation; yet interpretation (what Thomas and Znaniecki termed the subjective side of social reality or *attitudes*) was an inescapable part of empirical data. His processual and double-natured view of social reality lay at the heart of his vision of what the sociological imagination was and what role sociology had in society. It also informed his thoughts on data and methods for analysing them: his methodological viewpoints. In the appendix to *The Sociological Imagination* he outlines in much detail how social science studies can be carried out in order to collect and produce empirical material and how to analyse it in ways that shed light on the crucial questions of a particular period in history; identifying how *private troubles* and *public issues* are interconnected for people living in particular places at some defined period in history (ibid). Empirical material includes biographical accounts as told and interpreted by individuals themselves, in addition to information of a more factual kind; records and facts about life courses in general and about the society in which the individual lives unfold. He did in other words advocate the use of data from many different sources in order to understand the layers of context that people's lives are embedded in.

Mills' writings did not result in any revival of biographical research in his time. It took nearly two decades after the publication of *The Sociological Imagination* for this research tradition to re-emerge, this time in Europe.

METHOD DISCUSSIONS: CHANGES IN APPROACHES TO THE QUANTITATIVE-QUALITATIVE DIVIDE

As positivism came under close scrutiny and critique from philosophers and social scientists alike throughout the 1960s and 70s, mainstream social science debates were still stuck within the parameters of discussion defined by positivist notions of science: those of methods as techniques. Questions about validity and reliability of data, of generalisations and representativeness were argued over across the borders between qualitative and quantitative research.

The publishing of *The Discovery of Grounded Theory* (Glaser and Strauss 1967) was important for the development of qualitative research in its own right. The main thesis in this book challenged contemporary notions of theory and method both. Where surveys were analysed to test hypotheses based on theoretical assumptions formulated beforehand, grounded theory suggested a way of carrying out research and analysis starting from data and building concepts and theories

from the ground up[13]. Qualitative data, such as observation and interviews, was the main source of empirical evidence in this approach. It thus helped to develop a logic of method that was said to be particular to qualitative analysis[14].

Another approach that emerged in the 1970s was life course research, a quantitative way of analysing data with special attention to life course events seen in light of cohorts and historical periods. Age is of special relevance as social institutions in most societies are organised such that cohorts go through the same events at roughly the same chronological age, for instance the system of education (Elder 1974; Riley 1988; Giele and Elder 1998). This perspective, which is quantitative and owes much to both demographic studies and more macro-oriented social research as found in the classic texts as well as to Mills' approach to sociology, has been influential also in qualitative approaches in that both see *temporal* aspects of social processes, and the link between macro and micro, as central to social research (Giele and Elder 1998). Methodologically, life course research with its large datasets that can span generations of individuals is oriented towards debates on statistical analyses and methods as technique. Following Bryman's (2004) distinction between an approach to the quantitative-qualitative divide as one based on data and methods on the one hand, and the more epistemologically founded one on the other, quantitative life course research and qualitative biographical approaches can easily be combined if the former stance is taken. However, as will be seen in the following, this combination of data is not possible with all types of approaches to biographical material.

THE REVIVAL OF BIOGRAPHICAL APPROACHES

Oral history had by the early 1970s emerged as a tradition to be reckoned with in history (Thompson 1978). Biographical accounts played an important role in this research, and debates in this field to start with often centred on whether or not such data could be considered reliable sources of knowledge for historians; whether people's recollections of the past could be considered accurate enough for this to qualify as scientific data, and the retrospective element in such interviews was scrutinised (see, e.g. Gittins 1979). What distinguished oral history from the work of Thomas and Znaniecki was first and foremost the use of interviews. Wladek's autobiography was a written account, and therefore not the result of a life history interview[15].

The most important phase in biographical research started in the late 1970s with the work of Daniel Bertaux in France. The publication of a collection of papers from the first ad hoc workshop on biographical research at the World Congress in Sociology in 1978 in Uppsala, marks a revival of the interest for biographical research in sociology. The book, entitled *Biography and Society. The Life History Approach in the Social Sciences* contains papers that cover a broad spectrum of topics. Questions arising from written and oral biographical accounts were looked into, and perspectives from the social sciences and humanities were drawn on to explore them. Common to all papers in this volume is a concern with time, and life lived and interpreted in time. Questions about generalisations and representativeness are also explored but unlike earlier discussions they are set within a wider frame of understanding than a mere positivistic frame of reference[16].

Another influential work from the early days is Ken Plummer's *Documents of Life* (1983). In contrast to the volume edited by Bertaux, this book is a monograph that sets the biographical tradition within the frame of Chicago sociology in general and symbolic interactionism in particular. This book has also become a classic in biographical research because it was a first attempt to map the history of this particular sociological research tradition. Plummer's epistemological perspective in this book is realist, and he pays much attention to interviewing and analysis of interviews in order to grasp the meaning inherent in biographical accounts. This perspective is a contrast to his publication

of a follow-up volume of this book published in 2001. By then what could be called 'the linguistic turn' had taken hold in the social sciences, and most discussions related to methodology had taken on a new shape.

Epistemologically the discussions during the first revival phase of biographical research were carried out from a realist ontological position, e.g. underlying the debates was the notion that biographical material was able to give access to some form of *truth* about social life. When accounts were questioned it was from a perspective of reliability at a methodological level, whether people's stories could be relied upon; notions of truth itself were not the object of debate during this phase.

'THE LINGUISTIC TURN': POST-MODERNISM AND POST-STRUCTURALISM

In Europe hermeneutical approaches have become prominent in discussions that highlight differences between the humanities and the natural sciences[17]. Husserl's phenomenology was important for the development of the Heideggerian hermeneutics, but has also been influential in its own right in the social sciences, not least through Garfinkel's ethnomethodology which was developed in the intersection between Parsonian thought and A. Schutz's expanding of Husserl's work (Heritage 1984). Hermeneutics started out as a method to examine texts, and to try and read texts as part of the context they originated in – the hermeneutical circle. As this perspective gained more ground in social science methods debates, aspects of language and narrative structure in biographical accounts were highlighted.

Another important influence for this shift came from linguistics. As the structural linguistics of Lévi-Strauss was criticised by Foucault and Derrida, the grounds were laid for post-structuralism in language theory and social theory. But:

> Despite their differences, structuralism and post-structuralism both contributed to the general

displacement of the social in favour of culture viewed as linguistic and representational. Social categories were to be imagined not as preceding consciousness or culture or language, but as depending upon them. Social categories only came into being through their expressions or representations. (Bonnell and Hunt 1999, p. 9)

The semiotics of Roland Barthes, Foucault's critique of power and Lyotard's critique of 'grand narratives' were all influential for the direction social science research took throughout the 1980s. Methodological questions were replaced by epistemological debates; and these centred on whether there was reality beyond language.

When influence from the humanities became more pronounced throughout the 80s, a shift of focus also occurred in biographical research. From having been concerned with analyses of life stories and biographical accounts as empirical evidence of *lived life*, gradually more attention was given to the narrative itself, to *the told life* and to the different phases of interpretation of a biography. Questions about the role of the researcher in the production of the biographical account, whether this had originated as a written autobiography or was the outcome of an interview between an informant and a researcher, became important. Demands that the researcher be self-reflective in the writing up of biographical research material were frequently heard, and in many instances the biographical experiences of the researcher and his or her reactions to the story told by the informants, became topics of interest (Iles 1992). This shift also marked a change in epistemological focus towards a more constructionist standpoint which implies a line of questioning that is premised on *knowledge about* reality *as* reality (Lewis and Smith 1980). A belief that reality is a human construction alone can lead to extreme relativism in the approach to any research material. A blurring of the boundaries between fact and fiction, between truth and non-truth, between the factual and the non-factual, implies a very different approach to biographical research from that of the classic studies.

Norman Denzin was one of the most prominent advocates of a shift in biographical research towards narrative approaches and a focus on language. A former student of Blumer's, he changed the term used for his perspective from symbolic interactionism to *interpretive interactionism* (Denzin 1989a, 1989b).

The term 'interpretive interactionism [...] signifies an attempt to join traditional symbolic interactionist thought with participant observation and ethnographic research, semiotics and fieldwork, postmodern ethnographic research, naturalistic studies, creative interviewing, the case study method, the interpretive, hermeneutic, phenomenological works of Heidegger and Gadamer, the cultural studies approach of Hall, and recent feminist critiques of positivism. (Denzin 1989a, pp. 7–8)[18]

From this quote it becomes clear that biographical research epistemologically founded in realist pragmatist thought was no longer centre stage. A blending of many different – and in some instances incompatible – research approaches opened a wider field for biographical research, and also invited collaboration across disciplinary boundaries in ways that had earlier not been common. This was especially true in feminist biographical research[19].

Denzin's changed approach is symptomatic of the debates that occurred in biographical research during this period. From discussions about whether individuals' accounts could be regarded as reliable in the sense of people telling the truth about their lives, the interest was gradually shifted towards debates on ontological and epistemological issues (Nilsen 1994, 1996). In many instances the underlying epistemological notions were not taken up explicitly but informed research design and choices of methods for data collection and analysis in empirical studies.

In Chicago during the 20s a processual notion of the self as developed in the pragmatist thought of Peirce and Mead, underpinned Thomas and Znaniecki's research. A notion of self, and of life, as lived in time with access to memories of experiences in the past and the willingness and ability to recount these in some present, is central in classical biographical research[20]. In order for this approach to have merit, some form of realist epistemological position must bear upon the theoretical and methodological perspectives employed in research. *Experiences*[21] cannot be recalled if there is no such thing as reality beyond language. Indeed, a strong constructionist position seems to annihilate the notion of time as process and leaves only a present with no relation to past or future as discourse and language replace time and material practice. Where there was earlier a concern with time as process and self as developing in social relationships that changed over time, more attention has been paid to the concept of *identity*, also in biographical research.

Identity was earlier discussed in relation to development and particularly with reference to the life course phase of youth (Erikson 1980 [1959]). The epistemological shift towards constructionist approaches introduced terms such as 'fragmented identities' and identities as matters of choice (Giddens 1991; Plummer 2001). Such notions are more spatial than temporal since identities in this sense bear no relation to development in time but can be regarded as *constructed* in discourse and markers of *life style* rather than being related to the development over life course phases (Brannen and Nilsen 2005). Where Erikson saw identity as part of a wider notion of self, identity has in many instances replaced the notion of self as 'selves' are thought of in terms of being constructed in discursive fields rather than developed in social relationships (Bonnell and Hunt 1999, p. 22).

METHODOLOGY DISCUSSIONS BEYOND THE QUANTITATIVE-QUALITATIVE, THE POSITIVIST-INTERPRETIVE AND THE REALIST-CONSTRUCTIONIST DIVIDES?

Biographical research currently sweeps a wide array of approaches and perspectives. As the blurring of boundaries between disciplines within the social sciences and between the social sciences and the humanities has increased over the past decade, and cross-disciplinary studies have been encouraged[22], the debates over biographical and other methods of performing research are many and varied. The influence from hermeneutics and methodological approaches originating in humanistic disciplines, together with the epistemological shift towards constructionist/interpretive perspectives, has led some to subsume biographical material under the term *interpretive approaches*[23]. In doing so the story as a *told* story is put at the forefront of attention. It goes without saying that biographical accounts are told stories. However, whether one believes there is a reality beyond the account and hence some factual experiences informants talk about and make these part of the analysis, is an important distinction between a constructionist and a realist approach. In order to overcome the divide created by the epistemological debates, and for social science in general and biographical research in particular, to maintain its critical potential, a return to *agency* as a key sociological notion, is by some held as crucial (Bonnell and Hunt 1999; Chamberlayne et al. 2000).

Exploring the way people talk about their lives is important for many reasons. Understanding narrative structure can add immensely to the overall understanding of a biographical account, not only in terms of language used, but also with reference to the social positioning of individuals in society (Reissman 1991; Nilsen 1996). Moreover, it can also give insight into and draw attention to the *silences* in biographical accounts, and thus make visible the taken-for-granted aspects of people's lives that are more often than not structurally founded and thus important for understanding the informant in the context that the life unfolds within. In cross-national comparative research this aspect of biographical accounts is particularly important (Nilsen and Brannen 2002; Brannen and Nilsen 2005).

However, approaching biographical accounts from this perspective alone can render the more *material* structural contexts that surround and inform the *content* of the story an individual has to tell less important. It therefore seems significant for biographical research to be equally aware of the questions that were raised early in its history as those that are currently in vogue.

The ontological and epistemological foundations of the 'cultural turn' make it difficult to envisage a social science that can produce convincing evidence of, for instance, social disparities between groups of people (Nilsen 1994; Bonnell and Hunt 1999). If the notion of culture replaces that of social structure, and individual narratives *about* lives become the most important objects of analysis rather than *lived* experiences as expressions of social and collective being, the question of whether there is a place for social science research that highlights power and systematic differences and inequalities between people may rightfully be posed. Whether there will indeed be room for the potential of social science to provide critical analyses of trends and development at different levels of society is another question that can be asked. As Chamberlayne et al. point out in a critique of cultural studies without agency, ' "Cultural sociology" rather than "cultural studies" is what is needed' (p. 9).

To illustrate some implications of these questions a current strand of thought may be taken as an example. It also highlights the importance of discussing methods in relation to theoretical perspectives and ideas that address themselves to particular topics in social research.

The individualisation thesis as formulated by Beck (1992) and Beck and Beck-Gernsheim (1995) is informed by a life course perspective and a biographical approach. Arguing from a life course perspective Beck and Beck-Gernsheim (1995) maintain that a 'standard biography' is being replaced by a 'choice biography', and that life course phases no longer follow the same pattern they used to since structural characteristics such as age, gender and social class are not as significant for shaping individuals' lives as they once were. An individualisation is said to take place, where people are forced to

make *choices* to a much larger extent than in 'high modernity'. Individual choices become centre stage and the characteristics that form opportunity structures that make for systematic disparities in individuals' life chances are not recognised as such. If social scientists carry out empirical biographical research with this type of theoretical back cloth as the main conceptual apparatus, analyses are taken to a level of abstractions where indeed discourse and narratives are more meaningful starting points than the intersection of history and biography. For the latter to be included in studies, attention to the complex and many layered contexts that people's lives are embedded is needed. Empirical research has challenged the individualisation thesis on many fronts, especially the fact that it is not sensitive to variation but rather works as another 'Grand Narrative' that shapes the outlook on life rather than tells a sociological story about social diversity and inequality (Nilsen and Brannen 2002; Brannen and Nilsen 2005).

For biographical research it is especially important that the tradition which sets the stories informants tell into a multi-layered social framework rather than merely analysing them from a discourse and narrative approach, is upheld. As Daniel Bertaux observes in a paper that highlights biographical research as a tool for comparative analysis,

Whenever [life stories] are used for probing subjectivities, life story interviews prove able to probe deep; perhaps because it is much easier to lie about one's opinions, values and even behaviour than about one's own life. [...] it takes a sociological eye – some lay persons do possess it – to look through a particular experience and understand what is universal in it; to perceive, beyond described actions and interactions, the implicit sets of rules and norms, the underlying situations, processes and contradictions that have both made actions and interactions possible and that have shaped them in specific ways. It takes some training to hear, behind the solo of a human voice, the music of society and culture in the background. This music is all the more audible if, in conducting the interview, in asking the very first question, in choosing, even earlier, the right persons for interviewing, one has worked with sociological issues and riddles in mind. (Bertaux 1990, pp. 167–168)

This quote echoes Mills' visions for sociology – what it should be about and the role of sociologists in society. However, it also draws attention to some of the debates that biographical research initiated by the work of Thomas and Znaniecki; can life stories be relied upon? To what extent can this type of material hope to be seen as representative of more than the individual story? Far from being dismissed as mere 'positivist' lines of questioning, such issues are real and are routinely faced by researchers working within this tradition. The paradox is that both the positivist and interpretive sides of the divide question the validity of biographical research founded on a realist pragmatic starting point. From an extreme interpretive side of the divide debates about representativeness are easily rejected as irrelevant since they are considered positivist. Extreme positivism on the other hand would question biographical material because it does not qualify as objective data. This chapter has thus argued that a third position needs focusing on. In order to map out this third position the case has been made for a closer look into the ontological and epistemological standpoints that underpin methodological debates within biographical research. The parameters for the discussion have been the starting point in debates about 'method as technique' that highlighted the quantitative-qualitative divide, to the current situation that focuses on epistemological questions and discussions across the boundaries of a realist-constructionist divide.

NOTES

1 Definitions of biographical research will be discussed in a later section. In this chapter the focus will be on overall debates within this field, thus variations in traditions for making use of this perspective will not be the focus here.

2 The terms 'case' and 'case studies' are referred to in different ways in current sociology. For an overview of themes and topics in debates over case studies, see Gomm et al. 2000 and Yin 2003.

3 In Durkheim's original text the use of the term 'method' also encompasses what is being referred to here as methodology.

4 As pointed out by Platt (1996) the English terms for method and methodology create problems when used as adjectives; both are referred to as 'methodological'. This chapter is concerned with methodology in the wider sense, not to method in the strict sense of 'technique' or 'procedure' for studying the social world.

5 As Kaplan (1964) observes, the term 'methodology' is often used synonymously with epistemology by philosophers (p. 20). The definition of epistemology referred to in the context of this chapter is 'theory of knowledge'.

6 For other ways of classifying, see Miller 2000; Roberts 2002.

7 This study was carried out in Chicago where sociology was still very much influenced by American pragmatism. For a further discussion of this see Nilsen *American Pragmatism and Biographical Research* (work in progress).

8 See, e.g. Kaplan (1964) for a detailed discussion of different forms of positivism and their relevance for social science studies. Platt (1996) also gives a detailed account of different interpretations of positivism in relation to 'scientism': 'Its meaning overlaps with that now attached to 'positivism'. It is associated with a commitment to making social science like natural science, and thus with themes such as empiricism, objectivity, observability, operationalism, behaviourism, value neutrality, measurement and quantification' (Platt 1996, pp. 67–68).

9 This ontological position is in Lewis and Smith's (1980) terms a 'materialist social nominalism' (p. 8).

10 Theory in a strong positivist sense is aimed at building laws through hypothesis testing over time.

11 It should be kept in mind here that the situation in Hitler's extended Germany was one where positivist ways of doing social science was actually the most effective way to challenge racist beliefs that underpinned the Third Reich's ideology, and social scientists who advocated such research were persecuted and had to flee the country if they could. Paul Lazarsfeld was but one of these scientists who fled to the USA. The direct impact of the 'Vienna Circle' for the development of American and also European social science methods, is however one that must be seen in view of other simultaneous tendencies within American social science itself (see Platt 1996 for a detailed discussion of this topic).

12 The difference between Blumer and Mead on approach to method, where the latter saw no problems in combining qualitative and quantitative methods, is pointed out by Deegan 2001. Blumer's approach must be seen in view of the contemporary time of his writing, where the quantitative-qualitative divide was much more prominent than in Mead's time.

13 In one sense Glaser and Strauss took Blumer's notion of 'sensitising concepts' and developed it in a direction that 'operationalised' how to go about making use of sensitising concept in actual empirical studies.

14 Grounded theory has been criticised for being too positivist and quantitative in its approach to data and method (see, e.g. Christensen et al. 1998). However, at the time it was published it represented a more radical approach than what it is thought of today.

15 This is not to say that life history interviews had not been conducted before the 1960s; in psychology there was much interest in biographical interviewing. However, an account of this falls outside the scope of this paper.

16 See in particular papers by Bertaux, Ferrarrotti, Kohli and Thompson in the book.

17 Drawing on Dilthey's notions of understanding meaning in context and Heidegger's development of his ideas in *Being and Time*, Heidegger's student Gadamer published *Truth and Method* in 1960 (Gadamer 1989), which has since become a standard reference within hermeneutical approaches. These works are mainly concerned with the interpretation of texts and were subjects for the humanities rather than the social sciences to start with. This was to change as post-structuralism and post-modernism gained more ground in the social sciences in the 1980s.

18 References in Denzin's text are not included in this quote.

19 See Teresa Iles (1992) for an example of publications from meetings across disciplinary boundaries. Stanley (1992) also voices the need for more cross-disciplinary research in feminist biographical studies.

20 Pragmatist thought does not rest on a notion about truth as fixed, and thus a possibility to arrive at some final account of life. Events and individuals' experiences of them are recalled at different points in time which can make factual events take on different meanings in a personal life as time passes. This does, however, not mean events did not happen, or did not happen that particular way, rather that they are seen and *interpreted* in different ways depending on the present a story is told in and the context the interview takes place in (Nilsen 1996). The interview itself and the relationship between the interviewer and the informant, are also decisive of what aspects of factual events informants relate in their accounts. It is important to note here that this way of approaching interpretation does not imply a rejection of something 'true' and 'factual' in events, in personal lives as well as in historical and structural terms.

21 The notion of experience, for the very reasons mentioned here, came under debate and questions about experience itself were asked. It was not the 'truth' of people's accounts of experiences that were called into question, but the ontological foundation that the notion of experience rests on; whether there is independent reality.

22 This drift towards interdisciplinarity has its critics. As Bonnell and Hunt (1999, p. 14) observe: 'Dialogue among the disciplines depends in part on a strong sense of their differences from each other: exchange is not needed if everything is the same; interdisciplinarity can only work if there are in fact disciplinary differences'.

23 See, e.g. Plummer 2001.

REFERENCES

Beck, Ulrich 1992. *The Risk Society*. London: Sage.

Beck, Ulrich and Elisabeth Beck-Gernsheim 1995. *The Normal Chaos of Love*. Cambridge: Polity Press.

Bertaux, Daniel (ed.) 1981. *Biography and Society*. London: Sage.

Bertaux, Daniel 1990. 'Oral History Approaches to an International Social Movement' in Öyen E. (ed.) *Comparative Methodology*. London: Sage.

Bertaux, Daniel and Paul Thompson 1997. *Pathways to Social Class: A Qualitative Approach to Social Mobility*. Oxford: Clarendon Press.

Blumer, Herbert 1979 [1939]. *An Appraisal of Thomas and Znaniecki's 'The Polish Peasant in Europe and America'*. New Brunswick: Transaction Books.

Blumer, Herbert 1954. 'What is Wrong with Social Theory', *American Sociological Review* 19, 3–10.

Bonnell, Victoria E. and Lynn Hunt 1999. 'Introduction' in Bonnell V. and Hunt L. (eds) *Beyond the Cultural Turn*. Berkeley: University of California Press.

Bourdieu, Pierre et al. 1999. *The Weight of the World: Social Suffering in Contemporary Society*. Cambridge: Polity Press.

Brannen, Julia 1995. *Mixing Methods. Qualitative and Quantitative Research*. Aldershot: Avebury.

Brannen, Julia, Peter Moss and Ann Mooney 2004. *Working and Caring over the Twentieth Century. Change and Continuity in Four-Generation Families*. Basingstoke: Palgrave Macmillan.

Brannen, Julia and Ann Nilsen 2005. 'Individualisation, Choice and Structure: A Discussion of Current Trends in Sociological Analysis', *The Sociological Review* 53(3), 412–428.

Bryman, Alan 2004. *Social Research Methods*. Oxford: Oxford University Press.

Chamberlayne, Prue, Joanna Bornat and Tom Wengraf 2000. 'Introduction' in Chamberlayne et al. (eds) *The Turn to Biographical Methods in Social Science: Comparative Issues and Examples*. London: Routledge.

Christensen, Karen, Else Jerdal, Atle Møen, Per Solvang and Liv J. Syltevik 1998. *Prosess og methode (Process and Method)*. Oslo: Universitetsforlaget.

Deegan, Mary Jo 2001. 'Introduction: George Herbert Mead's First Book' in Mead, George Herbert (ed.) *Essays in Social Psychology*. New Brunswick: Transaction Publishers.

Denzin, Norman 1989a. *Interpretive Interactionism.* London: Sage.

Denzin, Norman 1989b. *Interpretive Biography.* London: Sage.

Durkheim, Emile 1972 [1895]. *Den sociologiske metode (Rules of Sociological Methods).* København: Fremad.

Elder, Glen 1974. *Children of the Great Depression: Social Change in Life Experience.* Chicago: University of Chicago Press.

Erikson, Erik 1980 [1959]. *Identity and the Life Cycle.* New York: Norton.

Gadamer, Hans-Georg 1989. *Truth and Method.* London: Sheed and Ward.

Giddens, Anthony 1991. *Modernity and Self-Identity.* Cambridge: Polity Press.

Giele, Janet and Glen Elder 1998. 'Life Course Research. Development of a Field' in Giele J. and Elder G. (eds) *Methods of Life Course Research. Qualitative and Quantitative Approaches.* London: Sage.

Gittins, Diana 1979. 'Oral History, Reliability, and Recollection' in Moss and Goldstein. (eds) *The Recall Method in Social Survey.* University of London Institute of Education: Studies in Education 9.

Glaser, Barney G. and Anselm L. Strauss 1967. *The Discovery of Grounded Theory: Strategies for Qualitative Research.* Chicago: Aldine.

Gomm, Roger, Martyn Hammersley and Peter Foster (eds) 2000. *Case Study Method.* London: Sage.

Harding, Sandra 1987. 'Introduction: Is There a Feminist Method' in Harding S. (ed.) *Feminism and Methodology.* Milton Keynes: Open University Press.

Heritage, John 1984. *Garfinkel and Ethnomethodology.* Cambridge: Polity Press.

Iles, Teresa (ed.) 1992. *Biography. All Sides of the Subject.* London: Pergamon Press.

Kaplan, Abraham 1964. *The Conduct of Inquiry. Methodology for Behavioral Science.* Scranton: Chandler Publishing Company.

Levin, Irene 2000. 'Forholdet mellom sosiologi og sosialt arbeid' (The relationship between sociology and social work), *Sosiologisk tidsskrift* (*Journal of Sociology*) 8(1), 61–71.

Lewis, David and Richard Smith 1980. *American Sociology and Pragmatism. Mead, Chicago Sociology and Symbolic Interactionism.* Chicago: The University of Chicago Press.

Miller, Robert 2000. *Researching Life Stories and Family Histories.* London: Sage.

Mills, C. Wright 1940. 'Methodological Consequences of the Sociology of Knowledge', *American Journal of Sociology* 46(3), 316–330.

Mills, C. Wright 1980 [1959]. *The Sociological Imagination.* London: Penguin Books.

Nilsen, Ann 1994. 'Life Stories in Context. A Discussion of the Linguistic Turn in Contemporary Sociological Life Story Research', *Sosiologisk Tidsskrift* 2(2), 139–153.

Nilsen, Ann 1996. 'Stories of Life – Stories of Living. Women's Narratives and Feminist Biographies in *NORA*', *Nordic Journal of Women's Studies* 1(4), 16–31.

Nilsen, Ann 1997. 'Great Expectations? Exploring Men's Biographies in Late Modernity' in Grønmo, Sigmund and Bjørn Henrichsen. (eds) *Society, University and World Community. Essays for Ørjar Øyen*, pp. 111–135. Oslo: Scandinavian University Press.

Nilsen, Ann and Julia Brannen 2002. 'Theorising the Individual-Structure Dynamic' in Brannen et al. (eds) *Young Europeans, Work and Family: Futures in Transition*, pp. 30–48. London: Routledge.

Nilsen, Ann and Julia Brannen 2005. *Consolidated Interview Report from the Transitions Research Project* for the EU Framework 5 funded study Gender, parenthood and the changing European workplace, printed by the Manchester Metropolitan University: Research Institute for Health and Social Change.

Nilsen, Ann (forthcoming) *American Pragmatism and Biographical Research* (work in progress).

Platt, Jennifer 1992. '"Case Study" in American Methodological Thought', *Current Sociology* 40(1), 17–48.

Platt, Jennifer 1996. *A History of Sociological Research Methods in America. 1920-1960* Cambridge: Cambridge University Press.

Plummer, Ken 1983. *Documents of Life. An Introduction to the Problems and Literature of a Humanistic Method.* London: Allen & Unwin.

Plummer, Ken 2001. *Documents of Life 2. An Invitation to a Critical Humanism.* London: Sage.

Reissman, Catherine Kohler 1991. 'When Gender is Not Enough. Women Interviewing Women' in Lorber, Judith and Susan Farrell. (eds) *The Social Construction of Gender.* London: Sage.

Riley, Mathilda W. (ed.) 1988. *Social Structures and Human Lives.* London: Sage.

Roberts, Brian 2002. *Biographical Research.* Buckingham: Open University Press.

Stanley, Liz 1992. *The Autobiographical I.* Manchester: Manchester University Press.

Thomas, William I. and Florian Znaniecki [1918–20] 1927. *The Polish Peasant in Europe and America.* New York: Knopf.

Thompson, Paul 1978. *The Voice of the Past, Oral History.* Oxford: Oxford University Press.

Yin, Robert 2003. *Case Study Research. Design and Methods.* Thousand Oaks: Sage.

Research Ethics in Social Science

Celia B. Fisher and Andrea E. Anushko

Unparalleled growth in the social and behavioral sciences in the last half of the twentieth century has and will continue to make significant contributions to society's understanding of persons as individuals, as members of familial and non-familial social groups, and participants within cultural, social, economic and political macrosystems. Increased public recognition of the value of social research has been accompanied by heightened sensitivity to the obligation to conduct social science responsibly. The formidable task of insuring ethical competence in social research depends upon sensitive and informed planning by ethically informed scientists and careful review by nationally mandated or independent Institutional Review Boards (IRBs) or Research Ethics Committees (REC). The broad language of national and international regulations and the diversity of expertise and wide latitude in decision-making given to IRBs is often intimidating to social scientists who are required to apply for IRB approval as a condition of conducting their research. Social scientists are additionally challenged because of the historical and biomedical bias in the language and scope of regulations governing IRBs in the United States and RECs in Europe, Latin America, India, Thailand, and Africa among other developing countries (e.g. Council for International Organizations of Medical Sciences, 2002; Indian Council of Medical Research, 2000; National Consensus Conference on Bioethics and Health Research in Uganda, 1997; National Research Council, 2003; Thailand Ministry of Public Health Ethics Committee, 1995; World Medical Association, 2000).

A BRIEF HISTORY OF RESEARCH ETHICS RULES AND REGULATIONS

Biomedical research ethics have a long history formally beginning with the Nuremberg Code (1946), the international response to the atrocities committed by the Nazi medical experimentation. However because the acts committed by the Nazi scientists seemed so far removed from standard medical and social research, the Nuremberg Code had little influence on medical or social science research (Steinbock et al., 2005). Biomedical research ethics continued to evolve slowly in the United States and abroad (*Declaration of Helsinki*, 1964). In the United States it was not until the 1970s, when revelations of subjects' abuse in the now infamous Tuskegee Syphilis

Study (Heller, 1972; Jones, 1993) prompted U.S. Public Law 93-348 to call for the establishment of the National Commission for the Protection of Human Subjects of Biomedical and Behavioral Research. The National Commission published recommendations, known as the Belmont Report (DHEW, 1978), that served as the basis for revised federal regulations published in the Federal Register in 1979 with continued revisions through 2001 (DHHS, Code of Federal Regulations Title 45-Part 46 Protection of Human Subjects 45 CFR 46, 2001). At the same time the Council for International Organizations of Medical Sciences (CIOMS) in association with the World Health Organization (WHO) set out to develop guidelines that applied the principles of the Declaration of Helsinki to the conduct of biomedical research, particularly in developing countries. The final product was the 1982, *Proposed International Ethical Guidelines for Biomedical Research Involving Human Subjects*. Since 1982 two revisions have been made to the CIOMS guidelines: one in 1993 and the most recent in 2002. National and international guidelines base research ethics regulation on three general ethical principles: (1) Beneficence: the obligation to maximize research benefits and minimize research harms; (2) Respect: the responsibility to ensure that research participation is informed, rationale, and voluntary; and (3) Justice: the obligation to ensure the fair distribution of research benefits and burdens across populations. While the conceptual and practical frameworks for research ethics in its present form are rooted in and largely dominated by Western culture (Ogundiran, 2004), these principles have retained their fundamental value in guiding the ethical conduct of contemporary research in the West and increasingly in developing countries. In Africa for example, the Pan African Bioethics Initiative (PABIN), was established in 2001 to foster the development of research ethics with special emphasis on the need to develop the capacity for reviewing the ethics of research conducted in Africa by nationals and internationals (see:http://www.pabin.net/en/index.asp).

Ethics in the social sciences

Problems identified in social science research did not produce the serious harms observed in medical studies during the period of national and international biomedical research regulations. Indeed, in the United States for example, prior to the National Commission's report, social science researchers rarely sought informed consent even when punishing stimuli were part of the research design and the use of deception and invasion of privacy was common place (Sieber, 1992). This is somewhat surprising since the American Psychological Association (APA) adapted its first ethics code covering research, teaching, and practice in 1953 (APA, 1953) and the American Anthropological Association officially approved their Statement on Problems of Anthropological Research and Ethics in 1967 (Nolan, 2002). One reason for the lack of ethical awareness within social science research at that time might have been the broad aspirational languages of the codes. For example, it was not until 1992 that specifically worded operational standards of conduct for research, teaching and professional practice were included in the APA Ethics Code (Canter et al., 1994) and this model was then adapted by other social sciences including the American Sociological Association, and the Canadian Psychological Association (ASA, 1999; CPA, 2000). The most recent revision of the APA Ethics Code (APA, 2003) includes a more protective standard on deception research, prohibiting such research if it leads to pain or substantial stress or discomfort and requiring investigators to respect a participant's request to withdraw data following debriefing (Fisher, 2003a).

Recognizing the strong biomedical basis for many of the previous guidelines governing research, some countries have shifted their focus to create statements of ethical conduct specific to the social sciences. Australia for instance, in revising their 1999 *National Statement on Ethical Conduct in Research Involving Humans* has drafted a new set of guidelines specifically for social scientists while still building upon the Nuremberg Code and the Declaration of Helsinki, highlighting such principles as research merit and integrity, justice, beneficence, and respect. Others have chosen to order their principles according to the weight they should receive when in conflict specific to the types of dilemmas social scientists often face. For example, Canada prioritizes their four principles for social science researchers in the order of: (1) Respect for the Dignity of Persons; (2) Responsible Caring; (3) Integrity in Relationships; and (4) Responsibility to Society (CPA, 2000).

This chapter now turns to four specific areas of continued and emerging ethical concern in social research: conflicts of interest, informed consent, cultural equivalence, and the use of monetary incentives. The chapter concludes with a call for ethical commitment, ethical awareness and active engagement in the ongoing development of courses of action reflecting the highest ideals of responsible social science.

CONFLICT OF INTERESTS

Social researchers should strive to establish relationships of trust with research participants, the scientific community, and the public. When conflicting professional, personal, financial, legal or other interests impair the objectivity of data collection, analysis or interpretation, such trust and the validity of the research is compromised. Ethical steps to avoid potentially harmful or exploitative conflicts of interest are critical to ensure that the objectivity of data analysis and interpretation is led by data and not other interests. Impairment of objectivity can harm participants, the public, institutions, funders, and the integrity of social science as a field.

Several national bodies and organizations have produced guidelines for conflict of interest decision-making relevant to the conduct of social science research. For example, in the United States the National Institutes of Health Office of Extramural Research requires every institution receiving federal research funds to have written guidelines for the avoidance and institutional review of conflict of interest. These guidelines must reflect state and local laws and cover financial interests, gifts, nepotism, political participation, and other issues (see: http://grants.nih.gov/grants/policy/emprograms/overview/ep-coi.htm).

Of relevance to investigators is the U.S. Public Health Service and National Science Foundation (NSF) requirement that any funding application must include a statement on whether there are any *significant* financial interests that could directly and significantly affect the design, conduct or reporting of the research. Such interests can include consulting fees, honoraria, ownership or equity options, or intellectual property (e.g. patents, copyrights, and royalties) where such values exceed $10,000. Academic institutional salaries and lectures sponsored by non-profit or public entities are exempt from this policy (see: http://www.nsf.gov/policies/conflicts.jsp, http://grants2. nih.gov/grants/policy/nihgps_2001/nihgps_2001.pdf). In addition, many IRBs in the United States are requiring researchers to include a conflict of interest statement in their informed consents and journals are requiring a statement describing the absence or existence of a potential conflict of interest. For example, APA publications require authors to reveal any possible conflict of interest (e.g. financial interests in a test procedure, funding by pharmaceutical companies) in the conduct and reporting of research. According to the International Committee of Medical Journal Editors (ICMJE) (2003) editors may use information disclosed in conflict of interest and financial interest statements as a basis for editorial decisions. Prompted in large part by concerns about conflicts of interest stemming from the relationship between pharmaceutical companies and independent clinical research organizations, India and other developing countries are beginning to call for adoption of international and establishment of national regulations for research conflicts of interest (Editorial, The Hindu, 2005; Pan African Bioethics Initiative, 2001).

Several professional codes of conduct, including the APA Ethics Code standard on conflict of interest (APA, 2002, Standard 3.06), the British Sociological Association Code of Ethics (BSA, 2002, Standard 42), the British Psychological Society Code of Ethics and Conduct (BPS, 2006, Standard 4.2), and the Canadian Code of Ethics for Psychologists (CPA, 2000, Standard III.31) are applicable for all social science researchers. As applied to research they prohibit conflict of interests if another personal, scientific, professional, financial or other interests or relationships could reasonably be expected to impair objectivity, competence or effectiveness of the psychologist to conduct the research, if it would expose his or her organization to harm, or if it would result in the harm or exploitation of research participants or research assistants. The ethics codes of other social science organizations have similar prohibitions against conflicts of interest (e.g. AAA, 1998; ASA, 1999 in the U.S.).

Examples of potentially harmful conflicts of interest

Examples of potential conflicts of interest can occur if: (a) a social scientist takes gifts from or has financial holdings in a company whose product she or he is investigating; (b) the research is sponsored by a company or organization that has a financial investment in the direction of results that might place pressure on the investigator; (c) the investigator or his or her institution will hold the patent for the researched instrument; or (d) scientists are reviewing a grant application or manuscript submission from a competitor.

Conflict of interest and industry sponsored research: Who owns the data?

In traditional academic contexts, social scientists have a responsibility to report on the results of their data, and to ensure that the report accurately represents the findings. Potentially unethical conflicts of interest can emerge when investigators sponsored by private industry or organizations do not consider in advance the implications of data ownership (Fried & Fisher, in press). Investigators working on independent projects funded externally need to ensure that they maintain all access to and ownership of data as well as the right to publish results without prior approval or interference from the sponsor. Sponsors with financial interest in the outcome of the research if provided the opportunity may deny investigators access to the final dataset, attempt to dictate analytic strategies, stall dissemination of negative findings, or insist on ghostwriting the scientific report. Failure to anticipate the consequences of, acquiescing to or naively signing a contract waiving these responsibilities can result in becoming an accomplice to letting a financial agenda rather than the data drive research results. In addition to resulting in a violation of avoidance of unethical conflicts of interest, such decisions can result in other violations within APA. For example, according to the APA Ethics Code (APA, 2002, Standards 1.01 Misuse of Psychologists Work and 5.01 Avoidance of False or Deceptive Statements) and the International Sociological Association Code of Ethics (ISA, 2001, Standard 3, Publication and Communication of data) investigators are prohibited from knowingly making public statements that are false, deceptive or fraudulent concerning their research and are responsible for preventing or correcting false statements about their work by others. For social scientists such public statements can include not only false statements in publications and professional presentations, but product endorsements, false statements concerning conflict of interest or delegation of research responsibilities on grant applications, and expert testimony about scientific data in legal proceedings.

Conflicts between ethics and organizational demands

Social scientists who are employees or consultants to an organization face a slightly different set of ethical challenges. In such contexts, the company or organization may have *a priori* ownership of any data produced by its employees. In such contexts the investigator's role is to provide the organization with the results and interpretation of data collected from well-designed studies that were conducted to provide information for organizational decision-making. The choice to make public the findings belongs to the organization. Unethical conflicts of interest can emerge in such settings. For example, if the researcher agrees to a request by the company or organization to design a study that will guarantee results are all biased in a particular direction, falsify results from previously collected data or write a report that provides an incomplete summary of the data or that intentionally misinterprets study results. When entering into an employment or contractual agreement with a company or organization, social scientists should anticipate and educate the company to the conflict of interest issues that may emerge and establish agreements about data collection, interpretation, and dissemination that permit the investigator to act ethically.

Conflicts of interest in social research: Unchartered territory

In summary, as industry and organizations increasingly recognize the value of social research for policy decisions and public relations, social scientists will increasingly be confronted with conflict of interest challenges. Not all conflicts of interest are unethical or avoidable. The ethical challenge for social scientists is to be vigilant in identifying such conflicts, assure the public that conflicts are eliminated when possible and effectively managed when necessary. As noted by the Office of Human Research Protections, 'Openness and honesty are indicators of integrity and responsibility, characteristics that promote quality research and can only strengthen the research process' (http://www.hhs.gov/ohrp/nhrpac/mtg12-00/finguid.htm).

INFORMED CONSENT

The principle of respect reflects a moral concern for the autonomy and privacy rights of those recruited for research participation. In its most fundamental form, it embodies the moral necessity of obtaining consent to participate in research that is informed, rationale and voluntary. The informed requirement requires that prospective participants are provided with all information about the study that would be expected to influence their willingness to participate. As embodied in U.S. federal regulations and the APA Ethics Code (APA, 2002, Standards 3.10 and 8.02; DHHS, 2001) as well as the Canadian Code of Ethics (CPA, 2000, Standard 1.24) and the EU Code of Ethics for Socio-Economic Research (Dench, Iphofen, Huws, 2004, Standard 4.3) such information includes: (1) the purpose, duration, and procedures; (2) the right to decline or withdraw from participation; (3) consequences of declining or withdrawing; (4) risks and potential discomforts or adverse effects; (5) any prospective benefits to participants or society; (6) extent and limits of confidentiality; (7) incentives for participation; (8) who to contact with questions regarding the research (usually the principal investigator) and their research rights (usually the Chair of the IRB); and (9) an opportunity to ask questions. Some forms of social research create consent challenges. Next we discuss informed consent within the context of three of these research methods: Qualitative, archival, and deception research.

Qualitative research

The exploratory and open-ended nature of semi-structured interviews, participant observation, or ethnographic work raises questions about whether truly informed consent for such research can be obtained (Marshall, 1992). Several Codes, including the Australian National Statement on Ethical Conduct in Human Research (National Health and Medical Research Council (NHMRC), 2007). Set out specific guidelines for qualitative research (Standard 3.1). The movement to view social sciences as 'hard science' and IRB unfamiliarity with qualitative research methods has also posed challenges to anthropologists, sociologists, and other social scientists whose research often strays from the classical scientific method because of unique research questions or the nature of their population (Marshall, 2003). Informed consent is also problematic when working with immigrant populations or in international settings for reasons ranging from language barriers and fear of exploitation or deportation to authority to consent resting with an individual other than the participants, e.g. in countries where women are not permitted to consent to research without prior male permission (Marshall, 2003).

In studies where informed consent is obtained, it is often difficult to ensure *fully* informed consent at the start of a project because researchers may not be able to anticipate the full extent of information that will emerge (Haverkamp, 2005). Risks to privacy and confidentiality emerge when the information leads to unanticipated revelations regarding illegal behaviors (crimes, child or domestic abuse, illegal immigration), health problems (HIV status, genetic disorder) or other information that if revealed could jeopardize participants' legal or economic status (Fisher & Goodman, in press; Fisher & Ragsdale, 2006). One way to address this issue is to develop in advance a re-consent strategy for situations in which unanticipated and sensitive issues emerge during the course of observation or discussion (Fisher, 2004; Haverkamp, 2005). The strategy can include a set of criteria to help the interviewer: (1) identify when unexpected information may lead to increased participant privacy and confidentiality risk; (2) determine whether the direction of the conversation is relevant to the research question; (3) if not relevant, find ways to divert the discussion; or (4) if relevant, alert the participant to the new nature of information and implement a mutually negotiated re-consent procedure.

Archival research

Similar, but more difficult issues emerge when consent is obtained for social research that will be archived. Social science has a prestigious history of archives (Young & Brooker, 2006). The purpose of archived data is to provide a rich set of data that can be used by future investigators to examine empirical questions about populations that may not be anticipated when information is first collected. Several organizations have begun to unite social science researchers and their data from around the world to create large and secure accessible databases of archived information. For instance, the Inter-University Consortium for Political and Social Research (ICPSR) has over 500 college or university members and has four major operations units, one of which is data security and preservation. The Harvard-MIT data center also archives and protects various social science data to allow access for future generations of social science researchers. Participant identity is protected in these archives through a very detailed process of individual de-identification. However, the racial, ethnic, cultural, health, or other demographic-based populations from which participants were recruited in most instances must remain identifiable for the research questions to be meaningful.

Within the continuously changing social-political context in which science and society evolve, some investigators have begun to question the validity of informed consent to ongoing secondary analysis by unknown third parties with research questions that may be inconsistent with the consent understandings of those who initially agreed to participation and preservation. This becomes of particular concern when secondary analysis of data from historically oppressed or disenfranchised communities is requested (Young & Brooker, 2006) or if the circumstances under which the original data was collected is questionable as in the 1968 Yanomami research conducted by Neel (http://members.aol.com/archaeodog/ darkness_in_el_dorado/documents/0081.htm).

Requiring individual participants to reconsent to the use of archival data can be both harmful and infeasible. First, it would require that records linking responses to individually identifiable information is preserved over decades, where confidentiality protections may be vulnerable over time.

Second, it would require locating individuals after years or decades which in many cases would be impossible and the unavailability of segments of the initial population would compromise the validity of the sample. In response to these challenges, the Council of National Psychological Associations for the Advancement of Ethnic Minority Interests (CNPAAEMI, 2000) has recommended that social research archives consider setting up standing community (broadly defined) advisory boards as a means of helping archive administrators determine when newly proposed analyses may violate the intent of the informed consent.

Deception research and the 'consent paradox'

In research using deceptive methods, the researcher intentionally misinforms participants about the purpose of the study, the procedures, or the role of individuals with whom the participant will be required to interact (Sieber, 1982). The use of deceptive techniques is not prohibited in any national research regulations and is explicitly permitted with stipulations in professional ethics codes including the American Psychological Association (2002), American Sociological Association (1999), Canadian Psychological Association (2000), British Psychological Society (2006), and the International Sociological Association (2001). Baumrind (1979) distinguished between *nonintentional deception,* in which failure to fully inform cannot be avoided because of the complexity of the information, and *intentional deception,* which is the withholding of information in order to obtain participation that the subject might otherwise decline. Simply not providing participants with specific hypotheses regarding the relationship among experimental variables does not in itself constitute deception.

Deception most obviously violates the principle of respect, by depriving prospective participants the opportunity to make an informed choice regarding the true nature of their participation. What Fisher (2005) has termed the 'consent paradox' underscores the moral ambiguity surrounding consent for deception research when the investigator intentionally gives participants false information about the purpose and nature of the study. In such contexts consent for deception research distorts the informed consent process, because it leads prospective participants to believe they have autonomy to decide about the type of experimental procedures they will be exposed to, when in fact they do not.

The deception debate

Debate on the ethical justification for deceptive research practices reflects a tension between scientific validity and respect for participants' right to make a truly informed participation decision (Fisher & Fyrberg, 1994). Arguments for deception emphasize the methodological advantage of keeping participants naïve about the purpose of the study to ensure responses to experimental manipulations are spontaneous and unbiased (Milgram, 1964; Resnick & Schwartz, 1973; Smith & Richardson, 1983). Arguments against deception emphasize the violation of participant autonomy, the potential to create public distrust in social science research in general and the harm resulting from infliction of self-knowledge that was unexpected, unwanted, shameful or distressful (Baumrind, 1964).

Sociologists have been at the center of deception controversy and have members who are stanch advocates and opponents of the practice. Allen (1997) falls into the latter category, criticizing sociologists for befriending groups of interest without letting on that they were subjects of sociological research, misrepresenting the motives of their research, and adopting a false persona to conduct research. Particularly disturbing to Allen is the defense that personal time and effort prevented the feasibility of other methods, thus in order to get the research done deception was necessary.

Ethical options

Bulmer (1982) concludes that completely disguising the intent of research can affect the quality of the data collected as well as exaggerate the unknown biases of the researcher. Instead he proposes such methods as retrospective participant observation in which a sociologist uses retrospective observations from previous experience when she was a total participant prior to any research interest. He also supports the use of native as stranger, in which an already established member of the group is trained as a sociologist. The covert outsider is another suggested method in which a legitimate role, such as a teacher in a prison, is taken on in order to observe behavior and gain access to an otherwise unreachable population (Bulmer, 1982).

According to U.S. federal guidance (OPRR, 1993), when considering the use of deception, investigators must first decide whether the information to be withheld during consent would, if known, influence the individual's desire to participate in research. However how to judge this prospectively is difficult. Some have argued that responses from previous participants during dehoaxing (revealing the true nature of the study at the end of participation) can be used to document the benign effects of different deceptive methodologies. This approach raises its own (debriefing) paradox (Fisher, 2005). Fisher and Fyrberg (1994) found that introductory psychology students (the most commonly recruited participants for deception studies) were likely to believe that the dehoaxing process was either simply a continued extension of the research or that the debriefing information was itself untrue. As a result, students reported they would be unlikely to reveal their true feelings to experimenters during the dehoaxing process; and some were concerned they would be penalized if they were truthful.

The APA Ethics Code (APA, 2002) attempts to balance the principles of beneficence, non-maleficence, and respect. First, the use of deceptive methods must be justified by the study's prospective value in scientific, educational or applied areas. Second, even if the research is determined to have value, deception is prohibited if it is reasonably expected that the procedures will cause any

physical pain or severe emotional distress. Third, the investigator must prove that the same hypotheses cannot be sufficiently explored and tested using non-deceptive designs. This standard thus prohibits the use of deception research if inconvenience or costs of performing non-deceptive research are the only reasons for proposing such methods (Fisher, 2003a). In addition, the true nature of the deception must be revealed to participants at the end of the study unless the debriefing might reasonably be expected to bias future participant responses; or withhold such information if the debriefing itself would cause participant harm (APA, 2002, Standard 8.08b).

While the APA and other organizations' ethics codes attempt to increase the ethical rigor of decisions to use deception methodologies, no guidance can erase the threat to participant autonomy that such procedures reflect. Neither, debriefing (even when believed to be valid by participants) nor the opportunity to withdraw their data, are a panacea for the ethical paradox of deception research. Consent can only be obtained prospectively (OPRR, 1993); subsequent procedures can never be considered an adequate substitute.

FAIR DISTRIBUTION OF THE BENEFITS AND BURDENS OF RESEARCH

The principle of justice is concerned with the fair and equitable distribution of research benefits and burdens. In social research, benefits are defined by the usefulness of data generated to help understand micro and macro social processes within and among different populations. The burdens of social research include exposure to research risks and required time and effort associated with participation. Justice in social research becomes a particular ethical challenge when racial or ethnic minority, disadvantaged, or disenfranchised populations are recruited for participation in research designs that fail to include consideration of unique population characteristics that may reduce the knowledge value of data generated or expose them to greater risk or financial burden (Fisher, 1999; Trimble & Fisher, 2006).

Population generalizability

The constantly changing demographic U.S. and international landscapes pose the risk that research findings from one participant population will be inappropriately generalized to other populations. This can occur in at least two ways. First, injustices may occur when populations are intentionally or unintentionally excluded from recruitment, but results of the study are inappropriately generalized to apply to their social or psychological characteristics and circumstances. This becomes particularly problematic for social science when the descriptions of ethnic/racial characteristics are vaguely described in journal articles. Typical descriptions that provide inadequate knowledge for assessing the relevance of the data to ethnic minority populations in the United States, for example are: 'the majority of participants were non-Hispanic white'; or 'eighty-percent of participants were non-Hispanic white; the remaining 20 percent were African American and Hispanic' (Fisher & Brennan, 1992).

Defining race, ethnicity, and culture

When participants' race, ethnicity, or culture are described in greater detail there is often an absence of definition of what these terms mean or how decisions to identify participants by 'race' (physical similarities assumed to reflect phenotypic expressions of shared genotypes), 'ethnicity' (assumed cultural, linguistic, religious, and historical similarities), or 'culture' (group ways of thinking and living based upon shared knowledge, consciousness, skills, values, expressive forms, social institutions, and behaviors that allow individuals to survive in the contexts within which they live) reflects assumptions about the underlying causal mechanisms driving similarities or differences found among populations (Fisher et al., 1997). Further, there is often little recognition that

social, economic, and political forces continuously shape and redefine these definitions for both individuals and society at large (Chan & Hume, 1995; Zuckerman, 1990). Investigators need to consider and explicitly describe the theoretical, empirical, and social frameworks driving the definitions of race, ethnicity, or culture used to select participant populations, to insure the scientific validity of the research question and to allow their research findings to be evaluated within the context of continuously changing scientific and societal conceptions of these definitions (Fisher et al., 2002).

Within group differences are also an important factor to consider when identifying population characteristics relevant to the study questions. Investigators often ignore the scientific implications of variation among populations described under broad panethnic labels. For example, failure to identify the national origins of participants categorized as 'Hispanic' (e.g. Mexico, Puerto Rico, Guatemala, Chile) can produce overgeneralizations that dilute or obscure moderating effects on social behavior resulting from national origin, immigration history, religion, and tradition. In addition, within even these more nationally defined categories, research participants may vary greatly in their identification with the ethnic group of family origin or with the degree to which they are acculturated to majority culture (Fisher et al., 1997).

Cultural equivalence of assessment measures

Investigators need to heed a second risk of producing research injustice: failure to recognize when a measure of a social construct established in one population when applied to another ethnic/cultural group may not yield similar psychometric properties nor reflect a social phenomenon that has similar behavioral or psychological patterns of relationships (Hoagwood & Jensen, 1997; Laosa, 1990). The use of such measures risks the over- or under-identification of socially meaningful characteristics, compromising the scientific benefits of the research and potentially resulting in harmful social labeling or maladaptive self-conceptions of members of the racial or ethnic group studied (Canino & Guarnaccia, 1997; Fisher et al., 2002; Knight & Hill, 1998). Thus, whenever possible, investigators should select surveys, interview techniques or instruments that have been standardized on members of the research participants' racial or ethnic group. When such measures have not yet been developed or sufficiently evaluated, investigators can evaluate the cultural validity of the measure by evaluating item equivalence and other psychometric properties.

Moving away from comparative and deficit approaches

Injustices in research can also occur when social research involving ethnic minority populations focuses only on population deficits rather than a more comprehensive analysis of both population vulnerabilities and strengths. This 'deficit' investigative approach often appears alongside another potential bias in social research design: the assumption that ethnic minority social constructs can only be understood when compared to non-minority standards (Fisher et al., 2002; Heath, 1997). To provide fair and equitable research knowledge benefits, social scientists need to apply the same principles of scientific inquiry to all populations studied (e.g. EU Code of Ethics for Socio-Economic Research, Standard 2.5, Dench et al., 2004). Cultural bias in social science has also been identified in developing countries. In India for example, the People's Science Movement (PSM) has drawn attention to the internalization of local cultural gender biases by scientists in developing countries (Varma, 1999).

DUE AND UNDUE RESEARCH INCENTIVES FOR DIVERSE SOCIOECONOMIC POPULATIONS

National guidelines and organizational ethics codes permit compensation for effort, time,

and inconvenience of research as long as no 'undue inducements' are offered to lure people into participating and incentives are not included as a 'benefit' in risk-benefit analyses (APA, 2002, Standard 8.06; BPS, 2006, Standard 3.3.4; CPA, 2000, Standard 1.14; NHMRC, 2007, Standard 2.2.9; National Advisory Council on Drug Abuse, 2000; OHRP, 1993). The science establishment thus recognizes that some inducement is necessary to insure sufficient sample size and that it is possible for investigators to distinguish between 'due' and 'undue' inducements (Dickert & Grady, 1991; Macklin, 1999). Selecting non-coercive incentives is critical to insuring the voluntary nature of participation and that research burdens are not born unequally by economically disadvantaged populations. Cash payments or other incentives may be considered coercive if they: (1) prompt participants to lie or conceal information that would disqualify them from the research or; (2) lure into participating those who would otherwise choose not to expose themselves to research risks (Macklin, 1999). The extent to which these criteria are met will vary across research populations.

Types of payments

Ethical decisions about the use of cash incentives to secure and retain participation in surveys on illegal and dangerous behaviors must include consideration of how monetary inducements will affect the quality of data as well as the equitable distribution of the benefits and burdens of research participation. Monetary incentives are often used for participant recruitment. Payments to research participants can be ethically justified as: (1) reimbursement for legitimate travel or other expenses accrued because of research participation; (2) fair compensation for time and inconvenience involved in research participation; (3) appreciation payments (e.g. in the form of cash, coupons, or gifts); and (4) incentive payments that offer money or the equivalence beyond those limited to reimbursement, compensation, or appreciation (Wendler et al., 2002).

Payments across research populations differing in financial need create a tension between fair compensation for the time and inconvenience of research participation and coercion.

Ideally monetary incentives for research participation should strengthen generalizability by providing a balanced representation of individuals from all economic levels appropriate to the research question (Giuffrida & Togerson, 1997; Kamb et al., 1998). However, individuals from different economic circumstances can have different responses to cash inducement as fair or coercive (Levine, 1986). Payments that are unnecessarily low can reduce the generalizability of data through under-recruitment of economically disadvantaged populations. Payments that are too high raise different concerns. For example, large financial incentives can jeopardize the voluntary nature of participation, undermine altruistic motivations for engaging in research, tempt prospective participants to provide false information to become eligible for study participation, or lie in response to experimental questions to comply with investigator expectations (Attkisson et al., 1996; Fisher, 2003b; Saunders et al., 1999). Grady (2001) argues that arbitrary or large sums of money to entice participants is poor practice, while modest payments help to minimize possible undue inducement. She proposes that the informed consent process in which participants are reminded of their freedom to refuse participation or withdraw their consent without repercussions is adequate protection against potential coercion (Grady, 2001).

Based on an analysis of compensation practices of a representative sample of biomedical and psychosocial research conducted in 1997 and 1998, Latterman and Merz (2001) reported research payments on average of $9.50/hour plus $12.00 for each additional task (U.S. dollars); larger compensation was related to longer participatory time, repeated interaction with the researcher, invasive tasks, and the number of tasks. From their small study these researchers concluded that payments in published studies are related to time and level of activity. In addition they found no evidence that participants of these studies were being enticed with large monetary inducements.

Payment for participation in illicit drug use research

Cash payment for participation in illicit drug use research can create an ethical paradox if it is used by participants to purchase illegal drugs, encourages them to maintain their drug habits to continue earning research money, or leads them to provide answers to experimental questions that distort evaluation of the social correlates and consequences of drug use (Fisher, 2003b; Koocher, 1991; McGrady & Bux, 1999; Shaner et al., 1995). On the other hand, for those who have difficulty obtaining and holding jobs, the money may be ethically justified as a legal means of obtaining payment for unskilled labor. Policies aimed at addressing this problem include spreading out the payment of full compensation over a period of time, using food coupons or vouchers for other health-related products, making payments to third parties on behalf of the participant, or withholding payment if a participant is intoxicated or in withdrawal (Fisher, 2004; Gorelick et al., 1999). Such alternatives raise their own ethical quandaries. First, there is no evidence that any substitute for non-cash incentives deters participants with illicit drug habits from using the monetary value of the incentives to purchase drugs. For example, informal observations by social scientists working in the field suggest that if need be vouchers are easily sold by participants for cash. Furthermore, a decision not to pay substance abusers can reinforce economic inequities between drug abusing and non-abusing populations or deny them the right to apply their own value system to life risk decisions (Fisher, 1999).

Ensuring fairness

Social scientists are challenged to determine payments that are perceived by all participants as equally attractive and legitimate for the time and effort contributed. To ensure fairness, some institutions adopt a standard compensation rate for all research participation. Others have defined fair financial inducements as the amount of money a normal, healthy volunteer would lose in work and travel time or by fair market value for the work involved (Dickert & Grady, 1991; Winslade & Douard, 1992). Obtaining the opinions of community representatives prior to research initiation provides another means of establishing fair and non-coercive research payments (Fisher, 2003b).

DOING GOOD SCIENCE WELL

The conduct of responsible social science depends upon investigators' commitment and lifelong efforts to act ethically. However, a desire to do the right thing must be accompanied by familiarity with national and international regulations, ethics codes, and laws essential to the identification and resolution of ethics-in-science challenges (Fisher, 2003a). Ethical commitment and consciousness in turn are necessary but not sufficient to anticipate and rightly address the array of ethical challenges that will emerge when social scientists work in diverse contexts with diverse populations. Doing good science well requires flexibility and sensitivity to the research context, the scientist's fiduciary responsibilities, and participant expectations unique to each study. The evaluation of risks and benefits, the construction of informed consent procedures, and the development of confidentiality and disclosure policies need to reflect a 'goodness of fit' between study goals and participant characteristics (Fisher, 2002, 2003c; Fisher & Goodman, in press; Fisher & Masty, 2006; Fisher & Ragsdale, 2006). Framing the responsible conduct of social science as a process that draws upon investigators' dual commitment to scientific validity and participant protection will nourish activities that reflect the highest ideals of science and merit participant trust.

REFERENCES

Allen, C. (1997). Spies like us: When Sociologists deceive their subjects. *Lingua franca, 7,* 31–39.

American Anthropological Association. (1998). *Code of ethics of the American Anthropological Association.* Retrieved March 10, 2006 from http://www.aaanet.org/committees/ethics/ethicscode.pdf.

American Psychological Association. (1953).*Ethical standards of psychologists.* Washington, DC: American Psychological Association.

American Psychological Association. (2002). Ethical principles of psychologists and code of conduct. *American Psychologist, 57,* 1060–1073.

American Sociological Association. (1999). *Code of ethics.* Washington, DC: American Sociological Association. Retrieved March 10, 2006 from http://www.asanet.org/galleries/default-file/Code%20of%20Ethics.pdf.

Attkisson, C. C., Rosenblatt, A., & Hoagwood, K. (1996). Research ethics and human subjects protection in child mental health services research and adolescent and parent studies. In K. Hoagwood, P. Jenson, & C. B. Fisher (eds.), *Ethical issues in research with children and adolescents with mental disorders* (pp. 43–58). Hillsdale, NJ: Lawrence Erlbaum Associates, Inc.

Baumrind, D. (1964). Some thoughts on ethics of research: after reading Milgram's 'Behavioral study of obedience.' *American Psychologist, 26,* 887–896.

Baumrind, D. (1979). IRBs and social science research: The cost of deception. *IRB: A Review of Human Subjects Research, 1,* 1–4.

British Psychological Society (2006). http://www.bps.org.uk/downloadfile.cfm?file_uuid=5084A882-1143-DFD0-7E6C-F1938A65C242&ext=pdf.

British Sociological Association. (2002). http://www.britsoc.co.uk/user_doc/Statement%20of%20Ethical%20Practice.pdf.

Bulmer, M. (1982). When is disguise justified? Alternatives to covert participant observation. *Qualitative Sociology, 5,* 251–264.

Canadian Psychological Association. (2000). *Canadian code of ethics for psychologists,* 3rd edition. Retrieved March 10, 2006 from http://www.cpa.ca/cpasite/userfiles/Documents/Canadian%20Code%20of%20Ethics%20for%20Psycho.pdf.

Canino, G., & Guarnaccia, P. (1997). Methodological challenges in the assessment of Hispanic children and adolescents.*Applied Developmental Science, 7,* 13–26.

Canter, M. B., Bennett, B. E., Jones, S. E., & Nagy, T. F. (1994). *Ethics for psychologists: A commentary on the APA ethics code.* Washington, DC: American Psychological Association.

Chan, K. S., & Hume, S. (1995). Racialization and panethnicity: From Asians in America to Asian Americans. In W. D. Hawley & A. W. Jackson (Eds.), *Toward a common destiny: Improving race and ethnic relations in America* (pp. 205–236). San Francisco: Jossey-Bass.

Council for International Organizations of Medical Sciences. (2002). International guidelines for ethical review of epidemiological studies Geneva: Council for International Organizations of Medical Sciences. Retrieved May 11, 2007 from http://www.cioms.ch/frame_guidelines_nov_2002.htm.

Council of National Psychological Associations for the Advancement of Ethic Minority Interests. (2000).*Guidelines for research in ethnic minority communities.* Washington, DC: American Psychological Association.

Dench, S., Iphofen, R., & Huws, U. (2004). *IES Report 412. An EU code of Ethics for Socio-economic Research.* Brighton, UK: The Institute for Employment Studies.

Department of Health, Education, & Welfare (DHEW). (1978). *The Belmont report: Ethical principles and guidelines for the protection of human subjects of research.* Washington DC: US Government Printing Office.

Department of Health and Human Services. (2001). Title 45 Public Welfare, Part 46, *Code of federal regulations, Protections of human subjects.*Washington, DC: Government Printing Office.

Dickert, N., & Grady, C. (1991). What's the price of a research subject: Approaches to the payment for research participation. *New England Journal of Medicine, 341,* 198–203.

Fisher, C. B. (1999). Relational ethics and research with vulnerable populations. *Reports on research involving persons with mental disorders that may affect decision-making capacity* (Vol. II, pp. 29–49). Commissioned Papers by the National Bioethics Advisory Commission, Rockville, MD. Retrieved March 21, 2006 from http://www.georgetown.edu/research/nrcbl/nbac/pubs.html.

Fisher, C. B. (2002). A goodness-of-fit ethic for informed consent. *Fordham Urban Law Journal, 30,* 159–171.

Fisher, C. B. (2003a). *Decoding the ethics code: A practical guide for psychologists.* Thousand Oaks, CA: Sage Publications.

Fisher, C. B. (2003b). Adolescent and parent perspectives on ethical issues in youth drug use and suicide survey research. *Ethics & Behavior, 13,* 302–331.

Fisher, C. B. (2003c). A goodness-of-fit ethic for child assent to nonbeneficial research. *The American Journal of Bioethics, 3,* 27–28.

Fisher, C. B. (2004). Informed consent and clinical research involving children and adolescents: Implications of the revised APA ethics code and HIPAA. *Journal of Clinical Child and Adolescent Psychology, 33,* 833–840.

Fisher, C. B. (2005). Deception research involving children: Ethical practices and paradoxes. *Ethics & Behavior, 15,* 271–287.

Fisher, C. B., & Brennan, M. (1992). Application and ethics in developmental psychology. In D. L. Featherman, R. M. Lerner, & M. Perlmutter (Eds.), *Life-span development and behavior* (pp. 189–219). Hillsdale, NJ: Lawrence Erlbaum Associates.

Fisher, C. B., & Fyrberg, D. (1994). College students weigh the costs and benefits of deceptive research. *American Psychologist, 49,* 417–426.

Fisher, C. B., & Goodman, S. J. (in press). Goodness-of-fit ethics for non-intervention research involving dangerous and illegal behavior. In D. Buchanan, C. B. Fisher, & L. Gable (Eds.), *Ethical & legal issues in research with high risk populations: Addressing threats of suicide, child abuse, and violence.* Washington, DC: APA Press.

Fisher, C. B., Hoagwood, K., Boyce, C., Buster, T., Frank, D. A., Grisso, T., Levine, R. J., Macklin, R., Spencer, M. B., Takanishi, R., Trimble, J. E., & Zayas, L. H. (2002). Research ethics for mental health science involving ethnic minority children and youth. *American Psychologist, 57,* 1024–1040.

Fisher, C. B., Jackson, J., & Villarruel, F. (1997). The study of African American and Latin American children and youth. In R. M. Lerner (Ed.), *Handbook of child psychology* (Vol. I, 5th ed., pp. 1145–1207). New York: Wiley.

Fisher, C. B., & Masty, J. K. (2006). A goodness-of-fit ethic for informed consent to pediatric cancer research. In R. T. Brown (Ed.), *Comprehensive handbook of childhood cancer and sickle cell disease: A biopsychosocial approach* (pp. 205–217). New York: Oxford University Press.

Fisher, C. B., & Ragsdale, K. (2006). A goodness-of-fit ethics for multicultural research. In J. Trimble and C. B. Fisher (Eds.),*The handbook of ethical research with ethnocultural populations and communities* (pp. 3–26). Thousand Oaks, CA: Sage Publications.

Fried, A. F., & Fisher, C. B. (in press). The ethics of informed consent for research in clinical and abnormal psychology. In D. McKay (Ed.), *Handbook of research methods in abnormal and clinical psychology.* Thousand Oaks, CA: Sage Publications.

Giuffrida, A., & Togerson, D. J. (1997).Should we pay the patient? Review of financial incentives to enhance patient compliance. *British Medical Journal, 315,* 703–707.

Gorelick, D. A., Pickens, R. W., & Bonkovsky, F. O. (1999). Clinical research in substance abuse: Human subjects issues. In H. A. Pincus, J. A. Lieberman, & S. Ferris (Eds.), *Ethics in psychiatric research* (pp. 177–192). Washington, DC: American Psychiatric Association.

Grady, C. (2001). Money for research participation: Does it jeopardize informed consent? *American Journal of Bioethics, 1,* 40–44.

Haverkamp, B. E. (2005). Ethical perspectives on qualitative research in applied psychology. *Journal of Counseling Psychology, 52,* 146–155.

Heath, S. B. (1997). Culture: Contested realm in research on children and youth. *Applied Developmental Science, 1,* 113–123.

Heller, J. (1972). Syphilis victims in the U.S. study went untreated for 40 years. *New York Times*, 26 July 1972, 1, 8.

Hoagwood, K., & Jensen, P. S. (1997). Developmental psychopathology and the notion of culture: Introduction to the special section on 'The fusion of cultural horizons: Cultural influences on the assessment of psychopathology in children and adolescents.' *Applied Developmental Science, 1,* 108–112.

Indian Council of Medical Research. (2000). Ethical guidelines on biomedical research involving human subjects New Delhi: Indian Council of Medical Research. Retrieved May 11, 2007 from http://www.icmr.nic.in/ethical.pdf.

International Committee of Medical Journal Editors. (2003). *Uniform requirements for manuscripts submitted to biomedical journals: Writing and editing for biomedical publication.* Retrieved April 2, 2004 from http://www.icmje.org/#conflicts.

International Sociological Association (2001). http://www.isa-sociology.org/about/isa_code_of_ethics.htm.

Jones, J. H. (1993). *Bad blood: The Tuskegee syphilis experiment*, new and expanded ed. New York: Free Press.

Kamb, M. L., Rhodes, F., Hoxworth, T., Rogers, J., Lentz, A., Kent, C., MacGowen, R., & Peterman, T. A. (1998). What about money? Effects of small monetary incentives on enrollment, retention, and motivation to change behavior in an HIV/STD prevention counseling intervention. *Sexually Transmitted Infection, 74,* 253–255.

Knight, G. P., & Hill, N. E. (1998). Measurement equivalence in research involving minority adolescents. In V. C. McLoyd & L. Steinberg (Eds.), *Studying minority adolescents: Conceptual, methodological, and theoretical issues* (pp. 183–211). Mahwah, NJ: Erlbaum.

Koocher, G. P. (1991). Questionable methods in alcoholism research. *Journal of Consulting and Clinical Psychology, 59,* 246–248.

Laosa, L. M. (1990). Population generalizeability, cultural sensitivity, and ethical dilemmas. In C. B. Fisher & W. W. Tryon (Eds.), *Ethics in applied developmental psychology: Emerging issues in an emerging field* (pp. 227–252). Norwood, NJ: Ablex.

Latterman, J., & Merz, J. F. (2001). How much are subjects paid to participate in research? *The American Journal of Bioethics, 1,* 45–46.

Levine, R. (1986). *Ethics and regulation of clinical research* (2nd ed.). Baltimore: Urban & Schwarzenberg.

Macklin, R. (1999). Moral progress and ethnical universalism. In R.Macklin (Ed.), *Against relativism: Cultural diversity and the search for ethical universal in medicine* (pp. 249–274). New York: Oxford University Press.

Marshall, P. L. (1992). Research ethics in applied anthropology. *IRB: A Review of Human Subjects Research, 14,* 1–5.

Marshall, P. L. (2003). Human Subjects Protections, Institutional Review Boards, and Cultural Anthropological Research. *Anthropological Quarterly, 76,* 269–285.

McGrady, B. S., & Bux, D. A. (1999). Ethical issues in informed consent with substance abusers. *Journal of Consulting and Clinical Psychology, 67,* 186–193.

Milgram, S. (1964). Issues in the study of obedience: A reply to Baumrind. *American Psychologist, 19,* 848–852.

National Advisory Council on Drug Abuse. (2000). *Recommended guidelines for the administration of drugs to human subjects.* DA-01-002. NIDA-CAMCODA. Retrieved January 11, 2004 from http://grants.nih.gov/grants/guide/noticefiles/NOT-DA-01-002.html.

National Consensus Conference on Bioethics and Health Research in Uganda. (1997). *Guidelines for the Conduct of Health Research Involving Human Subjects in Uganda.* Kampala, Uganda.

National Health and Medical Research Council (NHMRC). (2007). *National Statement on Ethical Conduct in Human Research.* http://www.nhmrc.gov.an/publications/synopses/_files/e72.pdf.

National Research Council. (2003). *Protecting participants and facilitating social and behavior sciences research.* In C. F. Citro, D. R. Ilgen, & C. B. Marret (Eds.). Washington, D.C.: The National Academies Press.

Nolan, R. W. (2002). *Anthropology in practice: building a career outside the academy (directions in applied anthropology).* Boulder: Lynne Rienner.

Nuremberg Code. (1946). *Journal of the American Medical Association, 132*, 1090.

Office for Protection From Research Risks, Department of Health and Human Service, National Institutes of Health. (1993). *Protecting human research subjects: Institutional review board guidebook.* Washington, DC: Government Printing Office.

Ogundiran, T. O. (2004). Enhancing the African bioethics initiative. *BMC Medical Education, 4*, 21.

Pan African Bioethics Initiative (PABIN). (2001). Terms of Reference. http://www.pabin.net/enindex.asp.

Resnick, J. H., & Schwartz, T. (1973). Ethical standards as an independent variable in psychological research. *American Psychologist, 28,* 134–139.

Saunders, C. A., Thompson, P. D., & Weijer, C. (1999). What's the price of a research subject? *New England Journal of Medicine, 341,* 1550–1552.

Shaner, A., Eckman, T. A., & Roberst, L. J. (1995). Disability income, cocaine use, and repeated hospitalization among schizophrenic cocaine abusers: A government-sponsored revolving door? *New England Journal of Medicine, 333,* 777–783.

Sieber, J. E. (1982). Ethical dilemmas in social research. In J. E. Sieber (Ed.), *The ethics of social research: Surveys and experiments* (pp. 1–30). New York: Springer-Verlag.

Sieber, J. E. (1992). *Planning ethically responsible research: A guide for students and internal review boards.* Thousand Oaks: CA. Sage Publications.

Smith, S. S., & Richardson, D. (1983). Amelioration of deception and harm in psychological research. *Journal of Personality and Social Psychology, 44,* 1075–1082.

Steinbock, B., Arras, J. D., & London, A. J. (2005). *Ethical issues in modern medicine.* New York, NY: McGraw-Hill Higher Education.

Thailand Ministry of Public Health Ethics Committee. (1995). Rule of the medical council on the observance of medical ethics. Thailand: Ministry of Public Health.

The Hindu. (2005). Editorial: A dangerous conflict of interest. *The Hindu.* Retrieved May 11, 2007 from http://www.hindu.com/2005/11/30/stories/2005113 002301000.htm.

Trimble, J. E., & Fisher, C. B. (2006). *The handbook of ethical research with ethnocultural population and communities.* Thousand Oaks, CA: Sage Publications.

Varma, R. (1999). Women and people's science movements in India. *Technology & Society: Historical, Societal, and Professional Perspectives Proceedings, 1999 International Symposium, 29-21,* 378–382.

Wendler, D., Rackoff, J. E., Emanuel, E. J., & Grady, C. (2002). The ethics of paying for children's participation in research. *Journal of Pediatrics, 141(2),* 166–171.

Winslade, W. J., & Douard, J. W. (1992). Ethical issues in psychiatric research. In L. K. G. Hsu & M. Hersen (Eds.), *Research in psychiatry: Issues, strategies, and methods* (pp. 57–70). New York: Plenum.

World Medical Association. (2000). Declaration of Helsinki: Ethical principles for medical research involving human subjects. Edinburgh: World Medical Association. Retrieved May 11, 2007 from http://www.wma.net/e/policy/pdf/17c.pdf.

Young, C. H., & Brooker, M. (2006). Safeguarding sacred lives: The ethical use of archival data for the study of diverse lives. In J. E. Trimble & C. B. Fisher (Eds.), *The handbook of ethical research with ethnocultural populations and communities.* Thousand Oaks, CA: Sage Publications.

Zuckerman, M. (1990). Some dubious premises in research and theory on racial differences: Scientific, social and ethical issues. *American Psychologist, 45,* 1297–1303.

PART II

Research Designs

This section of the handbook provides diverse perspectives on the design of social research. This section provides a sample of important issues in the design of qualitative and quantitative research rather than an integrated textbook approach to design. This approach allows a more in-depth exploration of topics that range from a detailed quantitative analysis of sample size planning for studies using multiple regression, to broader overviews of the conduct of qualitative case studies. The creation of randomized and quasi-experimental research designs is discussed in detail in the first two chapters. These chapters provide essential information on how to improve both of these research designs. From the in-depth quantitative perspective on sample size we move to a re-conceptualization of generalizability in qualitative research. The author of this chapter argues that correctly designed qualitative studies are as generalizable as representative sampling used in quantitative studies. An overview of the qualitative case study is provided in the following chapter. In the next chapter the similarities and differences in the design of qualitative and quantitative longitudinal and panel studies are discussed. The final chapter of this section discusses specific issues in the design of comparative and cross-national studies.

The first two chapters of this section deal with social science studies where an intervention is being tested to determine its impact. The priority for these research designs is to enhance the ability to draw valid conclusions about the attribution of cause. Howard Bloom's chapter on randomized experiments provides both a basic framework for understanding the design of experiments as well as a look at future developments and applications. Randomized designs require that individuals or aggregates such as organizations have an equal chance of being assigned to treatment or control groups. The major advantage of this design is that it is the best way to assure that the groups are equivalent on both measured and unmeasured variables at the start of the study. Properly implemented, this design eliminates most threats to internal validity, i.e. the factors that threaten the ability to demonstrate that the treatment caused the effect and not something else. Familiarity with randomized designs is increasingly important as the number of studies using these designs increases. For example, in the U.S. one federal research agency (Institute of Education Sciences) requires applicants for research grants to use a randomized design or justify why they did not. Randomized designs have been used in almost all substantive areas including such diverse topics as education, policing, and child care.

Bloom explains the five elements that need to be present in a randomized design. The research question must specify what treatment is being tested and with what condition it will be compared. Typically the comparison group will not be a no treatment group but a group receiving usual treatment. Second, the unit of randomization needs to be specified. One of the major advances in research has been the application of randomized designs to organizations and other aggregations such as schools or classes. The specification of the measurement methods is the third element. How will outcome and baseline characteristics be measured? The fourth element is of a practical nature. What is the implementation strategy? How will sites or individuals be recruited, randomly assigned and the treatment delivered? Fifth is the analysis plan that addresses whether randomization was successful and if the treatment delivered as planned.

Planning a randomized experiment is more complex than just these five elements. Bloom explains some of these complications and suggests actions that the researcher can take to prevent or deal with potential problems. For example he discusses the effects of non-compliance to the intervention and how to statistically adjust for it in the analysis. The chapter also suggests future directions for randomized designs.

The chapter by Tom Cook and Vivian Wong provides an excellent overview of experimental and quasi-experimental research designs, with a focus on the latter. The authors stress that while well-executed, randomized experiments are the best choice for drawing causal conclusions there are some quasi-experiments that are excellent alternatives. The first section of the chapter carefully examines two strong designs. Both the regression-discontinuity and the interrupted time series with a control series are good in reducing the plausibility of alternative explanations that threaten the internal validity of non-experimental designs. However, there are significant limitations to both approaches. The regression-discontinuity design requires that the treatment and comparison be assigned by a cut-off score from some assignment variable. This is feasible, for example, where there is screening before getting the intervention but

more difficult in other situations. This design is less powerful than a randomized design and thus is less likely to detect an effect if one is there. The interrupted times series design requires several data points before and after the intervention.

The authors also discuss in some detail how to strengthen the most widely used design – the non-equivalent control design. This design compares a treated group with an untreated control group using one pre-test and one post-test. Random assignment to conditions is not used in this design. Cook and Wong note that many dismiss quasi-experiments as being grossly inferior to randomized experiments. However, they describe studies that show that under some circumstances well-executed quasi-experiments' outcomes are comparable to randomized experiments' outcomes. One of the most important conditions is how well the groups match before the study on both measured and unmeasured variables.

One of the more recent approaches to matching groups to enhance their equivalency involves the use of propensity scores. These scores are usually constructed of variables found in pre-treatment scores that are good predictors of group membership. These scores represent the differences in selection between the two groups. The authors provide excellent examples of other ways to strengthen quasi-experiments such as the use of double pre-tests.

One of the first questions experimental researchers need to consider in planning a study is the sample size. The availability and feasibility of collecting data from the sample is of prime consideration, especially when the sampling units are not individuals but organizations such as schools or clinics. The cost collecting data and the number of units required will set the outer limit on the sample size. In planning a study two categories need to be considered. The first category is whether the research question is about an overall indicator (i.e. an omnibus test) or targeted effect. The second category is whether the goal is to determine a point estimate that requires the calculation of statistical power or if it is a confidence interval that requires the calculation of accuracy.

In the second category a power estimate is needed to test the null hypothesis, i.e. that a specific value is different from zero. Concern over power is driven by needing to demonstrate statistical significance or how probable the result (a point estimate) is due to chance. An alternate approach to research questions favored by some is the use of confidence intervals. Here the question is concerned with how wide is the band of uncertainty or error. The authors use the term 'accuracy' to describe the narrowness of confidence intervals. The smaller the confidence interval the better is the accuracy. Accuracy is a function of precision and bias.

Ken Kelley and Scott Maxwell provide an in-depth explanation of these concepts and how research questions can be categorized into a two by two table where the goal can be power verses accuracy and the effect can be targeted verses omnibus. They use this approach to help explicate how the determination of the sample size in multiple regression is dependent on these four factors. The chapter can be formidable for persons not well versed in statistical analysis. However, it provides an important way to conceptualize the decisions needed to determine sample size.

In the chapter 'Re-Conceptualizing Generalization in Qualitative Research' Giampietro Gobo makes the point that probability sampling cannot be advocated as the only model suited to the generalization of findings. On the other hand Gobo warns against the extreme postmodernist stance, which in fact agrees with and supports the positivist viewpoint that generalizability can only be based on random sampling. Instead, he promotes what he calls an idiographic sampling theory, which is in fact in use in several disciplines outside the human sciences. These are disciplines akin to qualitative research, for they work exclusively on few cases and have learnt to make a virtue out of necessity. Disciplines such as biology, astrophysics, genetics, paleontology, and linguistics work on non-probability samples regarded as being just as representative of their relative populations and therefore as producing generalizable results, because they start from the assumption that their objects of study possess quasi-invariant states on the properties observed. The (statistical) principle of variance is the key concept applied here. Under the variance principle, to determine the sample size, the researcher must first know the range of variance that one intends to measure. If the range of variance is high, the number of cases studied needs to be high, whereas if the range of variance is restricted, the number may be restricted as well. Gobo shows how the way in which representativeness is discussed and sought for in many traditions of qualitative research is in line with the variance principle. By applying a theory-driven strategy of choosing additional cases and by defining their units of analysis in a sensible way, researchers are able to assess the variability of the phenomenon and to make sure that extreme cases are taken into account. Thus the explanation given can be argued to be generalizable to the defined population, although probability sampling is not used.

Linda Mabry's chapter on case studies in social research provides an overview of the ways in which this approach has evolved and is used in the social sciences. Case studies are most useful for identifying and documenting the patterns of ordinary events in their social, cultural, and historical context. The case study is based on the inductive method and is a means to build a theoretical understanding of social phenomena. From this viewpoint, traditional hypotheses testing may restrict the researchers' vision and may foster a premature conclusion and thus miss a deeper understanding of the object of study. Mabry emphasizes that an attitude of openness should be maintained in conducting a case study.

The particular strength of the chapter by Jane Elliott, Janet Holland, and Rachel Thomson on longitudinal research is that they cover both qualitative and quantitative research traditions, which are both well established and typically discussed separately. The chapter focuses on panel and cohort studies where the same group of individuals is followed through time. Elliott et al. show that in terms of the objectives for carrying out longitudinal research, there isn't much difference between qualitative and quantitative researchers. Longitudinal social research is done because it offers unique insights into process, change and continuity over time in phenomena ranging from individuals, families, and institutions to societies.

Elliott et al. point out that both qualitative and quantitative traditions have their strengths, which may be complemented in mixed methods studies. Quantitative methods offer refined techniques to analyze causal relations, whereas qualitative researchers tend to be shy in talking about causal relations even though some argue that because of its attention to detail, process, complexity, and contextuality, qualitative research is particularly valuable for identifying and understanding multi-causal linkages. In quantitative longitudinal research a priority is placed on collecting accurate data from a large representative sample about the nature and timing of life events, circumstances, and behavior. In qualitative longitudinal research the emphasis is far more on individuals' understanding of their lives and circumstances and how these may change through time. While quantitative longitudinal analytic processes provide a more processual or dynamic understanding of the social world, they do so at the expense of setting up a static view of the individual. Quantitative longitudinal research provides a powerful tool for understanding the multiple factors that may affect individuals' lives, shaping their experiences and behavior. But there is little scope for understanding how individuals use narrative to construct and maintain a sense of their own identity. Without this element there is a danger that people are merely seen as making decisions and acting within a predefined and structurally determined field of social relations rather than as contributing to the maintenance and metamorphosis of themselves, and the culture and community in which they live.

Comparative research, especially when it is conducted cross nationally, is another important growth area in the social sciences in the context of the globalization of communications, technological progress, and growing internationalization. This is the focus of Chapter 15 by David de Vaus. As de Vaus concludes, such research raises the same methodological issues as other research, at least *in abstracto*. However because of the complexity involved in comparative research, especially when applied cross nationally, there are additional problems of how to deal with inter- and intra-societal differences of language and culture. The chapter explores the nature of comparative research and classifies it according to two broad types: case-based comparative studies and variable-based comparative research. The chapter explores their different logics and the problems that each confronts. The strength of case-based comparative methods lies in its understanding of specificities within the context of the whole case, a feature that is crucial to cross-cultural research. On the other hand, such research raises the problem of how to know the boundaries of the case, issues to do with the small number of cases that are typically involved, and issues around invariant causation. The problems of variable-based comparative studies, notably discussed with reference to cross-national surveys, also have their own problems related to equivalences of meanings and the standardization of procedures. However it is arguable that case-based comparative research also has to contend with these challenges.

The Core Analytics of Randomized Experiments for Social Research

Howard S. Bloom

INTRODUCTION

This chapter introduces the central analytic principles of randomized experiments for social research. Randomized experiments are lotteries that randomly assign subjects to research groups, each of which is offered a different treatment. When the method is implemented properly, differences in future outcomes for experimental groups provide unbiased estimates of differences in the impacts of the treatments offered. The method is usually attributed to Ronald A. Fisher (1925 and 1935), who developed it during the early 1900s[1]. After World War II, randomized experiments gradually became the method of choice for testing new drugs and medical procedures, and to date over 350,000 randomized clinical trials have been conducted (Cochrane Collaboration, 2002)[2].

Numerous books have been written about randomized experiments as their application has expanded from agricultural and biological research (e.g. Fisher, 1935; Kempthorne, 1952; Cochran and Cox, 1957; Cox, 1958) to research on industrial engineering (e.g. Box et al., 2005), to educational and psychological research (e.g. Lindquist, 1953; Myers, 1972) to social science and social policy research (e.g. Boruch, 1997; Orr, 1999; Bloom, 2005a). In addition, several journals have been established to promote advancement of the method (e.g. the *Journal of Experimental Criminology, Clinical Trials* and *Controlled Clinical Trials*).

The use of randomized experiments for social research has greatly increased since the War on Poverty in the 1960s. The method has been used in laboratories and in field settings to randomize individual subjects, such as students, unemployed adults, patients, or welfare recipients, and intact groups, such as schools, firms, hospitals, or neighborhoods[3]. Applications of the method to social research have examined issues such as child nutrition (Teruel and Davis, 2000); child abuse

(Olds et al., 1997); juvenile delinquency (Lipsey, 1988); policing strategies (Sherman and Weisburd, 1995); child care (Bell et al., 2003); public education (Kemple and Snipes, 2000); housing assistance (Orr et al., 2003); health insurance (Newhouse, 1996); income maintenance (Munnell, 1987); neighborhood effects (Kling et al., 2007); job training (Bloom et al., 1997); unemployment insurance (Robins and Spiegelman, 2001); welfare-to-work (Bloom and Michalopoulos, 2001); and electricity pricing (Aigner, 1985)[4].

A successful randomized experiment requires clear specification of five elements.

1 *Research questions:* What treatment or treatments are being tested? What is the counterfactual state (in the absence of treatment) with which treatments will be compared? What estimates of net impact (the impact of specific treatments versus no such treatments) are desired? What estimates of differential impact (the difference between impacts of two or more treatments) are desired?

2 *Experimental design:* What is the unit of randomization: individuals or groups? How many individuals or groups should be randomized? What portion of the sample should be randomized to each treatment or to a control group? How, if at all, should covariates, blocking, or matching (explained later) be used to improve the precision of impact estimates?

3 *Measurement methods:* What outcomes are hypothesized to be affected by the treatments being tested, and how will these outcomes be measured? What baseline characteristics, if any, will serve as covariates, blocking factors, or matching factors, and how will these characteristics be measured? How will differences in treatments be measured?

4 *Implementation strategy:* How will experimental sites and subjects be recruited, selected, and informed? How will they be randomized? How will treatments be delivered and how will their differences across experimental groups be maintained? What steps will be taken to ensure high-quality data?

5 *Statistical analysis:* The analysis of treatment effects must reflect how randomization was conducted, how treatment was provided, and what baseline data were collected. Specifically it must account for: (1) whether randomization was conducted or treatment was delivered in groups or individually (explained later); (2) whether simple randomization was conducted or randomization occurred within blocks or matched pairs; and (3) whether baseline covariates were used to improve precision.

This chapter examines the analytic core of randomized experiments — design and analysis, with a primary emphasis on design.

WHY RANDOMIZE?

There are two main reasons why well-implemented randomized experiments are the most rigorous way to measure causal effects.

They eliminate bias: Randomizing subjects to experimental groups eliminates all *systematic* preexisting group differences, because only chance determines which subjects are assigned to which groups[5]. It is therefore valid to attribute observed differences in future group outcomes to differences in the treatments they were offered. Hence, these causal inferences (impact estimates) are unbiased. Randomization of a given sample may produce experimental groups that differ by chance, however. These differences are random errors, not biases. Hence, the absence of bias is a property of the *process* of randomization, not a feature of its application to a specific sample. The laws of probability ensure that the larger the experimental sample is, the smaller preexisting group differences are likely to be.

They enable measurement of uncertainty: Experiments randomize all sources of uncertainty about impact estimates for a given sample (their internal validity). Hence, confidence intervals or tests of statistical significance can account for all of this uncertainty. No other method for measuring causal effects has this property. One cannot, however, account for all uncertainty about generalizing an impact estimate beyond a given sample (its external validity) without both randomly *sampling* subjects from a known population and randomly *assigning* them to experimental groups (which is rarely possible in social research)[6].

A SIMPLE EXPERIMENTAL ESTIMATOR OF CAUSAL EFFECTS

Consider an experiment where half of the sample is randomized to a treatment group that is offered an intervention and half is randomized to a control group that is not offered the intervention, and everyone adheres to their assigned treatment. Follow-up data are obtained for all sample members and the treatment effect is estimated by the difference in mean outcomes for the two groups, $\overline{Y}_T - \overline{Y}_C$. This difference provides an unbiased estimate of the average treatment effect (ATE) for the study sample, because the mean outcome for control group members is an unbiased estimate of what the mean outcome would have been for treatment group members had they not been offered the treatment (their counterfactual).

However, any given sample can yield a treatment group and control group with preexisting differences that occur solely by chance and can overestimate or underestimate the ATE. The standard error of the impact estimator $(SE(\overline{Y}_T - \overline{Y}_C))$ accounts for this random error, where:

$$SE(\overline{Y}_T - \overline{Y}_C) = \sqrt{\frac{\sigma^2}{n_T} + \frac{\sigma^2}{n_C}} \qquad (1)$$

given:

n_T and n_C = the number of treatment group members and control group members,

σ^2 = the pooled outcome variance across subjects within experimental groups[7].

The number of treatment group members and control group members are experimental design decisions. The variance of the outcome measure is an empirical parameter that must be 'guesstimated' from previous research when planning an experiment and can be estimated from follow-up data when analyzing experimental findings. For the discussion that follows it is useful to restate Equation 1 as:

$$SE(\overline{Y}_T - \overline{Y}_C) = \sqrt{\frac{\sigma^2}{nP(1-P)}} \qquad (2)$$

where n equals the total number of experimental sample members $(n_T + n_C)$ and P equals the proportion of this sample that is randomized to treatment[8].

CHOOSING A SAMPLE SIZE AND ALLOCATION

The first steps in designing a randomized experiment are to specify its treatment, target group, and setting. The next steps are to choose a sample size and allocation that maximize precision given existing constraints. For this purpose, it is useful to measure precision in terms of minimum detectable effects (Bloom, 1995, 2005b). Intuitively, a minimum detectable effect is the smallest true treatment effect that a research design can detect with confidence. Formally, it is the smallest true treatment effect that has a specified level of statistical power for a particular level of statistical significance, given a specific statistical test.

Figure 9.1 illustrates that the minimum detectable effect of an impact estimator is a multiple of its standard error. The first bell-shaped curve (on the left of the figure) represents a t distribution for a null hypothesis of zero impact. For a positive impact estimate to be statistically significant at the α level with a one-tail test (or at the $\alpha/2$ level with a two-tail test), the estimate must fall to the right of the critical t-value, t_α (or $t_{\alpha/2}$), of the first distribution. The second bell-shaped curve represents a t distribution for an alternative hypothesis that the true impact equals a specific minimum detectable effect. To have a probability $(1 - B)$ of detecting the minimum detectable effect it must lie a distance of t_{1-B} to the right of the critical t-value for the null hypothesis. (The probability $(1-B)$ represents the level of statistical power.) Hence the minimum detectable effect must lie a total distance of $t_\alpha + t_{1-B}$ (or $t_{\alpha/2} + t_{1-B}$) from the null hypothesis. The minimum detectable effect is either $t_\alpha + t_{1-B}$ (for a one-tail test) or $t_{\alpha/2} + t_{1-B}$ (for a two-tail test) times the standard error. These critical t-values depend on the number of degrees of freedom.

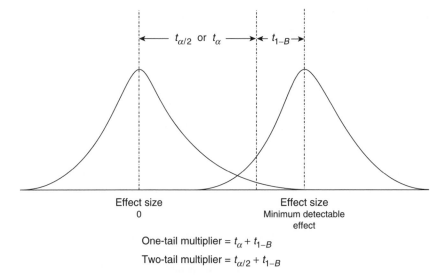

One-tail multiplier = $t_\alpha + t_{1-B}$

Two-tail multiplier = $t_{\alpha/2} + t_{1-B}$

Figure 9.1   The minimum detectable effect multiplier

A common convention for defining minimum detectable effects is to set statistical significance (α) at 0.05 and statistical power ($1 - B$) at 80 percent. When the number of degrees of freedom exceeds about 30, the multiplier equals roughly 2.5 for a one-tail test and 2.8 for a two-tail test[9]. Thus, if the standard error of an estimator of the average effect of a job-training program on future annual earnings were $500, the minimum detectable effect would be roughly $1,250 for a one-tail test and $1,400 for a two-tail test.

Consider how this applies to the experiment described above. The multiplier, M_{n-2}[10], times the standard error, $SE(\overline{Y}_T - \overline{Y}_C)$, yields the minimum detectable effect:

$$MDE(\overline{Y}_T - \overline{Y}_C) = M_{n-2}\sqrt{\frac{\sigma^2}{nP(1-P)}} \quad (3)$$

Since the multiplier M_{n-2} is the sum of two t-values, determined by the chosen levels of statistical significance and power, the missing value that needs to be determined for the sample design is that for σ^2. This value will necessarily be a guess, but since it is a central determinant of the minimum

detectable effect, it should be based on a careful search of empirical estimates for closely related studies[11].

Sometimes impacts are measured as a standardized mean difference or 'effect size,' (*ES*) either because the original units of the outcome measures are not meaningful or because outcomes in different metrics must be combined or compared. (There is no reason to standardize the impact estimate for the preceding job training example.) The standardized mean difference *ES* equals the difference in mean outcomes for the treatment group and control group, divided by the standard deviation of outcomes across subjects within experimental groups, or:

$$ES = \frac{\overline{Y}_T - \overline{Y}_C}{\sigma} \quad (4)$$

Some researchers use the pooled within-group standard deviation to define *ES*s while others use the control-group standard deviation. Standardized mean *ES*s are therefore measured in units of standard deviations. For example, an *ES* of 0.25 implies an impact equal to 0.25 standard deviation. When impacts are reported in *ES*, precision can be reported as a minimum detectable *ES* (*MDES*), where:

$$MDES(\overline{Y}_T - \overline{Y}_C) = M_{n-2}\sqrt{\frac{1}{nP(1-P)}} \quad (5)$$

Table 9.1 illustrates the implications of Equations 3 and 5 for the relationship between sample size, allocation, and precision. The top panel in the table presents minimum detectable effects for a hypothetical job training program, given a standard deviation for the outcome (annual earnings) of $1,000. The bottom panel presents corresponding *MDES*s.

The first main observation is that increasing sample size has a diminishing absolute return for precision. For example, the first column in the table illustrates how the minimum detectable effect (or *ES*) declines with an increase in sample size for a balanced allocation ($P = 0.5$). Doubling the sample size from 50 individuals to 100 individuals reduces the minimum detectable effect from approximately $810 to $570 or by a factor of $1/\sqrt{2}$. Doubling the sample size again from 100 to 200 individuals reduces the minimum detectable effect by another factor of $1/\sqrt{2}$

from approximately $570 to $400. Thus, quadrupling the sample cuts the minimum detectable effect in half. The same pattern holds for *MDES*s.

The second main observation is that for a given sample size, precision decreases slowly as the allocation between the treatment and control groups becomes more imbalanced. Equation 5 implies that the *MDES* is proportional to $1/\sqrt{P(1-P)}$, which equals 2.00, 2.04, 2.18, 2.50, or 3.33 when *P* (or its complement) equals 0.5, 0.6, 0.7, 0.8, or 0.9. Thus, for a given sample size, precision is best with a balanced allocation ($P = 0.5$). Because precision erodes slowly until the degree of imbalance becomes extreme (roughly $P \le 0.2$ or $P \ge 0.8$), there is considerable latitude for using an unbalanced allocation. Thus, when political pressures to minimize the number of control group members are especially strong, one could use a relatively small control group. Or when the costs of treatment are particularly high, one could use a relatively large control group[12].

One of the most difficult steps in choosing a sample design is selecting a target minimum detectable effect or *ES*. From an economic perspective, this target should equal the

Table 9.1   Minimum detectable effect and *ES* for individual randomization

Sample size n	Sample allocation P/(1 − P)				
	0.5/0.5	0.6/0.4 or 0.4/0.6	0.7/0.3 or 0.3/0.7	0.8/0.2 or 0.2/0.8	0.9/0.1 or 0.1/0.9
	Minimum detectable effect given σ = $1,000				
50	$810	$830	$880	$1,010	$1,350
100	570	580	620	710	940
200	400	410	430	500	660
400	280	290	310	350	470
800	200	200	220	250	330
1,600	140	140	150	180	230
	Minimum detectable effect size				
50	0.81	0.83	0.88	1.01	1.35
100	0.57	0.58	0.62	0.71	0.94
200	0.40	0.41	0.43	0.50	0.66
400	0.28	0.29	0.31	0.35	0.47
800	0.20	0.20	0.22	0.25	0.33
1,600	0.14	0.14	0.15	0.18	0.23

Source: Computations by the author.
Note: Minimum detectable effect sizes are for a two-tail hypothesis test with statistical significance of 0.05 and statistical power of 0.80.

smallest true impact that would produce benefits that exceed intervention costs. From a political perspective, it should equal the smallest true impact deemed policy-relevant. From a programmatic perspective, the target should equal the smallest true impact that exceeds known impacts from related interventions.

The most popular benchmark for gauging standardized *ES*s is Cohen's (1977/1988) prescription (based on little empirical evidence) that values of 0.20, 0.50, and 0.80 be considered small, moderate, and large. Lipsey (1990) subsequently provided empirical support for this prescription from a synthesis of 186 meta-analyses of intervention studies. The bottom third of *ES*s in Lipsey's synthesis ranges from 0.00 to 0.32, the middle third ranges from 0.33 to 0.55, and the top third ranges from 0.56 to 1.20. Both authors suggest, however, that their general guidelines do not apply to many situations. For example, recent research suggests that much smaller *ES*s are policy-relevant for educational interventions. Findings from the Tennessee Class Size Experiment indicate that reducing elementary school class size from 22–26 students to 13–17 students increased performance on standardized reading and math tests by 0.1 to 0.2 standard deviation (Nye et al., 1999). More recently, Kane's (2004) study of grade-to-grade improvement in math and reading on a nationally normed test suggests that one full year of elementary school *attendance* increases student achievement by roughly 0.25 standard deviation. These results highlight the importance of basing decisions about needed precision on the best existing evidence for the context being studied[13].

ESTIMATING CAUSAL EFFECTS WITH NONCOMPLIANCE

In most social experiments, some treatment group members ('no-shows') do not receive treatment and some control group members ('crossovers') do. This noncompliance dilutes the experimental treatment contrast, causing it to understate the average treatment effect.

Consequently, it is important to distinguish between the following two impact questions:

1 What is the average effect of offering treatment?
2 What is the average effect of receiving treatment?

The first question asks about the impact of a treatment offer. This impact — which can be estimated experimentally — is often called the average effect of 'intent to treat' (*ITT*). Since voluntary programs can only offer treatment — they cannot require it — the effect of *ITT* is a relevant consideration for making policy decisions about such programs. Furthermore, since even mandatory programs often have incomplete compliance, the effect of *ITT* can be an important consideration for judging them.

The second question above asks about the impact of treatment receipt. It is often called the average impact of 'treatment on the treated' (*TOT*) and is typically the question of interest for developers of interventions who want to know what they can achieve by full implementation of their ideas. However, in many instances this impact question may not be as policy-relevant as the first one, because rarely can treatment receipt be mandated.

There is no valid way to estimate the second type of effect experimentally, because there is no way to know which control group members are counterparts to treatment group members who receive treatment. To estimate such impacts, Bloom (1984) developed an extension of the experimental method, which was later expanded by Angrist et al. (1996)[14]. To see how this approach works, it is useful to adopt a framework and notation that is now conventional for presenting it. This framework comprises three variables: Y, the outcome measure; Z, which equals one for subjects *randomized* to treatment and zero otherwise; and D, which equals one for subjects who *receive* the treatment and zero otherwise.

Consider an experiment in which some treatment group members do not receive treatment (they become no-shows) but no control group members receive treatment (there are no crossovers). If *no-shows experience no effect* from the intervention (because they are not exposed to it) or from randomization per se, the average effect of *ITT* equals the weighted mean of *TOT* for treatment recipients and zero for no-shows, with weights equal to the treatment receipt rate ($[E(D|Z = 1])$) and the no-show rate ($1 − [E(D|Z = 1)]$), such that:

$$ITT = [E(D|Z=1)]TOT + [1 − E(D|Z=1)]0$$
$$= [E(D|Z=1)]TOT \qquad (6)$$

Equation 6 implies that:

$$TOT = \frac{ITT}{E(D|Z = 1)} \qquad (7)$$

The effect of *TOT* thus equals the effect of *ITT* divided by the expected receipt rate for treatment group members. For example, if the effect of *ITT* for a job training program were a $1,000 increase in annual earnings, and half of the treatment group members received treatment, then the effect of *TOT* would be $1,000/0.5 or $2,000. This adjustment allocates all of the treatment effect to only those treatment group members who receive treatment. Equation 7 represents the true effect of *TOT* for a given population. The corresponding sample estimator, $T\hat{O}T$, is:

$$T\hat{O}T = \frac{\overline{Y}_T − \overline{Y}_C}{(\overline{D}|Z = 1)} \qquad (8)$$

where $(\overline{D}|Z = 1)$ equals the observed treatment receipt rate for the treatment group. If no-shows experience no effect, this estimator is statistically consistent and its estimated standard error is approximately:

$$se(T\hat{O}T) \approx \frac{se(\overline{Y}_T − \overline{Y}_C)}{(\overline{D}|Z = 1)} \qquad (9)$$

Hence, both the point estimate and standard error are scaled by the treatment receipt rate.

The preceding approach does not require that no-shows be similar to treatment recipients. It requires only that no-shows experience no effect from treatment or randomization[15].

In addition, because of potential heterogeneity of treatment effects, the effect of *TOT* generalizes only to experimental treatment recipients and does not necessarily equal the average treatment effect for the full study sample.

Now add crossovers (control group members who receive treatment) to the situation, which further dilutes the experimental treatment contrast. Nonetheless, the difference in mean outcomes for the treatment group and control group provides an unbiased estimate of the effect of *ITT*. Thus, it addresses the first impact question stated above. To address the second question requires a more complex analytic framework with additional assumptions. This framework — developed by Angrist et al. (1996) — is based on four conceptual subgroups, which because of randomization comprise the same proportion of the treatment group and control group, in expectation. Figure 9.2 illustrates the framework and how it relates to the concepts of no-shows and crossovers. The first stacked bar in the figure represents all treatment group members (for whom $Z = 1$) and the second stacked bar represents all control group members (for whom $Z = 0$). Treatment group members who do not receive treatment (for whom $D = 0$) are no-shows, and control group members who do receive treatment (for whom $D = 1$) are crossovers.

Randomization induces treatment receipt for two of the four subgroups in the Angrist et al. framework — 'compliers' and 'defiers.' Compliers receive treatment only if they are randomized to the treatment group, and defiers receive treatment only if they are randomized to the control group. Thus, compliers add to the effect of *ITT*, and defiers subtract from it. Randomization does not influence treatment receipt for the other two groups — 'always-takers,' who receive treatment regardless of their randomization status, and 'never-takers,' who do not receive treatment regardless of their randomization status. Never-takers experience no treatment effect in the treatment group or control group, and always-takers experience the same effect in both groups, which cancels out

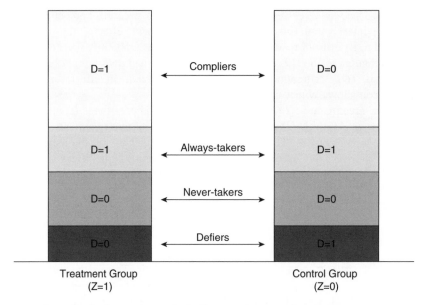

Figure 9.2   A hypothetical experiment including no-shows and crossovers
Source: **Bloom 2005a.**
Note: **D equals 1 if the treatment would be received and 0 otherwise.**

in the overall difference between treatment and control groups. Hence, always-takers and never-takers do not contribute information about treatment effects.

If defiers do not exist[16], which is reasonable to assume in many situations, the effect of treatment for compliers, termed by Angrist et al. (1996) the Local Average Treatment Effect (*LATE*) is[17]:

$$LATE = \frac{ITT}{E(D|Z=1) - E(D|Z=0)} \quad (10)$$

Thus to estimate the *LATE* from an experiment, one simply divides the difference in mean outcomes for the treatment and control groups by their difference in treatment receipt rates, or:

$$L\hat{A}TE = \frac{\overline{Y}_T - \overline{Y}_C}{(\overline{D}|Z=1) - (\overline{D}|Z=0)} \quad (11)$$

The estimated *LATE* is the ratio of the estimated impact of randomization on outcomes and the estimated impact of randomization on treatment receipt[18]. Angrist et al. show that this ratio is a simple form of instrumental variables analysis called a Wald estimator (Wald, 1940).

Returning to our previous example, assume that there is a $1,000 difference in mean annual earnings for a treatment group and control group; half of the treatment group receives treatment and one-tenth of the control group receives treatment. The estimated *LATE* equals the estimated impact on the outcome ($1,000), divided by the estimated impact on treatment receipt rates (0.5 – 0.1). This ratio equals $1,000/0.4 or $2,500[19].

When using this approach to estimate treatment effects, it is important to clearly specify the groups to which it applies, because different groups may experience different effects from the same treatment, and not all groups and treatment effects can be observed without making further assumptions. The impact of *ITT* applies to the full treatment group. So both the target group and its treatment effect can be observed. The *LATE*, which can be observed, applies to compliers, who cannot be observed. The effect of *TOT*, which cannot be observed, applies to all treatment group members who receive treatment (compliers plus always-takers), who can be observed.

USING COVARIATES AND BLOCKING TO IMPROVE PRECISION

The two main approaches for improving the precision of randomized experiments — covariates and blocking — use the predictive power of past information about sample members to reduce unexplained variation in their future outcomes. This reduces the standard error of the impact estimator and its corresponding minimum detectable effect[20]. To examine these approaches, it is useful to reformulate the impact of *ITT* as the following bivariate regression:

$$Y_i = \alpha + \beta_0 T_i + \varepsilon_i \qquad (12)$$

where:

Y_i = the outcome for sample member i

T_i = one if sample member i is randomized to the treatment group and zero otherwise

ε_i = a random error that is independently and identically distributed across sample members within experimental groups, with a mean of 0 and a variance of σ^2.

α is the expected mean outcome without treatment and β_0 is the average effect of *ITT*. Thus β_0 equals the difference in expected outcomes for the treatment group and control group, and its estimator, $\hat{\beta}_0$ equals the difference in mean outcomes for the treatment and control groups in the experimental sample.

Using k^* baseline characteristics, X_{ki}, as covariates to reduce the unexplained variation in Y_i produces the following

multiple regression model for estimating intervention effects:

$$Y_i = \alpha + \beta_0 T_i + \sum_{k=1}^{k^*} B_k X_{ki} + \varepsilon_i' \qquad (13)$$

Defining R_A^2 as the proportion of pooled unexplained variation in the outcome within experimental groups predicted by covariates, the *MDES* is[21]:

$$MDES(\hat{\beta}_0) = M_{n-k^*-2}\sqrt{\frac{1 - R_A^2}{nP(1 - P)}} \qquad (14)$$

There are two differences between the *MDES* in Equation 14 with covariates and Equation 5 without covariates. The first difference involves the multipliers, M_{n-2} and M_{n-k^*-2}, where the latter multiplier accounts for the loss of k^* degrees of freedom from estimating coefficients for k^* covariates. With roughly 40 or more sample members and 10 or fewer covariates, this difference is however negligible[22].

The second difference is the term $1 - R_A^2$ with covariates in Equation 14, instead of the value 1 in Equation 5 without covariates. The term $1 - R_A^2$ implies that the *MDES* decreases as the predictive power of covariates increases for a given sample size and allocation. In this way, covariates can increase effective sample size. For example, an R_A^2 of 0.25 yields an effective sample that is one-third larger than that without covariates; an R_A^2 of 0.50 yields an effective sample that is twice as large; and an R_A^2 of 0.75 yields an effective sample that is four times as large.

Several points are important to note about using covariates with experiments. First, they are not needed to eliminate bias, because randomization has done so already[23]. Thus, values for the term B_0 in Equations 12 and 13 are identical. Second, it is good practice to specify all covariates in advance of the impact analysis — preferably when an experiment is being designed. This helps to avoid subsequent data mining. Third, the best predictors of future outcomes are typically past outcomes. For example, past student achievement is usually the best predictor of future student achievement. This is because past outcomes reflect most factors that determine future outcomes. Fourth, some outcomes are more predictable than others, and thus covariates provide greater precision gains for them. For example, the correlation between individual standardized test scores is typically stronger for high school students than for elementary school students (Bloom et al., 2005).

The second approach to improving precision is to block or stratify experimental sample members by some combination of their baseline characteristics, and then randomize within each block or stratum. The extreme case of two sample members per block is an example of matching. Factors used for blocking in social research typically include geographic location, organizational units, demographic characteristics, and past outcomes. To compute an unbiased estimate of the impact of *ITT* from such designs requires computing impact estimates for each block and pooling estimates across blocks. One way to do this in a single step is to add to the impact regression a series of indicator variables that represent each of the m^* blocks, and suppress the intercept, α, yielding:

$$Y_i = \beta_0 T_i + \sum_{m=1}^{m^*} \gamma_m S_{mi} + \varepsilon_i'' \qquad (15)$$

where:

$S_{mi} =$ one if sample member i is from block (or stratum) m and zero otherwise.

The estimated value of B_0 provides an unbiased estimator of the effect of *ITT*. The *MDES* of this estimator can be expressed as:

$$MDES(\hat{\beta}_0) = M_{n-m^*-1}\sqrt{\frac{1 - R_B^2}{nP(1 - P)}} \qquad (16)$$

where:

$R_B^2 = $ the proportion of unexplained variation in the outcome within experimental groups (pooled) predicted by the blocks.

There are two differences in the expressions for minimum detectable effects with and without blocking (Equations 16 and 5). The first difference involves the multipliers, M_{n-m^*-1} versus M_{n-2}, which account for the loss of one degree of freedom per block and the gain of one degree of freedom from suppressing the intercept. With samples of more than about 40 members in total and 10 or fewer blocks, there is very little difference between these two multipliers. The second difference is the addition of the term $1 - R_B^2$ in Equation 16 to account for the predictive power of blocking. The more similar sample members are within blocks and the more different blocks are from each other, the higher this predictive power is. This is where precision gains come from. Note, however, that for samples with fewer than about 10 subjects, precision losses due to reducing the number of degrees of freedom by blocking can sometimes outweigh precision gains due to the predictive power of blocking. This is most likely to occur in experiments that randomize small numbers of groups (discussed later).

Another reason to block sample members is to avoid an 'unhappy' randomization with embarrassing treatment and control group differences on a salient characteristic. Such differences can reduce the face validity of an experiment, thereby undermining its credibility. Blocking first on the salient characteristic eliminates such a mismatch.

Sometimes researchers wish to assure treatment and control group matches on multiple characteristics. One way to do so is to define blocks in terms of combinations of characteristics (e.g. age, race, and gender). But doing so can become complicated in practice due to uneven distributions of sample members across blocks, and the consequent need to combine blocks, often in ad hoc ways. A second approach is to specify a composite index of baseline characteristics and create blocks based on intervals of this index[24]. Using either approach, the quality of the match on any given characteristic typically declines as the number of matching variables increases. So it is important to set priorities for which variables to match[25].

Regardless of how blocks are defined, one's impact analysis must account for them if they are used. To not do so would bias estimates of standard errors. In addition, it is possible to use blocking in combination with covariates. If so, both features of the experimental design should be represented in the experimental analysis.

RANDOMIZING GROUPS TO ESTIMATE INTERVENTION EFFECTS

This section introduces a type of experimental design that is growing rapidly in popularity — the randomization of intact groups or clusters[26]. Randomizing groups makes it possible to measure the effectiveness of interventions that are designed to affect entire groups or are delivered in group settings, such as communities, schools, hospitals, or firms. For example, schools have been randomized to measure the impacts of whole school reforms (Cook et al., 2000; Borman et al., 2005) and school-based risk-prevention campaigns (Flay, 2000); communities have been randomized to measure the impacts of community health campaigns (Murray et al., 1994); small local areas have been randomized to study the impacts of police patrol interventions (Sherman and Weisburd, 1995); villages have been randomized to study the effects of a health, nutrition, and education initiative (Teruel and Davis, 2000); and public housing developments have been randomized to study the effects of a place-based HIV prevention program (Sikkema et al., 2000) and a place-based employment program (Bloom and Riccio, 2005).

Group randomization provides unbiased estimates of intervention effects for the same reasons that individual randomization does. However, the statistical power or precision of group randomization is less than that for individual randomization, often by a lot. To see this, consider the basic regression

model for estimating *ITT* effects with group randomization:

$$Y_{ij} = \alpha + \beta_0 T_j + e_j + \varepsilon_{ij} \qquad (17)$$

where:

Y_{ij} = the outcome for individual i from group j

α = the mean outcome without treatment

B_0 = the average impact of *ITT*

$T_j = 1$ for groups randomized to treatment and 0 otherwise

e_j = an error that is independently and identically distributed between groups with a mean of 0 and a variance of τ^2

ε_{ij} = an error that is independently and identically distributed between individuals within groups with a pooled mean of zero and variance of σ^2.

Equation 17 for group randomization has an additional random error, e_j, relative to Equation 12 for individual randomization. This error reflects how mean outcomes vary across groups, which reduces the precision of group randomization.

To see this, first note that the relationship between group-level variance, τ^2, and individual-level variance, σ^2, can be expressed as an intra-class coefficient, ρ, where:

$$\rho = \frac{\tau^2}{\tau^2 + \sigma^2} \qquad (18)$$

ρ equals the proportion of total variation across all individuals in the target population $(\tau^2 + \sigma^2)$ that is due to variation between groups (τ^2). If there is no variation in mean outcomes between groups, $(\tau^2 = 0)$ ρ equals zero. If there is no variation in individual outcomes within groups, $(\sigma^2 = 0)$ ρ equals one.

Consider a study that randomizes a total of J groups in proportion P to treatment with a harmonic mean value of n individuals per group. The ratio of the standard error of this impact estimator to that for individual randomization of the same total number of subjects (Jn) is referred to as a design effect (DE), where:

$$DE = \sqrt{1 + (n-1)\rho} \qquad (19)$$

As the intra-class correlation (ρ) increases, the DE increases, implying a larger standard error for group randomization relative to individual randomization. This is because a larger ρ implies greater random variation across groups. The value of ρ varies typically from about 0.01 to 0.20, depending on the nature of the outcome being measured and the type of group being randomized.

For a given total number of individuals, the DE also increases as the number of individuals per group (n) increases. This is because for a given total number of individuals, larger groups imply fewer groups randomized. With fewer groups randomized, larger treatment and control group differences are likely for a given sample[27].

The DE has important implications for designing group-randomized studies. For example, with ρ equal to 0.10 and n equal to 100, the standard error for group randomization is 3.3 times that for individual randomization. To achieve the same precision, group randomization would need almost 11 times as many sample members. Note that the DE is independent of J and depends only on the values of n and ρ.

The different standard errors for group randomization and individual randomization also imply a need to account for group randomization during the experimental analysis. This can be done by using a multilevel model that specifies separate variance components for groups and individuals (for example see Raudenbush and Bryk, 2002). In the preceding example, using an individual-level model, which ignores group-level variation, would estimate standard errors that are one-third as large as they should be. Thus, as Jerome Cornfield (1978: 101) aptly observed: 'Randomization by group accompanied by an analysis appropriate to randomization by individual is an exercise in self-deception.'

Choosing a sample size and allocation for group-randomized studies means choosing values for J, n, and P. Equation 20 illustrates how these choices influence $MDES$ (Bloom et al., 2005).

$$MDES(\hat{\beta}_0) = M_{J-2}\sqrt{\frac{\rho}{P(1-P)J} + \frac{1-\rho}{P(1-P)Jn}} \qquad (20)$$

This equation indicates that the group-level variance (ρ) is divided by the total number of randomized groups, J, whereas the individual-level variance, $(1-\rho)$ is divided by the total number of individuals, Jn[28]. Hence, increasing the number of randomized groups reduces both variance components, whereas increasing the number of individuals per group reduces only one component. This result illustrates one of the most important design principles for group-randomized studies: *The number of groups randomized influences precision more than the size of the groups randomized.*

The top panel of Table 9.2 illustrates this point by presenting $MDES$s for an intra-class correlation of 0.10, a balanced sample allocation, and no covariates. Reading across each row illustrates that, after group size reaches about 60 individuals, increasing it affects precision very little. For very small randomized groups (with less than about 10 individuals each), changing group size can have a more pronounced effect on precision.

Reading down any column in the top panel illustrates that increasing the number of groups randomized can improve precision appreciably. Minimum detectable effects are approximately inversely proportional to the square root of the number of groups randomized once the number of groups exceeds about 20.

Equation 21 illustrates how covariates affect precision with group randomization[29].

$$MDES(\hat{\beta}_0)$$

$$= M_{J-g^*-2}\sqrt{\frac{\rho(1-R_2^2)}{P(1-P)J} + \frac{(1-\rho)(1-R_1^2)}{P(1-P)Jn}} \qquad (21)$$

Table 9.2 Minimum detectable effect size for balanced group randomization with $\rho = 0.10$

Total groups randomized (J)	Group size (n)				
	10	30	60	120	480
	No covariates				
10	0.88	0.73	0.69	0.66	0.65
30	0.46	0.38	0.36	0.35	0.34
60	0.32	0.27	0.25	0.24	0.24
120	0.23	0.19	0.18	0.17	0.17
480	0.11	0.09	0.09	0.08	0.08
	Group-level covariate ($R_2^2 = 0.6$)				
10	0.73	0.54	0.47	0.44	0.41
30	0.38	0.28	0.25	0.23	0.22
60	0.27	0.20	0.17	0.16	0.15
120	0.19	0.14	0.12	0.11	0.11
480	0.09	0.07	0.06	0.06	0.05

Source: Computations by the author.
Note: Minimum detectable effect sizes are for two-tail hypothesis tests with statistical significance of 0.05 and statistical power of 0.80.

where

$R_1^2 =$ the proportion of individual variance (at level one) predicted by covariates,

$R_2^2 =$ the proportion of group variance (at level two) predicted by covariates,

$g^* =$ the number of group covariates used (note: the number of individual-level covariates does not affect the number of degrees of freedom).

With group randomization, multiple levels of predictive power are at play — R_1^2 for level one (individuals) and R_2^2 for level two (groups)[30]. Group-level covariates can reduce the unexplained group-level variance (τ^2), whereas individual-level covariates can reduce both the group-level and individual-level variances (τ^2 and σ^2). However, because group-level variance is typically the binding constraint on precision, its reduction is usually most important. This is analogous to the fact that increasing the number of groups is usually more important than increasing group size. Thus, in some cases group-level covariates — which can be simple and inexpensive to obtain — provide as much gain in precision as do individual covariates (Bloom et al., 1999, 2005).

Because of group-randomization's large sample size requirements, it is especially important to use covariates to predict group-level variances. The bottom panel of Table 9.2 illustrates this point. It presents the *MDES* for each sample configuration in the top panel when a covariate that predicts 60 percent of the group-level variance ($R_2^2 = 0.6$) is included. For example, adding this covariate to a design that randomizes 30 groups with 60 individuals each reduces the *MDES* from 0.36 to 0.25, which is equivalent to doubling the number of groups randomized.

Widespread application of group randomization is only beginning, and much remains to be learned about how to use the approach effectively for social research. One of the most important pieces of information required to do so is a comprehensive inventory of parameter values needed to design such studies: ρ, R_1^2 and R_2^2. These values vary widely, depending on the type of outcome being measured, the type of group being randomized, and the type of covariate/s being used[31].

FUTURE FRONTIERS

During the past several decades, randomized experiments have been used to address a rapidly expanding range of social science questions; experimental designs have become increasingly sophisticated; and statistical methods have become more advanced. So what are the frontiers for future advances?

One frontier involves expanding the geographic scope of randomized experiments in the social sciences. To date, the vast majority of such experiments have been conducted in the United States, although important exceptions exist in both developed and developing countries[32]. Given the promise of the approach, much more could be learned by promoting its use throughout the world.

A second frontier involves unpacking the 'black box' of social experiments. Experiments are uniquely qualified to address questions like: what did an intervention cause to happen? But they are not well suited to address questions like: why did an intervention have or not have an effect[33]? Two promising approaches to such questions are emerging, which combine nonexperimental statistical methods with experimental designs.

One approach uses instrumental variables analysis to examine the causal paths between randomization and final outcomes by comparing intervention effects on intermediate outcomes (mediating variables) with those on final outcomes[34]. The other approach uses methods of research synthesis (meta-analysis or multilevel models that pool primary data) with multiple experiments, multiple experimental sites, or both to estimate how intervention effects vary with treatment implementation, sample characteristics, and local context[35]. It is especially important for this latter approach to have high-quality implementation research that is conducted in parallel with randomized experiments.

Perhaps the most important frontier for randomized experiments in the social sciences is the much-needed expansion of organizational and scientific capacity to implement them successfully on a much broader scale. To conduct this type of research well requires high levels of scientific and professional expertise, which at present exist only at a limited number of institutions. It is therefore hoped that this chapter will contribute to a broader application of this approach to social research.

ACKNOWLEDGMENTS

This chapter was supported by the Judith Gueron Fund for Methodological Innovation in Social Policy Research at MDRC, which was created through gifts from the Annie E. Casey, Rockefeller, Jerry Lee, Spencer, William T. Grant and Grable Foundations. Many thanks are due to Richard Dorsett, Carolyn Hill, Rob Hollister, and Charles Michalopoulos for their helpful suggestions.

NOTES

1 References to randomizing subjects to compare treatment effects date back to the seventeenth century (Van Helmont, 1662), although the earliest documented use of the method was in the late nineteenth century for research on sensory perception (Peirce and Jastrow, 1884/1980). There is some evidence that randomized experiments were used for educational research in the early twentieth century (McCall, 1923). But it was not until Fisher (1925 and 1935) combined statistical methods with experimental design that the method we know today emerged.

2 Marks (1997) provides an excellent history of this process.

3 See Bloom (2005a) for an overview of group-randomized experiments; see Donner and Klar (2000) and Murray (1998) for textbooks on the method.

4 For further examples, see Greenberg and Shroder (1997).

5 Absent treatment, the expected values of all *past, present, and future* characteristics are the same for a randomized treatment group and control group. Hence, the short-term and long-term future experiences of the control group provide valid estimates of what these experiences would have been for the treatment group had it not been offered the treatment.

6 Three studies that used national probability sampling *and* random assignment are the evaluations of Upward Bound (Myers et al., 2004), Head Start (Puma et al., 2006) and the Job Corps (Schochet, 2006).

7 The present discussion assumes a common outcome variance for the treatment and control groups.

8 Note that Pn equals n_T and $(1 - P)n$ equals n_C.

9 When the number of degrees of freedom becomes smaller, the multiplier becomes larger as the t distribution becomes fatter in its tails.

10 The subscript $n - 2$ equals the number of degrees of freedom for a treatment and control group difference of means, given a common variance for the two groups.

11 When the outcome measure is a one/zero binary variable (e.g. employed $= 1$ or not employed $= 0$) the variance estimate is $p(1 - p)/n$ where p is the probability of a value equal to one. The usual conservative practice in this case is to choose $p = 0.5$, which yields the maximum possible variance.

12 The preceding discussion makes the conventional assumption that σ^2 is the same for the treatment and control groups. But if the treatment affects different sample members differently, it can create a σ^2 for the treatment group which differs from that for the control group (Bryk and Raudenbush, 1988). This is a particular instance of heteroscedasticity. Assuming that these two standard deviations are equal to each other can produce a bias in estimates of the standard error of the impact estimator (Gail et al., 1996). Two ways to eliminate this problem are to: (1) use a balanced sample allocation and (2) estimate separate variances for the treatment and control groups (Bloom, 2005b).

13 Weisburd (1993) among others, found that large samples can sometimes provide less statistical power than small samples because large samples may have weaker treatment implementation. Researchers should consider this possibility when designing experiments, although there are no clear quantitative guidelines for doing so.

14 Angrist (2005) and Gennetian et al. (2005) illustrate the approach.

15 This is a specific case of the exclusion principle specified by Angrist et al. (1996).

16 Angrist et al. (1996) refer to this condition as monotonicity.

17 This formulation assumes that the average effect of treatment on always-takers is the same whether they are randomized to treatment or control status.

18 The expression for *LATE* in Equation 10 simplifies to the expression for *TOT* in Equation 7 when there are no-shows but no crossovers. Both expressions represent *ITT* divided by the probability of being a complier. When there are crossovers (but no defiers), the probability of being a complier equals the probability of receiving the treatment if randomized to the treatment group, minus the probability of being an always-taker. When there are no crossovers, there are no always-takers.

19 In the present analysis, treatment receipt is a mediating variable in the causal path between randomization and the outcome. Gennetian et al. (2005) show how the same approach (using instrumental variables with experiments) can be used to study causal effects of other mediating variables.

20 The remainder of this chapter assumes a common variance for treatment and control groups.

21 One way to estimate R_A^2 from a dataset would be to first estimate Equation 12 and compute residual outcome values for each sample member. The next step would be to regress the residuals on the covariates. The resulting r-square for the second regression is an estimate of R_A^2.

22 See Bloom (2005b) for a discussion of this issue.

23 Covariates can also provide some protection against selection bias due to sample attrition.

24 Such indices include propensity scores (Rosenbaum and Rubin, 1983) and Mahalanobis distance functions (http//en.wikipedia.org/wiki/Mahalanobis_distance).

25 One controversial issue is whether to treat blocks as 'fixed effects,' which represent a defined population, or 'random effects,' which represent a random sample from a larger population. Equations 15 and 16 treat blocks as fixed effects. Raudenbush et al. (2005) present random-effects estimators for blocking.

26 Bloom et al. (2005), Donner and Klar (2000), and Murray (1998) provide detailed discussions of this approach; Boruch and Foley (2000) review its applications.

27 The statistical properties of group randomization in experimental research are much like those of cluster sampling in survey research (Kish, 1965).

28 When total student variance $(\tau^2 + \sigma^2)$ is standardized to a value of one by substituting the intra-class correlation (ρ) into the preceding expressions, ρ represents τ^2 and $(1 - \rho)$ represents σ^2.

29 Raudenbush (1997) and Bloom et al. (2005) discuss in detail how covariates affect precision with group randomization.

30 The basic principles discussed here extend to situations with more than two levels of clustering.

31 Existing sources of this information include, among others: Bloom et al. (1999, 2005); Hedges and Hedberg (2005); Murray and Blitstein (2003); Murray and Short (1995); Schochet (2005); Siddiqui et al. (1996); and Ukoumunne et al. (1999).

32 Some other countries where randomized social experiments have been conducted include: the UK (Walker et al., 2006); Mexico (Shultz, 2004); Colombia (Angrist et al., 2002); Israel (Angrist and Lavy, 2002); India (Banerjee et al., 2005; Duflo and Hanna, 2005); and Kenya (Miguel and Kremer, 2004). For a review of randomized experiments in developing countries, see Kremer (2003).

33 Two studies that tried to open the black box of treatment effects experimentally are the Riverside, California Welfare Caseload Study, which randomized different caseload sizes to welfare workers (Riccio et al., 1994) and the Columbus, Ohio, comparison of

separate versus integrated job functions for welfare workers (Scrivener and Walter, 2001).

34 For example, Morris and Gennetian (2003), Gibson et al. (2005), Liebman et al. (2004), and Ludwig et al. (2001) used instrumental variables with experiments to measure the effects of mediating variables on final outcomes.

35 Heinrich (2002) and Bloom et al. (2003) used primary data from a series of experiments to address these issues.

REFERENCES

Aigner, Dennis J. 1985. 'The Residential Time-of-Use Pricing Experiments: What Have We Learned?' In Jerry A. Hausman and David A. Wise (eds.), *Social Experimentation*. Chicago: University of Chicago Press.

Angrist, Joshua D. 2005. 'Instrumental Variables Methods in Experimental Criminology Research: What, Why and How.' *Journal of Experimental Criminology* 2: 1–22.

Angrist, Joshua, Eric Bettinger, Erik Bloom, Elizabeth King, and Michael Kremer. 2002. 'Vouchers for Private Schooling in Colombia: Evidence from a Randomized Natural Experiment.' *The American Economic Review* 92(5): 1535–58.

Angrist, Joshua, Guido Imbens, and Don Rubin. 1996. 'Identification of Causal Effects Using Instrumental Variables.' JASA Applications invited paper, with comments and authors' response. *Journal of the American Statistical Association* 91(434): 444–55.

Angrist, Joshua D., and Victor Lavy. 2002. 'The Effect of High School Matriculation Awards: Evidence from Randomized Trials.' Working Paper 9389. New York: National Bureau of Economic Research.

Banerjee, Abhijit, Shawn Cole, Esther Duflo, and Leigh Linden. 2005. 'Remedying Education: Evidence from Two Randomized Experiments in India.' Working Paper 11904. Cambridge, MA: National Bureau of Economic Research.

Bell, Stephen, Michael Puma, Gary Shapiro, Ronna Cook, and Michael Lopez. 2003. 'Random Assignment for Impact Analysis in a Statistically Representative Set of Sites: Issues from the National Head Start Impact Study.' *Proceedings of the August 2003 American Statistical Association Joint Statistical Meetings* (CD-ROM). Alexandria, VA: American Statistical Association.

Bloom, Dan, and Charles Michalopoulos. 2001. *How Welfare and Work Policies Affect Employment and Income: A Synthesis of Research*. New York: MDRC.

Bloom, Howard S. 1984. 'Accounting for No-Shows in Experimental Evaluation Designs.' *Evaluation Review* 8(2): 225–46.

Bloom, Howard S. 1995. 'Minimum Detectable Effects: A Simple Way to Report the Statistical Power of Experimental Designs.' *Evaluation Review* 19(5): 547–56.

Bloom, Howard S. (ed.). 2005a. *Learning More from Social Experiments: Evolving Analytic Approaches*. New York: Russell Sage Foundation.

Bloom, Howard S. 2005b. 'Randomizing Groups to Evaluate Place-Based Programs.' In Howard S. Bloom (ed.), *Learning More from Social Experiments: Evolving Analytic Approaches*. New York: Russell Sage Foundation.

Bloom, Howard S., Johannes M. Bos, and Suk-Won Lee. 1999. 'Using Cluster Random Assignment to Measure Program Impacts: Statistical Implications for the Evaluation of Education Programs.' *Evaluation Review* 23(4): 445–69.

Bloom, Howard S., Carolyn J. Hill, and James A. Riccio. 2003. 'Linking Program Implementation and Effectiveness: Lessons from a Pooled Sample of Welfare-to-Work Experiments.' *Journal of Policy Analysis and Management* 22(4): 551–75.

Bloom, Howard S., Larry L. Orr, George Cave, Stephen H. Bell, Fred Doolittle, and Winston Lin. 1997. 'The Benefits and Costs of JTPA Programs: Key Findings from the National JTPA Study.' *The Journal of Human Resources* 32(3): 549–576.

Bloom, Howard S., and James A. Riccio. 2005. 'Using Place-Based Random Assignment and Comparative Interrupted Time-Series Analysis to Evaluate the Jobs-Plus Employment Program for Public Housing Residents.' *Annals of the American Academy of Political and Social Science* 599 (May): 19–51.

Bloom, Howard S., Lashawn Richburg-Hayes, and Alison Rebeck Black. 2005. 'Using Covariates to Improve Precision: Empirical Guidance for Studies that Randomize Schools to Measure the Impacts of Educational Interventions.' Working Paper. New York: MDRC.

Borman, Geoffrey D., Robert E. Slavin, A. Cheung, Anne Chamberlain, Nancy Madden, and Bette Chambers. 2005. 'The National Randomized Field Trial of Success for All: Second-Year Outcomes.' *American Educational Research Journal* 42: 673–96.

Boruch, Robert F. 1997. *Randomized Experiments for Planning and Evaluation*. Thousand Oaks, CA: Sage Publications.

Boruch, Robert F., and Ellen Foley. 2000. 'The Honestly Experimental Society: Sites and Other Entities as the Units of Allocation and Analysis in Randomized Trials.' In Leonard Bickman (ed.), *Validity and Social*

Experimentation: Donald Campbell's Legacy, vol. 1. Thousand Oaks, CA: Sage Publications.

Box, George E.P., J. Stuart Hunter, and William G. Hunter. 2005. 2nd ed. *Statistics for Experimenters: Design Innovation and Discovery*. New York: John Wiley and Sons.

Bryk, Anthony S., and Stephen W. Raudenbush. 1988. 'Heterogeneity of Variance in Experimental Studies: A Challenge to Conventional Interpretations.' *Psychological Bulletin* 104(3): 396–404.

Cochrane Collaboration. 2002. 'Cochrane Central Register of Controlled Trials Database.' Available at the Cochrane Library Web site: www.cochrane.org (accessed September 14, 2004).

Cochran, William G., and Gertrude M. Cox. 1957. *Experimental Designs*. New York: John Wiley and Sons.

Cohen, Jacob. 1977/1988. *Statistical Power Analysis for the Behavioral Sciences*. New York: Academic Press.

Cook, Thomas H., David Hunt, and Robert F. Murphy. 2000. 'Comer's School Development Program in Chicago: A Theory-Based Evaluation.' *American Educational Research Journal* 37(1): 535–97.

Cornfield, Jerome. 1978. 'Randomization by Group: A Formal Analysis.' *American Journal of Epidemiology* 108(2): 100–02.

Cox, D.R. 1958. *Planning of Experiments*. New York: John Wiley and Sons.

Donner, Allan, and Neil Klar. 2000. *Design and Analysis of Cluster Randomization Trials in Health Research*. London: Arnold.

Duflo, Esther, and Rema Hanna. 2005. 'Monitoring Works: Getting Teachers to Come to School.' Working Paper 11880. Cambridge, MA: National Bureau of Economic Research.

Fisher, Ronald A. 1925. *Statistical Methods for Research Workers*. Edinburgh: Oliver and Boyd.

Fisher, Ronald A. 1935. *The Design of Experiments*. Edinburgh: Oliver and Boyd.

Flay, Brian R. 2000. 'Approaches to Substance Use Prevention Utilizing School Curriculum Plus Social Environment Change.' *Addictive Behaviors* 25(6): 861–85.

Gail, Mitchell H., Steven D. Mark, Raymond J. Carroll, Sylvan B. Green, and David Pee. 1996. 'On Design Considerations and Randomization-Based Inference for Community Intervention Trials.' *Statistics in Medicine* 15: 1069–92.

Gennetian, Lisa A., Pamela A. Morris, Johannes M. Bos, and Howard S. Bloom. 2005. 'Constructing Instrumental Variables from Experimental Data to Explore How Treatments Produce Effects.' In Howard S. Bloom (ed.), *Learning More from Social Experiments:*

Evolving Analytic Approaches. New York: Russell Sage Foundation.

Gibson, C., Katherine Magnusen, Lisa Gennetian, and Greg Duncan. 2005. 'Employment and Risk of Domestic Abuse among Low-Income Single Mothers.' *Journal of Marriage and the Family* 67: 1149–68.

Greenberg, David H., and Mark Shroder. 1997. *The Digest of Social Experiments*. Washington, DC: Urban Institute Press.

Hedges, Larry V., and Eric C. Hedberg. 2005. 'Intraclass Correlation Values for Planning Group Randomized Trials in Education.' Working Paper WP-06-12. Evanston, IL: Northwestern University, Institute for Policy Research.

Heinrich, Carolyn J. 2002. 'Outcomes-Based Performance Management in the Public Sector: Implications for Government Accountability and Effectiveness.' *Public Administration Review* 62(6): 712–25.

Kane, Thomas. 2004. 'The Impact of After-School Programs: Interpreting the Results of Four Recent Evaluations.' Working Paper. New York: W.T. Grant Foundation.

Kemple, James J., and Jason Snipes. 2000. *Career Academies: Impacts on Students' Engagement and Performance in High School*. New York: MDRC.

Kempthorne, Oscar. 1952. *The Design and Analysis of Experiments*. Malabar, FL: Robert E. Krieger Publishing Company.

Kish, Leslie. 1965. *Survey Sampling*. New York: John Wiley.

Kling, Jeffrey R., Jeffrey B. Liebman, and Lawrence F. Katz. 2007. 'Experimental Analysis of Neighborhood Effects.' *Econometrica* 75(1): 83–119.

Kremer, Michael. 2003. 'Randomized Evaluations of Educational Programs in Developing Countries: Some Lessons.' *American Economic Review* 93(2): 102–06.

Liebman, Jeffrey B., Lawrence F. Katz, and Jeffrey R. Kling. 2004. 'Beyond Treatment Effects: Estimating the Relationship Between Neighborhood Poverty and Individual Outcomes in the MTO Experiment.' IRS Working Paper 493 (August). Princeton, NJ: Princeton University, Industrial Relations Section.

Lindquist, E.F. 1953. *Design and Analysis of Experiments in Psychology and Education*. Boston: Houghton Mifflin Company.

Lipsey, Mark W. 1988. 'Juvenile Delinquency Intervention.' In Howard S. Bloom, David S. Cordray, and Richard J. Light (eds.), *Lesson from Selected Program and Policy Areas*. San Francisco: Jossey-Bass.

Lipsey, Mark W. 1990. *Design Sensitivity: Statistical Power for Experimental Research*. Newbury Park, CA: Sage.

Ludwig, Jens, Greg J. Duncan, and Paul Hirschfield. 2001. 'Urban Poverty and Juvenile Crime: Evidence from a Randomized Housing-Mobility Experiment.' *The Quarterly Journal of Economics* 116(2): 655–80.

McCall, W.A. 1923. *How to Experiment in Education.* New York: MacMillan.

Marks, Harry M. 1997. *The Progress of Experiment: Science and Therapeutic Reform in the United States, 1900–1990.* Cambridge: Cambridge University Press.

Miguel, Edward, and Michael Kremer. 2004. 'Worms: Identifying Impacts on Education and Health in the Presence of Treatment Externalities.' *Econometrica* 72(1): 159–217.

Morris, Pamela, and Lisa Gennetian. 2003. 'Identifying the Effects of Income on Children's Development: Using Experimental Data.' *Journal of Marriage and the Family* 65(3): 716–29.

Munnell, Alicia (ed.). 1987. *Lessons from the Income Maintenance Experiments.* Boston: Federal Reserve Bank of Boston.

Murray, David M. 1998. *Design and Analysis of Group-Randomized Trials.* New York: Oxford University Press.

Murray, David M., and Jonathan L. Blitstein. 2003. 'Methods to Reduce the Impact of Intraclass Correlation in Group-Randomized Trials.' *Evaluation Review* 27(1): 79–103.

Murray, David M., Peter J. Hannan, David R. Jacobs, Paul J. McGovern, Linda Schmid, William L. Baker, and Clifton Gray. 1994. 'Assessing Intervention Efforts in the Minnesota Heart Health Program.' *American Journal of Epidemiology* 139(1): 91–103.

Murray, David M., and Brian Short. 1995. 'Intraclass Correlation among Measures Related to Alcohol Use by Young Adults: Estimates, Correlates and Applications in Intervention Studies.' *Journal of Studies on Alcohol* 56(6): 681–94.

Myers, David, Robert Olsen, Neil Seftor, Julie Young, and Christina Tuttle. 2004. *The Impacts of Regular Upward Bound: Results from the Third Follow-up Data Collection.* Washington, DC: Report prepared by Mathematica Policy Research for the U.S. Department of Education.

Myers, Jerome L. 1972. *Fundamentals of Experimental Design.* Boston: Allyn and Bacon.

Newhouse, Joseph P. 1996. *Free for All? Lessons from the RAND Health Insurance Experiment.* Cambridge, MA: Harvard University Press.

Nye, Barbara, Larry V. Hedges, and Spyros Konstantopoulos. 1999. 'The Long-Term Effects of Small Classes: A Five-Year Follow-Up of the Tennessee Class Size Experiment.' *Education Evaluation and Policy Analysis* 21(2): 127–42.

Olds, David L., John Eckenrode, Charles R. Henderson, Jr., Harriet Kitzman, Jane Powers, Robert Cole, Kimberly Sidora, Pamela Morris, Lisa M. Pettitt, and Dennis Luckey. 1997. 'Long-Term Effects of Home Visitation on Maternal Life Course and Child Abuse and Neglect.' *The Journal of the American Medical Association* 278(7): 637–43.

Orr, Larry L. 1999. *Social Experiments: Evaluating Public Programs with Experimental Methods.* Thousand Oaks, CA: Sage Publications.

Orr, Larry L., Judith D. Feins, Robin Jacob, Erik Beecroft, Lisa Sanbomatsu, Lawrence F. Katz, Jeffrey B. Liebman, and Jeffrey R. Kling. 2003. *Moving to Opportunity: Interim Impacts Evaluation.* Washington, DC: U.S. Department of Housing and Urban Development.

Peirce, Charles S., and Joseph Jastrow. 1884/1980. 'On Small Differences of Sensation.' Reprinted in Stephen M. Stigler (ed.), *American Contributions to Mathematical Statistics in the Nineteenth Century*, vol. 2. New York: Arno Press.

Puma, Michael, Stephen Bell, Ronna Cook, Camilla Heid, and Michael Lopez. 2006. *Head Start Impact Study: First Year Impact Findings.* (Prepared by Westat, Chesapeake Research Associates, The Urban Institute, American Institutes for Research, and Decision Information Resources, June.) Washington, DC: U. S. Department of Health and Human Services, Administration for Children and Families, Office of Planning, Research, and Evaluation.

Raudenbush, Stephen, W. 1997. 'Statistical Analysis and Optimal Design for Group Randomized Trials.' *Psychological Methods* 2(2): 173–85.

Raudenbush, Stephen W., and Anthony S. Bryk. 2002. *Hierarchical Linear Models: Applications and Data Analysis Methods,* 2nd ed. Thousand Oaks, CA: Sage Publications.

Raudenbush, Stephen W., Andres Martinez, and Jessaca Spybrook. 2005. *Strategies for Improving Precision in Group-Randomized Experiments.* New York: William T. Grant Foundation.

Riccio, James, Daniel Friedlander, and Stephen Freedman. 1994. *Benefits, Costs, and Three-Year Impacts of a Welfare-to-Work Program.* New York: MDRC.

Robins, Philip K., and Robert G. Spiegelman (eds.). 2001. *Reemployment Bonuses in the Unemployment Insurance System: Evidence from Three Field Experiments.* Kalamazoo, MI: W.E. Upjohn Institute for Employment Research.

Rosenbaum, Paul R., and Donald B. Rubin. 1983. 'The Central Role of the Propensity Score in Observational Studies for Causal Effects.' *Biometrika* 70(1): 41–55.

Schochet, Peter A. 2005. *Statistical Power for Random Assignment Evaluations of Education Programs.* Princeton, NJ: Mathematica Policy Research.

Schochet, Peter A. 2006. *National Job Corps Study and Longer-Term Follow-Up Study: Impact and Benefit-Cost Findings Using Survey and Summary Earnings Records Data.* Princeton, NJ: Mathematica Policy Research.

Scrivener, Susan, and Johanna Walter, with Thomas Brock and Gayle Hamilton. 2001. *National Evaluation of Welfare-to-Work Strategies: Evaluating Two Approaches to Case Management: Implementation, Participation Patterns, Costs, and Three-Year Impacts of the Columbus Welfare-to-Work Program.* Washington, DC: U.S. Department of Health and Human Services, Administration for Children and Families, and Office of the Assistant Secretary for Planning and Evaluation; and U.S. Department of Education, Office of the Under Secretary and Office of Vocational and Adult Education.

Sherman, Lawrence W., and David Weisburd. 1995. 'General Deterrent Effects of Police Patrol in Crime 'Hot Spots': A Randomized Control Trial.' *Justice Quarterly* 12(4): 625–48.

Shultz, Paul T. 2004. 'School Subsidies for the Poor: Evaluating the Mexican Progresa Poverty Program.' *Journal of Development Economics* 74(1): 199–250.

Siddiqui, Ohidul, Donald Hedeker, Brian R. Flay, and Frank B. Hu. 1996. 'Intraclass Correlation Estimates in a School-Based Smoking Prevention Study: Outcome and Mediating Variables, by Sex and Ethnicity.' *American Journal of Epidemiology* 144(4): 425–33.

Sikkema, Kathleen, J., Jeffrey A. Kelly, Richard A. Winett, Laura J. Solomon, Cargill, V.A., Roffman, R.A., McAuliffe, T.L., Heckman, T.G., Anderson, E.A., Wagstaff, D.A., Norman, A.D., Perry, M.J., Crumble, D.S., and Mercer, M.B. 2000. 'Outcomes of a Randomized Community-Level HIV Prevention Intervention for Women Living in 18 Low-Income Housing Developments.' *American Journal of Public Health* 90(1): 57–63.

Teruel, Graciela M., and Benjamin Davis. 2000. *Final Report: An Evaluation of the Impact of PROGRESA Cash Payments on Private Inter-Household Transfers.* Washington, DC: International Food Policy Research Institute.

Ukoumunne, O.C., Gulliford, M.C., Chinn, S., Sterne, J.A.C., and Burney, P.F.J. 1999. 'Methods for Evaluating Area-Wide and Organisation-Based Interventions in Health and Health Care: A Systematic Review.' *Health Technology Assessment* 3(5): 1–99.

Van Helmont, John Baptista. 1662. *Oriatrik or, Physick Refined: The Common Errors Therein Refuted and the Whole Art Reformed and Rectified.* London: Lodowick-Lloyd. Available at the James Lind Library Web site: www.jameslindlibrary.org/trial_records/17th_18th_Century/van_helmont/van_helmont_kp.html (accessed January 3, 2005).

Wald, Abraham. 1940. 'The Fitting of Straight Lines If Both Variables Are Subject to Error.' *Annals of Mathematical Statistics* 11(September): 284–300.

Walker, Robert, Lesley Hoggart, Gayle Hamilton, and Susan Blank. 2006. *Making Random Assignment Happen: Evidence from the UK Employment Retention and Advancement (ERA) Demonstration.* Research Report 330. London: Department for Work and Pensions.

Weisburd, David, with Anthony Petrosino and Gail Mason. 1993. 'Design Sensitivity in Criminal Justice Experiments.' In Michael Tonry (ed.), *Crime and Justice, An Annual Review of Research*, vol. 17. Chicago: University of Chicago Press.

Better Quasi-Experimental Practice

Thomas D. Cook and Vivian C. Wong

INTRODUCTION

Recent reviews comparing effect size estimates from randomized experiments and quasi-experiments that share the same treatment group have strengthened the view that randomized experiments provide the best approximation to a gold standard for answering causal questions (Glazerman et al., 2003; Bloom et al., 2005a). This is because the quasi-experiments in these reviews generally failed to attain the same effect sizes as their yoked experiments. The finding has prompted major funding institutions such as the Department of Labor and the Institute of Education Sciences to encourage those who apply to them for grants and contracts to use randomized experiments whenever possible.

We believe that the question of whether to use experiments or quasi-experiments is not closed. This is not just because well-designed randomized experiments are not always possible, but also because there are reasons to question the validity and generality of past research contrasting the effect sizes from experiments and quasi-experiments that

share the same treatment group and therefore only vary how the control group is created — randomly or not. Our doubt comes from two sources: the judgment that the majority of such studies are logically and empirically flawed in ways we will point out; and our demonstration that experiments and stronger quasi-experiments do indeed sometimes produce the same causal answers in ways that make theoretical sense.

This chapter is organized in three sections. The first highlights the strongest quasi-experimental designs, regression-discontinuity and interrupted time series, and discusses features that make these designs superior, including results from studies that empirically test their efficacy relative to experiments. The second section examines the difference-in-differences design, the most frequently used quasi-experimental design that contrasts two non-equivalent groups measured at pretest and posttest on the same scale. This section also uses details from recent empirical attacks on the difference-in-differences design to show how certain ways of selecting control groups and of measuring and analyzing selection can lead to very close approximations of experimental results. The third section offers suggestions for improving quasi-experimental design, not through the use of matching — the current dominant strategy — but through an alternative pattern-matching strategy that depends on generating and testing multiple empirical implications from the same causal hypothesis. We use examples from education and job training to illustrate the specific design attributes we discuss and recommend because the debate over experiment versus quasi-experiment is most heated in these fields. However, the design principles presented here apply elsewhere as well. Finally, it is worth mentioning that our intention is not to present a treatise on analytic methods for quasi-experimental designs, but is rather to showcase the strongest and best quasi-experimental designs and design features and to suggest common areas of weakness in current practice. For more technical and theoretical discussions on analytic methods described in this chapter as well as additional examples, we include a list of suggested readings in Appendix 1.

EFFICACY TESTS OF QUASI-EXPERIMENTS RELATIVE TO EXPERIMENTS: BETWEEN-STUDY VERSUS WITHIN-STUDY APPROACHES

Two approaches have been employed in studies that have assessed the validity of quasi-experimental designs. In the *between-study* approach, researchers compare estimated effects from the set of experimental studies done on a topic with the estimated effects from whatever quasi-experimental studies were available on the same topic. Aiken et al. (1998) summarized findings from this tradition. Across many domains of application, they concluded that the average effect sizes were sometimes similar across the experiments and quasi-experiments, but that they were also often different. And even when the means did not differ, the variance in effect

sizes tended to be greater among the quasi-experiments than experiments (Lipsey & Wilson, 1993; Glazerman et al., 2003). So, the average experiment and quasi-experiment cannot be relied on to generate the same causal conclusion.

In the *within-study* approach, researchers take the effect size from a randomized experiment and compare it to the effect size from a quasi-experiment that uses the same intervention group data as the experiment but compare it with data from a non-randomly formed control group. Most of the within-study comparisons conducted to date have been in the job training field, though some have involved educational topics. At first glance, the within-study approach seems a stronger empirical test of design type difference. After all, there is variation in whether a study is experimental or not, and settings, people, and treatments are more likely to be held constant by virtue of the shared experimental group[1]. In contrast, the between-study tradition can involve a set of experiments that differs in many ways on average from the comparison set of quasi-experiments, even though logic calls for variation in design types but not in anything else that might be correlated with study outcomes. This makes between-study results inherently ambiguous.

Our goal is to reexamine conclusions from the *within-study comparison* literature that have been most prominently discussed and cited in the fields of economics, job training, and education. We focus on studies that were included in Glazerman et al.'s (2002, 2003) meta-analysis of within-study comparisons, as well as comparisons that have been more recently published (see Appendix 1 for a list of within-study comparisons found in education, job training, and economics). However, since there are only 20 within-study comparison studies we acknowledge that basis for extrapolation is limited. Moreover, we discuss only a subset of these studies in detail — three with RD design, one with an abbreviated interrupted time series design, and four with a difference-in-differences design. Thus while the conclusions presented here are meant to spur further debate, discussion, and research, they are not meant to be the final word on the efficacy of quasi-experimental designs as assessed empirically from the results of within-study comparisons.

TYPES OF EXPERIMENTS: RANDOMIZED, NONEXPERIMENTS, AND QUASI-EXPERIMENTS

All experiments seek to test a causal hypothesis by demonstrating that the cause preceded the effect in time, that the two co-vary, and that there are no alternative interpretations of why they vary other than that the cause was responsible for the effect. Experiments in the social and behavioral sciences also have some similar structural attributes. There is always one or more outcome measure, plus groups of units that undergo either a treatment or some contrast experience. This last is often a no-treatment control group experience that seeks to function as a causal counterfactual — that is, as an assessment of what would have happened to units receiving the treatment if they had not in fact received it.

There are different types of experiments. The randomized experiment is characterized by assignment to treatment or control status on the basis of some equivalent of a fair coin toss. It creates two or more groups that are initially comparable within the limits of sampling error. This renders them valid as a no-treatment counterfactual, with the warrant for this judgment stemming from formal probability theory. Nonexperiments, in contrast, do not use random assignment. Quasi-experiments are the special subtype of nonexperiments that attempt to mimic randomized experiments in purpose and structure despite the absence of random assignment. In contrast to quasi-experiments, other nonexperiments do not directly manipulate treatments, nor do they have observations and comparison groups that are deliberately and originally designed to provide a causal counterfactual. Longitudinal observational studies are a common type

of nonexperiment used for testing causal hypotheses that do not have these last features and are therefore not quasi-experimental. This chapter is concerned with the efficacy of quasi-experimental designs relative to the randomized experiment.

In quasi-experiments, assignment to treatment or control status may be determined by self-selection or administrator decision, and so initial differences between groups may come to mimic treatment effects, thus confounding population differences between the treatment and control groups with possible effects of the treatment and so creating what is called a 'selection' problem. The perfectly implemented randomized-experiment rules out selection (and other alternative interpretations of why a potential cause and effect co-vary) by distributing these alternatives equally over the various experimental conditions. They are not removed from the research setting, as though by magic; they are merely removed as alternative interpretations by being equally represented in each of the groups under contrast.

A well-designed quasi-experiment can also rule out alternative explanations, but to do this requires more assumptions and less transparency, and consequently a more uncertain causal answer than the randomized experiment provides. In particular, the use of quasi-experiments requires close attention to three related issues. The first is to identify all plausible alternative interpretations to the hypothesis that the independent and dependent variables are causally related, these alternatives being called threats to internal validity (see Shadish et al. (2002) for extended discussion). While the randomized experiment takes care of these threats by distributing them equally across conditions, the quasi-experiment requires researchers to examine and assess the plausibility of each threat explicitly. The second is the assumption that experimental design principles enjoy a primacy over substantive theory or statistical adjustment procedures when it comes to ruling out validity threats. In practice, this entails reliance on carefully chosen comparison groups and/or pretest measures taken at multiple times. The third principle for ruling out alternative explanations is the use of coherent pattern matching. This requires that existing substantive theory be specific enough to predict the specific pattern of multivariate results that should result from a given causal hypothesis, a pattern that few alternative explanations can match. We begin by discussing designs that exemplify the best of what quasi-experimental theory has to offer.

REGRESSION-DISCONTINUITY DESIGN

The regression-discontinuity (RD) is still not widely used despite theoretical and empirical demonstrations of its ability to provide unbiased treatment effect estimates when its assumptions are met. Nonetheless, RD has gained prominence as an abstract alternative to experiments in health, economics, and education (for history of RD, see Cook, in press). Indeed, a recent request for proposal from the Institute of Education Sciences, a United States Department of Education agency that funds education research, stated that if a randomized experiment was not possible for addressing a causal question, then acceptable alternatives included 'appropriately structured regression-discontinuity designs' (Institute of Education Sciences, 2004). In this section, we examine the basics of a RD design, theoretical and empirical reasons for why RD is so special among quasi-experimental designs, and examples of RD in order to highlight practical considerations that are important for implementing the design.

The basics of RD

In a RD design, individuals are assigned to treatment and comparison groups solely on the basis of a cutoff score from some assignment variable. The assignment variable is any measure taken prior to the treatment intervention, and there is no requirement that the measure be reliable. The obtained fallible score suffices. Individuals who score on one side of the cutoff score are assigned to the treatment while individuals who score on the other side are assigned to the comparison. Thus, treatment assignment is completely observed and depends on one's score on the cutoff variable and on nothing else. Treatment effects then are estimated by examining the displacement of the regression line at the cutoff point determining program receipt.

Figures 10.1 and 10.2 show a hypothetical RD experiment with and without treatment effects. In both cases, the cutoff is a score of 50 — those scoring above 50 receive treatment and those scoring below it are the non-equivalent controls. The graphs show scatterplots of assignment scores against posttest scores, each depicting a linear, positive relationship between the two variables. In Figure 10.1, where a treatment effect is present, we see a vertical disruption — or discontinuity — at the cutoff, though treatments can obviously also cause an upward shift. The displacement in Figure 10.1 represents a change in the mean posttest scores, equivalent to a main effect of treatment. It is also possible for treatments to cause a change in slope at the cutoff, this being equivalent to a treatment by assignment statistical interaction, provided that the change in slope can be unambiguously attributed to the intervention rather than to some underlying non-linear relationship between the assignment and outcome. In Figure 10.1 that has linear and parallel regressions, we interpret the effect size to be a negative change of 5 units because there is a vertical displacement of 5 points at the cutoff. In Figure 10.2, there is no displacement at cutoff and the regression lines are again parallel. So we interpret this as no effect.

For a simple RD design one needs an assignment variable that has ordinal properties or better. Continuous measures such as income, achievement scores, or blood pressure work best, while nominal measurements such as race or gender do not work at all because they cannot lead to correct modeling of the regression line. However, the continuous assignment variable can take on any form. It can be a pretest measure of the

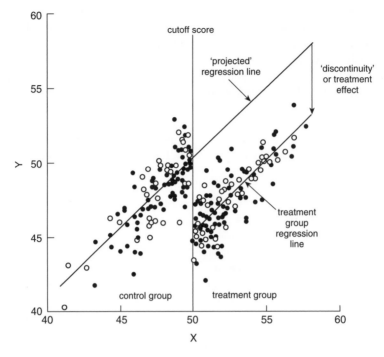

Figure 10.1   Regression-discontinuity with treatment effects
Source: Trochim, 1994.

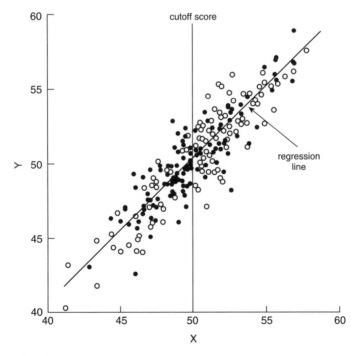

Figure 10.2   Regression-discontinuity without treatment effects
Source: Trochim, 1994.

dependent variable (Seaver & Quarton, 1976), a three-item composite measuring family material welfare in Mexico (Buddelmeyer & Skoufias, 2003), a composite of 140 variables predicting the likelihood of long-term unemployment (Black et al., 2005), a birth order of participants, or an order of individuals entering a room. When the assignment and outcome variables are not correlated, this is very much like what happens with a randomized experiment where, because of the coin toss, the process of assignment to conditions is not related to the outcome.

Second, a cutoff point must be carefully selected. Many considerations for choosing a cutoff point are beyond the scope of this chapter, but in general one should select a cutoff point that ensures adequate range and sample sizes in both the treatment and comparison groups so that the regression each side of the cutoff can be reliably estimated. This is potentially problematic if awards are given to the particularly meritorious or compensatory resources to those in very greatest need, thus creating a miniscule range on one side of the cutoff.

Third, the strict implementation of a cutoff score is what makes RD designs unique, and serves as the basis for this design's comparative advantage over other quasi-experimental designs. Assignment must be by the specific score on the assignment variable, and nothing else. As with randomized experiments, overriding the selection mechanisms by arbitrarily moving participants from one condition to another introduces the potential for bias because some persons whose scores place them on one side of the cutoff will in fact receive the treatment destined for those on the other side. This makes the assignment process more 'fuzzy' in practice than it is supposed to be in theory (Trochim, 1984). So, as with the randomized experiment, treatment assignment must be carefully planned and its implementation controlled, making many retrospective uses of the RD design problematic. The main exception here is when assignment is by birth dates (Angrist et al., 1996; Staw et al., 1974), or some other means that can be easily verified and carefully recorded.

$$O_1 \ C \ X \ O_2$$
$$O_1 \ C \quad \ O_2$$

Figure 10.3   Regression-discontinuity design

Taken together, the basic RD design can be represented as in Figure 10.3. Here O_1 represents the assignment variable, C is the units assigned to conditions on the basis of the cutoff score, X is the treatment, and O_2 is the posttest or outcome measure.

Unique characteristics of this design: Theoretical and empirical reasons

The most common question asked about RD is how the design can yield unbiased estimates when the pretest means of the treatment and control groups do not overlap. In an experiment, treatment effects are usually inferred by comparing treatment group posttest means with control group posttest means under the assumption that they would otherwise have been identical, given the perfect overlap that is initially achieved on both observed and unobserved variables. Similarly, causal inference in quasi-experiments is stronger the less the two group means initially differ (Cook et al., 2005). Yet in RD, the groups must maximally differ on the assignment variable.

In RD, treatment effects are not estimated by comparing posttest means or some form of difference in gains, but rather by extrapolating the relationship between the assignment variable and posttest on the untreated side of the cutoff into the treated side. The counterfactual is therefore a slope, and the simplest null hypothesis is that both treatment and comparison group regression lines have the same intercept at the cutoff. Should there be a difference and all other conditions for causal inference are met — especially the comparability of regression functions on each side of the cutoff — then an inference is drawn that the treatment caused the difference in the intercept.

A better way to think about RD design is that the selection process is perfectly known. It depends only on the obtained score on the assignment variable and so can be perfectly modeled. In other quasi-experiments, how units came to be assigned to treatment is usually not fully known. We cannot control for *all* the possible covariates that might discriminate between students who volunteer to participate in a dropout prevention program versus those who do not. Indeed, the methodology literature is replete with mostly unresolved debates about procedures that might control for selection in quasi-experiments other than RD. However, only in RD and the randomized experiment is the selection process completely known and measured. This is why strict adherence to assignment based on the cutoff is essential if RD is to yield unbiased results, just as strict adherence to the 'coin toss' allocation is crucial for interpreting a randomized experiment.

Goldberger (1972a, 1972b) proved that generalized treatment estimates obtained from RD are comparable to estimates from randomized-experimental designs. However, unbiased estimates require meeting the following key assumptions: that the cutoff is rigorously followed; that the functional form of the relationship between the assignment and posttest can be fully described; that there are enough assignment values to responsibly estimate the regression line each side of the cutoff; and that the assignment variable is continuous. Under these conditions, and when the assignment and outcome variables are linearly related, a single regression function or ANCOVA can be used to estimate treatment effects, with the group assignment variable and the cutoff being included as covariates. However, as Goldberger (1972a, 1972b) also showed, the RD analysis will have approximately 2.75 times less statistical power than an experiment with the same sample size when the cutoff is at the midpoint of the assignment variable.

Econometricians have extended the discussion of statistical analysis in RD by devising methods that bypass the questions of which variables are needed to model outcomes and their functional form. Hahn et al. (2001) have shown that treatment effects at the point of

discontinuity can be estimated using non-parametric regression techniques, and other economists have attributed the virtues of RD to the near randomness of allocation decisions around the cutoff point itself. So they use analytic methods that give greatest weight to observations closer to the cutoff on grounds that this is where random error is most likely to determine treatment status. The disadvantage of this assumption and its attendant analysis strategy is that treatment effects are identified only at the cutoff, thus limiting external validity over what would be the case when slopes on each side of the cutoff have similar values.

Adding to the theoretical case for the bias-free nature of perfectly implemented RD are the results of three empirical studies that compare effect sizes from RD and experimental benchmarks. Aiken et al. (1998) examined how students enrolled in a college remedial writing class performed in essay writing and on a Test of Standard Written English (TSWE) when compared to students without the remedial course. Before the study began, students at this university were assigned to the remedial class on the basis of a cutoff score either on the ACT or SAT. The RD design used this feature to create the treatment group consisting of all those students scoring below the cutoff, and the comparison group from all those scoring above it. In addition to the RD design, the authors included a randomized experiment that took a sample of volunteers from just below the cutoff and randomly assigned them to the remedial course or Standard English writing class. Despite differences in where treatment effects were estimated for both the experimental and RD studies, the authors found that both designs produced similar patterns of results in significance levels and effect size.

The second experiment RD contrast was by Buddelmeyer and Skoufias (2003). They reanalyzed data from PROGRESA, a large-scale Mexican program aimed at alleviating poverty through investments in education, nutrition, and health. The authors took advantage of the fact that Mexican villages were randomly assigned to PROGRESA, but that families within the experimental villages were then assigned into treatment conditions based on their score on a scale of material resources. For the experimental and RD studies, the authors examined whether PROGRESA improved school attendance and reduced labor force participation among girls and boys between the ages of 12 and 16. Overall, the authors found close correspondence in the experimental and RD results. However, there was one round of results where the RD and experimental findings diverged and, after additional analyses, the authors found evidence of spillover effects in the comparison group that produced dissimilar RD findings. This led the authors to conclude that, 'it is the comparison group rather than the method itself that is primarily responsible for the poor performance of the RD.'

The third direct comparison of experiment/ RD results is the most methodologically advanced. Black et al. (2005) reanalyzed data from a job training program in Kentucky that assigned those likely to exhaust unemployment insurance to mandatory reemployment services as a requirement for benefit receipt. The RD was claimants' assignment into job training programs based on a single score derived from a 140-item test predicting the likelihood of long-term unemployment. For each local employment office in each week, new claimants were ranked by their assigned scores. Reemployment services were given to those with the highest scores, followed by those with the next highest scores until the slots for each office each week were filled. When offices reached their maximum capacity, and if there were two or more claimants with the same profiling scores, then random number generators were used to assign the remaining claimants with the same profiling scores into treatment condition. Thus, only claimants with marginal profiling scores — the point at which capacity constraint was reached in a given week and in a given local office — were randomly assigned into experimental groups. This sampling procedure resulted in a true tie-breaking

experiment and ensured that the RD causal estimate was at the same average point on the assignment variable as the experiment, creating a more interpretable contrast of the two design types.

The experimental and RD analyses compared results for three outcomes — weeks receiving unemployment insurance (UI) benefits, amount of UI benefits received, and annual earnings. The RD analyses weighted data closer to the cutoff and examined how the correspondence between experimental and RD results varied with proximity to the cutoff. The assignment and outcome variables were not linearly related, but even so a close correspondence was obtained between the experimental and RD results in statistical significance patterns, magnitude of estimates, and in direct tests of differences between the RD and experimental impacts. This was especially true when the RD observations were closest to the cutoff. The implication of all three attempts to check RD results against experimental ones is that the design generates bias-free results, not just in theory, but also in complex research practice.

Black et al.'s (2005) study further illustrates that researchers can handle non-linearity in the relationship between the assignment variable and the outcome. They did this by varying the range of the assignment variable and putting an a priori faith in estimates with the least range. It is also possible to use non-parametric regression or to include a range of models using higher order terms, interactions, and/or transformations of variables in order to probe the stability of results across alternative specifications of functional form. Best of all, though, is to get measures of the outcome variable from a period prior to the intervention. Such a pretest helps describe the functional form of the assignment/outcome relationship independently of the influence of the treatment in order to permit an analysis that, in essence, differences the pre- and post-intervention slopes each side of the cutoff. This design response to the problem of possible non-linear relationships stands in stark contrast to statistical responses that are based on non-parametric regression, differential weighting, and willingness to limit the external validity of the causal relationship to just around the cutoff point.

Examples of RDs

Earlier, we suggested that RD is slowly becoming a more popular choice for evaluation in education, where standards-based reforms have allocated funds, resources, and penalties based on students' or schools' obtained scores on achievement tests. This section offers more examples for how RD can be used to evaluate treatment effects in education; and it also illustrates another common problem in RD that arises when the cutoff point is not the only criterion for treatment assignment and when other, more social or political factors, also enter into the allocation decision, making it fuzzy rather than sharp as is preferable for RD.

Trochim (1984) analyzed data to determine the effects of compensatory education on student achievement. He examined a second-grade compensatory reading program in Providence, Rhode Island where all children in the same pool were pre-tested using a reading test. Those who scored below the cutoff were assigned to a reading program while those who scored above the cutoff were not assigned treatment. His analysis of Rhode Island second-graders found that the program significantly improved children's reading abilities. However, few other state compensatory education programs that Trochim examined yielded similar positive effects (1984).

Jacob and Lefgren (2004a, 2004b) examined the effects of teacher training and summer school participation and retention on student achievement in Chicago Public Schools (CPS). We describe the design of the teacher training study in detail only. In 1996, CPS introduced a reform that placed schools on academic probation if fewer than 15 percent of students met the national norms on standardized reading exams. To improve academic achievement, CPS provided probation schools with funds and resources to buy teacher development services from external organizations. Schools that were below the 15 percent cutoff were assigned to the treatment condition (teacher development) while schools above the cutoff served as the comparison group. The independent variable was resources for teacher training; the assignment was the percentage of students who met national norms in reading; and the outcome was math and reading achievement among elementary school students. Results found that teacher training had no statistically significant effect on either students' math or reading achievement.

However, the cutoff for assignment in Jacob and Lefgren's (2002) study was not as clean as one would want. First, several schools that scored below the probation cutoff were waived from the policy (15 of the 77). Second, 25 schools originally placed on probation raised student achievement by enough to be removed from probation even before the treatment was completed. On the other hand, 16 schools that missed the probation cutoff in the first year were placed on probation in the next two years. Finally, there was substantial student mobility between schools. Including overrides to the cutoff in the analysis sample is likely to produce bias in treatment effect estimates, as is failure to take up the assigned treatment and attrition from the sample after assignment.

Several statistical procedures have been proposed to address fuzzy discontinuity. In the first approach, suggested by Trochim and Spiegelman (1980), an estimated assignment variable is constructed for each unit. Its distribution resembles, not the step function of a sharp discontinuity, but an ogive or spline whose slope value depends on how much mis-assignment has occurred. A simulation study by Trochim (1984) and an evaluation of Title I (Trochim, 1984) show the use of such functions as an unbiased method for dealing with fuzzy discontinuity. The second approach, employed by Jacob and Lefgren (2004a, 2004b) and others (Angrist & Lavy, 1999; van der Klauww, 2002), uses an instrumental variable (IV) framework. Here, fuzzy discontinuity is seen as an endogeneity issue, where the assignment variable is believed to be correlated with unobservables in the error term. An ideal instrument in RD is a variable that affects the outcome *only* through its association with the endogenous assignment term. In principle, the use of an instrument expunges correlation between the assignment variable and the error term. In practice, it may be difficult to know what a good IV is because one cannot test whether the IV in question is truly uncorrelated with unobservables in the error[2]. Jacob and Lefgren (2004a) used discontinuities in school test scores for predicting whether teachers received training or not, and then used the predicted term as their instrument for the assignment variable in the parametric RD models. They ran sensitivity tests to explore alternative pathways for how test scores could influence the outcome other than through its relationship with the assignment and found no such evidence. Thus, the authors concluded that they had a valid instrument for addressing fuzziness[3].

Finally, it is important with RDs to examine empirically the social dynamics of the cutoff. In the Irish school-leaving examination, it was discovered that scores just below the passing cutoff score were underrepresented in the frequency distribution, presumably because examiners did not want to hurt a student's chances by assigning them a 38 or 39 when 40 was the passing score. In other RD studies it is not unknown for social workers to misrepresent family income around cutoffs that determine eligibility for services. Researchers should control the assignment process as much as possible and observe the process directly, preferably in a pilot research phase so that potential problems can be addressed. This same advice holds for the experiment also. Its implementation needs to be directly examined and otherwise checked.

ABBREVIATED INTERRUPTED TIME SERIES DESIGN WITH A CONTROL SERIES

When a series of observations are available on the same variable, an interrupted time series (ITS) design can be used to assess whether a treatment administered at a known time during the series leads to a change in intercept or slope at the intervention point. In much social science practice, it is difficult to find studies with enough time points to estimate the error structure and provide responsible analysis at a district, school, class or student level (Box & Jenkins, 1970)[4]. Much more common are abbreviated ITSs with, say, 4 to 20 pretest time points. Indeed, standards-based reform in education has led to the repeated tracking of student test scores, providing many opportunities for abbreviated ITS design and analysis. This section discusses the design, the theory and empirical research supporting its validity, and examples of how it has been used.

The basics of controlled abbreviated ITS design

A time series requires repeated measurements made on the same variable over time. The observations can be made on the same units, as with multiple test scores on the same student, or on different but similar units, as with test scores from multiple cohorts of students within the same school. ITS also requires an intervention that is supposed to generate an interruption in the series at a known point in time corresponding to implementation of the treatment. The design also works better when a rapid response to the intervention is expected (or when the response interval is well known, as with 9 months in the case of the period from intercourse to birth), and when the intervals between observations are short. If a treatment is phased in slowly over time, or if it reaches different sections of the target population at differing times, then implementation is better described as a gradually diffusing process rather than as an abrupt intervention. In these cases of delayed intervention, the chance of other events influencing the outcome increases, making history a plausible threat to internal validity. At a minimum, the diffusion process should be directly observed and, where possible, modeled.

$$O_1 \quad O_2 \quad O_3 \quad O_4 \quad O_5 \ X \ O_6 \quad O_7 \quad O_8 \quad O_9 \quad O_{10}$$
$$O_1 \quad O_2 \quad O_3 \quad O_4 \quad O_5 \quad O_6 \quad O_7 \quad O_8 \quad O_9 \quad O_{10}$$

Figure 10.4   Interrupted time series design

Also, the inclusion of an untreated control group with multiple observations can help rule out plausible threats to validity such as history, maturation, and statistical regression that a simple ITS cannot rule out. So a quality-abbreviated ITS requires both treatment and control groups for which there are multiple and frequent observations before and after the intervention. A simple design with a control group and 10 observations is depicted in Figure 10.4.

Unique characteristics of this design: Theoretical and empirical reasons

There are several potential advantages of the abbreviated ITS for assessing treatment effects. Ashenfelter (1978) examined the effects of participation in a job training program on earnings for Blacks and Whites and for males and females. The treatment group consisted of individuals who began job training under the Manpower Development and Training Act in the first 3 months of 1964. The comparison sample was constructed from the 0.1 percent Work History Sample of the Department of Labor, a random sample of earnings records on American workers. The outcome was earnings at 11 time points for each of the groups. In addition to multiple posttest observations, Ashenfelter had four years of earnings for the treatment and comparison groups prior to the intervention. Posttest results suggested that participation in the job training program increased earnings for all the treatment groups by race and gender. However, Ashenfelter noted that treatment group members had lower earnings than the comparison group in the year before intervention. While comparison group members remained in the labor force, those eligible for job training in 1964 were required as a condition of acceptance into the program

to be out of work in 1963. So their reported earnings in 1963 had to be depressed.

Consider the numerous threats to validity if Ashenfelter had used only one pretest measure. First, he would not have been able to eliminate 'maturation' as an alternative explanation. Under the maturation hypothesis, training members' earnings increased at a faster rate than comparison members' but had started at a lower point than comparison units, even before 1963. With multiple years of earnings data, Ashenfelter was able to examine the data for group differences in maturation. Second, regression to the mean would have been difficult to discount. In this scenario, if unemployment of treatment group members in 1963 was temporary and necessary for program inclusion, then the increase in earnings after 1963 might have occurred even without participation in the treatment. Using multiple years of pre-intervention data, Ashenfelter (1978) found a small decrease in earnings for the treatment group between 1962 and 1963, but not enough that regression could have accounted for all treatment effects. Finally, history would have been another plausible alternative explanation. Under this threat, observed increases in earnings would have been due to upward trends in the economic cycle, and not to treatment effects. Multiple pretest observations allowed Ashenfelter to test for seasonal or cyclical patterns in the data. Note in this example that it is the length, number, and frequency of *pre-intervention* time points that permits the examination of common threats to validity. Multiple *posttest* observations help determine the temporal pattern of an effect, but they cannot rule out alternative explanations.

The second unique feature of ITS design is that treatment effects can be assessed along multiple dimensions. The next example demonstrates that treatment effects can be measured by the form of the effect (level,

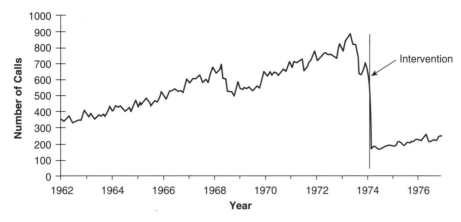

Figure 10.5   The effects of charging for directory assistance in Cincinnati
Source: Shadish et al., 2002. Copyright 2002 by Houghton Mifflin Company.

slope, and variance), its permanence (continuous or discontinuous), and its immediacy (immediate or delayed). In March 1974, Cincinnati Bell began charging 20 cents per call to local directory assistance. Figure 10.5 shows an immediate and large drop in local directory assistance calls when this charge began. But treatment effects can be described along dimensions other than their means. A continuous treatment effect persists over time, while a discontinuous effect tends to drift back to pre-intervention level after the initial effect wears off. Figure 10.5 shows a continuous treatment effect because the change in level persisted well into 1976. Effects can also be immediate or delayed. Immediate treatment effects are easier to interpret, while delayed effects are more problematic because plausible alternative explanations may be introduced in the time interval between intervention onset and the recorded response. Therefore, a strong theoretical justification that predicts the length of a delay is helpful when examining delayed effects, such as the expectation of increased births *nine months* after a citywide electricity blackout, not three months after the event. In the Cincinnati Bell case, the treatment response was immediate, with a large drop in directory assistance calls occurring on intervention day. When interpreting an ITS study, it is helpful to describe effects in terms of changes in level, slope, and variance, thus

assessing whether effects are immediate or not and continuous or not.

We are only aware of one study testing the validity of an abbreviated ITS design by comparing its results to those achieved from a randomized experiment that had the same intervention group. Bloom et al. (2005a; Michalopoulos et al., 2004) reanalyzed data from the 11-city NEWWS, a component of the Job Opportunity and Basic Skills (JOBS) program that mandated job training services for unemployed individuals. The study involved at least 8 pretest quarterly reports on earnings prior to intervention and 20 quarters of earnings post-intervention. Four cities — Oklahoma City, Riverside, Portland, and Detroit — included welfare recipients in one part of the city who were randomly assigned to treatment or control group, and the non-equivalent comparison group for the ITS study was composed of people from another part of the same city. In fact, comparisons had comprised of individuals who had served as controls in the same experiment. A fifth comparison was in-state rather than within-city, involving treatment and comparison groups from Detroit and Grand Rapids. All the data we report here are at the site mean level, aggregated up from longitudinal individual data collected at the same times and on the same measures for both the experimental and the abbreviated ITS samples. The general logic with empirical tests of the correspondence in results between an experiment and quasi-experiment is that the randomly formed control group and the non-randomly formed comparison group would have to be identical if they were to produce the same causal effect size, given that both groups would be analyzed with the same treatment data. In the ITS case, though, the logic is slightly different. The means and slopes can differ, but not the behavior of the control or comparison group around the intervention point. Any temporal changes observed there can masquerade as alternative interpretations of an immediate program impact.

Figure 10.6 displays the means over time for the control and comparison groups at each of the five sites, the intervention point being designated as 0 on the time scale. Visual inspection suggests no shift in the intercept at the intervention point in three sites — Oklahoma City (N controls = 831; N comparisons = 3,184), Detroit (N controls = 955; N comparisons = 1,187), and Riverside (N controls = 1,459; N comparisons = 1,501). There were no reliable differences in slopes either, though the possibility of such is indicated in the later lags in both Detroit and Riverside. However, these small differences had opposite signs and basically cancelled each other out. Indeed, neither the means nor trends reliably differed at any of these three sites and would not differ if they

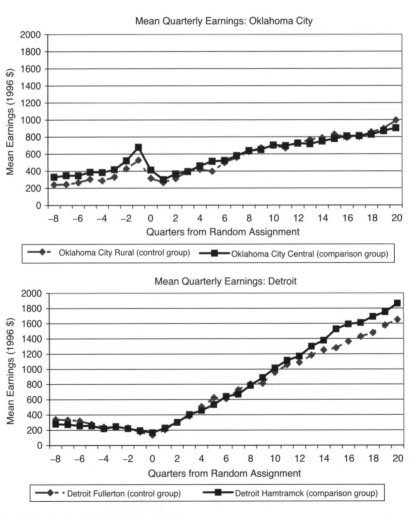

Figure 10.6   Mean quarterly earning by site
Source: Michalopoulos et al., 2004.

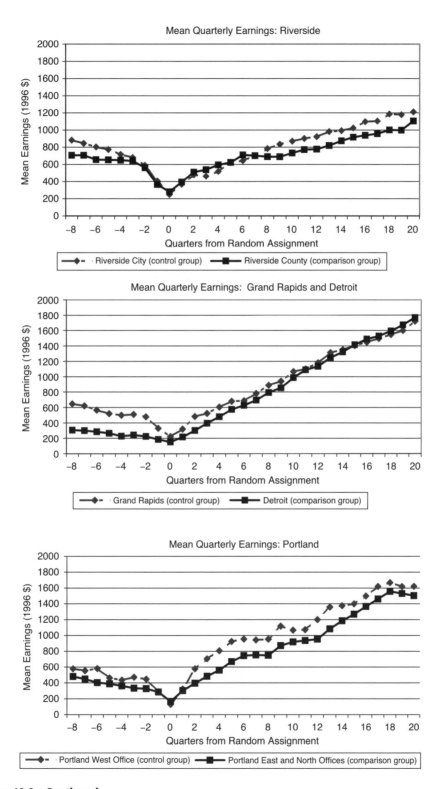

Figure 10.6　Continued

were aggregated into a single analysis. These results suggest that selecting these samples within cities induced so much comparability that further individual matching would hardly help control bias.

The comparability between control and comparison groups was not replicated in Portland, the smallest site where the randomized control cases were about a third of the next smallest control group (N controls = 328; N comparisons = 1,019). Figure 10.6 shows that while control and comparison groups were stably different at the series' very beginning and throughout most of the post-intervention period, one group exhibited a large earnings dip immediately prior to the intervention. Thus, the control and comparison groups did not act similarly pre- and post-intervention, as ITS requires. The same was true when Grand Rapids (N = 1,390) was compared to its within-state comparison, Detroit (N = 2,142). Here, the pre-intervention group means differed, but not the post-intervention ones. This again implies that different causal conclusions would arise between the randomized experiment and the abbreviated ITS quasi-experiment yoked to it. However, design and city differences were confounded in this last analysis. While Detroit and Grand Rapids are in the same state, they are not in the same city and so would likely have different local labor markets with their unique economic pressures at different times.

If we were to sum the four within-city comparisons and weight Portland appropriately less than the other sites, there would be little or no difference between the control and comparison groups around the intervention point and hence, there would be little causal bias. The same would likely be true if all five sites were summed. In this particular case, the abbreviated ITS would not be biased relative to the experiment. However, Bloom et al. (2005a; Michalopoulos et al., 2004) concluded that the within-state control and comparison groups did not closely approximate each other. Their analysis of absolute bias was predicated on computing the difference between the randomly and non-randomly formed comparison groups across

all 28 time points *irrespective* of the sign of these differences, thus capitalizing on random error of whatever source. By contrast, our analysis was of average bias, of the difference between the two types of comparisons across 28 time points per site when account is taken of the signs attached to each difference at each time point. Fortunately, Bloom et al. also compute average bias, reporting that the comparison and control group differed by between 1 percent and −3 percent at two years after the intervention and between 3 percent and −4 percent at five years, even when the less appropriate Grand Rapids/Detroit comparison was included in the calculation. Such a close correspondence between an experimental control group and a nonexperimental comparison group would lead to experimental and quasi-experimental effect sizes that do not differ when each is subsequently yoked to the same treatment group.

Even accepting Bloom et al.'s (2005a; Michalopoulos et al., 2004) analysis of absolute rather than average bias, we would still have reason to be concerned about generalizing the study's findings to other research domains. Despite the 8 pretest observations, the earnings measures were not highly correlated across a year (by our rough estimate, about 0.42). As a point of comparison, for example, student test scores tend to correlate on a magnitude of about 0.58 to 0.74 in math and 0.60 to 0.74 in reading (Bloom et al., 2005b). The relatively low annual correlations for earnings suggest that the pretests were limited in their usefulness as selection controls than would be the case when examining academic achievement, for example. Even so, the number of pretest observations still helps, for Bloom et al. report that constructing a pretest covariate out of pretest earnings data from varying numbers of waves led to less bias the more waves there were. The presumption is that creating a single pretest measure out of more waves leads to more reliable estimation of that pretest selection difference. Bloom et al. could not show, though, that constructing an individual level growth model helped reduce the selection threat they claimed to find when analyzing absolute bias. But even so, the lower correlations among adjacent earnings measures suggest that growth trends were not stably estimated in this project, the more so since quarterly data were analyzed and these are presumably even less stable than the 0.42 correlations for annual data.

To summarize, when we look at the four within-city comparisons, there were no differences between control and comparison groups at three of the sites. The only difference was in the smaller, less stable Portland comparison. For the fifth within-state comparison, labor markets between Grand Rapids and Detroit were different enough that we would expect these sites to produce inferior matches to those of truly local comparison and control groups. Even so, when results were summed across all sites, the average biases cancelled each other out, and the quasi- and experimental studies yielded estimates with close correspondence. Thus, we disagree with Bloom et al.'s (2005a; Michalopoulos et al., 2004) conclusion about different effects attributable to the experiment and quasi-experiment. Fortunately, it is easy for readers to judge for themselves. Just look at Figure 10.6 and see whether there is a control/comparison difference around the intervention point for most of the within-city cases.

Examples of ITS design

In this section, we use examples of abbreviated ITS to highlight two design features over and above those already mentioned — a longer pretest time-series and a control series selected from non-equivalent but matched units. The two features we emphasize are nonequivalent dependent variables and switching replications. When they are thoughtfully incorporated into quasi-experimental designs, many common threats to validity can be addressed.

In a study that assessed the effects of a 1989 media campaign to reduce alcohol use among students at a university festival, McKillip (1992) added two nonequivalent dependent variables to strengthen inference in a short time series. His main dependent variable was a time series of 10 observations on awareness of alcohol abuse among college students. The two nonequivalent dependent variables, good nutrition and stress reduction, were conceptually related to health, and thus would reflect changes if the treatment effect was due to a general improvement in attitudes toward health. However, since good nutrition and stress reduction were not targeted by the campaign, they would not show improvements if the effect resulted from the treatment alone. As Figure 10.7 shows, awareness of alcohol abuse clearly increased during the media campaign, but awareness of other health-related issues did not.

McClannahan et al. (1990) employed a switching-replications feature to assess the effects of providing married couples who supervised group homes for autistic children with regular feedback about the daily personal hygiene and appearance of the children in their home. The authors used a short time series (21 observations), with feedback introduced after Session 6 in Home 1, Session 11 in Home 2, and Session 16 in Home 3. Figure 10.8 shows that after each introduction, the personal appearance of the children in that home increased above baseline, and the improvement was maintained over time. Both examples, however, demonstrate one limitation of abbreviated time series data — the difficulty in knowing the duration of an effect. For example, Figure 10.7 shows an apparent decrease in alcohol abuse awareness after the two-week intervention.

Two additional features, removing a treatment at a known time and adding multiple replications of a treatment, can strengthen inference in an abbreviated ITS design. In the former, treatment effects can be demonstrated by not only showing that the effects occur with the treatment but also that the effects stop when the treatment is removed later in the time series, making this design akin to having two consecutive ITS. In multiple replications, the treatment is introduced, removed, and then introduced again according to a planned schedule. A treatment effect is suggested if the outcome responds similarly each time the treatment is introduced and removed, with the

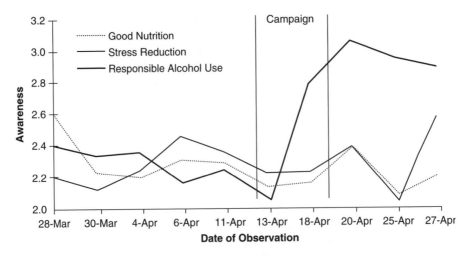

Figure 10.7   The effects of a media program to increase awareness of alcohol abuse
Source: McKillip, 1992. Copyright 1992 by Plenum Press.

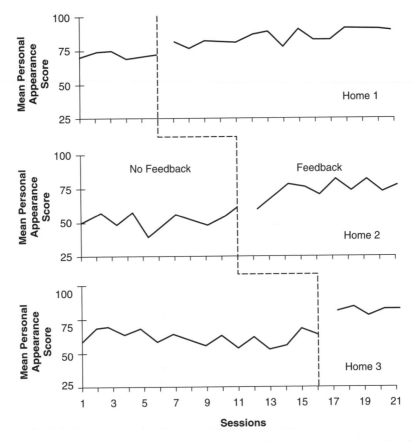

Figure 10.8   The effects of a parental intervention on the physical appearance of autistic children in three different homes
Source: McClannahan et al., 1990. Copyright 1990 by The Society for the Experimental Analysis of Behavior.

direction of responses being different for the introductions compared with the removals.

THE MOST FREQUENTLY USED QUASI-EXPERIMENTAL DESIGN: DIFFERENCE-IN-DIFFERENCES DESIGN

Probably the most widely used nonequivalent comparison group design compares a treated and an untreated comparison group at one pretest time point and at one posttest time, using the same units in each group at each time. Within the quasi-experimental tradition, this design is called the nonequivalent comparison group design (Campbell & Stanley, 1963; Cook & Campbell, 1979; Shadish et al., 2002), but in economics, the design is described as fixed effects or difference-in-differences. We use all three names interchangeably. The design is diagrammed in Figure 10.9. In quasi-experiments, because comparison groups are nonequivalent by definition, selection is a concern. Pretest measures can help researchers assess the direction and size of any bias directly observable at pretest. It can also help assess the threat of attrition if participants exit the study before it is finished, for those exiting may be different from those who remain. With a pretest one can directly examine group differences in those exiting and remaining, at least on the pretest variable.

A word of caution, however. A single pretest measure rarely eliminates all plausible threats to validity. The extent to which the pretest rules out selection can also depend on unmeasured variables that are correlated with both treatment receipt and outcome. When pretests show differences between groups, selection can also combine with other threats additively or interactively. Thus, the earlier Ashenfelter example demonstrated how selection can combine with such internal

$$O_1 \quad X \quad O_2$$
$$O_1 \qquad\quad O_2$$

Figure 10.9 Nonequivalent comparison group design

validity threats as maturation, regression, and history.

Evidence for this design's validity

The validity of the difference-in-differences design depends on how well the comparison group is matched to the treatment group. Ideal matches would not differ between treatment groups other than for participation in the intervention, thus ruling out selection as a threat to validity. Randomized experiments are based on this paradigm. Statisticians have routinely shown that, in a perfectly implemented randomized experiment, no differences are expected between treatment groups prior to intervention, and that this holds for both measured and unmeasured variables. Congruent with this analogy and Mill's canons (1856), finding better matches dominates much of the thinking about better quasi-experimental design.

Some studies have examined the validity of the difference-in-differences design by comparing estimates from it with those from an experimental benchmark that shares the same treatment group. One is by Shadish et al. (2007), and the second by Aiken et al. (1998). Each study exemplifies the most important requirement for a fair test of design types — that everything is identical between the experiment and quasi-experiment other than how units are assigned to treatment.

Shadish et al. (2007) present one of the best tests of the difference-in-differences design, though it is only one study, in the laboratory, and very short term. The authors looked at the effects of a group coaching intervention on math and vocabulary performances among college students. Participants were randomly assigned to either the experimental or quasi-experimental condition. Both designs were administered so that respondents underwent essentially the same experiences at the same time and in the same setting. Further, the same battery of measurements was used in the experiment and quasi-experiment, with all participants providing details at a pretest time point on personality scales, about their interest in math and reading, and about their performance on math and vocabulary topics close to those taught. School records were also examined to get their grades in math and language arts courses as well as their SAT scores. For students exposed to math coaching, their posttest math scores functioned as the intervention-relevant outcome while their vocabulary posttest results served as controls. For students who received the reading intervention, vocabulary performance was the intervention-relevant outcome and math performance served as controls. Half of the students were randomly assigned a vocabulary or math treatment, while students in the quasi-experimental design condition were able to choose which treatment they received. The pretest results indicated no treatment and control group differences in the experimental condition, but not in the quasi-experimental condition. Those who chose the vocabulary intervention had higher vocabulary pretest scores than those who chose the math intervention, and vice versa. Thus, the quasi-experimental groups were non-equivalent in a way that was originally intended by the authors.

Consider the ways in which Shadish et al.'s (2007) study meet our criterion for a strong test of design types. First, pretest scores for students in the experimental and quasi-experimental conditions indicate that there was variation between design types. Next, as we have already discussed, the random assignment of students into the experimental and quasi-experimental conditions and the uniformity in procedures for both conditions ruled out variation in features that were correlated with both design type and outcome. Third, the laboratory conditions meant that the random assignment process was entirely under experimenter control and its efficacy could be independently checked against the pretest means. The setting also prevented differential attrition from the two design type groups, and no treatment contamination from math to vocabulary coaching and vice versa. So we feel confident that results obtained from the experimental design served as a valid standard for which to compare estimates from the quasi-experiment.

We would also expect that a fair test of design types uses a sophisticated quasi-experimental design, and appropriate statistical procedures. At a minimum, a quality quasi-experiment minimizes selection by clearly measuring and modeling it. Note the pool from where comparison group members were drawn — not only were comparison matches 'local' to treatment members, but they also attended the same institution, were of similar ages, and exposed to similar experiences at the institution (a psychology course). In addition, the authors modeled a selection process where individuals' motivation for choosing a field of coaching was related to their interests and cognitive strengths, measured by pre-intervention, psychometrically sound multi-item questionnaires assessing students' motivation to learn about math and language arts, their test scores in math and language arts, past grades in math and language arts courses, and content-valid scales specifically constructed to assess math and vocabulary knowledge. This last was also used to measure post-intervention outcomes, with the expectation that pre- and post-intervention test scores would be highly correlated. In all, access to rich covariates that modeled the selection process, and strong overlap in background characteristics between treatment and comparison group members, enabled the authors to use a statistical procedure called propensity score matching.

Like other matching techniques, propensity scores seek to pair treatment and comparison group members on observable characteristics that are stably measured. One problem is that, as the number of matching variables increases, so does the dimensionality of matches, making it exponentially more difficult to find suitable matches for each treated unit. Propensity scores reduce this problem by creating a single index of the propensity to be exposed to the treatment through a first stage in the analysis where potential predictors of selection are used to see which ones are related to treatment exposure understood in binary fashion. A propensity score is the probability of receiving treatment conditional on these pretreatment covariates that are weighted and put into a single index. The advantage of propensity score matching is that it allows researchers to condition on a single scalar variable rather than multiple dimension spaces; this single variable is then used to analyze the outcome data in a number of different possible ways.

Because there is some art to the use of propensity scores, Shadish et al. (2007) consulted with one of the method's developers, Paul Rosenbaum. They then used his recommendations, first, to calculate propensity scores from the array of covariates collected and, then, to achieve good balance across the five equal strata computed from these scores. (Another analysis used the propensity scores as covariates, after testing and adjusting for possible non-linearities — this not being the analysis Rosenbaum recommended.)

Within-study comparisons results indicated that under the conditions built into this study, the experiment and quasi-experiment resulted in post-intervention effect sizes that corresponded for the experiment and quasi-experiment. Bias was not significantly reduced, however, when just the demographic variables—called predictors of convenience by the authors—were used and in one case may even have increased it. Later analyses showed that a measure of the strength of motivation to be exposed to math or language arts was the most important single covariate for reducing bias, particularly for the effects of instruction in mathematics, followed by the measures of math and language arts achievement. The key assumption is that, in this case, the selection process was driven largely, but not exclusively, by individuals self-selecting themselves into coaching on the subject matter about which they felt more comfort. It seems plausible to hypothesize, therefore, that the quality of the covariate structure played a role in reducing bias, and that this quality reflects how well the selection process was conceptualized and measured.

The second study we identified as a strong test of the difference-in-differences design is by Aiken et al. (1998). In addition to the RD design discussed earlier, the authors compared their experimental results on the efficacy of remedial English with estimates obtained from a carefully designed basic quasi-experiment. Their comparison group was of students who could not be contacted prior to the quarter they attended the university, or whose decision to enroll was made after information was collected for the RD study. Because the hard-to-reach and late-applying students still had SAT or ACT scores as requirements for admission, the authors were able to create a quasi-experimental comparison group that was restricted to those who scored within the same bandwidth as students in the randomized experiment.

Note that the matching took place within the sampling design and not ex post facto when cases from obviously different populations would have to be individually matched by taking advantage of where they overlap. Indeed, the match at the sampling level was so close, as in Bloom et al. (2005a) that the control and comparison groups did not differ on any observables correlated with the outcomes of interest—viz., on entry-level ACT/SAT scores or pretest essay writing and multiple choice exam scores. Moreover, the experimental and quasi-experimental samples underwent the same treatment and nontreatment experiences and the same measurement schedules in order to rule these out as sources of conceptually irrelevant variance. In all, this was a carefully constructed quasi-experiment despite the modest structure of just two non-equivalent groups and a single pretest measurement wave. The randomized experiment was also carefully managed. The authors demonstrated that pretest means did not differ and differential attrition did not occur. Given the close correspondence in means, the authors used ANCOVA to analyze the quasi-experiment, with each pretest outcome serving as a covariate for itself at a later date.

For the test of English knowledge outcome, effect size results were 0.57 standard deviations for the quasi-experiment and 0.59 for the randomized experiment, both being statistically different from zero. For the essay-writing outcome, the effect sizes were 0.16 and 0.06, neither being reliably different from zero. Thus, by criteria of both effect size magnitude and statistical significance patterns, the experimental and quasi-experimental design produced comparable results. Note that the close correspondence was achieved largely through careful selection of the non-equivalent comparison cases, prior to statistical adjustment that in this case served more to increase power than to control for selection.

We now briefly review within-study comparisons from the job training literature. These studies have had extraordinary influence over methodology choice in American evaluation policy, with conclusions from these studies suggesting that quasi-experiments fail to replicate benchmark experimental estimates (Glazerman et al., 2003). However, a close reading of these early papers (Cook et al., 2005; Smith & Todd, 2005) suggests that the experiments and quasi-experiments differed in many other ways than just in how treatments were assigned, thus making obscure why the experiments and quasi-experiments differed in obtained effect sizes. Was it due to the mode of treatment assignment, the issue at stake, or was it due to extraneous differences between the two study types — e.g. in how outcomes were measured?

The earliest within-study comparisons in job training took the effect size from a randomized experiment and compared it to the effect size from a quasi-experiment consisting of the same intervention group (Fraker & Maynard, 1987; LaLonde, 1986). Comparison group members were drawn selectively and systematically from large, national datasets, such as the Panel Study of Income Dynamics or the Current Population Study. Data from the quasi-experiments were then analyzed using various statistical models, including OLS and the Heckman selection models of the day. Here the emphasis was on selection adjustment via statistical manipulation rather than sample selection. When the resulting effect sizes were compared to the effect size from the yoked experiment, the authors concluded that the experimental and nonexperimental effect sizes were generally different whatever the mode of statistical adjustment for selection.

Unfortunately, the design comparisons were almost inevitably confounded with both location and manner of testing. In the quasi-experiments, unlike the experiments,

comparison cases came from national registries rather than from the same local venue as the experiments, and earnings were measured at different times in each study, thus confounding the type of design with the state of local labor markets as they varied over time (Smith & Todd, 2005). In addition, selection models were sometimes estimated using few demographic variables that did not even contain pre-intervention earnings assessments, though many later studies did include these measures. However, the pre-intervention variables were not analyzed in the abbreviated time-series fashion detailed earlier, but combined into a single propensity score. In fairness, the early job training studies were conducted by pioneers, many of whom were anxious to investigate matching strategies with databases that had already been collected for non-evaluation purposes and that would be much less expensive than constructing randomly formed control groups as in an experiment. So their interests were pragmatic as well as theoretical.

The early within-study comparisons spawned more studies similar in conception and overall structure but differing in some details. Later studies used newer statistical tools for handling selection, more experimental datasets were added, and different ways evolved for constructing quasi-experimental comparison groups, moving away from the use of national datasets to comparisons that were living quite locally to the treated (Smith & Todd, 2005). This was to unconfound the mode of treatment assignment with differences in location and testing in order to draw clearer conclusions about the effects of random assignment or not.

Overall, the job training literature yielded some important lessons about quasi-experimental design. We learned that 'technically better' designs had the following features: (1) pretests and longer pretest time series, especially those with higher pretest-outcome correlations; (2) local control groups, though this never went so far as to use twins, siblings or within-organization comparisons; (3) treatment and comparison groups assessed in exactly the same way at exactly the same time by exactly the same assessment procedure; (4) testing a causal hypothesis with several implications in the data; and (5) directly and comprehensively measuring and modeling the selection process in its own right.

Examples of difference-in-differences design

In this section, we discuss examples of the nonequivalent comparison group design. Because of the wide variation in *quality* of quasi-experimental designs that use this design model, we present two studies that Cook and Campbell (1979) would identify as 'generally uninterpretable,' and two that we believe are exemplars of the design. We begin with two studies that attempt to strengthen quasi-experiments almost exclusively through the use of statistical matching procedures, in this case matching through propensity scores.

The original intent of the Wilde and Hollister (2007) and Agodini and Dynarski (2004) studies was to compare impact causal estimates from a randomized experiment with those from a quasi-experimental design that used propensity scores to match what were evidently different populations. Using data from 11 schools in the Tennessee Project Star Study, Wilde and Hollister looked at class size effects on student achievement in each of the 11 sites. For their quasi-experimental study, the researchers matched students from treatment classrooms within a school to students from untreated classrooms from all other schools in the Project Start study. Their propensity score matches were constructed using data from multiple levels, including information about the student (especially free-lunch status) and about the teacher and school. No pretest achievement measures were used at the student, classroom, or school levels since none were collected in the original study. The authors concluded that results from the experimental and quasi-experimental designs generally failed to replicate, and that experimental results should be preferred on a priori grounds.

A closer look at the quasi-experimental design, however, suggests several weaknesses. First, because the original study was a randomized experiment with large samples of students, Project Star did not require pretest achievement measures. Most non-time series quasi-experiments are considered to be causally uninterpretable if they are without pretest measures because it is so difficult to rule out selection effects in any transparent fashion (Cook & Campbell, 1979). A second concern is that treatment students were matched with control students who attended schools from all over the state of Tennessee, thus reducing the degree of localness. Yet with little extra effort the researchers could have first selected schools or classrooms in terms of their average student race or free lunch status, then creating their individual student-level matches from within this prior school and/or classroom matching. Better yet, since prior achievement data is routinely available at the school level, and sometimes even at the classroom level, why did the researchers not match on prior aggregate level achievement before then matching on individual level propensity scores? The matching procedure used by Wilde and Hollister created treatment and comparison units from such different aggregate worlds that there was little overlap on measured variables. The alternative sampling design we propose permits propensity scores to be calculated from worlds that overlap much more from the start. We suspect that the lack of pretest achievement measures and weak matching procedure with samples of limited initial comparability led to a design that no sophisticated researcher would use if asked to create a quasi-experiment from scratch. In other words, a good experiment is being compared to a mediocre quasi-experiment in both design and analysis terms, thus confounding design type with quality of design in features other than the mode of treatment assignment.

Agodini and Dynarski (2004) is the second study we analyze. It examined how 16 middle and high school dropout prevention programs affected student dropout, absenteeism, and self-esteem two years later. They provided volunteer students with targeted services such as mentoring, tutoring, individual counseling, and smaller class sizes in order to reduce student dropout and absenteeism and increase self-esteem and educational aspirations over two years. In the experiment, controls were randomly selected students who had applied to the intervention or were referred to participate in it. Two data sources were used to construct the non-equivalent comparison groups from which propensity scores were computed. For the first, researchers matched treatment group members with students attending four comparison schools in a quasi-experimental study of school restructuring. These were 7th graders in two middle schools, 9th graders in one high school, and 10th graders in another. For the second, Agodini and Dynarski constructed matches from a national dataset, the National Educational Longitudinal Study (NELS). The researchers' original plan was to generate 128 propensity score matches across four outcomes, 16 schools and their matched comparisons, and two types of comparison groups (NELS versus the four comparison middle schools). The number of pre-intervention covariates used in the propensity score calculations varied by data source, but there were never fewer than 13, including prior test scores but not much dropout information since so few students drop out and then return to school.

Agodini and Dynarski (2004) concluded that their quasi-experimental and experimental designs produced different results when the two could be compared, but that they could be compared in only 29 of the 128 planned cases. At first glance, the quasi-experimental design appears strong due to the presence of pretest scores and extensive baseline measures. However, close inspection of both comparison group sources suggests serious limitations in the sampling design. For the first comparison, students were drawn from four schools not in the same school districts as the treatment schools, nor necessarily even in the same part of the country. In addition, treated students were from all the middle and high school grades whereas the comparison students were fewer in number

and restricted only to the 7th, 9th and 10th grades. Given the differences between the two groups in location and school age, and probably also in observed characteristics, it is understandable why so few acceptable matches were achieved between treatment students and comparison students from a few middle schools. The NELS comparison was likely no better. National datasets contain relatively few persons at risk for dropping out, and so the pool of potential matches was restricted to start with. Further, measurement specifics and geographic location vary between the treatment group and potential comparison students from NELS, making it all the more difficult to achieve suitable matches when using NELS for matching purposes.

Looking at Wilde and Hollister (2007) and Agodini and Dynarski (2004) together, one is reminded of the adage, 'You cannot put right by statistics what you have done wrong by design' (Light & Pillemer, 1984). Shadish et al. (2007) and Aiken et al. (1998) showed that the best nonequivalent group comparisons are from studies where matching was achieved through a careful sampling design and where statistical adjustment is relegated to the role of an auxiliary procedure to control for any remaining differences between groups. It is definitely not the first line of attack on initial group non-comparability. Below, we discuss other design features that improve causal conclusion-drawing from quasi-experiments over and above the careful sampling discussed above that antedates any individual case-matching.

Wortman et al. (1978) examined how a program that provided parents with educational vouchers to attend a local school of their choice affected students' reading test scores. The program's goal was to foster competition between schools in the system, and initial results by others suggested that vouchers decreased academic performance among students. However, Wortman et al. doubted these conclusions and so they followed groups of students from first to third grades in both voucher and non-voucher schools, and further divided voucher schools into those with and without traditional voucher programs.

The authors also reanalyzed the data using *double pretest* scores, which allowed them to compare pretreatment growth rates in reading with posttest change in rates. Results from Wortman et al.'s analyses found that the decrease in reading scores previously attributed to voucher schools could actually be attributed to nontraditional voucher programs. Further, traditional voucher and non-voucher groups showed no differential effects that could not be explained by a continuation of the same maturation rates which had previously characterized the traditional and voucher control schools.

Double pretests allowed researchers to assess the threat of selection-maturation on the assumption that the rates between the first two pretests will continue between the second pretest and outcome measure. However, this assumption is testable only for the untreated group, and within-group growth rates will be fallibly estimated given measurement error and possible instrumentation shifts that make measured growth between the two pretests different from the second pretest and outcome measure. Thus, while the double pretest design with nonequivalent groups is not perfect, it can help assess the plausibility of selection-maturation by describing pretreatment growth differences. The double pretest design can also assess regression effects by showing whether the second pretest for either group is atypically low or high compared to the first pretest. Finally, the second pretest measure can help with statistical analysis by providing more precise estimates of correlation between observations at different times. Without the extra pretest measure, the correlation in observations without the treatment would be unclear.

Hackman et al. (1978) strengthened the nonequivalent comparison group design by adding a reversed-treatment control group feature to investigate how changes in motivational properties of jobs affect worker attitudes and behaviors. In a reversed-treatment control design, one group receives a treatment (+) to produce an effect in one direction and the other group receives a conceptually opposite treatment (−) to produce the reverse effect. In Hackman et al.'s study, technological innovations in a bank resulted in some clerical jobs to be more complex and challenging (treatment +) and other jobs to be less so (treatment −). The job changes were made without telling the employees of their possible motivational consequences, and measures of job characteristics, employee attitudes, and work behaviors were taken before and after the jobs were reconstituted. An effect would be detected if a statistical interaction resulted from improved scores among employees who received treatment (+) and lower scores among those who received treatment (−).

Consider how the reversed-treatment design can strengthen a study's construct validity. In a design with only treatment (+) and no treatment controls, a steeper pretest-posttest slope in the enriched condition could be explained by employees' responding to novelty in their jobs, feelings of special treatment, or guessing the study's hypothesis. These alternatives are less plausible if the reversed-treatment group exhibits a pretest-posttest decrease in job satisfaction because it is thought that knowledge of being in a study tends to elicit socially desirable responses from participants. Thus, to explain both an increase in treatment (+) group and decrease in the reversed group, each set of respondents would have to guess the hypothesis and corroborate it in their own different way. Interpretation of this design then depends on producing two effects with opposite signs, and the design assumes that little historical and/or motivation changes are otherwise taking place.

STRENGTHENING WEAK QUASI-EXPERIMENTAL DESIGNS THROUGH THE USE OF PATTERN-MATCHING

The quasi-experimental designs we believe are weak causal tests should be apparent by now — those without a pretest measure on the same scale as the outcome, those without a comparison group, and those without baseline covariates that can be combined to create a plausible and well-measured selection model. Without a pretest, it is difficult to know whether a change has occurred and to rule out most threats to internal validity. Without a comparison group, it is difficult to know what would have happened in the treatment group had the intervention not been in place — the desired counterfactual. Finally, without relevant covariates to control for pre-intervention differences between groups, it is difficult to know whether selection is confounded with treatment effects. These factors point to the kinds of quasi-experiment that should be avoided because of the high risk of yielding results that Cook and Campbell (1979) have called 'generally non-interpretable.' However, what happens in circumstances where the ideal design conditions that Shadish et al. (2007) and Aiken et al. (1998) created are not possible (i.e. studies where pretest data is not available)?

The superiority of RD and ITS designs is based on an epistemology that is subtly different from the one that validates randomized experiments and most of the other quasi-experimental designs utilized today. There, the counterfactual is a single posttest mean or a form of 'gain' in the control group. In RD and ITS, on the other hand, the counterfactual is more complex and depends instead on a *pattern* match, on a causal hypothesis that predicts multiple implications in the data. Together, they form a multivariate pattern (Corrin & Cook, 1998; Shadish et al., 2007) that few if any alternative interpretations would be expected to create, though this last assertion has to be critically assessed.

Let us illustrate an example. Minton (1975) examined the effects of Sesame Street by comparing the cognitive performance of children who were exposed to the show in kindergarten with the performance of their own siblings when they were in the same kindergarten one or two years earlier and when they could not have seen the show since it was not yet on the air. To compare just these siblings is a weak design that fails to account for selection and history differences. However,

content analysis showed that Sesame Street taught predominantly letter skills in its first year, and so Minton hypothesized that the younger siblings should do better than their older siblings in letter recognition but not in five other cognitive areas that are part of a child's normal maturation. In other words, the difference between siblings should be greater in letter recognition than in other cognitive skills. She further hypothesized that children who watched the show more frequently would do better than their siblings on letter recognition to a degree that was different from among lighter viewers and that was different than what was found for non-letter recognition skills. Thus, the hypothesis was of a difference of differences of differences. OLS analyses showed that heavier viewers did indeed do better than their siblings on letter recognition to an extent not found with the lighter viewers, and that this difference of differences was not as pronounced on the five other cognitive tests as on letter recognition. Few alternative interpretations can be offered for this predicted pattern of difference of difference of differences.

Note that this study's finding appears valid even without pretests, and that measurement took place at different years for the treatment and comparison groups. Yet the design seems strong. Why? First, Minton compensated for some design weaknesses by having siblings in the treatment and comparison groups. They are not perfect matches, though, even if they do control for some environmental and family differences better than matches better than more distantly related individuals would. Second, the same general causal hypothesis about Sesame Street's effectiveness was made to have a number of substantive and testable implications in the data, not just a single implication. In particular, effect sizes should vary by the outcome measure and dosage level. This still does not make causal inference 'automatic.' A case still has to be made that no other causal hypothesis can explain the predicted and obtained complex data pattern; and one has to develop such designs with one's eyes wide open that the hypothesis involves a multi-way statistical analysis that requires large sample sizes and quality measurement to test well. Nonetheless and following Minton's example, we would like to see more use of patterned causal hypotheses when experiments or very high-quality quasi-experiments are not possible.

CONCLUSIONS

In some economics' contexts, quasi-experiments are lumped together with causal studies that do not have any direct intervention, and the whole is called 'nonexperiments.' However, one tradition (Campbell & Stanley, 1963; Cook & Campbell, 1979; Shadish et al., 2002) makes finer distinctions than this, distinguishing among experiments and nonexperiments — based mainly on deliberate intervention into an ongoing activity — and between different kinds (and qualities) of quasi-experiments. Widespread use of the generic 'nonexperiment' label loses all this subtlety. At best, it serves as the contrast to experiment; at its worst it lumps together methods that radically vary in their ability to approximate the results of experiments. It should be a concept rarely invoked, though we realize we cannot legislate this.

In this chapter, we have chosen to highlight the best designs that quasi-experimental theory has to offer. Empirical research has shown that RD studies give the same causal answer as experiments on the same topic; abbreviated ITS studies may also when there is a control time series; even the lowly workhorse design with two non-equivalent groups and a pretest and posttest may give a close approximation if the treatment and comparison groups are carefully selected initially. Certain design attributes seem particularly important, including: (1) pretests and longer pretest time series, especially when the pretest-outcome correlation is high; (2) local comparison groups — whether these be monozygotic twins, identical twins, same-sex siblings, opposite-sex siblings, within-organization controls, within-city matched controls, and so on; (3) treatment and comparison groups that are assessed in exactly the same way at exactly the same time by exactly the same person; (4) a causal hypothesis with several testable implications in the data that can be addressed with larger samples and quality measurement; and (5) a study component that empirically examines the selection process into treatment, and then measures this process very carefully.

Because of the randomized experiment's more elegant rationale and transparency of assumptions, no quasi-experiment provides a better warrant for causal inference. However, randomized experiments are not always possible, and so we ask, 'How can quasi-experiments be crafted and justified because, on empirical grounds, they are likely to produce similar results to an experiment?' A review of the empirical literature suggests that the best quasi-experiments tend to yield causal estimates close to those of the experiment, while the worst quasi-experiments do not. The time has come for us to move beyond the simplicity of the 'experiment versus nonexperiment' debate and to take a closer look at factors affecting the quality of quasi-experiments.

NOTES

1 Cook and Wong (in press) present the following seven criteria for conducting a high quality study of within-study comparisons:

1 There must be variation in the design types being compared — that is, random assignment in one group of units and a contrasting form of assignment in another group.
2 The assignment difference between the experiment and nonexperiment should not co-vary with theoretically irrelevant third variables that might be plausibly correlated with study outcome (Smith & Todd, 2005). For instance, in the earliest within-study comparisons, the randomly selected control cases came from the same sites as the intervention cases, but the non-random comparison cases came from national datasets like the Current Population Survey and hence from different physical locations than those in the experiment. The random and systematic controls also differed in many aspects of when and how outcome measurement occurred, thus also confounding the assignment variable of theoretical interest with measurement factors.

3 The experiment and nonexperiment should also estimate the same average or local average treatment effect. For example, in a RD study the causal impact is assessed at the cutoff point on the assignment variable. Comparability demands that the average treatment effect in the experiment should also be estimated at this point. Otherwise, differences in results might be attributed to differences in design type whereas they are due to differences in where the effect is estimated. This will not matter with linear effects in RD, but it will with non-linear ones.

4 The randomized experiment should demonstrably meet all the usual criteria for technical adequacy. That is, the treatment and control group should have been properly randomized; the correct randomization procedure should not have resulted in unhappy randomization by chance; there should be no differential attrition; nor should there be treatment crossovers. The importance of these features follows from the role the randomly formed control group is supposed to play as a benchmark of complete internal validity.

5 The type of nonexperiment under analysis should also meet all of its technical criteria for being a good example of its type. This is a difficult criterion, but necessary for avoiding the situation that results when a good experiment is contrasted with a poor example of a particular type of observational study. The key here is an explicit theory of what constitutes a quality observational study in terms of its design, implementation, and analysis. This is better known for RD than for the difference-in-differences design, largely because the assignment process is more transparent and better modeled in RD, directing major attention to how the functional form is specified and how fuzziness around the cutoff is handled. This is not to argue that unbiased inference is impossible with the difference-in-difference design. However, the requirement is then that assignment processes have to be perfectly modeled or the outcome totally predicted and, in actual research practice, uncertainties always remain about how well these requirements are met. Clues are also offered by the results identifying bias-reducing features in past reviews of the within-study comparison literature in job training. But as we have seen, these are incomplete and have never completely reduced selection bias. At most, common sense can help identify clear cases of poor design and analysis even if it cannot help discriminate among the alternatives currently thought to be better.

6 A within-study comparison should be explicit about the criteria it uses for inferring correspondence between experimental and nonexperimental results. Identical estimates are not to be expected. Even close replications of the same randomized experiment will not result in identical posttest sample means and variances. Assuming adequate statistical power, the same pattern of statistical significance will result in only 68 percent of comparisons — the probability of two significant findings across experiments is 0.80 × 0.80, and the probability of two non-significant findings is 0.20 × 0.20. Better than comparisons of significance test patterns are focused tests of the difference between mean estimates. But these are rare in the literature we review and require careful interpretation, especially when experimental and nonexperimental estimates with the same causal sign reliably differ from zero and are also reliably different from each other. Comparing magnitude estimates without significance tests is another option. But this is complicated by the need to determine what degree of difference is close enough to justify concluding that the experimental and nonexperimental estimates do or do not differ.

7 The persons analyzing the non-experimental data should be blind to the results of the experiment so as not to bias which non-experimental analyses are conducted or offered for publication.

2 One of the cleanest examples of IV is the use of random assignment as an instrumental variable in order to examine the effects of assignment as it actually occurred as opposed to how it was supposed to occur (see Angrist et al., 1996 for full explanation).

3 Hahn et al. (2001) offer a formal discussion of instrumental variable methods for addressing fuzzy discontinuities, and suggest local linear regression as a non-parametric IV procedure for estimating treatment effects.

4 It is important to note that when doing analysis using an interrupted time series design, one must adjust for possible correlation between observations. For example, ordinary statistical tests (i.e. t-tests) that compare pre- and post-treatment observations assume that observations are taken from independent and identical distributions. However, this assumption is often not met when analyzing time series data (think about autocorrelation of a student's test score from year to year). Estimating autocorrelation requires a larger number of observations to facilitate correct model identification.

REFERENCES

Agodini, R., & Dynarski, M. (2004). Are experiments the only option? A look at dropout prevention programs. *The Review of Economics and Statistics, 86*(1), 180–194.

Aiken, L. S., West, S. G., Schwalm, D. E., Carroll, J., & Hsuing, S. (1998). Comparison of a randomized and two quasi-experimental designs in a single outcome evaluation: Efficacy of a university-level remedial writing program. *Evaluation Review, 22*(4), 207–244.

Angrist, J., Imbens, G. W., & Rubin, D. B. (1996). Identification of causal effects using instrumental variables. *Journal of the American Statistical Association, 91*, 444–472.

Angrist, J. D., & Lavy, V. (1999). Using Maimonides' rule to estimate the effect of class size on scholastic achievement. *Quarterly Journal of Economics, 144*, 533–576.

Ashenfelter, O. (1978). Estimating the effects of training programs on earnings. *Review of Economics and Statistics, 60*, 47–57.

Black, D., Galdo, J., & Smith, J. C. (2005). Evaluating the regression discontinuity design using experimental data. *Working paper*.

Bloom, H. S., Michalopoulos, C., & Hill, C. J. (2005a). Using experiments to assess nonexperimental comparison-group methods for measuring program effects. In H. S. Bloom (Ed.), *Learning more from social experiments* (pp. 173–235). New York: Russell Sage Foundation.

Bloom, H. S., Michalopoulos, C., Hill, C. J., & Lei, Y. (2002). *Can nonexperimental comparison group methods match the findings from a random assignment evaluation of mandatory welfare-to-work programs?* Washington, DC: Manpower Demonstration Research Corporation.

Bloom, H. S., Richburg-Hayes, L., & Black, A. R. (2005b). *Using covariates to improve precision: Empirical guidance for studies that randomize schools to measure the impacts of educational interventions.* Washington, DC: Manpower Demonstration Research Corporation.

Box, G. E. P., & Jenkins, G. M. (1970). *Time series analysis: Forecasting and control.* San Francisco: Holden-Day.

Buddelmeyer, H., & Skoufias, E. (2003). *An evaluation of the performance of regression discontinuity design on PROGRESA.* Bonn, Germany: IZA.

Campbell, D. T., & Stanley, J. C. (1963). Experimental and quasi-experimental designs for research on teaching. In N. L. Gage (Ed.), *Handbook of research on teaching.* Chicago: Rand McNally.

Cook, T. D. (in press). 'Waiting for life to arrive': A history of the regression-discontinuity design in psychology, statistics and economics. *Journal of Econometrics.*

Cook, T. D., & Campbell, D. T. (1979). *Quasi-experimentation: Design and analysis for field settings.* Chicago, IL: Rand McNally.

Cook, T. D., Shadish, W. R., & Wong, V. C. (2005). Within-study comparisons of experiments and non-experiments: Can they help decide on evaluation policy? *Econometric evaluation of public policies: Methods and applications* Retrieved December 15, 2005, from www.crest.fr/conference/paper/cook.doc

Cook, T. D., & Wong, V. C. (in press). Empirical tests of the validity of the regression-discontinuity design. *Annales d'Economie et de Statistique.*

Corrin, W. J., & Cook, T. D. (1998). Design elements of quasi-experiments. In A. J. Reynolds & H. J. Walberg (Eds.), *Advances in educational productivity* (Vol. 7). Greenwich, CT: JAI Press, Inc.

Fraker, T., & Maynard, R. (1987). The adequacy of comparison group designs for evaluations of employment-related programs. *Journal of Human Resources, 22*(2), 194–227.

Glazerman, S., Levy, D. M., & Myers, D. (2003). Nonexperimental versus experimental estimates of earnings impacts. *The Annals of the American Academy, 589*, 63–93.

Goldberger, A. S. (1972a). *Selection bias in evaluating treatment effects: Some formal illustrations.* Madison, WI: Institute for Research on Poverty.

Goldberger, A. S. (1972b). *Selection bias in evaluating treatment effects: The case of interaction.* Madison, WI: Institute for Research on Poverty.

Hackman, J. R., Pearce, J. L., & Wolfe, J. C. (1978). Effects of changes in job characteristics on work attitudes and behaviors: A naturally occurring quasi-experiment. *Organizational Behavior and Human Performance, 21*, 289–304.

Hahn, J., Todd, P., & Van der Klaauw, W. (2001). Identification and estimation of treatment effects with a regression-discontinuity design. *Econometrica, 69*(1), 201–209.

Institute of Education Sciences (2004). Reading comprehension and reading scale-up research grants request for applications. Washington, DC: Department of Education.

Jacob, B., & Lefgren, L. (2004a). The impact of teacher training on student achievement: Quasi-experimental evidence from school reform efforts in Chicago. *Journal of Human Resources, 39*(1), 50–79.

Jacob, B., & Lefgren, L. (2004b). Remedial education and student achievement: A regression-discontinuity analysis. *Review of Economics and Statistics, LXXXVI*(1), 226–244.

Jacob, B. A., & Lefgren, L. (2002). The impact of teacher training on student achievement: Quasi-experimental evidence from school reform efforts in Chicago. *NBER working paper series #W8916.*

LaLonde, R. (1986). Evaluating the econometric evaluations of training with experimental data. *The American Economic Review, 76*(4), 604–620.

Light, R. J., & Pillemer, D. (1984). *Summing up: The science of reviewing research.* Cambridge, MA: Harvard University Press.

Lipsey, M. W., & Wilson, D. B. (1993). The efficacy of psychological, educational, and behavioral treatment. *American Psychologist, 48*(12), 1181–1209.

McClannahan, L. E., McGee, G. G., MacDuff, G. S., & Krantz, P. S. (1990). Assessing and improving child care: A personal appearance index for children with autism. *Journal of Applied Behavior Analysis, 23*, 469–482.

Michalopoulos, C., Bloom, H. S., & Hill, C. J. (2004). Can propensity-score methods match the findings from a random assignment evaluation of mandatory welfare-to-work programs? *The Review of Economics and Statistics*, 86(1), 156–179.

McKillip, J. (1992). Research without control groups: A control construct design. In F. B. Bryant, J. Edwards, R. S. Tindale, E. J. Posavac, L. Heath & E. Henderson (Eds.), *Methodological issues in applied psychology* (pp. 159–175). New York: Plenum.

Mill, J. S. (1856). *A system of logic: Ratiocinative and inductive.* Honolulu, Hawaii: University Press of the Pacific.

Minton, J. H. (1975). The impact of 'Sesame Street' on reading readiness of kindergarten children. *Sociology of Education, 48*, 141–151.

Seaver, W. B., & Quarton, R. J. (1976). Regression-discontinuity analysis of dean's list effects. *Journal of Educational Psychology, 68*, 459–465.

Shadish, W. R., Clark, M. H., & Steiner, P. M. (2007). Can nonrandomized experiments yield accurate answers? A randomized experiment comparing random to nonrandom assignment.

Shadish, W. R., Luellen, J. K., & Clark, M. H. (2006). Propensity scores and quasi-experiments: A testimony to the practical side of Lee Sechrest. In R. R. Bootzin (Ed.), *Measurement, methods and evaluation*. Washington, DC: American Psychological Association Press.

Smith, J. C., & Todd, P. (2005). Does matching overcome LaLonde's critique of nonexperimental estimators. *Journal of Econometrics, 125*, 305–353.

Staw, B. M., Notz, W. W., & Cook, T. D. (1974). Vulnerability to the draft and attitudes toward troop withdrawal from Indochina: Replication and refinement. *Psychological Reports, 34*, 407–417.

Trochim, W. (1994). *The regression-discontinuity design: An introduction.* Chicago, IL: Thresholds National Research and Training Center on Rehabilitation and Mental Illness.

Trochim, W. M. K. (1984). *Research design for program evaluation.* Beverly Hills, CA: Sage Publications.

Trochim, W. M. K., & Spiegelman, C. (1980). *The relative assignment variable approach to selection bias in pretest-posttest designs.* Alexandria, VA: American Statistical Association.

van der Klaauw, W. (2002). Estimating the effect of financial aid offers on college enrollment: A regression-discontinuity approach. *International Economic Review, 43*(4), 1249–1287.

Wilde, E. T., & Hollister, R. (2007). How close is close enough? Testing nonexperimental estimates of impact against experimental estimates of impact with education test scores as outcomes. *Journal of Policy Analysis and Management, 26*, 455–477.

Wortman, P. M., Reichardt, C. S., & St. Pierre, R. G. (1978). The first year of the education voucher demonstration. *Evaluation Quarterly, 2*, 193–214.

APPENDIX 1: SUGGESTIONS FOR FURTHER READINGS ON TOPICS COVERED IN THIS CHAPTER

Regression discontinuity design

Aiken, L. S., West, S. G., Schwalm, D. E., Carroll, J., & Hsuing, S. (1998). Comparison of a randomized and two quasi-experimental designs in a single outcome evaluation: Efficacy of a university-level remedial writing program. *Evaluation Review, 22*(4), 207–244.

Angrist, J. D., & Lavy, V. (1999). Using Maimonides' rule to estimate the effect of class size on scholastic achievement. *Quarterly Journal of Economics, 144*, 533–576.

Berk, R. A., & de Leeuw, J. (1999). An evaluation of California's inmate classification system using a generalized regression discontinuity design. *Journal of the American Statistical Association, 94*(448), 1045–1052.

Berk, R. A., & Rauma, D. (1983). Capitalizing on nonrandom assignment to treatments: A regression-discontinuity evaluation of a crime-control program. *Journal of the American Statistical Association, 78*(381), 21–27.

Black, D., Galdo, J., & Smith, J. C. (2005). Evaluating the regression discontinuity design using experimental data. *Working paper*.

Buddelmeyer, H., & Skoufias, E. (2003). *An evaluation of the performance of regression discontinuity design on PROGRESA.* Bonn, Germany: IZA.

Cook, T. D. (in press). 'Waiting for life to arrive': A history of the regression-discontinuity design in psychology, statistics and economics. *Journal of Econometrics*.

Goldberger, A. S. (1972a). *Selection bias in evaluating treatment effects: Some formal illustrations.* Madison, WI: Institute for Research on Poverty.

Goldberger, A. S. (1972b). *Selection bias in evaluating treatment effects: The case of interaction.* Madison, WI: Institute for Research on Poverty.

Hahn, J., Todd, P., & Van der Klaauw, W. (2001). Identification and estimation of treatment effects with a regression-discontinuity design. *Econometrica, 69*(1), 201–209.

Jacob, B., & Lefgren, L. (2004a). The impact of teacher training on student achievement: Quasi-experimental evidence from school reform efforts in Chicago. *Journal of Human Resources, 39*(1), 50–79.

Jacob, B., & Lefgren, L. (2004b). Remedial education and student achievement: A regression-discontinuity analysis. *Review of Economics and Statistics, LXXXVI*(1), 226–244.

Ludwig, J., & Miller, D. L. (2005). *Does head start improve children's life chances? Evidence from a regression discontinuity design.* Cambridge, MA: National Bureau of Economic Research.

Seaver, W. B., & Quarton, R. J. (1976). Regression-discontinuity analysis of dean's list effects. *Journal of Educational Psychology, 68*, 459–465.

Spiegelman, C. (1977). A technique for analyzing a pretest-posttest nonrandomized field experiment. *Statistics Report M435.*

Thistlewaite, D. L., & Campbell, D. T. (1960). Regression-discontinuity analysis: An alternative to the ex-post facto experiment. *Journal of Educational Psychology, 51*, 309–317.

Trochim, W. M. K. (1984). *Research design for program evaluation.* Beverly Hills, CA: Sage Publications.

Trochim, W. M. K., & Spiegelman, C. (1980). *The relative assignment variable approach to selection bias in pretest-posttest designs.* Alexandria, VA: American Statistical Association.

van der Klaauw, W. (2002). Estimating the effect of financial aid offers on college enrollment: A regression-discontinuity approach. *International Economic Review, 43*(4), 1249–1287.

Interrupted time series design

Ashenfelter, O. (1978). Estimating the effects of training programs on earnings. *Review of Economics and Statistics, 60*, 47–57.

Bloom, H. S., Michalopoulos, C., & Hill, C. J. (2005). Using experiments to assess nonexperimental comparison-group methods for measuring program effects. In H. S. Bloom (Ed.), *Learning more from social experiments* (pp. 173–235). New York: Russell Sage Foundation.

Bloom, H. S., Michalopoulos, C., Hill, C. J., & Lei, Y. (2002). *Can nonexperimental comparison group methods match the findings from a random assignment evaluation of mandatory welfare-to-work programs?* Washington, DC: Manpower Demonstration Research Corporation.

Braver, M. W. (1991). *The multigroup interrupted time-series design and analysis: An application to career ladder research.* Arizona State University, Phoenix.

McArdle, J. J., & Wang, L. (2006). Modeling age-based turning points in longitudinal life-span growth curves of cognition. In P. Cohen (Ed.), *Turning points research.* Mahwah, NJ: Erlbaum.

McClannahan, L. E., McGee, G. G., MacDuff, G. S., & Krantz, P. S. (1990). Assessing and improving child care: A personal appearance index for children with autism. *Journal of Applied Behavior Analysis, 23*, 469–482.

McKillip, J. (1992). Research without control groups: A control construct design. In F. B. Bryant, J. Edwards, R. S. Tindale, E. J. Posavac, L. Heath & E. Henderson (Eds.), *Methodological issues in applied psychology* (pp. 159–175). New York: Plenum.

Difference-in-differences studies that use propensity score methods

Agodini, R., & Dynarski, M. (2004). Are experiments the only option? A look at dropout prevention programs. *The Review of Economics and Statistics, 86*(1), 180–194.

Dehejia, R., & Wahba, S. (1999). Causal effects in nonexperimental studies: Reevaluating the evaluation of training programs. *Journal of the American Statistical Association, 94*(448), 1053–1062.

Heckman, J., Ichimura, H., & Todd, P. E. (1998). Matching as an econometric evaluation estimator. *Review of Economic Studies, 65*(2), 261–294.

Heckman, J., Imbens, I. H., & Todd, P. E. (1997). Matching as an econometric evaluation estimator: Evidence from evaluating a job training programme. *Review of Economic Studies, 64*, 605–654.

Heckman, J., & Navarro-Lozano, S. (2004). Using matching, instrumental variables, and control functions to estimate economic choice models. *Review of Economics and Statistics, 86*(1), 30–57.

Hirano, K., & Imbens, G. W. (2001). Estimation of causal effects using propensity score weighting: An application to data on right heart catheterization. *Health Services and Outcomes Research Methodology, 2*, 259–278.

Imbens, G. W. (2000). The role of the propensity score in estimating dose-response functions. *Biometrika, 87*(3), 706–710.

Michalopoulos, C., Bloom, H. S., & Hill, C. J. (2004). Can propensity-score methods match the findings from a random assignment evaluation of mandatory welfare-to-work programs? *The Review of Economics and Statistics, 86*(1), 156–179.

Rosenbaum, P. (2002). *Observational Studies*. New York: Springer-Verlag.

Rosenbaum, P., & Rubin, D. B. (1983). The central role of the propensity score in observational studies for causal effects. *Biometrika, 70*(1), 41–55.

Rosenbaum, P., & Rubin, D. B. (1984). Reducing bias in observational studies using subclassification on the propensity score. *Journal of the American Statistical Association, 79*, 516–524.

Rosenbaum, P., & Rubin, D. B. (1985). Constructing a control group using multivariate matched sampling methods that incorporate the propensity score. *The American Statistician, 39*(1), 33–38.

Rubin, D. B. (1977). Assignment to treatment group on the basis of a covariate. *Journal of Educational Statistics, 2*(1), 1–26.

Rubin, D. B., & Thomas, N. (1996). Matching using propensity scores: Relating theory to practice. *Biometrics, 52*, 249–264.

Shadish, W. R., Luellen, J. K., & Clark, M. H. (2006). Propensity scores and quasi-experiments: A testimony to the practical side of Lee Sechrest. In R. R. Bootzin (Ed.), *Measurement, methods and evaluation*. Washington, DC: American Psychological Association Press.

Wilde, E. T., & Hollister, R. (2002). How close is close enough? Testing nonexperimental estimates of impact against experimental estimates of impact with education test scores as outcomes, *Discussion paper no. 1242-02*. Madison, WI: Institute for Research on Poverty.

Zhong, Z. (2004). Using matching to estimate treatment effects: Data requirements, matching metrics, and Monte Carlo evidence. *The Review of Economics and Statistics, 86*(1), 156–179.

Within-study comparison papers

Agodini, R., & Dynarski, M. (2004). Are experiments the only option? A look at dropout prevention programs. *The Review of Economics and Statistics, 86*(1), 180–194.

Aiken, L. S., West, S. G., Schwalm, D. E., Carroll, J., & Hsuing, S. (1998). Comparison of a randomized and two quasi-experimental designs in a single outcome evaluation: Efficacy of a university-level remedial writing program. *Evaluation Review, 22*(4), 207–244.

Bell, S. H., Orr, L. L., Blomquist, J. D., & Cain, G. C. (1995). *Program applicants as a comparison group in evaluating training programs*. Kalamazoo, MI: Upjohn Institute for Employment Research.

Bloom, H. S., Michalopoulos, C., & Hill, C. J. (2005). Using experiments to assess nonexperimental comparison-group methods for measuring program effects. In H. S. Bloom (Ed.), *Learning more from social experiments* (pp. 173–235). New York: Russell Sage Foundation.

Bloom, H. S., Michalopoulos, C., Hill, C. J., & Lei, Y. (2002). *Can nonexperimental comparison group methods match the findings from a random assignment evaluation of mandatory welfare-to-work programs?* Washington, DC: Manpower Demonstration Research Corporation.

Bratberg, E., Grasdal, A., & Risa, A. E. (2002). Evaluating social policy by experimental and nonexperimental methods. *Scandinavian Journal of Economics, 104*(1), 147–171.

Buddelmeyer, H., & Skoufias, E. (2003). *An evaluation of the performance of regression discontinuity design on PROGRESA*. Bonn, Germany: IZA.

Dehejia, R., & Wahba, S. (1999). Causal effects in nonexperimental studies: Reevaluating the evaluation of training programs. *Journal of the American Statistical Association, 94*(448), 1053–1062.

Fraker, T., & Maynard, R. (1987). The adequacy of comparison group designs for evaluations of employment-related programs. *Journal of Human Resources, 22*(2), 194–227.

Friedlander, D., & Robins, P. (1995). Evaluating program evaluations: New evidence on commonly used nonexperimental methods. *American Economic Review, 85*(4), 923–937.

Glazerman, S., Levy, D. M., & Myers, D. (2002). *Nonexperimental replications of social experiments: A systematic review*. Washington, DC: Mathematica Policy Research, Inc.

Glazerman, S., Levy, D. M., & Myers, D. (2003). Nonexperimental versus experimental estimates of earnings impacts. *The Annals of the American Academy, 589*, 63–93.

Greenberg, D. H., Michalopoulos, C., & Robins, P. (2006). Do experimental and nonexperimental evaluations give different answers about the effectiveness of government-funded training programs. *Journal of Public Policy and Management, 25*(3), 523–552.

Gritz, M., & Johnson, T. (2001). *National Job Corps Study: Assessing program effects on earnings for students achieving key program milestones*. Seattle, WA: Battelle Memorial Institute.

Heckman, J. J., Ichimura, H., Smith, J. C., & Todd, P. (1998). Characterizing selection bias. *Econometrica, 66*(5), 1017–1098.

Hotz, V. J., Imbens, G. W., & Klerman, J. (2000). The long-term gains from GAIN: A re-analysis of the impacts of the California GAIN program. *NBER technical working paper #8007.*

Hotz, V. J., Imbens, G. W., & Mortimer, J. H. (1999). Predicting the efficacy of future training programs using past experience. *NBER technical working paper #238.*

LaLonde, R. (1986). Evaluating the econometric evaluations of training with experimental data. *The American Economic Review, 76*(4), 604–620.

Michalopoulos, C., Bloom, H. S., & Hill, C. J. (2004). Can propensity-score methods match the findings from a random assignment evaluation of mandatory welfare-to-work programs? *The Review of Economics and Statistics, 86*(1), 156–179.

Olsen, R., & Decked, P. (2001). *Testing different methods of estimating the impacts of worker profiling and reemployment services systems.* Washington, DC: Mathematica Policy Research, Inc.

Shadish, W. R., Luellen, J. K., & Clark, M. H. (2006). Propensity scores and quasi-experiments: A testimony to the practical side of Lee Sechrest. In R. R. Bootzin (Ed.), *Measurement, methods and evaluation.* Washington, DC: American Psychological Association Press.

Smith, J. C., & Todd, P. (2005). Does matching overcome LaLonde's critique of nonexperimental estimators. *Journal of Econometrics, 125*, 305–353.

Wilde, E. T., & Hollister, R. (2002). How close is close enough? Testing nonexperimental estimates of impact against experimental estimates of impact with education test scores as outcomes, *Discussion paper no. 1242-02.* Madison, WI: Institute for Research on Poverty.

Threats to internal validity

Shadish, W. R., Cook, T. D., & Campbell, D. T. (2002). *Experimental quasi-experimental designs for generalized causal inference.* Boston: Houghton Mifflin Company.

Sample Size Planning with Applications to Multiple Regression: Power and Accuracy for Omnibus and Targeted Effects

Ken Kelley and Scott E. Maxwell

ABSTRACT

When designing a research study, sample size planning is one of the key factors to consider. One aspect of sample size planning is whether the primary goal of the research study is to reject a false null hypothesis, the power analytic approach. Another primary goal may be to obtain a confidence interval that is sufficiently narrow, the accuracy in parameter estimation approach. Some questions of interest may pertain to a collection of parameters (i.e. an omnibus effect), whereas other questions may pertain to only a single parameter (i.e. a targeted effect). The issue of power or accuracy and the issue of an omnibus effect or a targeted effect leads to a two-by-two conceptualization for planning sample size. The power analytic and accuracy in parameter estimation approaches are discussed in the context of multiple regression

for the squared multiple correlation coefficient (an omnibus effect) and for a specific regression coefficient (a targeted effect). A discussion of statistical significance testing and confidence interval construction for the parameters of interest is provided. Whereas the power analytic approach is largely reviewed from existing literature, developments are made for the accuracy in parameter estimation approach.

At the heart of scientific research is the desire for understanding. Even though many methods exist for attempting to gain a better understanding of the phenomenon or phenomena of interest, statistical methods have proven to be the most useful way of extracting information from data. Given that the use of statistical methods is so vital to scientific research, ensuring that the statistical methods chosen provide the information of interest is an important step for scientific progress. Even though science is often laborious and slow, by designing a well-planned study researchers can be in the best position to maximize their chances for success, where the ultimate goal is gaining a better understanding of the phenomenon of interest.

Designing research studies is arguably the most important single phase of research. With a poorly designed study, little or no understanding of the phenomenon of interest may be gained. Given the high economic and professional costs of poorly designed research, motivation of the researcher should clearly be on the side of beginning an investigation with a well-designed study.

Many facets exist to research design and each one deserves attention. At a minimum, the following points must be considered when designing studies in the behavioral, educational, and social sciences:

(a) the question(s) of interest must be determined;
(b) the population of interest must be identified;
(c) a sampling scheme must be devised;
(d) selection of independent and dependent measures must occur;
(e) a decision regarding experimentation versus observation must be made;
(f) statistical methods must be chosen so that the question(s) of interest can be answered in an appropriate and optimal way;
(g) sample size planning must occur so that an appropriate sample size given the particular scenario, as defined by points a through f, can be used;
(h) the duration of the study and number of measurement occasions need to be considered;
(i) the financial cost (and feasibility) of the proposed study calculated.

Sample size planning (Point g) as it relates to the question(s) of interest (Point a) of an investigation is the focus of this chapter. Although sample size planning is an important part of research design, sample size planning cannot occur without some question of interest

first being defined. There are multiple ways to plan sample size for a single study. The way in which sample size is planned depends heavily on the question(s) of interest that the investigator has defined. Thus, not defining the question of interest implies that a method for choosing sample size, and thus the sample size itself, cannot adequately be defined[1].

For example, suppose a researcher wishes to examine the relationship between five regressor variables and a criterion variable in a multiple regression context. However, the process of deciding on an appropriate sample size cannot begin until the question of interest has been clearly defined. There are *at least* four scenarios in which sample size planning can proceed in a multiple regression context:

(a) desired degree of statistical power for the overall fit of the model (i.e. power for the squared multiple correlation coefficient);
(b) desired degree of statistical power for a specific regressor variable (i.e. power for the test of a particular population regression coefficient);
(c) statistical accuracy for the overall fit of the model (i.e. a narrow confidence interval for the population squared multiple correlation coefficient);
(d) statistical accuracy for a specific regressor variable (i.e. a narrow confidence interval for one or more population regression coefficients)[2].

Thus, an appropriate sample size depends very much on the goals of the researcher. Not surprisingly, given the fundamental differences between power and accuracy for omnibus and targeted effects, necessary sample size can be very different in the four scenarios. More general than the multiple regression example, sample size planning can be conceptualized in a two-by-two table, where the effect of interest, either an omnibus or a targeted effect, is on one dimension and the goal, either power or accuracy, is on the other dimension. Such a conceptualization is given in Table 11.1 for sample size planning

Table 11.1 Two-by-two conceptualization of possible scenarios when statistical power is crossed with statistical accuracy

		Effect	
		Omnibus	Targeted
Goal	Power	a	b
	Accuracy	c	d

for points a–d, where the effect is represented by the column dimension and the goal is represented by the row dimension.

Even though Table 11.1 has four cells, none of the cells are mutually exclusive, nor is any specific one necessary. That is to say, a researcher could have the goal of achieving power for the omnibus effect (cell a) and a specific effect (cell b). Likewise, a researcher could have the goal of accuracy for the omnibus effect (cell c) and a specific effect (cell d). A researcher most interested in the omnibus effect could desire both its power (cell a) and its accuracy (cell c). A researcher most interested in a specific effect could desire both power (cell b) and accuracy (cell d). Another possibility is for a researcher to desire a high degree of power for the omnibus effect (cell a) and to desire accuracy for a specific effect (cell d). Conversely, a researcher might desire a high degree of accuracy for the omnibus effect (cell c) and a high degree of power for a specific effect (cell b). Any combination of the cells in the table is possible, and given the goals of the researcher, multiple cells in Table 11.1 might be relevant.

What may not be obvious from Table 11.1 is that the sample size necessary to fulfill one of the scenarios of interest might also be large enough to fulfill one or more other scenario(s). We will discuss methods of planning sample size for each of the scenarios in upcoming sections of the chapter in the context of multiple regression. The next three sections provide overviews and rationales of statistical power,

statistical accuracy, and multiple regression, respectively. The overview sections are followed by methods for planning sample size given the goals of statistical power and statistical accuracy for omnibus and targeted effects, respectively, in the context of multiple regression analysis. The computer program R (R Development Core Team, 2007) is used throughout the article with the MBESS package (Kelley, 2007). R is a comprehensive statistics environment and language with powerful graphics capabilities. MBESS is an add-on package for R that has, among other things, numerous functions for assisting researchers planning an appropriate sample size. Both R and MBESS are Open Source and freely available[3]. The R code used throughout the chapter is distinguished from text by using a non-serif font (such as this). R examples are typeset in a gray box with 'R >' denoting an executable R command as follows:

R > mean (data)

which returns the mean of the values contained in the object 'data.'

We have synthesized a large amount of work done in the sample size planning literature and packaged it in what we hope is a conceptually appealing and readily comprehensible presentation, complete with easy to use computer commands for planning necessary sample size in each of the four scenarios described.

RATIONALE OF STATISTICAL POWER ANALYSIS

Statistical power is a function of four things: (a) the size of the effect; (b) the model error variance; (c) the Type I error rate (α); and (d) sample size (N)[4]. Power is defined as one minus the probability of a Type II error[5]. In most cases the size of the effect, Type I error rate (e.g. $\alpha = 0.01$ or $\alpha = 0.05$), and often the model error variance are considered fixed, leaving only the sample size as a quantity that is in the control of the researcher[6]. Given that power is in part a function of sample size, the sample size can be manipulated so that a desired degree of power is reached. Power has been discussed in numerous book length treatments for many statistical tests (e.g. Kraemer & Thiemann, 1987; Cohen, 1988; Lipsey, 1990; Murphy & Myors, 1998).

The use of null hypothesis significance testing has been under fire for some time (e.g. Nickerson, 2000, for a review; the works contained in Rozeboom, 1960; Bakan, 1966; Morrison & Henkel, 1970; Meehl, 1978; Cohen, 1994; Schmidt, 1996). Even though we sympathize with many of the critiques leveled against the use of null hypothesis significance testing, null hypothesis significance testing has its place in science and there is little question that it will continue to be widely used (e.g. Chow, 1996; Hagen, 1997; Harris, 1997; Wainer, 1999; Mogie, 2004). There are two main reasons why null hypothesis significance tests are valuable in research: they help researchers decide if the population value of some effect differs from a specified quantity (generally zero), and for many tests they allow the researcher to decide the direction of the effect. For some questions of interest, the use of null hypothesis significance tests is not especially helpful. In those situations other techniques can be used.

One common alternative to null hypothesis significance testing is the use of effect sizes and their corresponding confidence intervals (e.g. Schmidt, 1996; Thompson, 2002; Smithson, 2003; Hunter & Schmidt, 2004; Steiger, 2004; Grissom & Kim, 2005). Effect sizes and their corresponding confidence intervals can better address issues involving the magnitude of an effect than can null hypothesis significance tests. However, some research questions do not lend themselves to being framed as an effect where the magnitude is meaningful and of interest. This is especially true with some multiparameter and multivariate hypotheses, as such tests are more difficult to transform into an effect size and corresponding confidence interval that is readily interpretable. For example, multivariate analysis of variance

and covariance have omnibus effect sizes that are generally not easy to interpret. One option is to reduce such multivariate effects into simpler effects (e.g. pairwise, simple main effects, specific effects, etc.) and then report their corresponding effect sizes and confidence intervals. Even though such effects are readily comprehensible, such simplified hypotheses generally fail to consider the complexity and multivariate nature of the original research question, requiring the questions to be addressed with multivariate techniques that may not have readily interpretable effect sizes. We will discuss the benefits of confidence interval formation in the next section, but we acknowledge that confidence intervals are not adequate for addressing all substantively interesting questions. In cases where a research question is best addressed with a null hypothesis significance test, the a priori power of the test should be as important as the obtained probability value.

Even though the conceptual rationale of power analysis is generally well understood, not often discussed are the implications and importance of mapping a power analysis onto the research question(s) of interest. In a given study, there are often numerous statistical hypotheses evaluated. Given a particular sample size and holding everything else constant, each of the potential statistical tests has a population effect size and model error (or simply a standardized effect size which simultaneously considers both) that must be estimated, and an associated level of statistical power. Sample size can thus be determined so that power is at some desired level for one or several tests. If power is set to a value, such as 0.85, it is likely that a different sample size would be necessary for each of the statistical tests of interest. Depending on the exact question of interest (i.e. for which test is the appropriate sample size determined), necessary sample size to achieve some desired goal will generally be different. Thus, before sample size planning from a power analytic approach can proceed, the exact question of interest must be specified (Point a from the designing research list).

When statistical tests are conducted in situations of low power, the literature of an area can become awash with contradictory results (e.g. Sedlmeier & Gigerenzer, 1989; Rossi, 1990; Hunter & Schmidt, 2004; Maxwell, 2004). For example, suppose several researchers each replicate the same previously reported study using multiple regression with several regressor variables. Further suppose that the power was low for each of the several regressors. It is entirely possible that each of the researchers obtained a different set of statistically significant regression coefficients, none of which mirror the previously reported study! By having low power across multiple parameters, there is often a high probability of obtaining statistical significance somewhere (Kelley et al., 2003), but a small probability of replicating the same set of statistically significant regressors (Maxwell, 2000, 2004). Consistency of research findings is thus difficult if power is low for some or all of the effects examined. Without ensuring that an adequate degree of power is achieved, low-powered studies riddled with Type II errors can permeate the literature and scientific growth can falter because of inconsistencies regarding statistically significant effects across multiple studies that examine the same effects (Rosenthal, 1993; Schmidt, 1996; Kraemer et al., 1998; Hunter & Schmidt, 2004, chapter 1).

Many times when a study has important implications, such as those often conducted in the behavioral, educational, social, and medical sciences, ignoring issues of power is irresponsible and potentially even unethical. This is true, for example, when individuals are subjected to an inferior treatment condition in a study with low power. The individuals in such studies are put at risk with little chance of determining whether some treatments are truly superior to others. A more tangible reason for seriously considering power analysis is that grant funding review boards now generally require explicit consideration of design and power in grant proposals in order to receive funding (e.g. Allison et al., 1997; Kraemer et al., 1998). Thus, not only can ignoring power issues lead to a study with little chance of achieving statistical significance for the parameter(s) of interest, it can prevent the study from even being conducted because funding is not secured.

Power analysis is also an important tool for protecting valuable resources. For example, suppose a study was conducted with a sample size of $N = 20$. Further suppose that the statistical test on the parameter of interest did not yield a statistically significant result. Such a result might be disappointing, but such a result might have also been avoided. Suppose that a power analysis (e.g. based on an independent group t-test where the population standardized mean difference is thought to be 0.40 with the Type I error rate set to 0.05) would have revealed that a sample size of 100 would be necessary in order for the power to equal 0.80, the researcher's operational definition of 'adequate power.' Had such a power analysis been conducted by the researcher a priori, the researcher would have had at least three choices: (a) perform the study with $N = 20$ anyway, with the caveat that there would be only a small probability (specifically 0.23 under the anticipated effect size) of achieving statistical significance (i.e. low power); (b) modify the original design so that the sample size was changed to $N = 100$ in order for the researcher to have an adequate degree of power for detecting the effect of interest; or (c) realize that $N = 100$ is not practical given the difficulty of collecting data and conclude that the cost/benefit ratio is not worth conducting the study at the present time. Points b and c are both enlightening from a resource standpoint, because it may become apparent that $N = 20$ is not adequate and thus using a sample size of only 20 may not be a wise use of resources given the low probability of finding statistical significance.

RATIONALE OF ACCURACY IN PARAMETER ESTIMATION

In order for a piece of information to be meaningful, it is generally desirable for that piece of information to be accurate. In the context of parameter estimation, accuracy is defined in terms of the (square) root of the mean square error (RMSE), and is a function of precision and bias. Formally, the accuracy of an estimate $\hat{\theta}$ is defined as

$$
\begin{aligned}
\text{RMSE} &= \sqrt{E\left[\left(\hat{\theta}-\theta\right)^2\right]} \\
&= \sqrt{E\left[\left(\hat{\theta}-E\left[\hat{\theta}\right]\right)^2\right]+\left(E[\hat{\theta}-\theta]\right)^2} \\
&= \sqrt{\sigma_{\hat{\theta}}^2+B_{\hat{\theta}}^2},
\end{aligned}
\tag{1}
$$

where $E[\cdot]$ is the expected value of the quantity in brackets, θ is the parameter of interest with $\hat{\theta}$ as its estimate, $\sigma_{\hat{\theta}}^2$ is the population variance of the estimator $\left(\text{i.e. } E\left[\left(\hat{\theta}-E\left[\hat{\theta}\right]\right)^2\right]\right)$, and $B_{\hat{\theta}}$ is the bias of the estimator $\left(\text{i.e. } E[\hat{\theta}-\theta]\right)$ (Rozeboom, 1966, p. 500). Whereas precision reflects the repeatability of measurements and is thus inversely related to the sample-to-sample variability, bias is the systematic (i.e. average) discrepancy between an estimate and the parameter it estimates. Notice that when the bias equals zero, the estimate is unbiased and accuracy and precision are equivalent concepts[7]. However, precision alone does not imply an accurate estimate[8].

A narrow confidence interval has a tightly clustered set of plausible parameter values that will contain the parameter of interest with the degree of confidence specified. These plausible parameter values are those that *cannot* be rejected as the value of the population parameter. In the long run when the assumptions of the model are satisfied for an exact confidence interval procedure, $(1-\alpha)100\%$ of the confidence intervals formed under the same conditions will contain θ (Hahn & Meeker, 1991, p. 31). Holding the confidence level constant, the narrower the confidence interval width, the more values can be excluded from the plausible set of parameter values. The effect of this is a homing in on the population parameter. Because an appropriately constructed confidence interval will always contain the observed parameter

estimate and will contain the parameter $(1-\alpha)100\%$ of the time, as the width of the interval decreases the expected accuracy of the estimate improves (i.e. the RMSE is reduced).

The effect of increasing sample size potentially has two effects on accuracy. First, the larger the sample size generally the more precision the estimate will have (i.e. its variance decreases as N increases)[9]. For unbiased estimates, improving the precision necessarily improves accuracy. Estimators that are biased will many times become less biased as sample size increases. Indeed, for consistent estimators, regardless of whether the estimator is biased or unbiased, as sample size tends to infinity the probability that the sample estimate differs from the population quantity by any value tends to zero (Stuart et al., 1994, chapter 17). Thus, above and beyond any effect of precision, decreasing bias also improves accuracy. In fact, even for biased estimates, decreasing the confidence interval width can still be desirable. In such a scenario the point estimate itself might be biased but the range of plausible parameter values sufficiently small[10].

Sample size planning is almost always regarded as being synonymous with power analysis. However, as previously discussed, sample size planning can also proceed with the goal of obtaining a sufficiently narrow confidence interval. We call this method of sample size planning *accuracy in parameter estimation* (AIPE; Kelley & Rausch, in press; Kelley et al., 2003; Kelley & Maxwell, 2003; Kelley, 2006), because when the width of the $(1-\alpha)100\%$ confidence interval decreases — implying that there is a smaller range of plausible parameter values at a given confidence level — the expected accuracy of the estimate necessarily increases. Because accuracy can almost never be calculated for a single estimate, due to the fact that it depends on unknown population values, minimizing the confidence interval width to some acceptable value serves as a way to operationally define the expected accuracy of the estimate. Our usage of the term 'accuracy in parameter estimation' is consistent with that used by Neyman in his seminal work on the theory of confidence intervals: 'the accuracy of estimation corresponding to a fixed value of $1-\alpha$ may be measured by the length of the confidence interval' (1937, p. 358, notation changed to reflect current system).

It can be argued that obtaining an estimate that has a narrow confidence interval is more beneficial scientifically than obtaining an estimate that reaches statistical significance. It has even been recommended that statistical significance tests be banned and replaced with point estimates and their corresponding confidence intervals (Schmidt, 1996, p. 116). In many situations, especially in observational research, it is known a priori that the null hypothesis is almost always false (Bakan, 1966; Meehl, 1967; Cohen, 1994; Schmidt, 1996; Harris, 1997), and as such situations reaching statistical significance is simply a function of having a large enough sample size (of course, the direction of some effects is often of interest and importance; see our discussion in the previous section)[11]. However, when an effect is of interest, learning as much as possible about the size of the effect is almost always beneficial, and many times it can be more beneficial than learning only the direction and statistical significance of the parameter. Embracing the AIPE approach to sample size planning will help to facilitate the accumulation of scientific knowledge by yielding more accurate information about the parameter. Indeed, as Rosenthal (1993) discusses, there are really two results of interest: (a) the estimate of the magnitude of the effect; and (b) an indication of the accuracy of the effect 'as in a confidence interval around the estimate' (p. 521). Thus, rather than simply asking if an effect differs from some specified null value, in most cases it seems better to address the size of the effect, realizing that the more accurate the estimate of the effect the more information is learned.

Suppose there is no treatment effect in a two-group situation (i.e. the null hypothesis is true). Assuming its assumptions are met, the t-test will yield a p-value greater than α on $(1-\alpha)100\%$ of occasions. The corresponding confidence interval will, on $(1-\alpha)100\%$ of occasions, have its lower bound less than zero and its upper bound greater than zero (and thus the null value of zero is contained within the interval and cannot be rejected). Further suppose that the confidence interval contains zero, yet is wide relative to the scale of the measurement. Even though the null hypothesis of zero cannot be rejected, a large range of other plausible values (i.e. those values contained in the confidence limits) can also not be rejected. Contrast such a situation with one where zero is contained within the interval and the width of the confidence interval is narrow. In such a situation it is possible to exclude a wide range of values as being plausible (i.e. those not contained within the confidence limits) and thus narrow the range of plausible values.

When one wishes to show support for the null hypothesis (Greenwald, 1975), the accuracy of the obtained estimate as judged by the width of the corresponding confidence interval should be of utmost concern. The 'good enough' principle can be used and a corresponding 'good enough belt' can be formed for the null value, where the limits of the belt would define what constituted a nontrivial effect (Serlin & Lapsley, 1985, 1993). Suppose that not only is the null value contained within the good enough belt, but so too are the confidence limits. This would be a situation where all of the plausible values would be smaller in magnitude than what has been defined as a trivial effect (i.e. the confidence limits are contained within the good enough belt). In such a situation the limits of the $(1-\alpha)100\%$ confidence interval would exclude all effects of any 'meaningful' size. If the parameter is less in magnitude than what is minimally important, then learning this can be very valuable. This information may or may not support the theory of interest, but what is important is that valuable information about the size of the effect, and thus the phenomenon of interest, has been gained. Illuminating the size of the effect is something a null hypothesis test in and of itself cannot do. Furthermore, in order for future researchers to incorporate the study into a meta-analysis, the size of the effect is required (e.g. Hunter & Schmidt, 2004).

OVERVIEW OF MULTIPLE REGRESSION

Let Y_i be an observed score on some criterion variable for the ith individual ($i = 1, \ldots, N$) and X_{ij} be the observed score for the jth regressor variable ($j = 1, \ldots, p$) for the ith individual[12,13]. The general univariate linear model can be written as

$$Y_i = \beta_0 + X_{i1}\beta_1 + X_{i2}\beta_2 + \cdots + X_{ip}\beta_p + \varepsilon_i, \quad (2)$$

where β_0 is the population intercept, β_j is the regression coefficient for the jth regressor, and ε_i is the error in prediction for the ith individual generally assumed to be normally distributed with mean zero and variance σ_ε^2 [14]. The matrix analog of Equation 2 can be written as

$$\mathbf{y} = \beta_0 \mathbf{1} + \mathbf{X}\boldsymbol{\beta} + \boldsymbol{\varepsilon}, \quad (3)$$

where $\mathbf{y}$ is an N length vector of observed criterion variables, β_0 is the intercept, $\mathbf{1}$ is an N length column vector of 1s, $\mathbf{X}$ is an N by p matrix of fixed regressor variables, $\boldsymbol{\beta}$ is a p length vector of regression coefficients, and $\boldsymbol{\varepsilon}$ is an N length vector of errors[15]. The p regression coefficients in the vector $\boldsymbol{\beta}$ can be obtained by manipulation of the normal equations as

$$\boldsymbol{\beta} = \Sigma_{XX}^{-1}\sigma_{XY} = \Sigma_{XX}^{-1}\sigma_{YX}', \quad (4)$$

where Σ_{XX} is the p by p covariance matrix of the regressor variables with a minus one power representing the inverse of the matrix, σ_{XY} is the p length column vector of covariances of the p regressors with Y and σ_{YX} is the p length row vector of covariance of Y with the p regressors ($\sigma_{XY}' = \sigma_{YX}$, where prime denotes transposition). The intercept is defined as

$$\beta_0 = \mu_Y - \mu_X'\boldsymbol{\beta}, \quad (5)$$

where μ_Y is the population mean of Y and μ_X is the p length vector of population means for the regressor variables (see, for example, Graybill, 1976; Darlington, 1990; Pedhazur, 1997; Rancher, 2000; Cohen et al., 2003 for comprehensive coverage of multiple regression and the general linear model).

Throughout the chapter we assume that the regressor variables are fixed, which implies that in theoretical replications of the study the same $\mathbf{X}$ matrix would be obtained. This would be the case, for example, when the $\mathbf{X}$ matrix is literally developed as part of the study design. Theoretical replications of the study would then have the same $\mathbf{X}$ matrix and the only variation would be the values of the criterion variables (and thus the error). When the regressors are random, and thus in theoretical repetitions of the study different $\mathbf{X}$ matrices would be obtained, the discussion that follows would need to be modified to take into consideration the increased randomness of the design (e.g. Sampson, 1974; Gatsonis & Sampson, 1989; Rancher, 2000).

Often of interest in a multiple regression context is the squared multiple correlation coefficient, sometimes termed the coefficient of determination. Recall that the squared multiple correlation coefficient is the proportion of variance in Y that is accounted for by the p regressor variables. The population multiple correlation coefficient, denoted with an uppercase Greek rho, squared, is defined as

$$P_{Y \cdot X}^2 = \frac{\sigma_{YX} \Sigma_{XX}^{-1} \sigma_{XY}}{\sigma_Y^2}, \quad (6)$$

which is equivalent to the population squared product moment correlation coefficient between the observed scores (Y_i) and the predicted scores ($\hat{Y}_i$; i.e. $P_{Y \cdot X}^2 = \rho_{Y\hat{Y}}^2$) [16].

Equations 2–6 have used only population parameters. In practice, of course, only the sample means, variances, and covariances are known. The means and the variance/covariance matrix of the $p + 1$ variables (the outcome variable and the p regressor variables) are estimated with the usual unbiased estimates and substituted into Equations 4–6. The estimate of $\boldsymbol{\beta}$ corresponding to the p

regressor variables, **b**, can be obtained by substituting s_{YX} or s_{XY} and S_{XX} for their population analogs into Equation 4:

$$b = S_{XX}^{-1}s_{XY} = S_{XX}^{-1}s_{YX}'. \tag{7}$$

Likewise, the estimate of β_0 can be obtained by substituting the sample means for the population means and the vector of sample regression coefficients in Equation 5:

$$b_0 = \overline{Y} - \overline{X}'b. \tag{8}$$

The estimate of $P_{Y \cdot X}^2$, $R_{Y \cdot X}^2$, is obtained by substituting the sample estimates of the parameters into Equation 6:

$$R_{Y \cdot X}^2 = \frac{s_{YX}S_{XX}^{-1}s_{XY}}{s_Y^2}. \tag{9}$$

An obtained estimate will almost certainly not equal its population value. What is generally of interest is knowing if the population value differs from some specified null value (generally zero) or determining the plausible values of the parameter (i.e. the values contained within the $(1 - \alpha)100\%$ confidence interval). The next two sections discuss null hypothesis significance testing and confidence interval formation, respectively, first for the squared multiple correlation coefficient and then for regression coefficients. Null hypothesis significance tests and confidence interval formation are briefly discussed for regression parameters in order to form a basis for the methods of sample size planning that will be discussed in later sections of the chapter.

NULL HYPOTHESIS SIGNIFICANCE TESTS FOR REGRESSION PARAMETERS

The idea of a null hypothesis significance test is to infer if values at least as extreme as the observed value are sufficiently unlikely if in fact the population value were equal to the specified null value (usually zero). Of course,

when claiming statistical significance, there is always the possibility of a Type I error, but that is the price of rejecting a population value based on a sample value. The next two subsections discuss the two most common null hypotheses that are tested in the context of multiple regression: the test that $P_{Y \cdot X}^2 = 0$ and the test that $\beta_j = 0$.

The test of the null hypothesis that the squared multiple correlation coefficient equals zero

When $P_{Y \cdot X}^2$ is zero, by implication β is a p-length vector of zeros (i.e. $\beta = 0_p$). Of course, in any particular sample, $R_{Y \cdot X}^2$ will almost certainly be greater than zero. It is a task of the researcher to evaluate if enough evidence exists to reject the idea that $P_{Y \cdot X}^2$ is zero. When the null hypothesis that $P_{Y \cdot X}^2 = 0$ is true, a test statistic can be formed from $R_{Y \cdot X}^2$ that follows a central F-distribution. The statistic that is used to test the null hypothesis for the squared multiple correlation coefficient is

$$F = \frac{R_{Y \cdot X}^2 / p}{(1 - R_{Y \cdot X}^2)/(N - p - 1)}, \tag{10}$$

where the F-value has p and $N - p - 1$ degrees of freedom. Of course, this F-statistic has an associated probability value, and if the obtained p-value is less than the adopted Type I error rate (i.e. the α level), then the null hypothesis can be rejected.

When $P_{Y \cdot X}^2$ is not zero, implying that $\beta \neq 0_p$ (i.e. at least one element of the vector of regression coefficient is non-zero), the distribution of the F-statistic from Equation 10 follows a noncentral F-distribution, whereas the F-statistic when the null hypothesis is true follows a central F-distribution (the central F-distribution is the standard 'F-distribution' discussed in introductory and intermediate level statistics books). Rather than having only two parameters, the numerator and denominator degrees of freedom like the central F-distribution, the noncentral F-distribution also has a noncentrality parameter. The noncentrality parameter indexes the magnitude of the difference between the null and alternative hypotheses. The larger the difference between the null and alternative hypotheses, the larger is the noncentrality parameter.

It can be shown that the noncentrality parameter of the sampling distribution for the F-statistic of Equation 10 is given as

$$\Lambda = f^2 N, \tag{11}$$

where

$$f^2 = \frac{P^2_{Y \cdot \mathbf{X}}}{1 - P^2_{Y \cdot \mathbf{X}}} \tag{12}$$

and where f^2 has an interpretation as the signal-to-noise ratio (Cohen, 1988; Stuart et al., 1999; Rancher, 2000; Smithson, 2001). As can be seen, Λ is a function of $P^2_{Y \cdot \mathbf{X}}$ and N. As either of these quantities becomes larger, so too does Λ. The effect of a larger Λ is that the sampling distribution of the F-statistic in Equation 10 has a larger mean and for fixed sample size values will be more positively skewed. Thus, a larger proportion of the noncentral distribution will be larger than the critical value under the null hypothesis. This idea will become important in the discussion of power and for confidence interval formation.

The test of the null hypothesis that a regression coefficient equals zero

Let $P^2_{Y \cdot \mathbf{X}_{-j}}$ be the population squared multiple correlation coefficient when Y is predicted from $p - 1$ regressor variables with X_j excluded. Researchers are often interested in knowing if a specific regressor variable adds a statistically significant amount to the fit of the model, which translates into a test of $P^2_{Y \cdot \mathbf{X}}$ being larger than $P^2_{Y \cdot \mathbf{X}_{-j}}$. Such a test is equivalent to the test of the regression coefficient for X_j when all of the p variables are included in the model.

One of the ways to test the hypothesis that β_j is non-zero is to conduct a t-test directly on b_j from the full model. A null hypothesis significance test for a regression coefficient,

evaluated against a null value of zero, is based on a t-value with $N - p - 1$ degrees of freedom, and is given as

$$t = \frac{b_j}{s_{b_j}}, \tag{13}$$

where s_{b_j} is given as

$$s_{b_j} = \sqrt{\frac{1 - R^2_{Y \cdot \mathbf{X}}}{\left(1 - R^2_{X_j \cdot \mathbf{X}_{-j}}\right)(N - p - 1)}} \left(\frac{s_Y}{s_{X_j}}\right), \tag{14}$$

with $R^2_{X_j \cdot \mathbf{X}_{-j}}$ being the squared multiple correlation coefficient using the jth regressor as the criterion on the remaining $p - 1$ regressors. $R^2_{X_j \cdot \mathbf{X}_{-j}}$ is also indirectly available from $\mathbf{S}_{XX}$ as

$$R^2_{X_j \cdot \mathbf{X}_{-j}} = 1 - \left(s_j^2 c_{jj}\right)^{-1}, \tag{15}$$

where s_j^2 is the variance for the jth regressor and c_{jj} is the jth diagonal element of $\mathbf{S}_{XX}^{-1}$ (Harris, 2001).

Similar to the situation described previously when the null hypothesis that $P^2 = 0$ is false and the F-statistic of Equation 10 follows a noncentral distribution, so too does the test statistic of Equation 13 when $\beta_j = 0$. It can be shown that when the null hypothesis that $\beta_j = 0$ is false, the t-statistic in Equation 13 has a noncentrality parameter which can be written as

$$\lambda_j = f_j \sqrt{N}, \tag{16}$$

where

$$f_j = \beta_j \sqrt{\frac{1 - P^2_{X_j \cdot \mathbf{X}_{-j}}}{1 - P^2_{Y \cdot \mathbf{X}}}} \left(\frac{\sigma_{X_j}}{\sigma_Y}\right). \tag{17}$$

Because β_j can be written (e.g. Hays, 1994) as

$$\beta_j = \sqrt{\frac{P^2_{Y \cdot \mathbf{X}} - P^2_{Y \cdot \mathbf{X}_{-j}}}{1 - P^2_{X_j \cdot \mathbf{X}_{-j}}}} \left(\frac{\sigma_Y}{\sigma_{X_j}}\right), \tag{18}$$

f_j from Equation 17 can be rewritten as

$$f_j = \sqrt{\frac{P^2_{Y \cdot \mathbf{X}} - P^2_{Y \cdot \mathbf{X}_{-j}}}{1 - P^2_{Y \cdot \mathbf{X}}}}. \tag{19}$$

As mentioned, the test of a specific regression coefficient is equivalent to the test of no change in $P_{Y \cdot \mathbf{X}}^2$ when the jth regressor is removed from the regression equation (i.e. $P_{Y \cdot \mathbf{X}}^2 - P_{Y \cdot \mathbf{X}_{-j}}^2 = 0$). This is in turn equivalent to the test of the squared semi-partial (part) correlation of Y with the jth regressor being zero. Let $P_{Y \cdot (X_j \cdot \mathbf{X}_{-j})}^2$ be the correlation of Y with the independent part of X_j (i.e. the squared semi-partial correlation between Y and X_j). The definition of $P_{Y \cdot (X_j \cdot \mathbf{X}_{-j})}^2$ is given as

$$P_{Y \cdot (X_j \cdot \mathbf{X}_{-j})}^2 = P_{Y \cdot \mathbf{X}}^2 - P_{Y \cdot \mathbf{X}_{-j}}^2. \qquad (20)$$

Similar to the test of $P_{Y \cdot \mathbf{X}}^2$ from Equation 10, the test of $P_{Y \cdot (X_j \cdot \mathbf{X}_{-j})}^2$ can be written as an F-statistic with 1 and $N - p - 1$ degrees of freedom:

$$
F = \frac{\left(R_{Y \cdot \mathbf{X}}^2 - R_{Y \cdot \mathbf{X}_{-j}}^2\right)/(p - (p - 1))}{\left(1 - R_{Y \cdot \mathbf{X}}^2\right)/(N - p - 1)}
$$
$$
= \frac{R_{Y \cdot (X_j \cdot \mathbf{X}_{-j})}^2}{\left(1 - R_{Y \cdot \mathbf{X}}^2\right)/(N - p - 1)}, \qquad (21)
$$

The F-statistic of Equation 21 is the square of the t-statistic in Equation 13. The reason for rewriting the t-statistic for β_j as an F-test for the change in $P_{Y \cdot \mathbf{X}}^2$ when X_j is removed (i.e. $P_{Y \cdot \mathbf{X}}^2 - P_{Y \cdot \mathbf{X}_{-j}}^2$) from the prediction equation is to show the relationship between the omnibus F-statistic of Equation 10 and the targeted F-statistic of Equation 21. This relationship will become important later when discussing power.

It should be noted that the noncentrality parameter of the test of a single regression coefficient is very similar to the noncentrality parameter of the test of all regression coefficients tested simultaneously (i.e. the test of $P_{Y \cdot \mathbf{X}}^2 = 0$). The signal-to-noise ratio for the change in $P_{Y \cdot \mathbf{X}}^2$ when the jth regressor is removed is given as

$$f_{-j}^2 = \frac{P_{Y \cdot \mathbf{X}}^2 - P_{Y \cdot \mathbf{X}_{-j}}^2}{P_{Y \cdot \mathbf{X}}^2}, \qquad (22)$$

implying the noncentrality parameter for the jth regressor is

$$\Lambda_{-j} = f_{-j}^2 N. \qquad (23)$$

It should be kept in mind that all derivations have been for the case where the regressors are considered fixed. This and the previous section laid out the formal distributional theory of $R_{Y \cdot \mathbf{X}}^2$ and b_j. The derivations given in this section allow them to be used in a future section that deals with statistical power for the squared multiple correlation coefficient.

CONFIDENCE INTERVAL FORMATION FOR REGRESSION PARAMETERS

In order to understand how well an observed estimate represents its corresponding parameter, confidence intervals are necessary. Confidence intervals for some effects are simple and involve only the estimate, the standard error of the estimate, and the critical value from the test of the null hypothesis (e.g. the critical t, F, or χ^2 value). However, in certain cases the confidence interval is more complicated and involves the use of noncentral distributions.

Noncentral distributions, as will be discussed in a future section, are important for determining sample size in a power analytic context. These distributions are also important for confidence interval formation for certain effects, especially those that have been standardized or when the sampling distribution of the statistic does not follow a central distribution or a mean-shifted central distribution[17]. Effects that are standardized will *not* generally follow a central distribution, because such effects are not pivotal. Stuart et al. (chapter 23, 1999) provide a technical discussion of pivotal quantities, but in the context of effect sizes, a pivotal quantity is one where the confidence interval is a simple rearrangement of the test statistic (Cumming and Finch, 2001). Effects such as the squared multiple correlation coefficient (e.g. Smithson, 2003), the standardized mean difference (e.g. Steiger &

Fouladi, 1997; Cumming & Finch, 2001; Kelley, 2005), and standardized regression coefficients all require the use of noncentral distributions. The following subsection will discuss methods of forming confidence intervals when noncentral distributions are required.

Forming noncentral confidence intervals: Applications to regression parameters

Confidence intervals based on noncentral distributions are computed in a different manner than typical confidence intervals based on central distributions. Two principles, or their equivalent, are necessary and are described below. The description given here is largely based on Steiger and Fouladi (1997) and Steiger (2004).

The *confidence interval transformation* principle is beneficial for forming a confidence interval on a parameter that is monotonically related to another parameter, when the latter has a tractable method of obtaining the confidence interval whereas the former might not. Let $f(\theta)$ be a monotonic transformation of θ, some parameter of interest, with θ_L and θ_U being the lower and upper $(1 - \alpha)100\%$ ($\alpha = \alpha_L + \alpha_U$; generally $\alpha_L = \alpha_U = \alpha/2$) confidence limits for θ, where α_L and α_U define the lower and upper proportion of the distribution beyond the lower θ_L and upper θ_U, respectively. The $(1 - \alpha)100\%$ confidence limits for $f(\theta)$ are $f(\theta_L)$ and $f(\theta_U)$,

$$prob.[f(\theta_L) \leqslant f(\theta) \leqslant f(\theta_U)] = 1 - (\alpha_L + \alpha_U),$$

where *prob.* represents probability. Thus, for monotonic transformations the confidence interval for the transformed population quantity is obtained by applying the same transformation to the limits of the confidence interval for the population quantity (Steiger & Fouladi, 1997; Steiger, 2004).

The *inversion confidence interval principle* states that if $\hat{\theta}$ is an estimate of θ with a cumulative distribution that depends on some Ψ, the probability of observing an estimate of θ smaller than that obtained is

given as $p(\hat{\theta}|\Psi)$. Calculation of a confidence interval for θ based on the inversion confidence interval principle involves finding θ_L such that $p(\hat{\theta}|\theta_L) = 1 - \alpha_L$ for the lower limit and θ_U such that $p(\hat{\theta}|\theta_U) = \alpha_U$ for the upper limit. The confidence interval for θ has coverage of $1 - (\alpha_L + \alpha_U)$ and is given as

$$prob.[\theta_L \leqslant \theta \leqslant \theta_U] = 1 - (\alpha_L + \alpha_U).$$

The confidence interval is general and need not have equal rejection regions. For example, a one-sided confidence interval is obtained by setting α_L or α_U (whichever is appropriate for the specific situation) to zero (Steiger & Fouladi, 1997; Steiger, 2004).

The real benefit from the confidence interval transformation and inversion confidence interval principles, is that when the two principles are combined, confidence intervals for quantities that are not pivotal can be determined. In the context of effect sizes, Cumming & Finch (2001) describe pivotal quantities to be those that are of the form

$$\frac{\hat{\theta} - \theta^*}{s_{\hat{\theta}}},$$

where $\hat{\theta}$ is the estimate of the population quantity θ, θ^* is the null value of interest (usually zero), and $s_{\hat{\theta}}$ is the standard deviation of the sampling distribution of $\hat{\theta}$ (i.e. its standard error). What can be done in order to form confidence intervals for non-pivotal quantities is to use the inversion confidence interval principle to find a confidence interval for some noncentrality value (i.e. what values of the noncentrality parameter lead to the observed noncentrality parameter being the $1 - \alpha/2$ and $\alpha/2$ quantiles?). When these values are found, the noncentrality parameters (i.e. the confidence bounds of the noncentral value) are transformed into the statistic of interest, which then yields a $(1 - \alpha)100\%$ confidence interval for the parameter of interest. Stated another way, confidence intervals for non-pivotal quantities are found by determining the values of the noncentrality parameter that would lead to the observed noncentral value having probability $1 - \alpha/2$ and $\alpha/2$ for the lower and upper confidence limits, respectively. The values of the noncentrality parameter that would lead to the observed values occurring with the specified probabilities are then transformed into the quantity of interest. The resultant limits form the $(1 - \alpha)100\%$ confidence interval for the population quantity of interest. Although true for confidence intervals based on central distributions when $\alpha_L = \alpha_U$, there is no requirement that the lower confidence interval width, $\hat{\theta} - \theta_L$, will equal the upper confidence interval width, $\theta_U - \hat{\theta}$ for confidence intervals based on noncentral distributions. Throughout the chapter, 'width' refers to the full confidence interval width, $\theta_U - \theta_L$.

Confidence interval for the squared multiple correlation coefficient

The squared multiple correlation coefficient is one of the most widely used statistics. $R^2_{Y \cdot X}$ is almost always reported in the context of multiple regression, but in its various forms $R^2_{Y \cdot X}$ can be used to describe the proportion of variance accounted for in a wide variety of situations (e.g. between subjects analysis of variance and covariance designs; as a measure of cross validation; as an index of comparison in meta-analyses, etc.). As Steiger states, 'confidence intervals for the squared multiple correlation are very informative yet are not discussed in standard texts, because a single simple formula for the direct calculation of such an interval cannot be obtained in a manner that is analogous to the way one obtains a confidence interval for the population mean' (2004, p. 167). However, confidence intervals for the population squared multiple correlation coefficient are available with certain software (e.g. R2, an MS-DOS program written by Steiger and Fouladi, 1992; MultipleR2, a Mathematica package written by Mendoza and Stafford, 2001; MBESS, an R package written by Kelley (2007); and indirectly with SAS and SPSS, Smithson, 2003). Difficulties arise when forming a confidence interval for $P^2_{Y \cdot X}$ because when

$P^2_{Y \cdot X} \neq 0$, the test statistic given in Equation 10 follows a noncentral F-distribution with noncentrality parameter Λ, as given in Equation 11. In accord with the inversion confidence interval principle, $R^2_{Y \cdot X}$ must be converted into the estimated noncentrality parameter and then noncentral parameters must be found such that

$$p(\hat{\Lambda}|\Lambda_L) = 1 - \alpha/2 \qquad (24)$$

and

$$p(\hat{\Lambda}|\Lambda_U) = \alpha/2, \qquad (25)$$

where $\hat{\Lambda}$ is the observed noncentrality parameter, Λ_L and Λ_U are the noncentral values that have at their $1-\alpha/2$ and $\alpha/2$ quantiles $\hat{\Lambda}$ and are thus the lower and upper confidence limits, respectively (e.g. Mendoza and Stafford, 2001; Smithson, 2003; Steiger 2004).

The MBESS R package includes a function, ci.R2(), for confidence interval formation for $P^2_{Y \cdot X}$, for fixed (or random) regressor variables. Although other options can be specified, a straightforward call to the ci.R2() function for fixed regressor variables would be of the form

> R > ci.R2(R2 = $R^2_{Y \cdot X}$, N = N, p = p,
>
> conf.level = $1 - \alpha$,
>
> Random.Regressors = FALSE)

where $R^2_{Y \cdot X}$, N, p, and $1-\alpha$ are defined in the function in the same way as they have been defined previously and **Random. Regressors** identifies if the regressors are random **(TRUE)** or fixed **(FALSE)**. For example, suppose a researcher conducts a study with five regressor variables on 145 individuals and obtains a multiple correlation of $R^2_{Y \cdot X} = 0.7854$[18]. The ci.R2() function for 95% confidence interval coverage could be specified as

> R > ci.R2(R2 = 0.7854, N = 145,
>
> p = 5, conf.level = 0.95,
>
> Random.Regressors = FALSE)

which yields a confidence interval of $CI_{0.95} = [0.7165 \leqslant P^2_{Y \cdot X} \leqslant 0.8206]$, where $CI_{0.95}$ represents a 95% confidence interval with the limits given in the brackets for the parameter on interest. Thus, we can be 95% confident that the population squared multiple correlation coefficient in this situation is somewhere between 0.7165 and 0.8206.

Confidence interval for a regression coefficient

Before forming a confidence interval for a regression coefficient, the distinction has to be made whether or not the regression coefficient will be standardized. An unstandardized regression coefficient is a pivotal quantity, whereas a standardized regression coefficient is a non-pivotal quantity (in an analogous fashion as the difference between two group means is pivotal but the standardized difference between two group means is nonpivotal). Thus, a confidence interval for an unstandardized regression coefficient requires only a critical value from a central distribution whereas a standardized regression coefficient requires the critical values to be obtained from a noncentral distribution (analogous to forming a confidence interval for $P^2_{Y \cdot X}$). The following two sections discuss confidence intervals for unstandardized and standardized regression coefficients.

Confidence intervals for an unstandardized regression coefficient

The t-test for the unstandardized regression coefficient, Equation 11, is a pivotal quantity implying that the test statistic can be manipulated into a confidence interval. The confidence interval for the unstandardized regression coefficient is thus given as

$$prob.[b_j - t_{(1-\alpha/2; N-p-1)}s_{b_j} \leqslant \beta_j$$
$$\leqslant b_j + t_{(1-\alpha/2; N-p-1)}s_{b_j}] = 1 - \alpha. \quad (26)$$

The confidence interval given above is the confidence interval given in standard textbooks that discuss multiple regression.

The MBESS R package includes a function, ci.reg.coef(), for confidence interval formation for β_j. A confidence interval for an unstandardized regression coefficient can be obtained by specifying the standard deviations of the variables (with the arguments s.Y and s.X) and specifying Noncentral = FALSE. In the situation described for the unstandardized regression coefficients ($b_j = 4.4245$), where $s_Y = 150.0734$ and $s_{X_j} = 9.3605$, the ci.reg.coef() function could be specified as

```
R > ci.reg.coef( b.j = 4.4245,

    R2. Y_X = 0.7854,

    R2.j_X.without.j = 0.3607, N = 145, p = 5,

    s.Y = 150.0734, s.X = 9.3605,

    conf.level = 0.95, Noncentral = FALSE)
```

which yields a confidence interval of $CI_{0.95} = [2.8667 \leqslant \beta_j \leqslant 5.9823]$, where b.j is the unstandardized regression coefficient for the jth regressor variable, R2.Y_X is the squared multiple correlation coefficient, R2.j_X.without.j is the squared multiple correlation coefficient when the jth regressor variables are predicted from the remaining $p - 1$ regressor variables, conf.level is the confidence level specified (i.e. $1 - \alpha$), and Noncentral is an indicator of whether or not the noncentral method should be used (FALSE for unstandardized and TRUE for standardized regression coefficients).

Confidence intervals for a standardized regression coefficient

When a regression coefficient is standardized, the unstandardized regression coefficient is multiplied by the quantity $\frac{s_{X_j}}{s_Y}$ in order to remove the scale of X_j and Y. Such a quantity is no longer pivotal because of the process of standardization, implying that the confidence interval necessarily depends on a noncentral t-distribution. The difficulties that arise when forming a confidence interval for $_s\beta_j$, the population standardized regression coefficient for the jth regressor, arise because

b_j is multiplied by $\frac{s_{X_j}}{s_Y}$ (in order to obtain $_sb_j$, the sample standardized regression coefficient for variable j). The distribution of $_sb_j$ is not pivotal and it is necessary to form confidence intervals based on noncentral t-distributions. In accord with the inversion confidence interval principle, $_sb_j$ must be converted into the observed noncentrality parameter (via, Equation 13), and then the noncentral parameters must be found such that

$$p(\hat{\lambda}|\lambda_L) = 1 - \alpha/2 \qquad (27)$$

and

$$p(\hat{\lambda}|\lambda_U) = \alpha/2, \qquad (28)$$

where λ_L and λ_U are the lower and upper confidence limits for $_s\beta_j$ and are noncentrality parameters from t-distributions.

The MBESS R package includes a function, **ci.reg.coef()**, for confidence interval formation for $_s\beta_j$, technically assuming fixed regressor variables. Although other options can be specified, a straightforward call to the **ci.reg.coef()** function would be of the form

R > ci.reg.coef (b.j = $_sb_j$, R2.Y_X = $R^2_{Y \cdot \mathbf{X}}$,

R2.j_X.without.j = $R^2_{X_j \cdot \mathbf{X}_{-j}}$, N = N, p = p,

conf.level = $1 - \alpha$, Noncentral = TRUE).

For example, in the previous example where $N = 145$ and $R^2_{Y \cdot \mathbf{X}} = 0.7854$, suppose that $_sb_j = 0.2760$ and $R^2_{X_j \cdot \mathbf{X}_{-j}} = 0.3607$. The **ci.reg.coef()** function for 95% confidence interval coverage could be specified as

R > ci.reg.coef(b.j = 0.2760,

R2.Y_X = 0.7854,

R2.j_X.without.j = 0.3607, N = 145, p = 5,

conf.level = 0.95, Noncentral = TRUE)

which yields a confidence interval of $CI_{0.95} = [0.1739 \leqslant {}_s\beta_j \leqslant 0.3771]$. Notice the asymmetry between the confidence limits and the estimate for the standardized regression coefficient, whereas it was symmetric for the unstandardized regression coefficient. This asymmetric property about the point estimate generally holds for confidence intervals based on noncentral distributions.

SAMPLE SIZE PLANNING FOR MULTIPLE REGRESSION GIVEN THE GOAL OF STATISTICAL POWER

This section discusses methods to plan sample size for statistical power in multiple regression. We begin with an overview of sample size planning for a desired power for the omnibus effect (i.e. $P^2_{Y \cdot \mathbf{X}}$) and then provide an overview of sample size planning for a desired power for a targeted effect (i.e. β_j or $_s\beta_j$).

Power for omnibus effects in multiple regression: Obtaining statistical significance for the squared multiple correlation coefficient

When interest concerns the omnibus effect of the model, recall that the noncentrality parameter was previously shown (Equations 11–12) to equal

$$\Lambda = \left(\frac{P^2_{Y \cdot \mathbf{X}}}{1 - P^2_{Y \cdot \mathbf{X}}}\right) N. \qquad (29)$$

This implies that sample size is given as

$$N = \Lambda \left(\frac{1 - P^2_{Y \cdot \mathbf{X}}}{P^2_{Y \cdot \mathbf{X}}}\right). \qquad (30)$$

Thus, given $P^2_{Y \cdot \mathbf{X}}$ and Λ, sample size can be determined. Once $P^2_{Y \cdot \mathbf{X}}$ is specified, Λ is the only unknown parameter since N is unknown. If the Λ that satisfies a desired degree of power can be determined, then the equation can be solved for necessary sample size.

Power is based on Λ and the degrees of freedom, which are in turn based on N. Even though, N is unknown, it is the value of interest when planning a study with a desired degree of power. The way to plan an appropriate sample size is to use different values of N to update Λ and the degrees of freedom until the desired level of power is achieved for the test that $P^2_{Y \cdot \mathbf{X}} = 0$. This process of using different values of N, which occurs essentially by systematic trial and error, can be implemented using tabled values (e.g. Kraemer & Thiemann, 1987; Cohen, 1988; Murphy & Myors, 1998; Lipsey, 1990) or with a noncentral F computer routine (see also Gatsonis & Sampson, 1989; Green, 1991; Dunlap et al., 2004). The general idea of the power analysis procedure is to determine the sample size so that the proportion of the alternative distribution beyond the critical value under the null distribution is at or greater than the desired degree of power.

The **ss.power.R2()** function from MBESS can be used to determine sample size for the omnibus effect of the regression model $\left(\text{i.e., } P_{Y \cdot \mathbf{X}}^2\right)$. For example, suppose a researcher wishes to determine necessary sample size when it is believed $P_{Y \cdot \mathbf{X}}^2 = 0.25$ for the test of the null hypothesis that the squared multiple correlation coefficient is zero in order to have power of 0.80 when the Type I error rate is specified at $\alpha = 0.05$. The basic way in which the **ss.power.R2()** function from MBESS would be used is as follows:

R > ss.power.R2(Population.R2 = 0.25,

   alpha.level = 0.05,

   desired.power = 0.80, p = 5)

where **Population.R2** is the (hypothesized) value of $P_{Y \cdot \mathbf{X}}^2$, **alpha.level** is the Type I error rate, **desired.power** is the desired degree of power, and p is the number of regressor variables. Applying this function to the example yields a necessary sample size of 45.

Power for targeted effects in multiple regression: Obtaining statistical significance for a regression coefficient of interest

When the effect of interest concerns a single regression coefficient, the noncentrality parameter from the noncentral t-distribution

was previously shown (Equations 16–19) to equal

$$
\begin{aligned}
\lambda_j &= \beta_j \sqrt{\frac{1 - P_{X_j \cdot \mathbf{X}_{-j}}^2}{1 - P_{Y \cdot \mathbf{X}}^2}} \left(\frac{\sigma_{X_j}}{\sigma_Y}\right) \sqrt{N} \\
&= \sqrt{\frac{P_{Y \cdot \mathbf{X}}^2 - P_{Y \cdot \mathbf{X}_{-j}}^2}{1 - P_{Y \cdot \mathbf{X}}^2}} \sqrt{N}.
\end{aligned}
\tag{31}
$$

This implies that sample size is given as

$$
\begin{aligned}
N &= \left(\frac{\lambda_j}{\beta_j}\right)^2 \left(\frac{1 - P_{Y \cdot \mathbf{X}}^2}{1 - P_{X_j \cdot \mathbf{X}_{-j}}^2}\right) \left(\frac{\sigma_Y^2}{\sigma_{X_j}^2}\right) \\
&= \lambda_j^2 \left(\frac{1 - P_{Y \cdot \mathbf{X}}^2}{P_{Y \cdot \mathbf{X}}^2 - P_{Y \cdot \mathbf{X}_{-j}}^2}\right).
\end{aligned}
\tag{32}
$$

Thus, given the population parameters and λ_j, sample size can be determined. However, in order to plan an appropriate sample size, once the population parameters and the desired degree of certainty are specified, λ_j is the only unknown parameter because N is unknown. If the λ_j that satisfies a desired degree of power can be determined, then the equation can be solved for necessary sample size.

Power is based on λ_j and the degrees of freedom, which in turn are based on N. Different values of N can be used to update λ_j and the degrees of freedom until the desired level of power is achieved for the test that $\beta_j = 0$. As before, this process can be implemented with tabled values (e.g. Kraemer & Thiemann, 1987; Cohen, 1988; Lipsey, 1990; Murphy & Myors, 1998; see also Maxwell, 2000 for a comprehensive review) or with a noncentral t (or F) computer routine.

The **ss.power.reg.coef()** function from MBESS can be used to determine sample size for a targeted regression coefficient. For example, suppose a researcher believes that $P_{Y \cdot \mathbf{X}}^2 = 0.40$ and when the regressor of interest is removed $P_{Y \cdot \mathbf{X}_{-j}}^2 = 0.30$. Thus, the regressor of interest uniquely explains 0.10 of the proportion of variance in the criterion variable. Although several possibilities exist, the basic way that the **ss.power.reg.coef()**

function from MBESS can be specified is as follows:

R > ss.power.reg.coef(Rho2.Y_X = 0.40,
    Rho2.Y_X.without.j = 0.30, p = 5,
    desired.power = 0.80, alpha.level = 0.05)

where Rho2.Y_X is the population squared multiple correlation coefficient predicting Y from **X** and Rho2.Y_X.without.j is the population squared multiple correlation coefficient predicting Y from $\mathbf{X}_{-j}$. The necessary sample size in this example is 50.

SAMPLE SIZE PLANNING FOR MULTIPLE REGRESSION GIVEN THE GOAL OF STATISTICAL ACCURACY

AIPE for the omnibus effect in multiple regression: Obtaining a narrow confidence interval for the population squared multiple correlation coefficient

The way in which sample size can be determined in order for the expected width of the confidence interval for $P^2_{Y \cdot \mathbf{X}}$ to be sufficiently narrow is quite involved. The method is computationally tedious and can only be carried out with the use of an iterative computer routine that uses noncentral F-distributions. As elsewhere in the chapter, we have restricted the discussion to regressors that are fixed. The case of random regressors is fully developed in Kelley (2006)[19]. It should be noted that two methods are discussed. The first method discussed provides necessary sample size for the expected confidence interval width. The confidence interval width is a random variable that will vary from sample to sample. A modified approach will also be discussed so that the width will be sufficiently narrow with no less than some specified degree of certainty.

The values that must be specified in order to determine the necessary sample size given an expected confidence interval width that is sufficiently narrow are $P^2_{Y \cdot \mathbf{X}}$, p, and α.

The idea is to first use $P^2_{Y \cdot \mathbf{X}}$, p, and α in order to determine the width of the confidence interval given some minimal sample size. If the width is larger than desired, the current estimate of N is incremented by 1 and then the expected width is determined again. This iterative process continues until the sample size is just large enough so that the expected confidence interval width is sufficiently narrow. Two caveats with such an approach arise: $R^2_{Y \cdot \mathbf{X}}$ is a positively biased estimate of $P^2_{Y \cdot \mathbf{X}}$ and the sample size calculated is only for the expected width.

Even though $R^2_{Y \cdot \mathbf{X}}$ is the sample estimate of $P^2_{Y \cdot \mathbf{X}}$, $R^2_{Y \cdot \mathbf{X}}$ is positively biased. However, the confidence limits for $P^2_{Y \cdot \mathbf{X}}$, and thus its width, are based on $R^2_{Y \cdot \mathbf{X}}$. Even though the bias of $R^2_{Y \cdot \mathbf{X}}$ decreases as N increases, holding everything else constant, basing the necessary sample size on $P^2_{Y \cdot \mathbf{X}}$ directly would lead to inappropriate estimates of necessary sample size because the width of the computed confidence interval in part depends on $R^2_{Y \cdot \mathbf{X}}$. The way in which this complication is overcome is by using the expected value of $R^2_{Y \cdot \mathbf{X}}$ in place of $P^2_{Y \cdot \mathbf{X}}$. The expected value of $R^2_{Y \cdot \mathbf{X}}$ given P^2_Y, N, and p when regressors are fixed does not have a known derivation. However, the expected value of $R^2_{Y \cdot \mathbf{X}}$ given $P^2_{Y \cdot \mathbf{X}}$, N, and p when regressors are random is known and is used as an approximation to the case where predictors are fixed, which is given as

$$
\begin{aligned}
\mathrm{E}&\left[R^2_{Y \cdot \mathbf{X}} | (P^2_{Y \cdot \mathbf{X}}, N, p) \right] \\
&= 1 - \frac{N - p - 1}{N - 1} \left(1 - P^2_{Y \cdot \mathbf{X}} \right) \\
&\quad \times \mathrm{H}\left[1; 1; \frac{N+1}{2}; P^2_{Y \cdot \mathbf{X}} \right],
\end{aligned} \tag{33}
$$

where H is the hypergeometric function (Stuart et al., 1999, section 28.32; Johnson et al., 1995).

The sample size procedure is based on the expected value of $R^2_{Y \cdot \mathbf{X}}$ because it is the value expected to be obtained in the study. For a given α, p, and N, the confidence interval width depends only on $R^2_{Y \cdot \mathbf{X}}$. Thus, the expected confidence interval width can be determined by forming a confidence interval with the expected $R^2_{Y \cdot \mathbf{X}}$. The expected confidence interval width can be made sufficiently narrow by increasing sample size, implying that the expected value of $R^2_{Y \cdot \mathbf{X}}$ changes, until the expected confidence interval width is equal to or just narrower than the desired width. Once the sample size is found so that the expected confidence interval width is sufficiently narrow, using the sample size in a study will ensure that the expected width of the confidence interval will be sufficiently narrow.

For example, suppose a researcher wishes to determine necessary sample size so that the expected width of a 95% confidence interval for $P^2_{Y \cdot \mathbf{X}}$ is 0.20 for 5 regressor variables in a situation where $P^2_{Y \cdot \mathbf{X}} = 0.5$. The ss.aipe.R2() function from MBESS would be used as

```
R > ss.aipe.R2(Population.R2 = 0.50,

    conf.level = 0.95, width = 0.20, p = 5,

    Random.Regressors=FALSE),
```

which returns a necessary sample size of 152. Thus, using a sample size of 152 would provide an expected width for the confidence interval of 0.20.

Since the width of the confidence interval is a random variable, having a sample size such that the expected width is sufficiently narrow does not ensure that any particular sample will have a confidence interval that is sufficiently narrow (e.g. see Hahn & Meeker, 1991, or Kupper & Hafner, 1989, for a discussion of these issues in simpler situations). What can be done is to specify some desired degree of certainty that the obtained confidence interval will in fact be sufficiently narrow. The way in which this additional step proceeds is by using the sample size obtained from the previously discussed procedure and from two $\gamma 100\%$ one-sided confidence intervals for $P^2_{Y \cdot \mathbf{X}}$, where γ is the desired degree of certainty that the obtained interval will be sufficiently narrow. The limits from the $\gamma 100\%$ confidence intervals are then used to plan an appropriate sample size as

before, but now using the confidence limits in place of $P^2_{Y \cdot \mathbf{X}}$ from the first procedure. The rationale of this approach is to base the sample size procedure on the largest and smallest plausible value for the obtained $R^2_{Y \cdot \mathbf{X}}$ based on the original sample size and the degree of certainty specified.

The reason the upper and lower confidence limits are used is because, unlike many effects where the larger the noncentrality parameter the wider the confidence interval (holding everything else constant), there is a nonmonotonic relationship between $R^2_{Y \cdot \mathbf{X}}$ and the confidence interval width. Depending on the particular situation, a larger sample size may be necessitated by the lower limit or the upper limit from the two $\gamma 100\%$ one-sided confidence limits (or a value in between). The relationship between $R^2_{Y \cdot \mathbf{X}}$ and the corresponding confidence interval width is illustrated in Figure 11.1 for 95% confidence intervals where $p = 5$ and $N = 100$. The lack of monotonicity between the size of $R^2_{Y \cdot \mathbf{X}}$ and the confidence interval width implies that, depending on the particular situation, the upper limit, the lower limit, or values in-between the two one-sided $\gamma 100\%$ confidence interval limits will yield wider confidence intervals for $P^2_{Y \cdot \mathbf{X}}$. Even though Figure 11.1 is helpful to illustrate why upper and lower limits are required, recall that the procedure always uses the expected value of $R^2_{Y \cdot \mathbf{X}}$. Thus, an analog to the figure presented, and what is actually used in the procedure, is one where the values on the ordinate are a function of basing confidence interval width on the expected values of $R^2_{Y \cdot \mathbf{X}}$ for corresponding values of $P^2_{Y \cdot \mathbf{X}}$.

Two issues arise when basing the sample size procedure on limits from the $\gamma 100\%$ one-sided confidence intervals. First, it is possible that the point estimate itself requires a larger sample size than either of the confidence limits (e.g. suppose the corresponding point estimate is 0.35 from the figure). Second, the maximum confidence interval width could be between the limits (e.g. suppose the corresponding confidence limits are 0.2 and 0.6 from the figure). To ensure that an appropriate sample size is determined, an

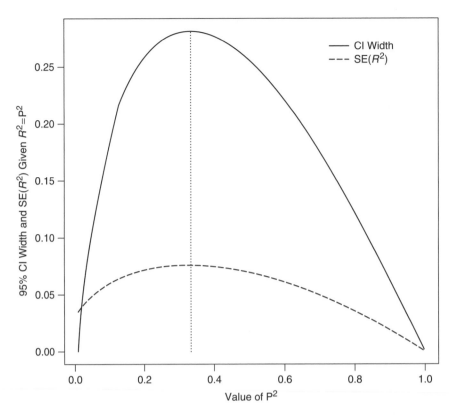

Figure 11.1   Relationship between the observed width of the 95% confidence interval for the population squared multiple correlation coefficient ($P^2_{Y \cdot X}$) as a function of the observed squared multiple correlation coefficient ($R^2_{Y \cdot X}$) when the total sample size is 100 and there are five regressors

optimization routine is used to determine if there is a value within the confidence limits that leads to a wider confidence interval than either of the limits. If not, the larger of the two sample sizes is used. If so, if the value that leads to the widest confidence interval is the value on which the original sample size is based, then the original sample size is used. If it is some other value between the confidence limits, then the $R^2_{Y \cdot X}$ value that occurs with probability $(1 - \gamma)/2$ less than the value leading to the maximum confidence width and the value that occurs with probability $(1 - \gamma)/2$ more than the maximum confidence width are used. The probabilities are determined from the appropriate noncentral F-distributions. Of the contending sample sizes, the largest one is used. Doing so ensures that no less than

$\gamma 100\%$ of the confidence intervals widths will be sufficiently narrow (Kelley, 2006, provides more detail on the procedure in the case of random regressors). It is important to remember that at every stage, the expected value of $R^2_{Y \cdot X}$ is used based on the particular population value. Depending on the particular situation, incorporating a degree of certainty parameter can yield only a small or a large increase in necessary sample size.

The method discussed in order to obtain a narrow confidence interval with some degree of certainty can be readily implemented with the **ss.aipe.R2()** function. Realizing that having only an expected width of 0.20 is not sufficient, further suppose that the researcher incorporates a 99% degree of certainty that the obtained confidence interval will be no wider than 0.20 units. The way in which the ss.aipe.R2() function is used in order to ensure a desired degree of certainty of 0.99 is given as follows:

R > ss.aipe.R2(Population.R2 = 0.50,
    conf.level = 0.95, width = 0.20, p = 5,
    degree.of.certainty = 0.99,
    Random.Regressors = FALSE),

which yields a necessary sample size of 189.

AIPE for targeted effects in multiple regression: Obtaining a narrow confidence interval for the population regression coefficient

Recall that when regression coefficients are unstandardized, the way in which confidence intervals are obtained is based on the central t-distribution. However, confidence intervals based on standardized regression coefficients require the use of noncentral distributions (since $_s b_j$ is not a pivotal quantity). Thus, the appropriate procedures are different for the two scenarios. The first procedure discussed will be for unstandardized regression coefficients followed by a procedure for standardized regression coefficients.

AIPE for unstandardized regression coefficients

Kelley and Maxwell (2003) discussed AIPE for a targeted regression coefficient. We will base the present discussion largely on an updated account of that work in the context of unstandardized regression coefficients. Recall from Equation 26 that the confidence interval for β_j is straightforward to calculate given b_j, s_{b_j} (which is a function of $N, p, R^2_{Y \cdot \mathbf{X}}, R^2_{X_j \cdot \mathbf{X}_{-j}}$), N, p, and α. The population variance for the jth regression coefficient is given as

$$\sigma^2_{b_j} = \left(\frac{\left(1 - P^2_{Y \cdot \mathbf{X}}\right)}{\left(1 - P^2_{X_j \cdot \mathbf{X}_{-j}}\right)/(N - p - 1)} \right) \left(\frac{\sigma^2_Y}{\sigma^2_{X_j}} \right). \tag{34}$$

Given $\sigma^2_{b_j}$, the sample size can be solved for, yielding the necessary sample size in

order for the expected width to be sufficiently narrow:

$$N = \left(\frac{t_{(1-\alpha/2; N-p-1)}}{\omega/2} \right)^2 \left(\frac{1 - P^2_{Y \cdot \mathbf{X}}}{1 - P^2_{X_j \cdot \mathbf{X}_{-j}}} \right) \times \left(\frac{\sigma^2_Y}{\sigma^2_{X_j}} \right) + p + 1, \tag{35}$$

where ω is the desired full width of the confidence interval. A complication is that the desired N is implicitly involved on the right side of the equation since the degrees of freedom of the t-value depend on N. It is thus necessary to solve Equation 35 iteratively.

Because the confidence interval width is itself a random variable, obtained values of $s^2_{b_j}$ larger than the population value used in the calculation of N will lead to confidence intervals wider than desired. In order to avoid obtaining a confidence interval wider than desired, the $\gamma 100\%$ confidence limit for the standard error can be used in place of the population standard error when solving for N. The $\gamma 100\%$ upper confidence limit for the population standard error of the jth regression coefficient, based on a chi-square distribution with $N - p - 1$ degrees of freedom, can then be substituted for the population variance from Equation 34. Doing so will ensure that the obtained confidence interval will be sufficiently narrow no less than $\gamma 100\%$ of the time. Since the only way for a confidence interval to be wider than desired is to obtain a standard error larger than the population standard error, using the upper $\gamma 100\%$ confidence limit of the standard error will ensure that the confidence interval will be sufficiently narrow no less than $\gamma 100\%$ of the time.

The way in which the upper limit for the variance of the regression coefficient is determined is given as

$$_\gamma \sigma^2_{b_j} = \frac{\left(1 - P^2_{Y \cdot \mathbf{X}}\right)}{\left(1 - P^2_{X_j \cdot \mathbf{X}_{-j}}\right)/(N - p - 1)} \left(\frac{\sigma^2_Y}{\sigma^2_{X_j}} \right) \times \left(\frac{\chi^2_{(\gamma; N-1)}}{N - p - 1} \right), \tag{36}$$

where $\chi^2_{(\gamma;N-1)}$ is the γth quantile from a χ^2 distribution with $N-1$ degrees of freedom and $_\gamma\sigma^2_{b_j}$ is the upper limit of the $\gamma100\%$ confidence interval for $\sigma^2_{b_j}$. Substituting $_\gamma\sigma^2_{b_j}$ from Equation 36 for $\sigma^2_{b_j}$ from Equation 34 yields the modified sample size,

$$
N_\gamma = \left(\frac{t_{(1-\alpha/2;N-p-1)}}{\omega/2} \right)^2 \left(\frac{1 - P^2_{Y\cdot\mathbf{X}}}{1 - P_{X_j\cdot\mathbf{X}_{-j}}^2} \right)
$$
$$
\times \left(\frac{\sigma^2_Y}{\sigma^2_{X_j}} \right) \left(\frac{\chi^2_{(\gamma;N-1)}}{N-p-1} \right) + p + 1,
$$

(37)

where N_γ is the modified sample size so that there is $\gamma100\%$ certainty that the obtained confidence interval will be sufficiently narrow.

The methods discussed can be readily implemented with the MBESS R function **ss.aipe.reg.coef()**. Suppose that $P^2_{Y\cdot\mathbf{X}} = 0.50$ and $P^2_{X_j\cdot\mathbf{X}_{-j}} = 0.20$, $\sigma^2_Y = 50$, $\sigma^2_{X_j} = 5$, $p = 5$, and $\beta_j = 3$. Further suppose that the desired width for the 95% confidence interval is 2 for the regressor of primary importance (the estimate plus and minus 1 unit). The way in which the **ss.aipe.reg.coef()** function can be used is given as

```
R > ss.aipe.reg.coef(Rho2.Y_X = 0.5,
  Rho2.j_X.without.j = 0.2, p = 5, b.j = 3,
  width = 2, sigma.Y = 50, sigma.X = 5,
  conf.level = 0.95.)
```

with the result of the function being 250. Further suppose that the researcher would like to be 85% certain that the 95% confidence interval is no larger than 2 units wide. The modified sample size can be obtained by specifying the degree of certainty parameter:

```
R > ss.aipe.reg.coef(Rho2.Y_X = 0.5,
  Rho2.j_X.without.j = 0.2, p = 5, b.j = 3,
  width = 2, sigma.Y = 50, sigma.X = 5,
  conf.level = 0.95,
  degree of certainty = 0.85)
```

which yields a necessary sample size of 278.

AIPE for standardized regression coefficients

Similar to the sample size for the expected confidence interval width being sufficiently narrow for an unstandardized regression coefficient, the sample size necessary in order for the expected width of a noncentral confidence interval for $_s\beta_j$ can be solved iteratively. Because the critical value cannot be written analytically since it is based on a noncentral t-distribution, the iterative nature for the necessary sample size of the standardized regression coefficients must also include a step for determining the expected confidence interval width given the particular sample size. Thus, the iterative nature necessary to determine the expected width is more difficult for standardized regression coefficients than it is for their unstandardized counterparts due to the necessary employment of the noncentral t-distribution. Although this requires a great deal more work in the actual algorithm to determine sample size, there is no conceptual difference compared to the method for the unstandardized regression coefficient.

The method has been implemented in the ss.aipe.reg.coef() function from MBESS when **Noncentral=TRUE** has been specified. For the situation described in the previous section, sample size for the standardized analog can be obtained as

```
R > ss.aipe.reg.coef(Rho2.Y_X = 0.5,
  Rho2.j_X.without.j = 0.2, p = 5, b.j = 0.3,
  width = 0.2, sigma.Y = 1, sigma.X = 1,
  conf.level = 0.95, Noncentral = TRUE)
```

which yields a necessary sample size of 264.

As in the unstandardized case, the confidence interval width is itself a random variable. At the present time, there has not been a satisfactory method developed for determining necessary sample size for confidence intervals for $_s\beta_j$ that incorporates a desired degree of certainty. The complication in developing such a method stems from the fact that the noncentrality parameter is based on two parameters: $_s\beta_j$ and $\sigma^2_{s_{b_j}}$.

Thus, an analog for the way a desired degree of certainty is incorporated into the unstandardized regression coefficient, where the confidence interval width depends on only one parameter, $\sigma_{b_j}^2$, is necessarily more difficult in the standardized case. Even though we believe that a method can and will be developed, at the present time a brute-force trial and error simulation-based method can be implemented in order to plan an appropriate necessary sample size. Such an approach would proceed by specifying the population parameters and simulating data based on a particular sample size. From there, confidence intervals could be performed for standardized regression coefficients as previously discussed. The proportion of confidence intervals that are less than the desired width can be determined for different sample size values. This could be done until the minimum sample size is found that yields no less than the desired degree of certainty specified.

The function **ss.aipe.reg.coef.sensitivity()** contained in the MBESS R package can be used to determine the appropriate sample size as well as perform general sensitivity analyses. When an estimated set of population parameters is specified (that differs from the true set), the sample size used is based on the estimated values, but the simulation is conducted based on the properties of the true set of parameter values. This allows one to perform a sensitivity analysis, where the effects of mis-specifying population parameters by varying amounts on the typical width and the percentage of confidence intervals narrower/wider than desired can be evaluated. Alternatively, a specific sample size can be used in order to evaluate the properties of the situation described by the true set of parameter values at the specified value of sample size. Using the specified sample size approach, one can run the simulation with different values of sample size until the percentage of confidence interval widths less than the desired width is equal to the degree of certainty of interest. Although generally more time consuming, the brute force method described works very well when one wants to incorporate a desired

degree of certainty parameter into the sample size procedure for standardized regression coefficients and for sensitivity analyses in general[20].

DISCUSSION

In the context of multiple regression, the question 'What size sample should I use?' does not have a simple answer. As this chapter has demonstrated, the answer is best addressed with the two-by-two conceptualization presented in Table 11.1. Specifically, the sample size that should be used depends on the goals of the study. If the goal is for the overall fit of the model, then interest concerns $P_{Y \cdot \mathbf{X}}^2$; if the goal is for a targeted effect, then interest concerns β_j (or $_s\beta_j$). Of course, both $P_{Y \cdot \mathbf{X}}^2$ and β_j (or $_s\beta_j$) might be of interest, which implies that the larger of the two sample sizes from the situations of interest should be used.

However, identifying only that one is interested in $P_{Y \cdot \mathbf{X}}^2$ and/or β_j (or $_s\beta_j$) is still not enough to determine the necessary sample size. It is also necessary to determine if the goal is to reject the null hypothesis that the effect is zero in the population or if the goal is to obtain an accurate parameter estimate via a narrow confidence interval for the population parameter (possibly both). In multiple regression, although the idea is much more general, choosing an adequate sample size is not generally possible until a particular cell in Table 11.1 has been identified as the scenario of interest. Once the particular scenario from the two-by-two conceptualization has been determined, then and only then can an appropriate sample size be planned (recall Point f from the designing research studies list in the introduction of the chapter).

Even after the scenario has been determined, it is still necessary to use an appropriate value of an effect size parameter. One thing that has been conspicuously absent from the chapter is ways to choose an appropriate value for the effect size parameter so that all the sample size procedures can be implemented. The effect size has been termed the 'problematic parameter' due to the difficulty in estimating this unknown but necessary quantity (Lipsey, 1990). Options include basing population values on values obtained in previous research, possibly using meta-analytic techniques, performing a pilot study to estimate the necessary population quantities, or basing the population values on a reasonable exchangeable correlation structure. An exchangeable correlation structure is one where the correlation between each regressor and the criterion is the same and the correlation among the regressors is the same (but the two correlation values may be different; Maxwell, 2000). Even though this may seem simplistic, it is often a reasonable alternative unless obvious reasons exist for why it should not be used (Maxwell, 2000; see also Green, 1977). Given the difficulty of estimating the effect size parameter, combined with the nonlinear relationship between the necessary sample size and the desired degree of power or accuracy, sensitivity analyses are almost always helpful.

The chapter has made use of the Open Source and freely available computer package MBESS for the R statistical language and environment. We believe that the user-friendly functions contained in this package will be helpful for researchers planning sample size for multiple regression from any of the cells within Table 11.1. Alternatively, when there are multiple goals, choosing the larger of the necessary sample sizes is suggested as a way to achieve the multiple goals.

It is our hope that this chapter has been helpful in synthesizing four very different methods of planning sample size. The correct choice, of course, depends on the goal(s) of the researcher. Before determining sample size, a necessary but not a sufficient task is to clearly identify the particular question of interest that the study would ideally accomplish. Unless the question of interest is clearly identified, sample size cannot be adequately planned. Perhaps the best answer to the question 'What size sample should I use?' is, 'Well, it depends.'

NOTES

1 One important complication not addressed in this chapter is the total financial cost of conducting a study. Some studies may require a necessary sample size so large that the cost of conducting the study with that sample size becomes prohibitively expensive (e.g. Kraemer, 1991; Allison et al., 1997).

2 With regards to the statistical power or accuracy of regression coefficients, we have approached the chapter as if interest is restricted to *either* the omnibus effect *or* a single targeted regression coefficient. Of course, a researcher might be interested in more than one regression coefficient or potentially all regression coefficients. When interest includes more than one regression coefficient or all regression coefficients, issues of multiple and simultaneous inference become important. These issues are beyond the scope of the present chapter and are not discussed.

3 R and MBESS, along with their respective manuals, can be downloaded from the following Internet address: http://www.cran.r-project.org/.

4 Some sources state that power is a function of only three things, but in those cases the work generally refers to the standardized effect size, which involves both the (unstandardized) effect size and the model error variance. An example of such a situation is when planning sample size to detect the difference between two independent group means. Either the mean difference and the common variance or the standardized mean difference, which is defined as the mean difference divided by the square root of the common variance, can be specified.

5 A Type I error occurs when the null hypothesis is true but the null hypothesis is rejected (this occurs with probability α). A Type II error occurs when the null hypothesis is false but the null hypothesis fails to be rejected.

6 At times the data analysis procedure can be modified so as to reduce the model error variance yet still address the same research question, which potentially increases power and/or accuracy. For example, analysis of covariance can be used instead of an analysis of variance in a randomized design. The same question is addressed (are there differences among the population group means?), yet the model error variance is reduced by an amount related to the squared correlation between the covariate and the dependent variable (e.g. Huitema, 1980; Cox & McCullagh, 1982; Maxwell & Delaney, 2004).

7 It should be noted that the terms accuracy and precision have often been (incorrectly) used synonymously in the literature, which has at times caused confusion (Stallings & Gillmore, 1971). We believe the definition used here is optimal, in the sense that accuracy is clearly a function of precision and bias. The term accuracy in parameter estimation, the term we use for planning sample size with the desire to have a narrow confidence interval, is also thought to be

ideal, as it conveys the goal of achieving a parameter estimate that is close to its population value.

8 As an extreme example, suppose that regardless of the observed data, a researcher always estimates the parameter to be a value that corresponds to an a priori theory irrespective of any observed data. In such a case there would be a high degree of precision but the accuracy would likely be poor due to the effect of bias in the estimation procedure unless the theory is perfect. Precision is thus a necessary but not a sufficient condition for achieving accurate parameter estimates.

9 A counter example is the Cauchy distribution, where the precision of the location estimate is the same regardless of the sample size used to estimate it (Stuart et al., 1994, pp. 2–3).

10 Some population parameters are typically estimated with biased estimators but have exact confidence interval procedures. Even though the estimator is biased, the point estimate may be necessary for calculation of the (exact) confidence interval, where the values within the interval represent plausible values and will contain the parameter with $(1 - \alpha)100\%$ confidence. Many such population parameters also have unbiased (or more unbiased) estimators. Examples include the standardized mean difference (e.g. Hedges & Olkin, 1985), the squared multiple correlation coefficient (e.g. Algona & Olenek, 2000), the standard deviation (e.g. Hays, 1994, for the confidence interval method and Boltzmann, 1950, for the unbiased estimate), and the coefficient of variation (e.g. Johnson & Welch, 1940 for the confidence interval method and Social & Baumann, 1980, for its nearly unbiased estimate). A strategy in such cases is to report the exact confidence interval and the unbiased estimate of the population parameter.

11 The direction of an effect is known if the upper and lower limits of the confidence interval are both in the same direction (i.e. both are positive or both are negative). Furthermore, the confidence limits determine whether or not a particular null hypothesis (such as zero) can be rejected. Confidence limits provide the same information as an infinite set of hypothesis tests. The values within the confidence limits are the values of the null hypothesis that would not be rejected. The values outside of the confidence limits are the values of the null hypothesis that would be rejected.

12 The term 'regressors' has been used throughout the chapter as a generic term for the A_x variables. A regressor variable is termed independent, explanatory, predictor, or concomitant variable in other contexts. The term criterion is used as a generic term for the Y variable. The criterion variable is termed dependent, outcome, or predicted variable in other contexts.

13 Notice that the regressor variables (i.e. the A_x variables) are not italicized in any of the equations. This is because we will regard the regressors as fixed throughout the chapter. Even though the distinction between fixed and random regressors is not often made in applied work, the sampling distribution of an estimated regression coefficient tends to depend on whether the regressors are fixed or random (e.g. Stuart et al., 1999; Rancher, 2000). Many applications of multiple regression implicitly or explicitly take the view 'given this **X**' so that the **X** variables can be considered fixed for purposes of the study (e.g. O'Brien & Mueller, 1993, p. 23). O'Brien and Mueller (1993) make the argument that the distinction is not important in the context of sample size planning for power in multiple regression by stating that 'the practical discrepancy between the two approaches disappears as the sample size increases' (p. 23). O'Brien and Mueller (1993) go on to say that 'because the population parameters are conjectures or estimates, strict numerical accuracy of the power computations is usually not critical' (p. 23). We will say more about the distinction between fixed and random regressors elsewhere in the chapter.

14 We use both standardized and unstandardized regression coefficients in various parts of the chapter. Observed standardized regression coefficients have at times been referred to as 'beta weights' in the behavioral and educational sciences. We will use β_j to represent the unstandardized population regression coefficient of variable j with b_j as its estimate. We use $_s\beta_j$ to represent the standardized population regression coefficient of variable j with $_sb_j$ as its estimate.

15 Notice that we have not used the standard general linear model equations, where the intercept is contained within β and X contains a vector of ones for the intercept. The notation used here is equivalent to the standard general linear model equations, but it is especially helpful for presenting the necessary information for each of the four approaches to sample size planning for multiple regression.

16 Throughout the chapter, multiple correlation coefficients will be denoted with a subscript that identifies the variable being predicted separated by a dot from one or more regressor variables. Thus, the criterion variable is on the left of the dot and the regressor variable(s) are to the right of the dot, where the dot can literally be read as 'regressed on,' 'predicted from' or 'explained by.'

17 A mean-shifted central distribution is one that follows a central distribution after subtracting the population value. For example, when comparing two independent group means, if there is a population mean difference between the two groups a priori, then that difference can be subtracted from the observed difference: $(\bar{Y}_1 - \bar{Y}_2) - (\mu_1 - \mu_2)$, where $\bar{Y}_1$ and $\bar{Y}_2$ are the observed means for groups one and two, respectively, and μ_1 and μ_2 are the population means for groups 1 and 2, respectively.

18 The illustrative data from Holzinger and Swineford's (1939) Grant-White School data (available in MBESS), where the criterion variable, *total*

score (the sum of all of the 26 measured variables included in the dataset), is modeled as a function of the regressor variables *flags*, *wordm*, *addition*, *object*, and *series*. The standardized and unstandardized regression coefficients, presented in the next section, are for the *series* variable, which was a test that measured students' ability to complete mathematical/numeric series. Notice that the squared multiple correlation coefficient is quite large by most behavioral, educational, and social science standards. The large squared multiple correlation coefficient is because the dependent variable is a sum of five positively correlated measures, where the zero-order correlations among the measures tended to be large.

19 Even though only fixed regressors are discussed in the chapter, The ss.aipe.R2() function in MBESS can be used for regressors that are fixed *or* random by specifying Random.Predictors=TRUE (for random predictors) or Random.Predictors=FALSE (for fixed regressors).

20 In addition to the ss.aipe.reg.coef.sensitivity() function described, there is also a ss.power.reg. coef.sensitivity() function that allows the effects of parameter mis-specification or selected sample size to be specified in order to assess empirical power, and other properties, for a targeted regression coefficient. These functions for confidence interval width and power have analogs for omnibus effect with the ss.aipe.R2.sensitivity() and the ss.power.R2.sensitivity() functions.

REFERENCES

Algona, J., & Olenek, S. (2000). Determining sample size for accurate estimation of the squared multiple correlation coefficient. *Multivariate Behavioral Research, 35*, 119–136.

Allison, D. B., Allison, R. L., Faith, M. S., Paultre, F., & F. X. Pi-Sunyer. (1997). Power and money: Designing statistically powerful studies while minimizing financial costs. *Psychological Methods, 2*, 20–33.

Bakan, D. (1966). The test of significance in psychological research. *Psychological Bulletin, 66*, 423–437.

Chow, S. L. (1996). *Statistical significance: Rationale, validity and utility*. Newbury Park, CA: Sage Publications.

Cohen, J. (1988). *Statistical power analysis for the behavioral sciences* (2nd ed.). Hillsdale, NJ: Lawrence Erlbaum Associates.

Cohen, J. (1994, December). The earth is round ($p < 0.05$). *American Psychologist, 49*, 997–1003.

Cohen, J., Cohen, P., West, S. G., & Aiken, L. S. (2003). *Applied multiple regression/correlation analysis for the behavioral sciences* (3rd ed.). Mahwah, NJ: Erlbaum.

Cox, D. R., & McCullagh, P. (1982). Some aspects of analysis of covariance. *Biometrics*, 541–561.

Cumming, G., & Finch, S. (2001). A primer on the understanding, use, and calculation of confidence intervals that are based on central and noncentral distributions. *Educational and Psychological Measurement, 61*, 532–574.

Darlington, R. B. (1990). *Regression and linear models*. New York, NY: McGraw-Hill.

Dunlap, W. P., Xin, X., & Myers, L. (2004). Computing aspects of power for multiple regression. *Behavior Research Methods, Instruments, & Computers, 36*, 695–701.

Gatsonis, C., & Sampson, A. R. (1989). Multiple correlation: Exact power and sample size calculations. *Psychological Bulletin, 106*, 516–524.

Graybill, F. A. (1976). *Theory and application of the linear model*. Pacific Grove, CA: Brooks/Cole.

Green, B. F. (1977). Parameter sensitivity in multivariate methods. *Multivariate Behavioral Research, 12*, 263–288.

Green, S. B. (1991). How many subjects does it take to do a regression analysis? *Multivariate Behavioral Research, 26*, 499–510.

Greenwald, A. G. (1975). Consequences of prejudice against the null hypothesis. *Psychological Bulletin, 82*, 1–20.

Grissom, R. J., & Kim, J. J. (2005). *Effect sizes for research: A broad practical approach*. Mahwah, NJ: Lawrence Erlbaum Associates.

Hagen, R. L. (1997). In praise of the null hypothesis statistical test. *American Psychologist, 52*(1), 15–24.

Hahn, G., & Meeker, W. (1991). *Statistical intervals: A guide for practitioners*. New York, NY: John Wiley & Sons, Inc.

Harris, R. J. (1997). Significance tests have their place. *Psychological Science, 8*, 8–11.

Harris, R. J. (2001). *A primer of multivariate statistics* (3rd ed.). Mahwah, NJ: Lawrence Erlbaum Associates.

Hays, W. L. (1994). *Statistics* (5th ed.). Belmont, CA: Wadsworth Publishing.

Hedges, L. V., & Olkin, I. (1985). *Statistical methods for meta-analysis*. Orlando, FL: Academic Press.

Boltzmann, W. H. (1950). The unbiased estimate of the population variance and standard deviation. *American Journal of Psychology, 63*, 615–617.

Holzinger, K. J., & Swineford, F. (1939). *A study in factor analysis: The stability of a bi-factor solution*. Chicago, IL: The University of Chicago.

Huitema, B. E. (1980). *The analysis of covariance and alternatives*. New York, NY: Wiley.

Hunter, J. E., & Schmidt, F. L. (2004). *Methods of meta-analysis: Correcting error and bias in research findings*. Newbury Park, CA: Sage.

Johnson, N. L., Kotz, S., & Balakrishnan, N. (1995). *Continuous univariate distributions* (Vol. 2). New York, NY: John Wiley & Sons, Inc.

Johnson, N. L., & Welch, B. L. (1940). Applications of the noncentral *t*-distribution. *Biometrika, 31*, 362–389.

Kelley, K. (2005). The effects of nonnormal distributions on confidence intervals for the standardized mean difference: Bootstrapping as an alternative to parametric confidence intervals. *Educational and Psychological Measurement, 65*(1), 51–69.

Kelley, K. (2006). Sample size planning for the squared multiple correlation coefficient: Accuracy in parameter estimation via narrow confidence intervals. *Manuscript under review.*

Kelley, K. (2007). MBESS version 0.0.9: An R package. [computer software and manual]. Retrievable from http://www.cran.r-project.org/

Kelley, K., & Maxwell, S. E. (2003). Sample size for multiple regression: Obtaining regression coefficients that are accurate, not simply significant. *Psychological Methods, 8*, 305–321.

Kelley, K., Maxwell, S. E., & Rausch, J. R. (2003). Obtaining power or obtaining precision: Delineating methods of sample size planning. *Evaluation and the Health Professions, 26*, 258–287.

Kelley, K., & Rausch, J. R. (2006). Sample size planning for the standardized mean difference: Accuracy in parameter estimation via narrow confidence intervals. *Psychological Methods, 11*, 363–385.

Kraemer, H., Gardner, C., Brooks, J. O., & Yesavage, J. A. (1998). Advantages of excluding underpowered studies in meta-analysis: Inclusionist versus exclusionist viewpoints. *Psychological Methods, 3*, 23–31.

Kraemer, H. C. (1991). To increase power in randomized clinical trials without increasing sample size. *Psychopharmacology Bulletin, 27*, 217–224.

Kraemer, H. C., & Thiemann, S. (1987). *How many subjects?* Beverly Hills, CA: Sage.

Kupper, L. L., & Hafner, K. B. (1989). How appropriate are popular sample size formulas? *American Statistician, 43*, 101–105.

Lipsey, M. W. (1990). *Design sensitivity: Statistical power for experimental research.* Newbury Park, CA: Sage.

Maxwell, S. E. (2000). Sample size and multiple regression. *Psychological Methods, 5*, 434–458.

Maxwell, S. E. (2004). The persistence of underpowered studies in psychological research: Causes, consequences, and remedies. *Psychological Methods, 9*, 147–163.

Maxwell, S. E., & Delaney, H. D. (2004). *Designing experiments and analyzing data: A model comparison perspective.* (2nd ed.). Mahwah, NJ: Lawrence Erlbaum Associates.

Meehl, P. E. (1967). Theory testing in psychology and in physics: A methodological paradox. *Philosophy of Science, 34*, 103–115.

Meehl, P. E. (1978). Theoretical risks and tabular asterisks: Sir Karl, Sir Ronald, and the slow progress of soft psychology. *Journal of Consulting and Clinical Psychology, 46*, 806–834.

Mendoza, J. L., & Stafford, K. L. (2001). Confidence intervals, power calculations, and sample size estimation for the squared multiple correlation coefficient under the fixed and random regression models: A computer program and useful standard tables. *Educational and Psychological Measurement, 61*, 650–667.

Mogie, M. (2004). In support of null hypothesis significance testing. *Proceedings of the Royal Society of London, Series B, Biology Letters, 271*, 82–84.

Morrison, D. E., & Henkel, R. E. (1970). *The significance test controversy: A Reader.* Chicago, IL: Aldine Publishing Company.

Murphy, K. R., & Myors, B. (1998). *Statistical power analysis: A simple and general model for traditional and modern hypothesis tests.* Mahwah, NJ: Erlbaum.

Neyman, J. (1937). Outline of a theory of statistical estimation based on the classical theory of probability. *Philosophical Transaction of the Royal Society of London. Series A, Mathematical and Physical Sciences, 236*, 333–380.

Nickerson, R. S. (2000). Null hypothesis significance testing: A review of an old and continuing controversy. *Psychological Methods, 5*, 241–301.

O'Brien, R., & Mueller, K. E. (1993). A unified approach to statistical power for *t*-tests to multivariate models. In L. Edwards (Ed.), *Applied analysis of variance in behavioral sciences* (pp. 297–344). New York, NY: Marcel Dekker.

Pedhazur, E. J. (1997). *Multiple regression in behavioral research: Explanation and prediction* (3rd ed.). New York, NY: Harcourt Brace College Publishers.

R Development Core Team. (2007). R version 2.5.0: A language and environment for statistical computing [computer software and manual], R foundation for statistical computing.

Rancher, A. C. (2000). *Linear models in statistics.* New York, NY: John Wiley & Sons, Inc.

Rosenthal, R. (1993). Cumulative evidence. In G. Keren & C. Lewis (Eds.), *A handbook for data analysis in the behavioral sciences: Methodological issues* (pp. 519–559). Hillsdale, NJ: Lawrence Erlbaum Associates.

Rossi, J. S. (1990). Statistical power of psychological research: What have we gained in 20 years? *Journal of Consulting and Clinical Psychology, 58*(5), 646–656.

Rozeboom, W. W. (1960). The fallacy of the null-hypothesis significance test. *Psychological Bulletin, 57*, 416–428.

Rozeboom, W. W. (1966). *Foundations of the theory of prediction*. Homewood, IL: The Dorsey Press.

Sampson, A. R. (1974). A tale of two regressions. *Journal of the American Statistical Association, 69*, 682–689.

Schmidt, F. L. (1996). Statistical significance testing and cumulative knowledge in psychology: Implications for training of researchers. *Psychological Methods, 1*, 115–129.

Sedlmeier, P., & Gigerenzer, G. (1989). Do studies of statistical power have an effect on the power of studies? *Psychological Bulletin, 105*, 309–316.

Serlin, R., & Lapsley, D. (1985). Rationality in psychological research: The good-enough principle. *American Psychologist, 40*, 73–83.

Serlin, R. C., & Lapsley, D. K. (1993). Rational appraisal of methodological research and the good-enough principle. In G. Keren & C. Lewis (Eds.), *Methodological and quantitative issues in the analysis of psychological data* (pp. 199–228). Mahwah, NJ: Lawrence Earlbaum Associates.

Smithson, M. (2001). Correct confidence intervals for various regression effect sizes and parameters: The importance of noncentral distributions in computing intervals. *Educational and Psychological Measurement, 61*, 605–632.

Smithson, M. (2003). *Confidence intervals*. Thousand Oaks, CA: Sage Publications.

Social, R. R., & Baumann, C. A. (1980). Significance tests for coefficients of variation and variability profiles. *Systematic Zoology, 29*, 50–66.

Stallings, W. M., & Gillmore, G. M. (1971). A note on 'accuracy' and 'precision'. *Journal of Educational Measurement, 8*, 127–129.

Steiger, J. H. (2004). Beyond the *F* test: Effect size confidence intervals and tests of close fit in the analysis of variance and contrast analysis. *Psychological Methods, 9*, 164–182.

Steiger, J. H., & Fouladi, R. T. (1992). R2: A computer program for interval estimation, power calculation, and hypothesis testing for the squared multiple correlation. *Behavior Research Methods, Instruments, and Computers, 4*, 581–582.

Steiger, J. H., & Fouladi, R. T. (1997). Noncentrality interval estimation and the evaluation of statistical methods. In L. L. Harlow, S. A. Mulaik, & J. H. Steiger (Eds.), *What if there where no significance tests?* (pp. 221–257). Mahwah, NJ: Lawrence Erlbaum Associates.

Stuart, A., & Ord, J. K. (1994). Kendall's advanced theory of statistics: Distribution theory (6th ed.). New York, NY: John Wiley & Sons.

Stuart, A., Ord, J. K., & Arnold, S. (1999). *Kendall's advanced theory of statistics: Classical inference and the linear model* (6th ed., Vol. 2A). New York, NY: Oxford University Press.

Thompson, B. (2002). What future quantitative social science research could look like: Confidence intervals for effect sizes. *Educational Researcher, 31*(3), 25–32.

Wainer, H. (1999). One cheer for null hypothesis significance testing. *Psychological Methods, 4*(2), 212–213.

Re-conceptualizing Generalization: Old Issues in a New Frame

Giampietro Gobo

INTRODUCTION

Even though qualitative methods are now recognized in the methodological literature, they are still regarded with skepticism by some methodologists, mainly those with statistical training. One reason for this skepticism concerns whether qualitative research results can be generalized, which is doubted not only because they are derived from only a few cases, but also because even where a larger number is studied these are generally selected without observing the rigorous criteria of statistical sampling theory. In this regard, the methodology textbooks still distinguish samples into two types: *probability* samples (simple random, systematic, proportional stratified, non-proportional stratified, multistage, cluster, area, and their various combinations), and *non-probability* ones (haphazard or convenience, quota, purposive, of the emblematic

case, snowball, telephone)[1]. With regards the latter is stated:

> the obvious disadvantage of nonprobability sampling is that, since the probability that a person will be chosen is not known, the investigator generally cannot claim that his or her sample is representative of the larger population. This greatly limits the investigator's ability to generalize his or her findings beyond the specific sample studied (…) A nonprobability sample may prove perfectly adequate if the researcher has no desire to generalize his or her findings beyond the sample. (Bailey, 1978: 92)

This position again tends to relegate qualitative research to the marginal role of furnishing ancillary support for surveys, which is precisely as it was conceived by Barton and Lazarsfeld (1955) and the methodologists of their time.

The aim of this study is to show that this methodological denigration of qualitative research is overly severe and unjustified, for three reasons. First, because the use of probability samples and statistical inference in social research often proves problematic. Second, because there are numerous disciplines, in both the social and human sciences, whose theories are based exclusively on research conducted on only a few cases. Third, because, *pace* the methodological orthodoxy, a significant part of sociological knowledge, is idiographic. My intention is therefore not to criticize sampling theory or its applications; rather, it is to remedy a situation where statistical inference is deemed the only acceptable method, and idiographic generalization as scientifically ill-founded. Finally qualitative researchers do not need to throw away the baby generalization with the bathwater of probability sampling, because we can have generalizations without probability.

THE PROBLEMATIC USE OF PROBABILITY SAMPLES IN SOCIAL RESEARCH

Several authors (among them Goode and Hatt, 1952; Chain, 1963; Galtung, 1967; Capecchi, 1972) have stressed that the application of statistical sampling theory in sociological contexts gives rise to various difficulties. This theory, in fact, requires the researcher to construct a probability sample (one, that is, where each subject's likelihood of being selected is known and also every item has an equal chance of being selected), and the cases must be selected in rigorously random manner. But these two requirements are not easy to satisfy in social research, because their fulfillment encounters a series of obstacles, not all of which can be overcome.

There is no space to describe in depth the problems and limits of statistical sampling theory (see Gobo, 2004). I will briefly examine three limits only:

1 *The difficulty of finding sampling frames* (lists of population) for certain population sub-sets, because these frames are often not available. How, for example, can a random sample of the unemployed be extracted if the whole list of unemployed people is not available beforehand? It is true that many unemployed people are enrolled at job placement offices, but it is equally true that not *all* unemployed people are so enrolled. Consequently, the majority of studies on particular segments of the population cannot make use of population lists: consider studies on blue-collar workers, the unemployed, home-workers, artists, immigrants, housewives, pensioners, football supporters, members of political movements, charity workers, elderly people living alone, and so on.

2 *The phenomenon of nonresponse.* The concept of random selection is theoretically very simple and, thanks to the ideal-typical image of the box, quite clear to the general public. This clarity is misleading, however, because human beings differ from balls in a ballot box in two respects: they are not immediately accessible to the researcher, and they are free to decide not to answer. In fact, account must be taken of the gap (which varies according to the research project) between the *initial* sample (all the individuals about whom we want to collect information) and the *final* sample (the cases about which we have been able to obtain information); the two sets may correspond, but usually some of the objects in the first sample are not surveyed. As Groves and Lyberg (1988: 191) pointed out, nonresponse error threatens the characteristic which makes the survey unique among research methods: its statistical inference from sample to population. If the sample is at odds with the probability model, nothing can be said about its general representativeness; that is, about whether it truly reproduces all the characteristics of the population.

3 *Representativeness and generalizability: two sides of the same coin?* The social science textbooks usually describe generalizability as the natural outcome of a prior probabilistic procedure. In other words, the necessary condition for carrying out a statistical inference is previous use of a probability sample. It is forgotten, however, that probability/representativeness and generalizability are not two sides of the same coin. The former is a property of the *sample*, whilst the latter concerns the *findings* of research. Put otherwise: between construction of a sample and confirmation of a hypothesis there intervene a complex set of activities which pertain to at least seven different domains: (1) the trustworthiness of operational definitions and operational acts; (2) the reliability of the data collection instrument;

(3) the appropriateness of conceptualizations; (4) the accuracy of the researcher's descriptions, categorizations, and/or measurements; (5) to be successful with observational (or field) relations; (6) the validity of the data; and (7) the validity of the interpretation. These activities, and their relative errors (called 'measurement errors' in the literature), may impair the connection between probability/representativeness and generalizability – a not infrequent occurrence in a complex activity like social research.

These drawbacks do not signify that probability sampling and statistical inference are instruments by their nature unsuited to social research. Rather, according to the research setting, they are instruments with certain practical disadvantages that can sometimes be remedied and sometimes cannot.

In light of these difficulties, probability sampling cannot be propounded as the only model suited to the generalization of findings. As Geertz (1973: 21) points out, it is not only statistical inference that enables the move from 'local truths to general visions.' Moreover, as we have seen, not all sociological phenomena can be studied with rigorous application of the principles of sampling theory, the consequence being that the adoption of other forms of generalization has been vital for social research: otherwise, an important part of sociological theory (that based on research conducted on a few cases or even on haphazard or convenience samples as in the cases of, for example, Gouldner, Dalton, Becker, Goffman, Garfinkel, Cicourel) would never have been produced.

GENERALIZATION AS SEEN BY QUALITATIVE METHODOLOGISTS

Qualitative researchers have taken up a variety of positions in reaction to the pronouncement that those who do not use probability samples cannot generalize. The most extreme of them have (paradoxically) on the one hand accepted the verdict but on the other dismissed sampling as 'a mere positivist worry' (Lincoln and Guba, 1979; Denzin, 1983).

Some have aptly pointed out that 'most social anthropological and a good deal of sociological theorizing has been founded upon case studies' (Mitchell, 1983: 188) or has been the product of exclusively theoretical inquiry (without, that is, being grounded on systematic research). The more moderate have complied with the injunction of the statisticians but reconceptualized the problem by claiming that there are two types of generalization (which they have termed in various ways): *enumerative* (statistical) vs. *analytic* induction (Znaniecki, 1934: 236; Mitchell, 1983: 191); *formalistic/scientific* vs. *naturalistic* generalization (Stake, 1978: 6); *distributive* vs. *theoretical* generalization (Hammersley, 1992: 186ff; Williams, 2000: 215; Payne and Williams, 2005: 296–7). The first type of generalization involves estimating the distribution of particular features within a finite population; the second, eminently theoretical, is concerned with the relations among the variables in any sample of the relevant kind (moreover, the population of relevant cases is potentially infinite). The latter is usually based on identifying causal or essential relations among particular categories, whose character is defined by those relations, so that it is inferred that all instances of those categories are involved in the specified type of relation.

Even though some qualitative researchers may privately agree with Znaniecki (1934: 236–7) that analytical induction is the true method of science and it is the superior method (because it discovers the causal relations of a phenomenon rather than only the probabilistic ones of co-occurrence), the idea that there exist two types of generalization represents acceptance of the statisticians' diktat. It also represents acceptance of a 'political' division into areas of competence: a compromise already envisaged by some members of the Chicago School, like Burgess (1927), who maintained that statistics and case studies were mutually complementary[2] with their own criteria of excellence.

The distinction between the two types of generalization has been drawn with exemplary clarity by Alberoni and colleagues, who wrote in their *Introduction* to a study on 108 political activists of the Italian Communist Party and the Christian Democrat Party as follows:

> if we want to know, for instance, how many activists of both parties in the whole country are from families of Catholic or Communist tradition, (this) study is useless. Conversely, if we want to show that family background is important in determining whether a citizen will be an activist in the Communist rather than Christian Democratic party, this research can give the right answer. If we want to find out what are and have been the percentages of the different 'types' of activists [...] in both parties, the study is useless, whereas if we want to show that these types exist the study gives a certain answer [...]. The study does not aim at giving a quantitative objective description of Italian activism, but it can aid understanding of some of its essential aspects, basic motivations, crucial experiences and typical situations which gave birth to Italian activism and help keep it alive. (1967: 13)

The two generalizations are therefore made in completely different ways[3].

This moderate stance has been adopted by the majority of qualitative methodologists, some of whom have sought to underscore the difference between statistical and 'qualitative' generalization by coining specific terms for the latter. This endeavor has given rise to a welter of terms: 'naturalistic generalization' (Stake, 1978: 6), 'transferability' (Lincoln and Guba, 1979), 'translatability' (Goetz and LeCompte, 1984), 'analytic generalization' (Yin, 1984), 'extrapolation' (Mitchell, 1983: 191; Alasuutari, 1995: 196–7), 'moderatum generalization' (Williams, 2000; Payne and Williams, 2005), and others.

Five concepts of generalization

At least five different positions on the generalizability of research results can be identified within the qualitative methodological tradition (see Ragin and Becker, 1992; Gomm, Hammersley and Foster, 2000).

The first position, the most radical of them, has been assumed by Lincoln and Guba (1979), Guba (1981), Guba and Lincoln (1982), and Denzin (1983). It adheres to the traditional position that qualitative research is

an idiographic account which lays no claim to generalization (see Burrell and Morgan, 1979). Norman K. Denzin is very explicit on the matter:

> The interpretivist rejects generalization as a goal and never aims to draw randomly selected samples of human experience. For the interpretivist every instance of social interaction, if thickly described (Geertz, 1973), represents a slice from the life world that is the proper subject matter for interpretative inquiry (...) Every topic (...) must be seen as carrying its own logic, sense or order, structure, and meaning. (Denzin, 1983: 133–4)[4]

Guba and Lincoln (1981: 62) likewise claim that 'it is virtually impossible to imagine any human behavior that is not heavily mediated by the context in which it occurs. One can easily conclude that generalizations that are intended to be context free will have little that is useful to say about human behavior.' However, Guba and Lincoln moderate their position by introducing two novel elements: a new formulation of the concept of *working hypothesis* proposed by Cronbach (1975), and the new concept of *transferability*.

According to Cronbach, 'when we give proper weight to local conditions, any generalization is a working hypothesis, not a conclusion' (1975: 125). Hence, Lincoln and Guba maintain,

> local conditions (...) make it impossible to generalize. If there is a 'true' generalization, it is that there can be no generalization. And note that 'working hypotheses' are tentative both for the situation in which they first uncovered and for other situations; there are always differences in context from situation to situation, and even the single situation differs over time. (1979, reprinted 2000: 39)

They now make their own proposal, which has become well-known in qualitative research:

> How can one tell whether a working hypothesis developed in Context A might be applicable in Context B? We suggest that the answer to that question must be empirical: the degree of *transferability* is a direct function of the *similarity* between the two contexts, what we shall call '*fittingness*'. Fittingness is defined as the degree of congruence between sending and receiving contexts. If Context A and Context B are 'sufficiently' congruent, then working

hypotheses from the sending originating context *may* be applicable in the receiving context. (Lincoln and Guba, 1979, reprinted 2000: 40)

However, transferability is not an inferential process performed by the researcher (who cannot know all the other contexts of research). Rather, it is a choice made by the reader, who on the basis of argumentative logic and a thick description (of the case study) produced by the researcher, may decide (on his/her own responsibility – see Gomm, Hammersley and Foster, 2000: 102) to *transfer* this knowledge to other situations that she/he deems similar (Lincoln and Guba, 1979, reprinted 2000: 40). The reader, basing this on the persuasive power of the arguments used by the researcher, decides on the similarity between the (sending) context of the case studied and the (receiving) contexts to which the reader him/herself intends to apply the results (Guba and Lincoln, 1982: 246).

To conclude, these authors are convinced that 'generalizations are impossible since phenomena are neither time- nor context-free'; however, 'some transferability of these hypotheses may be possible from situation to situation, depending on the degree of temporal and contextual similarity' (Guba and Lincoln, 1982: 238).

A second, more moderate, approach has been proposed by Stake (1978: 1994), who argues that the purpose of case studies is not so much to produce general conclusions as to describe and analyze the principal features of the phenomenon studied. If these features concern an emblematic case of political, social, or economic importance (for example, the decision-making procedures of a large institution like the US Department of Defense), the 'intrinsic case study' will *per se* produce results of indubitable intrinsic relevance[5], even though they cannot be generalized in accordance with the canons of scientific induction:

naturalistic generalization, arrived at by recognizing the similarities of objects and issues in and out of context and by sensing the natural covariations of happenings. To generalize this way is to be both intuitive and empirical, and not idiotic.

Naturalistic generalizations develop within a person as a product of experience. They derive from the tacit knowledge of how things are, why they are, how people feel about them, and how these things are likely to be later or in other places with which this person is familiar. They seldom take the form of predictions but they lead regularly to expectations (...) These generalizations may become verbalized, passing of course from tacit knowledge to propositional; but they have not yet passed the empirical and logical tests that characterize formal (scholarly, scientific) generalizations. (Stake, 1978: 6)

A third position, which is contiguous to the intrinsic case study, has been put forward by Connolly (1998). It starts from the distinction between extensive vs. intensive studies. The aim of the former (like case studies) is to identify statistically significant and therefore generalizable causal relations; the aim of the latter is to reconstruct in detail the mechanisms that connect cause and effect. Like Stake, Connolly relieves the case study of responsibility for formal generalization, but he gives it a task complementary to such generalization, explaining (via the mechanisms) correlations whose statistical significance has already been documented by other studies.

These three positions have a common basis consisting in the concept of 'theoretical sampling' proposed by Glaser and Strauss (1967), Schatzman and Strauss (1973) and Strauss (1987): when we do not possess complete information about the population, cases are selected according to their status on one or more properties identified as the subject matter for research. As Mason writes, 'theoretical sampling is concerned with constructing a sample which is meaningful theoretically because it builds in certain characteristics or criteria which help to develop and test your theory and explanation' (1996: 94). And Strauss and Corbin are very explicit on the concept of generalization:

in terms of making generalization to a larger population, **we are not attempting to generalize as such but to specify** [...] the condition under which our phenomena exist, the action/interaction that pertains to them, and the associated outcomes or consequences. This means that our theoretical formulation applies to these situation or circumstances but **to no others**. (1990: 191, bold in the original text)

In other words the aim is not to generalize to some finite population but to develop theoretical ideas that will have general validity.

More practical are authors who engage in 'evaluation research' (Cronbach, 1982; Pawson and Tilley, 1997). These ground their reasoning on the notion of the cumulability of knowledge: case study after case study, in the course of time in a particular sector of research, there accumulates a repertoire or inventory of the possible forms that a particular object of study may assume. As Pawson and Tilley (1997: 119–20) put it, in polemic with Guba and Lincoln, what can be transferred between studies are not 'lumps of cases' but 'sets of ideas' which enable understanding of general mechanisms. In other words, cumulability is the prelude for qualitative generalizability.

The final position, and perhaps the oldest of them, is represented by Znaniecki's method of analytic induction. The purpose of analytic induction is to uncover causal relations through identification of the essential characteristics of the phenomenon studied. To this end, the method starts not with a hypothesis but with a limited set of cases from which an initial explanatory hypothesis is then derived. If the initial hypothesis fails to be confirmed by one case, it is revised. Additional cases of the same class of phenomena are then selected. If the hypothesis is not confirmed by these further cases, the conceptual definition of the phenomenon is revised. The process continues until the hypothesis is no longer refuted and further study tells the researcher nothing new (Znaniecki, 1934: 236ff). The inner logic of analytic induction derives from Mill's 'method of agreement' and 'method of difference.'

There are several variants of Znaniecki's method of analytic induction. One of them is Mitchell's (1983) critical case study approach.

Analytic induction revisited has been also widely used in comparative studies based on a small numbers of cases 'when little more than a handful of nations or organizations – sometimes even fewer – are compared with respect to the forces driving a societal outcome such a political development or an organizational characteristic' (Lieberson, 1992, reprinted in 2000: 208).

The unavoidableness of generalization

Sampling and generalizing are unavoidable practices because, even before being scientific, they are everyday life activities deeply rooted in thought, language, and practice (Gobo, 2004). With regard to thought, cognitive psychologists have demonstrated the tendency of people to generalize on the basis of a few observed characteristics or events, a process called the *heuristic of representativeness* by Kahneman and Tversky (1972) and Tversky and Kahneman (1974). With regard to the world of language, the same function is performed, as Becker has stated, by 'synecdoche, a rhetorical figure in which we use a part for something to refer the listener or reader to the whole it belongs to' (1998: 67). Finally, in the world of action, the seller shows a sample of cloth to the customer; in a paint shop the buyer skims through the catalogue of color shades in order to select a paint; the buyer tastes in order to choose a wine or a cheese; the teacher asks a student questions to assess his or her knowledge about the syllabus. In everyday life, social actors constantly sample and generalize. As Gomm, Hammersley and Foster point out, 'we all engage in naturalistic generalizations routinely in the course of our life, and this may take the form of empirical generalization as well as of informal theoretical inference. Given this, there is no reason in principle why case study research should not provide the basis for empirical generalization' (2000: 104). This is also because the unavoidability of generalization is epistemologically and reflexively founded. As Gomm, Hammersley and Foster acutely observe:

the very meaning of the word 'case' implies that what it refers to is a *case* [instance or example] of something. In other words, we necessarily identify cases in terms of general categories (...) the idea that somehow cases can be identified independently of our orientation to them is false. It is misleading to talk of the uniqueness of cases (...) we can only identify their distinctiveness on the basis of a notion of what is typical or representative of some categorial group or population. (Gomm, Hammersley and Foster, 2000: 104)

The unavoidableness of generalizing is such that 'in practice, much case study research has in fact put forward empirical generalizations' (Gomm, Hammersley and Foster, 2000: 98) and 'current qualitative researchers often seem to produce [generalization] unconsciously' (Payne and Williams, 2005: 297).

FOR AN IDIOGRAPHIC SAMPLING THEORY

The thesis (which I have called 'moderate') that there are two types of generalization has had the indubitable merit of cooling the dispute with quantitative methodologists and of legitimating two ways to conduct research. However, this political compromise has also had a number of harmful consequences.

First, it has not stimulated reflection on how to emancipate 'qualitative' generalization from its subordination to statistical inference. Traditional methodologists continue to attribute inferior status to qualitative research, on the grounds that although it can produce interesting results, they have a limited extension only. This long-standing positivist prejudice has been recently reinforced by the extreme positions taken up by Lincoln and Guba (1979) and Denzin (1983). Their insistence that generalization in interpretative research is impossible, and that their work is not intended to produce scientific generalizations, paradoxically fits perfectly with the equally intransigent position of quantitative methodologists. As Gomm, Hammersley and Foster, observe, 'to deny the possibility of case studies providing the basis for empirical generalizations is to accept the views of their critics too readily' (2000: 98). Even though

it may be a coincidence, the fact that Egon Guba was a well-known statistician before he became a celebrated qualitative methodologist may have heightened the inflexibility of the debate. Consequently, an unexpected consequence of this paradox is that interpretivism has been just as positivist on qualitative generalization as quantitative methods have.

Second, the concept of theoretical sampling has failed to address the problem of sample representativeness which Denzin himself (1971) considered so important. Likewise, the concept of transferability provides 'no guidance for researchers about *which* case to study – in effect, it implies that any case may be as good as any other in this respect' (Gomm, Hammersley and Foster, 2000: 101). This omission has been pedagogically harmful because it has permitted several generations of qualitative researchers entirely to neglect – in the belief that 'anything goes' – this aspect of the investigative process.

Third, an opportunity has been missed to rediscuss the entire issue, addressing it in more practical (and not solely theoretical) terms with a view to developing a new sampling theory: an idiographic theory, joint and equal with statistical theory, and which remedies a series of ancestral misunderstandings:

denial of the capacity of case study research to support empirical [distributive] generalization often seems to rest on the mistaken assumption that this form of generalization requires statistical sampling. This restricts the idea of representation to its statistical version; it confuses the task of empirical generalization with the use of statistical techniques to achieve that goal. While those techniques are a very effective basis for generalization, they are not essential. (Gomm, Hammersley and Foster, 2000: 104)

Sampling in some contemporary sciences

The first step in this endeavor is to survey certain disciplines – paleontology, archaeology, geology, ethology, biology, astronomy, anthropology, cognitive science, linguistics (which for some scientists is more reputable than sociology) – and see how they have tackled the problems of representativeness and generalizability. In certain respects, these are disciplines akin to qualitative research, for they work exclusively on few cases and have learnt to make a virtue out of necessity. As Becker writes:

> Archeologists and paleontologists have this problem to solve when they uncover the remnants of a now-vanished society. They find some bones, but not a whole skeleton; they find some cooking equipment, but not the whole kitchen; they find some garbage, but not the stuff of which the garbage is the remains. They know that they are lucky to have found the little they have, because the world is not organized to make life easy for archeologists. So they don't complain about having lousy data. (1998: 70–1)

For reasons of space, it is not possible here to provide an exhaustive account of how these disciplines have dealt with the above issues. But by way of example, consider the following study, which is one of the dozens published on the subject. It appeared in the journal *Nature* on January 23, 2003.

The scientist Xing Xu and colleagues (2003) of the Institute of Vertebrate Palaeontology, Beijing, had found six fossils in the province of Liaoning, North China. The impression left in the rock was of two pairs of wings and a long feathered tail of what appeared to be a *Microraptor gui*: a dinosaur less than one meter in length which lived in that region of China around 130 million years ago. According to its discoverers, the fossil was the missing link between terricolous dinosaurs and modern birds, the intermediate evolutionary stage for which scientists had long been searching. The discovery has fuelled the debate among paleontologists on the origin of flight. Whilst the close kinship between birds and dinosaurs is accepted by almost all scientists, there is much disagreement on the evolutionary stages that led to winged flight. The predominant theory is that wings began to develop, not to enable flight but to help the ancestors of birds to run faster. The small dinosaur discovered in China instead appeared to support the opposite hypothesis, namely that the direct ascendants of birds were animals

which climbed trees and used wings to glide back to earth. This was the theory propounded, for example, by the American naturalist, William Beebe, who as early as 1915 had predicted the existence of feathered dinosaurs exactly like *Microraptor gui*. However, the British journal urged caution when evaluating the importance of the discovery: the *Microraptor* could also be an evolutionary blind ally which had not left descendants.

There are therefore numerous disciplines which work on a limited number of cases, and do so consciously; in fact, there is animated discussion within them on sampling and generalizability. Moreover, this procedure is adopted by other disciplines as well: for instance, biology, astrophysics, history, genetics, anthropology, linguistics, cognitive science, psychology (whose theories are largely based on experiments, and therefore on research conducted on non-probabilistic samples consisting of psychology students). Why, we may ask, is this procedure acceptable for monkeys, rocks, and cells but not for human beings? Why do the majority of disciplines work with/on non-probability samples (regarded as being just as representative of their relative populations and therefore as producing generalizable results) while in sociology this is not possible? Why can a geneticist like Luca Cavalli Sforza of Stanford University argue that the evolution of language has had a direct impact on our genetic heritage, while in sociology a similar claim would require very different methodological support? The majority of these disciplines start from the assumption that their objects of study possess quasi-invariant states on the properties observed: that is, their states with respect to a property (e.g. size of the brain or the physique of a hominid) vary little and slowly among members of the class. Consequently, these disciplines are unconcerned about their use of only a handful of cases to draw inferences and generalizations about thousands of people, animals, plants, and other objects. Moreover, science studies the individual object/phenomenon not in itself but as a member of a broader class of objects/phenomena with particular characteristics/properties.

FOUR PROPOSALS FOR AN IDIOGRAPHIC SAMPLING THEORY

The above survey of disciplines midway between the natural sciences and the social science yields a number of suggestions for formulation of an idiographic sampling theory. They can be summarized in the following four steps:

(a) abandon the (statistical) principle of probability;
(b) recover the (statistical) principle of variance;
(c) pay renewed attention to the units of analysis;
(d) identify social regularities.

Representativeness without probability

The use of probability samples does not automatically signify the use of representative samples. Random and representative are terms neither synonymous nor necessarily inter-related. 'Randomness' concerns a particular procedure used to select the cases to include in a sample, while 'representativeness' concerns the outcome of the selection. One may question whether the former is the obligatory path for the latter. Nor do representativeness and probability form a natural pair, since it may be possible to construct a representative sample using other procedures. Qualitative research (or at least a part of it) does not relinquish the aim of working with representative samples; it only rejects the obligatory nexus between probabilistic and representative (on the one hand), or between randomness and representativeness (on the other).

It is therefore not necessarily the case that a researcher must choose between an (approximately) random sample or an entirely subjective one – or between a sample which is (even only) partially probabilistic and one about whose representativeness absolutely

nothing can be said. Between the rationalism and the postmodern nihilism underlying these two positions, one may attempt to address the problem in practical terms, doing so by examining the nature of the units of analysis considered, rather than adhering to standard procedural rules. As stressed by Rositi (1993: 198), we may reasonably doubt the generalizability of findings from

> studies of 1,000–2,000 cases which claim to sample the whole population. We have to wonder if we should prefer such samples with such aims […]. Studies with samples of 100–200 conversational interviews, structured to 'describe' variables rather than a population are definitely more suitable for a new model of studying society. (1993: 198)

Variance: From (general) principle to (local) practice

The second step is to recover the (statistical) principle of variance, which has received less attention than the probability principle. Contrary to the latter's standardizing intent and automatist inclination (which are among the reasons for its success), variance is a criterion which requires the researcher to reason, to conduct contextual analysis, and to take local decisions. Under the variance principle,

> in order to determine the sample size, the statistics must first know the range of variance that the researcher intends to measure (at least in sufficiently close terms) because it is likely that, if the range of variance of variable X is high, n [the number of individuals to interview] will be high, whereas if the range of variance is restricted (for example to only two modalities), n may be very restricted as well. (Capecchi, 1972: 50)

Hence, it is more likely that a sample will be a miniature of the population if that population is tendentially homogeneous; and it is less likely to be so if the reference population is tendentially heterogeneous. Consequently, if the variance is high, the researcher will require a large number of cases (in order to include every dimension of the phenomenon studied in his/her sample). If, instead, the variance is low, the researcher will presumably need only a few cases, and in some instances only one. In other words,

> it is important to recognize that the greater the heterogeneity of a population the more problematic are empirical generalizations based on a single case, or a handful of cases. If we could reasonably assume that the population were composed of more or less identical units, then there would be no problem. (Gomm, Hammersley and Foster, 2000: 104)

As also Payne and Williams (2005: 306–7) point out:

> the *breadth* of generalization can be extensive or narrow, depending on the nature of the phenomenon under study and our assumptions about the wider social world (…) [hence] the generalization may claim high or lower levels of *precision of estimates* (…) [and it] will be conditional upon the ontological status of the phenomena in question. We can say more, or make stronger claims about some things than others. A taxonomy of phenomena might look like this: 1° physical objects and their social properties; 2° social structures; 3° cultural features and artefacts; 4° symbols; 5° group relationships; 6° dyadic relationship; 7° psychological dispositions/behaviour (…) This outline taxonomy demonstrates that generalizations depend on what levels of social phenomena are being studied.

The conversation analyst Harvey Sacks (1992, vol. 1: 485, quoted in Silverman, 2000: 109) reminds us of the anthropologist and linguist Benjamin Lee Whorf, who was able to reconstruct Navajo grammar by extensively interviewing only one native Indian speaker. Grammars usually have low variance. However, had Whorf wanted to study how the Navajo educated their children, entertained themselves, etc., he would (perhaps) have found greater variance in the phenomenon and would have needed more cases. On this logic, the formal criteria that guide sampling are more informed by and embedded in sociological (rather than statistical) reasoning based on contingent reflection about the dimensions specific to the phenomenon investigated and the knowledge objectives of the research.

Moreover, as said, an authoritative part of sociological theory and a large part of anthropological theory are based on the case study:

the quintessence of non-probability sampling. The research studies by Alvin G. Gouldner and Melvin Dalton belong to this category. For example, Gouldner (1954) studied a gypsum mine situated close to the university where he taught (a convenience sample, therefore[6]). In his methodological appendix, Gouldner reported that his team conducted 174 interviews – and therefore on almost all the population (precisely 77 percent). One hundred and thirty-two of these 174 interviews were conducted with a 'representative sample' of the blue-collar workers at the company, for which purpose Gouldner used quota sampling stratified by age, rank, and tasks. He then constructed another representative sample of 92 blue-collar workers, to whom a questionnaire was administered.

Dalton (1959), who was a company manager at that time, conducted covert observation at Milo and Fruhuling, the fictitious names of two American companies for which he worked as a consultant (again a convenience sample, therefore). The ethnologist De Martino (1961) observed 21 people suffering from tarantism disease; Goffman (1961) stayed for several months at a psychiatric hospital; the anthropologist Geertz (1972) attended 57 cock fights; Sacks and colleagues described the mechanics of conversational interaction by analyzing a few telephone calls; the anthropologist Crapanzano (1980) studied Moroccan social relations through the experience of Tuhami, a tilemaker. The anthropologist Griaule (1948) reconstructed the cosmology of the Dogon, a tribe in Mali, by questioning only a small group of informants; Bourdieu's book (1993) on professions was based on 50 interviews with policewomen, temporary workers, attorneys, blue-collar workers, civil servants, and unemployed workers.

Why, one may ask, have such circumscribed studies given rise to such wide-ranging theories? In other words, why have they been generalized to other contexts? I shall answer these questions later. For the moment I would stress (and avoid) the danger of the nihilistic or postmodern drift implied by this approach, where any sample may serve and it is not worth bothering too much about it. Instead, at a certain point of the inquiry, giving clear definition to the *units of analysis* (an operation performed before the cases are selected, and therefore before the sample is constructed) is of extreme importance if the research is not to be botched and empirically inconsistent. On analyzing a series of Finnish studies on 'artists,' Mitchell and Karttunen (1991) found that the results differed according to the definition given to 'artist' by the researchers, a definition which then guided construction of the sample. In some studies, the category 'artist' included (i) subjects who defined themselves as artists; (ii) those permanently engaged in the production of works of art; (iii) those recognized as artists by society at large; and (iv) those recognized as such by associations of artists. The obvious consequence was that it was subsequently impossible to compare the results of these studies.

Units of analysis

The standard practice in sociology and political science is to choose clearly defined and easily detectable individual or collective units: persons, households, groups, associations, movements, parties, institutions, organizations, regions, or states. The consistency of these collective subjects is vague. In practice, members of these groups are interviewed individually: the head of the family, the human resources manager, the statistics department manager, and so on.

This means that the *sampling* unit (e.g. the family) is different from the *observational* unit (i.e. the single respondent as a member of the family). Only a focus group can (at least to some extent) preserve the integrity of the collective subject. Instead, choosing individuals implies an atomistic rather than organic conception of society (Burgess, 1927), whose structural elements are taken for granted or reckoned to be mirrored in the individual (Galtung, 1967: 37), while the sociological tradition that gives priority to relations over individuals is neglected. As a consequence, the following more dynamic units are neglected as well:

- beliefs, attitudes, stereotypes, opinions;
- emotions, motivations;
- behaviors, social relations, meetings, interactions, ceremonies, rituals, networks;
- cultural products (such as pictures, paintings, movies, theatre plays, television programs);
- rules and social conventions;
- documents and texts (historical, literary, journalistic);
- situations and events (wars, elections).

Hence, 'a reliable sampling model that recognizes interaction must be adopted [so that sampling is conducted on] interactive units (such as social relationships, encounters, organizations)' (Denzin, 1971: 269).

The researcher should focus his/her investigation on these kinds of units, not only because social processes are more easily detectable and observable, but also because these units allow more direct and deeper analysis of the characteristics observed.

Consider the following illustrative example. Assume that we want to study work practices at call centers, which are technology-intensive workplaces. In Italy, it has been calculated that there were 1350 call centers in 2002. In order to construct a probability and representative sample, we may proceed in two ways: randomly extract a certain number of cases from the population list (which is possible because a complete list can be obtained from the Chambers of Commerce), or construct a proportional stratified sample. In this latter case, we must first classify call centers according to the properties that interest us:

- the ownership of the organization, so that we have private call centers (e.g. Vodafone), public ones (e.g. the 911 emergency helpline), and non-profit ones;

- the 'vocation,' so that we have call centers that are 'generalist' (in the sense that they provide a variety of services) or 'vertical' (i.e. dedicated to only one service, e.g. credit recovery);
- membership or otherwise of the organization for which the service is provided, so that we have call centers 'internal' to the company, or ones to which the work is outsourced;
- the classic variables such as size of the organization (small, medium, large), geographical location (north-west, north-east, centre, south, islands), etc.;
- the type of service furnished.

Note that many of these properties are mutually exclusive, so that the sampling decision must be carefully pondered. In these cases, the usual practice is for the researcher to base the probability sampling on the first property. However, this may be sociologically inadequate if the researcher's interest is in work practices, because these cannot be accessed via the variable 'ownership.' For some authors (e.g. Capecchi, 1972), representativeness does not seem to transfer from one property to another. Put otherwise: it is not the variance of the ownership of call centers that interests us here, but the variance of work practices. It might be more satisfactory to choose property (e). Experience of this sector of inquiry (but also the literature, previous research, interviews with experts or operators in the sector, etc.) shows that call centers mainly provide the following services: counseling, credit recovery, marketing, interviewing, and advertising. Constructing a probability sample on this classification is practically impossible because a population list for each of these activities does not exist. The only alternative is to use the method outlined in the previous section. Again on the basis of experience, we note that only the first of these five activities has substantial variance, while the four latter seem to have low variance. In fact, the counseling provided by call centers is multiform: it consists of information, technical assistance, psychological help or support, medical advice, or therapy. Consequently, in order to preserve the representativeness of the sample, we must sample several cases for the specific work practice of counseling. If we have insufficient resources to collect the necessary number of cases, we can restrict our research to only some activities. Other studies in the future will account for the rest.

It is evident that representativeness is not always possessed by the sample when research begins. It is a resource also acquired *ex post*, progressively and iteratively, research project after research project, with the gradual accumulation of expertise. This definition of representativeness seems somehow to tie this property to the relation between the results obtained by an individual research project and the experience of the researcher who conducts it.

In search of social regularities

I now turn to the final aspect of the entire question. There are three broad criteria which serve to orient the construction of a non-probability sample; and to each of them corresponds a particular form of reasoning alternative to inductive or statistical inference: deductive inference, comparative inference, and emblematic case.

The three criteria impose different cognitive objectives, and they are used according to the type of generalization that the researcher wants to make. The first two criteria are in some way opposed to each other: comparative inference maximizes the probability of extracting odd cases; deductive inference selects only odd (deviant) cases. Theoretical inference instead concentrates on emblematic cases, focusing on social similarities.

Deductive inference

The first criterion consists of the choice of a critical or deviant case which can be used (*à la* Popper) to prove the refutability of an accredited or standard theory. An outstanding example of its application is provided by Goldthorpe et al.'s study (1968) of workers in the town of Luton. The distinctive feature of this inferential process is that it starts from a theory of which it intends to prove the implausibility: in this case the embourgeoisement of the working class. The theory is tested against a case comprising the largest number (and the greatest intensity) of its founding properties or requirements of this theory. If, in these optimal conditions, the consequences foreseen by the theory do not ensue, it is extremely unlikely that the theory will work in all those empirical cases where those requirements are more weakly present. Hence the theory is falsified, and its inadequacy can be legitimately generalized. When the critical case study procedure is used, the cases are selected according to their explanatory power, rather than according to the criteria of probability theory or their typicality (Mitchell, 1983: 207, 209). Moreover, the legitimacy of the generalization (of the scant explanatory capacity of the theory just falsified) depends not only on the cogency of the rhetorical argument but also on the strength of the connections established between theory and observations.

There are many other important studies (which follow in a very broad sense the Popperian approach) which have focused on deviant cases in order to understand standard behavior: Goffman (1961) on ceremonies and rituals in a psychiatric clinic; Cicourel and Boise (1972) on the interpersonal communications of deaf children; Garfinkel (1967) on achievement of sex status in an 'intersexed' person; Pollner and Winkler (1985) on interactions in a family with a mentally retarded child; and many others.

This criterion can also be used to explore subcultures or emergent or avant-garde phenomena which may become dominant or significant in the future, although at present they are still marginal: see Festinger et al. (1956) on millenial groups after their predicted date for the end of the world had passes; Becker (1953) on marijuana smokers; Hebdige (1979) on style groups like mods, punks, skinheads; Fielding (1981) on right-wing political movements.

The deviant case can also be used to prove the refutability and falsifiability of a well-known and received theory, as in Rosenhan's (1973) study on the medical-organizational origin of psychiatric illness, or the already-cited study by Goldthorpe et al. (1968) on blue-collar workers in the town of Luton. This criterion (which is widely applied in biology, astrophysics, history, genetics, anthropology, linguistics, paleontology, archaeology, ethology, geology) does not determine the extent to which a phenomenon is widespread in the population. It only directs the scientific community's attention to the phenomenon's existence and the need to revise the dominant theory. The generalization to the population comes about by default: that is by virtue of the non-occurrence of the event foreseen by the theory under examination.

Obviously, the generalization must be carefully thought through. Otherwise, the danger arises of lapsing into the determinism to which Popper's falsificationism is susceptible. As Lieberson (1992: 212) emphasizes:

> it is very difficult to reject a major theory because it appears not to operate in some specific setting. One is wary of concluding that Max Weber was wrong because of a single deviation in some inadequately understood time or place. In the same fashion, we would view an accident caused by a sober driver as failing to disprove the notion that drinking causes automobile accidents.

Comparative inference

The second criterion is used to make generalizations similar to statistical inferences, but without employing probability criteria. This can be done by identifying cases within extreme situations as well as certain characteristics, or cases within a wide range of situations in order to maximize variation, that is, to have all the possible situations in order to capture the heterogeneity of a population. We can choose two elementary schools where, from press reports, previous studies, interviews or personal experiences, we know we can find two extreme situations: in the first school there are severe difficulties of integration between natives and immigrants, while in the second there are virtually none. We can also pick three schools: the first with severe integration difficulties; the second with average difficulties; and the third with rare ones. In the 1930s and 1940s, the American sociologist W. Lloyd Warner (1898–1970) and his team of colleagues and students carried out studies on various communities in the United States. When Warner set about choosing the samples, he decided to select communities whose social structures mirrored important features of American society. He chose four communities (given assumed names): a city in Massachusetts (Yankee City) ruled by traditions on which he wrote five volumes; a lonely county of Mississippi (Deep South, 1941); a Chicago black district (Bronzetown, 1945); and a city in the Midwest (Jonesville, 1949).

In comparative inferences, the cases are selected by making careful comparisons: first by seeking to find cases which represent all the forms of heterogeneity in a target population, and then by controlling whether they are sufficiently homogeneous with the type that one wants to represent. In this difficult but important analysis,

> it is necessary to compare the characteristics of the case(s) being studied with available information about the population to which generalization is intended (...) we are suggesting that where information about the larger population (or about overlapping populations) is available, it should be used. If it is not available, then the potential risks involved in generalization still need to be noted, preferably via specification of likely types of heterogeneity that could render the findings unrepresentative. (Gomm, Hammersley and Foster, 2000: 105–106)

We are therefore very distant from the concepts of naturalistic generalization and transferability, which are unsatisfactory in various respects, for they 'do not provide a sound basis for the design, or justification, of case study research' (Gomm, Hammersley and Foster, 2000: 102). They assign the reader a function which should also be performed by the researcher (assuming responsibility for affirming the generalizability of the study's findings). They therefore relieve the researcher of responsibility for the careful selection of cases on the basis of the variance principle, and not solely on the basis of the theoretical significance of theoretical sampling and of all research on variables (rather than cases). As Schofield (1990) notes, all too often cases seem to be chosen for reasons of convenience and are therefore atypical in various respects.

The emblematic case

If we bear the variance principle in mind, there emerges a third major criterion for

the construction of a sample: the typical or emblematic case.

Gouldner's case studies (1954) on bureaucratization in medium-sized firms, or that by Cicourel (1968) on the relational construction of the figure of the juvenile delinquent, have been considered amply generalizable (by both researchers and readers), probably because they were typical cases and consequently grasped structural aspects of the social action in the organizations studied. Nor should we forget that the question of generalizability is closely tied to the phenomenon being researched, according to the degree of variance in its states.

This means that it is possible to find cases which on their own can represent a significant feature of a phenomenon. Generalizability thus conceived concerns more general structures and is detached from individual social practices, of which they are only an instance. In other words, the scholar does not generalize the individual case or event, which as Weber stressed is unrepeatable, but the key structural features of which it is made up, and which are to be found in other cases or events belonging to the same species or class. As Becker has recently pointed out:

> in every city there is a body of social practices — forms of marriage, or work, or habitation — which don't change much, even though the people who perform them are continually replaced through the ordinary demographic process of birth, death, immigration, and emigration. (2000: 6)

On this view, the question of generalizability assumes a different significance: for example in the conclusions to his study on the relationship between a psychotherapist and a patient suffering from AIDS, Peräkylä writes:

> The results were not generalizable as descriptions of what other counselors or other professionals do with their clients; but they were generalizable as descriptions of what any counselor or other professional, with his or her clients, *can* do, given that he or she has the same array of interactional competencies as the participants of the AIDS counseling session have. (1997: 216, quoted in Silverman, 2000: 109)

Something similar happens in film and radio productions with noise sampling. The squeak of the door (which gives us the shivers when we watch a thriller or a horror film) does not represent all squeaks of doors, but we associate it with them. We do not think about the differences between that squeak and the one made by our front door; we notice the similarities only. These are two different ways of thinking, and most social sciences seek to find patterns of this kind.

While the verbal expressions of an inter-active exchange may vary, exchange based on the question-answer pattern features a for-mal trans-institutional (though not universal) structure. While laying a page of a newspaper on the floor and declaring one's sovereignty over it (Goffman, 1961) is a behavior observed in one psychiatric clinic only, the need to have a private space and control over a territory has been reported many times, albeit in different forms.

INTERACTIVE, PROGRESSIVE, AND ITERATIVE SAMPLING: SOME TIPS

Having outlined the theoretical premises of an idiographic sampling theory, I shall now describe its procedural aspects. However, there is no precise logical itinerary to set out, because methodological principles and rules do not have to stand on their own – as they are instead required to do in statistical sampling theory – in that they have only a weak relation to practice. It is instead necessary to approach the entire question of sampling sequentially, and it would be misleading to plan the whole strategy beforehand. In order to achieve representativeness, the sampling plan must be set in *dialogue* with field incidents, contingencies, and discoveries. This is what I mean by 'interactive, progressive, and iterative sampling.' An excellent instance of this procedure 'is given in Glaser and Strauss's (1964, 1968) studies on dying in the hospital, where hypotheses were developed hand in hand with data collection' (Denzin, 1971: 269). Another example of changing or adding to the sampling plan on the basis of something

the researcher has learnt in the field is provided by Becker:

> Blanche Geer and I were studying college students. At a certain point, we became interested in student 'leaders,' students who were heads of major organizations at the university (there were several hundred of them). We wanted to know how they became leaders and how they exercised their powers. So we made a list of the major organizations (which we could do because we had been there for a year and knew what those were, which we would not have known when we began) and interviewed twenty each of men and women student leaders. And got a great result — it turned out that the men got their positions through enterprise and hustling, while the women were typically appointed by someone from the university! (Howard Becker, 13/7/2002, personal communication)

Consistency must be given to the sampling reasoning, but not by mere application of procedural steps. The reasoning could be as follows.

1 The researcher usually starts from his/her research questions. Melvin Dalton's were:

> Why did grievers and managers form cross-cliques? Why were staff personnel ambivalent toward line officers? Why was there disruptive conflict between Maintenance and Operation? If people where awarded posts because of specific fitness, why the disparity between their given and exercised influence? Why among executives on the same formal level, were some distressed and some not? And why were there such sharp differences in viewpoint and moral concern about given events? What was the meaning of double talk about success as dependent on knowing people rather than on possessing administrative skills? Why and how were 'control' staffs and official guardians variously compromised? What was behind the contradictory policy and practices associated with the use of company materials and services? Thus the guiding question embracing all others was: what orders the schism and ties between official and unofficial action? (1959: 274)

> Research questions comprise the concepts and categories (behaviors, attitudes, and so on) that the researcher intends to study.

2 The researcher conducts *primary* (or 'provisional' and 'open'[7]: Strauss and Corbin, 1990: 193) sampling in order to collect cases in accordance

with the concepts. As Payne and Williams (2005: 295) suggest, 'research design should *plan* for anticipated generalizations, and that generalization should be more *explicitly formulated* within a context of supporting evidence.'

3 Because not every concept can be directly studied, when the researcher constructs the provisional sample, s/he considers the following aspects:

   (a) specificity (focusing on specific social activities with distinctive features, like rituals or ceremonies);
   (b) the field's degree of openness (open or closed places);
   (c) intrusiveness (the endeavor to reduce the researcher's visibility);
   (d) institutional accessibility (free-entry *versus* limited-entry situations *within* the organization);
   (e) significance (frequent and high organizational significance of social activities).

4 It is advisable to sample type of actions or events: 'not, then, men and their moments. Rather moments and their men' (Goffman, 1967: 3), 'not only people but moments of lived life' (Converse and Schuman, 1974: 1), '**incidents** and not persons per se!' (Strauss and Corbin, 1990: 177), in contrast with the common practice of sampling bodies, and of seeking information from these bodies about behaviors and events that are never observed directly (Cicourel, 1996). There are two reasons for this important recommendation: first, it serves to prevent the survey sampling mistake concerning the transferability of ideas about representativeness; second, the same person may be engaged in overlapping activities. For example, Dalton (1959), when studying power struggles in companies, found five 'types of cliques:' vertical (symbiotic and parasitic), horizontal (defensive and aggressive), and random. If we sample individuals, we find that they belong to more than one clique according to the situation, intention, and so on. If we consider activities, everything becomes simpler.

5 To date, four main types of sampling have been developed in social research: purposive, quota, emblematic, and snowball. When cases are selected, attention should be paid to the variance of concept, so that different voices or cases can be included in the sample.

6 As the research proceeds, the researcher will refine his/her ideas, categories and concepts, or come up with new ones. The important thing is to make connections among them, thus formulating working hypotheses. Even though not every hypothesis is testable (indeed the most interesting ones often are not), if the reader is to be persuaded, they must be formulated in a testable way.

7 When the researcher has formulated hypotheses, s/he restarts sampling in order to collect cases systematically relating to each hypothesis, and seeking to make his/her analysis consistent. Strauss and Corbin call this second sampling 'relational and variational: is associated with axial coding. It aims to maximize the finding of differences at the dimensional level' (1990: 176). They depict the research process as funnel-shaped: through three increasingly focused steps (open, axial, and selective) the researcher clarifies his/her statements because 'consistency here means gathering data systematically on each category' (Strauss and Corbin, 1990: 178). When the researcher finds an interesting aspect, she/he must always check whether it occurs in other samples.

8 Generalization must be ensured 'across and within cases (…) [because] the danger of error in drawing general conclusions from a small number of cases must not be underestimated' (Gomm, Hammersley and Foster, 2000: 98). This concept has been sometimes rubricated as 'internal generalization,' and it implies different strategies which take account of diverse dimensions: time, sites, days, and people. The researcher should collect cases of behavior recurring at different moments of time. Because the researcher cannot observe the case-study population twenty-four hours a day, s/he must take a decision on when and where s/he will observe the population (Schatzman and Strauss, 1973: 39–41; Corsaro, 1985: 28–32). Unfortunately,

case study researchers rarely make clear what they take to be the temporal boundaries of the cases they have studied (…) it is not unusual for case studies of schools to focus on one year-group or cohort of students and to assume that the experience of these students is representative of other cohorts, past and future. (Gomm, Hammersley and Foster, 2000: 109)

Social practices always occur in certain places and at certain times of the day. Only if the researcher knows all the rituals of the organization observed can s/he draw a representative sample.

A classic illustration is provided by Berlak et al.'s study of progressive primary school practice in Britain in the 1970s (Berlak and Berlak, 1981;

Berlak et al., 1975). They argued that previous American accounts had been inaccurate because observation had been brief and had tended to take place in the middle of the week, not on Monday or Friday. On the basis of these observations, the inference had been drawn that in progressive classrooms children simply chose what they wanted to do and got on with it. As Berlak et al. document, however, what typically happened was that the teachers set out the week's work on Mondays, and on Fridays they checked that it had been completed satisfactorily. Thus, earlier studies were based on false temporal generalizations within cases they investigated. (Gomm, Hammersley and Foster, 2000: 109–110)

Qualitative researchers do not seek to know the distribution of such behaviors (how many times); they only seek to know whether they are recurrent and significant in the organization under study. In addition, 'our concern is with representativeness of concepts' (Strauss and Corbin, 1990: 190). And finally, in regard to people and sites,

there is also likely to be variation in the behavior of both teachers and pupils across different contexts within a school. While most contact between members of the two groups probably occur in classrooms, they also meet one another in other places as well: in assembly halls, dining rooms, corridors, on game fields, and so on (…) Teacher-pupil relationships are likely to vary across mathematics classrooms, drama studios and science laboratories, for example. (Gomm, Hammersley and Foster, 2000: 111)

9   The researcher can sample new incidents or s/he can review incidents already collected: 'Theoretical sampling is cumulative. This is because concepts and their relationships also accumulate through the interplay of data collection and analysis [...] until theoretical saturation of each category is reached' (Strauss and Corbin, 1990: 178, 188).
10 This interplay between sampling and hypothesis testing is needed because

    (a) representative samples are not predicted in advance but found, constructed, and discovered gradually in the field;
    (b) it reflects the researcher's experience, previous studies, and the literature on the topic. In other words, the researcher will come to know the variance of a

phenomenon cumulatively, study by study. As Gomm, Hammersley and Foster (2000: 107) acknowledge:

> it is possible for subsequent investigations to build on earlier ones by providing additional cases, so as to construct a sample over time that *would* allow effective generalization. At the present, this kind of cumulation is unusual (...) the cases are not usually selected in such a way as to complement previous work;

    (c) representative samples are used to justify the researcher's statements.

It is therefore apparent that, although on the one hand 'generalization is not an issue that can be dismissed as irrelevant by case study researchers' (Gomm, Hammersley and Foster, 2000: 111), on the other it is not the impossible undertaking that survey researchers have always mocked. Finally, whilst probability sampling has a substantive aim – to construct a sample in order to extend the findings to the population – interactive sampling has a further task: to reflect, through its recursiveness, on the plausibility of generalizations.

CONCLUSION

Statistical inference (survey) and theoretical inference (experiment), as the two legitimate ways to draw general conclusions, continue to be used even though their application is fraught with difficulties; and they in fact end up by deviating from their theoretical principles and assumptions. Hence one fails to understand why it is not possible to resort to other forms of generalization which, though unsatisfactory, are no more unsatisfactory that those deemed superior to them. For that matter, contemporary social scientists do not have to choose between perfect and imperfect forms of generalization, but between forms of inference whose strengths and weaknesses depend on the researcher's cognitive aims, the research situation, and the nature of the phenomenon under study.

The central idea of this essay lies midway between two highly authoritative and well-known methodological proposals: Durkheim's (1912) *cas pur* (the 'pure case'), with positivist overtones, and Max Weber's (1904) theory of ideal types. Durkheim believed that the simplest society of all for study of the elementary forms of religious life was the Australian tribe of the Arunta. The Flemish statistician and sociologist Adolphe Quételet (1796–1874) looked to the crowd for his *homme moyen* (the average man), who represented the 'normality' of the species. He was prompted to do so by the discovery that certain characteristics (physical and biological) of individuals were distributed in the populations which he studied according to the 'normal' curve constructed by the mathematician Gauss.

Conversely, Weber maintained that 'feudal society,' 'bureaucracy,' 'charisma' were genetic concepts (developed with a view to a causal explanation) and limiting concepts. They consequently could not be evaluated in terms of their reality-describing adequacy, only in terms of their instrumental efficacy. For Weber (1904), an ideal type was *not a representation* of the real; rather, it was formed by a one-sided *accentuation* of *one or more* points of view and by the connection of a quantity of diffuse, discrete, more or less present and occasionally absent, *particular* phenomena. Given the conceptual purity of an ideal type, it could never be empirically detected in reality; it was a utopian entity.

The typical or emblematic case suggested as a criterion for the construction of sample stands midway between the claim to have discovered the pure case (the quintessence of the phenomenon studied) and renunciation of the empirical search for cases of interest because of their typicality.

At the end of the 1980s, in a study on the interview, I documented the rituals and rhetorical strategies used by an interviewer as he made telephone calls to 10 adolescents in order to arrange subsequent face-to-face interviews (Gobo, 1990, 2001). The research involved the recording of the telephone calls and subsequent discourse analysis. Some years later, Maynard and Schaeffer (1999) conducted very similar research in the United States. Comparison between the results of the two research studies showed that the three researchers had discovered almost identical patterns of behavior. The reason for this similarity was probably that the survey interviewers had been trained with textbooks widely used on both sides of the Atlantic, and that they had used artifacts – technological (telephone, keyboard), cognitive (questionnaires), and organizational (scripts or interview formats) – which made the social activities very similar. There are consequently numerous social research settings in which a few cases *may* suffice to make a generalization. Provided they are chosen carefully.

NOTES

1 To be stressed is that the distinction between probability and non-probability does not mark the boundary between qualitative and quantitative research: in fact, non-probability samples are also used for surveys (quota, telephone, and so on) and for experiments.

2 This compromise centered on the idea of complementarity is still accepted by numerous methodologists: see for instance Payne and Williams (2005: 297).

3 Indeed, there are some who maintain that *generalizability* is perhaps the wrong word for what qualitative researchers seek to achieve: 'Generalization is (…) [a] word (…) that should be reserved for surveys only' (Alasuutari, 1995: 156–7).

4 However, Denzin's (1971) position was very different at the end of the 1960s: he expressed himself in favor of operationalization ('this does not mean that operationalization is avoided – it merely suggests that the point of operazionalization is delayed until the situated meaning of concepts is discovered,' p. 268); he believed that the use of indicators was important ('a series of empirical indicators relevant to each data base and hypothesis must be constructed, and, last, research must progress in a formative manner in which hypotheses and data continually interrelate,' p. 269), and he argued that 'it is necessary for researchers to demonstrate the representativeness of those units in the total population of similar events' (p. 269).

5 Gomm, Hammersley and Foster (2000: 112, endnote 2) acutely point out: 'there is some ambiguity in Stake's position. He also recognizes that case studies can be instrumental rather than intrinsic, and in an outline of the 'major conceptual responsibilities' of case study inquiry he lists the final one as

'developing assertions or generalizations about the case (Stake, 1994, 244).'

6 For this reason, apparently too severe and without empirical justification is Payne and Williams' statement that: 'opportunistic site selection will normally be incompatible with even moderatum generalization' (2005: 310).

7 As Strauss and Corbin (1990: 176) explain: 'open sampling is associated with open coding. Openness rather than specificity guides the sampling choices.' Open sampling can be performed purposively (e.g. pp. 183–4) or systematically (e.g. p. 184), or it occurs fortuitously (e.g. pp. 182–3). It includes on-site sampling.

REFERENCES

Alasuutari, Pertti 1995 *Researching Culture*, London: Sage.

Alberoni, Francesco et al. 1967 *L'attivista di partito*, Bologna: Il Mulino.

Bailey, Kenneth D. 1978 *Methods in Social Research*, New York: Free Press.

Barton Allen H. and Lazarsfeld Paul F. 1955 Some functions of qualitative analysis in social research, *Frankfurter Beitrage zu Sociologie*, 1: 321–361.

Becker, Howard. 1953 Becoming a Marijuana Smoker. *American Journal of Sociology*, 59: 235–242.

Becker, Howard 1998 *Trick of the Trade*, Chicago and London: University of Chicago Press.

Becker, Howard 2000 *Italo Calvino as Urbanologist*, paper.

Bourdieu, Pierre. et al. 1993 *La Misere du monde*, Paris: Editions du Seuil, transl. *The Weight of the World: Social Suffering in Contemporary Society*, Cambridge: Polity, 1999.

Burgess, Ernest W. 1927 Statistics and case studies as methods of sociological research, *Sociology and Social Research*, 12: 103–120.

Burrell, Gibson and Morgan, Gareth 1979 *Sociological Paradigms and Organizational Analysis*, London: Heinemann.

Capecchi, Vittorio 1972 Struttura e tecniche della ricerca, in Pietro Rossi (ed.), *Ricerca sociologica e ruolo del sociologo*, Bologna: Il Mulino.

Chain, Isidor 1963 An introduction to sampling, in C. Selltiz and M. Jahoda (eds.), *Research Methods in Social Relations*, New York: Holt & Rinehart, pp. 509–45.

Cicourel, Aaron V. 1968 *The Social Organization of Juvenile Justice*, New York: Wiley.

Cicourel, Aaron V. 1996 Ecological Validity and White Room Effects, *Pragmatic and Cognition*, 4(2): 221–263.

Cicourel, Aaron V. and Boese, R. 1972 Sign language acquisition and the teaching of deaf children, in D. Hymes, Courtney B. Cazden, Vera P. John, and Dell Hymes (eds.), *Functions of Language in the Classroom*, New York: Teacher College Press.

Connolly, Paul 1998 'Dancing to the wrong tune': Ethnography, generalization, and research on racism in schools, in P. Connolly and B. Troyna (eds.), *Researching Racism in Education*, Buckingham: Open University Press, pp. 122–39.

Converse, Jean M. and Schuman, Howard 1974 *Conversations at Random: Survey Research as Interviewers See it*, New York: Wiley.

Corsaro, William A. 1985 *Friendship and Peer Culture in the Early Years*, Norwood, N.J: Ablex Publishing Corporation.

Crapanzano, Vincent 1980 *Tuhami. Portrait of a Moroccan*, Chicago: University of Chicago Press.

Cronbach, Lee J. 1975 Beyond the two disciplines of scientific psychology, *American Psychologist*, 30: 116–27.

Cronbach, Lee J. 1982 *Designing Evaluations of Educational and Social Programs*, San Francisco: Jossey-Bass.

Dalton, Melvin 1959 *Man Who Manage*, New York: Wiley.

De Martino, Ernesto 1961 *La terra del rimorso*, Milano: Il Saggiatore, transl. *The Land of Remorse: A Study of Southern Italian Tarantism*, London: Free Association Books, 2005.

Denzin, Norman K. 1971 Symbolic interactionism and ethomethodology, in J.D. Douglas (ed.), *Understanding Everyday Life*, London: Routledge and Kegan Paul, pp. 259–284.

Denzin, Norman K. 1983 Interpretive interactionism, in G. Morgan (ed.), *Beyond Method: Strategy for Social Research*, Beverly Hills, CA: Sage, pp. 129–46.

Durkheim, Emile 1912 Les formes élémentaires de la vie religieuse, Paris: Alcan, transl. *The Elementary Forms of the Religious Life,* London: G. Allen & Unwin, 1915.

Festingers, Leon, Riecken, Henry W. and Schachter, Sanley 1956 *When Prophecy Fails*, New York: Harper Torchbooks.

Fielding, Nigel 1981 *The National Front*, London: Routledge.

Galtung, John 1967 *Theory and Methods of Social Research*, Oslo: Universitets Forlaget.

Garfinkel, Harold 1967 *Studies in Ethnometodology*, Englewood Cliffs, NJ: Prentice Hall.

Geertz, Clifford 1972 Deep play: notes on the Balinese Cockfight, *Dedalus*, 101: 1–37.

Geertz, Clifford 1973 *The Interpretation of Culture*, New York: Basic Books.

Glaser, Barney G. and Strauss, Anselm L. 1967 *The Discovery of Grounded Theory,* Chicago: Aldine.

Gobo, Giampietro 1990 *The First Call: Rituals and Rhetorical Strategies in the First Telephone Call with Italian Respondents,* paper, Annual Meeting of the A.S.A., Washington D.C. August, 11–15.

Gobo, Giampietro 2001 Best practices: rituals and rhetorical strategies in the 'initial telephone contact,' Forum Qualitative Social Research, 2(1), http://www.qualitative-research.net/fqs-texte/1-01/1-01gobo-e.htm.

Gobo, Giampietro 2004 Sampling, representativeness and generalizability, in Seale C., Gobo G., Gubrium J.F., Silverman D. (eds.), *Qualitative Research Practice,* London: Sage, pp. 435–56.

Goetz, J.P. and LeCompte, Margaret D. 1984 *Ethnography and Qualitative Design in Education Research,* Orlando, FL, Academic Press.

Goffman, Erving 1961 *Asylums,* New York: Doubleday.

Goffman, Erving 1967 *Interaction Ritual,* New York: Doubleday Anchor.

Goldthorpe, John H., Lockwood, David, Bechhofer, Frank and Platt, Jennifer 1968 *The Affluent Worker: Industrial Attitudes and Behaviour,* Cambridge: Cambridge University Press.

Gomm, Roger, Hammersley, Martyn and Foster, Peter (eds.) (2000) *Case Study Method,* London: Sage.

Goode, William and Hatt, Paul, K. 1952 *Methods in Social Research,* New York: McGraw-Hill.

Gouldner, Alvin G. 1954 *Patterns of Industrial Bureaucracy,* New York: The Free Press.

Griaule, Marcel 1948 *Dieu d'eau: entretiens avec Ogotemmêli,* Paris: Éditions du Chêne.

Groves, Robert M. and Lyberg, Lars E. 1988 An overview of nonresponse issues in telephone surveys, in R.M. Groves, P.P. Biemer, L.E. Lyberg, J.T. Massey, W.L. Nicholls II and J. Waksberg (eds.), *Telephone Survey Methodology,* New York: Wiley.

Guba, Egon G. 1981 Criteria for assessing the trustworthiness of naturalistic enquiries, *Educational Communication and Technology Journal,* 2(29): 75–92.

Guba, Egon G. and Lincoln, Yvonna S. 1981 *Effective Evaluation: Improving the Usefulness of Evaluation Results Through Responsive and Naturalistic Approaches,* San Francisco: Jossey-Bass.

Guba, Egon G. and Lincoln, Yvonna S. 1982 Epistemological and methodological bases of naturalistic inquiry, *Educational Communication and Technology Journal,* 30: 233–252.

Hammersley, Martyn 1992 *What's Wrong with Ethnography?,* London: Routledge.

Hebdige, Dick 1979 *Subculture: The Meaning of Style,* London and New York: Routledge.

Kahneman, D. and Tversky, A. 1972 Subjective probability: A judgment of representativeness, *Cognitive Psychology,* 3: 430–454.

Lieberson, Stanley 1992 *Small N's and Big Conclusions: An examination of the Reasoning in Comparative Studies Based on Small Number of Cases,* reprinted in R. Gomm, Hammersley, M. and Foster P. (eds.) (2000), *op. cit.*

Lincoln, Yvonna, S. and Guba, Egon, G. 1979 *Naturalist Inquiry,* Beverly Hills, CA: Sage. (Reprinted partially in Gomm Roger, Hammersley, Martyn and Foster, Peter (eds.) 2000 *Case Study Method,* London: Sage, pp. 27–42.

Mason, Jennifer 1996 *Qualitative Researching,* Newbury Park: Sage.

Maynard, Douglas W. and Schaeffer, Nora Cate 1999 Keeping the gate, *Sociological Methods & Research,* 1: 34–79.

Mitchell, Clyde J. 1983 Case and situation analysis, *Sociological Review,* 31: 187–211.

Mitchell, R. and Karttunen, S. 1991 Perché e come definire un artista?, *Rassegna Italiana di Sociologia,* XXXII(3): 349–64.

Pawson Ray and Tilley Nick 1997 *Realistic Evaluation,* Sage: London.

Payne, Geoff and Williams, Malcolm 2005 Generalization in qualitative research, *Sociology,* 39(2): 295–314.

Peräkylä, Anssi 1997 Reliability and validity in research based upon transcripts, in David Silverman (ed.), *Qualitative Research,* London: Sage, pp. 201–19.

Pollner, Melvin and McDonald, Wikler Lynn 1985 The social construction of unreality: a case study of a family's attribution of competence to a severely retarded child, *Family Process,* 24: 241–254.

Ragin Charles C. and Becker Howard S. (eds.) 1992 *What is a Case?* Cambridge: Cambridge University Press.

Rosenhan, David L. 1973 On being sane in insane places, *Science,* 179: 250–8.

Rositi, Franco 1993 Strutture di senso e strutture di dati, *Rassegna Italiana di Sociologia,* 2: 177–200.

Sacks, Harvey 1992 *Lectures on Conversation,* Oxford: Blackwell.

Schatzman, Leonard and Strauss, Anselm L. 1973 *Field Research,* Englewood Cliffs, NJ: Prentice Hall.

Schofield Janet Ward 1990 Increasing the generalizability of qualitative research, in E.W. Eisner and A. Peshkin (eds.), *Qualitative Inquiry in Education: The Continuing Debate,* New York: Teachers College Press, pp. 201–232.

Silverman, David 2000 *Doing Qualitative Research,* London: Sage.

Stake, Robert 1978 The case study method in social enquiry, *Educational Researcher,* 7: 5–8 (Reprinted in Gomm Roger, Hammersley, Martyn and Foster, Peter (eds.) 2000 *Case Study Method,* London: Sage, pp. 19–26).

Strauss, Anselm 1987 *Qualitative Analysis for Social Scientists*, Cambridge: Cambridge University Press.

Strauss, Anselm and Corbin, Julet 1990 *Basics of Qualitative Research*, London: Sage.

Tversky, Amos and Kahneman, Daniel 1974 Judgment under uncertainty: Heuristics and biases, *Science*, 185: 1123–1131.

Weber, Max 1904 Die 'Objektivität' sozialwissenschaftlicher und sozialpolitischer Erkenntnis, Archiv für sozialwissenschaf und Sozialpolitik, XIX: 22–87, transl. On the methodology of the social sciences, Illinois: The Free Press of Glencoe, 1949.

Williams, Malcolm 2000 Interpretativism and generalization, *Sociology*, 34(2): 209–24.

Xing Xu, Zhonghe Zhou, Xiaolin Wang, Xuewen Kuang, Fucheng Zhang and Xiangke Du 2003 Four winged dinosaurs from China, *Nature*, 421: 335–339.

Yin, Robert K. 1984 *Case Study Research*, Thousand Oaks: Sage.

Znaniecki , Florian 1934 *The Method of Sociology*, New York: Farrar & Rinehart.

Case Study in Social Research

Linda Mabry

A case study is the empirical investigation of a specified or *bounded* phenomenon (Smith, 1978). The focus of study – the case – may be as minutely targeted as a single person, such as a clinical case of a patient's response to medical treatment or an investigation of whether the educational resources provided to a student eligible for special services meet legal requirements. More commonly, case study research in social science concentrates on instances of greater complexity, such as a community's approach to addressing a prevailing societal issue, a program's effectiveness, or a policy's implications. The case may be selected because of the researcher's interest in a particular instance or site or because of the case's capacity to be informative about a theory, an issue, or a larger constellation of cases.

This chapter will discuss case study as a research approach, its contribution to understanding social phenomena, its methodology, and related issues. Discussion will be illustrated with examples from social science, especially the field of education.

UNDERSTANDING CASES AND CASE STUDY

The *raison d'être* of case study is deep understanding of particular instances of phenomena. This overriding goal drives all practical decisions in conducting a case study: which site or sites might prove most revealing, which questions or issues might usefully guide investigation, which data collection methods might be helpful, which participants might be informative, which analyses might be revealing, which reporting style might be most accessible and compelling to interested audiences. Deep understanding is not easily achieved. Take, for example, a single-subject case of interest to each of us, the effort to understand *oneself*. Such self-study, if it may be called that, often takes a lifetime and, clearly, can go awry, as is evident from our encounters with people who, despite their unlimited access to data, appear to have either unjustifiably humble or inflated views of their own capacities or importance. Case study in social science involves careful methodology to avoid such error.

Case study researchers in social science commonly scrutinize not only the demographics and other statistics of a case, such as how many persons are involved or affected and how indicators of impact vary over time, but even more closely the experiences and perceptions of participants. Understanding a case almost always requires going beyond countable aspects and trends. Inquiry into the social phenomenon of homelessness, for example, may benefit from counting the number of persons dispossessed, comparing the current with a past census, and identifying the homeless by age group, gender, and location. But this is not enough for deep understanding. Grasping why people live on the streets and such things as whether sufficient resources are available to support any who might choose not to do so, whether there are cross-generational effects, which policies and social structures tend to push people into homelessness and which tend to protect them from it will significantly improve understanding. What do the homeless think their opportunities and barriers are? Do social workers and law enforcement officers agree with them? What do policy-makers think the homeless need, and what do they think their constituents or budgets will support? Because the social reality of homelessness is co-constructed by people who participate in the phenomenon, their experiences, beliefs, and values must be studied in order to understand the phenomenon of homelessness in any place that it occurs, the political and ideological contexts that sustain it, and the capacity of participants to imagine or accept potential solutions.

Historical and epistemological antecedents

Because social reality is created by people and because it is complex, dynamic, and context-dependent, its study required the development of a highly nuanced research approach. Eighteenth-century views of *natural science* and *social science* were contrasted by Kant (1781) as the study of *phenomena* or things-as-they-appear and the measurement of things-as-they-are or *nuomena*. As human beings were distinguished on the basis of their sense-making proclivities, *perception* emerged as an object of social science – how things appear to a participant in the scene (e.g. the homeless person, the manager of a soup kitchen, the police chief) and how they appear to an observer (e.g. the social scientist). To the extent that case study researchers work to document human perception and experiences, consciously using their own perceptions in the process, they engage in *phenomenology*.

The clashing motifs of natural science (sometimes referred to as hard science or quantitative or experimental research) and social science (contrastingly referred to as soft science or qualitative, interpretive, or hermeneutic research) may present themselves to case study researchers as a choice or may be resolved in mixed-methods inquiry. Resolution once seemed unlikely, and some still deem the two research paradigms incommensurable (Kuhn, 1962; Lincoln & Guba, 1985). Where case study researchers in social science choose between the two, their methodological choice is typically qualitative.

In this methodological distinction, differentiation has evolved over time. During the century after Kant, the Vienna School moved from *positivism*'s insistence on the measurability of an *objective* reality (Comte, 1822) and the notion that the truth of a statement depends upon its being in a one-to-one correspondence with an objective reality (David, 2005) to *logical positivism*'s less demanding requirement of the verifiability of real entities (Popper, 1935). Across the scientific aisle, simultaneously, Nietzsche (1882), urging *subjective* judgment, observed, 'We behold all things through the human head', and Dilthey (1883) advanced a general theory of understanding, *Verstehen*, whose research imperative involved subjective meaning-making, *Geisteswissenschaften*. From there, the Chicago School developed an urban sociology in the 1920s–30s employing ethnographic methods.

At the end of the next century, Erickson, describing qualitative methodology, was still encouraging researchers to 'put *mind* back in the picture' (1986, p. 127, italics original).

Qualitative or interpretivist study implies the *constructivist* theory that all knowledge is personally constructed (Piaget, 1955; see also Glassman, 2001; and Phillips, 1995). Personal experience, including the vicarious experience promoted in interpretivist case studies, provides the building blocks for the knowledge base constructed by each individual. In articulating a resonant interpretivist research methodology, Lincoln and Guba (1985) promoted an ontology of truth and a subjectivist epistemology in which meaning is personally or socially constructed (see Vygotsky, 1978). Similarly, hermeneutic methodology is marked by search for the meanings people attribute to phenomena (Guba and Lincoln, 1994; see also Guba and Lincoln, 2005; Schutz, 1967; Schwandt, 1994).

Interpretivist distinctions

Three additional contrasts help to distinguish interpretivist case study in the social sciences, with the caution that these characteristics are better understood as complementary than as conflicting with quantitative methodology. First, while large-scale quantitative studies sample from broad populations and produce grand generalizations, case studies provide deep understanding about specific instances. The contrast is one of *breadth* and *depth*, both needed for understanding complex social phenomena. For example, it may be helpful to know the correlations between exposure to the sun and the incidence of melanoma, treatment options, and survival rates; it may also be helpful to know how some patients deal with the effects of treatment and whether their personal strategies aided recovery and quality of life. For disaster planning, it may be helpful to know which community services are most frequently accessed during emergencies; it may also be helpful to know how a critical service agency mobilizes and rations access.

Second, the search for broad applicability of findings in quantitative research drives random sampling from large populations and data collection using standardized procedures. The quality of large-scale quantitative research depends largely on careful adherence to a prescriptive research design. In contrast to the *preordinate design* of quantitative studies, qualitative case studies employ *emergent design*. Rather than carefully adhering to a design specified at the outset, when relatively little is known about a case, a qualitative case researcher is expected to improve on the original blueprint as information emerges during data collection. For example, if unexpected sources of data become apparent or if unanticipated aspects of the case come to light, the researcher is expected to capitalize on the new opportunities and *progressively focus* the study on the features of the case which gradually appear to be most significant.

Finally, while large-scale quantitative studies reduce data to numbers for aggregation and statistical analysis, interpretivist case studies tend to expand datasets as new sources are discovered and questions articulated. The contrast is between the *reductionism* of quantitative studies and the *expansionism* of interpretivist studies. Reductionism allows quantitative researchers to utilize statistical analysis procedures; expansionism allows interpretivist case study researchers fuller access to a case's contexts, conditionalities, and meanings.

Contributions to knowledge and understanding

Such characteristics position case studies to contribute substantively to social science by offering intense focus on cases of interest, their contexts, and their complexity.

Selection of cases

Cases abound – micro-lending, public transportation, the westernization of indigenous cultures, consolidation of rural high schools, access of the uninsured to hospitals, a social worker's case load, an immigrant child's struggle to learn. The identification of a case to be studied will largely depend on the researcher's interest, his or her industry in identifying a case informative enough to be worth studying, and his or her skill in negotiating access to its site.

Where a case is thought to be representative of a larger population, a *typical case* study may be useful for identifying and documenting patterns of ordinary events, the social and political structures that sustain them, and the underlying perceptions and values of participants (e.g. Fine, 1991; Stake et al., 1991; Tobin et al., 1989). Through studies of typical cases, the *status quo* of a phenomenon can be revealed and understood.

Atypical cases can be especially enlightening about the conditionalities of a phenomenon, promoting not only understanding but also theory refinement. Often, cases which defy expectations, conflict with the ordinary, illustrate contrasting approaches, or suggest alternatives or possibilities for change prove most illuminating. Recognition of the uniqueness of each case positions case study researchers to appreciate the particularities of outliers, to attend to the *negative, discrepant,* or *deviant cases* and to the disconfirming data other researchers often dismiss as trivial or 'noise'. Studies of exceptional cases often challenge and assist theorizers to account for enigmatic counterexamples at the margins of generalized explanations, offering invaluable opportunities to improve abstracted representations of social phenomena.

For example, in the field of education, a study of drop-outs which documents their resistance to numbing curricula and dehumanizing conformities as well as efforts to expel them can focus attention on the discrepancy between policy goals and actual practices (Fine, 1991) in a way that study of typically performing students cannot. A study that shows a well-meaning teacher to be, in effect, the unwitting cultural enemy of Native American children attending a residential boarding school (Wolcott, 1987) can raise new sensibilities about the role of teachers in diverse communities. Single-subject case studies of students (Mabry, 1991; Spindler, 1997; Wolcott, 1994) can identify

pressure points in educational delivery to those students who struggle academically, psycho-emotionally, or socio-economically, and often invisibly.

When more than one instance is to be studied, the scope of the inquiry may include contrasting cases. Contexts, circumstances, and their effects on each case may provide a fuller picture of the larger phenomenon as different cases feature different aspects of interest. For example, cases exhibiting different degrees of success in implementing a statewide model of inclusion for disabled children in regular classrooms can clarify factors that support or hinder local efforts (Peck et al., 1993). Cases from different countries can surface a variety of approaches to early childhood education and generate useful questions regarding teacher-pupil ratios, locus of authority for social norms, and societal support for young children and their families (Tobin et al., 1989).

Complexity and contextuality of cases

Case study exhibits a profound respect for the complexity of social phenomena. Interpretivist methodology encourages the case study researcher to be alert to patterns of activities and the variety of meanings participants ascribe to their experiences. While portrayals sensitive to myriad details and factors may include quantitative data, in general, reducing experiences and perspectives to numbers representing a few preselected dimensions involves too great a loss of meaning for quantitative methods alone to satisfy the expectations of case study.

Contextuality is an aspect of the dynamism and complexity of a case. Case study researchers recognize that cases are shaped by their many contexts – historical, social, political, ideological, organizational, cultural, linguistic, philosophical, and so on. Relationships between contexts and cases (and among contexts) are interdependent and reciprocal. For example, the operations of a social service agency may reduce the neediness of its clients and generate public support, while client neediness and available funding affect how the agency operates.

METHODOLOGICAL APPROACHES AND ISSUES

'What is happening here, specifically? What do these happenings mean to the people engaged in them?' – responding to such key questions, qualitative case study addresses a '*need for specific understanding through documentation of concrete details*' (Erickson, 1986, p. 124, italics original). Detailed data can reveal 'the invisibility of everyday life' (p. 121) and exotic othernesses, layers of lived experience, and their implications.

Taking a phenomenological approach (Barritt et al., 1985; Kant, 1781; Schutz, 1967), case studies are generally *naturalistic* (Lincoln & Guba, 1985), sited in natural settings as undisturbed by the researcher as possible. Interest in cultural contexts typically leads to 'thick description' (Geertz, 1973), the recording and analyzing of experiences and meaning-making in detail. Thick descriptions provide understanding of social realities as they are subjectively perceived, experienced, and created by participants. Some case studies are *radical* or *postmodern*, revealing power structures, imbalances, and their effects – for example, in critical ethnography (Anderson, 1989).

Methods and trustworthiness

Consistent with constructivist understanding of the slipperiness of human conceptions of reality, interpretivist methods may not seek to resolve social ambiguities into nomothetic findings but may problematize them: to whom is this real or true? According to which notions of reality? An attitude of openness about truth or reality pushes toward depth of understanding, propelling investigation to a profound level.

As noted, case study in social science generally involves qualitative or mixed methods (Chatterji, 2005; Datta, 1997; Greene et al., 1989; Johnson & Onwuegbuzie, 2004; Mertens, 2005). As described in the literature of educational research by Denzin (1989, 1997), Denzin and Lincoln and their colleagues (1994, 2005), Eisner (1991), Erickson (1986), LeCompte and Preissle (1993), Lincoln and Guba (1985), Stake (1978, 2005), and Wolcott (1994, 1995), qualitative methods prominently feature three data collection techniques: *observation*, *interview*, and the review and analysis of site-generated or -related *documents*. These methods have been accepted as legitimate even in program evaluation (e.g. House, 1994; Mabry, 1998, 2003; Shadish et al., 1991; Worthen et al., 1997).

Direct observation and semi-structured interviews, which allow probative follow-up questions and exploration of topics unanticipated by the interviewer, facilitate development of subtle understanding of what happens in the case and why. These techniques facilitate rigorous penetration of the unknowns and depend on the researcher to recognize the importance of new input, to generate pertinent questions, and to maintain curiosity rather than jumping to interpretation – that is, on intuitiveness and on a methodological commitment to emergent design. Rather than searching for data to confirm or disconfirm an *a priori* theory or hypothesis, interpretivist case study researchers are expected to notice opportunities and to follow data wherever they lead.

The openness and judgment-intensivity which necessitates subjective interpretation in data collection carries into data analysis. Two approaches, each with many variations in different qualitative genres, exemplify this point. Intended to produce *grounded theory*, *constant-comparative method* involves continuous comparison of incoming data with emerging interpretation (Glaser & Strauss, 1967; Strauss & Corbin, 1990), new data igniting new realizations and new interpretive possibilities provoking more sensitive data collection. Case study, however, rarely produces *grand* grounded theory, seeking instead local theory or *petite generalizations* (Erickson, 1986). Second, *thematic analysis* involves the identification of emerging patterns and categories from iterative reviews of the dataset, a process which marshals evidence for developing and warranting findings.

The inherent subjectivity of these methods leaves researchers susceptible to challenge regarding *validity* by those who equate subjectivity more with bias than with sensitivity. Case study researchers generally employ ethnographic techniques which require more intimate (proximal) contact with research subjects than, for example, survey researchers. The issues of validity, generalizability, and proximity call for care and will each be considered later in the text.

Narrative reporting

The development of reports, usually in the form of narrative accounts, is the final step in a long analytic process. Narrative reporting offers at least three important advantages: conveyance of deep meaning, reader accessibility, and opportunity for readers to recognize and consider researcher subjectivity. Narratives carry complex meanings which are comprehensible to readers, narrative portrayals building on natural ways of understanding which have evolved across human history (Carter, 1993), as the endurance of Homerian and other sagas attest.

Story-like representations of cases promote wide accessibility for general and scholarly audiences. Human capacity to grasp nuanced understandings from stories has been confirmed by cognitive psychologists who urge case-based approaches to understanding multi-faceted, ambiguous, ill-structured phenomena (Spiro et al., 1987) to help readers transition from grasping empirical findings to applying them.

First-person case narratives, using 'I' judiciously so as not to deflect focus from the case to the researcher, subtly and continuously remind the reader that the narrative is the product of the researcher's mind. Detailed data presentation in narratives also invites readers to judge whether the data support the findings and to construct their own personal meanings. Readers' analyses of the data presented may differ – usefully or uncomfortably – from those of the researcher. When experiential details in narratives allow readers to engage in analysis that extends

researcher interpretations, as exemplified by Freudian interpretations of Shakespeare three centuries after the Bard's death, narratives reveal their special merits and contributions.

Experientiality

Learning from experience is important partly because human capacity to understand exceeds the capacity of language to convey meaning. A company president may choose to spend a day as an entry-level employee, not because of insufficient written information about procedures, profits, or personnel but because such an experience can tell something more. In attempting to encourage public support for famine victims, a journalist may report not only mortality rates but also the harrowing stories of some individuals that instantiate the human understanding of media consumers.

More than other types of empirical research reports, a case study tells the story of the case. Interpretivist case study researchers are expected to stimulate vicarious experience for readers, providing a sense of almost having been present to witness the events documented in case studies. Case studies foster deep understanding not only by presenting analytic details – Geertz's (1973) 'thick description' – but also by offering experiential reports. Recognizing that, for purposes of understanding, *experiential knowledge* is often superior to *declarative knowledge*, interpretivist case study researchers attempt to promote their readers' vicarious experience of the events described. By contrast, the declarative knowledge in statements of research findings may be less memorable and more easily dismissed.

Experiential portrayals enhance *tacit knowledge* (Polanyi, 1958), unspoken understandings or 'gut feelings' that may elude satisfactory expression in language yet be more influential for action. The power of tacit knowledge can be seen in a parent's – but few others' – ability to decode a teenager's 'Right, Mom' which may signal approval, compliance, malingering, or sarcasm. Perhaps not even Mom, despite understanding the intent, could explain *how* to derive the meaning. The experientiality of narratives intensifies the power of case study reports to deepen understanding because it promotes development of tacit knowledge.

There are trade-offs and drawbacks to case study as a research approach, including proximity, validity, and generalizability.

PROXIMITY

The psycho-socio-emotional distance between researchers and the cases establishes their *proximity*. Researchers are usually outsiders to the cases they study (but not always), observers rather than true members of a case. On a continuum of possible roles from *external observer* to *participant-observer*, a researcher's stance may be as passive as that of the proverbial fly on the wall or more active, like a participant in the case. In *ethnography*, researchers are sometimes cautioned against 'going native'. Contrastingly, in *action research* or *self-study*, the case researcher may be a native from the outset – project manager or a classroom teacher conducting research for the purpose of translating deeper understanding into making immediate improvements.

Externality

A case study researcher can promotes understanding by collecting and organizing information, focusing attention on meaningful aspects, and providing an external analytic perspective that may be helpful even to insiders intimately familiar with the case. Although researchers choose cases partly out of personal interest, externality suggests an absence of vested interest, one source of bias, which can promotes the credibility of findings.

On the other hand, externality implies limited lived experience of the case and the danger that case studies may fail to 'get it right' (Geertz, 1973; Wolcott, 1994). The contextuality of cases and the phenomenological impulse of case study research create special burdens for external researchers attempting to grasp and represent multiple insider perspectives and cases' complexity. Familiarity with the ethos helps outsiders attempt *etic*[1] representations of insiders' experiences and meanings, representations which should be accompanied by appropriate qualification.

Cultural competence

Cultures and subcultures develop singular histories and respond to overlapping contexts and unique personalities in highly nuanced ways. For external researchers, the cultural competence needed for grasping local meanings cannot be presumed. Even when external researchers share nationality and language with case participants, they may be unable to detect the subtle or hidden meanings suggested by a pause in conversation, the type of refreshments offered, who is present and who is absent in a gathering, the items found (or not) on a meeting agenda, who gives and who receives gifts, who makes decisions and how. Reliance on knowledgeable participants acting as *key informants* can help surface local meanings, although debriefings and other discussions for the purpose of cultural translation will inject key informants' own meanings into datasets and introduce new cautions for interpretation.

Where the researcher does not share the language(s) or dialect(s) indigenous to the case, dependence on translators is unavoidable. The transfer of meaning from speaker to hearer, never assured, is further compromised by introducing this mediating influence. Language structures and idioms are so culture-specific and dynamic that, even with highly competent and motivated translators, inaccuracies are difficult to avoid. These limitations, too, should be acknowledged in case reports.

Ethics

The misunderstandings which externality can generate has an ethical component. Participants have a stake in the accuracy of how they are presented and in whether case accounts are flattering or damning. For example, participants in Peshkin's case study of a Christian fundamentalist school (1986) may have thought it not only inaccurate but also unfair for a Jewish researcher to compare them to Nazis. A teacher in a California school, after agreeing to participate in a study about education in a socially stable community, did feel betrayed by a researcher who instead analyzed his classroom's lack of arts opportunities (Stake, 1991). These illustrations show how participants may suffer at the hands of an external other whom they have allowed into their communities.

Moreover, human subjects may sometimes forget that ever-present researchers are not their colleagues, neighbors, or friends. The close proximity, the access, the rapport case study researchers need in order to develop understanding can create special vulnerabilities for human subjects. Case study researchers are likely to learn a lot about participants, more even than participants may realize, and may anticipate some threats more quickly or clearly than participants might. The challenge here is to be appropriately alert and protective without lapsing into paternalism.

VALIDITY

Validity refers, essentially, to the accuracy of data and the reasonableness and warrantedness of data-based interpretations, to 'the *adequacy* and *appropriateness* of inferences' (Messick, 1989, p. 13, italics original). Whether the data and interpretations are infused with undue researcher bias, whether the methods of assuring trustworthiness are sufficient, whether limitations are fully explicated in reporting are critical validity considerations.

Important to all types of research, validity in interpretivist social science is complicated by subjectivity, so pervasive in interpretivist practice that some claim the researcher *is* the method. While subjectivity figures in all research, it is more obvious in qualitative than in quantitative methodology. The issue is complicated by interpretivist acknowledgment that social phenomena are perceived

differently not only by different participants but also by different researchers, preempting confirmatory replication of studies. Whether judgment-intensivity is a challenge for validity, an opportunity to seek information on a search-as-needed basis, or an insurmountable obstacle is a matter of paradigmatic controversy. The researcher's perspective has been described as more virtue than limitation (Peshkin, 1988), and it is researcher interest that compels the determined efforts resulting in deep understanding.

Although an interpretivist approach to case study assumes that each reader and each researcher will construct unique personal understandings of a case, substantial *intersubjective agreement* is desirable and expected – working agreement rather than absolute consensus on every point. Discussion of various interpretations about a case helps to maintain openness to meaning-making and to sustain the disequilibrium that presses toward ever deeper thinking and understanding.

Thus, while accepting the malleability of truth and the inherence of judgment in perception and interpretation, interpretivists do not approve unbridled subjectivity or absolute relativism. Typologies for understanding and encouraging validity in interpretive research include Lincoln and Guba's (1985) explication of *trustworthiness* and Maxwell's (1992) argument for *descriptive, interpretive, theoretical,* and *evaluative validity* – for accurate descriptive data, sufficient support for interpretations, and empirical justification of emergent theories and evaluative judgments.

Validation and triangulation

The validity of a case study would be suspect if participating human subjects rejected the report as completely false or if independent researchers familiar with the case or site did so. Consequently, case study and other interpretivist methods commonly include triangulation and validation (see especially Denzin, 1989) and articulate in reports their efforts to enhance validity. Although validity and credibility are separate properties, these efforts tend to improve both.

Triangulation

During data collection, *triangulation*[2] *by data source* involves collecting data from different persons or entities. Checking the degree to which each source confirms, elaborates, and disconfirms information from other sources honors case complexity and the perspectives among participants and helps ascertain the accuracy of each datum. *Methodological triangulation* involves checking data collected via one method with data collected using another, for example, checking whether direct observation can confirm interview testimony. *Triangulation by time* involves repeated return to the site to track patterns of events and their trends and permutations. Because different observers might see different things or might interpret the same things differently, *triangulation by observer* can help expand meaning-making, balance interpretations, and guard against undue researcher subjectivity.

Theoretical triangulation in data analysis involves recourse to different abstractions that might explain the data. Various theories, models, typologies, and categorization systems may suggest different meanings. For example, analysis of the productivity of a working unit according to an economic model may suggest an interpretation quite different from one suggested by analysis of the unit's procedures according to a model of democratic decision-making. Similarly, an analysis of classroom discussion regarding the degree to which the teacher's questioning prompts student knowledge gains may yield quite different results from an analysis regarding the degree to which ethnically diverse students participate meaningfully.

Validation

The notion that accounts may be 'made better by good readers and clearer by good opponents' (Nietzsche, 1879) underlies processes of validation in interpretivist social science. Research subjects can help assure the accuracy of data by *member-checking*,

a procedure in which groups representing those observed and interviewed are asked to confirm, elaborate, and disconfirm write-ups (Lincoln & Guba, 1985). In *comprehensive validation*, a more thorough approach, each human subject reviews data collected from his or her own interviews or observations prior to further dissemination (Mabry, 1998). Research subjects may be asked to validate interpretations as well as data.

In addition to triangulation and validation, peer review by critical friends, especially colleagues with expertise in the phenomenon or case or methodology, can provide a check on the sufficiency of the evidence, the logic of arguments, overall clarity and experientiality.

GENERALIZABILITY

Generalizability refers to the capacity of the case to be informative about a general phenomenon, to be broadly applicable beyond the specific site, population, time, and circumstances studied. The *understanding* that a single case studied in depth can offer is different from the generalizable *explanation*, often via theory or model, more easily provided by large-scale study (von Wright, 1971).

In quantitative research, generalizability, often referred to as *external validity*, drives design: hypothesis-testing to support a generalizable theory, random sampling to assure representativeness of a larger population, team training for *reliability* or consistency in administration of data collection instruments to allow aggregability. While researchers schooled in the quantitative tradition have considered case studies problematic in their determined focus on single cases (e.g. Campbell & Stanley, 1963), case study researchers have made different types of arguments regarding generalizing their work.

Acceptable interpretivist generalization

The *case-to-population generalizations* (Firestone, 1993) important in quantitative research may be more available from *multi-case studies* than from single cases, for example, a series of individual *lesson studies* (Lewis et al., 2006) or *scaling up* studies (McDonald et al., 2006) which pay specific attention to the particulars affecting wider application.

More appropriate to single case studies than grand generalizations are *petite generalizations* (Erickson, 1986) which apply within the case but do not go beyond the strongest possible interpretations warranted by the data from the case. Examples from Education are listed below:

- Henson Elementary School's implementation of a peer mediation program, despite missteps in training, empowered students to regulate and improve their interpersonal behaviors (adapted from Mahoney, 1999).
- Offering schooling in English and in the mother tongue forced parents in the communities of the remote highlands of Papua New Guinea to choose between their children's future economic prosperity and maintenance of their cultural identities (adapted from Malone, 1997).
- Local teachers' classroom assessments were more informative about their students' achievements but were sidelined by state tests (adapted from Mabry et al., 2003).

The temptation to generalize beyond a circumscribed case may be strong; for example, wouldn't peer mediation likely empower other children to regulate and improve their interpersonal behaviors? Firestone's (1993) concept of *analytic generalizations*, in which the 'theory in question is embedded in a broader web of theories … [used] to link specific study findings to the theory of interest' (p. 17) hints at the possibility of extension.

More common are *case-to-case generalizations* (Firestone, 1993), readers' links between case reports and cases of personal interest. Case study reports which include substantial data, even some relatively uninterpreted observation narratives and interview excerpts, not only convey vicarious experience but also present the evidentiary base. These *readerly* or *open texts* invite readers to construct individual interpretations and empower them to generalize to cases of interest to them.

Purposive sampling

Development of deep understanding does indeed take time, so few cases can usually be selected even for multi-case studies. The basis for making selections of cases and human subjects is consequently purposeful or *purposive*, since random selection might easily fail to yield the most informative sites or samples of human subjects, skewing findings because of sampling bias. Cases and subjects may be selected for their representativeness of a larger population but are more likely to be chosen for their or informativeness.

Exemplary cases, contrasting cases, deviant cases, or a range of cases illustrating different aspects or a phenomenon may be of interest. Selection may be based on reputation (e.g. the lowest-ranking school on California's accountability index, a school renowned for its focus on the arts) or location (e.g. a classroom in a juvenile detention center, one school per geographic area) or demographics (e.g. a school with a minority student population, a women's college) or other selection criteria. Such cases may not produce generalizable theory but are very capable of contributing to it.

Convenience sampling is inevitably a factor in any sampling strategy, reflecting subjects' willingness to participate or to grant access to a site, and suggesting two caveats. First, for case study or any other research, restricted access can diminish representativeness where typicality is desired. Second, researchers have more often chosen to study, for example, the impoverished than the rich, low-level workers rather than CEOs. This tendency may be related to a greater openness among the haves as opposed to the have-notes. The result is that, across cases, these methods have historically exhibited socio-economic lopsidedness.

Role of theory

Theory can be produced in small-scale studies but, more often, such generalizations result from large-scale research. Large-scale quantitative research often involves causal analysis for the purpose of prediction and control of future behaviour. For example, physicians may prescribing a drug to patients based on studies suggesting the drug alleviates their disease. Often, an experimental study begins with a hypothesis[3] derived from theory and tested empirically, a *deductive* approach in which theory propels data collection.

The inverse of this approach is more common to case study where theory development (if any) is *inductive*, following data collection and explaining the dataset. Theory may emerge, perhaps unexpectedly, through constant-comparative method, a dialogic cycle of data collection and interpretation which is incomplete until interpretations encompass all available data (Glaser & Strauss, 1967; Strauss & Corbin, 1990), as noted earlier. Small-scale studies can also refine existing theory, for example, physicians prescribing a drug to all patients except those from a specific ethnic group which tends to react negatively as revealed by prior case studies.

Whether or not research generates theory, personal theory plays a role in all research. Case study researchers who claim their work is 'merely descriptive' or 'atheoretical' inappropriately deny the effects of their own conceptualizations of the phenomena they study. From the outset of a case study, formation of a research question indicates an underlying personal theory, perhaps implicit, about the nature of the phenomenon. Even word choice signals theory, for example, 'active classroom' suggesting a theory that learners are active constructors of their knowledge bases; or 'chaotic' suggesting a theory that knowledge is delivered rather than constructed and that learning is passive. As part of the effort to discipline their subjectivities, interpretivist researchers may try to articulate their personal theories, making them explicit for readers as they consider the validity of descriptions and findings.

While theory development is not usually expected in small-scale studies, the use of theory to analyze data may nevertheless be a highly productive part of the interpretive process. Theoretical triangulation, noted earlier, facilitates interpretation by offering views of the data through different explanatory lenses. Different potential interpretations suggested by different theories help the interpretivist case study researcher to think deeply about meaning.

CONCLUSION

With deep understanding of a case as the prime goal of case study, an attitude of openness may be the most fortuitous item in a case study researcher's dispositional toolkit. There is always more that can be learned about a case, more potential interpretations of existing data, and new events that create alterations in the case. Premature conclusions can foreclose on deeper understanding. Curiosity to know more and to understand better encourages delving deeply into the meaning of the case. Link by link, case by case, construction of meaning by the researcher, by the reader, and by the research community is how case study contributes to social science and to society. As accumulated case studies refine understandings of social phenomena, accumulated practice of case study may continue to refine these methods, resulting in ever more careful and nuaneed social science.

NOTES

1 In contrast to a phenomenological *emic* approach to research is an *etic* approach in which an outsider's – rather than an insider's – perspective is offered to readers (see Seymour-Smith, 1986).

2 Triangulation, a term derived from nautical procedures for locating ships at sea based on three points, does not presume three sources (or methods, observers, data collection events, or theoretical perspectives). More or fewer, as needed and as available, may be consulted.

3 Actually, experimental studies generally begin with *null hypotheses*, testing to see whether the inverse of the actual hypothesis can be proved false – thus providing indirect evidence that the actual hypothesis is true. Note that this approach is essentially a matter of ruling out rival hypotheses to narrow the range of possible explanations for a phenomenon.

REFERENCES

Anderson, G. A. (1989). Critical ethnography in education: Origins, current status, and new directions. *Review of Educational Research, 59* (3), 249–270.

Barritt, L., Beekman, T., Bleeker, H. & Mulderij, K. (1985). *Researching educational practice.* University of North Dakota: Center for Teaching and Learning.

Campbell, D. T. & Stanley, J. C. (1963). *Experimental and quasi-experimental designs for research.* Boston: Houghton-Mifflin.

Carter, K. (1993). The place of story in the study of teaching and teacher education. *Educational Researcher, 22* (1), 5–12, 18.

Chatterji, M. (2005). Evidence on 'what works': An argument for extended-term mixed-method (ETMM) evaluation designs. *Educational Researcher, 33* (9), 3–13.

Comte, A. (1822/1970). *Plan des Travaux Scientifiques Nécessaires pour Réorganiser la Société.* Paris: Editions Aubier-Montaigne.

Datta, L. (1997). Multimethod evaluations: Using case studies together with other methods. In E. Chelimsky & W. R. Shadish (Eds.), *Evaluation for the 21st century: A handbook* (pp. 344–359). Thousand Oaks, CA: Sage.

David, M. (2005). The correspondence theory of truth. In E. N. Zalta (Ed.), *The Stanford encyclopedia of philosophy.* Retrieved May 22, 2006 from http://plato.stanford.edu/archives/fall2005/entries/truth-correspondence/.

Denzin, N. K. (1989). *The research act: A theoretical introduction to sociological methods* (3rd ed.). Englewood Cliffs, NJ: Prentice Hall.

Denzin, N. K. (1997). *Interpretive ethnography: Ethnographic practices for the 21st century.* Thousand Oaks, CA: Sage.

Denzin, N. K. & Lincoln, Y. S. (1994). *Handbook of qualitative research.* Thousand Oaks, CA: Sage.

Denzin, N. K. & Lincoln, Y. S. (2005). *Handbook of qualitative research* (3rd ed.). Thousand Oaks, CA: Sage.

Dilthey, W. (1883/1976). *Einleitung in die Geisteswissenschaften.* In H. P. Richman (Ed.), *W. Dilthey: Selected writings* (pp. 157–263). London: Cambridge University Press.

Eisner, E. W. (1991). *The enlightened eye: Qualitative inquiry and the enhancement of educational practice.* New York: Macmillan.

Erickson, F. (1986). Qualitative methods in research on teaching. In M. C. Wittrock (Ed.), *Handbook of research on teaching* (3rd ed., pp. 119–161). New York: Macmillan.

Fine, M. (1991). *Framing dropouts: Notes on the politics of an urban public high school.* Albany, NY: SUNY Press.

Firestone, W. A. (1993). Alternative arguments for generalizing from data as applied to qualitative research. *Educational Researcher, 22* (4), 16–23.

Geertz, C. (1973). *The interpretation of cultures: Selected essays.* New York: Basic Books.

Glaser, B. G. & Strauss, A. I. (1967). *The discovery of grounded theory.* Chicago, IL: Aldine.

Glassman, M. (2001). Dewey and Vygotsky: Society, experience, and inquiry in educational practice. *Educational Researcher, 30* (4), 3–14.

Greene, J. C., Caracelli, V. & Graham, W. F. (1989). Toward a conceptual framework for multimethod evaluation designs. *Educational Evaluation and Policy Analysis, 11* (3), 255–274.

Guba, E. G. & Lincoln, Y. S. (1994). Competing paradigms in qualitative research. In N. K. Denzin & Y. S. Lincoln (Eds.), *Handbook of qualitative research* (pp. 105–117). Thousand Oaks, CA: Sage.

Guba, E. G. & Lincoln, Y. S. (2005). Paradigmatic controversies, contradictions, and emerging confluences. In N. K. Denzin & Y. S. Lincoln (Eds.), *Handbook of qualitative research* (3rd ed., pp. 191–216). Thousand Oaks, CA: Sage.

House, E. R. (1994). Integrating the quantitative and qualitative. In C. S. Reichardt & S. F. Rallis (Eds.), *The qualitative-quantitative debate: New perspectives* (pp. 13–22). In W. R. Shadish (Ed.), *New Directions for Program Evaluation* (no. 61). San Francisco: Jossey-Bass.

Johnson, R. B. & Onwuegbuzie, A. J. (2004). Mixed methods research: A research paradigm whose time has come. *Educational Researcher, 33* (7), 14–26.

Kant, I. (1781/1996). *The critique of pure reason.* (trans. by W. S. Pluhar & P. Kitcher). Indianapolis, IN: Hackett.

Kuhn, T. (1962). *The structure of scientific revolutions.* Princeton, NJ: Princeton University Press.

LeCompte, M. D. & Preissle, J. (1993). *Ethnography and qualitative design in educational research* (2nd ed.). San Diego: Academic Press.

Lewis, C., Perry, R. & Murata, A. (2006). How should research contribute to instructional improvement? The case of lesson study. *Educational Researcher, 35* (3), 3–14.

Lincoln, Y. S. & Guba, E. G. (1985). *Naturalistic inquiry.* Newbury Park, CA: Sage.

Mabry, L. (1991). Nicole: Seeking attention. In D. B. Strother (Ed.), *Learning to fail: Case studies of students at-risk* (pp. 1–24). Bloomington, IN: Phi Delta Kappa.

Mabry, L. (1998). Case study methods. In H. J. Walberg & A. J. Reynolds (Eds.), *Evaluation research for educational productivity* (pp. 155–170). Greenwich, CT: JAI Press.

Mabry, L. (2003). In living color: Qualitative methods in educational evaluation. In T. Kellaghan & D. L. Stufflebeam (Eds.), *International handbook of educational evaluation* (pp. 167–185). Boston: Kluwer-Nijhoff.

Mabry, L., Poole, J., Redmond, L. & Schultz, A. (2003). Local impact of state-mandated testing. *Education Policy Analysis Archives, 11*(22). Available at: http://epaa.asu.edu/epaa/v11n22/

Mahoney, K. K. (1999). *Peer mediation: An ethnographic investigation of an elementary school's program.* Unpublished doctoral dissertation. Indiana University, Bloomington, IN.

Malone, D. L. (1997). *Namel manmeri: Language and culture maintenance and mother tongue education in the highlands of Papua New Guinea.* Unpublished doctoral dissertation. Indiana University, Bloomington, IN.

Maxwell, J. A. (1992). Understanding and validity in qualitative research. *Harvard Educational Review, 62* (3), 279–300.

McDonald, S.-K., Keesler, V. A., Kauffman, N. J. & Schneider, B. (2006). Scaling-up exemplary interventions. *Educational Researcher, 35* (3), 15–32.

Mertens, D. (2005). *Research and evaluation in education and psychology: Integrating diversity with quantitative, qualitative, and mixed methods* (2nd ed.). Thousand Oaks, CA: Sage.

Messick, S. (1989). Validity. In R. L. Linn (Ed.), *Educational measurement* (3rd ed., pp. 13–103). New York: American Council on Education, Macmillan.

Nietzsche, F. (1879/1996). *Human, all too human.* (trans. by R. J. Hollingdale). Cambridge, MA: Cambridge University Press.

Nietzsche, F. (1882/1974). *The gay science.* (trans. W. Kaufmann). London: Vintage Books.

Peck, C. A., Mabry, L., Curley, J. & Conn-Powers, M. (1993, May). Implementing integration at the preschool and kindergarten level: A follow-along study of Washington's efforts. Washington Office of the Superintendent of Public Instruction and Early Childhood Development Association of Washington's Infant and Early Childhood Conference, Seattle, WA.

Peshkin, A. (1986). *God's choice.* Chicago: University of Chicago Press.

Peshkin, A. (1988). In search of subjectivity—one's own. *Educational Researcher, 17* (7), 17–22.

Phillips, D. C. (1995). The good, the bad, and the ugly: The many faces of constructivism. *Educational Researcher, 24* (7), 5–12.

Piaget, J. (1955). *The language and thought of the child.* New York: World.

Polanyi, M. (1958). *Personal knowledge: Towards a post-critical philosophy.* Chicago, IL: University of Chicago Press.

Popper, K. R. (1935). *Logik der Forschung.* Vienna: Julius Springer Verlag.

Schutz, A. (1967). *Collected papers I: The problem of social reality.* The Hague: Martinus Nijhoff.

Schwandt, T. A. (1994). Constructivist, interpretivist approaches to human inquiry. In N. K. Denzin & Y. S. Lincoln (Eds.), *Handbook of qualitative research* (pp. 118–137). Thousand Oaks, CA: Sage.

Seymour-Smith, C. (1986). *Dictionary of anthropology.* Boston: G. K. Hall.

Shadish, W. R., Jr., Cook, T. D. & Leviton, L. C. (1991). *Foundations of program evaluation: Theories of practice.* Newbury Park, CA: Sage.

Smith, L. (1978). An evolving logic of participant observation, educational ethnography and other case studies. In L. Shulman (Ed.), *Review of research in education* (vol. 6, pp. 316–377). Itasca, IL: Peacock.

Spindler, G. D. (1997). Beth Anne—A case study of culturally defined adjustment and teacher perceptions. In G. D. Spindler (Ed.), *Education and cultural process: Anthropological approaches* (3rd ed., pp. 246–261). Prospect Heights, IL: Waveland Press.

Spiro, R. J., Vispoel, W. P., Schmitz, J. G., Samarapungavan, A. & Boerger, A. E. (1987). Knowledge acquisition for application: Cognitive flexibility and transfer in complex content domains. In B. C. Britton (Ed.), *Executive control processes* (pp. 177–199). Hillsdale, NJ: Erlbaum.

Stake, R. E. (1978). The case study method in social inquiry. *Educational Researcher, 7* (2), 5–8.

Stake, R. E. (2005). Qualitative case studies. In N. K. Denzin & Y. S. Lincoln (Eds.), *Handbook of qualitative research* (3rd ed., pp. 443–466). Thousand Oaks, CA: Sage.

Stake, R., Bresler, L. & Mabry, L. (1991). *Custom and cherishing: The arts in elementary schools.* Urbana, IL: Council for Research in Music Education, University of Illinois.

Strauss, A. & Corbin, J. (1990). *Basics of qualitative research: Grounded theory procedures and techniques.* Newbury Park, CA: Sage.

Tobin, J. J., Wu, D. Y. H. & Davidson, D. H. (1989). *Preschool in three cultures: Japan, China, and the United States.* New Haven, CT: Yale University Press.

von Wright, G. H. (1971). *Explanation and understanding.* London: Routledge & Kegan Paul.

Vygotsky, L. S. (1978). *Mind in society: The development of higher mental process.* Cambridge, MA: Harvard University Press.

Wolcott, H. F. (1987). The teacher as an enemy. In G. D. Spindler (Ed.), *Education and cultural process: Anthropological approaches* (2nd ed., pp. 136–150). Prospect Heights, IL: Waveland Press.

Wolcott, H. F. (1994). *Transforming qualitative data: Description, analysis, and interpretation.* Thousand Oaks, CA: Sage.

Wolcott, H. F. (1995). *The art of fieldwork.* Walnut Creek, CA: AltaMira Press.

Worthen, B. R., Sanders, J. R. & Fitzpatrick, J. L. (1997). *Program evaluation: Alternative approaches and practical guidelines* (2nd ed.). New York: Longman.

Longitudinal and Panel Studies

Jane Elliott, Janet Holland and
Rachel Thomson

INTRODUCTION

Longitudinal social research offers unique insights into process, change and continuity over time in phenomena ranging from individuals, families and institutions to societies. It helps to map the social world temporally, enabling us to make sense of changes that take place between generations, within the life course and through history. Longitudinal data can broadly be understood as any information that tells us about what has happened to a set of research cases over a series of time points. The majority of longitudinal data take human subjects as the unit of analysis, and therefore longitudinal data commonly record change at an individual or 'micro' level (Ruspini, 2002). They can be contrasted with cross-sectional data, which record the circumstances of individuals (or other research units) at just one particular point in time. Different traditions of longitudinal research seek to combine analyses of quantity (of cases) and the quality (of changes) in different ways, producing different types of data, privileging particular forms of understanding, and pursuing different logics of enquiry.

Both qualitative and quantitative longitudinal research traditions are well established, with quantitative longitudinal research having offered a powerful input into government policy in many societies. We indicate here some of the established quantitative longitudinal studies with their complex, cumulative datasets, which have made, and are making, considerable contributions in these areas, and discuss developments of analysis. The focus is on panel studies and cohort studies where the same group of individuals are followed through time. Trend studies, which focus on change over time by using repeated *cross-sectional* samples (for example opinion polls which track changes in the popularity of political parties) are beyond the scope of this chapter. Qualitative longitudinal work has been the mainstay of some social science disciplines and subsets of sociology, including anthropology, oral history, community studies, education studies and criminology. It is currently gaining ground in the social sciences more generally, and is also becoming valued by policy-makers concerned with issues where questions about what happens are seen to need the unique experiential and contextual elaboration of qualitative approaches. In this chapter we examine and review both qualitative and quantitative approaches to longitudinal social research. In some instances the problems and contributions are shared and similar. In others the specificities of quantitative and qualitative research raise particular issues, or create particular inflections on common issues. Commonalities can include overall research design (prospective, retrospective, cohort), and issues of attrition, archiving and ethics; differences include modes of data generation, type of data generated, methods of analysis and conceptualisation of the subject. Where issues are common they are merged in the chapter, with specific inflections indicated; where different they are discussed separately.

COLLECTING LONGITUDINAL DATA

Prospective and retrospective research designs

Longitudinal data are frequently collected using a *prospective* longitudinal research design, i.e. the participants in a study are contacted by researchers and asked to provide information about themselves and their circumstances on a number of *different* occasions. This is often referred to as a *panel study*. It is not necessary, however, to use a longitudinal research design in order to collect longitudinal data and a conceptual distinction between longitudinal data and longitudinal research should be maintained (Featherman, 1980; Scott and Alwin, 1998; Taris, 2000). Indeed, the one-off *retrospective* collection of longitudinal data is very common in both qualitative and quantitative research traditions. In quantitative approaches it has become an established method for obtaining basic information about the dates of key life course events such as marriages, separations and divorces and the birth of any children (i.e. event history data). This is clearly an efficient way of collecting longitudinal data and obviates the need to re-contact the same group of individuals over a period of time.

In qualitative approaches, such as life history research, individuals may be asked to report events spanning a lifetime.

A potential problem in quantitative research is that people may not remember the past accurately enough to provide good quality data. While some authors have argued that recall is not a major problem for collecting information about dates of significant events, other research suggests that individuals may have difficulty remembering dates accurately or may prefer not to remember unfavourable episodes or events in their lives (Dex, 1995; Dex and McCulloch, 1998; Jacobs, 2002; Mott, 2002). The techniques for helping respondents to remember accurately the dates of events of interest to the researcher can be similar to those used by some qualitative researchers. It is by linking together experiences across different life domains that it becomes easier to remember exactly when specific events took place. Qualitative researchers are generally interested in the meaning of events for participants and so might be less interested in the *accuracy* of descriptions of the past, but regard reflective accounts generated in interviews as reworking the past (Halbwachs, 1992). These reflective versions of self offered at different points in time can be compared to show for example how past events are reworked to validate or conform with current needs and future ambitions (Plumridge and Thomson, 2003).

Large-scale quantitative surveys often combine a number of different data collection strategies so that they do not always fit neatly into the classification of prospective or retrospective designs. In particular longitudinal event-history data are frequently collected *retrospectively* as part of an ongoing *prospective* longitudinal study. For example, the British Household Panel Survey (BHPS) is a prospective panel study. However, in addition to the detailed questions asked every year about current living conditions, attitudes and beliefs, in the 1992 and 1993 waves of the BHPS, respondents were asked to provide information about their past employment experiences and their relationship histories. This type of retrospective collection of information is also common in qualitative longitudinal studies.

A further type of prospective panel study is a linked panel, which uses census data or administrative data (such as information about hospital treatment or benefits records). This is the least intrusive type of quantitative longitudinal research study as individuals may well not be aware that they are members of the panel. Unique personal identifiers are used to link together data that were not initially collected as part of a longitudinal research study. For example a 1 percent sub-sample of records from the 1971 British Census has been linked to records for the same sample of individuals in 1981, 1991 and 2001. This is known as the Longitudinal Study of the British Census. A similar study linking the 1991 and 2001 Census records for 5 percent of the population of Scotland has recently been established.

Cohort studies

A cohort has been defined as an 'aggregate of individuals who experienced the same event within the same time interval' (Ryder, 1965: 845). The notion of a group of people bound together by sharing the experience of common historical events was first introduced by Karl Mannheim in the early 1920s. Mannheim argued that people are more sensitive to social phenomena that occur during their formative years and this may shape a cohort's future values and behaviour. The most straightforward type of cohort used in longitudinal quantitative research is the birth cohort, i.e. a sample of individuals born within a relatively short time period. We might also choose to study samples of a cohort of people who got married, or who were released from prison, in a particular month or year.

One major advantage of having longitudinal data on a series of separate cohorts is that it is possible to distinguish between 'age effects' (or lifecycle effects) and cohort effects. For example, we may discover, from a cross-sectional survey carried out in 2006 in Britain, that people over the age of 50 are more likely to vote for the Conservative Party than those under the age of 50. However,

it is not clear whether this is an age effect such that as individuals grow older they are more likely to vote Conservative or whether it is a cohort effect so that those born before 1956 are more likely to vote Conservative than those born after 1956. In a longitudinal cohort study we would be able to track the voting intentions of those who reached age 50 in 2006 throughout their adult lives to see whether their political allegiances were stable or whether they became more Conservative as they grew older. This data could then be compared with the information from cohorts born at earlier and later time periods to see whether there were stable cohort differences in political beliefs.

Cohort studies allow an explicit focus on the social and cultural context that frames the experiences, behaviour and decisions of individuals. For example, in the case of the 1958 British Birth Cohort Study (the National Child Development Study), it is important to understand the cohort's educational experiences in the context of profound changes in the organisation of secondary education during the 1960s and 1970s, and the rapid expansion of higher education, which was well underway by the time cohort members left school in the mid 1970s (Bynner and Fogelman, 1993). In a similar way, qualitative longitudinal studies, in following individuals, groups and institutions over time, can provide information on the impact of dramatic changes of policy on the lives and experiences of participants. Examples here are the 12–16 study, which provides insight into the consequences of changing policies in different kinds of schools and communities in Australia, and Pollard and Filer charting the effects of rapidly changing education policy on children through critical years of their primary and secondary education in the UK (McLeod and Yates, 2006; Pollard and Filer, 1999, 2002). Qualitative studies constructed in this way tend to avoid the danger of producing findings that are disembodied from particular times and places. A similar argument has been made for quantitative approaches, where the use of data from a single cohort coupled with an awareness of how the historical context could shape the experiences of that generation of individuals, has been argued to lead to a more 'narrative' understanding of the patterns of behaviour being investigated (Elliott, 2005). Comparisons between cohorts can also help to clarify how individuals of different ages may respond differently to particular sets of historical circumstances. This emphasis on the importance of understanding individuals' lives and experiences as arising out of the intersection of individual agency and historical and cultural context has become articulated as the life course paradigm. The term 'life course' refers to 'a sequence of socially defined events and roles that the individual enacts over time' (Giele and Elder, 1998: 22). Research adopting the life course paradigm tends to use both qualitative and quantitative data (Elder, 1974; Giele, 1998; Laub and Sampson, 1998).

Studies can combine qualitative and quantitative methods in different ways, and although advocating the need for both, a discussion of mixed methods is beyond the scope of this chapter, other than stating that the combination of methods varies considerably. For example predominantly quantitative studies may have qualitative 'add ons' (for example, see Gorell-Barnes et al., 1998), studies may integrate both approaches (Du Bois-Reymond, 1998), and studies may begin as primarily quantitative and become increasingly qualitative over time as sample size erodes (Dwyer and Wyn, 2001).

Table 14.1 provides a brief summary of a small selection of quantitative and qualitative studies that have used different longitudinal panel designs, focusing on those that are commonly used in Britain, North America and Europe. While some of these are individual research projects others are multipurpose studies that generate datasets that can be used as resources by other researchers.

GENERATING QUALITATIVE LONGITUDINAL DATA

We can see from the examples of qualitative longitudinal studies in Table 14.1 that the type of data generated and methods employed are very different from those in quantitative studies, and that they can vary by social science discipline. Imagine the wealth of detailed data on all aspects of the life and culture of the Isthmus Zapotec generated in an ongoing, 40-year study of their community (Royce, 2005). In general the methods used to generate data in qualitative longitudinal research depend on the research questions, the substantive research area and the perspective of the researcher/discipline. Anthropology and community studies are the lead social science disciplines employing long-term fieldwork that can be seen as qualitative longitudinal research. The approach is also relatively common in the education field, relevant studies including Pollard and Filer, 2002; Gordon et al., 2000; Walkerdine et al., 2001; Yates et al., 2002; Ball et al., 2000 and Kuhn and Witzel, 2000. Qualitative longitudinal work is particularly apposite in developmental psychology and health – key studies include Cutting and Dunn, 1999; Hughes and Dunn, 2002; Brown and Gilligan, 1992; Gilligan, 1993; Gulbrandsen, 2003 and Woodgate et al., 2003. There is increasing use of this approach in sociology (Du Bois-Reymond, 1998) and policy studies, dealing with policy development and evaluation, impact and process (Molloy et al., 2002; Mumford and Power, 2003). Other sociology sub-disciplines where qualitative longitudinal research is prevalent include criminology, covering criminal, drug use and sex work 'careers' (Farrall, 2004; Plumridge, 2001; Smith and McVie, 2003), life course/life history studies (Elder and Conger, 2000; Laub and Sampson, 2003) and childhood and youth studies (Henderson et al., 2007; Neale and Flowerdew, 2003; White and Wyn, 2004). Areas investigated include for example gender, families, parenting, child development, children and young people, changing health status, all manner of transitions in life, sexuality, employment and the impact of new technology.

Two collections of anthropological studies, themselves providing a review of the field over time, yield a fascinating picture of the

Table 14.1 Examples of longitudinal studies

Study	Type	Country	Date started	Frequency of data collection	Main focus	Key reference or website
Panel Study of Income Dynamics	Household	USA	1968	Annual	Income	http://psidonline.isr.umich.edu/ McGonagle and Schoeni, 2006
National Longitudinal surveys	Cohort	USA	1966, 1971 etc.	Annual	A series of cohort studies started at different times and with cohorts of different ages, with a primary focus on employment	http://www.bls.gov/nls/ NLS Handbook, 2005 http://www.bls.gov/nls/handbook/ nlshndbk.htm
Survey of Income and Program participation	Household	USA	1984	Every 4 months	Income support	http://www.bls.census.gov/sipp/ SIPP users Guide 2001 available in PDF at http://www.bls.census.gov/sipp/pubs.html
National Longitudinal Study of Children and Youth	Cohort of children aged 0–11	Canada	1994	Every 2 years	Well-being and development of children into early adult life	http://www.statcan.ca/english/sdds/
British Birth Cohort Studies: National Survey of Health and Development; National Child Development Study; British Cohort Study 1970; Millennium Cohort Study	Cohort	Great Britain	1946, 1958, 1970 and 2000	Varies, but generally every 2–3 years at early stages of children's development and every 4 years in adult life	Health and child development with a broader focus in adult life (the 1946 cohort study is more specifically focused on health)	http://www.cls.ioe.ac.uk/ http://www.nshd.mrc.ac.uk/ Dex and Joshi, 2005; Ferri et al., 2003
Longitudinal Study of the Census in England and Wales	Linked panel using census data	England and Wales	1971	Links decennial census data	Demographic and employment topics included in the census	http://www.celsius.lshtm.ac.uk/ Blackwell et al., 2003; Akinwale et al., 2005
German Socio-economic Panel	Household study	West Germany and now includes the former GDR	1984	Annual	Broad focus on living conditions, social change, education and employment	http://www.diw.de/english/sop/
EU Survey on Income and Living Conditions (EU-SILC) formerly the European Community Household Panel (ECHP)	Household study	European Community	2003 (ECHP from 1994 to 2001)	Annual	Living conditions, employment, income, health and housing	http://epunet.essex.ac.uk/EU-SILC_UDB.pdf http://www.iser.essex.ac.uk/epag/ dataset.php Berthoud and Iacovou, 2002

Study	Approach	Location	Start date	Focus	Timing	References
The Isthmus Zapotec	Anthropological, ethnographic includes dance, photography, art, artefacts, advocacy	Mexico (USA)	1967	Identity, language, culture, art; change/continuity	Varies, but between every 1–3 years	Royce, 1977, 1982, 1993, 2002
The Harvard Chiapas Project Tzotzil and Tzeltal Indians	Anthropological, controlled comparative, ethnographic team approach	Mexico (USA)	1957	Determinants and processes of cultural change, language, conceptual system	Continuous annually 1957–1980, more sporadic since	Vogt, 1957, 1969, 1994, 2002
Gwembe, Valley Tonga (Northern Rhodesia/Zambia)	Anthropological demographic census, ethnographic team approach	Northern Rhodesia/Zambia (UK)	1956	Resettlement post-dramatic environmental change (Kariba Dam) Cultural, social, political change	Initially 5-year intervals, then varies	Cliggett, 2002; Scudder and Colson, 1979, 2002
12–18 Project	Sociology/ Psychology. Interview study of 4 schools, ethos, effect on young people	Australia	1993	Gendered subjectivity, identity formation, interaction of institutional + social contexts	1993–2000 twice-yearly interviews	McLeod and Yates, 2006
Identity and Learning Programme	Educational ethnography, of 17 children through ages 4–16. Multi-perspective, collaborative approach	UK	1987	Identity, learning stance, dynamics of learning careers, differentiation	Annually scheduled activities over the period of research	Pollard and Filer, 1999
Growing up Girl	Multi-method psychosocial study of female subjectivities and transitions to womanhood	UK	1977	Education, families, gender, ethnicity and social class	Revisits ages 4, 10, 16, 21	Walkerdine and Lucey, 1989; Walkerdine et al., 2001
Inventing Adulthoods	Multi-method sociological study of 100 young people's transitions to adulthood	UK	1996	Values, identities, material & social resources	5/6 waves in 10 years	Henderson et al., 2007; Thomson, 2007
Middletown	First classic US community study. Many others followed up	USA	1924	To study synchronously the interwoven trends that are the life of a small American city	E.g. 1924, 1935, 1979, 1982, 2001	Caccamo, 2000; Caplow and Bahr, 1979; Caplow et al., 1982; Lynd and Lynd, 1929, 1935

range and complexity of qualitative longitudinal research undertaken in this field (Foster et al., 1979; Kemper and Royce, 2002). Each provides considerable insight into an established canon of long-term anthropological enterprise. This has involved the development of a necessarily flexible approach, adapting to changes in the nature of the community; in the needs, goals, options and world-views of community members; in the political landscape and in the relationships between researchers and community members. Importantly, it illustrates how projects need to be organised on the basis of personnel and project size. As Kemper and Royce indicate it is impossible to take on issues of time without the research coming into the frame, including practical questions of how to organise and maintain a team, the domestic politics of a research team, funding and job security issues and intellectual fashions. Many of these issues are also relevant for quantitative longitudinal research. The body of anthropological research and the issues taken into consideration provide models for other disciplines and illustrate some differences in the concerns of different disciplines. An example here is concern about anonymity and confidentiality that emerges for many qualitative researchers, inhibiting the sharing of data. Data sharing and participatory involvement with those studied are well established in anthropology, although perhaps in danger in a constrained funding climate.

Anthropological studies can in some ways be seen as community studies, but the community studies literature tends to straddle disciplinary boundaries, including sociology, anthropology and geography or urban studies, and many of the classic studies were conducted within these fields, often drawing on an ethnographic method in which time, and change through time were critical elements. Important here are the urban ethnographic tradition of the Chicago School (Lynd and Lynd, 1929, 1935; Whyte, 1943, 1955; Wirth, 1938) and family and community studies in the UK. Examples include Young and Wilmott's studies of the family in Bethnal Green (1957) and Stacey's Banbury studies (1960 and 1975). The temporal character of

community studies has been heightened by the growing trend of researchers to return to the site of earlier research. Follow-up studies have involved the same researcher(s) (Stacey et al., 1975) or others (Warwick and Littlejohn, 1992). In the 1990s for example, Fiona Devine returned to Luton where working-class car workers were first studied by Goldthorpe and his colleagues and described in *The affluent worker* (1968). Devine (1992) was interested to see what changes had occurred in the intervening period in relation to working-class lifestyles and political and social beliefs. The Lynd and Lynd study of Middletown became a benchmark for community studies that was revisited by the Lynds themselves and by many others up to the present day (Caccamo, 2000, see also Crow, 2002; Crow and Allen, 1994).

The types of methods used to generate data in qualitative longitudinal research, are those of qualitative research in general, and can be combined in various ways, including with quantitative methods (for example surveys of varying sizes and types, the collection of baseline descriptive statistical and demographic data to enable assessment of change over time, social mapping of geographical areas). The basic method in anthropology, although now widely used in other disciplines, is ethnography, itself constructed from multiple qualitative methods. Critically, however, ethnography involves social exploration, *protracted investigation* and the interpretation of local and situated cultures grounded in attention to the singular and concrete (Atkinson and Hammersley, 1994; Atkinson et al., 2001). Amongst specific methods used in qualitative longitudinal research are interviews on a continuum from semi-structured to depth. Increasingly favoured are biographical interviews, which can relate to specific episodes in, or aspects of, a life, or be more holistic as in life history approaches. Also employed are case studies, observation and documents including diaries kept specifically for the research (written, audio-, video, photodiaries etc.; Thomson and Holland, 2005). Various standard instruments can also be used, particularly in psychology. Visual, play and drawing methods have also been developed, the latter for example with children.

Further aspects of research design will also be influenced by the social science discipline or disciplines within which the investigation takes place. This includes the nature of the sample to be selected, the unit of analysis for the research (including individual, group, community, organisation, institution, events, time period, spatial or geographical entities) and the overall timeframe of the study (including time intervals if relevant).

A major value of qualitative longitudinal research is flexibility, with the potential for development and innovation to take place throughout the entire research process. For example, with technological development, types of visual data (photography, video and hypermedia) are becoming increasingly popular in qualitative longitudinal research as in qualitative research in general (Pink, 2004a, 2004b; *Qualitative Sociology*, 1997). Changing technology is enabling the development and enhancement of ways of storing, accessing and representing data. This flexibility can extend to sampling, methods, units of analysis and theorisation. Sampling in qualitative research tends to follow a theoretical, rather than a statistical logic and so is characteristically conceptually and purposively driven. There is less concern than in quantitative approaches for representativeness, and sample and sampling can change in the process of the research, even more so in the longer-term qualitative longitudinal research. Two major approaches are purposive and theoretical sampling. In the first, cases are chosen because they illustrate some feature or process in which the researcher is interested; in the second, samples are selected on the basis of their relevance to the research questions and theoretical position of the researcher, and characteristics or criteria which help to develop and test the theory underlying the work are built into the sample. In the course of ongoing research and analysis, purposively chosen confirming or negative cases can also be used to enrich the data and its analysis and interpretation (Mason, 2002; Morse, 1994; Patton, 1990).

Qualitative longitudinal research can generate and test theory, and both inductive and deductive approaches can be undertaken, the specific theory again depending on the discipline. Whatever the theoretical perspective of a qualitative longitudinal study, it requires a theorisation of temporal processes. The structure of a qualitative longitudinal study makes it possible to employ an iterative and reflexive approach through which theoretical interpretations can be revisited in subsequent contact with the participants leading to further development of the ideas. A view emerging in the field is that a qualitative longitudinal methodology might itself challenge or expose the static character of existing theoretical frameworks, and in this way might represent a theoretical orientation as much as a methodology (McLeod, 2003; Neale and Flowerdew, 2003; Plumridge and Thomson, 2003).

Vogt, an anthropologist who worked on the Harvard Chiapras Project for many years, notes some advantages of the qualitative longitudinal approach:

> The principal advantage of a continuous long-range project over a short-range one, or a series of revisits, is the depth, quality, and variety of understandings achieved – understandings of the basic ethnography and of the trends and processes of change. If the long-range project also involves a sizable team of students and younger colleagues who make one or more revisits and keep abreast of all the publications, then there is the added advantage of having a variety of fieldworkers with varied training and different theoretical biases who are forced to reconcile their findings and their analyses with one another. Vogt (2002: 145)

Problems of attrition

A major methodological issue for both qualitative and quantitative longitudinal studies with the individual as the unit of analysis is the problem of attrition, i.e. the drop-out of participants through successive waves of a prospective study. Each time individuals in a sample are re-contacted there is the risk that some will refuse to remain in the study, some will be untraceable, and some may have emigrated or died[1]. In the United States the National Longitudinal Study of Youth (1979) is regarded as the gold standard for sample retention against which other surveys are evaluated (Olsen, 2005). Olsen reports that in 2002, 23 years after the first data collection, there were 9,964 respondents eligible for interview and of these 7,724 (77.5 percent) were successfully interviewed.

The prospective nature of the majority of longitudinal studies means that information will have been collected in earlier sweeps about members of the sample who are not contacted, or refuse participation, in later sweeps. This makes it possible to correct for possible distortion in results due to missing cases. In quantitative research weights may be applied or models may be constructed explicitly to adjust for missing data. In both qualitative and quantitative studies new members of the panel may be brought in, and/or studies may over-sample particular groups from the outset in anticipation of uneven attrition.

There are a number of ways in which sample retention can be maximised in longitudinal studies. These include: using targeted incentive payments; allowing respondents to choose the mode in which they are interviewed, i.e. by telephone or in a face-to-face interview (Olsen, 2005); collecting 'stable addresses' such as the address of parents or other relatives who are less likely to move than the respondent themselves and can subsequently be used to trace the respondent; making regular contact with respondents and asking them to confirm their current address and notify the research group of changes of address. Some of these techniques are used in qualitative longitudinal studies, but an important element in retention here is the relationship that is built up between the researcher(s) and the participants. In studies where the unit of analysis is a group or community rather than an individual, these issues are not so important.

ARCHIVING AND RE-USE OF DATA

Archiving and the secondary analysis of longitudinal data are already well established in the context of quantitative research. In particular the relatively high cost of conducting quantitative longitudinal studies makes it important that the fullest possible use is made of the data resource. In the past, archiving and use of archived qualitative data for substantive and theoretical re-enquiry have been relatively limited, and proposals for such developments provoked mixed reactions, although attitudes are changing (Holland et al., 2004; Parry and Mauthner, 2004: 139). Again there are differences within social science, with anthropology and oral history leading the field in archiving and re-use particularly of longitudinal material (Sheridan, 2000; Webb, 1996). The iterative, processual nature of qualitative research and consequent re-formulation and refinement of research questions over time also makes clear definition of secondary, as opposed to primary, analysis difficult and may, to some extent, explain the relative lack of secondary analysis of qualitative data (Hinds et al., 1997). The literature on the ethical, methodological and epistemological re-use of qualitative data and practical support for its archiving is, however, growing. A recent review of secondary analyses of qualitative data in health and social care research identified 55 studies, mostly North American, and six different types of qualitative secondary analysis based on variations in the purpose of the secondary analysis, the extent to which the primary and secondary research question differed and differences in the number and type of datasets re-used (Heaton, 2000, 2004).

ETHICAL CONSIDERATIONS IN LONGITUDINAL RESEARCH

Many of the ethical issues in longitudinal research are similar to those in cross-sectional research. Major concerns, for both qualitative and quantitative research, are around consent, confidentiality, anonymity and the distortion of life experience through repeated intervention. Concerns around confidentiality and anonymity tend to be amplified in the context of longitudinal research, where typically more detailed information is held on participants, increasing the possibility of being able to identify individuals, even in large samples. Birth cohort studies where the dates of birth of those participating may be widely known are seen as posing additional risks for disclosure.

Informed consent in the context of longitudinal research is not a one-off event, but a process, with repeated consultation necessary at each new phase of data generation. In the context of qualitative longitudinal research this is frequently extended throughout all phases of the research, including data analysis and final reporting.

Ethical issues have been much more widely discussed in the qualitative literature than in the context of quantitative research. In particular qualitative researchers have highlighted concerns around the potential impact of the research on both researched and researchers, intrusion, dependency, emotional involvement and problems of closure and ownership and control of the data (Kemper and Royce, 2002; Mauthner et al., 1998; Royce, 2005; Ward and Henderson, 2003; Yates and McLeod, 1996). In the case of researching children and young people, or otherwise potentially vulnerable groups, the issues once again are intensified (France et al., 2000; Saldana, 2003).

ANALYSING QUANTITATIVE LONGITUDINAL DATA

There is an extensive literature on the statistical analysis of longitudinal data (Allison, 1984; Cox, 1972; Lancaster, 1990; Yamaguchi, 1991), and while some of the approaches described have their roots in engineering and bio-medical research there are an increasing number of social scientists and applied social statisticians working on methods which are specifically applicable to social data (Blossfeld and Rohwer, 1995; Dale and Davies, 1994; Tuma and Hannan, 1979; Yamaguchi, 1991). Here we can contrast traditional modelling strategies applied to event history data and more innovative approaches to analysis that aim to provide descriptions

or classifications of samples of narratives (Abbott, 1992). Given restrictions on space, we do not discuss methods such as OLS regression and logistic regression, which for example are commonly used in cohort studies to examine the links between experiences in early life and outcomes in adulthood (see Savage and Egerton, 1997; Schoon and Parsons, 2002). These methods are also frequently used to explore associations using quantitative *cross-sectional* data. Rather, the focus here is on methods that can only be used with longitudinal data.

Event history modelling

In many respects event history modelling resembles more widely understood regression techniques, such as ordinary least squares regression and logistic regression (where the dependent variable is dichotomous). The emphasis is on determining the relative importance of a number of independent variables or 'covariates' for 'predicting' the outcome of a dependent variable. However, event history modelling differs from standard multiple regression in that the dependent variable is not a measurement of an individual attribute (such as income or qualifications), rather it is derived from the occurrence or non-occurrence of an event, which is *temporally* marked. For example, age at first partnership or length of unemployment. Standard regression techniques are not appropriate in the case of event history data, which focus on the timing of events, for two reasons. First is the problem of what duration value to assign to individuals or cases that have not experienced the event of interest by the time the data is collected – these cases are termed 'censored cases'. A second problem, once a sample is observed longitudinally, is the potential for the values of some of the independent covariates to change. The issue then arises as to how to incorporate these 'time-varying' covariates into the analysis.

These two problems have led to the development of modelling techniques specifically intended for the analysis of event history data. In essence, these techniques allow us to evaluate the relative importance of a number of different variables, or 'covariates' for predicting the chance, or *hazard,* of an event occurring. The hazard is a key concept in event history analysis, and is sometimes also referred to as the hazard rate or hazard function. It can be interpreted as the probability that an event will occur at a particular point in time, given that the individual is at risk at that time. The group of individuals who are at risk of the event occurring are therefore usually referred to as the *risk set.*

Approaches to event history modelling

One of the most common approaches within the social sciences is to use Cox's proportional hazard models or 'Cox Regression' (Cox, 1972). This provides a method for modelling time-to-event data and allows the inclusion of predictor variables (covariates). For example, a model could be estimated for duration of marriage based on religiosity, age at marriage and level of education. Cox Regression will handle the censored cases correctly, and it will provide estimated coefficients for each of the covariates, allowing an assessment of the relative importance of multiple covariates and of any interactions between them. Cox regression is known as a continuous time approach because it is assumed that the time that an event occurs is measured accurately.

Even though the Cox model is one of the most popular and widely applied approaches it has two main disadvantages. First, it is relatively inflexible in terms of modelling duration dependence i.e. for specifying exactly how the hazard may change over time, and, second, it makes it difficult to incorporate time-varying covariates. For this reason, many researchers, with an explicit interest in how the probability of an event occurring changes over time, prefer to use a 'discrete-time' approach. This requires that the data have a specific format. A separate unit of analysis is created for each discrete time interval. Each record therefore corresponds to a person/month or person/year (depending on the accuracy with which events have been recorded). Once the data has been

reconfigured in this way, the unit of analysis is transferred from being the individual case to being a person-year and logistic regression models can be estimated for the dichotomous dependent variable (whether the event occurred or not) using maximum likelihood methods (Allison, 1984). This approach facilitates inclusion of explanatory variables that vary over time because each year, or month, that an individual is at risk is treated as a separate observation. It is also easy to include more than one measure of duration. Discrete time methods are therefore thought to offer a preferable approach when the researcher wants to include several time-varying covariates. A good example is provided by Heaton and Call's research on the timing of divorce (Heaton and Call, 1995). This analytic approach is also frequently used by those looking at recidivism and wanting to understand the timing and correlates of repeat offending (Baumer, 1997; Benda, 2003; Gainey et al., 2000).

Individual heterogeneity

A major limitation with the simple approach to the analysis of discretized longitudinal data described above, is that it does not take account of the fact that the unit of analysis is the 'person-year' and therefore the individual cases are not fully independent (as they should be for a logistic regression) but are clustered at the level of the person. For example, in an analysis modelling duration of marriage, an individual who had been married for 10 years would contribute 10 observations or 'person-years' to the dataset. Another way to understand this problem is to consider that there may be additional variables which have a strong association with the dependent variable but which are not included in the model. The existence of such 'unobserved heterogeneity' will mean that models are mis-specified and in particular spurious duration effects may be detected. The use of more sophisticated models including fixed or random effects models can overcome these problems and allow the researcher to produce more robust estimates of duration dependence. It is beyond the scope of this chapter to discuss these models but for a more detailed introductory treatment see Elliott (2002), Davies (1994) and Box-Steffensmeier and Jones (2004).

Repeated measures analysis

In some quantitative longitudinal research the focus is not on the timing of events but rather on change in an individual attribute over time, for example weight, performance score, attitude, voting behaviour, reaction time, depression etc. In particular, psychologists often use repeated measures of traits, dispositions or psychological well-being to examine which factors may promote change or stability for individuals. This approach can also be used to investigate what type of effect a particular life event may have on individual functioning. For example, several studies examining the potential consequences of parental divorce for children have compared behavioural measures and measures of performance in mathematics and reading in addition to other outcomes, before and after a parental divorce (Cherlin et al., 1991; Elliott and Richards, 1991; Ni Bhrolchain et al., 1994).

CAUSALITY IN CROSS-SECTIONAL AND LONGITUDINAL RESEARCH

Information about the temporal ordering of events is generally regarded as essential if we are to make any claims about a causal relationship between those events. Given the importance of establishing the chronology of events in order to be confident about causality it can be seen that longitudinal data is frequently to be preferred over cross-sectional data. In some substantive examples even when data is collected in a cross-sectional survey, it is clear that one event or variable, precedes another. For example, in an analysis that focuses on the impact of school-leaving age on occupational attainment there is unlikely to be confusion about the temporal ordering of the variables. However, there are a number of examples where the use of cross-sectional survey data prevents researchers

from determining the causal ordering of variables. For example, there is a considerable body of research that has shown a strong association between unemployment and ill health. This can either be interpreted to imply that unemployment causes poor health or that those who are in poor health are more likely to become unemployed and subsequently find it more difficult to find another job, i.e. there is a selection effect such that ill health might be described as causing unemployment (Bartley, 1991; Blane et al., 1993). In this case, longitudinal data would be needed to follow a sample of employed individuals and determine whether their health deteriorated if they became unemployed, or conversely whether a decline in health led to an increased probability of becoming unemployed (for examples which make use of longitudinal data to untangle this issue see Montgomery et al., 1996 and 1999).

In quantitative studies, longitudinal data is also valuable for overcoming the problems of disentangling maturational effects and generational effects. As Dale and Davies (1994) explain, cross-sectional data that examines the link between age and any dependent variable confounds cohort and life course effects. As was discussed above, using the example of political allegiances, one advantage of having longitudinal data on a number of separate cohorts is that it enables the researcher to disentangle these effects.

Perhaps the major advantage of longitudinal data over cross-sectional data in understanding the possible causal relationships between variables is its ability to take account of omitted variables. Quantitative longitudinal data enables the construction of models that are better able to take account of the complexities of the social world and the myriad influences on individuals' behaviour.

Qualitative researchers can be reluctant to use the term causality, seeing it as intrinsically part of a quantitative paradigm. Understanding phenomena in time enables a researcher to capture meaning, intention and consequence, rather than findings true for all times and places (Gergen, 1984). But some argue that because of its attention to detail, process, complexity and contextuality, qualitative research is particularly valuable for identifying and understanding causal and multi-causal linkages, especially in relation to the temporal dimension of the longitudinal approach (Mason, 2002; Miles and Huberman, 1994). Again, whilst this might be the case, qualitative longitudinal researchers would not necessarily refer to their findings in this way, for example in ethnography causal theories are common if implicit. The focus on the meaning of experience for a participant active in the construction of her/his own identity and reflexive narrative of self could lead to explanations that might identify 'causal' or 'multicausal' sequences. Pollard and Filer (1999) in a study of primary school children's identities and careers eschew a focus on the academic and social outcomes usually associated with school achievement, and what inputs would produce that output. Taking a holistic approach they highlight the dynamic, recursive nature of pupil experience, seeing these children as continuously shaping and maintaining their identity and status as a pupil as they move through different school settings, in a dynamic, fluctuating process, open to possibilities for change in varying degrees. Many elements are identified as contributing in various ways to this reflexive pupil identity – gender, social class and ethnicity, material, cultural and linguistic resources, physical and intellectual capability and potential and multiple and various experiences in school observed in the study. This is clearly a different understanding of causality than that found in quantitative approaches.

NARRATIVE POSITIVISM AND EVENT SEQUENCE ANALYSIS: A MORE QUALITATIVE APPROACH?

Even though the event history techniques described in the section on quantitative analysis above are powerful and flexible, they still have the disadvantage that they do not deal with sequences *holistically*. An alternative approach to the analysis of event history data

is not to attempt to model the underlying processes, but rather to establish a systematic description or typology of the most commonly occurring patterns or sequences within them (Abbott 1990, 1992). This approach has been termed 'narrative positivism'. Abbott introduced the set of techniques known as Optimal Matching Analysis into sociology from molecular biology, where it had been used in the study of DNA and other protein sequences. He has applied the method to substantive issues including the careers of musicians (Abbott and Hrycak, 1990), and the development of the welfare state (Abbott and DeViney, 1992). Following his lead, other sociologists have also begun to adopt this approach and in particular have found the method to be useful for the analysis of careers (Blair-Loy, 1999; Chan, 1995; Halpin and Chan, 1998; Stovel et al., 1996). However the technique is not as well developed or as widely used as the modelling approaches described above (Wu, 2000).

It is perhaps in this approach, which aims to provide a detailed description of the different types of pathways or trajectories followed by individuals, that qualitative and quantitative approaches to analysis of longitudinal data come closest. Abbott's approach uses large samples and utilises sophisticated software to construct clusters of cases with similar longitudinal profiles. However, the research question addressed using this technique mirrors the type of research questions that form the focus of many qualitative longitudinal studies, although the two approaches provide rather different types of data on such trajectories.

APPROACHES TO ANALYSIS IN QUALITATIVE LONGITUDINAL RESEARCH

The analysis of quantitative data largely involves statistical modelling of large datasets to identify patterns and relationships in the data at an aggregated level to be able to make probabilistic statements about particular populations. As we have just seen, more recent holistic approaches are attempting to deal with describing and classifying individual trajectories through time, through clustering techniques. Qualitative longitudinal data provides a different type of detailed information about processes through time for individuals or groups of varying sizes, requiring different analytic strategies. These methods of analysis will also vary, depending on the discipline, the theoretical approach and the unit of analysis. A key aspect of qualitative longitudinal analysis in general, however, is that it is theoretically driven, and is characterised by a focus on meaning.

Saldana highlights colourfully the problems of analysis for the qualitative longitudinal researcher:

> The challenge for qualitative researchers is to rigorously analyze and interpret primarily language-based data records to describe credibly, vividly, and persuasively for readers through appropriate narrative the processes of participant change through time. This entails the sophisticated transformation and integration of observed human interactions in their multiple social contexts into temporal patterns or structures. (Saldana, 2003: 46)

The analysis of qualitative longitudinal research must then engage with and capture time, process and change. It requires working in two temporal dimensions: diachronically, through time, and synchronically cross-cutting at one point in time, and the articulation of these two through a third, integrative dimension. This is recognised as crucial for analysing change through time (Saldana, 2003). Even though both qualitative and quantitative longitudinal traditions have realised such analyses, this remains a challenging task both to execute and to describe. Here are some of the general approaches mooted.

Wolcott (1994) suggests three stages of increasing abstraction for the analytic process: description, analysis and interpretation. Description involves recording, chronicling and describing what kinds of change occur, in whom or what, at what time and in what context. Analysis accomplishes 'the identification of essential features and the systematic interrelationships among them'

(Wolcott, 1994: 12). Finally, 'Explaining the nature and meaning of those changes, or developing a theory with transferability of the study's findings to other contexts, is the final stage of interpretation' (Saldana, 2003: 63).

Saldana elaborates the Wolcott schema in his guidebook for qualitative longitudinal research, providing framing, descriptive, analytic and interpretive questions to guide the analytic process. 'Framing questions' (p. 63) address and manage the contexts of the particular study's data, locating them in the process (e.g. what contextual and intervening conditions appear to influence and affect participant changes through time?). Descriptive questions (e.g. what increases or emerges through time? What kinds of surges or epiphanies occur through time?) generate information to help answer the framing questions, and the more complex analytic and interpretive questions. Analytic and interpretive questions integrate the descriptive information to guide the researcher to richer levels of analysis and interpretation (e.g. which changes interrelate through time? What is the through-line of the study? The through-line is 'a single word, a phrase, a sentence, or a paragraph with an accompanying narrative that describes, analyzes, and/or interprets the participant's changes through time by analyzing its thematic flow—its qualitative trajectory' (Saldana, 2003: 151, see too Saldana, 2005).

Thomson and Holland (2003) provide an example of an analysis attempting two of the dimensions suggested above in their 10-year study of 100 young people's transitions to and constructions of adulthood, Inventing Adulthoods. The cross-sectional analysis captures a moment in time in the life of the sample (at each interview or data generation point) to identify discourses through which identities are constructed. In this case the data was coded descriptively and conceptually (using NUD.IST[2]) to enable comparison across the sample on the basis of a range of factors, e.g. age, gender, social class, geographical location. These analyses form a repeat cross-sectional study on the same sample and analyses can be compared for change over time, and each contextualised in social and historical time. They highlight differences and similarities within the sample, and help identify the relationship between individual narratives and wider social processes. The longitudinal analysis consists of examining the development of a particular narrative for each case over the course of the study, following the complexity and contingency of individual trajectories, and identifying critical moments and change. This individual temporal analysis can also be related to social and historical time and change. More recently Thomson (2007) has described the process of constructing longitudinal case histories.

Drawing on a significant body of policy evaluation research, Lewis (2005) outlines a multi-dimensional approach to qualitative longitudinal data analysis built around the 'framework' approach to qualitative analysis developed by the National Centre for Social Research (Ritchie and Lewis, 2003). Changes in evaluation studies are identified as occurring at the individual, service and policy levels. Change is manifest in a literal way through the chronology of the account, yet it is also evident in how this chronology is reinterpreted by a research participant over time. Lewis suggests that qualitative longitudinal data are characterised by 'discordant data' where subsequent re-interpretations conflict with original accounts. To complicate matters further, not only does the participant reinterpret their story, but the researcher also reinterprets their analysis in the light of new revelation and the passage of time. Lewis maps each longitudinal case within a two-by-two frame that enables them to plot a series of interviews with a single participant (vertical axis) against themes (horizontal axis). In a similar way to that described by Thomson and Holland (2003), the analysis proceeds in two directions: horizontally across themes and vertically through a case over time, as well as 'zigzagging' between themes and interviews within a single case to trace the development of a theme over time. But in order to move away from the single case to the wider dataset, Lewis encourages an approach to working with whole cases: undertaking comparison between cases and between groups of cases, asking questions such as why and how might something that is present in one case (or group) be absent in another?

As we can see, qualitative longitudinal studies produce complex and multi-dimensional datasets, which in turn demand innovative strategies for data analysis and display that operate on more than two dimensions.

CONCLUSIONS: THE CONSTRUCTION OF THE INDIVIDUAL IN QUALITATIVE AND QUANTITATIVE LONGITUDINAL RESEARCH

As we discussed earlier, one of the main advantages of both qualitative and quantitative longitudinal research is the ability to track individual lives through time. In quantitative longitudinal research a priority is placed on collecting accurate data from a large representative sample about the nature and timing of life events, circumstances and behaviour. In qualitative longitudinal research the emphasis is far more on individuals' understanding of their lives and circumstances and how these may change through time.

Even though both qualitative and quantitative longitudinal research have the potential to provide very detailed information about individuals, what is obscured in the quantitative approach are the narratives that individuals tell about their own lives. While complex biographical case studies can be developed from survey data (Sampson and Laub, 1993; Singer et al., 1998), these accounts are clearly authored by the researcher and allow no access to the reflexivity of the respondents themselves. In contrast with qualitative longitudinal research, the whole emphasis of the study may be on understanding the reflexive process of identity work accomplished by individuals (Pollard and Filer, 1999; Thomson and Holland, 2003). It is important to be clear therefore that whereas the criticism that quantitative research is less detailed than qualitative research may be misplaced (particularly in the context of *longitudinal* research), there is a sense in which quantitative research can never provide access to the *reflexive* individual. The individual in quantitative research is seen as a unitary subject that has remained relatively impervious to postmodern deconstruction. Even when detailed longitudinal studies are used to construct case histories or biographies, the assumption is that those individuals have a clear, stable and coherent identity. Importantly, in quantitative research the description of the individual is provided by the researcher, and the resources available are variables which apparently allow no scope for ambiguity or inconsistency. The identity of individuals, and the meaning of variables such as gender and social class remain relatively fixed in quantitative research (Elliott, 2005).

While quantitative longitudinal analytic processes provide a more processual or dynamic understanding of the social world, they do so at the expense of setting up an overly static view of the individual. Quantitative longitudinal research provides a powerful tool for understanding the multiple factors that may affect individuals' lives, shaping their experiences and behaviour. But there is little scope for understanding how individuals use narrative to construct and maintain a sense of their own identity. Without this element there is a danger that people are merely seen as making decisions and acting within a pre-defined and structurally determined field of social relations rather than as contributing to the maintenance and metamorphosis of themselves, and the culture and community in which they live.

In contrast, a more post-modern understanding of the self fits easily within qualitative longitudinal research and, indeed, has engendered qualitative analysis that emphasises the role of narrative in the formation and maintenance of the self (e.g. Gubrium and Holstein, 1995; Ronai and Cross, 1998; Wajcman and Martin, 2002). As has been discussed in more detail elsewhere (Elliott, 2005) this provides a powerful argument for the need to use both quantitative and qualitative approaches to longitudinal research.

NOTES

1 In some cases in both qualitative and quantitative longitudinal research even those who have emigrated might be followed up and included.

2 NUD.IST (Non-numerical Unstructured Data Indexing Searching and Theorizing) is CAQDAS (Computer Assisted Qualitative Data Analysis Software). Others include The Ethnograph (now out of date), NVivo7 (a combination of the earlier NUD.IST6 and NVivo2), ATLAS.ti, HyperQual (CAQDAS for the Apple Mac OS).

REFERENCES

Abbott, A. (1990). 'Conceptions of Time and Events in Social Science Methods.' *Historical Methods* 23,4: 140–150.

Abbott, A. (1992). 'From Causes to Events: Notes on Narrative Positivism.' *Sociological Methods and Research* 20,4: 428–455.

Abbott, A. and DeViney, S. (1992). 'The Welfare State as Transnational Event.' *Social Science History* 16: 245–274.

Abbott, A. and Hrycak, A. (1990). 'Measuring Resemblance in Sequence Data: An Optimal Matching Analysis of Musicians' Careers.' *American Journal of Sociology* 96,1: 144–185.

Akinwale, B., Antonatos, A., Blackwell, L. and Haskey J. (2005). 'Opportunities for New Research Using the Post-2001 ONS Longitudinal Study.' *Population Trends* 121: 8–16.

Allison, P. D. (1984). *Event History Analysis: Regression for longitudinal event data*, Beverly Hills: Sage.

Atkinson, P., Coffey, A., Delamont, S., Lofland, J. and Lofland, L. (2001). *Handbook of ethnography*, London: Sage, pp. 248–261.

Atkinson, P. and Hammersley, M. (1994). 'Ethnography and Participant Observation,' in Denzin, N. K. and Lincoln Y. S. (eds) *Handbook of qualitative research*, London: Sage.

Ball, S. J., Maguire, M. and Macrae, S. (2000). *Choice, pathways and transitions post-16: New youth, new economics in the global city*, London: RoutledgeFalmer.

Bartley, M. (1991). 'Health and Labour Force Participation: Stress, Selection and the Reproduction Costs of Labour Power.' *Journal of Social Policy* 20,3: 327–364.

Baumer, E. (1997). 'Levels and Predictors of Recidivism: The Malta Experience.' *Criminology* 35: 601–628.

Benda, B. B. (2003). 'Survival Analysis of Criminal Recidivism of Boot Camp Graduates Using Elements from General and Developmental Explanatory Models.'

International Journal of Offender Therapy and Comparative Criminology 47,1: 89–110.

Berthoud, R. and Iacovou, M. (2002). *Diverse Europe: Mapping patterns of social change across the EU*, Economic and Social Research Council.

Blackwell, L., Lynch, K., Smith, J. and Goldblatt, P. (2003). 'Longitudinal Study 1971–2001: Completeness of Census Linkage' (Series LS No. 10) (PDF 841K), http://www.celsius.lshtm.ac.uk/2001_data.html

Blair-Loy, M. (1999). 'Career Patterns of Executive Women in Finance.' *American Journal of Sociology* 104: 1346–1397.

Blane, D., Smith, G. and Bartley, M. (1993). 'Social Selection: What Does it Contribute to Social Class Differences in Health.' *Sociology of Health and Illness* 15,1: 1–15.

Blossfeld, H.-P. and Rohwer, G. (1995). *Techniques of event history modeling: New approaches to causal analysis.* Mahwah, NJ: Lawrence Erlbaum Associates.

Box-Steffensmeier, J. and Jones, B. (2004). *Event history modeling*, Cambridge: Cambridge University Press.

Brown, L.M. and Gilligan, C. (1992). *Meeting at the crossroads: Women's psychology and girls' development*, Cambridge, MA: Harvard University Press.

Bynner, J. and Fogelman, K. (1993). Making the grade: education and training experiences, in Ferri, E. (ed.) *Life at 33: The fifth follow-up of the National Child Development Study*, London: National Children's Bureau, pp. 36–59.

Caccamo, R. (2000) *Back to Middletown: Three generations of sociological reflections*, Stanford: Stanford University Press.

Caplow, T. and Bahr, H. M. (1979) 'Half a Century of Change in Adolescent Attitudes: Replication of a Middletown Survey by the Lynds.' *Public Opinion Quarterly* 43,1: 1–17.

Caplow, T., Bahr, H. M., Chadwick, B. A., Hill, R. and Williamson, M. H. O. (1982). *Middletown families: Fifty years of change and continuity*, Minneapolis, MN: University of Minnesota Press.

Chan, T.-W. (1995). 'Optimal Matching Analysis.' *Work and Occupations* 22: 467–490.

Cherlin, A. J., Furstenberg, F., Chase-Landsdale, P. L. and Kiernan, K. (1991). 'Longitudinal Studies of Effects of Divorce on Children in Great Britain and the United States.' *Science Technology & Human Values* 252: 1386–1389.

Cliggett, L. (2002). 'Multigenerations and Multidisciplines: Inheriting Fifty Years of Gwembe Tonga Research,' in Kemper, R. and Royce, A. P. (eds) *Chronicling cultures: Long-term field research in anthropology*, Walnut Creek, CA: AltaMira, pp. 239–251.

Cox, D. R. (1972). 'Regression Models and Life Tables.' *Journal of the Royal Statistical Society* B 34: 187–202.

Crow, G. (2002) 'Community Studies: Fifty Years of theorization.' *Sociological Research Online* 7,3,http://www.socresonline.org.uk/7/3/crow.html

Crow, G. and Allen, G. (1994). *Community life: An introduction to local social relations*, London: Harvester Wheatsheaf.

Cutting, A. L. and Dunn, J. (1999). 'Theory of Mind, Emotion Understanding, Language and Family Background: Individual Differences and Inter-relations.' *Child Development* 70: 853–865.

Dale, A. and Davies, R. (1994). *Analyzing social and political change: A casebook of methods*, London: Sage.

Davies, R. B. (1994). 'From cross-sectional to longitudinal analysis,' in Dale, A. and Davis, R. B. (eds) *Analyzing social and political change: A casebook of methods*, London: Sage, pp. 20–40.

Devine, F. (1992) *Affluent workers revisited: Privatism and the working class*, Edinburgh: Edinburgh University Press.

Dex, S. (1995). 'The Reliability of Recall Data: A Literature Review.' *Bulletin de Methodologie Sociologique* 49: 58–80.

Dex, S. and Joshi, H. (2005). *Children of the 21st century: from birth to nine months*, Bristol: The Policy Press.

Dex, S. and McCulloch, A. (1998). 'The reliability of retrospective unemployment history data.' *Work Employment and Society* 12,3: 497–509.

Du Bois-Reymond, M. (1998). '"I don't want to commit myself yet": Young people's life concepts.' *Journal of Youth Studies* 1,1: 63–79.

Dwyer, P. J. and Wyn, J. (2001). *Youth, education and risk: Facing the future*, London: RoutledgeFalmer.

Elder, G. and Conger, R. D. (2000). *Children of the land: Adversity and success in rural America*, Chicago: University of Chicago Press.

Elder, G. H. (1974). *Children of the great depression: social change in life experience*, Chicago: University of Chicago Press.

Elliott, B. J. (2002). 'The Value of Event History Techniques for Understanding Social Processes: Modelling Women's Employment Behaviour After Motherhood.' *International Journal of Social Research Methodology* 5,2: 107–132.

Elliott, B. J. and Richards, M. P. M. (1991). 'Children and Divorce: Educational Performance and Behaviour Before and After Parental Separation.' *International Journal of Law and the Family* 5: 258–276.

Elliott, J. (2005). *Using narrative in social research: Qualitative and quantitative approaches*, London: Sage.

Farrall, S. (2004). 'Social Capital and Offender Reintegration: Making Probation Desistance Focussed,' in Maruna, S. and Immarigeon, R. (eds) *After crime and punishment: Ex-offender reintegration and desistance from crime*, Cullompton: Willan.

Featherman, D. L. (1980). 'Retrospective Longitudinal Research: Methodological Considerations.' *Journal of Economics and Business* 32: 152–169.

Ferri, E., Bynner, J. and Wadsworth, M. (2003). *Changing Britain, changing lives: three generations at the turn of the century*, London: Institute of Education.

Foster, G. M., Scudder, T., Colson, E. and Kemper, R. (1979). *Long-term field research in social anthropology*, New York: Academic Press.

France, A., Bendelow, G. and Williams, S. (2000) 'A "Risky" Business: Researching the Health Beliefs of Children and Young People,' in Lewis, A. and Lindsay, G. (eds) *Researching children's perspectives*, Buckingham: Open University Press, pp. 231–263.

Gainey, R. R., Payne, B. K. and O'Toole, M. (2000). 'The Relationship Between Time in Jail, Time on Electronic Monitoring, and Recidivism: an Event History Analysis of a Jail-Based Program.' *Justice Quarterly* 17,4: 733–752.

Gergen, K. J. (1984). 'An Introduction to Historical Social Psychology,' in Gergen, K. J and Gergen, M. M. (eds) *Historical social psychology*, London: NJ: Lawrence Erlbaum Associates.

Giele, J. Z. (1998). *Innovation in the typical life course. Methods of life course research: qualitative and quantitative approaches*. J. Z. Giele and G. H. Elder. London: Sage, pp. 231–263.

Giele, J. Z. and Elder, G. H. (1998). *Methods of life course research: qualitative and quantitative approaches*, Thousand Oaks, CA: Sage.

Gilligan, C. (1993). *In a Different Voice: Psychological Theory and Women's Development*, Cambridge, MA: Harvard University Press.

Goldthorpe, J. H., Lockwood, D., Bechofer, F. and Platt, J. (1968). *The affluent worker in the class structure*, Cambridge: Cambridge University Press.

Gorell-Barnes, L. G., Thompson, P., Barnes, P., Daniel, G. and Burchardt, N. (1998). *Growing up in stepfamilies*. Oxford: Oxford University Press.

Gordon, T., Holland, J. and Lahelma, E. (2000). *Making spaces: Citizenship and difference in schools*, London: Macmillan.

Gubrium, J. F. and Holstein J. A. (1995). 'Individual Agency, The Ordinary and Postmodern Life.' *Sociological Quarterly* 36,3: 555–570.

Gulbrandsen, L. M. (2003). 'Peer Relations as Arenas for Gender Constructions Among Young Teenagers.' *Pedagogy, Culture and Society* 11,1: 113–132.

Halbwachs, Maurice (1992). *On collective memory.* Translated and edited by Lewis A. Coser. Chicago: University of Chicago Press.

Halpin, B. and Wing Chan, T. (1998). 'Class Careers as Sequences: an Optimal Matching Analysis of Work-Life Histories.' *European Sociological Review* 14,2: 111–130.

Heaton, J. (2000). *Secondary analysis of qualitative data: a review of the literature,* Full Research report ESRC 1752 (8.00), Social Policy Research Unit, University of York

Heaton, J. (2004). *Re-working qualitative data,* London: Sage.

Heaton, T. B. and Call, V. R. A. (1995). 'Modeling Family Dynamics with Event History Techniques.' *Journal of Marriage and the Family* 57: 1078–1090.

Henderson, S., Holland, J., McGrellis, S., Sharpe, S. and Thomson, R. (2007). *Inventing adulthood: A biographical approach to youth transitions*, London: Sage.

Hinds, P., Vogel, R. and Clarke-Steffen, L. (1997). 'The Possibilities and Pitfalls of Doing a Secondary Analysis of a Qualitative Data Set.' *Qualitative Health Research* 7,3: 408–424.

Holland, J., Thomson, R. and Henderson, S. (2004). *Feasibility study for a possible qualitative longitudinal study*, Specification ad Discussion Paper for Economic and Social Research Council, UK.

Hughes, C. and Dunn, J. (2002). '"When I Say a Naughty Word". A Longitudinal Study of Young Children's Accounts of Anger and Sadness in Themselves and Close Others.' *British Journal of Developmental Psychology* 20, 515–535.

Jacobs, S. C. (2002). 'Reliabilty and Recall of Unemployment Events Using Retrospective Data.' *Work, Employment and Society* 16,3: 537–548.

Kemper, R. and Royce, A. P. (eds) (2002) *Chronicling cultures: Long-term field research in anthropology*, Walnut Creek, CA: AltaMira.

Kuhn, T. and Witzel, A. (2000). School-to-work Transition, Career Development and Family Planning – Methodological Challenges and Guidelines of a Qualitative Longitudinal Panel Study. *Forum: Qualitative Social Research* 1, 2: http://www.qualtative–research.net/fqs-texte/2-00/2-00kuehnwitzel-e.htm

Lancaster, T. (1990). *The econometric analysis of transition data*, Cambridge: Cambridge University Press.

Laub, J. H. and Sampson, R. J. (1998). 'Integrating Quantitative and Qualitative Data,' in Giele, J. Z. and Elder, G. H. (eds) *Methods of life course research: qualitative and quantitative approaches*, Thousand Oaks, CA: Sage, pp. 213–230.

Laub, J. H. and Sampson, R. J. (2003). *Shared beginnings, divergent lives: Delinquent boys to age 70*, Cambridge, MA: Harvard University Press.

Lewis, J. (2005). 'Qualitative Longitudinal Data for Evaluation Studies,' SPRU (University of York) and CASP (University of Bath), Friends Meeting House, London 11th November 2005.

Lynd, R. and Lynd, H. M. (1929). *Middletown. A study in American Culture*, New York: Harcourt Brace.

Lynd, R. and Lynd, H. M. (1935). *Middletown in transition: A study of cultural conflicts*, New York: Harcourt Brace.

Mannheim, Karl (1956). 'On the Problem of Generations,' in *Essays on the sociology of culture*. New York: Oxford University Press.

Mason, J. (2002) (2nd edn.). *Qualitative researching*, London: Sage.

Mauthner, N., Parry, O. and Backett-Milburn, K. (1998). 'The Data are Out There, or are They? Implications for Archiving and Revisiting Qualitative Data.' *Sociology* 32,4: 733–745.

McGonagle, K. A. and Schoeni, R. F. (2006). 'The Panel Study of Income Dynamics: Overview & Summary of Scientific Contributions After Nearly 40 Years.' Retrieved March 2006, from http://psidonline. isr.umich.edu/Publications/Papers/montrealv5.pdf

McLeod, J. (2003). 'Why We Interview Now – Reflexivity and Perspective in a Longitudinal Study.' *International Journal of Social Research Methodology* 6,3: 223–232.

McLeod, J. and Yates, L. (2006). *Making modern lives: Subjectivity, schooling and social change*, Albany: State University of New York Press.

Miles, M. B. and Huberman, A. M. (1994). *Qualitative data analysis: An expanded sourcebook* (2nd edn), London: Sage.

Molloy, D. and Woodfield, K. with Bacon, J. (2002). *Longitudinal qualitative research approaches in evaluation studies*, Working Paper No. 7, London: HMSO.

Montgomery, S. M., Bartley, M. J., Cook, D. G. and Wadsworth, M. (1996). 'Health and Social Precursors of Unemployment in Young Men in Great Britain.' *Journal of Epidemiology and Community Health* 50, 415–422.

Montgomery, S. M., Cook, D. G., Bartley, M. J. and Wadsworth, M. (1999). 'Unemployment Pre-dates Symptoms of Depression and Anxiety Resulting in Medical Consultation in Young Men.' *International Journal of Epidemiology* 28,1: 95–100.

Morse, J. M. (1994). 'Designing Funded Qualitative Research,' in Denzin, N. L. and Lincoln, Y. S. (eds) *Handbook of qualitative research*, London: Sage.

Mott, F. (2002). 'Looking Backward: Post hoc Reflections on Longitudinal Surveys,' in Phelps E., Furstenberg, F. and Colby A. (eds) *Looking at lives: American longitudinal studies of the twentieth century*, New York: Russell Sage.

Mumford, K. and Power, A. (2003). *East Enders: Family and community in East London*, Bristol: Policy Press.

Neale, B. and Flowerdew, J. (2003). 'Time, Texture and Childhood: The Contours of Longitudinal Qualitative Research.' *International Journal of Social Research Methodology: Theory and Practice* 6,3: 189–199.

Ni Bhrolchain, M., Chappell, R. and Diamond, I. (1994). 'Educational and Socio-demographic Outcomes Among Children of Disrupted and Intact Marriages.' *Population* 36: 1585–1612.

Olsen, R. J. (2005). 'The Problem of Respondent Attrition: Survey Methodology is Key.' *Monthly Labor Review* 128,2: 63–70.

Parry, O. and Mauthner, N. (2004). 'Whose Data are They Anyway? Practical, Legal and Ethical Issues in Archiving Qualitative Data.' *Sociology* 38,1: 139–152.

Patton, M. Q. (1990). *Qualitative evaluation and research methods* (2nd ed.), Newbury Park, CA: Sage.

Pink, S. (ed.) (2004a). *Visual images*, London: Routledge.

Pink, S. (2004b). *Home truths: Gender, domestic objects and the home*, Oxford: Berg.

Plumridge, L. (2001). 'Rhetoric, Reality and Risk Outcomes in Sex Work.' *Health, Risk and Society* 3,2: 119–215.

Plumridge, L. and Thomson, R. (2003). 'Longitudinal Qualitative Studies and the Reflexive Self.' *International Journal of Social Research Methodology* 6,3: 213–222.

Pollard, A. and Filer, A. (1999). *The social world of pupil career: Strategic biographies through primary school*, London: Cassell.

Pollard, A. and Filer, A. (2002). *Identity and secondary schooling project*. Full report to the ESRC.

Qualitative Sociology (Spring 1997) 20 (1) Special Issue: *Visual methods in sociological analysis.*

Ritchie, J. and Lewis, J. (2003). *Qualitative research practice: A guide for social science students and researchers*, London: Sage.

Ronai C. R. and Cross, R. (1998). 'Dancing With Identity: Narrative Resistance Strategies of Male and Female Striptusers.' *Deviant Behaviour* 19: 99–119.

Royce, A. P. (1977). *The anthropology of dance*, Bloomington: Indiana University Press.

Royce, A. P. (1982). *Ethnic identity: strategies of diversity*, Bloomington: Indiana University Press.

Royce, A. P. (1993). 'Ethnicity, Nationalism, and the Role of the Intellectual,' in Toland, Judith D. (ed.) *Ethnicity and the state, political and legal anthropology*, Vol. 9, New Brunswick, NJ: Transaction Press, pp.103–122.

Royce, A. P. (2002). 'Learning to See, Learning to Listen: Thirty-five Years of Fieldwork with the Isthmus Zapotec,' in Kemper, R. V. and Royce, A. P. (eds) *Chronicling cultures: Long-term field research in anthropology*, Walnut Creek: Altamira Press, pp. 8–33.

Royce, A. P. (2005). 'The Long and the Short of it: Benefits and Challenges of Long-Term Ethnographic Research.' Paper presented at Principles of Qualitative Longitudinal Research: An International Seminar, University of Leeds, UK, September 30, 2005.

Ruspini, E. (2002). *Introduction to longitudinal research*, London: Routledge.

Ryder, N. B. (1965). 'The Cohort as a Concept in the Study of Social Change.' *American Sociological Review* 30: 843–861.

Saldana, J. (2003). *Longitudinal qualitative research: Analyzing change through time*, Walnut Creek, Lanham, New York, Oxford: Altamira Press.

Saldana, J (2005). 'Coding Qualitative Data to Analyze Change.' Paper presented at Principles of Qualitative Longitudinal Research: An International Seminar, University of Leeds, UK, September 30, 2005.

Sampson, R. J. and Laub, J. H. (1993). *Crime in the making: pathways and turning points through life*, Cambridge, MA: Harvard University Press.

Savage, M. and Egerton, M. (1997). 'Social Mobility, Individual Ability and the Inheritance of Class Inequality.' *Sociology* 31,4: 465–472.

Schoon, I. and Parsons, S. (2002) 'Competence in the Face of Adversity: The Impact of Early Family Environment and Long-term Consequence.' *Children & Society* 16,4, 260–272.

Scott, J. and Alwin, D. (1998). 'Retrospective Versus Prospective Measurement of Life Histories in Longitudinal Research, in Giele, J. Z. and Elder, G. H. (eds) *Methods of life course research: qualitative and quantitative approaches*, Thousand Oaks, CA: Sage, pp. 98–127.

Scudder, T. and Colson, E. (1979). 'Long-term Research in Gwembe Valley, Zambia,' in Foster G. M., Scudder, T., Colson, E. and Kemper R. V. (eds) *Long-term field research in social anthropology*, New York: Academic Press, pp. 277–254.

Scudder, T. and Colson, E. (2002) 'Long-term Research in Gwembe Valley, Zambia,' in Kemper, R. V. and Royce, A. P. (eds) *Chronicling cultures: Long-term field research in Anthropology*, Walnut Creek, CA: AltaMira, pp. 197–238.

Sheridan, Dorothy (2000). 'Reviewing Mass-Observation: The Archive and its Researchers Thirty Years on,' *Forum Qualitative Sozialforschung/Forum: Qualitative Social Research*, 1,3. Available at: http://qualitative-research.net/fqs/fqs-eng.htm

Singer, B., C. D. Ryff, D. Carr and Magee, W. J. (1998). 'Linking Life Histories and Mental Health: A Person Centred Strategy.' *Sociological Methodology* 28: 1–51.

Smith, D. J. and McVie, S. (2003). 'Theory and Method in the Edinburgh Study of Youth Transitions and Crime.' *British Journal of Criminology* 43,1: 169–195.

Stacey, M. (1960). *Tradition and change: A study of Banbury*, Oxford: Oxford University Press.

Stacey, M., Batstone, E., Bell, C. and Murcott, A. (1975). *Power, persistence and change: A second study of Banbury*, London: Routledge & Kegan Paul.

Stovel, K., Savage, M. and Bearman, P. (1996). 'Ascription into Achievement: Models of Career Systems at Lloyds Bank, 1890–1970.' *American Journal of Sociology* 102,2: 358–399.

Taris, T. W. (2000). *A primer in longitudinal data analysis*, London: Sage.

Thomson, R. (2007). 'The QL 'Case History': Practical, Methodological and Ethical Reflections.' *Social Policy and Society* 6,4.

Thomson, R. and Holland, J. (2003). 'Hindsight, Foresight and Insight: The Challenges of Longitudinal Qualitative Research.' *International Journal of Social Research Methodology* 6,3: 233–244.

Thomson, R. and Holland, J. (2005). '"Thanks for the Memory": Memory Books as a Methodological Resource in Biographical Research.' *Qualitative Research* 5,2: 201–291.

Tuma, N. B. and Hannan, M. T. (1979). 'Dynamic Analysis of Event Histories.' *American Journal of Sociology* 84,4: 820–854.

Vogt, E. Z. (1957). 'The Acculturation of the American Indians.' *Annals of American Academy of Political and Social Science* 311: 137–146.

Vogt, E. Z. (1969) *Zinacantan: A Maya community in the Highlands of Chiapas*, Cambridge, MA: Bellknap Press of Harvard University Press.

Vogt, E. Z. (1994). *Fieldwork among the Maya: Reflections on the Harvard Chiapas Project*, Albuquerque: University of New Mexico Press.

Vogt, E. Z. (2002). 'The Harvard Chiapas Project; 1957–2000,' in Kemper, R. and Royce, A. P. (eds) *Chronicling cultures: Long-term field research in anthropology*, Walnut Creek, CA: AltaMira, pp. 135–159.

Wajcman J. and Martin B. (2002). 'Narratives of Identity in Modern Management: the Corrosion of Gender Difference?' *Sociology* 36: 985–1002.

Walkerdine, V. and Lucey, H. (1989). *Democracy in the kitchen: Regulating mothers and socialising daughters*, London: Virago.

Walkerdine, V., Lucey, H. and Melody, J. (2001). *Growing up girl: Psychosocial explorations of gender and class*, Houndmills: Palgrave.

Ward, J. and Henderson, Z. (2003). 'Some Practical and Ethical Issues Encountered While Conducting Tracking Research with Young People Leaving the "Care" System.' *International Journal of Social Research Methodology* 6,3: 255–259.

Warwick, D. and Littlejohn, G. (1992). *Coal, capital and culture: A sociological analysis of mining communities in West Yorkshire*, London: Routledge.

Webb, C. (1996) 'To Digital Heaven? Preserving Oral History Recordings at the National Library of Australia.' *Staff paper*, http://www.nla.gov.au/nla/staffpaper/archive/index1996.html

White, R. and Wyn, J. (2004). *Youth and society: Exploring the social dynamics of youth experience*, Oxford: Oxford University Press.

Whyte, W.F. (1943 2nd edition 1955). *Street Corner Society: The social structure of an Italian slum*, Chicago: University of Chicago Press.

Wirth, L. (1938). 'Urbanism as a Way of Life.' *American Journal of Sociology*, 44: 1–24.

Wolcott, H. F. (1994). *Transforming qualitative data: Description, analysis, and interpretation*, Thousands Oaks, CA: Sage.

Woodgate, R., Degner, L. and Yanofsky, R. (2003). 'A Different Perspective to Approaching Cancer Symptoms in Children.' *Journal of Pain and Symptom Management,* 26,3: 800–817.

Wu, L.L. (2000). 'Some Comments on "Sequence Analysis and Optimal Matching Methods in Sociology: Review and Prospect".' *Sociological Methods and Research* 29,1: 41–64.

Yamaguchi, K. (1991). *Event History Analysis.* Newbury Park, CA: Sage.

Yates, L. and McLeod, J. (1996). "'And How Would You Describe Yourself?" Researchers and Researched in the First Stages of a Qualitative, Longitudinal Research Project.' *Australian Journal of Education* 40,1: 88–103.

Yates, L., McLeod, J. and Arrow, M. (2002). *Self, school and the future: The 12 to 18 Project*, University of Technology, Sydney, Changing Knowledges Changing Identities Research Group.

Young, M. and Willmott, P. (1957). *Family and kinship in East London*, London: Routledge and Kegan Paul.

Comparative and Cross-National Designs

David de Vaus

It can be argued that virtually all social research is comparative in that descriptions and explanations are derived from comparisons of groups, cases, periods or some other unit of analysis (Przeworski and Teune 1966). This chapter focuses on one type of comparative research – that which is based on cross-national comparisons. The discussion concentrates on two main matters.

First it outlines the nature and purpose of comparative cross-national research designs and how this broad design relates to other major types of research design. The purpose of this discussion is to argue that while most research can be considered comparative, there are quite distinctive elements of comparative cross-national research that deserve special attention.

The second goal of the chapter is to describe and evaluate two broad forms of comparative cross-national research – case based and survey based. Apart from demonstrating that comparative cross-national designs come in two main forms, the purpose of this discussion is to show that most of the problems encountered by researchers engaged in cross-national comparative research are confronted in one way or another by those in other forms of research.

PART 1: WHAT IS COMPARATIVE CROSS-NATIONAL RESEARCH?

While the chapter is restricted to cross-national comparative research, even this focus is not without its definitional problems. As we shall see, one of the purposes of cross-national research is to assess the role of culture in shaping outcomes. The problem in comparing *nations* is that nations and cultures are not synonymous. On the one hand, many countries consist of quite distinct cultures within the same national border while the one culture is not necessarily constrained by national borders (see discussion p. 258).

Types of research design

At its simplest, cross-national comparative research is research in which nations are compared on some dimension (Przeworski and Teune 1966). The purpose of cross-national comparisons may either be simply to describe national differences or to draw on the logic of comparisons to *explain* cross-national similarities and differences. This chapter focuses on explanatory forms of comparative cross-national designs.

To understand the place of cross-national comparative designs within social science methods it is useful to review Smelser's (1972) fourfold classification[1] of methodological approaches.

The first approach is the *experimental method* which Smelser, like many others regards as the gold standard in research. The simplest experimental design involves the comparison of two groups at two time points. Initially these two groups are identical, a condition that is achieved by random allocation of cases to the two groups. Initial measures on an outcome variable are obtained from both groups prior to one of the groups (the experimental group) being exposed to an experimental intervention. The other group (the control group) is not exposed to the intervention. At some point following the intervention both groups are remeasured on the outcome variable. The effect of the intervention is measured by comparing the amount of change in the experimental group with that in the control group. Any significant difference in the amount of change between the two groups is attributed to the effect of the intervention since, ideally, this is the only difference between the two groups.

For ethical and practical reasons, the experimental method cannot be used for most social science research. This has led to many social scientists adopting what Smelser calls the *statistical method*. The logic of the statistical method is to simulate important aspects of the experimental method by ensuring that the groups that are comparable are as similar as possible except in relation to the causal and outcome variables. The statistical method relies on multivariate analysis to compare groups that differ in regard to the key independent variables and statistically to remove other relevant differences between

groups. Statistical techniques enable investigators to control or remove these differences to ensure group equivalence on specified characteristics.

Suppose a study was being planned to assess the impact of divorce on the educational performance of children. This would involve comparing *comparable* children from intact and divorced families. However, since children from certain types of circumstances are more likely than others to experience parental divorce it is necessary to distinguish between the effect of divorce and these other circumstances. This is achieved by statistically removing the effect of these other differences to then assess the impact of divorce – *other things being equal*. Statistical controls are an attempt to simulate the effect of random allocation to groups that is used in the experimental method.

A third approach outlined by Smelser is the *comparative method*. This approach can also be understood as simulating some of the features of the experimental method. This approach will be discussed in detail in Part 2.

The fourth approach that Smelser identifies is the *case study method*. This method can consist of either single cases or multiple cases. Where multiple case studies are used the logic of the case study method can be similar to that of the comparative method as outlined by Smelser.

While it is useful to view comparative cross-national *designs* within this framework of experimental, statistical comparative and case study designs this framework does not fully incorporate all the work covered by comparative or cross-national *studies*. Many studies that involve some comparisons between nations and cultures fit more readily under the heading of the statistical method. I will argue, along with Ragin, that there are at least two different approaches to comparative research – what Ragin (1987) calls the variable-based and the case-based methods. The variable-based method is equivalent to the statistical method outlined by Smelser and the case-based method is similar to Smelser's description of the comparative method.

Universal and particular

In 1963 Bendix summarized the role of comparative cross-national research as follows:

> Comparative sociological studies represent an attempt to develop concepts and generalizations at a level between what is true of all societies and what is true of one society at one point in time and space. (1963, p. 532)

This distinction is reflected in universalist and culturalist approaches to explanation to which writers such as Hantrais (1999) and Kohn (1987) draw attention.

Universalist approaches are those that search for general laws or uniform patterns (nomothetic explanation) that apply in all situations regardless of the cultural context being investigated. Ragin and Zaret (1983) refer to this approach as one in which the investigator seeks to identify 'permanent causes'. Using this approach, which was relatively popular in comparative studies in the 1950s and 1960s, the purpose of comparative cross-national research was to identify the commonalities across cultures and countries and thus to establish the universality of particular phenomena. Examples of this approach were those studies that sought to demonstrate principles such as the universality of the nuclear family, the incest taboo or the iron law of oligarchy.

The culturalist approach stands in direct contrast. It stresses the uniqueness of each event and circumstance and emphasizes the particular and unique set of historical and cultural conditions that lead to specific events and outcomes (ideographic explanation). This approach rejects the idea of being able to identify general patterns of behaviour or law-like principles that operate independently of their specific cultural and historical context.

A more useful approach takes a midway position between these extremes. Ragin and Zaret (1983) and Hantrais (1999) argue that this middle position is what makes comparative cross-national research unique and what, in different ways, characterized the vision and work of both Weber and Durkheim as founders of sociology. Both

Weber and Durkheim saw comparative sociology as a way of moving beyond the atheoretical focus on detail that characterized traditional history and the sweeping generalizations of the social philosophers (Ragin and Zaret 1983, p. 731). This midway approach argues that particular phenomena in any society can be the outworking of more or less universal principles *and* of the particular cultural and historical circumstances within which the phenomenon is placed.

Taking this approach, *the contribution of comparative cross-national research is to identify the extent to which social phenomena are shaped by universal system factors and the extent to which they are shaped by unique factors intrinsic to the specific time, place and culture in which they occur.*

PART 2: CASE-BASED CROSS-NATIONAL COMPARISONS

Ragin (1987) distinguishes between case-based comparative research and variable- (or survey-) based comparative research. While these two manifestations of comparative research may apply to a variety of types of comparative research the distinction is an apt way of describing the two major forms of cross-national comparative research. This section outlines the nature and logic of case-based cross-national comparative research while Part 3 will discuss survey-based cross-national comparative research.

Case-based cross-national comparative research is closest to the approach described above by Smelser as the comparative *method* and is similar to the multiple case study approach described by Yin (1989). It should be stressed however that the comparative cross-national method does not encompass all comparative cross-national *research*.

Case-based comparative cross-national research is distinguished by two features: the way in which it seeks to *understand* cases and the logic of the *causal* analysis employed.

Understanding

Case-based comparative cross-national designs seek to understand elements of a country (case) within the context of the *whole* case. It adopts a cultural and interpretive model in that it is taken for granted that any behaviour, attitude, indicator or event can only be understood within its historical, cultural and social context. Thus, rather than having a uniform meaning across all countries, the act of voting, living alone or civil unrest can only be understood within the context of its history, culture and society.

Case-based comparative cross-national research is based on the view that the whole is greater than the sum of the parts and that parts cannot be understood without reference to the whole. Rather than proceeding by isolating and measuring discrete variables in each country, case-based designs seek to build a rounded understanding of each country regarding the phenomenon being investigated. Each case (country) is treated as a unit in its own right that deserves to be understood as a coherent whole rather than simply the site to which variables are somehow attached.

Once each case is understood as a whole, causal analysis proceeds by then *comparing* the cases.

Causal explanation

The similarity or difference of selected countries lies at the heart of the logic by which comparative cross-national designs identify causes and develop explanations. In some comparative cross-national designs countries are selected for comparison because they are *similar* to one another in important respects. In other designs countries are selected for comparison specifically because they *differ* from each other.

Kohn (1987) argues that one of the key contributions of comparative cross-national designs is that they can help distinguish between phenomena that stem from universal principles and those that result from particular

historical and cultural contexts. Slomczynski et al. (1981) argue that:

> Insofar as cross-national analysis of social structure and personality yield *similar* findings in the countries studied, our interpretation can ignore whatever differences there may be in the cultures, political and economic systems, and historical circumstances of the particular countries, to deal instead with social structural universals. But when the relationships between social structure and personality *differ* from country to country, then we must look to what is idiosyncratic about particular countries for our interpretation. (p. 740, my emphasis)

Method of agreement (different cases)

This form of comparative cross-national design is built around comparing countries using the logic of J.S Mill's Method of Agreement. He formulated this method as follows:

> If two or more of the phenomenon [countries] under investigation have only one circumstance in common, the circumstance in which alone all the instances agree, is the cause (or effect) of the given phenomenon. (Mill 1879, Vol. 1, p. 451)

For the current purpose this may be translated as:

*If two or more countries being compared display the same phenomenon (e.g. high rates of solo living) and these countries **share only one other characteristic in common** (e.g. high levels of prosperity) then that characteristic is the cause of the phenomenon they have in common (i.e. high rates of living alone).*

This means that, apart from the phenomenon to be explained, where countries differ in all respects but one, the one factor they have in common is the cause of the phenomenon. This idea is expressed diagrammatically in Table 15.1.

In this case Countries A and B display similar behaviours (Y). On the basis that 'a circumstance that is not common to all instances cannot, by definition, be causally related to it' (Cohen and Nagel 1934) the only causal factor identified above is X_1 (Prosperity) because this is the only common factor between the cases. The countries differ in each other characteristics so these

Table 15.1 Method of agreement

Case	Y High rate of solo living	X_1 Prosperity	X_2 High value placed on privacy	X_3 Low levels of family solidarity	X_4 Ample housing suitable for solo living
Country A	1	1	1	0	1
Country B	1	1	0	1	0

All variables in this example are dichotomous and are coded 0 and 1. 0=not present; 1=present.

characteristics could not be responsible for the common outcome.

When comparative cross-national analysis uses this reasoning it usually proceeds by beginning with the observation of the same behaviour across countries (e.g. that the countries share a high rate of solo living) and then seek the single characteristic that the countries have in common that could explain this common behaviour.

This form of reasoning has important shortcomings which mean it must be used with care.

First, it is impossible to list and compare *every* possible characteristic of two countries. The method can, at best, concentrate on comparing *relevant* characteristics – in this case, characteristics that might affect national rates of solo living. But the selection of such factors is inevitably driven by theory or previous research and therefore risks missing factors not considered by the theories.

Second, the method is biased towards the concept of mono-causation – that an outcome has a single cause. In social life this is by no means true and many phenomena can have both multiple and alternative causes. While the example in Table 15.1 is consistent with prosperity (X_1) being *a* cause of living alone rates it certainly does not demonstrate that it is *the* only cause. It may be the only cause identified within a limited set of factors but the method cannot, in reality, exhaustively eliminate all other factors.

Third, the Method of Agreement is completely unable to identify interaction effects or what is called 'chemical causation' (Mill 1879, Vol. 8, pp. 204–8). That is, some effects will take place only when two characteristics are present in a particular combination.

For example, there is nothing in the example in Table 15.1 to preclude the argument that prosperity *plus* a high value placed on privacy *or* prosperity *plus* low levels of family solidarity result in high levels of solo living.

A final problem is the level of abstraction at which concepts are used. This point can be illustrated by the story of a man who, one evening, drank a great deal of scotch and soda and woke up the next morning with a hangover. The next evening he drank a great deal of brandy and soda and again woke up with a hangover. After drinking gin and soda the next evening and subsequently waking up with a hangover he concluded that the soda was causing the hangover. While this reasoning may appear logical by this method, the reasoning is flawed because of the conceptualization of the variables and the failure to recognize the common element of scotch, brandy and gin. Similarly, conceptualizing characteristics of a country at a highly specific level can cause an investigator to miss more abstract features that countries have in common. Alternatively, conceptualizing country characteristics at too general a level (e.g. democratic) may cause one to overstate the degree of similarity between the countries – a problem described by Ragin as the problem of 'illusory commonality'.

However, for all its dangers, the Method of Agreement can play a useful role by *eliminating* possible explanations. If 'nothing can be the cause of a phenomenon which is not a common circumstance in all instances of a phenomenon' (Cohen and Nagel 1934), the Method of Agreement can be used to eliminate explanations that do not meet this criterion.

Method of difference (similar cases)

Comparative cross-national studies that rely on the Method of Difference proceed by focusing on *countries that differ in regard to the outcome* (e.g. rates of solo living) and seek to find the one, and only one, other difference between those countries (Lijphart 1975). Where only one difference between countries can be found (apart from the outcome) and this difference corresponds to country differences on the outcome variable this characteristic is regarded as the cause or explanation of the outcome. This scenario is represented in Table 15.2 and is exemplified by Lipjhart (1971) who argues that comparative design must be based on selecting comparable or similar cases.

Ideally, when using the Method of Difference, all cases will be identical on each of the potential explanatory variables except for the actual causal variable. Where countries share the same characteristic a potential explanatory variable can be regarded as controlled. For example, in Table 15.2 the countries have different levels of solo living (Y) even when they are equally prosperous (X_1) and have equal levels of family solidarity (X_3). Therefore, these controlled variables cannot be causes of the variations in solo living.

The only explanatory variable that has *the same pattern of variation to the outcome variable* in Table 15.2 is the extent to which privacy is valued in the culture (X_2). In this example, it would be concluded that X_2 is the cause of differences in Y. The availability of suitable housing (X_4) would not be regarded as a cause of solo living since its variation between countries does not match variations in the rates of solo living.

This form of reasoning is the analogue of that used in the classic experiment. In experimental designs random allocation or matching are used to ensure that the control and experimental groups are identical on all variables except for the exposure to the experimental intervention (de Vaus 2001).

A similar logic applies to comparative cross-national designs where similar cases are selected. By selecting countries that have similar cultural political, economic and historical circumstances the aim is to control for these factors. If the countries then differ in relation to the phenomenon under investigation (e.g. rates of solo living) it is argued that the different rates of solo living *cannot* be attributable to the cultural political, economic and historical characteristics that the countries have in common. In other words, *differences* between countries cannot be attributed to characteristics that the countries have in *common*.

Of course it is impossible to select countries that are identical in all respects but one. In selecting countries the investigator will select countries that are similar in *relevant* respects – that is, similar in regard to factors that are potentially relevant to the phenomena to be explained.

However, since many unobserved differences will persist, it is impossible to know if there are factors that have been missed that explain the variation in the outcome variable. While this shortcoming is important, it is no more serious than in all survey-based statistical studies where all conclusions are based on models that contain just a small subset of the possibly relevant variables.

Table 15.2 Method of difference

Case	Y High rate of solo living	X_1 Prosperity	X_2 High value placed on privacy	X_3 Low levels of family solidarity	X_4 Ample housing suitable for solo living
Country X	1	1	1	0	1
Country Y	0	1	0	0	1
Country Z	0	1	0	0	0

All variables in this example are dichotomous and are coded 0 and 1. 0 = not present; 1 = present.

Difficulties with case-based comparative cross-national designs

Since case-based comparative cross-national designs largely rely on the logic of the Methods of Agreement and Difference the method encounters the problems inherent in these methods. Some of the problems associated with each of these particular forms of reasoning have been discussed above. There are additional difficulties with case-based comparative cross-national designs that apply to such studies regardless of whether the Method of Agreement or the Method of Difference is applied.

Reliance on categorical classifications

The Methods of Agreement and Difference are based on simple categorical classifications in which countries are classified as being similar or different. Whether or not countries are classified as similar or different can have a profound influence on the conclusions drawn from a comparative design. But for many variables similarity and difference is a matter of degree. At what point in continuous measures (e.g. rate of solo living) are two countries to be defined as similar? There is a danger that where the design requires that countries are similar the operational definition of 'similar' becomes so broad so that countries that are quite heterogeneous are nevertheless classified as similar. The reverse can be true when defining countries as different (Lieberson 1992).

Defelice (1986) argues for a more flexible approach to comparative design. Rather than classifying cases as similar or different he argues that Mill's Method of Concomitant Variation should be used so that the similarity and difference of countries is regarded as a continuum rather than a dichotomy. Instead of selecting countries that are only similar or only different he argues that the full range of countries should be selected and ranked in terms of similarity/difference on the independent variables (e.g. rapidity of economic development) and the dependent variables (e.g. rapidity of fertility decline). The comparative cross-national analysis then assesses the extent to which the rank ordering of the selected countries corresponds to the rank ordering of the countries on the outcome variable.

Assessing similarity and difference

When assessing similarity or difference it is important to interpret the meaning of indicators within their social and cultural context. For example, religion is expressed differently in different cultures. In one culture high levels of attendance at religious services might reflect religiousness while in another religiousness is expressed in high levels of personal and private piety. A culturally alert approach would investigate what constitutes religiousness in different countries and on that basis select countries that were religious or secular.

The reverse may also be true – something that appears the same in two cultures may have different meanings in different cultures. For example, we may observe increasingly high rates of solo living in a number of countries. However, solo living may mean different things in different countries. In one country it may reflect social breakdown, social isolation and loneliness associated with rapid urbanization. In another country, living alone may reflect an achievement that is only attainable because of a person's prosperity and may reflect the high value placed on privacy and personal autonomy. To treat living alone in such different contexts as though it was really the same thing would lead to serious misunderstanding and misleading explanations.

Type of causal explanation

A strong version of the causal reasoning that underlies the Methods of Agreement and Difference seeks to identify *invariant* patterns. Accordingly, any exception means that a particular causal explanation must be rejected. However, such a black and white approach should be avoided. Where a deviant case is inconsistent with a strong pattern, it is better to see what is peculiar about the deviant case. Rather than leading to the rejection of an idea the deviant case can be used to refine the understanding by helping specify the types of conditions under which a pattern applies.

Small numbers

Case-based comparative cross-national analysis that seeks to understand elements of the whole within their historical, cultural, social and economic context is time-consuming and difficult. The method limits the number of countries that can be thoroughly studied. In practice this means that case-based comparative designs frequently compare just two or three countries and this in turn results in the problem of too few cases (Lijphart 1971).

Clearly such a small number of cases precludes statistical generalization. But a small number of cases still allows for generalization based on the logic of replication – the same basis that is employed with most experiments. As findings are replicated and the range of conditions under which they apply are specified by repeated experiments (or comparisons between pairs of countries) the investigator becomes more confident about the results and can specify the range of situations to which they apply (de Vaus 2001).

The other problem with using such so few cases is that it becomes difficult to apply the logic of the Methods of Agreement or Difference (Lieberson 1991). With a very small number of cases the patterns can be highly ambiguous and indeterminate. For example, the Method of Agreement relies on finding one common factor across cases. But where only three or four countries are included in a comparative cross-national study there may be many characteristics that such a limited number of countries share. Only through the examination of further cases do patterns of agreement begin to come into focus.

PART 3: SURVEY BASED CROSS-NATIONAL COMPARATIVE RESEARCH

Survey-based comparative cross-national research employs a variable-based method of comparison. While the case-based approach described above uses variables these variables are placed and interpreted within the context of the whole case. The initial focus of the case-based approach is to understand the whole country so that specific attributes can be interpreted within the context of the whole. A variable-based approach pays little attention to the whole and largely uses variables without paying attention to the meaning of the attributes in particular cases. Attributes are more or less treated as meaning the same thing regardless of the country in which they are measured.

Two types of comparative survey studies

The two most important types of cross-national survey-based research designs are those in which the country is the unit of analysis and those in which individuals are the unit of analysis.

Country as the unit of analysis

With this design, data are collected about the country at an aggregate level. A set of characteristics of a country are delineated and each country is coded on each of these characteristics so that they are characteristics of nations/cultures rather than of the individuals in the nation/culture.

An example of this type of survey is the Human Relations Area File (http://www.yale.edu/hraf/). For each country or culture, codes are created to indicate the country's or culture's characteristics. The Human Relations Area File consists of a large number of variables that capture characteristics of each culture (e.g. kinship rules, marriage rules, language characteristics, religious characteristics, ways of thinking etc.). All these variables reflect the characteristics of the country or culture – not the individuals in the country.

Aggregate data of this type are also used widely by economists, criminologists, political scientists and others in comparative cross-national studies. While the nature of the variables differs the aggregate nature of the variables remains.

Individuals as the unit of analysis

In these survey-based comparative designs data are collected about and from *individuals* in each country. The profile of each country is the profile derived from the responses of each sample member.

A number of international survey programs ask comparable questions from comparable samples in a variety of countries. Examples of such survey programs include the International Social Science Survey Program (http://www.issp.org/data.htm), The Eurobarometer Survey (http://www.esds.ac. uk/International/access/eurobarometer.asp), the World Fertility Survey (http://opr. princeton.edu/archive/wfs/), the World Values Survey (http://www.worldvaluessurvey.org/) and the European Social Survey (http:// naticent02.uuhost.uk.uu.net/index.htm). Of these, The European Social Survey provides the best example of an international program that seeks to deal systematically and rigorously with many of the problems that confront cross-national survey designs.

The main way in which the analysis of survey data collected in cross-national surveys proceeds is by *pooling the surveys from each country* and testing for relationships between variables in the single dataset . Having established overall patterns, the investigator introduces country as a dummy variable into the statistical modelling to assess the extent of cross-national differences.

If the initial overall patterns remain unaffected by introducing country into the model it is reasonable for the investigator to conclude that the initial patterns are more or less international (universal) rather than national and that the patterns reflect regularities that transcend the particularities of time and place. If, on the other hand, the overall pattern changes once country controls are introduced and if different patterns of data are observed in different countries, the investigator will look to national characteristics to help account for the diverse national patterns.

Limitations of survey research in a comparative context

The survey-based approach to comparative research has a number of important strengths. Survey-based approaches provide the means of obtaining a systematic profile of each country and a formal way of evaluating the extent to which country differences exist. However, the approach encounters important challenges which, unless dealt with, limit the validity of cross-national comparisons. These problems fall into two broad categories: limitations related to the survey method itself and limitations due to the difficulty of obtaining equivalent information from each country.

An inherent bias in country-based surveys of individuals is that such studies equating interpret the sum of the responses of a sample of individuals as representing the country as a whole. This problem does not refer to the representativeness of samples but to two issues.

Individualist fallacy

Scheuch (1968) draws attention to the problem of the 'individualistic fallacy'. This problem, to which cross-national comparative research is especially vulnerable, is the opposite of Robinson's formulation of the ecological fallacy (1950). Essentially, the individualistic fallacy is the error of assuming that the whole is simply the sum of its parts. It is the error of drawing conclusions about a social unit such as a nation-state on the basis of measurements derived from the individuals in that social unit (Lazarsfeld and Menzel 1961).

For example, while a survey may indicate that most individuals value equality and democratic participation, it does not mean that the country exhibits equality or is democratic. Even though the character of a country may be affected by attitudes of individuals and the attitudes may be influenced by characteristics of the culture, one level (the national level) cannot be read off directly from the individual level. A country is also constituted by many factors including its institutions, its history, its physical environment and its location within larger international structures.

Furthermore, not all individuals contribute equally to shaping the national culture or mood. Verba (1993) suggests a variety of ways in which surveys might try to take into account the uneven impact of different types of individuals in shaping the national picture.

Instability of measurements

Survey research that discovers inter-country differences requires reliable measures. Long ago Scheuch (1968) reminded comparativists that many of the so-called differences between countries were in fact differences of only a few percentage points. To interpret these differences in terms of cultural characteristics requires that these inter-country differences are both real and persistent. However, given the many sources of measurement error in comparative research (see later discussion) it is a brave person who can confidently say that the observed differences between countries reflect real differences and are not simply an artefact of measurement error. Certainly one would want to be assured that the same pattern of inter-country differences persists over time and with alternative measures.

What is to be compared?

One of the purposes of cross-national research is to assess the role of culture in determining various outcomes. The problem confronted by cross-national survey research is that nation and culture are not synonymous. While country provides the frame from which survey data are collected (whether it be at the individual or aggregate level) these national boundaries do not necessarily correspond to cultural boundaries. Scheuch (1989) argues that 'there exists a German culture ...[but] this does not, nor ever did, coincide with the political boundaries of any one political entity'. Rokkan (1970) distinguishes between cross-national, cross-cultural and cross-societal comparisons. Dogan and Pelassy (1984) point out that 'Juan Linz delineated eight Spains, Erik Allardt four Finlands, and Stein Rokkan as many Norways. Anyone knows that there are three Belgiums, four Italys and five or six Frances'.

The lack of cultural homogeneity of most nations means that it is difficult to infer culture from nation. However, most comparative surveys are based on national boundaries and thus identify *national* rather than *cultural* differences. Given national heterogeneity any differences between countries may be due to the impact of a particular part of a nation rather than any *national culture*. Indeed cultural variations within a country may even be greater than those between nations and cross-country differences may simply be a statistical artefact. Care therefore is required when interpreting cross-national differences. The need to explore variations within countries as well as between countries is required if one is to avoid simplistic attributions of between-country differences to cultural differences.

There are, of course, valid reasons for using national rather than cultural boundaries. National boundaries are clearly defined and relate closely to the available statistical data. They also relate to policy and legislative frameworks and provide a means of evaluating the impact of national laws and policies – matters that are frequently of more interest to governments and funding agencies than the unique impact of particular cultures (Hantrais 1999).

The reverse problem, known as *Galton's problem*, can also complicate the interpretation of cross-national differences. 'Galton's Problem' is the problem of interpretation due to cultural diffusion whereby the culture of one country spreads to other countries and creates a degree of uniformity between countries. That is, each country is not truly independent of the other. Where this is the case comparative cross-national analysis may discover uniformity across nations (e.g. family forms or taboos), that is due to cultural diffusion rather than to the operation of universal principles.

Equivalence in cross-national comparisons

The goal of any cross-national survey is to collect data in such a way that any cross-national differences in survey findings can be attributed to real differences between the countries rather than to differences in data collection methods. There are two key sources of what can be called non-equivalence error in cross-national surveys: the adoption of non-equivalent methodologies and the non-equivalence of the meaning of the data that are collected. The issues of equivalence are covered in some detail in Hantrais (1999).

Methodological equivalence

Cross-national differences in survey results can be due to methodological differences such as non-equivalent samples, data collection methods and coding frames in different countries.

Achieving such equivalence is difficult (Harkness 1999). The European Social Survey (ESS) stands out for the diligence with which it minimizes methodological non-equivalence error in cross-national surveys. By adopting a centralized structure the ESS imposes the same methodology on each of the participating countries. This standardization includes such matters as the organization of the survey group in each country, sampling methods, fieldwork, the ways in which response rates are calculated, the level of survey documentation and many other detailed aspects of conducting and reporting the survey in each country. These detailed specifications are available in the ESS website (http://naticent02.uuhost.uk.uu.net/index.htm).

Since sample design and size affect the error of estimates the ESS provides detailed rules about the way in which samples are obtained and on providing information by which sample quality can be assessed (http://naticent02.uuhost.uk.uu.net/methodology/sampling_strategy.htm).

Methods of administration can affect responses to different types of questions and result in quite different levels of non-response and response bias. A good cross-national survey will therefore specify the mode of data collection and the specifics of exactly how that mode will be implemented (e.g.http://naticent02.uuhost.uk.uu.net/fieldwork/index.htm). Ways of evaluating the quality of the data in each country

are required. Common coding frameworks and ways of managing non-equivalent responses (e.g. political party supported) need to be specified. The ESS has made considerable advances in specifying the way in which equivalence in these areas can be achieved.

Until the ESS insisted on conformity to detailed survey requirements and established clear documentation standards, the information required to evaluate whether surveys conducted in different countries were actually comparable was frequently unavailable (Harkness 1999). This in turn has meant that we really do not know whether we can safely compare the data from many multi-country surveys. The use of ESS specifications will provide a major improvement in achieving methodological equivalence in comparative cross-national surveys.

However, even with detailed specifications and rules to achieve equivalence the reality remains that it is difficult to achieve equivalence in the implementation of surveys in different countries (Mitchell 1965). Not only are some countries better equipped to conduct quality surveys, countries vary in the types of sampling frames that are available, the methods of administration that are possible and even the level of survey 'literacy' of the population (Bulmer 1998; Harkness 1999). Furthermore, cultural differences in matters such as politeness can affect both response rates and the presence of acquiescent response sets (Jones 1963).

All these factors stem from the culture in which the survey is administered and therefore which in turn makes it difficult to standardize across cultures. Considerable work remains to be done to design ways of assessing the impact of these different methods of survey procedure in different contexts. Certainly, when using data from cross-national surveys investigators need to be aware of the survey design in each country and be aware of the way in which cultural practices may affect the way in which the survey is implemented. To use these datasets without this understanding, risks confusing *observed* cross-national differences with *real* differences and failing to consider that the differences are simply methodological artefacts.

Equivalence of meaning

It is one thing to enforce the same ways of collecting data in each country in a cross-national survey. It is another thing to ensure that the meaning of the data is equivalent in each country. The problem of the meaning of observations in different countries confronts all cross-national research. However, because survey responses are typically less contextualized than data collected with other methods, the problem of meaning is particularly acute in cross-national *survey* research.

Validity in different contexts.
Problems in assessing the meaning of observations relate to the validity and reliability of survey questions. Cross-national surveys produce special problems for validity since the way in which questions are understood can vary sharply in different cultural contexts. Validity problems in comparative cross-national surveys arise from the difficulty of ensuring that questions mean and measure the same thing in different countries.

The problem of equivalent meaning is obvious when the questionnaire needs to be administered in different languages. Where this is the case the first task is to ensure that the equivalent meaning is contained in the different translations. A common approach to ensuring that the language is equivalent is to use blind back-translation methods (Brislin 1970). This involves beginning with a base language (e.g. English) and then translating the questionnaire into each of the languages used in the survey. To check on the accuracy of the translation, the translation is then independently translated back into the base language and the two versions of the questionnaire in the base language are compared.

However, it is not always possible to achieve a neutral or an accurate translation. Since language is a carrier of culture, the words can reflect culturally specific meanings and concepts that may have no equivalent in another culture. For example, a common question in international surveys has been to ask people to indicate their political orientation on a left wing/right wing continuum. But the concept of left and right does not translate well to countries where the very *concept* is foreign. A similar problem arises when asking about religious beliefs in different countries where the concept of God does not always translate well (Jowell 1998).

Equivalence is not just a matter of arriving at equivalent *language* but of achieving equivalent *indicators*. Even when equivalent words are used the questions do not always work in the same way in different cultures. Most questions are used to tap more abstract concepts but the specific indicators of the concept can differ from one country to the next.

Even questions designed to measure behaviour or personal attributes encounter problems. Here the problem may be less a matter of achieving equivalent wording but in determining how to interpret responses. The same response will not necessarily have the same meaning in different cultures. Educational level is measured in most surveys but in cross-national surveys working out equivalent levels of education is confounded by different systems and qualifications. Even age is problematic (Verba 1993) especially where age is used as a proxy for other concepts such as stage in the life cycle. Depending on the culture and society, knowing that a person is 20 years old indicates different things.

These simple examples highlight the fundamental characteristic of all social measurement. The meaning of the measurement must be derived from the culture. This means that the same responses (e.g. years of education, voting behaviour, occupation or age) may not have the same meaning in different cultures.

Literal and functional equivalence.
One of the decisions any comparative survey researcher must make is whether to aim for *literal* or *functional* equivalence. Literal equivalence is achieved where identical stimuli are used in all countries and is exemplified in Almond and Verba's (1963) *The Civic*

Culture, a classic study in comparative politics. Using this approach, literal translations and the same indicators of concepts are used in each country. The shortcomings of literal equivalence have already been outlined above.

The alternative is to aim for functional equivalence (Przeworski and Teune 1966; Scheuch 1968). Functional equivalence is achieved where the goal is to measure the same construct but the specific means by which the construct is measured can vary from place to place. The notion of functional equivalence is based on Lazarsfeld's argument that indicators can be interchangeable. In cross-cultural research the argument is that measures must be culturally relevant and that therefore different measures will frequently be required to measure the same concept in different cultures.

The ESS seeks to achieve functional rather than literal equivalence of question wording. Rather than insisting on literal translations with the standard blind back-translation approach a Translation Panel works with the questionnaire design teams. This panel provides detailed annotations to the questionnaire that explain the purpose and meaning behind questions and concepts. The purpose of these annotations is to assist the translators in retaining the meaning of the concepts and to assist them in developing wordings that capture the meaning behind the question while freeing them from a strict literal translation (http://naticent02.uuhost.uk.uu.net/methodology/translation_strategy.htm).

The notion of functional equivalence is the most defensible approach in cross-national research as it recognizes that meaning derives from a context. However, the difficulty is in knowing whether one has achieved functional equivalence. It is one thing to accept that constructs can be measured in different ways in different cultures but it is quite another to demonstrate that the different ways *are* functionally equivalent. Przeworski and Teune (1966) proposed one method which they call the 'identity-equivalence' method for deriving functionally equivalent indices of concepts in different countries.

This method involves developing measures of concepts in each country that consist of a mixture of country-specific indicators and indicators that are common to all the countries being compared. In this way there is some capacity to evaluate the extent to which the country-specific indicators capture the same underlying concept as do the common cross-national indicators.

Improving equivalence

Equivalence is a continuum. While the goal in comparative cross-national survey research is to achieve full equivalence this goal is unlikely to be realized. Nevertheless, there are ways in which equivalence can be improved.

At the measurement level equivalence is much more likely to be achieved by aiming for functional than literal equivalence. While methods such as identity equivalence techniques can be useful they do not fully resolve the issue of establishing that different sets of indicators are functionally equivalent. Cognitive interviewing, by which means investigators try to access the meanings that respondents attach to questions and their answers can assist in evaluating whether different questions are functionally equivalent in different countries. Of course the traditional ways of assessing the validity of any measure can be used to improve the functional equivalence of measures in different cultures.

At the level of executing comparable surveys with comparable samples and comparable data collection methodologies there is room for considerable improvement (Lynn 2003). Much more careful specification of standards and requirements for surveys in each participating country is essential. While it will not be possible to implement identical procedures in all countries, some variation could be eliminated by more rigorous specification requirements such as those used in the ESS model. More thorough documentation will assist investigators in interpreting inter-country differences in results and assist in analyzing data so as to minimize the effect of these inter-country survey differences.

Other improvements can be achieved by better standardization in areas such as the way in which particular key questions are worded and coded. International efforts at achieving harmonization of key background variables have gone some way to obtaining consistent measures of key variables. The UK National Statistics Office provides an example of a set of harmonized questions used in government surveys (http://www.statistics.gov.uk/about/data/harmonisation/default.asp).

One of the criticisms of cross-national surveys is that variables are measured without context. One way in which both these dangers can be reduced is to ensure that data are collected about the structural and cultural elements of the country or region from which the individual comes. Thus, if national, regional and local characteristics can be added to individual records in survey datasets then it is much more likely that subsequent analysis can at least give some weight to these characteristics. The development of multi-level modelling techniques enables these macro characteristics to be taken into account in assessing individual data.

CONCLUSION

In 1989, Scheuch stated that 'in terms of [comparative] methodology *in abstracto* and on issues of research technology, most of all that needed to be said has already been published'. Nothing since then challenges the accuracy of his assessment. While comparative cross-national research continues, the main approaches and problems have been known for a long time. Little progress has been made in recent years in overcoming the basic problems.

In general, however, the problems faced in comparative cross-national research are encountered in one way or another in all other research designs.

Two main forms of comparative cross-national research have been outlined in this chapter. Case-based methods of comparative cross-national research share the same strengths and weaknesses of any case-based method (de Vaus 2001, 2006). The great strength of case-based comparative methods is that they seek to understand the specific within the context of the whole case. For cross-cultural research this is particularly important.

All case-based approaches encounter problems of knowing when the whole case, rather than just elements have been understood. All case-based methods rely on interpretation and this in turn leads to some difficulties in replication. The small number of cases that can be studied produce further problems for the methodology. Other difficulties include the shortcomings of the logic of the Methods of Agreement and Difference that have been outlined. The logic of the method is most suited to eliminating explanations than it is to 'proving' explanations. Case-based methods also encounter difficulties in that the logic of the method is to seek invariant causes, an aim which may be generally unachievable in social science research.

However, there is nothing unique about case-based methods in cross-national research. While cultural differences may be especially obvious in cross-national research the whole point of case-based approaches is to take the specific context into account. This applies to historical research and case studies as much as to cross-cultural research.

The second main form of cross-cultural comparative research is the cross-national survey. While there have been attempts to improve the comparability, the same problems apply to cross-national surveys as to national surveys. The differences are a matter of degree.

Any national survey faces problems associated with the meaning and equivalence of items. No nation is so homogenous that these issues are not important. While language may not be as obvious a factor within national surveys (or is conveniently ignored) the understanding of questions and the appropriateness of indicators will vary across a range of sub-cultural groupings within any nation (de Vaus 2002a, 2002b).

The equivalence of survey methodologies and the difficulties that non-equivalence creates for cross-national comparisons is a problem and has been recognized as such. But the problem is not unique to cross-national surveys. Precisely the same issue confronts repeated cross-sectional studies that attempt to track trends within countries. The non-equivalence of question wording, samples and methodologies confronts any survey analyst trying to interpret trend studies (Kulka 1982).

These shortcomings in case-based and survey-based methodologies in cross-national comparative research are not reasons for avoiding cross-national research any more than they are for avoiding these methods in national or sub-national contexts. As the world becomes increasingly globalized we can only anticipate a growth in the need and opportunity for cross-national research. An awareness of the challenges faced in conducting such research is part of the solution to reducing the effect of these problems and for evaluating the claims made on the basis of cross-national comparative research.

NOTES

1 Smelser actually identifies five types but one of these – the method of heuristic assumption – is not particularly relevant to this discussion.

REFERENCES

Almond, G. and S. Verba (1963). *The Civic Culture.* Princeton, Princeton University Press.

Bendix, R. (1963). 'Concepts and generalisations in comparative sociological studies'. *American Sociological Review* 28: 532–539.

Brislin, R. W. (1970). 'Back-translation for cross-cultural research'. *Journal of Cross Cultural Psychology* 1: 185–216.

Bulmer, M. (1998). 'The problem of exporting social survey research'. *American Behavioral Scientist* 42(2 Oct.): 153–167.

Cohen, M. R. and E. Nagel (1934). *An Introduction to Logic and Scientific Method.* New York, Harcourt Brace Inc.

Defelice, E. G. (1986). 'Causal inference and comparative methods'. *Comparative Political Studies* 19(3): 415–437.

de Vaus, D. A. (2001). *Research Design in Social Research.* London, Sage.

de Vaus, D. A. (2002a). *Surveys in Social Research,* 5th edn. London, Routledge.

de Vaus, D. A. (ed.) (2002b). *Social Surveys,* 4 volumes. London, Sage.

de Vaus, D. A. (ed.) (2006). *Research Design,* 4 volumes. London, Sage.

Dogan, M. and D. Pelassy (1984). *How to Compare Nations.* Chatham NJ, Chatham House.

Hantrais, L. (1999). 'Contextualization in cross-national comparative research'. *International Journal of Social Research Methodology* 2(2): 93–108.

Harkness, J. (1999). 'In pursuit of quality: issues for cross-national survey research'. *International Journal of Research Methodology* 2(2): 125–140.

Jones, E. L. (1963). 'The courtesy bias in South-East Asian survey'. *International Social Science Journal* 15(1): 70–76.

Jowell, R. (1998). 'How comparative is comparative research?' *American Behavioral Scientist* 42(2 Oct.): 168–177.

Kohn, M. L. (1987). *Cross-National Research as an Analytic Strategy. Cross-National Research in Sociology.* Newbury Park, Sage.

Kulka, R. A. (1982). 'Monitoring social change via survey replication: prospects and pitfalls from a replication survey of social roles and mental health'. *Journal of Social Issues* 38(1): 17–38.

Lazarsfeld, P. F. and H. Menzel (1961). 'On the relationship between individual and collective properties'. *Complex Organisations.* A. Etzioni. New York, Holt, Rinehart and Winston, pp. 422–440.

Lieberson, S. (1991). 'Small N's and big conclusions: an examination of the reasoning in comparative studies based on a small number of cases'. *Social Forces* 70: 307–20.

Lijphart, A. (1971). 'Comparative politics and the comparative method'. *American Political Science Review* 65(3): 682–693.

Lijphart, A. (1975). 'The comparable cases strategy in comparative research'. *Comparative Political Studies* 8: 158–177.

Lynn, P. (2003). 'Developing quality standards for cross-national survey research: five approaches'. *International Journal of Social Research Methodology* 6(4): 323–336.

Mill, J. S. (1879). *A System of Logic,* 8th edn. London, Longmans Green.

Mitchell, R. E. (1965). 'Survey materials collected in the developing countries: sampling measurement and interviewing obstacles to intranational and international comparisons'. *International Social Science Journal* 17(4): 665–685.

Przeworski, A. and H. Teune (1966). 'Equivalence in cross-national research'. *Public Opinion Quarterly* 30: 551–568.

Ragin, C. C. (1987). *The Comparative Method*. Berkeley, University of California Press.

Ragin, C. C. and D. Zaret (1983). 'Theory and method in comparative research: two strategies'. *Social Forces* 61(3): 731–754.

Robinson, W. S. (1950). 'Ecological correlations and the behavior of individuals'. *American Sociological Review* 15(June): 351–357.

Rokkan, S. (1970). *Cross-cultural, Cross-societal and Cross-national Research. Main Trends of Research in the Human and Social Sciences*. Paris, UNESCO.

Scheuch, E. K. (1968). The cross-cultural use of sample surveys: problems of comparability. *Comparative Research Across Cultures and Nations*. S. Rokkan. Paris, Mouton, pp. 176–209.

Scheuch, E. K. (1989). 'Theoretical implications of comparative survey research: why the wheel of cross-cultural research keeps on being reinvented'. *International Sociology* 4: 147–167.

Slomczynski, K. M., J. Miller, and M. Kohn. (1981). 'Stratification, work, and values: a Polish-United States comparison'. *American Sociological Review* 46(6): 720–744.

Smelser, N. J. (1972). The methodology of comparative studies. *Comparative Research Methods*. D. P. Warwick and S. Osherson. Englewood Cliffs, Prentice Hall, pp. 41–86.

Verba, S. (1993). 'The uses of survey research in the study of comparative politics: issues and strategies'. *Historical Social Research* 18(2): 55–103.

Yin, R. K. (1989). *Case Study Research: Design and Methods*. Beverley Hills and London, Sage Publications.

Data Collection and Fieldwork

This section of the handbook delves into several different ways to collect data and conduct fieldwork. Social science methodology is very rich in the choices it provides an investigator in conducting research. Matching the appropriate method to the research question sometimes makes this richness overwhelming. However, the choices provide the tools that are needed to conduct research. A sharper tool should provide a more clearly detailed answer. While most of the world focuses on the answer the trained social scientist is aware that how the question is answered can be as important as the question itself. This handbook section provides a range of such tools that include both introductory and intermediate approaches.

The chapter by Bovaird and Embretson on tests and measurement may be difficult to read but it is worth the effort. The chapter deals with a well-established approach to measure development that has recently received more visibility in the social sciences. Item response theory (IRT) can be applied to survey research, marketing, and health contexts in addition to most substantive areas in education and psychology. The authors argue that classical test theory (CTT), which is the primary social science approach to measurement, not only makes unrealistic assumptions about the characteristics of the data needed but also lacks several important advantages of IRT. The latter is more flexible and has an advanced framework that is model based that relates test items to examinee and item characteristics. IRT analysis produces an equation that describes the relationship between the respondent and item parameters.

Scores from CTT are dependent on the characteristics of the respondent and the specific test. These two characteristics cannot be separated in the CTT approach. The IRT model-based approach is not specific to the test or questionnaire used and the sample tested. With IRT different measures of the same trait can be used without expensive test-equating procedures. In CTT the reliability of the test increases with its length that produces long tests or questionnaires with redundant items. IRT allows the selection of items of varying and non-overlapping difficulty so that tests can be considerably shorter than those developed under CTT.

IRT is most advantageous when computer-based adaptive testing is used. In conventional testing everyone gets the same or parallel versions of a test. With IRT each test can be individualized by selecting items of varying difficulty from a pool of items. This approach provides a more accurate estimate of the person's ability in much less time. It is expected that the use of IRT will continue to grow and displace much of CTT.

Susan Speer's chapter provides an overview and critical evaluation of the debate on the relative advantages and disadvantages of 'natural' versus 'contrived' data, or 'unobtrusive' and 'obtrusive' methods. She concludes by saying that by adopting a reflexive approach to interviews or other contrived data collection procedures we can obtain rich insights into interactional issues and the workings of normativity in culture. On the other hand she stresses that we can never achieve an unmediated access to participants' realities, neutralize the context, or disinfect our data entirely of the researcher's presence, because the knower is always intimately bound up in and partially constitutive of what is known. Finally, what are natural data cannot be decided on the basis of their type and/or the role of the researcher within the data. Rather, the status of pieces of data as natural or not depends largely on what the researcher intends to 'do' with them.

Obtrusive questionnaires and interviews form the lion's share of the social research literature. The chapter by de Leeuw will help researchers plan their study using these approaches. One of the first problems researchers face is fewer people are willing to answer questions. In many cases the only way to assure an appropriate sample is to offer to pay the respondent. However, de Leeuw provides several suggestions for how to optimize response rates.

Another issue discussed in this chapter is how to write the questions. It seems obvious that the answer to the question needs to reflect what we wanted to know. However, respondents may not understand the question in the way the person who wrote it expects. Education, culture, experience all shape how we understand what we are being asked. Writing good questions requires pre-testing. The chapter introduces the use of cognitive psychology in question development.

The chapter also reviews several approaches to data collection. In person or face-to-face interviews are the most flexible and can help and motivate respondents. Telephone interviews are less flexible and do not possess the visual cues that can be used during an in-person interview to determine if the respondent appears to understand the question. Mail surveys have the advantage

of being relatively inexpensive but require accurate names and addresses. They are also subject to a low response rate. Internet- or Web-based survey are also relatively inexpensive, allow complex skip patterns that written questionnaires cannot do but are clearly limited to those persons who have easy access to the Internet. Finally, group administration of questionnaires, as in a classroom, can be used if appropriate. The author provides an excellent summary of the advantages and disadvantages of each of these techniques that will aid the researcher in making the correct choice in which method to use.

In qualitative research, the most common methods of data collection are in-depth and semi-structured interviews. Feminist researchers have been active in developing these methods in recent years. Doucet and Mauthner discuss qualitative interviewing from the standpoint of feminism and view the research interview as a way of constructing knowledge. They argue that feminists have problematized key issues in the use of interviews as a research tool: who produces knowledge, with what politics, and from which locations. The discussion covers issues around rapport and the relational aspects of interviewer-interviewee relationships. In discussing power differences they show how feminists have come to see the researcher as both 'outsiders' and 'insiders' in the way they relate to their interviewees and invest their identities in the research relationship but also in their relation to the data they produce. In referring to interview dynamics they point to the two-way nature of power between respondents and interviewers in the co-production of interview material. The discussion also moves to the power of researchers to represent the narratives of those they study including the links made with theory, the transcription, interpretation, and writing up.

While qualitative interviews are often directed to understanding the commonalities between those they study, biographical methods focus upon differences and upon the whole case. Biographical methods are enjoying a resurgence of popularity albeit, as Joanna Bornat shows in Chapter 20, a growing number of approaches have developed under this umbrella. Bornat's chapter is written from the perspective of an oral historian. Three main approaches are identified that have developed along rather different interdisciplinary lines: biographic-interpretive approach, oral history, and narrative analysis. The biographical interpretive method lends itself to more psychoanalytic interpretations of motivation and meaning; narrative analysis leans more toward socio-linguistics; while oral history draws from both sociology and history. Each gives centrality to the individual account and to individual agency in attempting to explain the changing nature and persistence of social relations and social structures; each makes use of the interview to generate data. They differ, Bornat argues, in three important respects: the dialogic or interactive aspects of the interview; the centrality of memories to their interpretation; and the role of the researcher in the interpretation of the data.

Reflecting her identification as an oral historian, Bornat argues that oral history places more emphasis on the dynamics of the interview process than the other two approaches. It also places more emphasis upon the importance of eliciting memories for their own sake so that the effects of time – a concern with 'pastness' is how she puts it – and an interest in change and continuity come to the fore. Oral history developed through a political concern to capture the unheard 'voices of the past' represents a rather more democratic approach to data analysis and interpretation. While narrative analysis and the biographic-interpretive approach provide for a deep analysis of subconscious as well as conscious processes – what may be unspoken or unacknowledged by the interviewee, oral historians maintain a greater interpretive distance and tighter boundaries around their role as interpreters than the two other approaches.

Janet Smithson's chapter on focus groups discusses practical and theoretical questions related to using focus groups in social research and suggests how to use them and analyse the data most effectively. According to her, the particular strength of the focus group method is that it enables research participants to discuss and develop ideas collectively, and articulate their ideas in their own terms, bringing forward their priorities and perspectives. The limitations of focus group research can be mitigated by awareness of the constraints, informed analysis, and by detailed consideration of the way the conversations are socially constructed in the group context.

Modern Measurement in the Social Sciences

James A. Bovaird and Susan E. Embretson

While item response theory (IRT) is a viable and well-established methodology for educational measures, it is still relatively unused in psychology and the rest of the social sciences. Despite its underutilization in the mainstream of social research, IRT is appropriate for consideration in any context that postulates the presence of a latent construct and involves constructing and/or analyzing a multicomponent instrument designed to measure that construct-including survey research, marketing, and health contexts in addition to most substantive areas of education and psychology. Some attractive features of IRT include the possibility of more flexible construction of alternative test forms, shorter and more efficient tests, equating, and interpretation of scores without norms. This chapter will review and emphasize the benefits of contemporary IRT, including the technical advances of IRT over methods based on classical test theory (CTT), the role of modern measurement methods in computer-based testing (CBT) and computerized adaptive testing (CAT),

and the potential of some IRT models to impact test design for targeted aspects of construct validity. We will begin with a brief discussion of what constitutes the area of testing and measurement followed by a direct contrast of IRT and CTT. The shortcomings of CTT will be used to illustrate the benefits of modern measurement techniques in the context of the characteristics of quality measurement. The chapter ends with a discussion of current trends and future directions.

TESTING AND MEASUREMENT

Most social scientists are interested in unobservable human attributes that are often referred to as *latent constructs*, raising the issue of imparting a clear meaning to the numbers that are assigned to represent levels of a construct, a process called *measurement* or *psychometrics*. *Testing* then refers to sampling the individual behavior that is observable at a given point in time. Unfortunately, measurement instruments cannot exactly represent the latent construct, so the quality of measurement is defined by the presence of four characteristics: a standardized mode of test administration, a meaningful metric for obtained scores, score reliability, and score validity. These four characteristics contribute to the interpretability (or lack thereof) of scores obtained in testing and will be expanded upon in subsequent sections as a means of distinguishing between CTT and IRT.

While some attributes such as age or weight can be precisely measured with a single measurement, most constructs are much harder to test with single measures. Consequently, most tests or scales contain multiple measures, each representing a single observation of the characteristic. In education, and testing in general, simple measures are often called *items*, in survey research they may be called *questions*, and in experimental psychology they may be referred to as *stimuli* or *cues*. Consistent with the testing background from which measurement has primarily developed, we will collectively refer to questions, items, and stimuli as items. The number of items required in a scale depends on the complexity of the characteristic. Individual items tend to be poor measures and often partially reflect attributes other than the targeted construct. Thus, the variability among responses to an individual item contains a portion attributable to the targeted construct, or *true score* variance, and a portion attributable to random error and unrelated systematic sources, or measurement *error*.

The numerical representation of an observable behavior requires a clear and definitive rule for associating *one and only one* number with the magnitude of an individual's construct level. Given a sample O of N distinct participants, any participant can be assigned a true score $t(o_s)$. A procedure is then devised for pairing each participant o_s with its imprecise numerical measurement, $m(o_s)$. Measurement scales can be classified as one of four *scales of measurement*: nominal, ordinal, interval, or ratio. Nominal and ordinal scales can be further classified as categorical data, and interval and ratio scales are often classified as continuous data.

In general, there are three basic item types in use in the social sciences. The first type is a response set that represents a range of trait levels ordered from low to high. Examples would be rating scales (often called Likert scales; Likert, 1932), physiological measurements, and any other 'continuous' measures. While not all of the response sets fully meet the requirements for interval level of measurement, there is an assumption of an underlying continuum. (See Goldstein & Hersen (1984) for a discussion of Likert-type items and interval properties.) The second type of item has a dichotomous (two response options) response format such as true/false questions or checklists (an endorsement constitutes the presence of the behavior, trait, event, etc. while the absence of endorsement indicates the absence of the behavior). The third item type is a dichotomous scoring of a polytomous (more than two response options) response set such as the case with multiple choice formats. Typically, there is a correct answer and a set of distractors and the resulting dichotomous data represents either a correct/incorrect response or a pass/fail decision.

CLASSICAL TEST THEORY AND MODERN MEASUREMENT

Historically, CTT has provided a general framework for the development, administration, and interpretation of assessment tools. Gulliksen (1950) is often referred to as the defining volume for CTT, but much of the work was first formalized by Spearman in the early 1900s, well before Lord and Novick (1968) laid the foundation for IRT. According to McDonald (1999), there are two views on the relationship between CTT and modern measurement. McDonald argues that CTT may be viewed as a reasonable approximation to IRT under certain conditions. Conversely, since the development of CTT occurred prior to the development of IRT, there exists the accurate impression that IRT represents a significant change in theoretical perspective from CTT. According to Embretson and Reise (2000), CTT can be best described as representing a set of 'Old Rules of Measurement' that have served applied psychologists and psychometricians for decades. Developed from common factor theory, CTT provides fairly accurate psychometric information for items resulting in continuous data. However, there are several inherent shortcomings involved when CTT is applied to categorical data that arise from polytomous response formats and dichotomous scoring. While CTT methods *may* provide reasonable approximations with binary data, it is only a *linear* approximation to a *nonlinear* system. As suggested by both the traditional label and the name given to them by Embretson and Reise, the old rules have been improved upon by two modern model-based frameworks for measuring abilities: the extension of biserial and tetrachoric correlation theory with the common factor model referred to as *item factor analysis* (Bock, Gibbons, & Muraki 1988; Knol & Berger, 1991), and the development of essentially a nonlinear common factor model suitable for conditional probabilities, or *item response theory*. Item factor analysis is best discussed in the context of structural equation modeling and confirmatory factor analysis and will not be covered further in this chapter. The interested reader is referred to Mislevy (1986), Muthén (1978), or Takane and de Leeuw (1987) for more information. The following sections will present a summary of the classical rules of measurement, contrast them with the 'new' rules of measurement, and illustrate how IRT better addresses some of the shortcomings of the classical methods, primarily when applied to binary data.

Historical development

Classical test theory is frequently cited as having its roots in Gulliksen (1950), however, the procedures upon which CTT is based were developed much earlier by Charles Spearman (1927) who described how to recognize that tests measure a common factor and determine the amount of error in test scores. The identification of a common factor gave rise to the concept of a true score and the common factor theory. Spearman's common factor theory was further developed and elaborated by Thurstone (see Thorndike & Lohman, 1990), Guttman (1957), Lawley (see McDonald, 1999), and Joreskog (see McDonald, 1985). Spearman also showed how a correlation between two alternate forms of a test could be used to estimate the amount of measurement error in test scores which became the primary purpose of CTT. Guttman (1945) introduced the concept of internal consistency by showing how items within a test could also be used to determine test reliability, and Cronbach (1951) continued the work to the extent that the most common CTT measure of internal consistency reliability is named after him, Cronbach's coefficient alpha (α).

IRT developed through the work of two traditions spanning both sides of the Atlantic Ocean. In the United States, Lazarsfeld (1950) introduced *latent structure analysis*, which eventually became known as IRT. IRT combines factor analysis with the *phi-gamma hypothesis*[1], one of the oldest laws in psychology that can be traced back as early as 1878 (see Guilford, 1954; McDonald, 1999). Another key development was Lord's (1952) demonstration that Spearman's single factor theory could be applied to binary items. Lord and Novick (1968) included four chapters from Allan Birnbaum on IRT. Bock and Aitken (1981) provided the elegant marginal maximum likelihood (MML) method for parameter estimation. In Europe, Rasch (1960) proposed what is now known as the Rasch model or 1-parameter logistic (1PL) model. Anderson (1972) elaborated on the MML estimation methods for Rasch item and person parameters. Gerhard Fischer (1973) extended the binary Rasch model to define parameters by incorporating stimulus properties, treatment conditions, etc. using a linear logistic latent trait model (LLTM). Others have progressed the field of IRT since this seminal work, but they are too numerous to name.

Classical test theory

The focus of CTT is to understand and improve the reliability of test scores. CTT is also synonymous with *true score theory* due to its decomposition of observed scores (X) into true score (T) and error (E). According to CTT, at the examinee level, any observation is a realization of a random variable X with a probability, or propensity, distribution. The examinee's true score is then the expectation of this propensity distribution. That is, if an examinee were observed an infinite number of times, the true score would be the average of the multiple observations. The difference between the actual observation and the true score is the error in measurement, where error is also a random variable but with an expectation of zero. CTT also assumes that errors are normally distributed and uncorrelated with other variables.

However, CTT is applied at the level of the test rather than the examinee level, so when examinees are randomly sampled, T becomes a random variable also. Reliability then is the ratio of variability in true scores to variability in observed scores, where the square root of reliability is the correlation between true and observed scores. There have been a number of methods developed to estimate CTT reliability, some of which will be discussed in a later section. For a more detailed discussion of CTT see McDonald (1999) or Crocker and Algina (1986) in addition to the classic Gulliksen (1950) and Lord and Novick (1968) texts.

Item response theory

IRT, also referred to as *latent trait theory*, *strong true score theory*, or *modern mental test theory*, represents a more flexible and more sophisticated testing framework than CTT by making CTT hypotheses more explicit. IRT represents a collection of related model-based psychometric theories that relate item responses to examinee and item characteristics. For a more thorough discussion of the principles of IRT than what is presented here, including additional technical details, see the excellent texts by Baker and Kim (2004); De Boeck and Wilson (2004); Embretson and Reise (2000); Hambleton, Swaminathan, and Rogers (1991); and van der Linden and Hambleton (1996).

The purpose of IRT is to provide an equation, called an *item response function* (IRF), to maximize the relationship between examinee and item parameters and the probability of a discrete response outcome such as endorsing an item or answering an item correctly. While the only explicit assumptions in CTT pertained to the distribution of measurement errors and their relationship with other variables, IRT makes two strong assumptions. The first assumption, *local independence,* requires that an examinee has a true location on at least one continuous latent dimension (true score) that can explain performance, resulting in responses that are statistically independent. In other words, proper specification of the latent dimension(s) explains any relationship between observed responses. There may be more than one dimension underlying performance, but all dimensions relevant to explaining performance are specified. Secondary factors are assumed to be mutually independent and collectively orthogonal (unrelated). In the event that not all relevant dimensions are specified, research has shown that IRT is robust to minor violations of this assumption as long as there is a strong dominant factor (Drasgow & Parsons, 1983; Tate, 2002).

The second assumption is that the relationship between performance and the underlying dimension has a specific form. In most IRT applications, including the most common models presented here, the item-trait relationship can be adequately described by a monotonically increasing IRF whereas the level of the trait increases, the probability of a correct response or item endorsement increases as well, in accordance with the phi-gamma hypothesis. Also referred to as an *item characteristic curve* (ICC), *item response curve*, or *trace line*, the IRF maps examinees' locations on the latent continuum across levels of a construct. Item characteristics, or parameters, determine the shape of the ICC and will be described shortly. IRT models and the corresponding IRFs differ in the mathematical form of the IRF and/or the number of parameters in the model, but all will have at least one examinee trait parameter and one item parameter. The reliance on an adequate model means that IRT models are falsifiable – they may or may not be appropriate for a particular set of test data and are testable – thus, model-to-data goodness of fit testing is essential (see Embretson & Reise, 2000). Evidence of poor model fit may be an indication of a heterogeneous population and will be discussed later in the chapter.

By relating the probability of an individual item response to both examinee and item parameters, the IRT model explicitly states that an examinee's response to a given item will be a joint function of examinee characteristics (i.e. level of the trait) and the characteristics of the item itself. When the model of examinee behavior is probabilistic, three fundamental problems with CTT exist when applied to categorical data (see McDonald, 1999). First, if the range of the construct is broad enough, CTT will result in a negative probability of response for examinees in the lower tail of the trait distribution and probability greater than 1.0 in the upper tail. Second, the linear common factor model used in CTT assumes that error variance is independent from true score variance, and this cannot be true for binary items. Third, CTT also assumes that measurement error (standard error of measurement) is constant over all levels of the trait, and this too is not realistic.

In order to represent probability, the IRF must be curvilinear since it is bounded by zero and one. The *logistic function, L(Z)*, where Z represents a linear combination of item and person parameters that varies across types of IRT models, is most commonly used as the *link function* to relate the linear function of the parameters to the nonlinear probability of the keyed response. The logistic link function is appropriate for a binomial dichotomous variable.

The fundamental item response model is the Rasch model (Rasch, 1960), or 1PL model,

$$P(X_{is} = 1|\theta_s, b_i) = \frac{e^{D(\theta_s - b_i)}}{1 + e^{D(\theta_s - b_i)}}, \quad (1)$$

where X_{is} is the response of person s to item i (0 or 1). The linear combination of parameters Z is the simple difference between the trait level for person s, θ_s, and the difficulty of item i, b_i. The person parameter, θ_s, is the *person location parameter* indicating a person's level of the trait. When estimating item parameters, a process referred to as *calibration*, the person parameter is assumed to be normally distributed, however non-normal distributions may be accommodated using a prior distribution in a Bayesian framework. The Rasch model is called a 1-parameter model since it contains only one item parameter, b_i. The difficulty parameter is sometimes referred to as the *item* location parameter indicating the item's position relative to the latent trait. Assuming that the latent trait metric is person-anchored, difficulty is interpreted in IRT as the point at which examinees have a 50 percent chance of answering the item correctly or endorsing the item. Thus, if an examinee's ability level is equal to the difficulty of the item (i.e. $\theta_s - b_i = 0$), they will have a probability that $X_{is} = 1$ (a correct response or item endorsement) of 0.50. An item's difficulty typically ranges from -2.0 to 2.0, where a negative value indicates an easier, more frequently endorsed item. In the ability context, an item with a negative difficulty parameter would be appropriate for an examinee of below-average ability. In a clinical context using a symptom checklist for depression (assuming that a high depression score indicates a depressed individual), an item with a negative difficulty parameter would indicate that a person who is below the average level of depression has a 50 percent chance of endorsing that item or exhibiting that symptom. The IRT difficulty parameter is comparable to the mean item response in CTT. The 1PL model assumes that all items have the same degree of relationship, or discrimination, with the construct. In CTT, this is referred to as parallel items (McDonald, 1999). The constant multiplier

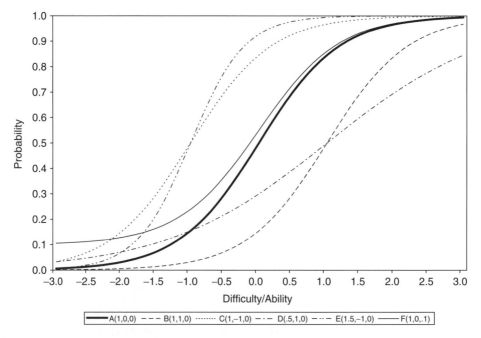

Figure 16.1 Item response functions for six hypothetical items. A, B, and C are 1PL models; D and E are 2PL models, and F is a 3PL model. The numbers in parentheses correspond with the discrimination, difficulty, and guessing parameter estimates, respectively

$D = 1.701$ is sometimes added to the logistic function to make it virtually indistinguishable from the cumulative normal-ogive function (McDonald, 1999).

IRFs A, B, and C in Figure 16.1 reflect three items that differ in difficulty or location, but are equal in discrimination. IRF A is appropriate for an examinee of average ability ($b_i = 0$), while IRFs B and C are appropriate for examinees who are above average on the trait ($b_i = 1.0$) and below average on the trait ($b_i = -1.0$), respectively. These items are equal in discrimination because they have the same shape or slope indicating the same relationship with the trait, just offset in location.

The most commonly used IRT model, the 2-parameter logistic (2PL) model allows items to vary in difficulty and in discrimination,

$$P\left(X_{is} = 1 | \theta_s, b_i, a_i\right) = \frac{e^{Da_i(\theta_s - b_i)}}{1 + e^{Da_i(\theta_s - b_i)}}, \quad (2)$$

where a_i is the discrimination parameter and is proportional to the slope of the IRF where $\theta_s = b_i$. Discrimination parameters typically range from 0.5 to 1.5. The IRF for an item with high discrimination looks like a step function. The IRT discrimination parameter corresponds to the CTT item-total correlation, and a discrimination of 1.0 corresponds to a common factor loading of 0.70. IRFs C and E and IRFs B and D in Figure 16.1 reflect the effect of unequal discrimination on the probability of a correct response or item endorsement. IRFs C and E have the same location ($b_i = -1.0$), but differ in the slope of the IRF at the location parameter with IRF E having a steeper slope indicating a more discriminating item. In CTT, one would say item E has a higher item-total correlation than item C. IRFs B and D also share the same location ($b_i = 1.0$), but IRF D has a lower slope at the location parameter and thus is a less discriminating item.

The 3-parameter logistic (3PL) model is represented as,

$$P\left(X_{is} = 1 | \theta_s, b_i, a_i, c_i\right)$$
$$= c_i + (1 - c_i)\frac{e^{Da_i(\theta_s - b_i)}}{1 + e^{Da_i(\theta_s - b_i)}}, \quad (3)$$

where c_i represents a lower asymptote, or guessing, parameter for the model to reflect the probability of a correct response by chance alone. IRF F in Figure 16.1 illustrates the impact of a guessing parameter on the IRF. Item F has a lower asymptote of $c_i = 0.10$, indicating that regardless of an examinee's ability or location on the trait, an examinee always has at least a 10 percent chance of responding correctly or endorsing that item due to chance alone. In comparison, examinees of low ability or trait level have a near 0 percent chance of responding correctly to items A–E. There is no equivalent to the guessing parameter under CTT.

Several extensions of the basic IRT models have been developed. Bock (1972) extended the 2PL model to the nominal response model in order to use all information contained in examinee responses. Thissen and Steinberg (1984, 1986) showed that all other non-ordered polytomous models are special cases of the nominal response model. The partial credit model (PCM; Masters, 1982) and its derivation, the rating scale model (Andrich, 1978), were introduced for the case where partial credit may be necessary as is often the case with math problems. The graded response model (Samejima, 1969) assumes available response categories can be ordered (i.e. Likert scales). The binomial trials model can be used for situations involving the probability that an examinee completes x of n trials such as making 8 of 10 free throws in a basketball game. The Poisson counts model is appropriate for measurement situations involving the number and difficulty of events (i.e. push-ups, sit-ups, etc.) completed per period of time must be considered.

Other examples of IRT models include the multidimensional extensions of the 1-, and 2-PL models: the multidimensional Rasch model (Reckase & McKinley, 1982) and the multidimensional 2PL model (Reckase, 1997). Fischer's LLTM has been extended to the multicomponent latent trait model (MLTM; Whitely, 1980), the general component latent trait model (GLTM, Embretson, 1984), and the multidimensional Rasch model for learning and change (MRMLC;

Embretson, 1991). Several models for continuous responses have been developed, such as Mellenbergh (1994), as well as models for exploring the multidimensionality of a scale akin to exploratory factor analysis, the exploratory multidimensional IRT model (Bock, Gibbons, & Muraki, 1988) and confirming the dimensionality of a scale akin to confirmatory factor analysis, the confirmatory IRT models for traits (Embretson, 1991, 1997; DiBello et al., 1995; Adams et al., 1997).

The benefits of a model-based approach

CTT has an advantage over IRT in that most CTT procedures have a closed form[2] and are computationally simple, with IRT requiring complex estimation procedures (MML, Empirical Bayes, etc.). It is also true that the correlation between IRT person ability and the CTT summed scale score is usually very high, and so an argument can be made that not much is gained through IRT. However, just because two scalings (CTT and IRT) are equivalent (or nearly so) does not mean that they will produce similar experimental and applied results. IRT separates examinees in the extreme ranges of the ability distribution rather than in the middle by providing optimal scaling of individual differences. For instance, in a bivariate scatterplot of CTT and IRT trait estimates, a Loess fit line would take on an ogive form with examinees having a high degree of correspondence around the average trait level and more variability at the extreme ranges of the ability distribution. Several authors have reported problems with using CTT scores as a metric for scaling individual differences or comparing groups (Maxwell & DeLaney, 1985; Yen, 1986; Bond & Fox, 2001), testing moderated effects (Embretson, 1996), and change (Bereiter, 1963; Embretson, 1998b, 2007; Fraley et al., 2000), where these problems were alleviated by IRT scaling. In addition, IRT's unique properties are necessary to facilitate advanced measurement applications such as CAT (Weiss, 1982), detecting item bias or differential item functioning (DIF; Lord, 1980), and test linking or equating (Cook & Eignor, 1983, 1989). Despite its historical popularity, CTT has many shortcomings. These shortcomings will be discussed in the context of the four characteristics of quality measurement: a meaningful metric for obtained scores, score reliability, score validity, and a standardized mode of test administration.

A meaningful metric

When constructs are considered latent (e.g. intelligence, depression, attitudes, etc.) and are not directly observable (e.g. pounds, liters, kilometers, etc.), they have no inherent metric. Under CTT, in many cases, construct scores have little or no meaning unto themselves unless they can be compared to a *normative* group. Normative information serves as a reference by which to evaluate how an individual compares to others who took the same test. IRT improves on this limitation by providing a sample-free metric for interpretation of performance.

Invariance. Perhaps the most significant characteristics of CTT are the dependency of the true score estimate on the specific test and population and the dependency of item characteristics on the specific sample from which they are derived. This means that examinee and test characteristics cannot be separated. That is, ability estimates apply only to items on a specific test or to items on a parallel test with equivalent item properties, and item characteristics depend on the group of examinees from which responses are obtained. Under CTT, the trait level is estimated by calculating the unit-weighted summed scale score. The meaning of the score is obtained by comparing the individual's performance to its position in a normative group in order to obtain a 'true score,' or the expected value of observed performance on the test of interest (Hambleton, Swaminathan and Rogers 1991). If an item is added or removed, the true score changes, resulting in a unique psychometric scale for every test. If a test is difficult, an examinee of average ability will appear to perform poorly, and if a test is easy, that same examinee will appear to perform at a high level. This is because the difficulty of a test, or individual items for that matter, is defined in CTT as the proportion of examinees in a group of interest who answers the item correctly. Thus, a difficult versus easy distinction depends on the examinees taking the test and performance depends on whether items are hard or easy.

IRT provides person-free item parameter estimation and item-free person parameter estimation that are invariant within a linear transformation, meaning that item parameters from one sample can be linearly transformed to be equal to parameters from a second sample. IRT places person ability and item difficulty on the same scale, explicitly estimating the joint relationship between person and item properties. Therefore, responses from items with known IRFs can be used to estimate trait levels for other samples. In CTT, the model does not include item properties, so the trait level applies only to particular items on that test. In contrast to CTT, the meaning of a trait level applies to any item where item characteristics are known. This is essential for *specific objectivity*: the case in which comparison of examinees is independent of the specific items or tests administered. In IRT, a number of item properties can be incorporated into the model including item difficulty, discrimination, susceptibility to guessing, the nature of the response alternatives, impact of substantive item features, average response time, etc.

It is important to note that even in IRT, careful consideration must be given when selecting the sample of examinees to be used for item calibration. As noted earlier, item parameter estimation assumes that the trait is person-anchored. If the calibration sample is not a representative sample of the population that an item bank is being developed for, the researcher will have difficulty in interpreting the meaning of the resulting item parameters. However, once the representative calibration sample is selected and IRFs are known, items from a calibrated bank can be used to estimate trait levels for other samples and the resulting trait estimates are comparable across samples, administrations, and studies.

Comparing groups. In order to compare the performance of groups of examinees, the items on the test must function the same for all examinees regardless of group membership. That is, the scale items must illustrate measurement invariance (Vandenberg & Lance, 2000). Under the IRT framework, an item exhibits DIF if the IRF is not equivalent when estimated separately for each group. Such an illustration is only possible because of the parameter invariance properties of IRT. Proper identification of DIF is hindered under the CTT framework by the lack of sample independent item statistics. DIF has increased in prominence, and will continue doing so, along with the increased emphasis on test fairness (see American Educational Research Association, American Psychological Association, & National Council on Measurement in Education, 1999). See Holland and Wainer (1993); Millsap and Everson (1993); Waller et al. (2000); or Reise et al. (2001) for further discussions and illustrations of DIF.

Comparing different measures of the same trait. Historically, when necessary to compare or relate test scores from two different administrations or test scores from two different measures of the same construct, test-equating procedures were necessary (see Doran & Holland, 2000; Embretson & Reise, 2000). The development and refinement of IRT procedures allows for a more powerful approach referred to as *scale linking* (Choi & McCall, 2002). Scale linking through IRT solves two classic problems experienced under CTT: respondent non-response resulting in a different set of items for different examinees, and different measures for different examinees (see Vale, 1986). Under CTT, when non-response occurs, the average item response may be used instead of the unit-weighted summed score, or a missing data procedure such as multiple imputation (MI; Schafer, 1997) may be used, although this rarely occurs or is recommended. Under IRT, examinee non-response is not a problem because the trait estimate can be estimated from any set of items with known IRFs. The need to link different measures for different examinees often occurs due to changing content over

time (i.e. revisions, short forms, etc.), different measures of a common construct, or the same measure administered in different languages. These situations are also easily remedied due to the invariance property of IRT.

Measurement of change. Under CTT, meaningful change scores can only be compared when initial score levels are equivalent as a small deviation from a high initial score on an easy test does not mean the same thing as a small score change from an average score, because an interval scale level of measurement is not achieved (Embretson & Reise, 2000). If an interval scale of measurement is achieved through transformations, then it is specific to that particular test administration. However, in IRT, change scores can be meaningfully compared even when the initial scores are unequal[3]. This is largely due to the interval scale nature of item difficulty parameters and individual trait parameters.

Bereiter (1963) indicated three basic problems with using a simple CTT difference score to indicate change: a paradoxical relationship between the test-retest correlation and the reliability of the change score, the initial score correlates negatively with the change score, and the fore-mentioned scaling issue. A fourth problem is whether the change score actually reflects change due to a condition or is simple error (Embretson, 1998a). A special Rasch-family model, the multidimensional Rasch model for learning and change (MRMLC; Embretson, 1991) addressed the four difficulties of CTT by resolving the scaling and reliability problems found with standard 'change' scores and removing some of the confounds that occur with initial status. Two of the problems are addressed by IRT in general. First, the Rasch model achieves interval scale properties (see Andrich, 1985; Fischer, 1995a). Second, the MRMLC, as an IRT model, provides individual standard error of measurement estimates. The MRMLC specifically addresses the two change score dilemmas: the issue of paradoxical reliabilities is addressed by modeling individual change directly in a model that explains changing test correlations, and the correlation between the initial score and the change score is resolved by achieving interval scale properties (Embretson, 1998b).

Reliability

Reliability refers to the accuracy or precision of a measurement instrument. That is, scores must be reliable before they can be valid. It is important to note that tests themselves are not reliable, the resulting scores are. It is possible for a given test to yield highly reliable scores in some circumstances but not others. Responsible reporting of test results should always include the reliability estimate in order to reflect the impact of sample-specific characteristics on score reliability.

Internal consistency. The second CTT shortcoming concerns the definition of reliability and its complement, the standard error of measurement (SEM). Under CTT, a measure is reliable, or *consistent*, if an individual examinee can hypothetically be measured a large number of times and achieve the same score each time. Reliability quantifies the proportion of true score variance in a set of scores. Even though the CTT model in Equation 1 specifies that there are two independent variables (IVs) per person (T and E), these IVs are not actually separable for an individual score. Instead, communalities (correlations) between items are used to infer population estimates of true and error variance. Reliability is estimated as the correlation between test scores on parallel forms of a test or as a function of inter-correlations among items on a test. As a test-level estimate under CTT, scale reliability, as well as the SEM, applies equally to all individuals in a sample that takes the test or all scores obtained from a particular test administration. Thus, CTT is relevant to reliability only at the population level and not at the individual level.

There are two primary sources of measurement error in observed scores: inconsistency across time and/or test forms (between-test variability), and inconsistency across items within a test (within-test variability). Spearman (1927) illustrated that the correlation between two alternate test forms could be used to estimate test reliability (Lord & Novick, 1968), thus between-test variability is often assessed by either repeated administrations of the same test (test-retest reliability) or by administrations of parallel forms (alternate forms reliability). Within-test consistency can be assessed with a single test administration either by use of split-half reliability or most commonly, coefficient alpha (Guttman, 1945; Cronbach, 1951).

Coefficient alpha, as the average inter-item correlation, quantifies the internal consistency within a test and is appropriate for multiple-item measures that measure a single common construct (i.e. are unidimensional). Coefficient alpha derivations assume that all items measure the same construct (i.e. the test is unidimensional), and all items are assumed to be equally related to the construct (i.e. parallel measures). For dichotomously scored items, the Kuder-Richardson Formula 20 (KR_{20}) is identical to coefficient alpha, and if all items have the same degree of difficulty, the Kuder-Richardson Formula 21 (KR_{21}) may be used. Several factors influence the reliability of test scores under CTT, including the heterogeneity of the sample, the level of the sample on the construct, and the number of items. Numerous other reliability coefficients have been developed for CTT that provide either lower bound estimates or estimates with unknown biases (see Hambleton & van der Linden, 1982).

Under CTT, the 'quality' of items or their relationship with the trait is evaluated based on the mean item response and the item-total correlation. The mean item response, or the proportion endorsing the item in the keyed direction, is a measure of the difficulty of the item, and the item-total correlation is an indication of how well the item taps the construct of interest. Such item statistics are not invariant across diverse samples and are thus sample dependent. Item difficulty changes depending on the average trait level of the respondent sample, and the item-total correlation is heavily influenced by the variability of scale scores on a given sample and changes depending on whether items are added or deleted from the test.

Unfortunately, coefficient alpha and the Kuder-Richardson formulas themselves can misestimate scale reliability. When items are not parallel, regardless of dimensionality, coefficient alpha is actually a lower-bound reliability estimate (i.e. reliability is under-estimated; see Lord & Novick, 1968; Raykov, 1997). Conversely, when unidimensionality is violated by the inclusion of subscales, methods factors, or strict time limits (causing the introduction of a speed of processing factor), coefficient alpha can result in an overestimate of the scale precision. Recently, newer methods have been proposed to more accurately estimate scale reliability and allow for establishing a confidence interval around the point estimate (see Raykov, 1997; Raykov & Shrout, 2002).

Information. The most significant difference between IRT and CTT is the conceptualization of measurement error. Under CTT, there is a single index of reliability for all examinees. Instead of item reliability, IRT uses an *item information function* (IIF),

where *information* reflects how well an item differentiates among respondents who are at different levels of the latent variable. Under IRT, the IIF and a *scale information function* (SIF) are calculated that allow measurement error to vary across levels of the trait. By allowing for non-uniform precision across the entire range of trait levels with extreme levels of a trait having more measurement error than the typical levels of the trait, IRT provides a more realistic and valid conceptualization of reliability.

Information is a function of item parameters at any given trait level. For the 1PL model, information is a product of the probability of a correct response, $p_i(\theta)$, and probability of an incorrect response, $q_i(\theta)$. Item information for the 2PL and 3PL models further incorporate the discrimination and guessing parameters. See Figure 16.2 for example IIFs relative to three of the IRFs presented in Figure 16.1. The IIF appears as a bell-shaped function with the maximum information provided at the location parameter. That is, information is greatest when the item's difficulty and the person's ability are matched. The shape of

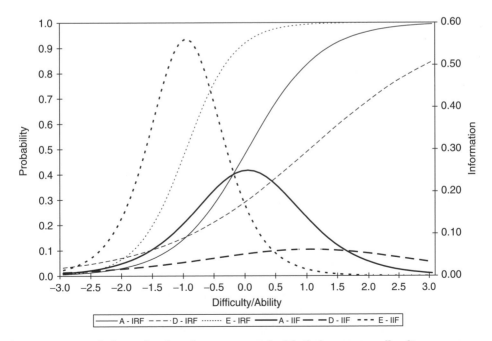

Figure 16.2   Item information functions contrasted with their corresponding item response functions for three of the items in Figure 16.1 differing in discrimination and difficulty

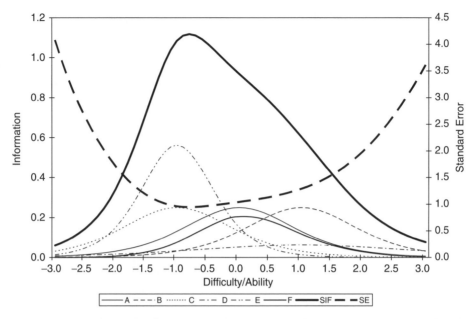

Figure 16.3 Item information functions, scale information function, and test standard error for a hypothetical test that includes the six items originally presented in Figure 16.1. Note that item E has the highest discrimination and thus the most information. Even though the average difficulty is 0.0, maximum precision is obtained for examinees that are approximately 0.80 standard deviations errors below 'average'

the IIF is indicated by the item discrimination, for models with varying discrimination parameters. Note that the highest IIF is for item E which also has the highest discrimination ($a_i = 1.5$). Highly discriminating items provide more information over a narrow range, while low discriminating items provide less information over a broader range. For instance, the IIF for item E shows a lot of information is available over a narrow range of abilities from about −2.0 to 0.0 centered at the item location parameter for that item ($b_i = -1.0$), while the IIF for item D shows that much less information is available for examinees with a much broader range of abilities.

Due to local independence (the latent variable explains any relationship between items), item information is additive, so test information represented by the SIF is a sum of item information. The SIF can be recomputed just as the CTT statistic of alpha-if-deleted is calculated. The standard error or measurement at a given trait level is then the reciprocal of

the square root of the SIF. Information in IRT allows the reliability of a test to be shaped for different ranges of ability. Figure 16.3 includes the SIF and SEM for a hypothetical test that includes the same six items illustrated in Figure 16.1. While the average difficulty of the 6 items is approximately 0.0, maximal precision is actually obtained for examinees $\theta_s/b_i = -0.80$ because of the additional information provided by item E at $b_i = -1.0$ and the relatively little information provided by item D at $b_i = 1.0$. Thus, this hypothetical test would yield the most precise measurement for individuals who are approximately 0.80 standard deviations below average on the trait of interest.

As a parallel to coefficient alpha, an empirical reliability coefficient can be computed as an average reliability across examinees. The empirical reliability coefficient (see du Toit, 2003) may be given as the ratio of the variance in estimated scores for the sample, σ_θ^2, to the sum of σ_θ^2 and the mean square SEM (σ_E^2).

Validity

While reliability is typically defined as consistency, *validity* is typically presented as accuracy, or the degree to which a test measures the construct it purports to measure. Validity generally involves either demonstrating a pattern of correlations with other variables that is consistent with theoretical expectations or demonstrating that some theoretically supported experimental manipulation of the construct results in the expected changes in the construct. For example, evidence of validity is established for a measure of depression if it positively correlates with other established measures of depression, negatively correlates with measures of positive affect, and does not correlate with measures of a theoretically unrelated construct. A measure of stress should result in higher levels of stress after examinees have been exposed to a stressor. Reliability is a necessary precondition for validity, as test scores can be reliable but not valid. For example, scores from a 'new' measure of depression may have high internal consistency or a high correlation with repeated administrations suggesting strong test-retest reliability, yet the same scores may not correlate at all with established measures of depression or show clinically meaningful differences in depression for diagnosed versus non-diagnosed patients.

IRT has a well-established place in testing research and applications, but CTT factor analytic models remain prevalent in most areas of social research despite their close association with IRT (McDonald, 1999) – factor loadings are comparable to item discriminations and factor thresholds are comparable to item difficulties, although thresholds are rarely used in factor analysis. IRT use may be more dependent on the underlying theoretical nature of the construct of interest rather than the discipline in which it is employed. For instance, IRT is appropriate for latent or reflective constructs but not formative or emergent constructs like social status or mental health (Reise & Henson, 2003). IRT is better suited for narrower constructs, rather than broad multidimensional constructs. In addition, IRT can be used to determine more precise subscores and then used to combine the subscores into a general score comparable to a second-order factor model (Thissen & Wainer, 2001). Birnbaum (1968) showed that IRT provides a weighted scaling that results in the smallest possible (most precise) SEM, but does IRT make a practical difference? The common answer (e.g. Reise & Henson, 2003) is 'maybe' as there is evidence on both sides. Interestingly, the split evidence parallels the two aspects of construct validity.

Construct validity. The traditional view of validity holds that there are three 'types' of validity information: how well the test represents the trait (*content validity*), how well the test predicts performance (*criterion-related validity*), and what scores on the test mean (*construct validity*). Currently, validity is viewed as consisting of only one type, construct validity, which has several aspects that apply to all tests (Messick, 1994). These aspects of validity are external validity, substantive validity, content validity, structural validity, generalizability, and consequential validity. External validity most closely reflects Cronbach and Meehl's (1955) emphasis on the nomological network of relationships to explicate construct validity.

Research to explicate the meaning of the nomological network of relationships examines individual differences relationships between the focal trait and other variables. The focal trait(s) should represent interpretable dimensions, account for the test's external validity, differentially predict learning under various treatments or in separate content areas, and generalize across tasks. Test scores show little difference in relative standing among examinees when determined by both CTT and IRT. In fact, the CTT raw score is a sufficient statistic for estimating the examinee trait parameter under the 1PL (Rasch) model. CTT raw scores and 2PL examinee trait estimates also tend to correlate in the upper 0.90s (Reise & Henson, 2003). In a well-designed instrument, item discriminations or weights do not differ widely, so a 2PL model would effectively employ unit weighting and be comparable to the 1PL model. Reise and Henson (2003) report that in personality research, there is no substantial evidence personality research to show that IRT increases the magnitude of the validity coefficient and thus external validity.

External validity, however, is not sufficient to elucidate construct meaning. The relationship between test scores and other variables elaborates the test's nomological network, but this confounds the meaning of a construct with its significance. Even though construct significance is elaborated by empirically established relationships, construct meaning is not (Bechtoldt, 1959). Establishing substantive validity (Messick, 1994) more directly involves construct meaning. Embretson (1983) suggested that the theory behind a construct must be brought into more of a central role in defining construct meaning by differentiating *construct representation* from *nomothetic span*. That is, the construct representation aspect of construct validity (see Embretson, 1983; Messick, 1994) is explained by understanding the cognitive processes and strategies that are involved in items, as well as by understanding the specific knowledge that is required for successful item completion. Even though nomothetic span is supported by individual differences relationships, construct representation is supported by studying the impact of item and task features on item responses. This distinction results in several advantages for test development, including the capacity to design items to reflect specific cognitive constructs and to select items for stimulus features that influence targeted processes.

IRT and CTT differ greatly in their potential for explicating construct representation and for guiding test design. Four general criteria can be applied to evaluate a psychometric methodology for construct validity: relating individual test performance to the characteristics of item stimuli, providing a comparison of alternative theories of the task constructs, establishing specific terms for theoretical construct quantification, and measuring individuals on the constructs involved. CTT does not meet these criteria because it is test-score oriented and does not link item

properties directly to the trait. Embretson (1983) noted that all four criteria could be met by multicomponent latent trait modeling which combines IRT with mathematical modeling. In this approach, task decomposition is applied to test items as a basis for estimating the theoretical parameters. Some early examples of this approach are the linear LLTM (Fischer, 1973), the multicomponent latent trait model (MLTM; Whitely, 1980), and the general component latent trait model (GLTM; Embretson, 1984).

Development of measures from cognitive principles. Even though researchers in psychological and educational measurement have been interested in developing tests based on cognitive principles for quite some time, little has been done to progress the interest. Aptitude and ability tests are frequently described using cognitive terms, but the real utility of cognitive theory has been widely ignored (Pellegrino, 1998). Cognitive psychology principles can be useful for test design because justifiable operational definitions are required for the construct measurement, the field frequently takes advantage of detailed task stimulus property descriptions, and they provide results on how item properties influence the cognitive processes involved in problem solving (Embretson, 1998a). Understanding the sources of cognitive complexity in items can lead to effective means of item generation. The stimulus features that are quantified to represent sources of cognitive demand potentially can be manipulated to develop items with specified sources and levels of cognitive complexity. Since the stimulus features are quantified in the cognitive model, item difficulty is predictable, depending on the strength of the model. This further leads to the possibility of quickly producing a large number of items that may require little or no empirical tryout, due to the priors from the model predictions (Mislevy, 1993). Effective cognitive models have been developed for many non-verbal intelligence tests (Bejar, 1993; Embretson & Gorin, 2001; Embretson, 2002) and several researchers have demonstrated the potential to generate test items based on a specific cognitive theory (Hornke & Habon, 1986; Bejar & Yocam, 1991; Embretson, 1994). Despite these successes, psychometric tests designed from cognitive theory have been rare. See Embretson (1995, 1998a), Kyllonen (1993), Kyllonen and Christal (1989, 1990), and Draycott and Kline (1994) for examples of cognitive design systems and efforts towards developing psychometric measures from cognitive principles.

Standardization

A measure is *standardized* if there are uniform procedures to ensure that the measure is administered and scored the same way each time it is used. If so, two individuals who receive the same score can be interpreted to possess the same amount of the attribute. However, there is a great degree of variability in the procedures that are used for standardization. Measures scored through CTT can be easily standardized, but some of the special qualities of IRT allow for major advances in test administration.

Computer-based testing. The development of the computer and its application to testing has brought with it several improvements in test standardization. In contrast to the traditional pencil-and-paper mode of test administration, CBT has become a common form of test delivery. Perhaps the most notable advantage of CBT over the pencil-and-paper and interview formats is the level of administrative control given over the testing conditions. CBT simplifies administration, requires fewer resources, provides faster results, may be less prone to testing-related errors, may minimize examinee cheating, and has become more cost-effective as the cost and prevalence of personal computers decreases (Mead & Drasgow, 1993). From a logistical perspective, CBT can reduce testing time, provide immediate scoring, allow more frequent testing, provide the opportunity for walk-in testing, allow individual administration, and increase test security by reducing the possibility that examinees can provide information to one another. More complex item types are available through increased capacity for expanded visualization, audition, and interaction, and the automated nature of computers can be capitalized to develop or compile, process, and score tests, including complex responses such as open-ended questions. Finally, from a substantive perspective, CBT has the potential to assess new skills, some even better than other testing formats, and can allow access to data that is not readily available from a pencil-and-paper format (e.g. response time).

CBT is not without its unresolved problems, however. Access to computer testing centers or the internet, item security, test-delivery system reliability, and the expense of development are of primary concern. The psychometric quality of the tests, the adequacy of the supporting theoretical models, and the issue of whether test bias occurs due to the effect of access to technology on performance are very active areas of inquiry. See Mills et al. (2002) for the current state of the art in CBT.

Computerized adaptive testing. CBT itself is not an advance attributable to the benefits of IRT over CTT. However, an important issue related to CBT is item selection. In a *conventional* test, every examinee receives the same (or parallel) test form, the same item set, and in the same (or counterbalanced) presentation order. Conventional tests are usually administered through the pencil-and-paper format, but a computer may be used to administer the test as well. Conventional tests are usually geared towards the average examinee, so they are not the best estimators of ability for examinees at the extremes of the ability continuum (low or high). These tests can be time-intensive for the examinee, but as group tests, they are relatively convenient for the administrator.

Adaptive tests tailor item selection to meet the examinee's individual ability levels by selecting from a pool of items that are the most appropriate for that particular examinee, so not all examinees will receive the same set of items. Traditional individual intelligence tests or subtests that require the administrator to determine a baseline ability level for the examinee and then administer increasingly more difficult items until a ceiling is reached are examples of adaptive tests. Individual versions of these tests are time-intensive on the part of the researcher and the examinee.

A *computer-adaptive test* (CAT) rapidly adjusts the difficulty level of the test to match the ability level of the examinee by using a computerized algorithm to select the items that are most appropriate for estimating the examinee's ability levels from a large pre-calibrated pool of items, an item bank, with pre-determined item characteristics (a set of items with known IRFs). A CAT starts at a difficulty level that is deemed most likely to be accurate for the examinee (usually 'average'). Depending on the accuracy of the initial response or set of responses, which is immediately scored by the computer, the item (or set of items) presented next is either more or less difficult than the last one. Thus the items administered are appropriate for the examinee's ability level. Based on the previous responses a trait estimate and standard error are estimated for the examinee, a new item is selected from the item bank, and so on. The iterative process is repeated until either a pre-specified number of items have been administered or a minimum standard error is achieved.

Through an iterative process of testing, updating the ability estimate, and retesting, a CAT can arrive at a more accurate ability estimate than what can be obtained by a non-adaptive test. Potentially, each examinee receives a different set of items that is tailored to provide the most efficient estimate of his or her ability. As a result, some of the notable advantages to a CAT beyond those that are inherent to any CBT are: fewer test items (as many as half when compared with pencil-and-paper tests; Wainer, 2000), less time required, enhanced test security because all examinees are potentially administered a different set of items, improved examinee test-taking motivation, and reduced average test score differences across ethnic groups.

Current focuses for research on CBT and CAT involve technical problems such as item bank maintenance, pre-testing items to obtain item statistics, and item and test security.

FUTURE DIRECTIONS AND TRENDS

IRT is rapidly being implemented in areas other than ability and achievement testing. A major effort in health measurement, the PROMIS project, is to provide common scaling for the diverse measures of subjectively reported patient outcomes (i.e. pain, depression, fatigue, etc.). The potential advantages for health-related studies include shorter and more efficient measures, common scaling between long forms, short forms and similar measures which lead to greater comparability between clinical studies and a rigorous comparison of item functioning from different tests of the same construct.

Current theoretical developments in IRT should permit an even greater role of existing substantive theories in the development and interpretation of measures. Perhaps the most important development is De Boeck and Wilson's (2004) book that introduces a family of explanatory item response models with estimates that are obtainable with commonplace statistical software. The explanatory models, like the LLTM described above, allow construct validity to be elucidated at the item level. Further, these explanatory models are also important for predicting the properties of newly generated items for ability and achievement tests, as described above. However, important applications in other areas with possibly structured item properties, such as personality, attitude, and psychopathology are feasible (see De Boeck & Wilson, 2004).

Another important theoretical direction is the development of new IRT models that incorporate response time in the estimation of the latent trait. For example, Tuerlinckx and De Boeck (2005) present alternative models to explain how response time impacts other IRT item parameters, such as item discrimination. Other research has been concerned with how to combine response time and accuracy into assessment (e.g. Glickman et al., 2005).

Finally, although computerized testing is rapidly becoming state of the art in many areas, internet testing has become an important variant. If internet testing occurs in a proctored laboratory, like computerized testing, no new issues emerge depending on the adequacy of the test administration programming. However, unproctored internet testing is quite controversial, prompting an American Psychological Association committee to outline the various issues involved in internet testing (see Naglieri et al., 2004). Even though unproctored testing cannot be generally recommended, research on the various issues is actively in progress.

SUMMARY AND CONCLUSIONS

This chapter has reviewed the principles of CTT and contrasted them with a modern measurement framework, IRT. IRT represents several important advances over classical methods, including the capacity to model the measurement process at the behavior level rather than at the instrument or person level; provide a meaningful and interpretable metric for comparing individual performance within a sample as well as between unrelated samples; provide a framework for acknowledging the non-uniform precision of measurement across the entire range of the trait; and provide the platform by which advances in computerized testing are possible.

IRT has its roots in educational testing and the general testing of mental abilities, and a vast majority of applications have been in these contexts. While CTT has historically been the dominant paradigm for measurement in the social sciences, and remains the preferred paradigm for a majority of applied researchers in the social sciences, the advances represented by IRT have been made apparent by this chapter, the numerous texts on the subject, and the rapidly expanding literature containing numerous applied examples. For instance, emerging work from a diverse set of applied research contexts is demonstrating the applicability of IRT in the broader social research context. Some emerging research contexts include personality assessment (Reise & Henson, 2003), stroke rehabilitation (Duncan et al., 1999; Andres et al., 2004), smoking cessation (Noel, 1999), attitude measurement (Roberts, 1995),

cultural linguistic differences (Alderman & Holland, 1981), and physical functioning (McHorney & Cohen, 2000). Through the continued expansion of available and user-friendly software and an increase in approachable references and applications, IRT will continue to become better-appreciated and further cemented in its status as the modern measurement framework.

NOTES

1 According to the phi-gamma hypothesis, when a series of stimuli are controlled to range in intensity from zero to high intensity, the probability that an observer can detect the increasing stimuli monotonically increases from zero to unity along a psychometric curve that can be represented by the cumulative normal distribution function. In modern measurement terms, as the difficulty of an item increases, the probability that an examinee will correctly answer the item increases according to the cumulative normal distribution function.

2 An equation is said to have a closed form if it can be expressed in terms of so-called 'elementary functions' such as addition, subtraction, multiplication, division, or exponentiation. In other words, it has a finite and exact solution. In contrast, estimation procedures such as MML and empirical Bayes require iterative procedures and result in an approximate solution that maintains a reasonably small amount of error.

3 Classical test theory suffers from the 'physicalism-subjectivism' dilemma that equal raw score differences do not necessarily correspond to equal differences in the true latent trait. This is related to the problem of ceiling and floor effects common in raw scores (Bereiter, 1963; Harris, 1963; Lord, 1963). It is considered well known that these dilemmas are solved or are at least less critical when using IRT (see Fischer, 1987, 1989, 1995b).

REFERENCES

Adams, R. A., Wilson, M., & Wang, W. C. (1997). The multidimensional random coefficients multinomial logit model. *Applied Psychological Measurement, 21,* 1–23.

Alderman, D. L., & Holland, P. W. (1981). *Item performance across native language groups on the Test of English as a Foreign Language* (Research Rep. No. 81-16). Princeton, NJ: Educational Testing Service.

American Educational Research Association, American Psychological Association, & National Council on Measurement in Education (1999). *Standards for educational and psychological testing.* Washington, DC: American Psychological Association.

Andersen, E. B. (1972). The numerical solution of a set of conditional estimation equations. *Journal of the Royal Statistical Society, Series B, 34*, 42–54.

Andres, P. L., Black-Schaffer, R. M., Ni, P., & Haley, S. M. (2004). Computer adaptive testing: A strategy for monitoring stroke rehabilitation across settings. *Topics in Stroke Rehabilitation, 11*, 33–39.

Andrich, D. (1978). A rating formulation for ordered response categories. *Psychometrika, 43*, 561–594.

Andrich, D. (1985). *Rasch measurement models.* Newbury Park, CA: Sage Publishers.

Baker, F. B., & Kim, S. H. (2004). *Item response theory: Parameter estimation techniques* (2nd ed.). New York: Marcel Dekker.

Bechtoldt, H. (1959). Construct validity: A critique. *American Psychologist, 14*, 619–629.

Bejar, I. I. (1993). A generative approach to psychological and educational measurement. In N. Frederiksen, R. J. Mislevy, & I. I. Bejar (Eds.), *Test theory for a new generation of tests* (pp. 323–359). Hillsdale, NJ: Erlbaum.

Bejar, I. I., & Yocam, P. (1991). A generative approach to the modeling of isomorphic hidden-figure items. *Applied Psychological Measurement, 15*, 129–138.

Bereiter, C. (1963). Some persisting dilemmas in the measurement of change. In C. Harris (Ed.), *Problems in measuring change* (pp. 3–20). Madison, WI: University of Wisconsin Press.

Birnbaum, A. (1968). Some latent trait models and their use in inferring an examinee's ability. In F. M. Lord & M. R. Novick (Eds.), *Statistical theories of mental test scores* (pp. 397–424). Reading, MA: Addison-Wesley.

Bock, R. D. (1972). Estimating item parameters and latent ability when responses are scored in two or more nominal categories. *Psychometrika, 37*, 29–51.

Bock, R. D., & Aitken, M. (1981). Marginal maximum likelihood estimation of parameters: An application of an EM algorithm. *Psychometrika, 45*, 443–459.

Bock, R. D., Gibbons, R., & Muraki, E. (1988). Full-information item factor analysis. *Applied Psychological Measurement, 12*, 261–280.

Bond, T. G., & Fox, C. M. (2001). *Applying the Rasch model: Fundamental measurement in the human sciences.* Mahwah, NJ: Lawrence Erlbaum Associates, Inc.

Choi, S. W., & McCall, M. (2002). Linking bilingual mathematics assessments: A monolingual IRT approach. In G. Tindal & T. M. Haladyna (Eds.), *Large-scale assessment programs for all students: Validity, technical adequacy, and implementation* (pp. 317–338). Mahwah, NJ: Lawrence Erlbaum Associates, Inc.

Cook, L. L., & Eignor, D. R. (1983). Practical considerations regarding the use of item response theory to equate tests. In R. K. Hambleton (Ed.), *Applications of item response theory* (pp. 175–195). Vancouver, BC: Educational Research Institute of British Columbia.

Cook, L. L., & Eignor, D. R. (1989). Using item response theory in test score equating. *International Journal of Educational Research, 13*, 161–173.

Crocker, L., & Algina, J. (1986). *Introduction to classical and modern test theory.* New York: Holt, Rinehart and Winston.

Cronbach, L. J. (1951). Coefficient alpha and the internal structure of tests. *Psychometrika, 16*, 297–334.

Cronbach, L. J., & Meehl, P. E. (1955). Construct validity in psychological test. *Psychological Bulletin, 52*, 281–302.

De Boeck, P., & Wilson, M. (2004). *Explanatory item response models.* New York: Springer.

DiBello, L. V., Stout, W. F., & Roussos, L. (1995). Unified cognitive psychometric assessment likelihood-based classification techniques. In P. D. Nichols, S. F. Chipman, & R. L. Brennan (Eds.), *Cognitively diagnostic assessment* (pp. 361–389). Hillsdale, NJ: Erlbaum Publishers.

Doran, N. J., & Holland, P. W. (2000). Population invariance and the equatability of tests: Basic theory and the linear case. *Journal of Educational Measurement, 37*, 281–306.

Drasgow, F., & Parsons, C. (1983). Applications of unidimensional item response theory models to multidimensional data. *Applied Psychological Measurement, 7*, 189–199.

Draycott, S. G., & Kline, P. (1994). Speed and ability: A research note. *Personality and Individual Differences, 17 (6)*, 763–768.

Duncan, P. W., Wallace, D., Min Lai, S., Johnson, D., Embretson, S., & Laster, L. J. (1999). The stroke impact scale version 2.0: Evaluation of reliability, validity, and sensitivity to change. *Stroke, 30*, 2131–2140.

du Toit, M. (Ed.) (2003). *IRT from SSI: BILOG-MG, MULTILOG, PARSCALE, TESTFACT.* Lincolnwood, IL: Scientific Software International.

Embretson, S. E. (1983). Construct validity: Construct representation versus nomothetic span. *Psychological Bulletin, 93*, 179–197.

Embretson, S. E. (1984). A general multicomponent latent trait model for response processes. *Psychometrika, 49*, 175–186.

Embretson, S. E. (1991). A multidimensional latent trait model for measuring learning and change. *Psychometrika, 56*, 495–516.

Embretson, S. E. (1994). Application of cognitive design systems to test development. In C. R. Reynolds (Ed.), *Cognitive assessment: A multidisciplinary perspective* (pp. 107–135). New York: Plenum.

Embretson, S. E. (1995). The role of working memory capacity and general control processes in intelligence. *Intelligence, 29*, 169–189.

Embretson, S. E. (1996). Item response theory models and spurious interaction effects in factorial ANOVA designs. *Applied Psychological Measurement, 20*, 201–212.

Embretson, S. E. (1997). Structured ability models in tests designed from cognitive theory. In M. Wilson, G. Engelhard, & K. Draney (Eds.), *Objective measurement III* (pp. 223–236). Norwood, NJ: Ablex.

Embretson, S. E. (1998a). A cognitive design system approach to generating valid tests: Application to abstract reasoning. *Psychological Methods, 3*, 380–396.

Embretson, S. E. (1998b). *Modifiability in lifespan development: Multidimensional Rasch Model for learning and change.* Paper presented at the annual meeting of the American Psychological Association, San Francisco, August.

Embretson, S. E. (2002). Generating abstract reasoning items with cognitive theory. In S. Irvine, & P. Kyllonen, (Eds.), *Generating items for cognitive tests: Theory and practice* (pp. 219–250). Mahwah, NJ: Erlbaum.

Embretson, S. E. (2007). Impact of measurement scale in modeling development processes and ecological factors. In T. D. Little, J. A. Bovaird, & N. A. Card (Eds.), *Modeling contextual effects in longitudinal studies.* Mahwah, NJ: Erlbaum.

Embretson, S. E., & Gorin, J. (2001). Improving construct validity with cognitive psychology principles. *Journal of Educational Measurement, 38*, 343–368.

Embretson, S. E., & Reise, S. P. (2000). *Item response theory for psychologists*. Mahwah, NJ: Lawrence Erlbaum Associates, Inc.

Fischer, G. H. (1973). The linear logistic model as an instrument in educational research. *Acta Psychologica, 37*, 359–374.

Fischer, G. H. (1987). Applying the principles of specific objectivity and generalizability to the measurement of change. *Psychometrika, 52*, 565–587.

Fischer, G. H. (1989). An IRT-based model for dichotomous longitudinal data. *Psychometrika, 54*, 599–624.

Fischer, G. H. (1995a). Derivations of the Rasch model. In G. H. Fischer, & I. W. Molenar (Eds.), *Rasch models: Foundations, recent developments and applications.* New York: Springer-Verlag.

Fischer, G. H. (1995b). Some neglected problems in IRT. *Psychometrika, 60*, 459–487.

Fraley, R. C., Waller, N. G., & Brennan, K. A. (2000). An item response theory analysis of self-report measures of adult attachment. *Journal of Personality and Social Psychology, 78*, 350–365.

Glickman, M. E., Gray, J. R., & Morales, C. J. (2005). Combing speed and accuracy to assess error-free cognitive processes. *Psychometrika, 70*, 405–425.

Goldstein, G., & Hersen, M. (1984). *Handbook of psychological assessment.* New York: Pergamon Press.

Guilford, J. P. (1954). *Psychometric methods* (2nd ed.). New York: McGraw Hill.

Gulliksen, H. (1950). *Theory of mental tests.* New York: Wiley.

Guttman, L. (1945). A basis for analyzing test-retest reliability. *Psychometrika, 10*, 255–282.

Guttman, L. (1957). Simple proofs of relations between the communality problem and multiple correlation. *Psychometrika, 22*, 147–157.

Hambleton, R. K., Swaminathan, H., & Rogers, H. J. (1991). *Fundamentals of item response theory.* Newbury Park, CA: Sage Publishers.

Hambleton, R. K., & van der Linden, W. J. (1982). Advances in item response theory and applications: An introduction. *Applied Psychological Measurement, 6*, 373–378.

Harris, C. W. (Ed.) (1963). *Problems in measuring change.* Madison: The University of Wisconsin Press.

Holland, P. W., & Wainer, H. (1993). *Differential item functioning.* Hillsdale, NJ: Lawrence Erlbaum Associates, Inc.

Hornke, L. F., & Habon, M. W. (1986). Rule-based item bank construction and evaluation within the linear logistic framework. *Applied Psychological Measurement, 10*, 369–380.

Knol, D. L., & Berger, M. P. (1991). Empirical comparison between factor analysis and multidimensional item response models. *Multivariate Behavioral Research, 26*, 457–477.

Kyllonen, P. C. (1993). Aptitude testing inspired by information processing: A test of the Four-Sources Model. *Journal of General Psychology, 120*, 375–405.

Kyllonen, P. C., & Christal, R. E. (1989). Cognitive modeling of learning abilities: A status report of LAMP. In R. Dillon, & J. W. Pellegrino (Eds.), *Testing: Theoretical and applied issues* (pp. 146–173). New York: Freeman.

Kyllonen, P. C., & Christal, R. E. (1990). Reasoning ability is (little more than) working-memory capacity?! *Intelligence, 14*, 389–433.

Lazarsfeld, P. F. (1950). The logical and mathematical foundation of latent structure analysis. In E. A. Schulman, P. F. Lazarsfeld, S. A. Starr, & J. A. Clausen (Eds.), *Studies in social psychology in World War II.*

Vol. 4: Measurement and prediction (pp. 362–412). Princeton, NJ: Princeton University Press.

Likert, R. (1932). A technique for the measurement of attitudes. *Archives of Psychology, 140*, 44–53.

Lord, F. M. (1952). A theory of test scores. *Psychometric Monograph*, No. 7.

Lord, F. M. (1963). Elementary models for measuring change. In C. W. Harris (Ed.), *Problems in measuring change* (pp. 21–38). Madison: The University of Wisconsin Press.

Lord, F. M. (1980). *Application of item response theory to practical testing problems*. Hillsdale, NJ: Erlbaum.

Lord, F. M., & Novick, M. R. (1968). *Statistical theories of mental test scores*. Reading, MA: Addison-Wesley.

Masters, G. (1982). A Rasch model for partial credit scoring. *Psychometrika, 47*, 149–174.

Maxwell, S. E., & DeLaney, H. (1985). Measurement and statistics: An examination of construct validity. *Psychological Bulletin, 97*, 85–93.

McDonald, R. P. (1985). *Factor analysis and related methods*. Hillsdale, NJ: Lawrence Erlbaum Associates.

McDonald, R. P. (1999). *Test theory: A unified treatment*. Mahwah, NJ: Lawrence Erlbaum Associates, Inc.

McHorney, C. A., & Cohen, A. S. (2000). Equating health status measures with item response theory: Illustrations with functional status items. *Medical Care, 38*, 43–59.

Mead, A. D., & Drasgow, F. (1993). Equivalence of computerized and paper-and-pencil cognitive ability tests: A meta-analysis. *Psychological Bulletin, 114*, 449–458.

Mellenbergh, G. J. (1994). A unidimensional latent trait model for continuous item responses. *Multivariate Behavioral Research, 29*, 223–236.

Messick, S. (1994). *Validity of psychological assessment: Validation of inferences from persons' responses and performances as scientific inquiry into score meaning*. Research Report RR-94-45. Princeton, NJ: Educational Testing Service.

Mills, C. N., Potenza, M. T., Fremer, J. J., & Ward, W. C. (Eds.) (2002). *Computer-based testing: Building the foundation for future assessments*. Mahwah, NJ: Erlbaum.

Millsap, R. E., & Everson, H. T. (1993). Methodology review: Statistical approaches for assessing measurement bias. *Applied Psychological Measurement, 17*, 297–334.

Mislevy, R. (1986). Recent developments in the factor analysis of categorical variables. *Journal of Educational Statistics, 11*, 3–31.

Mislevy, R. (1993). Foundations of a new test theory. In N. Frederiksen, R. Mislevy, & I. Bejar, (Eds.), *Test theory for a new generation of tests* (pp. 19–39). Hillsdale, NJ: Lawrence Erlbaum Associates.

Muthén, B. (1978). Contributions to factor analysis of dichotomous variables. *Psychometrika, 43*, 551–560.

Naglieri, J. A., Drasgow, F., Schmit, M., Handler, L., Prifitera, A., Margolis, A., & Velasquez, R. (2004). Psychological testing on the internet: New problems, old issues. *American Psychologist, 99*, 150–162.

Noel, Y. (1999). Recovering unimodal latent patterns of change by unfolding analysis: Applications to smoking cessation. *Psychological Methods, 4*, 173–191.

Pellegrino, J. W. (1998). Mental models and mental tests. In H. Wainer, & H. I. Brown (Eds.), *Test validity* (pp. 49–59). Hillsdale, NJ: Erlbaum.

Rasch, G. (1960). *Probabilistic models for some intelligence and attainment tests*. Chicago, IL: The University of Chicago Press.

Raykov, T. (1997). Estimation of composite reliability for congeneric measures. *Applied Psychological Measurement, 21*, 173–184.

Raykov, T., & Shrout, P. E. (2002). Reliability of scales with general structure: Point and interval estimation using structural equation modeling. *Structural Equation Modeling, 9*, 195–212.

Reckase, M. D. (1997). The past and future of multidimensional item response theory. *Applied Psychological Measurement, 21*, 25–36.

Reckase, M. D., & McKinley, R. L. (1982). Some latent trait theory in a multidimensional latent space. In D. J. Weiss (Ed.), *Proceedings of the 1982 item response theory and computerized adaptive testing conference* (pp. 151–177). Unpublished manuscript, Minneapolis, University of Minnesota, Department of Psychology.

Reise, S. P., & Henson, J. M. (2003). A discussion of modern versus traditional psychometrics as applied to personality assessment scales. *Journal of Personality Assessment, 81*, 93–103.

Reise, S. P., Smith, L., & Furr, R. M. (2001). Invariance on the NEO PI–R Neuroticism scale. *Multivariate Behavioral Research, 36*, 83–110.

Roberts, J. S. (1995). Item response theory approaches to attitude measurement. (Doctoral dissertation, University of South Carolina, Columbia, 1995). *Dissertation Abstracts International, 56*, 7089B.

Samejima, F. (1969). Estimation of latent ability using a response pattern of graded scores. *Psychometrika Monograph*, No. 17.

Schafer, J. L. (1997). *Analysis of incomplete multivariate data*. New York: Chapman & Hall.

Spearman, C. (1927). *The abilities of man*. New York: Macmillan.

Takane, Y., & de Leeuw, J. (1987). On the relationship between item response theory and factor analysis of discretized variables. *Psychometrika, 52*, 393–408.

Tate, R. (2002). Test dimensionality. In G. Tindal & T. M. Haladyna (Eds.), *Large-scale assessment programs for all students: Validity, technical adequacy, and implementation* (pp. 181–211). Mahwah, NJ: Lawrence Erlbaum Associates, Inc.

Thissen, D., & Steinberg, L. (1984). A response model for multiple choice items. *Psychometrika, 49,* 501–519.

Thissen, D., & Steinberg, L. (1986). A taxonomy of item response models. *Psychometrika, 51,* 567–577.

Thissen, D., & Wainer, H. (2001). *Test scoring.* Mahwah, NJ: Lawrence Erlbaum Associates, Inc.

Thorndike, R. M., & Lohman, D. F. (1990). *A century of ability testing.* Chicago: Riverside Publishers.

Tuerlinckx, F., & De Boeck, P. (2005). Two interpretations of the discrimination parameter. *Psychometrika, 70,* 629–649.

Vale, D. C. (1986). Linking item parameters onto a common scale. *Applied Psychological Measurement, 10,* 133–144.

Vandenberg, R. J., & Lance, C. E. (2000). A review and synthesis of the measurement invariance literature: Suggestions, practices, and recommendations for organizational research. *Organizational Research Methods, 3,* 4–70.

van der Linden, W. J., & Hambleton, R. K. (Eds.) (1996). *Handbook of modern item response theory.* New York: Springer-Verlag.

Wainer, H. (2000). *Computerized adaptive testing: A primer* (2nd ed.). Mahwah, NJ: Lawrence Erlbaum Associates, Inc.

Waller, N. G., Thompson, J., & Wenk, E. (2000). Black-white differences on the MMPI: Using IRT to separate measurement bias from true group differences on homogeneous and heterogeneous scales. *Psychological Methods, 5,* 125–146.

Weiss, D. J. (1982). Improving measurement quality and efficiency with adaptive testing. *Applied Psychological Measurement, 6,* 473–492.

Whitely, S. E. (1980). Multicomponent latent trait models for ability tests. *Psychometrika, 45,* 479–494.

Yen, W. M. (1986). The choice of scale for educational measurement: An IRT perspective. *Journal of Educational Measurement, 23,* 299–325.

Natural and Contrived Data

Susan A. Speer

INTRODUCTION

In recent years there has been considerable debate concerning the relative advantages and disadvantages of 'natural' versus 'contrived' data or 'unobtrusive' versus 'obtrusive' methods[1]. In this chapter I provide an overview and critical evaluation of these debates, illustrating my argument with analyses drawn from an empirical study conducted as part of my own research on the topic of 'gender talk' (Speer, 2002c, 2005). Gender represents a particularly interesting case for an analysis of the relative virtues of natural and contrived data, since most feminist research on gender frequently, if not habitually, studies talk generated using conventional social scientific research methods such as surveys, interviews and focus groups. Many feminists are of the view that since they deal with research topics that are often hidden from view, or are too sensitive or delicate to be accessed in random conversation (e.g. talk about gender identity, sex, infidelity, sexual harassment, rape and incest, for example), that they must artificially elicit talk about such topics from participants, just to render them studiable. In this chapter I highlight the kinds of gender-relevant evidence and insights that

close analysis of a relatively contrived dataset provides. Even though I use these analyses to argue *for* the virtues of analysing naturally occurring data, at the same time I urge caution in applying the 'natural/contrived' distinction too rigidly. In particular, I suggest that whether or not a piece of data is natural or contrived depends largely on what one is going to *do* with it. I consider the implications of this analysis for the way feminists and other researchers derive and analyse gender talk.

NATURAL AND CONTRIVED DATA

For some time now, social scientists have made a distinction between: (i) 'naturally occurring', 'natural' or 'naturalistic' data; and (ii) 'non-naturally occurring', 'researcher-provoked', 'artificial', or 'contrived' data, arguing that the former are somehow qualitatively different from, preferable to, and/or 'better' (for the purposes of analysis) than the latter (see Ten Have, 1999: 48ff; Heritage, 1984: 234ff; 1988; Heritage and Atkinson, 1984: 2–5; Potter, 2002, 2003: 612ff; 2004; Potter and Hepburn, 2005a; in press; Potter and Wetherell, 1995; Sacks, 1984;

Scheddloff, 1996a, 1996b; Silverman, 2006: 201).

Conversation analysts and discursive psychologists are among the chief advocates of this position, expressing a strong preference for working with 'tapes and transcripts of *naturally occurring interactions*' (Schegloff and Sacks, 1973: 291, emphasis added). Indeed, for many, this preference has become a requirement built into *definitions* of conversation analysis (CA). According to Hutchby and Wooffitt for example, CA is 'the study of *recorded, naturally occurring talk-in-interaction*' (1998: 14, emphasis in original). Similarly, Psathas argues that within CA 'data may be obtained from any available source, the only requirements being that *these should be naturally occurring*' (1995: 45, emphasis added). Others put this 'requirement' for natural data even more strongly. For example, Paul ten Have suggests that 'it is *essential* for the CA enterprise to study recordings of natural human interaction' (1999: 47, emphasis added) and that these recordings 'should catch "natural interaction" as fully and faithfully as is practically possible' (1999: 48). Likewise, Heritage and Atkinson assert that 'within conversation analysis there is an *insistence* on the use of materials collected from *naturally occurring* occasions of everyday interaction' (1984: 2, former emphasis added).

A variety of terms have been used alongside, and interchangeably with, references to 'naturally occurring data'. Researchers work with 'natural conversation' (Sacks et al., 1974: 698), 'natural conversational materials' (Schegloff and Sacks, 1973: 291), 'actual utterances in actual ordinary conversations' (Schegloff, 1988a: 61), 'actually occurring data' (Heritage and Atkinson, 1984: 18), and 'actual, empirical, naturally occurring garden variety actions' (Schegloff, 1996a: 166). Here, the 'natural' or 'actual' is implicitly or explicitly contrasted with data that are 'non-natural', 'contrived' or 'researcher-provoked'. So, Hutchby and Wooffitt argue that 'naturally occurring' refers to recorded interactions 'situated as far as possible in the ordinary unfolding of people's lives, *as opposed to being prearranged or set up in*

laboratories' (1998: 14, emphasis added). While naturally occurring data involve 'real interests, investments, interactional trajectories' which 'are at stake and serve as formative context' (Schegloff, 1998: 247), non-natural data are data that have been 'got up' by the researcher using an interview, an experiment, or a survey questionnaire (Potter, 2004: 205). Such data, then, 'would not exist apart from the researcher's intervention' (Silverman, 2006: 201).

The issue of 'researcher provocation' appears central here: According to Schegloff and Sacks (1973: 291), natural interaction is not 'coproduced with or provoked by the researcher' (ten Have, 1999: 48), and the materials are 'as uncontaminated as possible by social scientific intervention' (Heritage, 1988: 130). Ten Have (1999: 49) argues that 'the ideal is to (mechanically) observe interactions as they would take place without research observation', while Drew (1989: 96) goes even further, asserting that the data must not have been 'produced for the purpose of study', or collected 'for any pre-formulated investigative or research purposes'[2].

In what is still one of the clearest expositions of the ethnomethodological origins of CA, Heritage (1984) argues that CA's insistence on the use of naturally occurring data is matched by an avoidance of data sources that are deemed 'unsatisfactory' (1984: 236). These include data from interviews, where participants' reports of events are treated as an 'appropriate substitute' for a recording of the actual events; experiments and testing, which involve the 'direction or manipulation of behaviour'; observational methods, where data are recorded in field notes or using pre-coded schemas (and which rely on the researcher's post-hoc recollection or recall); and invented data (sentences, speech acts or exemplar dialogues) based on intuition or 'idealizations about how interactions work' (Heritage, 1984: 236; see also, Heritage and Atkinson, 1984: 2–5, ten Have, 1999: 53–4). In sum, advocates of 'natural data' overwhelmingly focus on 'the details of actual events' (Sacks, 1984: 26) and avoid the decontextualised kinds of data; the 'hypotheticalized, proposedly typicalized versions of the world' (1984: 25) commonly used in linguistic and philosophical approaches to language (see also Schegloff, 1988a).

Underlying this preference for natural data was Harvey Sacks' desire to produce a stable (and hence reproducible) natural observational science of society (Schegloff, 1995, vol. 1: xxx–xxxii). As part of this, Sacks and his colleagues aimed to produce an inventory of 'recognizable social actions in this culture … to find it and provide an account of it empirically and precisely, not imaginatively or typically or hypothetically or conjecturally or experimentally, and to use actual, situated occurrences of it in naturally occurring social settings to control its description' (Schegloff, 1996a: 167). Sacks' (1987: 54) argument was that if we are serious about producing empirically grounded descriptions of the social organisation of human interaction, then 'sequences [or talk] are the most natural sorts of objects to be studying'. And yet, according to Sacks (1995, vol. 2: 5), researchers do not 'have a strong intuition for sequencing in conversation'. Indeed, no matter how rich the researcher's imagination (Sacks, 1995, vol. 2: 419), if we work with idiosyncratic, invented or hypotheticalised-typicalised data examples, then we risk producing what Schegloff calls a 'sociology by epitome' (1988b: 101), overlooking precisely those features of interaction and its sequencing that might tell us something new or surprising about the phenomena we are studying. As Sacks notes, it is only 'from close looking at the world [that] you can find things that we couldn't, by imagination, assert were there' (1995, vol. 2: 419).

Likewise, where the researcher uses 'written texts, monologues, talk or writing produced under experimental or quasi-experimental conditions' (Schegloff, 1996b: 468), then the interactional practices which 'undergird' our 'natural phenomena' of interest may be 'largely or totally absent … suppressed by specially designed circumstances of production' (1996b: 468). Experimental control and standardisation 'of stimuli, conditions, topics, etc.' (Schegloff, 1996b: 468) suppress 'the very heart of the phenomena we

are trying to understand' (1996b: 468), and 'confront participants with quite distinctive, and potentially complicating, interactional exigencies' (1999: 419)[3]. And yet, ironically, even interviews and experiments rely in their design on the identification of relevant variables for study taken from the observation of naturally occurring interaction. As Heritage puts it, 'it is unlikely that an experimenter will be able to identify [control and manipulate] the range of relevant variables without previous exposure to naturally occurring interaction' (1984: 238, see also Schegloff, 2004).

FEMINIST PERSPECTIVES ON NATURAL AND CONTRIVED DATA

One group of researchers for whom this preference for naturally occurring data has proven especially problematic, is feminist researchers. Indeed, as I note above, most feminist research on gender frequently, if not habitually, studies talk generated using conventional social scientific research methods such as surveys, interviews and focus groups. As C. Kitzinger (2000: 170) observes, very little feminist research is conducted using naturalistic data where gender and sexuality 'just "happen" to be present'.

There are three main reasons why feminist researchers have been reluctant to stray far from the use of such 'contrived' materials: First, it seems to be a widely held, tacit assumption that since gender is, for most 'ordinary' members, taken for granted and thus background to interaction, the researcher must artificially elicit talk about gender from participants (i.e. they must 'topicalize' gender) just to make it visible. I made precisely this assumption in my early research on masculinity, where I asked my respondents questions like 'do you ever think you behave in a way that's not traditionally masculine?', and 'do you think the fact you're male affects your leisure in any way?' (Speer, 2001; for a discussion of related issues see C. Kitzinger, 2006). For researchers who adopt this approach, far from suppressing the kinds of 'natural' phenomena to which they wish to gain access, by exposing the phenomena to the researcher's view, contrived materials render them studiable.

Second, many feminist researchers deal with topics that they deem to be too sensitive, private or delicate to be accessed in their 'home' environments (e.g. talk about sex, infidelity, sexual harassment, rape, incest, and so on). They commonly assume that it is extremely difficult or impossible to gain access to settings where instances of the phenomena or talk *about* the phenomena, 'crop up' as a matter of course. As Tainio (2003: 173–4) remarks, 'It is seldom possible to get recordings of actual instances of "sexual harassment"'. Many feminists overcome these problems of access by obtaining members' *retrospective reports* on their experiences of the phenomena, using those reports as relatively unproblematic, unreconstructed evidence for the underlying experiential reality. For example, C. Kitzinger and Frith (1999, and for a recent overview of this study see Wilkinson and C. Kitzinger, 2007) collected focus group data of women's reported *accounts* of their difficulties in saying no to unwanted sexual advances, in order to help them understand the *actual* difficulties that women might experience in saying no to sex. As they note 'We are not aware of any research which has used as data actual naturalistically occurring acceptances – or refusals – of sexual interaction' (1999: 300). And yet, as Tainio (2003) has since shown, it *is* both possible and hugely illuminating, to access and analyse actual instances of sexual harassment and refusal *in action*.

Third, and relatedly, many feminists are of the view that certain topics are mentioned far too infrequently in random conversation to be captured through naturalistic means. For example, gender and language researchers have often found it difficult to obtain examples of 'sexist talk' in naturally occurring materials and have resorted to using made-up or remembered examples of talk in their place. In her classic and still much heralded study of gender and language, for example, Robin Lakoff (1973) justified using contrived

(hypothetical and anecdotal) examples of sexist talk, by referring to the pragmatics of obtaining and accessing a sizeable enough corpus of such data. She argued that:

> random conversation must go on for quite some time, and the recorder must be exceedingly lucky anyway, in order to produce evidence of any particular hypothesis, e.g. that there is sexism in language. If we are to have a good sample of data to analyze, this will have to be elicited artificially from someone; I submit I am as good an artificial source of data as anyone. (Lakoff, 1973: 47)

Although she was writing more than three decades ago, Lakoff's views are echoed frequently by contemporary gender and language researchers in order to justify the use of contrived materials. Mary Bucholtz (2004: 123), for example, commends Lakoff's use of an 'introspective methodology' and desire to 'locate herself so squarely within her text' as an example of feminist 'reflexivity'. Similarly, Livia (2003: 147) argues that the use of constructed dialogue or scripts, can 'allow us to see . . . what expectations speakers have of patterns of speech appropriate for each sex'[4]. Some feminist discourse analysts even suggest that contrived sources like interviews and focus groups may 'yield richer data' than naturally occurring talk, 'simply because the topic has been pre-set' (Sunderland, 2004: 183).

THE BIOGRAPHY OF A FEMINIST RESEARCH PROJECT

I began my own research career with a similar set of assumptions. My early interest was in the topic of gender and leisure, and specifically, people's views about men and women's participation in 'non-traditional' activities (such as men's ballet and women's rugby, for example). I knew, on the basis of both commonsense and my own experience as a member of this culture, that when confronted with instances of men and women breaking norms and engaging in activities considered 'inappropriate' for their sex, many people would express negative (sexist and homophobic) views. Therefore I thought that

if I could contrive it so that my participants would talk about their views on such
topics, and do so in a fairly naturalistic
and spontaneous manner, then I might be
able to say something productive about the
conversational and interactional practices that
members deploy in order to reproduce and
maintain restrictive gender norms within
society. In sum, I would be able to access
what sexism and heterosexism looks like
'in action'.

I considered a range of methods through
which I might be able to access such talk.
Given that I was driven by a feminist political
agenda, the issue for me was how to obtain
topic-focused information at the same time as
giving respondents a degree of control over
the research agenda. Indeed, as a feminist,
one of my primary methodological concerns
was to encourage non-hierarchical research
relationships and to avoid imposing my
own analytic categories and concepts on my
respondents[5]. Instead, I wanted to 'give voice'
to my participants (C. Kitzinger, 2003) and
have them, as far as possible, 'assert their
own interpretations and agendas' (Wilkinson,
1999: 233). I was acutely aware that the
more keenly my presence and direction
was felt by those present, and the more
'contrived' the research setting, the less likely
it was that the participants would respond
'in their own terms'. Conversely, if I was
to impose no structure or framework on
the discussion at all, I might be left with
a confusing array of incomparable, irrelevant
or 'off-topic' responses. So, my ultimate aim
was to adopt methodological procedures that
would facilitate the collection of relatively
naturalistic and spontaneous talk about my
phenomena of interest, but in a relatively
researcher controlled – and hence contrived,
fashion.

USING PROMPTS AS STIMULUS MATERIALS

Though not heralded as specifically feminist,
one method that is increasingly recommended
by feminists who want to collect spontaneous,
topic-focused data from within a non-
hierarchical, participant-centred framework,
is the use of prompts as 'stimulus materials'
(C. Kitzinger and Powell, 1995; J. Kitzinger
and Barbour, 1999; Wilkinson, 1999). I use the
concept of 'prompt' broadly to refer to audio
and video clips (Schlesinger et al., 1992), photographs, magazine images, advertisements
and newspaper clippings (J. Kitzinger, 1990,
1994), objects (Chiu and Knight, 1999),
vignettes (Finch, 1987; Hughes, 1998; Sleed
et al., 2002), sentence and story completion
exercises (C. Kitzinger and Powell, 1995;
Pollak and Gilligan, 1982), group exercises,
games, and set tasks (Snelling, 1999), concept
mapping (Campbell and Salem, 1999), and
the sorting and ranking of cards (J. Kitzinger,
1990). While some disadvantages of prompts
have been noted: stimulus materials 'can
make people feel uncomfortable ("it's like
being back at school")' (J. Kitzinger and
Barbour, 1999: 12), they are, nonetheless,
overwhelmingly regarded in a positive light.
Feminist researchers have argued that prompts
are 'a useful tool for stimulating discussion'
(J. Kitzinger, 1990: 323) and represent
'a very effective way of exploring people's
understandings' (1990: 330). This is primarily
because they take the focus away from
the researcher and allow the participants
themselves to set the agenda. As J. Kitzinger
and Barbour (1999: 12) note, prompts can
'engage people in discussion without the
researcher providing any vocabulary or terminology'. Prompts, then, seemed to provide
the ideal solution to the problems I was
facing.

I decided to use prompts in my research,
believing that they would provide an interesting, often provocative stimulus around
which to generate discussion about gender
issues. They would (I thought) encourage
respondents to produce 'gendered' views in
a relatively naturalistic, spontaneous fashion,
and with as little obvious direction from
myself as possible. However, as is so often
the case with the 'real life' application of
social science methods, things did not turn
out quite how I had first anticipated. Indeed,
it did not occur to me at the outset that

adopting these procedures might generate its own set of problems, or that my presence in the interactions would have the impact that it did.

I found that while the prompts were certainly useful and provocative, they did, nonetheless, often fail to work in the way I had intended them to work. In practice, the prompts did not seem to minimise my impact, encourage the respondents to set the priorities, or produce spontaneous or naturalistic 'gender talk'. In fact, it was not always clear to the participants how they were supposed to respond to the prompts, and it often took further work on my part, and follow-up questioning, before I could elicit their (gendered) view.

METHOD AND ANALYSIS

In the remainder of this chapter, I want to revisit some of the data I obtained from this study in order to demonstrate what actually happened when the prompts were shown, and to consider what this might tell us about the relative virtues of natural and contrive materials.

The four excerpts I discuss below derive from a series of prompted one-to-one and group discussions. Research participants were drawn from several 'naturally occurring' friendship and family groups, and included a diverse range of men and women ranging in age from 20 to 70+ years. Visual prompts were drawn mainly from newspapers and magazines and showed images of men and women engaging in a variety of 'non-traditional'

activities (men ballet dancing, and women boxing or playing rugby, for example). Some prompts showing men and women engaging in traditionally gendered activities were also used as a point of comparison (men playing rugby and women shopping, for example). All but one of the interviews and focus groups were moderated by myself. The remaining group was moderated by a second (female) moderator (referred to, respectively, as 'Mod 1' and 'Mod 2' below). All the data were transcribed verbatim in the first instance. Detailed transcripts were then worked up using conventions developed within CA by Gail Jefferson (2004a). A simplified version of these conventions is included in the Appendix.

In a search of the corpus I identified 58 occasions where a prompt was shown. In just under half of these instances the participants had no problems responding to the prompt, and engaging with the task set (for a discussion of some of these 'successful' instances see Speer, 2002c). However, in the remaining instances, the participants seemed to have some trouble identifying the content of the prompt. They sought clarification from the moderator of the grounds on which they were required to respond to the prompt, thus engaging her in work to disambiguate its content.

Consider the following two excerpts. In excerpt 1 (line 1) the moderator introduces a picture of a female football supporter in overlap with Keith and Alice's discussion of rugby (Donald [line 6] is the first participant to respond to the prompt). In excerpt 2 (line 1), the moderator shows a picture of two women dancing in a club.

```
    (1) SAS 28-12-97 A:22-3 Mealtime Discussion
1   Mod 1:    F   ->    [>Ah this one.<]
2   Keith                [is a different] [ket- (of-)] I [think ru]gby=
3   Alice.                                [r u g b y ]  [ra- pu-]
4   Keith:               =is-[is a di]fferent kettle of fish.
5   Alice:                   [soccer ]
6   Donald:   Fins->    I presume that is a (.) women- woman
7                        supporter of foot↓ball.
8   Mod 1:    Sins->    Yeah.
9                       (0.8)
10  Donald:   S   ->    We:::ll if that's what she likes doing she
```

```
11                  ->    can like it but I don't like the cigarette
12                  ->    hanging out of her mouth at a:ll.

      (2)  SAS 2-12-97 A: 8-9 Focus Group
 1    Mod 2:    F  ->   An' how about (1.2) that one.
 2    ?:                (       )
 3                      (1.8)
 4    Mod 2:       ->   °How do you react to that.°
 5                      (3.8)
 6    Sarah:    Fins->  °Is that two girls dancing together is
 7                ->    [it?]°=
 8    Carole:   Sins->  [Yeah.]=
 9    Mod 2:    Sins->  =Mm:.
10    (Sarah):          ((sniff))
11                      (1.2)
12    Carole:   S  ->   >I think that's prob'ly quite a normal (0.6)
13                ->    normal thing [because-] coz of all this (.)=
14    (Sarah)?:                      [((sniffs))]=
15    Carole       ->   =weird (.) kind of lighting eff[ect
16    ?:                                               [heh heh
17                      heh [.h h h ]
18    Carole: ->            [it makes] it look really quite biza:rre,
```

In both excerpts, when the moderator shows the prompt, she treats the task that the participants are engaged in as one that is already familiar to them. Additionally, as the 'first pair part' of the sequence, the turn that accompanies the showing of the prompt strongly implies that there is something 'comment-worthy' or 'notable' about the image that the recipients might be able to respond or react *to*. In other words, the showing of the prompt invites – or makes 'conditionally relevant' – an appropriately fitted 'second pair part' in which the recipients produce some sort of evaluative commentary on the prompt (for more on adjacency pairs see Schegloff, 2007: 13ff). However, in both instances, the recipients do *not*, initially at least, produce such an evaluative commentary. Instead, they defer their evaluations until later (excerpt 1, lines 10–12, excerpt 2, lines 12–13, 15, and 18) in order to first check with the moderator whether what they have seen in the prompt is what they are *supposed* to see.

In each case their checks take the form of a question-answer 'insertion sequence' (Schegloff, 2007: 97ff). Insertion sequences are sequences within a sequence: they come after the base first pair part (i.e. the showing of the prompt) and before the base second

pair part (i.e. the evaluation of the prompt). These insertion sequences are addressed 'to contingencies of what is to be done next' (2007: 100). In other words, they help the participants to establish the information and resources they need in order to appropriately evaluate the prompt and thus 'to implement the second pair part [the evaluation] which is [still] pending' (Schegloff, 2007: 106). The different parts of this sequence are marked in the left-hand margin of the transcripts, above.

In the first part of the insertion sequence (excerpt 1, lines 6–7 and excerpt 2, lines 6–7), the recipients ask a question which puts forward a possible candidate interpretation of what it is they see in the prompt and the grounds on which they might evaluate it. Notice that both Donald and Carole treat *gender* as the 'relevant thing' about the prompt (Edwards, 1998; Hopper and LeBaron, 1998). So, for Donald it is not just a supporter of football, but a 'woman supporter of foot↓ball' (said with emphasis on the repaired gender category, 'woman'), whereas for Carole it is not just *people* dancing, but 'two girls dancing together' (said with emphasis on the word 'girls'). In both cases the moderator (and in excerpt 2, another group member [line 8]) confirms these candidate interpretations as 'appropriate grounds' for response: 'Yeah.' (excerpt 1, line 8) and 'Mm:' (excerpt 2, line 9). Now they have secured the moderator's confirmation, the recipients in each case have the resources necessary to go on to produce their (non-gendered) evaluation of the prompt (i.e. the conditionally relevant base second pair part) -an evaluation that has been held in temporary abeyance by the insertion sequence.

The first two excerpts, then, are organised as follows:

[F] First pair part: Moderator shows the prompt and indicates that a response is a relevant next turn.

[Fins] First pair part of insertion sequence: Respondent asks a question which puts forward a possible candidate interpretation of what it is they see in the prompt and the grounds on which they might evaluate it. This candidate interpretation makes gender explicitly relevant.

[Sins] Second pair part of insertion sequence: Moderator confirms candidate.

[S] Second pair part. Respondent offers evaluative commentary on the prompt but does not follow up their prior gender noticing.

Insertion sequences are often found in environments of 'dispreference' (Pomerantz, 1984). Dispreference refers not to a psychological state but rather to an interactional one, and it concerns the kinds of alignment that a speaker of a second pair part takes up with respect to the first pair part (Schegloff, 2007: 59). In the data discussed here, the 'preferred response' (i.e. the alignment that the recipient should ideally take up with respect to the *action* that is initiated by the showing of the prompt) may be one in which they immediately identify what it is about the prompt that they are required to respond to, and evaluate it accordingly. However, in these excerpts, since the insertion sequence intervenes between the first and second pair parts of the sequence, it compromises the 'progressivity of the base sequence', and projects 'the possibility of a dispreferred response' (Schegloff, 2007: 100). Moreover, it indicates that the participants are somehow disaligned in this case, unable (or unwilling) to respond in the interactionally 'preferred' way to the showing of the prompt.

Other features of dispreference are evident in the lengthy delays both before the insertion sequence (the delay that coincides with the intervening talk on a separate matter in excerpt 1, lines 2–5, and the gaps in excerpt 2, lines 3 and 5), and after the insertion sequence, just prior to the evaluations proper (excerpt 1, line 9, excerpt 2, line 11). The evaluations themselves (excerpt 1, lines 10–12, and excerpt 2, lines 12–13, 15, and 18) are composed in a characteristically dispreferred format. So in both excerpts, even while the insert expansions serve to supply the information necessary for the respondents to proceed to their evaluative commentaries, those commentaries are nonetheless delayed (excerpt 1, line 9; excerpt 2, lines 10–11). Moreover, in excerpt 1, Donald's commentary on the prompt is prefaced with the elongated 'We:::ll', which indicates that his upcoming response may disaffiliate with, or provide a disfavourable interpretation of, the content of the prompt (for more on the function of turn-initial 'well' see Schegloff and Lerner, 2004). Similarly, in excerpt 2, Carole's evaluation is characterised by hedging (it is 'prob'ly quite a <u>normal</u> . . . . <u>thing</u> [lines 12–13] and 'quite biza:rre' [line 18]), disfluency and perturbations: she stops and then re-starts her utterance after the word '<u>normal</u>' pausing, mid-Turn Constructional Unit (TCU) (lines 12–13).

Notice that, in their evaluations of the prompt, neither Donald nor Carole expands on the 'gendered' grounds that they initially made relevant in their inserted question about the prompt. Indeed, they do not follow up on this prior gender noticing or mention anything at all about women football supporters or girls who dance. Thus although Donald's wonderfully circular 'if that's what she likes doing she can <u>like</u> it' (excerpt 1, lines 10–11) has a possibly slightly 'disgusted' tone which might be heard as evaluative and as indicative of some distaste for the (gendered) activity in question, the *design* of this turn is such that he does not so much *evaluate* the activity of women football supporting as pointedly *pass up* the opportunity to evaluate it. Likewise his contrastively negative 'but I don't like the cigarette hanging out of her mouth at a:ll' (lines 11–12) is not so much a negative evaluation of women football supporters as it is a personal view on an aspect of the image (cigarette smoking) that is seemingly unrelated (and built by Donald as unrelated) to the activity in question.

Similarly, in excerpt 2, the participants clearly take the task set by the moderator in which they are required to 'react' to the content of the prompt, as indicative of something potentially non-normative or incongruous about it. However, since, for them, they seem unable to find anything non-normative or 'newsworthy' about 'two girls dancing together', then rather than offer an evaluation which follows up on Sarah's gender noticing at lines 6–7 (a noticing confirmed by Carole and the moderator at lines 8 and 9), they simply comment on the 'normality' of what the prompt depicts ('>I think that's prob'ly quite a normal (0.6) normal thing' [lines 12–13]). Thus, their response is not so much an evaluation or commentary on the activity of 'girls dancing together' as it is an account for not having an evaluation. Indeed, the thing that seems most newsworthy about the image is not 'girls dancing together', but rather, non-normative features of the semiotics of the picture ('because- coz of all this (.) weird (.) kind of lighting effect … it makes it look really quite biza:rre' [lines 12–13, 15, and 18]).

In the two excerpts I've discussed so far the moderator responds to the inserted question about the prompt with the relevant second pair part in which she helps the recipients to disambiguate its content, thereby confirming that they have 'correctly' identified what the prompt depicts and the grounds on which they might appropriately evaluate it (excerpt 1, line 8, excerpt 2, line 9). One consequence of her participation in the insertion sequence is that the moderator helps progress the course of action toward her required interactional outcome – the respondent evaluations and the giving of (possibly gendered) views. However, at the same time, the help she provides may inadvertently reinforce the respondents' presumption that she is a social

science 'expert' with privileged access to, and knowledge about, the prompts. Indeed, in this context, the moderator's first turn may be hearable by the respondents as an 'exam' or 'test' question for which there is a 'right' or 'wrong' answer (Levinson, 1992)[6]. The trouble and dispreference evident in these excerpts – and the very necessity for the question posed by the recipients in the insertion sequence – displays strongly the respondents' presumption that the moderator *already knows* what is going on in the prompt, and that she has an expectation about what kind of reaction might be an 'appropriate' or the most 'correct' one.

This creates a paradoxical situation for the moderator. On the one hand, she uses picture prompts in order to generate non-hierarchical, participant-led discussion of topics that *they* draw out from the picture as relevant to them. On the other hand, the occasion is set up as one in which the prompt, and the moderator's accompanying question, is taken by the respondents to be a 'test question', where their answer is actually not a free and unencumbered one, but rather one that is going to be measured against the knowledge that they surmise the moderator may already have about it.

In the next excerpt we see a possible attempt by the moderator to manage this paradox and re-establish a non-hierarchical research relationship. There is a considerable amount of complexity here which would repay a detailed analysis. However, for our present purposes I want simply to note that just as in excerpts 1 and 2, the recipients appear to have some trouble ascertaining the grounds on which they are required to respond to or evaluate the prompt. This trouble appears especially acute in this case because it revolves around the delicate problem of assigning a gender to the person in the image (lines 10–11 and 14–15). This trouble, combined with the moderator's withholding of assistance at precisely those points where she could legitimately provide it (e.g. at lines 6, 8, 12, 16), provokes Alice to initiate the first pair part of an insertion sequence in which she reports her 'first thoughts' (Jefferson 2004b) on the gender of the person in the image (constructed in a way that indicates she thinks she may well be wrong) (lines 10–11). When the moderator does not respond, she seeks confirmation regarding the correctness of her interpration: 'is it a wo↑man ↑Su°san?' (lines 14–15). However, in this case, the moderator does not answer the inserted question, or confirm or disconfirm Alice's candidate interpretation of what is going on in the prompt. Instead, she initially resists answering the question by using a conversational 'counter' (marked as 'cnt' in the left-hand margin of the transcript), which serves to throw Alice's question about the prompt directly back to her for her to answer: 'What do you ↑think?' (line 17):

```
    (3) 26-12-97 A: 36-7 Mealtime Discussion
 1 Mod 1:  F    ->    Right. What's going [on in this one.]
 2 Eadie:                           [((Hearing aid whistles))]
 3 Jan:                                      [Oh:!]
 4 Alice:              What is going on:,=
 5 Mat:               =Whistles.
 6                     (0.4)
 7 Eadie:              .hhm hhh.
 8                     (0.8)
 9 Jan:                Oh.
10 Alice: Fins ->     >Oh it looks as if-< (.) ↑OOH I thought that
11            ->       was a woman to start with.
12                     (0.8)
13 Jan:                Oh::.
14 Alice:      ->      I ↑thought it was a woman so it- (.) is it a
15            ->       wo↑man ↑Su°san?°
16                     (.)
17 Mod 1: Fins cnt ->  What do you ↑think?
18                     (3.4)
19 Jan:                Ah [hah.]
20 Alice: Sins cnt ->     [ I ] thought it was a woman in a- playing
21                     [rugby.]
22 Mod 1: Sins ->      >[No it] is a woman<.
23                     (.)
24 Mod 1:      ->      It's a woman with a cigarette in her mouth
25            ->       and a can o' lager.
26 Alice:              Ye:s.
27 Mod 1:      ->      It's a football supporter I think.
28 Alice:              Oh: football supporter.
29                     (3.4)
30 Mod 1:              >Shall I pass it round?<
31 Alice:  S   ->      We::ll. .hhh
32 Jan:                Pass [(t  h  a t)]
33 (Alice):    ->           [(It's j'st)]
34 Eadie:                    [((clears throat))
35                     (1.2)
36 Alice:      ->      I mean probably, .hh (0.2) they dress up more
37            ->       (.) nowadays than [they did.]
38 Jan:       ->                        [That's all] put on though,
39            ->       that seems to me as if it's just a big act.
```

Where insertion sequences serve to defer the production of a second pair part which is conditionally relevant but temporarily held in abeyance, a counter serves to '*replace*' the second pair part 'with a question of their own. They thus reverse the direction of the sequence and its flow; they reverse the direction of constraint' (Schegloff, 2007: 17, emphasis in original). The interactional effect of this is that it is not the moderator who is now required to respond to the inserted question about the prompt, but the original questioner, Alice. In technical terms, the moderator essentially uses the counter to 'redistribute the responsibility for producing a base second pair part' (2007: 99).

Alice responds to the counter by reverting to the same first thoughts that she has already expressed twice (at lines 10–11 and 14) *before* asking her question about the prompt. This time she expands her candidate interpretation by adding the activity (rugby) to the gender element: 'I thought it was a wo̲man in a-playing rugby' (lines 20–21). This response, as it turns out, offers the 'wrong' candidate, as the moderator's subsequent turn – '>No it i̲s a woman<' (line 22), makes clear. Thus, although Alice has, in her reported first thoughts, correctly identified the *gender* of the person in the image, she has failed to correctly identify the *activity* that the woman is engaged in: it is not a woman *rugby* player but 'It's a woman with a ci̲garette in her mouth and a can o' lager…. It's a fo̲otball supporter I think.' (lines 24–5 and 27).

Note that the moderator's conversational counter at line 17 does not, at this point in the sequence, project that she will go on to answer Alice's question and provide the 'correct' interpretation of the prompt. Indeed, she could quite reasonably respond at line 22 with a further question: 'what makes you think that?', for example. However, as can sometimes happen with counters (see Schegloff, 2007: 17), in this case (and perhaps in part because Alice's past tense 'I thought it was' construction may indicate that she still thinks she may be wrong), the moderator *does* end up producing the response to the inserted question that she has just thrown back to Alice for Alice to answer[7].

So what should we make of the moderator's use of the conversational counter in this excerpt? It is quite possible that she uses it in order to minimise her control over the research agenda, and to encourage the participants to define what they see in the prompt 'in their own terms'. Indeed, the immediate effect of the counter is to return the conversational floor – and hence the responsibility for answering the question – directly to the recipients. However, one could argue that, in practice, by reversing the direction of the sequence and redirecting Alice's question back to her, the counter constrains the recipients still further, putting them 'on the spot'. Moreover, the positioning of the counter (after the first pair part of an insertion sequence) is doubly consequential in that, as I have already noted, insertion sequences tend to get launched in situations of dispreference. By throwing back a question to someone who asked it *because* they are already in the midsts of trouble answering a just prior question, one strongly risks exacerbating rather than rectifying that trouble[8].

Having finally established what it is about the prompt that they are responding *to*, the recipients turn their attention to providing the evaluation and/or commentary on the prompt that has so far been held in abeyance by the insertion sequence and conversational counter. As before, the respondent's reactions to and evaluations of the prompt are marked as 'dispreferred', and preceded by a lengthy delay (line 29). In response to this delay, the moderator demonstrates that an evaluation (the base second pair part) is still pending, by offering to pass the prompt around the table (line 30). Rather like Donald in excerpt 1, Alice reacts with what looks like the start of a negative evaluation that disaffiliates with the activity shown in the prompt (line 31). However there follows a further delay (e.g. line 35) before Alice unpacks what it is that she is getting at: 'I mean pro̲bably, .hh (0.2) they dress up more (.) no̲wadays than they did' (lines 36–7). Just as we have seen with the participants reactions in previous excerpts, even though her earlier identification problems revolved around assigning a gender to the person in the image, Alice's subsequent prompt-related commentary does not follow up on this gender relevance, or evaluate the activity depicted in the prompt in gendered terms. In fact, her response at lines 36–7 is not so much an evaluation and commentary on the activity of women football supporting, as it is a remark on an aspect of the image (what women football supporters wear nowadays) that is arguably only marginally related to the (gendered) activity in question. Similarly, Jan's commentary on the prompt, 'That's all put on though, that seems to me as if it's just a big act' (lines 38–9) is delivered as a *qualification* of Alice's evaluation (with the 'though' marking the qualification [Pomerantz, 1984: 97]), and instead of evaluating the activity depicted in the image 'on its own terms', Jan's assessment treats it as somehow 'staged' or 'non-genuine' and thereby as something that is possibly not worthy of her evaluation.

So far I have demonstrated how, when they are shown a prompt the respondents appear to have some significant difficulties both working out the grounds on which they are required to respond to it, and in making their evaluations proper. Instead of responding 'in their own terms' (and as I, as a feminist, might have wished), they tend to treat the moderator as an 'expert' with privileged access to the prompt, and engage her in additional interactional work in order to disambiguate its content. Even where the moderator works explicitly to avoid answering the respondents' questions about the prompt, and encourages them, through the use of a conversational counter, to put things in their own terms, she is still engaged in work to disambiguate the content of the prompt and progress the interaction towards her favoured interactional outcome (i.e. the production of [gendered] views or commentaries on the prompt). Finally, where evaluations *are* eventually elicited by the moderator, the participants do not follow up on the gender noticing made relevant in their own earlier candidate inquiries about the prompt's content.

So what might account for these inter-actionally 'troubled' responses in which participants do not follow up their own initial

indexing of gender? One possible explanation is that the participants may have picked up on what they take to be the researcher's 'elusive hypothesis' (that the showing of prompts will allow her to access the participants' gendered views) and that their responses to the prompt may therefore be used indirectly to reveal something negative about them as people that is not immediately evident or apparent. In other words, they may have correctly identified that what's 'up for grabs' is not whether the image depicted in the prompt is good or bad, but whether they're good or bad. It would hardly be surprising given this context, if the recipients were to anticipate and work to avoid producing the kind of 'identity implicative' commentary that they assume the moderator is pursuing. In sum, there may be a sense in which the respondents' apparent trouble with the prompt, the insertion sequences in which they seek clarification from the moderator, the delays, and the inexplicitness of their subsequent commentaries on, and evaluations of, the prompt may be part of *resisting* giving gendered views. If they do provide such views, then they could be labelled sexist or homophobic – and, as I will show below, this 'oriented to' possibility, creates the ideal environment for resistance.

Indeed, I want to propose that, in addition to fulfilling the task made relevant by the showing of the prompt, the design and delivery of participants' responses to the moderators' questions can perform resistive 'identity work'. We can find clear evidence for this resistance in sequence organisational terms.

In a search of the corpus I found 12 instances in which respondents actively resist the production of a gendered view. In these instances, the interactions do not progress through the kinds of sequences identified above. Instead, they are characterised by an extended 'series' of (moderator) questions and (respondent) answers concerning the prompt. The moderator is more or less dissatisfied with the response she gets in each case, and doggedly pursues her course of action until she either elicits some (gendered) commentary on, or evaluation of, the prompt or appears satisfied that none will be forthcoming[9]. Consider excerpt 4, below:

```
   (4) SAS 27-12-97 B: 20-21 Interview
 1 Mod 1:  F    ->      >What do you think o' that one then.<
 2                      (1.0)
 3 Ben:    S    ->      Lovely.
 4                      (0.8)
 5 Mod 1:  Fpost   ->   Well what's going on in it.
 6                      (0.6)
 7 Ben:    Spost   ->   It's a male ballet dancer.
 8                      (.)
 9 Mod 1:  SCT ->       Ri:ght.
10                      (1.4)
11 Mod 1:  F    ->      Would you do that?
12                      (0.8)
13 Ben:    S    ->      Uh:m,
14                      (1.4)
15 Ben:         ->      No I've got dodgy ankles.
16 Mod 1:               °Hhhh.°
17                      (2.2)
18 Ben:         ->      But if I could, (.) then I prob'ly would.
19                      (1.8)
20 Ben:         ->      If I: (1.0) was interested in it.
21 Mod 1:  Fpost a->    Do you think though that it breaks
22                      stereotypes at all.
23                      (.)
24 Ben:    Spost a->    No:.
25                      (0.4)
26 Mod 1:  Fpost b->    It doesn't.
27                      (.)
28 Ben:    Spost b->    [No,]
29 Mod 1:  Fpost c->    [I] mean some people would say that he's a
30                      'poof' or something.
31                      (0.3)
32 Ben:    Spost c->    I think that some people would.
33                      (0.6)
34 Mod 1:  Fpost d->    But you wouldn't.
35                      (.)
36 Ben:    Spost d->    ↑No.
```

As Schegloff (2007: 179–80) notes 'generally speaking, preferred second pair parts are "closure relevant" and dispreferred second pair parts are "expansion relevant"' (2007: 179–80). However, in certain types of sequences, called 'topic-proffering' sequences, 'preferred responses engender expansion and dispreferred responses engender sequence closure' (2007: 169). Despite some obvious differences (the prompt is an object shown to recipients in part for them to establish its 'topicality' or relevance), I want to suggest that the showing of the prompt,

accompanied as it is by the moderator's question, can be understood rather like a topic proffer. Examples of topic proffers include questions such as: 'How was the races last night?', 'So are you dating Keith?' and 'So, you're back?' (Schegloff, 2007: 170–1). These questions, like the showing of the prompt, are 'recipient oriented': they refer to (but do not themselves progress) topics 'about which the recipient is, or is treated as being, an/the authoritative speaker .... or on which their view has special weight or authority' (2007: 170). Indeed, in showing the prompt the moderator treats the recipient as having access to, and as able to display a stance toward, it (2007: 171). Finally, within topic proffering sequences, just like the prompted sequences shown here, the recipient 'is likely to carry the burden of the talking' (2007: 170).

If we consider the showing of the prompt as akin to the initiation of a topic proffering sequence, then the preferred response for this kind of sequence would be geared toward the expansion, rather than closure of the sequence. In each case, the recipients would display a stance toward the prompt that accepts, encourages, and embraces the proffered topic (they would literally talk about it) (Schegloff, 2007: 171), and their responses would be oriented toward being 'more than minimal'. By contrast, a dispreferred response to a prompted topic proffer would be one in which the recipient rejects, declines, or discourages it (2007: 171). Dispreferred responses would therefore be designedly minimal, and the sequence would move toward 'incipient closure' (2007: 180).

Right from the start, Ben refuses to embrace the possibility for discussion engendered by the showing of the prompt, or to produce the extended evaluative commentary that it makes procedurally relevant. Instead, he responds with a delayed and starkly minimal, unmit-igated, one-word answer to the moderator's opening question: 'Lovely' (line 3). This is said with final intonation, and does not yield to the 0.8 second silence which follows. This silence provides ample opportunity for Ben to resume talking and thereby expand, unpack, or account for his (minimal) response. It is worth noting that his evaluation *does* respond in a 'type conforming' (Raymond, 2003) way to the moderator's question (the question makes an assessment [what Ben 'thinks of' the prompt] relevant, and this is what Ben provides). However, it does not meet the requirement for expansion associated with the hitherto mentioned preference organisation for a topic proffer. Ben's bald response stands out as resistive here, not only because it is designedly minimal, patently 'not playing along with' the task set by the moderator, but also because he clearly does have direct access

to the thing he is being asked about (at least he has direct visual access to the image depicted in the prompt).

The moderator shows that she understands Ben's response to be disaligned with, and resistant of, the topic proffer. Her question 'Well what's going on in it' (line 5) is 'well' prefaced – something that we saw earlier, can signal disagreement or disaffiliation with the prior (Schegloff and Lerner, 2004). As a post-expansion, it orients to the starkly minimal nature of Ben's answer, and constitutes a 'second try' at the topic proffer. Although addressed to the same 'target' (the prompt), this question makes relevant a different class of answer to the prior – not an evaluation of the prompt, but a description of what is going on in the image – something Ben arguably needs to do *before* he can evaluate it.

Now Ben identifies the content of the prompt, and, like the participants in excerpts 1–3, he does so using a gender-marked term 'It's a male ballet dancer' (line 7). The moderator's third position, 'Ri:ght' (line 9) shows that he is now on the right lines, grasping the nature of the task she is setting in showing him the prompt and closes this part of the sequence.

The moderator continues by asking 'Would you do that?' (line 11), thus turning the focus away from the picture to Ben's own relationship to the activity it depicts – ballet dancing. After a lengthy delay (lines 12–14), Ben answers 'No', explaining that he would not do ballet because he has 'got dodgy ankles' (line 15). The moderator appears to laugh briefly here, and a series of gaps follow (lines 17 and 19) in which she withholds any further response, allowing Ben to incrementally unpack his account for why he would not do ballet (lines 18 and 20). There is much that could be said about the way Ben crafts this account. However, one of the most interesting features of it is that it seems designed so as to deflect the potential imputation that he would not want to do ballet for reasons of prejudice. Ben presents his reasons for not wanting to do ballet as due to his physical incapacity (his 'dodgy ankles' [line 15]) and lack of interest (line 20) rather than his conscious choice. As he makes clear: 'if I could, (.) then I prob'ly would' (line 18). (For more on 'inability' accounts see Drew, 1984.)

There follows a series of post-expansions where the moderator makes a concerted effort to elicit (or else initiate repair on) Ben's view about male ballet dancers (e.g. lines 21–22, 26, 29–30, and 34). However, Ben actively resists responding to each successive intervention on the moderator's terms, producing only minimal answers (lines 24, 28, 32, 36). Even where the moderator invites him to reconsider his response with the initiation of a disagreement implicative, other-initiated repair ('It doesn't'. [line 26], (For more on the conversation analytic concept of repair see Schegloff, 2007: 151 and Schegloff et al., 1997)). Ben does not work to resolve the misalignment by backing down, expanding his answer, or adjusting it to make it more acceptable to the moderator. Instead, he simply repeats his prior, bald 'No', response (line 28). That he does this is further evidence for resistance: He is pointedly refusing to 'play along' with the moderator's agenda.

Ben's resistance may be due, in part, to his being asked questions that may involve answers that could potentially place him in (what he takes to be) a negative identity category – as someone who is 'effeminate', 'gay' or 'homophobic', for example. His resistance to the latter is most obvious in his response to the moderator's '[I] mean some people would say that he's a 'poof' or something' (lines 29–30). This observation is clearly designed in continuity with the moderator's previous line of questioning, and in response to Ben's failure to repair his minimal answer. In citing others' hypothetical, prejudiced views, the observation is designedly provocative – placing Ben in a position where he might discuss his views on the normativity (or otherwise) of male ballet dancing. However, instead of treating the observation as something that is designed to elicit his view, or as another attempt by the moderator at a topic proffer, Ben simply agrees with the moderator's assertion, producing a second pair part to a factual

statement about what 'some people would' say (line 32). The grammatical construction of Ben's turn – in particular the repetition of 'some people would' is another way to embody a minimal response (Schegloff, 2007: 171). Indeed, this turn is designedly not adding anything to what the moderator's prior utterance has done, and does not progress or develop the course of action or prompt-related 'topic talk'. Finally, when the moderator pursues the question of his view: 'But you wouldn't' (line 34), he simply provides a further bald and final '↑No' response (line 36).

This excerpt neatly highlights some of the interactional contingencies that participants' responses to picture prompts may be designed to manage. In this instance, the prompt is not treated by Ben as a facilitator of talk in which he is free to set the priorities. Rather, his response is co-constructed within a context of mutual suspicion, and in which he exposes and seeks to manage what he takes to be the researcher's (hidden) agenda. Specifically, Ben orients to the moderators' questions, and his responses, as things that may reveal something negative about him (he may be effeminate, gay or prejudiced, for example). Instead of 'playing along with' the task set by the moderator by engaging in prompt-related topic talk (thus collaborating with the moderator in progressing the interaction toward the successful resolution of the sequence), Ben's answers seem dedicated to pre-empting, deflecting, and actively resisting inferences that he is a certain sort of person, and which may have negative implications for his identity.

DISCUSSION

I began this chapter by summarising some key issues at the heart of debates about natural and contrived data. I suggested in particular that the strong preference for natural data expressed by conversation analysts and discursive psychologists derives from a concern not to suppress fundamental features of the natural interactional phenomena to which they wish to gain access. I argued that this preference for natural data is especially problematic for feminist researchers who, for various reasons to do with assumptions about the observability, access to, and frequency of occurrence of the phenomena they wish to study, have tended to work with relatively contrived social science data sources such as surveys, interviews, and focus groups. For them, far from suppressing the kinds of 'natural' phenomena to which they wish to gain access, the artificially elicited 'topic talk' that they derive from contrived materials render those phenomena observable – and hence studiable.

In order to explore the kinds of gender-relevant evidence and insights that close analysis of a relatively contrived dataset provides, I revisited some data from my own early research on gender and leisure, in which I used picture prompts in order to access people's views about men and women's participation in 'non-traditional' activities (such as men's ballet and women's rugby, for example). I showed that, when we subject the actual use of relatively 'contrived' techniques involving prompts to a detailed analysis, that such techniques do not always work in the way the researcher might have intended them to work. Thus, in my data, the participants were invited to find something topical in, or 'comment-worthy' about the prompt. In just under half the instances in the corpus, what they were invited to see was obviously and immediately self-evident to them, and they engaged in lively discussion about the (gendered) content of the prompt. In other instances, including the first three excerpts discussed in this chapter, the participants seemed to have trouble seeing what they were supposed to see in the prompt. They sought clarification from the moderator (in the form of an 'insertion sequence'), of the grounds on which they were required to respond to it, engaging her in work to disambiguate its content. Thus, the participants routinely treated the moderator as 'expert' on the prompts and her opening question as a 'test' question for which there is a right or wrong answer. Even where the moderator tried to resist answering

the participants' questions about the prompt (through the use of a conversational counter, for example [as in excerpt 3]), she would often quickly re-engage in talk that would progress the course of action toward her favoured interactional outcome (i.e. the production of [gendered] commentary on/evaluations of the prompt). However, while the prompts initially appeared successful in getting the participants to notice gender, these initial gender noticings were rarely followed up in their subsequent evaluative commentaries.

Finally, in a number of instances (depicted here by excerpt 4), the participants strongly resisted seeing what they were supposed to see in the prompt, and it often took considerable constructive work on the moderator's part, and further follow-up questioning, in order to produce the kind of non-minimal reaction to the prompt that the moderator was after. In these instances, the participants seemed suspicious about (what they took to be) the researcher's 'elusive hypothesis', and oriented to the possibility that their responses might have negative implications for their identity. Far from being naive cultural dopes that passively accepted the doing of social science upon them, then, in these instances, participants would actively strive to subvert such an image. They resisted the potential inferences about their identities that were being imposed on them by researchers.

In sum, the prompts did not seem to minimise the researcher's impact, generate non-hierarchical research relationships, or encourage the respondents to set the priorities 'in their own terms'. As we have seen, their evaluations and commentaries on the prompt were rarely delivered in a spontaneous, unencumbered, or naturalistic fashion, and attempts to disguise researcher provocation as free-for-all opinion giving, or manipulation as complete freedom, did not work.

So what might these analyses tell us about the relative virtues of natural and contrived data? The interactional contingencies that I have shown the participants are oriented towards in their responses pose problems for researchers who treat prompts, or other 'contrived' techniques involving researcher intervention, as neutral resources for accessing some 'truth' or 'reality' beyond or beneath the data.

The data show how, even where the researcher tries to remove herself as far as possible from the data collection process – as in this case through the use of prompts – that her presence is still very much in evidence and that the data collected, just like the data from interviews and other more 'interventionist' techniques that involve the manipulation and control of variables, are thereby always collaboratively produced, interactional products. Indeed, the very business of doing research undercut the intended neutrality of the prompts and reinstated normative conversational procedures – procedures that were in this case bound up in the construction of the data and the nature of the 'gender talk' obtained.

In many ways prompts and other contrived techniques create an artificial situation in which respondents are asked to comment on things that in more mundane contexts are not typically brought to relevance in such an explicit way. Indeed, this may be one reason why the respondents in my data did not respond immediately to the stimuli in the way I had initially hoped. The situation was fundamentally *non-natural* for them. Prompts, interview questions, experiments and such like, are not neutral, non-invasive stimuli that help people formulate their thoughts and opinions on certain topics. Instead, the reality of 'contrived methods' is a socially constructed one and their use is embedded in collaborative, meaning-making activities.

Researchers have long since acknowledged that contrived methods cannot be neutral 'machinery for harvesting data from respondents' (Potter, 2004: 205). We can never achieve an unmediated access to participants' realities, neutralise the context, or disinfect our data entirely of the researcher's presence, because the knower is always intimately bound up in and partially constitutive of what is known. To assume otherwise is to deny the unavoidably social nature of data collection practices. As Holstein and Gubrium (1997: 114, see also, 2003) point out, 'any

technical attempts to strip interviews of their interactional ingredients will be futile' (see also Speer and Hutchby, 2003a, 2003b). Indeed, for feminists, such worries buy into the very illusion of objectivity and value neutrality that they have long since sought to expose and counter.

It is important to remember that views about gender are produced in thoroughly social and interactional contexts and that the use of prompts and/or more traditional social scientific methods does not make those contexts any the less contextual and interactional. It is for this reason that I am now of the view that prompted and other contrived techniques may not be the best way to gain access to talk about gender or to understand how people 'do gender' in everyday contexts. Indeed, we need to give serious thought to the extent to which artificially elicited 'topic talk' that involves putting members in a situation that explicitly requires them to comment on gender, is paradigmatic of, or will necessarily give us access to, how members routinely do gender in other settings. As C. Kitzinger and Wilkinson (2003, emphasis in original) observe, 'While this approach yields a great deal of talk *about* a category, it precludes any exploration of how people *use* categories interactionally in everyday life'.

It was precisely these concerns which encouraged me in my more recent work to collect examples of gender talk from settings where I was *not* present. I wanted to obtain 'naturally occurring' data in which gender crops up routinely as part of the day-to-day business of an institution, and where my own presence would not limit or constrain that gendered activity. In 2004 I began, in collaboration with Richard Green (a consultant psychiatrist and then Head of Charing Cross Hospital Gender Identity Clinic), a large-scale ESRC-funded study on the construction of transsexual identities in medical contexts (Speer and Green, forthcoming). This study involved me collecting more than 150 hours of audio and 20 hours of video-taped assessment sessions between psychiatrists and pre-operative transsexual patients. Unlike my own prior work, and much contemporary research on gender and language (which tends to ask members to comment on gender, seeks out their retrospective reports on how they do gender, or else is based on the researcher's own recollections and post hoc reports of gendered events), this new, naturally occurring dataset, has allowed me to examine examples of interactions in which members are currently engaged in the act of doing gender with the psychiatrist in the clinic. And once I began to look at this dataset, it became apparent that often the doing of gender (in particular – working to pass as 'authentically' male or female in this setting) does not involve its overt topicalisation at all (for more on this see Speer and Green, 2007; Speer and Parsons, 2006; and also C. Kitzinger, 2006, 2007).

Some researchers suggest that in the future, it is likely that the use of 'naturalistic materials' will become more common in qualitative research 'and interviews and focus groups will be mainly an adjunct to those naturalistic studies' (Potter, 2003: 614). In a recent debate Potter and Hepburn (2005a: 282) 'challenge the taken-for-granted position of the open-ended interview as the method of choice in modern qualitative psychology', suggesting that 'The ideal would be much less interview research, but much better interview research' (2005a: 282). They argue that in the future, it is likely that the use of 'naturalistic materials' will become more common in qualitative research 'and interviews and focus groups will be mainly an adjunct to those naturalistic studies' (Potter, 2003: 614). Indeed, Schegloff (1996b: 471, emphasis added), suggests that 'investigators *should* increasingly work with such [naturalistic] materials'.

Even though I would generally subscribe to these recommendations, and have used the data in this chapter to demonstrate the virtues of analysing naturally occurring data, one important caveat needs to be noted: I would not want to imply that existing feminist data collection practices and modes of analysis are wrong or bad, or that we should stop using contrived materials and other 'non-directive' techniques altogether. The rhetoric of social science data – just like essentialism – can be a useful tool in certain circumstances

(e.g. in a court of law). Nor would I want to imply that we will never obtain naturalistic talk, or gain access to general features of the 'doing' of gender in purportedly 'contrived' materials. Our inability to strip data of its context should not (necessarily) be adequate justification for abandoning the use of contrived materials altogether. As I have shown here, by adopting a reflexive approach to our data, and by being sensitive to the ways in which the researcher herself is bound up in the production of that data, we can obtain rich insights into respondents' ways of managing the interactional issues and dilemmas their participation throws up.

By turning what is commonly regarded as a 'resource' (albeit an inherently flawed one) into their 'topic', an increasing number of researchers using fine-grained analytic methods have been able to show how social science methods get done, identifying features which characterise, say, interview talk *as* interview talk, and which distinguish it from 'mundane conversation' (Drew et al., 2006; Maynard et al., 2002; Mishler, 1986; Suchman and Jordan, 1990). In such studies the researcher is treated – not as a potential 'contaminant' – but rather, as much of a 'member' as the other participants, and of equal status for the purposes of analysis.

Thus, I want to urge caution in applying the 'natural-contrived' distinction too rigidly. As I have argued elsewhere (Speer, 2002a, 2002b), from a discursive and CA perspective, it actually makes little theoretical or practical sense to map the natural/contrived distinction onto discrete 'types' of data or to treat the researcher as a potentially contaminating force. In this respect the natural-contrived distinction has been overplayed. What are natural data and what are not is not decidable on the basis of their type and/or the role of the researcher within the data. *All* data can be natural or contrived depending on what one wants to *do* with them.

Thus, it follows that it is fine if we, as feminist researchers, want to use contrived materials to explore how gender talk is derived in research contexts, paying close attention to the constructive processes involved (the data can be 'naturalised' – or treated as natural, as it has been in this chapter). However, if one wants to analyse contrived data where participants are asked to comment on gender in order to discover how people routinely do gender in 'everyday' settings, then such prompted 'gender commentary' may not be the best data for such purposes.

Ultimately, what is needed if we are to make well-informed choices about the data we use, and – perhaps more importantly – if we are to produce theoretically sound, analytically tractable justifications for those choices, is a more sophisticated understanding of the relationship between method, context and data. We need to be clearer and more consistent about what exactly constitutes the object of our analysis, and to establish why a particular research method is chosen over and above others. In sum, we need to have a greater awareness of how our data collection practices shape the phenomena to which we wish to gain access.

APPENDIX

TRANSCRIPTION NOTATION

See Jefferson (2004a) for further information about these transcription symbols.

.	A full stop indicates falling, or stopping intonation.
,	A comma indicates a continuing intonation.
?	A question mark indicates rising intonation.
-	A dash marks a sharp cut-off of the just prior word or sound.
↑	An upward arrow immediately precedes rising pitch.
↓	A downward arrow immediately precedes falling pitch.
LOUD	Capitals mark talk that is noticeably louder than that surrounding it.
°quiet°	Degree signs enclose talk that is noticeably quieter than that surrounding it.

Underline	Underlining marks parts of words that are emphasised by the speaker.
Rea::lly	Colons mark an elongation or stretch of the prior sound. The more colons, the longer the stretch.
huh/hah/heh	Marks full laughter tokens.
(h)	An 'h' in brackets indicates laughter particles.
.hhh	A dot before an 'h' or series of 'h's indicates an inbreath.
hhh	An 'h' or series of 'h's marks an out-breath.
>faster<	'More than' and 'less than' signs enclose speeded up talk.
=	An equals sign indicates immediate latching of successive talk.
(2.0)	The length of a pause or gap, in seconds.
(.)	A pause or gap that is hearable but too short to assign a time to.
[overlap]	Square brackets mark the onset and end of overlapping talk.
( )	Single brackets indicate transcriber doubt.
(brackets)	Content of single brackets represents a possible hearing.
((laughs))	Double brackets enclose comments from the transcriber.

ACKNOWLEDGEMENT

I would like to thank Victoria Clarke and Jim Holstein for their helpful comments on an earlier draft of this chapter.

NOTES

1 See, for example, the debates between Speer (2002a, 2002b) and ten Have (2002), Lynch (2002) and Potter (2002) in *Discourse Studies*; between Potter and Hepburn (2005a, 2005b) and Hollway (2005), Mishler (2005), and Smith (2005) in *Qualitative Research in Psychology,* and finally, between Griffin

(2007a, 2007b), Henwood (2007) and Potter and Hepburn (2007) in *Discourse Studies*.

2 Jonathan Potter suggests that, in order to judge whether a piece of data is natural or not, 'the test is whether the interaction would have taken place, and would have taken place in the form that it did, had the researcher not been born' (1996: 135; Potter and Wetherell, 1987: 162). The data must, in other words, pass the 'dead social scientist test': the interaction must have taken place even 'if the researcher got run over on the way to the university that morning' (Potter, 2003: 612). From this perspective, doctor–patient interaction, courtroom trials, calls to the police, business meetings, talk in the classroom, and conversations between friends are all 'natural' (Potter, 1997: 148–9; 2003).

3 For example, as Potter (1997: 150) notes, the social science interview 'is contrived; it is subject to powerful expectations about social science research fielded by participants; and there are particular difficulties in extrapolating from interview talk to activities in other settings'. This is not least because 'the interaction in interviews and focus groups is flooded by the expectations and categories of social science agendas' (2003: 613; see also Potter and Hepburn, 2005a).

4 For contemporary examples of the use of fictional data in research on gender and language, see Cameron (1998) and Hopper (2003).

5 For some recent discussions of feminist methodology see Harding and Norberg (2005), Lykke (2005), and Ramazanoglu and Holland (2002).

6 Such 'known answer' questions are conventionally associated with instructional or classroom settings, but can also be found in other contexts (Schegloff, 2007: 223–5): for example courtroom cross-examination, psychiatric assessment interviews, and even interactions around the dinner table.

7 Of course, the virtue of this response is that it allows the moderator to progress the interactional project toward sequence closure – eliciting recipients' commentaries on, and evaluations of, the prompt.

8 Moreover, it is worth noting that the insertion sequence is already deferring the base second pair part (the evaluation of the prompt). The counter – which reverses the sequence – thereby takes the speakers even further away from the resolution of the moderator's interactional project (i.e. progressing the sequence in the direction of prompt-related commentary and evaluation). As Schegloff (2007: 17) notes, a counter can end up 'having only deferred the answer, and inserted one question-answer exchange inside another'. In this case, the counter serves simply to delay the moderator's subsequent provision of the 'correct' answer.

9 This style of questioning is not dissimilar to the kinds of cross-examination one finds in legal settings (e.g. Drew, 1992).

REFERENCES

Bucholtz, M. (2004) 'Changing places: Language and woman's place in context'. In R. Lakoff. *Language and Woman's Place: Text and Commentaries* (revised and expanded edn, ed. M. Bucholtz, pp. 121–8). New York and Oxford: Oxford University Press.

Cameron, D. (1998) 'Is there any ketchup Vera? Gender, power and pragmatics', *Discourse & Society* 9(4): 437–55.

Campbell, R. and Salem, D.A. (1999) 'Concept mapping as a feminist research method: Examining the community response to rape', *Psychology of Women Quarterly* 23: 65–89.

Chiu, L. and Knight, D. (1999) 'How useful are focus groups for obtaining the views of minority groups?' In R.S. Barbour and J. Kitzinger (eds) *Developing Focus Group Research: Politics, Theory and Practice*, pp. 99–112. London: Sage.

Drew, P. (1984) 'Speakers' reportings in invitation sequences'. In J.M. Atkinson and J. Heritage (eds) *Structures of Social Action: Studies in Conversation Analysis*, pp. 129–51. Cambridge: Cambridge University Press.

Drew, P. (1989) 'Recalling someone from the past'. In D. Roger and P. Bull (eds) *Conversation: An Interdisciplinary Perspective*, pp. 96–115. Clevedon: Multilingual Matters.

Drew, P. (1992) 'Contested evidence in courtroom cross-examination: The case of a trial for rape'. In P. Drew and J. Heritage (eds) *Talk at Work: Interaction in Institutional Settings*, pp. 470–520. Cambridge: Cambridge University Press.

Drew, P., Raymond, G. and Weinberg, D. (eds) (2006). *Talk and Interaction in Social Research Methods.* London: Sage.

Edwards, D. (1998) 'The relevant thing about her: Social identity categories in use'. In C. Antaki and S. Widdicombe (eds) *Identities in Talk*, pp. 15–33. London: Sage.

Finch, J. (1987) 'Research note: The vignette technique in survey research', *Sociology* 21(1): 105–14.

Griffin, C. (2007a) 'Being dead and being there: Research interviews, sharing hand cream and the preference for analysing "naturally occurring data"', *Discourse Studies* 9(4): 246–69.

Griffin, C. (2007b) 'Different visions: A rejoinder to Henwood, Potter and Hepburn', *Discourse Studies* 4(9): 283–87.

Harding, S. and Norberg, K. (eds) (2005) 'New feminist approaches to social science methodologies', Special issue, *Signs* 30(4).

Have, P. ten (1999) *Doing Conversation Analysis: A Practical Guide.* London: Sage.

Have, P. ten (2002) 'Ontology or methodology? Comments on Speer's "natural" and "contrived" data: A sustainable distinction?' *Discourse Studies* 4(4): 527–30.

Henwood, K. (2007) 'Beyond hypercriticality: Taking forward methodological inquiry and debate in discursive and qualitative social psychology', *Discourse Studies* 4(9): 270–5.

Heritage, J. (1984) *Garfinkel and Ethnomethodology.* Cambridge: Polity Press.

Heritage, J. (1988) 'Explanations as accounts: A conversation analytic perspective'. In C. Antaki (ed.) *Analysing Everyday Explanation: A Casebook of Methods*, pp. 127–44. London: Sage.

Heritage, J. and Atkinson, J.M. (1984) 'Introduction'. In J.M. Atkinson and J. Heritage (eds) *Structures of Social Action. Studies in Conversation Analysis*, pp. 1–15. Cambridge: Cambridge University Press.

Hollway, W. (2005) 'Commentary 2', *Qualitative Research in Psychology* 2(4): 312–14.

Holstein, J.A. and Gubrium, J.F. (1997) 'Active interviewing'. In D. Silverman (ed.) *Qualitative Research: Theory, Method and Practice*, pp. 113–29. London: Sage.

Holstein, J.A. and Gubrium, J.F. (2003) 'Context: Working it up, down, and across'. In C. Seale, G. Gobo, J. Gubrium and D. Silverman (eds) *Qualitative Research Practice*, pp. 297–311. London: Sage.

Hopper, R. (2003) *Gendering Talk.* East Lansing, MI: Michigan State University Press.

Hopper, R. and LeBaron, C. (1998) 'How gender creeps into talk', *Research on Language and Social Interaction* 31(1): 59–74.

Hughes, R. (1998) 'Considering the vignette technique and its application to a study of drug injecting and HIV risk and safer behaviour', *Sociology of Health and Illness* 20(3): 381–400.

Hutchby, I. and Wooffitt, R. (1998) *Conversation Analysis.* Cambridge: Polity.

Jefferson, G. (2004a) 'Glossary of transcript symbols with an introduction'. In G.H. Lerner (ed.) *Conversation Analysis: Studies from the First Generation*, pp. 13–31. Amsterdam: John Benjamins.

Jefferson, G. (2004b) '"At First I Thought": A normalizing device for extraordinary events'. In G.H. Lerner (ed). *Conversation Analysis: Studies from the First Generation*, pp. 131–67. Amsterdam/Philadelphia: John Benjamins.

Kitzinger, C. (2000) 'Doing feminist conversation analysis', *Feminism & Psychology* 10(2): 163–93.

Kitzinger, C. (2003) 'Feminist approaches'. In C. Seale, G. Gobo, J. Gubrium and D. Silverman (eds) *Qualitative Research Practice*, pp. 125–40. London: Sage.

Kitzinger, C. (2006) 'Talking sex and gender'. In P. Drew, G. Raymond and D. Weinberg (eds) *Talk and Interaction in Social Research Methods*, pp. 155–170. London: Sage.

Kitzinger, C. (2007) Is 'woman' always relevantly gendered?, *Gender and Language* 1(1): 39–49.

Kitzinger, C. and Frith, H. (1999) 'Just say no? The use of conversation analysis in developing a feminist perspective on sexual refusal', *Discourse and Society* 10(3): 293–316.

Kitzinger. C. and Powell, D. (1995) 'Engendering infidelity: Essentialist and social constructionist readings of a story completion task', *Feminism & Psychology* 5: 345–72.

Kitzinger, C. and Wilkinson, S. (2003) 'Constructing identities: A feminist conversation analytic approach to positioning in action'. In R. Harré and A. Moghaddam (eds) *The Self and Others: Positioning Individuals and Groups in Personal, Political and Cultural Contexts*, pp. 157–180. New York Praeger/Greenwood.

Kitzinger, J. (1990) 'Audience understandings of AIDS media messages: A discussion of methods', *Sociology of Health and Illness* 12: 319–35.

Kitzinger, J. (1994) 'The methodology of focus groups: The importance of interaction between research participants', *Sociology of Health and Illness* 16: 103–21.

Kitzinger, J. and Barbour, R.S. (1999) 'Introduction: The challenge and promise of focus groups'. In R.S. Barbour and J. Kitzinger (eds) *Developing Focus Group Research: Politics, Theory and Practice*, pp. 1–20. London: Sage.

Lakoff, R. (1973) 'Language and woman's place', *Language in Society* 2: 45–79.

Levinson, S. C. (1992) 'Activity Types and Language'. In P. Drew and J. Heritage (eds) *Talk at Work: Interaction in Institutional Settings*, pp. 66–100. Cambridge: Cambridge University Press.

Livia, A. (2003) '"One man in two is a woman": Linguistic approaches to gender in literary texts'. In J. Holmes and M. Meyerhoff (eds) *The Handbook of Language and Gender*, pp. 142–58. Oxford: Blackwell.

Lykke, A. (ed.) (2005) 'Transformative methodologies in feminist studies', Special Issue, *European Journal of Women's Studies* 12(3).

Lynch, M. (2002) 'From naturally occurring data to naturally organized ordinary activities: Comment on Speer', *Discourse Studies* 4(4): 531–7.

Maynard, D.W., Houtkoop-Steenstra, H., Schaeffer, N.C. and van der Zouwen, J. (eds.) (2002) *Standardization and Tacit Knowledge. Interaction and Practice in the Survey Interview.* John Wiley: New York.

Mishler, E.G. (1986) *Research Interviewing: Context and Narrative*. Cambridge, MA: Harvard University Press.

Mishler, E. (2005) 'Commentary 3', *Qualitative Research in Psychology* 2(4): 315–18.

Pollak, S. and Gilligan, C. (1982) 'Images of violence in thematic apperception test stories', *Journal of Personality and Social Psychology* 42: 159–67.

Pomerantz, A. (1984) 'Agreeing and disagreeing with assessments: Some features of preferred/dispreferred turn shapes'. In J.M. Atkinson and J. Heritage (eds) *Structures of Social Action: Studies in Conversation Analysis*, pp. 57–101. Cambridge: Cambridge University Press.

Potter, J. (1996) 'Discourse analysis and constructionist approaches: Theoretical background'. In J.T.E. Richardson (ed.) *Handbook of Qualitative Research Methods for Psychology and the Social Sciences*, pp. 125–40. Leicester: BPS Books.

Potter, J. (2002) 'Two kinds of natural', *Discourse Studies* 4: 539–42.

Potter, J. (2003) 'Discourse analysis', in M. Hardy and A. Bryman (eds) *Handbook of Data Analysis*, pp. 607–24. London: Sage.

Potter, J. (2004) 'Discourse analysis as a way of analysing naturally occurring talk'. In D. Silverman (ed.) *Qualitative Research: Theory, Method and Practice*, pp. 200–21. London: Sage.Potter, J. and Hepburn, A. (2005a) 'Qualitative interviews in psychology: Problems and prospects', *Qualitative Research in Psychology* 2: 281–307.

Potter, J. and Hepburn A. (2005b) Action, interaction and interviews: Some responses to Hollway, Mishler and Smith, *Qualitative Research in Psychology* 2: 319–25.

Potter, J. and Hepburn, A. (2007) 'Life is out there: A comment on Griffin', *Discourse Studies* 9(4): 276–82.

Potter, J. and Wetherell, M. (1987) *Discourse and Social Psychology: Beyond Attitudes and Behaviour*. London: Sage.

Potter, J. and Wetherell, M. (1995) 'Natural order: Why social psychologists should study (A constructed version of) natural language, and why they have not done so', *Journal of Language and Social Psychology* 14(1–2): 216–22.

Psathas, G. (1995) *Conversation Analysis: The Study of Talk-in-Interaction*. London: Sage.

Ramazanoglu, C. and Holland, J. (2002) *Feminist methodology: Challenges and Choices*. London: Sage.

Raymond, G. (2003) 'Grammer and social organization: Yes/No type interrogatives and the structure of responding', *American Sociological Review* 68: 939–67.

Sacks, H. (1984) 'Notes on methodology'. In J.M. Atkinson and J. Heritage (eds) *Structures of Social Action: Studies in Conversation Analysis*, pp. 21–7. Cambridge: Cambridge University Press.

Sacks, H. (1987) 'On the preferences for agreement and contiguity in sequences in conversation'. In G. Button and J.R.E. Lee (eds) *Talk and Social Organisation*, pp. 54–69. Clevedon: Multilingual Matters.

Sacks, H. (1995) *Lectures on Conversation*, Vols. 1 & 2, ed. Gail Jefferson. Oxford: Blackwell.

Sacks, H., Schegloff, E.A. and Jefferson, G. (1974) 'A simplest systematics for the organization of turn-taking for conversation', *Language* 50(4): 696–735.

Schegloff, E.A. (1988a) 'Presequences and indirection: Applying speech act theory to ordinary conversation', *Journal of Pragmatics* 12: 55–62.

Schegloff, E.A. (1988b) 'Goffman and the analysis of conversation'. In P. Drew and A. Wootton (eds) *Erving Goffman: Exploring the Interaction Order*, pp. 89–135. Cambridge: Polity Press.

Schegloff, E.A. (1995) Introduction (Volume 1). In Sacks, H. (ed.) *Lectures on Conversation*. 2 vols. Edited by Gail Jefferson. pp. ix–lxii. Oxford: Basil Blackwell.

Schegloff, E.A. (1996a) 'Confirming allusions: Toward an empirical account of action', *American Journal of Sociology* 104(1): 161–216.

Schegloff, E.A. (1996b) 'Some practices of referring to persons in talk-in-interaction: A partial sketch of a systematics'. In B. Fox (ed.) *Studies in Anaphora*, pp. 437–85. Amsterdam: Benjamins.

Schegloff, E.A. (1998) 'Reflections on studying prosody in talk-in-interaction', *Language and Speech* 41(3–4): 235–63.

Schegloff, E.A. (1999) 'Discourse, pragmatics, conversation, analysis', *Discourse Studies* 1(4): 405–36.

Schegloff, E.A. (2004) 'Experimentation or observation? Of the self alone or the natural world?' *Behavioral and Brain Sciences* 27(2): 271–2.

Schegloff, E. A. (2007) *Sequence Organization in Interaction: A Primer in Conversation Analysis,* Vol 1. Cambridge: Cambridge University Press.

Schegloff, E.A., Jefferson, G. and Sacks, H. (1977) 'The preference for self correction in the organisation of repair in conversation', *Language* 53: 361–82.

Schegloff, E.A. and Lerner, G. (2004) 'Beginning to respond', Paper presented at the *Annual Meeting of the National Communication Association*, Chicago, IL, November.

Schegloff, E.A. and Sacks, H. (1973) 'Opening up closings', *Semiotica* 8: 289–327.

Schlesinger, P., Dobash, R.E., Dobash, R.P. and Weaver, C.K. (1992) *Women Viewing Violence*. London: British Film Institute.

Silverman, D. (2006) *Interpreting Qualitative Data: Methods for Analysing Talk, Text and Interaction*, 3rd edn. London: Sage.

Sleed, M., Durrheim, K., Kriel, A., Solomon, V. and Baxter, V. (2002) 'The effectiveness of the vignette methodology: A comparison of written and video vignettes in eliciting responses about date rape', *South African Journal of Psychology* 32(3): 21–8.

Smith, J. (2005) 'Commentary 1: Advocating pluralism', *Qualitative Research in Psychology* 2(4): 309–11.

Snelling, S.J. (1999) 'Women's perspectives on feminism: A Q-methodological study', *Psychology of Women Quarterly* 23: 247–66.

Speer, S.A. (2001) 'Reconsidering the concept of hegemonic masculinity: Discursive psychology, conversation analysis, and participants' orientations', *Feminism and Psychology* 11(1): 107–35.

Speer, S.A. (2002a) 'Natural and contrived data: A sustainable distinction?' *Discourse Studies* 4(4): 511–25.

Speer, S.A. (2002b) 'Transcending the natural/contrived distinction: A rejoinder to ten Have, Lynch and Potter', *Discourse Studies* 4(4): 543–8.

Speer, S.A. (2002c) 'What can conversation analysis contribute to feminist methodology? Putting reflexivity into practice', *Discourse and Society* 13(6): 801–21.

Speer, S.A. (2005) *Gender Talk: Feminism, Discourse and Conversation Analysis*. London: Routledge.

Speer, S.A. and Green, R. (2007) 'On passing: The interactional organization of appearance attributions in the psychiatric assessment of transsexual patients'. In V. Clarke and E. Peel (eds) *Out in Psychology: Lesbian, Gay, Bisexual, Trans and Queer Perspectives*, pp. 336–68. Chichester: Wiley.

Speer, S.A. and Hutchby, I. (2003a) 'From ethics to analytics: Aspects of participants' orientations to the presence and relevance of recording devices', *Sociology* 37(2): 315–37.

Speer, S.A. and Hutchby, I. (2003b) 'Methodology needs analytics: A rejoinder to Martyn Hammersley', *Sociology* 37(2): 353–9.

Speer, S.A. and Parsons, C. (2006) 'Gatekeeping gender: Some features of the use of hypothetical questions in the psychiatric assessment of transsexual patients', *Discourse & Society* 17(6): 785–812.

Suchman, L. and Jordan, B. (1990) 'Interactional troubles in face-to-face survey interviews', *Journal of the American Statistical Association* 85(409): 232–41.

Sunderland, J. (2004) *Gendered Discourses*. Basingstoke: Palgrave Macmillan.

Taino, L. (2003) '"When shall we go for a ride?" A case of the sexual harassment of a young girl', *Discourse & Society* 14: 173–90.

Wilkinson, S. (1999) 'Focus groups: A feminist method', *Psychology of Women Quarterly* 23: 221–44.

Wilkinson, S. and Kitzinger, C. (2007) 'Conversation analysis, gender and sexuality: A feminist perspective'. In A. Weatherall, B. Watson and C. Gallois (eds) *Language, Discourse and Social Psychology*, pp. 206–30. Basingstoke, UK: Palgrave: Macmillian.

Self-Administered Questionnaires and Standardized Interviews

Edith de Leeuw

INTRODUCTION

In the not too distant past there were only two survey methods to choose from: the face-to-face interview and the postal or mail questionnaire. The first scientific interview goes back to 1912 and Bowley's study of working-class conditions in five British cities, while the first postal survey is attributed to Sir John Sinclair in 1788 (for a historical overview, see De Heer et al., 1999). In the first part of the twentieth century face-to-face survey interviews were further developed in the United States and evolved from short and simple inquiries into complex and highly flexible research instruments (e.g. Hyman, 1954). At the same time, standardized instruments were developed to measure attitudes and opinions, but also to measure capacities (see also O'Muircheartaigh, 1997, pp. 9–12). Soon self-administered questionnaires and tests became the favourite data collection method in education and psychology.

In survey research however, self-administered mail surveys were mainly seen as a fallback method, until the publication of the 1978 Dillman book, which resulted in a rise in high-quality mail surveys. Around 1970 a third data collection method became a serious option: the telephone interview. This method was quickly adopted and telephone surveys became the predominant mode in the USA around 1980. Since then major advances in computer technology have launched computer-assisted methods for data collection, of which Computer Assisted Telephone Interviewing (CATI) is the oldest form, and the Internet or Web survey is the youngest.

Just as in the past, there are now basically two main forms of data collection: those with and those without an interviewer, or in other words standardized interviews and self-administered questionnaires. But there are many variations possible within each main form. Standardized interviews can either be in person (face-to-face) or over the phone, and computer-assisted equivalents are available for each version: Computer-Assisted Personal Interviewing (CAPI) and CATI. Self-administered questionnaires can be used in group settings (e.g. educational tests in classrooms), or in individual settings (e.g. postal sample survey). Again computer-assisted equivalents are available for different types of self-administered questionnaires. In educational research, the school computers and computer laboratories are being used to administer tests, in establishment surveys disk-by mail surveys and Web surveys are becoming popular, and Internet surveys for population surveys and panel research are the latest development (for an introduction and overview of computer-assisted data collection, see De Leeuw et al., 2003). Due to this variety, the choice for the optimal data collection method is far from simple!

SELF-ADMINISTERED QUESTIONNAIRES VERSUS STRUCTURED INTERVIEWS

There are two main differences between self-administered questionnaires and structured interviews. The first is the absence versus presence of the interviewer and its consequences for implementation, non-response and data quality. Interviewers may convince reluctant respondents, motivate respondents, and provide additional instruction or explanations during the data collection. However, at the same time the mere presence of the interviewer can influence responses and cause unwanted interviewer effects, especially when sensitive issues are being discussed. In other words, interviewers are assets and liabilities at the same time.

The second main difference is that in self-administered questionnaires, be it a psychological test, a postal survey or a Web questionnaire, the respondents *see* the questions, while during structured interviews respondents usually do not, although show material such as flash cards with response categories may be used. As a consequence, the visual presentation of questions and the general layout of the questionnaire are far more important in self-administered questionnaires and also different from the ones used in interviews.

Response and non-response

Response to surveys has been decreasing over the years. This is partly due to an increase in non-contacts and partly due to an increase in refusals (De Leeuw & De Heer, 2002). Besides non-contact and refusals there are also other sources of non-response, such as inability to cooperate (e.g. ill health, absence, language problems). These all influence response rates, and should be clearly defined. For clear definitions of response rates for face-to-face, telephone, mail, and Internet surveys, see the website of the American Association for Public Opinion Research (www.aapor.org), and the section of survey methods standards and best practices. Depending on the type of survey and the fieldwork organization, different sources of non-response play a more important role. For instance, in telephone surveys, it is relatively easy to keep trying to reach not-contacted respondents during the fieldwork period without raising the costs considerably. As a consequence, non-contacts are a small portion of the total non-response and the major part of non-response is due to refusals. However, in face-to-face interviews, the number of contact attempts is usually more limited, depending on budget and fieldwork procedures, and non-contacts can be a substantial part of the total non-response (De Heer, 1999). In mail surveys the number of non-contacted depends on the reliability of the mail system; usually the number of non-contacts due to non-delivery is small. Finally, for surveys of the general population the 'other' category, such as inability, will be small compared to the refusals. However, when special topics and populations are studied, such as health surveys of the elderly, this other category may become very important and special fieldwork measures should be taken to reduce this source. For an overview of non-response sources and design implications on response propensity, see Dillman et al. (2002).

In general, face-to-face surveys tend to obtain higher response rates than *comparable* telephone surveys, but both methods show a decrease in response over time. Mail surveys tend to have a lower response rate than comparable face-to-face and telephone surveys. However, there is no evidence for a decrease of response over time in mail surveys. Thus, the differences in response between survey methods have become smaller both in Europe and in the USA and Canada (e.g. Goyder, 1987; Hox and De Leeuw, 1994). In recent years telephone response rates have further decreased, partly due to technological changes, such as call-screening devices which increase the non-contacts, partly due to changes in attitude towards unwanted telephone calls (Curtin et al., 2005; Steeh and Piekarski, 2006). Systematic overviews of response rates in Internet surveys are scarce; studies comparing response rates among Internet, mail, and telephone surveys suggest that response rates are generally lower for online surveys (Matsuo et al., 2004). Empirical comparisons between e-mail and paper mail surveys of the same population indicate that response rates on e-mail surveys are lower than for comparable paper mail surveys (Couper, 2000); similar results are found for list-based Web surveys (Couper, 2001).

To reduce non-response in interview surveys, one has to reduce both the non-contact (e.g. through intensified field work), and the refusals. The fact that response rates in structured interviews are in general higher than in self-administered surveys, is mainly due to the role of the interviewer as persuader of reluctant respondents (cf. Groves and Couper, 1998). Interviewers may differ in their individual success rate, but all interviewers can be trained to do a good job of convincing respondents to cooperate, both for face-to-face surveys (National Centre for Social Research, 1999; Snijkers et al., 1999) and for telephone interviews (Groves and McGonagle, 2001). To achieve a high

response rate in mail surveys a respondent-friendly questionnaire and cover letter in combination with well-timed reminders is necessary (Dillman, 1978, 2000), while for Internet surveys a well-written invitation, in combination with reminders and a good lay out and respondent-friendly Web interface is essential (Dillman, 2000, 2007; Lozar et al., 2008). Two measures are effective in all forms of data collection, that is, both in interviews and in self-administered mail and Internet surveys. Advance letters or prenotifications do have a positive influence on the response for all types of surveys (De Leeuw et al., 2007). The same goes for incentives, which are effective in raising response in both self-administered and interview surveys (e.g. Singer, 2002). It should be noted that, in general, incentives sent in advance, the 'prepaid' incentives, work better than 'promised' incentives. Furthermore, there is no clear evidence that 'lotteries' are effective in increasing response.

Question development

A sound questionnaire is essential for data gathering in both self-administered questionnaires and structured interviews. The questions asked should cover the research objectives in order to avoid specification errors and to get valid answers. Specification error – a term from survey methodology – occurs when the final version of the question, as printed in the questionnaire, fails to collect information that is essential to answer the research question (cf. Biemer and Lyberg, 2003). In the social sciences this is usually referred to as construct validity: does the question measure what it is supposed to measure? Does it measure the intended theoretical construct? (See: Cronbach and Meehl, 1955; see also Embretson and Bovaird, this book, on measurement and scaling).

But a good question needs to do more than cover the construct, it should be understandable and the respondent should be able to answer it. When constructing questionnaires a researcher should start with following the basic rules for general questionnaire construction as outlined in handbooks such as Fowler (1995). These include the advice to use simple words, avoid ambiguity, ask one question at a time, etc. In the next stage the questions always should be tested. No one, not even the most renowned expert, can write a perfect questionnaire. Pre-testing is the only way of assuring that the questions as written do communicate to respondents as intended and that the respondent will be able to answer the questions. Besides performing checks, pre-tests may also provide valuable pointers on how to improve unsatisfactory questions.

Systematic pre-testing is a recent development. In the last three decades, cognitive psychology has strongly influenced survey methodology and questionnaire development. One of the most profound aspects of the effects of cognitive psychology on surveys are the insights into survey artefacts, for instance why do context effects occur, why do respondents satisfice and give only superficial answers, etc. For an overview, see Tourangeau et al. (2000) and Sudman et al. (1996). Another major contribution has been the development of intensive, small-scale methods for evaluating and testing questions, often called 'cognitive testing' or 'cognitive lab methods'. There is a variety of methods available (cf. Presser et al., 2004), but all have in common that a small group of respondents, who are similar to the intended subjects on important characteristics, like age and education, are studied in depth to determine if they understand the question and are able and willing to answer it. Usually a form of in-depth or 'cognitive' interviewing is used. For specific cognitive interview methods see Willis (2004). For a comprehensive overview and general introduction into systematic pre-testing, see Campanelli (2008).

A good guideline for both question writing and question testing is the question-answer process and its four stages: (1) comprehension and interpretation of the question being asked; (2) retrieval of relevant information from memory; (3) integrating this information into a summarized judgement; and (4) reporting this judgement by translating it to offered response options. Respondents first have to understand the question and decide what information the researcher asks for. In the second step, they need to recall all relevant information from memory. When it is simple factual or behavioural information respondents can retrieve this, when it is rare behaviour or refers to a long time ago, this is a difficult task and respondents have to rely on heuristic strategies. When the question asks for a strongly held attitude, it is relatively easy to retrieve, but if the question refers to more superficial opinions, respondents will rarely find a 'ready-for-use' answer stored in memory. Instead, they will need to form a judgement on the spot, based on whatever relevant information comes to mind. Once step 3 has been successfully completed and respondents have formed a judgement in their own minds, they have to report it. When an open question is used they can report it in their own words. However, more often a closed question is used and respondents need to format their answer to fit the response alternatives provided by the researcher. In this final reporting stage, respondents may hesitate to communicate their private judgement, due to reasons of social desirability and self-presentation. If so, they will either refuse to answer, offer a 'do-not-know' option, or in the case of a closed question may also opt for a more acceptable, but not necessarily true response category. For an in-depth discussion of the psychology of asking questions, see Schwarz et al. (2008) and Tourangeau et al. (2000).

From question to ready-to-use questionnaire or interview schedule

As stated in the section above, careful writing and testing of questions is important both for structured interviews and for self-administered questionnaires. But, a questionnaire is more than a collection of questions; it contains instructions and texts to keep the flow of information going and to keep the respondents motivated. It also should be pleasant to use, avoid unnecessary routing errors, and correctly guide from question to question. Visual design through the use of graphical tools and lay-out is very important to successfully transform a collection of questions into a well-designed questionnaire (see for instance Redline et al., 2003). It is important to note that structured interviews and self-administered questionnaires differ in necessary layout and in how the final questionnaire has to be constructed. The users are different and have different needs: interview schedules are designed for trained interviewers who have to guide a respondent through the question-answer process, while self-administered questionnaires should be totally self-explanatory to respondents.

Interview schedules constructed for structured interviews, both over the telephone or face-to-face, contain besides the questions also instructions for trained interviewers. As a consequence, a finalized interview schedule contains text to be read aloud by the interviewer, text that should never be read aloud at all, and text that only in certain situations should be read. Examples of texts that always are read out aloud by the interviewer are the questions themselves, texts to make the transition from one group of questions to the next (e.g. 'now I would like to ask you some question on …'), and instructions to respondents (e.g. 'I am going to read you a list of ... statements. For each, please indicate whether you think it is not important, somewhat important, or very important'). Examples of texts that are never read are specific interviewer instructions (e.g. 'probe if the respondent does not answer', or, 'skip to question 13'), or certain response and/or coding categories (e.g. 'refused, no opinion, does not apply'). An example of a text that is sometimes read aloud is: 'if you are not sure, please give me your best guess'. To avoid interviewer mistakes and to help interviewers read out aloud the correct information it is advised to use consistent graphical language, such as different fonts. Examples are using bold type for all questions, signalling that all text in bold should be read aloud. For other types of information, other styles should be used; for instance, instructions in italics, categories not to be read in capitals,

and placing explicit interviewer instructions in parentheses (Salant and Dillman, 1994, pp. 130–132). This is all for the benefit of interviewers, not for the eyes of the respondent. Exceptions are response cards printed with the major answer categories, which are shown to respondents when long lists of response categories are presented in face-to-face interviews.

In contrast, in a self-administered questionnaire everything must be tailored to the respondent. There is no interviewer to motivate or help out, and the questionnaire itself should do it all. Visual design is here of the utmost importance. Salant and Dillman (1994) and Dillman (2000, 2007) give clear instructions and numerous examples of how to order questions, give instructions, and motivate respondents. Numbers, symbols, and graphical layout (e.g. spacing, location, brightness, contrast, and figure/ground arrangements) all communicate meaning, and should be used to optimize a questionnaire for self-administered use. A good example of how this has been done in a consistent way is described by Dillman et al. (2005). For a theoretical background see Jenkins and Dillman (1997), and Redline et al. (2003).

FACE-TO-FACE INTERVIEWS

Face-to-face interviews are the most flexible form of data collection method. Main advantages of the face-to-face interview are the availability of an interviewer to structure the interview situation and help and motivate respondents. Furthermore, the face-to-face setting allows for optimal communication, as both verbal and non-verbal communication are possible. Structured or partly structured interview schedules with open questions can be used as the interviewer poses the questions, follows up with additional probes, bridges silences, and records answers. The presence of a well-trained interviewer also enables the researcher to use a variety of measurements besides simple question-answer sequences. For instance, respondents can be asked to sort objects or pictures, perform specific tasks, or the interviewer may even do some physical measurements, e.g. in health-related studies. Also, respondents can be presented with all kinds of visual stimuli, ranging from simple response cards listing the answer categories for a question to pictures, advertisement copy or video clips. Finally, highly complex questionnaires can be successfully implemented as a trained interviewer takes care of navigating through the questionnaire. In computer-assisted face-to-face interviews (CAPI), the interviewer is guided through the (complex) questionnaire by a computer program. This lowers error rates even more and gives the interviewer more opportunities to concentrate on the interviewer-respondent interaction. (For an overview see De Leeuw, 1992, 2004.)

When one is interested in studying the general population, the face-to-face survey also has the greatest potential. Sophisticated sampling designs for face-to-face surveys have been developed, which do not require a detailed sampling frame or a list of persons or households. For instance, area probability sampling can be used to select geographically defined units (e.g. streets or blocks of houses) as primary units and households within these areas. Therefore, a main advantage of face-to-face interviews is its potential for a high coverage of the intended population. Elaborate techniques based on household listings (e.g. inventories of all household members derived by an interviewer) can then be used to randomly select one respondent from those eligible in a household (e.g. Kish, 1965).

The presence of an interviewer is a great advantage, but it can also be a disadvantage. Respondents may feel inhibited to answer more sensitive questions in the presence of an interviewer, and in general, more socially desirable answers and conventional answers are given in interviews than when a self-administered questionnaire is being used. If some questions have a very sensitive nature, but a face-to-face interview is preferable for other reasons (e.g. coverage, additional questions) a good strategy is to combine an interview with a self-administered questionnaire

in a mixed-mode design (for more details, see De Leeuw, 2005). In general, interviewers affect respondents and their answers also when non-sensitive questions are being asked. Respondents that are interviewed by the same interviewer tend to have more similar answers; this is called the interviewer effect or interviewer variance. There are many reasons for this: interviewers vary in their capabilities of motivating respondents, they may use different probing techniques, or reword badly worded questions in different ways, etc. (for more detail see Japec, 2005). Well-tested questionnaires, standardized procedures, and thorough interviewer training is necessary to reduce unwanted interviewer effects.

Face-to-face interviews are the 'Rolls Royce' of data collection and just like the car they are extremely costly and take much care and time to get rolling. Interviewers have to be trained, not only in standard interview techniques, but also in how to implement sampling and respondent selection rules and in how to solve various problems that can arise when they are working along in the field. In addition, an extensive supervisory network is needed to maintain quality control. Finally, an administrative manager is needed to make sure that new addresses and interview material are mailed to the interviewers on a regular basis.

TELEPHONE INTERVIEWS

Telephone interviews are less flexible than face-to-face interviews. Their major drawback is the absence of visual cues during the interview; telephone is auditory only. This limits interviewers in their tools for communication. For instance, as no non-verbal communication is possible, they have to say explicitly 'thank-you' or 'yes', instead of nod or smile. The absence of a visual channel of communication also limits the researcher in the type of questions that can be asked. For instance, questions using graphical techniques, like smiley faces, and ranking and sorting techniques are not possible. Semantic differentials and other rating tasks with many potential response categories will be difficult to use. As no response cards with lists of answer categories are available in telephone interviews, the interviewer and respondent have to rely solely on the auditory channel of communication. The interviewer has to read out aloud the question along with the available answer categories and the respondent has to try to keep all possibilities in memory. As a consequence, only very familiar scales, such as 0 to 10 scales ('on a scale of 0 to 10 where …') or questions with a limited number of response categories can be used. This has led to the development of special question formats in which the answer categories are split up, for questions with seven or more response categories. An example is the two-step or unfolding procedure in which respondents are first asked if they are 'satisfied', 'dissatisfied' or 'somewhat in the middle', and depending on their answer, are asked specific follow-up questions (e.g. 'is this completely satisfied, mostly satisfied, or somewhat satisfied'). In general, over the telephone questions must be short and easily understandable.

However, just as in face-to-face interviews, well-trained interviewers are an advantage. In telephone surveys the interviewer can assist respondents in understanding questions, can administer questionnaires with a large number of screening questions, control the question sequence, and probe for answers on open questions. Again like in CAPI, the use of CATI makes these tasks easier for the interviewer.

The personnel requirements for a telephone survey are less demanding than in face-to-face surveys. Usually, telephone interviews are conducted from a central setting where supervisors and quality controllers follow the process closely. Because the interviews are being conducted from a central location over the phone and interviewers do not have to travel to respondents, fewer highly trained interviewers and supervisors are needed. Interviewers should, of course, be well trained in standard interview techniques and in telephone conversations and know how to use this auditive-only medium of communication, but the variety of interviewer skills needed in one person is less than in face-to-face interviews. The majority of telephone interviewers no longer have to be prepared for every possible emergency and can concentrate on standard, but high-quality interviewing. Special respondents or problem cases can be dealt with by the available supervisor or can be allocated to specially skilled and trained or bi-lingual interviewers.

Because of the potentials for close supervision and quality control, interviewer effects are in general smaller over the phone than in face-to-face interviews (e.g. Groves, 1989, chapter 8). Interviewers can effect the responses given in different ways, by the way they read the question and emphasize certain parts, by deviating from prescribed wording, by reacting in different ways to questions or problems of the respondents, and even by the way they look or sound. As interviewers are only a voice over the phone, many interviewer characteristics (e.g. those connected with appearance) will be less obvious. Furthermore, the close supervision and potential for immediate feedback on inadequate interviewer behaviour will lessen unwanted interviewers' influence over the phone.

Telephone interviews are only feasible if telephone coverage is high, in other words if the non-telephone part of the population can be ignored. To be sure that persons with unlisted telephones are also included, one can employ random digit dialling. Random digit dialling techniques, which are based on the sampling frame of all possible telephone numbers, make it feasible to use telephone interviews in investigations of the general population. A new challenge to telephone survey coverage is the increasing popularity of mobile (cell) phones. If mobile phones are additional to fixed landline phones (i.e. a person has a mobile phone, but also a landline phone at home), this will not pose a major problem for under-coverage. But, there is evidence that certain groups (e.g. the young, lower income, urban, more mobile) are over-represented in the mobile-phone-only proportion of the population. When mobile phones are excluded from telephone surveys, this may result in serious under-coverage of these groups. Some countries have good listings of all phone numbers, including mobile phones, others have not; customs associated with mobile phone use also differ from country to country. How mobile phones affect the efficacy of telephone surveys is therefore country dependent. For an overview see Nathan (2001) and Steeh (2008).

In telephone interviews, as in face-to-face interviews, the Kish procedure based on a complete household listing can in theory be used to select respondents within a household. However asking for a complete household listing over the phone, is a rather complex and time-consuming procedure and increases the risk of break-offs. A good alternative for the Kish procedure is the last birthday or the next birthday method. In the last birthday method, the interviewer asks to speak with that household member who most recently had a birthday. Even though, the birthday methods are very popular and seen as the standard to select a particular respondent from a household in telephone surveys, they are not as precise as the complete Kish method. For an overview see Ganziano, 2005.

One of the main advantages of telephone interviews, besides the close supervision of interviewers for quality control, is the relative low cost of telephone interviews both for completed interviews and for callbacks to non-respondents. As interviewers do not have to travel, a limited number of interviewers may call a large number of respondents in a relative short time period. This is especially important in sparsely populated areas or countries.

MAIL SURVEYS

Mail surveys require an explicit sampling frame of names and addresses, and have the advantage if only addresses and no telephone numbers are available. Often, telephone directories or other lists are used for mail surveys of the general population. Using the telephone directory as a sampling frame has the drawback that people without a telephone and people with an unlisted telephone cannot be reached, but the advantage that telephone reminders or follow-ups can easily be implemented. Another reason for the frequent use of the telephone directory as sampling frame is the relative ease and the low costs associated with this method.

A distinct drawback of mail surveys is the limited control the researcher has over the choice of the specific individual within a household who in fact completes the survey. There is no interviewer available to apply respondent selection techniques within a household and all instructions for respondent selection have to be included in the accompanying letter. As a consequence only simple procedures such as the male/female/youngest/oldest alternation or the last birthday method can be successfully used. The male/female/youngest/oldest alternation asks in a random 25 percent of the accompanying letters for the youngest female in the household to fill in the questionnaire; in a second random 25 percent of the letters the youngest male is requested to fill in the questionnaire, etc. When a complete list of the individual members of the target population is available, which can be the case in surveys of special groups or in countries with good administrative records, a random sample of the target population can be drawn regardless of the data collection method used. In that case, coverage and sampling will be as good as in interview methods.

The absence of an interviewer makes mail surveys the least flexible data collection technique when complexity of the questionnaire is considered. All questions must be presented in a fixed order, and only a limited number of simple skips and branches can be used. For routings special written instructions and graphical aids, such as arrows and colours, have to be provided; for a great example see Dillman et al. (2005). Furthermore, in a mail survey, all respondents receive the same instruction and are presented with the questions without added interviewer probing or help in individual cases. In short, a mail questionnaire must be totally self-explanatory. But, a big advantage is that visual cues and stimuli can be used, and with well-developed instructions fairly complex questions and attitude scales can be implemented. The visual presentation of the questions makes it possible to use all types of graphical questions (e.g. ladder, thermometer), and to use questions with seven or more response categories. Also, information booklets or product samples can be sent by mail with an accompanying questionnaire for their evaluation. However, open-ended questions are difficult to ask, as no interviewer is present to probe for more details.

In general, self-administered question-naires are less intrusive and allow for more privacy and less time pressure. The absence of an interviewer may in certain situations be a real advantage, especially when sensitive or socially desirable questions are being asked. Another advantage is that mail surveys can be completed when and where the respondent wants and is not dependent on interviewer time. A respondent may consult records if needed, which may improve accuracy. For an overview see de Leeuw (1992) and Dillman (2000).

From a logistic point of view mail surveys have two drawbacks: questionnaire length and turn-around time. The personal presence of interviewers in face-to-face interviews prohibits break-offs and allows for longer questionnaires than in mail surveys, although telephone interviews do not have this advantage. According to Dillman (1978, p. 55) mail questionnaires up to 12 pages, which contain less than 125 items, can be used without adverse effects on the response. Turn-around in mail surveys is slower than in most other modes. Mail surveys are locked into a definite time interval of mailing dates with rigidly scheduled follow-ups, and therefore take longer than other modes of data collection, with the exception of large, geographically dispersed face-to-face interviews, which take the longest. When speed of completion is really important and data are needed fast, telephone and Internet surveys are best. If the data are needed in a couple of weeks, mail surveys are a good choice.

Dillman (1978, p. 68) gives an example in which a survey unit of 15 telephones can complete roughly 3000 interviews during the 8 weeks it takes to perform a complete mail survey with reminders. Only if the telephone unit is smaller than 15 interviewers, or the number of needed completed interviews is larger than 3000, will a mail survey be faster.

Logistically, mail surveys also have two huge advantages: small staff and low costs. Organizational and personnel requirements for a mail survey are far less demanding than in interviews. Most of the workers are not required to deal directly with respondents, and the necessary skills are mainly generalized clerical skills (e.g. typing, sorting, response administration, and correspondence process-ing). Of course, a trained person must be available to deal with requests for informa-tion, questions, and refusals of respondents, but no interviewers or other field staff are needed. Thus, the number of different persons necessary to conduct a mail survey is far less than that required for interview surveys with equal sample sizes. Requirements for the organization and personnel do influence the cost of data collection; as a consequence mail surveys are among the least expensive and may be the only affordable mode in certain situations.

INTERNET SURVEYS

In Internet or Web surveys, coverage is still a major problem when surveying the gen-eral population (Couper, 2000, 2001). Even though Internet access is growing and around 70 percent of the US population has access to the Internet, the picture is diverse ranging from 75 percent coverage for Sweden to 4 per-cent in Africa (www.internetworldstats.com). Furthermore, those covered differ from those not covered, with the elderly, lower educated, lower income, and minorities less well-represented online.

As reaction to the differential coverage and the relative low response rates of Internet surveys, so-called 'access panels' gain in popularity in market research. In access panels, samples of panel members with Internet access are sent requests to fill in questionnaires at regular intervals. Panel research is not new, and the advantages and disadvantages of panel research have been well described (e.g. Kasprzyk et al., 1989); what is new is the potential of Internet to select and survey huge panels at low costs. A major quality criterion for Internet panels is how the Internet or access panels were composed. Is the panel based on a probability sample (e.g. RDD telephone invitation), or is it a non-probability sample, in other words is it based on self-selection (e.g. through banners or invitations on a website inviting people to become a panel member)? Only probability-based panels allow for sound statistical analysis. Non-probability panels may result in very large numbers of respondents, but those respondents are a convenience sample. As all statistics are based on the assumption of probability sampling, statistics (e.g. margin of errors, p-values) computed on non-probability samples, such as self-selected Internet panels, make no sense at all. Recently, propensity score adjustment has been suggested to reduce the biases due to non-coverage, self-selection, and non-response (Lee, 2006). In propensity weighting one ideally has access to a reference sample with high-quality data and low non-response. Like in all weighting schemes it is important that good auxiliary variables are available and that the variables used in the adjustment are both highly related to the 'outcome' variable and to the self-selection mechanism. It is the researchers' duty to be transparent on the weighting procedures and the predictive power of the propensity model used.

Like in mail surveys, the control of the interview situation is low in Internet surveys. This is often considered a disadvantage: one does not know if the intended respondent is completing the questionnaire. But this can also be seen as an advantage: the respondent is in charge and the interview situation may offer more privacy. Of course, to fully take advantage of this, potential privacy concerns of respondents should be met (see for instance the guideline of the world association of

market research (ESOMAR) on conducting market and opinion research using the Internet (http://www.esomar.org/web/show/id=49859).

Because an interview program determines the order of the questions, more complex questionnaires can be used than in a paper mail survey. In this sense – complexity of questionnaire structure – an Internet or Web survey is equivalent to an interview survey. In addition, Internet surveys share the advantages of mail surveys regarding visual aids, but the Web has far more potential than paper. Dillman (2007) gives a comprehensive overview of visual design and Web surveys. This is based on both theory and empirical studies (see also http://survey.sesrc.wsu.edu/dillman/papers.htm). Compared to mail surveys that are limited to questionnaires of low complexity, Web-based questionnaires allow for very complex questionnaires that on the screen may appear simple and attractive. This, together with the potential for using visual stimuli, the freedom for the respondent to respond at their chosen time or place, and the greater privacy, makes Internet a new and unique data collection procedure. However, Internet also has data drawbacks, it is a more perfunctory medium and people often just pay a flying visit. Respondents may have a stronger tendency to satisfies and give top-of-the head answers, or just peek and leave causing many early break-offs. In general, it is therefore wise to use only short questionnaires on the Web; 10–15 minutes is already a long time for an Internet survey.

Logistically, only a small number of staff is needed to implement and run Internet surveys. But, to design and implement an Internet survey highly skilled and specialized personnel are needed, who combine technical knowledge (e.g. operating systems, browsers, etc.) and knowledge on usability and visual design. These requirements for the organization and personnel do influence the cost of data collection. But, when a survey is implemented, it can be used for large numbers: a large sample does not cost more than a small sample in running the survey. This is what constitutes the attractiveness of Internet surveys: it can be used for the fast collection of large numbers of completed questionnaires at low costs. In addition, there are no data entry costs, an advantage Internet surveys share with all computer-assisted interview modes.

OTHER SELF-ADMINISTERED QUESTIONNAIRES

Mail and Internet surveys are only two forms in which self-administered questionnaires can be used. These forms are most often implemented in social sciences surveys and in polling. In psychology and education, other forms of self-administered question-naires are frequently used. In educational research, group-wise administration of self-administered questionnaires is common, be it in a paper form in the classroom, or in an electronic form in the school's computer laboratory (cf. Beebe et al., 1998; Van Hattum & De Leeuw, 1999). In psychological testing, self-administered tests are used either in an individual or a group setting. Again the administration can be either as paper-and-pen or computer-assisted testing (cf. Weisband and Kiesler, 1996).

Examples of individual administration are questionnaires that are handed out by a nurse or health officer in a hospital waiting room, or by a receptionist in a day care centre. Sometimes, self-administered questionnaires are used with an interviewer present. This is usually done when sensitive questions have to be asked and the interviewer hands over a questionnaire for the respondent to fill in privately. When computer-assisted interviewing or CAPI is used, the interviewer hands over the computer to the respondent for a short period. The respondent can answer the specific questions in privacy and the interviewer remains at a respectful distance, but also is available for instructions and assistance.

Just as in mail and Internet surveys, the questionnaires should be well tested and attention should be paid to graphical tools and layout. Just as in mail and Internet

surveys, these forms of self-administered questionnaires allow for more privacy and self-disclosure as no interviewer is *directly* involved in the question-answer process. But there are two main differences. The first is that it is the researcher and not the respondent who decides when and where the questionnaire has to be completed. The researcher also determines how long a session will take, and how much time subjects have to fill in the questionnaire. This may be a disadvantage when well-considered responses are needed, but an advantage when speed-tests or first associations are more appropriate. The second difference is that, although no interviewer is directly involved, usually a trained research assistant is present to give instructions, distribute the tests, and answer questions if necessary. Group-administered question-naires can be seen as a hybrid between interview and mail survey, combining the advantages of both methods: enough privacy for subjects to answer more freely, and available assistance when needed.

SUMMARY

In survey research there are two main forms of data collection: self-administered question-naires and standardized interviews. These are mainly characterized by the absence versus presence of an interviewer. But there are many variations possible, such as face-to-face and telephone interviews with their computer-assisted equivalents CAPI and CASI, and self-administered mail questionnaires and Internet surveys. Each method has its advantages and disadvantages, which are summarized below.

Deciding which data collection is best in a certain situation is often complex and depends on many factors, such as population under investigation, topic, types of questions to be asked, available time, and funds. This presents researchers with a difficult choice indeed. It is no wonder that recently multiple modes of data collection or mixed modes have become popular. In mixed-mode surveys, two or more modes of data collection are

Main Advantages and Disadvantages of Questionnaires and Interviews

Face-to-Face Interviews in Sum:

1   Face-to-face interviewing has the highest potential regarding types of questions asked, and complexity of questionnaires. To realize this potential one needs both well-trained interviewers and well-tested questionnaires. In addition a highly qualified field staff is necessary to make sure that all logistics are taken care of. Only then will a face-to-face interview really fulfill its potential. This is very costly and time-consuming and only worth it in some situations; researchers should carefully consider if all that potential is really needed to answer the research question.

2   Face-to-face interviewing has also the highest potential regarding coverage and sampling, but it can be very costly, especially if the country is large and sparsely populated. Cluster sampling may be needed, and if the sample dispersion is very high telephone surveys are often employed.

3   The greatest asset of the face-to-face interview – the presence of an interviewer – is also its greatest weakness. Their presence may influence the answers respondents give, especially when sensitive questions are being asked, and in general they may contribute to the total survey error, due to variance in interviewer ability and competence.

Telephone Interviews in Sum:

4   Telephone interviews have less potential regarding types of questions asked than face-to-face interviews, as no visual communication is possible. But interviewers are available to help and guide the respondent and complex questionnaires may be used. However, fewer questions can be asked and telephone interviews must be far shorter than face-to-face interviews.

5   Due to unlisted numbers and cell phones, coverage may be sub-optimal. However if good lists are available telephone interviewing is, from a sampling point of view, comparable to face-to-face interviewing. If the sample dispersion is very high telephone surveys are often the only interview mode feasible.

6   In telephone interviews quality control is high as interviewers can be closely monitored and immediate feedback is possible.

7   Many interviews can be completed in a relatively short time with a smaller number of interviewers than face-to-face. Also telephone interviews are less costly than face-to-face interviews.

Mail Surveys in Sum:

8   Mail surveys lack the flexibility and interviewer support of interview surveys, which limits the complexity of the questionnaire used. However, visual stimuli, such as pictures or graphics can be applied and examples or show material may be included.

9   Mail surveys are less intrusive than interviews: respondents may answer at leisure in their own time and there is no interviewer present who may inhibit free answers to more sensitive topics.

10   Lists with addresses of the target population should be available, but telephone numbers are not necessary.

11   Mail surveys have a longer turn-around than telephone surveys, but face-to-face interviewing usually takes longer.

12   Mail surveys are far less costly than both face-to-face and telephone interview surveys.

Internet Surveys in Sum:

13   Internet access varies strongly between countries and within countries. Lists with e-mail addresses of the target population should be available, and depending on the population under investigation large coverage problems may arise.

14   In Internet surveys complex questionnaires and visual stimuli can be applied, but questionnaires have to be very short.

15   Like mail surveys Internet surveys are less intrusive.

16   Large numbers of completed questionnaires can be collected in a very short time and at low costs.

combined in such a way that the disadvantages of one method are counterbalanced by the advantages of another; for instance combining a Web survey with a telephone interview to compensate for under-coverage of the elderly and lower educated on the Internet. Other examples of mixed-mode designs are the use of face-to-face interviews for those who cannot be reached by telephone, or telephone interviews among non-respondents in mail or Internet surveys. In longitudinal surveys, mixed-mode designs are common as data collection methods often vary between waves; for instance (face-to-face) surveys during recruitment and in the base-line survey and less expensive survey methods (e.g. mail, Internet, or telephone) in the subsequent waves. Of course, when mixing modes particular attention should be paid to equivalence of question format, comparability of answers and data integrity. (For extensive overviews see De Leeuw, 2005.)

Which data collection mode or mix of modes is chosen is the result of a careful consideration of quality and costs. But, certain survey design steps should always be taken, as they are extremely important for high-quality data. Among these are the careful construction and (pre)-testing of the questionnaire, the implementation of response-inducing features, such as advance letters, reminders, and if the budget allows the use of incentives. Finally, in the case of interviews a thorough training of interviewers is necessary in interview rules and non-response reduction.

SUGGESTED READINGS

On survey quality and data collection

Paul, P.B. and Lars, E.L. (2003). Introduction to Survey Quality. New York: Wiley (especially chapters 5 & 6).

On practical aspects of surveys

Czaja, R. and Blair, J. (2005). *Designing Surveys: A Guide to Decisions and Procedures.* Thousand Oaks:

Sage (Pine Forge Press series in research methods and statistics).

Don, A.D. (2007). *Mail and Internet Surveys (with 2007 update).* New York: Wiley (discusses establishment surveys and mixed mode too).

Floyd, J.F. (1995). *Improving Survey Questions: Design and Evaluation* (Vol. 38). Thousand Oaks: Sage Applied Social Research Methods Series (on question writing and testing).

For international studies

de Leeuw, E.D., Hox, J., and Dillman, D. (eds) (2008). *International Handbook of Survey Methodology.* Mahwah, N.J.: Erlbaum (especially chapters 9–14 & 16).

REFERENCES

Beebe, T.J., Harrison, P.A., McRae, J.A., Anderson, R.E., and Fulkerson, J.A. (1998). An evaluation of computer-assisted self-interviews in a school setting. *Public Opinion Quarterly*, 62: 623–632.

Biemer, P.P. and Lyberg, L.E. (2003). *Introduction to Survey Quality.* New York: Wiley.

Campanelli, P. (2008). Testing survey questions. In Edith de Leeuw, Joop Hox, and Don Dillman (eds) *International Handbook of Survey Methodology.* Mahwah, N.J.: Erlbaum.

Couper, M.P. (2000). Websurveys; A review of issues and approaches. *Public Opinion Quarterly*, 64, 4: 464–494. See also Couper (2000) the Good, the Bad, and the Ugly. University of Michigan, Institute for Social Research, Survey Methodology Program, Working paper series # 077.

Couper, M.P. (2001). The promises and perils of web surveys. Presentation at the ASC-Conference on the Challenge of the Internet. Available at www.asc.org.uk (accessed January, 2006).

Cronbach, L.J. and Meehl, P.E. (1955). Construct validity in psychological tests. *Psychological Bulletin*, 52: 281–302.

Curtin, R., Presser, S., and Singer, E. (2005). Changes in telephone survey nonresponse over the past quarter century. *Public Opinion Quarterly*, 69: 87–98.

de Heer, W. (1999). International response trends: results of an international survey. *Journal of Official Statistics, JOS*, 15, 2: 129–142. Also available on www.jos.nu.

de Heer, W., de Leeuw, E., and van der Zouwen, J. (1999). Methodological issues in survey research: A historical review. *BMS, Bulletin de Methodologie Sociologique*, 64: 25–48.

de Leeuw, E.D. (1992). *Data Quality in Mail Telephone and Face-to-face Surveys*. Amsterdam: TT-Publikaties. Available at http://www.xs4all.nl/~edithl/pubs/disseddl.pdf (accessed June 2006).

de Leeuw, E.D. (2004). *New Technologies in Data Collection, Questionnaire Design and Quality*. International Statistical Seminars Series # 44. San Sebastian: EUSTAT. Available at http://www.eustat.es/prodserv/datos/sem44.pdf (accessed June 2006).

de Leeuw, E.D. (2005). To mix or not to mix: data collection modes in surveys. *Journal of Official Statistics*, 21, 2: 233–255. Available at www.jos.nu (accessed June 2007).

de Leeuw, E.D., Callegaro, M. Hox, J.J., Korendijk, E., and Lensvelt-Mulders, G. (2007). The influence of advance letters on response in telephone surveys: A meta-analysis. *Public Opinion Quarterly*, 71, 3: 1–31.

de Leeuw, E.D. and de Heer, W. (2002). Trends in household survey nonresponse: A longitudinal and international comparison. In Dillman, D.A., Eltinge, J.L., Groves, R.M., and Little, R.J.A. (eds) *Survey Nonresponse*. New York: Wiley.

de Leeuw, E., Hox, J., and Kef, S. (2003). Computer-assisted self-interviewing tailored for special populations and topics. *Field Methods*, 15: 223–251.

Dillman, D.A. (1978). *Mail and Telephone Surveys. The Total Design Method*. New York: Wiley.

Dillman, D.A. (2000). *Mail and Internet Surveys. The Tailored Design Method*. New York: Wiley.

Dillman, D.A. (2007). *Mail and Internet Surveys. The Tailored Design Method (2007 Update with Appendix)*. New York: Wiley.

Dillman, D.A., Eltinge, J.L., Groves, R.M., and Little, R.J.A. (2002). Survey nonresponse in design, data collection and analysis. In Dillman, D.A., Eltinge, J.L., Groves, R.M., and Little, R.J.A. (eds) *Survey Nonresponse*. New York: Wiley.

Dillman, D.A., Gertseva, A., and Mahon-Taft, T. (2005). Achieving useability in establishment surveys through the application of visual design principles. *Journal of Official Statistics (JOS)*, 21, 2: 183–214. Also available at www.jos.nu.

Fowler, F.J. (1995). *Improving Survey Questions: Design and Evaluation* (Vol. 38). Thousand Oaks: Sage Applied Social Research Methods Series.

Ganziano, C. (2005). Comparative analysis of within-household respondent selection techniques. *Public Opinion Quarterly*, 69: 124–157.

Goyder, J. (1987). *The Silent Minority: Nonrespondents on Sample Surveys*. Cambridge: Policy Press.

Groves, R.M. (1989). *Survey Errors and Survey Costs*. New York: Wiley.

Groves, R.M. and Couper, M.P. (1998). *Nonresponse in Household Interview Surveys*. New York: Wiley.

Groves, R.M. and Mc Gonagle, K.A. (2001). A theory guided training protocol regarding survey participation. *Journal of Official Statistics (JOS)*, 17, 2: 249–265. Also available at www.jos.nu.

Hox, J.J. and de Leeuw, E.D. (1994). A comparison of nonresponse in mail, telephone, & face to face surveys: Applying multilevel modeling to meta-analysis. *Quality & Quantity*, 28: 329–344. Reprinted in: David de Vaus (2002) *Social Surveys*, part eleven, nonresponse error. London: Sage, Benchmarks in Social Research Methods Series.

Hyman, H.H. (1954). *Interviewing in Social Research*. Chicago: Chicago University Press.

Japec, L. (2005). *Quality Issues in Interviewer Surveys: Some Contributions*. Stockholm: Stockholm University: Department of statistics (ISBN 91-7155-155-7).

Jenkins, C. (now Cleo Redline) and Dillman, D.A. (1997). Towards a theory of self-administered questionnaire design. In Lyberg, L., Biemer, P., Collins, M., de Leeuw, E., Dippo, C., Schwarz, N., and Trewin, D. (eds) *Survey Measurement*. New York: John Wiley.

Kasprzyk, D., Duncan, G.J., Kalton, G., and Singh, M.P. (1989). *Panel Surveys*. New York: Wiley.

Kish, L. (1965). *Survey Sampling*. New York: Wiley.

Lee, S. (2006). Propensity score adjustment as a weighting scheme for volunteer panel web surveys. *Journal of Official Statistics (JOS)*, 22, 2: 329–349. Also available at www.jos.nu.

Lozar, M.K. and Vehovar, V. (2008). Internet surveys. In de Leeuw, E., Hox, J., and Dillman, D. (eds) *International Handbook of Survey Methodology*. Mahwah, N.J.: Erlbaum.

Matsuo, H., McIntyre, K.P., Tomazic, T., and Katz, B. The online survey: its contributions and potential problems. American Statitistical Association (ASA). Proceedings, 2004, ASA section on Survey Research Methods, pp. 3998–4000. Available at www.amstat.org/sections/srms/proceedings.

Nathan, G. (2001). Telesurvey methodologies for households: A review and some thoughts for the future. *Survey Methodology*, 27: 7–31.

National Centre for Social Research (1999). *How to Improve Survey Response Rates: A Guide for Interviewers on the Doorstep*. London, Thousand Oaks and New Delhi: Sage Publications.

O'Muircheartaigh, C. (1997). Measurement error in surveys: A historical perspective. In Lyberg, L., Biemer, P., Collins, M., de Leeuw, E., Dippo, C., Schwarz, N., and Trewin, D. (eds) *Survey Measurement and Process Quality*. New York: Wiley.

Presser, S., Rothgeb, J., M., Couper, M.P., Lessler, J.T., Martin, E., Martin, J., and Singer, E. (2004). *Methods for Testing and Evaluating Survey Questions*. New York: Wiley.

Redline, C.D., Dillman, D.A., Carley-Baxter, L., and Creecy, R. (2003). Factors that influence reading and comprehension in self-administered question- naires. Paper presented at the Workshop on Item-Nonresponse and Data Quality, Basel Switzerland, October 10, 2003. Available at http://survey.sesrc. wsu.edu/dillman/papers.htm (accessed June 2006).

Salant, P. and Dillman, D.A. (1994). *How to Conduct Your Own Survey*. New York: Wiley.

Schwarz, N., Knäuper, B., Oyserman, D., and Stich, C. (2008). The *Psychology of Asking Questions*. In Edith De Leeuw, Joop Hox, and Don Dillman (eds) *International Handbook of Survey Methodology*. Mahwah, N.J.: Erlbaum.

Singer, E. (2002). The use of incentives to reduce nonresponse in household surveys. In Dillman, D.A., Eltinge, J.L., Groves, R.M., and Little, R.J.A. (eds) *Survey Nonresponse*. New York: Wiley.

Snijkers, G., Hox, J.J., and de Leeuw, E.D. (1999). Interviewers' tactics for fighting survey nonresponse. *Journal of Official Statistics (JOS)*, 15, 2: 185–198 (available at www.jos.nu). Reprinted in: David de Vaus (2002), *Social Surveys*, part eleven, nonresponse error. London: Sage, Benchmarks in Social Research Methods Series.

Steeh, C. (2008). Telephone surveys. In de Leeuw, E., Hox, J., and Dillman, D. (eds) *International Handbook of Survey Methodology*. Mahwah, N.J.: Erlbaum.

Steeh, C. and Piekarski, L. (2006). Accommodating new technologies: the rejuvenation of telephone surveys. Paper Presented at the second International Conference on Telephone Survey Methodology (TSMII), Florida.

Sudman, S., Bradburn, N.M., and Schwarz, N. (1996). *Thinking About Answers. The Application of Cognitive Processes to Survey Methodology*. San Francisco: Jossey-Bass.

Tourangeau, R., Rips, L.J., and Rasinski, K. (2000). *The Psychology of Survey Response*. Cambridge: Cambridge University Press.

Van Hattum, M.J.C. and de Leeuw, E.D. (1999). A disk by mail survey of pupils in primary schools: Data quality and logistics. *Journal of Official Statistics (JOS)*, 15, 3: 413–429. Also available at www.jos.nu (accessed June 2006).

Weisband, S. and Kiesler, S. (1996). Self disclosure on computer forms: Meta analysis and implications. *CHI '96*. Available at http://acm.org/sigchi/chi96/ proceedings/papersWeisband/sw_txt.htm (accessed July 2006).

Willis, G.B. (2004). *Cognitive Interviewing. A Tool for Improving Questionnaire Design*. Thousand Oaks: Sage.

19

Qualitative Interviewing and Feminist Research

Andrea Doucet and Natasha Mauthner

INTRODUCTION

Over the past three decades, there have been multiple intersections between feminism and the fields of methodology and epistemology. While feminist scholars initially claimed the distinctiveness of 'feminist methods,' 'feminist methodologies,' and 'feminist epistemologies,' since the 1990s they have begun to map out significant feminist contributions to these domains rather than separate fields of study *per se* (see Doucet and Mauthner 2006). Nevertheless, feminist researchers have embraced particular characteristics in their work. First, they have long advocated that feminist research should be not just *on* women, but *for* women (DeVault 1990, 1996; Edwards 1990; Fonow and Cook 1991, 2005; Ramazanoglu and Holland 2002; Reinharz 1992; Smith 1987, 1989, 1999; Stanley and Wise 1983, 1993). Second, they have advocated that feminist research should be concerned with issues of broader social change and social justice (Fonow and Cook 1991, 2005). For example, Beverly Skeggs argues that feminist research is distinct

because it 'begins from the premise that the nature of reality in western society is unequal and hierarchical' (Skeggs 1997, 77) while Ramazanoglu and Holland (2002, 2–3) note that such research 'is imbued with particular theoretical, political, and ethical concerns that make these varied approaches to social research distinctive.' Third, feminist researchers have actively engaged with methodological innovation through challenging conventional or mainstream ways of collecting, analyzing, and presenting data (Code 1995; Gelsthorpe 1990; Lather 2001; Lather and Smithies 1997; Mol 2002; Naples 2003; Richardson 1988, 1997).

In the 1970s and 1980s, many feminists questioned whether positivist frameworks and quantitative methods could adequately capture women's experiences and everyday lives (Graham 1983; Oakley 1974; Reinharz 1979; Stanley and Wise 1990). Early feminist debates tended to draw a marked distinction between qualitative and quantitative approaches with the implication that qualitative methods were quintessentially feminist (Maynard and Purvis 1994). In particular, the in-depth face-to-face interview came to be seen as 'the paradigmatic "feminist method"' (Kelly et al. 1994, 34). The equation of feminist research with qualitative methods was criticized by a number of feminists early on (e.g. Jayaratne 1983). Since then, feminists have increasingly moved away from privileging particular methodological approaches and methods. There has been recognition that research methodologies and methods should reflect the specific research questions under investigation, and that key feminist concerns can usefully be addressed by adopting a range of different approaches and methods (Brannen 1992; Chafetz 2004a, 2004b; Kelly et al. 1994; Maynard 1994; McCall 2005; Oakley 1998; Westmarland 2001).

Whilst recognizing that current feminist research is characterized by the use of multiple and mixed methods and approaches, the focus of this chapter is specifically on the ways in which feminist scholars have sought to transform the classic social science interview in line with feminist aims. Just as feminist thinking around issues of method, methodology, and epistemology have had a profound effect on research practices and theories more generally, contributions that feminist scholars have brought to the *interview* as a site for knowing from and about women's lives have been influential in re-shaping the practice and theory of qualitative interviewing more broadly.

The aim of this chapter is therefore to examine feminist debates concerning the interview as a particular method of data collection. We begin by sketching out what we regard as some key historical trends in feminist approaches to interviewing, with a particular discussion of Ann Oakley's (1981) now classic piece on the importance of non-hierarchical interviewing practices. While Oakley's contribution initially stimulated discussions around the possibilities and limitations of creating rapport and friendliness within interviews, more recent challenges from black feminism, cultural studies, post-structural and postcolonial writing have questioned the extent to which 'others' can be

known at all through interviews or, indeed, through any other method (Wilkinson and Kitzinger 1996). Our chapter also addresses the increasingly topical and critical question of how one can come to know others who are different from ourselves (such as in cross-cultural interviewing and women interviewing men) and highlights the most recent contributions of feminist scholarship to contemporary understandings of the research interview.

FEMINIST CONTRIBUTIONS TO THE INTERVIEW: 1970s AND 1980s

In the 1970s, feminist researchers began to engage with the intersections between feminist theory and methodologies, and turned their attention to the ways in which the methods available for studying and understanding women's lives were flawed. As Dorothy Smith (1974, 2) noted, there was within sociology 'a disjunction between how women find and experience the world beginning (though not necessarily ending up) from their place and the concepts and theoretical schemes available to think about it in.' Early feminist sociological theory thus pointed to how women's exclusion mattered both theoretically and methodologically. Turning their gaze to dominant methods used to generate theory, many feminist scholars expressed unease about quantitative data collection methods across the social and natural sciences and, more specifically, gender bias in the collection and interpretation of data on sex differences in behavioral, biological, and bio-behavioral scientific research. Feminist scientists documented, in particular, the exclusive use of male subjects in both experimental and clinical biomedical research, the selection of male activity and concomitant male-dominant animal populations for study, and the blatant invisibility of females in research protocols (Haraway 1988, 1991; Keller 1983, 1985; Keller and Longino 1998; Longino and Doell 1983; Rose 1994).

Whilst feminist scientists made such observations on the basis of experiments conducted on rats and baboons, similar concerns were made across the social sciences and humanities on research processes and protocols with human beings. Feminist social scientists noted how masculine bias permeated research, as perhaps best revealed in the valuing and incorporation of traditional masculine characteristics of reason, rationality, autonomy, and disconnection (see Code 1981; Gilligan 1977, 1982; Keller 1985; Lloyd 1983; Miller 1976; Smith 1974). Also within the social sciences and humanities, feminists waged a long and wide epistemological critique of positivism as a philosophical framework and its detached and 'objective' scientific approach that objectified research subjects.

Feminist scholars raised three particular concerns within this epistemological critique. First, women's lives and female-dominated domains were largely absent in much social science research. Thus when Dorothy Smith argued that 'sociology ... has been based on and built up within the male social universe' (Smith 1974, 7), this was a 'social universe' that left unstudied and invisible the female-dominated social sites of domestic work and the care of children, the ill and the elderly (see also Finch and Groves 1983; Graham 1983, 1991). Second, these sentiments were even more profoundly felt by particular groups of women, especially by women of color who watched as feminist movements and feminism within the academy unfolded in ways that did not speak to them or about them. In the United States, this sense was aptly described as one of 'feelings of craziness' by the infamous Combahee River Collective's manifesto entitled: 'A Black Feminist Statement' (Combahee River Collective 1977/1986; see also Collins 1990; Hooks 1989, 1990; Lorde 1984). In Britain, women of African and Asian descent spoke to the invisibility of their experiences in public, political, and academic portrayals of women's lives (see Bryan et al. 1985; Mirza 1998; Wilkinson and Kitzinger 1996). A third concern was over the preferred tool for research within positivist frameworks, namely, the quantitative survey, and the extent to which it could adequately capture the complexity of women's lives. As Hilary Graham

lamented, women's experiences were being measured within surveys designed on the basis of men's lives; her provocative question, posed at the beginning of the 1980s, summed up the growing dissatisfaction with surveys for understanding women's experiences: '*Do her answers fit his questions?*' (Graham 1983).

It was against this backdrop that feminist social scientists turned their attention to the possibilities and practices of interviewing. During the 1980s feminist researchers, especially those working within sociology, began to engage with the issue of how to interview in ways that would adhere to widely recognized feminist goals of conducting non-hierarchical and egalitarian research. This critique began early in the decade with Ann Oakley's now highly cited article on 'non-hierarchical' relationships between female interviewers and interviewees (Oakley 1981). Her discussion sought to provide an alternative to what were presented as 'proper interviews' in sociological textbooks. More broadly, Oakley challenged positivist research methods that emphasized 'objectivity,' distance, and 'hygienic' research uncontaminated by the researcher's values or biases. In contrast to an objective, standardized and detached approach to interviewing, Oakley argued that 'the goal of finding out about people through interviewing was best achieved when the relationship of interviewer and interviewee is non-hierarchical and when the interviewer is prepared to invest his or her own personal identity in the relationship' (1981, 41). Janet Finch (1984), writing a few years later, echoed Oakley's concerns in emphasizing the rapport that could easily be struck between two women in an interview situation while others followed suit and argued for the importance of developing mutually reciprocal relationships during the interviewing stage (Mies 1983; Rheinharz 1992; Stanley and Wise 1983, 1993).

A central preoccupation for feminist researchers writing in the 1980s was an acute sensitivity to the relations between researcher and researched, and power relations more widely (see Maynard and Purvis 1994;

Ramazanoglu and Holland 2002). In the 1990s, however, feminist social scientists began to challenge the notion of non-hierarchical interviews, the idea that power differentials could be equalized between women, as well as the assumption that reciprocity and mutuality between women necessarily leads to 'better' knowing. Indeed, feminists began to display a growing appreciation of the 'dilemmas' and tensions involved in coming to know and represent the narratives, experiences, or lives of their interview subjects (e.g. Ribbens and Edwards 1998; Willkinson and Kitzinger 1996; Wolf 1992).

Western-based social scientists have exhibited profound 'worry' over resolving these tensions (Fine and Wiess 1996, 251; see also DeVault 1999). However, the ethical dilemmas around coming to know 'others' have been particularly clearly articulated by Black feminist scholars (Lewis 2000; Mama 1995; Reynolds 2002a) and by feminists working in contexts where inequalities are especially acute, such as in low-income communities and in Third World countries (Patai 1991; Wolf 1992). One of the most vocal scholars on this issue has been Daphne Patai who has insisted that, due to socio-economic and global inequalities, research relations between First World women interviewing Third World women are not only intrinsically hierarchical, but can be unethical (Patai 1991). Questions of who produces knowledge, with what politics, and from which locations (Mohanty 1988, 1991) have, furthermore, become increasingly critical and urgent in feminist, postmodern, and post-colonial research. Throughout the 1990s, women of color working within western contexts and feminists working in Third World settings have highlighted systemic processes of exclusion, racism, and ethnocentrism in research. Key and much-debated issues have included: intersections of global capitalism and feminist transnational identities (Ferguson 2004; Schutte 1993, 1998, 2000; Shohat 2001); the extent to which feminists in dominant cultures can ever *know* subaltern cultures (Alexander and Mohanty 1997; Ladson-Billings 2000;

Mohanty et al. 1991; Oyewumi 2000; Spivak 1993); the challenges of knowing transnational lesbian and gay identities (Bunch 1987; Stone 1991); and the role and representation of subordinate 'others' in the production of knowledge (Bernal 2002; Christian 1996).

A decade after Ann Oakley's celebration of non-hierarchical woman-to-woman interviewing, and its ability to yield greater insight into knowledge of women's lives, feminist work took a 360-degree turn and began to highlight the potential dangers associated with trying to pretend that interviews could be friendly or mutually beneficial for both researchers and interviewees. Judith Stacey (1991: 114) argued that the 'ethnographic method exposes subjects to far greater danger and exploitation than do more positivist, abstract, and "masculinist" research methods. And the greater the intimacy – the greater the apparent mutuality of the researcher/researched relationship – the greater is the danger.' Pamela Cotterill (1992: 597) similarly drew attention to the 'potentially damaging effects of a research technique which encourages friendship in order to focus on very private and personal aspects of people's lives.' These criticisms have continued into the new millennium, with feminists commenting on the irony that feminist researchers may be reproducing the very practices they have been seeking to challenge:

> It is perhaps ironic, then, that scholars are discovering that methodological changes intended to achieve feminist ends—increased collaboration, greater interaction, and more open communication with research participants—may have inadvertently reintroduced some of the ethical dilemmas feminist researchers had hoped to eliminate: participants' sense of disappointment, alienation, and potential exploitation. (Kirsch 2005, 2163)

Three decades of ardent reflection on the usefulness of interviews as the most appropriate, or even the best, way of gathering knowledge from and for women have paved the way for broader theoretical and epistemological debates about 'knowing' others. Beginning in the 1990s, feminists have turned their attention to the difficulties and challenges involved in creating knowledge from interview accounts.

FEMINIST CONTRIBUTIONS TO THE INTERVIEW: RECENT ISSUES AND CONCERNS (1990s–2000s)

While the issues raised by Oakley have been critiqued and displaced with other key concerns, it remains the case that her reflections on what was important to feminist interviewing still resonate as highly relevant in the new millennium. That is, issues of non-hierarchical relations, power, rapport, and empathy, and the investment of one's identity in the interview process continue to dominate discussions of feminist research practices. However, these discussions have grown more complex and nuanced, and have incorporated a number of other concerns including: interviews as sites for collaborative meaning-making (the 'how' of interviews); the interrogation of 'what' constitutes data; and the theoretical assumptions and under-pinnings of interviews, and research methods more generally.

Non-hierarchical relations in interviewing

Underlying early discussions of non-hierarchical interviewing was the assumption that differences between women could be muted or eliminated altogether. Decades of scholarship on differences between women, postmodern and post-structural critiques of the stability of a concept and identity such as 'woman,' and black feminist contributions to this debate have revealed the naivety and essentialism inherent within this position. Many feminist researchers have shown that structural characteristics other than gender, such as differences in class, ethnicity, age, sexuality, and global location can matter and that the ways in which power imbalances play out in the interview process are not straightforward. Tang, for example, in her interviews with peers – academic mothers

in both China and the UK – argues that both the interviewer's and interviewee's *perceptions* of social, cultural, and personal differences have an impact on the power relationship in the interview and that the relational dynamics between the interview pair can matter in what kind of information is divulged (Tang 2002; see also Garg 2004). Others have focused on how other aspects of the research relationship can influence the content and conduct of interview, including: shared proficiency by both interviewer and interviewee in the language of the interview (Garg 2004; Temple and Edwards 2002); generational differences between interviewers and interviewees (Casey 2003); shared racial position (such as Black women researchers conducting interviews with Black women on topics that are highly sensitive) (Few et al. 2003); and how class relations may influence the 'telling' of lesbian stories in research interviews (McDermott 2004).

Power relations in research have been discussed with an overwhelming focus on how interviews affect the researched. Recently, however, feminists have highlighted the ways in which research respondents can exercise power, creating a two-way flow of power relations between the researcher and the researched. Informed by Fou-cauldian understandings of power, Thapar-Bjorkert and Henry (2004) view power hierarchies in research as 'shifting, multiple, and intersecting' (Thapar-Bjorkert and Henry 2004, 364). Drawing on the multiple locations within which both researchers and research participants are located, they argue that their combined locations as 'non-white/non-western and non-white/western researchers in a non-western setting' enabled them to 'closely examine the operation of power as it flows and ebbs in the context of a multiplicity of potential identities of researchers and research participants' (2004, 363). They note, in particular, how age, generation, national location, and reciprocity during and after the interviews influence how these power relations play out. Similarly, drawing on her research with Black mothers,

Reynolds (2002b) questions the notion of the 'powerful researcher.' She notes that 'the power relations between the mothers and myself, as researcher, involved a dynamic, fluid and two-way interactive process' (2002b, 303). She found that power relations within her interviews shifted according to structural differences in race, class, age, and gender between researcher and researched. She writes:

'Where the researcher and research participant share the same racial and gender position, such as Black female researcher interviewing Black women, power between the two groups is primarily negotiated through other facts such as social class and age difference. This interaction between race, class and gender suggests that power in social research is not a fixed and unitary construct, exercised by the researcher over the research participant. Instead … power is multifaceted, relational and interactional and is constantly shifting and renegotiating itself between the researcher and the research participant according to differing contexts and their differing structural locations.' (2002b, 307–8)

Feminist reflections on the inevitability of hierarchy and power differences in interview settings and relationships do not suggest or imply abandonment of this method but rather invite researchers to be reflexive about their research practices by recognizing, debating, and working with these power differentials.

Empathy, rapport, and reciprocity

Feminists have deepened their reflections on issues of empathy, rapport, and reciprocity in interview situations, with a recent focus on how to navigate differences of social positioning. Questions about how much researchers should reveal about themselves, their situations and their views during interviews have continued to be asked (see Edwards 1993), particularly in cases of research on overtly political issues where researcher and researched may hold divergent perspectives. For example, in her research in the British Serbian community on Serbian liability for atrocities, Pryke (2004) challenges the methodological convention that the interviewer must never disagree with a respondent in qualitative research.

Issues of rapport and empathy in interviewing have tended to be discussed and conceptualized in relation to woman-to-woman interviewing. However, since the 1990s, feminists have increasingly been investigating the lives of men, thus raising questions around creating empathy and rapport with male research subjects. These challenges have emerged from the work of feminist researchers who, for example, have interviewed powerful, authoritative, and uniformed men (e.g. senior police officers) or violent male offenders (Campbell 2003; Presser 2004, 2005; Taylor and Rupp 2005). Researchers of fatherhood have further explored how feminist research relationships can be fostered with men. In recent research on divorced fathers, for example, Canadian feminists have reflected on the tensions in interviewing fathers in political climates where fathers' rights groups have been gaining momentum. They highlight how fathers' narratives can be heard as potentially damaging to women's traditional caregiving interests (see Doucet 2004, 2006; Mandell 2002). Feminist research on men's experiences demonstrates how the establishment of trustworthy relations in the interviewing setting can nevertheless exist within relations of considerable power inequities and conflict that can ultimately undermine larger feminist research objectives.

Investing one's identity in the research relationship

In the early work of Ann Oakley (1981), the idea of investing one's identity in the research relationship was marked by a tendency to frame a binary opposition between the researcher as an 'insider' or an 'outsider' to the research and to one's research subjects. Oakley, and many other feminist researchers who followed her, illustrated this tendency in the argument that where the researcher has an area of shared identity with her research subjects, there was a reduced likelihood of unequal, exploitative, or unethical research. In the case of

Oakley, shared motherhood was the entry point for the researcher to have 'insider' status in the research. Other feminists were quick to contest this notion by underlining how differing, as well as shared, structural characteristics could impede mutuality and reciprocity (Coterill 1992; Edwards 1990, 1993; Glucksmann 1994; Ramazanoglu 1989; Reynolds 2002b; Ribbens 1989; Song and Parker 1995). Feminist scholars also noted that even where researchers and respondents shared structural and cultural similarities of gender, ethnicity, class, and age, this did not guarantee mutual understanding or 'better' knowing. As Catherine Riessman pointed out, 'gender and personal involvement may not be enough for full "knowing"' (Riessman 1987, 189; see also Ribbens 1998). Since the early 1990s, feminist discussions of identity investment in interviews have, thus, debunked the view that any commonality in one's social positionality, structural location, and biographical experience can guarantee that these axes of shared identification will establish an open or 'better' research exchange (see Dyck 1997).

At the same time, feminists began to recognize that the identity of being an 'insider' was riddled with contradictions and that there were varied degrees of being *both* an insider and an outsider in the research relationship (e.g. Narayan 1993; Olesen 1998; Stanley 1994; Zavella 1993). In this vein, Patricia Hill Collins has referred to herself as the 'outsider within' (Hill Collins 1990, 1998) as a way of describing 'being on the edge' of 'intersecting power relations of race, gender and social class' (Hill Collins 1999, 85; see also Anzaldua 1987; Braidotti 1994). Furthermore, post-structuralist discussions of the complexity of the theoretical concepts and empirical constructs of subjectivity and identity have further strengthened the problematization of what it means to be an insider or an outsider, both theoretically and methodologically.

Two key issues have come to the fore in these debates. First, there is now fairly widespread consensus among feminists that '"outsiderness" and "insiderness" are not

fixed or static positions; rather they are ever-shifting and permeable social locations that are differentially experienced or expressed by community members' (Naples 2003, 373; see also Naples 1996). Ongoing reflections on the complexities of 'otherness' have highlighted the increasing set of challenges that face researchers as they attempt to know others who are different from themselves across multiples axes of identities and experiences (see Fawcett and Hearn 2004).

Second, the question of *who we are*, while engaged concretely in the practice of research interviews, is also viewed as neither unitary nor static. Shlulamit Reinharz, for example, in a book chapter entitled 'Who Am I,' reflects upon how she has 'approximately 20 different selves' (Reinharz 1997, 5) during her interviews and fieldwork. Recent feminist contributions to this debate have highlighted how the interview topics as well as the relational dynamics occurring in the research encounter influence *how we present ourselves* and *which parts of our identity we choose to emphasize*. Some researchers may adopt 'in-between positions' as they straddle different identities (Ghorashi 2005) while others have stressed the 'border-making process that occurs during the social constructionist interview' wherein 'various pre-assumed roles are created by researchers and by their respondents' (Gubrium and Koro-Ljungberg 2005, 690).

Interviews and an interrogation of 'what' constitutes data

Feminist researchers have also interrogated just 'what' emerges out of interview data. In the 1970s and 1980s, there was a tendency for feminist researchers, particularly those influenced by feminist standpoint theory (Harding 1987; Hartsock 1983, 1985; Smith 1987), to talk and write about seemingly coherent and transparent subjects whose experiences, voices, or subjectivities could be captured by well-formulated research questions. Going back to Hilary Graham's point about 'her answers' not fitting 'his questions,' there was an implicit assumption that if the questions could just be reformulated *better*, then 'her answers' would indeed provide pathways into understanding women's experiences. In ensuing years, however, the influence of postmodern and post-structural critiques has meant that feminists have begun to strongly challenge this view. Researchers have named this as the recurring 'transparent self problem' and the 'transparent account problem' (Hollway and Jefferson 2000, 3; see also Frith and Kitzinger 1998, 304–307) within interviews and their analysis.

An extensive scholarship on post-structuralist conceptualizations of subjects is now well incorporated into feminist research and feminist approaches to the interview. Most notable has been post-structural theorizing about a non-unitary, constantly changing subject where there is no 'core self' (e.g. Weedon 1987). Even feminist scholars who have been critical of post-structuralist approaches have been influenced by such critiques. Sandra Harding, for example, has moved beyond her originally narrow conception of a feminist standpoint to argue that 'the subjects of knowledge are … multiple, heterogeneous and contradictory or incoherent' (Harding 1993, 65). Other scholars have remained unconvinced by the linguistic turn and have continued to hold onto some notion of coherent subjectivities, or to 'knowing subjects' in their interviewing, as well as knowledge-construction practices (see Code 1993; Smith 1999; Stanley 1994). Dorothy Smith, for example, has argued persuasively that post-structuralism 'has rejected the unitary subject of modernity only to multiply it as subjects constituted in multiple and fragmented discourses' (Smith 1999, 108) while Linda Alcoff has maintained: 'Poststructuralist critiques pertain to the construction of *all* subjects or they pertain to none' (Alcoff 1988, 409). These debates on 'who' or 'what' is being accessed within interviews have continued in discussion of feminist research into the new millennium against a backdrop of larger theoretical work on post-structuralist and materialist/interpretivist conceptions of the subject (see Benhabib

1995; Butler 1995; Fraser and Nicholson 1988; Weeks 1998), debates on theorizing the concept of 'experience' (Holt 1994; Scott 1992, 1994) as well as feminist critiques of Foucault's varied conceptions of the subject (Deveaux 1994; McNay 1993; Sawicki 1991).

Interviews as collaborative meaning-making: The 'how' of interviews

Feminists, particularly those influenced by ethnomethodology, have highlighted the importance of the interview not only as a place to collect data, but also a site where data is co-constructed, where identities are forged through the telling of stories, and where meaning-making begins. Researchers have focused on how the research interview has particularly strong meanings for the research participant (Hiller and DiLuzio 2004; see also Brannen 1988). The research interview can be a site for the construction of one's 'moral' identity (Presser 2004) as well as a potential avenue for resistance and healing when topics are of a sensitive nature (Taylor 2002). In Presser's qualitative work with men who had committed 'serious violent crimes, including crimes again women – rape of girls and women and assault and murder of female partners' (2005, 2067), she examines how the interview itself acted as a context for the creation of men's narratives and their identities. Reflecting on her role as a researcher in these settings, she highlights how the men she interviewed presented themselves as 'good and manly' and 'decent' while simultaneously constructing her, the researcher, both as somebody 'needing strength and guidance concerning relations with men' as well as 'an object of fantasies of domination' (2005, 2086). Presser, thus, argues that feminist researchers need to pay closer attention to how power relations within the interview setting can become part of one's data and she calls for a 'close and deep (multilevel) examination of the "how" of talk and not just the "what'" (2005, 2087).

These issues have also received considerable attention in the expanding literature on focus groups. Focus group, or groups interviews, have come to be viewed as important ways of breaking down hierarchies between the interviewer and the interviewees, of providing insights into group-based discussion, and for allowing an interactive forum for negotiation around concepts and issues (see Doucet 2006; Frith and Kitzinger 1998; Kitzinger 1994; Munday 2006; Warr 2005; Wilkinson 1999). Kitzinger (1994, 119), for example, maintains that the interactive nature of group interviews 'enables the researcher to … explore how accounts are constructed, expressed, censured, opposed and changed though social interaction.' Hyams (2004), who utilized a 'feminist group discussion method' in her research on adolescent Latina gender identities noted that '(g)roup discussions are seen as potentially empowering in exploring and enabling group members' social agency and knowledge production while at the same time diminishing the unequal power relations between the researched and researcher.' A further example of the links between feminist research ideals and group interviews is in Pini's work (2002) on the Australian sugar industry where she argues that the effectiveness of focus groups for reaching feminist research goals can be demonstrated in at least four ways. These include: making visible to women that which was previously invisible; enabling connections between individual and collective experiences; challenging dominant beliefs; and allowing a space for ample discussion about gender issues (see also Wahab 2003). Others have argued for the complementarities of individual and group-based interviews (Pollack 2003; Wahab 2003). Given that a fundamental aim of feminist research has always been that of social change for women, focus groups have served the function of eliciting a rich dataset which can simultaneously complement individual interviews while also potentially facilitating 'consciousness raising' (see Wilkinson 1999).

Research methods as theoretical issues

While early feminist discussions of issues of identity, reciprocity, and power focused on the initial research stages, more recent feminist discussions have highlighted how these issues pervade the entire research endeavor, and particularly the post-interview processes of data analysis, writing up and dissemination. As Harrison writes: 'Every stage of the research process relies on our negotiating complex social situations' (Harrison et al. 2001, 323). For example, feminists have drawn attention to the ways in which race, class, and gender intersect during data analysis (Archer 2002); the influence of biographical and theoretical issues on the analysis and interpretation of interview transcripts (Mauthner and Doucet 1998, 2003); and the diverse ways in which interview stories can be presented and re-told (McCormack 2004; M. Wolf 1992).

These reflections serve to underline the ways in which power relations continue to shape the research process long after interviews have been completed. Feminists have noted that researchers and respondents have a 'different and unequal relation to knowledge' (Glucksmann 1994, 150) and that within most research projects, 'the final shift of power between the researcher and the respondent is balanced in favor of the researcher, for it is she who eventually walks away' (Cotterill 1992, 604; see also Reinharz 1992; Stacey 1991; Wolf 1992). We have argued that when interview accounts or narratives become 'transformed' into theory, the later stages of analysis, interpretation, and writing up are critical to feminist concerns with power, exploitation, knowing and representation (Doucet and Mauthner 2002; Mauthner and Doucet 1998, 2003; see also Glucksmann 1994). Researchers have also reflected on the dilemmas and power issues involved when contradictions arise between interviewer interpretations and interviewee understandings of their own stories (see Andrews 2002; Borland 1991; Ribbens 1994).

The move away from an overwhelming focus on the interview setting, to what happens after the interview is completed, transcribed, analyzed, and written up has meant that the issue of power in interviewing has shifted from the question of *whether* there are power inequalities between researchers and respondents, to consider *how, when, and where* power influences knowledge production and construction processes. These reflections on negotiating research relationships in the post-interview phase of research are part of a larger set of methodological and epistemological conversations on the intricate connections between 'doing and knowing' (Lather 2001; Letherby 2003, 2004) and on the critical ways in which methods, methodologies, and epistemologies are linked through all stages of the research process (e.g. Code 1995; Holland and Ramazanoglu 1994; Maynard 1994; Naples 2003; Ramazanoglu and Holland 2002). These feminist debates have highlighted how research methods are imbued with methodological, epistemological, and ontological assumptions that impact on the later interpretive stages of the research in terms of how and what knowledge gets constructed from them. As Jennifer Mason (2002, 225) writes, 'Asking, listening and interpretation are *theoretical projects* in the sense that how we ask questions, what we assume is possible from asking questions and from listening to answers, and what kind of knowledge we hear answers to be, are all ways in which we express, pursue and satisfy our theoretical orientations in our research.'

CONCLUSIONS

In 1990, feminist theorists and researchers Liz Stanley and Sue Wise (1990, 37) noted that 'feminist theorists have moved away from the "reactive" stance of the feminist critiques of social science and into the realms of exploring what "feminist knowledge" could look like.' Part of this task of generating feminist knowledge, and social science knowledge more generally, relates to the widely acknowledged contributions that feminist researchers have made to the theory and practice of qualitative research (see, for example, DeVault 1999; Hesse-Biber and Yaiser 2004; Olesen 1998, 2005; Stanley and Wise 1983, 1990, 1993). The issue of interviewing as a way of coming to know others and to construct knowledge about them has been a recurrent theme of debate for all qualitative researchers. As discussed in this chapter, it has also been a subject that has had particular salience for feminist scholars. Beginning with Ann Oakley's classic piece over two decades ago which argued that 'the goal of finding out about people through interviewing is best achieved when the relationship of interviewer and interviewee is non-hierarchical' (1981, 41), this chapter has traced some of the key feminist contributions to the theory and practice of interviewing over the past quarter century. While discussion initially focused on the potential and pitfalls of attempting to create rapport and friendliness within interviews, more recent challenges from cultural studies, post-structural sensibilities, and postcolonial writing have unsettled the idea that 'others' can be known through interviews or indeed through any method.

This chapter has also highlighted the most recent contributions of feminist scholarship to contemporary understandings of the research interview. These contributions include: attempts to render more complex earlier debates on non-hierarchical interviewing; empathy, rapport, reciprocity, and the investing of one's identity in the research relationship; interviews as sites for collaborative meaning-making (the 'how' of interviews); the interrogation of 'what' constitutes data; and the theoretical assumptions and underpinnings of interviews, and research methods more generally. Feminist scholars, due to their overarching focus on issues of power and a quest to dismantle systemic inequalities within social relationships more widely, have made – and will continue to make – important and rich contributions to the practice of interviewing as well as to the field of qualitative methods and methodologies more generally.

REFERENCES

Alcoff, Linda Martin. 1988. 'Cultural Feminism Versus Post-Structuralism: The Identity Crisis in Feminist Theory.' *Signs: Journal of Women in Culture and Society* 13: 405–436.

Alexander, Jackie and Chandra Talpede Mohanty. 1997. *Feminist Genealogies, Colonial Legacies, Democratic Futures.* New York: Routledge.

Andrews, Molly. 2002. 'Feminist Research with Non-Feminist and Anti-Feminist Women: Meeting the Challenge.' *Feminism and Psychology* 12: 55–77.

Anzaldua, Gloria. 1987. *Borderlands/La Frontera: The New Mestiza.* San Francisco: Spinsters/Aunt Lute.

Archer, Louise. 2002. '"It's Easier That You're a Girl and That You're Asian": Interactions of "Race" and Gender Between Researchers and Participants.' *Feminist Review* 72: 108–132.

Benhabib, Seyla. 1995. 'Feminism and Postmodernism.' In *Feminist Contentions: A Philosophical Exchange*, edited by S. Benhabib, J. Butler, D. Cornell, and N. Fraser. New York and London: Routledge.

Bernal, Dolores Delgado. 2002. 'Critical Race Theory, Latino Critical Theory, and Critical Raced-Gendered Epistemologies: Recognizing Students of Color as Holders and Creators of Knowledge.' *Qualitative Inquiry* 8: 105–126.

Borland, Katherine. 1991. '"That's Not What I Said": Interpretive Conflict in Oral Narrative Research.' pp. 63–75 in *Women's Words: The Feminist Practice of Oral History*, edited by S. B. Gluck and D. Patai. New York: Routledge.

Braidotti, Rosi. 1994. *Nomadic Subjects: Embodiment and Sexual Difference in Contemporary Feminist Theory.* New York: Columbia University Press.

Brannen, Julia. 1988. 'Research Note: The Study of Sensitive Subjects.' *The Sociological Review* 36: 552–563.

Brannen, Julia. 1992. 'Combining Qualitative and Quantitative Approaches: An Overview.' pp. 3–37 in *Mixing Methods: Qualitative and Quantitate Approaches*, edited by J. Brannen. Avebury: Aldershot.

Bryan, Beverly, Stella Dadzie, and Suzanne Scafe. 1985. *The Heart of the Race: Black Women's Lives in Britain.* London: Virago.

Bunch, Charlotte. 1987. *Passionate Politics: Feminist Theory in Action.* New York: St. Martin's Press.

Butler, Judith. 1995. 'Contingent Foundations.' In *Feminist Contentions: A Philosophical Exchange*, edited by S. Benhabib, J. Butler, D. Cornell, and N. Fraser. New York and London: Routledge.

Campbell, Elaine. 2003. 'Interviewing Men in Uniform: a Feminist Approach?' *International Journal of Social Research Methodology* 6: 285–305.

Casey, Emma. 2003. '"How do You Get a Ph.D. in That?" Using Feminist Epistemologies to Research the Lives of Working Class Women.' *International Journal of Sociology and Social Policy* 23: 107–123.

Chafetz, Janet Saltzman. 2004a. 'Bridging Feminist Theory and Research Methodology.' *Journal of Family Issues* 25: 963–977.

Chafetz, Janet Saltzman. 2004b. 'Reply to Comments by Walker, Baber, and Allen.' *Journal of Family Issues* 25: 995–997.

Christian, Barbara. 1996. 'The Race for Theory.' In *Contemporary Postcolonial Theory: a Reader*, edited by M. Padmini. New York: Arnold.

Code, Lorraine. 1981. 'Is the Sex of the Knower Epistemologically Significant?' *Metaphilosophy* 12: 267–276.

Code, Lorraine. 1993. 'Taking Subjectivity into Account.' In *Feminist Epistemologies*, edited by L. Alcoff and E. Potter. New York and London: Routledge.

Code, Lorraine. 1995. 'How Do We Know? Questions of Method in Feminist Practice.' In *Changing Methods: Feminists Transforming Practice*, edited by S. D. Burt and L. Code. Peterborough: Broadview.

Collins, Patricia Hill. 1990. *Black Feminist Thought: Knowledge, Consciousness, and the Politics of Empowerment.* London and New York: Routledge.

Collins, Patricia Hill. 1998. *Fighting Words: Black Women and the Search for Justice.* Minneapolis: University of Minnesota Press.

Collins, Patricia Hill. 1999. 'Reflections on the Outsider Within.' *Journal of Career Development* 26: 85–88.

Combahee River Collective. 1977. 'A Black Feminist Statement.' In *Capitalist Patriarchy and the Case for Social Feminism*, edited by Z. Eisenstein.

Cotterill, Pamela. 1992. 'Interviewing Women: Issues of Friendship, Vulnerability, and Power.' *Women's Studies International Forum* 15: 593–606.

DeVault, Marjorie L. 1990. 'Talking and Listening from Women's Standpoint: Feminist Strategies for Interviewing and Analysis.' *Social Problems* 37: 96–116.

DeVault, Marjorie L. 1996. 'Talking Back to Sociology: Distinctive Contributions of Feminist Methodology.' *Annual Review of Sociology* 22: 29–50.

DeVault, Marjorie. 1999. *Liberating Method: Feminism and Social Research.* Philadelphia, PA: Temple University Press.

Deveaux, Monique. 1994. 'Feminism and Empowerment: A Critical Reading of Foucault.' *Feminist Studies* 20: 223–247.

Doucet, Andrea. 2004. 'Fathers and the Responsibility for Children: A Puzzle and a Tension.' *Atlantis: A Women's Studies Journal* 28: 103–114.

Doucet, Andrea. 2006. *Do Men Mother? Fathering, Care and Domestic Responsibility*. Toronto: University of Toronto Press.

Doucet, Andrea and Natasha S. Mauthner. 2002. 'Knowing Responsibly: Linking Ethics, Research Practice and Epistemology.' In *Ethics in Qualitative Research*, edited by M. Mauthner, M. Birch, J. Jessop, and T. Miller. London: Sage.

Doucet, Andrea and Natasha S. Mauthner. 2006. 'Feminist Methodologies and Epistemologies.' In *Handbook of 21st Century Sociology*, edited by Clifton D. Bryant and Dennis L. Peck. Thousand Oaks, CA: Sage.

Dyck, Isabel. 1997. 'Dialogue with Difference: A Tale of Two Studies.' pp. 183–202 in *Thresholds in Feminist Geography: Difference, Methodology, Representation*, edited by J. P. I. Jones, H. Nast, and S. M. Roberts. Lanham, MD: Rowman and Littlefield.

Edwards, Rosalind. 1990. 'Connecting Method and Epistemology: A White Woman Interviewing Black Women.' *Women's Studies International Forum* 13: 477–490.

Edwards, Rosalind. 1993. 'An Education in Interviewing: Placing the Researcher and the Researched.' In *Researching Sensitive Topics*, vol. 181–196, edited by C. M. Renzetti and R. M. Lee. Newbury Park: Sage.

Fawcett, Barbara and Jedd Hearn. 2004. 'Researching Others: Epistemology, Experience, Standpoints and Participation.' *International Journal of Social Research Methodology* 7: 201–218.

Ferguson, Ann. 2004. 'Symposium: Comments on Ofelia Schutte's Work on Feminist Philosophy.' *Hypatia* 19: 169–181.

Few, April L., Dionne P. Stephens, and Marlo Rouse-Arnett. 2003. 'Sister-to-Sister Talk: Transcending Boundaries and Challenges in Qualitative Research with Black Women.' *Family Relations* 52: 205–215.

Finch, Janet. 1984. '"It's Great to Have Someone to Talk to": The Ethics and Politics of Interviewing Women.' In *Social Researching: Politics, Problems, Practice*, edited by C. Bell and H. Roberts. London: Routledge and Kegan Paul.

Finch, Janet and Dulcie Groves. 1983. *A Labour of Love: Women, Work and Caring*. London: Routledge.

Fine, Michelle and Lois Wiess. 1996. '"Writing the Wrongs' of Fieldwork: Confronting our Own Research/Writing Dilemmas."* Qualitative Inquiry* 2: 251–274.

Fonow, Mary M. and Judith A. Cook. 1991. *Beyond Methodology: Feminist Scholarship as Lived Research*. Bloomington: Indiana University Press.

Fonow, Mary M. and Judith A. Cook. 2005. 'Feminist Methodology: New Applications in the Academy and Public Policy.' *Signs: Journal of Women in Culture and Society* 30: 2211–2236.

Fraser, Nancy and Linda Nicholson. 1988. 'Social Criticism without Philosophy: An Encounter between Feminism and Postmodernism.' *Theory, Culture and Society* 5: 373–394.

Frith, Hannah and Celia Kitzinger. 1998. '"Emotion Work" as a Participant Resource: A Feminist Analysis of Young Women's Talk-in-interaction.' *Sociology* 32: 299–320.

Garg, Anupama. 2004. 'Interview Reflections: A First Generation Migrant Indian Woman Researcher Interviewing a First Generation Migrant Indian Man.' *Journal of Gender Studies* 14: 147–152.

Gelsthorpe, Lorraine. 1990. 'Feminist Methodology in Criminology: A New Approach or Old Wine in New Bottles.' In *Feminist Perspectives in Criminology*, edited by L. Gelsthorpe and A. Morris. Milton Keynes: Open University Press.

Ghorashi, Halleh. 2005. 'When the Boundaries are Blurred: The Significance of Feminist Methods in Research.' *European Journal of Women's Studies* 12: 363–375.

Gilligan, Carol. 1977. 'In a Different Voice: Psychological Theory and Women's Development.' *Harvard Educational Review* 47: 481–517.

Gilligan, Carol. 1982. *In a Different Voice: Psychological Theory and Women's Development*. Cambridge, Mass.: Harvard University Press.

Glucksmann, Miriam. 1994. 'The Work of Knowledge and the Knowledge of Women's Work.' In *Researching Women's Lives from a Feminist Perspective*, edited by M. Maynard and J. Purvis. London: Taylor and Francis.

Graham, Hilary. 1983. 'Do Her Answers Fit His Questions? Women and the Survey Method.' In *The Public and the Private*, edited by E. Gamarnikow. London: Tavistock.

Graham, Hilary. 1991. 'The Concept of Caring in Feminist Research: The Case of Domestic Service.' *Sociology* 25: 61–78.

Gubrium, Erika and Mirka Koro-Ljungberg. 2005. 'Contending with Border Making in the Social Constructionist Interview.' *Qualitative Inquiry* 11: 689–715.

Haraway, Donna. 1988. 'Situated Knowledges: The Science Question in Feminism and the Privilege of Partial Perspective.' *Feminist Studies* 14: 575–599.

Haraway, Donna. 1991. *Simians, Cyborgs and Women: The Reinvention of Nature*. New York: Routledge.

Harding, Sandra. 1987. 'Conclusion: Epistemological Questions.' pp. 181–190 in *Feminsm and Methodology*, edited by S. Harding. Bloomington, Indiana and Milton Keynes, UK: Indiana University Press and Open University Press.

Harding, Sandra. 1993. 'Rethinking Standpoint Epistemologies: What is Strong Objectivity.' In *Feminist Epistemologies*, edited by L. Alcoff and E. Potter. London: Routledge.

Harrison, Jane, Lesley MacGibbon, and Missy Morton. 2001. 'Regimes of Trustworthiness in Qualitative Research: The Rigors of Reciprocity.' *Qualitative Inquiry* 7: 323–345.

Hartsock, Nancy. 1983. 'The Feminist Standpoint: Developing the Ground for a Specifically Feminist Historical Materialism.' In *Discovering Reality: Feminist Perspectives on Epistemology, Metaphysics, Methodology and Philosophy of Science*, edited by S. Harding and M. Hintakka. Dordrecht: D. Reidel Publishing.

Hartsock, Nancy. 1985. *Money, Sex and Power: Toward a Feminist Historical Materialism*. Boston: Northeastern University Press.

Hesse-Biber, Sharlene Nagy, and Michelle L. Yaiser. 2004. *Feminist Perspectives on Social Research*. New York and London: Oxford University Press.

Hiller, Harry H. and Linda DiLuzio. 2004. 'The Interviewee and the Research Interview: Analysing a Neglected Dimension in Research.' *The Canadian Review of Sociology and Anthropology* 41: 1–26.

Holland Janet and Caroline Ramazanoglu. 1994. 'Coming to Conclusions: Power and Interpretation in Researching Young Women's Sexuality.' pp. 125–148 in *Researching Women's Lives from a Feminist Perspective*, edited by M. Maynard and J. Purvis. London: Taylor and Francis.

Hollway Wendy and Toni Jefferson. 2000. *Doing Qualitative Research Differently: Free Association, Narrative and the Interview Method*. London: Sage.

Holt, Thomas A. 1994. 'Experience and the Politics of Intellectual Inquiry.' In *Questions of Evidence: Proof, Practice and Persuasion across the Disciplines*, edited by J. Chandler, A. I. Davidson, and H. Harootunian. Chicago: University of Chicago Press.

Hooks, Bell. 1989. *Talking Back: Thinking Feminist, Thinking Black*. Boston: South End Press.

Hooks, Bell. 1990. *Yearning: Race, Gender and Cultural Politics*. Boston: South End Press.

Hyams, Melissa. 2004. 'Hearing Girls' Silences: Thoughts on the Politics and Practices of a Feminist Method of Group Discussion.' *Gender, Place and Culture* 11: 105–119.

Jayaratne, T. E. 1983. 'The Value of Quantitative Methodology for Feminist Research.' In *Theories of Women's Studies*, edited by G. Bowles and R. Duelli-Klein. London: Routledge and Kegan Paul.

Keller, Evelyn Fox. 1983. *A Feeling for the Organism: The Life and Work of Barbara McClintock*. New York: W.H. Freeman.

Keller, Evelyn Fox. 1985. *Reflections of Gender and Science*. New Haven and London: Yale University Press.

Keller, Evelyn Fox and Helen E. Longino. 1998. 'Feminism and Science.' Oxford and New York: Oxford University Press.

Kelly, Liz, Sheila Burton, and Linda Regan. 1994. 'Researching Women's Lives or Studying Women's Oppression? Reflections on what Constitutes Feminist Research.' pp. 27–48 in *Researching Women's Lives from a Feminist Perspective*, edited by M. Maynard and J. Purvis. London: Taylor and Francis.

Kirsch, Gesa E. 2005. 'Friendship, Friendliness, and Feminist Fieldwork.' *Signs: Journal of Women in Culture and Society* 30: 2163–2172.

Kitzinger, Jenny. 1994. 'The Methodology of Focus Groups: The Importance of Interaction between Research Participants. *Sociology of Health & Illness* 16(1): 103–121.

Ladson-Billings, G. 2000. 'Racialized Discourses and Ethnic Epistemologies.' pp. 257–277 in *Handbook of Qualitative Research*, 2nd edition, edited by N. K. Denzin and Y. S. Lincoln. Thousand Oaks, CA: Sage.

Lather, Patti. 2001. 'Postbook: Working the Ruins of Feminist Ethnography.' *Signs* 27: 199–227.

Lather, Patti and Chris Smithies. 1997. *Troubling the Angels: Women Living with HIV/AIDS*. Boulder, CO: Westview.

Letherby, Gayle. 2003. *Feminist Research in Theory and Practice*. Buckingham: Open University Press.

Letherby, Gayle. 2004. 'Quoting and Counting: An Autobiographical Response to Oakley.' *Sociology* 38: 157–189.

Lewis, Gail. 2000. *'Race,' Gender and Social Welfare*. London: Polity Press.

Lloyd, Genevieve. 1983. *Man of Reason*. London: Routledge.

Longino, Helen E. and Ruth Doell. 1983. 'Body, Bias, and Behaviour: A Comparative Analysis of Reasoning in Two Areas of Biological Science.' *Signs: Journal of Women in Culture and Society* 9: 206–227.

Lorde, Audre. 1984. *Sister Outsider: Essays and Speeches*. Berkeley, California: The Crossing Press.

Mama, Amina. 1995. *Beyond the Mask: Race, Gender and Subjectivity*. London: Routledge.

Mandell, Deena. 2002. *Deadbeat Dads: Subjectivity and Social Construction*. Toronto: University of Toronto Press.

Mason, Jennifer. 2002. 'Qualitative Interviewing: Asking, Listening and Interpreting.' pp. 225–241 in *Qualitative Research in Action*, edited by T. May. London: Sage Publications.

Mauthner, Natasha S. and Andrea Doucet. 1998. 'Reflections on a Voice Centred Relational Method of Data Analysis: Analysing Maternal and Domestic Voices.' In *Feminist Dilemmas in Qualitative Research: Private Lives and Public Texts*, edited by J. Ribbens and R. Edwards. London: Sage Publications.

Mauthner, Natasha S. and Andrea Doucet. 2003. 'Reflexive Accounts and Accounts of Reflexivity in Qualitative Data Analysis.' *Sociology* 37: 413–431.

Maynard, Mary. 1994. 'Methods, Practice and Epistemology: the Debate about Feminism and Research.' pp. 10–26 in *Researching Women's Lives from a Feminist Perspective*, edited by M. Maynard and J. Purvis. London: Taylor and Francis.

Maynard, Mary and June Purvis. 1994. *Researching Women's Lives from a Feminist Perspective*. London: Taylor and Francis.

McCall, Leslie. 2005. 'The Complexity of Intersectionality.' *Signs: Journal of Women in Culture and Society* 30: 1771–1799.

McCormack, Coralie. 2004. 'Storying Stories: A Narrative Approach to In-Depth Interview Conversations.' *International Journal of Social Research Methodology* 7(3): 219–236.

McDermott, Elizabeth. 2004. 'Telling Lesbian Stories: Interviewing and the Class Dynamics of 'Talk'.' *Women's Studies International Forum* 27: 177–187.

McNay, Lois. 1993. *Foucault and Feminism: Power, Gender and the Self*. Boston, MA: Northeastern University Press.

Mies. M. 1983. 'Towards a Methodology for Feminist Research.' In *Theories of Women's Studies*, edited by G. Bowles and R. Duelli Klein. London: Routledge and Kegan Paul.

Miller, Jean Baker. 1976. *Towards a New Psychology of Women*. London: Penguin Books.

Mirza, Heidi Safia. 1998. *Black British Feminism: A Reader*. London: Routledge.

Mohanty, Chandra Talpede. 1988. 'Under Western Eyes: Feminist Scholarship and Colonial Discourses.' *Feminist Review* 30: 61–88.

Mohanty, Chandra Talpede. 1991. 'Under Western Eyes: Feminism and Colonial Discourse.' In *Third World Women and the Politics of Feminism*, edited by C. T. Mohanty, A. Russo, and L. Torres. Bloomington: Indiana University Press.

Mohanty, Chandra Talpede, Ann Russo, and Lourdes Torres. 1991. *'Third World Women and the Politics of Feminism.'* Bloomington: Indiana University Press.

Mol, Annemarie. 2002. *The Body Multiple: Ontology in Medical Practice*. Durham, NC: Duke University Press.

Munday, Jennie. 2006. 'Identity in Focus: The Use of Focus Groups to Study the Construction of Collective Identity.' *Sociology* 40: 89–105.

Naples, Nancy A. 1996. 'A Feminist Revisiting of the 'Insider/Outsider' Debate: The 'Outsider Phenomenon' in Rural Iowa.' *Qualitative Sociology* 19: 83–106.

Naples, Nancy A. 2003. *Feminism and Method: Ethnography, Discourse Analysis, and Activist Research*. New York and London: Routledge.

Narayan, Kiran. 1993. 'How Native is a 'Native' Anthropologist?' *American Anthropologist* 95: 671–686.

Oakley, Ann. 1974. *Housewife*. London: Allen Lane.

Oakley, Ann. 1981. 'Interviewing Women: A Contradiction in Terms.' pp. 30–61 in *Doing Feminist Research*, edited by H. Roberts. London: Routledge and Kegan Paul.

Oakley, Ann. 1998. 'Gender, Methodology and People's Ways of Knowing: Some Problems with Feminism and the Paradigm Debate in Social Science.' *Sociology* 32: 707–731.

Olesen, Virgina. 1998. 'Feminism and Models of Qualitative Research.' In *The Landscape of Qualitative Research: Theories and Issues*, edited by N. K. Denzin and Y. S. Lincoln. Thousand Oaks, California: Sage.

Olesen, Virgina. 2005. 'Early Millennial Feminist Qualitative Research.' pp. 235–278 in *The Sage Handbook of Qualitative Research*, edited by N. K. Denzin and Y. S. Lincoln. Thousand Oaks, CA: Sage.

Oyewumi, Oyeronke. 2000. 'Family Bonds/Conceptual Binds: African Notes on Feminist Epistemologies.' *Signs: Journal of Women in Culture and Society* 25: 1093–1098.

Patai, Daphne. 1991. 'U.S. Academics and Third World Women: Is Ethical Research Possible?' pp. 137–153 in *Women's Words: The Feminist Practice of Oral History*, edited by S. B. Gluck and D. Patai. New York: Routledge.

Pini, Barbara. 2002. 'Focus Groups, Feminist Research and Farm Women: Opportunities for Empowerment in Rural Social Research.' *Journal of Rural Studies* 18: 339–351.

Pollack, Shoshana. 2003. 'Focus-Group Methodology in Research with Incarcerated Women: Race, Power, and collective experience.' *Affilia* 18: 461–472.

Presser, Lois. 2004. 'Violent Offenders, Moral Selves: Constructing Identities and Accounts in the Research Interview.' *Social Problems* 51: 82–101.

Presser, Lois. 2005. 'Negotiating Power and Narrative in Research: Implications for Feminist Methodology.' *Signs: Journal of Women in Culture and Society* 30: 2067–2090.

Pryke, Sam. 2004. '"Some of Our People Can Be the Most Difficult." Reflections on Difficult Interviews.' *Sociological Research Online* 9.

Ramazanoglu, Caroline. 1989. 'Improving on Sociology: The Problems of Taking a Feminist Standpoint.' *Sociology* 23: 427–442.

Ramazanoglu, Caroline and Janet Holland. 2002. *Feminist Methodology: Challenges and Choices.* London: Sage Publications.

Reinharz, Shulamit. 1979. *On Becoming a Social Scientist.* San Francisco: Jossey-Bass.

Reinharz, Shulamit. 1992. *Feminist Methods in Social Research.* Oxford: Oxford University Press.

Reinharz, Shulamit. 1997. 'Who Am I? The Need for a Variety of Selves in the Field.' pp. 3–20 in *Refelxivity and Voice,* edited by R. Hertz. Thousand Oaks, CA: Sage.

Reynolds, Tracey. 2002a. 'Re-thinking a Black Feminist Standpoint.' *Ethnic and Racial Studies* 25: 591–606.

Reynolds, Tracy. 2002b. 'On Relations Between Black Female Researchers and Participants.' pp. 300–310 in *Qualitative Research in Action,* edited by T. May. London: Sage Publications.

Ribbens, Jane. 1989. 'Interviewing – an Unnatural Situation?' *Women's Studies International Forum* 12: 579–592.

Ribbens, Jane. 1994. *Mothers and their Children.* London: Sage.

Ribbens, Jane. 1998. 'Hearing my Feeling Voice? An Autobiographical Discussion of Motherhood.' pp. 24–38 in *Feminist Dilemmas in Qualitative Research: Private Lives and Public Texts,* edited by J. Ribbens and E. Rosalind. London: Sage.

Ribbens, Jane and Rosalind Edwards. 1998. *Feminist Dilemmas in Qualitative Research: Private Lives and Public Texts.* London: Sage.

Richardson, Laurel. 1988. 'The Collective Story: Post-modernism and the Writing of Sociology.' *Sociological Focus* 21: 199–208.

Richardson, Laurel. 1997. *Fields of Play: Constructing an Academic Life.* New Brunswick, NJ: Rutgers University Press.

Riessman, Catherine. 1987. 'When Gender is not Enough: Women Interviewing Women.' *Gender and Society* 1: 172–207.

Rose, Hilary. 1994. *Love, Power and Knowledge: Towards a Feminist Transformation of the Sciences.* Cambridge: Polity Press.

Sawicki, Jana. 1991. *Disciplining Foucault: Feminism, Power and the Body.* New York: Routledge.

Schutte, Ofelia. 1993. *Cultural Identity and Social Liberation in Latin American Thought.* Albany: Suny Press.

—— 1998. 'Cultural Alterity: Cross-Cultural Communication and Feminist Thought in North-South Dialogue.' *Hypatia* 13: 53–72.

—— 2000. 'Negotiating Latina Identities.' In *Hispanics/Latinos in the United States: Ethnicity, Race and Rights,* edited by J. E. Gracia and P. De Grief. London: Routledge.

Scott, Joan W. 1992. 'Experience.' pp. 22–40 in *Feminists Theorize the Political,* edited by J. Butler and J. W. Scott. London: Routledge.

Scott, Joan W. 1994. 'A Rejoinder to Thomas C. Holt.' In *Questions of Evidence: Proof, Practice and Persuasion across the Disciplines,* edited by J. Chandler, A. I. Davidson, and H. Harootunian. Chicago: University of Chicago Press.

Shohat, Ella. 2001. 'Area Studies, Transnationalism and the Feminist Production of Knowledge.' *Signs: Journal of Women in Culture and Society* 26: 1269–1272.

Skeggs, Beverley. 1997. *Formations of Class and Gender.* London: Sage.

Smith, Dorothy. 1974. 'Women's Perspective as a Radical Critique of Sociology.' *Sociological Inquiry* 4: 1–13.

Smith, Dorothy. 1987. *The Everyday World as Problematic: A Feminist Sociology.* Milton Keynes, UK: Open University Press.

Smith, Dorothy. 1989. 'Sociological Theory: Methods of Writing Patriarchy.' In *Feminism and Sociological Theory,* edited by R. A. Wallace. London: Sage.

Smith, Dorothy. 1999. *Writing the Social: Critique, Theory and Investigations.* Toronto: University of Toronto Press.

Song, Miriam and Ian Parker. 1995. 'Commonality, Difference, and the Dynamics of Disclosure in In-depth Interviewing.' *Sociology* 29 :241–256.

Spivak, Gayatri Chakravorty. 1993. *Outside in the Teaching Machine.* New York: Routledge.

Stacey, Judith. 1991. 'Can There be a Feminist Ethnography?' pp. 111–120 in *Women's Words: The Feminist Practice of Oral History,* edited by S. B. Gluck and D. Patai. New York: Routledge.

Stanley, Liz. 1994. 'The Knowing Because Experiencing Subject: Narratives, Lives, and Autobiography.' pp. 132–149 in *Knowing the Difference: Feminist Perspectives in Epistemology,* edited by K. Lennon and M. Whitford. London: Routledge.

Stanley, Liz and Sue Wise. 1983. *Breaking Out.* London: Routledge and Kegan Paul.

Stanley, Liz and Sue Wise. 1990. *Feminist Praxis: Research, Theory and Epistemology in Qualitative Research.* London: Routledge.

Stanley, Liz and Sue Wise. 1993. *Breaking Out Again.* London: Routledge and Kegan Paul.

Stone, Sandy. 1991. 'The Empire Strikes Back: A Post-Transsexual Manifesto.' In *Body Guards,* edited by J. Epstein and K. Straub. New York: Routledge.

Tang, Ning. 2002. 'Interviewer and Interviewee Relationships Between Women.' *Sociology* 36: 703–721.

Taylor, Janette Y. 2002. 'Talking Back: Research as an Act of Resistance and Healing for African American Women Survivors of Intimate Male Partner Violence.' *Women and Therapy* 25: 145–160.

Taylor, Verta and Leila J. Rupp. 2005. 'When the Girls are Men: Negotiating Gender and Sexual Dynamics in a Study of Drag Queens.' *Signs: Journal of Women in Culture and Society* 30: 2115–2140.

Temple, Bogusia and Rosalind Edwards. 2002. 'Interpreters/Translators and Cross-Language Research: Reflexivity and Border Crossings.' *International Journal of Qualitative Methods* 1(2), Article 1.http://www.ualberta.ca/~ijqm/ Date of access: December 12, 2006.

Thapar-Bjorkert, Suruchi and Marsha Henry. 2004. 'Reassessing the Research Relationship: Location, Position and Power in Fieldwork Accounts.' *International Journal of Social Research Methodology* 7: 363–381.

Wahab, Stephanie. 2003. 'Creating Knowledge Collaboratively with Female Sex Workers: Insights from a Qualitative, Feminist, and Participatory Study.' *Qualitative Inquiry* 9: 625–642.

Warr, Deborah J. 2005. '"It Was Fun … But We Don't Usually Talk About These Things": Analyzing Sociable Interaction in Focus Groups.' *Qualitative Inquiry* 11: 200–225.

Weedon, Chris. 1987. *Feminist Practice and Poststructuralist Theory.* Oxford: Blackwell Publishers.

Weeks, Kathi. 1998. *Constituting Feminist Subjects.* Ithaca and London: Cornell University Press.

Westmarland, Nicole. 2001. 'The Quantitative/Qualitative Debate and Feminist Research: A Subjective View of Objectivity.' *Forum Qualitative Sozialforschung/Forum: Qualitative Social Research* 2.

Wilkinson, Sue. 1999. 'Focus Groups in Feminist Research: Power, Interaction and the Co-Construction of Meaning.' *Psychology of Women Quarterly* 23: 221–244.

Wilkinson, Sue and Celia Kitzinger. 1996. *Representing the Other: A Feminism and Psychology Reader.* London: Sage.

Wolf, Marjery. 1992. A Thrice Told Tale: Feminism, Postmodernism and Ethnographic Responsibility. Stanford: Stanford University Press.

Zavella, Patricia. 1993. 'Feminist Insider Dilemmas: Constructing Ethnic Identity with 'Chicana' Informants.' pp. 42–62 in *Situated Lives: Gender and Culture in Everyday Life*, edited by L. Lamphere, H. Ragone, and P. Zavella. London: Routledge.

20

Biographical Methods

Joanna Bornat

Had I been writing this chapter only a few years ago I would have had a much easier task. But now, in the first decade of the twenty-first century, containing developments in biographical methods in under eight thousand words, borders on the impossible. What was an area of work scarcely acknowledged beyond groups of committed oral historians, occasional sociologists, auto/biographers and ethnographers has become a vast and constantly changing and expanding ferment of creative work, drawing in new as well as career-old researchers. In critical pedagogy, cultural studies, critical race theory, gerontology, decolonising research, social policy, health studies, feminisms, identity theory, studies of sexuality, employment, family and management theory, the range of areas in which biographical methods have been taken up is vast. All reach for meaning and accounts in individual biographies to both confirm and complicate understandings of the working and emergence of social processes and relationships in place and through time. And this is only within academe. Telling your story, the public confessional, the personal account has become a totally pervasive form, as any quick check through the media will show.

Simply putting a term such as 'life story' into Google brings hundreds and thousands of hits. This is all good news, if difficult to assimilate.

Biographical methods thrive on invention and have changed and adapted to methodological, theoretical and technological change. The arrival of the small portable audio recording machine has undoubtedly played a leading role. Indeed it would be impossible to imagine much of what is now recognised as biographical work without it. Gone are the days when using a machine to record interviews was seen as a form of journalism, to be eschewed by sociologists and anthropologists in the field[1]. Now we have the capability to capture not only sounds but visual expression and to send the information round the world, or next door in a matter of seconds.

In this chapter, I focus on ways in which individual life experience is generated, analysed and drawn on to explain the social world. However generated, the common denominator is that accounts are solicited and told in the first person. I focus on three very different approaches, briefly outlining each in turn and finally look at some ways to distinguish each in a final, and unashamedly partisan argument for the contribution of oral history. There are, the biographical interpretive methods, oral history and narrative analysis.

BIOGRAPHICAL METHODS

'Biographical methods' is an umbrella term for an assembly of loosely related, variously titled activities: narrative, life history, oral history, autobiography, biographical interpretive methods, storytelling, auto/biography, ethnography, reminiscence. These activities tend to operate in parallel, often not recognising each other's existence, some characterised by disciplinary purity with others demonstrating deliberate interdisciplinarity. To explain and present such disparity feels like a demanding intellectual undertaking. History, psychology, sociology, social policy, anthropology, even literature and neurobiology at times, all have a part to play.

By their very nature, biographical methods encourage a universalistic and encompassing approach, encouraging understanding and interpretation of experience across national, cultural and traditional boundaries, better to understand individual action and engagement in society. See for example, Prue Chamberlayne and Annette King's comparative study of family caring in East and West Germany and Britain drawing on biographical interview data (Chamberlayne & King, 2000), James Hammerton and Alistair Thomson's life history interviews with UK migrants to Australia in the 1950s and 1960s (Hammerton & Thomson, 2005), and African-American women's accounts of their professional lives in Gwendolyn Etter-Lewis's study (1993).

The personal and individual nature of biographical data adds an additional layer of complexity. Biographical researchers work with a range of different types of data including diaries, notebooks, interactive websites, videos, weblogs and written personal narratives with methods of collection varying from the directly interventionist in, for example oral history interviewing, to a more detached encouragement and stimulation to write and record as in the collection of accounts through an archive like Mass Observation or on-line interactive websites.

How best then to give shape and meaning to this task? How to organise and communicate a framework which is an aid to understanding and which provides a manageable and yet inclusive approach to presenting biographical methods? In sorting through the various activities I looked for themes which would bring out the strengths of biographical approaches while highlighting what are for me the most innovative and creative aspects of the contribution they make to social research methods. On that basis the themes I will be working with are: interactivity, subjectivity and structuring. I'll explain briefly what I mean by each of these themes.

By interactivity I mean the generation of data through some kind of direct social interaction. This is likely to be an interview or at least a situation which involves, or has involved, face-to-face verbal exchange. This leads to the inclusion of biographical interpretive methods, oral history, reminiscence, storytelling, life history and narrative, but not autobiography, auto/biography or ethnography. By choosing subjectivity I am highlighting the extent to which the method leads to the expression of the self, a focus on feelings and emotions providing insight into individual perceptions and understandings of situations and experiences. All the activities I have identified could be included under this theme, though some, for example oral history, have at different times, and in varying settings shown less attention to the self, while for others, example auto/biography, see the positioning of the self, as generator or reader of the text as a main focus of attention (Stanley, 1994).

With structuring I intend to convey the idea that biographical methods aim to generate accounts or data which, either by means of direct questioning, or through the nature of individuals' own responses, have an obvious or implicit structure. Again, this feels all-inclusive as what account, either told or expressed, does not have some kind of narrative, a beginning or an ending? Or what story is not connected in some way to the bigger picture, be it childbirth, war, schooling or sexuality? This may indeed be the case; however, by structuring, I mean the idea that the methods used rely on some kind of prior theorising or framework of ideas on the part of the researcher. This is not to rule out informal structuring or the kind of everyday theorising people develop in order to explain their lives but for my purposes here to emphasise the contribution which the theorising and methods of particular disciplines, such as psychology, sociology or history make to the generation of the data. So, I would exclude storytelling and autobiography from this particular category.

Finally, context; by this I mean the ways in which an individual account, or set of accounts, is given meaning by its own framework of time and space and by those of the researcher and interpreter of the data. Context is not only to be seen in terms of setting or the historical time or social and political structures surrounding a particular account; it also includes the agency and agendas of researcher and researched, their biographical time. Autobiography and storytelling fit less well once again. Where the main source is the single-authored account generated independently *for* an audience, rather than *with* another, context has fewer dimensions for exploration.

The burgeoning of interest in the perspective of the individual, in what has been described as a more 'humanistic' approach in sociological research has resulted in review articles and books which in their different ways have helpfully sketched out origins and developments in work with biography (Plummer, 2001; Thompson, 2000; Roberts, 2002; Seale et al., 2004; Thomson, 2007). This is an exciting area in which to work. Biographical work engages with many of the most telling and enduring epistemological and methodological issues in the human sciences taking in debates on validity, memory, subjectivity, standpoint, ethics, voice and representivity amongst others (Chamberlayne et al., 2000, p. 3).

The three methods I have chosen to concentrate on have shared antecedents in

most respects, but with some individual differences which show the distinctiveness of each. In what follows I draw on several of the works cited above where these lineages and identities are drawn out. A familiar starting point is the group of sociologists known as the 'Chicago School' and their work in the first 40 years of the twentieth century. The focus on the collection of direct testimony and on observation under realistic conditions led to methodological innovation in a number of areas. Urban society came under scrutiny, with studies of poverty, street gangs, and high life. Alongside this strongly engaged and situated commitment came a new development in social psychology. Herbert Mead's idea of 'the self' (1934) stressed the significance of language, culture and non-verbal communication, with its focus on social interaction and reflection in the development of the individual's sense of who they are. His notion of the self as having its own meaning and sense of reality, identifiable and recognisable in relation to social or historical context, provided a challenge to arguments which gave primacy to the investigator's or commentator's perspective. Students, teachers and researchers associated with the Chicago School were to generate some of the most influential developments in sociology; amongst these were symbolic interactionism (Plummer, 1991) and grounded theory (Glaser & Strauss, 1968).

It is with this background in mind that I now go on to take a closer look at the first of the three methods I identified under the biographical 'umbrella': the biographical interpretive method.

Biographical interpretive method

Fritz Schütze, a sociologist writing in Germany in the 1980s is usually credited with the originating work which led to the development of the biographical interpretive method. He was greatly influenced by 'third generation Chicagoans' such as Anselm Strauss, Howard Becker, Erving Goffman and others (Apitzsch & Inowlocki, 2000, p. 58). The interview method and its subsequent analysis which he developed and which has been further refined by Gabriele Rosenthal (2004), who followed his theoretical and methodological lead, requires the separating out of the chronological story from the experiences and meanings which interviewees provide. The process depends on an understanding of the biographical interview as a process in which movement between past, present and future is constant and in which the interviewee may not be fully aware of contexts and influences in their life.

Rosenthal and her erstwhile collaborator Wolfgang Fischer, developed this approach into what is now usually known as 'biographical interpretive analysis' or 'biographic narrative interpretive analysis' (Wengraf, 2001). She had been interested in explaining work and life ethics in post World War II West German society being convinced that the sense which people made of their lives under the Third Reich played a central role (Rosenthal, 2004, p. 49). Since Rosenthal and Fischer's early development, the method has been given much more elaborated treatment, using individual case study analysis, based on interview transcripts, by Prue Chamberlayne and colleagues. Their particular interest has been to theorise and explain the impact of social welfare policies through embracing the subjectivity and agency of welfare recipients, linking private and public spheres, as these are experienced, expressed and represented through individual accounts (Chamberlayne & King, 2000; Chamberlayne et al., 2000, 2004).

The systematisation inherent in this approach requires the elaborate codification of the interview in such a way as to identify themes, having separated out the 'lived life' from the 'told story' in the transcribed interview (Wengraf, 2001, p. 231). This distinction separates the chronological sequence of the events of a life from the way that the story is told. By identifying how someone relates to their story, in the telling, labelling text segments as to whether they are descriptive, argumentative, reporting, narrative or evaluative, biographical interpretive analysis addresses the qualitative data with hypotheses which draw on significant segments of text. Wengraf (2001) details the procedure for interpreting biographical data, showing with a detailed account, how hypotheses are arrived at and then worked through, as the life story is explored. Life events, as told by the interviewee, are looked at and hypotheses and counter hypotheses drawn up and explored, preferably by groups of people working together, as to likely effects on someone's later life.

This phenomenological approach to understanding biographical data focuses on the individual's perspective within an observable and knowable historical and structural context, and what it is like to be the person describing their lives and the various decisions, turns and patterns of that life (Wengraf, 2001, pp. 305–6).

At one level what Wengraf is describing is a complex process of interpretation, a shared and carefully documented practice of searching for themes in data typical of a grounded theory approach (Wengraf, 2001, p. 280). However, at quite another level the analysis expects a deep level of explanation and interpretation, one which looks for hidden and explicit meanings in the transcript. Just how this differs from the other two approaches I've identified, I will come back to this later in this chapter.

Oral history's distinctive characteristic is its use of sociological approaches to data generation and analysis in what is an historical pursuit. Even though the development of the interview as a tool of investigation has a much longer history, the significance of the Chicago School, as Paul Thompson points out in his seminal text, *The Voice of the Past,* was its effect on the idea of the life history (2000). The interview became more than simply extraction of information around specific topics; it became an object in itself with shape and totality given by the individual's told life events.

In an early essay, the Italian oral historian Alessandro Portelli, argues 'What makes oral history different'. Having identified oral history's particular qualities as 'the orality of oral sources' arguing for attention to the sounds and turns of speech as opposed to the written transcript and as 'narrative', pointing out variations in narrative forms and styles, he goes on to argue oral history's unique qualities. These are, he suggests, 'that it tells us less about *events* than about their *meaning*' (his emphases) and that 'the unique and precious element which oral sources possess in equal measure is the speaker's subjectivity' (1981, p. 67). From this, he argues that, 'oral sources' have a '*different* credibility' (p. 100, his emphasis) and that 'today's narrator is not the same person as took part in the distant events he or she is relating' (p. 102). It follows, therefore that, 'Oral sources are *not objective*' they are '*artificial, variable and partial*' (p. 103, his emphases).

Portelli's position has been taken up subsequently in studies of ethnicity, class, gender, colonialism, tradition, displacement, resistance, exclusion, by oral historians who see the method as particularly suited to understandings of oppression and marginalisation. With this unashamedly political and partisan approach to history, a contribution to the histories of elites was always going to be less likely, though there have been some exceptions, for example Courtney & Thompson's study of business elites in the city of London (1997) and Seldon and Pappworth's case studies of elites in their handbook of elite oral history (1983).

Oral history in its early and subsequent development drew sociology for methods of structuring data collection. Writing and researching in the context of the sociology department at the University of Essex in the mid 1960s (Thompson & Bornat, 1994), Thompson was familiar with the development of grounded theory as a solution to sampling from a population of survivors (2000, p. 151). While some studies have rested on only a handful of interviewees, for example Alessandro Portelli's investigation into local memory of a massacre of civilians by German troops occupying Tuscany in 1944 (Portelli, 1997), or Al Thomson's use of four life histories in his exploration

of the legend of Anzac solidarity amongst Australian World War I veterans (Thomson, 1994), oral historians more typically seek ways of representivity through theoretical sampling, with contacts made opportunistically or through snowballing (see for example Thompson, 1975; Bertaux, 1981; Lummis, 1987; Bornat, 2002; Hammerton & Thomson, 2005, Merridale, 2005). As for data analysis, a range of approaches, some more familiar to historians and some to sociologists, are typically followed by oral historians, who tend to take a more eclectic approach methodologically than researchers using the biographical interpretive method. In the main these would be recognisable as thematic in approach, drawing directly or indirectly on the type of constant comparative analysis and theme searching typical in grounded theory (Glaser & Strauss, 1968).

Given oral history's early commitment to a form of history-making which seeks to give expression to marginalised voices with emphasis on the importance of language, emotions and oral qualities generally, data analysis presents something of a moral challenge as Thompson and others have pointed out (Borland, 1991; Portelli, 1997, pp. 64&ff; Thompson, 2000, p. 269&ff; Bornat & Diamond, 2007). The tension lies in a commitment to the presentation of the actual words of interviewees while seeking a way to generalize from a number of stories without creating too much distance between the original recording or text and the resulting publication, be it hard copy, electronic or sound and vision presentation.

Narrative analysis

The third area of biographical activity I have identified, narrative analysis, also traces its origins back to the Chicago School. The move towards the subject as author and source of evidence, through the telling of their story became its defining feature in the 1920s. However, where those early sociologists of the city were intent on capturing reality from accounts, narrative theorists see the story as a greater sum of parts than the particularities of events, atmospheres, environments and relationships described. Catherine Kohler Riessman, a leading narratologist, explains how narratives interpreted through use of language, symbolic representations and cultural forms, provide access to understanding the workings across and within time of gender, class, culture, ethnicity, place and age, to name but a few social divisions and differences (1993, p. 5). This plurality does, however, mean that as she also points out: 'There is considerable disagreement about the precise definition of narrative' (1993, p. 17).

A focus on story or narrative sees telling, relating and recounting as a central and universal human activity. Lives, it is argued, are constructed, and presented to listeners in storied forms. As Widdershoven argues: '... a story is never a pure ideal, detached from real life. Life and story are not two separate phenomena. They are part of the same fabric, in that life informs and is formed by stories' (Widdershoven, 2003, p. 109). For Polkinghorne, narrative has special significance for the human sciences. He argues that it is, '... the linguistic form uniquely suited for displaying human existence as situated action'. This very generality presents problems of definition he goes on to admit (1995, pp. 5–7).

Riessman's solution to the problem of definition is to account for narratives in terms of genre. Narratives are to be recognised to the extent to which they relate to a 'narrative genre' with its own 'persistence of certain elements'. She argues that the conventional idea of a story having characters acting in various ways and moving towards some kind of conclusion is not a sufficiently broad enough definition. Her narrative genre includes accounts where the same event is described repeatedly – 'habitual narratives' – or which are 'topic-centred' where particular kinds of events are linked through a common theme or shared characteristic. She also includes 'hypothetical narratives' of events which never happened. What is distinctive, she seems to be arguing, is that there is a 'teller', an account of 'a situation'

and an audience: 'us' (Riessman, 1993, pp. 18–19).

When it comes to analysing narrative data, Riessman and others point out (Andrews et al., 2004) '... there is no *one* (her emphasis) method' (1993, p. 5). Indeed the pervasiveness of narrative studies with use in, for example, medicine (Greenhalgh & Hurwitz, 1998), anthropology (Skultans, 1998), psychology (Sarbin, 1986; Crossley, 2000), media studies (Ryan, 2004), feminist studies (Personal Narratives Group, 1989), linguistics (Bamberg, 1997), organisation studies (Denning, 2005), history (Roberts, 2001), and literature (Hawthorn, 1985) suggests a plethora of possible analytical procedures.

As a way to manage this diversity, to pull it within range of some reliable analytical framework which others can respond to and which for her preserves acknowledges the performative and interactive nature of the interview Riessman advocates use of poetic and literary forms as analytical tools. These, she argues, enable her to identify how a narrative is put together and to see what are its particularities in terms of characteristics of speech and discourse (1993, pp. 50–51). Seeking to keep 'the teller' in the centre of her analysis is 'starting from the inside' looking for meanings shown in the way the words are presented, not ignoring issues of power which may determine what is said and how (Riessman, 1993, p. 61). The perspective of the interpreter, their particular theoretical stance and even their personal history, is bound to play a part. Like the oral historians, this presents a dilemma for her but one which she feels can be resolved through a process of open reflection and questioning, as she puts it: 'the comfort of a long tradition of interpretive and hermeneutic enquiry' (1993, p. 61).

In these very brief sketches, I've identified what I see as the distinctive features of the biographical interpretive method, oral history and narrative method, focusing mainly on their antecedents and rather different approaches to the interpretation of personal accounts. To begin with, I used four themes and on the basis of these selected the three approaches I've just been outlining from amongst all those which come under the heading: 'biographical'. The themes were: interactivity, subjectivity and structuring and context.

Before I go on to look at some differences between the three approaches, with the aid of these themes, I want to consider what are the innovative and creative contributions of the biographical interpretive method, oral history and narrative analysis to social research methods generally. In my view, each approach highlights the interview as an example of social interaction in ways that draw on ideas of reflexivity and with reference to the significance of difference, each foregrounds the subjectivity, expressed feelings and meanings of the respondent, interviewee or subject. Yet for each, the structuring of the dialogue through the disciplinary antecedents of the particular approach is methodologically relevant. Finally, context, remembered, observed, researched, told and immediate, plays a significant role in each of the three methods. All of them, part of the 'biographical turn' in social science, are in different ways positioned '… within the shifting boundaries between history and sociology … (and there) some of the most telling and stimulating debating issues have emerged' (Chamberlayne et al., 2000, p. 3).

DRAWING OUT THE DIFFERENCES

In the last part of this chapter I will take the comparison further, emphasising what are, in my opinion, three specific areas of difference using examples from interviews. However, this time I won't conceal my preference and standpoint. In identifying the interview as interrogative, emphasising the role of memory as a source for 'pastness' and by questioning levels of interpretive influence, I will argue that all these issues have been most effectively dealt with by oral historians. I will deal first with the interview as interrogative.

The interview as interrogative

To argue that the interview, the most typical source of biographical data is interrogative may appear to be a statement of the obvious (Bornat, 1994). After all, an interview involves questioning and the soliciting of answers, most effectively between two people though occasionally more. Why emphasise its obvious interrogative qualities? My reason for doing so is to draw attention to the dialogic qualities of an interview, to the significance of the relationship which develops, and to emphasise the intentions and perspective of the interviewer.

The approach taken in biographical interpretation is to use an initial question, and then to stand back, as it were. Having posed that initial question, where interest in a particular topic is expressed, the interviewee in the biographical interpretive interview is then left to relate a life narrative, if possible without interruption. A second phase then follows in which questions are asked as a means to expanding on themes, to clarify points made or to ask for more detail about aspects of the life portrayed in the narrative.

In the oral history interview in contrast questioning drives the dialogue along in a quite deliberate way. As Ken Plummer argues, oral history and life history interviews draw on 'researched and solicited stories … (which) do not naturalistically occur in everyday life; rather they have to be seduced, coaxed and interrogated out of subjects' (Plummer, 2001, p. 28). The questioning and answering builds on itself, so that the interviewers have the complex task of listening while questioning, holding at least two, sometimes more, foci of interests, as the interviewees pursues their own story, sometimes surprised at what they have remembered or have found themselves saying in response to a question or opportunity to reflect. While the topic of the oral history interview will have been clear initially it is never possible to be certain how it will turn out as the dialogue develops.

I'll illustrate this with an excerpt from an interview I carried out in the early 1990s with Pat Hanlon (1915–1998), a well-known

UK cyclist when I interviewed her and four other women for an edited collection of writing on older women (Bornat, 1993). I invited her to tell me her life story, as a cyclist and businesswoman (unusually for the cycling world she ran her own shop). She began with an unbroken account of her early years as a cyclist, replete with technical terms related to cycle racing and bike parts. I was keen to guide her towards talking more about the social world of cycling and took this opportunity with a question about her first husband:

So was your first husband a cyclist as well?

Yes, he was a cyclist, yes. But he used to go out with another club. We didn't go out with our club, because there wasn't any women in that club. I used to go out with the Actonia CC … But I also belonged to the Clarion, which was a union all over the country, the Clarion were. Supposed to be Labour club, but I mean, I didn't go to it because it was a Labour club. Because they used to threaten to throw me out all the time, because I used to – didn't agree with what they said. You know, you're supposed to be Labour, you know, and half of them were communists. They used to go preaching down on the Dorking, on the hills and things like that. And I thought, I mean, wasting my time down there, you know, with that lot! So I used to go out on my own then.

Were they strict then, about that?

They were very strict about whether you were Labour or not, yes. Because if the heads there found you talking about you were – I mean, I wasn't anything really, but I used to annoy them, you know, when I said, I'm not Labour, I don't want to be Labour and all this. And they used to get ever so annoyed. And they said, well, we're going to get you chucked out, you know. I says, I don't care, you know. But, er, they never did.

I suppose cycling was, it was quite a kind of what you might call a more working-class sort of leisure thing.

It was mostly, oh yes, mostly poor people. I mean, there was never a car on the road when you raced. Only the time-keeper was the only car. I mean if you looked for the car, that was the start of your race …

And they'd all be people who would be, what working all week, like you, and spending all their weekends –

Oh yes, there was, oh, it took years and years for wealthy people to start cycling. Their sons might cycle, and they used to come out n their big cars, you know, and watch their son racing. But that kind of thing didn't happen for years and years.

Did you feel that it was a sort of – was that a part of the feel of it, do you think, that you were with people who were, you know, you were like a kind of group who were rather the same, or – ?

Well, there wasn't very many wealthy people around in those days. If there were they were nothing to do with us. You know, they'd be in a different society. There was sort of two societies, wealthy people and poor people. Or moderately poor. But there was never all running into one like they do now these days.

Did it feel like that did it? That you were very separate somehow?

Well yes. Because they never did the things we did. You'd hear about them going to these dinners and things up the town, but it never, you didn't even know them, half of them. It was a different world. I mean, if we went to a dinner, it was only the one year dinner, our club dinner, that was the only dinner we ever went to. And I hadn't got any clothes to go out in. I had nothing, only cycle clothes, that was all I had. I worked in them, I did the housework in them. The milkman would knock the door and I was in my shorts, you know …

As she answered my question about her husband I realised that she was beginning to talk about social and political divisions in the cycling world. This was something that interested me very much. Leaving behind, for the moment, the events of her life story, I began on a series of questions which I hoped would lead her into talk about the class politics of cycling between the two world wars in the UK. As is obvious from the transcript, I used various strategies. In the end she comes back to talk about herself as a cyclist, positioning herself as a cyclist first, then as a woman. It seems that for her, class and politics were an irrelevance, or in the case of the socialist Clarion movement, a means to an end: more cycling.

If I had used no prompts I might not have heard this particular account of her life, and the social world of cycling might well not have appeared at all. Biographical purists might argue that I was guilty of distorting Pat's story. In fact I would argue the opposite, that I was encouraging her to develop it and to reframe it through my interrogative dialogue. She would have told her story differently on another occasion, to another listener or interviewer. Undoubtedly I was bringing my particular 'cultural habitus'

(Hammersley, 1997) to that interview with all that this entailed. In oral history the idea that somehow it might be possible to render oneself invisible or non-interfering is regarded as mythical and certainly not desirable (Portelli, 1997, chapter 1; Thompson, 2000, p. 227; Bornat, 2004).

I make this point to contrast with both biographical interpretive and narrative approaches. As I have already shown the preferred approach in the biographical interpretive method is for a contained non-interventionist initial interview to be followed by questioning led by the interviewer. This separation of interviewer and interviewed through the privileging of the interviewee's account in the first interview and of the interviewer's interests in the second, excludes the possibility of a responsive interaction with joint initiative taking on both sides. In a contrasting way, though narrative approaches vary in their attitude to the part played by questions, their focus on the structure of the account in order to draw out the individual's perspective, similarly gives little weight to the dialogic possibilities of the interview. Context is relevant as Riessman emphasises, 'The text is not autonomous of its context' (1993, p. 21) and she rejects the model of a narrativist such as Labov who leaves out the interviewer-interviewee relationship in their analysis (cited in Riessman, 1993, p. 20). However, even in her hands, context, both historical and immediate is presented more as a framework than as part of the data and evidence of the interviewer's presence is typically excised from the text being analysed.

Memory as a source for 'pastness'

Elizabeth Tonkin, an anthropologist and oral historian, prefers the term 'representations of pastness' to 'history'. She argues that though it is less elegant, it conveys more of a sense of movement between past and present as people speak and others listen (Tonkin, 1992, p. 2). The active role of memory in oral history making again distinguishes it from biographical interpretive and narrative research. However, while memory gives us access and to experience before our own time, to experience which might otherwise be unreachable since it may not be recorded in documentary formats, it is not necessarily always accurate. For Portelli this is one of its very strengths. Confronted by old communists whose tales of the past were sometimes partial, even plainly false, he turns the tables in a celebration of oral history's ability to reveal what really mattered to people, '… uncovering the contradiction between reality and desire' (Portelli, 1991, p. 116).

Memory also plays a function in the present and is as much about future hopes and intentions as it is about telling stories, bearing witness or confessing to past involvements and actions. It draws on and engages with collective representations and can change according to audience, stimuli and time of life (Coleman et al., 1998; Rose, 2003; Draaisma, 2004). Indeed the reliance of oral history on older people's memories means being aware of the psychological tasks facing older people towards the end of life (Bornat, 2001). 'Pastness' for older people therefore needs to be seen as a multidimensional remembering, but none the less valuable for that. I'll take this point further with an excerpt from an interview carried out for Margot Jefferys' research into the founders of geriatric medicine (Ogg et al., 1999; Jefferys, 2000).

Dr Ronald Dent, one of Jefferys' interviewees, was in his mid eighties at the time of his interview:

What do you think of the new developments in the National Health Service? Do you have any views about that?

Well, I'm a bit scared that a vulnerable group like the elderly sick might not benefit as much as they should. In fact I think they might be neglected a bit again. And that's what frightens me. One wouldn't like to feel that the work that all of us who had been in geriatric medicine, the work we've done to make it a good thing to do, might find, find that our work has been let down a little bit because hospitals are so quick, so busy doing routine ops — operations — which they get paid a lot for rather than looking after strokes and other problems of the elderly which take a lot longer and need more resources. One hopes it's not like that[2].

Some of Jefferys' interviewees had worked since before the NHS and in its very early days. Medical care of older people had been much neglected and was a major challenge for the health service. At the end of their careers these doctors were looking back at success, medically, and in policy terms. They had established a specialty and could point to a much better standard of care for older people, in hospital and in the community than they had witnessed in the ex Poor Law hospitals at the start of their careers. However, they were being interviewed at a time of change for the health service. Many expressed concern at the introduction after 1979 of a market model and business methods into health care. To add another contextual layer, these doctors were now themselves old. Contemplating the possible end to what they had achieved had specific personal resonance for their own healthcare. 'Pastness' is thus represented through multiple time frames, in this interview as in other oral history interviews: remembered time; the time of the interview; the 'time' of the interviewee and of the interviewer and our own time in looking back at these particular archived interviews (Bornat, 2005).

Memory as an individual and social practice and a process with known and observable features and effects is of central interest to oral historians in ways that it does not appear to be in biographical interpretive and narrative analysis. It enables a perspective which includes the effect of time and the influence of change and continuity while maintaining the agency of the individual as the central focus of interest.

Interpretive influence

The last of the three areas of difference I identify here is interpretive influence. By this I am drawing attention to the ways in which the three approaches I've been looking at position the interpreter of the data in relation to its originator, the interviewee. Oral history's early commitment to a democratic purpose has led to some pointed debates

about ownership and partnership (see for example Frisch, 1990). Some feminist oral historians have led the way in questioning assumptions as to any essential understanding or solidarity across the microphone, as I have argued elsewhere (Borland, 1991; Bornat & Diamond, 2007; see also Armitage & Gluck, 2002). The result for many oral historians is a practice which seeks to maintain the integrity of the original interview, and of the interviewee, by maintaining interpretive distance.

To identify the subjectivity of the interview, to put oneself in their place, to draw out understandings which are not necessarily articulated in the words of the transcript, are all recognisable and shared interpretive practices. To look and listen for silences, experiences or relationships which are unspoken or unexpressed, is acknowledged as appropriate and rewarding, but to go beyond this and to seek out unconscious motivations, or ways of thinking, is perhaps to be guilty of over-interpretation. The researcher, who may or may not be the original interviewer, has a duty to ask questions of the data, to theorise about it and about the people and experiences represented in it, and to become more deeply embedded in it, but this, risks distancing the interviewee from their own words. I'll use one final example to show where I feel that the line is drawn between oral history and biographical interpretive and narrative approaches.

I spent more than two hours with Pat Hanlon recording her life history. She gave me a detailed account of her progression as a cyclist to becoming one of the best wheel builders in the country, owning a shop and being married twice, once early in her life and then again much later, as she retired. What she didn't tell me was that she had a son, from whom she was estranged. She didn't tell me and I didn't ask her. She only finally told me when I gave her the book chapter in which she appears to check for accuracy and representation. She then let me know that it might be better to mention her son as otherwise her friends might was a little strange.

To be silent about such a defining experience as motherhood, could be attributed to some deep personal flaw. I might turn to some psychological explanations for this apparent pathology on her part; I could look back through the transcript for clues as to her mindset and evidence of suppression of maternal instincts, her predilection for wearing shorts perhaps, or an apparently obsessive interest in mileage. I could hypothesise as to her decision-making and her reflection on her life from the way she accounts for the events in her life. I could counterpose her lived life to her told life, drawing out inferences as to her motivations and tendencies as a mother and a woman. But, in the end I find this to be a process of distancing and indeed of subjecting Pat to an over-interpreted reconstruction of her life. She may have actively chosen not to mention her son because to mention him would be upsetting. She may have decided to focus exclusively on her life as a cyclist; indeed she made few references to other aspects of her personal life, and only when prompted by me. She may have retold the narrative of her life for herself so that her son was given no role. She might also have felt, as a public person, that her private life would be of little interest to me. Least possible, she may simply have forgotten to mention her son. Whatever the reason, I can't know and though I could speculate and develop a theory relating to some developmental deficiency I can see no advantage in this. To carry out more interviews with older women cyclists might give me a better idea of Pat's life in context. As it is, I have only her testimony to go on. Perhaps what I can draw out of this experience is a sense of inadequacy as an interviewer. For once my interrogative powers failed me.

But there is also another angle to interpretive influence and this is the question of ethics. How far is it ethical to subject another person's life to interpretation if the process and outcome are likely to be unrecognisable to them? How acceptable is an interpretation in which there is no possibility of continuing dialogue and discussion, particularly where the data originated in an interview relationship?

These are difficult questions to answer, complicated by new debates about the ethics of the secondary analysis of archived data (Bornat, 2005).

CONCLUSION

The three biographical methods I have discussed in this chapter each has a distinctive practice and, though they share origins in the Chicago School of Sociology, they have developed along rather different interdisciplinary lines. Where the biographical interpretive method lends itself to more psychoanalytic interpretations of motivation and meaning, narrative analysis leans more towards sociolinguistics, while oral history draws across both sociology and history. Each gives centrality to the individual account in attempting to explain the changing nature and persistence of social relations and social structures. While each makes use of the interview to generate data, only oral history continues to focus on the dynamics of the interview through the process of interpretation and discussion. I have admitted a partisan position in my relationship with oral history but that is not to ignore the contribution of the other two approaches. In looking for ways to pin down the process of interrogating the data they force us to pay attention to explaining our thinking and analytical procedures, highlighting the detail which a phenomenological approach demands. My only concern is that in doing so we risk an over-interpretation which rather than emphasising the qualities of the original teller, eclipses them and puts the interpreter in a position of authority and control.

NOTES

1 Fieldwork training for some trainee sociologists in the 1960s involved making notes after the interview or observation. Taping was definitely frowned on as a poor substitute for skills in observation and recall (Graham Fennell, personal communication).

2 Margot Jefferys Interview number 306, deposited at the British Library Sound Archive.

REFERENCES

Andrews, M., Day Sclater, S., Squire, C. & Tamboukou, M. (2004) 'Narrative research', in C. Seale, G. Gobo, J. Gubrium eds, *Qualitative Research Practice*, London, Sage, pp. 109–124.

Apitzsch, U. & Inowlocki, L. (2000) 'Biographical analysis: a "German" school?', in P. Chamberlayne, J. Bornat & T. Wengraf eds, *The Turn to Biographical Methods in Social Science*, London, Routledge, pp. 53–70.

Armitage, S. H. & Berger Gluck, S. (2002) 'Reflections on women's oral history: an exchange', in S. H. Armitage, P. Hart & K. Weathermon eds, *Women's Oral History: the Frontiers Reader*, Lincoln, University of Nebraska Press, pp. 75–86.

Bamberg, M., ed. (1997) 'Oral versions of personal experience–Three decades of narrative analysis: A special issue of the *Journal of Narrative and Life History*', Mahwah, USA, Lawrence Erlbaum.

Bertaux, D. (1981) 'Life stories in the baker's trade', in D. Bertaux ed., *Biography and Society*, London, Sage.

Borland, K. (1991) ' "That's not what I said": Interpretive conflict in oral narrative research', in S. B. Gluck & D. Patai eds, *Women's Words: the Feminist Practice of Oral History*, London, Routledge, pp. 63–75.

Bornat, J. (1993) 'Life Experience', in Bernard, M. and Meade, K. eds. *Women Come of Age: Perspectives on the Lives of Older Women*, London, Edward Arnold, pp. 23–42.

Bornat, J. (1994) 'Is oral history auto/biography?' *Auto/Biography* 3.1/3.2, 17–30.

Bornat, J. (2001) 'Reminiscence and oral history: Parallel universes or shared endeavour?' *Ageing and Society* 219–241.

Bornat, J. (2002) 'Doing life history research', in A. Jamieson & C. Victor eds, *Researching Ageing and Later Life*, Buckingham, Open University Press, pp. 117–134.

Bornat, J. (2004) 'Oral History', in C. Seale, G. Gobo & J. Gubrium eds, *Qualitative Research Practice*, London, Sage, pp. 34–47.

Bornat, Joanna (2005) 'Recyling the evidence: different approaches to the reanalysis of gerontological data [37 paragraphs]'. *Forum Qualitative Sozialforschung/Forum: Qualitative Social Research* [On-line Journal], 6(1), Art. 42. Available at: http://www.qualitative-research.net/fqs-texte/1-05/05-1-42-e.htm.

Bornat, J. & Diamond, H. (2007) 'Women's history and oral history: Developments and debates', *Women's History Review* 16(1), 19–39.

Chamberlayne, P., Bornat, J. & Apitzsch, U. eds (2004) *Biographical Methods and Professional Practice*, Bristol, The Policy Press.

Chamberlayne, P., Bornat, J. & Wengraf, T. eds (2000) *The Turn to Biographical Methods in Social Science*, London, Routledge.

Chamberlayne, P. & King, A. (2000) *Cultures of Care: Biographies of Carers in Britain and the Two Germanies*, Bristol, The Policy Press.

Coleman, P. G., Ivani-Chalian, C. and Robinson, M. (1998) 'The story continues: persistence of life themes in old age'. *Ageing and Society* 18(4), 389–419.

Courtney, K. & Thompson, P. (1997) *Changing Lives: the Changing Voices of British Finance*, London, Methuen.

Crossley, M. L. (2000) *Introducing Narrative Psychology: Self, Trauma, and the Construction of Meaning*, Buckingham, Open University Press.

Denning, S. (2005) *The Leader's Guide to Storytelling: Mastering the Art and Discipline of Business Narrative*, San Francisco, Jossey-Bass.

Draaisma, D. (2004) *Why Life Speeds up as you Get Older: How Memory Shapes our Past*, Cambridge, Cambridge University Press.

Etter-Lewis, G. (1993) *My Soul is My Own: Oral Narratives of African American Women in the Professions*, New York, Routledge.

Frisch, M. (1990) *A Shared Authority: Essays on the Craft and Meaning of Oral and Public History*, Albany, State University of New York Press.

Glaser, B. & Strauss, A. (1968) *The Discovery of Grounded Theory*, London, Weidenfeld & Nicholson.

Greenhalgh, T. & Hurwitz, B. (1998) *Narrative Based Medicine: Dialogue and Discourse in Clinical Practice*, London, BMJ Books.

Hammersley, M. (1997) 'Qualitative data archiving: some reflections on its prospects and problems', *Sociology* 31(1), 131–142.

Hammerton, A. J. & Thomson, A. (2005) *Ten Pound Poms: Australia's Invisible Migrants*, Manchester: Manchester University Press.

Hawthorn, J. (1985) *Narrative: From Memory to Motion Pictures*, London, Edward Arnold.

Jefferys, M. (2000) 'Recollections of the pioneers of the geriatric medicine specialty', in Bornat, J., Perks, R., Thompson, P. & Walmsley J. eds, *Oral History, Health and Welfare*, London, Routledge, pp. 75–97.

Lummis, T. (1987) *Listening to History*, London, Hutchinson.

Mead, G. H. (1934) *Mind, Self and Society from the Standpoint of a Social Behaviorist*, Chicago, University of Chicago Press.

Merridale, C. (2005) *Ivan's War: the Red Army 1939–45*, London, Faber and Faber.

Ogg, J., Evans, G., Jefferys, M. & MacMahon, D. G. (1999) 'Professional responses to the challenge of old age', in Bernard, M. & Phillips, J eds, *The Social Policy of Old Age: Moving into the 21st Century*, London, Centre for Policy on Ageing, pp. 112–127.

Personal Narratives Group (1989) *Interpreting Women's Lives: Feminist Theory and Personal Narratives*, Bloomington: Indiana University Press.

Plummer, K. (1991) *Symbolic Interactionism, vols 1&2*, Aldershot, Edward Elgar.

Plummer, K. (2001) *Documents of Life 2*, London, Sage.

Polkinghorne, D. E. (1995) 'Narrative configuration in qualitative analysis', in Hatch, J. A. & Wisniewski, R. eds, *Life History and Narrative*, London, Falmer.

Portelli, A. (1981) 'What makes oral history different', *History Workshop*, 12, 96–107.

Portelli, A. (1991) *The Death of Luigi Trastulli and Other Stories: Form and Meaning in Oral History*, New York, State University of New York Press.

Portelli, A. (1997) 'The massacre at Civitella val di Chiani (Tuscany, June 29, 1944): myth and politics, mourning and common sense', in Portelli, A. ed., *The Battle of Valle Giulia: Oral History and the Art of Dialogue*, Madison, University of Wisconsin Press, pp. 140–160.

Riessman, C. K. (1993) *Narrative Analysis*, Newbury Park, Sage.

Roberts, B. (2002) *Biographical Research*, Buckingham, Open University Press.

Roberts, G. (2001) *The History and Narrative Reader*, London, Routledge.

Rose, S. (2003) *The Making of Memory: from Molecules to Mind*, London, Vintage, 2nd edition.

Rosenthal, G. (2004) 'Biographical research', in Seale, C., Gobo, G. & Gubrium, J. eds, *Qualitative Research Practice*, London, Sage, pp. 48–64.

Ryan, M.-L. ed. (2004) *Narrative across Media the Languages of Storytelling*, Lincoln, USA, University of Nebraska Press.

Sarbin, T.R. (1986) 'The Narrative as a Root Metaphor for Psychology', in T. R. Sarbin (ed) *Narrative Psychology: The Storied Nature of Human Conduct*, New York, Praeger, pp. 3–21.

Seale, C., Gobo, G., Gubrium, J. & Silverman, D. (2004) *Qualitative Research Practice*, London, Sage.

Seldon, A. & Pappworth, J. (1983) *By Word of Mouth: Elite Oral History*, London, Methuen.

Skultans, V. (1998) 'Anthropology and narrative', in Greenhalgh, T. & Hurwitz, B. eds, *Narrative Based Medicine: Dialogue and Discourse in Clinical Practice*, London, BMJ Books.

Stanley, L. (1994) 'Sisters under the skin? Oral histories and auto/biographies', *Oral History*, 22(2), 88–89.

Thompson, P. (1975) *The Edwardians*, London, Weidenfeld & Nicholson.

Thompson, P. (2000) *The Voice of the Past*, Oxford, Oxford University Press, 3rd edition.

Thompson, P. & Bornat, J. (1994) 'Myths and memories of an English rising 1968 at Essex', *Oral History* 22(2), 44–54.

Thomson, A. (1994) *Anzac Memories: Living with the Legend*, Melbourne, Oxford University Press.

Thomson, A. (2007) 'Four paradigm transformations in oral history', *Oral History Review*.

Tonkin, E. (1992) *Narrating our Pasts: The Social Construction of Oral History*, Cambridge, Cambridge University Press.

Wengraf, T. (2001) *Qualitative Research Interviewing*, London, Sage.

Widdershoven, G. A. M. (2003) 'The story of life: Hermeneutic perspectives on the relationship between narrative and life history', in R. Miller ed., *Biographical Research Methods*, Vol. IV, London, Sage, pp. 108–123.

Focus Groups

Janet Smithson

INTRODUCTION

This chapter sets out some of the main issues, both practical and theoretical, of using focus groups in social research, together with suggestions on how to use and analyse the groups most effectively. First the history and reasons for using focus groups in social research are considered, taking note of some of the different epistemological and theoretical positions underpinning focus group research. Then, design and procedure are considered, including sampling and selecting participants, the logistics of recording and managing the data, and ethical considerations. Third, the role of the moderator, including strategies for moderating focus groups, and acknowledgement of the impact of the moderator, is discussed. In the section entitled 'Analysing focus group data', some of the specific issues which arise in analysis of focus groups are highlighted, with particular reference to the importance of the group context. Finally, the section entitled 'Using focus groups in specific contexts' looks at the use of focus groups in specific contexts: within feminist research, organisational research, in cross-cultural and cross-national research, in

action research, and the growing use of online focus groups.

THE HISTORY OF FOCUS GROUPS IN SOCIAL SCIENCE RESEARCH

Focus groups originated in sociology in the 1920s (Merton and Kendall 1946), but were primarily used by market researchers for several decades (Templeton 1987), before regaining popularity in the social sciences in the 1990s (Wilkinson 1998), as well as becoming widely used as a marketing and political tool for gathering 'opinions'. They are increasingly being used as a research tool throughout the social sciences, as well as in a wide range of other academic fields – for example health studies, education, political science and geography.

Even though focus groups comprise face-to-face interaction of crucial interest to social scientists, and are increasingly being used as a research tool (Wilkinson 1998), there is a significant lack of literature on the analysis of the conversational processes and structures involved in them, although various researchers have called attention to this lack

(Kitzinger 1994, Agar and MacDonald 1995, Myers 1998, Wilkinson 1998), and there have been some recent considerations of interactive patterns within focus groups (e.g. Myers 1998, Kitzinger and Frith 1999, Puchta and Potter 1999). Wilkinson (1998) concludes that 'there would seem to be considerable potential for developing new – and better-methods of analysing focus group data' (1998: 197). The regularly occurring lack of theoretical and analytical discussions in the focus group literature, even in academic contexts, is perhaps partially explained by the roots of focus group usage as a market research tool. The perception that focus groups are a quick and useful way of gathering 'opinions' still informs mainstream debate on focus groups and focus group manuals, and affects how they are used – for example, they are often viewed as (only) suitable for the initial stages of a research project.

WHAT IS A 'FOCUS GROUP'?

A focus group is generally understood to be a group of 6–12 participants, with an interviewer, or moderator, asking questions about a particular topic. Some researchers, such as Hughes and DuMont (1993: 776) characterise focus groups as group interviews: 'Focus groups are in-depth group interviews employing relatively homogenous groups to provide information around topics specified by the researchers'. Others define them as group discussions: 'a carefully planned discussion designed to obtain perceptions on a defined environment' (Kreuger 1998: 88) or 'an informal discussion among selected individuals about specific topics' (Beck et al., 1986). These definitions show a tension between participant-researcher interaction and interaction between participants, with interactions between participants in the group being a particularly distinctive characteristic of focus group methodology, although this is not always apparent from analysis of focus group data. The data obtained in this method is neither a 'natural' discussion of a relevant topic, nor a constrained group interview with

set questions, but it has elements of both these forms of talk. The different definitions of focus groups, as well as the origins of focus group methodology in very varied contexts, demonstrate some of the variations within this methodology; even within the social research context, focus groups are used by researchers with very different theoretical and analytical backgrounds, and these have implications for the use and analysis of focus groups.

REASONS FOR USING FOCUS GROUPS IN SOCIAL RESEARCH

A growing literature on the reasons for using focus groups in the social sciences, together with practical advice and how to organise them and run them, is now available, for example by Kitzinger (1995), Vaughn et al. (1996), Greenbaum (1998), Morgan and Kreuger (1998) and Bloor et al. (2000). One often-stated advantage of using focus groups lies in the fact that they permit researchers to observe a large amount of interaction on a specific topic in a short time. They are sometimes viewed as a quick and easy way to gather data. However, there are often problems with setting up and organising groups and obtaining the right number and mix of people to groups. In practice, groups tend to be based on availability rather than representativeness of sample. Moderating focus groups can be complex, and the data obtained can be difficult to transcribe and analyse (Pini 2002).

From a practical perspective, the feasibility of arranging focus groups needs to be considered. For example, if interviewing people who are geographically distant, or who have very little time, or who will be interviewed in a second language, then focus groups may prove impossible (though telephone and online focus group methods are being developed, see the section entitled 'Using focus groups in specific contexts'). Focus groups have been described as particularly useful at an early stage of research as a means of eliciting general viewpoints, which can be used to inform design of larger studies (Vaughn et al., 1996). They are often used in conjunction with another method, such as individual interviews or survey questionnaires. While perceived convenience is a regularly cited reason for using focus groups, from a methodological perspective, the question should rather be whether focus groups will produce the best sort of data for the research question.

One of the perceived strengths of focus group methodology is the possibility for research participants to develop ideas collectively, bringing forward their own priorities and perspectives, 'to create theory grounded in the actual experience and language of [the participants]' (Du Bois 1983). Morgan (1988) views the hallmark of a focus group as 'the explicit use of the group interaction to produce data and insight that would be less accessible without the interaction found in a group' (Morgan 1988: 12). A central feature of focus groups is that they provide researchers with direct access to the language and concepts participants use to structure their experiences and to think and talk about a designated topic. 'Within-group homogeneity prompts focus group participants to elaborate stories and themes that help researchers understand how participants structure and organize their social world' (Hughes and DuMont 1993). Focus groups with children have been shown to be a very effective approach for collecting data in a setting which children feel comfortable with (Ronen et al., 2001).

DESIGN AND PROCEDURE

Sampling and selecting participants

In focus group methodology, the unit of analysis is taken to be the group (Morgan 1988, Kreuger 1998), and groups are typically homogenous – for example, students on a certain course, or a group with a similar medical condition. Participants are chosen to fit in with the group's demographic. According to the prescriptions about focus group methodology in the literature

should be relatively homogenous membership (Kreuger 1994, Ritchie and Lewis 2003). Guides of focus group research typically advocate having single sex groups, and several groups with members with comparable characteristics, to permit cross-group comparability. There are many other variables which may need to be taken into consideration, such as nationality, sexuality and ethnic background. Having people at similar life stages, or working in similar jobs, can be particularly relevant. However, heterogeneous groups can produce very interesting discussions. For example, mixed sex groups can challenge the typical male and female discourses on these topics (Smithson 2000). Recruitment of group members has been shown to affect the group dynamics, for example Agar and MacDonald (1995) point out how the ways in which respondents are recruited come to condition the group talk.

Organisation and dynamics of focus groups

While the literature often (e.g. Vaughn 1996) recommends focus groups of up to 12 participants, there are practical and methodological reasons why many focus groups are smaller. Practically, it can be difficult to get an exact number of participants to turn up to a focus group, especially if trying to get a specific sub-group, for example new parents working in specific jobs, or expectant mothers of a particular age. In larger groups, there is a likelihood that some participants will remain silent or speak very little, while smaller groups (say 4–8 participants) often provide an environment where all participants can play an active part in the discussion. Smaller groups often yield interesting and relevant data, giving more space for all participants to talk and to explore the various themes in detail (Brannen et al., 2002). Ritchie and Lewis (2003) suggest that if groups are smaller than four they can lose some of the qualities of being a group, while they see triads and dyads as an effective hybrid of in-depth interviews.

The practicalities of organising focus groups are covered in various guides, for example Vaughn et al. (1996) and Morgan and Kreuger (1998). Practicalities of setting up focus groups include considering the issues of how you are going to obtain a sufficiently large (but not too large) group of people at a specific place and time. Will childcare, travel expenses or renumeration be provided, and if not will this exclude certain groups of participants? Moreover, as with recruitment, the way in which the focus group is presented and conducted – whether refreshments are offered, whether the group is being paid to participate, the perceived formality of the occasion – will, as with all research methods, have an impact on the participants' responses and interactions.

The focus group procedure is typically to follow a relatively unstructured interview guide, which generates a list of topics for discussion. The aim is to cover the topics set by the research agenda, but with some flexibility to allow related topics to emerge in this context. The focus group moderator (who may or may not be the researcher) guides the discussion, making sure that all topics are covered, and that all group members are given the chance to speak. Groups will ideally last from 1 to 2 hours. Just as with other forms of semi-structured interview, testing the guide on a pilot group is highly recommended. In social science research, focus groups are usually recorded either aurally and/or using video facilities. This contrasts with market research where notes are made during the focus group by the moderator or a colleague.

Morgan (2002) makes a distinction between the more structured approach to focus groups which originated in market research, and a less structured approach which has emerged from social research using focus groups. In marketing research, moderators are usually being paid to find out some specific answers for a client, and there is therefore a need for the moderator to be active and visible in the group, performing for the satisfaction of a paying client. In this context, the moderator of a fairly structured focus group is likely to refocus off-topic discussions, and stick to a structured interview schedule. In this context, most interaction is likely to be between the moderator and the participants, and there is little discussion besides answering the set questions. In contrast, a less structured approach is typical in much social research; whether the goal is more typically to understand the participants' thinking, the moderator is primarily aiming to facilitate discussion rather than direct it, and participants are encouraged to talk to each other rather than just respond to the moderator's questions. As Morgan (2002) points out, both of these focus group types can be used within social research, depending on the research topic and theoretical approach.

Agar and MacDonald (1995) argued that focus groups are usually too structured and not as useful as more in-depth qualitative ethnographic interviews. However, as described in this chapter, focus groups can be conducted in a less structured way, and have been found useful in postmodernist and feminist research, for example, as a way of uncovering discourses and narratives in a way which can feel less structured to participants. It is vital to remember in focus group research that the data obtained is different to the data which would emerge in a different research context, such as individual interviewing. This can be viewed as hearing different stories in the different research contexts, or as getting both public and private accounts.

Ethical considerations

A particular concern with using focus group methodology is the ethical issues involved of having more than one research participant at a time. This has two implications: first people may be uncomfortable with talking about their concerns in a group context, whether with strangers or with people they know. Sometimes group members may not respond appropriately to other members' disclosures. The moderator can try and move the discussion on or change the topic if group members appear uncomfortable with sensitive issues.

Second, the researcher cannot guarantee that all discussion in this context will remain totally confidential. A useful strategy is to start the focus group with a list of 'dos and don'ts', including asking participants to respect each others' confidences and not repeat what was said in the group; however this cannot be enforced. The moderator can guarantee from a personal perspective that the things said in a focus group context will be kept anonymous and confidential, but cannot guarantee that co-participants will not discuss the group, which can be a problem, especially in an institutional setting, such as in a workplace, or health care setting.

When are focus groups not appropriate?

Certain topics are commonly understood to be unsuitable for the focus group context. In particular, topics which participants may view as personal or sensitive are often better left for other methods, for example individual interviews. These may include people's personal experiences or life histories, their sexuality, and topics such as infertility or financial status. What is viewed as a private issue varies between different cultural groups (and also depends on age, gender and other contexts). In institutional contexts, such as workplaces, or schools, people may be particularly wary of presenting their views or talking about their personal experiences in front of colleagues, managers or peers. Focus groups may also be inappropriate when the aim of the research is to obtain in-depth personal narratives, for example of the experience of illness. The methodology may also be inappropriate for topics where people have strong or hostile views. However, in all these cases, much depends on the questions asked and the group dynamics.

There are perspectives which rarely come out in 'mainstream' groups, though these vary in different cultural contexts, and are affected by age, gender and background of the participants, as well as the setting and context of the focus group. Perspectives which rarely come out in focus groups unless specifically designed groups, include gay and lesbian views, and other non-standard family set-ups, and also ethnic minority and religious minority perspectives. Separate focus groups can cover some aspects of these perspectives, and for other aspects, more 'private' methods such as individual interviews may be more suitable. However, the limitations of what is discussed and what is omitted vary and it is possible to get unexpected and extremely interesting discussions about topics which are not always 'recommended' in focus group manuals. Groups may be happy to discuss sensitive topics such as sexual orientation and parenting in a general way, but not to give personal details about their own lives. Sensitive topics can be discussed in a general way in a focus group context, but with the emphasis on general discussion rather than individual experience.

THE ROLE AND IMPACT OF THE MODERATOR

In market research moderators tend to be specifically trained and employed to perform this task, while in the social sciences researchers often moderate the group themselves. Specific issues that the moderator is expected to deal with include dealing with disagreement and arguments in the groups, including all participants, noticing when participants are uncomfortable with a discussion and dealing with this appropriately, ensuring that essential topics are covered in the time available. The moderator is expected to strike a balance between generating interest in and discussion about a particular topic, while not pushing their own research agenda ending in confirming existing expectations (Vaughn et al., 1996, Sim 2002). They should be trying to ensure that discussion is between participants rather than between them and the moderator (Sim 2002).

In qualitative social science research, the role and subjectivity of the researcher is a vital part of the research context, and in this paradigm, the role and positioning of the focus group moderator is understood to make a difference to the group dynamic, as well as to the data obtained. For example, when considering single sex groups, the sex of the moderator also needs to be taken into account. The moderator's impact as a gendered and embodied being needs to be considered both in the set-up of the groups, and in the analysis. This is not unique to focus group research: surveys, questionnaires and individual interviews have all been shown to sometimes result in respondents giving accounts perceived as acceptable to the researcher (Bradburn and Sudman 1979, Bryman 1988). The problem may be exacerbated in focus group research by fear of peer group disapproval.

While focus group literature may sometimes give the impression that the ideal moderator is a neutral person with the ability to encourage the discussion, and pick up on participants' responses and narratives, in practice the moderator can never be a neutral bystander, and should instead aim for reflexivity and awareness of the way their characteristics and behaviour may be influencing the group (Wilkinson and Kitzinger 1996, Stokoe and Smithson 2002). Moreover, it is possible for the moderator to make explicit use of their own experience as a way of encouraging the discussion, for example a moderator with young children, or with experience of a specific life event or illness, may give examples from their own experience as a way of encouraging the group to discuss an issue.

Group dynamics and interaction

The role and impact of focus group participants on each other and on the perspectives which emerge have been relatively little studied. There is wide variation in focus group research in type and size of group, with corresponding effects on the group dynamics. For example, some groups consist of people who have worked together or know each other well; others are made up of complete strangers. While the literature stresses the importance of homogeneity in groups, there is little attention to how

groups of strangers, friends or colleagues, respectively, affect each others' contribution to the research.

Participants' use of groups

Morgan (1996) highlights the need for focus group organisers to consider more carefully both the concerns and the priorities of the participants. In qualitative social research paradigms, research participants are understood to be active co-researchers or participants rather than passive subjects. An important question for focus group methodology is how do participants use the focus groups? Focus groups are not simply a means of eliciting knowledge from participants, but are often reported to be quite creative experiences for the participants themselves (Madriz 2000, Brannen 2004). People can use the context to become particularly reflective, exploring themselves and their relationships in tentative and thoughtful ways. Groups can become a space for participants to discover new things about their condition or organisation, or to make contact with other people with similar experiences.

ANALYSING FOCUS GROUP DATA

Even though focus groups comprise face-to-face interaction of crucial interest to social scientists, and are increasingly being used as a research tool (Wilkinson 1998), there was, until recently, a significant lack of literature on the analysis of the conversational processes and structures involved in them, although various researchers have called attention to this lack (Kitzinger 1994, Agar and MacDonald 1995, Myers 1998, Wilkinson 1998), and there have been some recent considerations of interactive patterns within focus groups (e.g. Myers 1998, Kitzinger and Frith 1999, Puchta and Potter 1999). Wilkinson (1998) concludes that 'there would seem to be considerable potential for developing new – and better-methods of analysing focus group data' (1998: 197).

Groups as the unit of analysis

As mentioned earlier, an important characteristic of focus group data is that groups, rather than individuals within groups, are usually viewed as the unit of analysis. However, the unit of analysis depends on the interpretative framework (and attendant underlying assumptions) that the researcher leans on. Wilkinson (1998) argues that many articles based on focus group research appear to be treating the data as identical to individual interview data, and the unique aspects of focus groups are habitually ignored in the analysis.

The many variables in setting up and conducting focus groups touched on earlier can make systematic analysis tricky. Sample populations in the focus groups are small and non-representative. Topics are not all discussed in equal depth in all groups. Some information is volunteered in some groups and not others, some individuals are more forthcoming than others, and the group interactions will determine the discussion. If a systematic analysis is needed for the research agenda, then there will be a fairly structured approach to the use of focus groups, as described earlier (c.f. Morgan 2002), with a strict control on the number and mix of participants, a limited set of questions, and a more guided approach to moderation. The use of systematic coding, or content analysis, which has been historically popular in focus group research (Morgan 1988, Wilkinson 1998) tends to fit with the more structured approach to focus groups found in market research, and often reflects a more positivist epistemological stance.

In contrast, focus group researchers coming from a postmodernist research perspective, place less (or no) emphasis on 'systematic analysis', as groups are viewed as producing locally situated accounts – 'collective testimonies' (Madriz 2000) – which are not necessarily directly comparable. From this approach, size of groups and the exact discussion of set topics may be less essential, and the research agenda may be better met by a fairly unstructured approach which permits a participant-led discussion.

As with all social research, the researcher needs to consider whether the status of the data (for example, realist or postmodernist approach) fits with the methodological approach, and with the analytical techniques employed, as well as fitting the research concerns. The variation in focus group methodologies and uses demonstrates that this methodology is not uniquely tied to one theoretical perspective; focus groups are popular with researchers from a wide range of epistemological positions, as well as across a range of disciplines, but the way they are used and analysed is likely to be very different.

Natural discussion or artificial performance?

The central feature of focus groups, as a site of social interaction, is rarely picked up on in focus group analysis, with some notable exceptions (for example Myers 1998, Puchta and Potter 1999). A key issue for researchers is the complex relation of focus group talk to everyday talk. Agar and MacDonald doubt the 'lively conversation' called for in the focus group handbooks – 'in fact a judgement as to whether a conversation occurred, lively or not, is a delicate matter that calls for some close analysis of transcripts' (1995: 78). Focus groups can be viewed as performances in which the participants jointly produce accounts about proposed topics in a socially organised situation. Participants and moderator are 'operating under the shared assumption that the purpose of the discussion is to display opinions to the moderator' (Myers 1998: 85). However, 'natural' discussion is also a performance (Goffman 1981); there is not a 'simple opposition of the institutional and the everyday, the artificial and the real' (Myers: 107). Rather, 'natural' conversation and various forms of institutional talk, including classroom, courtroom, workplace and research-generated talk, are all part of a range of situations for talk(Drew and Heritage 1992). Silverman argues that 'neither kind of data [artificial and naturally occurring] is intrinsically better than the other; everything depends on the method of analysis' (Silverman 1993: 106). Focus groups, then, should not be analysed as if they are naturally occurring discussions, but as discussions occurring in a specific, controlled context.

There have been numerous critiques of qualitative techniques which appear to offer an 'authentic gaze' into participants' views or lives (Silverman 2000). Focus group researchers have typically extolled the group context as one which limits the role and impact of the moderator, thereby permitting a more 'natural' discussion to emerge. This view needs to be treated with caution; the group context does not obliterate the role of the moderator, or the research context of the talk.

Consensus and disagreement

The emergence of dissonant views and opinions between participants – what Kitzinger (1994) calls 'argumentative interactions' is a distinctive feature of the focus group method and often makes an important contribution to the richness of the data obtained (Sim 2002). However, there are limitations to how disagreements are expressed in this peer group context. The group context of this methodology, while appropriate for uncovering group discourses and stories, is, meanwhile, likely to reproduce the socially accepted, normative discourse for that group. People with unpopular views, or less confident group members, may be reluctant to air their views in a group context. People are often (though not always – see shortly) reluctant to disagree openly with a stated view, especially in groups of strangers. It is important therefore not to assume consensus just because no one has disagreed openly (Sim 2002). If a divergence of views emerges, it is safe to assume that participants do hold different views; however if no divergence appears, this does not indicate consensus.

General questions can often elicit socially acceptable responses when it is likely that in fact the individuals in the group hold stronger views than this. The timing and stage of the focus group can also make a difference – a question asked in the first few minutes of the focus group may elicit a different response if asked later on when people are more comfortable with the group. Overall, a focus group is likely to elicit 'public' accounts (Smithson 2000, Sim 2002) in contrast to the private accounts which might emerge in individual interviews or in everyday interactions.

But detailed study of group data suggests the opposite can also happen and they can be a forum for contrasting opinions to emerge and develop (Smithson 2000, Pini 2002). There are various powerful counter-examples to the expected 'rule' that focus groups replicate the dominant discourse. Sometimes participants make gentle, or overt challenges to the status quo, and there are particular strengths in the challenging of views by other participants, rather than by the moderator. Kitzinger (1994) shows how difference can be examined in the focus group context, and how the method can be used as a way of studying how differences are negotiated and understood.

One of the strengths of the method (Smithson 2000, Pini 2002) is the way focus group discussions often range between discussion of personal experiences, and collective experiences. Kitzinger and Farquhar (1999) contend that focus groups sometimes provide an opportunity for 'sensitive' topics to be raised, as there is the space for discussion and reflection and time to explore issues in a more in-depth way than might be the case in more routine dialogue. They argue that focus groups can be used to unpack the social construction of sensitive issues, uncover different layers of discourse, and illuminate group taboos and the routine silencing of certain views and experiences. Through attention to sensitive moments, researchers can identify unspoken assumptions and question the nature of everyday talk. Focus group talk, like everyday talk can include many contradictions, norms, and both official and unofficial perspectives on a sensitive topic.

One of the claims made in favour of focus groups as a methodology is that they can be a powerful method for minority groups or groups which are often ignored in other research methods to express their views and experiences (Wilkinson 1998, Smithson 2000). In these cases, the group perspective and concerns can dominate, rather than the interviewer's pre-set agenda.

Silences and omissions in focus groups

All research methods have in-built omissions – things that a specific methodology is unlikely to pick up on. Inevitably, some participants speak freely in the groups and others remain silent, or need encouragement to speak. It is not necessarily a problem if some people remain silent. Silence is an 'enduring feature of human interaction', present in research communicative contexts as elsewhere (Poland and Pederson 1998: 308). Silences and pauses are issues both for focus group moderation, and for analysis. Silences after a specific question can be an indicator to the moderator that the group is not comfortable with talking about a particular issue (Myers 1998).

Emergent themes and discourses

While researchers construct the focus group schedules around their research topics, a particularly interesting feature of focus group methodology is the way in which groups take up these discourses or themes in ways unanticipated by the researchers. It is also common for groups to introduce new themes unanticipated in the research design. Literature on analysing focus groups stresses the key issue that the analytic focus is not on what individuals say in a group context but on the discourses which are constructed within this group context (e.g. Wilkinson 1998, Smithson 2000, Sims 2002). For this reason, analytical approaches which explicitly consider interactive effects and group dynamics are particularly appropriate (Myers 1998, Puchta and Potter 1999, 2002, Stokoe and Smithson 2002). These approaches all focus on how discourses, or themes, are constructed jointly by participants in a group context.

Conversational interaction is viewed as the prime locus for the development, or co-construction (Jacoby and Ochs 1995) of sense-making. Disagreements, challenges and resistances are seen as important parts of the construction of collective opinions. From this perspective, social realities and identities are understood to be socially constructed, fluid and context-dependent, so focus groups are a particularly appropriate method. For example, Munday (2006) has argued that the use of focus groups provides a method particularly suited to researching the construction of collective identity. Puchta and Potter (1999) consider the contradiction in focus group methodology between the requirement that the talk should be both highly focused on predefined topics and issues, and at the same time spontaneous and conversational.

USING FOCUS GROUPS IN SPECIFIC CONTEXTS

Using focus groups in cross-cultural and cross-national research

Focus groups are being increasingly suggested as a good method for understanding cultural variations and differences. The involvement of minority community groups through focus groups has been shown to be a powerful tool in developing culturally appropriate methods (Hughes and DuMont 1993, Pollack 2003, Willgerodt 2003), and in including culturally diverse perspectives in research. There are issues in the running of focus groups in different cultural contexts – in some cultures dissent is not expressed in public, some cultures have more subjects which are not discussed in public, and in some cultures variables such as gender will be a bigger concern. There are topics which tend not to work well in the focus group context, though these vary greatly in different contexts and cultures.

As with any cross-national research, there are issues of translation of research tools and data between languages. With qualitative research methodologies cross-national research also needs to take note of cultural differences in emotional tone, feelings and reflexivity, which are particularly noticeable in focus group research. In some cultures it is not usual to directly disagree in a group situation, or to overtly criticise authority. Ways of interacting are of course cultural as well as responses to a particular method and the result of particular factors such as gender and status. For example, in a cross-European study of new parents' orientations to work, focus groups in Sweden were described by the national research team as 'consensual', with turn taking easily managed. In the same cross-national study, focus groups in the UK were notable for high levels of criticism and outspokenness, while in the Bulgarian focus groups in the same study there was little cross talking or butting in (Brannen 2004).

Using focus groups in feminist research

Focus groups have been widely used in recent feminist research, and feminist social scientists have elaborated on the ways in which the methodology can be used to further feminist aims of giving various minority groups a voice through the research process. For example, Madriz (2000) starts an account of feminist focus group research with a quotation from a Dominican woman telling how she prefers the focus group context as she finds it less intimidating than being alone with an interviewer. Focus groups have been taken up as an appropriate method by both post modernist and feminist standpoint researchers (Wilkinson 1998, Madriz 2000, Olesen 2000). They are seen as a way of lessening the impact of the researcher and permitting minoritised groups to develop and elaborate their own perspective on a research topic, in a 'safe' environment. Madriz argues that 'the focus group is a collectivist rather than an individualistic research method that focuses on the multivocality of participants' attitudes, experiences and beliefs' (Madriz 2000: 836).

However, other feminist researchers are more cautious about the use of focus groups. In practice, while focus groups can be less directive and perhaps less intimidating than traditional research methods, there is wide variation in this, as described elsewhere in this chapter. The moderator is still exerting a strong influence over the group, and still retaining a high degree of control, typically, over the recruitment, procedure and subsequent analysis and reporting of the group. Using focus groups does not in itself make the research 'collectivist', or empower participants. A postmodernist feminist approach which views accounts gathered in a research process as stories, or narratives, can be well suited to focus group methodology, but the questions of how to represent these stories, which questions to ask and which replies to prioritise in analysis, and how to interpret or analyse these stories, are as pertinent for focus group research as for other feminist qualitative methodologies. A priority for feminist focus group researchers is how to make participants' voices heard without being exploited or distorted, and taking account of 'unrealised agendas' of class, race and sexuality (Oleson 2000). Focus groups are not a 'solution' for highlighting the views of oppressed or minority groups, but can, used sensitively, help to facilitate listening to these narratives.

Ethnographic research and focus groups

Ethnographic researchers have made use of small group discussions for many years, although rarely using the term 'focus groups'. Focus groups methodology can fit neatly with certain streams of ethnographic thought, which place the research encounter in a wider social context, and emphasise the social and processual nature of experiences (Tedlock 2000). As with feminist research, focus groups have been viewed within ethnography as a way of emphasising the collective nature of experience, and the social context of accounts.

Focus groups in organisational research

Conducting focus groups in an organisational context has particular implications. While it can be an advantage having people from the same departments and work teams, who have shared experiences and are often comfortable talking together, there can be problems with how freely people feel they can express themselves in a workplace situation. Shared workplace experiences such as restructuring, management experiences, enthusiasm or resistance to work-life initiatives, can encourage feelings of solidarity among team members. Groups can share common knowledge about relevant issues in the company even when the people were strangers. For example, in a study of new parents in organisations (das Dores Guerreiro 2004), everyone had a strong view about the change from formal to informal flexi-time, and there had clearly been a great deal of discussion over the past months about it which was continued in lively focus group discussion.

Possible drawbacks of using focus groups in organisational settings include people feeling unable to speak out in front of superiors or people from different parts of the organisation. It is generally not recommended to place managers and employees in the same group, although this will vary with the nature of the organisation. Privacy and ethical issues are of particular importance in an organisational context, where people are encouraged to talk freely in front of colleagues.

Online focus groups

The use of online interviewing, including group interviewing, is being increasingly taken up in social science research. Online focus group research methods are part of this rapid expansion of online methodologies (e.g. Murray 1997, Chappell 2003). There are various reasons for this. It can be a good way of including in research hard-to-reach groups. An online focus group method can bring together geographically distant participants in one, online forum. It can also be used to bring together people with disabilities or illnesses who would not otherwise find it easy to participate in research, especially in group contexts. For example, Kralik et al. (2006) brought together people to explore experiences of chronic illness. It is also a potentially useful way of talking in a group context about sensitive or embarrassing issues, in a relatively anonymous context. Other reasons for the growing popularity of online focus group methods include cost savings, and attracting people who would otherwise have little time to participate (Edmunds 1999).

There are two main discussion options available when running an online focus group – synchronous and asynchronous (Chappell 2003). Synchronous discussions occur in 'real time' with the moderator and participants all logged onto a discussion at the same time, posting their comments on a joint board. While this is a close simulation of a face-to-face focus group, one of the advantages of an online method (the ability to participate at one's own convenience) is no longer available. Additional drawbacks of this method are that the conversation can become hard to follow and participants tend to answer questions with short, 'I agree'-type responses because they feel pressured to answer quickly. This can also pose problems for the moderator. It can become difficult to keep track of the conversations and responses of group members, as there is often more than one track of conversations running simultaneously (Montoya-Weiss et al., 1998). The other main online focus group option is asynchronous discussions, which do not occur in real time. Messages are posted in response to the moderator and the group members at the participants' convenience. Participants do not have to be logged on at the same time and can participate at any point during the day or night.

Edmunds (1999) points out that online groups can lead to greater anonymity for participants, which can lead to greater openness. The downside of this, and a particular issue for online groups is the possibility of 'fake' participants – people joining in with false personas or providing false information (a regular problem on internet chat rooms, for example). While online methods might seem to be particularly susceptible to this sort of misinformation, it is useful to remember that in 'real' focus groups, as with other forms of research, the participant is an actor constructing a performance (Goffman 1981). Newhagan and Rafaeli (1996) pointed out that using electronic media affected how people communicated. While it is important to be aware of the ways in which different media affect people's communication patterns, this is an issue for all qualitative social research, and all focus group situations, not just for online groups.

There are ways of regulating participation to limit possible misuse, for example making contact individually with the focus group participants before the online group occurs. There is a growing literature on chat room behaviour and discourses, and the use of online methods in social science, which is particularly relevant when considering the use and analysis of online focus groups (Rezabek 2000).

CONCLUSIONS

The diverse nature of focus group research reflects the origins of focus groups, first in social science research before being taken up mainly by market researchers for several decades, and more recently becoming widely and increasingly popular in various social research fields. The method is used by researchers from very varied epistemological and theoretical research traditions, which is reflected in the variations of approaches, and specifically the techniques and approaches to analysing the talk produced in this context.

There are conceptual, methodological and ethical issues in focus group research. As with other qualitative research methods, there are opportunities for consciously or unconsciously manipulating the participants' responses, and it is perhaps a feature of focus group methodology, with its seeming emphasis on 'natural discussion' and 'collective accounts', for there to be relatively little explicit awareness of the constructed nature of the discussion, and the salience of the moderator and research agenda throughout the process. The 'collective stories' which

are produced in this way perhaps mitigate the awareness that the interactions occurring in this formalised research setting will differ in many ways from interactions in other contexts. As well as differing from individual interview data, focus group talk will also be substantially different from 'natural' conversation.

Focus groups have specific dilemmas, both ethical and procedural, such as respect for individuals' privacy, and the difficulties of dealing with inappropriate group behaviour (for example, insensitive comments or reactions to another participant's contribution), as well as the more ubiquitous dilemmas of qualitative research concerning respect for participants' voices, and concerns for misrepresenting the experiences and discussions of vulnerable groups.

The focus group method does have particular strengths. It enables research participants to discuss and develop ideas collectively, and articulate their ideas in their own terms, bringing forward their own priorities and perspectives. Not only can a wide variety of opinions be given and considered, but also a wide variety of interactive techniques can be observed. Participants engage in a range of argumentative behaviours, which results in a depth of dialogue not often found in individual interviews. Moreover, some of these limitations can also be viewed as possibilities for the method. Myers suggests that 'the constraints on talk do not invalidate focus group findings; in fact, it is these constraints that make them practicable and interpretable' (Myers 1998, p. 107). Focus groups permit some insights into rhetorical processes, or contemporary discourses. Another plus is that participants often report that joining in a focus group has been an enjoyable and creative experience (Wilkinson 1998, Madriz 2000, Smithson 2000, Pini 2002).

The effects of group dynamics in the focus groups can therefore be of benefit in social research for exploring issues from the perspective of the participants, in a way that is culturally sensitive to participants' priorities and experiences. While there are some limitations of focus group research, these can be partially overcome by awareness of the constraints, by informed analysis, and by detailed consideration of the way the conversations are socially constructed in the group context, and are narratives produced jointly by the co-participants and also by the moderator.

REFERENCES

Agar, M. and MacDonald, J. (1995) Focus groups and ethnography. *Human Organization* 54: 78–86.

Beck, L. C., Trombetta, W. L. and Share, S. (1986) Using focus group sessions before decisions are made. *North Carolina Medical Journal* 47(2): 73–4.

Bloor, M., Frankland, J., Thomas, M. and Robson, K. (2000) *Focus groups in social research*. Sage: London.

Bradburn, N. M. and Sudman, S. (1979) *Improving interview method and questionnaire design*. San Francisco: Jossey-Bass.

Brannen, J. (2004) *Methodological issues in the consolidated case studies*. Research Report #5 for the EU Framework 5 funded study 'Gender, parenthood and the changing European workplace'. Printed by the Manchester Metropolitan University: Research Institute for Health and Social Change.

Brannen, J., Lewis, S., Nilsen, A. and Smithson, J. (eds) (2002) *Young Europeans, work and family: Futures in transition. London: Routledge.*

Bryman, A. (1988) *Quantity and quality in social research*. London: Unwin Hyman.

Chappell, D. (2003) *A procedural manual for the online work-family focus group*. Centre for Families, Work and Well-being, Guelph, Canada.

Das Dores Guerreiro, M. (2004) *Case studies report*. Research report #3 for the EU Framework 5 funded study 'Gender, parenthood and the changing European workplace'. ISBN 1-900139-46-4. Printed by the Manchester Metropolitan University: Research Institute for Health and Social Change.

Drew, P. and Heritage, J. (eds) (1992) *Talk at work*. Cambridge: Cambridge University Press.

Du Bois, B. (1983) Passionate Scholarship: Notes on values, knowing and method in feminist social science. In G. Bowles and R. D. Klein (eds) *Theories of women's studies*. London: Routledge.

Edmunds, H. (1999) *The focus group research handbook*. Lincolnwood, IL: NTC Business Books/Contemporary Publishing.

Goffman, E. (1981) *Forms of talk*. Oxford: Blackwell.

Greenbaum, T. (1998) *The handbook for focus group research*. Sage: London.

Hughes, D. and DuMont, K. (1993) Using focus groups to facilitate culturally anchored research. *American Journal of Community Psychology* 21(6): 775–806.

Jacoby, S. and Ochs, E. (1995) Co-construction: An introduction. *Research on Language and Social Interaction* 28(3): 171–183.

Kitzinger, J. (1994) The methodology of focus groups: The importance of interaction between research participants. *Sociology of Health and Illness* 16(1): 103–121.

Kitzinger, J. (1995) Introducing focus groups. *British Medical Journal* 311: 299–302.

Kitzinger, J. and Farquhar, C. (1999) The analytical potential of 'sensitive moments' in focus group discussions. In Barbour, Rosaline S. and Kitzinger, Jenny (eds) *Developing focus group research: Politics, theory and practice*. London: Sage.

Kitzinger, C. and Frith, H. (1999) Just say no? The use of conversation analysis in developing a feminist perspective on sexual refusal. *Discourse and Society* 10/3: 293–316.

Kralik, D., Price, K., Warren, J. and Koch, T. (2006) Issues in data generation using email group conversations for nursing research. *Journal of Advanced Nursing* 53/2: 213–220.

Kreuger, R. A. (1994) *Focus groups: A practical guide for applied research*, 2nd edition. Newbury Park: Sage.

Kreuger, R. A. (1998) *Analyzing and reporting focus group results. Focus group kit, Volume 6*. California: Sage.

Madriz, E. (2000) Focus groups in feminist research. In N. K. Denzin and Y. S. Lincoln (eds) *Handbook of qualitative research*. California: Sage.

Merton, R. K. and Kendall, P. L. (1946) The focused interview. *American Journal of Sociology* 51: 541–557.

Montoya-Weiss, M. M., Massey, A. P. and Clapper, D. L. (1998) On-line focus groups: Conceptual issues and a research tool. *European Journal of Marketing* 32: 713–723.

Morgan, D. L. (1988) *Focus groups as qualitative research*. Newbury Park, CA: Sage.

Morgan, D. L. (2002) Focus group interviewing. In J. F. Gubrium and J. A. Holstein (eds) *Handbook of interviewing research. Context and method*. Thousand Oaks, California: Sage.

Morgan, D. L. and Kreuger, R. A. (1998) *The focus group kit*. California: Sage.

Munday, J. (2006) *Identity in focus: The use of focus groups to study the construction of collective identity*. *Sociology* 40/1: 89–105.

Murray, P. J. (1997) Using virtual focus groups in qualitative research. *Qualitative Health Research* 7(4): 542–554.

Myers, G. (1998) Displaying opinions: topics and disagreement in focus groups. *Language in Society* 27: 85–111.

Newhagen, J. E. and Rafaeli, S. (1996) Why communication researchers should study the internet: a dialogue. *Journal of Communication* 46(1): 4–13.

Oleson, V. L. (2000) In N. K. Denzin and Y. S. Lincoln (eds) *Handbook of qualitative research*. California: Sage.

Pini, B. (2002) Focus groups, feminist research and farm women: opportunities for empowerment in rural social research. *Journal of Rural Studies* 18/3: 339–351.

Poland, B. and Pederson, A. (1998) Reading between the lines: interpreting silences in qualitative research. *Qualitative Inquiry* 4/2: 293–312.

Pollack, S. (2003) Focus-group methodology in research with incarcerated women: race, power, and collective experience. *Affilia* 18/4: 461–472.

Puchta, C. and Potter, J. (1999) Asking elaborate questions: focus groups and the management of spontaneity. *Journal of Sociolinguistics* 3: 314–335.

Puchta, C. and Potter, J. (2002) Manufacturing individual opinions: market research focus groups and the discursive psychology of attitudes. *British Journal of Social Psychology* 41: 345–363.

Rezabek, R. (January, 2000) Online focus groups: electronic discussions for research. *Forum for Qualitative Social Research* [On-line Journal], 1(1). Available at: *http://qualitative-research.net/fqs* [2007, 08,08].

Ritchie, J. and Lewis, J. (eds) (2003) *Qualitative research practice: a guide for social science students and researchers*. Thousand Oaks, California: Sage.

Ronen, G. M., Rosenbaum, P., Law, M. and Streiner, D. L. (2001) Health-related quality of life in childhood disorders: a modified focus group technique to involve children. *Quality of Life Research* 10(1): 71–79.

Silverman, D. (1993) *Interpreting qualitative data: methods for analysing talk, text and interaction*. London: Sage.

Silverman, D. (2000) Analyzing talk and text. In N. K. Denzin and Y. S. Lincoln (eds) *Handbook of qualitative research*. California: Sage.

Sim, J. (2002) Collecting and analysing qualitative data: issues raised by the focus group. *Journal of Advanced Nursing 28(2): 345–352.*

Smithson, J. (2000) Using and analysing focus groups: limitations and possibilities. *International Journal of Methodology: Theory and Practice* 3(2): 103–119.

Stokoe, E. H. and Smithson, J. (2002) Gender and sexuality in talk-in-interaction: considering conversation analytic perspectives. In P. McIlvenny (ed.) *Talking gender and sexuality*. John Benjamins: Amsterdam.

Tedlock, B. (2000) Ethnography and ethnographic representation. In N. K. Denzin and Y. S. Lincoln (eds) *Handbook of qualitative research*. California: Sage.

Templeton, Jane F. (1987) *A guide for marketing and advertising professionals*. Chicago: Probus.

Vaughn, S., Shay Schumm, J. and Sinagub, J. (1996) *Focus group interviews in education and psychology.* California: Sage.

Wilkinson, S. (1998) Focus group methodology: a review. *International Journal of Social Research Methodology, Theory and Practice* 1(3): 181–204.

Wilkinson, S. and Kitzinger, C. (1996) *Representing the other*. London: Sage.

Willgerodt, M. A. (2003) Using focus groups to develop culturally relevant instruments. *Western Journal of Nursing Research 25(7): 798–814.*

PART IV

Types of Analysis and Interpretation of Evidence

This section inevitably only covers some of the many analytic strategies available. It covers a number of types of analysis available in relation to quantitative and qualitative data and issues that the researcher will encounter. It also has a number of chapters that focus on the analysis of data derived via different methods.

ANALYSIS OF PRIMARY QUANTITATIVE DATA

Three chapters focus on quantitative data: one on the analysis of change; a second on the analysis of latent variables (variables that cannot be measured); and a third on the biases that are introduced into analysis when there are no comparison groups or control groups as in evaluation research.

Analysing change is difficult. Only in the past 35 years have approaches to statistical measures of change been developed. Chapter 22 by Graham, Singer and Willett provides an introduction to one approach to the analysis of quantitative longitudinal data. The chapter goes into enough depth to provide a basic understanding of longitudinal modelling but does not become so technical that it is difficult for a person who is not familiar with the terminology and concepts to follow.

One of the problems for the student in this field is the surfeit of terms for similar approaches: individual growth modelling, random coefficient modelling, multilevel modelling, mixed modelling, and hierarchical linear modelling, together with the range of statistical packages that can be used. The term the authors use is multilevel modelling. This approach has several advantages that include: its ability to deal with any number of time points; that each wave of data can be collected with different time schedules and; that no data need be discarded because they are missing. The approach can be applied to linear, non-linear and discontinuous trends. The analysis can include both time-invariant predictors such as gender and race as well as ones that do change with time such as attitudes. Moreover, these predictors can be fixed or randomly varied across persons.

In Chapter 23, Hoyle addresses the analysis of complex quantitative data, focusing on latent variable modelling, which examines the presence or influence of constructs that cannot be measured. The chapter discusses the use of linear structural equation modelling (SEM) to evaluate social models, an approach that has many uses in the social sciences: in particular the evaluation of measurement models, mediated effects, moderator effects and longitudinal data using several approaches including latent growth curve models. In all these cases a predicted model is compared to actually observed data to determine if the predicted model is a good fit with the data. The predicted model describes the relationships among constructs and can be regarded as a hypothesis of the mechanisms that produced the data. The use of latent variables is especially useful in decreasing the number of variables that need to be tested and in increasing the reliability of measurement. SEM's measurement component is used to test the relationship among latent variables and their indicators. The structural component is concerned with the directional relationship. While the latter appears to be causal, because the path model specifies direction, Hoyle is quick to point out that unless the data are longitudinal then causal conclusions cannot be made. The measurement component can be used to test if the model is consistent across time or samples, which would indicate measurement invariance. He notes that although this is a very valuable function of SEM it is rarely used that way. Hoyle sets out six limitations of SEM including requiring a sample size of a minimum of 400 in order to obtain stable estimates but he also predicts that SEM's use will grow because of its many advantages compared to other techniques.

In Chapter 24 West and Thoemmes address the issue of having appropriate control or comparison groups in research using an intervention or a programme evaluation, especially when the question being addressed is the effectiveness of an intervention. These techniques, even though they have important limitations, provide a safety net for experimental social research. The authors provide valuable advice for research where the design is intended to have non-equivalent groups or where there is a failure of random assignment, as well as research that sets out to have random assignment. They discuss several techniques that can be used in an attempt to deal with groups that are not equivalent at the start of the study. However, even when the design is labelled as random assignment, the implementation of the design may result in obtaining non-comparable groups. Unfortunately, West and Thoemmes conclude from their literature review that it is not clear whether the bias introduced by having non-equivalent groups will make the comparison between the two groups appear smaller or larger. The chapter also deals with the following issues: the importance of lack of bias in the assignment; the importance of delivering the intervention to everyone in the treatment group; issues of attrition; and questions concerning the information given to intervention and non-intervention groups.

ANALYSIS OF PRIMARY QUALITATIVE DATA

Five chapters focus on the analysis of primary qualitative data. Three chapters are devoted to the analysis of talk: a chapter on discourse analysis and conversation analysis; a chapter on the analysis of narrative and storytelling; and a chapter on grounded theory.

Charles Antaki's chapter (25) on how to analyse discourse covers a lot of ground not only by talking about different varieties of discourse analysis (DA) but also by including conversation analysis (CA). Even though these approaches are often seen as separate or even belonging to opposing camps, both types of analysis address the organization of talk and text as 'speech acts' thereby emphasizing their agentic dimension. Among the plethora of methods used for analysing discourse, Antaki also discusses narrative analysis, critical discourse analysis, interactional sociolinguistics, membership category analysis, discursive psychology, and ethnomethodologically inspired DA. Social interaction as revealed through the lens of CA is similar to other ways in which discourse is analysed: it can discover things about interaction and language use that the participant did not suspect, or which have effects or functions which did not figure in the original aims of the encounter or speaker. Such revelations, whatever the method used in teasing them out, are the ultimate criteria for the right to claim to have carried out an analysis. As Antaki stresses, any researcher who claims to be a discourse analyst must 'add value' to what can be read or heard in speech and claims must be backed up by evidence grounded in the words used (or not used). Thus the 'argumentative steps' leading to the conclusion must be available to the reader and fellow-scholar.

In discussing the analysis of narrative Hyvarinen makes a very rich contribution to the Handbook. The chapter 26 starts with a wide-ranging account of the different definitions of narrative, many of which have been potentially confusing including ordinary talk to accounts that are 'narratives' and those that 'possess narrativity'. The chapter goes on to suggest that narrative analysis includes as many genres as the term narrative itself and picks out two developments that have had great impact on social research: grand narratives and the notion of 'life as narrative'. The discussion then turns to the methods of analysis that have been applied to different genres of narrative, in particular the Proppian model in which Russian wonder tales were analysed in terms of the basic functions of actions performed by their different characters in the plots and the textual approach adopted by Labov and Waletsky who sought to identify the basic elements of narrative. The chapter then moves to recent developments: to the study of narratives as *practices* and in *context*, thereby making a distinction between the story and the storying process. The last part of the chapter discusses how narrative practices are transformed into cultural scripts, shape individual action and narration, and lead to breach and discordance.

Grounded theory has been an extremely important development in the analysis of talk although it does not need to be limited to such a form of data. In Chapter 27, Kathy Charmaz provides an illuminating analysis of its development according to its originators – Glaser and Strauss in their book *The Discovery of Grounded Theory* published in 1967. She discusses the development of their ideas from her own position as a long-time exponent and developer of the method. Her argument is that its clear appeal lay in the fact that *The Discovery of Grounded Theory* was the first methodological text to set out explicit

systematic procedures for the analysis of qualitative data. Hitherto such strategies were largely learned by researchers in the field. In a context and time in which US research was largely quantitative or rather status was accorded largely to quantitative research, the systematization of its approach bestowed on qualitative research some legitimacy. However, as Charmaz argues, in their enthusiasm followers of the approach sought to project a rigidity on to it, in particular a belief that disallowed macro social processes or structures that are left untapped at the interactional level, while a second considerable benefit of a grounded approach – namely to generate theory – was rarely exploited. Both developments are ironic, Charmaz notes, given grounded theory's original openness to methodological innovation and development. On the other hand, this chapter represents an inspiring account of grounded theory and encouragement for its further use notably for those who wish 'by interrogating and following content, ..[to] construct form for their inquiry, rather than solely creating content from form used as a recipe for generating research' (Charmaz Chapter 27).

Two chapters focus on the analysis of qualitative material of a different kind, the first on the analysis of documents and the next on the analysis of visual material.

Documents are a key source of data but methodological guidance to their analysis and use is rare. Typically documents are used by researchers as resources for trawling content. The grounded theorist distinction between form and content is taken up by Lindsay Prior in Chapter 28 on documentary research. Prior argues they can also be seen as a topic in their own right in which the focus is on documents as 'informants' that perform functions in social interaction. In arguing in favour of a focus upon discourse (as well as content) Prior gives a striking example of how the scientific discovery of DNA came to be represented in text as something that was endowed with creative action. Without the use of metaphors drawn from communication this would not have been possible to convey and hence for the public to comprehend.

Documents are also read and understood – as in Bernstein's terms (Bernstein 2000[1]) they are the object of recontextualization. They may 'act', as in the case of a will, and they may form part of a network of actors, as in the case of a genre of literature, and they are used in social interaction to structure and pattern their readers.

Like documentary methods visual methods are a relatively ignored field of methodology with the exception of social anthropology where visual data have been used for some time. In Chapter 29, Christian Heath and Paul Luff set out a case for a particular approach within sociology that draws upon ethnomethodology and conversation analysis and directs analytic attention towards the social and interactional accomplishment of everyday activities and events. In their chapter, they draw upon their own study of auctions and auction houses, to provide some practical guidance to using video recordings to address the social and interactional organization of naturally occurring events.

SECONDARY AND META-ANALYSIS

Three chapters are concerned with the secondary analysis of data: the first on qualitative data, the second on quantitative data, while the third is a discussion of meta-analysis.

The re-use of qualitative data is not established practice in social research, as Janet Heaton suggests in Chapter 30. However, it is a developing methodology, and the re-use of qualitative data is becoming more common, partly due to computer technology and partly due to the promotion of data sharing. Social researchers can access qualitative data for secondary analysis in three ways: through data archives, through informal data sharing, and by re-using data from their own previous research. The latter is still the most common alternative, despite the increasing availability of qualitative data collected by others. Heaton lists several ways in which qualitative data can be re-used. In supra analysis, the focus of the secondary analysis transcends the primary data analysis in that new theoretical, empirical

or methodological questions are explored. Supplementary analysis involves the in-depth investigation of an issue, or one aspect of the data, that was not addressed, or was only partly covered, in the original research. Instead, the purpose of re-analysis is to verify and corroborate the findings of previous work. In amplified analysis, two or more datasets are utilized to form a larger dataset, or used to compare different populations. Finally in assorted analysis, secondary analysis of qualitative data is combined with additional primary research. Despite recent advances in the re-use of qualitative data, Heaton stresses that further work is needed to explore and outline different strategies for re-using qualitative data, and to examine the acceptability of these strategies to research participants and the public.

Angela Dale and colleagues in Chapter 31 provide a mine of useful information about the secondary analysis of quantitative data. They present an excellent overview of the types of data available that are collected by academics, governments and supra-national organizations such as the European Union. These include: administrative datasets, national cohort and panel studies, international and national surveys, pooled samples from several surveys (where no one source provides sufficient numbers of a particular group that is of interest), and micro datasets that link together administrative records for the same individuals. The secondary analysis of large-scale datasets is moreover occurring in a context in which attempts are being made to take a more global view of available datasets. For example, the UK's Economic and Social Research Council is now taking a strategic approach by providing a national map that will enable researchers to find their way through the myriad resources available. The chapter is highly practical and includes some tips on how to gain access to these datasets, with a particular focus upon data archives. It has the added advantage of covering datasets in a range of countries. It also makes reference to ways in which such datasets may be used in combination with qualitative methods as part of a mixed-methods strategy. The last three sections of the chapter offer cautionary advice about using data collected for different purposes to those of the secondary analyst and discuss a variety of good practices. The chapter also raises ethical issues stressing how secondary data analysts inherit responsibilities at the point of access to these data. A section is importantly devoted to advances in access to data via e-social science (grid technology).

Meta-analysis is the integration of data from similar studies that leads to a quantitative summary of the results of these studies. In Chapter 32 Patall and Cooper provide a comprehensive framework for understanding meta-analysis that is increasingly used to make literature reviews of quantitative research more systematic, replacing the more traditional narrative review. However they suggest that informed social scientists need to be aware of both the advantages and disadvantages of meta-analysis, regardless of their own use of this approach. They discuss a range of issues that include: the identification of studies for inclusion; coding frames, calculation of effect sizes; sample weighting and so on. They also identify the problems to do with testing the same relationship in all the studies under review, issues concerning the independence of findings, and the variable quality of the studies included. This chapter provides an excellent way to obtain competence in addressing these issues.

INTEGRATING ANALYSES OF DATA FROM DIFFERENT SOURCES

Finally, we come to the key issue of how to integrate the analysis of data from different sources. One of the central themes of this section, to which three chapters are devoted, is the combination of different data collected through different methods. In Chapter 33, Jane Fielding and Nigel Fielding discuss the integration of qualitative and quantitative data, that which is most commonly described as mixed-methods research. They emphasize that what is important is not the choice of design and use of different data sources

per se but the logic that underlies the integration of data within the analysis, and the extent to which the combination of methods strengthens the validity of that analysis. As the authors put it, data integration should act as quality control. This does not in their view mean ignoring the epistemological assumptions underlying each method but recognizing that there are several ways of interpreting a research question, while being open to the benefits and constraints of each type of data.

The authors point to several different possible mixed-method research designs and discuss their own study in some depth in which both qualitative and quantitative methods were equally important. They show how in their study of public responses to flood warning, how one method (a survey) revealed that many of those identified according to external measures and perspectives as being at risk of flooding were unaware of the risks, while the qualitative method they used explained this lack of awareness. They conclude that, rather than seeing the different methods as generating competing findings, the complex social phenomena under investigation required the coordination of different perspectives and their associated methodologies.

Cronin et al. in Chapter 34 take a similar view about the integration of different types of data. Their concern is to describe the processes involved in analytic integration. Drawing upon their own research, this discussion is about research in which no one method is dominant. Through the use of in-depth interviews, life histories and visual methods they explored the meaning of vulnerability and safety in everyday life. They broadly defined these different data sources as qualitative. The process of analysis they describe is one in which they followed 'different threads': using one method they picked out one thread of the analysis, generated either inductively or imported from external theory, that they then pursued in the analysis of data produced by the other methods. The chapter is particularly useful in giving a very detailed account of the steps in the analytic process while at the same time demonstrating close attention to epistemological and theoretical issues and the intrinsic form of the data. Thus it identifies how the researchers sought to preserve the integrity of the individual narrative accounts and cautions against the translation of one set of data into another – in this study the translation of visual data into textual data.

In Chapter 35, Max Bergmann considers what data 'are', the reasons for using more than one dataset for a research question and how these reasons connect differently to various parts of the research process. The chapter reviews issues concerned with the analysis of different sources of largely quantitative data and discusses how data are always contingent and shaped by analytic strategies; analyses of data provide only partial answers to research questions. In making this case a number of arguments are presented for using a number of different (quantitative) data sources: verification, convergence, complementarity and holism, rationales that apply equally in research that combines quantitative and qualitative data. These ways of combining data are played out at different phases of the research process so that data in a qualitative form may be transformed into quantitative format at the point of data collection, for example through CAPI technology. Such processes of transformation Bergman refers to as 'a form of taming and disciplining' data for a particular type of analysis. The chapter begins and ends with a reference to Segal's law that does not propose that it is better to

have just one watch instead of two; instead, it may simply be less confusing.

The Handbook's last chapter is about writing and presenting social research. Amir Marvasti (Chapter 36) suggests alternative ways of writing social science and argues that during the second half of the twentieth century a 'third culture' of representation has challenged the necessity of treating science and literature as mutually exclusive realms of knowledge. This means that in the social sciences there is a growing awareness of the rhetorical dimensions of writing and representing facts, so that efforts to inscribe social reality also involve linguistic constructive practice. As a consequence, in recent decades alternative forms of writing have emerged. These Marvasti classifies into six genres: (1) writing with pictures; (2) performative writing; (3) writing factual fiction; (4) poetic representation; (5) writing the author; and (6) post-colonial writing. Marvasti also discusses the ways in which alternative texts have been criticized. The chapter provides the reader with a map of an ever-changing terrain and suggests that many territories are still to be discovered.

NOTES

1 Bernstein, B. (2000) Pedagogy, Symbolic Control and Identity Theory: Research Critique, Lanham Maryland: Rowman and Littlefield.

An Introduction to the Multilevel Model for Change

Suzanne E. Graham, Judith D. Singer and
John B. Willett

Researchers often examine how individual change over time depends on selected predictors by fitting a *multilevel model for change*. Generations of behavioral scientists have been interested in measuring and investigating individual change, but for decades, the prevailing view was that it was impossible to do well (Cronbach and Furby, 1970). During the 1980s, however, methodologists working within a variety of different disciplines developed a class of appropriate methods—known variously as *individual growth modeling, random coefficient modeling, multilevel modeling, mixed modeling*, and *hierarchical linear modeling*—that permit the effective investigation of change. Today we know that it is indeed possible to model change, and to do it well, as long as you have *longitudinal data* available (Rogosa et al., 1982; Willett, 1988).

A multilevel model for change can be fit successfully to longitudinal data of many different kinds. The research design that generated the data can be either experimental or observational, prospective or retrospective. Time can be measured in whatever units make

the most sense to the research question—from seconds to years, sessions to semesters. The data collection schedule can be fixed (everyone has the same periodicity) or flexible (each person has a unique schedule); the number of waves of data collected can be identical or vary from person to person. And don't let the term 'growth model' fool you—these models are also appropriate for outcomes that *decrease* over time (e.g. weight loss among dieters) or exhibit complex trajectories that include plateaus and reversals.

Furthermore, fitting a multilevel model for change can be used to address research questions posed across many substantive disciplines. In medicine, we study change over time in aspects of health status, such as alcohol consumption among adolescents (Curran et al., 1997). In education, we examine changes in student academic achievement over time, for example, the development of the understanding of mathematical concepts during secondary school (Ai, 2002). In psychology, we investigate changes in behavioral outcomes, such as externalizing behaviors or depressive episodes, over time (Keiley et al., 2000).

Perhaps the most intuitively appealing way of understanding how a multilevel model for change is postulated is to link its specification to two distinct substantive questions about change, each arising from a particular level in a natural hierarchy:

- At *level-1*—the 'within-person' or intra-individual level—we can ask questions about each person's *individual change trajectory*. Does a particular student's mathematics achievement improve rapidly during secondary school? Does another student's achievement increase less rapidly? Might yet another student's mathematics achievement actually decrease over time? Are these changes linear or non-linear? The goal of addressing a level-1 research question is to interrogate the trajectory of each person's individual growth over time.
- At *level-2*—the 'between-person' or inter-individual level—we can ask how other variables may predict differences among the change trajectories of many individuals. On average, do girls' and boys' mathematics achievement trajectories start at the same initial level? Do boys and girls have the same rates of change over time? Do the change trajectories differ systematically by other important individual characteristics, such as a student's race or socio-economic background? The goal of addressing a level-2 research question is to interrogate any heterogeneity in change among individuals in order to determine the *relationship* between predictors and the growth trajectories.

These two types of questions are natural precursors of the statistical models that together form an overall *multilevel model for change*.

In this chapter, we illustrate these ideas using five waves of mathematics achievement data collected as part of the *Longitudinal Study of American Youth* [LSAY], a national longitudinal study of U.S. secondary school students (Miller et al., 2000). LSAY data were collected from 5,945 students over the course of seven years, beginning in the fall of 1987 when the students were in either 7th or 10th grade. A primary focus of the LSAY investigation was on the measurement of students' mathematics achievement over time,

using items from the National Assessment of Educational Progress. Here, in our example, we present analyses of the mathematics achievement data from a sub-sample of 1,322 White and African-American students between 7th grade and 11th grade. We begin by examining the effects of race on changes in the students' mathematics achievement over time. Then, we investigate whether individual mathematics achievement growth trajectories differ for students from different socio-economic backgrounds and whether girls' trajectories differ from those of boys.

Level-1 model for individual change

In the left-hand panel of Figure 22.1, we plot the mathematics achievement (MATHACH) of one African-American girl from our dataset against her grade, between 7th and 11th grade. Notice the upward trend in the empirical growth record, which we have summarized in the figure by superimposing an ordinary least squares (OLS) 'achievement on grade' linear regression line, fitted for this girl. With few waves of data, it is difficult to argue that anything except a linear model is suitable for representing change, within-person. Here, with five waves of data, we need not be limited to thinking only in terms of linear trajectories, but for simplicity we begin here by focusing on linear growth over time. Later in the chapter we consider non-linear growth trajectories.

A level-1 statistical model, or *individual growth model*, can be specified to represent the change that we hypothesize each member of the population will experience during the time period under study. Assuming that true individual change is a linear function of grade, for instance, a reasonable level-1 model may be:

$$Y_{ij} = \left[\pi_{0i} + \pi_{1i}(GRADE_{ij} - 7)\right] + \varepsilon_{ij} \quad (1)$$

This model asserts that, in the population from which this sample was drawn, Y_{ij}, the value of *MATHACH* for student i at time j is constituted from two important parts.

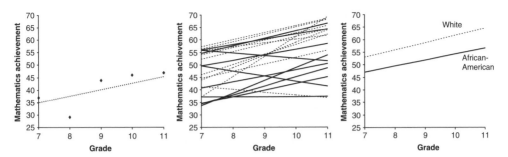

Figure 22.1 Developing a multilevel model for change using data on mathematics achievement over time. Left-hand panel contains the empirical growth record of one African-American girl plotted against her grade in school. Middle panel presents exploratory OLS-fitted trajectories for a random sample of 10 White and 10 African-American students (coded using dashed lines for White students and solid lines for African-American students). Right-hand panel presents fitted change trajectories for White and African-American students, obtained by substituting prototypical predictor values into the fitted multilevel model for change

The first part — in brackets in equation (1) — describes the underlying true change for this individual as a linear function of his (or her) grade in school on that occasion ($GRADE_{ij}$). In our case, the model implicitly assumes that a straight line adequately represents the student's true change trajectory over time. The second part of the individual growth model is a random error (ε_{ij}), which is intended to account for the scatter of the observed data around the individual true change trajectory. Even though everyone in our example was assessed on the same five occasions (grades 7, 8, 9, 10, and 11), this basic level-1 model can be used in a wide variety of other datasets, even those in which the timing and spacing of waves varies across people.

The brackets in equation (1) identify the model's important structural component, which represents our hypotheses about each person's true trajectory of change in mathematics achievement over time. The model stipulates that this linear trajectory is characterized by two critical individual growth parameters, π_{0i} and π_{1i}, which determine its shape for the ith student in the population. If the model is appropriate, these parameters represent the fundamental features of each student's true growth trajectory, and as such, become the objects of prediction in the linked level-2 model that we specify below.

An important feature of the level-1 specification is that the researcher controls the substantive meaning of these parameters by choosing an appropriate metric for the temporal predictor. For example, in this level-1 model, the intercept, π_{0i}, represents student i's true mathematics achievement in 7th grade. This interpretation applies because we *centered GRADE* in the level-1 model by subtracting the constant '7' from it, to provide the level-1 predictor ($GRADE-7$). Had we not centered the predictor in this way, the intercept π_{0i} would represent individual i's true value of mathematics achievement at grade 0, which, corresponding with kindergarten, predates the onset of data collection! Centering the level-1 time predictor on the first wave of data collection, as we have done here, is a popular approach because it allows us to interpret π_{0i} easily: it is student i's true 'initial' status, at the beginning of the study.

Perhaps a more important individual growth parameter is slope, π_{1i}, which represents the rate at which student i's true mathematics achievement changes over time. Since time is measured in grades, in our example, individual growth parameter π_{1i} represents student i's true annual rate of change in mathematics achievement. During the investigation—from 7th grade to 11th grade—her achievement is hypothesized to change by π_{1i} *per grade*. Because we hypothesize that each individual in the population has his (or her) own rate of true change, this growth parameter has the subscript i.

In specifying a level-1 model, we implicitly assume that all the true individual change trajectories in the population have a common algebraic form. But because each person has his or her own value of the individual growth parameters, everyone does not need to follow exactly the same trajectory. Students' true mathematics achievement levels in 7th grade may vary, as may their rates of true change in achievement. Some students may begin 7th grade with lower mathematics achievement than others, and some students' mathematics achievement may improve more rapidly over time than others. Yet other students may have mathematics achievement trajectories that actually *decrease* over time. Specifying the level-1 model appropriately allows us to specify the trajectories of different participants using only the values of their individual growth parameters. This leap is the cornerstone of the growth curve modeling approach to analyzing longitudinal data because it means that we can study inter-individual differences in individual growth *trajectories* by studying inter-individual variation in growth *parameters*. Our general questions about predictors of 'change' then become questions about the relationship between the individual growth parameters and those predictors.

Level-2 model for inter-individual differences in change

Once the level-1 model has been specified, a level-2 statistical model can then codify the hypothesized relationship between the inter-individual differences in the change trajectories (as embodied in the individual growth parameters) and time-invariant characteristics of individuals, such as race and gender. For instance, we can use a level-2 model to address questions like: On average,

do African-American 7th graders have lower mathematics achievement than their White peers, or do they have different rates of change in achievement from 7th grade to 11th grade?

To develop intuition about the level-2 model, examine the middle panel of Figure 22. 1, which represents an exploratory analysis in which we plot fitted OLS individual growth trajectories for a random subset of 10 White and 10 African-American students in our example (coded using solid lines to represent African-American students and dashed lines for White students). As noted for the single student in the left panel, mathematics achievement appears generally to increase over time. In addition, African-American students seem to have generally lower mathematics achievement scores in 7th grade than do White students, and their rate of increase in achievement over time may not be as great. In other words, their intercepts may be lower and their slopes shallower. Also note the substantial inter-individual heterogeneity in growth trajectories *within* groups. Not all African-American students have lower intercepts than do White students; many of them have higher mathematics achievement in 7th grade than many White students. Similarly, not all African-American students have less steep slopes; some of them have very rapid increases in mathematics achievement over time. Furthermore, within both groups there are students whose mathematics achievement actually *decreases* over time. Our level-2 model must simultaneously account for both these general patterns (the evident between-group differences in intercepts and slopes) *and* any inter-individual heterogeneity that remains within groups.

This suggests that an appropriate level-2 model would have outcomes that are the level-1 individual growth parameters themselves (the π_{0i} and π_{1i} parameters from equation (1)). In addition, the level-2 model must specify the relationship between each of the individual growth parameters and the predictor of interest (here, *AFAM*, which takes on only two values: $0 =$ White, $1 =$ African-American). Finally, the level-2 model must allow even individuals who share common predictor values to differ stochastically in their individual change trajectories, by permitting random variation in the individual growth parameters across people. These considerations suggest that the following level-2 model may be a useful specification for the inter-individual differences in change:

$$\pi_{0i} = \gamma_{00} + \gamma_{01}AFAM_i + \zeta_{0i}$$
$$\pi_{1i} = \gamma_{10} + \gamma_{11}AFAM_i + \zeta_{1i} \qquad (2)$$

Like all level-2 models, equation (2) has more than one component; but, taken together, they simultaneously treat the intercept (π_{0i}) and the slope (π_{1i}) of an individual's growth trajectory as level-2 outcomes that are associated with predictors (here, $AFAM$). As in multiple regression analysis, we can modify the level-2 model to include other predictors, adding, for example, socio-economic status and gender. Each component of the level-2 model also has its own residual—here, symbolized by ζ_{0i} and ζ_{1i}—that permits stochastic variation in the level-1 parameters, after the impact of the predictor has been accounted for. The stochastic part of the level-2 model allows the individual intercepts and slopes to differ across individuals, in the population.

The structural parts of the level-2 model in (2) contain four level-2 parameters— which we have labeled γ_{00}, γ_{01}, γ_{10}, and γ_{11}—that are known collectively as the *fixed effects*. These fixed effects capture the *systematic* inter-individual differences in change trajectories. Later, in our example, we estimate them all. In equation (2), γ_{00} and γ_{10} are level-2 intercepts; γ_{01} and γ_{11} are level-2 slopes. As in simple and multiple regression analysis, the level-2 slopes are of greater interest because they represent the effect of predictors (here, $AFAM$) on the individual growth parameters. We interpret the level-2 parameters much like linear regression coefficients, except that they describe variation in 'outcomes' that are themselves the level-1 individual growth parameters. For example, γ_{00} represents the average true initial status (mathematics achievement in 7th grade) among White students in the population, while γ_{01} represents the hypothesized population *difference* in average true initial status between African-American and White students. Similarly, γ_{10} represents the average true annual rate of change in mathematics achievement for White students, in the population, while γ_{11} represents the hypothesized population difference in average true annual rate of change between African-American and White students. The level-2 slopes, γ_{01} and γ_{11}, then jointly capture the effects of $AFAM$. If γ_{01} and γ_{11} are non-zero, the average population trajectories in true mathematics achievement differ between the two ethnic groups; on the other hand, if γ_{01} and γ_{11} are both 0, then the trajectories do not differ by race. These two level-2 slope parameters therefore address the following research question: What is the difference in the average trajectory of true change in mathematics achievement between White students and African-American students?

An important feature of both the level-1 and level-2 models is the presence of requisite stochastic terms—the residuals ε_{ij} at level-1, and ζ_{0i} and ζ_{1i} at level-2. In the level-1 model, residual ε_{ij} accounts for the difference between individual i's true and observed value of the outcome, on occasion j. For our example, each level-1 residual represents that part of student i's value of MATHACH at time j not predicted by his (or her) grade level. The level-2 residuals, ζ_{0i} and ζ_{1i}, on the other hand, allow each person's individual growth parameters to be deviated from their relevant population averages. They represent those portions of the level-2 outcomes—the individual growth parameters—that remain 'unexplained' by the level-2 predictor(s). For our example, ζ_{0i} represents the difference between student i's true mathematics achievement in 7th grade and the population average true mathematics achievement in 7th grade for this student's racial group. Similarly, ζ_{1i} represents the difference between student i's rate of true change in mathematics achievement and the population true slope for her racial group.

As is the case with most residuals, we are usually less interested in their specific values than in their *variability*. Level-1 residual variance, σ_ε^2, for instance, summarizes the scatter of the level-1 residuals around each person's true change trajectory, in the population. The level-2 residual variances, σ_0^2 and σ_1^2, summarize the population inter-individual variation in true individual intercept and slope around their averages that is *left over* after controlling for the effect(s) of any predictors included in the corresponding level-2 model. Conditional on adjusting for the impact of the level-2 predictors, therefore, σ_0^2 represents population residual variance in true initial status and σ_1^2 represents population residual variance in true annual rate of change, across all individuals in the population. The level-2 variance components therefore allow us to address the research question: how much heterogeneity in true initial status and true rate of change remains among students after accounting for the effects of race?

There is a final complication at level-2. In practice, it is entirely possible that there may be an association between initial status and rate of change across individuals in the population. For instance, students who begin 7th grade with higher mathematics achievement may have higher (or lower) rates of change. To permit this possibility, we must permit the level-2 residuals to be correlated. Since ζ_{0i} and ζ_{1i} represent the deviations of the individual growth parameters from their population averages, their population covariance, σ_{01}, summarizes the association between true individual intercept and slope across all members of the population. Again because of their conditional nature, this population covariance, σ_{01}, summarizes the association between true initial status and true annual rate of change, *controlling for race*. This parameter then allows us to address the question: controlling for race, are the true mathematics achievement in 7th grade and the true rate of change in achievement related across students?

To fit any statistical model to data, including the multilevel model for change, we must make appropriate distributional assumptions about the residuals. At level-1, the situation is relatively simple. In the absence of evidence suggesting otherwise, we usually begin by invoking the classical normal-theory assumption that the level-1 residuals are independently and identically distributed with homoscedastic variance, $\varepsilon_{ij} \sim N(0, \sigma_\varepsilon^2)$. At level-2, the presence of two (or sometimes more) residuals necessitates that we describe their underlying distribution using a *bivariate* (or *multivariate*) assumption, such as:

$$\begin{bmatrix} \zeta_{0i} \\ \zeta_{1i} \end{bmatrix} \sim N \left(\begin{bmatrix} 0 \\ 0 \end{bmatrix}, \begin{bmatrix} \sigma_0^2 & \sigma_{01} \\ \sigma_{10} & \sigma_1^2 \end{bmatrix} \right) \quad (3)$$

This complete set of residual variances and covariances—both the level-1 residual variance, σ_ε^2 and the level-2 error variance-covariance matrix—are jointly referred to as the model's *variance components*. Later, in our example, we estimate them all.

The composite multilevel model for change

This 'level-1/level-2' format is not the only way to specify the multilevel model for change. A more parsimonious representation results if you collapse the level-1 and level-2 models together into a single *composite* statistical model. The composite representation of the multilevel model for change, while identical to the level-1/level-2 specification mathematically, provides an alternative way of codifying hypotheses about change and is the specification utilized by many dedicated statistical software programs. To derive the composite specification—also known as the *reduced form* growth curve model—notice that any pair of linked level-1 and level-2 models share terms in common. Specifically, the individual growth parameters specified on the right-hand side of the 'equals' sign in the level-1 model become the outcomes on the left-hand side of the 'equals' sign in the level-2 model. We can therefore collapse the submodels together by substituting for π_{0i} and π_{1i} from the level-2 model in equation (2) into the level-1 model in equation (1), as follows:

$$Y_{ij} = \pi_{0i} + \pi_{1i}TIME_{ij} + \varepsilon_{ij}$$
$$= (\gamma_{00} + \gamma_{01}AFAM_i + \zeta_{0i})$$
$$+ (\gamma_{10} + \gamma_{11}AFAM_i + \zeta_{1i})TIME_{ij} + \varepsilon_{ij} \tag{4}$$

Where we have replaced the level-1 predictor, $(GRADE_{ij}-7)$, by the generic temporal representation, $TIME_{ij}$, for simplicity. Multiplying out and rearranging terms yields the *composite multilevel model for change*:

$$Y_{ij} = \left[\gamma_{00} + \gamma_{10}TIME_{ij} + \gamma_{01}AFAM_i \right.$$
$$\left. + \gamma_{11}(AFAM_i * TIME_{ij})\right]$$
$$+ \left[\zeta_{0i} + \zeta_{1i}TIME_{ij} + \varepsilon_{ij}\right] \tag{5}$$

Where we once again use brackets to distinguish the model's structural and stochastic components.

Even though the composite specification of the multilevel model for change in (5) appears more complex than the level-1/level-2 specification, the two forms are logically and mathematically equivalent. The level-1/level-2 specification is more substantively appealing; the composite specification is algebraically more parsimonious. In addition, the fixed effects—the γ's—capture the patterns of change in the ways that we have described, but they function in the composite model in a different way. Rather than *first* postulating how *MATHACH* is related to *TIME* and individual growth parameters, and *second* how the individual growth parameters are related to *AFAM*, the composite specification postulates that *MATHACH* depends *simultaneously* on: (1) the level-1 predictor, *TIME*; (2) the level-2 predictor, *AFAM*, and (3) their *cross-level* interaction, *AFAM*TIME*. From this perspective, the composite model's structural portion resembles a multiple regression model with two predictors, *TIME* and *AFAM*, that appear as both main effects (associated with parameters γ_{10} and γ_{01}, respectively) and in a *cross-level* interaction (associated with parameter γ_{11}).

How did this cross-level interaction arise, when the level-1/level-2 specification of the multilevel model for change appears to have no similar term? Its genesis is in the 'multiplying-out' procedure used to generate the composite model. When we substitute the level-2 model for individual growth parameter π_{1i} into its appropriate position in the level-1 model, level-2 parameter γ_{11}, previously associated only with level-2 predictor *AFAM*, gets multiplied by level-1 predictor *TIME*. In the composite model, then, this parameter becomes associated with the interaction term, *AFAM*TIME*. This association makes perfect sense if you consider the following logic. When γ_{11} is different from zero in the level-1/level-2 specification, the *slopes* of the true change trajectories differ according to values of *AFAM*. In other words, the effect of *TIME* (whose effect is represented by the slopes of the change trajectories) differs by race. However, generically, when the effects of one predictor (here, *TIME*) differ by the levels of another predictor (here, *AFAM*), we say that the two predictors *interact*. The cross-level interaction in the composite specification codifies this effect, modeling any difference in the average rate of true change in mathematics achievement between African-American and White students.

Another distinctive feature of the composite model is its 'composite residual,' the three terms in the second set of brackets on the right-hand side of equation (5) that combine together the effects of the single level-1 residual and the two level-2 residuals that appeared in the earlier level-1/level-2 specification:

Composite residual: $\left[\zeta_{0i} + \zeta_{1i}TIME_{ij} + \varepsilon_{ij}\right]$

Even though the components that make up the composite residual have the same meaning under both the level-1/level-2 and composite specifications of the multilevel model for change, the composite residual provides valuable insight into our assumptions about the behavior of residuals over time in longitudinal data. Instead of being a simple sum, the second level-2 residual, ζ_{1i}, in the composite residual is multiplied by level-1 predictor, *TIME*. Despite this unusual construction, the interpretation of the composite residual is straightforward: it describes the difference between the observed and predicted value of Y for individual i on occasion j. Inspection of the mathematical form of the composite residual, however, reveals two important properties of the occasion-specific residuals not readily apparent in the level-1/level-2 specification for the multilevel model for change: the composite residuals can be both *autocorrelated* and *heteroscedastic* within-person. Fortunately, these are exactly the kinds of properties that you would expect among residuals associated with repeated measurements of a changing outcome over time, within-person.

When residuals are heteroscedastic, the unexplained portions of each person's outcome have unequal variances from occasion to occasion. Even though heteroscedasticity has many roots, one cause is the effects of omitted predictors—the consequences of failing to include variables that are, in fact, related to the outcome. Because their effects have nowhere else to go, they are bundled together, by default, into the residuals. If their impact differs across occasions, the residual's magnitude may differ as well, creating heteroscedasticity. The composite model allows for heteroscedasticity via the level-2 residual ζ_{1i}. Because ζ_{1i} is multiplied by *TIME* in the composite residual, its contribution can differ (linearly, at least, in a linear level-1 submodel) across occasions. If there are systematic differences in the *magnitudes* of the composite residuals across occasions, there will be accompanying differences in residual *variance*, and hence heteroscedasticity.

When residuals are autocorrelated, the unexplained portions of each person's outcome are correlated with each other across repeated occasions. Once again, omitted predictors, whose effects are bundled into the residuals, are a common cause of this phenomenon. Because their effects may be present identically in each residual over time, an individual's residuals may become linked across occasions. The presence of the time-invariant level-2 residuals, ζ_{0i} and ζ_{1i}, in each of the composite residuals defined in equation (5) allows them to be autocorrelated. Because they have only an 'i' subscript (and no 'j'), they feature identically in each individual's composite residual on every occasion, generating the required autocorrelation across time.

Fitting the multilevel model for change to data

Many different statistical software programs can be used to fit the multilevel model for change to data. Some are specialized packages written expressly for this purpose (such as HLM, MlwiN, and MIXREG). Others are part of popular multipurpose software packages including SAS (PROC MIXED and PROC NLMIXED), SPSS (MIXED), STATA (xtmixed, xtreg, and gllamm) and SPLUS (NLME). At their core, each program does the same job: it fits the hypothesized multilevel model for change to data and generates parameter estimates, measures of precision, diagnostics, and so on. All of the different packages tend to produce the same, or very similar, answers to a given problem, regardless of their method of model-fitting and parameter-estimation (Kreft and De Leeuw, 1998). So, in one sense, it does not matter which computer program you choose for your data analysis. But, the packages do differ in many important other ways, including the 'look and feel' of their interfaces, their ways of entering and pre-processing data, their approach to model specification (whether they require the multilevel model for change be specified in the level-1/level-2 or composite formats), their estimation methods (e.g. full vs. restricted maximum likelihood methods), their strategies for hypothesis testing, and their provision of diagnostics. It is beyond the scope of this chapter to discuss these details. Instead, we illustrate some of them by turning to the results of fitting the multilevel model for change that we have specified above to data on our example, using SAS

Table 22.1   Results of fitting a multilevel model for change to data ($n = 1,322$). This model predicts mathematics achievement between grades 7 and 11 as a function of (GRADE-7) at level-1 and race (AFAM) at level-2

			Parameter	Estimate (s.e.)
Fixed effects				
Initial status, π_{0i}	Intercept		γ_{00}	53.02***
				(0.26)
	AFAM		γ_{01}	-5.93***
				(0.80)
Rate of change, π_{1i}	Intercept		γ_{10}	2.87***
				(0.80)
	AFAM		γ_{11}	-0.48*
				(0.23)
Variance components				
Level-1:	Within-person, ε_{ij}		σ_ε^2	37.17***
				(0.86)
Level-2:	In initial status, ζ_{0i}		σ_0^2	59.05***
				(3.23)
	In rate of change, ζ_{1i}		σ_1^2	3.19***
				(0.29)
	Covariance between ζ_{0i} and ζ_{1i}		σ_{01}	6.18***
				(0.69)

$\sim p < 0.10$; * $p < 0.05$; *** $p < 0.001$
Note: Full ML, SAS Proc Mixed.

PROC MIXED. Estimates are presented in Table 22.1.

INTERPRETING A FITTED MULTILEVEL MODEL FOR CHANGE

In any analysis of change, the fixed effects parameters—the γ s of equations (2) and (4)—quantify the impact of time-invariant predictors on the individual change trajectories. In our example, for instance, they characterize the relationship between the individual growth parameters and race. We interpret these estimates much as we do any regression coefficient, with one key difference: the level-2 'outcomes' that these fixed effects describe are the level-1 individual growth parameters built into the multilevel model for change. As is usual in any regression analysis, we can conduct a hypothesis test on each fixed effect using a single parameter test (most commonly to examine the null hypothesis $H_0 : \gamma = 0$). As shown in Table 22.1, we reject all four such null hypotheses, suggesting that each parameter plays an important role in the story of how race

is related to student mathematics achievement in secondary school.

Substituting the estimated fixed effects — the $\hat{\gamma}'s$— from Table 22.1 into the hypothesized level-2 model in equation (2), we have the following fitted level-2 model:

$$\hat{\pi}_{0i} = 53.02 - 5.93AFAM_i$$
$$\hat{\pi}_{1i} = 2.87 - 0.48AFAM_i \tag{6}$$

The first part of this fitted model describes the estimated effects of *AFAM* on true initial status; the second part describes its estimated effects on the annual rates of true change in mathematics achievement. Begin with the first part of the fitted model, for true initial status. In the population from which this sample was drawn, we estimate that the true initial status (*MATHACH* at grade 7) for the average White student is 53.02; for the average African-American 7th grader, we estimate that initial true mathematics achievement is 5.93 points lower (47.09). In addition, in rejecting (at the 0.001 level) the null hypotheses on γ_{00} and γ_{01}, we conclude that the average White student had non-zero true mathematics achievement in 7th grade (hardly surprising!)

and that there is a statistically significant difference in the average true mathematics achievement of White students compared with their African-American peers.

Next examine the second part of the fitted model, for the annual rate of true change. In the population from which this sample was drawn, we estimate the annual rate of true change in mathematics achievement for the average White student is 2.87 points per year; for the average African-American student, we estimate it to be nearly half a point lower (at 2.39). In rejecting (at the 0.001 level) the null hypothesis on γ_{10}, we conclude that the average White student experienced a statistically significant increase in true mathematics achievement over time. Because we also reject (at the 0.05 level) the null hypothesis on γ_{11}, we conclude that differences between African-American and White students in their annual rates of true change are also statistically significant. The estimated mathematics achievement for the average White student increased 11.48 points from 7th grade to 11th grade, while the increase for African-American students was two points lower (9.56). African-American students begin 7th grade with lower average mathematics achievement than their White counterparts, and the achievement gap increases over time.

Another way of interpreting the estimated fixed effects is to plot fitted trajectories for prototypical individuals. For this particular model, only two prototypes are possible: an African-American student ($AFAM=1$) and a White student ($AFAM=0$). Substituting these predictor values into equation (6) yields the estimated initial status and annual growth rates for each:

When $AFAM = 0$:

$$\hat{\pi}_{0i} = 53.02 - 5.93(0) = 53.02$$
$$\hat{\pi}_{1i} = 2.87 - .48(0) = 2.87$$

When $AFAM = 1$:

$$\hat{\pi}_{0i} = 53.02 - 5.93 = 47.09$$
$$\hat{\pi}_{1i} = 2.87 - .48(1) = 2.39$$
\hfill (7)

We then substitute these estimates into the hypothesized level-1 model in equation (1) to obtain the fitted individual change trajectories:

When $AFAM = 0$:

$$\hat{Y}_{ij} = 53.02 + 2.87(GRADE_{ij} - 7)$$

When $AFAM = 1$:

$$\hat{Y}_{ij} = 47.09 + 2.39(GRADE_{ij} - 7) \quad (8)$$

These fitted trajectories are plotted in the right-hand panel of Figure 22.1, and reinforce the numeric conclusions articulated above. In comparison to White students, the average African-American student has lower mathematics achievement in 7th grade and a slower rate of increase in mathematics achievement.

The estimated variance components assess the amount of outcome variability left—at either level-1 or level-2—after including the specified predictors. Because the variance components are harder to interpret in absolute terms, many researchers rely on the associated hypothesis tests, for at least they provide some benchmark for comparison. Some caution is necessary, however, because a null hypothesis on a variance necessarily falls at the border of the available parameter space (by definition, variances cannot be negative) and as a result, the asymptotic distributional properties that hold in simpler settings may not apply (Snijders and Bosker, 1999). The level-1 residual variance, σ_ε^2, summarizes the population variability in an average person's outcome values around his or her own true change trajectory. Its estimate here is 37.17. Rejection of the associated null hypothesis test (at the 0.001 level) suggests the existence of additional outcome variation at level-1 (within-person) that may be predictable in subsequent analyses by time-varying predictors other than time itself.

The level-2 variance components, σ_0^2 and σ_1^2, summarize the variability in true initial status and rate of true change that remains after controlling for level-2 predictors (here, $AFAM$). Tests associated with these variance components evaluate whether there is any remaining *residual* outcome variation that could potentially be explained by further predictors at level-2. For these data, we reject both of these null hypotheses (at the 0.001 level). Because these are level-2 variance components (describing the residual variation in true initial status and rate of true change), we would consider adding further time-invariant predictors to the multilevel model for change. Finally, let's turn to the level-2 covariance component, σ_{01}. Since we reject the null hypothesis on this parameter too, we can conclude that the intercepts and slopes of the individual true change trajectories are indeed correlated in the population, controlling for student race—there is a positive association between true initial status and annual rate of true change, once the effects of *AFAM* have been removed. On average, African-American and White students who have higher true mathematics achievement in 7th grade also have greater rates of increase in true mathematics achievement between 7th and 11th grade.

Adding further predictors to the multilevel model for change

Our discussion to this point has focused on developing the foundation for understanding the multilevel model for change by comparing the average trajectories of two populations of students, African-American and White. We have seen that true change in both groups is positive, on average, with White students enjoying a more rapid increase in true mathematics achievement over time. However, through the analysis of the associated variance components, we have found that heterogeneity remains at level-1 and in the true intercepts and slopes, even after the effect of time and race have been partialled out. This suggests that it is important to consider the addition of further predictors to the model. Here, as we fit selected additional models, it is important to remain aware of the complexities involved, of which there are: (1) *multiple level-2 outcomes* (the individual growth parameters), *each* of which can be

related to predictors; and (2) *multiple kinds of effects,* both the fixed effects and the variance components. Hypothesizing a level-1 linear individual growth model has provided two level-2 outcomes; a more complex level-1 submodel specification may provide more. One simple strategy in specifying the level-2 models is to include each level-2 predictor simultaneously in all level-2 submodels. However, as we show below, they need not all remain. Each individual growth parameter can have its own predictors at level-2, and one goal of model specification is to identify which level-2 variables are important predictors of which level-1 individual growth parameters. So, too, although each level-2 submodel may contain both fixed and random effects, both are not necessarily required. Sometimes hypothesizing a model that has fewer random effects will provide a more parsimonious representation of the data and clearer substantive insights into the research questions being posed.

In the data-analytic example that follows, we continue to ask whether race has an impact on change in mathematics achievement between 7th grade and 11th grade, but we now expand our analyses to include socio-economic status and gender as important controls. Model B in Table 22.2 includes *SES* as a level-2 predictor of both true initial status and rate of true change in mathematics achievement. Model C then removes the effect of race on the rate of true change. In Model D, the effect of *FEMALE* on both true initial status and rate of true change is included in the level-2 model, and in Model E, the model is again simplified by removing the effect of *FEMALE* on the rate of true change.

Interpreting the additional fitted models

We have already discussed fitted Model A, which includes *AFAM* as a predictor of both true initial status and rate of true change. In Model B, we now add *SES* to the level-2 model, including it as a predictor of both true initial status and rate of true change. There are therefore now six fixed effects

Table 22.2 Results of fitting a taxonomy of multilevel models for change to the mathematics achievement data($n = 1,322$)

	Parameter	Model A	Model B	Model C	Model D	Model E
Fixed effects						
Initial status						
Intercept	γ_{00}	53.02***	52.81***	52.82***	52.39***	52.40***
		(0.26)	(0.25)	(0.25)	(0.35)	(0.35)
AFAM	γ_{01}	−5.93***	−4.66***	−4.77***	−4.80***	−4.80***
		(0.80)	(0.77)	(0.77)	(0.77)	(0.77)
SES	γ_{02}		3.62***	3.61***	3.62***	3.62***
			(0.34)	(0.34)	(0.34)	(0.34)
FEMALE	γ_{03}				0.84~	0.82~
					(0.48)	(0.48)
Rate of change						
Intercept	γ_{10}	2.87***	2.85***	2.81***	2.85***	2.81***
		(0.08)	(0.08)	(0.07)	(0.11)	(0.07)
AFAM	γ_{11}	−0.48*	−0.35			
		(0.23)	(0.24)			
SES	γ_{12}		0.37***	0.40***	0.40***	0.40***
			(0.10)	(0.10)	(0.10)	(0.10)
FEMALE	γ_{13}				−0.08	
					(0.146)	
Variance components						
Level-1:	Within-person σ_{ε}^{2}	37.17***	37.17***	37.16***	37.17***	37.16***
		(0.86)	(0.86)	(0.86)	(0.86)	(0.86)
Level-2:	In initial status σ_{0}^{2}	59.05***	52.46***	52.46***	52.30***	52.30***
		(3.23)	(2.98)	(2.98)	(2.97)	(2.97)
In rate of change	σ_{1}^{2}	3.19***	3.13***	3.14***	3.14***	3.14***
		(0.29)	(0.29)	(0.29)	(0.29)	(0.29)
Covariance	σ_{01}	6.18***	5.50***	5.50***	5.51***	5.51***
		(0.69)	(0.66)	(0.66)	(0.66)	(0.66)

~ $p < 0.10$; * $p < 0.05$; *** $p < 0.001$
Note: Full ML, SAS Proc Mixed.

to interpret. We begin by interpreting the parameter estimates in the fitted level-2 submodel for initial status. The estimated intercept for this first part of the level-2 model provides an estimate of true initial mathematics achievement when *all* predictors in that part of the level-2 model are set to zero. As we know, when *AFAM* equals 0 we are dealing with White students. *SES* equals 0 for students of average socio-economic status since this measure was standardized in preliminary analysis to a mean of zero. Therefore, we estimate that the average 7th grade mathematics achievement for White students of average socio-economic status is 52.81. The next parameter, γ_{01}, represents the effect of race on true initial status, controlling for socio-economic status. Here, we estimate that, controlling for the effects of *SES*, the true mathematics achievement of the average African-American 7th grader is 4.66 points lower than that of the average White 7th grader (p<.001). Therefore, while the effect of *AFAM* is slightly attenuated by controlling for *SES*, there remains a statistically significant effect of race on 7th grade true mathematics achievement. The final parameter in the level-2 submodel for true initial status is γ_{02}, representing the effect of *SES*, controlling for race. This parameter describes the difference in 7th grade true mathematics achievement for a one-unit difference in *SES*, for students of either race. We are not surprised to find a positive effect of *SES*—controlling for race, we estimate that average true mathematics achievement is 3.62 points higher for students whose *SES* is one point greater (p<0.001).

Turning now to parameter estimates associated with the rate of true change in Model B, we find that the estimated rate of true change in mathematics achievement for White students of average *SES* is 2.85 (p<0.001). While adding *SES* to the slope submodel has not impacted its estimated intercept, the effect of *AFAM*, while still negative, is no longer statistically significant. Controlling for *SES*, the average rate of true change no longer differs for African-American and White students. Our final parameter estimate,

$\hat{\gamma}_{13}$, represents the estimated effect of *SES* itself, controlling for race. Again we are not surprised that this estimate is positive—for students of either race, on average, those with *SES* one point higher have true growth rates that are .37 points per year greater (p<0.001).

Now examine the variance components associated with Model B. The statistically significant within-person variance component $(\hat{\sigma}_{\varepsilon}^2)$ for Model B is identical to that of Model A, reinforcing the need to explore the potential inclusion of time-varying predictors at level-1. We anticipated stability like this in our estimates because we have added no additional predictors at level-1 between Models A and B (although estimates may vary inadvertently because of uncertainties arising from iterative estimation). The estimated level-2 variance components, however, do differ: $\hat{\sigma}_0^2$ declines by 11.2 percent from Model A (from 59.05 to 52.46). Because it is still statistically significant, however, potentially explainable residual variation in true initial status remains. The estimated variation in rate of true change declines only minimally from 3.19 to 3.13, and also remains statistically significant, suggesting the continued presence of explainable residual variation in rates of true change.

Because the average rate of true change in mathematics achievement does not differ for African-American and White students once SES is controlled, in Model C we remove *AFAM* as a predictor of rate of true change, while retaining it as a predictor of true initial status. The parameter estimates associated with both the fixed and random effects are essentially unchanged with the removal of *AFAM* as a predictor of rate of true change. In including the effect of predictor gender, we use a similar approach, first adding *FEMALE* as a predictor of both true initial status and true slope (Model D), then, because we find no differences in the average rate of true change for girls and boys, we remove *FEMALE* as a predictor of rate of true change (Model E).

In interpreting Model E, we begin again by interpreting the model's fixed effects. With *FEMALE* now a predictor of true initial status, the interpretation of the intercept term for the initial status submodel has changed yet again. Now γ_{00} represents the average true mathematics achievement for White, male (*FEMALE* = 0) students of average SES. Therefore, we estimate that the average 7th grade mathematics achievement for White male students of average socio-economic status is 52.40. The next parameter, γ_{01}, models the effect of race on true initial status, controlling for socio-economic status and now gender as well. We estimate that the 7th grade mathematics achievement of an African-American male from an average socio-economic background is 4.80 points lower than that of a comparable White student (p<0.001). The effect of *AFAM* is essentially unchanged when we control for *FEMALE* in addition to *SES*. Similarly, the effect of *SES* on true initial status does not change when controlling for *FEMALE*. The final parameter in the level-2 submodel for true initial status is γ_{03}, representing the effect of *FEMALE*, controlling for race and socio-economic status. Average 7th grade mathematics achievement is almost one point higher for girls than boys of comparable race and socio-economic status, but since the *p*-value is slightly larger than 0.05, the effect is not statistically significant at the conventionally accepted 0.05 level. Nevertheless, we choose to retain *FEMALE* as a predictor of true initial status in our model, given its substantive importance as a predictor of mathematics achievement and the fact that the *p*-value is less than 0.10.

In Model E, *FEMALE* is not a predictor of rate of true change, a substantively interesting finding that suggests that the rate of change in mathematics achievement from 7th to 11th grade does not differ by gender. Our rate of true change submodel now includes only *SES*

as a predictor. We estimate that the rate of true change in mathematics achievement for a student of average *SES* is 2.81 (p<0.001), and that students whose *SES* is one unit higher have rates of change in mathematics achievement that are greater by 0.4 point per year (p<0.001).

Finally, examining the associated variance components for Model E, we see that the only thing that has changed is the estimated variation in true initial status, which has declined only slightly from 52.46 in Model C to 52.30 in Model E. Because all of the variance components remain statistically significant, potentially explainable residual variation in true initial status and rate of true change remain for future consideration.

Displaying prototypical trajectories of change

For longitudinal analyses, we find that graphs of fitted trajectories for prototypical individuals are more powerful tools than numerical summaries for communicating our findings. In Figure 22.1, we presented plots of fitted individual growth trajectories for prototypical African-American and White students, using the estimates of the fixed effects from Model A to obtain estimates of true initial status and rate of true change for the two populations of students (equation (7)). We can extend these strategies to models with multiple predictors, as we have in Model E.

Figure 22.2 presents fitted trajectories derived from Model E for four prototypical students—African-American and White students of different *SES*. We have selected prototypical values of *SES* that correspond to the sample mean plus and minus one standard deviation (0.735 and −0.693, respectively)

Table 22.3 Fitted values of the individual growth parameters from Model E for four prototypical individuals

AFAM	SES	Initial status ($\hat{\pi}_{0i}$)	Rate of change ($\hat{\pi}_{1i}$)
White	Low	52.401−4.798(0)+3.616(−0.693)+0.818(1)=50.713	2.808+0.395(−0.693)=2.534
White	High	52.401−4.798(0)+3.616(0.735)+0.818(1)=55.877	2.808+0.395(0.735)=3.098
African-American	Low	52.401−4.798(1)+3.616(−0.693)+0.818(1)=45.915	2.808+0.395(−0.693)=2.534
African-American	High	52.401−4.798(1)+3.616(0.735)+0.818(1)=51.079	2.808+0.395(0.735)=3.098

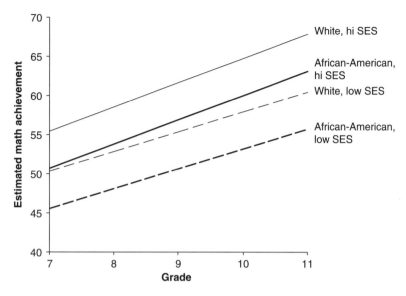

Figure 22.2 Fitted growth trajectories for prototypical African-American and White students of high and low socio-economic backgrounds

and chose to present trajectories for females only. Since the gender effect is small, the plot would be essentially identical for males. We compute the fitted values of the individual growth parameters for these prototypical individuals as follows: shown in Table 22.3.

Notice that the fitted trajectories of mathematics achievement differ by both race and socio-economic status, as anticipated. At each level of *SES*, the fitted trajectory for White students is consistently elevated above that of African-American students, and the differential in mathematics achievement between White and African-American students of the same *SES* does not differ over time. The effect of *SES* is more complex. Within racial groups, the trajectory for students of high socio-economic status is above that of students of low socio-economic status across all grades. Furthermore, the increase in mathematics achievement over time is more rapid for the high socio-economic status students than for their low socio-economic status peers, with the difference in estimated mathematics achievement between high and low *SES* 11th graders of the same race over 40 percent higher than the difference between these students in 7th grade.

Extensions of the multilevel model for change

While it permits considerable complexity in analysis, as evidenced in Table 22.2, the example that we have presented in this chapter has two structural features that simplify analysis. The example is both balanced and time-structured—all students are assessed on exactly five occasions and these occasions (7th grade to 11th grade) are identical across individuals. Our analyses are also straightforward in that we have used only: (1) time-invariant predictors that describe immutable characteristics of the students (except for *TIME* itself); and (2) a representation of *TIME* that forces the level-1 individual growth parameters to represent 'initial status' and 'linear rate of change.' However, the multilevel model for change is very flexible and can be used to address more complex problems, as we now describe.

Variably spaced measurement occasions

Researchers often collect longitudinal data in which the actual measurement occasions differ across individuals. These differences may result from the realities of fieldwork and data collection. For example, when studying the psychological consequences of unemployment, Ginexi et al. (2000) designed a time-structured study, with interviews scheduled at 1, 5, and 11 months after job loss. Once in the field, however, the interview times varied substantially around these targets, so Ginexi and colleagues chose to use the number of days since job loss as a metric for the measurement of time in their study. Each individual in their study, therefore, had a unique data collection schedule: 31, 150, and 365 days for the first person in the dataset; 23, 162, and 401 days for the second person; and so on.

Differences in the actual measurement occasions across individuals may also occur by design. This is the case, for example, in *accelerated cohort* or *accelerated longitudinal* designs, in which multiple cohorts of different ages are followed longitudinally. Each cohort must have at least one age that overlaps with another cohort and then a single growth trajectory is estimated, extending from the youngest age to the oldest (Collins, 2006). The advantage of an accelerated cohort design is that change can be modeled over a longer temporal period using fewer waves of data. The disadvantage is that the researcher must rely more heavily on assumptions about the shape of the change trajectory. Miyazaki and Raudenbush (2000) discuss important assumptions of the analysis of data from accelerated longitudinal designs.

Varying numbers of measurement occasions

A major advantage of the multilevel model for change is that it is easily fit to unbalanced data. In our mathematics achievement data, the analytic sample used included only students with five waves of data; however, in the original dataset there are many additional students with fewer waves of data. It is straightforward to fit the multilevel model for change in the larger unbalanced dataset. With severely unbalanced datasets, however, there can be problems of convergence in the iterative methods used by standard computer packages to fit the models to the data. Practical problems that may arise when analyzing such

datasets are described in Singer and Willett (2003).

The impact of time-varying predictors

A time-varying predictor is a variable whose *values* may differ over time. Some time-varying predictors have values that change naturally; others have values that change by design. For example, in the mathematics achievement data, students' *attitudes toward mathematics* change naturally over time. We would expect students with more positive attitudes about mathematics to also have higher levels of mathematics achievement. In specifying a multilevel model for change that includes a time-varying predictor, we add the time-varying predictor to the level-1 submodel either as a main effect or as an interaction with time, or both. Thus, conceptually, we may still interpret the effects of the time-varying predictor in terms of its impact on true initial status and/or rate of true change. However, since the time-varying predictor is added to our level-1 submodel, we can also specify any additional main effect and interaction with time as either a fixed or a random effect, thereby allowing us to investigate whether these effects are constant or vary across members of the population.

While time-varying predictors offer exciting analytic possibilities to researchers, many present interpretive difficulties stemming from the problem of reciprocal causation (endogeneity), as in the case of our example of mathematics achievement and attitudes toward mathematics: if X is correlated with Y, can you conclude that X *causes* Y or is it possible that Y causes X? To address this problem it is important to first assess whether inferences are clouded by reciprocal causation. Second, if your data allow, consider coding time-varying predictors so that their values in each record of the person-period dataset refer to the *previous* point in chronological time.

Modeling discontinuous individual change

Not all individual change trajectories are continuous functions of time. If you believe that individual change trajectories might suddenly shift in elevation and/or slope, your level-1 model can reflect this hypothesis. Doing so allows you to test ideas about how the trajectory's shape might be disrupted, with time. To postulate a discontinuous individual change trajectory, it is important to hypothesize not just why the shift might occur, but also when. The level-1 individual growth model can then include one (or more) time-varying predictor(s) that describe whether and, if so, when each person experiences the hypothesized shift. In some studies, the precipitating event occurs at the same exact moment for everyone. In other studies, the precipitating event occurs at different times for different people and some participants may not experience the event at all. Discontinuities can immediately affect a trajectory's elevation, slope, or both, and may be modeled as either fixed or random effects. Furthermore, each person's trajectory can be divided into discrete epochs by adding multiple discontinuities, allowing the trajectories to differ in elevation (and perhaps slope) during each epoch.

Modeling nonlinear individual change

In addition to using the multilevel model for change to model discontinuous change, we may also use it to model smooth nonlinear individual change trajectories. The easiest strategy for fitting such models is to transform either the outcome, or *TIME*, in the level-1 submodel so that a growth model that specifies linear change in the transformed outcome or predictor will suffice. You can also model curvilinear change by including several level-1 predictors to collectively represent a polynomial function of time, which can capture a wide array of complex patterns of change over time. Finally, it is possible to specify and fit individual growth models that are fully nonlinear in the parameters themselves, such as the logistic and hyperbolic trajectories of change. Singer and Willett (2003) provide strategies for selecting optimal transformations, polynomial functions, and fully nonlinear individual growth models.

Modeling change using covariance structure analysis

The multilevel model for change can also be mapped directly onto the general mathematical framework provided by covariance structure analysis, an analytic approach known as *latent growth modeling*. At its core, a latent growth model is essentially a multilevel model for change. But, not only does the mapping of the multilevel model for change onto the general covariance structure model provide an alternative approach to model specification and estimation, the flexibility of the general covariance structure model permits the modeling of simultaneous change in several dimensions, and other important extensions. See Singer and Willett (2003), Willett and Sayer (1994), and Curran (2003) for detailed descriptions of latent growth modeling.

Concluding comments

The multilevel model for change offers empirical researchers a wealth of data-analytic opportunities with their longitudinal data. The approach can accommodate any number of waves of longitudinal data, the occasions of measurement need not be equally spaced, and different participants can have different data collection schedules. Individual change can be represented by a variety of substantively interesting hypothesized trajectories, not only linear functions presented but also curvilinear and discontinuous functions. In addition to time-invariant predictors of change, we can also estimate the effects of time-varying predictors, whose effects may either be fixed or allowed to vary randomly across individuals in the population. Not only can multiple predictors of change be included in a single analysis, change in multiple domains can be investigated simultaneously. Finally, the multilevel model for change can be used to analyze intensive longitudinal data, where there may be nearly continuous records of outcomes (Collins, 2006). Readers wishing to learn more about the multilevel model for change should consult recent books devoted to the topic, including Diggle et al. (2002); Fitzmaurice et al. (2004); Hedeker and Gibbons (2006); Raudenbush and Bryk (2002); Singer and Willett (2003); Snijders and Bosker (1999); Verbeke and Molenberghs (2000); Walls and Schafer (2006); and Weiss (2005).

REFERENCES

Ai, X. (2002). Gender differences in growth in mathematics achievement: Three-level longitudinal and multilevel analyses of individual, home, and school influences. *Mathematical Thinking and Learning, 4*, 1–22.

Collins, L. M. (2006). Analysis of longitudinal data: The integration of theoretical model, temporal design, and statistical model. *Annual Review of Psychology, 57*, 505–528.

Cronbach, L. J., & Furby, L. (1970). How should we measure 'change'—or should we? *Psychological Bulletin, 74*, 68–80.

Curran, P. J. (2003). Have multilevel models been structural equation models all along? *Multivariate Behavioral Research, 38*, 529–569.

Curran, P. J., Stice, E., & Chassin, L. (1997). The relation between adolescent and peer alcohol use: A longitudinal random coefficients model. *Journal of Consulting and Clinical Psychology, 65*, 130–140.

Diggle, P., Liang, K.-Y., & Zeger, S. (2002). *Analysis of longitudinal data*, 2nd edition. New York, NY: Oxford.Fitzmaurice, G.M., Laird, N. M., & Ware, J. H. (2004). *Applied longitudinal analysis.* New York, NY: Wiley.

Ginexi, E. M., Howe, B. W., & Caplan, R. D. (2000). Depression and control beliefs in relation to reemployment: What are the directions of effect? *Journal of Occupational Health Psychology, 5*, 323–336.

Hedeker, D., & Gibbons, R. D. (2006). *Longitudinal data analysis.* New York, NY: Wiley.

Keiley, M. K., Bates, J. E., Dodge, K. A., & Pettit, G. S. (2000). A cross-domain growth analysis: Externalizing and internalizing behavior during 8 years of childhood. *Journal of Abnormal Child Psychology, 28*, 161–179.

Kreft, I. G. G., & de Leeuw, J. (1998). *Introducing multilevel modeling.* Thousand Oaks, CA: Sage.

Miller, J. D., Kimmel, L., Hoffer, T. B., & Nelson, C. (2000). *Longitudinal study of American youth: User's manual.* Chicago, IL: International Center for the Advancement of Scientific Literacy, Northwestern University.

Miyazaki, Y., & Raudenbush, S. W. (2000). Tests for linkage of multiple cohorts in an accelerated longitudinal design. *Psychological Methods, 5*, 44–63.

Rogosa, D. R., Brandt, D., & Zimowski, M. (1982). A growth curve approach to the measurement of change. *Psychological Bulletin, 90*, 726–748.

Singer, J. D., & Willett, J. B. (2003). *Applied longitudinal data analysis: Modeling change and event occurrence.* New York, NY: Oxford.

Snijders, T. A. B., & Bosker, R. J. (1999). *Multilevel analysis: An introduction to basic and advanced multilevel modeling.* London: Sage.

Raudenbush, S. W., & Bryk, A. S. (2002). *Hierarchical linear models: Applications and data analysis methods*, 2nd edition. Thousand Oaks, CA: Sage.

Verbeke, G., & Molenberghs, G. (2000). *Linear mixed models for longitudinal data.* New York, NY: Springer.

Walls, T. A., & Schafer, J. L. (2006). *Models for intensive longitudinal data.* New York, NY: Oxford.

Weiss, R. (2005). *Modeling longitudinal data.* New York, NY: Springer.

Willett, J. B. (1988). Questions and answers in the measurement of change. In E. Rothkopf (Ed.), *Review of research in education (1988–1989)* (pp. 345–422). Washington, DC: American Education Research Association.

Willett, J. B., & Sayer, A. G. (1994). Using covariance structure analysis to detect correlates and predictors of individual change over time. *Psychological Bulletin, 116*, 363–381.

23

Latent Variable Models of Social Research Data

Rick H. Hoyle

During the writing of this chapter, Rick Hoyle was supported by grant P20-DA017589 from the National Institute on Drug Abuse.

LATENT VARIABLE MODELS IN SOCIAL RESEARCH

Latent variable models concern the presence, definition, and/or influence of constructs that either cannot be observed or characteristics that are, in principle, observable but that have not been directly observed in a given dataset (Bollen, 2002; MacCallum & Austin, 2000; Sobel, 1994). The focus of this chapter is recent advances in the use of linear structural equation modeling with continuous variables to evaluate such models in social research. Alternative approaches to evaluating latent variable models not covered in the chapter include latent class analysis (Clogg, 1995), latent transition analysis (Collins & Wugalter, 1992), latent profile analysis (Gibson, 1959), latent logit modeling (McCutcheon, 1994), and growth mixture modeling (Muthén &

Shedden, 1999). Variants of most of the models described in the chapter could, in principle, be evaluated using one or more of these alternative strategies.

After presenting a brief history of structural equation modeling, I provide an overview of the technique, with a particular focus on the representation of models in diagrams. I do not provide technical details or outline the steps involved in implementing a structural equation modeling analysis. Rather, I use the brief overview as a foundation for presenting, in conceptual terms, specific latent variable models relevant for social research. Even though I touch on basic models, the primary focus is more complex models that take full advantage of the capabilities of structural equation modeling. I conclude the chapter with a brief section on the limitations of the technique.

History

The origin of structural equation modeling typically is traced to the work of population geneticist, Sewall Wright, best known as a pioneer in the synthesis of genetics and evolutionary theory (e.g. Wright, 1968). Wright invented the statistical method of path analysis, a graphical model in which the linear relations between variables are expressed in terms of coefficients that are derived from the correlations between them (Wright, 1934). Even though Wright's approach was limited by the availability of suitable estimators of those coefficients in complex models, he foreshadowed many important developments in structural equation modeling that did not come into wide use for another 50 years (Tomer, 2003).

The potential value of Wright's model for social research was not immediately recognized; it was not until the 1960s that applications of path analysis to social research data were described. The principle figures in early applications of path analysis to social research data were sociologists Blalock (1961, 1964) and Duncan (1966, 1969). Duncan and Goldberger, an econometrician, integrated the sociological approach to path analysis with the simultaneous equations approach in economics (e.g. Goldberger & Duncan, 1973) and the factor analytic approach in psychology (e.g. Duncan, 1975; Goldberger, 1971), yielding the integrated approach to data analysis now known as structural equation modeling.

This general model was formalized and extended in the 1970s by Jöreskog (1973), Keesling (1972), and Wiley (1973), producing what became known as the LISREL (*L*inear *S*tructural *REL*ations) model. This model includes two parts: one specifying the relations between indicators and latent variables—the measurement model; and the other specifying the relations between latent variables—the structural model (Anderson & Gerbing, 1988). The LISREL model served as the basis for the LISREL software program, which, by the release of Version 3 in the mid-1970s, allowed substantively oriented social researchers to specify, estimate, and test latent variable models.

Since the mid-1970s, most significant developments in structural equation modeling have involved improvements to or extensions

of the framework developed by Jöreskog, Keesling, and Wiley[1]. These include estimators for non-normal and categorical data (e.g. Bentler, 1983; Browne, 1974, 1984; Muthén, 1984), and various approaches to evaluating model fit (e.g. Bentler, 1990; Bentler & Bonett, 1980; Browne & Cudeck, 1993; Steiger & Lind, 1980). Also, various notation systems (e.g. Bentler & Weeks, 1980; Jörskog, 1973; McArdle & McDonald, 1984) and software programs (e.g. Arbuckle, 2003; Bentler, 1995; Jörskog & Sörbom, 1999; Muthén & Muthén, 2006) now offer multiple approaches to specifying and communicating about structural equation models.

Current status

The use of structural equation modeling in the social sciences is now widespread. Social researchers have access to a growing number of social science-oriented textbooks and reference volumes targeting beginning (e.g. Hoyle, 1995; Kline, 2005; Maruyama, 1998; Schumacker & Lomax, 2004; Tenko & Marcoulides, 2000), intermediate (e.g. Bollen & Long, 1993; Hancock & Mueller, 2006; Kaplan, 2000; Wansbeek & Meijer, 2000), and advanced users (e.g. Bollen, 1989; Marcoulides & Schumacker, 2001), as well as volumes focused on applications (e.g. Bollen & Curran, 2006; DuToit et al., 2001) and software (e.g. Byrne 2001, 2006; Diamantopoulos & Siguaw, 2000).

OVERVIEW

Because latent variable models often include many variables and parameters, fully specifying and describing them can be a challenge. The principal 'languages' of structural equation modeling are path diagrams and statistical equations, the latter often involving matrix equations and extensive use of Greek characters. For our purposes, path diagrams, described in the next section, provide a relatively straightforward and efficient means of presenting latent variable models suitable for estimation using structural equation modeling. This material is followed by a brief description of estimation and the logic of model fit in applications of structural equation modeling.

Path diagrams

A convenient and informative means of depicting a latent variable model is the path diagram (McArdle & McDonald, 1984; McDonald & Ringo Ho, 2002). An example appears in Figure 23.1. This path diagram includes all the elements necessary for depicting even the most complex models. The ovals represent latent variables, sources of influence not measured directly. The large ovals correspond to substantive latent variables, or factors. The large oval labeled, F1, is an independent variable—it is not influenced by other variables in the model. The large ovals labeled, F2 and F3, are dependent variables—their variance is, in part, accounted for by other variables in the model. Paths run from each of these latent variables to their indicators, represented by squares labeled x_1 to x_{10}. These paths are either labeled '1,' which means the factor loading has been fixed at this value, or *, indicating that the factor loading is to be estimated from the data. Variance in each indicator not attributable to the latent variable is allocated to measurement error, or uniqueness, indicated by the small ovals labeled u_1 to u_{10}. Associated with each of

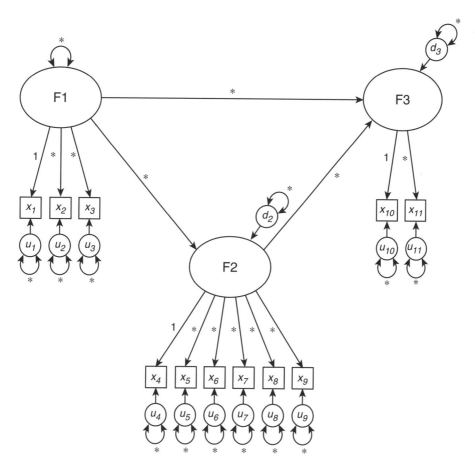

Figure 23.1   Path diagram illustrating the specification of latent independent and dependent variables and the designation of free parameters

these ellipses is a curved, two-headed arrow and an*, which indicates a variance. The three latent variables are connected by directional arrows. Associated with each is a path coefficient, accompanied by a * indicating the magnitude and direction of influence of one latent variable on another. Small ovals also are associated with the latent dependent variables. These indicate variance in the latent variables, labeled d_2 and d_3, not accounted for by other latent variables in the model. Finally, there is a variance, indicated by *, associated with the latent independent variable.

As is true of most models, this model includes a combination of free and fixed parameters. Free parameters are indicated by *s. The location of fixed parameters is less obvious. It is apparent that there is a single fixed loading on each latent variable (Steiger, 2002, provides a clear discussion of the rationale behind this aspect of the specification). The remaining fixed loadings involve paths that could have been included but were not. For instance, there is no path from F1 to $x_4{}^2$. Implicitly, this path has been fixed to zero. Also, there are no covariances between uniquenesses, meaning these parameters are implicitly fixed at zero as well. Fixed parameters in the form of excluded paths are desirable in a model, for they contribute to parsimony. They also can explain the inadequacy of a poor fitting model. Hence, when processing path diagrams, it is important to take note of paths that haven't omitted, indicating that the accompanying parameters have been fixed to zero.

The model displayed in Figure 23.1 is a covariance structure model, the most common type of model estimated using structural equation modeling. The focus of such models is accounting for the covariances among variables. As will become evident later in the chapter, it also is possible, and often desirable, to attempt to account for the observed variable means as well. Models with this focus include a structured means component (e.g. Thompson, 2006). Two examples of models with structured means components are presented later in the chapter.

Estimation and testing

The particular construal of observed and latent variables in combination with the array of free and fixed parameters shown in Figure 23.1 constitutes a model specification. The specified model is a hypothesis regarding the mechanisms that produced the data. In this instance, it is a parsimonious account of those mechanisms. Whereas the observed data encompasses 66 parameter estimates (55 covariances and 11 variances), the specified model encompasses only 25 (8 loadings, 11 uniquenesses, 1 variance, 3 directional paths, and 2 disturbances). Other models could be specified that include more or fewer latent variables, a different number and pattern of directional paths, and/or covariances among uniquenesses. It would be important to establish not only that the hypothesized model provides a suitable account of the data, but that it provides a better fit than plausible alternative (MacCallum, 2003).

Even though a specified model might have a strong grounding in theory and offer a compelling conceptual model of the mechanisms that produced the observed data, there is no guarantee that, statistically speaking, it does. The statistical tenability of a model is evaluated by using observed data to estimate values for free parameters, then evaluating the degree to which the data implied by the model including these parameter estimates, corresponds to, or fits, the observed data. Parameter estimates typically are obtained using the maximum likelihood estimator, which produces values that maximize the likelihood of the data given the specified model (Myung, 2003).

In most applications of structural equation modeling, the relevant data are elements in the variance-covariance matrix of the observed variables. This matrix is compared to a theoretical matrix produced by substituting the estimated values for the free parameters in the structural equations and solving for the covariances and variances (Bollen, 1989). To the extent that the observed and implied covariance matrices do not, within sampling error, differ, the specified model is said to fit the data. Because the assumptions of the basic statistical test of whether these matrices differ are rarely met in practice, a host of adjunct fit indices have been developed and informal criteria for applying them proposed (Hu & Bentler, 1995, 1999). When, by well-justified criteria, a model yields an acceptable account of the data, parameter estimates can be interpreted in a manner not unlike the interpretation of regression coefficients or factor loadings.

Before turning to a presentation of specific model specifications of potential interest to social researchers, it is important to establish that not all models that are specified can be estimated. For a model to be estimated, it must be specified in such a way that it is identified. Conceptually speaking, identification concerns the integrity of estimates of free parameters in a model. If a model is identified, a unique estimate for each and every free parameter can be obtained given the criteria of the estimator. If no value, or more than one value, of one or more free parameters can be obtained, then the model is unidentified and estimates of parameters are not valid. Eve though most applications typical of social research yield models that are identified, it is wise to evaluate the identification status of a model before estimating. Even though application of a number of relatively straightforward identification rules can provide some assurance that the model is identified, the definitive evaluation of the identification status of individual free parameters and the model as a whole requires solving the structural equations using the variances and covariances (Bollen, 1989).

SPECIFIC MODELS FOR SOCIAL RESEARCH DATA

In this section I present a series of specific latent variable models relevant for social research. The models are presented in three groups: measurement models, which focus on latent variables but not the relations between them; models appropriate for cross-sectional data; and models appropriate for longitudinal

data. Even though the focus is on innovative models that are not yet in wide use in social research, the presentation of each group is prefaced by a description of basic models of that type.

Measurement

As noted earlier, model specifications might comprise one or both of two components—measurement and structural (Anderson & Gerbing, 1988). The measurement component concerns the relations between latent variables and their indicators, and the structural component concerns the directional relations between the latent variables. Models need not include both components and, in fact, models that include only the measurement equations are relatively common. A focus strictly on the measurement component typically is motivated either by a desire to test specific hypotheses about the latent structure of a set of indicators or a need to ensure the integrity of a set of latent variables before testing hypotheses about the relations between them. The use of structural equation modeling in this way is referred to as confirmatory factor analysis (Hoyle, 2000).

Basic model

The most basic application of structural equation modeling to matters of measurement is the first-order factor model. In this model, one or more latent variables are predicted to explain the commonality among a set of indicators. Returning to Figure 23.1, if the directional paths between latent variables were replaced by curved arrows indicating covariance, the model would be a basic first-order measurement model. Because there are no directional paths between latent variables, all latent variables are, in effect, independent variables. To illustrate, Funk (1999) used data from the National Election Studies to investigate the latent structure of trait ratings of presidential nominees. The hypothesized three-factor model proved superior to one- and two-factor models and held across all nominees for which data were available.

An advantage of this basic application over traditional methods such as exploratory factor analysis is that competing models can be formally compared, specific aspects of models (e.g. correlations ‣between factors) can be formally evaluated, and adjustments can be made to accommodate covariation among indicators not explained by the latent variables (i.e. correlated uniquenesses) or indicators influenced by more than one latent variable (i.e. cross loadings). Even though this approach to factor analysis is sometimes portrayed as contrasting sharply with exploratory factor analysis, it is possible to relax many of the restrictions on the standard confirmatory factor model (e.g. simple structure) and, in so doing, approximate applications of exploratory factor analysis (Hoyle & Duvall, 2004).

Higher-order factor models

For measurement models that specify four or more first-order factors, it is possible to test hypotheses about sources of commonality that underlie correlations among the factors. In so doing, one, in effect, combines a confirmatory factor analysis of the observed variables with a confirmatory factor analysis of the factors. As would be the case for factors at the first order, factors at the second order are a function of commonality—in this instance, commonality among the first-order factors. Also, as would be the case in terms of observed variables at the first-order level, at least four first-order factors are necessary in order to allow for a test of that portion of the model[3]. For example, Hoyle (1991) examined the second-order structure of a 20-item measure of self-esteem designed to yield four first-order factors corresponding to self-esteem domains (e.g. social competence, physical appearance). He reasoned that the correlation among the first-order factors could be attributed to a general self-esteem factor, which would be evidenced by a single second-order factor. The analyses indicated that the second-order model provided a good account of the data and, importantly, provided a better account than a first-order

model with correlated factors. In principle and with enough indicators and factors, one could estimate third-order or higher models; however, in practice, such models are rare.

Models of measurement invariance

When relations between latent variables or mean levels on constructs represented by those latent variables are to be compared across samples or within a sample across time, a key concern is whether the meaning of the latent variables is consistent across levels of the dimensions on which they are to be compared such as nationality (e.g. Steenkamp & Baumgartner, 1998), measurement modality (e.g. Deutskens et al., 2006), and age (Pentz & Chou, 1994). To the extent that the measurement model for a latent variable is consistent across samples or time, it is invariant with respect to measurement. Despite the obvious importance of measurement invariance, it is rarely evaluated (Vandenberg & Lance, 2000).

In order to illustrate the various aspects of measurement invariance and how they are evaluated, it is useful to consult a path diagram. Displayed in Figure 23.2 is a single model with two correlated latent variables that is specified for two levels, *a* and *b*, of some dimension of interest (e.g. ethnicity, age). Note the presence of paths that are not present in the model shown in Figure 23.1. In the typical application of structural equation modeling, all variables are rescaled as deviations from their means, thereby setting intercepts in the measurement equations and means of the latent variables to zero. In tests of measurement invariance, the estimated values of these constants often are of interest. The triangle in the center of the two-factor model is a constant affecting the indicators and the latent variables. Paths running from the constant to the indicators correspond to intercepts. Paths running from the constant to the latent variables correspond to means.

Note that every parameter in the two-factor model on the left and has a corresponding parameter in the two-factor model on the

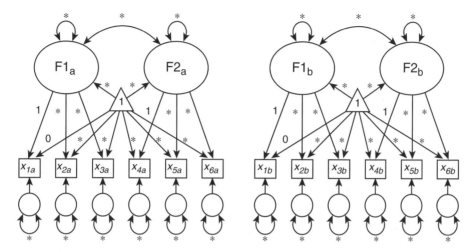

Figure 23.2   Path diagram illustrating parameters that can be compared in studies of measurement invariance

right. These parameters are estimated from the augmented moment matrix, which adds means to the covariance matrix, and adds the mean structure to the standard covariance structure in the model. If the model were fully invariant for a and b, every pair of parameters would be equivalent. Rather than comparing each pair of parameters individually, invariance analyses usually involve comparing sets of parameters and doing so in a systematic manner (Widaman & Reise, 1997). The result is a determination of whether the observed variables reflect similar constructs, and therefore can be compared, across groups or time (Byrne et al., 1989; Steenkamp & Baumgartner, 1998).

Multitrait-multimethod models

The measurement models described to this point decompose variance in observed variables into two components: variance shared with other indicators of a single latent variable and uniqueness. It is, however, possible to further decompose variance by accounting for multiple sources of commonality. Such is the case in latent variable models of multitrait-multimethod data (Campbell & Fiske, 1959), which allow for the disentanglement of variance in observed variables attributable to

what they represent from variance attributable to how they were measured. The multitrait-multimethod matrix is a covariance matrix comprising data on two or more characteristics obtained using two or more methods. For instance, McPherson and Rotolo (1995), in a study of the composition of voluntary groups, obtained data on four characteristics of such groups (e.g. group size, age composition) provided by three sources (e.g. group member, observer). Using the language of multitrait-multimethod analysis, in this example, group characteristics are 'traits' and sources are 'methods.' In the prototypic model specification, each observed score is influence by a trait factor, a method factor, and a uniqueness component (Marsh & Grayson, 1995). Variance in the observed variables is decomposed into a portion attributable to the construct regardless of how it is measured (monotrait-heteromethod), a portion attributable to how it was measured without reference to the constructs (heterotrait-monomethod), and a portion attributable neither to the trait nor the method (uniqueness). Obtaining estimates of parameters in the prototypic model can be difficult, but alternative, more robust specifications have been proposed (Kenny & Kashy, 1992). Latent variable models of multitrait-multimethod data provide useful information about the reliability and validity of observed variables.

Trait-state-error models

Like multitrait-multimethod models, trait-state-error models posit the influence of two latent variables on each observed variable (Cole et al., 2005; Kenny & Zautra, 1995). The univariate trait-state-error model is a sophisticated measurement model that, in effect, decomposes variance in a construct measured on four or more occasions into three components. The trait component is that part that does not change over time—the autoregressive component in panel and time-series designs. The state component is that portion of the variance that is reliable but variable over time. The error component is that portion of variance that is not reliable over time. For example, Zautra et al. (1995) obtained 10 monthly measures of pain and psychological distress. Their trait-state-error model revealed that 60 percent of the variance in pain and 75 percent of the variance in psychological distress was stable and therefore trait-like over the year of their study. Importantly, however, 35 percent of the variance in pain and 18 percent of the variance in psychological distress could be attributed to reliable variance at each assessment. In a bivariate form of the model, they were able to study the directional influences of pain and distress on each other, focusing only on reliable variance in the variables subject to change over time (i.e. states). The trait-state-error model is valuable both for the information it provides regarding the nature of variability on a construct and as a means of examining the causal influence of components of constructs subject to change over time.

Cross-sectional

I now turn to latent variable models that focus on the relations between latent variables. In such models, we assume that the specification of the relations between indicators and latent variables has been evaluated and deemed adequate, allowing the focus to shift to the structural portion of the model. Referring back to Figure 23.1, this focus concerns the directional relations between the latent variables, estimated by the *s on the directional paths, and the disturbance terms, d_1 and d_2. In the remainder of this section, I focus on models for data gathered at a single point in time.

Basic model

The most basic structural model includes one latent independent and one latent dependent variable (e.g. F1 and F3 in Figure 23.1). Such a model is equivalent to a simple regression model except that both the predictor and outcome do not reflect sources of error that vary across the indicators (DeShon, 1998). Thus, latent variable models overcome a critical shortcoming of traditional approaches to modeling directional effects. Latent variable models also provide a means of evaluating the effects of independent variables on multiple dependent variables while also evaluating the effects of dependent variables on each other. For instance, in Figure 23.1, F1 affects both F2 and F3, which are specified as related due to the directional influence of F2 on F3. Importantly, however, latent variable models do not overcome the significant limitation of cross-sectional data for tests of directional effects. For instance, if data on the 11 observed variables in Figure 23.1 were gathered at a single point in time, the arrows between the latent variables could be reversed with no change in model fit (MacCallum et al., 1993). Thus, it is not possible to test in a definitive manner the direction of influence between variables measured at a single point in time (Gollob & Reichardt, 1991). This raises the question of why one would use structural equation modeling on cross-sectional data when more familiar models are available. Even though the ability to model predictors and outcomes as latent variables cannot address the directionality criterion association with causal inferences, it provides significant benefits for addressing the two remaining criteria: association and isolation (Bollen, 1989). In terms of association, the removal of some forms of error from constructs between estimating their association ensures that the association is not underestimated. In terms of isolation, the ability to model extraneous influences as latent variables operating at different points in a model optimizes statistical control when random assignment to levels of causal constructs is not feasible.

With this background, I now describe two useful latent variable models of cross-sectional data.

Mediated effects

Mediators are variables that represent constructs proposed to explain the association between two variables (Hoyle & Robinson, 2003). In social research, mediational hypotheses typically are evaluated using the measurement-of-mediation design (Spencer et al., 2005). In this design, the causal variable is either manipulated or measured and mediators and outcomes are measured. In cross-sectional designs the mediators and outcomes are assessed simultaneously despite the fact that mediators are presumed to exert a causal influence on the outcomes. The evaluation of a mediated effect involves partitioning the effect of a causal variable on an outcome into two portions: the direct effect and the indirect effect. The direct effect is that portion of the effect that is not transmitted through the mediator. Referring back to Figure 23.1, the path from F1 to F3 is the direct effect. In the three-variable case, the remaining portion of the effect is transmitted through the mediator as an indirect effect. In the model shown in Figure 23.1, the mediator is F2 and the magnitude and direction of the indirect effect is expressed in the product of the parameter estimates for the F1-F2 and F2-F3 relations. Statistically speaking, F2 mediates the relation between F1 and F3 if the indirect effect is significant. If the F1-F3 relation remains significant in the presence of the significant indirect effect, then the mediation is only partial; if the F1-F3 relation is nonsignificant, then the mediation is full. For example, using structural equation modeling in this way, Deardorff et al. (2003) found that the effect of stress on depressive symptoms among inner-city youth is mediated by control beliefs.

A key concern in tests of mediated effects is the reliability of the mediator. The more unreliable the mediator, the more the indirect effect is underestimated and the direct effect overestimated (Hoyle & Kenny, 1999). Thus, with an unreliable mediator, it is possible to conclude partial or no mediation of an effect when mediation is, in fact, full. For this reason, it is advisable to always model mediators as latent variables in tests of mediated effects.

Moderated effects

The evaluation of a moderated effect, in conceptual terms, involves an evaluation of the effect (direct or indirect) of an independent variable on an outcome at different levels of a moderator variable. In social research, moderated effects are sometimes referred to as interaction effects and evaluated as a matter of course in research involving factorial designs, from which data typically are analyzed using analysis of variance. When the independent variable and/or moderator variable are measured on a continuum rather than manipulated, the data are best analyzed using techniques that do not evaluate interaction effects as a matter of course (e.g. multiple regression). In such cases, researchers must manually construct interaction terms and evaluate them in strategically specified predictive equations.

Tests of moderated effects involving latent variables are rarer still. This is unfortunate because, as with tests of mediated effects, tests of moderated effects are adversely affected by measurement error (Busemeyer & Jones, 1983; McClelland & Judd, 1993). Even though the adverse effect of measurement error could be overcome by specifying the interaction term as a latent variable, historically this strategy has not been accessible to most social researchers because the loadings and uniqueness terms associated with these latent variables are nonlinear transformations of their counterparts in the latent variables for the independent and moderator variables (Kenny & Judd, 1984). This nonlinearity can be incorporated into the specification of the latent variable representing the interaction term; however, if the number of indicators of the independent and moderator variables exceeds three, the specification becomes prohibitively complex. Fortunately, ignoring the theoretical nonlinearity in these parameters produces results that, in practical terms, are equivalent to results obtained using the more complex specification (Marsh et al., 2004). Published examples of moderated effects involving latent variables are rare; a substantive example can be found in Ping (1996).

Longitudinal

Well-designed longitudinal studies offer significant inferential advantages over cross-sectional studies, the foremost being the possibility of definitive tests of directionality (Halaby, 2004). In this section, I focus on latent variable models of data from studies involving at least two assessments.

Basic model

In the basic longitudinal latent variable model, variables are positioned in a model according to when they were assessed. Thus, for example, the specific arrangement of the latent variables in the model shown in Figure 23.1 would suggest a three-wave longitudinal design in which F1 was assessed in the first wave, F2 in the second wave, and F3 in the third wave. This rudimentary longitudinal model is an example of the sequential strategy of longitudinal research, in which the temporal order in which constructs are assessed corresponds to the presumed causal order of constructs in the model (Hoyle & Robinson, 2003). Data from this design are an improvement over data from the cross-sectional design because the directional paths can logically only go in the direction they are specified; however, the improvement is modest. This is because, using terminology from the trait-state-error model described earlier, the latent variables include both trait (i.e. stable) and state (i.e. time-specific)

components. Thus, for instance, if F1-F2 relation is significant, the inference regarding directionality is nonetheless ambiguous because it might reflect nothing more than correlation between the stable components of F1 and F2. This inferential ambiguity is overcome through the use of a replicative strategy, in which all variables are assessed and included in the model at each wave. This strategy allows for the evaluation of lagged effects from which temporal stability in constructs has been removed.

Cross-lagged panel models

In the simplest latent variable cross-lagged panel model, two constructs are measured using multiple indicators at two points in time. The name derives from the fact that, in addition to autoregressive effects—the effect of each construct on itself at subsequent waves (i.e. stability)—the model specifies an effect of each construct on the other construct at the next wave. These latter effects, which are the focal part of the model, are the cross-lagged paths. As with tests of mediated and moderated effects, controlling for measurement error is vital in cross-lagged panel models. In such models the adverse effect of measurement error extends beyond the attenuation of associations. Because hypotheses about causal priority concern the relative magnitude of the cross-lagged paths, it is critical that the reliability of the variables be equivalent. By modeling them as latent variables, the reliability of each variable is 1.0 and, therefore, differences in the cross-lagged path coefficients cannot be attributed to differences in the reliability of the measures.

In latent variable models of cross-lagged panel data, the primary concern is the absolute and the relative magnitudes of the coefficients associated with the cross-lagged paths. In absolute terms, the concern is whether, after control for stability in the constructs, there is evidence of an association between them. In relative terms, the concern is whether one cross-lagged path coefficient is larger than the other over the same span of time. If one cross-lagged path coefficient is larger than the other, particularly if the smaller coefficient is not significantly different from zero, then the evidence supports an inference of a causal relation in the direction of the path associated with the larger coefficient. Sher et al. (1996) used this strategy to investigate the association between alcohol outcome expectancies and alcohol use. In a two-wave study across three years, they found evidence that alcohol expectancies and use are associated and that the direction of prospective influence is from expectancies to use.

Latent growth curve models

An alternative strategy for modeling repeated observations of a sample is latent growth curve modeling, by which trajectories of means are modeled and potentially included as predictors or outcomes in structural models (Duncan et al., 1999). Because the focus is on modeling means rather than covariances, these models are fit to the augmented moment matrix (described in the earlier section on measurement invariance). Models of latent growth require at least three, preferably four, repeated observations on a sample. As with trend analysis in repeated measures analysis of variance, one can model up to k-1 trajectory shapes (e.g. four observations would allow fitting of linear, quadratic, and cubic trajectories). In unconditional models, determining the best-fitting trajectory for one or more samples is the primary focus. The basic specification for an unconditional latent growth model is shown in Figure 23.3. Free parameters are omitted; only the essential fixed parameters are shown. Note that the paths from the intercept latent variable are fixed to 1, and the paths from the linear latent variable are fixed to values that begin with zero and increase linearly[4]. Also note that, as in Figure 23.2, the latent variables are influenced by a constant, which produces estimates of the latent variable means. Thus, this model yields estimates of the mean intercept and linear slope. Variances also are estimated for these latent variables, which can be treated as Level 2 variables in a

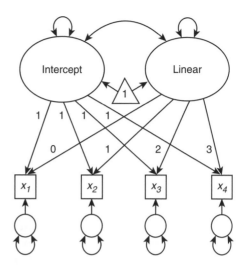

Figure 23.3 Path diagram of an unconditional latent growth model in which linear growth is modeled across four, equally spaced assessments

multilevel model. For instance, if person-level (i.e. Level 2) data on other constructs are available, the influence of those constructs on the intercept and linear growth latent variables can be estimated in a conditional growth model (Willett & Sayer, 1994). An instructive example of latent growth modeling is provided by Reynolds et al. (2005), who modeled linear and quadratic change in cognitive abilities in adult twins from their early fifties into their mid-sixties.

An innovative longitudinal latent variable model combines cross-lagged panel and latent growth models in an autoregressive latent trajectory model (Bollen & Curran, 2004). Even though this model can be estimated with as few as three repeated observations, the ideal design would include at least five. A strength of this model is the simultaneous and integrative approach to modeling associations (i.e. covariances) and trajectories (i.e. means) over time.

LIMITATIONS

Structural equation modeling is a flexible and general approach to latent variable modeling in social research; however, as with any statistical model, it is not without limitations. These limitations are well documented in the literature (for general discussions, see Breckler, 1990; MacCallum & Austin, 2000), and increasingly are understood and acknowledged by social researchers. Six of these limitations are described in the remainder of this section.

Sample size

The maximum likelihood estimator can be expected to evince theoretical properties in arbitrarily large samples. Not all social research yields large samples, raising the question of how large a sample must be in order to produce valid estimates and tests. Even though there are qualifying factors, and the number is somewhat variable as a function of the particular outcome in question (e.g. parameter estimates, fit indices), simulation studies point to about 400 as the number of observations at which the outcomes of maximum likelihood estimation correspond to expectation (e.g. Bentler, 1990). The stability of parameter estimates is questionable in all but the simplest models (i.e. fewer than 10 variables) with fewer than 200 observations (Loehlin, 1992). This number increases as the distributions of the variables depart from normality and as models become more complex. The minimum number is substantially larger for estimators that do not assume normality and/or continuous measurement.

Measurement scale

Another fundamental assumption of the maximum likelihood estimator is continuous measurement of variables (Jöreskog, 1994). Strictly speaking this assumption is not met by most measures in social research. Typically, research participants are provided a relatively small number of response options arrayed along a continuum defined by the two extreme options. Such response formats produce variables that, at best, evince interval-scale properties. Even though violation of this assumption seems almost certain in the typical

application of structural equation modeling in social research, the consequences of violating the assumption in the manner typical of such research (e.g. 5- or 7-point Likert scales) do not appear to be severe (e.g. Tepper & Hoyle, 1996). Nonetheless, the more coarsely categorized a measurement scale, the greater the cause for concern, and estimation from data gathered on response scales with fewer than five options is best carried out using an estimator for ordered categorical variables (e.g. Muthén, 2001).

Model fit

A fundamental concern in applications of structural equation modeling is the determination of whether a given model offers a suitable explanation for a set of data. As noted earlier in the chapter, the determination of whether the covariance matrix implied by a model differs from the observed covariance matrix is not straightforward. The standard hypothesis of no difference between these two matrices is increasingly recognized as unreasonable (Browne & Cudeck, 1993). Moreover, the traditional test of this hypothesis is, in practice, dependent on sample size, ironically favoring models estimated from small samples. This ambiguity in the evaluation of fit is compounded by concerns stemming from how a model was estimated. For instance, it is not unusual for social researchers to specify an initial model that does not meet fit criteria. The model is then re-specified and estimated and new fit statistics produced. These statistics must be interpreted with caution, because they were produced by a model modified after having consulted the data. In such cases, the likelihood of producing a model that would not replicate in a new sample from the same population is unacceptably high (MacCallum et al., 1992).

Equivalent models

The interpretation of results from estimation of a model also must take into account the possibility that other models would provide an equally tenable account of the data (MacCallum et al., 1993). For instance, one might posit a second-order factor model in which a general factor accounts for the correlations among three first-order factors. Even though suitable absolute fit of this model would be consistent with the hypothesis, the fit of this model would be identical to the fit of a model in which the three factors were simply allowed to correlate. This issue is of greater concern in structural models estimated from cross-sectional data, for which plausible equivalent models often can be generated that reverse the specified direction of effects. For this reason, structural equation modeling alone cannot determine the direction of association between two constructs. The advantages structural equation modeling offers over other statistical approaches in this regard are the capacity to model relations between latent variables and, in quasi- or nonexperimental studies, to isolate putative causes and effects from extraneous variables.

Measurement error correction

As noted throughout the chapter, a significant advantage of latent variable models is the capacity for modeling relations between variables from which the effects of certain sources of measurement error have been removed. It is not uncommon, however, for social researchers to overstate the degree to which latent variables are error free (DeShon, 1998). In the typical case (cf. Bollen & Lennox, 1991) latent variables are a function of the commonality across all their indicators. Variance in indicators not shared with the remaining indicators is termed measurement error, or uniqueness, and potentially includes random and systematic components. Of relevance to measurement error correction is the fact that the measurement errors do not— and therefore the latent variables do—contain variance that is common to all the indicators. As such, if all indicators are subject to the same source of measurement error, the latent variable, in fact, is not free of the influence of that source of error. For instance, if error attributable to self-reports is a concern but all indicators are operationally defined as

self-reports, that error is reflected in the latent variable rather than the measurement error terms. Only the influence of those sources of error that vary across indicators, as in multitrait-multimethod models, is removed from latent variables (DeShon, 1998).

Software

Historically, software programs for estimating structural equation models could be described as a limitation because their use assumed familiarity with statistical theory and notation at a level uncommon among social researchers. Ironically, the relative ease with which software programs can now be used for estimating structural equation models has introduced a new concern—that social scientists can specify and estimate models without adequate understanding of what they are doing. Steiger (2001) notes that, because of the ease with which such software can be used (e.g. specification through diagrams), 'the newcomer is led to believe that there is this impressive, but easy-to-use technique that allows modeling of causality in a kind of flow diagram' (p. 338). Given the many ways in which a structural equation modeling analysis can go awry, the complexity in evaluating model fit, and the caveats associated with inferences about models and parameters, the likelihood of misuses of structural equation modeling by novice users is higher than ever.

FUTURE DIRECTIONS

As the use of structural equation modeling has become more commonplace across the social sciences, the gap between what can legitimately be accomplished using the technique in its traditional form and the questions social scientists wish to ask of their data has become increasingly apparent. In effect, the direction of influence between statistical methodology and research application has reversed. From the mid-1970s to the late-1990s, as social researchers came to appreciate the potential of latent variable modeling, they were inspired to address more complex research questions in a more holistic manner. At the dawn of the twenty-first century, with structural equation modeling having become more familiar to social scientists, they began contemplating research questions beyond the reach of standard specification and estimation strategies. Thus, an alternative direction of influence, from social researchers to statistical methodologists, has emerged. Spurred by the increasingly complex demands of social research data and questions, statistical methodologists are extending the boundaries of what traditionally would have been considered appropriate applications of structural equation modeling.

Three primary fronts on which this extension is taking place concern qualities of social research data. As noted earlier, the standard estimator in structural equation modeling, maximum likelihood, assumes multivariate normality and continuous measurement. In practice, these conditions often are not met. Even though the maximum likelihood estimator is reasonably robust to violations of these assumptions, the extent of non-normality or coarseness of measurement in social research data sometimes clearly exceeds the limits of this robustness. Advances in estimation from non-normal and categorical data that perform well in practice are increasingly available to social researchers (e.g. Muthén, 1984). A third characteristic of data with which social researchers often have to contend is missingness. Considerable progress has been made in the understanding and implementation of strategies for managing missingness that are not specific to a particular statistical strategy (e.g. Schafer & Graham, 2002). Also, however, statistical software for estimating latent variable models is increasingly likely to include an estimator that allows for the management of missingness within the context of specific models (Arbuckle, 1996; Enders, 2001). Because meeting minimum sample size recommendations for applications of structural equation modeling is a challenge in some social science literatures, the availability of a strategy for keeping all research participants in the analysis sample is critical.

Advances in the capacity for estimating from non-normal and categorical data have paved the way for advances in terms of the kinds of latent variable models that can be specified and estimated. For instance, a focus by methodologists on estimators and specification strategies for modeling nonlinear effects promises to increase the ease with which such effects can be incorporated into models such as the ones described in this chapter (Schumacker & Marcoulides, 1998). A particularly promising advance concerns the modeling of latent variables that are categorical. These latent variables can reflect latent classes in the traditional sense or reflect distinctive classes of latent growth trajectories (Muthén, 2001). Such applications illustrate the increasing generality of statistical models for estimating latent variable models in social research, potentially including in a single model continuous and categorical indicators, continuous and categorical latent variables— of which some are latent classes, and multiple levels of analysis—of which one might be a latent growth model of individual-level data.

CONCLUSION

Structural equation modeling is a flexible and general statistical approach to specifying and evaluating latent variable models in social research. In this chapter, I described and provided examples of basic and advanced applications of structural equation modeling relevant to social research. Measurement models focus strictly on the relations between observed variables and the latent variables they are assumed to reflect. They can be used to decompose variance in observed variables in ways that both increase understanding of the observed variables and produce latent variables that are relatively pure representations of the constructs the observed variables are assumed to reflect. Even though structural equation modeling is not a viable solution to the primary limitation of cross-sectional data—the inability to determine direction of influence—it is nonetheless useful for modeling such data by enabling some control over the effects of measurement error on directional relations and the inclusion of multiple dependent variables and the relations among them. The ability to eliminate some sources of measurement error is particularly beneficial in 'third-variable' models such as mediation and moderation, in which the effects of such error are compounded. The full benefits of structural equation modeling are apparent in latent variable models of longitudinal data. In traditional autoregressive models, structural equation modeling allows for simultaneous estimation of directional effects across waves controlling for measurement error. In latent growth curve models, structural equation modeling allows for the estimation of patterns of change and the prediction of variation in those patterns across individuals. These models are illustrative of the broad range of latent variable models relevant to social research. A burgeoning didactic literature on applied structural equation modeling coupled with software updated frequently to reflect the latest developments in estimation and testing make these models more appealing than ever.

NOTES

1 An important exception is Muthén's more general framework, implemented in the Mplus software program (Muthén & Muthén, 2006).

2 Readers familiar with exploratory factor analysis will recognize this specification as corresponding to simple structure, which, in the exploratory case, is sometimes achieved through rotation. By forcing many loadings to zero, confirmatory factor analysis avoids the indeterminacy of parameter estimates in exploratory factor analysis.

3 With only two or three first-order factors, although a second-order factor could be specified, such a model would yield identical fit to a first-order model with correlated factors. Thus, although adequate fit of such models would suggest that a second-order model is consistent with the data, a first-order model with correlated factors would be equally consistent with the data. Nonetheless, if the loadings of a set of first-order factors on a second-order factor are high, the data favor interpretation of the second-order model.

4 As with orthogonal polynomials in analysis of variance or multiple regression analysis, the values corresponding to the various trajectory shapes must take into account the relative time lapses between waves. In Figure 23.3, the use of 0, 1, 2, and 3 for the coefficients corresponding to a linear trajectory indicates an assumption of equal spacing between waves. If, for example, there were six months between the first three waves and a year between the last two waves, the coefficients corresponding to a linear trajectory would be 0, 1, 2, 3, and 5.

REFERENCES

Anderson, J. C., & Gerbing, D. W. (1988). Structural equation modeling in practice: A review and recommended two-step approach. *Psychological Bulletin, 103*, 411–423.

Arbuckle, J. L. (1996). Full information estimation in the presence of incomplete data. In G. A. Marcoulides & R. E. Schumacker (Eds.), *Advanced structural equation modeling techniques* (pp. 243–277). Mahwah, NJ: Erlbaum.

Arbuckle, J. L. (2003). *AMOS 5.0 update to the AMOS User's Guide*. Chicago, IL: SPSS.

Bentler, P. M. (1983). Simultaneous equation systems as moment structure models. *Journal of Econometrics, 22*, 13–42.

Bentler, P. M. (1990). Comparative fit indices in structural models. *Psychological Bulletin, 107*, 238–246.

Bentler, P. M. (1995). *EQS structural equations program manual*. Encino, CA: Multivariate Software.

Bentler, P. M., & Bonett, D. G. (1980). *Significance tests and goodness-of-fit in the analysis of covariance structures. Psychological Bulletin, 88*, 588–606.

Bentler, P. M., & Weeks, D. G. (1980). Linear structural equations with latent variables. *Psychometrika, 45*, 289–308.

Blalock H. M. (1961). Correlation and causality: The multivariate case. *Social Forces, 39*, 246–251.

Blalock, H. M. (1964). *Causal inferences in nonexperimental research*. Chapel Hill: University of North Carolina Press.

Bollen, K. A. (1989). *Structural equations with latent variables*. New York: Wiley.

Bollen, K. A. (2002). Latent variables in psychology and the social sciences. *Annual Review of Psychology 53*, 605–634.

Bollen, K. A., & Curran, P. J. (2004). Autoregressive latent trajectory (ALT) models: A synthesis of two traditions. *Sociological Methods and Research, 32*, 336–383.

Bollen, K. A., & Curran, P. J. (2006). *Latent curve models: A structural equation perspective*. Hoboken, NJ: Wiley.

Bollen, K. A., & Lennox, R. D. (1991). Conventional wisdom on measurement: A structural equation perspective. *Psychological Bulletin, 110*, 305–314.

Bollen, K. A., & Long, J. S. (Eds.) (1993). Testing structural equation models. Thousand Oaks, CA: Sage Publications.

Breckler, S. J. (1990). Applications of covariance structure modeling in psychology: Cause for concern? *Psychological Bulletin, 107*, 260–273.

Browne, M. W. (1974). Generalized least squares estimators in the analysis of covariance structures. *South African Statistical Journal, 8*, 1–24.

Browne, M. W. (1984). Asymptotic distribution free methods in analysis of covariance structures. *British Journal of Mathematical and Statistical Psychology, 37*, 62–83.

Browne, M. W., & Cudeck, R. (1993). Alternative ways of assessing model fit. In K. A. Bollen & J. S. Long (Eds.), *Testing structural equation models* (pp. 136–162). Thousand Oaks, CA: Sage Publications.

Busemeyer, J. R., & Jones, L. D. (1983). Analysis of multiplicative combination rules when the causal variables are measured with error. *Psychological Bulletin, 93*, 549–562.

Byrne, B. M. (2001). *Structural equation modeling with AMOS: Basic concepts, applications, and programming.* Mahwah, NJ: Erlbaum.

Byrne, B. M. (2006). *Structural equation modeling with EQS: Basic concepts, applications, and programming.* Mahwah, NJ: Erlbaum.

Byrne, B. M., Shavelson, R. J., & Muthén, B. (1989). Testing for the equivalence of factor covariance and mean structures: The issue of partial measurement invariance. *Psychological Bulletin, 105*, 456–466.

Campbell, D. T., & Fiske, D. W. (1959). Convergent and discriminant validation by the multitrait-multimethod matrix. *Psychological Bulletin, 56*, 81–105.

Clogg, C. C. (1995). Latent class models. In G. Arminger, C. C. Clogg, & M. E. Sobel (Eds.), *Handbook of statistical modeling for the social and behavioral sciences* (pp. 311–359). New York: Plenum.

Cole, D. A., Martin, N. C., & Steiger, J. H. (2005). Empirical and conceptual problems with longitudinal trait–state models: Introducing a trait-state-occasion model. *Psychological Methods, 10*, 3–20.

Collins, L. M., & Wugalter, S. E. (1992). Latent class models for stage-sequential dynamic latent variables. *Multivariate Behavioral Research, 27*, 131–157.

Deardorff, J., Gonzales, N. A., & Sandler, I. N. (2003). Control beliefs as a mediator of the relation between stress and depressive symptoms among inner city adolescents. *Journal of Abnormal Child Psychology, 31*, 205–217.

DeShon, R. P. (1998). A cautionary note on measurement error corrections in structural equation models. *Psychological Methods, 4*, 412–423.

Deutskens, E., de Ruyter, K., & Wetzels, M. (2006). An assessment of equivalence between online and mail surveys in service research. *Journal of Service Research, 8*, 346–355.

Diamantopoulos, A., & Siguaw, J. A. (2000). *Introducing LISREL: A guide for the uninitiated.* London: Sage Publications.

Duncan, O. D. (1966). Path analysis: Sociological examples. *American Journal of Sociology, 74*, 119–137.

Duncan, O. D. (1969). Some linear models for two-wave, two-variable panel analysis. *Psychological Bulletin, 72*, 177–182.

Duncan, O. D. (1975). *Introduction to structural equation models.* New York: Academic Press.

Duncan, T. E., Duncan, S. C., Strycker, L. A., Li, F., & Alpert, A. (1999). *An introduction to latent variable growth curve modeling.* Mahwah, NJ: Erlbaum.

DuToit, S., Cudeck, R., & Sörbom, D. (Eds.) (2001). *Structural equation modeling: Present and future.* Lincolnwood, IL: Scientific Software International.

Enders, C. K. (2001). A primer on maximum likelihood algorithms available for use with missing data. *Structural Equation Modeling, 8*, 128–141.

Funk, C. L. (1999). Bringing the candidate into models of candidate evaluation. *Journal of Politics, 61*, 700–720.

Gibson, W. A. (1959). Three multivariate models: Factor analysis, latent structure analysis, and latent profile analysis. *Psychometrika, 24*, 229–252.

Goldberger, A. S. (1971). Econometrics and psychometrics: A survey of commonalities. *Psychometrika, 36*, 83–107.

Goldberger, A. S., & Duncan, O. D. (Eds.) (1973). *Structural equation models in the social sciences.* New York: Academic Press.

Gollob, H. F., & Reichardt, C. S. (1991). Interpreting and estimating indirect effects assuming time lags really matter. In L. M. Collins & J. L. Horn (Eds.), *Best methods for the analysis of change* (pp. 243–259). Washington, DC: American Psychological Association.

Halaby, C. N. (2004). Panel models in sociological research: Theory into practice. *Annual Review of Sociology, 30*, 507–544.

Hancock, G. R., & Mueller, R. O. (Eds.) (2006). *Structural equation modeling: A second course.* Greenwich, CT: Information Age Publishing.

Hoyle, R. H. (1991). Evaluating measurement models in clinical research: Covariance structure analysis of latent variable models of self-conception.

Journal of Consulting and Clinical Psychology, 59, 67–76.

Hoyle, R. H. (Ed.) (1995). *Structural equation modeling: Concepts, issues, and applications.* Thousand Oaks, CA: Sage Publications.

Hoyle, R. H. (2000). Confirmatory factor analysis. In H. E. A. Tinseley & S. D. Brown (Eds.), *Handbook of applied multivariate statistics and mathematical modeling* (pp. 465–497). New York: Academic Press.

Hoyle, R. H., & Duvall, J. L. (2004). Determining the number of factors in exploratory and confirmatory factor analysis. In D. Kaplan (Ed.), *Handbook of quantitative methodology for the social sciences* (pp. 301–315). Thousand Oaks, CA: Sage Publications.

Hoyle, R. H., & Kenny, D. A. (1999). Sample size, reliability, and tests of statistical mediation. In R. H. Hoyle (Ed.), *Statistical strategies for small sample research* (pp. 195–222). Thousand Oaks, CA: Sage Publications.

Hoyle, R. H., & Robinson, J. I. (2003). Mediated and moderated effects in social psychological research: Measurement, design, and analysis issues. In C. Sansone, C. Morf, & A. T. Panter (Eds.), *Handbook of methods in social psychology* (pp. 213–233). Thousand Oaks, CA: Sage Publications.

Hu, L.-T., & Bentler, P. M. (1995). Evaluating model fit. In R. H. Hoyle (Ed.), *Structural equation modeling: Concepts, issues, and applications* (pp. 76–99). Thousand Oaks, CA: Sage Publications.

Hu, L.-T., & Bentler, P. M. (1999). Cutoff criteria for fit indexes in covariance structure analysis: Conventional criteria versus new alternatives. *Structural Equation Modeling, 6,* 1–55.

Jöreskog, K. G. (1973). A general method for estimating a linear structural equation system. In A. S. Goldberger & O. D. Duncan (Eds.), *Structural equation models in the social sciences* (pp. 85–112). New York: Academic Press.

Jöreskog, K. G. (1994). On the estimation of polychoric correlations and their asymptotic covariance matrix. *Psychometrika, 59,* 381–389.

Jöreskog, K. G. & Sörbom, D. (1999). *LISREL 8: Structural equation modeling with the SIMPLIS command language.* Lincolnwood, IL: Scientific Software International.

Kaplan, D. (2000). *Structural equation modeling: Foundations and extensions.* Thousand Oaks, CA: Sage Publications.

Keesling, J. W. (1972). *Maximum likelihood approaches to causal analysis.* Unpublished doctoral dissertation, University of Chicago.

Kenny, D. A., & Judd, C. M. (1984). Estimating the nonlinear and interactive effects of latent variables. *Psychological Bulletin, 96,* 201–210.

Kenny, D. A., & Kashy, D. A. (1992). Analysis of the multitrait-multimethod matrix by confirmatory factor analysis. *Psychological Bulletin, 112,* 165–172.

Kenny, D. A., & Zautra, A. (1995). The trait-state-error model for multiwave data. *Journal of Consulting and Clinical Psychology, 63,* 52–59.

Kline, R. B. (2005). *Principles and practice of structural equation modeling* (2nd ed.). New York: Guilford Press.

Loehlin, J. C. (1992). *Genes and environment in personality development.* Thousand Oaks, CA: Sage Publications.

MacCallum, R. C. (2003). Working with imperfect models. *Multivariate Behavioral Research, 38,* 113–139.

MacCallum, R. C., & Austin, J. T. (2000). Applications of structural equation modeling in psychological research. *Annual Review of Psychology, 51,* 201–226.

MacCallum, R. C., Roznowski, M., & Necowitz, L. B. (1992). Model modifications in covariance structure analysis: The problem of capitalization on chance. *Psychological Bulletin, 111,* 490–504.

MacCallum, R. C., Wegener, D. T., Uchino, B. N., & Fabrigar, L. R. (1993). The problem of equivalent models in applications of covariance structure analysis. *Psychological Bulletin, 114,* 185–199.

Marcoulides, G. A., & Schumacker, R. E. (Eds.) (2001). *Advanced structural equation modeling: New developments and techniques.* Mahwah, NJ: Erlbaum.

Marsh, H. W., & Grayson, D. (1995). Latent variable models of multitrait-multimethod data. In R. H. Hoyle (Ed.), *Structural equation modeling: Concepts, issues, and applications* (pp. 177–198). Thousand Oaks, CA: Sage Publications.

Marsh, H. W., Wen, Z., & Hau, K.-T. (2004). Structural equation models of latent interactions: Evaluation of alternative estimation strategies and indicator construction. *Psychological Methods, 9,* 275–300.

Maruyama, G. M. (1998). *Basics of structural equation modeling.* Thousand Oaks, CA: Sage Publications.

McArdle, J. J., & McDonald, R. P. (1984). Some algebraic properties of the reticular action model for moment structures. *British Journal of Mathematical and Statistical Psychology, 37,* 234–251.

McClelland, G. H., & Judd, C. M. (1993). Statistical difficulties of detecting interactions and moderator effects. *Psychological Bulletin, 114,* 376–390.

McCutcheon, A. L. (1994). Latent logit models with polytomous effects variables. In A. von Eye & C. C. Clogg (Eds.), *Latent variables analysis: Applications for developmental research* (pp. 353–372). Thousand Oaks, CA: Sage Publications.

McDonald, R. P., & Ringo Ho, M.-H. (2002). Principles and practice in reporting structural equation analyses. *Psychological Methods, 7*, 64–82.

McPherson, J. M., & Rotolo, T. (1995). Measuring the composition of voluntary groups: A multitrait-multimethod analysis. *Social Forces, 73*, 1097–1115.

Muthén, B. O. (1984). A general structural equation model with dichotomous, ordered categorical and continuous latent variable indicators. *Psychometrika, 49*, 115–132.

Muthén, B. O. (2001). Second-generation structural equation modeling with a combination of categorical and continuous latent variables: New opportunities for latent class/latent growth modeling. In L. M. Collins & A. Sayer (Eds.), *New methods for the analysis of change* (pp. 291–322). Washington: American Psychological Association.

Muthén, L. K., & Muthén, B. O. (2006). *Mplus user's guide* (4th ed.). Los Angeles, CA: Muthén & Muthén.

Muthén, B. O., & Shedden, K. (1999). Finite mixture modeling with mixture outcomes using the EM algorithm. *Biometrics, 55*, 463–469.

Myung, J. (2003). Tutorial on maximum likelihood estimation. *Journal of Mathematical Psychology, 47*, 90–100.

Pentz, M. A., & Chou, C.-P. (1994). Measurement invariance in longitudinal clinical research Assuming change from development and intervention. *Journal of Consulting and Clinical Psychology, 62*, 450–462.

Ping, R. A., Jr. (1996). Estimating latent variable interactions and quadratics: The state of this art. *Journal of Management, 22*, 163–183.

Reynolds, C. A., Finkel, D., McArdle, J. J., Gatz, M., Berg, S., & Pedersen, N. L. (2005). Quantitative genetic analysis of latent growth curve models of cognitive abilities in adulthood. *Developmental Psychology, 41*, 3–16.

Schafer, J. L., & Graham, J. W. (2002). Missing data: Our view of the state of the art. *Psychological Methods, 7*, 147–177.

Schumacker, R. E., & Lomax, R. G. (2004). *A beginner's guide to structural equation modeling* (2nd ed.). Mahwah, NJ: Erlbaum.

Schumacker, R. E., & Marcoulides, G. A. (Eds.) (1998). *Interaction and nonlinear effects in structural equation modeling*. Mahwah, NJ: Erlbaum.

Sher, K. J., Wood, M. D., Wood, P. K., & Raskin, G. (1996). Alcohol outcome expectancies and alcohol use: A latent variable cross-lagged panel study. *Journal of Abnormal Psychology, 105*, 561–574.

Sobel, M. E. (1994). Causal inference in latent variable models. In A. von Eye, & C. C. Clogg (Eds.), *Latent variables analysis: Applications for developmental research* (pp. 3–35). Thousand Oaks, CA: Sage Publications.

Spencer, S. J., Zanna, M. P., & Fong, G. T. (2005). Establishing a causal chain: Why experiments are often more effective than mediational analyses in examining psychological processes. *Journal of Personality and Social Psychology, 89*, 845–851.

Steenkamp, J. E. M., & Baumgartner, H. (1998). Assessing measurement invariance in cross-national consumer research. *Journal of Consumer Research, 25*, 78–90.

Steiger, J. H. (2001). Driving fast in reverse: The relationship between software development, theory, and education in structural equation modeling. *Journal of the American Statistical Association, 96*, 331–338.

Steiger, J. H. (2002). When constraints interact: A caution about reference variables, identification constraints, and scale dependencies in structural equation modeling. *Psychological Methods, 7*, 210–227.

Steiger, J. H., & Lind, J. C. (1980, May). *Statistically based tests for the number of common factors.* Paper presented at the Annual Meeting of the Psychometric Society, Iowa City, IO.

Tenko, R., & Marcoulides, G. (2000). *A first course in structural equation modeling*. Mahwah, NJ: Erlbaum.

Tepper, K., & Hoyle, R. H. (1996). Latent variable models of need for uniqueness. *Multivariate Behavioral Research, 31*, 467–494.

Thompson, M. S. (2006). Evaluating between-group differences in latent variable means. In G. R. Hancock, & R. O. Mueller (Eds.), *Structural equation modeling: A second course* (pp. 119–169). Greenwich, CT: Information Age Publishing.

Tomer, A. (2003). A short history of structural equation models. In B. H. Pugesek, A. Tomer, & A. Von Eye (Eds.), *Structural equation modeling: Applications in ecological and evolutionary biology* (pp. 85–124). Cambridge, UK: Cambridge University Press.

Vandenberg, R. J., & Lance, C. E. (2000). A review and synthesis of the measurement invariance literature: Suggestions, practices and recommendations for organizational research. *Organizational Research Methods, 3*, 4–70.

Wansbeek, T., & Meijer, E. (2000). *Measurement error and latent variables in econometrics*. Amsterdam: Elsevier Science.

Widaman, K. F., & Reise, S. P. (1997). Exploring the measurement invariance of psychological instruments: Applications in the substance use domain. In K. J. Bryant, M. Windle, & S. G. West (Eds.), *The science of prevention: Methodological advances from alcohol and substance abuse research* (pp. 281–323). Washington, DC: American Psychological Association.

Wiley, D. E. (1973). The identification problem for structural equation models with unmeasured variables. In A. S. Goldberger & O. D. Duncan (Eds.), *Structural equation models in the social sciences* (pp. 69–83). New York: Academic Press.

Willett, J. B., & Sayer, A. G. (1994). Using covariance structure analysis to detect correlates and predictors of individual change over time. *Psychological Bulletin, 116*, 363–381.

Wright, S. (1934). The method of path coefficients. *Annals of Mathematical Statistics, 5*, 161–215.

Wright, S. (1968). *Evolution and the genetics of populations* (vol. 1). Chicago: University of Chicago Press.

Zautra, A. J., Marbach, J. J., Raphael, K. G., Dohrenwend, B. P., Lennon, M. C., & Kenny, D. A. (1995). The examination of myofascial face pain and its relationship to psychological distress. *Health Psychology, 14*, 223–231.

24

Equating Groups

Stephen G. West and Felix Thoemmes

EQUATING GROUPS

One of the most central tasks of both basic and applied behavioral science is to estimate the size of treatment effects. The basic procedure is conceptually very straightforward. The researcher identifies a treatment (T) of interest such as a new drug treatment or a new cognitive approach to psychotherapy. In our illustration T is designed as a possible means of reducing depression in a clinical population. The researcher then identifies a comparison (C) condition to which the treatment is to be compared. In the case of the new drug treatment, the researcher might choose a placebo which has no pharmaceutical effect on depression or another drug that is the current standard drug prescribed to help relieve depression. Similarly, in the case of the new psychotherapy, the researcher might choose no psychotherapy, psychotherapy without the new cognitive elements, or the standard psychotherapeutic treatment that is commonly delivered (standard of practice). Each patient's level of depression is then measured following treatment. The difference between the mean level of depression in the treatment and control groups, $\overline{Y}_T - \overline{Y}_C$, is then

taken as the estimate of the treatment effect. However, the estimate of the treatment effect will be valid *if and only if* the two groups have been successfully equated prior to the implementation of the treatment. Otherwise stated, only if the groups are equated will $\overline{Y}_T - \overline{Y}_C$ be an unbiased estimate of the causal effect of the treatment.

This chapter will examine some major methods of equating groups. We will draw from insights in statistics (Holland, 1986; Rosenbaum, 2002; Rubin, 1974, 1978, 2005), psychology (Reichardt, 2006; Shadish et al., 2002; West et al., 2000), public health (Little & Rubin, 2000), and sociology and econometrics (Winship & Morgan, 1999). We will focus on comparisons of a treatment and comparison group in two commonly used research designs: the randomized experiment and the observational study (i.e. nonequivalent control group design). The key feature that distinguishes these two designs is the process through which units are assigned to the T and C groups (Judd & Kenny, 1981). The randomized experiment uses some random process (e.g. flipping a coin, a random number generator) to determine assignment of the units to the T and C groups. The units are typically individual participants, but they may be larger aggregations such as schools or entire communities. This process implies that the expected mean of the units in the T group will equal the expected mean of the C group on any conceivable measured or unmeasured baseline variable so that $\overline{Y}_T - \overline{Y}_C$ may be taken as an unbiased estimate of the treatment effect. In contrast, the observational study uses an unknown process to assign participants to the groups. Participants may choose to receive the T versus C, or participants may receive the treatment because they are located in a single community, school, hospital, or other larger unit that has agreed to participate in the study. The process through which participants end up in the T versus C groups is unknown, implying that researchers should expect that there are potential mean differences on background variables between the T and C groups at baseline, even before treatment commences. Now $\overline{Y}_T - \overline{Y}_C$ no longer represents an unbiased estimate of the causal effect of the treatment, but rather a confounded estimate reflecting some combination of the true causal effect of treatment and preexisting differences between the groups on measured or unmeasured variables at baseline (Reichardt, 2006). Only by carefully assessing critical participant characteristics at baseline and developing methods to equate the T and C groups prior to the beginning of treatment can the researcher even approximately estimate the desired effect of the treatment.

We begin this chapter by briefly reviewing the randomized experiment. The randomized experiment is often described as the 'gold standard' design and it serves as an important benchmark for the observational study. We identify some ways in which even randomized experiments can be enhanced through the use of additional procedures designed to more closely equate the groups at baseline. We then briefly review studies comparing the treatment effect estimates from randomized experiments to those of observational studies studying similar treatments, to provide information about the conditions under which these two designs may lead to different estimates

of the treatment effect. We then introduce modern methods of adjusting treatment effects in observational studies for measured differences at baseline. These methods can substantially reduce any bias in the estimate of the treatment effect. Other approaches attempt to bracket the size of the treatment effect so that it represents a reasonable estimate even if there are variations on important unmeasured differences at baseline. Finally, we consider design enhancements that help rule out likely effects of unmeasured variables that may provide alternative explanations for the observed effect of treatment.

RANDOMIZED EXPERIMENTS

Randomization approximately equates the T and C groups at baseline. More formally, randomization produces two important results (Holland, 1986; West et al., 2000). First, as we observed above, the *expected* mean on any participant characteristic at baseline will be equal in the T and C groups, $E\left(Y_{T_{baseline}}\right) = E\left(Y_{C_{baseline}}\right)$, where $E(\ )$ is the expected value of the variable in parentheses. Second, the binary variable X ($1 = T$; $0 = C$) indicating the treatment condition, is expected to be unrelated to all possible participant characteristics at baseline, $E\left(r_{XY_{baseline}}\right) = 0$. These two results imply that $\overline{Y}_T - \overline{Y}_C$ at post test will be an unbiased estimate of the treatment effect so that no adjustment of this effect is needed. Note, however, that these results are expectations. They will hold exactly only given very large sample sizes or across a large number of exact replications of the same experiment conducted on a single population. In any single experiment using more modest sample sizes—'unfortunate randomization'—in which the T and C groups differ at baseline on some subset of important background variables can be expected to occur with some regularity. For this reason many journals in the public health area formally require that means of the T and C groups on important baseline measures be reported as a check on the success of the randomization in the experiment. Following our presentation of additional requirements for randomized field experiments, we will discuss procedures that use these baseline measures to equate groups more adequately prior to treatment in order to provide more statistically powerful tests of the treatment effects.

Additional requirements

Randomized experiments involve additional requirements that must be met for valid estimation of the treatment effect (see Chapter 8). These requirements are routinely met in most laboratory experiments, but can be easily violated in community settings. Failure to meet these requirements may necessitate the use of special procedures, the inclusion of additional design features, or the use of special analysis procedures that adjust for the potential bias (Barnard et al., 1998). Four requirements over which the experimenter may only have limited control are of particular importance in randomized field experiments[1].

1 *Proper Randomization.* The randomization process must be properly carried out and adhered to. Treatment providers must not be permitted to alter the assignment of participants to the T and C conditions. Kopans (1994) presents evidence that reassignment of high-risk women to the treatment condition apparently occurred in a large national randomized trial evaluating the effectiveness of screening mammography. Connor (1977) provides other examples of experiments in which randomization failed or was not maintained by treatment providers. He suggests procedures that potentially minimize the likelihood of such randomization failures. Robins (1989) and Hernán et al. (2001) present methods of adjusting treatment effect estimates in complex longitudinal studies, for example, when participants are reassigned to another treatment, as in certain medical studies in which the patient does not respond to the assigned treatment.

2 *Treatment Compliance.* The participants must receive the intended treatment. In randomized experiments studying mammography screening, some participants have refused screening (T). Other participants in the C group have sought out mammography screening outside the experiment (Baker, 1998). West and Sagarin (2000; see also Angrist et al., 1996; Jo, 2002) review statistical procedures that can provide proper estimates of the treatment effect when there is treatment noncompliance.

3 *Absence of Attrition.* All participants who are assigned to T and C conditions must be measured on the outcome variable. Even though randomization serves to equate participants on average at baseline, this equating is potentially lost if some participants are *not* measured at posttest. Of most concern is differential attrition in which participants with different characteristics drop out of the two groups. For example, in an experiment investigating a new method of mathematics instruction, less mathematically talented students might find the new course too challenging and withdraw prior to the collection of the outcome measure. $\overline{Y}_T$ would only be based on the scores of the more talented students assigned to the T condition, leading to an overestimate of the effectiveness of the course.

Modern missing data techniques (Little & Rubin, 2002; Schafer & Graham, 2002) can improve the estimation of the treatment effect, particularly if variables that are highly related to the outcome (e.g. baseline measures on the outcomes of interest), to missingness, or ideally both are measured at baseline. Full information maximum likelihood estimation (FIML), now available in several statistical packages (e.g. Mplus), combines all of the observed data to produce optimal estimates and standard errors for the treatment effect and other parameters of interest in the statistical model. Multiple imputation (MI), also available in several statistical packages (e.g. SAS), makes multiple copies of the dataset. In each copy, the optimal predicted value for each missing datum is calculated, then random error matching that in the complete data is added. The step of adding random error ensures that the original variability of the observed data is retained in the values that are imputed. The statistical model testing the treatment effect is then estimated in each copy of the dataset. Finally, the estimates of the treatment effects (and other parameters of interest) in each copy of the dataset are recombined. FIML and MI will both produce unbiased estimates of the treatment effect with proper standard errors if missingness is related to measured variables in the dataset, but not if there are other aspects of the missing variables that are not captured by other variables in the dataset. Consider two potential reasons why participants might be missing from a measurement session in a study of health outcomes in a large company. In the first case, each participant's baseline measure of health (e.g. number of days of illness the previous year) is the only variable that systematically predicts whether the participant will be present for the session. In the second case, several of the participants in a division of the company are missing because they are suffering health problems from working day and night on an intensive new project. In the first case, either FIML or MI will produce unbiased estimates because the source(s) of missingness were measured at baseline and are present in the dataset. In the second case, both FIML and MI will produce biased estimates of the treatment effect unless information about project participation and the current project-related health problems are present in the dataset. Suppose, however, that the researchers had used available substantive theory and research to select an extensive set of baseline variables that were expected to be related to the outcome variables, missingness, or both. Once again, information about project participation and project-related health problems are not available in the dataset. In this case, the use of FIML or MI will typically lead to estimates of the treatment effect that are *less* biased, perhaps substantially so, than methods that ignore missing data or that use traditional approaches such as listwise deletion, pairwise deletion, and mean imputation to address missing data.

4 *Stable-Unit-Treatment-Value Assumption.* The response of the participant should not be affected by the treatments (or the participant's knowledge thereof) that other participants receive. This condition is known as the stable-unit-treatment-value assumption (SUTVA); its purpose is to ensure that each participant can only have one true response in the treatment condition (see Rubin, 1978, 1980). Otherwise, the outcomes of the participants in the C group are likely to be atypical. For example, if cancer patients learn that other participants have been assigned to a more promising treatment condition, they may give up hope and stop performing their normal health supportive practices (e.g. proper diet) so that they will have worse outcomes than they would have had in the absence of this knowledge.

Some effects of improving group comparability at baseline

Randomization combined with meeting the four requirements outlined above assures that the estimate of the treatment effect

is unbiased. Unfortunately, this only means that the treatment effect will be correct on average. There is no guarantee that unfortunate randomization will not occur in a particular experiment. If the T and C groups can be closely equated at baseline on variables thought to be important predictors of the outcome, then the likelihood of unfortunate randomization can be substantially reduced. Equating procedures thus reduce the potential of an incorrect estimate of the treatment effect in *a specific experiment*. Equating procedures can also have the benefit of increasing the statistical power of the test, the probability that a true treatment effect of a specified size can be detected. Finally, they may help reduce some of the uncertainty associated with statistical methods of correcting treatment estimates when the four additional requirements are not met. The use of equating procedures is particularly important when the number of units to be assigned is small, the units are not homogeneous, or the treatment effect is not constant, but rather differs in magnitude as a function of the variable(s) on which equating is based.

Consider the following example that captures the importance of equating with a small number of non-homogeneous units. Suppose a randomized experiment is conducted in which the units are six different US cities. Each city receives either an intensive mass media campaign of anti-smoking public service announcements (T) or it does not receive any smoking-related messages in the media (C). The cities chosen for study are from three groups: (a) large cities: Chicago, IL, Los Angeles, CA; (b) medium-sized cities: Baltimore, MD, Portland, OR; and (c) small cities: Terre Haute, IN and San Angelo, TX. Three cities are to be assigned to T and three cities to C. Assume that size of the city is known to be strongly related to the effectiveness of mass media campaigns in health. Following Cochran and Cox (1957), when there are equal numbers (n) of units in the T and C groups, there are $\binom{2n}{n}$ possible randomizations. In the present example, there are $\binom{6}{3} = \frac{6 \times 5 \times 4 \times 3 \times 2 \times 1}{(3 \times 2 \times 1)(3 \times 2 \times 1)}$ or 20 possible randomizations. A randomization that compared Chicago, Baltimore, and Terre Haute to Los Angeles, Portland, and San Angelo would be desirable. In contrast, a randomization that compared Chicago, Los Angeles, and Baltimore to Portland, Terre Haute, and San Angelo would be unfortunate. To avoid this problem, the researcher could match the two large cities, the two medium cities, and two small cities. Within each matched pair, one city would be randomly assigned to T and one to C, leading to a randomization in which the T and C groups will be more adequately balanced, particularly on the critical baseline variable of the size of city.

This procedure of pair matching followed by randomization is very general. For example, in a randomized experiment evaluating a new math instruction program, students could be assessed on a baseline measure of math ability that is expected to be highly related to the outcome variable, here math achievement. The students could be ranked based on their scores and pairs formed (the two highest; the next two highest; … down to the two lowest). Once again, within each pair students would be randomly assigned to T and C groups. This procedure ensures that the T and C groups will be closely equated on the important baseline variable of pretest math ability, preventing any possibility of unfortunate randomization with respect to this critical variable. A second advantage of this procedure is that it can lead to far more statistically powerful tests of the treatment[2]. For example, Student (1931) showed that an early randomized experiment on 10,000 children studying the effects of pasteurized (T) versus raw (C) milk on height and weight gains could have achieved the same level of statistical power with 50 pairs of identical twins. Matching followed by randomization may also lead to a third benefit, providing a stronger foundation for addressing failures to adequately meet the additional requirements of randomized experiments (presented above). For example, the existence of well-matched pairs may provide a stronger basis for modeling the effects of treatment non-compliance and attrition, particularly in experiments in which sample sizes are moderate rather than extremely large and the size of the treatment effect is not constant, but rather depends on the level of the baseline variable (i.e. a baseline × treatment condition interaction). Conceptually, matching followed by randomization may also have other potential advantages in certain contexts as it implicitly identifies a specific comparison participant with which each treatment recipient may be compared. For example, many clinicians would ideally like to understand the effects of treatments on single cases rather than the average effect of the treatment on patients in general. The matching and randomization procedure can permit a closer approximation of this ideal than simple randomization.

When many measures are collected at baseline, matching becomes more difficult. In some cases the multiple measures can be combined a priori into a single composite variable on which matching can occur. For example, in research related to breast cancer, a set of measures including age at menarche, number of first-degree relatives (mother, sister) with breast cancer, number of previous breast biopsies, and age are combined into a single risk score using a formula based on prior epidemiological research (Gail et al., 1989). Alternatively, measures can be collected on the entire sample prior to randomization. The researcher can generate several thousand different possible randomizations and calculate Hotellings T^2 for each randomization *using the key variables measured at baseline*. Hotellings T^2 describes the magnitude of the multivariate difference between the groups, here on the baseline variables. The randomizations are sorted from low to high in terms of the values of Hotellings T^2. From the 5 percent or 10 percent of the randomizations with the lowest values of Hotellings T^2, a randomization is chosen, thereby minimizing potential problems of unfortunate randomization. More complicated blocking and randomization procedures to achieve these same goals in other specialized experimental contexts (e.g. trickle flow randomization in which participants are recruited over an extended period of time) are described in Friedman et al. (1998) and Matthews (2000).

RESEARCH COMPARING THE RESULTS OF RANDOMIZED EXPERIMENTS AND OBSERVATIONAL STUDIES

As a starting point for studying methods to improve the results of observational studies, it is useful to review literature comparing the results of randomized experiments with those of observational studies. Properly implemented randomized experiments serve as the 'gold standard'—they typically provide the best, unbiased estimates of the magnitude of the treatment effect. In contrast, the unknown rules through which participants in observational studies are assigned to the T or C conditions lead to far greater uncertainty about the treatment effect estimate. The researcher would like to claim that some aspect of the treatment caused the observed results; however, it may be possible that a failure to successfully equate the groups at the beginning of the experiment provides a strong alternative explanation (Reichardt, 2006). Even when adjustments in the treatment effect can be made on the basis of measures collected at baseline, there may be less than complete certainty that the T and C groups have been properly equated.

Statistical theory clearly identifies failure to equate the T and C groups on important variables at baseline as an important plausible problem that may occur in observational studies. However, it provides little guidance as to the likely frequency of this problem in practice, nor to the contexts in which estimates of treatment effects are most likely to be biased. To gain some insights into this issue, below we briefly review literature comparing the results of randomized experiments with observational studies that employed similar treatments. We then turn to an examination of modern statistical and design solutions that attempt to address these issues.

Two types of comparisons have been made: (a) single investigations of parallel randomized experiments and observational studies using similar (possibly identical) treatments; and (b) extensive meta-analyses of research areas investigating the effect of a treatment. Of note, exact agreement of the estimates of treatment effects in randomized experiments and observational studies should not be expected—given sampling error, even exact replications of a randomized experiment using the same population would not be expected to produce identical treatment effects. In addition, other differences between the studies representing the two designs may exist. For example, the populations sampled in the two designs, the treatment delivery, the research setting, or other methodological features (e.g. a less adequate control condition is constructed in the observational study) may differ in addition to the focal difference of randomized versus non-randomized design (Cook et al., 2006; Reichardt, 2006; West et al., 2007).

Single comparative studies

Studies comparing treatment effect estimates from randomized experiments and observational studies have produced diverse results. A classic example is Meier's (1972) large-scale evaluation of the effectiveness of the Salk polio vaccine in the US. In some states, a randomized experiment was used; in others, an observational study. Even though both designs led to the conclusion that the Salk vaccine was effective, the effect size in the randomized experiment was substantially larger. Gilbert et al. (1975) suggested that the difference in effect sizes primarily resulted from the different populations on which the polio rates were based in the C conditions. In the randomized experiment, the comparison group included only children who had permission to be vaccinated in contrast to the observational study in which the full population was represented.

Cook et al. (2006) reviewed a unique subset of investigations in which a single randomized treatment group was compared with both a randomized control group (randomized experiment) and a second non-randomized comparison group (yoked observational study). Those observational studies that created a high-quality comparison group produced comparable results to those of the yoked randomized experiment. Investigations with a poorly selected comparison group, poor statistical adjustment for baseline differences, or which differed in other procedural or design features between the observational study and yoked randomized experiment often produced discrepant findings.

Meta-analyses

Across diverse substantive research areas, such as skill training, organizational development, psychotherapy, and medical interventions, meta-analyses have produced heterogeneous outcomes in which randomized experiments have shown larger, smaller, and no difference in treatment effect estimates relative to observational studies. An early influential meta-analytic investigation by Sacks et al. (1983) identified six medical therapies that had been studied using both randomized experiments and observational studies. Sacks et al. concluded that observational studies produced biased results in comparison to randomized controlled trials. Attempts to adjust treatment effects in observational studies for available prognostic factors did not remove this bias. More recently, Ioannidis et al. (2001) conducted meta-analyses of 45 medical interventions (e.g. vaccines for meningitis; local versus general anesthesia) involving a total of 240 randomized trials and 168 observational studies. Overall, there was no consistent pattern of over- or under-estimation of treatment effects by the observational studies relative to the randomized experiments Significant differences between the randomized experiments and observational studies were found in only a small proportion of the meta-analyses . Ioannidis et al. provided evidence of smaller between-study variance in the randomized experiments than in the observational studies, an important finding

that suggests that the effect size estimates of observational studies may be associated with more uncertainty than randomized experiments.

Reviews of other areas also suggest that the direction of mean bias is by no means certain. Lipsey and Wilson (1993) analyzed 74 meta-analyses of behavioral and educational interventions, finding no difference in the mean effect sizes of randomized experiments and observational studies. Heinsman and Shadish (1996) analyzed four meta-analyses in the areas of drug-use prevention, psychosocial interventions for surgery, coaching for the SAT, and ability grouping in secondary schools. They found a larger effect size for randomized experiments than for observational studies. Taken together, the meta-analytic results suggest that the magnitude of bias resulting from the use of an observational study rather than a randomized is typically not large and its direction is uncertain. They also suggest that area-specific choices of samples and methodological features (e.g. type of comparison group) may be important determinants of any bias that is observed.

Methodological features

Heinsman and Shadish (1996) coded methodological features that might potentially account for the observed difference in effect sizes between randomized experiments and observational studies in four behavioral science research areas (e.g. SAT coaching, drug use prevention). Of importance, they found in a regression analysis that *not* allowing self-selection into T versus C conditions in observational studies, using a control group from the same population as the treatment group, minimizing the baseline effect size difference between the T and C groups, and minimizing both overall attrition and differential attrition made the treatment effect estimates more comparable in the two designs. Shadish and Ragsdale (1996) found similar results in a meta-analysis of randomized experiments and observational studies of marital or family psychotherapy. Consistent with these findings, Heckman and Robb (1986) also point to conceptual and statistical reasons why allowing participants to self select into T and C groups is particularly likely to lead to biased estimates. These results suggest that it may be possible to improve estimates of treatment effects in observational studies through the careful use of design and analysis strategies.

Adjustment strategies for equating groups at baseline

Matching

Matching is used in observational studies to identify a set of participants in the T and C groups that are comparable. To illustrate, consider two small school classrooms, labeled A and B, one of which implements an innovative new math curriculum, whereas the other implements a standard math curriculum in 6th grade. Table 24.1 illustrates the basic process of simple 1:1 matching. All students in both classrooms are given an IQ test at the beginning of the school year. For each

Table 24.1 Illustration of simple matching of two small classroom on baseline IQ scores

Pair	Classroom A	Classroom B
	130	
1	125	124
2	120	120
3	119	119
4	119	118
5	117	116
6	115	115
7	109	109
8	107	107
9	107	106
10	104	102
11	101	101
12	96	96
		90
		89

Note: Scores were ordered within units and represent pretest IQ scores of participants. Pairs of participants on the same line represent matched pairs. One person in Classroom A and two persons in Classroom B have no matched pairs. The mean IQ score for all participants in Classroom A is 113; the mean IQ score for all participants in Classroom B is 108. The mean difference $(\overline{Y}_A - \overline{Y}_B)$ for the full unmatched sample is 5. The mean for the matched pairs of Classroom A is 111.6 and for Classroom B is 111.1, yielding a mean difference of 0.5. $n_A = 13$ and $n_B = 14$ for the full sample

student in the classroom A, an attempt is made to identify a student in classroom B who is closely equated on IQ. This matching process diminishes the mean difference in baseline IQ between the two groups in our example from $M_A - M_B = 5$ in the full unmatched sample to $M_A - M_B = 0.5$ in the reduced, matched sample. A variety of computer algorithms are available that match T and C participants to produce the minimum discrepancy on the pretest variable (see Ming & Rosenbaum, 2001; Rosenbaum, 2002). These computer algorithms are particularly useful when both the T and C groups are large, are of dramatically different sizes, or both. For example, observational studies of initial trials of innovative programs (T) may involve a relatively small number of participants, whereas there are a substantially larger number of participants in the standard program (C) that serve as the comparison. In such cases, the algorithm will select a variable number of optimal matches (e.g. up to 5) for each participant[3]. These variable matching procedures lead to more adequate equating of the groups on the matching variable and greater statistical power for the T versus C comparison, given the larger sample size (Ming & Rosenbaum, 2000).

Researchers are encouraged to measure many variables at baseline, particularly those that may be related to treatment group assignment or the outcome variable. Substantive theory and prior research can provide guidance in the selection of a set of measures that will capture as fully as possible potential baseline differences between the T and C groups. However, the availability of a large number of baseline variables makes matching far more complex. In rare cases, a composite variable can be created (e.g. the Gail score for breast cancer risk described earlier). More commonly, propensity scores are used. Propensity scores provide an estimate of the probability that a participant will be assigned to the treatment group (Rosenbaum, 2002; Rosenbaum & Rubin, 1983, 1984; Rubin, 1997; Shadish et al., 2006; Smith, 1997). The researcher uses all baseline variables (or a subset containing the most important ones if this number is very large) and predicts the probability that the participant will be in the T group. This probability is known as the propensity score.

There are two major issues in the creation of propensity scores. The first is to make sure that subject matter expertise in the form of prior research and theory has been used to select baseline measures that will capture as fully as possible important baseline differences between the T and C groups. The second is to choose a statistical model that adequately represents the form of the relationship between the variables and each participant's propensity score. Rosenbaum and Rubin (1983) used simple linear logistic regression to produce these estimates. Dehejia and Wahba (1999) used more complicated logistic regression models involving specification of interactions and curvilinear effects of baseline variables. McCaffrey et al. (2004) used automated stepwise nonparametric regression tree methods to model possible complex relationships between the variables and the propensity score. In each case the goal is to achieve T and C groups that are balanced on all important baseline variables and for which the error of prediction in the sample has been minimized (Shadish et al., 2006). As an important check on the success of this procedure, the data are divided into five strata and the balance of the baseline variables within each stratum is compared. When balance is achieved, there is a strong basis for comparing the groups. If balance is not achieved within one (or more) stratum, the comparison of the treatment and control groups is carried out only over those strata on which balance has been achieved.

Each participant's propensity score may then be taken as the best summary of the baseline information. The propensity score is used as the basis for equating the groups. The groups may be equated using the standard 1 to 1 or variable many to 1 matching procedures described above. Alternatively, analysis of covariance or blocking on the strata may be used (but see footnote 3). As an illustration of the matching strategy, Wu et al. (in press) constructed propensity scores for retention in first grade from a large set of baseline variables

measured early in the school year. In the full sample ($n = 769$) of children at risk for grade retention, there were large differences between students on the Woodcock Johnson reading score at baseline. Students who were later retained in first grade had substantially lower scores than students who were later promoted to second grade, $\overline{Y}_{baseline-retained} = 420$ $versus$ $\overline{Y}_{baseline-promoted} = 438$. Optimal 1 to 1 matching on propensity scores yielded 97 matched pairs with $\overline{Y}_{baseline} = 422.4$ for the retained students and $\overline{Y}_{baseline} = 423.4$ for the promoted students. Similar reductions in baseline differences were achieved for other variables measured at baseline. Theoretically, propensity scores will provide a proper adjustment for the unknown assignment rule if all important baseline variables have been included and the form of the propensity model has been correctly specified.

Matching has substantial strengths in that it does not require specification of the form of the relationship between the baseline and outcome variables, it clearly delimits the range of the baseline variables over which T and C can be appropriately compared, and it leads to efficient estimates of the treatment effect because of the small number of parameter estimates that are involved. Hypothesized treatment group x baseline level interactions can also be examined within the matched propensity score framework. There are two primary limitations of the matched propensity score framework. First, it does not adjust the treatment effect for measurement error in the baseline variables giving rise to potential regression to the mean effects if very reliable and stable measures of important baseline variables are not available. Second, it does not adjust for other important variables (hidden variables) that are not measured at pretest, again emphasizing the importance of selection of the full range of potential baseline variables based on subject matter expertise.

Statistical adjustment strategies based on measured baseline differences

A variety of statistical models may be developed that attempt to adjust for baseline differences in measured variables. Perhaps, the simplest is analysis of covariance (Huitema, 1980; Reichardt, 1979) which is used to provide an adjustment of the treatment effect for one or more baseline variables. Typically, a simple linear model is used, $\hat{Y} = b_0 + b_1 COV + b_2 X$, where Y is the outcome variable, COV is the covariate measured at baseline and X is the binary treatment indicator. This model can be extended to include multiple covariates, other parametric relationships (e.g. addition of a $b_3 COV^2$ term to represent a quadratic relationship between X and Y), and treatment x covariate interactions (Cohen et al., 2003; Huitema, 1980; Reichardt, 1979). Nonparametric methods can be used to model more complex relationships between X and Y (see Little et al., 2000). The primary limitation of ANCOVA methods is that their success in equating the T and C groups depends heavily on the correct specification of the adjustment model. For example, if the relationship between COV and Y is nonlinear and a simple linear ANCOVA model is used, the treatment effect estimate will be biased.

The basic ANCOVA approach shares the limitation with matching that baseline variables may be measured with less than perfect reliability. This problem is most serious when the T and C groups are selected from different populations, so that regression to the mean will occur (see Campbell & Kenny, 1999; Shadish et al., 2002). Even if the statistical adjustment model is otherwise correctly specified, measurement error will typically lead to under-adjustment of the treatment effect for baseline differences. Huitema (1980) provides an introduction and Fuller (1987) provides a more advanced treatment of methods for correcting for measurement error in the context of ANCOVA. Alternatively, when multiple indicators are available for each important construct measured at pretest, structural equation models can be used to provide measurement error-free estimates of the treatment effect. Aiken et al. (1994) provide a good discussion of the use of this approach and apply it to the evaluation of a drug treatment program. One limitation of the structural equation modeling approach is

that the models to date have specified a linear relationship between the baseline measures and the outcome. Lee et al. (2004), Marsh et al. (2004), and Wall and Amemiya (2007) describe extensions of structural equation models that may account for curvilinear and interactive effects.

Correction for measurement error can also be desirable when treatment participants are selected on the basis of a variable that is unstable over time. For example, if T participants are selected based on high scores on a measure of depression (or because they are seeking treatment because of a severe depressive episode), it is likely that some of the participants are in a temporary state of high depression and would return to their typical level of depression in the absence of any treatment simply given the passage of time. Reliability correction methods that adjust the estimate of the treatment effect for the test-retest reliability for the time interval between the baseline and outcome measures in the absence of treatment can improve the estimate of the treatment effect. If repeated measures are collected on multiple indicators of the outcome variable at baseline and multiple other time points, special structural equation models can be used that partition the variance at each time point into state (temporary) and trait (true score) components (cf. Khoo et al., 2006; Steyer et al., 1992).

Adjusting for unmeasured baseline differences (hidden variables)

The matching and the statistical adjustment strategies described above can provide appropriate correction of the estimate of treatment effect for variables measured at baseline. However, it is also possible that variables that are *not* measured at baseline could account for all or part of the estimated treatment effect. Three general strategies exist for addressing this problem.

First, a variety of methods have been proposed for conducting sensitivity analyses of treatment effect estimates (Marcus, 1997; McCafferty et al., 2004; Rosenbaum, 2002). As an illustration of one simple method, imagine a researcher has found a

0.8 standard deviation difference (large effect size) between the T and C groups on the outcome variable. The researcher would then identify the largest standardized difference between the T and C groups on the set of variables measured at baseline. Suppose the largest baseline difference were $d = 0.5$ standard deviations. Then the researcher identifies the maximum correlation between any of the baseline measures and the posttest measure of the outcome of interest. Suppose the maximum correlation were $r = 0.6$. The product of these two quantities, $adjustment = \frac{\overline{Y}_{baseline_T} - \overline{Y}_{baseline_C}}{SD} r_{baseline-outcome}$, here adjustment $= 0.5 \times 0.6 = 0.3$, provides a rough estimate of the maximum extent that this estimate of the standardized treatment effect would need to be reduced given what is a 'worst case scenario' for an important hidden variable. If the standardized treatment effect were reduced by this amount, to $0.8 - 0.3 = 0.5$ in our example, we would have a plausible estimate of its lower bound. If this value were still statistically significant, it would provide evidence that the treatment effect is robust. Note that there is no theoretical reason why the actual adjustment required for hidden variables could not exceed this value. However, in practice, if a number of variables are measured at baseline and they can be presumed to be representative of important hidden variables, the adjustment will nearly always be an *overestimate* of the adjustment needed in practice.

Econometric approaches (e.g. Barnow et al., 1980; Heckman, 1979, 1989, 1990; Muthén & Jöreskog, 1983) have been proposed that adjust for the effects of both measured and unmeasured variables at baseline. Two separate equations are used in these models. The first (selection model) equation uses measured baseline variables to predict the assignment of the participant to the treatment or control group. The second uses this selection probability, an indicator variable (T = 1; C = 0) for treatment condition, and potentially other covariates to estimate the outcome. A key feature of this approach is the requirement of an instrumental variable[4], a variable that strongly predicts treatment assignment in the first equation but which has no separate relationship to the outcome (see Figure 24.1). In essence, the instrument can be thought of as a naturally occurring randomization (Heckman, 1996). The instrumental variable can only affect the outcome indirectly through its effect on treatment assignment, an assumption known as the exclusion restriction. If the assumptions of this approach are met, the treatment effect estimate will include proper adjustment for both measured and unmeasured baseline variables. However, in practice, this method is extremely sensitive to violations of its underlying assumptions, particularly the exclusion restriction (Heckman, 1997; Stolzenberg & Relles, 1990; Winship &

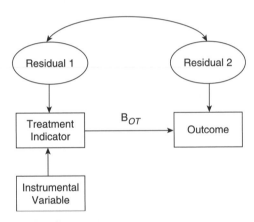

Figure 24.1 Illustration of econometric selection bias model
Note: **The instrumental variable directly affects only the Treatment Indicator (T = 1; C = 0). This condition is known as the exclusion restriction. Residual 1 is the error of the prediction of the Treatment Indicator including error produced by hidden variables. The hidden variables may also be associated with the residual of the Outcome (Residual 2). If the model is correctly specified, an adjustment of the regression coefficient B_{OT} will yield an unbiased estimate of the treatment effect controlling for the hidden variables. If the assumptions of the model are violated (notably the exclusion restriction), the estimate of the treatment effect may be severely biased.**

Mare, 1992). When assumptions are violated, the treatment effect estimates of econometric models can be far more biased than those based on simpler approaches like ANCOVA or matching. In addition, even if the assumptions of the approach are met, the standard errors of the estimate of the treatment effect can be extremely large if the instrument is not very strongly related to treatment assignment. Finally, the econometric approach assumes that the treatment effect is constant across all participants.

A third approach suggested by Manski (1994), Manski and Nagin (1998), Manski and Pepper (2000) has explored the effects of making weaker assumptions about instrumental variables in econometric selection models. This approach results in the estimation of a plausible range of values for the treatment effect within upper and lower bounds. However, in some cases, the bounds may be very large so that little information is conveyed about the size of the treatment effect.

Adjusting for growth

A final issue occurs when participants show different rates of natural growth (e.g. young children in math skills) or decline (e.g. Alzheimer's patients in memory) on the outcome variable of interest. With observations taken only at baseline, no measure of the natural growth rate in the absence of treatment is available for the participants. Change score analysis (Judd & Kenny, 1981) can be used to estimate the treatment effect. Participants are measured on the same measure at baseline and outcome. These baseline and outcome measures are then transformed so that their variances are equated (see Huitema, 1980). The mean change in the T group is then compared with the mean change in the C group to provide an estimate of the treatment effect. This approach adequately models special situations in which growth is occurring at a constant rate across all participants or is of the fan spread variety in which growth is occurring at a rate proportional to the participant's baseline score (e.g. those advantaged at baseline gain more). Treatment effects for other forms of growth are not

well represented using this approach. More adequate modeling of growth requires the collection of additional data at multiple time points, ideally both before and after the treatment (Shadish et al., 2002; West et al., 2000). If sufficient additional time points are collected, the natural pattern of growth prior to treatment can be estimated; this pattern can be compared to the pattern of growth following the introduction of treatment in the T group. Singer and Willett (2002) describe multilevel modeling methods that estimate the treatment effect while allowing for differences between participants in growth rates.

Design enhancements

In line with the topic of this chapter, we have focused on methods of equating the T and C groups at baseline. However, we would be remiss if we did not remind readers of an important alternative strategy emphasized by Shadish and Cook (1999) and Shadish et al. (2002). This strategy involves adding design features that address specific threats to validity that arise in observational studies. Shadish and Cook (1999) argue that the use of design enhancements will often be preferable to the use of statistical adjustment strategies. We present three methods of enhancing the design of the basic observational study here (see Shadish & Cook, 1999, for an extensive list).

Multiple control groups

When a treatment and control group are selected in an observational study, they will be similar at baseline in some respects and different in others. This feature gives rise to the possibility that some hidden variable may be accounting for the result. If multiple control groups can be identified and the estimates of the treatment effects are similar when different control groups are used, the researcher's confidence that the treatment effect is not biased is increased. For example, using a large database, Roos et al. (1978) compared children receiving tonsillectomies (T) with two different comparison groups: (a) children having a matched history of respiratory illness; and (b) untreated siblings of the *T* child who were similar in age. Rosenbaum (2002) presents several examples of the use of this strategy.

Nonequivalent dependent variables

Other dependent variables that would be expected to be affected by the same factors as the outcome of interest, but not by the treatment can sometimes be identified. Reynolds and West (1987) studied the effect of a promotional campaign (*T*) versus no campaign (*C*) on the sales of state lottery tickets in convenience stores. The sales of lottery tickets increased in the T stores relative to the *C* stores. However, sales of other classes of items (e.g. groceries, gasoline) did not change appreciably, providing support that the increase in ticket sales resulted from the promotional campaign rather than other factors (e.g. greater increase in customer traffic in T stores).

Multiple pretreatment measures over time

We noted earlier that the collection of multiple measurements over time prior to treatment permits estimation of the pattern of growth or decline in the absence of treatment. In one design reported by Reynolds and West (1987), sales figures were available from each store for each of the 12 weeks of the lottery game. Sales declined each week during the lottery. The sales campaign was introduced into the T stores during the middle of the lottery permitting a strong basis for estimating the treatment effect despite different rates of decline in the individual participating stores.

SUMMARY AND CONCLUSIONS

In this chapter we have considered methods of equating groups at baseline in randomized experiments and in observational studies. In randomized experiments, groups are equated to avoid unfortunate randomization and to maximize statistical power. Equating groups at baseline can also be helpful in interpreting the results when there is a breakdown of the original randomization, for example

through treatment noncompliance or attrition. In observational studies, groups are equated to help assure that the estimate of the treatment effect is unbiased and not the result of baseline differences on measured or unmeasured variables.

Initial attempts to compare the effect sizes of observational studies and randomized experiments studying the same treatment have suggested that the direction of bias, if any, observed in the observational study is not consistent, but rather depends on the research area and features of the design. Research by Shadish and colleagues suggests that three related factors—(a) larger measured baseline differences; (b) self-selection into treatment; and (c) the use of comparison groups selected from a different population than the treatment group—are all associated with bias in treatment effect estimates in observational studies.

A variety of statistical adjustment and design approaches were considered to minimize the influence of these factors. Matching strategies, including matching on propensity scores, provide a strong basis for equating the T and C groups on measured variables. Key determinants of the success of this strategy include the use of content area expertise to select reliable variables that will capture baseline differences between groups as fully as possible and careful checking that the propensity score model leads to balance of the baseline variables within each stratum on the propensity score. Analysis of covariance and structural equation modeling can also properly equate the T and C groups of measured variables at baseline variables and can also provide adjustment for measurement error. The key determinant of the success of these strategies is whether the relationships between the baseline variables and the outcome variable have been properly specified. For example, structural equation models have only recently been extended beyond examination of linear relationships. Econometric approaches provide appropriate adjustment for both measured and unmeasured variables, but the results may be fragile as they are dependent on meeting strong statistical assumptions. Other econometric methods make weaker assumptions and provide upper and lower bound estimates of treatment effects; however, if the bounds are large, there will be considerable uncertainty as to the true size of the treatment effect. Change score analyses can estimate models for the special case in which there is constant or fan spread growth (or decline) in the absence of treatment. Addressing more complex forms of growth requires the collection of additional measurements over time both pre- and post-treatment.

A complementary and often preferable approach to statistical adjustment is the inclusion of design enhancements that address specific threats to internal validity that arise in observational studies. Potential nonequivalence can be addressed during the design of the study, ensuring that the participants in the T and C conditions are sampled from populations that are as comparable as possible. The use of additional design features that rule out specific threats to internal validity can often increase the confidence with which inferences about treatment effects may be made. These include the use of multiple control groups that address different threats to validity, nonequivalent dependent variables that would be expected to be affected by potential threats to validity, but not the treatment, and multiple pretreatment measures over time which permit estimation of patterns of natural growth and decline.

As researchers move from the ideal randomized experiment to weaker designs such as broken randomized designs involving noncompliance or attrition, to designs in which participants are assigned to T versus C conditions on the basis of a quantitative measure (Reichardt, 2006; see also Cook & Wong, this volume), and finally, to the observational studies that have unknown assignment rules, the estimate of the magnitude of the treatment effect becomes associated with increasing uncertainty. To the extent that researchers can bring substantive knowledge, additional design features that address specific validity threats, and good measurement to bear, this uncertainty can be reduced. Rosenbaum

(2002) and Shadish et al. (2002) offer useful advice for planning studies to achieve this end.

NOTES

1 Other threats to internal validity are also possible, as when the experimenter uses different equipment or different observers to measure the outcome variable in the T and C conditions.

2 Blocking or analysis of covariance may also be used to increase statistical power. A priori matching is often preferred because it does not assume a specific form of relationship between the variable(s) on which participants are matched and the outcome variable. Matching can also make it easier to detect unexpected interactions between the matching variable(s) and treatment. Maxwell and Delaney (2004, pp. 448–452) provide a comparative discussion of the conditions under which matching, blocking, and analysis of covariance may be preferred.

3 As the ratio of the number of participants in the C to the T group approaches 5 or 6 to 1, the statistical power of the test approaches asymptote. Adding additional C participants will lead to only very minimal increases in statistical power.

4 Earlier work within the econometric tradition proved that selection models were identified so that treatment effects could be estimated without an instrument. However, these models require the assumption of a specific distribution of the variables in the population. Theoretical work by Little (1985) showed that these models are extraordinarily sensitive to the specific distributional assumptions that were made. More recent work by Heckman (1997) has emphasized the importance of having a good instrument in producing unbiased estimates of treatment effects.

REFERENCES

Aiken, L. S., Stein, J. A., & Bentler, P. M. (1994). Structural equation analysis of clinical subpopulation differences and comparative treatment outcomes: Characterizing the daily lives of drug addicts. *Journal of Consulting and Clinical Psychology*, 62, 488–499.

Angrist, J. D., Imbens, G. W., & Rubin, D. B. (1996). Identification of causal effects using instrumental variables (with commentary). *Journal of the American Statistical Association*, 91, 444–472.

Baker, S. G. (1998). Analysis of survival data from a randomized trial with all-or-none compliance: Estimating the cost-effectiveness of a cancer screening program. *Journal of the American Statistical Association*, 93, 929–934.

Barnard, J., Du, J., Hill, J. L., & Rubin, D. B. (1998). A broader template for analyzing broken randomized experiments. *Sociological Methods and Research*, 27, 285–317.

Barnow, L. S., Cain, G. G., & Goldberger, A. S. (1980). Issues in the analysis of selection bias. In E. S. Stromsdorfer & G. Farkas (Eds), *Evaluation studies review annual* (Vol. 5, pp. 53–59). Beverly Hills, CA: Sage.

Campbell, D. T., & Kenny, D. A. (1999). *A primer on regression artifacts*. New York: Guilford.

Cochran, W. G., & Cox, G. M. (1957). *Experimental designs* (6th ed.). New York: Wiley.

Cohen, J., Cohen, P., West, S. G., & Aiken, L. S. (2003). *Applied multiple regression/correlation analysis for the behavioral sciences* (3rd. ed.). Mahwah, NJ: Erlbaum.

Conner, R. F. (1977). Selecting a control group: An analysis of the randomization process in twelve social reform programs. *Evaluation Quarterly*, 1, 195–244.

Cook, T. D., Shadish, W. R., Jr., & Wong, V. C. (2006). Within-study comparisons of experiments and non-experiments: What the findings imply for the validity of different kinds of observational study. Unpublished Manuscript, Northwestern University. Available at: http://www.metheval.uni-jena.de/projekte/symposium2006/contributions.php

Dehejia, R. H., & Wahba, S. (1999). Causal effects in nonexperimental studies: Reevaluating the evaluation of training programs. *Journal of the American Statistical Association*, 94, 1053–1062.

Friedman, L. M., Furberg, C. D., & DeMets, D. L. (1998). *Fundamentals of clinical trials* (3rd ed.). New York: Springer.

Fuller, W. A. (1987). *Measurement error models*. New York: Wiley.

Gail, M. H., Brinton, L. A., Byar, D. P., Corle, D. K., Green, S. B., Schairer, C., & Mulvihill, J. J. (1989). Projecting individualized probabilities of developing breast cancer for White females who are being examined annually. *Journal of the National Cancer Institute*, 81, 1879–1886.

Gilbert, J. P., Light, R. J., & Mosteller, F. (1975). Assessing social innovations: An empirical base for policy. In C. A. Bennett & A. A. Lumsdaine (Eds), *Evaluation and experiment: Some critical issues in assessing social programs* (pp. 39–193). New York: Academic.

Heckman, J. J. (1979). Sample bias as a specification error. *Econometrica*, 46, 153–162.

Heckman, J. J. (1989). Causal inference and nonrandom samples. *Journal of Educational Statistics*, 14, 159–168.

Heckman, J. J. (1990). Varieties of selection bias. *American Economic Review*, 80, 313–318.

Heckman, J. J. (1996). Randomization as an instrumental variable. *Review of Economics and Statistics*, 77, 336–341.

Heckman, J. J. (1997). Instrumental variables: A study of implicit behavioral assumptions used in making program evaluations. *Journal of Human Resources*, 32, 441–462.

Heckman, J. J., & Robb, R. (1986). Alternative methods for solving the problem of selection bias in evaluating the impact of treatments on outcomes. In H. Wainer (Ed.), *Drawing inferences from self-selected samples* (pp. 63–113). New York: Springer-Verlag.

Heinsman, D. T., & Shadish, W. R. (1996). Assignment methods in experimentation: When do nonrandomized experiments approximate answers from randomized experiments? *Psychological Methods*, 1, 154–169.

Hernán, M. A., Brumbach, B., & Robins, J. M. (2001). Marginal structural models to estimate the joint causal effect of nonrandomized treatments. *Journal of the American Statistical Association*, 96, 440–448.

Holland, P. W. (1986). Statistics and causal inference (with discussion). *Journal of the American Statistical Association*, 81, 945–970.

Huitema, B. E. (1980). *The analysis of covariance and alternatives*. New York: Wiley.

Ioannidis, J. P. A., Haidich, A.-B., Pappa, M., Pantazi, N., Kokori, S. I., Tektonidou, M. G., Contopoulous-Ioannidis, D. G., & Lau, J. (2001). Comparison of evidence of treatment effects in randomized and nonrandomized studies. *Journal of the American Medical Association*, 286, 821–830.

Jo, B. (2002). Statistical power in randomized intervention studies with noncompliance. *Psychological Methods*, 7, 178–193.

Judd, C. M., & Kenny, D. A. (1981). *Estimating the effects of social interventions*. New York: Cambridge.

Khoo, S.-T., West, S. G., Wu, W., & Kwok, O.-M. (2006). Longitudinal methods. In M. Eid and E. Diener (Eds), *Handbook of multimethod measurement in psychology* (pp. 301–317). Washington, DC: American Psychological Association.

Kopans, D. B. (1994). Screening for breast cancer and mortality reduction among women 40–49 years of age. *Cancer*, 74 (Supplement.), 311–322.

Lee, S. Y., Song, X. Y., & Poon, W. Y (2004). Comparison of approaches in estimating interaction and quadratic effects of latent variables. *Multivariate Behavioral Research*, 39, 37–67.

Lipsey, M. W., & Wilson, D. B. (1993). The efficacy of psychological, educational, and behavioral treatment: Confirmation from meta-analysis. *American Psychologist*, 48, 1181–1209.

Little, R. J. (1985). A note about models for selectivity bias. *Econometrica*, 53, 1469–1474.

Little, R. J., Hyonggin, J., Johanns, J., & Giordani, B. (2000). A comparison of subset selection and analysis of covariance for the adjustment of confounders. *Psychological Methods*, 5, 459–476.

Little, R. J., & Rubin, D. B. (2000). Causal effects in epidemiological studies via potential outcomes: Concepts and analytical approaches. *Annual Review of Public Health*, 21, 121–145.

Little, R. J., & Rubin, D. B. (2002). *Statistical analysis with missing data* (2nd ed.). New York: Wiley.

Manski, C. F. (1994). The selection problem. In C. Sims (Ed.). *Advances in econometrics* (Vol. 1, pp. 147–170). Cambridge, UK: Cambridge University Press.

Manski, C. R., & Nagin, D. S. (1998). Bounding disagreements about treatment effects. *Sociological Methodology*, 28, 99–137.

Manski, C. R., & Pepper, J. V. (2000). Monotone instrumental variables: With an applications to the return to schooling. *Econometrica*, 68, 997–1010.

Marcus, S. (1997). Using omitted variable bias to assess uncertainty in the estimation of an AIDS education treatment effect. *Journal of Educational and Behavioral Statistics*, 22, 193–202.

Marsh, H. W., Wen, Z. L., & Hau, K. T. (2004). Structural equation models of latent interactions: Evaluation of alternative estimation strategies and indicator construction. *Psychological Methods*, 9, 275–300.

Matthews, J. N. S. (2000). An introduction to randomized clinical trials. New York: Oxford.

Maxwell, S. E., & Delaney, H. D. (2004). *Designing experiments and analyzing data: A model comparison perspective* (2nd ed.). Mahwah, NJ: Erlbaum.

McCaffrey, D. F., Ridgeway, G., & Morral, A. R. (2004). Propensity score estimation with boosted regression for evaluating causal effects in observational studies. *Psychological Methods*, 9, 403–425.

Meier, P. (1972). The biggest public health experiment ever: The 1954 field trial of the Salk poliomyelitis vaccine. In J. M. Tanur, F. Mosteller, W. H. Kruskal, R. F. Link, R. S. Pieters, & G. R. Rising (Eds), *Statistics: A guide to the unknown* (pp. 120–129). San Francisco: Holden Day.

Ming, K., & Rosenbaum, P. R. (2000). Substantial gains in bias reduction from matching with a variable number of controls. *Biometrics*, 56, 118–124.

Ming, K., & Rosenbaum, P. R. (2001). A note on optimal matching with variable controls using the assignment algorithm. *Journal of Computational and Graphical Statistics*, 10, 455–463.

Muthén, B., & Jöreskog, K. G. (1983). Selectivity problems in quasi-experimental studies. *Evaluation Review*, 7, 139–174.

Reichardt, C. S. (1979). The statistical analysis of data for nonequivalent group designs. In T. D. Cook and D. T. Campbell (Eds), *Quasi-experimentation: Design and analysis issues for field studies* (pp. 147–205). Boston: Houghton-Mifflin.

Reichardt, C. S. (2006). The principle of parallelism in the design of studies to estimate treatment effects. *Psychological Methods*, 11, 1–18.

Reynolds, K. D., & West, S. G. (1987). A multiplist strategy for strengthening nonequivalent control group designs. *Evaluation Review*, 11, 691–714.

Robins, J. M. (1989). The analysis of randomized and nonrandomized AIDS trials using a new approach to causal inference in longitudinal studies. In L. Sechrest, H. Freeman, & A. Mulley (Eds), *Health services research methodology: A focus on AIDS* (pp. 113–159). Washington, DC: US Public Health Service.

Roos, L. L., Jr., Roos, N. P., & Henteleff, P. D. (1978). Assessing the impact of tonsillectomies. *Medical Care*, 16, 502–518.

Rosenbaum, P. R. (2002). *Observational studies* (2nd ed.). New York: Springer-Verlag.

Rosenbaum, P. R., & Rubin, D. B. (1983). The central role of the propensity score in observational studies for causal effects. *Biometrika*, 70, 41–55.

Rosenbaum P. R., & Rubin, D. B. (1984). Reducing bias in observational studies using subclassification on the propensity score. *Journal of the American Statistical Association*, 79, 516–524.

Rubin, D. B. (1974). Estimating causal effects of treatments in randomized and nonrandomized studies. *Journal of Educational Psychology*, 66, 688–701.

Rubin, D. B. (1978). Bayesian inference for causal effects: The role of randomization. *Annals of Statistics*, 6, 34–58.

Rubin, D. B. (1980). Discussion of 'Randomization analysis of experimental data in the Fisher randomization test,' by D. Basu. *Journal of the American Statistical Association*, 75, 591–593.

Rubin, D. B. (1997). Estimating causal effects from large data sets using propensity scores. *Annals of Internal Medicine*, 127, 757–763.

Rubin, D. B. (2005). Causal inference using potential outcomes: Design, modeling, decisions. *Journal of the American Statistical Association*, 100, 322–331.

Sacks, H. S., Chalmers, T. C., & Smith, H. (1983). Sensitivity and specificity of clinical trials: Randomized

v. historical controls. *Archives of Internal Medicine*, 143, 753–755.

Schafer, J. L., & Graham, J. W. (2002). Missing data: Our view of the state of the art. *Psychological Methods*, 7, 147–177.

Shadish, W. R., & Cook, T. D. (1999). Design rules: More steps towards a complete theory of quasi-experimentation. *Statistical Science*, 14, 294–300.

Shadish, W. R., Cook, T. D., & Campbell, D. T. (2002). *Experimental and quasi-experimental designs for generalized causal inference.* Boston: Houghton-Mifflin.

Shadish, W. R., Luellen, J. K., & Clark, M. H. (2006). Propensity scores and quasi-experiments: A testimony to the practical side of Lee Sechrest. In R. R. Bootzin, & McKnight, P. E. (Eds), *Strengthening research methodology: Psychological measurement and evaluation* (pp. 143–157). Washington, DC: American Psychological Association.

Shadish, W. R., & Ragsdale, K. (1996). Random versus nonrandom assignment in controlled experiments: Do you get the same answer? *Journal of Consulting and Clinical Psychology*, 64, 1290–1305.

Singer, J. D., & Willett, J. B. (2002). *Applied longitudinal data analysis: Modeling change and event occurrence.* New York: Oxford.

Smith, H. L. (1997). Matching with multiple controls to estimate treatment effects in observational studies. *Sociological Methodology*, 27, 325–353.

Steyer, R., Ferring, D., & Schmitt, M. J. (1992). States and traits in psychological assessment. *European Journal of Psychological Assessment*, 8, 79–98.

Stolzenberg, R. M., & Relles, D. A. (1990). Theory testing in a world of constrained research design. *Sociological Methods and Research*, 18, 395–415.

Student (W. S. Gosset). (1931). The Lancashire milk experiment. *Biometrika*, 23, 398–406.

Wall, M. M., & Amemiya, Y. (2007). A review of nonlinear factor analysis and nonlinear structural equation modeling. In R. Cudeck & R. C. MacCallum (Eds), Factor analysis at 100: Historical developments and future directions (pp. 337–361). Mahwah, NJ: Erlbaum. West, S. G., Biesanz, J. C., & Pitts, S. C. (2000). Causal inference and generalization in field settings: Experimental and quasi-experimental designs. In H. T. Reis & C. M. Judd (Eds), *Handbook of research methods in social and personality psychology* (pp. 40–84). New York: Cambridge.

West, S. G., Duan, N., Pequegnat, W., Gaist, P., DesJarlais, D., Holtgrave, D., Szapocznik, J., Fishbein, M., Rapkin, B., Clatts, C., & Mullen, P. (2007). Alternatives to the randomized controlled trial. Manuscript under review, Arizona State University.

West, S. G., & Sagarin, B. J. (2000). Participant selection and loss in randomized experiments. In L. Bickman (Ed.), *Research design: Donald Campbell's legacy* (Vol. 2, pp. 117–154). Thousand Oaks, CA: Sage.

Winship, C., & Mare, R. D. (1992). Models for sample selection bias. *Annual Review of Sociology*, 18, 327–350.

Winship, C., & Morgan, S. L. (1999). The estimation of causal effects from observational data. *Annual Review of Sociology*, 25, 659–707.

Wu, W., West, S. G., & Hughes, J. (in press). Short-term effects of grade retention on the growth rate of Woodcock-Johnson III broad math and reading scores. *Journal of School Psychology*.

Discourse Analysis and Conversation Analysis

Charles Antaki

ANALYSING DISCOURSE

'Discourse' means what people say or write. Scholars might want to look into what people say or write for many reasons, and their particular reason will play a large part in deciding just what sort of saying and writing they choose to study, and what methods they use to do so.

Students of history, cultural and media studies and politics, among other disciplines, will want at times to identify a 'discourse' as a collection of metaphors, allusions, images, historical references and so on that populate some cultural phenomenon (the *discourse of modernity*, for example, or the *discourse of cyberculture*, or the *discourse of Human Resource Management*; all current scholarly projects). That way of looking at discourse is more static than those I review in this chapter, where discourse is taken to be social action made visible in language. The sort of discourse analyst I talk about in this chapter is a social scientist: she or he sees discourse as an organisation of talk or text that *does*

something, in the broad social world, or in the immediate interaction, or in both.

What is it that discourse is supposed to do? It varies, according to the interests of the analyst. The familiar way of setting out this difference is to range the interests from global to local. As we shall see later on, this distinction is itself a matter of dispute. But for the moment let us keep with it. At the more global end, discourse analysts can be interested in actions at the overarching level of social regulation, expressed through official and unofficial discourses like laws, media coverage or advertising texts; actions that have their effect not just in what is explicitly said, but what the analyst finds left unsaid. At that level, those doing the action (and those suffering it) may be classes of people, or 'society' in general. At the local end, the analyst might be interested in discourse that acts at the level of interaction, through conversationalists' activities, realised in the allocation, organisation and internal design of turns at talk. Here, doers and sufferers are visible in the scene.

METHODS

There is no lack of methods available to discourse analysts once they have decided where their interests lie. Since the 'linguistic turn' in the social sciences of the nineteen seventies, qualitative methods textbooks have laid out an increasingly varied menu of discourse analytic methods, which have over the years moved from novel and marginal to familiar and central. Picking a method among these is apparently straightforward, once analysts have a clear idea of what interests them. In Table 25.1, I range interests alongside appropriate methods.

Students of discourse analysis (DA) will recognise that the column headings in Table 25.1 should only be used as a convenience, because I have pretended that one can just start with a simple notion of 'what actions are to be revealed', list them, then read off the corresponding theory, method and data. In fact, of course, theory and method have a large say in calling something an 'action' in the first place, and what counts as evidence for that action; so these three apparently solid columns are better thought of as fuzzy threads twined around each other. Indeed, not even the rows are discrete; they too are harder to separate than the simple table suggests. All that will become clearer as we see examples of discourse analytic work in practice.

FOUR CORE FEATURES OF DA

The table below shows a variety of named discourse analytic methods, but I have reserved an entry for unadorned 'discourse analysis'. That is useful for two reasons: it prompts us to ask what the core features are that makes something recognisable as DA, and reminds us that many scholars are happy to use just these features without committing themselves to one or other specific variant.

The four core features of any DA are these:

- The talk or text is to be **naturally found** (in the sense of not invented, as it might be in psycholinguistics, pragmatics or linguistic philosophy; some analysts admit interview data into this natural category, while others do not);
- The words are to be understood in their **co-text** at least, and their more distant context if doing so can be defended;
- The analyst is to be sensitive to the words' **non-literal** meaning or force;
- The analyst is to reveal the social **actions** and consequences achieved by the words' use – as enjoyed by those responsible for the words, and suffered by their addressees, or the world at large.

Before I give an account of some specific examples of discrete sorts of discourse analysis, it would be as well to recall that many social scientists find a serviceable use for what we might call 'generic'

Table 25.1 Discourse analytic methods and data according to researcher's interests

What actions are to be revealed	Candidate theory/method	Typical data
Personal meaning-making	Narrative Analysis, Interpretative Phenomenological Analysis	Interviews, diaries, autobiographies, stories
Imposing and managing frames of meaning and identities	Interactional Sociolinguistics, Ethnography of speaking	Audio and video recordings, ethnographic observations
Accomplishing interactional life in real time	Conversation Analysis	Audio and video recordings
Displaying and deploying psychological states; describing the world and promoting interests	Discursive Psychology	Audio and video recordings, texts
Constituting and representing culture and society	[Generic] Discourse Analysis	Texts, interviews
Constituting and regulating the social and the political world; the operation of power	Critical Discourse Analysis	Official and unofficial texts, speeches, media accounts and representations, interviews

discourse analysis. This is work done without a strong commitment to the sorts of epistemologies and ontologies of the schools of analysis we shall see later on: it is a sort of working procedure, inspired by the four basic principles of discourse analysis, and brought off in bespoke ways to make sense of one particular topic or domain of experience. The method of choice in such work is often an inspection of textual material (e.g. news media reports) or interview transcripts (e.g. researchers' interviews with informants chosen for their particular experiences). The author or speaker is not, however, taken to be a simple informant, reporting unvarnished facts; he or she is seen as producing (or reproducing) themes or representations (sometimes called 'interpretative repertoires', after the influential use made of the term, originating in Gilbert and Mulkay (1984), by Potter and Wetherell (1987)). The job of the analyst is to sift carefully among the material to extract these themes or repertoires, and thus uncover the underlying dimensions along which the author or interviewee makes sense of their experiences, or, if the interest is less psychological, to uncover the imprint that society has left on their lives. Generic discourse analysis is, however, difficult to illustrate with a given empirical example, precisely because different studies take a great deal of colouring from their topic of interest (which might be media reports of political events, or people's experiences of health and illness, or organisational change, or educational practice, to name three typical examples).

We shall be on firmer ground if we turn now to see how particular styles of discourse analysts address the texts in front of them. In what follows, I won't be able to describe all the varieties of DA that I list in Table 25.1, still less those which haven't quite yet joined the canon. I have chosen five influential varieties that have been successful (and controversial) in different ways: narrative analysis, critical discourse analysis (CDA), interactional sociolinguistics, conversation analysis and discursive psychology. I have also appended a further example to illustrate

the sort of eclectic analysis that borrows from more than one school. I have allocated space to these six according to their influence as I see it, acknowledging that other reviewers may see things differently. Setting them out in series will reveal, I think, that the differences between them are instructive about what is at stake in the discourse analytic project as a whole.

NARRATIVE ANALYSIS

The origins of narrative analysis lie in literary anatomies of folk stories. Since the publication of Vladimir Propp's *The Morphology of the Folktale* (1928), folklorists and literary analysts have had an interest in discerning the underlying and possibly universal patterns in what seem to be discrete and individual stories (for example, in one of Propp's most basic templates, the underlying pattern of 'the quest' or 'the restitution of an object lost at the start of the tale'). Social scientists, as opposed to literary and folklore scholars, have seized on the idea of structure, but shied away from looking for universal primitives as such. Their interest is in finding how the narrator finds a pattern and chronology that makes sense of her or his own unique life and the events in it (see, for example, the work collected in Schiffrin et al., 2006). Such patterns and chronologies might be shared among a like-minded group, but can equally be wholly particular to the individual.

As illustration we may consider the work of Michelle Crossley, whose *Introducing narrative psychology: self, trauma and the construction of meaning* (2000) crystallised the application of narrative DA to the study of psychology, especially the psychology of health and wellbeing. Crossley analyses, among other kinds of narrative, the self-reflections of people who have undergone traumatic changes in their health. Here is an excerpt from such a reflection, in an autobiography:

> Without even realising it, before my diagnosis I had been living in an open, expansive, interior space.

Now the walls and ceilings had moved uncomfortably close. Limits were everywhere I looked … Gone was my sense of feeling protected or secure. Gone, too, was any feeling of certainty about the future. As my treatment progressed, these invisible losses were to become more painful, in some ways, than the outward, physical losses and privations of the disease and its remedies. (Mayer, 1994, p. 54, cited in Crossley, 2000)

Crossley's analysis points us towards the realisation that in words such as these, we see how psychologically important it is for the individual to have an articulable 'story-line' which maintains continuity and integrity: the trauma is destructive insofar as it radically disturbs one's sense of trajectory and sense of selfhood. As Crossley puts it: 'This sense is severely disrupted in the face of trauma, which demonstrates a devastating capacity to "unmake the world"', (Crossley, 2000, p. 541). The promise of this sort of discourse analysis is that it will recast 'facts' as constructions, reveal heretofore unsuspected and perhaps marginalised experiences, give voice to those whose experiences are not well understood, and perhaps feed into policy-making in the domains of health and education: two areas where narrative analysis has a strong presence.

CRITICAL DISCOURSE ANALYSIS

The umbrella term 'Critical Discourse Analysis' shelters a broad family of analysts, but all have this in common: they approach texts from a certain prior point of departure, often an avowedly political one. That is the 'critical' in the term. 'The way we approach these questions', says van Dijk, one of the doyens of CDA, 'is by focussing on *the role of discourse in the (re)production and challenge of dominance*. Dominance is defined here as the exercise of power by elites, institutions or groups, that results in social inequality, including political, class, ethnic, racial and gender inequality' (van Dijk, 1993, p. 249; emphasis in the original). To be aware of the exercise of power, and its resulting social inequality, requires a political theory about social life; and to have such a theory is vital. Without such a theory, the CDA argument runs, one risks wasting time on non-problems or trivialities, or telling only part of the story, and missing its political significance. In the worst case, one's mere technical analysis, by refusing to recognise political forces at work in the data, may implicitly condone or perpetuate them.

Within this broad family of analysts there are those who come from a post-structuralist background, to some degree independent of the linguistics traditions which inform a good deal of critical discourse work. In the post-structuralist tradition much use is made of Michel Foucault's insights into the operation of power in discourses, and, increasingly, psychoanalytical concepts from the school of Jacques Lacan. An example of this sort of CDA can be found in the work of Ian Parker (see, for example, his programmatic statement, Parker, 2003), and in the narrative analysis of Wendy Hollway (see, for example, Hollway and Jefferson, 2000), among many others. Other critical discourse analysts come from linguistics background, and bring with them an array of linguistic tools with which to unfold their data.

For an illustration of the more linguistically oriented kind of CDA, consider this exemplary analysis, taken from a joint account of CDA by two of its best-known (but of course not uniquely representative) proponents and theorists, Norman Fairclough and Ruth Wodak (1997). They give a 125-line-long extract from a question-and-answer radio interview with Margaret Thatcher during her time as Britain's Prime Minister. It is not an event-led news interview; she is being asked generally, if I can offer a rough gloss, about her political beliefs and aspirations. Fairclough and Wodak present their analysis in eight facets, of which I select the two most emblematic examples. Inevitably this will impoverish what they say, but it will give a flavour of these authors' CDA style, on two central CDA themes: power and ideology. I will quote part of the transcript to help illustrate their analysis.

Extract 1: From Fairclough and Wodak, (1997, pp. 269–270) (MT = Prime Minister Margaret Thatcher.)

```
61  MT [...] then you turn to internal
        security
62      and yes you HAVE got to be strong on
        law and order
63      and do things that only governments
        can do but
64      there it's part government and part
        people because
65      you CAN'T have law and order
        observed unless it's
66      in partnership with people then you
        have to be strong
67      to uphold the value of the currency
        and only
68      governments can do that by sound
        finance and then
69      you have to create the framework for
        a good
70      education system and social security
        and at that point
71      you have to hand over to people
        people are inventive
72      creative and so you expect PEOPLE to
        create thriving
73      industries thriving services yes you
        expect people
74      each and every one from whatever
        their background
75      to have a chance to rise to whatever
        level their own
76      abilities can take them [...]
```

Power

Fairclough and Wodak see Thatcher's display of power in a number of discourse features: her use of longish monologues; her interruption of her interviewer (not illustrated in the extract above); and her use of linguistic devices such as parallel constructions ('it has to be strong to have defence'… 'you HAVE got to be strong on law and order'… 'you have to be strong to uphold the value of the currency'). Such rhetorical devices, the authors claim, are 'the prerogative of professional politicians' (ibid., p. 272). CDA's willingness to use extra-textual claims (in this case, about what generally politicians do) is shared by many, but not all, kinds of DA.

Using their knowledge of the political scene, the authors are able to say that by using such privileged talk, Thatcher not only 'circumvents and marginalises [the radio presenter's] power as interviewer', but also exercises her power over the radio audience. They go on to observe that 'Thatcherism can … be partly seen as an ongoing hegemonic [power] struggle in discourse and over discourse, with a variety of antagonists - "wets" in the Conservative part, the other political parties, the trade unions, and so forth' (p. 273). This is a good illustration of how CDA is able to make the kind of generalisation that allows it to link the immediate data back to the analysts' prior political commitments.

Ideology

The authors note that, in the extract above, Margaret Thatcher formulates a free-market ideology explicitly; but their analysis aims to add value by showing how she expresses the ideology more subtly. This stretch of her words (and some 20 further lines not shown here), they say, 'is actually' (i.e. not as one might first naively think, without analytic help) 'built around a contrast between government and people which we would see as ideological: it covers the fact that "people" who dominate the creation of "thriving industries" and so forth are mainly the transnational corporations, and it can help to legitimise existing relations of economic and political domination' (pp. 265–266).

Fairclough and Wodak do not specify exactly where in the extract Thatcher's failure to mention transnational corporations was significant (that it is a 'fact' that her words 'cover'). This is an important analytic point. Claiming that something is a fact, and that it is significantly absent from a stretch of discourse, is a harder claim to ground than pointing to something that is significantly present (after all, there is an infinity of things that may be facts, and which are absent from any given stretch of talk or text; whereas what is there is at least there). Different DA traditions solve the problem in different ways. CDA notices absence not by working it out from the logical or pragmatic implications of the utterances around it, or from of the reaction of those who are there to hear it, as other schools of analysis do. It works it out by virtue of prior theorising about the political or social nature of the world to which the utterance refers. In this case, Fairclough and Wodak have a prior theory or account of what is happening in the British economy, what 'thriving industries' refer to, that these industries are owned by transnationals, and that this ownership is important in the discussion that Thatcher is currently having with her interviewer. They have a further belief, or expectation, that if given an opportunity, a speaker should express the politically relevant facts of the matter (as the analysts see them, and whether they are logically or pragmatically implied or not, or whether the speaker's local interlocutors hold them to it or not). Margaret Thatcher was given the opportunity, and did not mention transnationals; therefore, it is analytically safe, as well as useful, to claim that she is masking their role in the economy.

If we translate these snippets of analysis back into the four core features of DA (data found naturally; interpreted in co-text; non-literally understood; actions achieved), we see that CDA will insist on a very wide sense of 'co-text' in its interpretation, and on drawing out implications which may not be visible to those who do not share the analyst's prior political commitments, or hesitate to apply them to the data. Its prime candidate for 'social action' is the action, taken to be unequally shared in society, of constituting the social world. CDA is attractive to scholars who have the view that DA must ally itself to a social theory, and must be aware of inequalities in society. This is shared, in a more dilute form, in the next influential DA I shall look at.

INTERACTIONAL SOCIOLINGUISTICS

Interactional sociolinguistics emerged from quantitatively minded variation sociolinguistics of the 1960s (and which still continues today) which sought to correlate features of speech (like a glottal stop or a truncated verb form) with demographic factors like geographic location or socioeconomic class, or situational variables like the formality or informality of the speech setting. As interest shifted into what those features of speech might actively be doing in interaction, researchers dropped the survey method in favour of a close qualitative look at what was going on in the scene – what the founders of interactional sociolinguistics, Dell Hymes and John Gumperz, called the 'ethnography of communication'.

Like CDA, interactional sociolinguistics means to explore the way that social and cultural forces (including power differentials) cash out in the details of talk. Unlike CDA, its proponents do not normally require a specific prior theory of politics or society, beyond a generic belief that society is structured along class, gender and cultural or ethnic lines, and an expectation that this structure will reveal itself in interaction. A further difference is interactional sociolinguistics' preference for a great deal of ethnographic knowledge of the local scene in which the discourse takes place, and a fairly particular set of codes with which to analyse it.

To the degree that working interactional sociolinguists draw on pioneering work by John Gumperz, they will see people achieving their local goals (or being thwarted from doing so) by offering each other (and taking up, or failing to take up) 'contextualisation cues'. These are various sorts of hints, codes and signals as to what speakers mean. (The requirement to call such things 'contextualisation cues' has been progressively relaxed as interactional linguistics becomes more widespread, but remains important for core proponents of the method.) To get a sense of what these contextualisation cues are doing, the interactional sociolinguist is committed to knowing something about the local ethnography of the speakers' situation: what jobs they do, what their goals are and so on.

Here is an illustrative analysis, taken from an account meant to show off interactional sociolinguistics against a number of other discourse approaches (Stubbe et al., 2003).

Before turning to the transcribed recording, the authors give us some background:

> The discussion takes place between a senior public service manager, Tom, and an analyst, Claire, who is two ranks below him in the organisational hierarchy. From the ethnographic fieldwork that was done at the time of the data collection, we know that Claire is annoyed that she was overlooked for the shared acting manager position she believes she was promised by her own manager, and that she and some of her female colleagues interpret this as another example of gender discrimination within the organisation. We also know that she has expressed the intention to raise the issue with Tom [... continues ...]. (Stubbe et al., p. 359).

The authors then invite us to read over the following lines to see how Claire gets across to Tom a way of framing what she is about to say or do in the interaction:

Extract 2: From Stubbe et al., p. 381 (transcription conventions in this extract: '+' is a pause of up to one second; sloping lines indicate overlapping speech).

```
<#1:CT> yeah um yeah i want to talk to
        you about um oh it's a personal
        issue um + well i- the decision to
        make um jared acting manager while
        //joseph\ is away
<#2:TR> /mm\\
```

The authors point to certain speech features (the intonation, the ums, the false starts) that suggest that Claire is nervous. The interactional sociolinguist means to ask why this might be so in this local scene, and what it might prefigure for the conduct of the interaction, We can infer, the authors tell us, that one cause of her nervousness is the fact that she is lower in the hierarchy than is her interlocutor (something they have established prior to this recording). Furthermore, she is nervous because she is doing what women do not do: 'she is behaving in a direct, competitive way which is not stereotypically associated with women. This may help to explain some of the apparent tension in itself, as well as the likelihood that, given that her addressee is a senior male, her utterance may be heard as an implicit accusation of gender bias'. (ibid., p. 360). So the interaction

starts off with the 'contextualisation cues' of a complaint involving gender bias, and the authors can then proceed to see how these two interlocutors bring it off.

Interactional sociolinguistics' version of the four core features of DA (data found naturally; interpreted in co-text; non-literally understood; actions achieved) gives generous place to the wider ethnographic context. It is willing to use information from prior scenes to guess at what participants are feeling and intending in this one. It admits into its analysis inferences from prior theories, or common assumptions, about interaction. In the extract above, for example, a speaker was judged to be 'nervous', and her nervousness was partly ascribed to a common-sensical fear that a woman risks being heard as making a gender-based complaint. Such theorising is less particular and explicit than is required by CDA, yet still contrasts starkly with conversation analysis' distaste for what they consider to be 'going native'.

CONVERSATION ANALYSIS

Conversation analysis (henceforth, CA) is the study of social action as achieved through the medium of talk in interaction. Its genesis was in the dissatisfaction of some sociologists in the late 1960s with the dominant quantitative methodologies of their discipline, which were silent about how people actively realised the social world, in real time. In the 40 years since the pioneering work of the group around Harvey Sacks (whose lectures were published posthumously as Sacks, 1992), CA has attracted a good deal of attention within sociology and outside it, and has developed into a multidisciplinary enterprise (for an account of the history of CA, see Heritage, 1984; for a more recent overview of its methods and style, see Hutchby and Wooffitt, 1998; and for an account of its relation to other modes of DA, see Wooffitt, 2005).

CA abides by the four generic DA criteria of looking for natural data, setting it in its co-text, watching for its non-literal meaning, and identifying the social actions performed.

Perhaps its most obvious departure from this basic platform is its insistence on seeing social actions performed through the very close organisation, as well as the content, of talk. In describing those actions, CA – again unlike generic DA – wants to stay as close as possible to the speakers' own understandings of the actions without imposing interpretation from above or speculation about motives from below. Its 'added value' is teasing out the what and the how, while shying away from the why, and leaving off anything not made 'live' by the participants in the scene.

The currency that CA trades in might be structures on a chronologically minute scale (for example, the binding relation between speakers' adjacent utterances, and the injunction to keep their separation brief) or extensive (the overall shape of a story delivered over many turns), but they are all *normative*. That is to say, speakers are expected to follow them, or risk (or invite) listeners to draw implications when they do not. We can see an example of such a normative structure in the simple example below, where the second utterance meets the expectation of a prompt acceptance of the first:

Extract 3: Holt: 1988 Undated: Side 2: Call 1 (original transcription much simplified; for full list, see appendix)

```
1    Les: ((material not shown)) now we're
2         feeling a bit freer.
3         (.)
4    Arn: [Ye:s.
5    Les: [.hhhhhh So we wondered if you'd
6         like to meet us.hh
7 →  Arn: Yes certainly.
```

To show how strong the normative expectation is that the response be positive and prompt, consider this variant. Here the speaker's non-normative silence in line 3 invites the listener to draw a significant implication.

Extract 4: From Levinson (1983), p. 320

```
1    A: So I was wondering would you be
2       in your office on Monday (.) by any
3       chance
```

```
4 →    (2.0)
5    A: Probably not.
```

Note that it is A who is responsible for both turns – so why does s/he answer his or her own question, and answer it with a negative? Because B has done the unexpected thing of not answering, and thus allowed the implication that the answer is 'no'. A then makes plain that this has been understood. The interaction can proceed, with both parties now having disposed of the possibility that A visit B's office on Monday, without A having had explicitly to say no. The 'action' has been achieved by exploiting the regularities of talk.

CA has been applied productively to a variety of institutional activities otherwise accessible only in retrospect (by interviews with participants) or in simulation, or through comparatively coarse contemporary observation. For example, CA has been used in research on how talk in interaction achieves business meetings (Boden, 1994), educational testing (Maynard and Marlaire, 1992) and survey interviewing (Houtkoop-Steenstra, 2000), to take a few notable examples.

What can CA reveal about such working interactions? Peräkylä and Vehviläinen (2003) put it neatly. Members of a trade or profession (they were talking about psychotherapists, but it's true of anyone who routinely has dealings with clients) may have 'stocks of interactional knowledge' – fairly clear ideas of what they do with the people they work with. CA can check these accounts, correct them, or go beyond them. In going beyond lay accounts, CA can discover things about the interaction that the practitioners didn't suspect, or which have effects or functions which don't figure in (or indeed may be counter to) the official aims of the encounter.

As an example of CA's illumination of professional practice, consider Maynard's work on clinicians' delivery of a diagnosis. He inductively finds a pattern in which the clinician prefaces the actual diagnosis (*you have X*) by evidence (from test results, and so on). The typical sequence is like this, in which a doctor in a developmental difficulties clinic is talking to a mother about her five-year-old son:

Extract 5: From Maynard (2004, p. 63)

```
 1   Dr Y:  From the:: _test results (0.3)
 2          he seems to function (0.6)
 3          comfortably (0.2) you know and
 4          (achieve) some kind of you
 5          know happy and responsive
 6          (0.2)
 7   Mrs R: Ye [e:s ]
 8   Dr Y:     [ .h ]hh ON THE LEVEL of
 9          about you know three
10          (0.1) and
11          a half year old child
12   Mrs R: mm
```

The doctor is describing evidence: the boy *seems to function comfortably at the level of a three and a half year old*. She is not (yet) giving a diagnosis. The next extract follows the first (though some intervening talk has been omitted). But notice how the doctor manages to avoid actually stating the child's condition even as she makes her recommendation.

Extract 6: From Maynard (2004, p. 63)

```
 1   Dr Y:  I feel very strongly that, you
 2          know, because he (0.4) tests
 3          some kind you know, functions
 4          between mildly retarded and
 5          borderline level [.hhhhh ] he
 6          needs special class placement.
 7   Mrs R:                  [Mm hmm]
 8   Dr Y:  (Yeah) the (.) class for (0.2)
 9          .hh educable mentally retardet
10          (0.2) will be the best (.) for
11          his (0.8) you know?
12          functioning and emotional, he's
13          still not ready you know
14          enough [to be more- ]
15→  Mrs R:    [Are y- are you tr]yin' ta
16          tell me that you feel he
17          is: s:lightly mentally re
18          [tard]ed?
19   Dr Y:  [Yes.]
```

What the doctor has done is to glide from a statement of the evidence (from the tests) to a recommendation for treatment, passing over actually naming the child's condition. It falls to the mother (at line 9) to make explicit what has so far been implicit. Maynard has noted this pattern in his work on news delivery in

mundane conversation (Maynard, 2003). The news deliverer organises their hints at bad news in such a way that it is the recipient who is prompted actually to pronounce it. In ordinary social life that hinting has a set of implications which we might interpret as being to do with the complexities surrounding death and other taboo issues; in the clinic, it has all those, but also has more prosaic consequences as well. If the patient (or their representative, as in the case above) is the one who comes out with the news, it shows that he or she has been attending to what the doctor said, at least enough to work things out for themselves; it puts patient and doctor on something of an equal footing. Certainly it is more equal (or more equal-*looking*) than would be the case if the doctor simply pronounces the condition straight off.

CA AND 'MEMBERSHIP CATEGORIES'

My account of CA so far has focused on sequential analysis. There is another strand of CA, traceable back to Sacks' work in the early seventies, which, although it is alive to sequence and placement of utterances, is concerned with them insofar as they sustain the speaker's version of events; and specifically, the speaker's choice of *identity* or *person categories*. This is sometimes called Membership Category Analysis (though many in CA prefer to see it as merely a part of the broader CA project); but in any case, it is very different from other discourse work on identities. A generic DA of identities would look at material which explicitly names a given identity category (say, 'asylum seeker'), and chart the ways in which that category is constructed. The aim of that sort of analysis would be to draw up a picture of 'asylum seeker' as it appears, explicitly and subtly, in the materials. Then a further stage of analysis takes over, and speculation is made about what interests such a picture serves in a general way in society. For CA, there is no need to go to such an abstract level and separate the use of the category from its consequences.

The speaker or writer's use of (or hint at) an identity category is locally effective. If you call someone an asylum seeker (or hint that she or he is one) then you are doing it for local consumption, and the consequences will be interactionally visible. And this is true for mundane categories (like, say, 'daughter') as much as it is for more politically charged ones.

In the case of politically charged identities, consider what is happening here, in this extract from Dennis Day's (1998) account of 'ethnification'. Here, some workers in a factory in Sweden are in a coffee break and planning an upcoming works party.

Extract 7: Day, 1998, p. 163 (English translation from the Swedish)

```
 1    L:  that one has wine and normal
 2        drinks too,
 3        right, of course like a party
 4        ((writing))
 5  → L:  that's what we have at least
 6        here in
 7  →     Sweden one drinks wine, that's
 8        of course
 9        what [one wants
10    R:       [of course, it's like
11        different that
12        [to drink
13    L:  [what does one drink in what
14        does one drink
15    L:  ((points))
16    X:  [don't drink wine but light beer
17        or just (soda)
```

Speaker 'X', Day tells us, is categorisable on sight as not ethnically white-Swedish; she is (or looks) Chinese. But notice that we hardly need even this minimal piece of ethnography (and the reader might compare it with the thick description and inference required by interactional sociolinguistics; see above). See how, in lines 4 and 5, it is one of the participants himself (L) who introduces the notion that Otherness is a live issue. *That's what (drink) we have*, he says; *at least here in Sweden one drinks wine*. It is the 'we' and the 'here in Sweden' that do the work of setting national or ethnic identities on the table. From the CA point of view, the minimal observation is that L has 'ethnified' *X* to the extent that he has called into question what

drinks should be made available at the staff party. But there is more. He has explicitly excluded *X* from 'we … here in Sweden'. The effect is to exclude her not only from the fellow-national category but the locally operative category of fellow member of the current social group.

Both Day's work, and that of Maynard that I described above, are examples of CA's claim to deliver the substance of large-scale social phenomena. Their claim is that if we want to say that, for example, agreement between patient and clinician is at a premium in US consulting rooms; or that people can exclude fellow-workers from joint ventures by subtly casting them into ethnic categories; then CA will provide the evidence – unaffected, its adherents say, by prior theorising about context or social forces.

DISCURSIVE PSYCHOLOGY

The epistemological commitment of conversation analysis – to begin with what the participants in the scene make visible to each other – is shared by Discursive Psychology. This is a movement, impelled by a number of hands, to make Psychology treat the traditional psychological topics of perception and cognition (seeing, remembering, knowing and so on) not, in the first place, as mental and individual matters, but as resources that people use: a person will avow a belief, challenge another's veracity, test a third person's knowledge, admit a faulty memory and so on. This branch of DA, like others we have covered, comes in various versions. I will pick an illustrative example from what has probably been the most empirically productive form, the Discursive Psychology developed by Derek Edwards and Jonathan Potter (for programmatic statements of their project, see Edwards, 1997, Edwards and Potter, 1992, and Potter, 2003).

Consider Edwards' work on emotions (see, for example, Edwards, 1999). At first sight, emotions find a natural home in traditional Psychology: they are (surely?) subjective, directly experienced, irrational, stimulated by events in the world, and liable to vary in intensity and character according to classic psychological variables such as social and physical stimuli, mood, age, gender and so on. Yet, Edwards argues, to say all this is to put the cart before the horse. All these things are true not necessarily about emotions-in-the-head, but about emotions-as-traded-in-interaction. People (who, after all, predate psychologists) treat them as all of the above things, and psychologists have fallen into the trap of thinking they are all true. Edwards does not mean we should therefore replace a scientific study of emotions with a study of people's folk theories about emotion, or by asking them survey questions about what they think emotions are, or by recording their spontaneously offered definitions of emotions in natural talk and so on. Such things are of secondary importance. What is of prime importance is how people bring emotion terms into conversations (which may be mundane chat, or consequential events like police interrogations, marital counselling, psychotherapy, courtroom testimony and so on) actually to achieve their ends. To be sure, such ends will be served by the presumption that an emotion is internal, not rational and so on and so forth (or some distortion of this list, as circumstances demand) but that in no way guarantees the truth of the presumption, still less persuade us to give up the study of emotions in talk in favour of a possibly chimerical survey of emotions in the head.

We can put flesh on that argument by looking at a stretch of talk that Edwards reports from a marital therapy session, where one person's descriptions of their spouse's emotions have, of course, a high premium. Early in the session, 'Mary' describes what happened when she told her husband 'Jeff' of an affair she had had:

Extract 3 (DE-JF:C1:S1:4)

```
1   Mary:   (. . .) so that's when I decided
2           to (.)
3           you know to tell him. (1.0)
4           U::m (1.0)
5           and then::, (.) obviously
6           you went
7           through your a:ngry stage,
8           didn't you?
9           (.)
10          Ve:ry upset obviously, .hh
11          an:d uh,
12          (0.6) we: started ar:guing a
13          lot, an:d
14          (0.6) just drifted awa:y.
```

Edwards invites us to notice how Mary trades on the presumptions of emotion terms to accomplish a number of rhetorically powerful moves. Jeff's reaction to Mary's revelation was (according to her account) to be *angry*; she does not report his state of mind as a matter of reasoned appreciation, but of visceral reaction. Moreover she portrays this anger as *your angry stage*. This implies that Jeff is prone to a predictable chain-reaction of emotions that are sparked, then run their course. These two undercurrents, heavily implied but never stated, bear Mary's narrative into the rhetorically clear waters of inevitable separation. As Edwards puts it:

> … while Jeff's anger is proper in its place, one would not expect it to go on forever, to endure unreasonably, beyond its 'stage'. Mary has made rhetorical room for something she goes on to develop, which is the notion that Jeff's reactions are starting to get in the way of progress, starting to become (instead of her infidelity, as Jeff insists) 'the problem' they have in their relationship. Indeed, the next thing she says in her narrative (and implicationally, therefore, what not only follows but follows from Jeff's reactions) is how 'we started arguing a lot, and just drifted away' (…) Their problems are now joint ones, arguments, and a kind of non-agentive, non-blaming, 'just' drifting apart. (Edwards, 1999, p. 277)

In other words, Mary's description of events, in just that way and at just that time, has socially important consequences for how her relationship is to be read, how her spouse's role in proceedings is to be understood, and perhaps how the counselling will proceed. Deploying an emotion term was not a neutral matter of describing the world as it is and was, but a rhetorically charged choice of a term that packed a punch, as any choice of description always does.

Edwards' analysis here of the emotion term *angry* is a good example of the respecification that Discursive Psychology intends for the entire realm of 'the mental'. It reminds psychologists that emotions, like any other ostensibly mental state of mind, may be allegedly owned in private, but are manifestly traded in public. This makes Discursive Psychology especially attractive for application to any discourse in which play is made of psychological terms, and that of course is a wide field. But we should notice that Discursive Psychology is not limited to the study of the use of psychological terms, common though such usage is. Discursive Psychology's radical anti-cognitivism aligns it with other discourse analyses which take discourse to be constitutive of social (and not just social) reality – see, for example, Potter's Representing Reality (1996). Were space to permit, it would have been instructive to describe its close, ethnomethodologically – and Conversation Analytically – inspired investigation of people's interested descriptions and accounts of events, for example in such charged encounters as the police interrogation (Edwards, 2006). In its concern for unpacking descriptions of reality, Discursive Psychology is applicable to discourse in its widest remit.

AN EXAMPLE OF AN ECLECTIC DA

I want to turn for my last example to a DA inspired – if distantly – by ethnomethodology. If ethnomethodology has a place in a survey such as this one, it is an uncomfortable one at best. Most practitioners of ethnomethodology would not describe themselves as doing DA. Their aim – as the term 'ethno-methodology' suggests – is to explicate the reasoning practices or rules that ordinary people display in prosecuting their ordinary lives. While some of those practices are made visible in their use of language, many others are embodied in the props and resources which furnish the daily scene; in the temporal organisation of people's comings and goings; in the artefacts and documents available for

people to consult or refer to; and in the affordances of the physical sites they live and work in. Thus if one wanted to find out how people solve the problem of (say) taking turns to be served (Garfinkel, 2002, ch. 8), one would not limit oneself to analysing people's language, but would analyse the ebb and flow of bodily movement, synchronised occupation of space, gestures, gaze and so on, to see how queues form and are oriented to and policed. Much more than language needs to be mastered by the person who wants competently to join a line for service – as many of us who have tried the experience in unfamiliar places, perhaps when in foreign lands, can testify.

Nevertheless, ethnomethodology has inspired a kind of DA which, while wanting to explicate people's public reasoning processes, privileges talk in its ethnographic setting. Perhaps the best label for such work is 'eclectic', since it combines the four canonical principle of DA with a concern for the physical and temporal location in which the event takes place. For an example of such work, I have chosen a much-anthologised study by Hugh Mehan (1996) on how children are sorted into various categories by educators. This picks up the theme of identities in the section on CA above, and shows how an eclectic discourse analyst can use non-talk elements of the scene.

Mehan follows the career of one nine-year-old boy ('Shane'). Our first sight of him is when a teacher spots him behaving in a way that concerns her. He then becomes a case for the educational psychologist, who tests him, and the language in which he is described changes from the teacher's common-sensical, teacherly talk ('he's very apprehensive about approaching anything …', 'whenever he's given some new task to do it's always like, too hard, "no way I can finish it"') to technical, quantitative norm-based terms ('he was given the WISC-R and his IQ was slightly lower, full scale of 93 …').

Mehan's set-piece for analysis is a recording of a subsequent meeting of educators (teachers, educational psychologists and so on) and parents. At this point Shane's fate, as is that of a list of children who have to come to the school's attention as possibly needing special education, is to be decided. Each case will be decided by talk; and as the outcomes are quite dramatically different (the child might be classified then and there as 'learning disabled' and sent to one kind of school, or as 'educationally handicapped' and sent to another), the power of discourse is all too visible.

It is up to the Board to hear the various descriptions of Shane available from his teacher, his parents, the school nurse and the psychologist, and meld them into a decision as to just what kind of schoolboy he is. Mehan describes the props (for example, the psychologist's thick bundle of forms, test scores and reports) or the lack of them (the child's mother has no notes) as part of the action. The props round out his observations about the talk: that, for example, the psychologist refers to her official notes while delivering her account uninterrupted, while the mother's unsupported account is drawn out by others' questioning; or that the psychologists' document-based story, although freighted with obscure jargon, is not challenged, whereas the mother is asked to explain what she means by her common-sense claims about her son's behaviour (claims that would pass unremarked in a more mundane setting; for example, that 'lots of times he comes home and he'll write or draw'). Mehan 'adds value' of a startling kind when he claims that

> The psychologist's report gains its authority by the very nature of its construction. The psychologist's discourse obtains its privileged status *because* it is ambiguous, *because* it is shot full of technical terms, *because* it is difficult to understand (p. 357; emphasis in original)

Mehan's point is that the technicality of the psychologist's claims meant that they could not easily be challenged, so her conclusions were never subject to the sort of test that the mother's or the teacher's could be. Because of its permitted obscurity, it is the psychologist's report that carries the day, and Shane is classified as having a learning

disability; he has been set on a career which may have profound consequences (for good or ill). Mehan has not simply noted that different sorts of evidence have been brought forward to reach this decision; by careful note of how descriptions are phrased and received he has offered us the analysis that (as he puts it) 'these modes of representation are not equal' (p. 356). It is a DA that delivers the generic promise not merely of describing talk but of explaining social action, and adds specific ethnomethodological value by charting participants' treatment of each other and the distributions of powers and expertise that they allow themselves.

CONCLUDING COMMENTS: DISCOURSE ANALYSIS MEANS DOING ANALYSIS

A word is in order to remind the reader that this account of DA has been selective. Each example, in the sections above, elbowed its way past a dozen equally significant competitors. Some styles of analysis were crowded out entirely, and a longer chapter may well have found space for interpersonal phenomenological analysis (Smith, 2004), psychoanalytically oriented Marxist critical discursive psychology (Parker, 2002), Foucauldian discursive psychology (Wetherell and Edley, 1999), free-association narrative inquiry (Hollway and Jefferson, 2000), and action-implicative discourse analysis (Tracy, 2005), among others. And I ought to say that many working discourse analysts claim no specific rules beyond the four canonical DA features of looking for social action in natural data, non-literally understood in its co-text. Indeed some discourse analysts have made an explicit virtue of keeping their independence from restrictive technicality. An eloquent defence of this way of thinking is Billig's case in favour of critical scholarship over narrow method (Billig, 1988, 1999). It is better, on his argument, to have the core discourse analytic sentiments in mind, be guided by a critical spirit, and to avoid particular methodological practices which might miss as much as they catch.

However, whether one flies under the flag of a particular kind of DA or sails alone, it is not the case that 'anything goes'. The editor of one of the principal, indeed defining, journals of the field sounds a clear warning in his editorial instructions: 'Articles should provide a detailed, systematic and theoretically based analysis […]. It is insufficient to merely quote, summarise or paraphrase such discourse' (Teun van Dijk, in the instructions on 'Preferred Papers for *Discourse & Society*' which has appeared in the journal since March 2002). A useful expansion of that injunction can be found in a joint paper by Antaki et al. (2003) who, although as individual authors vary in their theoretical allegiances, nevertheless insist together that, as they put it, 'discourse analysis means doing analysis'. Any discourse analyst who claims to be analysing, they argue, must 'add value' to what is readable or hearable in the words straight off, beyond simple paraphrase or glossing; they must be able to back up their claims with some evidence grounded in the words used or warrantably not used; and they must reach their conclusions by argumentative steps available to a fair-minded fellow-scholar.

To use a DA 'method', or not, and which method to use, is not a simple matter of bloodless fashion; there are strong forces at work which push new methods onto the agenda (and indeed resist them). I haven't been able to do justice to such forces in this chapter; for an excellent recent survey of the general ebb and flow in the tides of discourse methods, see de Beaugrande's useful short account (de Beaugrande, 1997), Wood and Kroger's book-length overview (Wood and Kroger, 2000) and Denzin and Lincoln's thoughtful introduction to their recent *Handbook of Qualitative Research* (2005). DA is a particularly unsettled method of working in the social sciences – probably because, to its adherents, who want to understand (and sometimes unmask) social action, the stakes are high.

TRANSCRIPTION SYMBOLS FOR THE CONVERSATION ANALYSIS EXTRACTS

`(.)`	Just noticeable pause
`(.3), (2.6)`	Examples of timed pauses
`word [word`	
`      [word`	The start of overlapping talk.
`.hh, hh`	In-breath (note the preceding full stop) and out-breath respectively.
`wo(h)rd`	(h) shows that the word has 'laughter' bubbling within it
`wor-`	A dash shows a sharp cut-off
`wo:rd`	Colons show that the speaker has stretched the preceding sound.
`(words)`	A guess at what might have been said if unclear
`( )`	Very unclear talk.
`word=`	
`=word`	No discernible pause between two sounds or turns at talk
`word, WORD`	Underlined sounds are louder, capitals louder still
`°word°`	Material between 'degree signs' is quiet
`>word word<`	Faster speech
`<word word>`	Slower speech
`↑ word`	Upward arrow shows upward intonation
`↓ word`	Downward arrows shows downward intonation
`→`	Analyst's signal of a significant line
`((sniff))`	Attempt at representing something hard, or impossible, to write phonetically

FURTHER READING

The sources cited in the References (at the end of this chapter) will take the reader further along the particular paths sketched out in the text. Those who would like to follow up issues and topics I have only mentioned fleetingly may like to pick among the following further readings.

Interpersonal phenomenological analysis

An approach to individual meaning-making through a discursive analysis of interviews.

Smith, J.A. (2004) Reflecting on the development of interpretative phenomenological analysis and its contribution to qualitative research in psychology. *Qualitative Research in Psychology, 1*, 39–54.

Feminist discourse analysis

For a variety of examples of discourse analytic research projects that offer a specifically feminist approach, see:

Lazar, M. (Ed.) (2005). *Feminist Critical Discourse Analysis: Gender, Power and Ideology in Discourse.* Basingstoke: Palgrave.

Varieties of critical discourse analysis

There is broad range within Critical Discourse Analysis. These sources, along with those cited in the text, will give an indication of the variety.

Rogers, R. (Ed.) (2003). *An Introduction to Critical Discourse Analysis in Education.* Mahwah, NJ: Lawrence Erlbaum.

Toolan, M. (Ed.) (2002). *Critical Discourse Analysis: Critical Concepts in Linguistics* (Vols 1–4). London: Routledge.

Wodak, R. & Meyer, M. (Eds.) (2001). *Methods of Critical Discourse Analysis.* London: Sage.

van Dijk, T. (1993) Principles of CDA. *Discourse and Society, 4*, 249–83.

Debate between conversation analysis and critics

This exchange is often cited as a useful crystallisation of the debate – not always temperate – between Conversation Analysts and their discourse analytically minded critics. I list the papers in their chronological order.

Schegloff, E. A. (1997) Whose text? Whose context? *Discourse and Society, 8*, 165–87.

Wetherell, M. (1998) Positioning and interpretative repertoires: conversation analysis and post-structuralism in dialogue. *Discourse and Society, 9*, 387–412.

Schegloff, E. A. (1998) Reply to Wetherell. *Discourse and Society, 9*, 413–6.

Billig, M. (1999) Whose terms? Whose ordinariness? Rhetoric and ideology in Conversation Analysis. *Discourse and Society, 10*, 543–558.

Schegloff, E. A. (1999) 'Schegloff's texts' as 'Billig's data': a critical reply. *Discourse and Society, 10*, 558–72.

Billig, M. (1999) Conversation analysis and the claims of naivety. *Discourse and Society, 10* (4), 572–6.

Schegloff, E. A. (1999) Naiveté vs. sophistication or discipline vs. self-indulgence: a rejoinder to Billig. *Discourse and Society, 10*, 577–82.

Kitzinger, C. (2000) Doing feminist conversation analysis. *Feminism and Psychology, 10*, 163–93.

REFERENCES

Antaki, Charles, Billig, Michael, Edwards, Derek, and Potter, Jonathan (2003). Discourse analysis means doing analysis: A critique of six analytic shortcomings. Discourse Analysis On Line, 1(1). Available at: <http://www.shu.ac.uk/daol/articles/v1/n1/a1 antaki2002002.html>.

Billig, M. (1988). Methodology and scholarship in understanding ideological explanation. In C. Antaki (Ed.), *Analysing Everyday Explanation: A Casebook of Methods.* London: Sage.

Billig, M. (1999). Whose terms? Whose ordinariness? Rhetoric and ideology in conversation analysis. *Discourse and Society, 10*, 543–558.

Boden, D. (1994). *The Business of Talk.* Oxford: Polity.

Crossley, M. L. (2000). Narrative psychology, trauma and the study of self/identity. *Theory & Psychology, 10*, 527–546.

Day, D. (1998). Being ascribed, and resisting, membership of an ethnic group. In C. Antaki and S. Widdicombe (Eds.), *Identities in Talk.* London: Sage, pp. 151–170.

de Beaugrande, R. (1997). The story of discourse analysis. In T. van Dijk (Ed.), *Discourse as Structure and Process.* London: Sage, pp. 35–62.

Denzin, N. K., and Lincoln, Y. (2005). The discipline and practice of qualitative research. In N.K. Denzin, and Y. Lincoln (Eds.), *The Sage Handbook of Qualitative Research.* London: Sage.

Edwards, D. (1997). *Discourse and Cognition.* London: Sage.

Edwards, D. (1999). Emotion discourse. *Culture and Psychology, 5*, 271–291.

Edwards, D. (2006). Discourse, cognition and social practices: The rich surface of language and social interaction. *Discourse Studies, 8*, 41–49.

Edwards, D., and Potter, J. (1992). *Discursive Psychology.* London: Sage.

Fairclough, N., and Wodak, R. (1997). Critical discourse analysis. In T. van Dijk (Ed.), *Discourse Studies A Multidisciplinary Introduction, Volume 2: Discourse as Social Interaction*. London: Sage.

Garfinkel, Harold (2002). Ethnomethodology's program: Working out Durkheim's aphorism. Edited and introduced by Anne Rawls. Lanham, MD: Rowman & Littlefield.

Gilbert, G. N. and Mulkay, M. (1984). *Opening Pandora's Box: A Sociological Analysis of Scientists' Discourse*. Cambridge, UK: CUP.

Heritage, J. (1984). *Garfinkel and Ethnomethodology*. Cambridge: Polity Press.

Hollway, W. and Jefferson, T. (2000). *Doing Qualitative Research Differently: Free Association, Narrative and the Interview Method*. London: Sage.

Houtkoop-Steenstra, H. (2000). *Interaction and the Standardised Survey Interview: The Living Questionnaire*. Cambridge: Cambridge University Press.

Hutchby, I. and Wooffitt, R. (1998). *Conversation Analysis*. Oxford: Polity Press.

Levinson, S. C. (1983). *Pragmatics*. Cambridge, UK: Cambridge University Press.

Mayer, M. (1994). *Examining Myself: One Woman's Story of Breast Cancer Treatment and Recovery*. Winchester, MA: Faber & Faber.

Maynard, D. W. (2003). *Bad News, Good News: Conversational Order in Everyday Talk and Clinical Settings*. Chicago & London: University of Chicago Press.

Maynard, D. W. (2004). On predicating a diagnosis as an attribute of a person. *Discourse Studies*, *6*, 53.

Maynard, D. W. and Marlaire, C. (1992). Good reasons for bad testing performance: The interactional substrate of educational testing. *Qualitative Sociology*, *15*, 177–202.

Mehan, H. (1996). The construction of an LD student: A case study in the politics of representation. In M. Silverstein and G. Urban (Eds), *Natural Histories of Discourses*. Chicago: University of Chicago Press. Reprinted in M. Wetherell, S. Taylor and S. Yates (2001) (Eds), *Discourse Theory and Practice*. London: Sage Publications.

Parker, I. (2002). *Critical Discursive Psychology*. London: Palgrave.

Parker, I. (2003). Psychoanalytic narratives: Writing the self into contemporary cultural phenomena. *Narrative Inquiry*, *13* (2), 301–15.

Peräkylä, A. and Vehviläinen, S. (2003). Conversation analysis and the professional stocks of interactional knowledge. *Discourse & Society*, *14* (6).

Potter, J. (1996). *Representing Reality*. London: Sage.

Potter J. (2003). Discursive psychology: Between method and paradigm. *Discourse & Society*, *14*, 783–794.

Potter, J., and Wetherell, M. (1987). *Discourse and Social Psychology*. London: Sage.

Sacks, H. (1992). *Lectures on Conversation* (Vols 1 and 2). Oxford: Basil Blackwell.

Schiffrin, D., De Fina, A., and Bamberg, M. (Eds.) (2006). *From Talk to Identity: Methodological and Theoretical Issues in Identity Research*. Cambridge University Press.

Stubbe, M., Lane, C., Hilder J., Vine E., Vine B., Marra M., Holmes J., and Weatherall, A. (2003). Multiple discourse analyses of a workplace interaction. *Discourse Studies*, *5*, 351–388.

Tracy, K. (2005). Reconstructing communicative practices: Action-implicative discourse analysis. In K. Fitch and R. Sanders (Eds), *Handbook of Language and Social Interaction* (pp. 301–319). Mahwah, NJ: Lawrence Erlbaum.

van Dijk, Teun A. (1993). Principles of critical discourse analysis. *Discourse & Society*, *4*, 249–283.

Wetherell, M., and Edley, N. (1999). Negotiating hegemonic masculinity: Imaginary positions and psycho-discursive practices. *Feminism & Psychology*, *9*, 335–356.

Wood, L. A., and Kroger, R. O. (2000). *Doing Discourse Analysis*. Thousand Oaks: Sage Publications.

Wooffitt, R. (2005). *Conversation Analysis and Discourse Analysis*. London and New York: Sage.

Analyzing Narratives and Story-Telling

Matti Hyvärinen

Narrative inquiry has established itself as a broad and polymorphous research orientation within the social sciences. The most varied personal, political, institutional, organizational and conversational stories are currently collected and studied, yet the term 'narrative analysis' remains replete with innate tensions. Does the research material as such qualify the narrativity of the analysis, or is it also required that these narratives are studied *as* narratives?

The use of narratives in social research may be characterized by three separate, but by no means straightforwardly successive moments. At the first stage, narratives were used as *factual resources*. The second moment was characterized by the study of *narratives as texts* with a particular form. The third moment includes a movement beyond a separate narrative text, into the study of *narratives and storytelling* as polymorphous phenomena *in context*.

Narratives bring into the open rich, detailed and often personal perspectives. Therefore, it is easy to misunderstand narrative simply as a *method*, and narratives *as resources* with which to investigate the phenomena of which the narratives make an account. A more ambitious version of narrative analysis draws from the social constructionist notion that narratives already always are part of the constitution of the social, cultural and political world (Bruner 1991; Gergen and Gergen 1993). 'From a hermeneutic point of view', Guy Widdershoven maintains, 'human life is a process of narrative interpretation', quite independently and before any narrative analysis (Widdershoven 1993, 2). These notions motivate theoretical investigation on *how* narratives are constituted, what their place is in human life, who is entitled to tell them and when, how they are received, and how they work in the social world. Narrative analysis is thus inseparable from concerns of the narrative constitution of selves, identities and social realities.

This chapter first discusses the concept of narrative and then proceeds to outline the use of narratives before what has been termed 'the narrative turn'. Instead of one narrative turn, three partly separate turns are discussed. As early versions of narrative analysis, the models of Vladimir Propp (1968) and William Labov and Joshua Waletsky (1997) will be introduced next. The Labovian model will be systematically used as a comparative backdrop for further developments: the move from text to context and the contribution of recent semantic and cognitive studies for the analysis of narratives. The last section suggests expectation analysis as a way to connect the Labovian heritage, contextual orientation and the idea of positioning. The focus of the chapter is on the analytic procedures, not on the interpretive alternatives.

THE NOTION OF NARRATIVE

Social scientists have seldom considered definitions of narrative (cf. Brockmeier and Harré 1991; Riessman 1993, 17–18). Many scholars simply repeat Aristotle's characterization of a good tragedy having a *beginning*, *middle* and *end* (Aristotle 1968, 1450b). For open, conversational or artistic narratives this is a far too compelling formula, emphasizing the clear sequence of events; on the other hand the terms are far too broad to reveal anything fundamental in the nature of what narratives actually do.

Barbara Herrnstein Smith (1981, 228) offers a useful, rhetorically oriented definition: 'Someone telling someone else that something happened'. With a slight revision we can also include sensitivity to the context: 'Somebody telling somebody else on some occasion and for some purpose(s) that something happened' (Phelan 2005b, 18). The next step taken in this chapter is to suggest that one can also turn the term 'somebody' into the plural form, making shared tellership visible (Ochs and Capps 2001).

Cultural studies may be criticized for two confusing ways of discussing narrative. In the first case, all kinds of interview talk is understood as narrative, narration or story. In such manner, the whole term of narrative is itself at risk of becoming redundant. Ordinary talk may as well include different genres

of speech such as argumentation, instruction and narration (Linde 1993; Fludernik 2000). In the second case, narrative is a substitute for a general assumption, theory or ideological stance without temporal organization (Rimmon-Kenan 2006). Clive Seale, for example, suggests a far broader notion of narrative:

> I understand narratives to be constructed through many things, including acts of consumption, for example, which can be made symbolically to tell stories about tastes, relationships (whether real or desired) or social standing. (Seale 2000, 37)

Seale points out convincingly how narrativity and narrative understanding are not something that only accounts for social action in retrospect. He also rejects, in a useful way, the too narrow textualist ways of understanding narrative and opens new areas for narrative analysis. Narrativity is woven into acting and planning in ways discussed more thoroughly a moment later. But yet, in order to ward off the tendency of 'narrative imperialism' (Strawson 2004; Phelan 2005a), the elegant solution suggested by Mari-Laure Ryan might be more sustainable:

> The narrative potential of life can be accounted for by making a distinction between 'being a narrative', and 'possessing narrativity'. (Ryan 2005, 347)

Narrativity may be understood as an aspect of texts, experiences and action; an aspect that invites more or less direct narrative responses. Narrativity is a matter-of-degree, rendering texts and speech more or less narrative. A wish for analytic clarity does not imply that narratives would exist as pure and distinct objects. It would be hopeless and misleading to assume that narratives are formally similar, always complete and always neatly distinct from other kinds of discourse (Ochs and Capps 2001). 'Narrative is first and foremost a prodigious variety of genres', asserts Ronald Barthes (1966/1977, 79). This means that no definition will fit all narratives and that the desire for a conceptual consensus may be rather counter-productive.

NARRATIVES BEFORE NARRATIVE ANALYSIS

Many kinds of narratives were used as research material long before any narrative analysis. William I. Thomas and Florian Znaniecki (1984) used hundreds of more or less storied letters and other life documents in their classical work *The Polish Peasant in Europe and America*, originally published 1918–1920. In their analysis, letters and other documents constitute 'life records'.

The Polish Peasant demonstrates the power of individual story for the sociological imagination. The belief in the factual, referential transparency of these documents of life is tangible while the authors read the letters as *illustrations* of attitudes, life situations or their own conclusions. While the authors introduced new kinds of material to social research, they were still convinced that their field of study was sociology. No less than 50 years later, when Norman K. Denzin (1970) revisited the heritage of life history method, he shared this sociological point of departure. Denzin points out that 'the life history presents the experiences and definitions held by one person, one group or one organization as this person, group or organization interprets those experiences' (ibid, p. 220).

Daniel Bertaux' anthology *Biography and Society* (1981b) is an important threshold publication. It can be read as an early example of narrative studies; yet most of its articles discuss biography without any explicit narrative vocabulary. Bertaux himself recommends a far-reaching shift from the study of 'life history' to 'life stories', believing that the two kinds of data 'might well involve a distinction between two different approaches' (Bertaux 1981a, 7).

Martin Kohli (1981) explicitly offers the vision of narrative analysis. Kohli approaches biographical data from the perspective of its terms of production and wants to notice the 'codes', or 'textual schemata which are available for the production of meaningful biographical accounts' (p. 62). But this is a new research problem, and 'one has to rely not only on sociological approaches, but also on those of linguistics and literature' (p. 62). Where 'life records' orient the analysis towards registering past events, Kohli already addresses the relevance of the present moment and expectations of the future in the creation of biographical materials. Kohli notices the relevance of literary analysis for sociology by asserting that 'both literature and sociology are dealing with texts' (ibid., 67). The tone and point of view of his analysis is explicitly textualist: life stories should be analyzed as texts like literary artefacts.

The use of stories in social research thus has a much longer history than narrative analysis. Erik H. Erikson (1956, 118) had even suggested the systematic study of biographies of 'ordinary people'. However, narrative was not theorized as such, and it received no entries in the index sections of the early works.

THE NARRATIVE TURNS

Instead of one narrative turn and one new attitude towards narrative, we can rather speak of at least *three* different turns and attitudes. Within *literary* studies, the narrative turn began as early as the 1960s and signified a structuralist, scientific and descriptive rhetoric in the study of narrative. In *historiography*, the turn to narrative theory indicated criticisms of naive narrative historiography and more generally 'the value of narrative in representing reality' (Mink 1987; White 1987). The narrative turn in *social sciences* began later, in the early 1980s and encompassed entirely different issues: positive appraisal of narratives as such, a general anti-positivist and often humanist approach to the study of human psychology and culture (Plummer 1983, 2001; Bruner 1991; Riessman 1993). Several historical accounts of narrative turns are currently available (Fludernik 2005; Herman 2005; Kreiswirth 2005; Riessman 2001; Hyvärinen 2006b), yet the diversity of histories of different disciplines is seldom addressed.

But why is it a *turn* in the first place? Aristotle wrote on tragedy; epics, biographies and folktales had been studied for ages. But the new theoretical landscape was neither normative nor Aristotelian. What was new in the 1960s narrative inquiry was what Martin Kreiswirth identifies as 'the institutional study of narrative for its own sake, as opposed to the examination of individual narratives' (2005, 377–378). Marie-Laure Ryan (2005, 344) points out the birth of the new *concept* of narrative: 'it is only in the past fifty years that the concept of narrative has emerged as an autonomous object of inquiry'. The abstract, theoretically rich, flexible, and thus quickly moving concept of narrative was a new thing even in literature and linguistics in the 1960s. Roland Barthes's famous passage has been used to characterize the ubiquity of narrative:

> Able to be carried by articulated language, spoken or written, fixed or moving images, gestures, and the ordered mixture of all these substances; narrative is present in myth, legend, fable, tale, novella, epic, history, tragedy, drama, comedy, mime, painting [...], stained glass windows, cinema, comics, news item, conversation. (Barthes 1977, 79)

Looking from another angle, this passage indicates the existence of a new kind of *concept of narrative*. Structuralist narratology nurtured scientific ambitions and rhetoric. Its imagery 'projects the illusion that narrative is knowable and describable, and therefore that its workings can be explained comprehensively. Narratology promised to provide guidelines to interpretation uncontaminated by the subjectivism of traditional literary criticism' (Fludernik 2005, 38).

In education, psychology and sociology the narrative turn properly took place in the early 1980s, and often implied qualitative, humanistically oriented research – in stark contrast to the scientific, descriptive tenor of structuralist narratology and the growing post-structuralist discourse in cultural studies. The narrative turn signified both a new prospect and a new dilemma: many kinds of research materials were now to be theorized and analyzed as narratives – but often without the smallest consensus on what it actually meant.

Two major theoretical moves had huge impact on social research. Critical reception of Jean-Francois Lyotard's (1993[1983]) rejection of *grand narratives* was emblematic for the gradual rehabilitation of the alternative, small, forgotten and untold stories, often first in feminist studies. If quantitative research foregrounded dominant trends, stories were to theorize the particular. The post-modern suspicion of authoritative professional, scientific and institutional truths legitimated the search for new voices. Second, the new metaphoric discourse on '*life as narrative*' suggested that narratives should have a unique role in the study of human lives, action and psychology (MacIntyre 1984; Ricoeur 1984; Carr 1986; Sarbin 1986; Bruner 1987; McAdams 1988, 1993; Polkinghorne 1988; Ochberg and Rosenwald 1992; Widdershoven 1993; Brockmeier and Harré 2001; Plummer 2001; Bamberg 2004a; Hyvärinen 2006b).

The new theoretical perspective was not easily reconciled with the inherited structuralist, formal and scientifically oriented methods of reading. In many a case, the adopted way to interpret narratives might duly be characterized as the *hermeneutic re-telling* of the stories, or narrative 'criticism' (e.g. Freeman 1993, 2004; Josselsson 2004). There is always the point to which good stories are informative as such, and able to evoke strong reader responses.

The metaphorical impulse for narrative studies created a huge *search for methods*. Here the story of narrative turn is not so much progressive as often explicitly regressive: methods and theories were searched out from earlier decades and from other disciplines. Vladimir Propp (1968) and William Labov and Joshua Waletsky (1997 [1967]), for example, became widely topical in the 1980s. These retroactive moves of reception created substantial inconvenience between dominantly structuralist methods and often post-structuralist, phenomenological and hermeneutic theorizing. Yet, many authors have tried to overcome this tension and have written introductions to narrative analysis, including for example Kohler Riessman (1993, 2001); Lieblich et al. (1998); Clandinin and Connelly (2000); Czarniawska (2004); Daiute and Lightfoot (2004).

The metaphoric understanding of life as narrative sometimes incorporated the idea of one, ideally coherent, and encompassing story of life, as for example in McAdams (1993, 5, italics MH) '(I)n the modern world in which we all live, *identity is a life story*. A life story is a personal myth that an individual begins working on in late adolescence and young adulthood in order to provide his or her life with unity or purpose [...]' (see also Polkinghorne 1988, 150). Narrative is thus adopted as a way to re-theorize too static conceptions of self and identity. However, a kind of sweeping phenomenology and a rush to totalize the narrative aspect of life seems to characterize parts of the early theorizing: it is indeed the undivided and unquestioned 'we' who is having these narrative identities and narrative selves. Despite considerable diversity among authors regarding how normative the tone was, two major conclusions seemed to appear repeatedly: life as a whole is, or is in search of, a narrative while narrative implies first and foremost a unity of life (McAdams 1988, 1993). Discursive, post-structuralist analyses of personal narrative of course rejected this unitary vision. 'From this perspective, the storyteller is not a unitary self, making holistic sense of his/her life in the telling. Instead, the stories that people tell about themselves are about many selves, each situated in particular contexts, and working strategically to resist those contexts' (Squire 2004, 116).

The metaphoric discussion of life as narrative seems to have four equally important consequences. First of all, it makes the collection and study of life narratives vitally important; second, it privileges the 'big' narratives of life (see Bamberg 2004a, 2006; Freeman 2006; Georgakopoulou 2006); third, it gives a strong impetus towards reading life narratives as coherent and unitary; and finally, the emphasis on the expressive nature of life narratives encourages us to envisage them as self-sufficient wholes, waiting for 'externalization', and not primarily interactionally occasioned utterances within institutional and cultural contexts.

THE PROPPIAN MODEL

Propp studied one distinctive genre of narratives empirically – the Russian *wonder-tales*. He found out that 'in the wonder-tale different characters perform identical actions, or, what is the same thing, that identical actions can be performed in very different ways' (Propp 1984, 73). Within this formulaic genre, therefore, there are basic *functions* that can be actualized in different ways but which still occur in the tales in the same order. 'So, for example, if the hero leaves home in quest of something, and the object of his desires is far away, he can reach it by magic horse, eagle, flying carpet, flying ship, astride the devil' and so on (Propp 1984, 73).

Propp takes a remarkable variety of actions and condenses them into basic 'functions'. On the other hand, the number of key actors in fairy tales was also reduced into basic categories. He identified the roles of villain, donor, helper, princess and her father, dispatcher and hero (Propp 1968, 77–83). The power of the model lies in this compression of the seemingly unlimited number of agents and their possible moves into a limited number of alternatives, and in arranging the functions into a sequence.

Propp intended a bottom-up, empirical and strictly inductive approach in the study of wonder-tales. The reception of the book in the French discussion of the early 1960s turned his project upside down (Propp 1984, 69–74). As a consequence, the model was primarily used in a top-down way: trying fit parts of whatever narratives into wonder-tale categories. The merit of the model is to suggest that well-established cultural genres may privilege certain categories of agents, repertoires of actions and processes.

THE LABOVIAN PERSONAL NARRATIVE

Few other models of narrative analysis have ever had such huge impact in social research as the one presented by William Labov and Joshua Waletsky (1997 [1967]).

The formative role of the model was reflected in the 1997 special issue of *Journal of Narrative and Life History*.

Emerging from the linguistic discourse, the model provided social research with one of the first tools to approach the studied narratives in a detailed way. Textually, the model offered clear criteria to recognize narrative, and recognize its difference from other forms of talk (description, argument or question).

Labov and Waletsky tried to find the smallest, most elementary, oral version of narrative. Following the main trend of the time, their approach is formal, trying to locate the *structural* model of narrative. But in addition to this, there is a conscious *functional* element: narratives are for 'recapitulating experience', but this is not the only function. A sheer experiential narrative would be pointless, they argue, without the function of 'evaluation' (Labov & Waletsky 1997, 4).

The basic element of the model is a 'narrative clause'. Narrative clauses are ordered sequentially, and the change in their order would change the whole narrative. Thus, 'I fell in love with Paula. My wife left me' would be an entirely different story if the order of clauses had been reversed. But still, only very elementary narratives are exclusively built on these narrative clauses; 'free' and 'restricted' clauses are needed as well. The model is based on sequence, narratives being 'one method of recapitulating past experience by matching verbal sequence of clauses to the sequence of events that actually occurred' (Labov and Waletsky 1997, 12). The model has the following parts (Labov 1972, 370):

1. Abstract;   4. Evaluation;
2. Orientation;   5. Result;
3. Complicating action; 6. Coda.

As Hymes (1996, 193) notes, this structure resembles models created earlier in literary studies. In comparison with the very theoretical discussion of life as narrative, it steered interest towards more empirically based problems. Labovian approach and such influential works as Elliot Mishler's (1986) *Research Interviewing* informed narrative studies in practice, and offered the means to approach fairly small stories in a detailed way.

Mishler, however, was among the first to voice a key problem with the Labovian model, when he 'pointed to its relative inattention to the interview context in the production of narratives' (Mishler 1997, 71). In a typically structuralist way, the model portrays stories as independent and fully formed texts, and 'appears to take the story or narrative as already formed, as waiting to be delivered' (Schegloff 1997, 100). Schegloff points out that nothing is told about the recipients during the telling or afterwards, no silences or hesitations are reported (Ibid., 100–101).

The strong emphasis on sequence is another problem. Mishler (1997, 72) conveys a broadly shared experience in noticing how 'in intensive life history interviews, respondents rarely provided chronological accounts'. In other words, the model, strictly based on clause level narrative sequence, was all too narrow actually to capture the complex narration so typical in interview situations. This seems to lead to a marginalization in the model of other aspects such as place, by rendering it only as a static element of orientation. But from life stories to fiction, place may have a much more central and constitutive role in the narrative (e.g. Herman 2002; Georgakopoulou 2003).

FROM TEXT TO NARRATIVE PRACTICE

The changing reception of the Labovian model exhibits a more profound change from studying narratives as separate, complete and self-sufficient *texts* towards a study of narratives *in context* and interaction and the study of *narrative practices* (Gubrium and Holstein 2008). Within this emerging understanding, 'emphasis is on narrative activity as sense-making *process* rather than as a finished product in which loose ends knit together into a single story-line' (Ochs and Capps 2001, 15).

The work of Elinor Ochs and Lisa Capps (2001, 3) marks, in various ways, the end of the dominance of the Labovian *form* in narrative analysis. Instead of full narratives, proceeding through the six steps, the authors suggest conversational narratives, many of which 'seem to be launched without knowing where they will lead' (Ibid., 2). If narrative, as 'a cognitively and discursively complex genre' often incorporates the elements of description, chronology, evaluation and explanation, then the conversational story-telling completes and complicates this picture with the respective elements of *question, clarification, challenge* and *speculation* (Ibid., 18–19). What seemed to be formal and stable elements are transformed into processes.

Jaber F. Gubrium and James A. Holstein (2008) argue for a similar shift from strictly textual study of stories towards investigating the storying process, or 'narrative ethnography', as they call their approach. They recognize the relevance of the conceptual distinction between the story and storying process, which offers 'grounds for thinking about narrativity as something interesting on its own' (Ibid., 1). The observation has profound consequences. When the interest moves from narratives as separate texts into storytelling and narrative practice within social institutions, the social functions of narrativity can be theorized in a new way. This move out from the confines of narrative structure invokes a whole new array of questions, and the authors emphatically invoke even larger contexts than Ochs and Capps, seeing them embedded like nested dolls:

> Concern with the production, distribution, and circulation of stories in society requires that we step outside of narrative material and consider questions such as who produces particular kinds of stories, where are they likely to be encountered, what are their consequences, under what circumstances are particular narratives more or less accountable, what interests publicize them, how do they gain popularity, and how are they challenged? (Ibid., 19)

Distinctive for the work of Gubrium and Holstein is the recognition of two different layers of control: interactional and institutional (Ibid., 30–41). Within this approach, they welcome the study of 'narrative environments', which 'challenge as well as affirm various stories' (Ibid., 26) and 'narrative control'. Arthur W. Frank's influential study *The Wounded Storyteller* (1995) portrays 'restitution narrative' as one of the three basic models of illness narratives, but as the model that is heavily supported by medical institutions, advertising and media. (Frank 1995, 78–79).

Events, states and narrative genres

Catherine Riessman (1990, 75–78) identifies three separate narrative genres in the interviewed divorce talk she studied, calling them 'proper' stories, 'habitual narratives', and 'hypothetical narratives'. In her discourse, 'story' is reserved for the kind of oral narratives Labov and Waletsky studied. Indeed, how representative is the Labovian narrative?

Paul Ricoeur (1984) discusses 'the semantics of action', suggesting a strong relationship between the vocabularies of narrative and action (Hyvärinen 2006a). The narrative theorist David Herman takes this point further and unpacks the key Labovian terminology of 'complicating action' in his *Story Logic* (2002). Drawing on the work of language philosophers and semantics, he suggests a far-reaching distinction between *states, activities/processes, accomplishments* and *achievements* (Herman 2002, 29–37):

> [Zeno] Vendler [...] proposed a fourfold distinction between *activity* terms (e.g. used to describe someone running or pushing a cart), *accomplishment* terms (used to describe someone running a mile or drawing a perfect circle), *achievement* terms (used to describe someone reaching the top of a hill), and *state* terms (used to describe someone as female, North-American, or in debt). (Herman 2002, 30)

Each of these categories presumes a different extension of time. For processes, the implied period of time is not definite, as it is for accomplishments. 'Growing old takes a certain unspecified amount of time, whereas finishing a peanut butter sandwich entails a sequence of action that falls within a definite temporal span' (Ibid., 30). States (being in debt, being pregnant, being ill) apparently hold true over variable stretches of time.

This plurality helps to recognize new kinds of narratives. Frank (1995, 77), for example, briefly summarizes the restitution narrative: 'Yesterday I was healthy, today I'm sick, but tomorrow I'll be healthy again'. Does this narrative qualify at all as a story in the Labovian model? One could reasonably argue that states – states of mind, states of illness, states of body – figure more prominently within genres such as illness narratives. Herman suggests that different narrative genres have different 'preference-rules'.

As an example of different preference-rules, one can take the difference between 'epic' and 'psychological novel', (Ibid., 37):

Epic	Accomplishment>achievement> activities>states
Psychological novel	States>activities> accomplishments>achievements

It is easy to see that the Labovian model prefers the 'epics' over the 'psychological novel'. If the original question was about life-threatening situations, this inclination to see adventurous stories as paradigmatic narratives is not surprising. The concept of 'state' is obviously of great importance for positional analysis of storytelling. Actions, activities and states can also be either *bounded* or *unbounded* – Riessman's habitual narratives being a good example of the use of unbounded verbal forms.

Herman's discussion of Halliday's functional grammar, different verbal processes and semantic roles is of particular interest (Ibid., 140–148). Instead of approaching the whole range of verbal processes in terms of complicating action, Halliday's grammar offers useful new distinctions. His model portrays six verbal processes:

Process Types (adapted from Halliday 1994 via Herman 2002):

Process type	Role types
Material (Dispositive, Creative)	Agent,Goal
Mental (Perceptive, Affective, Cognitive)	Senser, Phenomenon
Relational	Carrier, Attribute, Identified, Identifier
Behavioural	Behaver
Verbal	Sayer, Receiver, Target
Existential	Existent

By simplifying Herman's discussion, this variety of process types may be condensed into three semantic roles of *agent*, *experiencer/witness* and *patient*. In comparison with the Labovian model, the accounted *mental* processes and the corresponding roles of the *experiencers* are considered on equal footing with material actions. Perception, affection and cognition may be the action privileged by particular genres, say in illness narratives. Genres, in turn, are far from exclusively textual phenomena, they are entirely socially conditioned (Bakhtin 1986). Gubrium and Holstein (2008, 34–37), for example, compare the narratives from *Alcoholics Anonymous groups* and *Secular Sobriety Groups* (SGS) as examples of different institutionally fostered ways of talking about alcoholism. While the SGS genre privileges the roles of *agent* and experiencer, the AA-narratives in contrast privilege the other end of the continuum, *experiencer* and *patient*. The grammar thus provides a basic semantic matrix for the study of narrative positioning.

SCRIPTS, STORIES AND NARRATIVITY

The shift in attention from strictly defined narrative *texts* and their inner structures to cover broader narrative *practices*, as Gubrium, Holstein, Ochs, Capps and many others have suggested, invite closer scrutiny of 'narrativity' as a theme. Many narratologists have argued for understanding narrativity as a matter of degree (Fludernik 1996; Abbott 2002, 22; Herman 2002). 'She drove the car to work' is unequivocally a narrative clause, yet its narrativity is almost nonexistent.

When children begin to narrate experiences at about the age of two, their way of telling is particular, because

...children's earliest personal narratives depict routine rather than particular, novel events. In addition,

> when young children recount *routine, scripted events*, their narratives tend to be more detailed than those of depicting less common incidents. (Ochs and Capps 2001, 78; Nelson 2003, 28)

It is as if these routines and scripts were still, for children, an open and exciting world to be learned and accounted for. But it does not take many years to learn to focus on the unforeseen, exceptional; the diversions from routine. Mark Turner (1996, 19) calls these routine sequences stories, and argues that 'most of our actions consist of executing small spatial stories: getting a glass of juice from the refrigerator, dressing, bicycling to the market. Executing these stories, recognizing them, and imagining them are all related because they are all structured by the same image schemas'. Turner is perfectly right in arguing for the relevance of such spatial sequences in organizing and perceiving human action. However, it is argued that these sequences are not yet stories.

Cognitive theorists have discussed scripts, frames and schemata as mental ways of understanding new and old situations (Schank and Abelson 1977). The famous restaurant script informs us about understandings of choosing a table, having a menu, ordering food and paying the bill as relatively permanent parts of the script. Scripts organize shopping, political campaigning and sexual relationships. Scripts, in addition to being cognitive, cultural and normative, also seem to be future oriented as well. It is possible to think that in both *following* such scripts in practice, and in *telling* stories on visiting restaurants, that each teller contributes to the construction of a script, or as I suggest, a *master narrative* on the issue. Michael Bamberg (2004a, 361) expresses a similar thought without explicitly making the connection between master narratives and scripts:

> I would like to catch up with the concession that speakers constantly invoke master narratives, and that many, possibly even most, of the master narratives employed remain inaccessible to our conscious recognition and transformation. Master narratives structure how the world is intelligible, and therefore permeate the petit narratives of our everyday talk.

An interesting interplay occurs above, involving slightly different horizons of a *cultural script* or (at least partly) shared cultural knowledge, *master* narratives presenting normatively privileged accounts, *counter* narratives that resist and take distance from such culturally privileged ways of telling, and *high narrativity* of good stories that do not simply recount the cultural scripts. Because master narratives are seldom explicitly told by anyone, the more formulaic term 'script' is preferred here to refer to the cultural and situational impacts on narration.

As Jens Brockmeier and Rom Harré (2001) argue, very little is known about how exactly cultural scripts impose their models on individual action or narration. There seems to be two different ways to reckon with cultural-cognitive scripts. One is conscious reflection, resisting or affirmation of what has been called 'master narratives' (Andrews 2004; Bamberg 2004a; Jones 2004).

But what should be said about the master narratives, which 'remain inaccessible to our conscious recognition and transformation' (Bamberg 2004a, 361)? One answer is that the human capacity of narrativity processes this scripting level in an automatic way. As a child, we start recounting the formulaic, normal course of events but learn step by step – in telling, listening and monitoring responses – to report on the exceptional. Our skill as narrators is established on expert understandings of such cultural scripts as 'going to a restaurant'. Herman suggests 'a direct proportion between a sequence's degree of narrativity' and the richness of 'world knowledge' that it triggers by using scripts. A clear paradox is made manifest here: narratives should invoke a rich density of scripts to provide thick narration, yet narration cannot merely constitute the repetition of these scripts:

> Just as there is a lower limit of narrativity, past which certain 'stories' activate so few world models that they can no longer be processed as stories at all, refusing to be configured into action structures drawing on pre-storied scripts and frames, so there is an upper limit of narrativity, past which the tellable gives way to stereotypical, and the *point* of

a narrative, the reason for its being told, gets lost or at least obscured [...]. (Herman 2002, 103)

Important conclusions can be drawn from this discussion. Narrativity is based on the processing of numberless cultural scripts. Scripts as such are *not* stories or narratives, because narrativity requires both 'canonicity and breach', as Jerome Bruner (1991) has put it. Scripts and formulaic narratives are used as resources both in living and telling; yet the whole point of narrativity grows out of surprise, betrayal of expectations, the 'discordance' of life (Ricoeur 1984). Beyond early childhood, there is no social telling of script-like sequences. But the told narratives can never be entirely individual, devoid of script-like resources. Narratives and narrativity thus move between cultural scripts ('canonicity') and totally idiosyncratic babble (breach in every moment).

If scripts and master narratives are vital parts of narrativity, so is the *expectation* they necessarily carry along. Labov and Waletsky (1997) noticed that recounted experiences are regularly contrasted with expectations. Reading, watching or listening to narratives trigger expectations that the stories either confirm or betray.

EXPECTATION ANALYSIS

Bakhtin (1986) not only understands all language use as response to earlier utterances, he also includes the aspect of expectation in every utterance: 'As we know, the role of the others for whom the utterance is constructed is extremely great. [...] From the very beginning, the speaker expects a response from them, an active responsive understanding. The entire utterance is constructed, as it were, in anticipation of encountering this response' (Bakhtin 1986, 94).

Expectation analysis presumes that oral life stories essentially recount the story of changing, failing or realized expectations (in other words, they reflect 'cononicity'). While experiences may be thought as mainly

personal and subjective, expectations are always social, local and conventional. The analysis of expectations focuses on the dialectics of recognizing, following and deviating from scripts. Originally presented by Hyvärinen (1994, 1998), the practice has been further elaborated by Komulainen (1998) and Löyttyniemi (2001).

The detailed way of reading owes much to Labov and Waletsky (1997) who already recognized the cognitive relevance of negative expressions, which paradoxically do not tell what happened, but what did not. In a closer examination, there are a good many linguistic expressions reckoning expectations, not the actual experience. Deborah Tannen (1993) has summarized the following list of what she calls 'evidence of expectation':

(1) Repetition; especially repetition of whole utterances; (2) False starts; (3) Backtracks, breaking-down of the temporal order of telling; (4) Hedges that flavour the relation between what was expected and what finally happened; indeed, just, anyway, however; (5) Negatives. As a rule negative is only used when its affirmative is expected (Labov, 1972, 380-381); (6) Contrastives; (7) Modals; (8) Evaluative language; (9) Evaluative verbs; (10) Intesifiers; including laughter. (Löyttyniemi 2001, 181)

The point of the list is to illustrate the way narrative is accounting for and making relevant past futures and past expectations rather than just piecing together action sequences. The claim behind the analysis is that the key turning points of life stories exhibit *thickness of expectation* and a strong presence of the 'I'. The examples below are from a study on the 1970s *Socialist Student Union* (SOL) in Finland (Hyvärinen 1994, 1998). The female interviewee, 'Kirsi', used to be a secretary general in a local university organization and member of the national central government of the SOL at the end of her career as an activist (Hyvärinen 1994, 164–167):

1   I guess it has been the same year when I've been in the Central Government that
2   I was totally stuck up
3   that I knew that now everything will go totally wrong
4   but I couldn't say it in a way that I'd believed

5 and probably the guys of SOL also loathed me […]

6 but I sulked there

7 To me, the visits to the government were horrible. Yuk.

8 But … the reason why I really had the horrible feeling

9 was that I was in a deadlock. In a way there was nothing to do

As a narrator, Kirsi is normally very determined and strongly enacts her identity as regards the interviewer. The problem here is that she cannot position herself anymore as an agent within the received horizon of expectations. In the above, she takes the position of *affective experiencer* who is not able to be a competent *reflective experiencer* in the situation. This is also a habitual narrative: it is about *the state* of being stuck, and unbounded emotional processes (sulking, loathing). The whole section is full of intensified, colourful expressions. She hates the situation; it is almost unbearable, but it is against her expectations of being a 'good comrade' to withdraw. The conflict of expectations is dramatized on lines (3–4): she sees that everything is going totally wrong but she cannot explain it – that is, she cannot solve the conflict within the frame of enduring expectations, since she cannot take her position as a brave speaker of truths.

A bit later she talks about leaving the position in the organization. The usual dilemma in those days was to find a replacement for the post to achieve a loyal exit:

1 It was a horrible task

2 I just said that in any case I'll quit

3 because I'd next start to go haywire

4 it was that tough

5 because I was [p]

6 afterwards one learned a lot, in a way, though

7 but it was a high price to pay

8 it was the worst situation I've gotten into in my life including my divorce

At last, Kirsi is able to reassume the role of an agent, in the verbal form of speaker. The conflict of expectations and the old structure of expectations as a dutiful activist are broken down on lines (2–3), where her words 'in any case' indicate that she no longer cares about the old expectations, whatever happens. There is still the balancing role of a loyal ex-activist and reflecting experiencer on line (6) appreciating the experience as such but quickly counterbalanced again by the price of its learning. Kirsi moves to Helsinki, where no one knows her, and is able to experience a new teenage with dancing and partying. The exhilaration is contrasted with the old expectation: 'I really had hobbies no Bolshevik would have ever […] believed' a secretary general to have. It is easy to see how this play with expectations signifies her re-positioning as regards the organization and the Communist movement.

A SECOND NARRATIVE TURN?

The map of narrative analysis is changing rapidly. Textual and structuralist models of analysis are giving way to more contextual approaches that focus on narrative practices and storytelling. Semantic theories and cognitive narratology offer new tools to connect the vocabularies of action and narrative in productive ways. Recent theories of narrative offer a new sensitivity to stories that are incomplete or foreground mental events (of observation, feeling, and cognition) instead of physical action. Expectation and positioning analysis alike direct attention to the fact that narratives not only account for past experiences but position speakers within networks of social and cultural expectations (Bamberg 2004b). The dialectics of 'master' and 'counter' narratives highlight the continuous move between cultural canon and individual expression. The rich flow of post-classical literary theory of narrative accentuates the need to realize the original, interdisciplinary ethos of narrative studies. Considering all these new and dynamic elements, it is indeed plausible to argue for a 'second narrative turn', as Alexandra Georgakopoulou (2006) does. The key to the realization of this promise, more than ever, seems to reside in realizing the interdisciplinary mission of the narrative turn.

REFERENCES

Abbott, H. Porter. 2002. *The Cambridge Introduction to Narrative*. Cambridge: Cambridge University Press.

Andrews, Molly. 2004. Opening to the original contributions. Counter-naratives and the power to oppose. In *Considering Counter-Narratives*, edited by M. Bamberg and M. Andrews, pp. 1–26. Amsterdam and Philadelphia: John Benjamins.

Aristotle. 1968. *Poetics*. Oxford: Clarendon Press.

Bakhtin, M.M. 1986. *Speech Genres and Other Late Essays*. Translated by V. W. McGee. Austin: Texas University Press.

Bamberg, Michael. 2004a. Considering counter narratives. In *Considering Counter-Narratives*, edited by M. Bamberg and M. Andrews. Amsterdam and Philadelphia: John Benjamins.

Bamberg, Michael. 2004b. Positioning with Davie Hogan. Stories, tellings, and identities. In *Narrative Analysis. Studying the Development of Individuals in Society*, edited by C. Daiute and C. Lightfoot. Thousand Oaks, London, New Delhi: Sage.

Bamberg, Michael. 2006. Stories: Big or small – Why do we care? *Narrative Inquiry* 16 :1, 139–147.

Barthes, Roland. 1977. Introduction to the structural analysis of narrative. In *Image, Music, Text. Roland Barthes*, edited by S. Heath. New York: Hill and Wang. Original edition, 1966.

Bertaux, Daniel. 1981a. From the life-history approach to the transformation of sociological practice. In *Biography and Society. The Life History Approach in the Social Sciences*, edited by D. Bertaux. Beverly Hills and London: Sage.

Bertaux, Daniel. 1981b. Introduction. In *Biography and Society. The Life History Approach in the Social Sciences*, edited by D. Bertaux. Beverly Hills and London: Sage.

Brockmeier, Jens, and Rom Harré. 2001. Narrative. Problems and promises of an alternative paradigm. In *Narrative Identity. Studies in Autobiography, Self and Culture*, edited by J. Brockmeier and D. Carbaugh. Amsterdam & Philadelphia: John Benjamins.

Bruner, Jerome. 1987. Life as narrative. *Social Research* 54 (1):11–32.

Bruner, Jerome. 1991. The narrative construction of reality. *Critical Inquiry* 18:1–21.

Carr, David. 1986. Time, narrative, and history. In *Studies in Phenomenology and Existential Philosophy*, edited by J.M. Edie. Bloomington & Indianapolis: Indiana University Press.

Clandinin, D. Jean, and F. Michael Connelly. 2000. *Narrative Inquiry. Experience and Story in Qualitative Research*. San Francisco: Jossey-Bass Publishers.

Czarniawska, Barbara. 2004. *Narratives in Social Science Research. Introducing Qualitative Methods.*

Series editor: David Silverman. London, Thousand Oaks & New Delhi: Sage.

Daiute, Colette and Lightfoot, Cynthia. 2004. *Narrative Analysis. Studying the Development of Individuals in Society*. Thousand Oaks, London and New Delhi: Sage.

Denzin, Norman K. 1970. The research act. A theoretical introduction to sociological methods. In *Methodological Perspectives*, edited by R. J. Hill. Chicago: Aldine Publishing Company.

Erikson, Erik H. 1994 [1956]. The problem of ego identity. In *Identity and the Life Cycle*, edited by E.H. Erikson. New York and London: W. W. Norton & Company.

Fludernik, Monika. 1996. *Towards a 'Natural' Narratology*. London and New York: Routledge.

Fludernik, Monika. 2000. Genres, text types, or discourse modes? Narrative modalities and generic categorization. *Style* 34 (1):274–292.

Fludernik, Monika. 2005. Histories on narrative theory (II): From structuralism to the present. In *A Companion to Narrative Theory*, edited by J. Phelan and P.J. Rabinowitz. Malden, MA: Blackwell.

Frank, Arthur W. 1995. *The Wounded Storyteller. Body, Illness, and Ethics*. Chicago & London: The University of Chicago Press.

Freeman, Mark. 1993. Rewriting the self. History, memory, narrative. In *Critical Psychology*, edited by J. Broughton, D. Ingleby and V. Walkerdine. London and New York: Routledge

Freeman, Mark. 2004. Data are everywhere: narrative criticism in the literature of experience. In *Narrative Analysis. Studying the Development of Individuals in Society*, edited by C. Daiute and C. Lightfoot. Thousand Oaks, London and New Delhi: Sage.

Freeman, Mark. 2006. Life 'on holiday'? In defence of big stories. *Narrative Inquiry* 16 (1):131–138.

Georgakopoulou, Alexandra. 2003. Plotting the 'right place' and the 'right time': place and time as interactional resources in narratives. *Narrative Inquiry* 13:413–423.

Georgakopoulou, Alexandra. 2006. Thinking with small stories in narrative and identity analysis. *Narrative Inquiry*, 16 :1, 122–130.

Gergen, Mary M., and Kenneth J. Gergen. 1993. Narratives of gendered body in popular autobiography. In *The Narrative Study of Lives*, edited by R. Josselsson and A. Lieblich. Newbury Park, London & New Delhi: Sage.

Gubrium, Jaber F., and James A. Holstein. (2008). Narrative ethnography. In *Handbook of Emergent Methods*, edited by S. Hesse-Biber and P. Leavy. New York: Guilford Press.

Halliday, M.A.K. 1994. *An Introduction to Functional Grammar*. Second ed. London, Melbourne & Auckland: Edward Arnold.

Herman, David. 2002. *Story Logic. Problems and Possibilities of Narrative*. Lincoln and London: University of Nebraska Press.

Herman, David. 2005. Histories of narrative theory (I): A genealogy of early developments. In *A Companion to Narrative Theory*, edited by J. Phelan and P.J. Rabinowitz. Malden, MA: Blackwell.

Hymes, Dell. 1996. Ethnography, linguistics, narrative inequality. In *Critical Perspectives on Literacy and Education*, edited by A. Luke and J. Cook. London: Taylor & Francis.

Hyvärinen, Matti. 1994. *Viimeiset taistot [The Last Battles]*. Tampere: Vastapaino.

Hyvärinen, Matti. 1998. Thick and thin narratives: Thickness of description, expectation, and causality. In *Cultural Studies: A Research Volume*, edited by N.K. Denzin. Stamford: JAI Press.

Hyvärinen, Matti. 2006a. Acting, thinking, and telling: Anna Blume's Dilemma in Paul Auster's *In the Country of Last Things. Partial Answers* 4 (2):59–77.

Hyvärinen, Matti. 2006b. Towards a conceptual history of narrative. In *The Travelling Concept of Narrative*, edited by M. Hyvärinen, A. Korhonen and J. Mykkänen. Helsinki: Helsinki Collegium for Advanced Studies.

Jones, Rebecca L. 2004. 'That's Very Rude, I Shouldn't be Telling You That'. Older women talking about sex. In *Considering Counter-Narratives. Narrating, Resisting, Making Sense*, edited by M. Bamberg and M. Andrews. Amsterdam/Philadelphia: John Benjamins.

Josselson, Ruthellen. 2004. The hermeneutics of faith and the hermeneutics of suspicion. *Narrative Inquiry* 14 (1):1–28.

Kohli, Martin. 1981. Biography: account, text, method. In *Biography and Society. The Life History Approach in the Social Sciences*, edited by D. Bertaux. Beverly Hills and London: Sage.

Komulainen, Katri. 1998. *Kotihiiriä ja ihmisiä*. Vol. 35, *Joensuun yliopiston yhteiskuntatieteellisiä julkaisuja*. Joensuu: Joensuun yliopisto.

Kreiswirth, Martin. 2005. Narrative turn in the humanities. In *Routledge Encyclopedia of Narrative Theory*, edited by D. Herman, M. Jahn and M.-L. Ryan. London and New York: Routledge.

Labov, William. 1972. *Language in the Inner City*. Oxford: Basil Blackwell.

Labov, William, and Joshua Waletsky. [1967] 1997. Narrative analysis: oral versions of personal experience. *Journal of Narrative and Life History* 7 (1–4): 3–38.

Lieblich, Amia, Rivka Tuval-Mashiach, and Tamar Zilber. 1998. *Narrative Research. Reading, Analysis, and Interpretation*. Vol. 47, *Applied Social Research Methods Series*. Thousand Oaks, London & New Delhi: Sage.

Linde, Charlotte. 1993. *Life Stories. The Creation of Coherence*. New York, Oxford: Oxford University Press.

Lyotard, Jean-Francois. 1993 [1983]. *The Postmodern Condition*, edited by W. a. J. S.-S. Godzich, *Theory and History of Literature*. Minneapolis: University of Minnesota Press.

Löyttyniemi, Varpu. 2001. The setback of a doctor's career. In *Turns in the Road. Narrative Studies of Lives in Transition*, edited by D. P. McAdams, R. Josselsson and A. Lieblich. Washington, DC: American Psychological Association.

MacIntyre, Alasdair. 1984. *After Virtue. A Study in Moral Theory*. Second ed. Notre Dame: University of Notre Dame Press.

McAdams, Dan P. 1988. *Power, Intimacy, and the Life Story. Personological Inquiries into Identity*. New York, London: The Guilford Press.

McAdams, Dan P. 1993. *The Stories We Live By. Personal Myths and the Making of the Self*. New York and London: The Guilford Press.

Mink, Louis O. 1987. *Historical Understanding*, edited by Brian Fay, Eugene O. Golob and R. T. Vann. Ithaca and London: Cornell University Press.

Mishler, Elliot G. 1986. *Research Interviewing. Context and Narrative*. Cambridge, MA: Harvard University Press.

Mishler, Elliot G. 1997. A matter of time: when, since, after Labov and Waletsky. *Journal of Narrative and Life History* 7 (1–4):61–68.

Nelson, Katherine. 2003. Narrative and the emergence of a consciousness of self. In *Narrative and Consciousness. Literature, Psychology, and the Brain*, edited by G.D. Fireman and T.E. McVay Jr. Oxford and New York: Oxford University Press.

Ochberg, Richard L., and George C. Rosenwald. 1992. *Storied Lives:The Cultural Politics of Self-understanding*. New Haven and London: Yale University Press.

Ochs, Elinor, and Lisa Capps. 2001. *Living Narrative. Creating Lives in Everyday Storytelling*. Cambridge, MA: Harvard University Press.

Phelan, James. 2005a. Editor's column. *Narrative* 13 (3):205–210.

Phelan, James. 2005b. *Living to Tell about It. A Rhetoric and Ethics of Character Narration*. Ithaca: Cornell University Press.

Plummer, Ken. 1983. *Documents of Life. An Introduction to the Problems and Literature of a Humanistic Method, Contemporary Social Science Series*. London: Allen & Unwin.

Plummer, Ken. 2001. *Documents of Life 2. An Invitation to a Critical Humanism*. London, Thousand Oaks, New Delhi: Sage.

Polkinghorne, Donald E. 1988. Narrative knowing and the human sciences. In *SUNY Series in Philosophy of the Social Sciences*, edited by L. Langsdorf. Albany: State University of New York Press.

Propp, Vladimir. 1968. *Morphology of the Folktale*. Translated by L. Scott. 2nd ed. Austin: University of Texas Press.

Propp, Vladimir. 1984. The structural and historical study of the wondertale. In *Theory and History of Folklore*, edited by A. Liberman. Manchester: Manchester University Press.

Ricoeur, Paul. 1984. *Time and Narrative 1*. Translated by K. McLaughlin and D. Pellauer. 3 vols. Vol. 1. Chicago and London: The University of Chicago Press.

Riessman, Catherine Kohler. 1990. *Divorce Talk. Women and Men Make Sense of Personal Relationships*. New Brunswick and London: Rutgers University Press.

Riessman, Catherine Kohler. 1993. *Narrative Analysis, Qualitative Research Methods Volume 30*. Newbury Park, London & New Delhi: Sage.

Riessman, Catherine Kohler. 2001. Analysis of personal narratives. In *Handbook of Interview Research*, edited by J.F. Gubrium and J.A. Holstein. Thousand Oaks, London & New Delhi: Sage.

Rimmon-Kenan, Shlomith. 2006. Concepts of narrative. In *The Travelling Concept of Narrative*, edited by M. Hyvärinen, A. Korhonen and J. Mykkänen. Helsinki: Helsinki Collegium for Advanced Studies, University of Helsinki.

Ryan, Marie-Laure. 2005. Narrative. In *Routledge Encyclopedia of Narrative Theory*, edited by D. Herman, M. Jahn and M.-L. Ryan. London and New York: Routledge.

Sarbin, Theodor. 1986. Narrative as a root metaphor for psychology. In *Narrative Psychology. The Storied Nature of Human Conduct*, edited by T. Sarbin. New York: Praeger Press.

Schank, Roger, and Robert Abelson. 1977. *Scripts, Plans, Goals and Understanding*. New York: John Wiley & Sons.

Schegloff, Emanuel A. 1997. 'Narrative Analysis' thirty years later. *Journal of Narrative and Life History* 7 (1–4):97–106.

Seale, Clive. 2000. Resurrective practice and narrative. In *Lines of Narrative. Psychosocial Perspectives*, edited by M. Andrews, S.D. Sclater, C. Squire and A. Treacher. London and New York: Routledge.

Smith, Barbara Herrnstein. 1981. Narrative version, and narrative theories. In *On Narrative*, edited by W.J.T. Mitchell. Chicago: University of Chicago Press.

Squire, Corinne. 2004. Narrative genres. In *Qualitative Research Practice*, edited by C. Seale, G. Gobo, J.F. Gubrium and D. Silverman. London, Thousand Oaks, New Delhi: Sage.

Strawson, Galen. 2004. Against narrativity. *Ratio (New Series)* XVII (4):428–452.

Tannen, Deborah. 1993. What's in a frame? In *Framing in Discourse*, edited by D. Tannen. Oxford: Oxford University Press. Original edition, Freedle, R.O. (Ed.) 1979 New Directions in Discourse Processing.

Thomas, William I., and Florian Znaniecki. 1984. *The Polish Peasant in Europe and America*, edited by E. Zaretsky. Urbana and Chicago: University of Illinois Press. Original edition, 1918–1920.

Turner, Mark. 1996. *The Literary Mind. The Origins of Thought and Language*. Oxford and New York: Oxford University Press.

White, Hayden. 1987 [1981] The value of narrativity in the representation of reality. In *The Content of the Form. Narrative Discourse and Historical Representation*, edited by H. White. Baltimore & London: The Johns Hopkins University Press.

Widdershoven, Guy A.M. 1993. The story of life. Hermeneutic perspectives on the relationship between narrative and life history. In *The Narrative Study of Life, Volume I*, edited by R. Josselsson and A. Lieblich. Newbury Park and London: Sage.

Reconstructing Grounded Theory

Kathy Charmaz

In the 40 years since Barney G. Glaser and Anselm L. Strauss (1967) wrote their pioneering book, grounded theory has become a general qualitative method that cuts across disciplines and professions. The method consists of several distinctive strategies; however, scholars vary in what they adopt and major proponents differ on which strategies they see as integral to the method (see Charmaz, 2006; Clarke, 2005, 2006; Glaser, 1998, 2001; Strauss, 1987; Strauss and Corbin, 1990, 1998). What then is grounded theory? What does it include? The term refers to both a method of theory construction, my focus here, and the product of this construction, a theory that explains or elucidates a particular process or phenomenon.

The grounded theory method provides systematic, successive strategies for developing fresh ideas to collect, study, and analyze empirical data (see also, Atkinson et al., 2003; Clarke, 2005, 2006; Glaser, 1978; Glaser and Strauss, 1967). Grounded theory starts with an inductive logic and emphasizes simultaneous data collection and analysis to construct middle-range theories.

Those who subscribe to grounded theory would accept this definition of the method.

Yet which grounded theory strategies to adopt, what they entail and how to put them into practice have undergone change and reconstruction, even by the originators themselves (see Glaser, 1998, 2001; Strauss 1987; Strauss and Corbin 1990, 1998). Major differences among proponents arise from varied assumptions about what constitutes theory and from contrasting epistemological allegiances. These allegiances result in different constructions of the research process, the practice of theorizing, and what stands as erosion or evolution of the method (see Baker et al., 1992; Boychuk Duchscher and Morgan, 2004; May, 1996; Mills et al., 2006; Stern, 1994).

Throughout the chapter, I show how grounded theory, and its various iterations, have shifted and changed. I also address the following objectives: (1) to situate the original methodological contribution of grounded theory; (2) to look at the history and development of the method; (3) to outline postmodern challenges to the method and discuss its constructivist reconstructions; and (4) to analyze grounded theory as method and practice. I attend to debates about grounded theory and show how they are played out as various proponents reconstruct the method and note its potential for creating imaginative interpretations.

SITUATING THE USE AND METHODOLOGICAL IMPORT OF GROUNDED THEORY

To understand why and how scholars, including its originators, have reconstructed grounded theory, one needs to know about the situations surrounding its development and current directions. These situations transcend the method itself as they include its followers and critics. Both followers and critics tend to have limited visions of the method. Followers commonly identify the version of grounded theory they first learned as representing the method in its entirety (Urquhart, 2007). Some followers and critics have scarcely read beyond Glaser and Strauss' (1967) original exegesis. Critics often conflate the way the originators used the method as mirroring inherent characteristics of the method (see, for example, Burawoy, 1991; Layder, 1998). They argue that grounded theory cannot account for macro social processes or structures left untapped at the interactional level.

Grounded theory made its methodological mark by proposing explicit guidelines for theorizing from data. From Glaser and Strauss' original treatise to recent major statements by Adele E. Clarke (2003, 2005) and Kathy Charmaz (2000, 2006), grounded theorists have emphasized constructing theory from inductive qualitative data through using successive analytic strategies. Grounded theory methods have appealed to diverse researchers from varied disciplines and professions who have claimed allegiance to using them. By now, spokespersons have emerged in a variety of disciplines, such as psychology (see for example, Charmaz, 2003; Charmaz and Henwood, 2007; Henwood and Pidgeon, 1995; 2003; Pidgeon and Henwood, 1996, 2004; Rennie et al., 1988), management (Goulding, 2002; Locke, 2001), nursing (Benoliel, 1996; Chenitz and Swanson, 1986;

Schreiber and Stern, 2001; Stern, 1980; Wilson and Hutchinson, 1996; Wuest, 1995, 2001) and information systems (Bryant, 2002, 2003; Urquhart, 2003). Specialists are beginning to appear within subfields (LaRossa, 2005), and have become established in grounded theory computer applications (see, for example, Fielding and Lee, 1998; Lonkila, 1995; Kelle, 2004).

The logic and explicit strategies of grounded theory have contributed to its wide appeal. Unlike earlier twentieth-century field research, Glaser and Strauss made simultaneous data collection and analysis an integral part of grounded theory. They proposed ways of focusing and integrating data collection while advancing the theoretical analysis of the collected data. The logic of grounded theory relies on starting with inductive data and subjecting them to close scrutiny through specific coding and analytic practices, while collecting data (see Charmaz, 2003, 2006; Glaser, 1978, 1998). Grounded theory coding practices lead to developing analytic categories, and then refining these categories and checking them empirically, as the analysis becomes increasingly theoretical. Thus, the logic of grounded theory means that researchers retain strong empirical foundations in their work and offer abstract, conceptual theories of the studied empirical phenomena.

Glaser and Strauss' original statement was revolutionary for four reasons. First, they took discussion of qualitative inquiry beyond data collection techniques and field research roles. Instead, they explained how to streamline data collection by asking analytic questions and developing theoretical rendering of the data—from the very beginning of the research endeavor. Second, they outlined inductive guidelines for coding data and developing emergent abstract categories. Third, Glaser and Strauss argued that their methodological strategies could advance data analysis to construct middle-level theories. Fourth, they provided powerful legitimation for conducting inductive qualitative research at a time when most social scientists were enamored with the promise of rigorous quantitative inquiry.

This last reason led social scientists to claim that they adopted grounded theory methods when they had conducted some sort of qualitative research or had only followed one or two grounded theory strategies but did not aim for theory development. Other researchers' claims of adopting grounded theory strategies may have been more consistent with the method but their reductionist, mechanistic application of it undermined its potential for open-ended, creative theorizing. Miller's (2000) argument still holds: the full potential of grounded theory methods for generating theory remains untapped. Researchers can profit from the flexible, open-ended strategies of grounded theory to conduct systematic, directed inquiry and to engage in imaginative theorizing from empirical data.

HISTORY AND DEVELOPMENT OF GROUNDED THEORY

The emergence of grounded theory

The history and development of grounded theory are intertwined with larger currents in social scientific inquiry, and particularly with tensions between qualitative and quantitative research in sociology in the United States. During the early decades of the twentieth century, sociologists, particularly at the University of Chicago, began building an empirical foundation in life histories and case studies[1]. By mid-century this foundation had weakened due to the development of quantitative methods. Unlike strong British and European sociological traditions in critical debate and praxis in theorizing, U.S. sociology advanced quantification of various sorts and abstract macro theories devoid of solid empirical roots. As Jennifer Platt (1996) states, leading quantitative methodologists often borrowed procedures from other disciplines and some sociologists quantified measures to persuade outside audiences, not because they believed quantification to be necessary. At that time, however, the divide between theory and research deepened and the gap between inductive qualitative and deductive quantitative

research widened. U.S. sociology steadily adopted more quantitative techniques and the distance between theory and methods grew (Charmaz, 2000, 2006).

Grounded theory methods arose from Glaser and Strauss (1967) efforts to explicate the strategies they had followed while conducting their qualitative studies of the social organization of dying in hospitals (Glaser and Strauss, 1965, 1968). Their efforts brought renewed attention to qualitative research at a pivotal point in time. Platt (1996) points out that the development of public opinion research and statistical techniques during World War II and the institution building of Kurt Lewin and Paul Lazarsfeld afterwards established the hegemony of the survey and the dominance of its proponents' departments. Meanwhile, inductive qualitative inquiry in sociology in the United States had shifted from the case study to participant observation. This methodology had not been theorized, explicated, or codified in accessible ways. Nor, as Platt notes, did proponents talk about field methods. Paul Rock (1979) points out that novices learned Chicago school field research through a combination of mentoring and becoming immersed in field research settings. What researchers actually did while in the field and afterwards remained opaque. Early methodological texts emphasized data gathering and field work roles and relations rather than qualitative analytic strategies (see, for example, Adams and Preiss, 1960; Junker, 1960; Kahn and Cannell, 1957)[2].

By 1965, quantification with its positivist underpinnings framed methodological discussions in United States sociology[3]. Methods textbooks of the day outlined methodological objectives and procedures that did not fit qualitative research. Some mid-century quantitative researchers saw qualitative inquiry as a precursor to constructing quantitative instruments but most viewed qualitative studies as impressionistic, anecdotal, and biased. As such, qualitative research could not meet mid-century canons for reliability and validity. The inability of qualitative researchers to replicate their studies further marginalized qualitative research.

The arrival of grounded theory sparked growing interest in qualitative methods beyond Chicago school sociologists and their students and subsequently changed the way American researchers learned these methods. Given the hegemony of quantitative research, the *Discovery* book probably remained unnoticed by leading quantitative researchers. Yet it commanded enormous symbolic and practical influence among U.S. qualitative researchers and graduate students with qualitative inclinations. Grounded theory methods made qualitative methods accessible. By adopting grounded theory methods, professors could impart specific data collection and analytic strategies to their students. From its beginning, grounded theory spread beyond sociology. Strauss' doctoral students in nursing brought grounded theory to new graduate students as the nursing profession began to establish its own doctoral programs.

The *Discovery* book legitimated inductive qualitative research. Glaser and Strauss challenged positivistic proclivities to apply the logic of quantitative research to qualitative studies. In opposition to narrow positivistic ideals, Glaser and Strauss proposed that qualitative inquiry had its own logic and could be conducted systematically. In short, they rejected the frame that quantitative methodologists imposed on research design and practice. Glaser and Strauss refuted quantitative researchers' claim to own exclusive rights on rigor. They also challenged the established—and growing—division of labor between theory and research. Mid-century theorists and methodologists had pursued different problems. At that time, theorizing emphasized grand theories that explained the social order of whole societies but exhibited scant study of empirical research. Glaser and Strauss saw such theorizing as far removed from worlds of everyday action. Instead of arising from human action, grand theory of the day took a logico-deductive form which reasoned from abstract concepts down to empirical instances. Meanwhile quantitative methodologists increasingly turned to refining instruments, developing statistical measures, and investigating concrete problems despite the rhetoric of operationalizing theoretical concepts into testable concepts through deductive reasoning.

Glaser and Strauss intended to wrest theorizing from exclusive domain of elite armchair macro theorists and to join theory and methods through proposing arguments and providing methodological strategies. They aimed to have empirical research inform theory construction and advocated an egalitarian approach to it: ordinary researchers could construct useful grounded theories.

The originators' construction of the method

The *Discovery of Grounded Theory* stands as a pioneering book that spawned generations of qualitative researchers, many of whom read no further works on grounded theory but claimed to use it. Perhaps most researchers cited the *Discovery* book to legitimize qualitative inquiry rather than to demonstrate adherence to the method. Glaser's lesser-known book, *Theoretical Sensitivity* (1978), provided the most definitive early exegesis of the logic of the method and instructions on how to use it. Nonetheless, the dense writing and the assumption of the reader's familiarity with the grounded theory method made *Theoretical Sensitivity* most accessible to those already schooled in this method (but see Melia, 1987, 1996). In this book, Glaser's concept-indicator approach and inductive reasoning took explicit form and his positivist assumptions became more visible.

Mid-century qualitative research also became an object of Glaser and Strauss' scrutiny. With the notable exception of Erving Goffman (1959, 1961, 1963), inductive qualitative studies of the time had largely remained descriptive[4]. Goffman wove stunning theoretical insights throughout his descriptions and essays but seldom organized them in explicit theoretical frameworks. From the start, Glaser intended to take description apart and treat it in analytic, abstract, general, and parsimonious concepts. Where Goffman's work was rich in both detail and context, Glaser (1978), in contrast, aimed for streamlined, general abstract statements removed from context. Goffman's metaphor of the drama permitted readers to see social life anew. In keeping with his empirical emphasis, however, Glaser (1978) contended that Goffman relied too heavily on this metaphor. Glaser and Strauss called on qualitative researchers to raise their description to a theoretical level and to develop explicit theoretical statements.

The Discovery of Grounded Theory attacked reigning theoretical and methodological assumptions of the day and led the charge to win a new and renewed place for qualitative inquiry—for everyone. In this sense, Glaser and Strauss democratized qualitative research. For them, it consisted of a set of skills that students beyond elite Chicago circles could learn. Simultaneously, they demystified qualitative analysis by offering flexible guidelines. This combination of democratization and demystification struck a responsive chord among diverse audiences.

Grounded theory combined two competing traditions in mid-century American sociology in an unlikely marriage. Glaser wished to codify qualitative inquiry in an analogous way that his mentor, Paul Lazarsfeld (Lazarsfeld & Rosenberg, 1955) had codified quantitative research[5]. Glaser's Columbia University intellectual heritage in structural-functionalism, rigorous quantitative methods, and the quest for middle-range theories gave grounded theory its rigor, language, direction, and objectives. He borrowed terms from quantitative research design but gave them new, often inverted, meanings. Thus qualitative coding became something that emerged from data rather than applied to it; sampling became a strategy to fill out theoretical categories rather than to seek population representativeness, and core variables arose from tentative categories not from deduced operations from abstract concepts. The language itself spawned confusion that has lasted until the present. When does grounded theorists' coding emerge from their study of data rather than serving as codes applied to data? When, if ever, might representational

sampling and theoretical sampling become blurred? How does a budding grounded theorist reconcile Glaser's notion of a single core variable with the search for meanings and actions in a field of inquiry?

For Strauss, the search for meanings and actions formed the core of sociological research. Pragmatists John Dewey, George Herbert Mead, and Charles S. Peirce had left a lifelong imprint on him. During his doctoral studies Strauss' immediate intellectual influences at the University of Chicago included Herbert Blumer, Everett Hughes, and Robert Park. Thus, Strauss brought symbolic interactionism, and ethnographic field research to grounded theory and an emphasis on work to his empirical research. Strauss' pragmatist heritage gave grounded theory its emphases on agency, emergence, meaning, and action. Both Glaser and Strauss aimed to study social and social psychological processes. They first planned to generate substantive theories that explicated and explained a fundamental social or social psychological process within a social setting or a particular experience such as dying in hospitals. They argued that the resulting grounded theory could explain the major categories in the studied process, explicate their properties, demonstrate the causes and conditions under which these categories emerged and varied, and delineate their consequences. As Glaser and Strauss (1965, 1968) developed categories such as 'mutual pretense,' 'open awareness,' 'closed awareness,' and 'time expectations,' they began to move into formal theorizing because their categories and processes reached across substantive areas and could be further explored in these new areas. Thus, as Glaser and Strauss' theories reached this level of generality, they advocated refining their emerging theories by seeking relevant data in varied settings that moved across substantive areas. The researchers would then refine the categories of the emerging formal theory, as informed by the new data these categories subsumed.

Glaser and Strauss' arguments in the *Discovery* book contributed much to revitalizing qualitative research and to maintaining and extending Chicago school ethnographic traditions in sociology. They inspired new scholars in diverse fields to pursue qualitative research and trained doctoral sociology and nursing students in grounded theory. They offered innovative strategies to move qualitative inquiry beyond description and into explanatory theory that conceptualized the studied phenomena in theoretical categories and demonstrated abstract relationships between these categories. And they contended that a completed grounded theory was useful, unlike mid-century grand theory. Glaser and Strauss proposed that a finished grounded theory would meet the following criteria: a close fit with the data, usefulness, density, durability, modifiability, and explanatory power (Glaser, 1978, 1992; Glaser and Strauss, 1967).

Procedures versus emergence in the reconstruction of grounded theory

Strauss' publication of *Qualitative Analysis for Social Scientists* (1987) sowed the seeds of the first reconstruction of grounded theory. These seeds matured in his co-authored book with Juliet Corbin, *Basics of Qualitative Research* (1990, 1998) because in significant ways it revised grounded theory and set a new course for it. In his 1987 book, Strauss began to move grounded theory toward verification. His co-authored works with Corbin further this direction. In addition, Strauss and Corbin created several new technical procedures to be applied to the data rather than emerging from analyzing them. Glaser's (1992) acrimonious response to the first edition of *Basics* disavows Strauss and Corbin's innovations and proclaims his version of grounded theory to be the only authentic statement of the method. Glaser argues that Strauss and Corbin's procedures force data and analysis into preconceived categories and, thus, contradicted essential grounded theory guidelines based on comparative analysis and emergent categories. Glaser saw Strauss and Corbin's innovations as usurping the method and imposing unnecessary complexity on the analytic process. At that time, Glaser

remained consistent with his 1978 exegesis of the method, which relied on comparative approaches at each step of the analytic process, avoidance of extant theories, a delayed literature review, and on a direct and, often, narrow empiricism.

To an extent, Strauss and Corbin's technical applications foster a formulaic approach rather than developing Glaser's type of emergent analysis. They introduce axial coding as part of a complex 'coding paradigm' and the conditional matrix as techniques for viewing data and producing an analysis. In axial coding, researchers (1) treat a category as an axis; (2) specify the properties and dimensions of this category; (3) relate categories to their subcategories; and (4) delineate relationships between them (Strauss and Corbin, 1998, p. 123). Strauss and Corbin argue that axial coding brings the data back together again into a coherent whole after fracturing them during initial line-by-line coding (Charmaz, 2006, p. 186). In addition to forcing data into preconceived frameworks, Glaser (1992, 1998) viewed axial coding as sidestepping his families of theoretical codes that he laid out in *Theoretical Sensitivity*. Glaser views these codes as supplying the latent links and theoretical explanations that hold a researcher's inductive categories together. He insists that theoretical codes must earn their way into the analysis; however, whether or not these codes constitute another form of forcing data remains ambiguous. Applying them mechanically would result in forcing data—and forcing one's categories into a particular configuration, as Glaser (1992) acknowledges. Seeing and pursuing which theoretical directions, issues, and, possibly, concepts the data suggest makes more sense. These theoretical directions may spawn original ideas that move beyond Glaser's theoretical codes or Strauss and Corbin's axial coding.

Strauss and Corbin designed their other procedural innovation, the conditional/ consequential matrix, to provide a technique for coding to make the intersections of micro and macro conditions/consequences on actions visible and to clarify connections between them. By creating the conditional/consequential matrix, Strauss and Corbin intended to make connections between levels of analysis more visible.

Kelle (2005) reduces the controversy between Glaser and Strauss and Corbin to whether a researcher follows the coding paradigm systematically—perhaps rigidly?—or adopts *ad hoc* theoretical codes from Glaser's coding families. Even though Kelle's view makes sense, it undermines Glaser's approach to constructing emergent categories. Kelle sees Glaser's emphasis on emergence as a problematic methodological concept imbedded in Glaser's exhortations to study data without adopting a preconceived theoretical frame. True, Glaser views emergence as contingent on not forcing data into extant theories and his resounding 'Trust in emergence' has the ring of a slogan. Yet an emphasis on emergence means more than a slogan. An apt approach combines Dey's (1999) view of bringing an open mind to data with Henwood and Pidgeon's (2003) notion of theoretical agnosticism. This approach is consistent with an injunction from the abductive logic that has always characterized grounded theory: remain open to all kinds of theoretical possibilities and gather more data to check the most plausible explanation (Peirce, 1938/1958; Rosenthal, 2004). Kelle correctly takes Glaser to task about assuming that facts stand alone, and that a theory-free observer can see them but also notes the conflicting assumptions about possessing 'theoretical sensitivity' (Glaser and Strauss, 1967, p. 3; Glaser, 1978).

A major difference between Glaser and Strauss and Corbin may lie in how and when each imports their respective form of coding into the analysis. For Glaser, theoretical coding comes after the grounded theorist has advanced tentative categories; for Strauss and Corbin axial coding is a means of developing categories. Glaser and Strauss and Corbin each contend that their respective forms of coding put the previously fractured data back together in conceptual ways. A second difference lies in their use of comparisons. Glaser sticks to comparing data with data, data

with code, code with code and so forth as the researcher moves up levels of abstraction.

The potential tensions between Glaser's positivism and Strauss' pragmatism are perhaps greater than their respective grounded theory books indicate. Strauss' strong pragmatist roots are more evident in his early works (e.g. 1959/1969, 1961; Glaser and Strauss, 1965, 1967, 1968) and in *Continual Permutations of Action* (1993) than in his co-authored grounded theory texts with Juliet Corbin, *Basics of Qualitative Research* (1990, 1998), which contain positivist undercurrents. Both Strauss and Corbin's and Glaser's versions of grounded theory assume an external reality independent of the observer, a neutral observer, and the discovery of data. Notions about what researchers see, define, and describe as data do not permeate their texts. Glaser ignores the vital roles of perspectives and language for what we define as data and Strauss and Corbin state, 'Although we do not create data, we create theory out of data' (1998, p. 56). Such approaches do not acknowledge the position from which the observer sees and speaks much less how grounded theory is an inherently interactive method during every step of the process.

Whether or not researchers use axial coding or adopt the conditional/consequential matrix, Strauss (1987) and Strauss and Corbin (1990, 1998) have made diagramming an integral part of the method for their followers. Diagramming representations of relationships between categories fosters developing analytic complexity with multiple categories. In this sense, Strauss and Corbin's reconstruction moves beyond Glaser's variable analysis of one core variable and also provides a foundation for Adele E. Clarke's (2003, 2006) postmodernist revision of grounded theory and methodological strategy of mapping empirical situations and positions. She creates positional maps that not only chart discourses but also locate silences and paths not taken as well as those taken.

In keeping with his positivist heritage, Glaser assumes an expert observer who makes neutral, unproblematic observations and offers slogans such as 'All is data'

(2001, p. 145) that gloss what researchers may define as 'all.' Glaser explicitly promotes theorizing from outside the studied experience rather than from within it. For years he argued that study participants will tell researchers their main concern about what's happening in their setting (see, for example, Glaser, 1992). Beyond any intent to focus an observer's gaze on some issues and away from others, relying on participants' directives can still result in an outsider's analysis. Participants often take for granted the fundamental processes and conditions that shape their lives. Following participants' overt statements may lead to unwitting acceptance of a public relations rhetoric and subsequent analysis of an outsider rather than insider's viewpoint. Interestingly, in a significant shift, Glaser later (2001, p. 51) acknowledges that the researcher identifies and conceptualizes participants' main concern.

Overall, Glaser's epistemology has remained consistent over the years. Yet he, too, has reconstructed grounded theory practice in both major and minor ways. Unlike Strauss and Corbin's (1990, 1998) reconstructions, Glaser's shifts are incremental and buried in the dense texts of his self-published books. He also presents his shifts as contributions to an evolving method. But who decides what represents its evolution, reconstruction or erosion? Glaser has disavowed his quest to define and analyze a basic social process or basic social psychological process because he now sees such a quest as forcing the data. This change is fundamental because earlier Glaser built grounded theory practice on the analytic explication of these processes. Similarly, another major change in methodological practice concerns initial coding. Glaser (1992, 2001) disavows his earlier prescription to do line-by-line coding to fracture the data and to see beyond the immediate story during the initial coding. Instead, he advocates seeking a core variable through comparisons of incidents. Minor shifts include adding more families of theoretical codes, changing the rules for memo-making, and narrowing the definition of theorizing to 'a theory of a core category' (2001, p. 206).

Since Glaser and Strauss' (1967) original statement, several major grounded theorists have aimed beyond middle-range theories. Strauss (1987, 1993), independently as well as with co-author Juliet Corbin (Strauss and Corbin, 1990, 1998), began to move from the micro level of analysis to meso and macro levels, an effort that Clarke (2003, 2005, 2006) has extended. Elsewhere I have initiated a discussion of taking grounded theory methods into structural analysis with an explicit emphasis on social justice (Charmaz, 2005).

POSTMODERN CHALLENGES AND CONSTRUCTIVIST RECONSTRUCTIONS OF GROUNDED THEORY

By 1990, publication of Strauss' *Qualitative Methods for Social Scientists* (1987) and Strauss and Corbin's *Basics of Qualitative Research* had made the method immensely popular throughout the social sciences and professions. The qualitative revolution had spread widely and *Basics* gave researchers a way to conduct qualitative research. Simultaneously, however, the positivist residues of early grounded theory statements came under increased scrutiny and postmodern and narrative turns undermined the method. Some scholars (see for example, Conrad, 1990; Ellis, 1995; Richardson, 1993) viewed grounded theory as clinging to an outdated modernist epistemology. For them, grounded theory fragmented the respondent's story, relied on the authoritative voice of the researcher, blurred difference, and accepted Enlightenment grand metanarratives about truth, universality, human nature, and world views. Such critiques melded grounded theory strategies with the originators' early statements and how they used the method.

A reconstructed grounded theory can take into account many of the criticisms that varied critics have raised. Researchers can adopt–and may adapt—the flexible strategies that Glaser and Strauss (1967; Glaser, 1978, 2001) originally delineated. These strategies remain enormously helpful in producing analyses that offer useful interpretations of studied life. A growing number of scholars, including myself, have sought to loosen key grounded theory strategies from their positivist foundations evident in both Glaser's and Strauss and Corbin's versions of the method (see, for example, Bryant, 2002, 2003; Castellani et al., 2003; Charmaz, 2000, 2002, 2005; Clarke, 2003, 2005; Henwood and Pidgeon, 2003; Seale, 1999).

Researchers can use grounded theory strategies without endorsing mid-century assumptions of an objective external reality, a passive, neutral observer, or a detached, narrow empiricism. If, instead, we start with the assumption that social reality is multiple, processual, and constructed, then we must take the researcher's position, privileges, perspective, and interactions into account as an inherent part of the research reality. It, too, is a construction. As Clarke (2005, 2006) stresses, the research reality arises within a situation and includes what researchers and participants bring to it and do within it. Thus, relativism characterizes the research endeavor rather than objective, unproblematic prescriptions and procedures. Research acts are not given; they are constructed. Viewing the research as constructed rather than discovered fosters researchers' reflexivity about their actions and decisions.

This perspective shreds notions of a neutral observer and value-free expert. Not only does that mean that researchers must examine rather than erase how their privileges and preconceptions may shape the analysis, but it also means that their values shape the very facts that they can identify. Like the Marxist view of history, this approach treats research as a construction but acknowledges that it occurs under specific conditions—of which we may not be entirely aware and of which may not be of our choosing.

Thus, the major reconstruction of grounded theory derives from wresting grounded theory from its earlier objectivist roots and, instead, adopting constructivist epistemologies with their respective implications for research practice (Charmaz, 2000, 2006).

The objectivist-constructivist dichotomy between grounded theory approaches juxtaposes their respective assumptions, logics, and objectives (see Figure 27.1).

This dichotomy provides a heuristic device for increasing the visibility of starting assumptions and for assessing proponents' innovations and reconstructions of the original method. This dichotomy also helps researchers to examine their starting assumptions and research actions. In practice, grounded theory inquiry ranges from objectivist to constructivist.

Constructivist grounded theorists refute notions of unproblematic selection, collection, and representation of data. Data and their meanings are neither singular nor self-evident; instead, researchers interpret and categorize data but their potential meanings are multiple. Constructivists look for multiple meanings and complexity and thus, limit the simplifying, generalizing impulse, and resist decontextualizing the analysis, as advocated in earlier grounded theory statements. Constructivists argue for locating both the grounded theory process and product in time, space, and social conditions. That means a completed grounded theory must be evaluated in light of its specific origins rather than viewed as separate and distant from its construction. Constructivists also favor aiming for abstract understanding rather than pursuing earlier positivist goals of explanation and prediction. In short, grounded theory strategies foster the researcher taking an active stance throughout data collection and analysis and constructivist approaches further this stance and combine it with reflexivity and relativity (Charmaz, 2006).

In her constructivist revision of classical grounded theory, Clarke (2003, 2005, 2006) explicitly builds on its pragmatist foundations and incorporates postmodern perspectives. When emphasizing the compatibility of pragmatism and symbolic interactionism with contemporary epistemological developments including feminist theory, Clarke reminds us that pragmatism's relativistic view of truth, assumption of a multiplicity of perspectives, and emphasis on partial views,

Objectivist Grounded Theory	Constructivist Grounded Theory
Assumes an external reality	Assumes multiple realities
Assumes discovery of data	Assumes mutual construction of data
Assumes conceptualizations emerge from data	Assumes researcher constructs categorizations
Views representation of data as unproblematic	Views representation of data as problematic, relativistic, situational, and partial
Assumes the neutrality, passivity, and authority of the observer	Assumes the observer's values, priorities and positions, and actions affect views
Views data analysis as an objective process	Acknowledges subjectivities in data analysis, recognizes co-construction of data; engages in reflexivity
Gives priority to researcher's views	Seeks participants' views and voices as integral to the analysis
Aims to achieve context-free generalizations	Views generalizations, as partial, conditional, and situated in time, space, positions, action, and interactions
Focuses on developing abstractions	Focuses on constructing interpretations
Aims for parsimonious explanation	Aims for interpretive understanding

Figure 27.1   Comparison of objectivist and constructivist grounded theory*

***See Charmaz, 2000, 2006.**

situated actions, and positional knowledge already aligns it with constructivist grounded theory. Clarke (2006) sees grounded theory and symbolic interactionism as fitting what Star (1989) calls a theory-method package in which ontology and epistemology are co-constitutive and non-fungible. To provide a research practice that builds on her perspective, Clarke (see especially 2003, 2005, 2006) offers situational analysis as a way to map positions, discourses, actions, and to capture silences at meso and macro levels.

GROUNDED THEORY AS METHOD AND PRACTICE

Properties of the method

Many qualitative researchers are familiar with the flexible guidelines constituting the grounded theory method. But what are its fundamental properties? To turn grounded theory logic on itself, which analytic properties distinguish the method and make it distinctive? Grounded theory is an inductive-abductive, comparative, emergent, and interactive method (Charmaz, 2006). These properties take full form in its constructivist versions and shape how researchers invoke its strategies.

From the beginning, Glaser and Strauss (1967) have treated grounded theory as an inductive and fundamentally comparative method. They align grounded theory with its practical applicability as consistent with John Dewey's pragmatism, but they do not mention Peirce (1938/1958) or abductive reasoning. Strauss (1987), however, acknowledges the debt that grounded theory owed to George Herbert Mead and Charles S. Peirce. In his teaching, Strauss routinely described grounded theory as an abductive method[6]. As such, researchers begin with inductive cases and define an intriguing finding, which they attempt to explain. Abductive reasoning involves the imaginative interpretation of accounting for this finding by entertaining all possible theoretical interpretations, and then checking these interpretations against experience until arriving at the most plausible theoretical explanation (Hildebrand, 2000/2004; Peirce, 1938/1958; Reichert, 2000/2004; Rosenthal, 2004). Abductive logic builds checks into the research process and, therefore keeps an emerging theory grounded in the data that it attempts to explain.

For Glaser (1992, 1998, 2001, 2003), the comparative methodology consists of a set of successive strategies for developing theoretical categories and renders these categories objective through abstraction of their properties. For Strauss and Corbin (1998), the comparative method corrects 'possible distortion of meaning' (p. 137). Their 'far-out' comparisons leap beyond the data but hearken back to Everett Hughes' (1958) seemingly incongruent comparisons such as the similarities between psychiatrists and prostitutes, a comparison that long entranced American sociologists.

In the early years, both Glaser and Strauss treated grounded theory as an emergent method. It is ironic that Strauss' methodological texts with Corbin became increasingly procedural. Mead's (1932) philosophy of time and conception of the emergent present had profoundly affected Strauss' methodological practice and theoretical perspective. His methodology books do not fully portray the fluidity of his thinking or the creativity enacted in his co-authored research with both Glaser and Corbin (see, for example, Corbin and Strauss, 1988; Glaser and Strauss, 1968).

A procedural approach to grounded theory dampens its emergent strengths and diminishes possibilities for theoretical innovation. Researchers have long associated grounded theory as having a particular form, but have not explicated the vital role of content for directing this form. They can become mired in following procedures and subsequently produce description rather than theoretical interpretation. Such an approach adopts a preconceived form for the method without attending to how the content of the research can re-form the form. Form and content shape each other, particularly in constructivist versions of grounded theory. Researchers study and focus data collection and analytic in a dialectical process. Therefore, the method itself becomes constructed and reconstructed throughout the research process. Maintaining this dialectic requires active, reflective researchers, whose reasoning directs their enactment of this method.

The fundamental property of emergence in grounded theory relies on active researchers who interact with their data and interpret these data—and their research practices. The image of neutral, passive researchers who discover data and theory is a mirage. Moving from data to theory requires researchers' sustained interaction and actions with their data and emerging analyses. In short, grounded theorists study emergent processes—and the method itself is an emergent process.

Grounded theory guidelines

Several basic grounded theory guidelines have become standard fare in qualitative inquiry. Nonetheless, the grounded theory emphasis on action and process, its comparative approach, and its particular coding and sampling strategies make the method unique—and sometimes misunderstood. Because these guidelines have been discussed at length elsewhere (Charmaz, 2003, 2005, 2006; Glaser, 1978, 1992, 1998, 2001, 2003; Glaser and Strauss, 1967; Locke, 2001; Strauss, 1987; Strauss and Corbin, 1990, 1998) I merely outline them here.

Unlike most qualitative approaches, grounded theory provides explicit strategies for defining and studying processes: this method places priority on action. Glaserian versions of grounded theory build action into the analysis from the earliest coding. The comparative study of actions and codes advances an inductive analysis. By invoking comparative methods throughout the analysis grounded theorists define analytic properties of their codes. Essentially from the start grounded theorists code and analyze to illuminate actions, process, and potential theoretical meaning (Glaser, 1978). In brief grounded theory guidelines include the following comparative research practices:

- Comparing data with data
- Labeling data with active, specific codes
- Selecting focused codes
- Comparing and sorting data with focused codes
- Raising telling focused codes to tentative analytic categories
- Comparing data and codes with analytic categories
- Constructing theoretical concepts from abstract categories
- Comparing category with concept
- Comparing concept and concept[7]

Objectivist grounded theorists who follow Glaser's aim to use comparative methods without preconceptions. Thus they prescribe entering the research setting and analysis uncontaminated by prior theory and disciplinary knowledge. Constructivist grounded theorists use their prior knowledge and disciplinary perspectives to sensitize them to conceptual issues at the beginning but seek new theoretical interpretations as they interrogate their data and emerging analyses.

At least two phases of coding characterize grounded theory: open, or initial, and selective, or focused. During the initial phase, line-by-line coding prompts the researcher's active involvement in the analysis. To do line-by-line coding at all, researchers must view the data in greater depth than passively perusing it or looking for themes, as qualitative researchers generally do. Even though Glaser has jettisoned line-by-line coding, it remains an excellent heuristic strategy for scrutinizing data and for examining one's preconceptions about the data as well as becoming aware of tacit alignments or shared assumptions with participants. By constructing active, specific, and short initial codes, the grounded theorist creates handles for making comparisons between data and between codes.

Focused or selective coding follows scrutiny of the initial codes. Focusing on both the most frequent and the most telling codes provides tentative leads to explore and check during subsequent data collection. Researchers use focused codes to sort large amounts of data and to construct tentative categories in their emerging theories.

Memo-writing is the crucial stage of analysis between coding and writing sections of a first draft of the study. In grounded theory practice, researchers write memos from the very beginning of their research and continue to write progressively more focused and analytic memos as they proceed. Memos lend form to fleeting ideas, take codes and categories apart, make comparisons explicit, mine descriptions, stories, and incidents for their analytic import, raise and discuss conjectures, and identify gaps and unanswered questions in the data. Writing memos becomes a means of actively engaging one's data, codes, and categories. By including data in the memo, researchers build clear links to categories. Much comparative analysis occurs while memo-writing from comparing data with data and codes early on to comparing category with category as researchers develop their theories. An emergent fit of the categories may then become apparent through writing memos.

Grounded theory builds checks on the analysis throughout the process. Memo-writing fosters checking hunches and keeping the analysis grounded. Theoretical sampling, offers another pivotal, but often misunderstood strategy for grounding the analysis and increasing its incisiveness. Theoretical sampling means sampling to flesh out or refine theoretical categories to increase the precision of the emerging theory. In short, this strategy invokes abductive reasoning because researchers test their tentative ideas. Theoretical sampling arises from researchers' analyses, not from any representation of population traits or status attributes.

When does the iterative process of moving between collecting and analyzing data end? The standard grounded theory answer is when categories are saturated. That means that the researcher has explicated the properties of each theoretical category and has sought data that fill each property. The emphasis on categories and properties makes saturation a *theoretical* concern, not merely a methodological measure indicating redundancy of data as in conventional qualitative research. Yet the concept of theoretical saturation remains problematic in grounded theory. Like the assumption that grounded theorists share definitions of 'theory,' the standard answer of saturation does not address what constitutes a category, nor does it explain how one knows that all salient properties and their variations have been defined, much less been given adequate coverage. Grounded theorists usually assert that they have saturated the properties of a category rather than demonstrating it (Morse, 1995).

The last major grounded theory strategy involves integrating the analysis. How does one accomplish it? By this time grounded theorists should have a set of well-developed analytic memos on their categories and concepts. Integrating them becomes part of theorizing and, thus, researchers next engage in theoretical sorting to best present the relationships between categories and concepts. Sorting memos occurs first in service to the emergent grounded theory and then, perhaps later, for presentation to an audience. The explanation of the sorting helps to integrate the theory and makes the analytic argument visible for the written report. Strauss (1987) and Strauss and Corbin (1990, 1998) propose diagramming major ideas and relationships, and Clarke (2003, 2005, 2006) offers a means of making structure and process visible.

ART AND SCIENCE IN GROUNDED THEORY STUDIES

Art and science in the originators' works

Strauss and Corbin (1998) treat their approach as both science and art but their overlay of technical procedures and objectivist assumptions undermine its interpretive elements

and their scientistic language undercuts its potential artfulness. Their dual emphases on science and art are also evident in their shared empirical works. They develop such concepts as 'biographical body conceptions (or BBC) ... [which] represents those three concepts—biographical time, body, and conceptions of self' (p. 252) and the 'BBC chain,' (Corbin and Strauss, 1987, p. 253), 'the combination of the three working together.' These concepts provide analytic tools that dissect experience but distance it from how people live it. Within the same paper, however, Corbin and Strauss, offer some artful narrative descriptions that bring the experience to life. Below they discuss questions arising when people first receive a diagnosis of chronic illness and describe the properties of this temporal turning point:

> ... [W]hen past and future come crashing into the undesirable or dreaded present. This identity shock is followed by future images of what the illness will mean in terms of biographical performances such as: 'I will be crippled.' 'I will no longer be able to,' 'I might die soon.' The degree to which identity is jolted depends upon the number of aspects of self lost, their salience, and the possibility of comeback – regaining lost aspects of self. (p. 272)

Glaser's version of grounded theory sticks to conventional social science. He does not take into account the potential power of artful interpretation and advises against attending to writing (2001). For Glaser, the 'conceptual grab' of the analysis trumps the writing of it (2001, p. 80). Not surprisingly, Glaser has expressed disdain for both qualitative researchers who aim to tell the overarching story in their research and the stories that support it. His remarks endorse a unitary treatment of grounded theory reportage, untouched by either the narrative turn in the social sciences or the demands of varied writing genres and publishing venues.

Artful interpretations in grounded theory works

Grounded theorists' published works range from neutral reports to imaginative interpretations written with style and grace. Much work conducted under the banner of grounded theory consists of routine description couched in academic conventions. Numerous analytic writings are stilted and mechanical. How might grounded theorists produce artful interpretations?

Typical grounded theory writing fosters making categories explicit in linear form. These categories represent authors' construction of their respective research participants' actions. This writing strategy can shrink the substance of a study to a list of mundane, loosely related processes or descriptors. When, however, authors present both the central idea and its major categories in vivid terms, they simultaneously integrate their analyses and engage readers in their theoretical renderings. Geralyn A. Meyer (2002) titles her articles, 'The Art of Watching Out: Vigilance in Women Who Have Migraine Headaches,' and then posits 'owning the label' and 'making the connections' as the two major conditions for her core category, 'watching out,' to occur. She aims to provide a substantive analysis of the vigilance she finds in her 22 interviews.

Meyer breaks down both the conditions and the core category into sub-categories. Watching out included these subcategories: *'assigning meaning to what is, calculating the risk, staying ready, and monitoring the results'* (p. 1225). The names of the categories and sub-categories alone carry substantial weight and create the form of the analysis. Thus these categories may require less detailing and supporting evidence than more opaque categories because their analytic rendering aims for limited theoretical reach but makes sound intuitive sense. Meyer's analysis resonates with readers' experience. She keeps the analysis simple, the categories crisp, and the relationships between them sequential.

In the following passage from a much larger project, Susan Leigh Star (1989) adopts a different and more difficult analytic objective and writing strategy. She sets high analytic stakes by making a major theoretical argument about relationships between scientific work and shifts in scientific theorizing. Her argument challenges Thomas Kuhn's

contention that a critical mass of anomalies eventually cause change in scientific theorizing. In contrast, Star proposes that theoretical shifts in science are continual and routine and argues that brain localizationists' victory over brain diffusionists in the late nineteenth century provides a case in point. She weaves description throughout the narrative to support her theoretical perspective and argument. For Star, abstract theorizing about scientific reasoning arises from the whole of her analysis rather than the disparate parts. In this sense, she reunites the fragmented data into a coherent—and fascinating—analytic story but she does so in a way that its grounded theory underpinnings recede into the background and her theoretical points emerge in the foreground. In the passage below, Star explores her category 'the contradictions' [in the localizationists' position] and also builds her case about how these scientists reconstruct the exigencies of their work to fit their theoretical proclivities. Star writes:

THE CONTRADICTIONS

Localizationists recognized that material and immaterial realms could not, without serious philosophical difficulties, simply be posited as causing action in one another. They also recognized that in principle 'correlation is not causation,' although they sometimes used correlation as proof. The major conceptual difficulties thus caused by parallelism ['the doctrine that the mind and body operate as two separate but parallel realms' (Star, 1989, p. 155)] were *how* the two realms (mind and brain) were brought together and *by what mechanisms* they were made to operate in tandem. Again, it is not surprising to find that the localizationists' responses of these problems were neither unified nor consistent. They were facing multiple incommensurate audiences: philosophy, medicine, physiology, antivivisection, and evolutionary biology. In addition their everyday work posed serious technical difficulties and uncertainties.

In order to resolve the conflicting demands of the several audiences, localization of adopted several general strategies. The first strategy was to refer philosophical problems to an expert *within their ranks*. This was someone who understood their daily work concerns but who would speak as a philosopher for them. The person elected to do this was John Hughlings Jackson. Because he addressed many of the contradictions posed by parallelism and the mind/brain relationship, Jackson became a kind of symbolic leader for the localizationists....

The second strategy was to develop theories and concepts that could act as plausible bridges between the realms of the mind and the brain. These explanations were not, strictly speaking, philosophically accurate. However they were good enough as theoretical explanations to allow work to continue respectably.

As a final resort, when problems cannot be resolved, localizationists would simply jettison intractable problems into other lines of work. That is, those difficulties that could not easily be addressed by some physical or medical model were relegated to 'mind'—related lines of work, such as psychiatry and psychology. In this way, psychophysical parallelism was reinforced on an organizational level. Such a division of labor effectively obscured many of the epistemological problems arising from the mind/brain gap. The contradictions were thus eradicated from immediate concern. (pp. 162–163)

Star crafts a convincing argument. Note how she weaves her evidence through the narrative to support her theoretical argument. She creates smooth transitions between description and her category of 'contradictions' that simultaneously directs the reader and builds her case.

construction nor in its seeming substance. Layers of meaning and action underlie both its construction and substance, which means researchers have rich soil to excavate. Doing grounded theory may simplify methodological decisions but it fosters developing complex and layered analyses, as the excerpt above from Star suggests. Given Glaser and Strauss' (1967) original openness to methodological innovation and development, it is ironic that grounded theory has become a methodological template—of whichever version—for some researchers who seek mechanical means to stamp out qualitative studies.

Yet by interrogating and following content, grounded theorists can construct form for their inquiry, rather than solely creating content from form used as a recipe for generating research. Grounded theory gives researchers sufficient strategies that they can assume control of their research practice and advance their original ideas. Thus, the present points the way for future reconstruction of grounded theory to open further possibilities for making original theoretical contributions.

CONCLUSION

Researchers have reconstructed grounded theory to fit their work and fulfill their objectives. As in the past, many researchers still claim grounded theory to legitimatize some support of inductive inquiry although it may bear faint resemblance to grounded theory strategies. Those who adopt grounded theory strategies tend to select among them and may remain unaware that their selections represent a partial use of the method. Still, the wide acceptance of versions of grounded theory attest to the usefulness of the method and the current debates about its construction and direction affirm its vibrancy.

How researchers reconstruct grounded theory matters. The strength of the method lies in its recursive practice in which content shapes form. As I have argued above, this content is neither straightforward in its

NOTES

1 What became known as the 'Chicago school' typically includes a symbolic interactionist theoretical perspective and ethnographic field research methodological tradition. As Abbott (1999) points out, consensus on theory and method did not exist at Chicago in the 1940s, when the 'second Chicago school' emerged. Some Chicago graduate students were influenced by Herbert Bulmer; others saw themselves as field researchers, but not necessarily symbolic interactionists, and, simultaneously, as Bulmer (1984) states, traditional methodologists pursued a vigorous quantitative agenda.

2 Platt (1996, 253) notes that the 'case-study method' held sway as a key concept before World War II, but what it meant was often not clear.

3 Platt (1996, 14–17) charts increased numbers of technical works addressing topics such as surveys, sampling, scaling, and measurement between 1945 and 1960 in her table of American methodological monographs. Of the 29 cited volumes, only four address distinctively qualitative methods. Several works focused on interview techniques, which Platt

correctly points out overlap quantitative and qualitative research.

4 Some blurring between theoretical treatises and empirical studies occurs when anything without numbers counts as 'qualitative.' Not all macro qualitative works are empirical.

5 Lazarsfeld also pursued qualitative methods but his contribution to quantitative methods became more widely known.

6 My comments here derive from my days as a student of both Glaser and Strauss and a long friendship with Strauss thereafter.

7 This list is congruent with Glaser's comparative approach. For further details see Charmaz (2006) and Glaser (1978, 1992, 1998).

REFERENCES

Abbott, A. (1999). *Department & Discipline: Chicago Sociology at One Hundred.* Chicago: University of Chicago Press.

Adams, R. N. & Preiss, J. J. Eds. (1960). *Human Organization Research.* Homewood, IL: Dorsey Press.

Atkinson, P., Coffey, A., & Delamont, S. (2003). *Key Themes in Qualitative Research: Continuities and Changes.* New York: Rowan and Littlefield.

Baker, C., Wuest, J. & Stern, P. (1992). Method slurring: The grounded theory, phenomenology example. *Journal of Advanced Nursing, 17*:1355–1360.

Benoliel, J. Q. (1996). Grounded theory and nursing knowledge. *Qualitative Health Research, 6(3)*: 406–428.

Boychuk Duchscher, J. E. & Morgan, D. (2004). Grounded theory: Reflections on the emerging vs. forcing debate. *Journal of Advanced Nursing, 48(6)*:605–612.

Bryant, A. (2002). Re-grounding grounded theory. *Journal of Information Technology Theory and Application, 4(1)*:25–42.

Bryant, A. (2003, January). A constructive/ist response to Glaser. *FQS: Forum for Qualitative Social Research, 4(1)*, www.qualitative-research. net/fqs/-texte/1-03/1-03bryant-e.htm [Accessed 03-14-2003].

Bulmer, M. (1984). *The Chicago School of Sociology.* Chicago: University of Chicago Press.

Burawoy, M. (1991). The extended case study. In M. Burawoy, A. Burton, A. A. Ferguson, K. Fox, J. Gamson, N. Gartrell, L. Hurst, C. Kurzman, L. Salzinger, J. Schiffman, & S. Ui (Eds.), *Ethnography Unbound : Power and Resistance in the Modern Metropolis* (pp. 271–290). Berkeley: University of California Press.

Castellani, B., Castellani, J., & Spray, S. L. (2003). Grounded neural networking: Modeling complex quantitative data. *Symbolic Interaction, 26(4)*: 577–589.

Charmaz. K. (2000). Constructivist and objectivist grounded theory. In N. K. Denzin & Y. Lincoln (Eds.), *Handbook of Qualitative Research, 2nd ed.* (pp. 509–535). Thousand Oaks, CA: Sage.

Charmaz, K. (2002). Grounded theory analysis. In J. F. Gubrium & J. A. Holstein (Eds.), *Handbook of Interview Research* (pp. 675–694). Thousand Oaks, CA: Sage.

Charmaz, K. (2003). Grounded theory. In Jonathan A. Smith (Ed.), *Qualitative Psychology: A Practical Guide to Research Methods* (pp. 81–110). London: Sage.

Charmaz, K. (2005). Grounded theory in the 21*st* century: A qualitative method for advancing social justice research. Forthcoming in N. Denzin & Y. Lincoln (Eds.), *Handbook of Qualitative Research, 3rd ed.* Thousand Oaks, CA: Sage.

Charmaz, K. (2006). *Constructing Grounded Theory: A Practical Guide Through Qualitative Analysis.* London: Sage.

Charmaz, K. & Henwood, K. (2007). Grounded theory. In C. Willig & W. Stainton-Rogers (Eds.), *Handbook of Qualitative Research in Psychology.* London: Sage 240–259.

Clarke, A. E. (2003). Situational analyses: Grounded theory mapping after the postmodern turn. *Symbolic Interaction, 26*, 553–576.

Clarke, A. E. (2005). *Situational Analysis: Grounded Theory After the Postmodern Turn.* Thousand Oaks, CA: Sage.

Clarke, A. E. (2006). Feminism, grounded theory, and situational analysis. In S. Hess-Biber & D. Leckenby (Eds.), *Handbook of Feminist Research Methods.* Thousand Oaks, CA: Sage.

Conrad, P. (1990). Qualitative research on chronic illness: A commentary on method and conceptual development. *Social Science & Medicine, 30*, 1257–1263.

Corbin, J. & Strauss, A. L. (1987). Accompaniments of chronic illness: Changes in body, self, biography, and biographical time. In J. A. Roth & P. Conrad (Eds.), *Research in the Sociology of Health Care,* Vol. 6. *The Experience and Management of Chronic Illness* (pp. 249–281). Greenwich, CT: JAI Press.

Corbin, J. & Strauss, A. L. (1988). *Unending Work and Care: Managing Chronic Illness at Home.* San Francisco: Jossey-Bass.

Dey, I. (1999). *Grounding Grounded Theory.* San Diego: Academic Press.

Dey, I. (2004). Grounded theory. In C. Seale, G. Gobo, J. F. Gubrium, & D. Silverman (Eds.), *Qualitative Research Practice* (pp. 80–93). London: Sage.

Ellis, C. (1995). Emotional and ethical quagmires of returning to the field. *Journal of Contemporary Ethnography, 24(1)*: 68–98.

Fielding, N. G. & Lee, R. M. (1998). *Computer Analysis and Qualitative Data.* London: Sage.

Glaser, B. G. (1978). *Theoretical Sensitivity.* Mill Valley, CA: The Sociology Press.

Glaser, B. G. (1992). *Basics of Grounded Theory Analysis.* Mill Valley, CA: The Sociology Press.

Glaser, B. G. (1998). *Doing Grounded Theory: Issues and Discussions.* Mill Valley, CA: Sociology Press.

Glaser, B. G. (2001). *The Grounded Theory Perspective: Conceptualization Contrasted with Description.* Mill Valley, CA: The Sociology Press.

Glaser, B. G. (2002). Constructivist grounded theory? Forum qualitative Sozialforschung/ Forum: *Qualitative Social Research [On-line Journal], 3.* Available at: http://www.qualitative-research.net/fqs-texte/3-02/3-02glaser-e-htm

Glaser, B. G. (2003). *Conceptualization Contrasted with Description.* Mill Valley, CA: Sociology Press.

Glaser, B. G. & Strauss, A. L. (1965). *Awareness of Dying.* Chicago: Aldine.

Glaser, B. G. & Strauss, A. L. (1967). *The Discovery of Grounded Theory.* Chicago: Aldine.

Glaser, B. G. & Strauss, A. L. (1968). *Time for Dying.* Chicago: Aldine.

Goffman, E. (1959). *The Presentation of Self in Everyday Life.* Garden City, NY: Doubleday Anchor Books.

Goffman, E. (1961). *Asylums.* Garden City, NY: Doubleday Anchor Books.

Goffman, E. (1963). *Stigma.* Englewood Cliffs, NJ: Prentice-Hall.

Goulding, C. (2002). *Grounded Theory: A Practical Guide for Management, Business, and Market Researchers.* London: Sage

Henwood, K. & Pidgeon, N. (2003). Grounded theory in psychological research. In P. M. Camic, J. E. Rhodes, & L. Yardley (Eds.), *Qualitative Research in Psychology: Expanding Perspectives in Methodology and Design* (pp. 131–155). Washington, DC: American Psychological Association.

Hildebrand, Bruno. (2000/2004). Anselm Strauss. In U. Flick, E. Von Kardorff, & I. Steinke (Eds.), *A Companion to Qualitative Research* (pp. 17–23). London: Sage.

Hughes, E. C. (1958). *Men and Their Work.* Glencoe, IL: Free Press.

Junker, B. H. (1960). *Field work: An introduction to the social sciences.* Chicago: University of Chicago Press.

Kahn, R. L. & Cannell, C. F. (1957). *The Dynamics of Interviewing.* New York: Wiley.

Kelle, U. (2004). Computer assisted qualitative data analysis. In Clive Seale, Giampietro Gobo, Jaber F. Gubrium, & David Silverman (Eds.), *Qualitative Research Practice* (pp. 479–483). London: Sage.

Kelle, U. (2005, May). 'Emergence' vs. 'forcing': A crucial problem of 'grounded theory' Reconsidered [52 paragraphs]. *Forum Qualitative Sozialforsung/ Forum Qualitative Sociology* [On-line journal] 6,2 Art. 27. Available at http/www.qualitative-research. net/fqs.texte-2-05/05-2-27-e.htm [Accessed: 05-30-2005].

LaRossa, R. (2005). Grounded theory methods and qualitative family research. *Journal of Marriage and Family 67 (November):*837–857.

Layder, D. (1998). *Sociological practice: Linking theory and social research.* London: Sage.

Lazarsfeld, P. & Rosenberg, M. (Eds.). (1955). *The Language of Social Research: A Reader in the Methodology of Social Research.* Glencoe, IL: Free Press.

Locke, K. (2001). *Grounded Theory in Management Research.* Thousand Oaks, CA: Sage.

Lofland, Lyn H. (1980). Reminiscences of classic Chicago. *Urban Life, 9:*251–281.

Lonkila, M. (1995). Grounded theory as an emerging paradigm for computer-assisted qualitative data analysis. In Kelle, U. (Ed.), *Computer-aided Qualitative Data Analysis: Theory, Methods and Practice* (pp. 41–51). London: Sage.

Maines, David R. (2001). *The Faultline of Consciousness: A View of Interactionism in Sociology.* New York: Aldine de Gruyter.

May, K. (1996). Diffusion, dilution or distillation? The case of grounded theory method. *Qualitative Health Research, 6(3):*309–311.

Mead, G. H. (1932). *Philosophy of the present.* LaSalle, IL: Open Court Press.

Melia, K. M. (1987). *Learning and Working: The Occupational Socialization of Nurses.* London: Tavistock.

Melia, K. M. (1996). Rediscovering Glaser. *Qualitative Health Research, 6(3):*368–378.

Meyer, G. A. (2002). The art of watching out: Vigilance in women who have migraine headaches. *Qualitative Health Research, 12(9):*1220–1234.

Miller, D. E. (2000). Mathematical dimensions of qualitative research. *Symbolic Interaction, 23:*399–402.

Mills, J., Bonner, A. & Francis, K. (2006). The development of constructivist grounded theory. *International Journal of Qualitative Methods, 5(1):*1–10.

Morse, J. M. (1995). The significance of saturation. *Qualitative Health Research, 5:*147–149.

Peirce, C. S. (1938/1958). *Collected Papers.* Cambridge: Harvard University Press.

Pidgeon, N. F. & Henwood, K. L. (1995). Grounded theory: Practical implementation. In J. T. E. Richardson

(Ed.), *Handbook of Qualitative Research Methods for Psychology and the Social Sciences* (pp. 86–101), Leicester: British Psychological Society Books.

Pidgeon, N. F. & Henwood, K. L. (2004). Grounded theory. In M. Hardy & A. Bryman (Eds.), *Handbook of Data Analysis* (pp. 625–648). London: Sage.

Platt, J. (1996). *A History of Sociological Research Methods in America, 1920–1960*. New York: Cambridge University Press.

Reichert, J. (2000/2004). Abduction, deduction and induction in qualitative research. In U. Flick, E. Von Kardorff, & I. Steinke (Eds.), *A Companion to Qualitative Research* (pp. 159–164). London: Sage.

Rennie, D., Phillips, J. R., & Quartaro, G. K. (1988). Grounded theory: A promising approach to conceptualisation in Psychology. *Canadian Psychology, 29(2)*:139–150.

Richardson, L. (1993). Interrupting discursive spaces: Consequences for the sociological self. In N. K. Denzin (Ed.), *Studies in Symbolic Interaction,* Vol. 14 (pp. 77–83). Greenwich, CT: JAI Press.

Rock, P. (1979). *The Making of Symbolic Interactionism.* London: Macmillan.

Rosenthal, G. (2004). Biographical research. In C. Seale, G. Gobo, J. F. Gubrium, & D. Silverman (Eds.), *Qualitative Research Practice* (pp. 48–64). London: Sage.

Schreiber, R. S. & Stern, P. N. (Eds.) (2001). *Using Grounded Theory in Nursing*. New York: Springer Publication Company.

Seale, C. (1999). *The Quality of Qualitative Research.* London: Sage.

Star, S. L. (1989). *Regions of the Mind: Brain Research and the Quest for Scientific Certainty.* Stanford, CA: Stanford University Press.

Stern, P. N. (1980). Grounded theory methodology: its uses and processes. *Image,* 12, 20–23.

Stern, P. N. (1994). Eroding grounded theory. In J. Morse (Ed.), *Critical issues in qualitative research methods* (pp. 212–223). Thousand Oaks, CA: Sage.

Strauss, A. (1987). *Qualitative Analysis for Social Scientists.* New York: Cambridge University Press.

Strauss, A. (1993). *Continual Permutations of Action.* New York: Aldine de Gruyter.

Strauss, A. L. (1959/1969). *Mirrors and Masks.* Mill Valley, CA: The Sociology Press.

Strauss, A. L. (1961). *Images of the American city.* Chicago: University of Chicago Press.

Strauss, A. & Corbin, J. (1990). *Basics of Qualitative Research: Grounded Theory Procedures and Techniques.* Newbury Park, CA: Sage.

Strauss, A. & Corbin, J. (1998). *Basics of Qualitative Research: Grounded Theory Procedures and Techniques, 2nd edn.* Thousand Oaks, CA: Sage.

Urquhart, C. (2003). Re-grounding grounded theory- or reinforcing old prejudices?: A brief response to Bryant. *Journal of Information Technology Theory and Application, 4*:43–54.

Urquhart, C. (2007 forthcoming). The evolving nature of the grounded theory method: The case of the information systems discipline. In A. Bryant & K. Charmaz (Eds.), *Handbook of Grounded Theory.* London: Sage.

Wilson, H. S. & Hutchinson, S. A. (1996). Methodologic mistakes in grounded theory. *Nursing Research, 45(2)*:122–124.

Wuest, J. (1995). Feminist grounded theory: An exploration of the congruency and tensions between two traditions in knowledge discovery. *Qualitative Health Research, 5(1)*:125–137.

Wuest, J. (2001). Precarious ordering: Toward a formal theory of women's caring. *Health Care for Women International, 22(1–2)*:167–178.

28

Documents and Action

Lindsay Prior

Tis writ, 'In the beginning was the Word'.
I pause, to wonder what is here inferred. …
The spirit comes to guide me in my need,
I write, 'In the beginning was the Deed'.
Goethe, *Faust, Part One*.

The dynamic connection between words, writing, and action that is highlighted in the extract from Goethe's *Faust* constitutes the central theme of this chapter. Oddly it is a theme that is rarely taken up with issues relating to social research, despite the fact that writing plays such a large part in everyday culture. Indeed, in our age and our world, writing is more often than not seen as being somewhat divorced from action – as something static, immutable and isolated from human deed – lodged as it is in books, libraries and archives. Yet the plain fact is that writing is itself a form of action and can even serve to structure significant features of interaction.

Writing is not of course co-terminus with documentation; rather it is contained within documentation (along with numerous other human creations such as maps, architectural plans, film, photographs and electronic web pages). However, in this chapter I will not be overly concerned with drawing distinctions between writing, text, records and documentation, but will merely refer to documents in a generic sense – that is, as readable matter.

As someone who has called upon and extensively used documents in social research, it seems to me that they always enter into social affairs in two distinct modes: (a) as receptacles of content; and (b) as agents in networks of action. In what follows I intend to illustrate by the use of examples how a researcher might relate to these two modes. My examples are drawn mostly from my own work and therefore concern matters affecting health, illness and medicine – the areas in which I do my research. However, the discerning reader should not be misled by the specificity of the examples, and should be able to see how an investigator in other fields of inquiry might extend the strategies discussed herein to their own areas of interest.

As far as the social sciences are concerned, most of the research that uses or calls upon documents focuses mainly on the collection and analysis of document content – and that is where our own starting point is to be found. Indeed, a focus on documents as containers for content is well established in the social sciences. Documents in this frame can be approached as sources of information, and the writing and images that they contain scoured for appropriate data. Thus, letters, texts, photographs, adverts, biographies and autobiographies, as well as documents containing statistical data are typically regarded as a resource for the social science researcher – see, for example, Plummer (2001) and Scott (1990, 2006). Usually, various kinds of content analysis are adopted for such approaches – see Bryman (2004), Krippendorf (2004) and May (2001). Content analysis can also blend into discourse analysis – a form of analysis that examines how objects and relations between objects are represented and structured by means of text and talk (Wood, 2000).

On occasion, these relatively static forms of analysis can be extended so as to study documents as 'topic', rather than resource – in which case the focus is, in part, on the ways in which any given document came to assume its actual content and structure. This latter approach is akin to what Foucault (1972) might have called the 'archaeology of documentation' – looking, for example, at the first points at which certain objects in the world are mentioned and come into being via documentation, or revealing the ways in which systems of classification of things in the world – birds, flowers, viruses and the like – change at specific points in time. Some implications of this style of research will also be examined in the following section.

Approaching documents as topic rather than resource can, however, open up a further dimension of analysis. It concerns an examination of the ways in which documents are used in social interaction and how they function. Indeed, in this vein it is evident that during recent decades new approaches to the study of documents have emerged. In the field of sociology these new visions may be seen to relate, in part, to developments in actor-network theory or ANT (Law and Hassard, 1999). In history and the history of science they relate to the newly emergent 'geographies of knowledge' (Livingstone, 2005). In all cases the key theme involves a consideration of documents as objects and actors in a web of activity. This kind of

strategy will be discussed in the section entitled 'Studying documents in action'.

Examining the role of documents in a network generates questions about what documents 'do', rather than what they 'say' – though in the messy way of the world such distinctions hold only at a conceptual rather than an empirical level. Yet, by focusing on 'doing' we come to see that documents not only enter into human affairs as actors, but can also structure such affairs – often in fine detail. Consequently, in the section entitled 'Documents in interaction' I will concentrate on word and deed – showing how documents can influence episodes of human interaction and thereby enter into the research frame as active agents and something other than mere containers of content.

STUDYING CONTENT

Given that documents are normally viewed as little more than containers of content, the study of the material lodged within documents usually takes pride of place in relevant social scientific research strategies. Thus, letters, diaries, wills, biographies, newspaper stories, or whatever, can be scrutinised for their rhetoric, their syntax or even just for 'themes'. In this respect, Glaser and Strauss (1967: 163), argued that, in matters of sociological research, documents ought to be regarded as akin 'to an anthropologist's informant or a sociologist's interviewee'.

Naturally, the use of documents as 'informants' stretches much further back into the social sciences than the 1960s. For example, in one of the earliest sociological studies of the twentieth century Thomas and Znaniecki (1958; orig. 1918) collected together and analysed letters written by Polish immigrants to the USA. The use of immigrant letters as a source of social scientific data was probably not original – even in 1918 when the first volume of the *'Polish Peasant'* was published – but it was, nevertheless, insightful. W. I. Thomas, in particular, was concerned with individual attitudes – towards possessions, the family, social relationships and the like. The immigrant letter in this respect was seen to function as a repository of attitudes. For instance, the very fact that such letters were written at all, indicated that Polish immigrants were ready to invest a considerable amount of time and effort in maintaining family links across two continents. On the other hand, the actual content of the letters suggested to Thomas that in many key respects social solidarity was breaking down in the Polish community. Thus, the letters were said to reveal a considerable degree of conflict about such matters as marriage partners and other family relationships. As with many researchers Thomas and Znaniecki can be accused of finding in the data only what they wished to see – a common failing in analyses of content – and it is clear that theme of 'social disorganisation' was already firmly implanted in the sociology of W. I. Thomas well before he had looked at any letters. It is not surprising, therefore, that social disorganisation in the American urban Polish community is what Thomas saw the letters to reveal, but the *Polish Peasant* nevertheless gave a spur to the use of such documents in the study of contemporary culture and history. In sociology and anthropology during subsequent decades there were a sizeable number of studies that used diaries, letters, biographies and autobiographies as life histories and as important sources of social scientific data (Angrosino, 1989). Plummer (2001) provides an excellent overview of the field and indicates how the use and study of such materials came to be associated with distinct methods of social scientific inquiry (as is the case with 'biographical' methods, for example).

Scouring newspapers and other documents for supportive stories or evidence is one way of approaching document content, but a more systematic approach would require both an appreciation of the 'population' of documents that may be available for sampling (Hill, 1993), and of the entire content of the documents selected – looking at the segments that fail to fit hypotheses and theories as well as those that support hypotheses and theories. In that respect Glaser and Strauss (1967) were probably among the first to suggest a rigorous

approach to the study of documentation as 'informant'. Insofar as rigour applies to content analysis – whether it is from a newspaper story, a life history, a police report on a crime scene or a social work report on a person with multiple problems – such analysis can take any one of a number of routes. In my own case, I usually like to begin by identifying all of the words used in a document as well as the number of times that any given word is used. (This can be achieved through the use of simple concordance programmes that are freely available on the WWW.) By implication, content analysis necessitates both enumeration and understanding of the various words lodged within a text. For example, in Table 28.1, I have provided an indication of the number of times that particular words appeared in a patient support group leaflet for people who suffer from chronic fatigue syndrome – CFS (also known in the UK as 'M.E'. and in the USA as CFIDS). Given the name of the condition, the appearance in the document of 'fatigue' and 'chronic' over 50 times apiece is not perhaps surprising. However, it is interesting to note that viruses seem to be associated with whatever is going on in the document (23 citations), as well as an entity referred to as fibromyalgia (18 citations), depression (14), genes (4)

Table 28.1   Occurrence of selected words in a 2315-word patient-support group leaflet on Chronic Fatigue Syndrome

Fatigue	55
Chronic	51
Illness	50
Syndrome	46
Research	29
Virus/Viral/Virology	23
Disease	19
Fibromyalgia	18
Depression	14
Immune/Immune-related/Immunology	9
Genetic	4
Psychology/psychological	4
Neurology/neurological	4
Psychoneuroimmunology	2
Psychiatric/ Psychiatrists	2
Mental	1
Mind	1

Source: Prior, 2003.

and something called psychoneuroimmunology (2). The simple presence of these words is worthy of note and for someone who knows the arguments and debates associated with the diagnosis and treatment of CFS they are all highly significant. In general, however, rather than a focus on individual words, it is usually more important for the researcher to grasp (a) how the words relate to each other and (b) what is being implied by their use. Let us consider a brief example, by moving up a level and looking at sentences and phrases rather than just words. Here is an extract from the aforementioned WWW document.

'Is CFS genetic?
    The cause of the illness is not yet known. Current theories are looking at the possibilities of neuroendocrine dysfunction, viruses, environmental toxins, genetic predisposition, or a combination of these. For a time it was thought that Epstein-Barr virus (EBV), the cause of mononucleosis, might cause CFS but recent research has discounted this idea. The illness seems to prompt a chronic immune reaction in the body, however it is not clear that this is in response to any actual infection – this may only be a dysfunction of the immune system itself.

A number of things are evident from the passage – such as the cause of the illness being unknown; the possibility of the illness being caused by toxins, viruses, or endocrine disorder; and the fact that the illness might be 'genetic', or caused by immune dysfunction. Indeed, the suggestion is that whatever the cause might be, it is likely to be a physiological (possibly neurological) rather than, say, a psychological cause. Indeed later on in the document we get the following statement:

Emerging illnesses such as CFS typically go through a period of many years before they are accepted by the medical community, and during that interim time patients who have these new, unproven illnesses are all too often dismissed as being "psychiatric cases". This has been the experience with CFS as well.

So it is also clear that somebody somewhere has argued that CFS might be related in some way to psychological or psychiatric conditions – but the author of this document rejects such a claim because that would be to suggest that CFS is being 'dismissed' or not 'accepted' as a real illness simply because it is 'unproven'. In fact, were I to produce the document in full it would be reasonably easy to see that throughout the text there is a tension between the claims of the writer – who asserts variously that CFS is a 'real' and essentially 'physical disease' – and some unknown others who have claimed that CFS is related to depression, anxiety and other psychological problems. (Similar tensions are evident in debates concerning the nature of fibromyalgia – also cited above.) By examining such tensions in the chosen text, the analyst is drawn into an examination of a rhetoric of illness – concerning the ways in which a disorder of unknown cause is represented and understood by different parties. It is at that point, however, that content analysis tends to drift into discourse analysis.

Unlike content analysis, discourse analysis is an awkward concept to capture. It has essentially concerned the ways in which things and our knowledge of things are structured and represented through text and talk. For instance, there is a considerable tradition within social studies of science and technology for examining the role of scientific rhetoric in structuring our notions of 'nature' and the place of human beings within nature. The role and structure of scientific rhetoric in text has, for example, figured in the work of Bazerman (1988), Gross (1996), Latour and Woolgar (1979), Myers (1990) and Woolgar (1988); and even been extended beyond text and into the realm of visual representations (Lynch and Woolgar, 1990) and everyday talk (Gilbert and Mulkay, 1984). And in this vein there have been numerous studies examining how the objects of science, medicine and technology have been, and are, structured through discourse. One particularly interesting set of studies have been those that have concentrated attention on the concept of the 'gene' and the human genome. For example, Lily Kay (2000) analysed the role of metaphors of the gene and genetics in genetic science between the 1950s and the twenty-first century – indicating how the image of DNA as a code or text of instructions (recipe) or plan (blueprint) emerged only gradually during the second half of the twentieth century. Thus, she points out how, in the famous April 1953 *Nature* paper by Crick and Watson on DNA, the authors referred only to the *structure* of DNA – and she then investigates how the idea of using concepts of grammar and semantics to describe genetic processes emerged during the 1960s – particularly relating to work on 'messenger' RNA. Indeed, the first 'word' of the genetic code (the UUU of RNA) was not identified until 1961. Kay subsequently argues that the Nobel prize-winning work of Nirenberg and Mathei (who discovered the first word) would simply not have been possible without calling upon and utilising metaphors of communication and information science such as we have referred to above. Other writers have chosen to focus on genetic discourse in everyday culture (as reflected through news stories and the like) with equally interesting results. Thus Nelkin (2001), for instance, has noted how, in popular culture, DNA is not simply regarded as a 'code' – carrying and expressing information – but that it is also endowed with executive action. In short, DNA is represented through text as something that 'makes things' (humans, cancers, and so forth), in a deterministic system. In the following paragraph I present some of my own data (derived from talk between a doctor and a client of a cancer genetics service) to illustrate some possibilities of this kind of approach. Even though the data are derived from talk (rather than text per se), they serve to illustrate how analysis of a discourse can reveal detail about the ways in which, in any given culture, the world and the objects within it are represented and structured.

200 *Doctor*: And the genes are broken up into sections and so a gene that
201 controls a protein function in a body is not just one long coding
202 instruction it is in fact broken up into sections that then get joined
203 together. And those sections you can think of them as being volumes of
204 an encyclopaedia. Basically between the two genes there are effectively

205 50 volumes. And it takes our laboratory a week to check each one,
206 which you can then work out quite quickly that that is effectively a year
207 to check every single one. That is just the practicality of the time scale.
208 The other problem though, if you are dealing with something as big as
209 something like an encyclopaedia and you are looking for a mistake and
210 effectively what you dealing with is just a code, a series of letters, then
211 you are looking for something like a missing paragraph or sometimes just
212 a missing word, or sometimes just a missing letter. And right down to
213 just a change on one letter can be all that is needed to have disastrous
214 effects.
215 *Patient*: Yeah.

A number of issues deserve attention here. The first is the extensive use of metaphor in this exchange. In particular, genes are referred to as 'coding instructions' (lines 201–02, 210), 'volumes of an encyclopaedia' (203–04), a 'series of letters' (210), and words and/or paragraphs (211–12). And in accord with such rhetorical forms, mutations are referred to as 'missing' words, letters or paragraphs, as 'mistakes' possibly brought about by a 'change in just one letter' (213). The second issue of interest is in what may be called the actional components of the sentences that link genes to human physiology. Of particular significance is the way in which genes are said to 'control' protein functions (line 201), and genetic re-arrangements of DNA sequences (letters) are argued to be capable of having 'disastrous effects' (lines 213–14) on the human body. Such attention to the ways in which the use of tropes (such as metaphor) and syntax operate in text lead us to consider how 'things' and events in the world are structured through discourse.

It could be said that with both content and discourse analysis, researchers are essentially seeking to use documentation as 'resource' – that is as a source of data for social scientific theorising (of varying degrees of complexity). It is, however, possible to approach document content as 'topic'. The very useful distinction between resource and topic was first introduced by Zimmerman and Pollner (1971), and picking up on this distinction can encourage us to ask a different set of questions about documentation. So instead of focusing merely on what documents contain we can begin to ask how the documentation that we elect to examine came to assume the form that it did. This line of inquiry can be especially useful in the examination of the ways in which people 'sort things out' (Bowker and Star, 1999). For instance, it is often instructive in matters of social research to ask how things come to be classified in a particular way (and not other ways) and what rules are to be used to allocate objects to one realm rather than another. Thus we might, for example, ask questions concerning the 'causes' of death, disease and illness – such as what can one die of? The answer to that question is invariably constrained by the content of a World Health Organization (WHO) manual – namely, *The International Classification of Diseases and Related Health Problems* (WHO, 1992). It is often referred to in an abbreviated form as the ICD. The current edition of the manual is the tenth, and so the abbreviation is, more accurately, ICD-10. ICD-10 provides a list of all currently accepted causes of death, and they are classified into 'chapters'. Thus, there are chapters relating to diseases and disorders of the respiratory system, the circulatory system, the nervous system and so on. In different decades different diseases and causes of death are added and deleted from the manual. HIV/AIDS is an obvious case of an addition and it appears as a cause of death only in ICD-10, whilst 'old age' as a cause of death was eliminated in ICD-6. Such taxonomies reflect aspects of human culture and researching the 'archaeology' of such documents can be instructive in itself. A related publication – *The Diagnostic and Statistical Manual of Mental Disorders* (American Psychiatric Association, 2000) or DSM – is available for the classification of psychiatric (mental) conditions. One might say that the DSM provides the conceptual architecture in terms of which western culture comprehends disorders of the mind. Post-Traumatic Stress

Disorder is, for instance, recognised as a disorder only in DSM-III (first published in 1974), whilst multiple personality disorder (MPD) has undergone a few transformations and is no longer listed in the 4th-revised edition of the DSM. The inclusion and deletion of such diagnostic categories can be used as key indicators of not merely how professional and technical discourse might have altered, but also how political, legal and socio-economic processes impinge on the affairs of science and medicine (for a detailed example of the relationships between a form of scientific classification and styles of professional practice see Keating and Cambrosio, 2000).

The manufacture and standardisation of taxonomies – as well as the deployment of rules for allocating 'cases' to appropriate categories – is important for various reasons, but not least because they are indispensable to generating images of the world. For example the ways in which events relating to crime, the economy, illness and disease or education are classified and counted, is fundamental to our understanding of long-term trends and our image of contemporary happenings. And as numerous analysts of official statistical accounts of the world have demonstrated (see for example, May, 2001; Prior, 2003), for any given society we can have as much or as little illness, crime, 'success' and 'failure' as we want – depending on how, exactly, we sort things out.

Unfortunately, once we are engaged with the routine messiness of the empirical world many of these distinctions between content and discourse, topic and resource are difficult to hold to. For documents, as with most phenomena are fluid, messy and somewhat slippery objects for analysis. More importantly, and as I shall demonstrate in the next two sections, documents often appear as active agents in a universe of deeds.

STUDYING DOCUMENTS IN ACTION

A focus on documents in action tends to encourage a focus on how documents are used (function) and how they are exchanged and circulate in various communities. Naturally, documents carry content – words, images, plans, ideas, patterns and so forth – but the ways in which such content is actually called upon and how it functions cannot be determined (though it may be constrained) by an analysis of its content. Indeed once a text or document is sent out into the world there is simply no predicting how it is going to circulate and how it is going to function in specific social and cultural contexts. For this reason alone, a study of what the author(s) of a given document (text) 'meant' or intended can only ever add up to limited examination of what a document 'is'. Indeed, as the literary theorist De Certeau (1984: 170) has argued, 'Whether it is a question of newspapers or Proust, the text has a meaning only through its readers; it changes along with them; it is ordered in accordance with codes of perception that it does not control'. In this regard an interest in the reception and reading of text has formed the focus for recent histories of knowledge that seek to examine how the 'same' documents have been received and absorbed quite differently into different cultural and geographical contexts (see, for example, Burke, 2000; Livingstone, 2005).

One possible starting point for inquiries into the dynamics of documentation rests in Latour's notion of an 'immutable mobile' (1987). An immutable mobile is something that can move around, whilst – at the same time – holding its essential shape. Thus a book, or set of instructions, or a recipe, or map, can hold its shape in the ordinary everyday sense of such words, and it can also hold its shape in a relational manner. That is to say, a book has shape in (three-dimensional) space, but it also has shape as a member of a specific type of literature (say a science text, or a work of fiction, or work of science-fiction, or philosophy, or poetry or history of art). Yet for the book to retain its shape in this relational sense, a dynamic network of actors is needed. Such a network might include, for instance, authors and literary critics to identify the book as a work of science-fiction, book catalogues to classify the work, libraries in which to hold

the book, librarians to identify the literary genre of the book, readers to search out the book as science-fiction and so forth. It is in such a way that we can begin to see the book as an object within a network. More importantly, however, it is likely that our mysterious book (or text) will not simply be at the mercy of the various 'actors' in such a network but will also become an actor itself.

Perhaps the clearest image of a document as an actor arises in the case of a legally constituted 'last will and testament', which on the occasion of its final 'reading', acts. Or consider the role of various books of the *Bible* in the history of social and religious controversy – which have also served as actors (as sources of authority, as witness to evidence and so forth). And as with human actors, documents as actors can be recruited, suppressed, enrolled into the service of various interest groups – some examples of which are referred to in Prior (2003). Unfortunately, one of the problems with the concept of immutable mobiles is its emphasis on stasis. For as the objects in a network move they often become mutable and metamorphose into new objects.

A consideration of objects in a network is usually associated with a somewhat amorphous group of writers who favour what is called actor-network-theory or ANT (see, Law and Hassard, 1999). ANT is of concern to us insofar as it opens a new dimension for social research – analysing how documents are positioned in actor-networks and also how they function (act) in such networks. (In terms of ANT, non-human agents are commonly referred to as actants rather than as actors.) From our point of view, the key research questions revolve around the ways in which documents are integrated into networks and how they influence the development of the network. This kind of focus has, in some cases, led to developments in research software to explore the relational aspects of humans and documentation. In what follows I shall outline a few examples. I shall concentrate first on WWW pages as documents and sketch out how they can be approached in a variety of social scientific frameworks.

In the first instance, of course, it is clear that WWW pages can be scoured for their content alone – that is, used and interrogated as informant. For example, in a 2002 study of anti-vaccination web sites, Wolfe et al. (2002) identified 22 such WWW sites and noted that in all cases the documentation asserted that vaccines caused idiopathic illness, in 95 percent of cases that vaccines erode immunity, and in 91 percent of cases that vaccination policy was driven by profit motives rather than cares about health. These and other details concerning document content were acquired by the use of relatively simple coding techniques. The authors also noted that anti-vaccination sites used specific tactics for transmitting their messages. Thus, one favoured strategy involved the use of personal stories – often from parents who served as witnesses to the fact that vaccination caused severe illness in their children. Analysis of story structure would, of course, inveigle us into a specific style of discourse analysis – in this case perhaps one that focused on narrative rather than on rhetoric. However, there remains a further strategy for the examination of anti-vaccination sites and it involves looking at the networks that emerge out of the relations between such sites.

The possibility for examining relations between web sites is, of course, built into web sites ordinarily, for web sites contain hyperlinks (to other web pages), and by concentrating on the outlinks of the web pages it becomes possible to study how internet documents relate one to another. In recent years the task of tracing the links between such sites has been facilitated by the use of web crawlers. However, Richard Rogers, who has designed one such crawler (www.govcom.org), refers to issue networks and issue spaces rather than WWW networks, (see, Marres and Rogers, 2005). An issue network is a network of pages that acknowledge each other by way of hyperlinks. I have provided a simple example of such a network in Figure 28.1. The figure traces links between web pages of organisations who work with people with HIV/AIDS in Uganda. The starting point for the web

crawl necessitated the identification of WWW addresses for two Ugandan non-governmental organisations (NGOs) working with people with HIV/AIDS. The results of this initial crawl indicate a number of features. I have highlighted only a few of these in Figure 28.1. They concern the centrality of international organisations such as the UN, Unicef and the World Health Organisation in the document network. Surrounding those organisations are the pages of various Ugandan government organisations (such as health.go.ug), and on the periphery are the local NGOs, whilst at the very edge is the page for the Ugandan parliament.

The links between such documentation may be considered as data in themselves – and they certainly point to factors such as position (degrees of centrality, for example), density of contact, directions of contact and so forth. The links could also be considered as a map for exploring the relationships between local NGOs, international organisations and the Ugandan government. Naturally, the exploration of such links would need to be supplemented by the use of other methods and techniques (such as interview techniques or a range of ethnographic techniques), nevertheless the provision of the web map provides both a starting point and ground on which hypotheses might be generated concerning notions of, say, 'partnership' in the field of HIV/AIDS in Africa. There is, however, a feature of social activity that is only touched upon – rather than confronted – by the use of a web crawler. It involves the fact that actor-networks contain human as well as non-human actors.

By tradition, a focus on relationships between people in a network has been associated with social network analysis. Such analysis concentrates on the number of links between specific individuals, the degree to which an individual is central or peripheral to a given network, the density of interactional or contact nodes and so forth (see, Scott, 1999). However, as actor-network theorists emphasise, social networks cannot be reduced to relations between humans. Consequently, what is usually needed is an analysis of

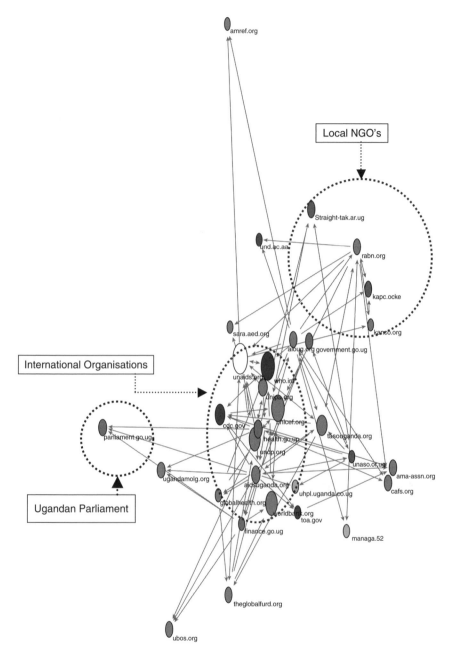

Figure 28.1 WWW links between organisations in Uganda concerned with HIV/AIDS (generated using Issuecrawler.net)

relationships between humans, organisations, and 'things' (such as documents, machines, germs or whatever). For example, Cambrosio et al. (2004) studied the nature of collaborative research networks and innovation in a specific field of biomedicine. The researchers were interested in how the people in the network collaborated, as well as the role of such things as antigen, antibody reagents (contained in bottles) and antibodies in a research network. One component of their investigation concentrated on the relationships between research workshops and research laboratories in the development of particular (HLDA) antibodies, and Cambrosio et al. sought to designed a network map of the relations that linked the institutions and workshops to the antibodies. In doing that they designed a network map – reproduced as Figure 28.2. In the context of this figure the points T, M and B represent different research workshops. The outer points represent the laboratories or research centres and the size of the circles and squares are proportional to the number of antibodies submitted by each laboratory to each workshop. We can see immediately

from the map how the relationships fan out, the relative importance of each of the three workshops and which institutions are linked to which antibodies. Antibodies are not documents, of course, but the network map illustrates how documents could be mapped into a scheme of social relations and how it could be the documents that form the focus of attention rather than the human beings. However, such maps require dedicated software that can generate visual traces of actor-networks. In the case discussed the relevant technology was provided by Réseau-Lu (see, Mogoutov et al., 2005).

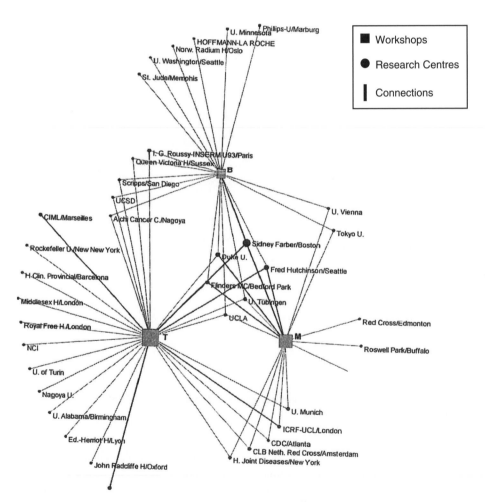

Figure 28.2 Human leucocyte differentiation antigens (HLDA) workshops research centres and antigens
Source: **Cambrosio et al., 2004.**

DOCUMENTS-IN-INTERACTION

A concern with documents-in-action does not, however, necessitate a commitment to any concept of network; whether it be of the ANT variety or otherwise. For it is possible to focus on documents-in-action in terms of traditional interactional frameworks. That is to say, it is plausible and possible to focus the research effort on examining how documents enter into ordinary everyday episodes of social interaction and how the presence of such documents influences such interaction. Sociological and other social scientific studies of schools, workplaces, hospitals, and the like are littered with observations concerning these influences but they are rarely picked up or emphasised in any coherent way. In what follows I shall provide a few simple examples of the manner in which documents can (a) enter into episodes of human interaction and (b) structure the activities of humans.

My first example arises out of consideration of an essay written by George Psathas (1979) on maps. In that essay, Psathas looked at how maps are used in everyday contexts. His specific focus was on the kind of maps that people draw and dispense for and to others so as to find the forthcoming party at 'our house' or some such. His sociological interest was on the reasoning that was implicated in the drawing of such maps. For example, he pointed out how direction maps are always drawn with reference to a destination rather than, say, to the topography of a given neighbourhood. More importantly, the use of such maps clearly implicates readers as well as writers (or in this case amateur cartographers). For readers of such maps are invariably inveigled into following the sequences drawn on the map. They are obliged, as it were, to 'perform' the route that is drawn on the map. Thus, in reading and using the map, the map reader moves herself or himself from point A to point B in a manner dictated above all by the mapmaker. Such use provides a good example of a process referred to as action-at-a-distance. It also serves to demonstrate how documents in use can structure and pattern their readers – tell the readers how to act.

In this respect, documents-in-action often take on qualities similar to those of the broom set in motion by Goethe's *Sorcerer's Apprentice*, or the monster unleashed on the world by Mary Shelley's *Frankenstein* – that is to say they take on the qualities of human creations that act back on their creators. Exactly how documentation can influence performances of this nature is a focus that is rarely given any emphasis in qualitative research, yet the detail of my next example underlines how central the role of documentation can be.

My second example is drawn from my own work and illustrates how documentation can form the occasion for talk and interaction; how documentation is drawn into interactions and, again, how it has effects on the performance of the interaction. The data are provided in Figure 28.3. The talk therein was gathered from a study of work in a cancer genetics clinic. In this instance a clinical geneticist (designated CG) and nurse counsellors (designated NC) are discussing their understanding of the degree to which a given patient is at risk of inheriting a certain type of cancer mutation. The episode begins with one of the NCs reading a letter (lines 1–9) of referral to the clinic, and the letter frames the ensuing discussion. A second document enters into the frame at line 11 – it's a family history, or pedigree as it is known in clinical genetics. The pedigree traces the ancestry of the patient who is the focus of the discussion, and it does so in a drawing that contains symbols for males and females and lines linking those who are related (see lines 12–13 of the data extract). In this case, the drawing has been composed by what Latour (1987) would refer to as an 'inscription device' (known here as 'Cyrillic'). Cyrillic has also calculated the numerical risk (line 19) of inheritance. Both documents are clearly central to the manner in which the interaction is sequenced and structured. Thus documents are read (lines 1–9) whilst others listen; they are referred to as the occasion for the talk (lines 11–19); they are pointed at (line 14); and used as evidence and counter evidence (lines 14–19). What's more the documents are linked to the speakers in distinct ways

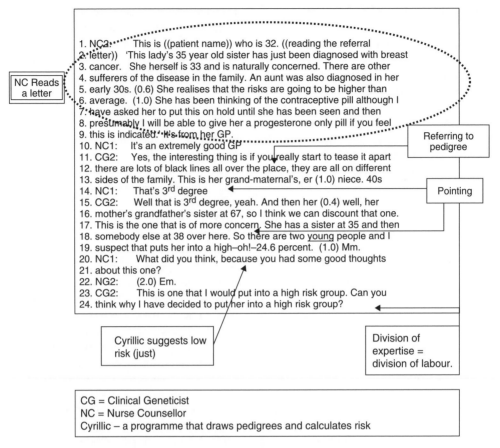

1. NC2:   This is ((patient name)) who is 32. ((reading the referral
2. letter))   'This lady's 35 year old sister has just been diagnosed with breast
3. cancer.   She herself is 33 and is naturally concerned. There are other
4. sufferers of the disease in the family. An aunt was also diagnosed in her
5. early 30s. (0.6) She realises that the risks are going to be higher than
6. average. (1.0) She has been thinking of the contraceptive pill although I
7. have asked her to put this on hold until she has been seen and then
8. presumably I will be able to give her a progesterone only pill if you feel
9. this is indicated.' It's from her GP.
10. NC1:   It's an extremely good GP
11. CG2:   Yes, the interesting thing is if you really start to tease it apart
12. there are lots of black lines all over the place, they are all on different
13. sides of the family. This is her grand-maternal's, er (1.0) niece. 40s
14. NC1:   That's 3rd degree
15. CG2:   Well that is 3rd degree, yeah. And then her (0.4) well, her
16. mother's grandfather's sister at 67, so I think we can discount that one.
17. This is the one that is of more concern. She has a sister at 35 and then
18. somebody else at 38 over here. So there are two young people and I
19. suspect that puts her into a high–oh!–24.6 percent. (1.0) Mm.
20. NC1:   What did you think, because you had some good thoughts
21. about this one?
22. NG2:   (2.0) Em.
23. CG2:   This is one that I would put into a high risk group. Can you
24. think why I have decided to put her into a high risk group?

NC Reads a letter

Referring to pedigree

Pointing

Cyrillic suggests low risk (just)

Division of expertise = division of labour.

CG = Clinical Geneticist
NC = Nurse Counsellor
Cyrillic – a programme that draws pedigrees and calculates risk

Figure 28.3   Text & documentation underpin the division of labour

and in clear sequences, and finally serve to underline the ways in which the division of labour (between 'doctors' and 'nurses') is underpinned in both this episode and the clinic at large (lines 23–24).

This second example also raises a number of other important issues that lay beyond the scope of this chapter; namely, how talk is to be transcribed and translated into writing (as has been done in Figure 28.3), and what conventions are to be deployed so as to render active talk into inert text.

CONCLUSIONS

The closing example – as shown in Figure 28.3 – illustrates the multidimensional features of documentation in the social world.

Documents have content – words, sentences, phrases – and content can be counted and classified and compared (one document to another). A study of document content can form an excellent starting point for social researchers – illustrating how 'things' are described and linked. Social researchers may also be interested in how those same things are represented and structured through language – in which case the researcher is drawn into various forms of discourse analysis. These days of course there are various types of software that can be called upon and used as aids to content and discourse analysis. At the most basic level a researcher can use a simple concordance programme. Such a programme would commonly provide a list and count of words used in a text (together with a facility for locating word use in sentence context). More sophisticated text analysis programmes also offer ways to recognise and extract 'concepts' out of a text and to undertake a conceptual analysis of content. (For some pointers on such programmes, see: http://caqdas.soc.surrey.ac.uk/bibliography.htm.) As with all forms of data analysis, however, the software cannot provide a substitute for thinking or for social scientific insight, and it is clear from some of the aforementioned references that the most imaginative forms of analysis rely on concepts that emerge from the sociological imagination rather than from simple data mining exercises.

These two broad kinds of analysis – content and discourse – in various guises tend to dominate in the collection and analysis of documents and documentary evidence. For the most part, both styles of research tend to treat the text as a static object – as something to be read and understood. Another way of putting this is to say that both styles of analysis use documents as 'resource' rather than 'topic'. In other words, text and documentation are there to be scoured for evidence or for facts. Consideration as to how the text assumes the shape that it does or, indeed, what the text does is left in abeyance. Yet during recent years there has been an emergent emphasis on the relational properties of documentation – in the manner described previously. These interests have been driven by the development of theoretical concerns (such as in ANT) and developments in technology that enable us to examine the traces that documentation produce. The clearest example of this trend relates to the links between WWW pages – which, with the use of web crawlers, can be seen to form a network. One could also extend this kind of analysis to citations of published work (citation networks); to an examination of links between e-mail messages, or possibly to telephone text messages (although the data for the latter would need to be derived form verbal answers to questions about networks rather than from electronic traces). The use of software such as *Réseau-Lu* also enables us to visualise networks of humans and things – including documents as things.

However, as I have demonstrated, a focus on documents as 'actors' need not be constrained by thinking about networks, and research into documentation can be allied to a variety of interactional approaches. Indeed, in the modern world, documents enter into almost all episodes of human interaction. Given such omnipresence it remains puzzling why social science relies so heavily on 'talk' rather than text as the key source of research data.

REFERENCES

American Psychiatric Association. (2000) *Diagnostic and Statistical Manual of Mental Disorders. DSM-IV-TR*. Washington, DC: American Psychiatric Association.

Angrosino, M.V. (1989) *Documents of Interaction. Biography, Autobiography, and Life History in Social Science Perspective*. Gainsville, FL: University of Florida Press.

Bazerman, C. (1988) *Shaping Written Knowledge. The Genre and Activity of the Experimental Article in Science*. Madison, WI: University of Wisconsin Press.

Bowker, G.C. and Star, S.L. (1999) *Sorting Things Out. Classification and its Consequences*. Cambridge: MA: MIT Press.

Bryman, A. (2004) *Social Research Methods. 2nd Ed*. Oxford: Oxford University Press.

Burke, P. (2000) *A Social History of Knowledge. From Guttenberg to Diderot*. Cambridge: Polity Press.

Cambrosio, A., Keating, P. and Mogoutov, A. (2004) Mapping collaborative work and innovation in biomedicine. *Social Studies of Science*, 34:3: 325–364.

De Certeau. M. (1984) *The Practice of Everyday Life*. Tr. S. Rendall. London: University of California Press.

Foucault, M. (1972) *The Archaeology of Knowledge*. Tr. A. Sheridan. NY: Pantheon.

Gilbert, G.N. and Mulkay, M. (1984) *Opening Pandora's Box. A Sociological Analysis of Scientists' Discourse*. Cambridge: Cambridge University Press.

Glaser, B.G. and Strauss, A.L. (1967) *The Discovery of Grounded Theory. Strategies for Qualitative Research*. New York: Aldine De Gruyter.

Goethe, J.W. (1949) Faust. Part One. Trans. P. Wayne. Harmondworth: Penguin.

Gross, A.G. (1996) *The Rhetoric of Science*. Cambridge, MA: Harvard University Press.

Hill, M. (1993) *Archival Strategies and Techniques*. London: Sage.

Kay, L.E. (2000) *Who Wrote the Book of Life? A History of the Genetic Code*. Stanford, CA: Stanford University Press.

Keating, P. and Cambrosio, A. (2000) '"Real compared to what?" Diagnosing leukemias and lymphomas', in M. Lock, A. Young and A. Cambrosio (eds.) *Living and Working with the New Medical Technologies. Intersections of Inquiry*. Cambridge: Cambridge University Press. pp. 103–134.

Krippendorf, K. (2004) Content analysis. *An Introduction to its Methodology*. 2nd *Ed.* London: Sage.

Latour, B. (1987) *Science in Action. How to Follow Scientists and Engineers Through Society*. Milton Keynes: Open University Press.

Latour, B. and Woolgar, S. (1979) *Laboratory Life. The Social Construction of Scientific Facts*. London: Sage.

Law, J. and Hassard, J. (eds.) (1999) *Actor-Network Theory and After*. Oxford: Blackwell.

Livingstone, D.N. (2005) Text, talk, and testimony: geographical reflections on scientific habits. An afterword. *British Society for the History of Science*, 38:1:93–100.

Lynch, M. and Woolgar, S. (eds.) (1990) *Representation in Scientific Practice*. Cambridge, MA: MIT Press.

Marres, N. and Rogers, R. (2005) Recipe for tracing the fate of issues and their publics on the web, in B. Latour and P. Wiebel (eds.) *Making Things Public. Atmospheres of Democracy*. Cambridge, MA: MIT Press. pp. 922–935.

May, T. (2001) *Social Research. Issues, Methods and Process*. 3rd *Ed.* Buckingham: Open University Press.

Mogoutov, A., Cambrosio, A. and Keating, P. (2005) Making collaborative networks visible, in B. Latour and P. Wiebel (eds.) *Making Things Public. Atmospheres of Democracy*. Cambridge, MA: MIT Press. pp. 342–345.

Myers, G. (1990) *Writing Biology. Texts in the Construction of Scientific Knowledge*. London: University of Wisconsin Press.

Nelkin, D. (2001) Molecular metaphors. The gene in popular discourse. *Nature Reviews*, 2:555–559.

Plummer, K. (2001) *Documents of Life.2. An invitation to critical humanism*. London: Sage.

Prior, L. (2003) *Using Documents in Social Research*. London: Sage.

Psathas, G. (1979) Organizational features of direction maps, in G. Psathas (ed.) *Everyday Language. Studies in Ethnomethodology*. New York: Irvington Publishers. pp. 203–225.

Scott, J. (1990) *A Matter of Record. Documentary Sources in Social Research*. Cambridge: Polity Press.

Scott, J. (1999) *Social Network Analysis*. London: Sage.

Scott, J.P. (ed.) (2006) *Documentary Research*. 4 Vols. London: Sage.

Thomas, W.I. and Znaniecki, F. (1958) *The Polish Peasant in Europe and America*. New York: Dover.

Wolfe, R.M., Sharp, L.K. and Lipsky, M.S. (2002) Content and design attributes of anti-vaccination websites. *Journal of the American Medical Association*, 287:24:3245–3248.

Wood, L.A. (2000) *Doing Discourse Analysis. Methods for Studying Action in Talk and Text*. London: Sage.

Woolgar, S. (1988) *Science: The Very Idea*. London: Tavistock.

World Health Organisation. (1992) *International Statistical Classification of Diseases and Related Health Problems. 10th Revision*. London: HMSO. 3 Vols.

Zimmerman, D.H. and Pollner, M. (1971) The everyday world as a phenomenon, in J.D. Douglas (ed.) *Understanding Everyday Life*. London: Routledge and Kegan Paul. pp. 80–103.

29

Video and the Analysis of Work and Interaction

Christian Heath and Paul Luff

If society is conceived as interaction among individuals, the description of the forms of this interaction is the task of the science of society in its strictest and most essential sense. (Simmel, 1950: 21–2)

INTRODUCTION

It has long been recognised that video, and before that film, provide the social sciences with an unprecedented opportunity to analyse human culture and social organisation. As early as the 1880s, A.C. Haddon used film as part of his studies of the Torres Strait Islands, and in a very different vein Edward Muybridge, encouraged by Leland Stanford, used instantaneous photography to explore, amongst other things, the structure of human movement and coordination. (Prodger, 2003). Since these early beginnings we have witnessed a burgeoning interest, in particular within social anthropology in using video in qualitative research (Marks, 1995). There is for example a well-established tradition of ethnographic film that powerfully portrays

cultural organisation and everyday practice and a growing range of anthropological, and more recently sociological, research that uses video and more generally visual media, to reflect on, illustrate, and in some cases analyse, the social and institutional forms that arise in contemporary society. In this regard, it is worthwhile differentiating the substantial corpus of research and methodological reflection concerned with the use of visual media in social science research (consider for example Banks and Murphy, 1997; Curry and Clarke, 1978; Emmison and Smith, 2000; Pink, 2001a, 2001b; Rose, 2001; Ruby, 2000), from the relative paucity of material that address the ways in which video can be used to analyse everyday activities and social interaction (for instance Goodwin, 1981; Heath, 1986; Heath and Luff, 2000; Kendon, 1982; Knoblauch et al., 2006).

Rather than review the diverse ways in which the visual, and to a lesser extent video, can inform qualitative research, in this chapter we wish to briefly sketch a particular approach, a methodological orientation, that enables the analysis of audio-visual recordings of everyday activities and events. The approach draws upon methodological developments within sociology, namely ethnomethodology and conversation analysis. It directs analytic attention towards the social and interactional accomplishment of everyday activities and events. Even though this analytic orientation is only one way in which video is used in social science research, it is an approach that has proved highly productive and is of growing significance within various disciplines including sociology, anthropology and linguistics. It is an approach that has begun to throw a new and distinctive light on a variety of long-standing topics and issues in the social sciences and an approach that provides the analytic resources to address the organisation of social action across a broad and complex range of everyday and institutional environments. In recent years for example, we have seen the emergence of studies of scientific practice, surveillance, medical consultations, children's play, museum visits, the household, computer-mediated communication, conversational interaction, political discourse, surgical operations and architectural practice (see for example Engeström and Middleton, 1996; Goodwin, 1981, 1995; Goodwin, 1990; Goodwin and Goodwin, 1994, 1996; Heath, 1986; Heath and Luff, 2000; Knoblauch et al., 2006; LeBaron and Koschmann, 2003; Luff et al., 2000; Mondada, 2003; Streeck and Kallmeyer, 2001; Suchman, 1987; Whalen, 1995, Whalen et al., 2002). In this chapter, we draw on materials from a study of auctions and auction houses, to provide some practical guidance to using video recordings to address the social and interactional organisation of naturally occurring events.

WORKPLACE ORGANISATION & SOCIAL INTERACTION

An increasing body of video-based, qualitative research is concerned with work; in particular the social and interactional accomplishment of complex forms of organisational activity. This burgeoning corpus of research is very different from more traditional studies of work and occupational practice. However, in various ways it can be seen to evolve from some of the key methodological and analytic concerns that underpinned the emergence of organisational ethnographies. It is perhaps worthwhile providing a little background and raising one or two points that might give a sense of the potential contribution of video and this particular approach.

Work and workplace organisation have formed a pervasive concern for sociology and more generally the social sciences from their significant beginnings in the late nineteenth century. It has long been recognised that social interaction in the workplace produces and reproduces organisational forms and the various rules, procedures and dispositions that inform the daily transactions that arise between people in organisations. Parsons' (1951) analysis of the 'situation of medical practice' is exemplary in this regard, and though commonly known more for its exposition of the sick role rather than the organisational structure of the professional-client consultation, it powerfully demonstrates the ways in which patterned forms of social interaction, governed by expectations and dispositions, underpin medical work. The character of this interaction however, and the practices that enable its concerted and contingent accomplishment, remain largely unexplicated. Indeed, despite the wide-spread recognition that social interaction forms the foundation to work and occupational practice, there is a long-standing neglect in many forms of organisational analysis, of what Goffman (1983) refers to as the 'interaction order'. In turn, by neglecting the interactional foundations of organisations, we not infrequently find a disregard for the ways in which work is accomplished by participants themselves (Barley, 1996; Barley and Kunda, 2001; Silverman, 1970, 1997a, 1997b).

There are important exceptions. Since their early beginnings many qualitative studies of work and organisation have placed social interaction at the heart of analytic agenda. For example, in his insightful discussion of the methodological commitments that informed what came to be known as the post-war Chicago school, Everett Hughes suggests that the principal aim of the studies is to 'discover patterns of interaction' and that 'the subject matter of sociology is interaction' (Hughes, 1971). These methodological commitments, and in particular, the recognition that work and occupational performance evolves in, and is sustained through, interaction, gave rise to a rich and insightful body of sociological and in particular ethnographic studies of work and organisation (see for example Becker, 1963; Goffman, 1963; Roth, 1963; Strauss et al., 1964). These studies have had a profound influence on successive generations of workplace ethnography including for example Barley, 1989; Hochschild, 1983; Star, 1996; Strong, 1978; Van Maanen, 1991, and directly and indirectly given rise to parallel developments in cognitive science, anthropology and emerging fields such as Computer Supported Cooperative Work. Despite these methodological commitments, the richness and insightfulness of these ethnographies, the interaction that arises in, and sustains, organisations, the interaction through which work is accomplished in collaboration with others, can remain under-explored and sometimes unexamined. Indeed, many of the concepts that inform this ethnographic tradition: concepts such as negotiation, bargaining, career, and the like, tend to draw attention away from the details of organisational conduct – the talk, visible and material action through which people, in collaboration with others, produce and coordinate their workplace activities. Moreover, the concepts and methodological precepts that pervade qualitative studies of work and related forms of ethnography, whilst powerfully resonating with field studies and naturalistic observation, do not necessarily lend themselves to the analysis of video and in particular to examining the wealth of detail made available through audio-visual recordings of everyday events.

Over the past few decades however the social and interactional foundations of workplace activities has received sustained sociological attention. Perhaps the most significant contribution in this regard are studies that draw upon ethnomethodology and conversation analysis and form 'part of a programme of work undertaken ... to explore the possibility of achieving a naturalistic observation discipline that could deal with the details of social action(s) rigorously, empirically, and formally' (Schegloff and Sacks, 1973:233). Building on the analysis of conversation, we have witnessed the emergence of a broad range of studies of talk in institutional settings, primarily based on audio-recordings, that address the organisation of a range of workplace activities including legal interrogation, news interviews, political oratory, diagnosis in medical consultations, the delivery of bad news, counselling and therapy and classroom instruction and teaching (see for example Atkinson, 1984; Atkinson and Drew, 1980; Boden, 1994, Boden and Zimmerman, 1991; Clayman and Heritage, 2002; Drew and Heritage, 1992; Heritage and Maynard, 2006; Maynard, 2003; Peräkylä, 1995; Silverman, 1997a, 1997b; Whalen et al., 1988; Zimmerman, 1992). As Heritage (1984, 1997) points out, the sequential and turn organisation of talk has provided a critical resource for these studies as they explicate the ways in which highly specialised forms of activity embody a re-specification of the interactional practices that inform conversational organisation; a re-specification that enables 'institutional realities and their unique characteristics to be talked into being'.

Not withstanding the significant contribution of these studies to our understanding of work and organisation, it is recognised that the interactional accomplishment of social actions and activities involves the interplay of talk and visible conduct such as gesture and bodily comportment. It is recognised that objects and artefacts, tools and technologies, play a critical part in many activities and that the use of material resources are a pervasive and integral feature of almost all human activities not least of which those that arise in the workplace. In the last decade or so, audio-visual recordings of naturally occurring events have provided researchers with unprecedented access not just to talk, but the bodily and material conduct of participants and enabled the detailed, repeated examination of social actions and activities and their situated accomplishment. Ethnomethodology and conversation analysis provide the resources that enable the analysis of video and in particular the detailed examination of the ways in which talk, gesture, the use of tools and artefacts and the like, inform the practical interactional accomplishment of work and organisation.

EXAMINING A FRAGMENT

This approach to the analysis of video recordings of naturally occurring events is driven by three principal methodological commitments that direct analytic attention towards the local, practical accomplishment of social actions and activities. In the first instance, it is concerned with the 'situated' character of practical action and in particular the ways in which the accomplishment of social actions and activities is inseparable from, and inextricably part of, the context in which they arise. In other words the sense and significance of social actions or activities is accomplished within the circumstances and context of their production. Second, the concern with the situated character of practical action directs attention to the ways in which social actions and activities are ongoingly and contingently accomplished by participants themselves; how actions and activities are produced moment by moment with regard to emerging circumstances at hand and in particular, the real time contributions of others. The emergent, interactional accomplishment of social action and activity is perhaps most manifest in talk in conversation, in which each next utterance, or a turn at talk, is produced with regard to the immediately preceding action(s) and in turn, implicates, and provides the framework for subsequent action; as Heritage (1984) suggests action

in interaction is both 'context-sensitive and context-renewing'. Third, analysis is directed towards explicating the social organisation, the methods in and through which participants themselves accomplish their actions and activities in concert and collaboration with others, that is, the socially organised practices and reasoning on which people rely to produce their own actions and make sense of the contributions of others – the practices and reasoning that inform the concerted, collaborative accomplishment of practical action.

With the focus on the situated accomplishment of practical action, analysis proceeds therefore on a 'case-by-case' basis. It involves the detailed examination of particular events and the ways in which they are accomplished by the participants themselves, within the practical circumstances in which they arise. It addresses the talk, the visible, and the material conduct of participants, their use of objects and artefacts, tools and technologies, and considers the ways in which particular actions and activities are accomplished, in and through interaction.

It is helpful to consider an example. The following fragment is drawn from a corpus of video recordings of auctions of fine art and antiques. The following fragment involves the sale of a small nineteenth-century silver porringer. It is one of six hundred or so lots for sale over a couple of days at a leading provincial auction house. The sale of the lot lasts no longer than thirty seconds. It involves a rapid and complex interaction through which the price is systematically escalated and the goods sold on the fall of the hammer to the highest bidder. This type of interaction is repeated numerous times during the auction and can provide some useful insights – not only into the organisation of sales, but the work and practices of a particular occupational group, namely auctioneers. Here, therefore is a fragment of organisational activity, involving a particular occupation, where work is accomplished through social interaction; interaction that involves the interplay of talk and visible conduct and a form of interaction that determines the price and exchange of goods worth some billions of pounds each year.

To simplify matters we use '{B1 bids}' to represent the bidding, the number giving an indication of the order at which different participants enter the bidding. Where the auctioneer (A) bids on behalf of a buyer who cannot attend the sale – what is known as a 'commission bid' – we have used '{A bids}'. Commission bids are where the buyer leaves a price with the auction house and the auctioneer bids on their behalf until they reach the maximum price of the commission.

FRAGMENT 1: TRANSCRIPT 1

```
A:   Lot number: (0.2) Four Three
     Three (.) Four Three Three the lot
     number: now. Bidding here at one
     hundred pounds now.
     (.) {A bids}
A:   A hundred pounds I'm bid straight
     away for this, at a hundred pounds:,
     (.) One hundred pounds (will do it)
     One hundred one ten (.) n_ow:? (0.3)
     A hundred pounds only. One hundred
     pounds, one hundred pounds. One ten
     now quickly?
     (0.3) {B1 bids, B2 raises hand}
A:   One ten is that. One ten I'm bid.
     One ten. One twenty on commission now.
     One thirty now:? One twenty   still
     with me, at one twenty.
     {B2 bids}
A:   One thirty bid there: fresh bid,
     one thirty, one thirty. Forty now:?
     (0.2)
A:   At a hundred an thirty pounds (.)
     bids there at one thirty. Do show
     if you happen to have an extra bid.
     At one thirty over there.
     {knock}
A:   One thirty that's yours sir.
     The buyer number is?
```

Talk is transcribed using an orthography developed by Gail Jefferson and commonly used in ethnomethodology, conversation analysis and cognate approaches such as discourse analysis. The transcription system is designed to capture aspects of the articulation of the talk and in particular the interactional position and production of the participants' utterances. Very briefly: talk is laid out turn by turn,

the length of pauses or silences are captured in tenths of a second, for example, '(0.3)'. Pauses of less than two tenths of a second are represented by '(.)'; words or parts of words that are emphasised by the speaker are underlined, 'is that'. Sounds that are elongated are captured by colons, the number of colons representing the length of the elongation, 'number:'; and intonation is captured by punctuation marks, for example, for rising intonation: 'One thirty now:?'. More detailed versions of the orthography can be found in various books and collections including for example Boden and Zimmerman (1991), Drew and Heritage (1992) and Maynard (2003).

Before considering the visible or nonverbal aspects of the participants' conduct, we can begin to generate some initial observations concerning the talk that arises in the fragment. In the first place, we can see that the talk is primarily produced by one party, namely the auctioneer. He briefly introduces the lot and then repeatedly announces a series of figures. These figures escalate in terms of increments of ten pounds – beginning at one hundred pounds, with the goods finally being sold at one hundred and thirty pounds. Bidding appears to alternate between the auctioneer, bidding on behalf of a commission buyer ('bidding here at one hundred' and 'one twenty on commission'), and buyers in the room (B1 bids 'one ten', B2 bids 'one thirty bid there:'). In the first instance, the auctioneer appears to take a bid from B1 rather than B2 who also attempts to bid by raising his hand. The auctioneer not only takes bids from particular participants, but displays those bids to all who are present, for example announcing that the bid is 'here' at one hundred pounds, 'there' at one hundred and thirty, and 'still with me' at one twenty. It also appears that the auctioneer goes to some trouble to elicit bids from people in the audience and before finally selling the goods; attempting to maximise the opportunities for anyone present to bid.

Whilst the auctioneer does most, if not all, of the speaking during the sale of the lot, the transcript begins to reveal the ways in which sequences of action are critical to the structure of the activity. For example, the auctioneer's repetition of a particular increment, such as one hundred pounds, involves an attempt to elicit a bid from a member of the audience. Once the bid is received, in this case by a participant raising his hand, it is acknowledged by the auctioneer with 'one ten is that'. In turn, the auctioneer produces the next bid, on behalf of his commission buyer, 'one twenty on commission now' and invites a subsequent bid from the floor, 'one thirty now:?'. The participant's bid, indeed the attempt by both B1 and B2 to bid, are sensitive to the auctioneer's invitation, 'one ten now quickly?', and in turn, the auctioneer accepts a bid from B1 and is able to announce the next bid, namely 'one twenty'. In turn, the announcement of the commission bid at 'one twenty still with me' is followed by the auctioneer looking for a next bid at one hundred and thirty pounds. We can see therefore how particular actions of the auctioneer serve to elicit bids from members of the audience, just as those bids enable the auctioneer to announce the price and produce a subsequent bid. Each action is sensitive to the prior, indeed, may be elicited by the prior action, and in each case forms the basis to subsequent action and activity. These actions are organised with regard to distinct forms of sequential and interactional organisation that underpins the escalation of price. Where no further bids are forthcoming, the auctioneer is able to bring the sale to a successful completion with the fall of the hammer.

Transcribing talk provides the opportunity to become more familiar with the actions that arise within a particular activity and to begin to scrutinise not only what is said and how, but the location of particular utterances or actions and how they are produced with regard to the contributions of others. It enables the researcher to address why specific actions arise at particular moments within the emerging course of the activity. As Schegloff and Sacks suggest:

> a pervasively relevant issue (for participants) about utterances in conversation is 'why that now,' a question whose [...] analysis may also be relevant to find what 'that' is. That is to say, some utterances may derive their character as actions entirely from placement considerations. (1974)

For instance, whilst the auctioneer repeatedly reiterates the first bid, one hundred pounds, it is only when he announces the next increment with a rising intonation that participants attempt to bid, in this case two at the same time. Transcription also begins to reveal the complexity of the action that arises even within a very brief fragment such as this, and provides the resources to begin to draw some preliminary observations concerning the structure and arrangement of the actions. In this case, the transcript also points to some more general features of interaction, be it within the workplace or any other environment for that matter – how the event contingently emerges, moment by moment, and the ways in which each contribution is sensitive to the actions of others, or the withholding of particular actions, and oriented to a determinate range of possibilities.

THE VISIBLE AND THE MATERIAL

It is clear that a range of actions that arise within the sale of the lot are not available through inspection of the talk alone and that the talk is accompanied by, and sensitive to, various visible and material actions. For example, at least two people bid using nonverbal or visible actions and these bids are critical to the escalation of the price and the final sale of the goods. How these actions arise with regard to the visible and accompanying talk of the auctioneer is not available using this limited transcript. Moreover, these gestured turns or bids, are attributed by the auctioneer to particular individuals in the room, or even an absentee buyer, and yet their ascription of actions to the participants, for example 'one ten is that', 'bids there at one thirty', 'bidding here at one hundred pounds now' remain ambiguous without reference to the visible aspects of the activity. These gestured turns and their revelation are critical to the escalation of price and the sale of the goods and feature in the sequence of action through which bids are elicited and acknowledged. Various artefacts also play an important role in the event. The fall of the gavel for example finalises the sale of the goods and their transfer of ownership. The auctioneer's book not only provides information concerning commission bids, reserves and the like, but is referenced and referred to by the auctioneer during the course of the sale. Without taking the visible aspects of the participants seriously, their gestures, bodily orientation, use of artefacts and the like, it is difficult to address the organisation of the activity and the practices upon which the auctioneer relies upon to conduct the sale.

To examine how the visible, as well as talk feature in the accomplishment of the activity, we need to develop our transcript to enable us to begin to encompass various aspects of the participants' visible conduct. Unfortunately, but not surprisingly, there is no general or widely accepted transcription system for the visible and material aspects of social interaction. Over some years however, those undertaking video-based studies informed by ethnomethodology and conversation analysis, have developed ways of working with video that enables them to transcribe aspects of the participants' bodily conduct in particular with regard to the talk (see for example Goodwin, 1981; Heath, 1986). There is some individual variation in how this is done, but it ordinarily includes identifying the onset and completion of particular actions, such as a gesture and demarcating significant aspects of its articulation – such as for example, where it reaches its acme. These transcripts are primarily concerned with delineating the occurrence and position of particular aspects of the participants' visible conduct. They may include details of head nods, gestures, visual orientation, changes in body position, the use of particular artefacts, and the like; indeed whatever arises within the developing course of a fragment. The transcript provides a resource to begin to discover the geography and organisation of action within a fragment and to document certain features of the participants' conduct and interaction.

The following is a highly simplified version of a more complex transcript that is included later in the chapter, but it provides a sense of the ways in which we can begin to map out the participants' conduct and identify some features of actions' organisation.

Transcribing the visible, as well as the spoken aspects of the fragment, provides an important resource with which to begin to examine the participants' conduct and to identify the potential relationship between particular actions. For example, in this fragment, we can notice that as he announces the current increment 'one twenty on commission' the auctioneer turns and gestures towards the first bidder, B1, inviting him to bid at the next increment, namely one hundred and thirty pounds. However, even as he voices the next increment 'one thirty now:?', he turns away from the first bidder and looks for an alternative participant who may be prepared to bid. The auctioneer's actions reveal that the first bidder has declined the next increment and that 'one thirty now:?' serves as a generalised invitation for anyone in the room to bid. As he undertakes the search for a new bidder, he not only announces that the bid is 'still with me' but reveals the source of that bid, dramatically pointing first to the book that contains the commission bid and second to himself bidding on behalf of the absentee participant. A new bidder raises his hand and the bid is accepted 'one thirty'. The bid is produced as the auctioneer announces 'it's still with me' and in particular when the auctioneer's search around the room arrives at the area where the bidder is sitting. In other words, both the auctioneer's announcement 'it's still with me' and his visual orientation, serve to encourage the participant to bid and to bid at a particular moment. As he announces the bid, 'one thirty', the auctioneer gestures towards the bidder, and displays both to the bidder and all those present, who has the bid of 'one thirty'.

Such transcripts are far more detailed than the diagram shown above. They are primarily used by the researcher and enable a range of potentially relevant details of conduct

FRAGMENT 1: TRANSCRIPT 2

Auctioneer

Orientation   looks
     B1   around room   B2

Gesture

   open palm   points
    at B1   at book   at self   at book   at B2
    ↓   ↓   ↓   ↓   ↓

One twenty on commission. One thirty now: It's still with me. At one twenty. One thirty
                                       ↑

to be identified, clarified and documented. They form the basis to generating notes and ideas about particular fragments and the organisation of particular actions and activities. The transcript below is part of the original from which our observations of this fragment are drawn and illustrates the ways in which such transcripts are primarily designed as a vehicle for the individual researcher to examine and document observations concerning a fragment. Transcription is an important, if not the critical resource, for the analysis of particular events with video recording remaining the principal source of data.

FRAGMENT 1 TRANSCRIPT 3

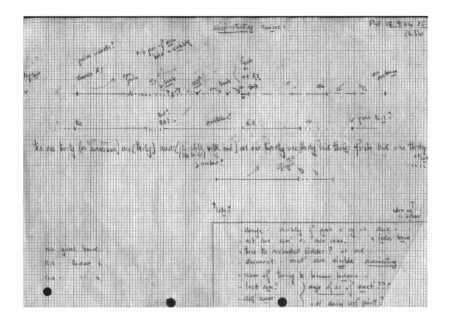

Video, coupled with an appropriate methodological framework, enables the researcher to begin to unravel the complex range of action that arises within a seemingly transient activity. In the case at hand, from a single fragment, one can begin to understand a little more of auctions and the practices through which the auctioneer and participants accomplish the valuation and sale of goods. We find for example, that the auctioneer juxtaposes bids from different members of the audience with commission bids from the book, and when one of those bidders withdraws, initiates a search to discover a new bidder. We also see how, through talk and gesture he ascribes values or increments to particular individuals, even absent individuals, and thereby enables bidders to know where they stand with regard to the escalating price of the goods. It is also interesting to note, that in eliciting and ascribing bids to particular individuals, the auctioneer enables all those present to see and to witness, who has the bid at any point within the developing course of the proceedings. In various ways therefore, despite the seeming, slightness of the actions revealed when scrutinising the video recording of naturally occurring events such as auctions, we can begin to discern the ways in which the character of the participants' conduct might be pertinent to our understanding of particular form of work and the organisation of markets as well as associated issues such as trust and legitimacy (see for example Heath and Luff, 2007; Smith, 1989).

Examination of a single case, in this instance a brief fragment from a sale by auction, can provide a rich array of observations concerning the organisation of an activity. It enables the researcher to scrutinise action, to consider the ways in which participants collaboratively accomplish an activity, and to reflect upon the resources, the competencies, on which they rely. It also enables a researcher to respect and to recognise the significance of seemingly slight, even trivial actions, and to discover how they feature in the activity's accomplishment. In this way, we can use video to address one of the basic methodological concerns that underlie much qualitative social science, that is, to take the participant's perspective seriously and to consider how their conduct serves to produce particular actions within the practicalities of accomplishing everyday, socially organised, activities, in concert, with others.

DATA COLLECTION

This particular form of analysis has a significant bearing on the type of data that needs to be gathered and the ways in which we record and document action and activities within particular environments. Every setting poses its own unique demands on data collection and can raise particular difficulties for undertaking video recording. In almost every setting it is critical therefore that the researcher undertakes a period of field observation before considering the introduction of cameras and microphones. Fieldwork provides an opportunity for the researcher to become familiar with the setting – the socio-physical environment, the sorts of activities that arise and patterns of interaction and the like. It also enables the researcher to see the ways in which various material resources feature in particular activities, be they computers, paper documents, or even as in previous fragment, hammers, and to reflect upon the ways in which they constrain and of course provide opportunities for particular activities. Last but not least, a period of fieldwork enables the researcher to engage, where relevant, with the participants themselves, and to establish a relationship that can form the basis to securing their willingness to be video recorded and to clarify the ethical requirements that participants themselves see as important.

There are a number of practical issues that have to be addressed in undertaking video recording of naturally occurring activities. Each setting poses its own unique demands and it is unusual that one is able to gather quality data on the first occasion that one records. The lighting, the physical arrangement of the space, the position and movement of the participants, the ambient noise, the location of particular objects and technologies and the necessity to remain, as far as possible, unobtrusive, can all raise difficulties that

have to be managed. Moreover, with the interest in exploring the social interactional organisation of naturally occurring activities, it is critical, as far as practically possible, to encompass the actions of all participants. In some settings, where there are two or three participants involved in what Goffman (1971) refers to as a 'focused gathering' it may well be possible to gather analytically fruitful data using a single camera with a built-in microphone. Settings that involve numerous participants, and in some cases a diverse range of material resources, settings such as classrooms, control rooms and operating theatres, may necessitate the use of multiple cameras and separate microphones placed in a number of locations. It is unlikely, even after a period of fieldwork, that the first recordings will provide the necessary quality or access to the action, and in many cases, the researcher will find that it is necessary to gather recorded data over a series of occasions before finding the most useful and appropriate position and perspective for recording. Indeed, it is not unusual during the course of a project to gather data from rather different positions to enable particular phenomena to be investigated. These phenomena, and the decision to collect particular forms of data, may change as the analysis develops during the course of a study; data collection is an iterative process in which materials may be progressively gathered in the course of examining, transcribing and analysing data.

While the audio-visual recordings are likely to form the principal data on which analysis is developed, fieldwork, and in some cases the fieldwork that accompanies the actual recording, remains an important, if not critical, part of the research. If we take the workplace for example, there are a range of practices, conventions and resources that bear upon, and inform the accomplishment of particular activities, and it may well be necessary to augment video analysis with field observation and even interviews. In many cases it is necessary to gain access to the relevant material resources, such as records, work sheets, diagrams, plans and the like, and become familiar with the ways in which they are used. In this regard, screen-based technologies can pose particular difficulties, since it may be necessary to record the contents of the screen. There are a number of solutions. In some circumstances it is possible to video record the screen with a camera (for some screens this may require the frame rate to be appropriately adjusted). The data that are gathered depends not only on the analytic approach that has been adopted but also the sorts of phenomena that are addressed. Data, including audio-visual recordings, are always constrained by practicalities and resources. It is critical however that the materials that underpin the research can legitimately serve the insights and phenomena that are addressed in the analysis. In particular, we need to demonstrate the ways in which participants themselves orient to and rely upon the practices that inform the accomplishment of the action and activities at hand.

SUMMARY

Despite numerous calls for the social sciences to take the visual seriously, video remains a surprisingly neglected resource, relegated to a marginal role in some qualitative research and absent from most. When video is used, it often forms an accompaniment to others forms of data collection that prioritises fieldwork, and is used to illustrate events and activities that have been primarily identified and analysed using conventional ethnographic observations. Yet video provides a more significant opportunity for social science research, a resource that enables analysts to scrutinise social actions and activities in ways that hitherto were not possible, to begin to discover phenomena and aspects of socially organised practice unavailable to conventional fieldwork and ethnography. Moreover, audio-visual recordings of naturally occurring activities and events provide the opportunity of building a more cumulative data corpus than is possible within many other forms of qualitative research and to engage in forms of collaborative research and analysis that is unavailable within much ethnography

or field research. The technology, and the analytic opportunities it affords, however, raises important methodological challenges for the social sciences and demands distinctive approaches to the study of social action and interaction.

Perhaps the most substantial corpus of video-based, naturalistic studies to emerge within sociology over the past couple of decades or so have been informed by ethnomethodology and conversation analysis. These studies have addressed the social and interactional organisation of a broad range of actions and activities and delineated ways in which seemingly mundane events are accomplished in, and through, the complex, yet systematic, interplay of talk, visible and material conduct. They have revealed the order and organisation that underlies and informs the production of everyday activities and begun to delineate the resources on which participants rely to make sense of and coordinate the actions in which they engage. In this regard, the emergence of workplace studies – studies of work, interaction and technology in complex organisational environments – is of particular interest. These studies provide the resources to address and re-specify some key concepts and ideas that inform more conventional analyses of occupational practice and institutional environments. Indeed, in various ways, these video-based studies of the workplace draw on, and transform, the long-standing recognition that social interaction underpins and preserves institutional arrangements, and enables a reorientation of studies of organisational practice. They also provide a vehicle for taking the object seriously, and reshaping the ways in which we address and reveal how the material, the environment, technology, artefacts and the like, feature in the practical accomplishment of social action and activity. The significance of video therefore is not simply that it provides another way of gathering data, but rather, with an appropriate methodological framework, enables the social sciences to build a rigorous and systematic analysis of the organised production of social action as it occurs in its everyday, natural environments.

REFERENCES

Atkinson, J. M. (1984). *Our Master's Voices: The Language and Body Language of Politics.* London: Methuen.

Atkinson, J. M., & Drew, P. (1980). *Order in Court: The Organisation of Verbal Interaction in Judicial Settings.* London: Macmillan.

Banks, M., & Murphy, H. (1997). *Rethinking Visual Anthropology.* New Haven: Yale University Press.

Barley, S. (1996). Technicians in the workplace: ethnographic evidence for bringing work into organisational studies. *Administrative Science Quarterly,* 41, 404–444.

Barley, S., & Kunda, G. (2001). Bringing work back in. *Organization Science,* 12 (1), 76–95.

Barley, S. R. (1989). Careers, identities and institutions: The legacy of the Chicago School of Sociology, in Arther, M., Hall, T., & Lawrence, B. (eds) *The Handbook of Career Theory* (pp. 41–65). Cambridge: Cambridge University Press.

Becker, H. (1963). *The Outsiders: Studies in the Sociology of Deviance.* New York: The Free Press.

Boden, D. (1994). *The Business of Talk: Organizations in Action.* Oxford and Cambridge, MA: Polity Press.

Boden, D., & Zimmerman, D. H. (eds). (1991). *Talk and Social Structure: Studies in Ethnomethodology and Conversation Analysis.* Cambridge: Polity Press.

Clayman, S., & Heritage, J. C. (2002). *The News Interview: Journalists and Public Figures on the Air.* Cambridge: Cambridge University Press.

Curry, T. J., & Clarke, A. C. (1978). *Introducing Visual Sociology.* Dubuque: Kendall Hunt.

Drew, P., & Heritage, J. C. (eds). (1992). *Talk at Work: Interaction in Institutional Settings.* Cambridge: Cambridge University Press.

Emmison, M., & Smith, P. (2000). *Researching the Visual.* London: Sage.

Engeström, Y., & Middleton, D. (eds) (1996). *Cognition and Communication at Work.* Cambridge: Cambridge University Press.

Goffman, E. (1963). *Asylums: Essays on the Social Situation of Mental Patients and other Inmates.* New York: Doubleday.

Goffman, E. (1971). *Relations in Public.* Harmondsworth: Penguin.

Goffman, E. (1983). The interaction order. *American Sociological Review,* 48 (February), 1–17.

Goodwin, C. (1981). *Conversational Organisation: Interaction between Speakers and Hearers.* London: Academic Press.

Goodwin, C. (1995). Seeing in depth. *Social Studies of Science,* 25 (2), 237–274.

Goodwin, C., & Goodwin, M. H. (1994). Professional vision. *American Anthropologist,* 96 (3), 606–633.

Goodwin, C., & Goodwin, M. H. (1996). Seeing as a situated activity: Formulating planes, in Y. Engeström, & D. Middleton (eds) *Cognition and Communication at Work* (pp. 61–95). Cambridge: Cambridge University Press.

Goodwin, M. H. (1990). *He-Said-She-Said: Talk as Social Organisation Among Black Children.* Bloomington, IN: Indiana University Press.

Heath, C. C. (1986). *Body Movement and Speech in Medical Interaction.* Cambridge: Cambridge University Press.

Heath, C. C., & Luff, P. K. (2000). *Technology in Action.* Cambridge: Cambridge University Press.

Heath, C. C., & Luff, P. (2007) Ordering competition: the interactional accomplishment of the sale of art and antiques at auction. *British Journal of Sociology,* 58 (1), 63–85.

Heritage, J. (1997). Conversation analysis and institutional talk: Analysing data, in S. D. Silverman (ed) *Qualitative Research: Theory, Method and Practice* (pp. 161–182). London: Sage.

Heritage, J., & Maynard, D. W. (eds) (2006). *Communication in Medical Care: Interaction between Primary Care Physicians and Patients.* New York and Cambridge: Cambridge University Press.

Heritage, J. C. (1984). *Garfinkel and Ethnomethodology.* Cambridge: Polity Press.

Hochschild, A. R. (1983). *The Managed Heart: The Commercialisation of Feeling.* Berkeley and Los Angeles, California: University of California Press.

Hughes, E. C. (1971). *The Sociological Eye: Selected Papers on Institution and Race (Part I) and Self and the Study of Society (Part II).* Chicago: Aldine Atherton.

Kendon, A. (1982). The organisation of behaviour in face to face interaction: Observation on a development of a methodology, in K. Scherer, & P. Ekman (eds) *Handbook of Methods of Nonverbal Behaviour Research.* Cambridge: Cambridge University Press.

Knoblauch, H., Schnettler, B., Raab, J., & Soeffner, G. (eds) (2006) *Video Analysis: Methodology and Methods.* Berlin: Peter Lang.

LeBaron, C., & Koschmann, T. (2003). Gesture and the transparency of understanding, in P. Glenn, C. LeBaron, & J. Mandelbaum (eds) *Studies in Language and Social Interaction in Honor of Robert Hopper* (pp. 119–132).Mahwah, NJ: Lawrence Erlbaum Associates.

Luff, P., Hindmarsh, J., & Heath, C. C. (eds) (2000). *Workplace Studies: Recovering Work Practice and Informing System's Design.* Cambridge: Cambridge University Press.

Marks, D. (1995) Ethnographic film: from Flaberty to Asch and after. *American Anthropologist*, 97 (2), 337–347.

Maynard, D. W. (2003). *Bad News, Good News: Conversational Order in Everyday Talk and Clinical Settings*. Chicago: University of Chicago Press.

Mondada, L. (2003). Working with video: how surgeons produce video records of their actions. *Visual Studies*, 18, 58–73.

Parsons, A. S. (1951). *The Social System*. Glencoe: Free Press.

Peräkylä, A. (1995). *Aids Counselling: Institutional Interaction and Clinical Practice*. Cambridge: Cambridge University Press.

Pink, S. (2001a). *Doing Ethnography: Images, Media and Representation in Research*. London: Sage.

Pink, S. (2001b) More visualising, more methodologies on video, reflexivity and qualitative research. *Sociological Review*, 49 (1), 586–599.

Prodger, P. (2003). *Time Stands Still: Muybridge and the Instantaneous Photography Movement*. Oxford: Oxford University Press.

Rose, G. (2001). *Visual Methodologies: An Introduction to the Interpretation of Visual Materials*. London: Sage.

Roth, J. A. (1963). *Timetables: Structuring and the Passage of Time in Hospital Treatment and other Careers*. Indianapolis: Bobbs Merrill.

Ruby, J. (2000). *Picturing Culture: Explorations of Film and Anthropology*. Chicago: University of Chicago Press.

Schegloff, E. A., & Sacks, H. (1973). Opening up closings. *Semiotica*, 7, 289–327.

Schegloff, E. A., & Sacks, H. (1974). Opening up closings, in R. Turner (ed.) *Ethnomethodology* (pp. 233–264). Harmondsworth, U.K. and Baltimore, MD: Penguin.

Silverman, D. (1970). *The Theory of Organisation*. London: Heinemann.

Silverman, D. (1997a). Studying organisational interaction: ethnomethodology's contribution to the 'new institutionalism'. *Administrative Theory and Praxis*, 19 (2), 1.

Silverman, D. (1997b). *Discourses of Counseling: HIV Counseling as Social Interaction*. London: Sage.

Simmel, G. (1950). *The Sociology of George Simmel*, Wolf, K. (ed). Glencoe, Illinois: Free Press.

Smith, C. W. (1989). *Auctions: The Social Construction of Value*. London: Harvester Wheatsheaf.

Star, S. L. (1996). Working together: Symbolic interactionism, activity theory and information systems, in Engeström, Y. & Middleton, D. (eds) *Cognition and Communication at Work* (pp. 296–318). Cambridge: Cambridge University Press.

Strauss, A., Schatzman, L., Bucher, R., Ehrlich, D., & Sabshin, M. (1964). *Psychiatric Ideologies and Institutions*. London: Free Press.

Streeck, J., & Kallmeyer, W. (2001). Interaction by inscription. *Journal of Pragmatics*, 33, 465–490.

Strong, P. (1978). *The Ceremonial Order of the Clinic: Patients, Doctors and Medical Bureaucracies*. London: Routledge Kegan Paul.

Suchman, L. (1987). *Plans and Situated Actions: The Problem of Human Machine Interaction*. Cambridge: Cambridge University Press.

Van Maanen, J. (1991) The smile factory: Work at Disneyland, in Frost, P. J., Moore, L. F., Louis, M. L., Lundberg, C. C., & Martin, J. (eds) *Reframing Organisational Culture* (pp. 58–76). London: Sage.

Whalen, J. (1995). Expert systems vs. systems for experts: Computer-aided dispatch as a support system in real-world environments, in P. Thomas (ed) *The Social and Interactional Dimensions of Human-Computer Interfaces* (pp. 161–183). Cambridge: Cambridge University Press.

Whalen, J., Whalen, M., & Henderson, K. (2002). Improvisational choreography in a teleservice work. *British Journal of Sociology*, 53 (2), 239–259.

Whalen, J., Zimmerman, D. & Whalen, M. (1988). When words fail: a single case analysis. *Communication Yearbook,* 11, 406–432.

Zimmerman, D. H. (1992). The interactional organization of calls for emergency assistance, in P. Drew & J. Heritage (eds) *Talk at Work: Interaction in Institutional Settings* (pp. 418–469). Cambridge: Cambridge University Press.

30

Secondary Analysis of Qualitative Data

Janet Heaton

INTRODUCTION

Secondary analysis of qualitative data is an emerging methodology in social research that involves the re-use of data originally collected in primary studies. Such data include field notes, transcripts of interviews and group discussions and observational records. The analysis of other 'found' or more 'naturalistic' types of qualitative data, such as personal diaries, autobiographies, letters, documents and photographs, is better known as 'documentary analysis' (Plummer, 1983, 2001; Scott, 1990). That said, some types of qualitative data, notably life stories, may be more or less naturalistic, depending on how they were produced, and hence the distinction between 'secondary' and 'documentary' analysis is not always clear-cut.

Unlike secondary analysis of quantitative data, the re-use of qualitative data is not established practice in social research. There are few qualitative multi-purpose or longitudinal datasets for researchers to access, no published manuals on 'how to do' qualitative secondary analysis, and limited funding dedicated for such studies. However, since the mid-1990s, there has been growing interest in the methodology, particularly in the UK, Europe and North America. This is indicated by the growing number of studies involving secondary analysis of a wide range of qualitative data, as well as commentaries on the possibilities and problems of re-using these data (for example, see Corti and Thompson, 2004; Fielding, 2004; Hammersley, 1997; Heaton, 1998, 2004; Hinds et al., 1997; Mauthner et al., 1998; Parry and Mauthner, 2004, 2005; Thorne, 1994, 1998).

In the first part of this chapter, I examine the current state of the methodology, describing sources of qualitative data available for secondary analysis, ways in which these could be and have been re-used, and key issues emerging from debates on the methodology. In the second part, I discuss three questions which have implications for future policy and practice concerning the collection, archiving, and re-use of qualitative data in social research. The chapter draws on and updates previous work exploring epistemological, methodological and ethical issues in qualitative secondary analysis (Heaton, 1998, 2000, 2004). It focuses on developments in the UK, where there has been considerable work to promote the archiving and re-use of qualitative data, and describes examples of secondary analysis carried out internationally in social research (but not social research of a more historical nature). Most of the examples are from health-related research, where the vast majority of studies involving the re-use of qualitative research data have been published to date.

STATE OF THE ART

Accessing qualitative data

There are three ways in which social researchers can access qualitative research data for secondary analysis: through data archives, by informal data sharing and by re-using data from their own previous research (Heaton, 2004). These approaches, and some illustrative examples of studies using different sources of data, are described below.

Data archives

Many countries have national and other data archives which preserve datasets from the social sciences and make them available for further use by other researchers. Archived data tends to be quantitative rather than qualitative in nature, although some longitudinal studies include a qualitative component. Where archives do hold qualitative data, these tend to be collections of life stories retained for use in historical research, rather than other types of qualitative data often collected in social research. Information on worldwide archives is available through the Council of European Social Sciences Data Archives (CESSDA) website[1]. In Europe, there are a number of archives where qualitative datasets are already deposited, or which are planning to accept this type of data[2]. They include: the UK Data Archive (UKDA); the Finnish Social Science Data Archive (FSD); the Danish Data Archives (DDA); the Sociological Data Archive in The Czech

Republic; the Norwegian Social Science Data Services (NSD); the Swedish Social Science Data Services (SSD); and the Institute für Geschichte und Biographie in Germany. In the USA, the Murray Research Center (A Center for the Study of Lives at Harvard University) holds over 270 datasets from research on human development and social change, including longitudinal datasets containing qualitative data (James and Sørensen, 2000).

Particular advances in qualitative data archiving have been made in the UK, where formal sharing of all types of qualitative data across the social sciences has been heavily promoted since the mid-1990s by a major funder of social research, the Economic and Social Research Council (ESRC). In 1994, the ESRC established the world's first and only Qualitative Data Archiving Resource Centre (Qualidata), based at the University of Essex in England and directed by Paul Thompson. The role of this service has evolved over time (Corti, 2000, 2003; Corti and Backhouse, 2005; Corti and Thompson, 2004). Originally, Qualidata was set up to promote and facilitate the archiving of qualitative datasets in existing repositories across the UK. In 2003, Qualidata became part of the new Economic and Social Data Service (ESDS), an initiative jointly funded by the ESRC and Joint Information Systems Committee (JISC). Renamed ESDS Qualidata, the service is now based within the UKDA. Following a consultation carried out for the ESRC on the use of qualitative research resources (Henwood and Lang, 2003), ESDS Qualidata has sought to improve the accessibility of archived material by making selected datasets available via the web, and by creating web-based samplers of a larger number of datasets so that researchers can more easily assess the potential for using them in teaching and/or for secondary research purposes.

The ESRC has further promoted qualitative data archiving and re-use through a number of related policy and funding initiatives. Since 1995, the ESRC has had a Datasets Policy making it a condition of its awards that researchers make available for archiving qualitative datasets arising from their work; in applying for funding researchers also have to demonstrate that the proposed primary research cannot be carried out using existing archived datasets[3]. In addition, following the aforementioned consultation on qualitative research resources, the ESRC funded a feasibility study on the possibility of a qualitative longitudinal study (Holland et al., 2004). This, in turn, has been followed up with funding for a programme of work intended to develop resources for qualitative secondary analysis. This includes funding for a series of demonstration studies to investigate the value of innovative models of archiving, sharing and re-using qualitative data, commissioned in 2005 as part of the ESRC's Qualitative Archiving and Data Sharing Scheme (QUADS)[4]. It also includes funding for a major qualitative longitudinal study, called *Changing Lives and Times*, commencing in 2006[5].

As a result of the above strategies, there has been an increase in the availability of archived qualitative datasets in the UK, as well as an improvement in the cataloguing of these resources. By 2002, Qualidata had facilitated archiving of 140 qualitative datasets and added details of a further 150 existing collections to its catalogue (Corti, 2003; see also Corti and Backhouse, 2005)[6]. However, there have been difficulties collating figures on usage of these resources (Corti, 2000), and little is known about the extent to which existing datasets have been accessed[7]. Of course, many archived datasets have only just become available and work is ongoing to improve the accessibility of some of these, hence it will take time for researchers to complete work based on these resources and for resulting secondary studies to be published. Nonetheless, as Parry and Mauthner (2005) have argued, the ongoing case for qualitative data archiving (and different models for this) needs to be supported by information on the extent to which these datasets are accessed and re-used, by whom and for what purposes.

In a bid to examine whether and how researchers have re-used qualitative research data, in 1997 I began a review of secondary studies published in the international health and social care literature, which has been updated over time (Heaton, 1998, 2000, 2004). While this work is limited in that it focuses on one area of social research, it provides an indication of how researchers have re-used qualitative data in practice, and I have not found evidence to suggest that numerous secondary studies have been published in other areas of social research to date[8]. The review found that that only nine (14%) of the 65 secondary studies identified involved the re-use of datasets collected by other researchers, and were carried out independently of the primary researchers (Heaton, 2004). Of these, two studies utilised publicly archived datasets. One was a study by Bloor (2000) of communal understanding of, and responses to, the disease popularly known as 'Miners' Lung', using oral history material from South Wales Miners' Library at the University of Wales Swansea. The other was a study by Bevan (2000) of the career choices of general practitioners, using life histories deposited with the British Library National Sound Library. Another two publications were based on data that Julius Roth had left with Paul Atkinson and which were used for teaching and in research. These data were re-used in a study of the cultural aspects of tuberculosis (Weaver, 1994), and also to illustrate a book on micro-computing and qualitative data analysis (Weaver and Atkinson, 1994).

Notable secondary studies which have been carried out using archived datasets in other areas of social research include Fielding and Fielding's (2000) secondary analysis of Cohen and Taylor's (1972) research on the long-term imprisonment of men in a maximum security prison (archived at the Institute of Criminology, Cambridge). And data from the 'Affluent Worker' study (available via Qualidata, at the University of Essex) have been re-used in a secondary study by Savage (2005a; see also Savage 2005b). Thompson (1998) has also reported that oral histories collected for 'The Edwardians' study (held at the University of Essex) have been re-used in numerous publications and for teaching.

Informal data sharing

An alternative approach to accessing data for secondary analysis is through informal data sharing. Here, researchers share their data directly with other researchers. One or more of the primary researchers who collected the data can be involved in the secondary analysis (and others may act as advisers). Single or multiple datasets can be shared, and re-used in full or in part, depending on the aims and scope of the secondary research.

While informal data sharing has not been officially promoted in the UK or elsewhere, this source of data has been used in secondary studies carried out in health-related research. In the aforementioned review, 20 (32%) of the secondary studies were by researchers who had informally shared their data with others (Heaton, 2004). These studies were by researchers based in North America. Examples include a secondary study by Yamashita and Forsyth (1998), which came about after the two researchers met at a conference and found that they had both carried out research on families' reactions to a relative's mental illness in Canada and the USA. Angst and Deatrick (1996) also drew on data from studies that they had independently carried out, to compare and contrast the involvement of children with different conditions in healthcare decision-making.

Self-collected data

Researchers also have the option of re-using datasets that they personally have collected and retained over the course of their career. This may be data which were not originally analysed, or data which are rich enough to support further analysis – either as a secondary study in its own right, or in conjunction with additional primary research designed to collect more data required to address the new study aims.

In the aforementioned review, over half the studies identified (36, 55%) were by researchers who had re-used their own data (Heaton, 2004). The majority were by authors based in the USA and Canada, while the remainder were from the UK and Sweden.

A more recent example illustrating this approach to qualitative secondary analysis, this time from the field of education, is provided by Nelson et al. (2004). They were part of a larger primary research team that carried out a study of family and professional partnerships in special education in the USA. Feedback on the original research findings highlighted issues regarding boundaries in families' relationships with professionals. A secondary analysis was carried out to examine this topic in more depth, in which some of the codes developed for the primary analysis (using Ethnograph) were re-used for this purpose.

Secondary uses of qualitative data

Various claims have been made about the ways in which qualitative data could be re-used in social research (for example, see Corti and Thompson, 2004; Hinds et al., 1997; Thorne, 1994). In one of the first articles dedicated to the topic of qualitative secondary analysis, Sally Thorne (1994) outlined five possibilities. In 'analytic expansion', she suggested researchers could make use of their own data to answer new or extended questions; in 'retrospective interpretation', new questions which were raised by, but not addressed in, the primary research could be examined; in 'armchair induction', inductive methods of textual analysis could be applied to data collected by others for purposes of theory development; in 'amplified analysis', several distinct and theoretically representative datasets could be compared; and in 'cross-validation', data collected by others could be re-analysed and alternative findings and links with other research explored.

Ten years later, Corti and Thompson (2004) were able to provide some examples of secondary studies carried out in the meantime to illustrate their view that archived qualitative data could be used for purposes such as: descriptive work; comparative research; re-study or follow-up study; reanalysis or secondary analysis; research design and methodological advancement;

verification; and for teaching and learning (no example of verification was provided, which the authors acknowledge researchers have not yet pursued, despite the availability of resources).

In my review of the health and social care literature, which looked in detail at how and why researchers had re-used qualitative datasets in published studies, I found that there were five main types of qualitative secondary analysis (Heaton, 2004). These are summarised below, together with a few examples of relevant studies drawn from the review and from a more recent search of the social research literature carried out to update the findings for this chapter.

Supra analysis

In this type of secondary analysis, the focus of the secondary study transcends that of the primary work. New theoretical, empirical or methodological questions are explored that are distinct from the aims of the original research. For example, three of the secondary studies reviewed focused on the use of metaphors in participants' accounts of medical encounters (Jairath, 1999; Jenny and Logan, 1996; Pascalev, 1996). Another three studies used secondary analysis in methodological work concerning micro-computing and qualitative data analysis (Weaver and Atkinson, 1994), different methods of textual analysis (Atkinson, 1992), and the value of different approaches to biographical analysis (Jones and Rupp, 2000).

Supplementary analysis

Supplementary analysis was the most common type of secondary analysis identified in the review. This approach involves the in-depth investigation of an issue, or aspect of the data, that was not addressed, or was only partly covered, in the original research. The focus may be on a particular issue or theme that emerged from the primary work, or on a sub-set of the data. Unlike supra analysis, the subject of this type of secondary analysis is more closely related to that of the primary work. As a result, in some cases it may be difficult to distinguish

where primary research stops and secondary analysis starts, particularly when the supplementary analysis is carried out by the same researchers who carried out the primary research.

An example of supplementary analysis is provided by Brownlie and Howson's (2005) secondary analysis of two datasets on professional and parental views of the measles, mumps and rubella (MMR) vaccination. These data were collected in studies carried out by an independent research agency for the Health Education Board for Scotland (HEBS, now NHS Health Scotland) in 1999 and 2001. These organisations agreed to provide the secondary researchers with access to the datasets after they had been anonymised by the research agency. The secondary analysis focused on 'emergent themes of trust and parental anxiety about risk' (Brownlie and Howson, 2005: 223).

Re-analysis

Whereas the above types of secondary analysis involve the investigation of new questions or emergent issues, the purpose of re-analysis is to verify and corroborate the findings of previous work. Only one example approximating this type of secondary analysis was identified in the review. This was a study by Popkess-Vawter et al. (1998), where alternative methods of analysis were used, in a form of methodological triangulation, to re-examine data originally collected by the first author on women's experiences of losing and gaining weight after dieting ('weight-cycling'). Whereas the primary analysis was based on 'reversal theory', the secondary analysis was a content analysis performed by two independent coders 'with no consideration for reversal theory' (Popkess-Vawter et al., 1998: 71). The authors claim that secondary analysis was carried out to provide 'a validity check for the primary coding and an accuracy check for complete interpretation' (Popkess-Vawter et al., 1998: 71), although in reporting their results they do not comment on how the coding and findings from the secondary analysis related to those previously applied and obtained.

Amplified analysis

Secondary studies vary not only in terms of the extent to which their aims diverge from, or converge with, the primary studies from which they are derived, but also according to the number and type of primary studies involved. In amplified analysis, two or more qualitative datasets are utilised. These data may be aggregated to form a larger dataset, or used to compare different populations. An example illustrating this approach (and supra analysis) is Bloor and McIntosh's (1990) study, in which they re-used two datasets to examine forms of surveillance in professional-client relationships, and associated strategies of resistance, from a Foucauldian perspective. In another, more recent example, data from a series of studies carried out between 1995 and 2001 were re-used to examine how family doctors conceptualised chronic illness and its management in their consultations with patients (May et al., 2004).

Assorted analysis

In assorted analysis, secondary analysis of qualitative data is combined with additional primary research and/or documentary analysis of relevant materials. For example, Thorne (1990a) re-used data from multiple datasets, and carried out additional interviews, in a study of non-compliance with advice in chronic illness. In other studies, re-use of qualitative research data was combined with analysis of more naturalistic data in the form of autobiographies (Cohen, 1995; Thorne, 1988).

Key issues

The development of qualitative secondary analysis has been accompanied by a growing debate over the epistemological, practical, ethical and legal problems connected with the re-use of qualitative data. Some of the key issues in this debate are highlighted below.

Epistemological and practical concerns

A major topic of debate has been whether or not secondary analysis of qualitative data is compatible with some of the basic tenets of qualitative inquiry. For example, one concern is whether research questions can be addressed using data which were originally collected for other purposes (Heaton, 2004; Szabo and Strang, 1997; Thorne, 1994, 1998). This problem of data 'fit' is seen as a particular problem in qualitative research where, for instance, data collection can be refined during a study in response to emerging findings. Use of open-ended topic guides in interviews can also result in a rich but relatively unstructured dataset, where a range of topics are covered in varying degrees of depth depending on the direction of the interviews. However, others have argued that secondary analysis allows for unexpected topics that emerge from primary research to be followed up, and that these are worthy topics of investigation precisely because they have emerged spontaneously, without being directly solicited by researchers (Corti and Thompson, 2004). It has also been suggested that secondary analysis allows primary researchers to 'salvage' data that could not be used for the original purposes intended (Sandelowski, 1997: 129).

Another matter of concern is whether researchers can effectively re-use qualitative data that other researchers have collected (Corti and Thompson, 2004; Hammersley, 1997; Heaton, 2004; Hinds et al., 1997; Mauthner et al., 1998; Parry and Mauthner, 2005; Thorne, 1994). When re-using other researchers' data, secondary analysts have the problem of not having 'been there' at data collection, which means that they do not have the benefit of personal knowledge and experience of being involved in the fieldwork that produced the data. As a result, they lack the primary researcher's detailed understanding of the context in which the data were collected, and have a relatively cold and distant relationship to the data (which may be compounded by the dataset having being anonymised and stripped of other identifying features). However, it has been pointed out that this problem is not particular to secondary analysis, as some qualitative studies are carried out by teams of primary researchers whose members are variously involved in the fieldwork (Heaton, 1998, 2004). Some archivists and researchers have also argued that this problem can be reduced by primary researchers fully documenting their dataset, and by secondary analysts consulting the researchers who collected the data (Corti and Thompson, 2004; Fielding, 2004; Hinds et al., 1997).

Yet another concern is whether one suggested use of secondary analysis – re-analysis in order to confirm or discount previous research findings – is a realistic ambition or accordant with the principles of qualitative inquiry (Hammersley, 1997; Heaton, 2004). However, others support the concept of preserving data for replication in both quantitative and qualitative research (Schneider, 2004).

Discussion of technical issues has tended to focus more on issues of how to archive qualitative data than how to do qualitative secondary analysis. For example, there has been some discussion of how best to anonymise qualitative data while preserving the integrity of datasets (Thomson et al., 2005), and when best to obtain consent for archiving and re-using qualitative data (see below). However, unlike the literature on secondary analysis of quantitative data, there are no textbooks on how to re-use qualitative data and there has been only preliminary discussion of issues such as: how to design secondary studies re-using qualitative data; how to find and select relevant datasets; how to analyse secondary qualitative data; how to assure and assess the quality of secondary studies; and what to include in reports of such studies (Heaton, 2004; Hinds et al., 1997; Thorne, 1994, 1998). There is an urgent need for further research on these topics.

Ethical and legal concerns

Another set of concerns relate to the ethical and legal aspects of re-using qualitative data. These include the issue of whether and, if so, when researchers should seek consent to re-use data in secondary studies (Alderson, 1998; Corti et al., 2000; Heaton, 2004; Hood-Williams and Harrison, 1998; Parry and Mauthner, 2004; Richardson and

Godfrey, 2003; Thorne, 1998). This could be done at the time data are collected. However, information on exactly how data will be re-used, by whom and for what purpose, is likely to be scant at this time. Alternatively, consent could be sought retrospectively, as and when particular secondary studies are planned. But this requires that participants' identity and contact details are known and can be used for this purpose. Re-contacting participants also presents researchers with logistical and ethical difficulties where people have changed address or may have died; being re-contacted may also be unwelcome to some former participants. In addition, whether or not researchers decide to seek fresh consent for a secondary study may depend on who collected the data and on the type of qualitative secondary analysis planned; for example, in the case of a supplementary analysis carried out by the same researchers who collected the primary data, and where the aims of the secondary and primary research are relatively congruent, this may not be required (for example, see Brownlie and Howson, 2005).

From a legal perspective, data may be re-used in research in the UK under the Data Protection Act 1998 providing it has been anonymised. However, copyright law also has to be considered when publicly archiving and re-using qualitative data. Under the Copyright, Designs and Patents Act 1988, copyright of 'original works' (which include interview transcripts), is owned by the interviewee. While some use can be made of such material by non-copyright holders, researchers in the UK have been advised to have ownership of copyright of qualitative data transferred in writing from participants to themselves or an archive if the dataset is to be archived for re-use by others (Allen and Overy, 1998).

QUESTIONS FOR FUTURE POLICY AND PRACTICE

Ongoing developments in the secondary analysis of qualitative data raise a number of questions for future policy and practice concerning the collection, archiving and re-use of qualitative data. Three of the most critical questions are discussed below.

Which qualitative datasets should be archived?

As we have seen, great advances in qualitative data archiving have been made in the UK, driven by policies of a major funder of research in the social sciences, the ESRC. Since 1995, the ESRC has had a Datasets Policy that requires researchers to provide qualitative datasets for archiving and possible use by third parties as a condition of their funding, although applicants may make a case for exemption or request access to their datasets is made subject to conditions. Qualidata helped inform development of the ESRCs Datasets Policy and has discussed archiving policies with other funders (Corti and Backhouse, 2005). While commending the ESRC's policy lead, staff from ESDS Qualidata have recommended that the ESRC improves implementation of its Datasets Policy, to make it more 'robust, systematic and accountable' – for example, suggesting that penalties could be introduced for non-compliant researchers (Corti, 2003: 424; see also Corti and Backhouse, 2005). But what is the case for such a mandatory policy of data archiving? And what are the possible alternatives to this model of promoting secondary analysis of qualitative data?

Parry and Mauthner (2005: 338) have argued that, so far as the demand for archived data goes, the 'jury are still out'. As they point out, there is no clear evidence of support for formal archiving of qualitative datasets. On the one hand, Qualidata carried out a survey of academics and researchers in the UK in 1999, which found that 92% of over 550 respondents wanted access to qualitative datasets (Corti and Thompson, 2004)[9]. On the other hand, a report of a consultation on ESRC Data Policy and Archiving found mixed support for, and highlighted 'considerable concerns within the research community' about, the archiving and re-use of qualitative data (Boddy, 2001). The report recommended that archiving policy

should concentrate on retention of 'classic' or 'key' qualitative datasets and suggested the ESRC explore 'alternative approaches to the re-use of qualitative data in order to demonstrate the possibilities' (Boddy, 2001). But, as Parry and Mauthner (2005) point out, this begs the question of how some datasets come to be defined as 'classic' and selected for archiving. Furthermore, as we have seen, there is little evidence of the extent to which researchers have made use of qualitative datasets that have been officially archived so far across the UK. So far, reviews have shown that most of the (non-historical) secondary analyses of qualitative data published to date have been by researchers who have informally shared their data or re-used their own data.

Adoption of a blanket mandatory rather than, say, an elective or invited, policy of formal data archiving, would mean that all researchers would have to aim to meet minimum criteria for archiving datasets to a standard that could be used by third parties – regardless of the nature of the study, the potential value of the dataset as a secondary resource (which may be hard to predict in advance), and the associated work and costs involved in meeting this standard. The requirement to archive could also impact upon the conduct of primary qualitative research when consent for archiving data is sought at the time of data collection, adding to the amount of information that needs to be given and explained to potential research participants by primary researchers. While ESDS Qualidata provide guidelines on how to do this[10], it is not known whether prolonging and complicating the process of getting informed consent at this stage affects participants' agreement to take part. Nor is it known if, having agreed to take part and have their contribution to the dataset deposited in an archive, participants' disclosure to the primary researcher(s) is affected by the knowledge that the information will be available, albeit anonymously, to unknown third parties. In short, there is little research on this topic to help researchers, peer reviewers of grant applications, funding organisations, ethics committees, and the public, decide whether or not archiving is, per se, a desirable scientific and personal option in social research.

Different models of quantitative and qualitative archiving have been previously discussed (see Boddy, 2001; Corti, 2000). In contrast to a mandatory qualitative data archiving policy, I would like to propose an alternative fourfold strategy, subject to support by the research community, including research participants and the public. First, this strategy would focus on making widely available datasets that have value for historical and/or contemporary secondary research. Where this differs from current policy and practice is that what counts as an 'exemplary' study would be decided retrospectively and by independent peer review, using agreed criteria for selecting studies which demonstrate value for teaching and/or secondary research purposes across social science disciplines. The selection of datasets for archiving would be a mark of prestige for the researchers involved, and include a financial award for their help in documenting and preparing the dataset for deposit.

Second, in support of the requirement of some funding organisations, and many publishers, that datasets are retained for a minimum period of time after work has been completed and/or published, funders would make available resources for the adequate in-house preparation and retention of qualitative datasets. At present, there is little provision in research grants, and limited facilities in university workplaces, for data to be adequately retained even for a limited period and to a lower standard than that required in formal data archiving (that is, where data are not purposely made available for use by third parties). Third, services such as Qualidata and data archives would provide advice and guidelines for researchers on protocols for informal data sharing and researchers' re-use of their self-held datasets, as well as procedures for depositing and re-using qualitative datasets in official archives. Finally, funds would be dedicated for projects, such as longitudinal studies, designed to supply qualitative data for use in secondary research. These studies would be the equivalent of multi-purpose statistical surveys, and funding would include provision for archiving and associated costs. Both 'exemplary' and multi-purpose qualitative datasets would be available to registered users via the web.

Whereas the first and last points are being advanced through the aforementioned ESRC initiatives on formal data sharing, less is being done to investigate, support and develop informal data sharing, or the private retention and re-use of qualitative datasets.

Whose qualitative data should be re-used?

As the availability of public and privately retained qualitative datasets grows, researchers will increasingly have a choice of not only whether to do primary or secondary research, but whether to re-use datasets available in dedicated archives, via informal data sharing, or from their own oeuvre. The advantages and limitations of re-using qualitative data varies depending on whose data are re-used.

The main advantages of re-using formally archived datasets are that these will have been specially prepared for use by third parties. Thus, issues of consent, copyright ownership, anonymity of data, meta-documentation of datasets and conditions of access to and use of the material, should have been dealt with and be clear to potential secondary users. The main limitations are that these datasets will have been collected by other researchers, which presents two major problems for secondary analysts. One is how they can recapture the context in which the original study was devised and the data collected. As we have seen, some researchers believe that intimate knowledge of 'being there' in the field and 'immersing' oneself in data processing and analysis, are integral and essential to the process of doing qualitative research and making sense of people's experiences. While the meta-documentation of datasets provides some background and insight, this can only ever be an approximation (Mauthner et al., 1998). The other problem, which is related to this, concerns the relative distance that secondary analysis of formally archived datasets imposes between the researcher and the researched (Thorne, 1994). Here, the researcher's relationship to the data is reduced to (most likely) anonymised data, perhaps offset by wider personal experience of doing primary research with similar groups of people, and/or by contact with the primary researcher(s) who collected the data. While there may be some advantages to having this distance in some secondary studies (for instance, where re-analysis is the goal), nevertheless it is a different, less intimate, relationship compared to that of primary researchers and their subjects[11].

Where datasets are informally shared between colleagues, and primary researchers are also involved in the secondary analysis, here the secondary research team have the advantage of jointly holding and sharing the tacit, as well as the documented, knowledge of the researcher(s) who collected the data. In this situation, the process of doing secondary analysis is arguably no different to that of doing primary research in teams where interviews may be carried out and analysed by different members (Heaton, 1998, 2004). The co-involvement of the primary researchers means that, compared to re-using archived data, there may be greater awareness of the context of the primary work, and sensitivity to the feelings of the researched (and any other researchers who carried out the primary work). Other advantages are that secondary researchers may be able to gain quicker access to informally shared datasets, rather than have to wait for them to be processed and become available via an archive. They may also have access to and be able to re-use any electronic coding that was employed in the original analysis, carried out using software designed to assist qualitative data analysis. And where primary researchers are involved in the secondary research, they may retain direct control over the re-use of the dataset rather than rely on an archive.

The main disadvantages of informal data sharing are that datasets may not be prepared to be as high a standard as in an archive, nor may all the aforementioned protocols be fully satisfied. For example, secondary researchers may have to re-contact participants for consent to re-use data where this is required. In addition, where primary researchers share their data but are not involved in the secondary analysis, the disadvantages of re-using formally archived data apply and may be compounded by the relatively poor documentation of datasets if they have not been prepared for sharing with third parties.

Many of the advantages and limitations of informal data sharing apply to secondary research carried out by researchers who choose to re-use their own data. Additional advantages are that researchers who have worked on related projects in their careers can draw on and utilise material from this work (for example, see Thorne, 1990a, 1990b and 1990c). Researchers may also identify and follow up spontaneous topics of analysis that emerge unexpectedly in the course of research and which otherwise may go unanalysed if they are not germane to the aims of the primary research, or if the data are not shared with others or archived for further use. However, this practice raises new issues. Where does primary research stop and secondary analysis start? At what point is further consent required from participants to re-use data for spontaneous studies, even if these are to be carried out by the same researcher(s) who collected the data? Finally, researchers who re-use their own data may also find that their memory of the original study changes over time, and that their perspective shifts as their own life experiences inform their subsequent analysis of the data (Mauthner et al., 1998).

Of course, the above are just some of the pros and cons of working with qualitative data drawn from different sources. Many other factors, including the accessibility of datasets, preference for data format, quality of the original study, degree of 'fit' between the aims of the secondary research and the content of the dataset(s), trust between researchers, compatibility of shared datasets, and availability of any electronic coding used in the primary research (and secondary analyst's preferred software), will influence the decision as to whether or not to do secondary analysis and, if so, using which source of data.

(How) do research participants want qualitative data to be re-used?

The third and final important topic for debate concerns the involvement of research participants in helping to shape future policy and practice in the secondary analysis of qualitative data. Some research has been carried out examining public attitudes to consent for secondary use of mainly statistical data collected for administrative or research purposes in health services research[12]. This has shown support for data sharing, although with appropriate consent and safeguards in place. However, little is known about participants' and public views on whether and, if so, how, qualitative data is obtained, anonymised, shared and re-used for secondary purposes in social research (Heaton, 2004). Some related work on methods of anonymisation in primary research has been carried out. For example, Grinyer (2002) has discussed participants' views on anonymisation and use of pseudonyms in connection with her primary research with families of young people who have cancer. This showed that respondents can have different views on whether or not they would like to be personally identified in research reports. A small study of participants' views on the use of verbatim quotations in qualitative research, including how speech should be edited, attributed and reported in research reports, showed that anonymisation was important to the people who took part, and also revealed a dislike of being identified as belonging to certain groups or categories that might be perceived negatively by others (Corden and Sainsbury, 2005). Hopefully, the aforementioned QUADS studies will provide an insight into participants' experiences of being involved in, for example, longitudinal research, where datasets are to be retained for use by third parties, and their views on the

appropriateness of approaches used to obtain and preserve data for sharing with others.

CONCLUSION

While an increasing number of secondary studies are being published, together with commentaries debating the pros and cons of re-using different types of qualitative data from different sources, secondary analysis of qualitative data is still an emerging and intricate methodology. There are, however, a number of things that researchers can do to further develop and establish the value of re-using qualitative data. In reports of their work, secondary analysts could usefully describe their methods in more depth and reflect on the strengths and limitations of the particular approach they used. Further work is also needed to explore and outline different strategies for re-using qualitative data, and to examine the acceptability of these strategies to research participants and the public. And primary researchers need to be mindful of the possibility of data being re-used, through data archiving, informal data sharing or secondary analysis of self-preserved datasets, when collecting qualitative data in the course of primary research. Finally, the ongoing development of secondary analysis of qualitative data has implications for the principles and practices in qualitative research generally. Ethical protocols, data processing, data analysis, reporting, and criteria for assessing the quality of qualitative research, need to keep pace with these developments so that they are inclusive of the possibilities and practice of secondary analysis of qualitative data.

NOTES

1 The CESSDA website address is: http://www.nsd.uib.no/cessda/ [accessed 28/2/2006].

2 International developments in qualitative data archiving are reported in an issue of *Forum: Qualitative Social Research* [Online Journal], 200, 1 (3). Available at: http://www.qualitative-research.net/fqs/fqs-e/inhalt3-00-e.htm [accessed 1/3/2006].

3 ESRCs Datasets Policy is set out in Annex C of '2005 ESRC Research Funding Guide Post fEC', available at: http://www.esrcsocietytoday.ac.uk/ESRCInfoCentre/opportunities/research%5Ffunding/ [accessed 28/2/2006].

4 Information on QUADS is available at the UKDA website: http://quads.esds.ac.uk/about/introduction.asp [accessed 28/2/2006].

5 'Changing Lives and Times qualitative longitudinal initiative'. Call for outline proposals on ESRC website: http://www.esrcsocietytoday.ac.uk/ESRCInfoCentre/opportunities/current_funding_opportunities/index28.aspx [accessed 28/2/2006].

6 The ESDS Qualidata catalogue currently lists 162 datasets (and details of others remain to be transferred from the older Qualicat catalogue). Available at: http://www.data-archive.ac.uk/search/allSearch.asp?q1=qualidata&zoom_page=1&zoom_per_page=10&zoom_cat=-1&zoom_and=1&zoom_sort=1&ct=xmlAll [accessed 28/2/2006].

7 There is some public information on this, produced by JISC on ESDS performance and published on its website: http://www.mu.jisc.ac.uk/servicedata/esds/data/ [accessed 28/2/2006].

8 Provisional searches of ASSIA and selected electronic databases of research on criminology and education carried out by myself and independently by two colleagues (Rachel Pitman and Janette Colclough, University of York) in February 2006 provided little evidence of such studies. However, there are difficulties searching for secondary studies because there are no established key words for classifying such studies, and authors' own definitions of secondary analysis vary. A renewed search of the health-related literature, using similar search strategies, did result in further studies been identified. In total, over 100 secondary studies in health, criminology and education have been identified to date.

9 A different response figure (99%) and date of the survey (2000) have been reported elsewhere (Corti, 2000). I have quoted the most recently published.

10 Guidelines on creating and depositing qualitative datasets are available on the ESDS Qualidata website: http://www.esds.ac.uk/qualidata/create/ [accessed 28/2/2006].

11 There are parallels here with concerns over the use of computer software in qualitative data analysis (see Gilbert, 2002).

12 See essays published in a special supplement of the *Journal of Health Services Research and Policy*, 2005, 8 (1).

REFERENCES

Alderson, P. (1998) 'Confidentiality and consent in qualitative research', *Network – Newsletter of the British Sociological Association*, 69: 6–7.

Allen and Overy (1998) 'Copyright/confidentiality: final report to the Economic and Social Research Council'. Retrieved from: ftp://ftp.esrc.ac.uk/pub/guide.doc [accessed 14/9/1998].

Angst, D.B. and Deatrick, J.A. (1996) 'Involvement in health care decisions: parents and children with chronic illness', *Journal of Family Nursing*, 2 (2): 174–94.

Atkinson, P. (1992) 'The ethnography of a medical setting: reading, writing and rhetoric', *Qualitative Health Research*, 2 (4): 451–74.

Bevan, M. (2000) 'Family and vocation: career choice and the life histories of general practitioners', in Bornat, J., Perks, R., Thompson, P. and Walmsley, J. (eds.), *Oral History, Health and Welfare*. London: Routledge. pp. 21–47.

Bloor, M. (2000) 'The South Wales Miners Federation, Miners' Lung and the instrumental use of expertise, 1900–1950', *Social Studies in Science*, 30 (1): 125–40.

Bloor, M. and McIntosh, J. (1990) 'Surveillance and concealment: a comparison of techniques of client resistance in therapeutic communities and health visiting', in Cunningham-Burley, S. and McKeganey, N.P. (eds.), *Readings in Medical Sociology*. London: Tavistock/Routledge. pp. 159–81.

Boddy, M. (2001) *Data Policy and Data Archiving: Report on Consultation for the ESRC Research Resources Board*. Bristol: University of Bristol.

Brownlie, J. and Howson, A. (2005) ' "Leaps of faith" and MMR: an empirical study of trust', *Sociology*, 39 (2): 221–39.

Cohen, M.H. (1995) 'The triggers of heightened parental uncertainty in chronic, life-threatening childhood illness', *Qualitative Health Research*, 5 (1): 63–77.

Cohen, S. and Taylor, L. (1972) *Psychological Survival: The Effects of Long-Term Imprisonment*. London: Allen Lane.

Corden, A. and Sainsbury, R. (2005) 'Research participants' views on use of verbatim quotations'. Final report to ESRC, ref 2094. York: Social Policy Research Unit (SPRU), University of York.

Corti, L. (2000) 'Progress and problems of preserving and providing access to qualitative data for social research – the international picture of an emerging culture', *Forum: Qualitative Social Research* [Online Journal], 1 (3): 58 paragraphs. Available at: http://www.qualitative-research.net/fqs-texte/3-00/3-00corti-e.htm [accessed 1/3/2006].

Corti, L. (2003) 'Infrastructure services and needs for the provision of enhanced qualitative data resources', *International Social Science Journal*, 55 (3): 417–32.

Corti, L. and Backhouse, G. (2005) 'Acquiring qualitative data for secondary analysis', *Forum: Qualitative Social Research* [Online Journal],

6 (2): 31 paragraphs. Available at: http://www. qualitative-research.net/fqs-texte/2-05/05-2-36-e.htm [accessed 1/3/2006].

Corti, L., Day, A. and Backhouse, G. (2000) 'Confidentiality and informed consent: issues for consideration in the preservation of and provision of access to qualitative data archives', *Forum: Qualitative Social Research* [Online Journal], 1 (3): 46 paragraphs. Available at: http://www.qualitative-research.net/fqs-texte/3-00/3-00cortietal-e.htm [accessed 1/3/2006].

Corti, L. and Thompson, P. (2004) 'Secondary analysis of archived data', in Seale, C., Gobo, G., Gubrium, J.F. and Silverman, D. (eds.), *Qualitative Research Practice*. London: Sage. pp. 327–43.

Fielding, N. (2004) 'Getting the most from archived qualitative data: epistemological, practical and professional obstacles', *International Journal of Social Research Methodology*, 7 (1): 97–104.

Fielding, N.G. and Fielding, J.L. (2000) 'Resistance and adaptation to criminal identity: using secondary analysis to evaluate classic studies of crime and deviance', *Sociology*, 34 (4): 671–89.

Gilbert, L.S. (2002) 'Going the distance: 'closeness' in qualitative data analysis software', *International Journal of Social Research Methodology*, 5 (3): 215–28.

Grinyer, A. (2002) 'The anonymity of research participants: assumptions, ethics and practicalities', *Social Research Update*, Issue 36, University of Surrey.

Hammersley, M. (1997) 'Qualitative data archiving: some reflections on its prospects and problems', *Sociology*, 31 (1): 131–42.

Heaton, J. (1998) 'Secondary analysis of qualitative data', *Social Research Update*, Issue 22, University of Surrey.

Heaton, J. (2000) 'Secondary analysis of qualitative data: a review of the literature'. Final report to ESRC, ref R000222918. York: Social Policy Research Unit (SPRU), University of York.

Heaton, J. (2004) *Reworking Qualitative Data*. London: Sage.

Henwood, K. and Lang, I. (2003) *Qualitative Research Resources: A Consultation with UK Social Scientists*. Swindon, UK: ESRC.

Hinds, P.S., Vogel, R.J. and Clarke-Steffen, L. (1997) 'The possibilities and pitfalls of doing a secondary analysis of a qualitative data set', *Qualitative Health Research*, 7 (3): 408–24.

Holland, J., Thomson, R. and Henderson, S. (2004) 'Feasibility study for a possible qualitative longitudinal study: discussion paper'. Available at: http://www. lsbu.ac.uk/inventingadulthoods/feasibility_study.pdf [accessed 23/2/2006].

Hood-Williams, J. and Harrison, W.C. (1998) ' "It's all in the small print ...": archiving and qualitative research', *Network – Newsletter of the British Sociological Association*, 70: 8–9.

Jairath, N. (1999) 'Myocardial infarction patients' use of metaphors to share meaning and communicate underlying frames of experience', *Journal of Advanced Nursing*, 29 (2): 283–89.

James, J.B. and Sørensen, A. (2000) 'Archiving longitudinal data for future research: why qualitative data add to a study's usefulness', *Forum: Qualitative Social Research* [Online Journal], 1 (3): 57 paragraphs. Available at: http://www.qualitative-research.net/fqs-texte/3-00/3-00jamessorensen-e.htm [accessed 1/3/2006].

Jenny, J. and Logan, J. (1996) 'Caring and comfort metaphors used by patients in critical care', *Image: Journal of Nursing Scholarship*, 28 (4): 349–52.

Jones, C. and Rupp, S. (2000) 'Understanding the carers' world: a biographical-interpretive case study', in Chamberlayne, P., Bornat, J. and Wengraf, T. (eds.), *The Turn to Biographical Methods in Social Science: Comparative Issues and Examples*. London: Routledge. pp. 276–89.

Mauthner, N.S., Parry, O. and Backett-Milburn, K. (1998) 'The data are out there, or are they? Implications for archiving and revisiting qualitative data', *Sociology*, 32 (4): 733–45.

May, C., Allison, G., Chapple, A., Chew-Graham, C., Dixon, C., Gask, L., Graham, R., Rogers, A. and Roland, M. (2004) 'Framing the doctor-patient relationship in chronic illness: a comparative study of general practitioners accounts', *Sociology of Health & Illness*, 26 (2): 135–58.

Nelson, L.G.L., Summers, J.A. and Turnbull, A. (2004) 'Boundaries in family-professional relationships: implications for special education', *Remedial and Special Education*, 25 (3): 153–65.

Parry, O. and Mauthner, N.S. (2004) 'Whose data are they anyway? Practical, legal and ethical issues in archiving qualitative research data', *Sociology*, 38 (1): 139–52.

Parry, O. and Mauthner, N.S. (2005) 'Back to basics: who re-uses qualitative data and why?', *Sociology*, 39 (2): 337–42.

Pascalev, A. (1996) 'Images of death and dying in the intensive care unit', *Journal of Medical Humanities*, 17 (4): 219–36.

Plummer, K. (1983) *Documents of Life: An Introduction to the Problems and Literature of a Humanistic Method*. London: George Allen & Unwin.

Plummer, K. (2001) *Documents of Life 2: An Invitation to a Critical Humanism*. London: Sage.

Popkess-Vawter, S., Brandau, C. and Straub, J. (1998) 'Triggers of overeating and related intervention strategies for women who weight cycle', *Applied Nursing Research*, 11 (2): 69–76.

Richardson, J.C. and Godfrey, B.S. (2003) 'Towards ethical practice in the use of archived transcripted interviews', *International Journal of Social Research Methodology*, 6 (4): 347–55.

Sandelowski, M. (1997) ' "To be of use": enhancing the utility of qualitative research', *Nursing Outlook*, 45: 125–32.

Savage, M. (2005a) 'Working-class identities in the 1960s: revisiting the Affluent Worker study', *Sociology*, 39 (5): 929–46.

Savage, M. (2005b) 'Revisiting classic qualitative studies', *Forum: Qualitative Social Research* [Online Journal], 6 (1): 43 paragraphs. Available at: http://www.qualitative-research.net/fqs-texte/1-05/05-1-31-e.htm [accessed 1/3/2006].

Schneider, B. (2004) 'Building a scientific community: the need for replication', *Teachers College Record*, 106 (7): 1471–83.

Scott, J. (1990) *A Matter of Record: Documentary Sources in Social Research*. Cambridge: Polity Press.

Szabo, V. and Strang, V.R. (1997) 'Secondary analysis of qualitative data', *Advances in Nursing Science*, 20 (2): 66–74.

Thompson, P. (1998) 'Sharing and reshaping life stories: problems and potential in archiving research narratives', in Chamberlain, M. and Thompson, P. (eds.), *Narrative and Genre*. London: Routledge. pp. 167–81.

Thomson, D., Bzdel, L., Golden-Biddle, K., Reay, T. and Estabrooks, C.A. (2005) 'Central questions of anonymization: a case study of secondary use of qualitative data', *Forum: Qualitative Social Research* [Online Journal], 6 (1): 33 paragraphs. Available at: http://www.qualitative-research.net/fqs-texte/1-05/05-1-29-e.htm [accessed 1/3/2006].

Thorne, S.E. (1988) 'Helpful and unhelpful communications in cancer care: the patient perspective', *Oncology Nursing Forum*, 15 (2): 167–72.

Thorne, S.E. (1990a) 'Constructive noncompliance in chronic illness', *Holistic Nursing Practice*, 5 (1): 62–9.

Thorne, S.E. (1990b) 'Mothers with chronic illness: a predicament of social construction', *Health Care for Women International*, 11: 209–21.

Thorne, S.E. (1990c) 'Navigating troubled waters: chronic illness experience in a health care crisis'. Unpublished thesis, The Union Institute of Advanced Studies: Cincinnati.

Thorne, S.E. (1994) 'Secondary analysis in qualitative research: issues and implications', in Morse, J.M. (ed.), *Critical Issues in Qualitative Research Methods*. London: Sage. pp. 263–79.

Thorne, S.E. (1998) 'Ethical and representational issues in qualitative secondary analysis', *Qualitative Health Research*, 8 (4): 547–55.

Weaver, A. (1994) 'Deconstructing dirt and disease: the case of TB', in Bloor, M. and Taraborrell, P. (eds.), *Qualitative Studies in Health and Medicine*. Aldershot: Avebury. pp. 76–95.

Weaver, A. and Atkinson, P. (1994) *Microcomputing and Qualitative Data Analysis*. Aldershot: Avebury.

Yamashita, M. and Forsyth, D.M. (1998) 'Family coping with mental illness: an aggregate from two studies, Canada and United States', *Journal of the American Psychiatric Association*, 4 (1): 1–8.

31

Secondary Analysis of Quantitative Data Sources

Angela Dale, Jo Wathan and
Vanessa Higgins

INTRODUCTION

Secondary analysis is generally understood as the analysis of data originally collected and analysed for another purpose (Hakim, 1982; Kielcolt and Nathan, 1986; Dale et al, 1988; Firebaugh, 1997). It is a method that has increased in popularity with the increasing availability of high-quality data through national data archives. Secondary analysis enables researchers to analyse datasets that they would not dream of being able to collect themselves. Examples include surveys and census data collected by government, or surveys conducted by academics but then made available for others to use. Here, we also discuss the increasing number of surveys which are collected specifically as a research resource for others. Secondary analysis is sometimes used to refer to the analysis of data sources such as published reports or newspaper articles. This may be better considered as primary analysis of secondary sources and is not discussed here.

The data sources discussed in this chapter are primarily those collected through some kind of survey, with a focus on microdata: typically individual-level data where there is one case for each respondent. However, we also mention data obtained from administrative records (for example vital registration, taxation records or records relating to those who have claimed benefits), as well as aggregate data – for example tables extracted from official sources such as the census of population, or the Office of Economic Cooperation and Development (OECD).

The chapter reviews the range of data available for secondary analysis and includes some tips on how to find data sources, with a particular focus on the data archives that play a key role in facilitating data access. We discuss some of the major benefits of secondary analysis and highlight ways in which it can be used to complement other methods, such as qualitative interviews. We then go on to stress the role of informed consent in the re-use of data and the importance of good practice. Good practice has two aspects – ensuring data are used in a responsible way that maintains the confidentiality of the respondents, and also good practice in terms of analysis. Finally, we review some of the new developments in access that have resulted from web technologies.

DATA AVAILABILITY

In this section we discuss what a data archive does, what types of data are available and provide some generic advice on how to find a dataset.

Data archives

Data archives play a fundamental role in making data available for secondary analysis. A data archive is a storehouse of digitised data. The archive performs a set of related functions which include obtaining data, assessing its suitability for release, checking the data, adding the necessary data description and documentation and preserving the data for future use. All archives have some form of catalogue. Large archives usually have sophisticated search facilities that allow you to browse through major studies, search abstracts for keywords and so forth.

Many countries now have either a national archive, or a small number of major archives. This development can be traced back to the establishment of the Roper Center in the United States in 1957 (Dale et al, 1988) which continues to be a major source of public opinion datasets. The Inter-University Consortium of Public and Social Research (ICPSR) followed in 1962 and houses a broad range of social data, mainly from academic and government sources. The UK Data Archive was formed in 1967 and has been centrally funded by the Economic and Social Research Council throughout this period. By the start of the century archives were widespread as illustrated in Box 31.1.

This list, which is far from comprehensive, illustrates the extent to which archives are found world-wide. More extensive lists of national archives can be found from the websites of the International Federation of Data Organisations (IFDO see http://www.ifdo.org/) and Council of European Social Science Data Archives (CESSDA see http://www.cessda.org).

The archives listed in Box 31.1 are typically created in an academic environment with academic re-use in mind. However, many data collectors are also involved with data distribution. In the United States a range of microdata are available directly from the website of the Census Bureau, whilst many other statistical offices, such as the UK Office for National Statistics (ONS) and the National Institute for Statistics and Economic Studies (INSEE) in France, make summary statistics available online. The United Nations Statistics Division provides a listing of national statistics offices as well as links to other statistical databases (http://unstats.un.org/unsd/methods/internatlinks/sd_natstat.htm (last accessed 06/02/07).

What data are available?

The range of data that is available for a specific country will vary with historical and cultural factors but may include many of the types described in Box 31.2. Data from private sector sources, or business surveys may also be available.

Locating a dataset

The following points provide some guidance on how to search for a dataset.

1 **Searching your local data archive**
    The most obvious place to search for a dataset is in the archives of your own country. Such archives will almost certainly have a website with a searchable catalogue. The CESSDA (for Europe) or IFDO websites are helpful in locating national archives.
2 **Looking for data from data collectors**
    If you know a dataset exists but cannot find it in your local data archive it is worth finding out who collected or commissioned the data. National statistical organisations and other major social survey organisations may be able to provide

Box 31.1   Some key national, and other, major data archives

Country	Archive	Web address[1]
Australia	Australian Social Science Data Archive	http://assda.anu.edu.au/
Austria	Wiener Institut für Sozialwissen-schaftliche Dokumentation und Methodik (WISDOM)	http://www.wisdom.at/
Czech Republic	Sociologický datový archiv (SDA)	http://archiv.soc.cas.cz/
France	Reseau Quetelet	http://www.centre.quetelet.cnrs.fr/
Germany	Zentralarchiv für Empirische Sozialforschung	http://www.gesis.org/ZA/
Ireland	Irish Social Science Data Archive (ISSDA)	http://www.ucd.ie/issda/
Israel	Israeli Social Sciences Data Center (ISDC)	http://isdc.huji.ac.il/
Japan	Information Center for Social Science Research on Japan (SSJ)	http://ssjda.iss.u-tokyo.ac.jp/en/index.html
Norway	Norsk samfunnsvitenskapelig datatjeneste	http://www.nsd.uib.no/
South Africa	South African Data Archive (SADA)	http://www.nrf.ac.za/sada/
United Kingdom	UK Data Archive – a member of the Economic and Social Data Service (ESDS). ESDS is a good entry point for new researchers.	http://www.data-archive.ac.uk http://www.esds.ac.uk
USA	Inter-university Consortium of Political and Social Research	http://www.icpsr.umich.edu/
USA	Minnesota Population Center	http://www.pop.umn.edu/
USA	Roper Center	http://www.ropercenter.uconn.edu/

[1]*Note*: urls given as at 6th February 2007.

you with access to the data or direct you to another organisation that disseminates data on their behalf.

3 **Using a dataset from another country**
Some datasets are restricted to users within the country of origin. However, the archive website will usually describe access conditions. Often your local data archive will be able to help you to obtain the dataset. CESSDA has an international data browser and search facility which enables users to explore a range of data published by major European national archives.

4 **Does a dataset exist?**
A literature search on your research topic is a good way to find out about data availability. If a major data source is available it is likely that someone will already have used it. A good knowledge of the literature will help you to identify the sorts of data sources that may be available.

5 **Other information sources**
You may find that there are other resources (often web-based) that can help with your search. The United Kingdom, for example, has a range of resources that can help you to locate potential data sources. A list of these is given in Box 31.3.

Microdata based on administrative records

There are a growing number of datasets that are constructed by linking together administrative records for the same individuals. However, they may not be listed in a data archive catalogue and will almost certainly only be available under restricted conditions. The use of administrative records for research has been pioneered by countries such as Norway, Denmark, Finland and the Netherlands. In these countries a single identification number which is used across a wide range of official records provides a basis of record linkage. In Denmark a unique ID is allocated to individuals at birth and is used by government departments responsible

Box 31.2 Types of data available to secondary analysts

Type of data	Example
Summary statistics for small areas	*Neighbourhood Statistics (United Kingdom)* These data are drawn from a mixture of census and administrative record sources. They provide summary statistics (e.g. counts) for small administrative areas and are available directly from the Office for National Statistics.
Large cross-survey series collected on behalf of government departments	*Enquete Emploi (France)* The European Union required member states to conduct regular labour force surveys. Some countries make the survey microdata available to secondary researchers. In France, the Enquete Emploi is conducted annually in March. A sample containing data on approximately 135,000 individuals is available from Réseau Quetelet
Large longitudinal datasets	*The Panel Study of Income Dynamics (United States)* The PSID is one of the longest running longitudinal studies, which started in 1968 with a sample of approximately 4,800 households. It focuses on family income and the determinants of changes in income. Microdata files are available from the ICPSR.
Academic studies	*Social Change and Economic Life Initiative (United Kingdom)* The SCELI study was a programme funded by the UK's Economic and Social Research Council. Around 6,000 interviews were conducted in four areas and collected work histories and attitudes to work. The data and its associated follow-up studies are available from the Economic and Social Data Service.
International comparative studies	*The European Social Survey (Europe)* The European Social Attitudes survey is conducted simultaneously in a large number of countries. Data are available from ESS data website at: http://ess.nsd.uib.no/
Census microdata	*The International Public Use Microdata Sets (USA/International)* Some countries make samples of microdata drawn from census output databases available for reanalysis. These data have small sampling fractions and are anonymised to protect confidentiality. The IPUMS is a major international collection of such files which are held at the University of Minnesota. Individual countries may also make census microdata available through national archives or statistical offices.

for employment, taxation, benefits, education, housing and health. This has enabled the Danish statistical office to create a research database by linking together records for each individual in the country (Smith et al, 2004). This has, for example, been used to model the effect of proposed tax and benefit changes on different sections of the population. Similarly, Sweden has a longitudinal database for education, income and employment that was set up to support research on changes in the Swedish labour market during the 1990s. In Norway, Sweden and Denmark, and also England and Wales, linked records have long been used for analysis of the social

determinants of mortality. These studies have all been based on evidence from death records, linked to other information from vital statistics and, in some cases, census data. In the UK these is a growing focus on realising the research benefits of record linkage across a much wider range of topic areas, although the absence of single reliable ID which is used across all administrative records hampers progress.

In all cases, where administrative records are used for research there are major concerns over protecting the anonymity and confidentiality of the individuals in the database. This means that databases are very carefully

Box 31.3   Information sources for UK secondary analysts

Economic and Social Data Service (ESDS)
http://www.esds.ac.uk
This service supports the work done by the UK Data Archive in making data available. There are
four specialist functions which support secondary analysis of: government surveys, longitudinal data,
international comparative data and qualitative data.

Census of Population Programme
http://www.census.ac.uk
Census data is accessible through a separate service designed for academic users.

Question Bank
http://qb.soc.surrey.ac.uk
This service contains information on survey content and survey questions. There are also links to the
Survey Link Scheme which enables researchers to attend a survey briefing, and often to shadow an
interviewer in the field.

Office for National Statistics
http://www.statistics.gov.uk
The National Statistics Office of the UK is responsible for collecting many key data series. It provides
information on their surveys, summary statistics and published reports.

Intute
http://www.intute.ac.uk
Intute is a general resource which provides links to key websites.

---

controlled by the relevant national statistical offices and research access is subject to very tight security measures (see section entitled 'Advances in access to data and support').

ANALYTICAL AND RESEARCH VALUE

The quantitative data sources available for secondary analysis offer enormous potential for research on a wide range of topics. Whilst tabular data provide an excellent source of material for many purposes (for example, national censuses of population provide essential information on the structure of the population and, in particular, the characteristics of small areas), these aggregate sources do not allow the analyst the flexibility available with microdata. For example, access to microdata provides a much more extensive range of variables, usually in a great deal of detail. This allows the creation of new categorisations and new definitions appropriate to the research question, rather than using those defined by the survey commissioner. It also

means that the data can be used in much more sophisticated analyses than is possible with tabular outputs.

Large quantitative surveys tend to be collected by agencies with well-established reputations for quality research, for example, the US Census Bureau or the UK Office for National Statistics. Rigorous methodologies and sophisticated sampling methods are employed and interviewers are trained extensively to ensure good quality data. Usually the survey process is well documented and data are carefully checked and edited. Access to these very expensive resources provides considerable benefit to secondary analysts. In the following paragraphs we briefly review some of the key research benefits from secondary analysis of microdata files.

Large and nationally representative samples

Secondary analysis can provide the basis for making generalisations to the population as a whole. Large government surveys are usually designed to be nationally representative and may contain weighting factors which gross up the sample to provide population estimates.

In the US, large surveys such as the Survey of Income and Program Participation (SIPP) (www.bls.census.gov/sipp) provide comprehensive information about the income and program participation of individuals and households in the US. In the UK, government surveys such as the Labour Force Survey provide detailed information on topics related to employment, education and training and earnings. In both examples sample sizes are very large and designed to be nationally representative; all adult members of the household are interviewed, and the surveys have been repeated, usually annually, over more than two decades.

Samples of microdata drawn from the census also provide large and nationally representative samples. The US Public-Use Microdata Samples (PUMS) are samples of individual records from the US decennial census of population. The files contain records representing 5 percent or 1 percent samples of the occupied and vacant housing units in the US and the people in the occupied units. Similarly, the UK Samples of Anonymised Records (SARs) are samples of individual records from the 1991 and 2001 censuses. The 1991 SARs represent 2 percent of enumerated individuals in the UK and 1 percent of enumerated households, whilst in 2001 the individual-level SAR file increased to 3 percent. The PUMS and SARs sample sizes are much larger than most national surveys thus permitting analysis of small groups and sub-national areas. Both cover the full range of census topics including housing, education, health, transport, employment and ethnicity and, in the US, income.

International comparisons

Secondary analysis plays an important role in supporting international comparisons. Sometimes it is possible to locate data sources from different countries with sufficient similarity in the topics and questions asked to support comparative research. The Luxembourg Income Study (LIS) (see http://www.lisproject.org/) brings together economic, social, demographic, and labour market data from about 30 different countries in Europe, America, Asia and Oceania and is widely used in comparative studies of income inequality and poverty. For example, Rainwater and Smeeding (2003) have used comparative data from LIS to ask what it means to be poor in a prosperous nation, especially for children. They compare the situation of American children in low-income families with their counterparts in 14 other countries – including Western Europe, Australia, and Canada, thus providing a powerful perspective on the dynamics of child poverty in the US. Their book also contains a valuable section on how to use the LIS.

The Luxembourg Employment Study (LES) provides a similar set of data files based on Labour Force Surveys for a range of countries. In both LIS and LES the support teams do a great deal of preparative work to make the studies comparable. Because most of the surveys come from national statistical offices and are not usually distributed internationally, a system of remote access has been devised so that no microdata actually leave the secure LIS/LES setting (see section entitled 'Advances in access to data and support').

In other situations comparative analysis may be based on separate analyses of different data sources but asking the same, or similar, questions. Breen (2005) reports results from a large international comparative study of social mobility based on 11 different European countries over more than 20 years (from the mid-1970s to the mid-1990s). Data were coded to common international class and education schemes. An early chapter brings together all the datasets to make a cross-country comparative analysis of social mobility in Europe between 1970 and 2000. Subsequent chapters provide an analysis for each country, by an expert from that country. These country-specific chapters provide the context needed to understand the differences found in the international comparative analyses.

The European Social Survey (ESS) provides a contrast in that it is explicitly designed to support international comparison. The survey started in 2001 and has been conducted every two years since. It covers over 20 nations and is designed to chart and explain the interaction between Europe's changing institutions and the attitudes, beliefs and behaviour patterns of its diverse populations. Achieving equivalence across all countries participating in the study is a principle that is applied to sample selection, translation of the questionnaire, and to all methods and processes. All procedures and outcomes are comprehensively documented in a standard way. More information and direct download of data is available from:www.europeansocialsurvey.org.

Clark and Lelkes (2005) used the 2002–2003 ESS to show that religion acts as a buffer between stressful life events and the ensuing economic and social implications. All denominations suffer less psychological harm from unemployment than the non-religious. Catholics and Protestants are less hurt by marital separation than the non-religious but, while Protestants are protected against divorce, Catholics suffer a greater fall in life satisfaction than other groups.

Historical comparisons and change over time

Many of the examples in the earlier section also included a time dimension and secondary analysis may be the only means by which historical comparisons can be made for information that cannot be collected retrospectively. Data archives allow the researcher to go back in time and find sources of information on, for example, what people thought, how they voted and how much they earned. Many surveys, such as the British General Household Survey (GHS), which collects data on a range of topics covering household, family and individual information, have now been running for 30 years or more. These surveys have retained a high degree of consistency in their core questions and therefore support time series analyses

(e.g. Dickens et al, 2000, Marmot, 2003) or before-and-after policy analysis (Gregg et al, 2005).

The General Social Survey has been conducted in the US by NORC since 1972 and provides information on the changing attitudes of the US population. In a similar vein, the British Social Attitudes Survey has been conducted annually since 1983 and provides a unique insight into how attitudes in Britain have changed over this time period. Both studies form part of a larger programme: the International Social Science Programme (ISSP) which provides comparative data for up to 41 countries world-wide www.issp.org.

Cross-sectional surveys do not follow the same individual over time so they cannot be used to analyse individual level change over time. However, change across aggregated groups can be analysed. For example, Payne and Payne (1994) used the Labour Force Survey for 1979–1989 to model trends in the work chances of unemployed people relative to the chances of people in work. Longitudinal data such as cohort studies or panel studies are required to compare individuals at different points in time.

Cohort studies

In the UK a succession of birth cohorts have studied people born in 1946, 1958, 1970 and, most recently, 2000–2001. These studies have been repeated at intervals since birth and thus grow richer as the respondents grow older. For example, the 1958 cohort study sampled all those children born in Great Britain during one week in March 1958 and conducted follow-up surveys of sample individuals at key stages (e.g. ages 7, 11, 16, 23, 33, 42). It is expected that all these cohort studies will continue throughout the lifetime of their members.

Longitudinal birth cohort studies are valuable for investigating the lifetime processes of individuals. For example, using the 1958 cohort, Butler et al (1971) identified the effect of smoking on low-birth weight and perinatal mortality; Hobcraft and Kiernan (2001) showed that any experience of childhood poverty is clearly associated with adverse outcomes in adulthood; and Elias and Blanchflower (1988) demonstrated the impact of early school achievement on occupational attainment.

A single cohort study is clearly limited in its ability to say anything about how outcomes vary between different cohorts. However, the ability to compare a number of cohorts born at time intervals from 1946 to 2000 becomes a very powerful analysis tool. Ferri et al (2003) provide an accessible account of cohort differences based on analysis of the 1946, 1958 and 1970 cohorts. Topics include: family and parenting, qualifications and employment, income and living standards, physical and mental health, lifestyles, health and citizenship. An account of the first findings from the Millennium cohort (births from 2000 to 2001) is given by Dex and Joshi (2005).

Panel studies

Panel studies such as the US Panel Study of Income Dynamics (PSID) and the British Household Panel Study (BHPS) cover all ages, and are repeated at frequent intervals, usually annually. Whereas cohort studies are primarily suited to understanding developmental processes over a life course, a panel study is able to show the effect of short-term changes in levels of income, household composition and changes in the economy. For example, Jarvis and Jenkins (1999) use the BHPS to show the impact of marital break-up on income whilst Jenkins and Van Kerm (2006) examine trends in income inequality and income mobility. The similarity between PSID and BHPS lends support to comparative analyses between the US and Britain – for example Banks et al's (2003) comparison of financial wealth inequality between these two countries. Both PSID and BHPS provide a wealth of information to support users and have published collections of papers that demonstrate very fully some of the research strengths of the data. Five Thousand American Families captures the first 13 years of PSID and is now available on-line from: www.psidonline.isr.umich.edu,

whilst Berthoud and Gershuny (2000) provide analyses based on the first seven years of BHPS.

Small population sub-groups

Secondary analysis can provide a means of obtaining data on small groups within the population for whom there is no obvious sampling frame. However, a dataset must be large enough to ensure that sufficient numbers of the sub-group can be located, and should also be able to provide a representative sample. Some surveys occasionally have special boost samples for sub-groups; for example, the Health Survey for England contained ethnic minority boosts in 1999 and 2004 (Erens et al, 2001; Sproston and Mindell, 2006). The survey results highlighted some interesting ethnic differences in health outcomes. Bangladeshi and Pakistani men and women, and Black Caribbean women, were more likely than the general population to report that they had bad or very bad health. In relation to the general population (set at 1.0) the risk ratios for bad or very bad health were 3.77 for Bangladeshi men, 4.02 for Bangladeshi women, 2.33 for Pakistani men, 3.54 for Pakistani women, and 1.90 for Black Caribbean women (Sproston et al, 2006).

Additionally, datasets with comparable questions and data collection methods can be pooled to increase sample sizes. For example Ginn and Price (2002) pooled a number of annual GHS datasets to look at the subpopulations of divorcees. Many analysts pool a number of years from the Labour Force Survey to allow analysis of ethnic minorities (Dale et al, 2006). When data are being pooled over successive years it is vitally important to check that there are no changes in sampling design, question wording or categorisation.

Relationships within households

Many datasets collect information about all members in the household, for example most of the UK government surveys, BHPS, PSID and the SIPP. This is valuable for analysing intra-household relationships and supports research concerned with, for example, the impact of a partner's characteristics on women's employment. Other levels of analysis may also be possible, for example it is often possible to identify a family unit or, in the case of the UK Family Resources Survey, a social-security benefit unit.

Combining survey analysis with qualitative research

New data dissemination and analysis tools make it easier than in the past to conduct secondary analysis as part of a mixed methods approach. There are many ways in which this might be undertaken (Bryman, 1988).

- Secondary analysis can provide evidence to help in planning a qualitative study. For example analysis of census data can help to target which geographical areas to use in an interview-based study.
- Secondary data can provide a nationally representative context for a small-scale study, such as a locality-based study or a study of divorcees or lone fathers.
- Qualitative studies are often very important in explaining relationships which are identified by quantitative analysis (for example, the low levels of economic activity amongst some groups of South Asian women in the UK; see Dale et al, 2006).
- Secondary analysis can often be used to test theories generated as the result of qualitative studies.

WHAT ARE THE METHODOLOGICAL ISSUES ASSOCIATED WITH SECONDARY ANALYSIS?

One of the earliest examples of secondary analysis is Durkheim's classic study of suicide – routinely cited as the archetype of positivistic research in which the administrative records of suicides were treated as 'social facts' to be studied as 'things, that is as realities external to the individual' (Durkheim, 1952: 38). Whilst Durkheim's study demonstrated that evidence on suicide rates showed relationships with particular characteristics of the individuals concerned, interpretivists pointed out that these social 'facts' were, in themselves, artefacts that resulted from socially mediated processes. For example, whether a suicide is recorded is influenced by legislation and coroner decisions (Atkinson, 1977). This prototype of secondary analysis not only came to be associated with positivism but also with a lack of reflection on data sources.

However, critical secondary analysts should now be aware that survey data are socially constructed artefacts of the processes that produced them. In this sense, secondary analysis is no different from other forms of social research. The results of a qualitative study based on in-depth interviews are, similarly, a product of the relationship between the subject and researcher, the researcher's interpretation of that interaction, and the choices made over which aspects of the research to report.

However, secondary analysis is usually undertaken by researchers who did not conduct the primary data collection. For this reason they have a more distant relationship to the data and may not, therefore, fully appreciate the processes by which the data were constructed. Therefore it is vital that analysts find out as much detail as possible about how the survey was conducted and the strengths and limitations of the dataset. Axinn and Pearce (2006: 23) make a number of valuable suggestions for ways in which the secondary analyst can learn about the process of collecting the data. These include using a copy of the survey questionnaire to interview someone and then getting them to interview you and visiting the organisation that collected the data and inspecting fieldwork notes to learn about the problems that occurred during fieldwork.

The secondary analyst is usually trying to answer a rather different research question than the primary data analyst. For example, data may have been collected by a government department to address a particular policy requirement and concepts will, therefore, reflect this. The secondary analyst needs to work through their own conceptual definitions before starting the study rather than accepting, uncritically, those of the primary data collector. Often it is possible to combine data elements in new ways to construct the desired definitions. Where the data are less than ideal it is valuable to explain the shortcomings and seek evidence of how this may affect the results.

One of the benefits of secondary analysis is that documentation and data are available for others to use. This means that the research results can be critically assessed by other researchers and analyses replicated, perhaps using alternative assumptions or different models.

ETHICS IN SECONDARY ANALYSIS

At first sight secondary analysis may appear to bypass all the ethical issues that arise at the data collection stage of a study. The primary investigators will have been responsible for obtaining appropriate ethical approval for the study and made decisions about their procedures for informed consent and for protecting the confidentiality of the respondent. Data collection agencies take great care to ensure that procedures conform to high ethical standards. Many national statistical offices collect data under statutory requirement and, in these cases, the security of the data is governed by law. However, for all data collection agencies, maintaining the confidentiality of their respondents is of huge importance and a breach of confidentiality may have negative consequences for the respondent as well as a negative impact on the public's willingness to participate in such studies.

Even though secondary analysts may not face these obligations at the point of data collection, they inherit responsibilities as a result of access to the data and must cooperate in ensuring the confidentiality of the data. In some cases this means that a researcher will not be able to obtain as much detailed data as wished. The relationship between the amount of detail released and the restrictions on access are discussed further in the section entitled 'Advances in access to data and support'.

A further set of obligations arises with respect to professional conduct. Even though there are no specific guidelines on secondary research, the codes of professional organisations, whose remit covers secondary analysts, share some common features. Table 31.1 gives the common features of the codes of the British Social Research Association (SRA) (e.g. 2003), British Sociological Association (BSA) (e.g. 2002) and the Royal Statistical Society (RSS) (1993). These include maintaining awareness of necessary law and legislation, reporting the limitations of your data and method, respecting privacy and maintaining confidentiality of data.

Table 31.1 A comparison of the ethical codes of the British Sociological Association, Royal Statistical Society and Social Research Association

Conduct	RSS	BSA	SRA
Ensure that you know the relevant law & regulations – abide by these	✓	✓	✓
Freely given informed consent wherever possible; be aware of power issues, explain the research fully and uses of data produced	✓	✓	
Do not produce misleading research; honestly & proportionately state problems and limitations of your data and method. Distinguish interpretation of results from opinion. Give readers enough information to assess the quality of work	✓	✓	✓
Seek to upgrade your own skills	✓		
Only do research work that you are competent to do	✓	✓	
Respect privacy – don't unnecessarily intrude on subjects		✓	✓
Consider the effects of your research, including publication; minimise harm to research participants and self		✓	✓
Maintain confidentiality of data – and inform research participants about the use to which data will be put	✓	✓	✓

GOOD PRACTICE

In this section we review issues around good practice in looking after data and using it in a responsible way that will produce research of high quality – both important aspects of the ethical use of data.

Looking after data

The secondary analyst is usually asked to accept the conditions laid down in some kind of agreement or licence that relates to the data to be used. Typically these require that you do not pass the data on to anyone else – unless they have already agreed to these same conditions – and not to try to identify any individual or household from the data. These are basic conditions to protect the interests of the individuals who take part in the study. However, it is also important that data are seen as a valuable commodity that needs to be treated with respect. This means that they should be stored securely and, when a project is finished, disposed of securely. For example, CDs containing data should be physically destroyed. Data files should not be left on your PC so that they may be accessible to the next person who uses it. UK guidelines for good practice in storing and deleting data are available from http://www.esds.ac.uk/news/microDataHandlingandSecurity.pdf.

Use of documentation

Good practice also extends to ensuring that data are used in an appropriate way. This entails reading all the relevant documentation so that you know, for example, what population the data refer to, how the information was collected and compiled and what biases and inaccuracies there may be in the data. Good datasets will have extensive documentation.

Analysis issues: Sampling

In the case of a sample survey you need to establish how the sample was drawn; whether some people (e.g. students, the homeless, high earners) were not included in the sampling frame; what the level of response was; and, most importantly, how this varied between different groups in the population.

If a survey has a complex sampling design, information on sampling design needs to inform analysis. For example where the population is stratified and a different sampling fraction is used for different strata, the sample needs to be adjusted before it is proportionate to the population. A sample may be stratified by ethnic group, and a larger sampling fraction used for minority groups than for the majority group. Disproportionate sampling may also occur where households are sampled and only one person in each household selected for interview. In this case people in small households have a disproportionate chance of being sampled by comparison with people in big households. Usually sample design weights will be supplied with the dataset so that weighting can correct for the effects of sampling design and thus the dataset can reflect the target population. If this is not done results will at best be biased and, in the examples given above, meaningless. Most analysis packages (e.g. SPSS version 13 onwards, STATA, SAS) support the use of these kinds of survey weights.

Analysis issues: Non-response

It is becoming increasingly difficult to obtain high response rates to social surveys (Groves and Couper, 1998; Groves et al, 2002; Couper and De Leeuw, 2003). The key concern for the secondary analyst is the fact that non-respondents almost invariably differ from respondents with obvious consequences for the validity of the results of any analysis. However, it is not just the level of non-response that matters but how it is distributed. If, in a survey with a 30 percent response rate, the 70 percent of non-respondents were allocated at random from the set sample then, apart from small numbers, the low response rate would not matter. However, if, in a survey with a response rate of 80 percent, the 20 percent of non-respondents came almost entirely from the top 20 percent of earners, we would have serious concerns about drawing inferences from the 80 percent of respondents, despite the high response rate. It is therefore important not just to establish the extent of non-response for the overall population but how non-response is distributed across population groups.

In some surveys weights are available to correct for non-response. Non-response weights give a differential weighting to each respondent depending on the likelihood of non-response for people with their characteristics. For example, we know that young single men tend not to respond to surveys and therefore young single men who were in the survey would have a higher weight than, say, older women who have higher response rates.

In longitudinal data, response rates are also of concern not just in the first survey sweep but in all subsequent sweeps. However, unlike cross-sectional surveys, valuable information is available from earlier sweeps on the characteristics of subsequent non-responders.

Generally it is accepted that using non-response weights reduces bias in the estimates and thus provides greater accuracy than not using them. However, Plewis (2004) points out that this may not be the case if the outcome is related to the sources of the non-response and the probability of response is related to the outcome. For example, if the outcome of interest is voting, where young men in inner cities are also known to have very low turn-out rates, then weighting may increase the non-response error rather than reduce it.

For many of the UK government surveys post-stratification or population weights are also calculated to allow weighting to the latest Census. Typically weights are based on variables such as age, sex and local authority. Applying these weights will mean that descriptive statistics from the survey correspond with the relevant population figures on the variables used to derive the weights.

Information about the use of weights may be available through various support services. In the UK a guide to weighting has been published by the ESDS. A broader account of the impact of sample design including non-response (see below) is given in the Practical Exemplars in Analysing Surveys web resource (see http://www.napier.ac.uk/depts/fhls/peas/).

Analysis issues: Item non-response

It is often the case that questions have missing information and this may apply particularly to some questions – for example questions about income. It is important that this is not ignored. First, it is valuable to explore the dataset to find out more about those who are missing on some questions – for example, are non-respondents on income more likely to be working or not-working? Young or old? These simple analyses can help to indicate whether dropping cases with missing data will bias the analysis. Kenward and Carpenter (2005) give examples where the use of imputation to correct for missing data made a radical difference to the results of an analysis on gender differences in children's literacy. Generally, it is worthwhile to use imputation methods to deal with missing data. Guidance on the range of options for dealing with item non-response is available at: www.missingdata.org.uk.

Modelling and causality

One of the strengths of survey analysis is the ability to conduct multivariate analysis (e.g. regression analysis) that includes all the variables which theory suggests are influential in producing a given outcome. This allows us to assess the effect of, say, qualifications on outcomes such as earnings whilst controlling for the individual's age, gender, full-time or part-time working; size of organisation; work experience; and other related factors. Almost always such models have an implicit or explicit assumption of causality. However, Cox and Wermuth (2001: 70) provide a very important reminder that single studies – whether based on cross-sectional or longitudinal data – cannot bear the weight needed for assumptions of causality. They emphasise the need for caution in attributing causality and the importance of having an a priori explanation or 'causal narrative', rather than a retrospective explanation. They also warn against reading too much into small effects, even if statistically significant, and emphasise the importance of replication to see whether the explanatory variable in question is found repeatedly in independent studies.

ADVANCES IN ACCESS TO DATA AND SUPPORT

The technical developments of the web and remote access to data are mirrored in moves towards distributed services: that is, a service that is located at more than one physical site. The UK ESDS is one such service with specialist functions run by teams at two universities which are 200 miles apart. This geographical distance should not be apparent to users who access a single website and who are supported by a joined up helpdesk. However the ability to run a distributed service means that it can benefit from specialist groups irrespective of their geographical location. This has the potential to add more expertise to the service than would be possible if all staff were required to be in the same institution. In this sense ESDS might be considered to set a new standard in data services.

A second area of development builds on the potential for networked technology to provide linkages without the constraints of geography. Grid technology moves beyond the internet and provides the means for users to benefit from increased data storage facilities and processing power. The Grid offers the potential for researchers to link data from different sources, held at a range of locations (perhaps still within the control of the data collector), with prescribed access conditions, and then to analyse these using data processing power from one or more servers. In the UK, the academic community has made some investment in pilot projects to establish areas of potential development. Grid technology has been used to provide virtual meeting spaces called 'access grid nodes' which have been used for meetings between partners in the ESDS distributed data service. From a secondary analysis

perspective, the potential of the grid might be to provide a controlled environment within which disclosive data could be analysed without the need to distribute the microdata to users. The processing capacity can also be harnessed for processing very large datasets and conducting very power-hungry analyses (Smith, 2004). These and other functions are being championed by the UK National Centre for E-social Science (www.ncess.ac.uk).

The increased power of the web, including its search facilities, and the increased level of data availability in general, has led to growing concerns over ensuring the confidentiality of data for secondary analysis. This applies particularly to microdata where a great deal of information about an individual may be contained in a single record. By contrast, it is much harder to identify someone using aggregate statistics (e.g. a table from the Census).

We can define two interacting dimensions when considering access to data – the level of safety associated with the dataset and the level of safety associated with the access setting. The level of safety associated with the dataset will depend heavily on the degree of detail in the data; the proportion of the population in the sample and the ease of identifying the data – either through matching or spontaneous recognition. Thus a small sample with very restricted individual detail and little geographical information will be much 'safer' than a very large sample containing detailed individual information (e.g. occupation, educational qualification, ethnic group) and also information on the locality of residence. The level of safety associated with the access setting will range from a safe setting within a statistical office at one extreme, to unrestricted access to data by any user, at the other extreme.

The two dimensions interact so that, at one extreme, if the data are judged to be entirely safe, then the access arrangements can be very open. This is exemplified by the Public Use Microdata Files produced by the US Bureau of the Census, which can be downloaded without restriction from the website of the US Bureau of the Census. These files are samples – 1 percent and 5 percent – where the amount of both individual detail and geographical information has been restricted to preserve confidentiality (Census Bureau, 2005).

By contrast, if the data are very detailed and/or contain information that could be readily used to identify someone, then greater safety needs to be built into the access conditions. An example is the ONS Longitudinal Study that contains data with a great deal of individual and geographical detail drawn from the census and from vital events (e.g. birth and death records). For this dataset access is only available within a secure setting inside the Office for National Statistics. An alternative is a remote access facility such as that used for the Luxembourg Income Study. Here researchers send requests for analysis (in the form of SPSS or STATA programs) which are run and checked before the non-disclosive results are emailed to the researcher.

In practice most data are made available under some kind of licence whereby the user agrees to a set of conditions designed to ensure the confidentiality of the data. However, as researchers need more detailed data, for example including information on locality, or more datasets are produced by linking administrative records, then they will be subject to tighter controls.

NEW DEVELOPMENTS IN METHODS

Developments in statistical analysis now provide more opportunities for building models that reflect some of the complexities of social life – for example, analysis of children's attainment in school. Multilevel models allow one to define children by the class they are in (and the characteristics of their class teachers); the school they attend (and the characteristics of the school); and also the catchment area of the school. All these different levels are known to affect a child's attainment and their impact can be modelled. Similarly, multilevel models can improve analyses of unemployment, for example, by allowing information about the local labour market to be included in the model. Software for

multilevel modelling is now readily available (e.g. MLWin, STATA, SAS) and there is abundant provision of training to help the new user (see www.ncrm.ac.uk/database).

Structural equation modelling (SEM) allows much greater flexibility in defining models than standard multiple regression. It introduces the concept of the latent variable which has multiple indicators and can correct for some of the measurement error in standard regression analysis. Models tested may have complex causal pathways, often with a two-way direction of causality. SEM allows specific pathways in the model to be tested as well as an overall test of a model. As for multilevel modelling, software for using SEM is becoming much more widely available and, for both, there are a growing number of courses and on-line resources.

Other developments in secondary analysis relate to the linkage of additional data sources to supplement or augment individual level records collected by a survey. The simplest example is where aggregate information about a respondent's locality is attached to that individual (for example, area-level statistics from the census) and this can then be used to explain variation at the level of the locality in a multilevel model. In addition, external data may be matched to an individual, for example tax returns may be used to provide accurate information on earnings. This has been introduced in the Canadian Survey of Living and Income Dynamics (SLID), where respondents can choose between providing detailed information on income or allowing this to be obtained from their tax return. This uses an exact matching method where it is vitally important to have identical keys in both data sources. An alternative that is used where income data cannot be obtained from the respondent is to add an estimated value to each individual. For example, a survey which *does* contain the required income information may be used to identify a set of explanatory variables that predict income well. If these explanatory variables are also contained in the dataset without income, then they can be used as a basis for predicting the expected income of each individual.

CONCLUSION

This chapter has demonstrated the breadth of high-quality data available from secondary sources and some of the exciting research areas that are opened up through secondary analysis. The increased ease of locating and accessing the data (and the accompanying documentation) means that secondary analysis can be readily used in its own right and also to complement other forms of research. It is very cost-effective in terms of both time and money and may therefore be particularly valuable to graduate students or to researchers with very limited funding. However, we have also argued that, despite not having participated in the first-hand collection of the data, the analyst nonetheless has an obligation to ensure that the data are used responsibly and the data subjects' confidentiality is protected. Finally, exciting new developments in access to data, data support and statistical methods are enhancing opportunities and potential for secondary analysis.

REFERENCES

Atkinson, M. (1977) Coroners and the classification of deaths as suicide, in C. Bell & H. Newby (eds) *Doing Sociological Research*. London: Unwin Hyman.

Axinn, W., & Pearce, L. (2006) *Mixed Methods Data Collection Strategies*. New York: Cambridge University Press.

Banks, J., Blundell, R., & Smith, J.P. (2003) Financial wealth inequality in the United States and Great Britain, *The Journal of Human Resources*, Vol. 38, No. 2, pp. 241–279.

Berthoud, R., & Gershuny, J. (eds) (2000) *Seven Years in the Lives of British Families*. Bristol: The Policy Press.

Breen, R. (ed.) (2005) *Social Mobility in Europe*. Oxford: Oxford University Press.

British Sociological Association (2002) *Statement of Ethical Practice*. Durham: BSA.

Bryman, A. (1988) *Quantity and Quality in Social Research*. London: Routledge.

Butler, N.R., Goldstein, H., & Ross E.M. (1971) Cigarette smoking in pregnancy: Influence on birth and perinatal mortality, *British Medical Journal*, Vol. 1, pp. 127–130.

Census Bureau (2005) Public use microdata sample: 2000 Census of Poplulation and Housing technical

Documentation, http://www.census.gov/prod/cen2000/doc/pums.pdf, accessed 20.09.07

Clark, A.E., & Lelkes, O. (2005) *Deliver Us From Evil: Religion As Insurance*, Paris, PSE, http://www.pse.ens.fr/document/wp200543.pdf, accessed 11.3.07.

Couper, M., & De Leeuw E. (2003) Non-response in cross-cultural and cross-national surveys, in Janet A. Harkness, Fons J.R. van de Vijer and Peter Mohler (eds) *Cross-cultural Survey Methods*. New Jersey: John Wiley.

Cox, D.R., & Wermuth, N. (2001) Some statistical aspects of causality. *European Sociological Review*, Vol. 17, No. 1, pp. 65–74.

Dale, A., Arber, S., & Procter, M. (1988) *Doing Secondary Analysis*. London: Unwin Hyman.

Dale, A., Lindley, J., & Dex, S. (2006) A life-course perspective on ethnic differences in women's economic activity in Britain, *European Sociological Review*, Vol. 22, No. 4, pp. 459–476.

Dex, S., & Joshi, H. (eds) (2005) *Children of the 21st Century: From Birth to Nine Months*. Bristol: The Policy Press.

Dickens, R., Gregg, P., & Wadsworth, J. (2000) *New Labour and the Labour Market*, Centre for Market and Public Organisation working paper series 00/19.

Durkheim, E. (1952) *Suicide - A Study in Sociology*. London: Routledge & Kegan Paul.

Elias, P., & Blanchflower, D. (1988) *The Occupations, Earnings and Work Histories of Young Adults – Who Gets the Good Jobs?* Department of Employment Research Paper No. 68, London: Department of Employment.

Erens, B., Primatesta, P., & Prior, G. (eds) (2001) *Health Survey for England 1999 – the Health of Minority Ethnic Groups, Vol 1: Findings*. London: TSO.

Ferri, E., Bynner, J., & Wadsworth, M. (eds) (2003) *Changing Britain, Changing Lives: Three Generations at the Turn of the Century*. London: Institute of Education.

Firebaugh, G. (1997) *Analyzing Repeated Surveys*. Thousand Oaks, CA: Sage.

Ginn, J., & Price, D. (2002) Do divorced women catch up in pension building, *Child and Family Law Quarterly*, Vol. 14, No. 2, 157ff.

Gregg, P., Waldfogel, J., & Washbrook, E. (2005) *Family Expenditures Post-Welfare Reform in the UK: Are Low Income Families Starting to Catch Up?* Centre for Market and Public Organisation working paper series 05/119.

Groves, R., & Couper, M. (1998) *Non-response in Household Interview Surveys*. New York: John Wiley.

Groves, R., Dillman, D., Eltinge, J., & Little, R. (2002) *Survey Non-response*. New York: John Wiley and Sons.

Hakim, C. (1982) *Secondary Analysis of Social Research.* London: George Allen and Unwin.

Hobcraft, J., & Kiernan, K.E. (2001) Childhood poverty, early motherhood and adult social exclusion, *British Journal of Sociology,* Vol. 52, No. 3, pp. 495–517.

Jarvis, H., & Jenkins, S.P. (1999) Marital splits and income changes: Evidence from the British Household Panel Survey, *Population Studies,* Vol. 53, No. 2, pp. 237–254.

Jenkins, S.P., & Van Kerm, P. (2006) Trends in income inequality, pro-poor income growth and income mobility, *Oxford Economic Papers,* Vol. 58, No. 3, pp. 531–548.

Kenward, M., & Carpenter, J. (2005) Missing Data Methodology for Multilevel Models, *Methods Briefing* 5, www.ccsr.ac.uk/methods/publications/documents/kenward_000.pdf.

Kielcolt, K.J., & Nathan, L.E. (1986) *Secondary Analysis of Survey Data.* London: Sage.

Luxembourg Income Study Project http://www.lisproject.org/.

Marmot, M. (2003) *Monitoring Socio-economic Differences in Health*, presentation to the Health Surveys User Group, RSS, London, 11/07/03, slides available at www.esds.ac.uk

Payne, J., & Payne, C. (1994) Recession, restructuring and the fate of the unemployed: Evidence in the underclass debate, *Sociology,* Vol. 28, No. 1, pp. 1–19.

Plewis, I. (2004) Weighting for Non-response: Illustrative Examples www.ccsr.ac.uk/esds/events/2004-03-12/documents/plewisexamleshandout.doc

Rainwater, L., & Smeeding, T.M. (2003) *Poor Kids in a Rich Country: America's Children in Comparative Perspective.* New York: Russell Sage Foundation.

Royal Statistical Society (1993) *Royal Statistical Society Code of Conduct.* London: RSS.

Samples of Anonymised Records: http://www.ccsr.ac.uk/sars

Smith, S. (2004) *Grid Enabling the SARs.* Manchester: Centre for Census and Survey Research, http://www.ccsr.ac.uk/sars/publications/

Smith, G., Noble, M., Anttila, C., Gill, L., Zaidi, A., Wright, G., Dibben, C., & Barnes, H. (2004) *The Value of Linked Administrative Records for Longitudinal Analysis, Report to the ESRC National Longitudinal Strategy Committee.*

Social Research Association (2003) *Ethical Guidelines.* London: Social Research Association.

Sproston, K., & Mindell, J. (eds) (2006) *Health Survey for England 2004. Volume 1: The Health of Minority Ethnic Groups.* London: The Information Centre.

32

Conducting a Meta-Analysis

Erika A. Patall and Harris Cooper

A literature review typically summarizes results of past studies, suggests potential reasons for inconsistencies in past research findings, and directs future investigations. Researchers often use a narrative approach to summarize and integrate research on a specific topic. The traditional narrative reviewer identifies articles relevant to the topic of interest, examines the results of each article to see whether the hypothesis was supported, and provides an overall conclusion.

Traditional narrative reviews have been criticized because, although they can provide a meticulous list of multiple tests of a hypothesis, they often fail to fully and accurately integrate the conclusions contained in them (Hunt, 1997). Narrative reviews are prone to allowing the biases of the reviewer to enter into conclusions, because information in the original studies can be discarded or improperly weighted.

More recently, systematic research syntheses that include meta-analyses have taken the place of purely narrative reviews of empirical literature. Meta-analysis is 'the statistical synthesis of the data from separate but similar, i.e. comparable studies, leading to a quantitative

summary of the pooled results' (Last, 2001). Even though meta-analysis has the same goals as the traditional narrative review, many limitations of the narrative review can be addressed by using statistical procedures to combine the results of previous studies. For example, one advantage of quantitative synthesis was demonstrated empirically in a study by Cooper and Rosenthal (1980). Faculty members and graduate students were asked to draw summary conclusions using either a meta-analytic or narrative approach about studies that tested whether females showed greater persistence at tasks than males. Results showed that narrative review procedures led to inaccurate or imprecise characterizations of the cumulative research results; in particular, reviewers using a qualitative approach underestimated the size of the effect.

In this chapter we provide a framework for understanding meta-analysis. First, major meta-analytic procedures are described. This is followed by a discussion of the major challenges that face the meta-analyst and some new directions in the development of meta-analytic methods.

PROCEDURES OF META-ANALYSIS

Much like primary research, a rigorous research synthesis involves several stages, including problem formulation, data collection or the literature search, data evaluation, analysis and interpretation, and public presentation (Cooper, 1998). A detailed description of each stage of the research synthesis process is beyond the scope of this chapter. Rather, we focus on the statistical analysis and interpretation stage. For a full discussion of methods involved at each stage of a research synthesis, the interested reader may refer to Cooper's *Synthesizing Research* (1998) or Cooper and Hedges' *The Handbook of Research Synthesis* (1994).

As we begin, it is important to note three assumptions crucial to the validity of the conclusions of a meta-analysis. First, each finding used in the calculation of average effect sizes and their associated statistics is assumed to be testing the same relationship. Second, individual findings used in a cumulative analysis must be independent from each other. Finally, a meta-analysis is only as good as the primary research it is cumulating. Therefore, the meta-analyst must believe that the primary researchers made valid assumptions when they computed the results of their statistical tests.

To make some of the procedures involved in meta-analysis more concrete, we will use a fictional example of a research synthesis. This synthesis attempts to answer the question, 'What is the impact of playing pool with friends on well-being?' We will assume that the (hypothetical) synthesist was able to

locate eight studies, each of which randomly assigned participants to play pool with friends or to a control condition and then measured well-being. Information relevant to our fictional example can be found in Table 32.1.

Estimating effect sizes

Often in a meta-analysis, answering the questions 'Does playing pool with friends have an effect on well-being?' and 'How much of an effect does playing pool with friends have on well-being?' are the questions of greatest importance. To answer these questions, meta-analysts will (a) calculate an effect size for the outcomes of hypothesis tests in every study; (b) average these effect sizes across hypothesis tests to estimate general magnitudes of effect and calculate confidence intervals as a test of the null hypothesis; and (c) compare effect sizes to discover if variations in outcomes exist and, if so, what features of comparisons might account for them.

Cohen (1988) defined an effect size as 'the degree to which the phenomenon is present in the population, or the degree to which the null hypothesis is false' (pp.9–10). There are many different metrics to describe an effect size. Generally, each metric is associated with particular research designs. We discuss three primary metrics to describe effect sizes. Even though there are others, we limit our discussion to those most amenable to single degree of freedom tests involving combinations of variables that are continuous or dichotomous.

Table 32.1 The effect of playing pool with friends on well-being

Study	Sex	Treatment group Sample size	Comparison group Sample size	Direction of the effect	Effect size (d)	Probability (p)
1	Female	23	25	positive	0.90	0.003
2	Male	42	46	positive	0.51	0.019
3	Male	18	18	positive	0.13	0.595
4	Female	32	45	negative	0.18	0.437
5	Female	36	24	positive	0.90	0.001
6	Female	48	48	positive	0.16	0.282
7	Male	66	64	negative	0.35	0.048
8	Male	27	27	positive	0.71	0.011

The d-index

Cohen's d-index[1] is a scale-free measure of the difference between two group means. It is used when one variable in the relations is dichotomous and the other is continuous. Calculating the basic d-index for any comparison involves dividing the difference between the two group means by either their pooled standard deviation or the standard deviation of the control group. The result is a measure of the difference between the two group means expressed in terms of their common standard deviation. The formula is as follows:

$$d = \frac{X_1 - X_2}{s_p}$$

where X_1 and X_2 represent the two group means and s_p is the pooled standard deviation defined as:

$$s_p = \sqrt{\frac{(n_1 - 1)s_1^2 + (n_2 + 1)s_2^2}{(n_1 - 1) + (n_2 + 1)}}$$

where n_1 and n_2 represent the number of subjects in each group and s_1 and s_2 represent the standard deviation of each of the groups.

Because the d-index is scale free, the standard deviation adjustment in the denominator of the formula means that studies using different measurement scales can be compared or combined. Reporting of effect sizes, such as the d-index, in primary research is not yet universal.

To illustrate how the d-index should be interpreted, Figure 32.1 presents three hypothetical d-indexes. Figure 32.1A presents a null relationship; $d = 0$ and there is no difference between participants randomly assigned to play pool with friends and participants who do not play pool with friends. In Figure 32.1B, the participants who play pool have an outcome score that is four-tenths of a standard deviation above the control group. Here $d = 0.40$. In Figure 32.1C, $d = 0.85$, indicating an even greater separation between the two group means.

In many instances, synthesists will find that primary researchers do not report

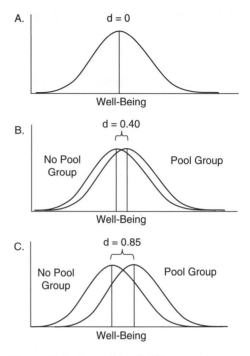

Figure 32.1   Examples of differences in standard deviation units

the means and standard deviations of the separate groups. For such cases, Rosenthal (1984, 1994) has provided a computational formula for the d-index that does not require the meta-analyst to have means and standard deviations. The formula is as follows:

$$d = \frac{2t}{\sqrt{df_{error}}}$$

where t represents the value of the t-test for the associated comparison and df_{error} represents the error degrees of freedom associated with the t-test. In fact, the d-index can be computed from a variety of statistical data. For a complete listing of algebraically equivalent formulas that can be used to compute an effect size from various statistical information, the interested reader should see Lipsey and Wilson's (2001) *Practical Meta-Analysis*.

The r-index

Another effect size metric is the r-index, or the Pearson product-moment correlation coefficient. Typically, it is used to measure the degree of linear relation between two variables. The correlation coefficient is familiar to most researchers and is most appropriate when describing the relationship between two continuous variables.

Information, such as variances and covariances necessary to calculate a correlation coefficient are rarely provided in primary research reports. Luckily, most researchers provide r-indexes in cases where they apply. When only the t-value associated with the r-index is given, the r-index can be calculated with the following formula:

$$r = \sqrt{\frac{t^2}{t^2 + \mathrm{df}_{\mathrm{error}}}}$$

where all terms are defined as before. However, it should be noted that this formula will always produce a positive value. Consequently, the researcher should seek additional information in the primary research report, such as a verbal description of the relationship, which would allow the direction of the relationship to be determined.

The odds ratio

The odds ratio is applicable when both variables are dichotomous and findings are presented as frequencies or proportions. This measure of effect is used most in medical sciences, in which the researcher is often interested in the effect of a treatment on mortality or the appearance or disappearance of disease. It also appears frequently in studies of educational interventions when the outcome of interest is drop-out or retention rates or criminal justice studies where the outcome is recidivism. Take for example, a case in which we are interested in whether playing pool with friends led to subsequent arrest. Suppose that the meta-analyst came across a study in which 200 people either played pool with friends or did not and then examined evidence for arrests later that night. The results of the study could have looked like the fictional data presented in Table 32.2.

First, the odds that a participant was arrested must be determined for each condition. When participants played pool, the

Table 32.2 An example of odds ratio estimation

	Pool playing	Control
Arrested	a = 75	b = 60
Not arrested	c = 25	d = 40

odds of arrest were 3 to 1 (75 to 25). When participants did something else, the odds of arrest were 1.5 to 1 (60 to 40). The meta-analyst then simply forms the ratio of the playing-pool odds over the control activities odds. In this case, the odds ratio is 2, meaning the odds of arrest are twice as large in the pool-playing condition as in the placebo condition. The odds ratio can also be calculated by dividing the product of the main diagonal elements by the product of the off-diagonal elements. In this example, using the previously described formula,

$$OR = \frac{ad}{bc} = \frac{75 \times 40}{60 \times 25} = 2$$

where all terms are defined in Table 32.2.

Identifying independent samples

A statistical problem arises when a single study contains multiple effect size estimates taken on the same sample of participants. There are several approaches meta-analysts use to handle such dependent effect sizes. Some treat each effect size as independent, regardless of the number of effect sizes that comes from the same sample of people. The strength of this technique is that it does not lose any of the within-study information regarding potential moderators. However, this strategy violates the assumption that the estimates are independent. This may cause the standard error associated with the overall effect to be underestimated and the robustness of the effect to be exaggerated. Further, the results of studies will not be weighted equally in any overall conclusion about results. Rather, studies will contribute to the overall effect in relation to the number of statistical tests contained in it.

Other meta-analysts use the study as the unit of analysis. They calculate the mean effect size, or take the median result, or identify a preferred outcome measure, and use this value to represent the study. This strategy ensures that the assumption of independence is not violated and that each study contributes equally to the overall effect. However, some within-study information may be lost in this approach.

Sophisticated statistical models also have been suggested as a solution to the problem of dependent effect size estimates (Gleser & Olkin, 1994; Raudenbush et al., 1988) but due to their complexity they are yet rarely found in practice.

A compromise solution is to use a shifting unit of analysis (Cooper, 1998). In this procedure, each effect size is coded into the dataset as if it were an independent estimate. For example, if a study of playing pool used both the Satisfaction with Life Scale (Diener et al., 1985) and the Subjective Happiness Scale (SHS) (Lyubomirsky & Lepper, 1999) to measure well-being, two separate d-indexes would be calculated. In the shifting unit of analysis approach, for estimating the overall relation between playing pool with friends and well-being, statistical independence is maintained by averaging these two d-indexes prior to entry into the analysis, so that the study only contributed one effect size. However, in an analysis that examined the effect of measurement characteristics on effect size, each sample would contribute one estimate to the effect size for life satisfaction measures and one to the effect size for happiness measures. This shifting unit of analysis approach retains as much data as possible from each study while holding to a minimum violations of the assumption that data points are independent.

Averaging effect sizes

The most pivotal outcomes of a meta-analysis are the average effect sizes and measures of dispersion that accompany them. Both unweighted and weighted procedures are typically used to calculate average effect sizes across comparisons. In the unweighted procedure, each effect size is given equal weight in calculating the average effect. In the weighted procedure, each independent effect size is first multiplied by the inverse of its variance and the sum of these products is then divided by the sum of the inverses. The weighting procedure is generally preferred because it gives greater weight to effect sizes based on larger samples and larger samples provide more precise estimates of the population value. Also, confidence intervals are calculated for weighted average d-indexes and used as a test of the null hypothesis that no relation exists in the population. Hedges and Olkin (1985), Shadish and Haddock (1994), and Lipsey and Wilson (2001) provide procedures for calculating the appropriate weights and confidence intervals.

For the d-index this procedure requires the meta-analyst to calculate a weighting factor, w_i, which is the inverse of the variance associated with each d-index estimate:

$$w_i = \frac{2(n_{i1} + n_{i2})n_{i1}n_{i2}}{2(n_{i1} + n_{i2})^2 + n_{i1}n_{i2}d_i^2}$$

where n_{i1} and n_{i2} represent the number of data points in Group 1 and Group 2 of the comparison and d_i represents the d-index of the comparison under consideration. Table 32.3 presents the group samples sizes, d-indexes, and w_i associated with each comparison from our fictional pool-playing and well-being example. The next step in obtaining a weighted average effect size involves multiplying each d-index by its associated weight and dividing the sum of these products by the sum of the weights. The formula is:

$$d_\bullet = \frac{\sum_{i=1}^{N} d_i w_i}{\sum_{i=1}^{N} w_i}$$

where all terms are defined as before. Table 32.3 shows the average weighted d-index for the eight comparisons was found to be $d = 0.21$.

Finally, the confidence interval around the average effect size estimate can be calculated.

Table 32.3 An example of *d*-index estimation and tests of homogeneity

Finding	n_{i1}	n_{i2}	d_i	w_i	$d_i^2 w_i$	$d_i w_i$	Grouping
1	23	25	0.90	10.88	8.81	9.79	Female
2	42	46	0.51	21.26	5.53	10.84	Male
3	18	18	0.13	15.96	0.28	2.12	Male
4	32	45	−0.18	18.62	0.60	−3.35	Female
5	36	24	0.90	13.12	10.63	11.81	Female
6	48	48	0.16	47.32	1.16	7.40	Female
7	66	64	−0.35	32.00	3.92	−11.20	Male
8	27	27	0.71	12.70	6.40	9.02	Male
Σ	292	297	2.78	171.89	37.34	36.44	

$$d_\bullet = \frac{36.44}{171.89} = 0.21$$

$$CI_{d_\bullet 95\%} = 0.21 \pm 1.96\sqrt{\frac{1}{171.89}} = 0.21 \pm 0.15$$

$$Q_t = 37.34 - \frac{36.44^2}{171.89} = 29.62$$

$$Q_w = 13.89 + 14.72 = 28.61$$

$$Q_b = 29.62 - 28.61 = 1.01$$

First, the inverse of the sum of the w_is is found. Then, the square root of this variance is multiplied by the z score associated with the confidence interval of interest. Thus, the formula for a 95% confidence interval would be:

$$CI_{d_\bullet 95\%} = d_\bullet \pm 1.96\sqrt{\frac{1}{\sum_{i=1}^{N} w_i}}$$

where all terms are defined as before. The 95% confidence interval for the eight pool-playing comparisons includes values of the d-index 0.15 above and below the average d-index. Thus, we expect 95% of estimators of this effect to fall between $d = 0.06$ and $d = 0.36$. Note that the interval does not contain the value $d = 0$. It is this information that can be taken as a test of the null hypothesis that no relation exists in the population. In this example, we would reject the null hypothesis that there is no difference in well-being between people who play pool with friends and those who do not.

A parallel procedure is conducted to find the average weighted r-index and confidence interval. However, because the sampling distribution for r is not symmetrical except when ρ equals 0, first r is transformed to its corresponding z score (Hedges & Olkin, 1985; Lipsey & Wilson, 2001; Rosenthal, 1994), z_i using the following formula:

$$z_i = 1/2 \log_e \left[\frac{1+r}{1-r}\right]$$

where r is the correlation coefficient and $\log_e$ is the natural logarithm. Next, the following formula is applied to compute the average weighted z:

$$z_\bullet = \frac{\sum_{i=1}^{N} (n_i - 3)z_i}{\sum_{i=1}^{N} (n_i - 3)}$$

where n_i represents the total sample size for the ith comparison and all other terms are defined as before. For the confidence interval, the formula is:

$$CI_{z_\bullet 95\%} = z_\bullet \pm \frac{1.96}{\sqrt{\sum_{i=1}^{N} (n_i - 3)}}$$

where all terms are defined as before. Finally, to present results, z is transformed back to the original r metric using the inverse of Fisher's z to r transformation (Lipsey & Wilson, 2001):

$$r = \frac{e^{2z_i} - 1}{e^{2z_i} + 1}$$

where e is the base of the natural logarithm (2.718) and all other terms are defined as before.

Like the correlation coefficient, the odds ratio must also be transformed by taking the natural logarithm (Haddock et al., 1998; Lipsey & Wilson, 2001):

$$LOR = \log_e (OR)$$

Next, a weighting factor, w_i, which is the inverse of the variance associated with each logged odds ratio is calculated using the following formula:

$$w_i = \frac{abcd}{ab(c+d) + cd(a+b)}$$

where all terms are defined in Table 32.2 illustrating the odds of being arrested after playing pool with friends.

The next step in obtaining a weighted average effect size involves multiplying each logged odds ratio by its associated weight and dividing the sum of these products by the sum of the weights. The formula to calculate the weighted average logged odds ratio is:

$$LOR_{\bullet} = \frac{\sum\limits_{i=1}^{N} LOR_i w_i}{\sum\limits_{i=1}^{N} w_i}$$

where LOR_i represents the logged odds ratio for the ith comparison and all other terms are defined as before. For the 95% confidence interval, the formula is:

$$CI_{LOR_{\bullet} 95\%} = LOR_{\bullet} \pm 1.96 \sqrt{\frac{1}{\sum\limits_{i=1}^{N} w_i}}$$

where all terms are as defined before. Finally these summary statistics can be converted back to the original odds ratio metric by taking the antilogarithms.

$$OR = e^{LOR}$$

It should be noted that if any of the cell frequencies equal zero, 0.5 should be added to every cell. Even though this solution solves

the problem of having cell frequencies equal to zero, this strategy will bias the estimate such that the strength of the relationship will be slightly underestimated (Fleiss, 1994). When only a few contingency tables contain zeros, this solution is acceptable. However, if there are many cases in which cell frequencies are equal to zero, the Mantel-Haenszel method of combining odds ratios should be used (Hauck, 1989). The interested reader may refer to Lipsey and Wilson (2001) or Shadish and Haddock (1994) for a full discussion of this method.

Models of error

Another aspect of conducting a meta-analysis that has recently received considerable attention involves the decision about whether a fixed effects or random effects model of error underlies the generation of study outcomes. In a fixed effects model, all studies assumed to be drawn from a common population are therefore, estimating a common population effect. As such, variance in effect sizes is assumed to reflect only sampling error, that is, error solely due to participant differences. This type of error is the only error taken into account using the procedures just described for weighting effect sizes by sample size. However, sometimes other features of studies can be viewed as random influences. For example, studies that look at the impact of pool playing on well-being might vary in the types of pool halls in which the studies were conducted, in the length of play, and in the game of pool being played. In this case, it may be most appropriate to consider pool halls as randomly sampled from all pool halls and pool games randomly sampled from all games. That is, in a random-effect analysis, study-level variance is assumed to be present as an additional source of random influence.

The question each meta-analyst must ask is whether the effect sizes in a dataset are affected by a large number of these study-level random influences. If it is the case that the meta-analyst suspects a larger number of these additional sources of random error in effect sizes then a random effects model is most appropriate in order to take these sources of variance into account. If the meta-analyst suspects that the data are most likely little affected by other sources of random variance, then a fixed effects model can be applied. Alternatively, Hedges and Vevea (1998; p. 3) state that fixed-effect models of error are most appropriate when the goal of the research is 'to make inferences only about the effect size parameters in the set of studies that are observed (or a set of studies identical to the observed studies except for uncertainty associated with the sampling of subjects).' A further statistical consideration is that in the search for moderators, fixed effect models may seriously underestimate error variance and random effects models may seriously overestimate error variance when their assumptions are violated (Overton, 1998).

In view of these competing sets of concerns, we recommend that the meta-analyst consider applying both models (e.g. Cooper et al., 2006). Specifically, all analyses could be conducted twice, once employing fixed effect assumptions and once using random effect assumptions. Differences in results based on which set of assumptions is used can be incorporated into the interpretation and discussion of findings.

Formulas to calculate random effects estimates of the mean effect size, confidence intervals, and homogeneity statistics are complex and involve a two-stage process. As such, the interested reader should refer to Hedges and Olkin (1985), Raudenbush (1994), and Lipsey and Wilson (2001) for a full discussion of random effects computation. In addition, several statistical packages have recently been developed specifically for meta-analysis that allow the meta-analyst to easily conduct analyses using both fixed and random effects assumptions (e.g. Comprehensive Meta-Analysis; Borenstein et al., 2005). For the remainder of this chapter, random effect estimates will be presented for our running example, although formulas and computations will not be shown.

In our fictional meta-analysis of the effect of playing pool with friends on well-being, the effect size estimate under a fixed effects model was $d = 0.21$ with a 95% confidence interval from 0.06 to 0.36. However, when a random effects model was used, the estimate was $d = 0.31$ with a 95% confidence interval from -0.01 to 0.63. Note that the mean estimate of d changes using the random-effect error model, because of a changed (lesser) effect of weighting studies by sample size on the result. Note also that in the random-effects error model, the variance around the mean estimate increases and the combined result of pool-playing studies no longer rejects the null hypothesis. In this case then, caution must be taken when considering the interpretation of the result that playing pool with friends has a positive effect on well-being, given that the effect is statistically different from zero only when a fixed-effects model is assumed.

Homogeneity of effect sizes

In addition to the confidence interval as a measure of dispersion, meta-analysts usually carry out *homogeneity analyses*. Homogeneity analyses allow the meta-analyst to explore if effect sizes vary from one study to the next. A homogeneity analysis compares the amount of variance in an observed set of effect sizes with the amount of variance that would be expected by sampling error alone and provides calculation of how probable it is that the variance exhibited by the effect sizes would be observed if only sampling error was making them different. If there is greater variation in effects than would be expected by chance, then the meta-analyst can begin the process of examining moderators of comparison outcomes. If the observed variance is not significantly different from that expected by sampling error alone, many statisticians advise the meta-analyst to stop the analysis there and not look for moderators. After all, chance is the most parsimonious explanation for the variation in effect sizes. We recommend that the meta-analyst may search for moderators in the absence of a statistically significant homogeneity analysis if there are good theoretical reasons for doing so.

An alternative approach to examining if effect sizes vary across studies also compares the observed variation in obtained effect sizes with the variation expected due to sampling error, that is, the expected variance in effect sizes given that all observed effects are estimating the same underlying population value (Hunter & Schmidt, 2004). However, a formal statistical test of the difference between these two values is typically not carried out. Rather, the meta-analyst adopts a critical value for the ratio of observed-to-expected variance to use as a means for rejecting the null hypothesis. In this approach, the meta-analyst might also adjust effect sizes to account for methodological artifacts such as sampling error, range restrictions, or unreliability of measurements. This method has been applied most often in the areas of industrial and organizational psychology. However, given the more widespread use of the inverse-variance method deriving from Hedges and Olkin (1985), the techniques described here follow this perspective.

To test whether a set of d-indexes is homogenous, the synthesis must calculate a statistic that Hedges and Olkin (1985) called Q_t.

$$Q_t = \sum_{i=1}^{N} w_i d_i^2 - \frac{\left(\sum_{i=1}^{N} w_i d_i\right)^2}{\sum_{i=1}^{N} w_i}$$

The Q statistic has a chi-square distribution with $N-1$ degrees of freedom, or one less than the number of d-indexes. If the obtained value of Q_t is greater than the critical value for the upper tail of a chi-square at the chosen level of significance, the meta-analyst rejects the hypothesis that the variance in effect sizes was produced by sampling error alone.

In our fictional meta-analysis of the effect of playing pool with friends on well-being, we find a highly significant homogeneity statistic $Q(7) = 29.62$, $p < 0.001$ (please see Table 32.3 for calculations). This suggests that we should reject the hypothesis that the d-indexes are all estimating the same

underlying population value, or that sampling error alone was responsible for the variation in effects. We would continue our analysis of the effect by looking for variables that may potentially moderate the effect of playing pool with friends on well-being.

An analogous procedure is followed for performing a homogeneity analysis on transformed r-indexes and odds ratios. The following formula illustrates how Q_t is calculated using the z transformation of r.

$$Q_t = \sum_{i=1}^{N} (n_i - 3)z_i^2 - \frac{\left(\sum_{i=1}^{N} (n_i - 3)z_i\right)^2}{\sum_{i=1}^{N} (n_i - 3)}$$

The following formula illustrates how Q_t is calculated using the transformed log-odds ratio.

$$Q_t = \sum_{i=1}^{N} w_i LOR_i^2 - \frac{\left(\sum_{i=1}^{N} w_i LOR_i\right)^2}{\sum_{i=1}^{N} w_i}$$

All terms are defined as before.

Just as with the d-index, these Q statistics are compared to a chi-square distribution with $N-1$ degrees of freedom. If the obtained value of Q_t is greater than the critical value of a chi-square at the chosen level of significance, the meta-analyst rejects the hypothesis that the variance in effect sizes was produced by sampling error alone.

Testing for moderators of effect sizes

The search for why the outcomes of hypothesis tests differ is often the most interesting and informative part of conducting a meta-analysis. As previously suggested, homogeneity analysis allows the meta-analyst to test whether sampling error alone accounts for variation in effect sizes or whether features of studies, samples, treatment designs, or outcome measures also play a role. The meta-analyst calculates average effect sizes for subsets of studies, comparing the average effect sizes for different methods, types of programs, outcome measures, and partici- pants and compares these to determine if they provide insight into what influences the strength and/or direction of the relationship. In fact, a major strength of meta-analysis is that the meta-analyst can ask questions about variables that moderate outcomes even if no individual study has included the moderator variable. In our example, we can ask whether the relationship between playing pool with friends and well-being differs for females compared to males, even if no single study has included both groups. The results of such a comparison of average effect sizes can suggest whether gender would be important to look at in future research.

The procedure to test whether a method- ological or conceptual distinction between comparisons explains variance in effect sizes involves several steps. First, a Q_t statistic is calculated using the formula just presented. Then, a Q statistic is calculated separately for each subgroup of studies. Then the values of these Q statistics are summed to form a value called Q_w. This value is then subtracted from Q_t to obtain Q_b.

$$Q_b = Q_t - Q_w$$

This Q_b statistic is used to test whether the average effects from the groupings of studies are homogenous. It is compared to a chi- square table using degrees of freedom one less than the number of groupings. If Q_b exceeds the critical value, then the grouping variable is a significant contributor to variance in effect sizes and remains a plausible moderator of effect. This test is analogous to conducting an analysis of variance in that a significant Q_b indicates that at least one group mean differs from the others.

We use our example, illustrated in Table 32.3, to demonstrate how a search for moderators of outcomes might proceed. Let us compare effect sizes calculated from female samples compared to effect sizes using male samples, given in the last column. First, we find that using a fixed-effect error model the

effect of playing pool with friends has a significant impact on well-being for females, $d = 0.29$ (95% CI $= 0.08/0.79$) but not males, $d = 0.13$ (95% CI $= -0.09/0.35$). As shown in Table 32.3, the Q_t statistic for the eight studies was 29.61. The Q_w statistic for females was 13.89 and for males was 14.72 and the total Q_w for both groups is 28.61. From here, the Q_b statistic comparing males to females can be calculated, $Q_b(1) = 1.01, p = 0.32$. This result was not significant with 1 degree of freedom. Using a random-effect error model, the impact of playing pool with friends does not have a significant effect on either females, $d = 0.41$ (95% CI $= -0.08/0.89$), or males $d = 0.23$ (95% CI $= -0.26/0.72$). Further, the Q_b statistic comparing males to females under random effects assumptions indicated that there was not a significant difference in the average weighted d-index between the groups, $Q_b(1) = 0.26, p = 0.61$.

In this way, the meta-analyst employs a formal means for testing whether different features of studies explain variation in their outcomes. This is an extension of the same rules of inference required of primary researchers. If reliable differences do exist, the average effect sizes corresponding to these differences will take on added meaning and will help the meta-analyst to guide future research or make policy recommendations. Further, in meta-analysis, tests of moderation may allow for the examination of certain forms of research bias. For example, modera- tor tests can be employed to explore whether stronger effects are more likely to come from certain researchers or whether allegiance effects in clinical research are present. Specif- ically, allegiance effects can be examined by using the preference researchers have for a particular treatment over others as a grouping variable when exploring explanations for the variation in study outcomes.

An alternative strategy for examining whether particular characteristics of studies are related to the sizes of the treatment effect is meta-regression. Unlike the strategy previously discussed, meta-regression allows the meta-analyst to explore the relationship between continuous, as well as categorical, characteristics and effect size, and allows the effects of multiple factors to be investigated simultaneously (Thompson & Higgins, 2002). In our example, imagine that our studies ranged in the duration of the manipulation of playing pool with friends. One option would be to group studies into several distinct categories of duration of pool playing and continue with subgroup moderator analyses as previously discussed. However, an alternative would be to employ meta-regression, leaving this characteristic continuous. The interested reader may refer to Thompson and Higgins (2002) or Higgins and Thompson (2004) for a full discussion of this method.

Sensitivity analysis

An additional step in meta-analysis is the performance of sensitivity analyses. A sensitivity analysis is used to determine if and how the conclusions of an analysis might differ if it was conducted using different statistical procedures or assumptions. There are numerous points at which a meta-analyst might decide a sensitivity analysis is appropriate. For example, there might be a set of comparisons that fall at the edge of the conceptual definition of what constitutes an acceptably reliable measure of well-being. The effects of playing pool with friends might be tested with and without the inclusion of these comparisons. Or, some evaluations of the relation between playing pool with friends and well-being might have missing data. These comparisons might be omitted from one analysis and included in another analysis that makes conservative assumptions about what those values might be. The calculation of weighted, unweighted, and median effect sizes can be considered a form of sensitivity analysis. Lastly, averaging effect sizes and conducting homogeneity and moderator tests using both fixed and random effects models is another form of sensitivity analysis. In each case, the meta-analyst is seeking to determine whether a particular finding is robust across different sets of assumptions. If the answer is 'conclusions do not change under different sets of assumptions' then greater confidence can be placed in the conclusion.

THE ISSUE OF DATA CENSORING

Many meta-analysts go to great lengths to locate as much relevant research as possible. However, even after careful planning, searching, and coding of research reports, missing data can influence the conclusions drawn from the meta-analysis. Just as biases in the selection of study participants threaten the validity of primary research, data censoring threatens the validity of the meta-analysis (Rothstein et al., 2005). When data are systematically missing, not only is the size of the sample gathered for the research synthesis reduced, but the representativeness of the sample and the validity of the results are compromised, regardless of the quality of the meta-analysis in all other respects (Rothstein et al., 2005).

Types of data censoring

Data censoring occurs when primary researchers, journals, or publishers censor what research gets into print or what specific findings or aspects of the research are reported. This data censoring can often cause the research included in a meta-analysis to be systematically unrepresentative of the population of completed studies. As suggested by Pigott (1994), there are three kinds of missing data that can result from data censoring.

First, entire studies may be unavailable to include in a dataset. In particular, unpublished research findings are frequently missing from meta-analyses. The research synthesist can take extra precautions to include unpublished research that may be difficult to locate. For example, search techniques that include contacting professional networks and listservs, using conference programs, or searching databases that include dissertation and masters theses (Dissertation Abstracts) can improve the inclusiveness of the studies in the meta-analysis. However, inevitably, there will be relevant studies left undiscovered. This form of data censoring is problematic because it frequently reflects the bias against the null hypothesis found in published research. That is, published articles tend to report statistically significant results, whereas, unpublished research is less likely to include statistically significant results.

Evidence suggests that bias against the null hypothesis is present in the decisions made by both reviewers and primary researchers (Cooper, 1998). For example, Atkinson et al. (1982) found that significant results were more than twice as likely as non-significant results to be recommended for publication in two APA journals in counseling psychology even when research designs of studies were identical. Greenwald (1975) found that researchers said they were inclined to submit significant results for publication approximately 60% of the time. However, they would submit the study for publication only 6% of the time if the results failed to reject the null hypothesis. When examining actual decisions made by researchers, Cooper et al. (1997) found that approximately 74% of researchers submitted significant results for publication, but only 5% submitted non-significant results.

Second, even if all relevant studies have been uncovered, individual studies may be missing relevant information necessary in order to calculate an effect size. Missing effect sizes will occur when the primary researcher does not report adequate statistics or descriptive information needed to calculate an effect size. The consequence of missing an effect size is similar to missing an entire study. That is, a study with a missing effect size cannot be included in the estimate of the average effect. Consequently, the generalizability of the results may be limited to the sample of studies which had complete data. Further, similar to reasons why entire studies may be missing from a review, effect sizes are frequently unreported in published reports when the relationship was not significant, and thus, the author fails to report the precise values of the means, standard deviations, statistical test, and/or p values (Pigott, 1994).

Finally, information about study characteristics used to examine moderators of an effect may be missing from individual reports. For example, when examining the effect of playing pool with friends on well-being, had particular studies failed to report the gender makeup of their participant sample, those studies could not have been included in the moderator analysis.

Detecting missing data

A number of graphical and statistical tests can be used to assess the possible presence of data censoring and the implications of this threat to the validity of the conclusions drawn from the meta-analysis. One way a meta-analyst can evaluate whether data censoring has affected a distribution of effect sizes is to create a funnel plot (Light & Pillemer, 1984). A funnel plot graphically depicts a measure of the sample size of studies, such as their given weight or precision, against their associated effect sizes (Greenhouse & Iyengar, 1994). If the meta-analyst has captured all the relevant studies, the funnel plots should be symmetric around the mean and approximate the shape of the normal distribution. However, publication biases can restrict the range of the distribution, resulting in overrepresentation of studies in one tail of the distribution (Sterne et al., 2005). In addition to graphical displays, regression methods such as the Rank Correlation Test (Begg & Mazumdar, 1994) and Egger's Test (Egger et al., 1997) can be used to detect whether a bias is present (see Sterne & Egger, 2005 for full discussion of these strategies).

Figure 32.2 presents the funnel plot illustrating the distribution of effect sizes from our example meta-analysis on the effect of playing pool with friends on well-being. Our plot suggests the presence of bias, as the bottom of the plot shows a higher concentration of studies on the right side of the mean compared to the left.

Another way to explore for possible data censoring is by using publication status as a moderator variable in a homogeneity analysis. As previously discussed, homogeneity analysis allows the meta-analyst to test whether sampling error alone accounts for variation in effect sizes or whether features of studies, in this case, publication status,

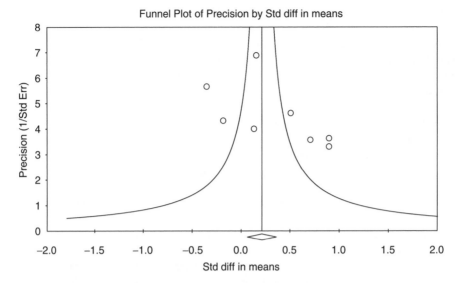

Figure 32.2   Funnel plot of *d* indexes for example meta-analysis

influences the observed effect sizes. In this way, the meta-analyst can use observed studies to assess whether publication status moderates an overall effect. Briefly, the meta-analyst calculates average effect sizes for published and unpublished studies and compares these to determine if there is a significant difference in the strength and/or direction of the relationship. A description of the procedure used to conduct a homogeneity analysis was discussed in the section 'Testing for moderators of effect sizes'.

Strategies for imputing missing data

There are a number of strategies that meta-analysts can use to deal with data censoring. Rothstein et al. (2005) provide an in-depth treatment of numerous approaches. One way is to try to estimate the missing value using one of a number of imputation techniques. Vote-counting is one strategy that can be used to generate an effect size estimate (see Bushman, 1994; Hedges & Olkin, 1985 for a discussion of vote-counting techniques). That is, the underlying magnitude of a treatment's effect can be estimated from the proportions of studies showing positive and negative directional outcomes. However, this approach requires that the vote-counter knows the

direction of each test of the treatment and the sample size associated with each condition, treatment and control.

Pigott (1994) outlined several methods of imputing an estimate for missing values. One strategy is to assume that missing values are equivalent to a very conservative estimate, such as zero. Another option is to replace missing values with the mean value calculated from available cases for that variable. Regression techniques can also be used to impute missing values. Complete cases are used to generate a regression equation that can be used to estimate missing values. A final alternative that appears to be promising are multiple imputation procedures (Rubin, 1987). Multiple imputation techniques use information from complete cases in the review to generate multiple estimates for each missing value. The advantage of using multiple imputation is that a range of estimates are provided for each missing observation. Therefore, results using each of the estimates can be compared.

Even though imputing an estimate for missing values allows the meta-analyst to include in the synthesis cases with missing data, data imputation methods force the meta-analyst to make assumptions that may not be accurate and can result in other types of bias. In particular, when using single-value imputation methods, the assumption that missing values may be either smaller than or similar to observed values may simply be incorrect. Further, using single-value imputation methods can result in an artificially reduced variance for those variables for which values were imputed. This reduced variance is particularly problematic when testing the homogeneity of effect sizes. In fact, one advantage of the regression imputation technique is that an adjustment can be applied to correct for this underestimation of the sampling variance (Little & Rubin, 1987). While all but the zero imputation technique provide a reasonable estimate for the mean when information is missing completely at random, when information is missing for reasons related to the value itself or other observed or unobserved variables, these imputation results fail to generate an unbiased estimate (Sutton & Pigott, 2005). Given the growing awareness of publication bias, imputation techniques seem destined to remain an important area for the development of new meta-analytic techniques.

Regardless of which method is employed, meta-analysts are obligated to discuss how much data was missing from their reports, how they handled it, and why they chose the methods they did. Finally, it is becoming increasingly common practice for meta-analysts with large amounts of missing data to conduct their analyses using more than one strategy and determining whether their findings are robust across different missing data assumptions (see Greenhouse and Iyengar, 1994).

The Trim-and-Fill procedure

There is an interesting imputation method that is gaining popularity because of its simplicity and ease of use. Duval and Tweedie, (2000a, 2000b) have recently developed a Trim-and-Fill method that, through an iterative process, fills in possible values for effect sizes from studies that are not represented in the dataset. The Trim-and-Fill procedure tests whether the distribution of effect sizes used in the

analyses are consistent with variation in effect sizes that would be predicted if the estimates were normally distributed. The method first examines whether the distribution of observed effect sizes is skewed, indicating a possible bias created either by the study retrieval procedures or by data censoring on the part of authors. Then it provides a way to estimate the values from missing studies that need to be present to approximate a normal distribution. It imputes these missing values, permitting an examination of an estimate of the impact of data censoring on the observed distribution of effect sizes and the statistics resulting from including the imputed values.

More specifically, the Trim-and-Fill technique uses a nonparametric method that initially removes the asymmetric studies from the right side of the funnel plot (those indicating a positive effect) in order to compute an unbiased estimate of the effect. Missing effect sizes from the left side of the plot (those that would reduce the size of the positive effect) are then estimated based on the normal distribution. Finally, both removed and imputed studies are placed into the funnel plot and a new combined effect that includes these imputed effect sizes is computed. Consequently, the Trim-and-Fill method provides a sensitivity analysis in which the meta-analyst can compare the observed combined effect size to the hypothetical combined effect size when imputed missing effect sizes are included.

Figure 32.3 depicts the asymmetric funnel plot of effect sizes from our fictional meta-analysis with effect sizes imputed using the Trim-and-Fill method included to make the funnel plot symmetric. When looking for missing studies on the left side of the distribution (and based on a fixed-effect model), the Trim-and-Fill technique suggests that there are three missing studies. Recall that the fixed effects observed point estimate and 95% confidence interval for the combined studies is 0.21 (95% CI = 0.06/0.36). Using Trim-and-Fill, the imputed fixed effects point estimate is 0.04 (95% CI = −0.09/0.18). The random effects observed point estimate and 95% confidence interval for the combined

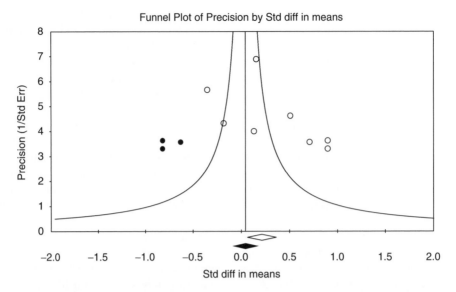

Figure 32.3   Funnel plot of observed and imputed *d* indexes for example meta-analysis
Note: Black dots represent imputed effect sizes, making the distribution symmetrical.

studies is 0.31 (95% CI = −0.01/.63). Using the Trim-and-Fill method the imputed random effects point estimate is 0.05 (95% CI = −0.29/0.38). Thus, this imputation technique changes our finding both in the statistical significance and magnitude of effect. Therefore, we may not be confident that the positive finding of our meta-analysis on the observed eight studies testing the effect of playing pool with friends on well-being is robust against a plausible assumption about data censoring. In such a case, we would certainly discuss the implications of this finding and take care to caution the reader about this important limitation.

NEW DIRECTIONS IN META-ANALYSIS

Alternative indices of heterogeneity

We have seen that studies addressing a common question will generally vary in terms of their design, interventions or other manipulations, sample characteristics, and/or outcomes. And, as previously mentioned, the most common way of assessing heterogeneity in a set of effect sizes is the Q test. A significant Q statistic indicates that the sample

of effect sizes is heterogeneous, that the differences between study outcomes exceed that which may have been found by chance alone. In contrast, a non-significant Q statistic indicates that the differences underlying the results of studies can be accounted for by sampling error alone.

However, the Q statistic itself has power characteristics. That is, it may fail to detect meaningful heterogeneity in the case in which just a few studies are being meta-analyzed, or it may detect 'unimportant' heterogeneity when a large number of studies are being synthesized (Hardy & Thompson, 1998). Consequently, it may be advisable for the meta-analyst to report another statistic, I^2, which provides a way to quantify the heterogeneity among effect sizes included in a synthesis. I^2 describes the percentage of total variation across studies that is due to heterogeneity rather than chance (Higgins & Thompson, 2002; Higgins et al., 2003). It can be derived from the Q test using the following formula:

$$I^2 = 100\% \times (Q - df)/Q$$

where all terms are as previously defined. Negative values for I^2 should be assumed to be equivalent to zero and indicate no heterogeneity. Non-zero I^2 values represent the extent to which heterogeneity is present in the sample of studies, with 100% being the maximum value. For example, in our fictional meta-analysis examining the effect of playing pool with friends on well-being, $I^2 = 100\% \times (29.616 - 7)/29.616 = 76.364$, indicating that over 76% of the variability between our eight studies cannot be explained by sampling error alone.

As suggested by Higgins and colleagues (2003), there are several important advantages of I^2. First, I^2 overcomes many of the drawbacks of the Q test because it does not depend directly on the number of independent effects included in the meta-analysis. Second, given that I^2 is a percentage, it can be easily compared across meta-analyses, even when they may differ in the number of studies included, the outcome being assessed, or effect size metric used. Finally, I^2 is easily computed from statistical tests that are normally conducted in a meta-analysis. Currently, I^2 is rarely reported in published meta-analyses outside of medicine, but its clear advantages, as well as the ease by which it can be interpreted, suggest it will soon be reported regularly in social science meta-analyses as well.

Combining slopes from multiple regressions

Up to this point, the procedures for combining and comparing study results have generally assumed that the measure of effect is a mean difference, correlation, or odds ratio. However, regression analysis is a commonly used technique in the social sciences, particularly for non-experimental studies. Like the standardized mean difference or correlation coefficient, the regression coefficient, b, or the standardized regression coefficient, β, are also measures of effect size. β will typically be used in meta-analyses because, like the d-index and r-index, it standardizes effect size estimates when different measures are used in different studies. β represents the standardized score change in a predictor

variable, controlling for all other predictors, given one unit change in the criterion variable.

Syntheses of regression analyses are difficult to conduct for a variety of reasons. First, models using multiple regression generally differ from study to study. Each study may include different predictors in the regression model and therefore, the slope for the predictor of interest will represent a different partial relationship in each study (Wu & Becker, 2004). Second, the scale of the predictor of interest and outcome may vary across studies (Wu & Becker, 2004). In some cases, a predictor such as SAT scores or monetary expenditures may have a common scale. However, in most cases the scale of both the predictor and outcome variable will vary, making comparisons across studies difficult. Still, this problem can be overcome by using β, the fully standardized estimate of the slope for a particular predictor when the scaling of both the predictor and outcome variable differ across studies. 'Half-standardizing' is an alternative way to create similar slopes when only outcomes are dissimilar (Greenwald et al., 1996).

If slopes are independently and identically distributed, we can apply standard methods for meta-analysis. Slopes will be identically distributed across studies when the outcome and predictor of interest are measured in a similar fashion, the other predictors in the model are the same across studies, and when predictor and outcome scores are similarly distributed (Becker, 2005). If these conditions are met, weighting can be accomplished by multiplying each effect size by the inverse of its variance and then the sum of these products is divided by the sum of the inverses. Standard tests can be then computed, including the mean effect, confidence intervals, and homogeneity tests.

However, it is rare that datasets meet the assumption of being identically and independently distributed (Becker, 2005). Typically, measures differ across studies and regression models are diverse in terms of which additional variables are included in them. And, because few studies provide descriptive statistics on the variables measured and included in the regression model, it remains difficult to assess whether the assumption that scores are distributed similarly across studies has been met. Given the current limitations, a common method for summarizing the results of the regression analyses has been to use a vote-count strategy (see Cooper et al., 2006; Hanushek, 1989; or Patall et al., 2007, for examples). What remains clear is that techniques for synthesizing results from multiple regression analyses need to be more extensively developed and studied.

CONCLUSIONS

In this chapter, the major meta-analytic procedures, challenges that face the meta-analyst, and new directions of meta-analysis were discussed. What should be evident is that meta-analysis is a powerful tool that can be used to inform future social science research, as well as social policy decision-making. While meta-analysis is not without limitation, meta-analyses help to meet rigorous standards that allow us to be more confident when drawing conclusions about the cumulative state of evidence on relationships in our social world.

NOTES

1 Hedges (1980) showed that the d-index may slightly overestimate the size of an effect in the entire population. However, the bias is minimal if the sample size is more than 20. If a meta-analyst is calculating d-indexes from primary research based on samples smaller than 20, Hedges' (1980) correction factor should be applied.

REFERENCES

Atkinson, D. R., Furlong, M. J., & Wampold, B. R. (1982). Statistical significance, reviewer evaluations and scientific process: Is there a (statistically) significant relationship? *Journal of Counseling Psychology, 29*, 189–194.

Becker, B. J. (2005, November). *Synthesizing Slopes in Meta-analysis.* Paper presented at the meeting on Research Synthesis and Meta-Analysis: State of the Art and Future Directions, Durham, NC.

Begg, C. B. & Mazumdar, M. (1994). Operating characteristics of a rank correlation test for publication bias. *Biometrics, 50,* 1088–1101.

Borenstein, M., Hedges, L., Higgins, J., & Rothstein, H. (2005). *Comprehensive Meta Analysis (Version 2.1) [Computer software].* Englewood, NJ: BioStat.

Bushman, B. J. (1994). Vote-counting procedures in meta-analysis. In H. Cooper & L.V. Hedges (Eds.). *Handbook of Research Synthesis.* New York: Russell Sage.

Cohen, J. (1988). *Statistical Power Analysis in the Behavioral Sciences.* Hillsdale, NJ: Erlbaum.

Cooper, H. M. (1998). *Synthesizing Research: A Guide for Literature Reviews* (3rd ed.). Thousand Oaks, CA: Sage.

Cooper, H., DeNeve, K., & Charlton, K. (1997). Finding the missing science: The fate of studies submitted for review by a human subjects committee. *Psychological Methods, 2,* 447–452.

Cooper, H. & Hedges, L. V. (1994). *Handbook of Research Synthesis.* New York: Russell Sage.

Cooper, H., Robinson, J. C., & Patall, E. A. (2006). Does homework improve academic achievement?: A synthesis of research, 1987–2003. *Review of Educational Research, 76,* 1–62.

Cooper, H. M. & Rosenthal, R. (1980). Statistical versus traditional procedures for summarizing research findings. *Psychological Bulletin, 87,* 442–449.

Diener, E., Emmons, R. A., Larsen, R. J., & Griffin, S. (1985). The stisfaction with life scale. *Journal of Personality Assessment, 49,* 71–75.

Duval, S. & Tweedie, R. (2000a). A nonparametric 'trim and fill' method of accounting for publication bias in meta-analysis. *Journal of the American Statistical Association, 95,* 89–98.

Duval, S. & Tweedie, R. (2000b). Trim and fill: A simple funnel plot-based method of testing and adjusting for publication bias in meta-analysis. *Biometrics, 56,* 276–284.

Egger, M., Davey Smith, G., Schneider, M., & Minder, C. (1997). Bias detected in meta-analysis detected by a simple, graphical test. *British Medical Journal, 315,* 629–634.

Fleiss, J. L. (1994). Measures of effect size for categorical data. In H. Cooper & L. V. Hedges (Eds.). *Handbook of Research Synthesis.* pp. 245–260. New York: Russell Sage.

Gleser, L. J. & Olkin, I. (1994). Stochastically dependent effect sizes. In H. Cooper & L. V. Hedges

(Eds.). *Handbook of Research Synthesis.* New York: Russell Sage.

Greenhouse, J. B. & Iyengar, S. (1994). Sensitivity analysis and diagnostics. In H. Cooper & L. V. Hedges (Eds.). *Handbook of Research Synthesis.* pp. 383–398. New York: Russell Sage.

Greenwald, A. (1975). Consequences of prejudice against the null hypothesis. *Psychological Bulletin, 82,* 1–20.

Greenwald, R., Hedges, L. V., & Laine, R. D. (1996). The effect of school resources on student achievement. *Review of Educational Research, 66,* 361–396.

Haddock, C. K., Rindskopf, D., & Shadish, W. R. (1998). Using odds ratios as effect sizes for meta-analysis of dichotomous data: A primer on methods and issues. *Psychological Methods, 3,* 339–353.

Hanushek, E. A. (1989). The impact of differential expenditures on school performance. *Educational Researcher, 18,* 45–51.

Hardy R. J. & Thompson, S. G. (1998). Detecting and describing heterogeneity in meta-analysis. *Statistics in Medicine, 17,* 841–856.

Hauck, W. W. (1989). Odds ratio inference from stratified samples. *Communications in Statistics, 18A,* 767–800.

Hedges, L. V. (1980). Unbiased estimation of effect size. *Evaluation in Education: An International Review Series, 4,* 25–27.

Hedges, L. V. & Olkin, I. (1985). *Statistical Methods for Meta-analysis.* Orlando, FL: Academic Press.

Hedges, L. V. & Vevea, J. L. (1998). Fixed and random effects models in meta-analysis. *Psychological Methods, 3,* 486–504.

Higgins, J. P. T. & Thompson, S. G. (2002). Quantifying heterogeneity in a meta-analysis. *Statistics in Medicine, 21,* 1539–1558.

Higgins, J. P. T. & Thompson, S. G. (2004). Controlling the risk of spurious findings from meta-regression. *Statistics in Medicine, 23,* 1663–1682.

Higgins, J. P. T., Thompson, S. G., Deeks, J.J., & Altman, D. G. (2003). Measuring inconsistency in meta-analyses. *British Medical Journal,* 327, 557–560.

Hunt, M. (1997). *How Science Takes Stock: the Story of Meta-analysis.* New York: Russell Sage Foundation.

Hunter, J. E. & Schmidt, F. L. (2004). *Methods of Meta-analysis: Correcting Error and Bias in Research Findings* (2nd ed.). Thousand Oaks, CA: Sage.

Last, J. M. (2001). *A Dictionary of Epidemiology.* Oxford: Oxford University Press.

Light, R. J. & Pillemer, D. B. (1984). *Summing Up: The Science of Reviewing Research.* Cambridge, MA: Harvard University Press.

Lipsey, M. W. & Wilson, D. B. (2001). *Practical Meta-analysis.* Thousand Oaks, CA: Sage.

Little, R. J. A. & Rubin, D. B. (1987). *Statistical Analysis with Missing Data.* New York: Wiley.

Lyubomirsky, S. & Lepper, H. S. (1999). A measure of subjective happiness: Preliminary reliability and construct validation. *Social Indicators Research, 46,* 137–155.

Overton, R. C. (1998). A comparison of fixed-effects and mixed (random-effects) models for meta-analysis tests of moderator variable effects. *Psychological Methods, 3,* 354–379.

Patall, E. A., Cooper, H., & Robinson, J. C. (2007). Parent involvement in homework: A research synthesis. Manuscript submitted for publication.

Pigott, T. D. (1994). Methods for handling missing data in research synthesis. In H. Cooper & L. V. Hedges (Eds.). *Handbook of Research Synthesis.* New York: Russell Sage.

Raudenbush, S. W. (1994). Random effects models. In H. Cooper & L. V. Hedges (Eds.). *Handbook of Research Synthesis.* pp. 301–322. New York: Russell Sage.

Raudenbush, S. W., Becker, B. J., & Kalaian, H. (1988). Modeling multivariate effect sizes. *Psychological Bulletin, 103,* 111–120.

Rosenthal, R. (1984). *Meta-Analytic Procedures for Social Research.* Beverly Hills, CA: Sage.

Rosenthal, R. (1994). Parametric measures of effect size. In H. Cooper & L. V. Hedges (Eds.). *Handbook of Research Synthesis.* New York: Russell Sage.

Rothstein, H. R., Sutton, A. J., & Borenstein, M. (2005). *Publication Bias in Meta-analysis: Prevention, Assessment and Adjustments.* Chichester, UK: John Wiley & Sons, Ltd.

Rubin, D. B. (1987). *Multiple Imputation for Nonresponse in Surveys.* New York: Wiley.

Shadish, W. R. & Haddock, C. K. (1994). Combining estimates of effect size. In H. Cooper & L. V. Hedges (Eds.). *Handbook of Research Synthesis.* pp. 261–282. New York: Russell Sage.

Sterne, J. A. C., Becker, B. J., & Egger, M. (2005). The funnel plot. In H. R. Rothstein, A. J. Sutton, & M. Borenstein (Eds.). *Publication Bias in Meta-analysis: Prevention, Assessment and Adjustments.* pp. 75–98. Chichester, UK: John Wiley & Sons, Ltd.

Sterne, J. A. C. & Egger, M. (2005). Regression methods to detect publication and other bias in meta-analysis. In H. R. Rothstein, A. J. Sutton, & M. Borenstein (Eds.). *Publication Bias in Meta-analysis: Prevention, Assessment and Adjustments.* pp. 99–110. Chichester, UK: John Wiley & Sons, Ltd.

Sutton, A. J. & Pigott, T. D. (2005). Bias in meta-analysis induced by incompletely reported studies. In H. R. Rothstein, A. J. Sutton, & M. Borenstein (Eds.). *Publication Bias in Meta-analysis: Prevention,*

Assessment and Adjustments. pp. 223–240. Chichester, UK: John Wiley & Sons, Ltd.

Thompson, S. G. & Higgins, J. P. T. (2002). How should meta-regression analyses be undertaken and interpreted? *Statistics in Medicine, 21,* 1559–1573.

Wu, M. & Becker, B. J. (2004, April). *Synthesizing Results from Regression Studies: What can we Learn from Combining Results from Studies Using Large Data Sets?* Paper presented at the annual meeting of the American Educational Research Association, San Diego, CA.

33

Synergy and Synthesis: Integrating Qualitative and Quantitative Data

Jane Fielding and Nigel Fielding

THE DEVELOPMENT OF SOCIAL SCIENCE PERSPECTIVES ON METHODOLOGICAL INTER-RELATION

The origins of multiple-method research

Research designs systematically relating multiple methods originated in the context of mainstream psychology (Campbell and Fiske 1959), initially being termed 'triangulation'. Multiple method research designs ('MMRD') remain prominent amongst mainstream methodological practices (Campbell and Russo 1999). Heuristics for relating results from substantially different methods were a theme from the outset. Campbell wrote that, when he decided to study psychology, while working on a turkey ranch for the summer, 'my notion of science was already of the experimental physics sort, whereas [a magazine article that inspired his choice of discipline] was solely about humanistic

psychology' (Campbell 1981: 456). Discussing his initial elaboration of triangulation by way of the 'multitrait-multimethod matrix' technique, Campbell wrote that it grew from lectures at Berkeley on measurement artefacts in the study of individual differences. Campbell used correlational matrices crossing different methods in his dissertation and thus had found his way to what he dubbed 'methodological triangulation' before his collaboration with Fiske.

The original conception was that triangulation would enhance validity, understood as agreement in the outcomes of more than one independent measurement procedure, relative to studies employing a single procedure. The position assumes that there are realities that exist independently of the observer, that have stable properties that can be measured, and that can be mutually related as the basis of internally consistent explanations of social phenomena. These assumptions are necessary because in relating findings from different methods, triangulation must assume that variations in findings arise from the phenomenon or the particularities of the methods being combined rather than methods haphazardly producing different findings on different occasions, or there being no predictable consistencies in the working of given methods. The latter is especially important in the convergent validation approach to triangulation, as it is premised on the combined methods having different and distinctive biases; if methods are susceptible to the same biases, combining them may simply multiply error. Further implied is that these sources of error can be anticipated and their effects can be traced during analysis. It is in this sense that Levins' (1966: 423) declaration that 'our truth is the intersection of independent lies' is so apt.

The doctrine of convergent validation therefore requires agreement of results from diverse but systematic uses of methods, data sources, theories and investigators (Denzin 1989). Some maintain that combining methods or drawing on different data sources only enhances validity where each is associated with compatible ontological and epistemological perspectives (Blaikie 1991). Post-positivists have somewhat sidestepped the ontological/epistemological critique with the argument that datasets are open to interpretation from a range of theories. Another perspective is that combining different methodologies does not necessarily enhance validity but can extend the scope and depth of understanding (Fielding and Fielding 1986; Denzin and Lincoln 2000; Fielding and Schreier 2001).

Triangulation has also been informed by rationales for the methodological 'division of labour' (Sieber 1973). For Sieber, qualitative work can assist quantitative work in providing a theoretical framework, validating survey data, interpreting statistical relationships and deciphering puzzling responses, selecting survey items to construct indices and providing case studies. Quantitative data can identify individuals, groups and settings for qualitative fieldwork and indicate representative and unrepresentative cases. Quantitative data can

counteract the 'holistic fallacy' that all aspects of a situation are congruent, and can demonstrate the generalisability of limited-sample observations. Qualitative research sometimes succumbs to 'elite bias', concentrating on respondents who are articulate, strategically placed and have a status that impresses researchers. Quantitative data can compensate by indicating the full range that should be sampled. Qualitative data can contribute depth to quantitative research, and suggest leads that the more limited kinds of quantitative data cannot address.

As well as combining methods, triangulation can also involve using a number of data sources (self, informants, other commentators), several accounts of events, or several researchers. Denzin's (1970) original conceptualisation, which was related to Webb et al's (1966) work on 'unobtrusive measures', not only involved multiple methods ('data triangulation') but multiple investigators ('investigator triangulation') and multiple methodological and theoretical frameworks ('theoretical and methodological triangulation'). Each main type has a set of subtypes. Data triangulation may include time triangulation, exploring temporal influences by longitudinal and cross-sectional designs; space triangulation, taking the form of comparative research; and person triangulation, variously at the individual level, the interactive level among groups and the collective level. In investigator triangulation, more than one person examines the same situation. In theory triangulation, situations are examined from different theoretical perspectives. Methodological triangulation has two variants: 'within-method', where the same method is used on different occasions (without which one could hardly refer to 'method' at all), and 'between-method', where different methods are applied to the same subject in explicit relation to each other.

While the classical approach represented by Campbell's work seeks convergence or confirmation of results across different methods, the triangulation term has accumulated so many renderings that it is now clearer to use the terms 'convergence' or 'confirmation' when seeking cross-validation between methods. In reality the classic goal of seeking convergence has always been relatively unusual. One reason is the difficulties caused when results fail to converge, but another is the effort required to pursue the goal of producing convergent findings. Morgan (1998) argues that researchers often cannot afford to put so much effort into finding the same thing twice. Moreover, the complex topics of social research make apparent the different strengths of different methods, supporting a more flexible approach to methodological combination than in classic triangulation.

The fact that there are different constructions of triangulation implies there are varying degrees of rigour in operationalising triangulation. We might, for example, regard as relatively weak the idea that validity will be enhanced simply by drawing on data collected by different researchers using the same method, while approaches based on combining different methods might be regarded as more rigorous. For triangulation to be credibly founded and implemented, we must identify in advance the characteristic weaknesses or types of error associated with the chosen methods so that we can discount the danger that they might be susceptible to the same threats to validity. Thus, much depends on the logic by which researchers derive and mesh together data from different methods. 'What is involved in triangulation is not the combination of different kinds of data *per se*, but rather an attempt to relate different sorts of data in such a way as to counteract various possible threats to the validity of (their) analysis' (Hammersley and Atkinson 1995: 199).

Triangulation in itself is no guarantee of internal and external validity. Its real value is not that it guarantees conclusions about which we can be confident but that it prompts in researchers a more critical stance towards their data. Too often, research attracts the criticism that its conclusions simply confirm what everyone already knew. Evaluative criteria for qualitative methods are particularly problematic, with much recourse

to 'ethnographic authority' (Hammersley and Atkinson 1995), the defence of interpretations not by adherence to systematic, externally tested analytic procedures but because the researcher 'was there' and so must have the best sense of what the data mean. Validity queries may be met by reference to the amount of time spent in fieldwork, the rapport achieved and so on. Such criteria contrast sharply with the warrant for inferences from quantitative data, where statistical procedures are used whose steps are standardised, so that adherence to each stage can be checked, and whose criteria for drawing a particular conclusion are not only explicit but precisely define the conditions under which it can be expected to hold. Triangulation enables qualitative researchers to adopt the stance often characteristic of the quantitative researcher, for whom conclusions are always 'on test', hold only under specified conditions, and whose relationship to the data is not uncritical 'immersion' but measured detachment.

It is not suggested that qualitative researchers should transform their approach to resemble that of quantitative researchers, but we can certainly argue that the value of triangulation lies more in 'quality control' than any guarantee of 'validity'. The approach promotes more complex research designs that oblige researchers to be more clear about what relationships they seek to study, what they will take as indicators of these relationships and so on. Diffusely-focused exploratory research will always have a place but as qualitative research tackles more precisely-specified topics and becomes more prominent in policy-related research its audiences want to know how confident in the findings they can be. Even in exploratory work researchers cannot be indifferent to accuracy.

Moreover, when findings from independent methods converge, it is not simply a matter of identifying points of agreement. We also have to identify the conditions under which findings are invariant, explain failures of invariance and determine why given conditions apply. The differences between findings from different knowledge sources can be as illuminating as their points of agreement. Triangulation helps address the tendency to focus on data fitting preconceptions or that is conspicuous at the expense of less exotic, but possibly more indicative, data. While the rigidity of quantitative methods helps researchers resist such faults, their work is not immune to such problems either. However, such faults can more readily be traced because quantitative methodologies necessitate clarity about hypotheses, make the researcher's assumptions more explicit and sediment these assumptions in research instruments that cannot generally be adjusted after they are deployed. Deploying qualitative methods alongside quantitative methods in multiple-method research designs helps qualitative research gain some of these benefits. Similarly, it can bring to quantitative elements of the research more refinement and analytic depth.

From convergent validation to the celebration of diversity

As well as taking a convergent validation perspective, the original literature on combining methods usually involved one method taking precedence (Creswell 2003). Qualitative components rarely held this role and were mostly used for pilot work or follow-up with a sub-sample. More recent approaches suggest more even-handed combinations, as in Caracelli and Green's (1997) classification of mixed-method research into component designs (such as 'complementary' or 'comparative' designs) and integrated designs, which include iterative designs, nested designs and holistic designs. Caracelli and Green (1993) identify four different strategies through which qualitative and quantitative data might be integrated. The first, data transformation, requires data of one type being converted into that of another so they may be analysed together. Typological development, the second strategy, involves the use of conceptual categories emergent from the analysis of one type of data to the analysis of a contrasting data type. Third, extreme case analysis requires the researcher

to focus on exceptional examples found in one type of data and refine their explanation of it via analysis of data of another type. The final strategy, data consolidation, extends the data transformation strategy in that data are converted into another form, but the emphasis is on assimilating multiple forms of data to produce a new dataset.

These strategies enable numerous types of multiple method research design. Green et al. (1989) identified six main dimensions of methodological design. When combining two methods the nature of the relationship between the methods can be categorised along each dimension (see Figure 33.1). Thus, combining a survey with qualitative interviewing – two distinct *methods* – can be categorised as using different *paradigms* to explore different aspects of the same phenomenon, in *sequence* (e.g. first the survey, then the interviews); with the methods being *independent* but with each method having equal *status*.

Moreover, the research *designs* must be distinguished from the reported *rationale* or practical purpose of the research (see Table 33.1).

Other attempts at definitive typologies arrive at different numbers of main types of methodological combination (Creswell 2003; Niglas 2004; Tashakkori and Teddlie 1998), some of which proliferate to the point of intellectual indigestion (Johnson and Onweugbuzie 2004). The most exhaustive typology can never capture all potential combinations; the essential thing is having a considered but open stance in deriving a design that captures the research question. Over-concentration on choosing exactly the right permutation at the outset can make for an unhelpfully rigid approach, but this is not to sideline preliminary reflection. Rather, it is to say that precisely specifying the research question is the key thing, and from this a sense of the best methodological combination will emerge, with the proviso that researchers must always be ready to adjust the design in light of what is found. Research design is not a stage, it is a process.

Broadly, strategies for interrelating findings from multiple methods fall into two

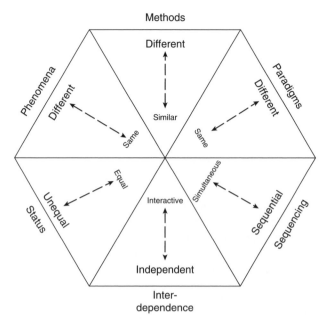

Figure 33.1   Dimensions of methodological design (Original figure, drawing on Green et al., 1989)

Table 33.1   Purpose of mixed-method research designs

Classification	Purpose
Triangulation	Convergence, corroboration and correspondence of results from different methods
Complementarity	Elaboration, illustration and clarification from one method with the results of the other
Development	The results of one method are used to help develop or inform the other (this may include sampling, implementation or measurement issues)
Initiation	Discovery of paradox – used to recast the questions or results of one method with the results of the other
Expansion (parallel design)	Expand the breadth of study using different methods for different components of the study.

Source: Adapted from Green et al. (1989), Table 1, p. 259

types: 'combination' and 'conversion' (Bazeley 2006). An instance of combination is when categorical or continuous variables are the basis both of statistical analysis and for comparison of coded qualitative data. Textual and numerical data may have been collected together, as where questionnaires mix fixed and open response items, or in sequence, such as where surveys are followed by interviews. Conversion involves changing one type of data to another, such as where the coding applied to qualitative data is used in statistical analysis, or where quantitative data contributes to narrative analyses or a life

history (Elliott 2005). Bazeley (2006) notes that strategies involving the consolidation, blending or merging of data tend to involve both conversion and combination.

A well-established case for inter-relating quantitative and qualitative methods is that the qualitative element can suggest types of adaptation or experience for which the quantitative element can then test, thus enabling conclusions concerning the statistical frequency of types in a population. Qualitative research is good at identifying types but is seldom sufficiently comprehensive to indicate for what share of the sample a given type may account. In combination, qualitative and quantitative methods can reveal more about the extent of regularities and the dimensions of the types. Numerous hybrid techniques interrelate quantitative and qualitative procedures. Where codes derived from qualitative data are recorded separately for each case, the presence/absence of each code can be used to create variables, from which case-by-variable matrices can be derived. Such matrices enable hypothesis testing, predictive modelling and exploratory analyses.

Statistical techniques like cluster analysis, correspondence analysis and multidimensional scaling can be applied to such 'quantitised' qualitative data. For example, non-standardised interviews documenting types of adaptation to labour force position can be used as the basis of a probabilistic cluster analysis. The proximity and probability of classification of each respondent towards the centre of the relevant cluster (i.e. type) can thus be visualised and categories reduced to fewer dimensions by multiple correspondence analysis. Kuiken and Miall (2001) used this technique to specify experiential categories derived from interview response in a study comparing different readers' impressions of the same short story. Having identified attributes qualitatively, categories were specified by a quantitative cluster analysis that systematically varied the presence of individual attributes. Subsequent qualitative inspection of the clusters further differentiated the types. In her study of mixed-methods projects, Niglas (2004) used scales to capture variation amongst them on various characteristics of research design. Cluster analysis of variables from her quantitative content analysis produced eight distinctive groups and identified the characteristics best differentiating them. The findings were compared to discursive notes from her initial reading of the study to produce summary descriptions of each group. The descriptions were used to make the final assignment of studies into categories representing variables for further statistical analysis. These alternating quantitative and qualitative procedures do not challenge the

essential integrity of the quantitative and qualitative components of the method. They represent moves to interrelation rather than juxtaposition of different forms of data.

CORE PRINCIPLES OF MULTIPLE-METHOD RESEARCH DESIGN

Epistemology and pragmatism

The advantages of combining methods do not require that we ignore that different approaches are supported by different epistemologies. Accepting the case for interrelating data from different sources is to accept a moderate relativistic epistemology, one that justifies the value of knowledge from many sources, rather than elevating one source. Taking a triangulation or multiple-method approach is to accept the continuity of all data-gathering and analytic efforts. Proponents are likely to regard all methods as both privileged and constrained: the qualities that allow us to access and understand one kind of information close off other kinds. A full understanding flows from tackling the research question in several ways.

Results from different methods founded on different assumptions may then be combined for different purposes than that associated with convergent validation. Theoretical triangulation does not necessarily reduce bias, nor does methodological triangulation necessarily increase validity. Combining results from different analytic perspectives or methods may offer a fuller picture but not a necessarily more 'objective' or 'valid' one. When we combine theories and methods we do so to add breadth or depth to our analysis, not because we subscribe to a single and 'objective' truth. In the social realm it is beyond our capacities to achieve absolute objectivity or axiomatic truth, but this is not the same as rejecting the attempt to be objective or the standard of truth. It is merely to accept that our knowledge is always partial and incomplete. We can make it less so by expanding the sources of knowledge on which we draw. When we accept an empirically based conclusion with identifiable and defined limits, such as that educational achievement is generally related to social class but the relationship is more pronounced for ethnic minority people (discussed in Becker 1986), we implicitly accept the 'constant and unevadable necessity for interpretation and change of aspect' (Needham 1983: 32). That is the ultimate warrant for the triangulation paradigm.

A rounded picture: data in tandem and data in conflict

We comment later on the extent to which MMRD is practised in applied research. Our principal example is taken from applied research for the UK Environment Agency (EA). One project, *Flood Warning for Vulnerable Groups* (FWVG) (Burningham et al., 2005) was designed to explore the social distribution of flood risk and variation in public awareness and the ability to respond to flood warning, especially for those seen as more 'vulnerable'. The second project, *Public Response to Flood Warning* (PRFW)

(Fielding et al., 2007), aimed to provide a detailed understanding of the ways in which the 'at flood risk' public understood, interpreted, and responded to flood warnings. Both projects consisted of qualitative and quantitative components whose results fed back into the subsequent phases of the project but also provided explanations for anomalies or actions reported in previous phases.

Figures 33.2 and 33.3 outline the projects' research designs. The vulnerable groups project consisted of two phases. The first involved secondary analysis of existing quantitative data to establish the social distribution of flood risk and identify groups that were particularly at risk. In parallel, qualitative interviews were conducted with key informants. Results from both techniques defined the sample for the second phase: focus groups with vulnerable groups. The public response project consisted of three phases: (i) a secondary analysis of existing data running in parallel to; (ii) a qualitative enquiry using focus groups and individual interviews; and followed by (iii) a primary quantitative survey. Phase 1, the secondary analysis, explored reported actions taken by flood

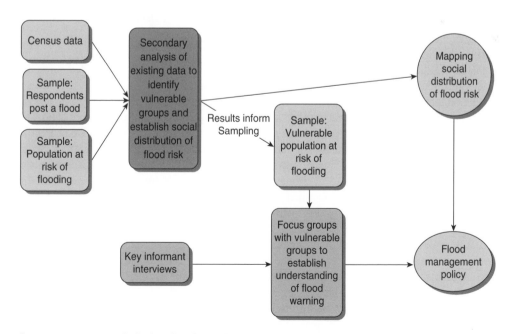

Figure 33.2   Research design for the *Vulnerable Groups Project*

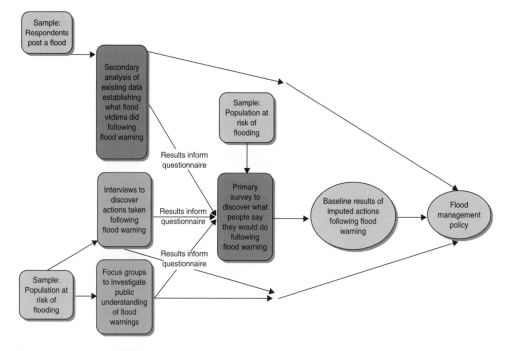

Figure 33.3 Research design for *Public Response to Flood Warning Project*

victims following the Autumn 2001 floods. Phase 2 consisted of two qualitative components: focus group discussions and individual interviews. While the focus groups concentrated on public *understanding* and *interpretation* of the Environment Agency's warning codes, the in-depth interviews explored how individuals said they would *act* in response to warnings. Another important difference was that while focus groups largely rely on the interaction between group members and a shared experience, the individual interviews were conducted in respondents' own homes, with the potential to provide situational cues prompting responses. In the final phase, the survey used a questionnaire instrument developed from the responses obtained in phases 1 and 2. This was designed, using hypothetical flood scenarios, to establish how the public would respond to flood warning in the event of an emergency.

Note that the conventional sequence of pilot qualitative work enabling design of a survey instrument is here augmented by preliminary secondary analysis, and that the qualitative components were in two modes chosen

because group discussions were thought best able to access people's thinking about the issue while action was thought most reliably to be accessed by interviewing individuals.

Identification of risky places and risky people

The EA projects had multiple aims and outcomes but centrally depended upon the identification of risky places and risky people. Respondents were defined as those 'at risk' from tidal or fluvial flooding but who may never have actually experienced a flood event. The study's multiple-method design enabled us to negotiate the controversies associated with identifying this population and their understanding of their risk. The 'at risk' samples were identified by the use of flood plain maps. It may seem obvious that residents within the flood plains are most at risk from flooding but measuring the extent of the flood plains and quantifying the likelihood of floods is a contentious exercise exacerbated by many factors ranging from climate change to the involvement of the insurance industry.

The EA maps identified the 'risky places' but were also used to identify the 'at risk' population living within them. Thus the quantitative data was used to define the sample for subsequent qualitative and quantitative analyses, exemplifying a 'development' strategy in research design (Green et al., 1989). This 'at risk' population was then targeted by the EA 'awareness campaigns' designed to educate the vulnerable public about flood facts. A potential five million people and two million homes and businesses were targeted. However, the flood maps were an *etic*, outsider measure of those at risk and recognition of their risk by those affected was clearly important for appropriate public action in preparation for any future disaster. This dichotomy of meaning and measurement, in terms of outsider (etic) and insider (*emic*) perspectives, will now be discussed.

Emic and etic conceptualisation of vulnerability

A useful conceptual framework for thinking about vulnerability to flood is in terms of 'emic' and 'etic' approaches (see Spiers 2000; Fielding and Moran-Ellis 2005). These concepts, re-interpreted from linguistics and anthropology, refer to two complementary perspectives. The etic perspective represents the 'outsider' viewpoint and the emic an 'insider' viewpoint. Pike (1967) linked emic and etic linguistic analysis to emic and etic perspectives on human behaviour, developing a methodology for cross-cultural comparisons. Pike regards emic and etic perspectives as being like the two images of a matching stereoscopic view. They may initially look alike but on close inspection are different, and, when combined, give a 'startling' and 'tridimensional understanding' of human behavior instead of a 'flat' etic one (Pike 1967: 41). The payoff from combination is key: 'emic and etic data do not constitute a rigid dichotomy of data, but often present the same data from two points of view' (ibid).

An etic viewpoint defines vulnerable individuals as those at greater risk based either on where they live (in vulnerable places) or on demographic characteristics (vulnerable people). These characteristics are usually seen as those which increase social dependence; i.e. old age, ill-health, disability and ethnicity (due to language barriers). Quantitative methods are nearly always used to identify vulnerable places (measuring the likelihood of an event occurring) and are also often used to identify vulnerable people. One negative consequence of this approach is that individuals may become stereotyped based on their defining functional 'deficit'. Another problem is that such defined 'vulnerable groups' are not homogenous.

In contrast, an emic viewpoint seeks to identify vulnerability on the basis of meanings held by individuals arising from their lived experience and tends to be aligned with qualitative methodology. Emic vulnerability is founded on a person's/family's/community's sense of their own resilience and ability to respond in the face of a flood. Emic vulnerability can only be determined by the person experiencing it. So, a person who may be defined as belonging to an at-risk group (etic vulnerability) may only *feel* vulnerable if they consider some threat to their self to exceed their capacity to adequately respond, despite 'rationally' acknowledging their possession of vulnerable characteristics. They need to recognise that they are at risk before they can effectively prepare.

Public awareness of risk

Quantitative analysis of the 'at risk' population based on a survey administered in 2001 (Fielding et al., 2005) and more recently reported by the EA[1], where 49 percent of residential respondents (41 percent in 2005) were not aware that their property was in a flood risk area, made it clear that the EA's message was not getting through. Nearly half those defined as 'at risk' were not aware of their risk. Thus, while the quantitative measurement of the extent of the flood plains had been used to identify the 'at risk' population, other quantitative analysis identified a differing perception of reality. The imposed, outsider view defining risky places was at odds with the lived experience of those defined 'at risk'. The fact that

Table 33.2   Factors that influence awareness of flood risk of own property

		% aware property in flood risk	Total N	Significance[a]
Age	16–24	31%	49	**
	25–34	43%	207	
	35–44	55%	193	
	45–54	57%	150	
	55–64	56%	141	
	65+	52%	201	
Class	A	86%	29	***
	B	62%	160	
	C1	49&	259	
	C2	47%	175	
	D	49%	144	
	E	43%	175	

Source: At Risk 2001 survey
[a] Chi Square test significance ***$p < 0.001$; **$p < 0.01$

an emic perspective (risk awareness) was captured using an etic measure illustrates that the etic/emic perspectives are not simply questions of method.

Why were those who are vulnerable according to etic measures not aware of their risk? This was initially explored using the survey data relating other variables to 'explain' variation in the dependant variable, awareness. However, the other variables chosen, generally those indicating, in line with the literature, a social or financial dependency, drew on etic, or outsider, analysis to explain lack of awareness. This did establish a clear social class gradient, with the lower social classes, the young and the old least aware of their flood risk (see Table 33.2). One use made of the focus groups and interviews was to establish whether these most vulnerable groups *feel* most at risk, and to see whether there were other explanations for lack of awareness. Thus the qualitative data was used to complement and 'explain' the findings from the quantitative analysis: an example of 'complementarity' in the Green et al., typology.

Flood researchers regularly encounter respondents who deny that they live within the flood plains identified by the EA. Indeed, some actively campaign against their properties being included (possibly because it affects their insurance premiums and thus house prices). In their experience, and

possibly their parents' experience, they may not have suffered flooding and therefore feel perfectly safe. EA public safety materials, including targeted letters and leaflet drops about the 'objective' risk, simply reinforce a belief that the authorities do not know what they are talking about. Analysis of response to flood warnings and of relevant survey data (Fielding et al., 2005) found that the most influential factor on flood awareness and likely action in the event of a flood was previous flood experience. Evidence of scepticism based on local knowledge and experience was found not only in verbatim responses in the survey but in elaborated form in the individual interviews.

In response to why no action was taken upon receiving a flood warning, verbatim responses in the survey included:

'Lived in [town] all my life and know where it floods and where it doesn't'.
'We were not flooded the first time so we did not expect to be flooded again'.
"I don't want to be ignorant but it is absolute trash to say that this property is at risk of being flooded. I have lived in [riverside town] all of my life and I am 84 years old, and this area has never been flooded in that time, and I am saying that with 30 years experience in the fire brigade. Whoever put this address on the at risk register was very wrong, if the flooding ever got to this area [town] would not exist'.
(Post Events Survey 2001 verbatim responses)

While interviews yielded similar responses, e.g. TD: No, I've lived 'ere thirteen years and I've never felt [at risk], never (*Parent Interview*, FWVG Project), the finer-grained data also contained indications that ignorance was a factor.

I knew about floodplains but I didn't imagine for one minute that where we're located was on a [floodplain], in fact I didn't even know [...] there was a bloody river, that was a surprise, I knew the hump back bridge [I] go over [it] every day but I didn't know there was a river in that proximity.
(New residents focus group (FWVG Project))

Interviews suggested that experience could negate 'objective' awareness:

F: I don't actually feel at risk. I mean I'm quite kind of aware that I live on

[a floodplain because], ... we have had leaflets through saying you're in a blue zone and ... knowing environmentally I could see there was a rise and you know floods that happened like ... Lewes and Cornwall.
(Owner occupier focus group (PRFW Project))

This respondent was aware of the flood risk but discounted it from lack of experience of flooding.

F: I think that's it, I think because I haven't actually experienced anything either.

Several respondents recognised their lack of awareness but blamed it on lack of official warning when they moved into the area, which in turn was blamed on the long time lapse, and therefore reduced risk, since the last flood:

...It's just ignorance on all of our parts because nobody had told us in the first place you know, if you only get flooded in the last time in 1968 everyone sort of forgets about it and if we'd have probably known that there was a chance that we were going to get flooded you might have done something about it sooner.
    F: And [property] searches ... you only have to give the last twenty years history.
(Families focus group (FWVG Project))
[Second participant] I looked for it you know because I phoned my solicitor up and gave him a piece of my mind and he said well ... it does show up in your search and he told me the page it was on but he said it is 1968, it's quite a long time ago so he said I never really mentioned it to you because I thought that ... perhaps [because] that was a long

time ago it's not worth worrying about ... Which I could understand.
(New residents interview (FWVG Project))

There is indeed 'objective' cause for scepticism about flood risk information. Flood plain maps underestimate risk in the case of flooding caused by inadequate storm-drains or groundwater and surface water runoff, and overestimate where flood defences or local topography have not been accounted for. In addition, the EA's own literature concedes the maps '... cannot provide detail on individual properties'[2]. There was evidence of disbelief in the integrity of the maps among 'at risk' respondents, who had taken no action when warned:

'Being on first floor flat didn't worry'
'Because property is not in flood area'
(Post Events Survey 2001 verbatim)

There were hints of conspiracy between the EA and insurers from respondents:

But as soon as you give your postcode they immediately know you're in a high risk flood area. [...]
Participant 1: Even if you're not, I mean I notice on the list of roads that you gave us one of those was ... Hill, well I mean that's literally up on the Downs, how can you possibly flood up there? [Laughter] [...] And yet as far as ... the insurance companies are concerned, all they have is your postcode [...] The Environment Agency's stated that you are in that area.[...] Participant 3: And in the harbour there are seven storey blocks ... so if you live in the top of the storey [...]
You're still going to be penalised.
(Owner occupier focus group (PRFW Project))

Depending on personal circumstances, recognition of vulnerability to flood risk, *according to the 'etic' flood maps*, may either be accepted and acted upon, a situation where the emic and etic perspective coincide, or rejected where etic and emic viewpoints are at variance. In the latter case there are two possibilities. First, the respondent is *not* actually at risk – due either to an error in the flood maps (the respondent lives on a hill or recent flood defences have not been taken into account) or personal circumstance (the respondent lives above the ground floor). Second, the respondent *is* at risk but does not perceive this risk to be significant. Reasons for this are diverse: they may lack information about the risk; through past experience and local knowledge their perception of their coping ability may outweigh perceived risk; acknowledging the risk may have negative impacts (psychological and/or economic); or they may distrust the flood maps.

So, while there is value in identifying those 'at risk' to target awareness campaigns or to explore the environmental justice agenda, it must also be recognised that vulnerability is a quality of experience and produces different responses in different individuals. Rather than regard emic and etic perspectives as competing versions, complex social phenomena require coordination of the perspectives and their associated methodologies. The principal social science tool enabling such an approach is a mixed-method design that assigns different roles to different methods.

THE STANDING, USES AND FUTURE OF METHODOLOGICAL COMBINATION

The contemporary practice of multiple-method research

The status of MMRD contrasts in the academic and applied research spheres. MMRD remains controversial in the academic sphere. Since the canonical formulation of 'triangulation' in the 1950s, the social sciences have developed a range of considered objections on grounds of epistemology and incommensurability of methods. The situation contrasts with that in applied research, where many regard MMRD as a practical necessity. Bryman (2005) compared planned research design and actual practice in studies claiming MMRD, finding substantial divergence from the kind of planned use of MMRD that we might expect if the concept of MMRD was firmly established as part of the methodological canon. Researchers sometimes employed multiple methods without any rationale for why this was superior to using a single method; other researchers who

declared such a rationale did not use multiple methods in the study itself, and yet other researchers who declared both a rationale and followed it through by using multiple methods actually relied on a single method for their analysis. These divergences reflect the fact that MMRD is not a technique, like calculating tests of significance or running a cross tabulation, but an attitude of inquiry, an approach to quality standards and to what constitutes adequate explanations of social phenomena.

The policy community – government, voluntary organisations and interest groups – is a growing consumer of social science research. In the UK and USA those engaged in commissioning research have increasingly construed adequate research as multiplemethod research. At root, MMRD is a growing orthodoxy because of the 'common sense' appeal of the underlying logic (combined with either a measure of ignorance or indifference to the epistemological differences between methods), but the trend is also related to the increasing promotion of 'evidence-based policy', which has engendered significant institutional moves towards standardisation of research methods, manifest in professional reviews of research capacity, such as the Rhind Report in the UK (2003).

To overcome what are regarded as the constraints on the representativeness and generalisability of qualitative research, government has initiated both topic-specific reviews of quality standards for research (such as in health) and generic reviews of quality standards for particular methods, such as qualitative research (e.g. the Spencer Review for the UK's Cabinet Office; Spencer et al., 2003). Such reviews tend to result in checklists of ingredients for reliable and valid research, and are uncomfortable reading for those who do not construe social research as a matter of following recipes, but there is no doubting the significance of such developments. In particular, qualitative research may have 'arrived', but it is welcome at the platform only provided its findings can be associated with findings from research using other methods.

Long before checklists emerged for qualitative research they were already a familiar part of the environment for quantitative researchers. Criteria in that area reflect the tidier characteristics of quantitative methodology and benefit from the benchmark standards that are intrinsic to work with statistical data, such as expected sample sizes, accepted tests of association and standard measures of effect size. So the checklist approach emerged earlier in relation to quantitative research and attracted less controversy. A major application of large-scale quantitative research is to health research and much of the heuristic associated with quality standards for quantitative research was laid down in the context of epidemiological research, which is associated with large samples and experimental/control designs. This approach is sufficiently embedded in the apparatus of policy-making that it has taken institutional form in organisations like the 'Campbell collaboration[3]' in criminal justice and the 'Cochrane collaboration[4]' in health. Membership represents a kind of official seal of approval to conduct research in this area and members must produce research that adheres to inflexible quality standards.

Ill-considered multiple-method research can lead to real methodological traps. We might take an example from the health field, concerning the UK controversy over the Measles, Mumps and Rubella (MMR) vaccine, a combined vaccination against common childhood diseases. A small sample study conducted by a medical researcher suggested a link between the vaccine and autism, and received considerable publicity. During the 1990s parental resistance to MMR vaccination grew, and many parents demanded that the National Health Service instead provide single vaccines against the various diseases. Other parents refused all vaccination. Both forms of parental resistance increased the incidence of the diseases. Health policy researchers were asked to address these problems. They wanted to add qualitative understanding to epidemiological and survey data. They proposed a 'meta-analysis' of qualitative studies. Initially their idea was to simply add together the samples from a number of qualitative studies of parental resistance until they had what they regarded as a large enough sample size from which to draw inferences. These researchers had no direct expertise in qualitative research. Their background was in epidemiology. It had to be explained that simply 'adding together' a cluster of qualitative studies would be to ignore the different modes of eliciting parental views, different analytic techniques, different degrees of experience of vaccination amongst the respondents and so on. 'Adding together' would do little more than multiply error.

Technological transformations

While the institutional frames within which multiple-method research is conducted cast a strong influence over what is understood as legitimate methodological practice, social research methodology is also responsive to new techniques, particularly those emergent from the computational field. In this section we consider some current and potential 'transformative technologies' for their potential impact on the future of multiple-method research.

A recent means of interrelating qualitative and quantitative data that embraces Caracelli and Green's integrated approach has emerged largely by stealth. This is the development of quantification routines within computer-assisted qualitative data analysis ('CAQDAS'). Most qualitative software counts 'hits' from specified retrievals (e.g. all single female interviewees who commented on divorce), and encourages triangulation by offering a port to export data to SPSS and import quantitative data tables. Some argue that such facilities represent a hybrid methodology transcending the quantitative/qualitative distinction (Bazeley 1999; Bourdon 2000). These claims relate to software that enables statistical information to be imported into qualitative databases and used to inform coding of text, with coded information then being exported to statistical software for further quantitative analysis. For example, NUD*IST's table import and export functions enable manipulation of exported data either as information about codes that have been applied to the text or a matrix built from cross-tabulated coded data. Some packages also have a command language for automating repetitive or large-scale processes, allowing autocoding of data. Quantitative data can be imported to inform interpretation before detailed coding, such as divisions within the sample that emerged from survey response.

Possibilities for interrelating data range from sorting qualitative comments by categorical or scaled criteria to incorporating the results of qualitative coding in correspondence analysis, logistic regression or other multivariate techniques. Categorised response sets exported to a statistics package for analysis are still linked to the qualitative data from which they were developed. For example, a table in N-Vivo provides access to qualitative data from each cell of the matrix produced when a cross-tabulation-type search is performed across data files. This enables users to show any number of socio-demographic characteristics against any number of selected codes. Supplementing counts of hits, colour-graduation of table cells flags the density of coding in each cell. Analytic searches can thus be composed of combinations of interpretive coding and coding representing socio-demographic details.

Since the emergence of Grid and High Performance computing in the late 1990s, a suite of new research tools has become available to social scientists (see Fielding 2003). Large gains in computing resource offer new data-handling capacities and analytic procedures, and new facilities to archive, curate and exploit social science data. A development relevant to methodological integration is in 'scaling up' findings from small-scale studies, which often have small sample sizes, non-standardised definitions and non-cumulative patterns of inquiry, in such a way that inquiries by cognate qualitative researchers can build on each other, and

so that findings from integrated qualitative studies can in turn be related to findings from quantitative research, exploiting meta-analysis strategies. Studies of family formation, the household economy and health-related behaviour are amongst areas where a number of qualitative studies, rich in themselves, have proved unable to 'talk to each other' due to varying conceptualisations addressing fundamentally rather similar characteristics. XML protocols provide the basis of a meta-data model to integrate individual analyses from cognate small-scale studies. In other words, we increasingly have just the tools the medical researchers wanted in the MMR example above. By creating a translation protocol between researchers, data, contexts and interpretations, using an XML data model and wrappers around each individual study, the meta-data model can access and query individual datasets. An ontology is used to specify a common vocabulary for both methodological and substantive facets. The ontology is in effect a practical conciliation of quantitative and qualitative epistemology. Defining it draws out and reconciles different constructions of the features of the same phenomenon. The procedure of matching up the disparate terminologies employed by different researchers in a number of independent studies enables a 'scaling up' of findings without the problem of multiplying error. The ontology 'translates' between projects (so that what study A calls 'conflict over shared space' is matched to 'kids fight over bathroom rights' in study B etc.), enabling generalisations and heuristics derived from the different studies to be reliably combined while genuine differences are identified and highlighted.

Another e-Research tool relates to the under-exploitation of archival data, particularly in the qualitative field. The capacity to link data is a key issue in exploiting archived data: linking qualitative and quantitative data, and linking material like personal biographies to census data, maps and so on. 'Data Grids' enable researchers to share annotations of data and access multimodal, distributed archival material with a view to producing multiple, inter-linked analytic narratives. A given data event can be represented by multiple streams and captured using multiple tools (for sound, image, transcript, statistics). 'Asset management' software such as 'Extensis Portfolio' and 'iVIEWMEDIA Pro' enable a range of data types to be held in an integrated environment that supports data collection, analysis and authoring. Such an approach was used in a multimedia ethnographic study of a heritage centre (discussed in Fielding 2003). Grid computing resources were used to distribute large audio and video datasets for collaborative analysis. For example, 'Hypercam' software was used to record 'physical' interaction within a 3D graphical environment as a way of annotating and modelling different visitor behaviours in heritage centres. The 3D files could be streamed over networks via the Internet, enabling researchers at other centres to comment on and modify the behavioural models in real time. Data Grids also enable researchers to access image, statistical or audio files held in remote archives and to work on them over networks (e.g. collaboratively, or using specialist software not available locally) or download them. Thus, an image database compiled in one study can be systematically compared to those from others.

Technology opens up new types of mode comparison. The oldest 'research' technique is pure observation and we still gain much from carefully watching what people do. Multimedia tools like THEME combine multivariate methods to detect behaviour patterns over time (Koch and Zumbach 2002). THEME searches for syntactical real-time patterns based on probability theory. Applying it to digital film, interaction patterns relating to complex behaviours can be found that are not detectable by 'eyeballing' the data. Comparisons can then be made between what is found using observation recorded in conventional field notes and using THEME. Since MMRD is all about making connections, technologies that allow researchers to derive comparator datasets, open up their own data to collation with that gathered by others and

detect points of disparity have a helpful part to play.

The potential analytic yield of multiple-method research from fully exploiting expensively gathered social science data and drawing on the analytic affordances of computational technologies is very attractive. Such applications interest several disciplines, including anthropologists working with visual archives, linguists with sound archives and humanities and social researchers interested in multimedia work. More significantly, the ability to interrelate a host of data sources offers the potential for multimethod research to address social science 'grand challenges', such as the relationship between social exclusion and educational achievement in a mixed economy, in such a way that the kind of predictive capacity and causal explanation associated with the natural sciences comes into frame for the social sciences.

NOTES

1 http://www.environment-agency.gov.uk/news/ *Environment Agency launches campaign to tackle flood apathy* (12/10/2005) Accessed 20/02/2006.

2 http://www.environment-agency.gov.uk/subjects/flood/826674/829803/858477/862632/?version=1&lang=_e#3

3 http://www.campbellcollaboration.org/index.html

4 http://www.cochrane.org/index.htm

REFERENCES

Bazeley, P. (1999) 'The bricoleur with a computer', *Qualitative Health Research* **9** (2): 279–287.

Bazeley, P. (2006) 'The contribution of qualitative software to integrating qualitative and quantitative data and analyses', *Research in the Schools* **13** (1): 63–73.

Becker, H. (1986) *Writing for Social Scientists*, Chicago: University of Chicago Press.

Blaikie, N. (1991) 'A critique of the use of triangulation in social research', *Quality and Quantity* **25** (2): 115–136.

Bourdon, S. (2000) 'QDA software: Enslavement or liberation', *Social Science Methodology in the New Millennium: Proceedings of the Fifth International*

Conference on Logic and Methodology, Köln: Zentralarchiv fur Empirische Sozialforschung.

Bryman, A. (2005) 'Why do we need mixed methods?'. Presented at 'Mixed-methods: Identifying the issues', Manchester, 26–27 October 2005.

Burningham, K., Fielding, J., Thrush, D. and Gray, K. (2005). *Flood Warning for Vulnerable Groups: Technical Summary*. Bristol: Environment Agency.

Campbell, D.T. (1981) 'Comment: another perspective on a scholarly career', in M. Brewer and H. Collins, eds., *Scientific Inquiry and the Social Sciences*, San Francisco: Jossey Bass, pp. 454–486.

Campbell, D.T. and Fiske, D.W. (1959) 'Convergent and discriminant validity by the multi-trait, multi-method matrix', *Psychological Bulletin* **56**: 81–105.

Campbell, D.T. and Russo, M.J. (1999) *Social Experimentation*, Thousand Oaks CA: Sage.

Caracelli, V. and Green, J. (1993) 'Data analysis strategies for mixed-method evaluation designs', *Educational Evaluation and Policy Analysis* **15**: 195–207.

Caracelli, V. and Green J. (1997) 'Crafting mixed method evaluation designs', in J. Green and V. Caracelli, eds., *Advances in Mixed Method Evaluation*, San Francisco CA: Jossey Bass.

Creswell, J.W. (2003) *Research Designs*, Thousand Oaks, CA: Sage. Second edition.

Denzin, N. (1970) *The Research Act*, Chicago: Aldine.

Denzin, N. (1989) *The Research Act*, New York: McGraw Hill. Second edition.

Denzin, N. and Lincoln, Y.S. (2000) 'Introduction: the discipline and practice of qualitative research', in N. Denzin and Y. Lincoln, eds., *Handbook of Qualitative Research*, Thousand Oaks, CA: Sage, pp. 1–28.

Elliott, J. (2005) *Using Narrative in Social Research*, London: Sage.

Fielding, Jane and Jo Moran-Ellis (2005) '*Synergies and tension in using multiple methods to study vulnerability*'. Presented at 'Mixed-methods: identifying the issues'; Manchester, 26–27 October 2005.

Fielding, J., Burningham, K., Thrush, D. and Catt, R. (2007) *Public Response to Flood Warning*', Bristol, Environment Agency.

Fielding, J., Gray K., Burningham K. and Thrush D. (2005) *Flood Warning for Vulnerable Groups: Secondary Analysis of Flood Data*, Bristol: Environment Agency.

Fielding, N. (2003) '*Qualitative research and E-Social Science: Appraising the potential*', Swindon: ESRC, pp. 43.

Fielding, N. and Fielding, J. (1986) *Linking Data*, Beverly Hills: Sage.

Fielding, N. and Schreier, M. (2001, February). Introduction: On the Compatibility between Qualitative and Quantitative Research Methods [54 paragraphs]. *Forum Qualitative Sozialforschung/Forum: Qualitative Social Research* [On-line Journal], *2*(1). Available at: http://www.qualitative-research.net/fqs-texte/1-01/1-01hrsg-e.htm [accessed 6 August 2007].

Green, J., Caracelli, V. and Graham, W. (1989) 'Towards a conceptual framework for mixed-method evaluation design', *Educational Evaluation and Policy Analysis* **11** (3): 255–274.

Hammersley, M. and Atkinson, P. (1995) *Ethnography: Principles in Practice*, London: Routledge. 2nd edition.

Johnson, R.B. and Onweugbuzie, A.J. (2004) 'Mixed methods research', *Educational Researcher* **33** (7): 14–26.

Koch, S.C. and Zumbach, J. (2002, May). The Use of Video Analysis Software in Behavior Observation Research: Interaction Patterns in Task-oriented Small Groups [37 paragraphs]. *Forum Qualitative Sozialforschung/Forum: Qualitative Social Research* [On-line Journal], *3*(2). Available at: http://www.qualitative-research.net/fqs-texte/2-02/2-02kochzumbach-e.htm [accessed 6 August 2007].

Kuiken, D. and Miall, D.S. (2001, February). Numerically Aided Phenomenology: Procedures for Investigating Categories of Experience [68 paragraphs]. *Forum Qualitative Sozialforschung/Forum: Qualitative Social Research* [On-line Journal], *2*(1). Available at: http://www.qualitative-research.net/fqs-texte/1-01/1-01kuikenmiall-e.htm [accessed 6 August 2007].

Levins, R. (1966) 'The strategy of model building in population biology', *American Scientist*, **54**, 420–440.

Morgan, D. (1998) 'Practical strategies for combining qualitative and quantitative methods', *Qualitative Health Research* **8** (3): 362–376.

Needham, R. (1983) *The Tranquillity of Axiom*, Los Angeles: University of California Press.

Niglas, K. (2004) '*The combined use of qualitative and quantitative methods in educational research*', Tallinn, Estonia: Tallinn Pedagogical University.

Pike, K.L. (1967) *Language in Relation to a Unified Theory of Human Behavior*, The Hague: Mouton.

Rhind, D. (2003) *Great Expectations*, London: Academy of Learned Societies in the Social Sciences.

Sieber, S. (1973) 'The integration of fieldwork and survey methods', *American Journal of Sociology* **78** (6): 1335–1359.

Spencer, L., Ritchie, J., Lewis, J. and Dillon, L. (2003) 'Quality in qualitative evaluation: a framework for assessing research evidence', *Government Chief*

Social Research Office Occasional Paper 2. London, Cabinet Office.

Spiers, J. (2000) 'New perspectives on vulnerability using emic and etic approaches', *Journal of Advanced Nursing* **31** (3): 715–721.

Tashakkori, A. and Teddlie, C. (1998) *Mixed Methodology*, Thousand Oaks CA: Sage.

Webb, E., Campbell, D., Schwartz, R. and Sechrest, L. (1966) *Unobtrusive Measures*, Chicago: Rand McNally.

The Analytic Integration of Qualitative Data Sources

Ann Cronin, Victoria D. Alexander, Jane
Fielding, Jo Moran-Ellis and Hilary Thomas

INTRODUCTION

In recent times there has been a considerable
growth in research projects using more than
one method (see for example, Corden and
Sainsbury, 2006; Dicks et al, 2006; Mason,
2006). This has led to renewed debate about
the issues involved in using multiple methods
in a single study, including questions concerning the different ways in which methods
and data could or should be brought together
(see for example, Caracelli and Greene, 1997;
Moran-Ellis et al, 2006; Pawson, 1995). However, within these debates there is a tendency
to focus attention on designs which bring
together qualitative and quantitative methods,
leaving aside research designs which utilise
multiple qualitative methods, perhaps on the
assumption that 'qualitative data' is a homogeneous category. In this chapter we examine the
issues involved in integrating different *types*
of qualitative data generated through three
qualitative methods: 'conventional' in-depth
interviews, photo-elicitation interviews and

narrative interviews. Drawing on data from
the PPIMs project[1] (Practice and Process
in Integrating Methodologies project), which
explored the methodological issues that arise
in multi-method and multi-level approaches to
investigating the management of vulnerability
in everyday life, we specifically focus on
the process of achieving integration across
these sets of data at the point of analysis
and document an approach we call 'following
a thread' (Moran-Ellis et al, 2004).

We begin the chapter with a brief overview
of the concept of integration before moving on
to an outline of our research design. We then
set out the framework we developed – 'following a thread' – to achieve the integration
of linked but separately generated qualitative
datasets at the point of analysis.

CONCEPTUALISING INTEGRATION

In our own work (Moran-Ellis et al, 2006)
we have argued for the importance of the

conceptualisation of integration as a specific *relationship* between different methods (and methodologies) which accords equal weight to the findings of all the methods used for answering the research question, does not violate the epistemological or ontological assumptions that underpin them, but does not necessarily lead to any particular knowledge claims concerning validity or complexity. This differs from triangulation approaches which are concerned with the accuracy or interpretive complexity of research findings (see for example Bryman, 2004). Integration of data may be necessary for triangulation, but it is a *process* of bringing research methods (or datasets) together, whereas triangulation is an epistemological claim. It also differs from other uses of multiple methods: for example research designs where one method is given explanatory precedence and the data from other method(s) are used to support and elaborate on those findings; and those designs where one method is employed to develop the other such as in the use of focus groups to inform questionnaire design. In both these examples the different methods do not contribute equally to the production of explanations of the phenomenon (see Greene et al, 1989 for a more comprehensive review of the different ways in which multiple methods may be used). In effect, our conceptualisation of integration in multiple methods research is analogous to an integrated transport system where buses, trains and perhaps planes are linked together by terminals, connections and timetables. Passengers use different transportation modes for different parts of their journey as appropriate, and each form of transportation retains its own nature whilst also interfacing in a coordinated way with the other means of transport needed for the journey (Moran-Ellis et al, 2006).

Key to this conceptualisation of integration in research is the requirement that each method used retains its own character: different data types are not transformed into one type and then analysed using one analytic method. This retention of methodological character allows the findings of each dataset or method to contribute equally to answering the research question in their own paradigmatic terms, and the methods interface with each other through some kind of designed and systematic juxtaposition.

Integration can be achieved at various points in the research process, from research instrument design to interpretation of findings (see Brannen, 2004; Moran-Ellis et al, 2004). However, it is frequently the case that integration is deferred until the analysis stage either for pragmatic or theoretical reasons. Such 'analytic integration' is distinct from integration at other stages of the research process, and it is this that we discuss in this chapter. Using data from our PPIMs project we illustrate how analytic integration might be achieved using the framework of 'following a thread'.

THE PPIMS PROJECT

The PPIMs project used a number of methods to explore the complex dimensions of vulnerability in the everyday lives of a wide range of people living in Hilltown[2]. The project also examined the methodological issues involved in implementing a mixed-methods research design.

The project consisted of small-scale studies that explored participants' understandings, experiences and management of everyday vulnerability. Table 34.1 provides an overview of each of the *qualitative* small-scale studies (the project also included a small-scale study that used secondary quantitative data but this is not discussed in this chapter).

The concept of vulnerability has been used extensively in both the physical and social sciences to investigate and theorise factors and processes that lead to individuals or groups having raised levels of risk concerning specific negative phenomena or events. Even though recent work has begun to take account of the socially constructed nature of vulnerability, it remains the case that much of the research on vulnerability has been underpinned by a deficit model which assumes that some groups of people are more vulnerable than others because they

Table 34.1 Overview of the PPIMs qualitative small-scale studies

Households	21 in-depth individual interviews and 3 paired sibling interviews with each member of 6 households containing children/young people and at least one parent.
Individuals	28 individual in-depth interviews with 10 people living on their own and 21 people living with at least one other adult.
People with experience of homelessness	1 focus group discussion with 6 people who had all been homeless at some time. Individual interviews using a life history approach with 7 participants.
Visual follow-on study	Photo elicitation interviews with 13 people, based on photographs they took for the study. Video-recorded neighbourhood journeys with 8 people. Participants had already participated in one of the first three parts of the research.

lack something. For example, people may be classified as 'vulnerable' because they are homeless, children are assumed to be essentially vulnerable and older people are seen as vulnerable when they lack power and capacity. Undoubtedly the uneven distribution of economic, social and political power in society leads to certain groups of people being at greater risk of adverse events such as ill-health, trauma or material loss. However, this one-sided approach tells us very little about the experiential nature either of being a member of such a group or of feeling vulnerable. Furthermore, designating specific groups of people 'vulnerable' and implying others are 'not vulnerable' leaves us unable to examine how people (regardless of their situation) experience and manage vulnerabilities in everyday life. As Wisner (1991: 128) argues, research on vulnerability needs to 'create ways of analysing the vulnerability implicit in daily life', and the coping strategies that people develop to manage these. This conceptualisation of vulnerability points towards the research methods which can capture these experiential aspects.

In the PPIMs project we used three methods to generate qualitative data in respect of the experiential nature of vulnerability: in-depth interviews, life histories, and visual methods. These different methods have the potential to tap into different dimensions of vulnerability. For example, verbal accounts of vulnerability elicited through in-depth interviews allow exploration of meanings of vulnerability whereas accounts generated through photo-elicitation interviews may connect with constructions connected to the visual realm. Similarly, accounts generated in interviews may emerge with different co-constructions of vulnerabilities than those generated through life history interviews. Critical reflection on these possibilities points towards the potentially heterogeneous nature of our qualitative datasets and the implications of this for integration of these particular data. One implication concerned analytic approaches to different sets of data, and the question of how to analyse each dataset using an approach appropriate to the nature of that data, so that its epistemological contribution to understanding the phenomenon is realised, whilst also being able to integrate the analyses to produce explanations and understandings which were greater than the sum of the parts.

The in-depth interviews were based on conventional practices of using a broad schedule of topics to guide the interview, and being responsive to participants' own accounts of their experiences and meanings with regard to questions asked. On the basis of this, we considered that the most appropriate analytic approach to the dataset generated through in-depth interviews was that of a grounded thematic analysis. For this the researcher typically begins by examining the data line by line, identifying themes and coding these (see Coffey and Atkinson, 1996), then developing these codings to capture multiple meanings, coding convergence and divergence, and the relationship of codes to broader categories. The process is iterative, and involves segmenting the data. Analysis then proceeds through consideration of codes and categories to develop a thematic level of analysis.

The practicalities of the process of comparison of segments of data leads to an enduring problem of this type of analysis, namely that the segments are to some extent removed from the contexts of their occurrences within the interview. The development of the thematic analysis requires the research to re-connect segments to contexts in order to derive legitimate interpretations of the data.

The visual study component of the project was based on two visually rooted methods: photo-elicitation interviews based on photographs, and video-recorded neighbourhood tours. In this chapter we focus on the verbal dataset generated through the photo-elicitation interviews. Photo-elicitation interviews involve participants discussing photographs with the researcher. In our study, participants themselves generated the photos about which they were interviewed. Collier (1967), an early advocate of this technique, suggests that the use of photographs during interviews helps frame and focus the discussion, sharpen memory, evoke rich descriptions and set the informant at ease. The interview enables participants to discuss their interpretation and meaning of the photographs and to provide an explanation for why they chose to photograph what they did. We felt that for this dataset a thematic approach to the photo-elicitation interviews was also appropriate. However, the presence in the photo-elicitation interview data of references to the photographs, and hence to the visual realm, both by participants and by the researcher, created a framing of participants' experiences to which the thematic analysis also had to attend.

The third set of qualitative data was generated via interviews with people who were, or had recently been, homeless. Our experience of running a focus group with previously homeless individuals indicated that although participants were willing to engage in interactive discussion about their experiences of homelessness, they were concerned to present their own life accounts, or *stories*, of homelessness. Taking this into account, subsequent individual interviews specifically used a life history approach which enabled participants

to narrate their experiences and thus situate the issue of vulnerability in a broader context. Consequently, these accounts required a different analytic approach. To have analysed such accounts through thematic analysis – which pulls short segments out of the whole interview, fragmenting it – would not have maintained the integrity of the participants' stories. Accordingly they were analysed using a sociologically informed narrative analysis approach.

Narrative analysis focuses on the social construction of the story and the role that stories play in the construction and presentation of identity (Rosenweld and Ochburg, 1992). Moving beyond the idea that a story is representative of an individual life, attention is focused on the 'joint actions' involved in the production of the story. Plummer's (1995) tri-partite model of the producers (those who tell their story), the coaxers (those who encourage and enable the story to be told) and the consumers (those who read/hear the story) is illustrative of this mode of thinking. Even though the producer (teller), encouraged by the coaxer, draws on real events and experiences to tell the story, the story is only ever an interpretation of the significance of past events and experiences. Finally the consumer will add another layer of meaning and interpretation onto the story. As Riessman (1993) notes, representation is ambiguous and always open to different interpretations. Thus, both the meaning and consequences of a story is always contingent upon first, the social location of those involved in the production and consumption of the story and second, the wider social context in which the story is told. For our purposes here we focus on the producers (the participants) who tell their stories.

In contrast to thematic analysis, narrative analysis begins by identifying the 'sequence' of a story. While 'sequencing' can take many forms, including chronological, consequential or thematic sequencing, it focuses attention on the socially constructed nature of the story. Thus analysis moves beyond the mere identification of past events and experiences to concentrate on trying to understand the contemporary significance or meaning they hold for the individual telling the story. Only when a skeleton structure has been completed for each story included in the dataset is it possible to begin to make comparisons between the stories.

To summarise, then, it was epistemologically most appropriate to analyse the in-depth interviews and photo-elicitation studies using a grounded thematic approach, whilst the life history accounts were best analysed through a sociologically informed narrative analysis approach. Even though both the thematic and narrative approaches are located in a social constructionist paradigm, the former focuses on identifying conceptual themes and issues raised by the participants, while the latter attends to the social construction of the story and the role that stories play in the construction and presentation of identity. This represented a potential point of tension for integration in as much as one mode of analysis consists of extracting information from the whole, while the other seeks to maintain the 'wholeness' of the story. Where the goal is analytic integration, a means must be found for reconciling this tension without undermining the contribution of each method to understanding the phenomenon being researched.

Achieving an integrated analysis

There has been little written about the practicalities of integrating multiple datasets within the parameters of each achieving an equal contribution (with the exception of Coxon, 2005 and Pawson, 1995). To address this challenge in our own research with respect to the heterogeneity of our three qualitative datasets we developed an approach to enable us to be systematic and rigorous which we called 'following a thread' (Moran-Ellis et al, 2004, 2006). This consisted of four steps. The first step entailed each dataset being initially analysed using the analytic method appropriate to that data (as described earlier) resulting in the identification of emergent findings and further analytic questions.

Having undertaken this initial analysis of each dataset, the second step focused on identifying a 'promising' finding within a dataset which could be picked up as a thread to be followed through into the other datasets. The identification of a promising emergent finding may be sparked by the relationship between it and the over-arching research question, or by the resonance of it with one or more of the other datasets. This established a lead for further analysis involving an iterative interrogation of all the datasets.

This led to the third step whereby emergent findings, categories, and codes concerning the thread that was followed into each dataset were juxtaposed to create a data 'repertoire'[3]. This repertoire was then further analysed to refine and extend the analysis of the relationship between the thread and the over-arching research question.

Finally, in the fourth step, the findings that Step 3 generated for a particular thread were synthesised with other threads that were similarly picked up and followed. This can be undertaken without predetermining whether the phenomenon being researched is multi-faceted, complex or singular, and without prejudicing the contribution each research method can make to the overarching research question.

The following section looks in more detail at this approach in practice. Even though we focus on our qualitative datasets in this chapter, in practice we used this approach to integrate all the PPIMs' data including the quantitative data.

AN EXEMPLAR: FOLLOWING THE 'PHYSICAL SAFETY' THREAD

In team discussions of the initial analytic findings from our qualitative datasets it became apparent that a particular finding from the visual component – that of the significance of physical safety as a vulnerability to be managed in everyday life – resonated strongly with emergent analytic findings in the homeless data and in the sub-set of interviews with the children and young people in our study. On this basis we moved to Step 2 and took it up as a 'promising' thread, systematically identifying and analysing 'physical safety' in these and the other datasets we had generated. Through this we identified codes and categories, and generated emergent findings on 'physical safety' for each dataset. This led on to Step 3 where we juxtaposed these to create a data repertoire. This repertoire was then analysed further, with particular emphasis on analytic questions such as whether issues concerning vulnerability and physical safety were persistent features of experiences of vulnerability, the different facets that were revealed by different research methods, and the importance of contexts for how this form of vulnerability was experienced.

Whilst it is interesting that two of our sets of participants – people who are homeless, and children and young people – are usually classified as 'vulnerable' in policy terms, or categorised as members of a vulnerable group in objective measures and conceptualisations of their social position, they were not selected for particular analytic attention on this basis. Rather their data have been given prominence here because of the strong resonances we found between the emergent findings in the analysis of the photo-elicitation interviews, which were conducted with a range of people, and the initial analyses of the data generated with these two groups of participants. Our orientation to all the participants in the study was to their subjective understandings and constructions of vulnerability in their everyday lives, and their accounts of how they strategically manage these vulnerabilities. This precludes any assumptions being made about essentialised or inevitable vulnerabilities for any group of participants in our studies. In this respect, the use of multiple *qualitative* methods was particularly valuable as it enabled us to gain an extensive and intensive exploration of vulnerability as a subjective interpretive phenomenon. This allowed for people's own understandings and agency and moved away from the overarching deterministic discourses which

tend to characterise notions of vulnerable groups and individuals at an objective level.

Step 1 – Initial analysis

The photo-elicitation interview data

Thematic analysis of the photo-elicitation interviews suggested that participants associated a threat to physical safety with specific places, groups of people or hazards, with a distinction being made between physical assault and accidents. Photographs of dark alleyways, deserted paths, and graffiti were taken by respondents to represent unsafe places where assaults could occur. Participants often said that they avoided these places, especially at night. Photographs of a fast lorry, a dark street and a blind curve represented potential traffic hazards. Even though participants said that they had to exercise due care, these hazards were constructed as being beyond the control of the individual and responsibility was seen to rest with 'the Council'. In relationship to a photo (of a blurry lorry), one participant commented:

> I hate the lorries using this as a rat run to the industrial estate at the end because they make the house shake. The whole road is up in arms about that. (Jane, 37 years old)

Participants made a further distinction between potential threats (either malicious or accidental) to their own safety and threats to other people. In the latter case, participants talked about the threat to specific groups of people – children, the elderly or the disabled – suggesting they saw vulnerability as being an inherent characteristic of these particular groups. One respondent, for example, photographed an uneven pavement which she saw as a potential tripping hazard. She was not concerned for her own safety, but referenced 'vulnerable old people', perhaps with walking sticks, who could easily trip. The same respondent photographed the detritus of drug use but focused her concern on this being found near a primary school:

> … it's literally about 50 yards from the back end of the school field and there is a gate that goes from the junior school, to this. It is literally about 50 yards

and you go down there and they have got, they have made, bits of furniture that have been chucked away, like that was a table and all around there there is paraphernalia, what I call paraphernalia. There is drink cans, there is coke cans where they have made bombs to smoke drugs, there's even silver foil where they have actually, we did have a look and it looked as though they had been smoking heroin and that is a concern, obviously, to the whole of the neighbourhood because any kids of any age can go down there. (Alice, aged 56-65)

Certain types of public space, represented by photographs of alleyways, overgrown passages between buildings and a subway were considered intrinsically unsafe, particularly at night time, due to the potential for physical assault. The canal had a more 'fluid' status as a safe/unsafe place, seen as a recreational amenity during the day but dangerous after dark. In addition, specific groups of people (the homeless, drunk people, local youth gangs) were labelled 'trouble' or 'scary', generally because they represented a potential threat to an individual's safety. Even though participants did not take photographs of people whom they feared – participants cited safety reasons for not photographing these threatening people, but also said that they did not feel comfortable invading the privacy of such individuals – other means were used to indicate the sense of threat felt by participants. For one respondent, a photograph of graffiti was emblematic of a gang of youths who were considered unstoppable due to the support they enjoyed from older male relatives. In contrast, participants took images of graffiti to suggest that crime was generally prevalent in the area where it was found.

Photographs of CCTV cameras were presented as either representing the dual sword of security and surveillance or, in one instance, given that an old man had been physically assaulted twice under the photographed camera, used to question the notion of security implicit in the use of CCTV cameras. In contrast to these examples, photographs of personal spaces – homes, gardens or bedroom – were taken to indicate safe, comfortable places.

Whilst experiences and perceptions of vulnerability were represented visually in the photographs as well as elaborated in the accompanying photo-elicitation interviews, it was only in the latter interviews that people talked about how they managed potential threats to their physical safety. From this verbal data we identified three key strategies which participants used to minimise either actual risk or their perception of risk. The first strategy was to avoid places or people categorised as unsafe. The second was related to the degree of familiarity participants felt about their local environment. While a high degree of familiarity could be used to aid decisions about which places or groups of people to avoid, it was also used to 'offset' feelings of insecurity or a lack of safety. One woman, for example, claimed that she felt safe living in the neighbourhood despite knowing that other people had been assaulted there. She had lived in the neighbourhood for a long time and was familiar with it, and so felt it was safe. This links to the third strategy of displacing the perception of risk to oneself onto groups of people already designated vulnerable.

Step 2 – Picking up the promising thread of 'physical safety'

The accounts of children and young people

Picking up the thread of physical safety in the interviews with children and young people, the analysis showed that these participants were often making decisions, and taking actions in relation to their safety, based on *other people's* worries and concerns rather than their own. In particular they were subject to the worries and concerns of their parent(s), which varied in terms of what the worry was, and how strongly it was a factor in parental moves to constrain their child's actions:

I: Are there any [...] rules that your parents set [about using the internet]?

P: Not really but they don't let us have hotmail because of the chat room, my sister had it but I don't know what she did but then they banned it ... so I don't get the benefit which I think is really unfair as all my friends have it and I'm the only one who doesn't have it

I: Do you understand the reasons why you can't have it?

P: Not really, I asked but they wouldn't tell me.

(Tom, age 13 years)

The children in our study, aged 10–13, indicated they were constrained concerning their actions, the places they could go, and how they got there. In general they accepted these limitations whilst also wishing for, and indeed trying to gain, greater autonomy in their movement in public spaces. Two of the children who had recently started cycling into the town centre on their own identified this as an extension of their usual domains beyond the house and garden. Undertaking this venture was accompanied by an acute awareness that they needed to guard their safety in respect of being in the town unaccompanied by an adult. Thus the threat, and their physical vulnerability, was associated with being in a particular place without the protection of an adult rather than the hazard of cycling on the roads (the latter being a safety issue they did not mention). Another child spoke of his sense of a particular threat to his safety when he was not in the company of a protective adult:

I: What is it about strangers that you worry about?

P: Kidnapped.

(Jack, 13 years old)

Indeed for some children the threat of being kidnapped or murdered framed their reflections on whether there were places in the town that they might not go, or where they had to be careful. These threats were 'monstrous' but at the same time the children outlined their strategies for maximising their safety, primarily through being able to identify people who might pose such a threat:

P: If I like see someone who doesn't, if it's late or something and I find, if I see someone who doesn't look like normal than I just walk off with my mates and go somewhere else.

I: [...]what kind of things do you look for when you're trying to decide if someone's OK or a bit?

P: It's just like if he doesn't look right, they're watching and things.

(Stuart, age 12 years)

Constraints related to safety were also often contingent on time of day. The arrival of 'the dark' was a particularly important marker of a shift from a safe time to an unsafe time. In this respect, the temporality of safety and threat resonated with a similar framing by adults as well as children in the visual data accounts. However, in the visual data it was named places that became less safe with the arrival of night time, whilst in the interviews with the children parental fears were understood as being simply about 'the dark':

I: What about when you are outside playing? Are there rules about where you can go or what time?

P: Sometimes I am not allowed to go to the park I have to stay right in front [garden]. And we are not allowed to come home really late.

I: What is late, what would be late?

P: Well, when it gets dark. When it gets dark.

(Yasmin, 11 years old)

In contrast young people, generally aged 14–18, felt that these worries about safety belonged really to their parents and did not reflect the safety issues that they actually had to deal with when they were out and about in public spaces. These young people identified having to deal with threats of violence: some of the places they went – the amusement arcade, the town centre – opened up the possibility that they might encounter individuals who wanted to fight, gangs or general violence. Thus, it was important to know when to leave a place and who to avoid. Furthermore, young people often worked to manage their parents so they did not find out about these hazards, for example by withholding information as to their true whereabouts or by presenting themselves in ways designed primarily to reassure their parents:

I go to my friend's house and we'll go out, and I'll just text my parents and say we've gone here, there or wherever. If I'm staying at a friend's house, I will go out with them but won't tell my parents. (Lucy, 14 years old)

While space does not permit a full discussion here, one of the girls in the study also talked about managing gendered threats to her safety from men, whilst another indicated that this was a parental worry that she had to negotiate in order to be allowed out with her friends or on her own.

Young people who articulated a definition of vulnerability tended to associate it with the ability or inability to defend oneself physically from attack.

The narrative data: Stories of homelessness

Picking up the thread in the narrative interviews with people who were homeless, the analysis revealed the ways in which the topic of physical safety in the accounts of people who had experienced homelessness was a salient factor in both the construction of identity, and the material practices of daily life. Physical safety – the lack of it, the search for it, the meaning of it – was an integral part of individual stories.

Many participants presented biographical, chronologically structured accounts of their lives which highlighted the lived experience of vulnerability and its links to (a lack of) physical safety. This included, for example, physical, sexual and emotional abuse in childhood, experiences of being street homeless, the physical dangers inherent in alcohol and/or drug abuse or the transient nature of many homeless people's lives. At the individual level it was evident that the majority of the stories were structured around the 'quest' for physical safety; taken collectively it was possible to chart the different 'stages' involved in homelessness, the strategies developed at each stage to deal with the experience, and the subsequent impact on identity.

One young man – David – for example, had become homeless in his home town and had lived for a short period of time in a car, yet had felt safe doing so because of his familiarity with the area and the people. This contrasted sharply with his recent experiences of living in a night shelter. His lack of familiarity with the area, coupled with his perception that local people were actively hostile to homeless people not only led him to reflect on the salience of this new identity for him but also to develop strategies to publicly

hide this identity: he avoided mixing with other homeless people in public therefore hoping to 'pass' as a general member of the public, thus remaining safe. Another resident of the night shelter – Tom, a man in his late thirties and homeless since the age of 14 – had developed additional strategies to cope with the physical threats that arise from being street homeless. On arriving in a new and unfamiliar environment he applied knowledge gained in previous locations to the new location, in short constructing a 'universalised' safety 'map'. For example, previous experiences had taught him that the chances of being physically attacked were higher if he slept in the centre of a town as opposed to the outskirts, thus he routinely avoided the centre of all towns.

Participants who had been through drug and/or alcohol rehabilitation and were currently living in residential move-on accommodation, from which they hoped to move to individual permanent accommodation, were at a different stage and this was reflected not only in the telling of their stories but also in their reflections on physical safety. While producing in-depth accounts of past threats to physical safety, the majority felt physically safe in the present although recognising that this was contingent upon remaining alcohol and/or drug free. Looking to the future, participants expressed concerns that they might be housed in areas populated by drug users and dealers, which would constitute a new threat to their physical safety.

These participants adopted a number of strategies to reduce threats to their physical safety, including avoidance, 'invisibility' and 'passing'. Additionally, recovery from alcohol and/or drug abuse was often talked about in terms of a long-term strategy to reduce the risk of physical harm, in as much as the ultimate goal is permanent accommodation and reintegration into 'mainstream' society. In addition, participants' explanations for why they left home could be construed as a strategic act of resistance, whereby being homeless was considerably preferable to being subjected to further abuse at home.

In the discussion of the previous two datasets it was possible to use data extracts from the interviews to illustrate our analysis. Unfortunately, a combination of a lack of space and methodological considerations does not permit the inclusion of data extracts from the homeless accounts – one 'extract' ran to some 12 pages of transcription. In order to do justice to the data we would need to present extended data extracts to demonstrate the narrative nature of the accounts and the presentation of identity. One man, for example, began his interview by asking if the interviewer wanted the story of his life and then proceeded to provide a very detailed chronologically ordered account of his life, which attempted to provide a socially situated explanation for his homelessness. Drawing on the notion of 'discredited identities' (Goffman, 1963) it is possible to see how the interview provided the homeless participants with the opportunity to provide an alternative account of homelessness from the negative one traditionally portrayed in society.

Step 3 – Creating a data repertoire

The third step of this process of analytic integration involved juxtaposing both the initial analytic findings of the individual datasets and the data segments/elements that had been coded in the initial analysis to create a data repertoire for the theme of 'physical safety'. This was then subjected to further analysis and interpretation, looking for commonalities and differences, convergences and divergences. Effectively this repeats the process of inductive analysis with the data identified as salient to the thread of physical safety whilst remaining mindful of the implications of the nature of the data and its origin. It is through the development of the analysis of the data repertoire that findings can be integrated to produce a more complex understanding of the thread and its relationship to the overall research question.

In relation to physical safety and vulnerability, further analysis of our data repertoire led us to understand physical safety as both a present *and* an embedded past feature of the lives of people who were homeless, a present but negotiable hazard for young people not

living with violence and a visually locatable phenomenon for all participants. For young children the concept was often related to extraordinary events (kidnap, murder) rather than more ordinary or frequent threats to physical safety such as road traffic accidents, muggings or assault.

Contingent features of vulnerability also emerged out of the analytic integration of the three datasets. These included vulnerabilities associated with physical safety which were contingent on time of day/night as well as being linked to material-spatial-architectural aspects of public spaces. In terms of dealing with situations and locations which increased perceptions or senses of physical vulnerability, all participants identified strategies which they used to manage their (potential) vulnerability.

It became clear that perceptions, constructions and experiences of vulnerability also diverged in different domains for different groups of participants. For people who were homeless, vulnerability was closely tied to the biographies that had led them to be without a home. They identified physical assault as a recurrent feature of their childhood homes, their temporary homes in their adult lives, and of their times living on the street. In addition, threats to their physical safety were encountered, or anticipated, when moving into new areas or new towns and occasioned the need to make decisions about where they would stay and where they would locate themselves. Physical vulnerability was tied into the identity of being homeless in a profoundly biographical and narrative way.

In contrast the physical safety issues that concerned children and young people in our study reflected the ways in which they are positioned between structures which constrain their actions on the basis of their age, and their own desires, opportunities, and abilities to be (relatively) autonomous social actors (see Hutchby and Moran-Ellis, 1998; James and Prout, 1990). In this regard their constructions of physical safety and vulnerability were linked to the relative distributions of power between adults and children/young people, and the ways in which these distributions intersect with their social worlds. For the children in the study, their sense of vulnerability in physical terms related to extending their usual geographical range from their immediate localities with known adults nearby to being unaccompanied in public spaces at a further distance from home. They managed their vulnerability by adhering to parental rules which they understood to be designed to maximise their safety, and by developing their own readings of other people in their vicinity in terms of whether or not they might present a threat. For the young people in the study their social worlds were already more extended both geographically and temporally, but they sought greater control and autonomy in their movements and activities. With this came an increased likelihood of having to deal with physical safety issues, with threats presented by others in the form of fights, gang actions, violent encounters, and possible sexual harassment or assault. Key for the young people in the study was managing parental concerns so that the young people could exercise physical autonomy in the face of other people's worries about their vulnerability whilst balancing this with managing the potential risk of actual violence when they were in the public arena. Their perception of their own physical vulnerability was framed in the context of their strength or weakness relevant to their potential assailant.

Physical safety and vulnerability took on a different dimension in the domain of the visual as represented in the photo-elicitation interviews. Here it was the material fabric of places which were invoked visually and verbally as increasing or decreasing vulnerability to physical hazards and assaults. The built environment was taken to be a context in which a person's vulnerability may be accentuated – for example that of older people who might trip over loose paving, or children who were at secondary risk to the hazards of drug taking near their school. This material context intersected with ideas of time of day and sources of responsibility to produce physical vulnerability as a product

of ecology on the one hand and an inherent characteristic for some on the other. Physical vulnerability can be understood in visual terms as readings of present dangers, future dangers, and attributed responsibility for causing the vulnerability to outside agents such as the Council, or a local group of youths. Strategies for managing safety were not manifested in the visual domain, emerging instead as accounts of actions including avoidance of the location.

In summary then, physical safety emerges as a dimension of vulnerability but how it emerges is contextual to the social worlds of the participants. How people experience vulnerability, and how they act on that, varies considerably whilst the environment presents different degrees of threat. For the homeless people in the study physical safety was a key strand in their narratives, interweaving with their identities and biographies. For the young people and children it was a site around which the relationship between their structural position in their families, and in society more generally, and their status as social actors is played out. Visually, the notion of physical safety can be framed by participants as a material, ecologically located phenomenon.

Uniting these dimensions brought us to considerations of vulnerability and safety which suggested that, whilst there were commonalities of dimensions across different genres of experience and perception, such as the significance of time and place, this form of vulnerability also intersected with individuals' notions of their own and others' identities. This led us towards theorising how this aspect of vulnerability and its intersection with (or contribution to) individual identities fits with other forms of vulnerability. To address this question we returned to the data to identify other 'promising threads' and followed those analytically across the datasets. The final goal was to synthesise these findings with other themes, to create multi-faceted understandings of vulnerability and its management in everyday life across a broad range of dimensions that emerged from our research. At the end our theoretical understandings of vulnerability was a picture woven from these different threads.

CONCLUSION

Challenges in this approach

Our goal in this chapter has been to demonstrate how integration of different qualitative datasets, through an examination of each set of findings relating to safety and vulnerability, increased our *understanding* of the experience of vulnerability. Each dataset contributed an equal share to the analysis of vulnerability and physical safety, and as the analysis proceeded, we were able to reflect on the complex nature of vulnerability in this regard.

This process for generating analytic integration is time-intensive and entails a number of challenges. The first is identifying 'promising' threads. There are a number of strategies used in single dataset analyses which can be drawn on: inductive leads may arise from within the project, through reference to the research question or sensitivity to the content of the data, or it may be sparked externally, so to speak, by the stimulus of theoretical work and other empirical studies. In addition, team discussions about dataset contents, emergent findings, and puzzling questions are essential for establishing resonances between the datasets. Thus it is important that team research includes team members with a range of expertise, allows for appropriate methodological divisions of labour, and includes sufficient opportunities for good communication within the team.

Another key challenge is to allow each dataset its own integrity throughout the integration process. Creating a data repertoire of systematically identified initial analyses, assembled for further analysis to produce an integrated story about a particular aspect of the phenomenon (such as we have in done in this chapter with respect to physical safety and vulnerability), might seem to privilege a thematic approach to analysis. If this were the case, it would be problematic for data more appropriately handled by other analytic approaches. In respect to this, the PPIMs team critically examined what happened to the narrative accounts of the homeless people when the data repertoire was created. Our conclusion was that the data repertoire could encompass narratives provided effort is made to preserve their integrity by constantly re-examining the links between the themes and the narratives. In our case, the overarching structural narrative feature, which was paramount to our understanding of the homeless participants' accounts, draws on notions of identity as a homeless person. The theme of physical safety extended beyond specific instantiations to form a cornerstone of identity. We suggest that the salience of identity in these accounts complements those produced by other participants and resulted in an increased understanding of the theme of physical safety and the overall theme of vulnerability.

Nevertheless, the potential 'risk' of some types of data being 'translated' into other types remains. We successfully retained the narrative quality of the homeless data; however, we were unable to convey a sense of the story-ness of the data in a short chapter such as this. Similarly, in this chapter we described photographs, thereby translating visual data into verbal, and relied on the transcriptions of the photo-elicitations (textual data) leaving aside actual visual analysis which was also part of the study. The photo-elicitation draws on the visual knowledge of the study participants and is therefore distinct from the other interview data. We believe that visual data itself, as with narrative data, can be part of analytical integration; however, conventional reporting and publishing formats provide challenges in presenting such data in their own terms.

In this chapter we have argued, drawing on our earlier work, that integration should be thought of as a process which creates, and analytically exploits, a particular relationship between different sets of data. We have also argued that since all qualitative data are not alike attention must be paid to the processes by which research generating multiple qualitative datasets will achieve integration, where that is the purpose of having a multiple methods research design. To this end we have presented a model for the practical accomplishment of integration at the level of analysis – 'following the thread' – which focuses on ensuring that the integrity of each type of dataset is preserved in the process of integration, and hence the epistemological contribution of each set of data is maintained. We also argue that this approach offers the opportunity for synergies between datasets in order to achieve one of the goals of multiple-methods research: the generation of an overall analysis which is greater than the sum of the (methodological) parts.

NOTES

1 ESRC Award H333250054 Investigating Practice and Process in Integrating Methodologies (PPIMs). The project is funded by the ESRC under the Research Methods Programme http://www.ccsr.ac.uk/methods/.

2 A pseudonym for a small town in the South of England. All participants are anonymised.

3 This alludes to a repertoire of dance or music pieces, rehearsed and developed, which provide a pool from which a selection is made to create a particular conceptual performance. We use this to capture the assemblage of initial analyses which are not 'raw' data, have their own (methodological) integrity, and which can be brought together to produce a coherent 'story'. We would not, however, wish the metaphor to be taken too far: the intention is to provide some language to describe this part of the process of integrated analysis.

REFERENCES

Brannen, J. (2004). 'Mixing methods: the entry of qualitative and quantitative approaches into the research process', *International Journal of Social Research Methodology*, 8(3):173–184.

Bryman, A. (2004). *Social Research Methods*, second edition. Oxford: Oxford University Press.

Caracelli, V.J. and Greene, J. (1997). *Advances in Mixed-Method Evaluation: The Challenges and Benefits of Integrating Diverse Paradigms*, New Directions for Evaluation, No. 74. San Francisco, CA: Jossey-Bass.

Coffey, A., and Atkinson, P. (1996). *Making Sense of Qualitative Data Analysis: Complementary Strategies*. Thousand Oaks, CA: Sage.

Collier, J. (1967). *Visual Anthropology: Photography as a Research Method*. New York: Holt, Rinehart and Winston.

Corden, A., and Sainsbury, R. (2006). 'Exploring 'quality': research participants' perspectives on verbatim quotations', *International Journal of Social Research Methodology*, 9(2):97–110.

Coxon, T. (2005). 'Integrating qualitative and quantitative data: What does the user need?' *FQS (Forum: Qualitative Social Research)*. 6 (2): e-paper. http://www.qualitative-research.net/fqs/fqs-eng.htm. Accessed July 2006.

Dicks, B., Soyinka, B., and Coffey, A. (2006). 'Multimodal ethnography', *Qualitative Research*, 6(1): 77–96.

Goffman, Erving. (1963). *Stigma: Notes on the Management of Spoiled Identity*. Englewood Cliffs, NJ: Prentice Hall.

Greene, J.C., Caracelli, V.J., and Graham, W.F. (1989). 'Toward a conceptual framework for mixed-method evaluation designs', *Educational Evaluation and Policy Analysis*, 11:225–274.

Hutchby, I., and Moran-Ellis, J. (eds) (1998). *Children and Social Competence: Arenas of Action*. London: Falmer Press.

James, A., and Prout, A. (eds) (1990). *Constructing and Reconstructing Childhood*. London: Falmer Press.

Mason, J. (2006). 'Mixing methods in a qualitatively driven way', *Qualitative Research*, 6(1): 9–25.

Moran-Ellis, J., Alexander, V.D., Cronin, A., Dickinson, M., Fielding, J., Sleney, J., and Thomas, H. (2004). *Following a Thread – An Approach to Integrating Multi-method Data Sets*, paper given at ESRC Research Methods Programme, Methods Festival Conference, Oxford, July 2004.

Moran-Ellis, J., Alexander, V.D., Cronin, A., Dickinson, M., Fielding, J., and Thomas, H. (2006). 'Triangulation and integration: Processes, claims and implications', *Qualitative Research*, 6(1): 45–59.

Pawson, R. (1995). 'Quality and quantity, agency and structure, mechanism and context, dons and cons', *BMS, Bulletin de Methodologie Sociologique*, 47:5–48.

Plummer, K. (1995). *Telling Sexual Stories: Power, Change and Social Worlds*. London: Routledge.

Riessman, C.K. (1993). *Narrative Analysis*. London: Sage.

Rosenweld, G.C. and Ochberg, R.L. (1992). *Storied Lives: The Cultural Politics of Self-understanding*. London: Yale University Press.

Wisner, B. (1991). 'Rural livelihoods in Kenya, 1971–1990: Further reflections on justice and sustainability'. Paper presented to the Association of American Geographers, Miami.

35

Combining Different Types of Data for Quantitative Analysis

Manfred Max Bergman

A man [sic.] with a watch knows what time it is.
A man [sic.] with two watches is never sure.
Segal's Law

INTRODUCTION

Data do not occur naturally, nor do data ever speak for themselves, nor does there exist an obvious interpretation for a datum. Instead, data are manufactured and interpreted to fit a particular research purpose or line of argumentation. Empirical detection and interpretation of presences or absences, patterns, order, structure, or change, regardless of whether inductively or deductively derived, are the outcome of theoretical models and assumptions underlying analysis, of which data are an integral part. Already in 1964, Coombs wrote: 'knowledge is the result of theory – we buy information with assumptions – "facts" are inferences, and so also are data and measurements and scales' (1964: 5). If data production is part of the constitutive process of research, then from where do they come and of what are they made? And if

data are indeed thus produced, what are the advantages of using more than one dataset for a particular research purpose?

This chapter is about what and how data are detected and used, and, as a consequence, how certain limitations thus arising may be overcome by using more than one dataset. Of particular interest are different types of data and how they are selected and combined in modern research designs. For this objective, it is necessary, first, to conceptualize data and their integral position within the research process, second, to understand the process of data production, and, third, to explain the possibilities and limits of using more than one dataset for a research project. This chapter will not deal with data analysis issues specifically but will nevertheless cover reasons for which more than one dataset could be used in quantitative research. In addition, while many of these issues could be applicable to qualitative or mixed-methods analysis, the explicit focus here is on quantitatively oriented research. Finally, there exists an excellent literature on validity and reliability, which connects in many ways to the use of more than one dataset for a particular research purpose. In this text, however, such issues are not covered in detail. The utility of using multiple datasets transcends quality issues relating to classical validity concerns but tends to be under-theorized. This chapter addresses this omission.

DATA AND THE RESEARCH PROCESS

Prompted by various introductory texts and lectures on research methods and methodology, most people understand empirical research as a tripartite process: the conceptualization of a research question, the collection of data, and the analysis of these data, from which the research results emanate.

The conventional view of the research process

The conventional model about the research process connects the four principal research components, i.e. research question, data collection, data analysis, and the research results[1], in a specific way. Figure 35.1 illustrates this conventional view of the research process.

There are three fundamental problems with this research model: chronology, fragmentation, and apparent inevitability:

- *Chronology*: This conventional model implies a chronological ordering of the different parts of the research process such that researchers appear to have settled on a research question before they collect or select appropriate data, and only then would they consider how these data are to be analyzed. Thus, the model strongly implies a deductive approach to research, while inductive research, including data exploration and visualization, are either ignored or spurned[2]. In

practice, researchers often either formulate or at least adjust their research questions according to the characteristics of the available data. This is particularly the case with secondary analysis of existing data, where researchers often create proxies from variables that may be related to, but do not fully connect with, a construct under investigation, or they adjust their research questions or models to create a more adequate fit between the constructs embedded in the research question and the data available. Moreover, few researchers are unclear about what analytic techniques they will use, at least in general terms, before they have collected their data, often selecting the analytic strategies and methods according to their analytic competences and habits. Quite often, specialists in multidimensional scaling, correspondence analysis, latent class analysis, etc. tend to stick with the technique with which they are familiar.

- *Fragmentation*: Due to the conventional tripartite division of the research process, researchers tend to focus on the details relating to the components of the research process – research question, data collection, and data analysis, while neglecting the intricate relations between them. However, the quality of the research process and its results are at least as dependent on the interconnectedness between the components as they are on the components themselves. Due in part to this fragmented research design, many research results are unconvincing or incommensurable with other research findings, despite the availability of appropriate data and the application of sophisticated analytic techniques. This connects to some extent to John Tukey's suggestion that there exists an error source far more treacherous than the Type I or Type II error: the greatest threat to validity, the 'Type III error,' is asking the wrong questions of the data (cited in Raiffa, 1968).

- *Inevitability*: This model also implies a certain inevitability of the results that emerge from the research question. The research results are believed to be an inevitable consequence of the research question because the data were collected

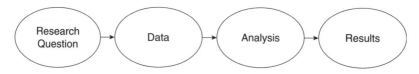

Figure 35.1   The conventional view of the research process

or selected based on their suitability for answering a particular research question, and the analytic technique was selected according to the data at hand and in line with the research question. However, this is not necessarily the case. Just because a dataset is analyzed adequately, i.e. the analysis conforms to established standards and that its output provides an answer to the research question, it does not mean that no other analyses are equally adequate for this dataset and research question. A different analytical model with the same data or a similar statistical model with different data is likely to produce variations in the results, even if the research question remains the same. What is neglected in this tripartite research process with one dataset and one analytic strategy is the awareness of equally suitable alternatives, i.e. other suitable datasets or analytic strategies, which could have served equally well to answer the research question. Due to the implied causal chain – from research question via a dataset to the research results, variations in results due to alternative data choices or analytic strategies are rarely considered.

An alternative view of the research process

Experienced researchers are not taken in by this traditional model and its implications. They are aware that the components of the research process are far more integrated, that many decisions about data analysis have been taken long before data have been collected, and that there exist many options to answer a particular research question. All research findings are contingent. The intricate interconnectedness between research results, research question, data, and analysis is illustrated in Figure 35.2.

Even though this model is less parsimonious than the research model presented in Figure 35.1, it is more comprehensive, making explicit the complex interactions between different parts of the research process. As a more realistic representation of the research process, it implies that:

- The research question, data collection, and data analysis are interconnected reciprocally and are thus not connected to one anther chronologically. For example, experienced researchers formulate precise research questions or hypotheses based on part or the data that can be or have been collected. They furthermore collect data such that they are suitable for a particular set of analyses. This does not only refer to the kind of data necessary to answer research questions but also to the 'shape' data needs to have in order to be analyzed according to various analytical techniques.
- The intricate relations between the components of the research process make it necessary to consider the research process within a larger research framework, within which the relations between the components are as important as the components themselves. Thus, there may exist

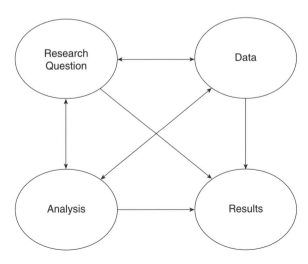

Figure 35.2   Interdependence between the research question, data, analysis, and results

different ways to analyze a particular dataset or there may exist many different datasets relevant for a research question. The criteria for data and analytic selection are not only based on the suitability in relation to the research question, but also on familiarity with the data or analytic technique, contemporary fashions and trends, institutional politics, access and cost, political and economic context, etc.

- The research results are a function of not only the research question, but also of choices relating to the selection and preparation of data and analysis. As different datasets and different analytic techniques respond to different parts of a particular research question, so will the results be a function of not only the research question *per se*, but also of the selection of the dataset (including how key concepts were operationally defined before data were collected, as well as the context within which these data were collected) and the analytic technique (including how data were prepared for analysis and which analyses were conducted). In other words, regardless of whether researchers frame their work in a materialist-realist or a constructivist paradigm, empirical research always has a constructivist slant to it because no objective manner exists to, for instance, define, measure, or analyze a cultural value, an attitude, a social class, a policy, an education level, or a poverty line. Empirical research results are framed by the way a research question has been phrased and operationally defined, as well as what and how empirical phenomena were selected and prepared as data. They are framed furthermore by how and in what context these data have been collected and prepared for analysis, how they have been analyzed, and how the results from the analysis have been interpreted and qualified.

While both models indicate that data should be collected or selected according to their suitability for the research question, the second model also shows – via the double arrows – that any specific dataset will only partially answer a research question. An example will clarify the arguments above. The European Social Survey (ESS, 2004) includes 21 items of a 56-item scale to measure ten 'universal cultural values,' as developed by Schwartz (1999). It should thus be possible to test Schwartz's hypothesis that the 10 values indeed exist within a particular configuration among the countries participating in the survey. However, as only 21 items of the scale were included in the ESS survey, some aspects of the theory cannot be tested fully (Schwartz, 2005). An inclusion of the entire scale or a different subgroup of items, a different sample of individuals within the participating countries, a different set of participating countries, etc. may have changed the results generated by the testing of the hypothesis regarding the universal nature and structure of cultural values. Furthermore, values are studied in many other ways. For example, Schwartz labeled the value associated with prestige and social status 'Power.' Two items measure Power on a six-point ordinal scale in the ESS: 'important to be rich, have money and expensive things' and 'important to get respect from others.' It is debatable whether these two survey items adequately measure prestige and social status and to what extent prestige and social status encapsulate power as a desirable and trans-situational goal for survey respondents. For instance, Treiman (1977), Coxon and Jones (1978), and Ganzeboom and Treiman (1992, 1996) propose markedly different ways to conceptualize and measure prestige. Returning to the research model, it should be clear from this example that cultural value theory can indeed be tested with the ESS data, but always only partially. Other data could be used for the same theory and associated hypothesis, which may not only produce different results, but might also address a different aspect of the research question. For instance, including one of the omitted items relating to Power in the ESS, i.e. authority ('the right to lead or command,' Schwartz, 1997) may have not only changed the result in relation to the presence of this value in the participating countries, but also have had implications for the way Power was assessed with this item. Thus, the research question not only has obvious implications for the selection of data but, less obviously, the actual data selected have implications for what part of the research question is being answered. Accordingly, the relationship between the research question and data is reciprocal in nature.

It is a matter of purpose and debate, whether empirical research ought to begin with basic laws or theory, whether it should start with empirical observations from which laws and theory are deduced, or whether research iteratively vacillates between data and theory (e.g. Bryman, 2001). Nevertheless, empirical research is irreducibly connected with both theory and data. Indeed, it is argued here that no datum can be conceived of or understood in the absence of explicit or implicit theoretical assumptions, and that data can be understood and evaluated in terms of their suitability and quality only with regard to their relationship with a research question and how they are to be analyzed. In order to substantiate this argument, it is necessary to examine how the term 'datum' is used and in what way assumptions and interpretations are part of this usage when conducting research. To explain how and why different types of data can be used for empirical research, it is necessary to explore: first, what data are made of; second, the reasons for using more than one dataset for a research question; and, third, how these reasons connect differently to various parts of the research process.

WHAT ARE DATA MADE OF?

Etymologically, a datum, past participle of the Latin word *dare*, i.e. 'to give,' implies that a datum is something given or something that exists, and that in some way it reflects or at least is connected with an understanding of what colloquially is referred to as reality. Most students taking an introductory course in statistics may get the impression that social science data originate from spreadsheets, readymade and conveniently organized into rows and columns that correspond to cases and variables, respectively. But data are of course the result of a very long production chain, which includes operationalization, selection, translation, and transmogrification processes (e.g. Marsh, 1982).

By either habit or misconception, only certain kinds of data, usually the rows-and-columns kind, are believed to be suitable for statistical analysis. To pursue this problematic argument and, thus, shed light on why and how multiple datasets could be used for quantitatively oriented research, it is necessary to explore how data are classified more generally.

Qualitative vs. quantitative data

One of the most widespread and misleading classification systems divides data into quantitative and qualitative data. Within this tradition, there are three different practices relating to this nomenclature. First, it is used to differentiate between variables measured on so-called continuous and discrete scales. The age of respondents in months or years, the precise net annual household income, the estimated percentage of time dedicated to specific leisure activities, etc. are habitually presented as continuous and are thus considered quantitative variables, while place of residence, religious affiliation, ethnicity, etc. are often considered discrete and thus qualitative variables. Setting aside a critique of this particular practice, it should be evident that data thus coded have already gone through a theoretical and analytic process such that using the terms 'qualitative' and 'quantitative' in this narrow sense is most useful for the selection of a particular statistical technique with which these data may be analyzed. Second, the bifurcation of data into qualitative and quantitative data often refers to a more general form in which observations have been recorded, e.g. numbers vs. words or numerical vs. textual data. The problem with this form of classification is that, on the one hand, numbers often stand for words, concepts, or positions on axes of judgment and that, on the other hand, textual data could be easily, and often are, transformed into numerical form. Furthermore and related to this point, numbers and text do not share the same level of abstraction in that numbers often stand for text. Finally, dividing data into numbers and text does not do justice to the tremendous variety of data used in the social sciences, such as visual and audio data. Depending on the research question and design, such data can be transformed into numerical or other kinds of data. Third, this bifurcation often reflects the way in which data are analyzed. Accordingly, quantitative data are ostensibly analyzed statistically, while qualitative data are not. However, any so-called qualitative data, e.g. texts, audio and video recordings, symbols, photos, drawings, etc. could be transformed into numerical form and then analyzed statistically. Quantitative content analysis is one of the numerous techniques, in which non-numeric data are analyzed statistically. As such, one would add to the confusion by proposing that 'qualitative data' are analyzed quantitatively.

From these arguments, the terminology 'qualitative data' and 'quantitative data' should be considered misnomers, and they should be avoided because these three practices are confusing and misleading. The terms 'qualitative' and 'quantitative,' if they must be used, should be restricted to how data are analyzed, though even this usage is not entirely unproblematic.

Data as a product of the data collection method

Beyond dividing data into qualitative and quantitative data, another typical way to classify data is to associate them with the method with which they were collected. Accordingly, interviews, focus groups, participant observations, indirect measurement, surveys, experiments and quasi-experiments, etc. generate interview data, focus group data, observational data, experimental data, etc. This classification is far less problematic but neither makes a clear statement about data types or of their content, nor about how these data will be analyzed. Despite the incorrect assumption that interview data or data from participant observations, e.g. will be submitted to some form of qualitative analysis, it is not only conceivable but occasionally of particular interest to statistically analyze data from interviews or participant observations (e.g. Johnson, 1978; Bernard, 2005). Similarly, while it is usually assumed that

data collected from surveys or experiments will be subjected to statistical analysis, it may be of interest to explore interactions between researchers and respondents in survey research or (quasi-) experiments non-statistically.

Sense data, objective data, and subjective data

A more elaborate way to classify data connects to its relation to a presumed external reality, dividing data into sense data, objective data, and subjective data. The most obvious way to think about where data come from and what they are made of relates to sense perception, i.e. acquiring and processing sensory information not only through the five senses – vision, audition, gestation, olfaction, and tactition, as proposed by Aristotle in *De Anima*, Book II, but also thermoception (heat), nociception (pain), equilibrioception (balance), and proprioception (body awareness), etc. (Hurley, 1998). More usual are empirical data that are derived from sense data. Derived data can be based on memory or experience such as attitude or value statements, or data that are inferred from sense or other derived data. Particularly the latter form of data gives rise to the central constructs in the empirical social sciences such as poverty, exclusion, class, networks, identity, family, household, etc. A further distinction of these indirect derivatives is termed 'objective and subjective data.'

No longer requiring the perceived information to represent faithfully the external objects, objective data nowadays are more likely to refer to data that may be observed and possibly verified by more than one person. Duncan et al. state that '[o]bjective phenomena are those that can be known by evidence that is, in principle, directly accessible to an external observer. Often that evidence is actually a matter of record, although the relevant records may not be easily sampled for the population of interest' (1984: 8). Experimental data or answers to survey questions relating to name, gender, age, commuting distance to work, annual gross income from work, marriage status, number of unprotected sexual encounters in the past month, etc. are examples of objective data in that the information conveyed by the data could be verified by someone other than the respondent. However, whether confirmation by others would indeed render data truly objective is questionable. On the one hand, convergence between the respondents' answers and an external observer about the phenomenon under investigation does not guarantee objectivity as the respondent and the external observer may misperceive or misjudge the phenomenon in a similar way. On the other hand, divergent information from verification through alternative sources may not automatically falsify the respondents' declarations. In contrast, subjective data are data that ostensibly cannot be verified by external observers. In this vein, '[s]ubjective phenomena are those that, in principle, can be directly known, if at all, only by persons themselves' (Duncan et al., 1984: 8). Examples of subjective phenomena are answers to questions relating to attitudes, values, preferences, judgments, etc. However, if this were true, i.e. if attitudes and values exist only in the minds of the persons in question, then they would be of little significance to social science research. Attitudes and values, e.g. often have behavioral and symbolic correlates such that they can be inferred by external others. Hence, Duncan et al. add the qualification that 'a person's intimate associates or a skilled observer may be able to surmise from indirect evidence what is going on "inside"' (ibid).

It should have become evident from these typologies that, contrary to habits and frequent misconceptions, all types of data presented above could be analyzed quantitatively, i.e. statistically. Indeed, it is important to differentiate between what data one wants to use and how these data need to be prepared for statistical analysis; the former is connected most closely to the research question, the latter to the statistical technique that will be performed. The typologies presented so far are based on the origin and uses of

data but none captures sufficiently how data should be integrated in the research process more generally and in quantitative research more specifically. Another conceptualization of data is needed in order to make a convincing argument about why and how more than one dataset should be used in quantitative analysis. If it is not possible to make a convincing case about the use of data from existing typologies, then it needs to be made with regard to their purpose in the different stages of the research process.

FOUR GENERAL REASONS FOR COMBINING DATASETS IN QUANTITATIVE RESEARCH

There are four general reasons for using more than one dataset in one research project, particularly in quantitatively oriented research: verification, convergence, complementarity, and holism.

- *Verification*: Using data for the purpose of verification can take a number of different forms. Generally, verification here means to assess some form of fit, whether empirical or theoretical, between an ostensibly established dataset or theory and another, less well-established dataset. Verification is part of what is often referred to as convergent validity. However, this form of 'validation,' i.e. convergence, differs from verification, in that using more than one dataset for the purpose of convergence goes beyond a comparison of results with some empirically or theoretically established baseline.
- *Convergence*: Researchers often consider findings from different datasets and different studies in order to examine how results between different time periods, contexts, or samples converge. Convergence can be of importance with regard to data quality, changes across time periods, regional and situational variations, etc. The idea of convergence connects to convergent (and divergent) validity. Derived from measurement theory and well established in psychometrics, convergent validity relates to the extent to which items or sets of items that should be associated with one another theoretically indeed can be observed to relate to each other statistically (Campbell & Fiske, 1959). When using

unconnected dataset, i.e. when it is not possible to correlate items or sets of items with each other, it is more difficult to assess convergence.

- *Complementarity*: In essence, complementarity stands for the use of more than one dataset for the purpose of finding additional but directly related aspects that can be discerned only in their combination. There may exist theoretical and empirical reasons for combining different conceptualizations and empirical findings in order to get an additional perspective on a particular theory or research finding. Important here is that researchers do not simply examine additional data that in some way relate to the research topic as practically any additional dataset would provide further insights or qualifications. Instead, the use of an additional dataset should go beyond the desire for an 'additional perspective.' It should be either theory driven or at least pursue a specific purpose. As with the first two reasons for using more than one dataset, here too, complementarity is often not mutually exclusive from the other reasons.
- *Holism*: Holism is an extension of complementarity but goes one step further. It is based on a classical view of empirical research and stands for the aim of studying the phenomenon under investigation as it exists 'in reality,' i.e. beyond the limits of research-related errors, biases, and subjectivity. Thus, each dataset and results associated with it is considered a piece of the puzzle that will eventually, if combined correctly, reveal the true phenomenon and its dynamics (Brewer & Hunter, 2006). The extent to which findings from many different datasets, often collected for different purposes and in different contexts, are able to eliminate all kinds of errors and provide insight into how things really are 'out there' are questionable. While holism explicitly aims at depicting reality by piecing together evidence from different data sources, complementarity merely uses different datasets for establishing, expanding, or testing an idea or theory. Nevertheless, the use of multiple datasets in the pursuit of holism has been practiced widely in the past although, with Kuhn (1970, 1983) and Rorty (1991), one wonders whether a belief in the idea of objectivity and convergence of scientific progress toward some external reality is necessary for even classical approaches to science.

The use of more than one dataset in a research project may be justified based on these four general reasons. While these reasons were presented as if they are mutually exclusive, researchers may actually pursue a combination of these reasons within one or more research phases. What remains to be accomplished is to connect these general reasons with the different phases in quantitatively oriented research in order to show that, on the one hand, different reasons could be employed in the same research phase, or that the same reason could be employed fruitfully for very different purposes, depending on the particular research step and research aim.

REASONS FOR USING MULTIPLE DATASETS AND THE FOUR RESEARCH COMPONENTS

With regard to the term 'data,' Coombs (1964) distinguishes between recorded observations and that which is analyzed. More precisely, his theory of data, implicitly emphasizing inductive and exploratory approaches to quantitative research, includes three phases: the selection and recording of observations from a universe of potential observations; the production of data by interpreting, classifying, and labeling these observations; and, by applying the data to an analytic model, the identification of relations, order, and structure. Given that the results from an analytic model do not speak for themselves but must be interpreted, one could propose a fourth phase: the transformation from the relations, order, and structure as emergent from the analysis into research results, usually by an interpretive process that links these to theories and research questions. While Coombs' Data Theory is predominantly concerned with the process of identifying patterns and structures from existing data, this chapter is an extension in three ways: it explores how and why more than one dataset could be used in quantitative analysis; it examines the research process beyond the identification of structures and patterns from existing data; and it emphasizes the non-chronological ordering and interconnectedness of the research components.

All four research components are embedded in creative and interpretive processes. In the absence of objective guidelines with regard to how researchers get from the conceptualization of the research question to the interpretation of the statistical results, each step requires creative decisions that are forced upon the researcher. Hence, each phase delimits the research results in a particular way, where different types of data and different types of analysis could be used for different purposes. The four research components and the four general reasons for using more than one dataset allow for 16 possible combinations, i.e. using more than one dataset for verification, convergence, complementarity, and holism in relation to identification/selection of observations, recording/transforming them into data, identifying analytically patterns/structures, and interpreting patterns/structures meaningfully. This section will not cover all 16 possibilities but only provide examples on how more than one dataset can be used for different reasons and different components. For the following, it is also important to realize that it is only possible in principle to separate the four general reasons for using more than one dataset across the different research components. In practice, the line of demarcation between categories can be rather difficult to identify.

Links between data and their patterns

For most of those conducting quantitatively oriented research, the relations within the research process between raw data and their patterns and structures are the most accessible, and so I will begin by outlining reasons for using more than one dataset within this phase. Data are either explored for patterns, or the fit between theory-guided patterns and the data are analyzed. Often, data are also prepared for further analysis, e.g. by creating compound variables or components. For example, variables relating to income, debts, savings, etc. of individuals living in a household may be used to produce a compound variable reflecting household net income, which will then be used for further analysis. Some transformations are so complicated that authors publish conversion tools that allow users to recode certain variables according to such a key (e.g. Ganzeboom & Treiman, 1992). But rather than using existing compound variables or using a conversion tool, one may want to adapt or test these instruments by, e.g. introducing or omitting variable, or by weighing the importance of a variable differently.

With regard to convergence, for instance, researchers may not be satisfied with using only a subset of an established scale to test a theory, such as the example about the universal cultural values as described above, and may therefore collect additional data. Within limits, they may also want to verify whether the ESS data from the subset of Schwartz's value scale are adequate to assess values as proposed by the full 56-item scale, as discussed earlier. Researchers may also want to verify the universality of Schwartz's theory on values by collecting and analyzing data for a country not part of the ESS. Verification may also include an examination of the suitability of a shortened scale or the representativeness of a dataset with regard to some demographic indicators, e.g. gender, ethnic composition, age, etc., by comparing them with national census data, for instance. With regard to complementarity, researchers may be interested in testing or qualifying the universality of value systems or Schwartz's value structure by exploring alternative cross-cultural datasets on values (e.g. Hofstede, 2001).

There are numerous problems associated with comparing the results of an analysis, including the compatibility of the contexts within which data were collected, the compatibility of the sample, the compatibility of the variables, etc. (Kiecolt & Nathan, 1985; Dale et al., 1988).

Beyond these, there are also problems associated with combining micro and micro data. In short, the social sciences often attempt to connect micro-level data such as individual behaviors or family dynamics with macro-level data such as social norms and power structures. For example, Alexander and Giesen (1987) identified the five main approaches to micro-macro analysis in the social sciences. According to the major strands in social theory, society is created by (a) rational individuals, (b) interpretive individuals, (c) socialized individuals acting as a collective force, (d) socialized individuals who reproduce the existing social environment on a micro-level, and (e) rational individuals who acquiesce due to external forces of social control (cf. Münch & Smelser, 1987). However, it should be noted that there is nothing intrinsic about a level to be identified as micro or macro, i.e. they represent relative points on a continuum. In other words, interactions, families, or neighborhoods could represent the micro or macro level, depending on their integration into a model. What is important, however, is that there are more micro-level units than macro-level units, and that the micro units can be assigned to a macro unit. The computational complexity of assessing the interrelation of systems that are formed concurrently between micro units, between macro units, and between micro-macro units is tremendous (Saam, 1999), but the greater problem is the lack of unity between theoretical and computational models. Consequently, some researchers, particularly those engaged in empirical research, often argue that the levels cannot be combined, i.e. that macro-level data follow a different set of laws and logics than micro-level data. Theorists, on the other hand, have long been involved in conceptualizing the relationship so central to social science (e.g. Mill, 1961; Luhmann, 1982; Giddens, 1991; Collins, 2000), but have difficulties with finding convincing empirical evidence for their sophisticated arguments. While the combination and analysis of micro- and macro-level data, either separately or pooled, may provide important insights into the complex relations between and within the levels, it is likely that the gap between empirical results and theory will remain. Combining micro- and macro-level data for verification,

convergence, and complementarity may nevertheless play an important role in advancing theory and empirical support thereof, without necessarily providing (or needing to provide) the 'real' model of complex social systems.

Links between patterns and their interpretation

The complex relations between patterns and structures on the one hand, and their interpretation, on the other, is also part of the main focus in statistically oriented research. An analysis of presences or absences, patterns, order, structure, etc. within datasets still needs to be interpreted. A mere statistical description thereof is insufficient because coefficients do not speak for themselves but must be linked meaningfully to the research question and the underlying theories. Convergence can play an important role at this state. For instance, in our study on intergenerational social mobility in Switzerland, we examined all large-scale data available in Switzerland that contained information about social position between parents and their children (Joye et al., 2003). Convergence was important in three respects: first, with regard to data quality, data collected during approximately the same period, including census data, should converge in order to cross-validate the datasets in relation to their representativeness of the population under investigation. Convergence of datasets from different time periods was examined in order to explore how intergenerational social mobility has changed in Switzerland over time. Finally, the chronological trends identified in this study were compared to those of other countries in order to explore how social mobility in Switzerland converged with other European countries.

When using unconnected dataset, i.e. when it is not possible to correlate items or sets of items with each other, it is more difficult to assess convergence. Meta-analysis is an area of research, where multiple research findings are compared with each other. There often exist many different studies with their own data, all pursuing a similar research question. Even though the first meta-analysis was performed to merely increase statistical power (Pearson, 1904), data and findings of related studies can be pooled and compared with each other in relation to a substantive theory. Meta-analysis, the 'analysis of analysis' (Glass, 1976) attempts to identify and partially correct artifacts and variations in findings due to sampling and measurement error, range restriction, correlation bias etc. over a series of studies (Hunter & Schmidt, 1990). With variations, this is basically accomplished by identifying a set of studies for meta-analysis that are relevant to a research question, determining the suitability for inclusion in a meta-analysis in terms of the research respondents, variables, time period, research design, etc., assessing the effect size of the different studies with regard to the qualities and quantities under investigation (e.g. group mean differences, correlations, proportions, etc.), creating comparability between the effect sizes by a coefficient, and then examining the convergence and variability between the studies and their respective data (Lipsey & Wilson, 2001). A further variant is that of pooled data, i.e. combining data collected at multiple sites, different time periods, or a combination thereof (Beck, 2001; Halaby, 2004). However, it is often argued that pooling data is fraught with error due to heterogeneity problems across datasets (Maddala, 1999). Another problem is the issue of which studies to include: some argue that methodologically weaker studies should also be included, albeit with a different weighting, while others propose to include only methodologically sound studies (Abrami et al., 1988). The 'file-drawer effect' is yet another problem because meta-analyses often exclude non-significant findings as these are usually not published.

Combining datasets and their analysis is also often practiced in search of holism. For example, some researchers interested in voting behavior may use a multitude of available data in order to pursue complex theories, e.g. a general theory on public opinion (e.g. John Zaller, 1992) or the role of cognitive intelligence in society (Herrnstein & Murray, 1994). An appeal toward holistic research is also made by Brewer and Hunter (2006), who even argue that by integrating the 'four major research styles' – fieldwork, surveys, experiments, and non-reactive research – it would be possible to take advantage of the strength of each of these methods and, thus, arrive at 'valid' research results. The attractiveness of this approach is an underlying quest for systematization of the many competing and conflicting theoretical and empirical approaches. For numerous reasons elaborated in this chapter, however, theories and empirical findings on a research topic are bound to be conflicting and contradictory. Rather than attempting to isolate the one set of social science theories and empirical findings that are superior according to some set of criteria, presumably because they are closer to reality, social science research may indeed be marked not only by systematic thought and analysis, but also by eternal ambiguity about the validity, utility, and context dependence of different approaches. This may not necessarily be a bad thing. It could be argued that it is precisely this ambiguity, the competition between theories and empirical approaches that can be considered a way of doing science; not necessarily a closing in of how things really are in a mind-independent reality but a negotiation of questions and their pursuit between different stake holders in a particular time and space.

Links between recorded observations and data

Statistically oriented research is often not directly involved in problems associated with transformation between recorded observations and data. Nevertheless, a considerable information loss occurs during the recording of an observation, e.g. from the attitude of voters at the moment of recording to the recorded attitude statements in the questionnaire, from the lived experience of the interview situation to the interview transcript, etc. This loss, however, should not only be considered as a potential source of bias in a classical sense, but also as a necessary step in the focusing of empirical phenomena to a set of relevant aspects as defined by the researcher's focus and research question. Once observations have been recorded in whatever crude form, e.g. photos, ticks on questionnaires, piles of items sorted by respondents, interview recordings, etc., they must be turned into data before they can be analyzed quantitatively. At times, this is done simultaneously, such as in the encoding of responses with CAPI or CATI, where the interviewers encode responses directly into preexisting response categories, often with significant freedom and error when reinterpreting respondents' answers (Elias, 1997a, 1997b). Turning the recorded observations into meaningful categories is an art in itself, as the following quote illustrates:

> In the field one has to face a chaos of facts, some of which are so small that they seem insignificant; others loom so large that they are hard to encompass with one synthetic glance. But in this crude form they are not scientific facts at all; they are absolutely elusive, and can be fixed only by interpretation, by seeing them sub specie aeternitatis, by grasping what is essential in them and fixing this. (Malinowski, 1948: 238)

Turning observations into data is a form of taming and disciplining them, turning them into a form that is suitable for a particular type of analysis. Far too little attention is paid to this process, which, ultimately, includes a type of analysis at least as important as the subsequent analysis with the thus derived data. For example, before a quantitative content analysis can be performed, non-numeric material needs to be coded meaningfully. While there are some tentative suggestions about how to derive and verify these codes, e.g. via iterative procedures (Glaser & Strauss, 1967; Glaser, 2005) and inter-rater reliability (Gwet, 2001), the processes suggested in the literature are at best guidelines and recommendations. In this case, producing different datasets from the same set of recorded observations could

be used for verification, convergence, or complementarity.

Links between potential observations and recorded observations

Despite the fact that the transformation from a potential observation to a recorded observation is so crucial to the research process, most quantitatively oriented researchers have not considered its complexity sufficiently. Thus, a brief transgression into related fields will shed light on the complexity, within which potential observations are ultimately transformed into data via their selection and recording. Originally explored by pre-Socratic philosophers in conjunction with the limits of our senses to provide us with true knowledge about the world (White, 1991; Dancy & Sosa, 1992), this first transition – from potential to recorded observations – has occupied a prominent position in cognitive and social psychology as well as social anthropology and ethnography.

Termed 'sense data' by twentieth-century philosophers, information from our senses appears to reproduce external objects in the mind via perception. According to sense-theorists such as Russell (1927) and Moore (1953), the book you are reading is represented by sense information relating to shape, texture, weight, color, etc. such that the object is represented by the mind according to this perceived sense information. Thus, sense data reflect the attributes that an object is believed to have. But sense data also relate to the awareness of perception and are, thus, always also mind dependent. From a materialist-realist perspective, even though the size and shape of this book varies if viewed from different angles or distances, these changes are variations in perspectives of the same external object. As part of cognitive development of infants, this and related issues have been studied by developmental psychologists such as Piaget (1955) under the heading of conservation and persistence. However, a number of philosophers (e.g. Austin, 1962;

Jackson, 1977) question the possibility of representation of external objects through sense data, listing in particular phenomena relating to illusions, hallucinations, double vision, and the time delay between existence and perception. Furthermore, sense data such as color, taste, smell, and sound do not exist in the external world but are recognized as attributes due to specific interactions between stimuli, physiology, and mind. As such, the perception of objects is fundamentally influenced by human physiology and psychology. More precisely, research in social cognition has revealed that perception and memory are shaped by prior knowledge and current context. Asch proposed two competing models for impression management (1946): according to Asch's configurational model, individual elements of perception are aligned to form an overall impression such that these can be changed according to context and expectations. His algebraic model proposes that individuals assemble all elements of perception and then come up with a combined impression thereof. Both of these models have received wide attention, while the latter has had a strong influence on attitude and value research (e.g. Fishbein & Ajzen, 1975). Heider's balance theory (1944) is related to Asch's in that perceived elements tend to be changed in people's minds, if they do not fit an existing model. Apparently, sense information is adapted to fit existing thought structures in order to maintain unified, overall impressions and knowledge structures. Less socially oriented, Bartlett (1932) explored how past behaviors and experiences are organized into patterns such that they facilitate future cognitions and behavior.

While psychological studies about social cognition and impression management focus on general human processes including cognition, motivation, and behavior, the findings from these studies could well be applied to researchers and the research process. Researchers make sense of a confusing and complex environment and, here too, researchers may have the tendency to adjust and adapt elements to fit existing schemas, i.e. theories and ideas. It is quite likely that many data collectors, coders, and researchers are subject to similar tendencies when they are identifying, sorting, and interpreting as relevant a small subset of observations in the pursuit of a particular research question.

Indeed, social anthropologists and ethnographers initially attempted, and later contested the possibility of, an objective description of meaning structures. Social anthropologists and ethnographers initially attempted to, and later contested the possibility of, objectively encode and present meaning structures. Malinowski, the first modern anthropological explorer and specialized fieldworker, outlined the tools with which to understand the complexities of meaning structures external to one's own mental context. Empathy and insight, acquired in part through long-term exposure to a socio-cultural environment of concern, are the tools that were believed to assist in the understanding of the meaning of such phenomena.

But careful and systematic empirical observations and detailed descriptions of socio-cultural phenomena have created inconsistencies and, ultimately, doubts about the feasibility of precisely this undertaking. At least since the 1970s, a time period marked by what Geertz named the 'crisis of representation,' it was clear that a reproduction of meaning or, more generally, the transport of meaning from one meaning system to another, is at least problematic. As Geertz states:

> There is a lot more than native life to plunge into if one is to attempt this total immersion approach to ethnography. There is the landscape. There is the isolation. There is the local European population. There is the memory of home and what one has left. There is the sense of vocation and where one is going. And, most shakingly, there is the capriciousness of one's passions, the weakness of one's constitution, and the vagaries of one's thoughts: the nigrescent thing, the self. It is not a question of going native.... It is a question of living a multiplex life: sailing at once in several seas. (1988: 77)

Clifford (1983, 1986) goes so far as to consider insights acquired through observations as highly intersubjective engagements, i.e. where observations are 'orchestrated' within politically charged situations, far better reflecting the ethnographer's view and position than that of the people and situations observed. While this position represents an extreme view in the social sciences, it nevertheless stresses correctly the intersubjective nature and selectivity of phenomena, long before these phenomena are recorded, transformed into analyzable data, and analyzed. From a practically infinite number of possible empirical phenomena, in themselves only a subgroup of all potential empirical phenomena that could have been chosen, researchers select as empirical evidence for their project that which they believe to be suitable, based on specific social, economic, political, cultural, etc. considerations (Bergman, 2002). In other words, even before a shred of empirical evidence has been conceived of as a potential source of data, the research results have been 'compromised.'

The social sciences deal with this problem in three ways. The first entails a call for the abandonment of empirical research altogether, supported by the claim that research thus tainted would not yield what is often called objectivity or, in epistemology and the philosophy of science, is considered true knowledge or truth, i.e. knowledge that is not subject to argument and perspective. In this vein, Tyler (1986) proposes that the aims of science in general, and ethnography in particular, are now an evocation of an imagined reality between the author and the reader of scientific texts for therapeutic and aesthetic effect. The second, far more frequently practiced way to deal with this problem, particularly by quantitatively oriented research, is to ignore it. Concerns outlined above are drowned out by comfortable routines engrained in the craft and habits of doing research. These include: the formulation of a research question or hypothesis in line with the literature of respectable authors and journals, the operational definition of key constructs relating to the research question or hypothesis, data collection according to these definitions and with well-established

tools, and the analysis, interpretation, and presentation of research results, also within the limits of well-established tools and forms. Inconsistencies between research findings, if detected at all, are usually attributed rather vaguely to differences in theoretical approaches, data collection and analysis methods, interpretations, etc. Sooner or later, the self-correcting nature of science, so it is hoped, will take care of these inconsistencies. The third way begins with the recognition that all knowledge derived from empirical research is partial, subject to argument, verification, and revision. This third option also paves the way for using more than one dataset for quantitative research, not merely for purposes relating to verification or convergence, but also for complementarity and holism.

All four reasons for the use of more than one dataset could be relevant in this permanently transitional phase. A researcher could use additional data to verify whether a construct has been adequately conceptualized and captured by existing studies. Similarly, convergence and complementarity could motivate a researcher to propose an alternative, shorter, or otherwise more convenient way to collect data, which would either test or elaborate on an existing study or theory. For example, values have been studied cross-nationally not only by Schwartz and his colleagues, but also by, for example, Hofstede (2001), Triandis (e.g. 1995) and Abramson and Inglehart (1995). There may exist theoretical and empirical reasons for combining different conceptualizations and empirical findings in order to get an additional perspective on how values are distributed across nations and in which combination they are distributed between regions or social groups. Finally, this third way also reconnects researchers to the human-made artifacts within research, e.g. that a 'value' is a complex construct and that it is part of a form of shorthand that allows researchers to explain to their public a set of phenomena, which they have crafted and identified as relevant within a particular space and time.

CONCLUSION

Research results are a function of not only the research question and how it is embedded in its socio-cultural, political, economic, and situational context, but also of the choices that are made in relation to data selection and analytic strategies. Given the chapter's focus on the use of more than one dataset in a quantitatively oriented research project, it was necessary to dispel some misconceptions about data and about which kind of data are used for statistical analysis. Next, four general reasons were presented for using more than one dataset in such studies: verification, convergence, complementarity, and holism. In the final part of this chapter, four phases of the research process were examined in order to illustrate different reasons for using more than one dataset. Overall, research results will remain contingent, and they will always only provide partial answers to a research question. What is argued here is to abandon both the relativistic and the positivistic approach; neither is it satisfactory any longer to attribute inconsistencies in findings to differences in methods and approaches, nor are efforts sustainable that aim at identifying objective structures behind the varying results. It is difficult to outline a third alternative at this time because most ontological and epistemological approaches seem to force researchers chose sides. Nevertheless, using more than one dataset to explore, verify, complement, or qualify may point to a solution. As such, integrating this research strategy into quantitatively oriented projects can be considered an important development for modern social science practices well beyond classical validity issues. This possibility is supported by the expansion and user-friendliness of data archives, the availability of a tremendous number of datasets, the cost-efficiency and popularity of secondary data analysis, etc.

There are of course also disadvantages associated with the use of more than one dataset. Beyond economic and other resource-related constraints, it is always easier to tell a coherent story about one set of statistical results from one dataset. Indeed, studies using more than one dataset, particularly those that focus on complementarity, often appear rather disjointed. Such studies can give the impression that they consist of a set of loosely related research findings without sufficient connection to each other. However, Segal's law, cited at the beginning of this chapter, does not propose that it is better to have just one watch; instead, it may simply be less confusing. But an absence of confusion due to divergent research findings should not be equated with coherence and the notion of truth in a scientific sense. Instead, divergences and inconsistencies are formidable sources for the elaboration and qualification of theory and research findings. Rather than ignoring complexities and inconsistencies, which experienced researchers are aware of anyway, a greater explicit attention to these, for instance by using more than one dataset in quantitatively oriented studies, would be an important development toward a more critical and differentiated approach to post-postmodern social science research.

ACKNOWLEDGMENTS

I would like to thank Eugène Horber, Bernhard Kittel, and two anonymous reviewers for their incisive comments on an earlier draft of this paper.

NOTES

1 Even though models relating to the research process vary in terms of their individual components and complexity, e.g. Leedy (1989) also includes, among other things, 'identification of the problem' and 'statement of the problem' as separate components, while Walliman (2005) adds the theoretical background and ethical issues among 14 components of the research process, they almost always share the four main components.

2 While many textbooks on research methods divide research approaches into inductive and deductive research, sometimes even connecting deductive research to quantitative research and inductive research to qualitative research, research practices differ. Indeed, while most exploratory

data analyses tend to emphasize induction and hypothetico-deductive research, exploratory analysis needs some form of 'container' that provides a minimal theoretical underpinning from which explorations are conducted. On the other hand, most statistical modeling, which formally is based on hypothesis testing, includes model adjustments for various theoretical and empirical reasons. Hence, empirical research in practice is rarely purely inductive or deductive (see also Bryman, 2001).

REFERENCES

Abrami, P.C., Cohen, P.A., & d'Apollonia, S. (1988). Implementation problems in meta-analysis. *Review of Educational Research*, 58, 2, 151–179.

Abramson, P.R., & Inglehart, R. (1995). *Value Change in Global Perspective*. Ann Arbor, MI: Michigan University Press.

Alexander, J.C., & Giesen, B. (1987). From reduction to linkage: The long view of the micro-macro debate. In J.C. Alexander, B. Giesen, R. Munch, N.J. Smelser (Eds.), *The Micro-Macro Link*. Berkeley: University of California Press.

Asch, S.E. (1946). Forming impressions of personality. *Journal of Abnormal and Social Psychology*, 41, 1230–1240.

Austin, J.L. (1962). *Sense and Sensibilia*. Oxford: Clarendon.

Bartlett, F.A. (1932). *A Study in Experimental and Social Psychology*. Cambridge: Cambridge University Press.

Beck, N. (2001). Time-series cross-section data: What have we learned in the past few years? *Annual Review of Political Science*, 4, 271–293.

Bergman, M.M. (2002). Reliability and validity in interpretative research during the conception of the research topic and data collection. *Sozialer Sinn*, 2, 317–331.

Bernard, H.R. (2005). *Research Methods in Anthropology: Qualitative and Quantitative Approaches* (4th ed.). Walnut Creek, CA: Alta Mira.

Brewer, J., & Hunter, A. (2006). *Foundations of Multimethod. Research: Synthesizing Styles* (2nd ed). Thousand Oaks, CA: Sage.

Bryman, A. (2001). *Social Research Methods*. Oxford: Oxford University Press.

Campbell, D.T., & Fiske, D.W. (1959). Convergent and discriminate validity by the multitrait-multimethod matrix. *Psychological Bulletin*, 54, 297–312.

Clifford, J. (1983). On ethnographic authority. *Representations*, 1, 2, 118–146.

Clifford, J. (1986). Introduction: Partial truths. In J. Clifford & G.E. Marcus (Eds.), Writing Culture: *The Poetics and Politics of Ethnography*. Berkeley, CA: University of California Press.

Collins, R. (2000). Situation stratification: A micro-macro theory of inequality. *Sociological Theory*, 18, 1, 17–43.

Coombs, C.H. (1964). *A Theory of Data*. New York: Wiley.

Coxon, A.P.M., & Jones, C.L. (1978). The Images of Occupational Prestige. London: Macmillan.

Dale, A., Arbor, S., & Proctor, M. (1988). *Doing Secondary Analysis (Contemporary Social Research Series No. 17)*. London: Unwin Hyman.

Dancy, J., & Sosa, E. (1992). A Companion to Epistemology. Oxford: Blackwell.

Duncan, O.D., Fischhoff, B., & Turner, C.F. (1984). Domain of the study: Objective and subjective phenomena. In C.F. Turner & E. Martin (Eds.), *Surveying Subjective Phenomena* (vol. 1). New York: Sage.

Elias, P. (1997a). Social class and the standard occupational classification. In D. Rose & K. O'Reilly (Eds.), *Constructing Classes: Towards a New Social Classification for the UK*. Swindon: ESRC/ONS.

Elias, P. (1997b). Occupational Classification: Concepts, Methods, Reliability, Validity, and Cross-National Comparability. Occasional Papers, 20, OECD, Warwick: Institute for Employment Research.

ESS (2004). ESS documentation report 2002/2003. The ESS Data Archive. Norwegian Social Science Data Services. http://www.europeansocialsurvey.org/

Fishbein, M., & Ajzen, I. (1975). *Belief, Attitude, Intention, and Behavior: An Introduction to Theory and Research*. Reading, MA: Addison-Wesley.

Ganzeboom, H.B.G., & Treiman, D.J. (1992). *International Stratification and Mobility File: Conversion Tools*. Utrecht: Department of Sociology.

Ganzeboom, H.B.G., & Treiman, D.J. (1996). Internationally comparable measures of occupational status for the 1988 international standard classification of occupations. *Social Science Research*, 25, 201–239.

Geertz, C. (1988). *Works and Lives: The Anthropologist as Author*. Stanford, CA: Stanford University Press.

Giddens, A. (1991). *Modernity and Self-Identity: Self and Society in the Late Modern Age*. Stanford: Stanford University Press.

Glaser, B.G. (2005). *The Grounded Theory Perspective III: Theoretical Coding*. Mill Valley, CA: Sociology Press.

Glaser, B.G., & Strauss, A. (1967). *Discovery of Grounded Theory: Strategies for Qualitative Research*. Chicago: Aldine.

Glass, G.V. (1976). Primary, secondary, and meta-analysis of research. *Educational Researcher*, 5, 3–8.

Gwet, K. (2001). *Handbook of Inter-Rater Reliability*. Gaithersburg, MD: StatAxis.

Halaby, C. (2004). Panel models in sociological research: Theory into practice. *Annual Review of Sociology*, 30, 507–544.

Heider, F. (1944). Social perception and phenomenal causality. *Psychological Review*, 51, 358–374.

Hofstede, G. (2001). *Culture's Consequences: Comparing Values, Behaviors, Institutions, and Organizations across Nations*. Thousand Oaks, CA: Sage.

Herrnstein, R.J. & Murray, C. (1994). *The Bell Curve: Intelligence and Class Structure in American Life*. New York: Simon & Schuster.

Hunter, J.E., & Schmidt, F.L. (1990). *Methods of Meta-Analysis: Correcting Error and Bias in Research Findings*. Newbury Park, CA: Sage.

Hurley, S. (1998). *Consciousness in Action*. Cambridge, MA: Harvard University Press.

Jackson, F.C. (1977). *Perception: A Representative Theory*. Cambridge: Cambridge University Press.

Johnson, A.W. (1978). *Quantification in Cultural Anthropology*. Stanford: Stanford University Press.

Joye, D., Bergman, M.M., & Lambert, P. (2003). Intergenerational educational and social mobility in Switzerland. *Swiss Journal of Sociology*, 29, 2, 263–291.

Kiecolt, K.J., & Nathan, L.E. (1985). *Secondary Analysis of Survey Data (Quantitative Applications in the Social Sciences)*. Newbury Park, CA: Sage. .

Kuhn, T.S. (1970). *The Structure of Scientific Revolutions* (2nd ed.). Chicago: Chicago University Press.

Kuhn, T.S. (1983). Rationality and theory choice. *Journal of Philosophy*, 80, 10, 563–570.

Leedy, P.D. (1989). *Practical Research: Planning and Design* (4th ed.). London: Collier Macmillan.

Lipsey, M.W., & Wilson, D.B. (2001). *Practical Meta-Analysis (Applied Social Research Methods)*. Thousand Oaks, CA: Sage.

Luhmann, N. (1982). *The Differentiation of Society*. New York: Columbia University Press.

Maddala, G.S. (1999). On the use of panel data methods with cross-country data. *Annales d'économie et de statistique*, 55–56, 429–448.

Malinowski, B. (1948/1916). *Magic, Science and Religion, and Other Essays*. Boston: Beacon.

Marsh, C. (1982). *The Survey Method: The Contribution of Surveys to Sociological Explanation*. Winchester, MA: Allen & Unwin.

Mill, J.S. (1961[1843]). *A System of Logic*. London: Longmans, Green & Co.

Moore, G.E. (1953). *Some Main Problems of Philosophy*. London: George, Allen and Unwin.

Münch, B., & Smelser, N.J. (1987). Relating the micro and macro. In J.C Alexander, B. Giesen, R. Münch, N.J. Smelser et al. (Eds.), *The Micro-Macro Link*. Berkeley: University of California Press.

Pearson, K. (1904). Report on certain enteric fever inoculation statistics. *British Medical Journal*, 3, 1243–1246.

Piaget, J. (1955). *The Construction of Reality in the Child*. London: Routledge and Kegan Paul.

Raiffa, H. (1968). *Decision Analysis*. Reading, MA: Addison-Wesley.

Richard, R. (1991). *Objectivity, Relativism, and Truth*. Cambridge: Cambridge University Press.

Russell, B. (1927). *The Analysis of Matter*. New York: Harcourt, Brace.

Saam, N.J. (1999). Simulating the micro-macro link: New approaches to an old problem and an application to military coups. *Sociological Methodology*, 29, 43–79.

Schwartz, S.H. (1999). A theory of cultural values and some implications for work. *Applied Psychology – an International Review*, 48, 23–47.

Schwartz, S.H. (2005). Universalism values and the inclusiveness of our moral universe. In A.-M. Pirttilä-Backman, M. Ahokas, L. Myyry, & S. Lähteenoja (Eds.), *Values, Morality and Society: Change and Diversity*. Helsinki: Gaudeamus.

Schwartz, S. H., Verkasalo, M., Antonovsky, A., & Sagiv, L. (1997). Value priorities and social desirability: Much substance, some style. *British Journal of Social Psychology*, 36, 3–18.

Treiman, D.J. (1977). *Occupational Prestige in Comparative Perspective*. New York: Academic Press.

Triandis, H.C. (1995). *Individualism and Collectivism*. Boulder, CO: Westview.

Tyler, S.A. (1986). Post-modern ethnography: from document of the occult to occult document. In J. Clifford & G.E. Marcus (Eds.), *Writing culture: The Poetics and Politics of Ethnography*. Berkeley: University of California Press.

Walliman, N. (2005). *Your Research Project* (2nd ed.). London: Sage.

White, N.P. (1991). Plato's epistemological metaphysics. In R. Kraut (Ed.), *Cambridge Companion to Plato*. Cambridge: Cambridge University Press.

Zaller, J.R. (1992). *The Nature and Origin of Mass Opinion*. Cambridge: Cambridge University Press.

36

Writing and Presenting Social Research

Amir Marvasti

Traditionally, there has been a divide between 'science' and 'literature,' mostly due to the belief that representing 'scientific facts' requires a method of writing that is free from aesthetic whimsy and emotions. A procedural approach to writing was first developed by natural scientists (e.g. physicists) and later adopted by social scientists (e.g. sociologists) as the ideal model for disseminating facts. Thus grew the two representational cultures of science and literature, with the former presiding over the domain of 'universal truths' and the latter being relegated to the world of fiction and individualistic self-expression.

The divide between science and literature went unchallenged well into the second half of the twentieth century. However, a 'third culture' of representation (Shaffer 1998) is now questioning the necessity of treating science and literature as mutually exclusive realms of knowledge. This emerging interdisciplinary field focuses on the reflexive relationship between the two worlds of representation where literature influences science and science informs literature.

In the social sciences, while some remain devoted to the traditional divide, there is a growing awareness of the rhetorical dimensions of writing and representing facts, particularly among qualitative researchers (see, for example, Alasuutari 1995 and Gubrium and Holstein 1997). This reflexive or rhetorical turn, as it is often called, centers on the recognition that any effort to inscribe social reality invariably involves linguistic constructive practices as well. Perhaps the work that is most widely cited in connection with this movement in the social sciences is James Clifford and George Marcus's *Writing Culture: The Poetics and Politics of Ethnography* (1986). This edited volume calls for social scientists, particularly ethnographers, to see writing as a craft that involves culture, aesthetics, and politics. As stated in this book's introduction, 'the making of ethnography is artisanal, tied to the worldly work of writing' (p. 6).

Another important work in this area is John Van Maanen's *Tales of the Field* (1988). This book is also concerned with ethnography and its stylistic conventions. Through secondary analysis, Van Maanen identifies different genres of ethnographic texts (e.g. realist, confessional, and impressionist). He argues that rather than describing a single social reality seen from multiple perspectives, variations in writing construct realities of their own. For Van Maanen, '[T]here is no way of seeing, hearing, or representing the world of others that is absolutely, universally, valid or correct' (p. 35).

In the analysis of writing as representational practice, some of the greatest contributions come from feminist scholars who have documented the absence or distortion of female subjectivity in dominant textual paradigms (e.g. Irigaray 1985 and Butler 1990). At the same time, feminists have turned our attention to the linguistic nuances and conventions of texts and their gendered tones. For example, Laurel Richardson (1990, 2000) shows the prevalence of literary devices (e.g. metaphors) in social science texts. For her, scientific writing is never neutral but is invariably embedded in practices of power and oppression. As she writes, 'power is, always, a sociohistorical construction. No textual staging is ever innocent. We are always inscribing values in our writing. It is unavoidable' (1990, p.12).

As a whole, the textual shift in the social sciences relates to a larger movement that explicitly and intensely questions the value and presumably benign character of all scientific knowledge. This movement largely referred to as 'postmodernism' or 'post-structuralism' challenges the very authority and linguistic structures of science and their representations of 'truth.' For example, the renowned sociologist and postmodern thinker, Norman Denzin (1993), states

[i]f there is a center to recent critical poststructural thought, it lies in the recurring commitment to strip any text of its external claims to authority. Every text must be taken on its own terms. The desire to produce a valid and authoritarian text is renounced. Any text can be undone in terms of its internal-structural logic. (p. 136)

While some have dismissed the textual shift as a passing fad, others have embraced it as the new logic of social science and have proposed writing strategies for texts that are sensitive to postmodern sentiments. It has been suggested that these experiments or alternative representational forms expand the representational space of 'value-free' research, provide strategies for challenging dominant texts, and convey fresh perspectives on old questions. Alternative forms of writing also have been the subject of considerable criticism, which I take up in the conclusion.

In the remainder of this chapter, I offer a brief survey of these alternative writing practices by focusing on the following six genres: (1) writing with pictures, (2) performative writing, (3) writing factual fiction, (4) poetic representation, (5) writing the author, and (6) post-colonial writing. I end the chapter with a critical assessment of these genres.

WRITING WITH PICTURES

The old saying 'a picture speaks a thousand words' is now considered theoretically naïve—pictures, like written texts, are seen as constructive of the realities they represent. Gillian Rose's *Visual Methodologies* (2001) offers an excellent postmodern analysis of the place of the visual in contemporary society and social research. According to Rose, rather than simply providing 'realistic' representations, the visual creates the reality under observation. Images provide ways of seeing social issues from particular cultural standpoints. Thus a given image can be interpreted in different ways depending on the viewers and their cultural sensibilities.

While the visual has always had a place in the social sciences, its use and analysis have fluctuated over the history of various disciplines. For example, more than a hundred years ago, the *American Journal of Sociology*, the flagship journal of the discipline, published a number of articles that used photos as data (Stasz 1979). According to Elizabeth Chaplin (1994: 201), the first manuscript of this type was F. Blackmar's 'The Smoky Pilgrims' published in 1897. The study depicted poverty in rural Kansas using posed photographs. Yet, this earlier interest in the visual waned as the written word accompanied with numerical analysis became the dominant mode of sociological analysis. In a way, statistical figures, charts, and tables became the visual centerpieces of professional sociological publications (Marvasti 2003). It is worth noting that this trend was not followed in the related discipline of anthropology where the visual has remained a strong and legitimate component of the discipline's representational practice.

In the different editions of the *Handbook of Qualitative Research*, Douglas Harper offers thorough surveys of the growing field of visual research. In the most recent edition (2005), he notes, for example, that *Contexts*, a relatively new journal of the American Sociological Association, makes use of visual images in three ways. First, images can be used to illustrate the text. Second, they are used as part of visual essays where the images dominate the discussion and the text for the most part describes the images. Third, *Contexts* articles sometimes use images to visually depict the process of social change (748–749).

In the broader context of writing in the social sciences, one can think of the visual in two ways: (1) writing about pictures and (2) writing with pictures (as is the case with most typologies, these categories are not mutually exclusive). Writing about pictures involves the analysis of existing images, often for the purpose of cultural critique. For example, in his landmark sociological study, *Gender Advertisements* (1979), Erving Goffman analyzed how gender roles and expectations are reflected in magazine ads. Using over 500 photos, he critiqued taken-for-granted nature of gender relations in Western societies. Goffman showed how magazine ads in the late 1970s, depicted men in active roles (doing things like helping patients or playing in sports), whereas the women were depicted as mere spectators, passively watching the men's activities.

Similarly, in *Images of Postmodern Society* (1991) and *Cinematic Society: The Voyeur's Gaze* (1995), Norm Denzin rejects the notion

that cinematic representations are mere entertainment with no social value. Instead, he argues that we understand and express ourselves and our social settings through Hollywood films. According to Denzin, cinematic representations both describe social realities and mandate a way of seeing or accepting these realities. Consider, for example, his analysis of the movie *When Harry Met Sally*:

> The movie … is a 'Field Guide to Single Yuppies'. … As such it takes a stand on and defines the following problematic terms; being single versus being married; sexuality and women's orgasms; love, sexuality, and friendship; life after divorce, or after breaking up with a lover. These terms are presented as obstacles. … The solutions are gender specific. Women must not be single, must learn how to fake orgasms, so that males think they have sexual power. … Men, on the other hand, must have a woman who lets them think they can make them sexually happy. They need male friends to talk to, because women don't understand male sexuality. In this battle between the sexes, sex must be overcome, before love and friendship can be achieved. (Denzin 1995: 117)

According to this analysis, such cinematic representations mandate a way of thinking about male-female relationships. *When Harry Met Sally* becomes a sort of how-to guide on heterosexual relations, constructing and describing the reality of how men and women should relate to one another. Over time cinematic representations become taken-for-granted truths that both construct and validate gender stereotypes.

In the field of anthropology, Catherine Lutz and Jane Collins' *Reading National Geographic* (1993) offers a brilliant critique of the representations of non-Western cultures in the *National Geographic*. This analysis connects the magazine's photographs with Western assumptions about 'savage' cultures and their exotic lifestyles. As Lutz and Collins put it, 'Non-Westerners draw a look, rather than disattention or interaction, to the extent that their difference or foreignness defines them as noteworthy yet distant' (188). The authors show how such 'looks' are reflected in the *National Geographic's* representations of 'foreignness.' The magazine's photos can thus be seen as 'gazes' that construct the exotic other.

Aside from analyzing existing images, writing with pictures could also involve creating first-hand visual material for the purpose of illustrating, complementing, or transcending the written text. In the social sciences, anthropology is a leader of the use of pictorial and filmic materials for illustrative purposes. For example, G. Bateson and Margaret Mead's *Balinese Character: A Photographic Study* (1942) juxtaposes text and the visual in a complementary way so that one would enhance the meaning of the other. In the words of the authors,

> We are attempting a new method of stating the intangible relationship among different types of culturally standardised behavior by placing side by side mutually relevant photographs. ... By the use of photographs, the wholeness of each piece of behavior can be preserved. (Bateson and Mead 1942: xii, as quoted in Harper 1994: 404)

For example, by placing a series of photos of a given native ritual on one page and related text on the opposite page, Bateson and Mead encourage their readers to see and read the story simultaneously.

In sociology, one of the most recognized voices of the visual has been Howard Becker, who in a 1975 article called for advancing beyond photography as an art form to seeing it as a mode of representing and analyzing social reality. He also promoted greater appreciation for the role of social theory in the production and analysis of photographic images (Harper 1994: 406). Becker subsequently published *Exploring Society Photographically* (1981), an edited book with a visual presentation style similar to that of Bateson and Mead.

Photographs can also be incorporated in writing personal narratives. For example, Richard Quinney (1996) uses photographs from his father's trip to California in the 1920s to tell the intimate, nostalgic story of his relationship with his father. Even though Quinney's photographs are interspersed with a good deal of writing, he gives greater weight to the visual impact of his work. In his words, 'photographs are not to be subjected to "scientific" and "professional" discourse. Photography resists a language of analysis. The image speaks in silence. We give ourselves up to that which is beyond language and rational thought' (p. 381). In a sense, Quinney uses photographs in the same way some social scientists use poetry to transcend the limits of scientific and ordinary language (poetic representations are discussed later in this chapter).

The use of photographs is most common in multidisciplinary fields like cultural studies. For example, *Crossing the Divide: Strangers, Neighbors, Aliens in New America* presents interviews with people from the multiethnic communities of Queens, New York. Here is how the authors describe the project:

> We decide to become travelers in our own backyard. For three years we trek between the shadows of the block-long superstores that now dominate most of the major boulevards in Queens, down the side streets, into the bodegas, family-owned restaurants, homes, places of worship, libraries, and community rooms—looking for migrations stories, culture, and soul. (Lehrer and Sloan 2003: 12–13)

The still photos in this book show the interviewee's faces, the places where they live and work, and the cultural artifacts that define their ethnic background. Even the written text itself is manipulated for visual effect with different font types, sizes, and colors adding more layers of textuality and meaning to the work.

Similarly, *Body Type: Intimate Messages Etched in Flesh* (Saltz 2006) tells the stories of tattoos and the people who wear them. The written text plays a minimal role in this book. Instead, the photographs of tattooed body parts dominate the book. Each photograph is accompanied with a direct quote explaining its significance for the tattooed person. Interestingly, the book does not contain any facial images; the respondents are identified only through their tattoos.

Writing with the visual continues to expand. As Douglas Harper (2005) notes, emerging computer technologies are revolutionizing the use of visual material in social research. Particularly, multimedia texts can now easily combine pictures and written material in the same context, thanks to technology that is exceedingly affordable. Additionally, multimedia texts can be posted on internet websites accessible to users virtually from any location in the world. A key feature of internet-posted multimedia text (e.g. 'hypertext') is that the material does not have to be read or viewed linearly like a bound book. So-called 'hot links' or 'hyperlinks' allow the readers to jump from one passage to another. For example, while reading a hypertext ethnography, the reader can click on pictures from the field, see an image of a respondent, and click on his name to see excerpts from an interview with that respondent.

Sarah Pink (2001) suggests that hypertext brings a sort of reader-oriented coherence to ethnographic research. In her words, 'The coherence of ethnographic hypermedia is created in the relationship between the design of the text and how it is interpreted. It depends on authors' creativity for the former and users' for the latter' (169). Pink also notes that hypertext allows for continuous revisions of the original work:

> Theoretically, this means neither knowledge itself nor representations of knowledge are ever complete. ... Practically, this means that, unlike printed books and finished films, on-line hypermedia texts may be up-dated, added to, or altered. Video sequences may be re-edited, photographs manipulated in new ways, written words changed, and the hyperlinks between them modified. (p. 167)

For an example of hypermedia ethnographies discussed in Pink (2001), visit the following website: http:anthropology.ac.uk/Bhalot

PERFORMATIVE WRITING

This genre of writing is the most aesthetically conscious (Ellis and Bochner 1992; Paget 1995; Mienczakowski 1996; Denzin 1997, 2000, 2003). Like other genres discussed thus far, the goal here is to transcend the limits of ordinary language and to, overtly or covertly, rebel against mainstream academia

and its conventions. In Sarah Finely's words, 'art-based research'

> is an act of political emancipation from the dominant paradigm of science for new paradigm researchers to say "I am doing art" and to mean "I am doing research" – or vice versa. In either utterance, that art and research are common acts makes a political statement. (Finely 2003: 90, cited in Finely 2005: 685)

There are many variations to this approach where the author becomes an acting voice or body in evocative texts. For the purpose of this discussion, I present a research example that literally involves a staged performance. Specifically, I use Gray Ross et al's 'Making a Mess and Spreading It Around: Articulation of an Approach to Research-Based Theater' to offer a summary of how social research is transformed into theater. The original research data for the staged performances discussed in this work come from Ross et al's studies of cancer patients (i.e. women with breast cancer and men with prostate cancer).

The first step in staging research is preparing a script. The authors recommend avoiding 'representations that fail to deliver the promise of an engaging and visceral connection with the research material' (Ross et al 2002: 62) by consulting expert directors, scriptwriters, set designers—generally people with expertise about what does or does not work on stage. Additionally, Ross et al suggest that the following groups be included in the development of the script: (1) researchers who are familiar with the nuances of the data; (2) research participants whose stories are being told; and (3) people who are 'naïve to the area under study' (p. 63) and can provide insight about how outside audiences might respond to the performance.

The script itself can incorporate: (1) the original research findings; (2) a 'second research process' (64) where new insights emerge through secondary analysis and examination of the original data; and (3) invented scenes from rehearsals and improvisations. The script should then be read, reread, rehearsed, and revised.

Finally, the cast could include both original research participants and actors who have become intimately familiar with the roles. To encourage audience participation a traditional viewing can be followed by a discussion and question-and-answer session with the actors, researchers, and director.

Of course, this entire process involves deliberate choices about what is included and what is excluded from the research. For example, an important research finding may not be dramatically and aesthetically powerful and thus cannot be included in the script. Ross et al advise against improvising the material to the point where the original research participants no longer recognize themselves on the stage. This commitment to 'real' people seeing themselves on the screen serves two purposes. On a practical level, if a dramatization of a tragedy does not connect with the very people who endured the suffering, then there might be reason to believe that the work has failed theatrically. On a more analytical level, the matter of authenticity takes center stage here, so to speak. That is, we are once more faced with the question: To what extent does the performance represent 'real' life experience? As this example indicates, alternative practices do not necessarily resolve representational dilemmas; sometimes they simply transport the questions to a different arena. In the case of research-as-theater, as the written text is set aside in favor of bodily performance, the problem of representing 'authentic selves' migrates onto the stage.

WRITING FACTUAL FICTION

Despite the apparent contradiction in the phrase, factual fiction or what is known as 'creative nonfiction' outside the social sciences, is an exciting and influential school of writing with a long and distinguished history of transgressing the divide between objective truth and imagination (see, for example, Truman Capote's 1966 novel *In Cold Blood*). As Michael Agar notes (1995), although largely ignored by social scientists, creative nonfiction and literary journalism in many respects could serve as

pedagogical and theoretical models for the kind of alternative writing or 'creative analytical practices' (Richardson and St. Pierre 2005: 962) that are now gaining momentum in the field. The same frustrations about the limitations of objectivity and the need to 'bring the text to life' inspired journalists to experiment with innovative modes of representing the stuff of everyday life and find ways of 'writing about oneself *in relation* to the subject at hand' (Brett Lott, cited in Moore 2007: 280). The sociological emphasis on the reflexive relationship between the self and the social world is echoed in the pedagogy of creative nonfiction. For example, in his introductory text for English courses about this genre, Dinty Moore delineates the link between reality and the imaginative author in this way:

> A subject becomes noteworthy, in other words, because the author takes close notice, and then finds a way to transmit his or her own fascination with the subject to the curious reader. Moreover, a writer of creative non-fiction is not asked to be invisible .... In fact, voice and point of view are fundamental to what is creative about creative non-fiction. (2007: 11)

Creative nonfiction writers have offered insightful analyses of topics that are the mainstay of the social sciences. For example, through 'total immersion' (the equivalent of what Adler and Adler (1987) call 'complete participant role'), Lee Gutkind explores the 'humanistic aspects of the high-tech medical world' (1998: 6). His book *Many Sleepless Nights* looks at the lives and practices surrounding organ transplantations. Gutkin observes that in their single-minded devotion to 'saving lives' surgeons become detached from the emotional health of the very lives they are saving:

> I once listened to a prominent surgeon impatiently interrupt a resident who was carefully explaining a procedure to a family member, prompting him to "save lives first—answer questions later." Another surgeon told me, in defense of his insensitive behavior, "Psychologic [sic] trauma and all that stuff is important, but it doesn't make a goddamn difference if you are well-adjusted and dead." (p. 7)

In contrast, Gutkind's study of veterinary medicine titled *An Unspoken Art* notes that touch and emotions ironically play a more important role in the business of healing animals. He recounts a surgical procedure on a race horse where,

> Eight exhausted veterinarians and nurses, all women, remained in the recovery area with Cam Fella (the horse), sitting in a circle, elbow to elbow, keeping him calm. Touching him. Kissing him. Talking to him. Until he was awake enough to stand on his own and navigate the winding path back to his stall. (p. 8)

A good example of the social science version of creative nonfiction can be found in Paul Rosenblatt's 'Interviewing at the Border of Fact and Fiction.' This author relies on fictional and literary tropes for soliciting and narrating life experiences. Rosenblatt's interview data, for example, are explicitly solicited in search of stories that are 'good enough to be fiction' (Rosenblatt 2002: 898). Likewise, his composition and narration styles do not just report the facts or present interview experts and analysis; rather, Rosenblatt's text is constructed around aesthetic and reader-response priorities. He quite deliberately engages in the kind of character and plot building that one finds in the best of fiction:

> I talk about how people sit as they talk, what they ask me, how they smell, how their language changes as who as present changes, how their dogs are players are in family experience, their use of facial tissues when they cry, how they slide by family disagreements during a family interview, the ways they can blithely and unapologetically be inconsistent, and how much they seem trapped by culture, neighbors, property, ownership, and much else into thinking along certain lines and not others. (Rosenblatt 2002: 901)

To the degree that the social scientific genre can be viewed as different from 'creative nonfiction' is that the former has different disciplinary ties and is more explicitly committed to systematic and scholarly research. For example, Rosenblatt writes that at the end even the most creative social science writer 'must still be a craftsperson, a consummate interviewer, a doubter,

a systematic explorer, and a careful reporter in ways that are responsive to a community of researchers' (Rosenblatt 2002: 907).

POETIC REPRESENTATION

At first glance representing science through poetry may seem impractical and contrary to the aphorisms regarding objectivity and detachment. Conventional wisdom suggests that poetry is the language of emotions and science the language of facts. The synthesis of the two, as in the phrase 'poetic science,' thus seems oxymoronic. Yet, as suggested throughout this chapter, such divisions are linguistic constructions in their own right and do not reflect inherent properties of texts. Indeed, the proponents of the third culture (alluded to earlier in the chapter) have noted that literary movements like Romanticism were directly influenced by scientific thought. For example, Joanne Merrison's (1998) 'The Death of the Poet: Coleridge and the Science of Logic' highlights Samuel Coleridge's appreciation for logic and empirical observation. According to Merrison, Coleridge was adamantly opposed to divorcing the 'essence' of 'nature' from lived experience and the social contexts that make it meaningful. This is shown in the following excerpt from a Coleridge poem:

> In nature there is nothing melancholy!
> But some night-wandering man, whose heart was pierced
> With the remembrance of a grievous wrong,
> Or slow distempter, or neglected love,
> (Coleridge, *Poetical Works*, p. 264, cited in Merrison 1998: 177–178)

Similarly, the famed Persian poet Omar Khayam was considered an important astronomer and mathematician, and his poetry in the *Rubaiyat* is as much about the physical wonders of the universe as it is about aesthetics and self-exploration per se. So the recent attempt by social scientists to use poetry in conveying their observations is not entirely without precedent, nor is it entirely 'new.'

The social scientist most widely associated with use of poetic prose in qualitative texts is Laurel Richardson, who argues,

> Poetic representation … is a practical and powerful, indeed transforming, method for understanding the social, altering the self, and invigorating the research community that claims knowledge of our lives. (Richardson 2002: 888)

It is worth noting that this method of writing does not imply an anything-goes approach to writing. Formal training and conventions still apply. In fact, Richardson recommends poetry classes for anyone interested in creative writing of social science. She reminds her would-be followers that writing poetry involves learning the basics of a craft like any other. Richardson draws attention to the importance of 'sound, sight, and ideation' (p. 881) (i.e. tone, imagery, and symbolism) in poetic representations and chides,

> A line
> break does
> not
> a poem
> make. (p. 882)

The task of writing or rewriting research findings into poetic forms requires familiarity with the conventions of the form and a good deal of practice. Like traditional poetry, this kind of writing begins with an object or a thing in the real world but then tries to transcend the object through masterful description. The poetry is intended to be a condensed and more powerful version of the original text. For example, Richardson rewrote the transcripts from a five-hour interview with a Southern woman into a five-page poem. Here is an excerpt from the poeticized interview:

> Well, one thing that happens
> growing up in the South
> is that you leave. I
> always knew I would
> I would leave. (p. 888)

The goal here is to convey the woman's life narrative without losing its emotional tone to the very words that describe the experience. Like other social scientific texts, the basic objective is still representing human experience. The genre simply gives the author greater creative latitude in telling the story. As Richardson notes about the above poem, 'The speech style is Louisa May's, the words are hers, but the poetic representation, including the ordering of the material, are my own' (883).

Again, initially, this kind of writing may seem a radical departure from mainstream representational practices in the social sciences, but in some ways it is simply an extension of existing practices. In particular, qualitative researchers have always had the discretion to use some material and not others. Arguably, the choices that shape the 'final report' have never been completely detached from aesthetic concerns. To the degree that ethnographers strive to tell a coherent story their field experiences, they all engage in poetic revisions. Surprisingly, this observation equally applies to quantitative writing. I recently attended a job interview in which the candidate presented several colorful graphs of a regression analysis. In a sense, the statistical logic of the numbers projected on the screen was complemented by aesthetically pleasing colors and shapes (e.g. a continuous green line for one dependent variable and fragmented red line for another). At one point, the candidate was openly complimented for his 'nice graphs,' making explicit the aesthetic criteria for the assessment of the quantitative representation of research findings.

WRITING THE AUTHOR

A few decades ago, including the subjective voice of the author in the scientific text was considered antithetical to the very essence of science. Today, at least in the realm of ethnographic texts, writing the author into the field notes, or autoethnography, has become an established method of representing research findings. There are many flourishing forms in this genre and a good deal of empirical and pedagogical literature.

A thorough survey of this type of writing can be found in the introductory chapter of Deborah Reed-Danahay's *Auto/Ethnography*.

Stylistic variations notwithstanding, one can gather form Reed-Danahay's discussion that most experts concede that autoethnographic writing is a self-reflexive account of social experience. The central criterion for autoethnographic text appears to be that the explicit voice of the author must be embedded in a broader social context. Autoethnographic text is expected to tie idiosyncratic stories with a larger universe of experiences and meanings. Reed-Danahay makes this point explicit in her definition of autoethnography as 'self-narrative that places the self within a social context' (1997: 9).

Having said that, how this is achieved and for what purposes is the subject of considerable debate and contention. In Reed-Danahay's chapter there seems to be a continuum of representational strategies for autoethnographers. On the one end, there is the minimally self-referential text that simply adds the author's own subjective voice to the many voices and observations from the field. On the other end, there is 'pure,' 'native' experience represented with little or no intervention from academic sources. For example, John Dorst's *The Written Suburb* (1989, cited in Reed-Danahay 1997) treats suburbanites' artistic creations (i.e. arts and crafts) as autoethnographic representations. For Dorst, autoethnography is a sort of 'self-documentation' done by ordinary people. In this context, expert social scientific description is unnecessary because in a postmodern society anyone can be an informed author of culture: 'If the task of autoethnography can be described as the inscription and interpretation of culture, then postmodernity seems to render the professional ethnographer superfluous' (Dorst 1989: 2, cited in Reed-Danahay 1997: 8).

Other advocates of autoethnography, who fall somewhere in the middle of the two extremes on the continuum, emphasize neither academic nor ordinary dimensions of this genre but its potential for political action and change. For example, Stacy Holman Jones (2005) introduces her paper titled 'Autoethnography: Making the Personal Political,' in this way: 'This is a chapter about how looking at the world from a specific, perspectival, and limited vantage point can tell, teach, and put people in motion' (2005: 763).

In the field of autoethnography, the works of Carol Ronai are exemplary because of her ability to combine the best analytical innovations of this genre with superior aesthetic sensibility. Ronai's writing is both informative and politically brave. The story of how her father sexually abused her, titled 'My Mother is Mentally Retarded,' is a classic example of what she calls a 'multi-layered account.' In this particular form of autoethnography, the author's experiential account is juxtaposed against academic and popular discourses. The descriptions are layered and deliberately disjointed using a set of asterisks. To better appreciate the potency of Ronai's writing, consider the following excerpt:

> I resent the imperative that all is normal with my family, an imperative that is enforced by silence, and "you don't talk about this to anyone" rhetoric. Our pretense is designed to make event flow smoothly, but it doesn't work. Everyone is plastic and fake around my mother, including me. Why? Because no one has told her to her face that she is retarded. We say we don't want to upset her. I don't think we are ready to deal with her reaction to the truth. … Because of [my mother] and because of how the family as a unit has chosen to deal the problem, I have compartmentalized a whole segment of my life into a lie. (1996: 115)

As this excerpt shows, autoethnographic text can be a powerful method of representing a social issue. Ronai's gripping and 'authoritative' voice compels the reader to engage the topic. For many readers of ethnography, this representation of Ronai's suffering has become an inescapable memory.

POSTCOLONIAL (RE)WRITING

This method of representation in some ways is as much about rewriting or un-writing the canonical texts as it is about writing per se. In some ways, postcolonial writing has been the analytical engine of the many alternative forms of representation in the social sciences. The seminal contributions of postmodernists and poststructuralists have played a crucial role in forming this body of knowledge. In particular, Jacques Derrida's direct assault on the authority of the text in *Writing and Difference* (1978) and Michel Foucault's analyses of the constructive power of text and discourse (1966, 1977) have been instrumental in defining the field of postcolonialism.

The postmodern critique of the authority of language enabled postcolonial writers to question the validity of so-called 'scientific' texts about *others*. For example, Edward Said's *Orientalism* (1978) challenges Western representations of Arab or Eastern others. According to Said, the 'Orient' is textually constructed as the mirror opposite of the 'Occident' in support of Western stereotypes (e.g. where the West is rational, the Arab world is irrational and childlike). For Said, colonial dichotomies are primarily constructed and maintained through textual practices.

Similarly, in *Nations and Narration* (1990), Homi Bhabha advances the critique of colonialism by suggesting that the very idea of 'nation' is textually sustained through selective memories and a sort of textual amnesia where the errors (or horrors) of the empire are erased. Thus, it is not a factual history that defines the relationship between the colonists and the colonized but a set of self-serving myths that conveniently validate colonial authority and its oppression of others. But unlike Said, Bhabha is careful not to inadvertently reify the 'self-other' dichotomy through his own text. Instead, Bhabha argues that colonialism and its culture are 'hybrid' and fluid; they are constantly rearticulated through multiple discursive sources.

In addition to broad critiques of Western imperialism, postcolonial writing sometimes focuses on retelling particular stories of the colonized. For example, in 'Inscribing Emptiness: Cartography and the Construction of Australia,' Simon Ryan (1994) shows how aboriginal inhabitants of Australia were made virtually invisible through cartographic texts that represented the continent as vacant space, ready for Western occupation. Ryan states

'constructing maps as innocently mimetic ignores the fact that maps are productions of complex social forces; they create and manipulate reality as much as they record' (1994: 115–116). Ryan empirically demonstrates the constructive power of cartography through his analysis of maps and related texts, such as the following:

> The soft, blue, harmless sky of Australia, the pale, white unwritten atmosphere of Australia. *Tabula rasa*. The world a new leaf. And on the new leaf nothing. The white clarity of the Australian, fragile atmosphere. Without a mark, without a record. (D. H. Lawrence 1950: 365, cited in Ryan 1994: 129)

Finally, postcolonial writing can be used to question mainstream culture. For example, in *Anthropology as Cultural Critique*, Marcus and Fischer offer 'defamiliarization' (1999: 137–164) as a writing strategy for challenging the dominant culture. This method of writing sometimes involves exoticizing the West's representations of itself to underline the fact that any culture can be textually constructed as 'irrational' or 'primitive.' A famous example of this kind of textual subversion is 'Body Ritual among the Nacirema.' In this article, through a clever reversal of spelling (i.e. 'American' into 'Nacirema'), Horace Miner (1956) transforms the familiar Western culture and selves into an exotic tribe. For example, he rewrites the significance of familiar Western hygiene rituals, as seen in the following excerpt:

> In addition to the private mouth-rite, the people seek out a holy-mouth-man once or twice a year. These practitioners have an impressive set of paraphernalia, consisting of a variety of augers, awls, probes, and prods. The use of these objects in the exorcism of the evils of the mouth involves almost unbelievable ritual torture of the client .... In the client's view, the purpose of these ministrations is to arrest decay and to draw friends. The extremely sacred and traditional character of the rite is evident in the fact that the natives return to the holy-mouth-men year after year, despite the fact that their teeth continue to decay. (pp. 504–505)

By casting the ordinary practices (e.g. a visit to a dentist) in an exotic light, Minor exposes the textual 'tricks' underpinning the construction of the 'savage' other.

As a whole, postcolonial writing argues that that the power of 'the empire' is mostly created and maintained through textual representations; therefore, it is through alternative texts that this power can be undone. As Chris Tiffin and Alan Lawson state in their book, aptly titled *De-Scribing Empire*:

> just as fire can be fought with fire, textual control can be fought with textuality, the post-colonial is especially and pressingly concerned with the power that resides in discourse and textuality; its resistance, then, quite appropriately takes place in –and from—the domain of textuality .... The contestation of post-colonialism is a contest of representation. (1994: 10)

Two words of caution are in order in this discussion of postcolonialism. First, postcolonial writing is not synonymous with a naïve image of natives speaking for themselves, or an 'essentialist Third World consciousness' (Tiffin and Lawson 1994: 8, see also Griffiths 1994). While such works are important in adding complexity to the understanding of subaltern identities (see for example, Yasmin Hussain's *Writing Diaspora* 2005), we cannot assume that they are inherently 'authentic' and textually 'innocent' because they are written by the 'natives' themselves. Such a conceptualization would contradict the core argument of rhetoric theorists that all texts are embedded in culture and discourse.

Second, despite its apparent phrasing, postcolonialism is not an analysis of events and practices of the past. This point is passionately made by Robert Ashcroft in the following passage:

> How many times must we insist that "postcolonialism" does not mean "after colonialism," that it begins from the moment of colonization? Indeed, how often must we insist that postcolonialism *exists*? ... How often must we wait for the occasional applause attending post-colonial theory to be matched by some small textual application by the applauders? (1994: 34–35)

CONCLUSION

The methods of writing discussed in this chapter overlap and there are many other forms that are not included. For example, much can be said about 'collaborative ethnography' and its inclusion of research participants in writing and editing of the findings (see, for example, Lassiter 2005). Likewise, entire books can and have been devoted to the feminist influence on writing (see, for example, Behar and Gordon 1995). Given these shortcomings, this chapter should be read as a necessarily selective map of an ever-changing terrain with many undiscovered territories. The topics discussed here can be thought of as relatively known landmarks in an otherwise elusive territory. Specifically, representational choices, authorship and authority debates, and the need and moral compulsion to 'give voice' to marginal groups, as discussed in relation to various writing forms in this chapter, continue to be the central themes that fuel the engine of textual experimentation in the social sciences.

Of course, the status of 'alternative' does not exempt these texts from critical assessment. Critics point out that some representational experiments result in bad writing. For example, in her review of Ellis's *The Ethnographic I: A Methodological Novel about Autoethnography*, Pamela Moro writes:

> The real question is, perhaps, whether Ellis is a good enough writer to pull off this heartfelt endeavor. Writing good fiction is hard; writing compelling dialogue is extremely hard. I am not entirely sure if what Ellis has written is a "novel." ... It is as though she has taken the shell of a novel and poured into it the material of textbook. (2006: 266)

Other critics question whether alternative writing forms are effective in achieving their emancipatory goals. For example, Atkinson and Delamont caution that some writing experimentations inadvertently (1) re-center the social scientist as the all-knowing author and (2) promote an individualized rather than an interactive view of social experience:

> we warn against the wholesale acceptance of aesthetic criteria in the reconstruction of social life.

In many contexts, there is a danger of collapsing the various forms of social action into one aesthetic mode—that is, implicitly revalorizing the authorial voice of the social scientist—and of transforming socially shared and culturally shaped phenomena into the subject matter of an undifferentiated but esoteric literary genre. (2005: 823)

Of course, these criticisms signal the fact that alternative or experimental forms are becoming 'in and of themselves, valid and desirable representations of the social' (Richardson and St. Pierre 2005: 962). However, as avant-garde writing becomes institutionalized, it has to contend with its own epistemological inconsistencies. Concurrently, the mainstream academic establishment could change its strategy from dismissing the alternative forms to appropriating and formalizing them on its own terms (for example, see Leon Anderson's (2006) article on 'analytical autoethnography' and the response from Ellis and Bochner (2006)).

Writers of alternative texts find themselves the target of attack from three fronts: (1) positivists who see their work as lacking scientific objectivity; (2) progressive sociologists with their warnings against individualism and self-absorption; and (3) the would-be literary who simply find the text lacking in craft, style, and substance. The response is sometimes moderate and sometimes decidedly oppositional, as in Denzin's declaration of 'guerrilla warfare' (1999) on mainstream academia.

This tension and conflict may be unnecessary. Again, creative nonfiction could serve as an instructive example. Rather than opposing science, some creative nonfiction writers are in fact inspired and intrigued by the language of science. For example, Allison H. Deming (1998) uses scientific observations and terms in her poems. The following is a commentary on the scientific fascination with the wonders of nature:

When the naturalists
See a pile of scat,
They speed toward it
As if a rare orchid
Bloomed in their path
…
An Ancient music they try
to recall because,

although they can't quite
hear the tune, they know
if they could sing it
that even their wild
rage and lust and death
terrors would seem
as beautiful as the
endolithic algae
that releases nitrogen
into rocks so that
junipers can milk them. (p. 18)

For writers like Deming, as languages that attempt to describe 'the unknown,' science and poetry are not mutually exclusive. On the contrary, she argues that 'What science bashers fail to appreciate is that scientists, in their unflagging attraction to the unknown, love what they don't know. It guides and motivates their work; it keeps them up at night; and it makes that work poetic' (p. 15). Accordingly, the language of science, in its own peculiar way, is transcendental and poetic. Conversely, poetry often relies on the material objects that science tries to explain. Instead of opposition, Allison speaks of an 'edge effect,' a term that in the field of ecology describes the border between two ecosystems where new life forms flourish (p. 23).

Ultimately, what is indisputable is that writing is an ongoing and socially embedded practice. It is about 'textwork' (Van Maanen 2006: 14), or the practice, art, and craft of writing. Writing is also what Pertti Alasuutari calls a 'literary process' that:

resembles riding a bicycle. Not in that once you have learned it you'll master it, but because riding a bike is based on consecutive repairments of balance. The staggerings or whole detours of the text have to be repaired over and over again so that they do not lead the story line in the wrong direction; and the rambling of the first draft cannot be seen in the final product. (1995: 178)

The best advice for writing 'good' social science may be to keep writing and always be open to constructive criticism. A social scientist committed to writing should be prepared to relentlessly improve her craft. Often adjustments may be necessary depending on the writing terrain in which one is traveling.

ACKNOWLEDGMENTS

I would like to thank Jaber Gubrium, Pertti Alasuutari, and anonymous reviewers for their comments on the earlier drafts of this chapter. I am particularly indebted to Jay Gubrium for providing the basic outline for this chapter.

REFERENCES

Adler, P. and P. Adler. 1987. *Membership Roles in Field Research.* Thousand Oakes, CA: Sage.

Agar, M. 1995. 'Literary Journalism as Ethnography: Exploring the Excluded Middle.' In *Representation in Ethnography*, edited by J. Van Maanen. Thousand Oaks, CA: Sage. pp. 112–129.

Alasuutari, P. 1995. *Researching Culture: Qualitative Method and Cultural Studies.* London: Sage.

Anderson, L. 2006. 'Analytic Autoethnography.' *Journal of Contemporary Ethnography* 35: 373–395.

Ashcroft, B. 1994. 'Excess: Post-Colonialism and the Verandahs of Meaning.' In *De-Scribing Empire: Post-Colonialism and Textuality*, edited by C. Tiffin and A. Lawson. London: Routledge. pp. 33–44.

Atkinson, P. and S. Delamont. 2005. 'Analytic Perspectives.' In *The Handbook of Qualitative Research* (3rd ed.), edited by N. Denzin and Y. S. Lincoln. Thousand Oaks, CA: Sage. pp. 821–840.

Bateson, G., and M. Mead. 1942. *The Balinese Character: A Photographic Analysis.* New York: New York Academy of Sciences.

Becker, H. 1975. 'Photography and Sociology.' *Afterimage* 3: 22–32.

Becker, H. 1981. *Exploring Society Photographically.* Chicago: University of Chicago Press.

Behar, R. and D. Gordon. 1995. *Women Writing Culture.* Berkeley, CA: University of California Press.

Bhabha, H. 1990. *Nations and Narration.* London: Routledge.

Blackmar, F. W. 1897. 'The Smoky Pilgrims.' *American Journal of Sociology* 2: 485–500.

Butler, J. 1990. *Gender Trouble: Feminism and the Subversion of Identity.* New York, NY: Routledge.

Capote, T. 1965. *In Cold Blood.* New York: Random House.

Chaplin, E. 1994. *Sociology and Visual Representation.* New York: Routledge.

Clifford, J. and Marcus G. (Eds.). 1986. *Writing culture: The poetics and politics of ethnography.* Berkeley, CA: University of California Press.

Deming, A. H. 1998. 'Science and Poetry: A View from the Divide.' *Creative Nonfiction* 11: 11–29.

Denzin, N. 1991. *Images of Postmodern Society.* Newbury Park, CA: Sage.

Denzin, N. K. (1993). 'Rhetoric and Society.' *The American Sociologist,* 24,135-146.

Denzin, N. 1995. *The Cinematic Society: The Voyeur's Gaze.* Thousand Oaks, CA: Sage.

Denzin, N. 1997. 'Performance Texts.' In *Representation and the Text: Re-framing the Narrative Voice*, edited by W. G. Tierney & Y. S. Lincoln. Albany, NY: State University of New York Press. pp. 179–217.

Denzin, N. 1999. 'Two Stepping in the 90's.' *Qualitative Inquiry* 5: 568–572.

Denzin, N. 2000. 'Aesthetics and the Practices of Qualitative Inquiry.' *Qualitative Inquiry* 6: 256–265.

Denzin, N. 2003. *Performance Ethnography: Critical Pedagogy and the Politics of Culture.* Thousand Oaks, CA: Sage.

Derrida, J. 1978. *Writing and Difference.* London: Routledge.

Dorst, J. 1989. *The Written Suburb: An American Site, an Ethnographic Dilemma.* Philadelphia: University of Pennsylvania Press.

Ellis, C. and A. P. Bochner. 1992. 'Telling and Performing Personal Stories: The Constraints of Choice in Abortion.' In *Investigating Subjectivity: Research on Lived Experience*, edited by C. Ellis and M. Flaherty. Thousand Oaks, CA: Sage Publications. pp. 79–101.

Ellis, C. and A. Bochner. 2006. 'Analyzing Analytic Autoethnography: An Autopsy.' *Journal of Contemporary Ethnography* 35(4): 429–449.

Finely, S. 2005. 'Arts-Based Inquiry: Performing Revolutionary Pedagogy.' In *The Handbook of Qualitative Research* (3rd ed.), edited by N. Denzin and Y. S. Lincoln. Thousand Oaks, CA: Sage. pp. 681–695.

Foucault, M. 1966. *The Order of Things.* London: Tavistock.

Foucault, M. 1977. *Discipline and Punish: The Birth of the Prison.* London: Allen Lane.

Goffman, E. 1979. *Gender Advertisements.* New York: Harper.

Grifiths, G. 1994. 'The Myth of Authenticity: Representation, Discourse and Social Practice.' In *De-Scribing Empire: Post-Colonialism and Textuality*, edited by C. Tiffin and A. Lawson. London: Routledge. pp. 70–85.

Gubrium, J. and J. Holstein. 1997. *The New Language of Qualitative Method.* New York: Oxford University Press.

Gutkind, L. 1998. 'Introduction: Doctors and Writers.' *Creative Nonfiction* 11: 1–10.

Harper, D. 1994. 'On the Authority of the Image: Visual Methods at the Crossroads.' In *Handbook of Qualitative Research*, edited by N. Denzin and Y. Lincoln. Thousand Oaks, CA: Sage. pp. 403–412.

Harper, D. 2005. 'What's New Visually?' In *The Handbook of Qualitative Research* (3rd ed.), edited by N. Denzin and Y. S. Lincoln. Thousand Oaks, CA: Sage. pp. 747–762.

Hussain, Y. 2005. *Writing Diaspora: South Asian Women, Culture and Ethnicity*. Burlington, VT: Ashgate.

Irigaray, L. 1985. *This Sex Which is Not One*. Ithaca, NY: Cornell University Press.

Jones, S. H. 2005. 'Autoethnography: Making the Personal Political.' In *The Handbook of Qualitative Research* (3rd ed.), edited by N. Denzin and Y. S. Lincoln. Thousand Oaks, CA: Sage. pp. 763–791.

Lassiter, L. E. 2005. *The Chicago Guide to Collaborative Ethnography*. Chicago: The University of Chicago Press.

Lawrence, D. H. 1950. *Kangaroo*. Middlesex, England: Penguin Press.

Lehrer, W. and J. Sloan. 2003. *Crossing the Divide: Strangers, Neighbors, Aliens in a New America*. New York: W. W. Norton & Company.

Lutz, C. A. and J. Collins. 1993. *Reading the National Geographic*. Chicago: The University of Chicago Press.

Marcus, E. M. and M. Fischer. 1999. *Anthropology as Cultural Critique: An Experimental Moment in the Human Sciences* (2nd ed.). Chicago: The University of Chicago Press.

Marvasti, A. 2003. *Qualitative Research in Sociology*. London: Sage.

Merrison, J. 1998. 'The Death of the Poet: Coleridge and the Logic of Science.' In *The Third Culture: Literature and Sciences*, edited by E. S. Shaffer. Berlin: Walter de Gruyter. pp. 170–181.

Mienczakowski, J. 1996. 'An Ethnographic Act: The Construction of Consensual Theater.' In *Composing Ethnography: Alternative Forms of Qualitative Writing*, edited by C. Ellis and A. Bochner. Walnut Creek, CA: AltaMira Press. pp. 244–266.

Miner, H. 1956. 'Body Ritual among the Nacirema.' *American Anthropologist* 58(3): 503–507.

Moore, D. 2007. *The Truth of the Matter: Art and Craft in Creative Nonfiction*. New York: Pearson Longman.

Moro, P. 2006. 'It Takes a Darn Good Writer: A Review of Ethnographic I.' *Symbolic Interaction* 29(2): 265–269.

Paget, M. A. 1995. 'Performing the Text.' In *Representation in Ethnography*, edited by J. Van Maanen. Thousand Oaks, CA: Sage. pp. 222–244.

Pink, S. 2001. *Doing Visual Ethnography*. London: Sage.

Quinney, R. 1996. 'Once My Father Traveled West to California.' In *Composing Ethnography: Alternative Forms of Qualitative Writing*, edited by C. Ellis and A. Bochner. Walnut Creek, CA: AltaMira Press. pp. 357–382.

Reed-Danahay, D. 1997. *Auto/Ethnography: Rewriting the Self and the Social*. Oxford, UK: Berg.

Richardson, L. 1990. *Writing Strategies: Researching Diverse Audiences*. Thousand Oaks, CA: Sage.

Richardson, L. 2000. Writing: A method of inquiry. In *Handbook of Qualitative Research,* edited by N. Denzin, and Y. Lincoln. Thousand Oaks, CA: Sage. pp. 923–948.

Richardson, L. 2002. 'Poetic Representation of Interviews.' In *The Handbook of Interview Research: Context & Method*, edited by J. Gubrium and J. Holstein. Thousand Oaks, CA: Sage. pp. 877–891.

Richardson, L. and E. A. St. Pierre. 2005. 'Writing: A Method of Inquiry.' In *The Handbook of Qualitative Research* (3rd ed.), edited by N. Denzin and Y. S. Lincoln. Thousand Oaks, CA: Sage. pp. 959–978.

Ronai, C. 1996. 'My Mother is Mentally Retarded.' In *Composing Ethnography*, edited by C. Ellis and A. Bochner. Walnut Creek, CA: Altamira Press. pp. 109–131.

Rose, Gillian. 2001. *Visual Methodologies*. London: Sage.

Rosenblatt, P. C. 2002. 'Interviewing at the Border of Fact and Fiction.' In *The Handbook of Interview Research: Context & Method*, edited by J. Gubrium and J. Holstein. Thousand Oaks, CA: Sage. pp. 893–909.

Ross, G., V. Invonoffski and C. Sinding. 2002. 'Making a Mess and Spreading It Around: Articulation of an Approach to Research-Based Theater.' In *Ethnographically Speaking*, edited by A. Bochner and C. Ellis. Walnut Creek: Altamira Press. pp. 57–75.

Ryan, S. 1994. 'Inscribing the Emptiness: Cartography, Exploration, and the Construction of Australia.' In *De-Scribing Empire: Post-Colonialism and Textuality*, edited by C. Tiffin and A. Lawson. London: Routledge. pp. 115–130.

Said, E. 1978. *Orientalism*. London: Routledge.

Saltz, I. 2006. *Body Type: Intimate Messages Etched in Flesh*. New York: Harry N. Abrams.

Shaffer, E. S. 1998. *The Third Culture: Literature and Sciences*. Berlin: Walter de Gruyter.

Stasz, C. 1979. 'The Early History of Visual Sociology.' In *Images of Information: Still Photography in the Social*

Sciences, edited by J. Wagner. Beverly Hills, CA: Sage. pp. 119–136.

Tiffin, C. and A. Lawson. 1994. 'Introduction: The Textuality of Empire.' In *De-Scribing Empire: Post-Colonialism and Textuality*, edited by C. Tiffin and A. Lawson. London: Routledge. pp. 1–14.

Van Maanen, J. 1988. *Tales of the Field*. Chicago: University of Chicago Press.

Van Maanen, J. 2006. 'Ethnography Then and Now.' *Qualitative Research in Organizations and Management* 1(1): 13–21.

Index